lon

Eastern USA

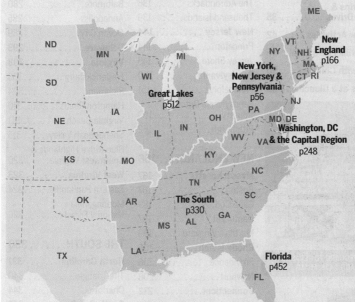

ME

ND

MN

MI

New England
p166

NY VT NH
MA
New York,
New Jersey &
Pennsylvania
p56

SD

WI

CT RI

Great Lakes
p512

IA

OH

NJ

PA

NE

IL IN

MD DE
Washington, DC
& the Capital Region
p248

WV

KS

MO

KY

VA

TN

NC

OK

AR

The South
p330

SC

MS AL

GA

TX

LA

Florida
p452

FL

Benedict Walker, Kate Armstrong, Carolyn Bain, Amy C Balfour, Robert
Balkovich, Ray Bartlett, Gregor Clark, Michael Grosberg, Ashley
Harrell, Adam Karlin, Brian Kluepfel, Kevin Raub, Simon Richmond,
Regis St Louis, Mara Vorhees, Karla Zimmerman

Contents

PLAN YOUR TRIP

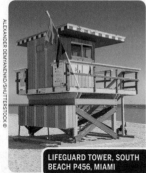

LIFEGUARD TOWER, SOUTH
BEACH P456, MIAMI

ALEXANDER DEMYANENKO/SHUTTERSTOCK ©

KING NEPTUNE STATUE BY
PAUL DIPASQUALE, VIRGINIA
BEACH P311

RITU MANOJ JETHANI/SHUTTERSTOCK ©

ON THE ROAD

Contents

UNDERSTAND

SURVIVAL
GUIDE

Welcome to Eastern USA

Flanked by megacities New York and Chicago, landscaped with dune-backed beaches, smoky mountains and gator swamps, and steeped in musical roots, the East rolls out a sweet trip.

Mighty Metropolises

Brimming with 8.4 million people, the megalopolis of New York looms like an alien mother ship over the East, offering a mind-blowing array of culture, cuisine and entertainment. Cloud-poking Chicago, power-brokering Washington, DC and fiery, Latin-infused Miami rise up close on its heels as other one-of-a-kind cityscapes. Look deeper to find the captivating old quarters of New Orleans, reborn from waterlogged ashes, and raw-edged Detroit, where young DIY devotees are flocking to transform the abandoned city.

Beaches & Back Roads

The East Coast is where America gets its beach on, from the wild dunes and whale-rich waters of Cape Cod to the taffy-shop-lined boardwalks of Ocean City or the coral reefs of the Florida Keys. Inland, nature puts on a show in the swampy Florida Everglades, wolf-howling Boundary Waters, mist-tipped Appalachian Mountains and New England's forests, which blaze red, orange and yellow each fall. Slowpoke byways unfurl throughout so you can soak up the landscapes, from historic Civil War battlefields to kitschy roadside attractions.

Chowhounds' Smorgasbord

Good eatin' reaches epic proportions here: hulking steamed lobsters with melted butter in Maine's seafood shacks, bagels and lox in Manhattan's delis, saucy barbecue ribs in Memphis' roadhouses, butter-smothered biscuits in North Carolina's diners, hot-spiced gumbo in New Orleans' cafes...and for dessert, thick slices of berry pie in the region's supper clubs. You'll certainly work up a thirst – which you can slake with the region's sweet white wines, microbrewed beers and home-grown bourbon.

Cultural Cradle

The museums here are the nation's greatest hits – the Smithsonian, housing everything but the kitchen sink; the Metropolitan Museum of Art, a city-state of treasures; and the Art Institute of Chicago, hanging Impressionists by the roomful. Explore the roots of the blues, jazz, and rock and roll at musical meccas such as Memphis' Sun Studio, where Elvis got his groove on; Cleveland's Rock and Roll Hall of Fame, for artifacts like Jimi Hendrix' Stratocaster; and the juke joints of Clarksdale, where blues slide guitar first pierced the air. For sky-high designs, Chicago and New York are drawing boards for the modern era's great architects.

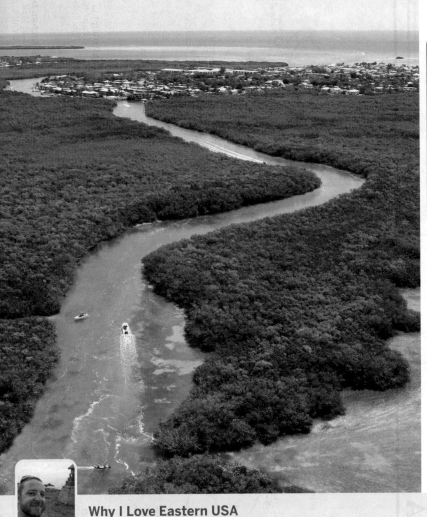

Why I Love Eastern USA

By Benedict Walker, Writer

I first came to the USA's inimitable east from my native Australia in my early twenties and was drawn to Oprah and Frank Lloyd Wright's Chicago and the gritty, giddy rush of Manhattan, pre-September 11. Two decades later, I keep coming back, called by gorgeous New England's less-touristed enclaves, Nashville's musical heart, the dulcet drawl of the sultry south and my love affair with sunny Florida. The magnificent Gulf coast – oft-maligned and misunderstood – feels simultaneously so like home, yet poles apart. Hit the backroads, meet the peeps and you too will fall for the mighty east.

For more about our writers, see p672

For more about our writers, see p672

Above: Florida Keys (p482)

Eastern USA

ELEVATION

16,000ft
12,000ft
9000ft
5000ft
2000ft
1000ft
500ft
Sea Level
-500ft

Chicago
Bluesy beats and superstar eats (p516)

Niagara Falls
North America's most voluminous cascade (p142)

New York City
Loud, fast, pulsating, dizzying metropolis (p57)

Boston
Follow the footprints of colonial rebels (p167)

Acadia National Park
Wild cliffs & wave-bashed beaches (p245)

Philadelphia
Chowhounds' and history buffs' delight (p151)

Washington, DC
National Mall: cultural epicenter (p249)

CANADA

500 km
300 miles

Appalachian Trail
Trek from
Georgia to Maine (p43)

Blue Ridge Parkway
Sublime drive through
the Appalachians (p35)

Great Smoky Mountains
Misty, forested USA's
most visited park (p350)

Walt Disney World® Resort
The world's
greatest theme park (p505)

Miami
Chic, sexy,
Latin-spiced culture (p453)

Florida Keys
Coral reefs and
a helluva party (p482)

Everglades National Park
Seek alligators
in the swamp (p477)

New Orleans
Sazerac-soaked
Cajun banquet (p430)

ATLANTIC
OCEAN

BAHAMAS

★ NASSAU

Gulf of Mexico

Eastern USA's
Top 25

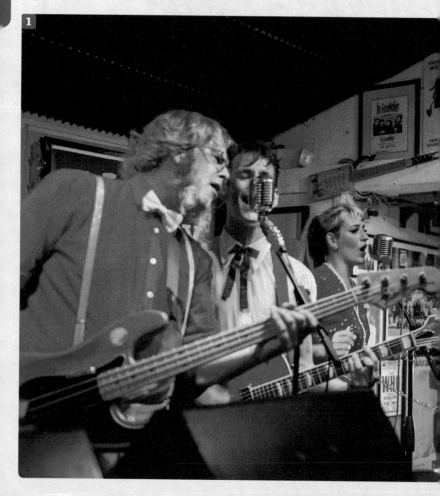

Florida Keys

1 This island chain drifts as far south as you can get in the continental USA. Except for drinking and partying, people come to the Keys (p482) to fish, snorkel, dive, kayak, hike, cycle, fish some more, snorkel again. North America's best coral reefs percolate under the jade-green water and provide brag-worthy expeditions. Then there's Key West, the gloriously unkempt, bawdy, freak-loving exclamation point at the end of the line. Hippies, fire-jugglers, artists and other free spirits converge on its carnival atmosphere after dark. Below left: A band performing in the Green Parrot bar (p487), Key West

New York City

2 Home to striving artists, hedge-fund moguls and immigrants from every corner of the globe, New York City (p57) is constantly reinventing itself. It remains one of the world centers of fashion, theater, food, music, publishing, advertising and finance. A staggering number of museums, parks and ethnic neighborhoods are scattered through the five boroughs. Do as every New Yorker does: hit the streets. Every block reflects the character and history of this dizzying kaleidoscope, and on even a short walk you can cross continents. Below: High Line park (p68), New York City

Chicago

3 The Windy City (p516) will blow you away with its architecture, lakefront beaches, top-notch dining scene and world-class museums. But its true mojo is its blend of high culture and earthy pleasures. Is there another metropolis that dresses its Picasso sculpture in local sports-team gear? Where residents queue for hot dogs in equal measure to North America's top restaurants? Winters are brutal, but come summer, Chicago fetes the warm days with food and music festivals that make fine use of its waterfront.
Below: Navy Pier (p523)

New England Fall Foliage

4 It's a major event, and one approaching epic proportions in New England (p166): watching the leaves change color. You can do it anywhere – all you need is one brilliant tree. But if you're most people, you'll want *lots* of trees. From the Berkshires in Massachusetts and the Litchfield Hills in Connecticut to the Green Mountains in Vermont, entire hillsides blaze in brilliant crimsons, oranges and yellows. Covered bridges and white-steeple churches with abundant maple trees put Vermont (pictured) and New Hampshire at the forefront of leaf-peeping heaven.

National Mall

5 Nearly 2 miles long and lined with iconic monuments and hallowed marble buildings, the National Mall (p249) is the epicenter of Washington, DC's political and cultural life. In the summer, massive music and food festivals are staged here, while year-round visitors wander the halls of America's finest museums lining the green. For exploring American history, there's no better place to ruminate, whether tracing your hand along the Vietnam Veterans Memorial or ascending the steps of the Lincoln Memorial, where Martin Luther King Jr gave his famous 'I Have a Dream' speech. Left: The Martin Luther King Jr Memorial (p253), National Mall

New Orleans

6 Reborn after Hurricane Katrina in 2005, New Orleans (p430) is back. Caribbean-colonial architecture, Creole cuisine and a riotous air of celebration seem more alluring than ever in the Big Easy. Nights are spent catching Dixieland jazz, blues and rock amid bouncing live-music joints, and the city's riotous annual festivals (Mardi Gras, Jazz Fest) are famous the world over. 'Nola' is also a food-loving town that celebrates its myriad culinary influences. Feast on lip-smacking jambalaya and Louisiana *cochon* before hitting the bar scene on Frenchman St. Below top: Mardi Gras (p436)

Boston

7 From cobbled colonial lanes to crazed sports fans, Boston (p167) brews a colorful scene. It is arguably the USA's most historic city: site of the Boston Tea Party, Paul Revere's ride and the first battle of the Revolutionary War – all of which you can trace on the 2.5-mile, red-brick Freedom Trail. Harvard University's campus lets you be a little rebellious yourself at its edgy music clubs. Boston's oyster houses, cafes and trattorias (especially thick in the Italian North End) fortify you for the evening's exploits. Below bottom: Acorn Street, Beacon Hill (p172)

APPALACHIANVIEWS/GETTY IMAGES ©

TRPHOTOS/SHUTTERSTOCK ©

Miami

8 How does one city get so lucky? Most content themselves with one or two highlights, but Miami (p453) seems to have it all. Beyond the stunning beaches and Art Deco Historic District, there's culture at every turn. In cigar-filled dance halls, Havana expats dance to *son* and *boleros;* in exclusive nightclubs stiletto-heeled, fiery-eyed Brazilian models shake to Latin hip-hop; and in the park old men clack dominoes. To top it off, street vendors and restaurants dish out flavors from the Caribbean, Cuba, Argentina and Spain.

Acadia National Park

9 Acadia National Park (p245) is where the mountains meet the sea. Miles of rocky coastline and even more miles of hiking and biking trails make this wonderland Maine's most popular destination, and deservedly so. The high point (literally) is Cadillac Mountain, the 1530ft peak that can be accessed by foot, bicycle or vehicle; early risers can catch the country's first sunrise from this celebrated summit. Later in the day, after working up an appetite on the trails and beaches, indulge in tea and popovers at Jordan Pond.

Niagara Falls

10 Crowded? Cheesy? Well, yes. Niagara (p142) is short too – it barely cracks the top 500 waterfalls worldwide for height. But c'mon, when those great muscular bands of water arch over the precipice like liquid glass and roar into the void below, and when you sail toward it in a misty little boat, Niagara Falls impresses big time. In terms of sheer volume, nowhere in North America beats its thundering cascade, with more than one million bathtubs of water plummeting over the edge every second.

DAN ANDERSON/GETTY IMAGES ©

Walt Disney World® Resort

11 Want to set the bar high? Call yourself the 'Happiest Place on Earth.' Walt Disney World® Resort (p505) does, and then pulls out all the stops to deliver the exhilarating sensation that you are the most important character in the show. Despite all the frantic rides, entertainment and nostalgia, the magic is watching your own child swell with belief after they have made Goofy laugh, been curtsied to by Cinderella, guarded the galaxy with Buzz Lightyear, and battled Darth Maul like your very own Jedi knight. Above left: Magic Kingdom, Walt Disney World® Resort

Everglades National Park

12 The Everglades (p477) unnerve. They don't reach majestically skyward or fill your heart with the aching beauty of a glacier-carved valley. They ooze, flat and watery, a river of grass mottled by hammocks, cypress domes and mangroves. You can't hike them, not really. To properly explore the Everglades – and meet its prehistoric residents, like the snaggle-toothed crocodile – you must leave the safety of land. Push a canoe off a muddy bank, tamp down your fear, and explore the waterways on the Everglades' own, unforgettable terms.

Route 66

13 Known as the Mother Road, this fragile ribbon of concrete was the USA's original road trip, launched in 1926. It begins in Chicago, at the iconic Route 66 Sign (p519), from where the 300-mile stretch onward through Illinois offers classic, timewarped touring. Fork into thick slabs of pie in small-town diners; snap photos of roadside attractions like the Gemini Giant, a sky-high fiberglass spaceman; and motor on past neon signs, drive-in movie theaters and other Americana. From here it's 2100 miles more to the end of the route in Los Angeles.

Mississippi River

14 As Old Man River traces through the country from its Northwoods beginning in Minnesota to its palmetto-fringed end in Louisiana, it meanders past eagles' nests and juke joints, pine forests and plantations. Covering more than 2000 miles, it churns through major cities like Memphis, Minneapolis and New Orleans. There are still riverboats, as in Mark Twain's heyday, but they're more likely to be casinos or tour vessels now. Road trippers heed the call of the mythic Great River Road (p36), as it edges the waterway throughout its duration.

Musical Roots

15 Name the genre, and it probably began here. The Mississippi Delta birthed the blues, while New Orleans opened the door to jazz. Rock and roll arrived the day Elvis Presley walked into Sun Studio in Memphis. And country made its way from fiddle-and-banjo Appalachian hamlets to Nashville's Grand Ole Opry (p378). The Mississippi River took the music north, where Chicago and Detroit riffed into the electric blues and Motown sound, respectively. It all translates into great live music wherever you are in the region. Below bottom: Sun Studio (p365), Memphis

Great Lakes

16 Together, the five Great Lakes (p512) – Superior, Michigan, Huron, Ontario and Erie – that extend across the region's north possess about 20% of the earth's fresh water and 95% of America's. They offer miles of beaches, dunes, resort towns and lighthouse-dotted scenery. Add in wave-bashed cliffs, islands freckling the shore, and freighters chugging in to busy ports, and you can see how the region earned its 'Third Coast' nickname. Anglers, kayakers and even surfers will find their sweet spot here. Below top: Kitesurfers at Montrose Beach, Lake Michigan

The Deep South

17 Steeped in history and regional pride, the antebellum South is about grand homes and cotton plantations, moss-draped trees and azalea-choked gardens. Absorb the vibe in Charleston (p353), while strolling, admiring the architecture and lingering over dinners on the verandah. Fall under the spell of Savannah's live oaks (pictured), shady boulevards, seafood and humid nights. Or ogle the mansions of genteel Natchez, the oldest town on the Mississippi River – you'd be hard-pressed to see more sweeping staircases per square mile anywhere else.

MATT MUNRO/LONELY PLANET ©

BHOFACK2/GETTY IMAGES ©

Appalachian Trail

18 The country's longest footpath (p43) is over 2100 miles in length, crosses six national parks and slices through 14 states from Georgia to Maine. Deep woods, alpine peaks, cow-dotted farms and foraging bears are all part of the landscape. It's estimated that two to three million people trek a portion of the trail every year, inhaling the fresh air and admiring the spectacular scenery. Fewer than 600 hikers persevere all the way through. Got six months and fortitude to spare? The reward is sublime – true for shorter stretches too.

Blue Ridge Parkway

19 Take in sublime sunsets, watch for wildlife and lose all sense of the present while staring off at the vast wilderness surrounding this 469-mile roadway (p35) traversing the southern Appalachian Mountains of Virginia and North Carolina. Hikes take you deeper into nature, from easy lakeside trails to challenging scrambles up to eagles'-nest heights. Camp or spend the night at forest lodges, and don't miss the bluegrass and mountain music scene of nearby towns such as Asheville, North Carolina and Floyd and Galax in Virginia.

Philadelphia

20 Philly (p151) is often overlooked in the pantheon of great American cities, and that's a shame. It's a beautiful place, its streets dotted with gracious squares and linked by cobbled alleys. As the 'birthplace of American government' – where the founding fathers signed the Declaration of Independence in 1776 – history abounds (the Liberty Bell! Ben Franklin's office!). But it's not all about the past: the dining scene has heated up way beyond the famed cheesesteak sandwich (pictured). Chowhounds' eateries lurk on every corner, and most are reasonably priced.

ARJUNA RAVIKUMAR/500PX ©

Great Smoky Mountains

21 Named after the heather-colored mist that hangs over the peaks, the Smokies (p350) comprise a national park that receives more visitors than any other. The pocket of deep Appalachian woods straddles Tennessee and North Carolina, protecting thickly forested ridges where black bears, white-tailed deer, antlered elk, wild turkeys and over 1600 kinds of flowers find sanctuary. Nearly 10 million people a year come to hike, camp, ride horses, cycle, raft and fly fish, though it's easy to lose the crowds if you're willing to walk or paddle.

New England Beaches

22 Summer in New England can get quite humid, so the region's population flocks to the coast for cool ocean breezes. In Massachusetts, great beaches ring Martha's Vineyard, the area's largest island. At nearby Cape Cod National Seashore, salt marshes and wild dunes dot the landscape, while humpback whales spout offshore. Unspoiled Block Island (p211) offers simple pleasures such as rolling farms, uncrowded beaches and quiet hiking and cycling trails – all just a short float from Rhode Island. Top right: Provincetown coastline, Cape Cod National Seashore (p196)

Civil War Sites

23 Sites are scattered over swaths of the eastern USA, from Pennsylvania to Louisiana. Renowned places to connect with some of America's darkest hours are at Antietam, Maryland, site of the bloodiest day in American history, where 23,000 soldiers died; Gettysburg, Pennsylvania (the battlefield and cemetery where President Lincoln delivered his 'Four score...' address); and Vicksburg (pictured; p418), Mississippi, a must for history buffs, with a 16-mile driving tour through the areas General Grant besieged for 47 days. In summer many sites host battle re-enactments.

Amish Country

24 Life slows way down in the Amish communities of northeast Ohio (p560), southeast Pennsylvania and northern Indiana – the USA's three largest Amish clusters. Little boys in straw hats steer horse-drawn buggies, long-bearded men hand-plow the tidy fields, and demurely dressed women and girls carry shoofly pies to market. The 'Plain People,' as they're known, are a centuries-old sect who live a simple life without electricity, telephones or motorized vehicles.

Boardwalk Empire

25 Strolling along the East Coast's beach boardwalk is a rite of passage, be it in Rehoboth Beach, Delaware; Ocean City, Maryland; Virginia Beach, Virginia; or Atlantic City (p148; pictured below), New Jersey. It doesn't matter where. The point is to enjoy the all-star roster of summer indulgence that inevitably lines the walkway: funnel cakes, go-karts, pizza shacks, glow-in-the-dark mini golf and saltwater taffy shops. Parents push strollers, tots lick ice-cream cones and teenagers check each other out. Don't get so caught up you forget to take in the sea views!

Need to Know

For more information, see Survival Guide (p639)

Currency
US dollar ($)

Language
English, Spanish

Visas
Visitors from Canada, the UK, Australia, New Zealand, Japan and many EU countries do not need visas for less than 90 days, with ESTA approval. For other nations, see www.travel. state.gov or www.usa. gov/visas-and-visitors.

Money
ATMs widely available. Credits cards accepted at most hotels, restaurants and shops.

Cell Phones
Foreign phones operating on tri- or quad-band frequencies will work in the USA. Or purchase inexpensive cell phones with a pay-as-you-go plan.

Time
Eastern Time Zone (GMT minus five hours): NYC, New England, Miami; Central Time Zone (GMT minus six hours): Chicago, Nashville, New Orleans.

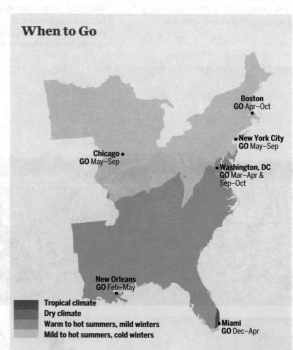

When to Go

Boston
GO Apr–Oct

New York City
GO May–Sep

Chicago
GO May–Sep

Washington, DC
GO Mar–Apr &
Sep–Oct

New Orleans
GO Feb–May

Miami
GO Dec–Apr

Tropical climate
Dry climate
Warm to hot summers, mild winters
Mild to hot summers, cold winters

High Season
(Jun–Aug)

➡ Warm, sunny days across the region

➡ Accommodation prices peak (30% up on average)

➡ Big outdoor music festivals abound: Milwaukee's Summerfest, Newport's Folk Fest, Chicago's Lollapalooza etc

Shoulder Season (Apr–May, Sep–Oct)

➡ Milder temperatures; can be rainy

➡ Wildflowers bloom, especially in May

➡ Fall foliage areas (ie New England, Blue Ridge Parkway) remain busy

Low Season
(Nov–Mar)

➡ Dark, wintry days, with snowfall in the north

➡ Lowest prices for accommodations (aside from ski resorts and warmer getaway destinations like Florida, for which it's peak season)

➡ Attractions keep shorter hours or close for the winter

Useful Websites

Lonely Planet (www.lonely planet.com/usa/eastern-usa) Destination information, hotel bookings, traveler forum and more.

Eater (www.eater.com) Foodie insight into two-dozen American cities.

National Park Service (www. nps.gov) Gateway to America's greatest natural treasures: its national parks.

New York Times Travel (www. nytimes.com/section/travel) Travel news, practical advice and engaging features.

Roadside America (www. roadsideamerica.com) For all things weird and wacky.

Thrillist (www.thrillist.com) Food, drink, travel and entertainment, from New York.

Important Numbers

To call a number within the USA, dial 1, followed by the area code and the seven-digit number.

USA country code	☏1
International access code	☏011
Emergency	☏911
Directory assistance	☏411
International directory assistance	☏00

Exchange Rates

Australia	A$1	$0.75
Canada	C$1	$0.75
Eurozone	€1	$1.12
Japan	¥100	$0.89
New Zealand	NZ$1	$0.72
UK	UK£1	$1.26

For current exchange rates see www.xe.com.

Daily Costs

Budget: Less than $100

➡ Dorm bed: $20–40

➡ Campsite: $15–30

➡ Room in a budget motel: $60–80

➡ Lunch from a cafe or food truck: $6–10

➡ Travel on public transit: $2–3.50

Midrange: $150–250

➡ Room in a midrange hotel: $80–200

➡ Dinner in a popular restaurant: $20–40

➡ Car hire per day: from $30

Top End: More than $250

➡ Room in a top hotel/resort: from $250

➡ Dinner in a top restaurant: $60–100

➡ Big night out (plays, concerts, clubs): $60–200

Opening Hours

Typical opening times are as follows:

Banks 8:30am to 4:30pm Monday to Friday (and possibly 9am to noon Saturday)

Bars 5pm to midnight Sunday to Thursday, to 2am Friday and Saturday

Nightclubs 10pm to 3am Thursday to Saturday

Post Offices 9am to 5pm Monday to Friday

Shopping Malls 9am to 9pm

Stores 9am to 6pm Monday to Saturday, noon to 5pm Sunday

Supermarkets 8am to 8pm, some open 24 hours

Arriving in Eastern USA

JFK International (New York) From JFK take the AirTrain to Jamaica Station and then LIRR to Penn Station, which costs $12 to $16 (45 minutes). A taxi to Manhattan costs around $60, plus toll and tip (45 to 90 minutes).

O'Hare International (Chicago) The CTA Blue Line train ($5) runs 24/7. Trains depart every 10 minutes or so; they reach downtown in 40 minutes. Airport Express shuttle vans cost $32 to $34 (approximately 60 minutes); taxis cost around $55 (30 minutes or so).

Miami International Super-Shuttle to South Beach for $22 (50 to 90 minutes); taxi to Miami Beach for $36 (40 to 60 minutes); or take the Metrorail to downtown (Government Center) for $2.50 (15 minutes).

Getting Around

Car Driving is the main way to access the region. In big cities (New York, Chicago) it can be a hassle, though, with traffic gridlock and hefty parking fees (upward of $40 per day). Car rentals are available in every town.

Train Outside the Boston–Washington, DC, corridor train travel is mostly for scenic journeys. Amtrak (www.amtrak. com) is the national carrier.

Bus Short-haul carriers such as Megabus (www.megabus.com/ us) and Bolt Bus (www.boltbus. com) are popular for getting between main cities (eg New York to DC) – this is typically the cheapest way to travel. Tickets must be purchased online in advance.

For much more on **getting around**, see p651

If You Like...

Big Cities

New York City You can't get bigger than NYC – 8.4 million people strong, loud, fast, pulsing with energy, symphonic and always evolving. (p57)

Chicago The Great Lakes' metropolis is a cultural stew of skyscrapers, public art, vast museums, indie clubs and a delirious number of eats. (p516)

Baltimore The gritty port city has morphed into a hip beauty, sporting world-class museums, trendy shops and boutique hotels. (p280)

Philadelphia History is everywhere in the USA's first capital, but Philly's urbane side comes out in its energetic food, music and arts scenes. (p151)

Detroit A case study of how cities rise and fall, and maybe – just maybe – rise again. (p568)

National Parks

Great Smoky Mountains Heather-colored mist clings to the peaks, while black bears, elk and wild turkeys prowl the USA's most-visited park. (p350)

Acadia Maine's unspoiled wilderness offers surging coastal mountains, towering sea cliffs, surf-pounded beaches and quiet ponds. (p245)

Shenandoah Spectacular vistas unfurl along the Blue Ridge Mountains, with great hiking and camping, including along the Appalachian Trail. (p317)

Everglades South Florida's watery wonderland is home to snaggle-toothed crocodiles, stealthy panthers, pink flamingos and mellow manatees. (p477)

Isle Royale Floating in Lake Superior's midst, it's devoid of roads, cars and crowds, giving moose and loons room to roam. (p585)

Fabulous Food

Maine lobster, Philly cheesesteaks, Memphis barbecue, Wisconsin cheddar – you'll need to loosen the belt wherever you are in the East.

New Orleans Hot-spiced gumbo, fresh-shucked oysters and bourbon-soaked bread pudding highlight the Creole menu in America's most food-centric city. (p430)

New York City Whether you crave steak *frites*, sushi, chicken tikka masala or gourmet hot dogs, globe-trotting Gotham has you covered. (p57)

Chicago The Windy City plates an unapologetically rich clash of high gastronomy and comfort food, plus neighborhoods packed with ethnic eats. (p516)

Charleston The well-bred, gardenia-scented city brings on decadent, Lowcountry fare such as shrimp and grits and she-crab soup. (p353)

Minneapolis It has been called 'America's next great food city' for its creative, sustainable, Scandinavian-tinged eateries. (p598)

Old-Fashioned Americana

Wellfleet Drive-In Flash back to the 1950s at this movie theater in Cape Cod. (p193)

Arcade Tuck into thick pancakes at the classic Memphis diner that Elvis used to frequent. (p369)

Route 66 Mom-and-pop motels, neon-lit pie shops and oddball roadside attractions – and that's just along Illinois' 300-mile stretch of road. (p519)

Architecture

Chicago Birthplace of the skyscraper, Chicago has magnificent works by many of the great 20th-century architects. (p516)

Newport Mansions Newport, Rhode Island's ostentatious

clifftop mansions ushered in an era of opulence at the turn of the 20th-century. (p208)

Miami Miami's Art Deco Historic District is a Technicolor dream come to life. (p453)

Columbus Believe it: there's big architecture in small Columbus, Indiana – thanks to the town's forward-thinking industrialists. (p549)

Savannah This Southern belle never fails to turn heads with her striking antebellum buildings. (p404)

Museums

Smithsonian Institution The nation's premier treasure chest is actually a group of 19 museums. Best of all, they're all free. (p249)

Metropolitan Museum of Art The top-draw attraction in NYC is like a cultural city-state, boasting a trove of two million artworks. (p82)

Art Institute of Chicago The nation's second-largest art museum (after the Met) hangs masterpieces aplenty, especially Impressionist paintings. (p518)

Rock and Roll Hall of Fame & Museum It has Jimi Hendrix's Stratocaster and John Lennon's Sgt Pepper suit, all in Cleveland. (p555)

National Civil Rights Museum Moving exhibits set across the street from where Martin Luther King Jr was assassinated in Memphis. (p365)

Newseum Celebrating freedom of expression and tracing the history of journalism, this fun, sparkling new museum is hard to resist. (p262)

Top: Brooklyn Bridge (p57), New York City

Bottom: Red squirrel at Isle Royale National Park (p585)

Theme Parks

Walt Disney World® Resort
Plunge into the fairytale world of the 'Happiest Place on Earth' and get swept up in miles of nostalgia and thrill rides. (p505)

Dollywood A paean to the much-loved country singer Dolly Parton, with Appalachian-themed rides and attractions in the hills of Tennessee. (p382)

Cedar Point Home to several of the globe's tallest and fastest roller coasters, like the 120mph Top Thrill Dragster. (p558)

Universal Orlando Resort Famed home of Universal Studios and the new Wizarding World of Harry Potter. (p507)

Busch Gardens Epic roller coasters and rides, animal encounters and oodles of live entertainment await in this African-themed mega-park. (p496)

Outdoor Activities

Appalachian Trail Even if you choose not to walk all 2160 miles, hop on for a day hike to experience the sublime scenery; 14 states provide access. (p324)

Boundary Waters Canoe deep into Minnesota's northern wilderness to camp under the stars and perhaps glimpse the aurora borealis. (p609)

New River Gorge National River Legendary white water froths in West Virginia, ripping through a primeval forest gorge that's utterly Eden-like. (p326)

Long Island Surf's up in New York, from Montauk's waves to Nassau County's Long Beach. (p123)

Stowe Mountain Vermont practically invented snowboard-ing. The state's premier crag is *the* place to shred. (p45)

Presidential Range Challenging trails, lofty peaks and an excellent hut-to-hut system in New Hampshire's White Mountains. (p233)

History

The north has Colonial and Revolutionary hot spots, while the mid-Atlantic and south hold the majority of Civil War battlefields.

Independence National Historic Park Highlights include the Liberty Bell and Independence Hall, where America's founders signed the Constitution. (p151)

Boston's Freedom Trail Visit Paul Revere's home, an 18th-century graveyard and 14 other Revolutionary War sites along the 2.5-mile path. (p181)

Henry Ford Museum/Greenfield Village These two museums hold US history's greatest hits: the bus Rosa Parks sat in, the Wright Brothers' airplane workshop and more. (p575)

Washington, DC See the sites where Lincoln was assassinated, Martin Luther King Jr gave his most famous speech and Nixon's presidency was undone. (p249)

Vicksburg The Mississippi bluffs that General Grant besieged for 47 days are ground zero for Civil War enthusiasts. (p418)

Williamsburg Step back into the 1700s in this preserved town, the largest living history museum on the planet. (p308)

Harpers Ferry A fascinating open-air museum of 19th-century village life framed by mountains and rivers. (p324)

Nightlife

New Orleans Go beyond Bourbon St into the neighborhoods where Sazerac swirls in glasses and jazz, Dixieland and zydeco spill from clubs. (p430)

New York City As Sinatra sang, it's the city that doesn't sleep, with bars and clubs throughout town staying open till 4am nightly. (p57)

Athens, Georgia The compact little college town boasts a mighty music scene that launched the B-52s and R.E.M. (p402)

Nashville Everyone strums the guitar here, and there are bars and honky-tonks aplenty for boot-stompin' shows into the wee hours. (p371)

Key West A lot of booze goes down the hatch in this raucous, free-spirited, carnival of a town. (p485)

Offbeat America

NashTrash Tours Nashville's tall-haired 'Jugg Sisters' take visitors on a deliciously tacky journey through the city's spicier side. (p375)

Spam Museum Try your hand at canning the sweet pork magic in Austin, Minnesota, the blue-tinned meat's revered birthplace. (p606)

American Visionary Art Museum Peruse outsider art (including pieces created by the clinically insane) at this Baltimore gem. (p282)

World's Largest Ball of Twine It's a 17,400lb behemoth sitting in a Minnesota gazebo. (p606)

Art Deco buildings on Ocean Dr, Miami (p453)

Theater

New York City and Chicago are the stars, while smaller cities such as Minneapolis give voice to emerging talents.

Broadway It doesn't get more iconic than the bright lights and glittering marquees along this most famous Midtown Manhattan street. (p73)

Steppenwolf Theatre John Malkovich, Gary Sinise and other now-famous actors launched Chicago's scene here more than four decades ago. (p538)

Guthrie Theater Minneapolis has so many theaters it's nicknamed 'the Mini Apple.' The uber-cool Guthrie leads the pack. (p603)

American Players Theatre Stages Shakespeare and other classics outdoors amid the woodlands of Spring Green, Wisconsin. (p594)

Grand Ole Opry There's more than country music under the lights – it's a full-fledged, footstompin' variety show. (p378)

Beaches

South Beach The world-famous strand is less about wavefrolicking than taking in the parade of people on Miami's favorite playground. (p456)

Cape Cod National Seashore Massive sand dunes, picturesque lighthouses and cool forests invite endless exploring on the Massachusetts cape. (p196)

Michigan's Gold Coast Endless stretches of sand, dunes, wineries, orchards and B&B-filled towns blanket the state's western shoreline. (p578)

Outer Banks North Carolina's isolated barrier islands offer everything from popular beaches to remote strands where wild ponies run free. (p334)

Month by Month

January

The New Year starts off with a shiver as snowfall blankets large swaths of the northern regions. Ski resorts kick into high gear, while sun-lovers seek refuge in warmer climes (especially Florida).

🌟 Mummers Parade

Philadelphia's biggest event is this brilliant parade (www.mummers.com) on New Year's Day, for which local clubs spend months creating costumes and mobile scenery in order to win top honors. String bands and clowns add to the general good cheer.

🌟 Chinese New Year

In late January or early February, you'll find colorful celebrations and feasting anywhere there's a Chinatown. NYC and Chicago each ring in the occasion with a parade, floats, firecrackers, bands and plenty of merriment.

🌟 St Paul Winter Carnival

Is it cold in Minnesota in late January? You betcha. That doesn't stop denizens from bundling up in parkas and snow boots to partake in 10 days of ice sculptures, ice skating and ice fishing (www.wintercarnival.com).

February

Despite indulging in winter mountain getaways, many Americans dread February for its long, dark nights and frozen days. For foreign visitors, this can be the cheapest time to travel, with ultra-discount rates for flights and hotels.

🌟 Mardi Gras

Held in late February or early March, on the day before Ash Wednesday, Mardi Gras (Fat Tuesday) is the finale of Carnival. New Orleans' celebrations (www.mardigrasneworleans.com) are legendary as colorful parades, masquerade balls and feasting rule the day.

☆ Groundhog Day

Made famous by the eponymous 1993 film, the little town of Punxsutawney, PA steals the nation's attention at sunrise on 2 February, when Punxsutawney Phil, the world's best-known marmot, makes his predictions about the coming of winter's end.

☆ Mix NYC Experimental Fim Festival

New York's longest running queer film festival (www.mixnyc.org) is a stalwart on the global LGBT film festival circuit and a must-attend for avant-garde and experimental film buffs.

☆ North Carolina Jazz Festival

Since 1980, this volunteer-run not-for-profit festival (www.ncjazzfestival.com) has been warming winter hearts with the magic of world-renowned jazz musicians, over three days in February.

March

The first blossoms of spring arrive – at least in the south (the north still shivers in the chill). In New England's mountains, it's still ski season. Meanwhile, the Spring Break masses descend on Florida.

✤ National Cherry Blossom Festival

The brilliant blooms of Japanese cherry blossoms around DC's Tidal Basin are celebrated with concerts, parades, taiko drumming, kite-flying and loads of other events during the three-week fest (www.nationalcherryblossomfestival.org). More than 1.5 million people go each year, so don't forget to book ahead.

☆ Maple Syrup Tasting

Vermont's maple-syrup producers invite the public to their 'sugarhouses' to see the sweet stuff being made during the Vermont Maple Open House Weekend (www.vermontmaple.org) in late March. Maine producers do the same on the last Sunday of the month.

☆ Baseball Spring Training

Throughout March, Florida hosts Major League Baseball's spring training 'Grapefruit League' (www.floridagrapefruitleague.com): 15 pro baseball teams train and play exhibition games, drawing fans to the Orlando, Tampa Bay and southeast areas.

🍷 St Patrick's Day

On the 17th, the patron saint of Ireland is honored with brass bands and ever-flowing pints of Guinness. Huge parades occur in New York, Boston and Chicago (which goes all-out by dyeing the Chicago River green).

April

The weather is warming up, but April can still be unpredictable, with chilly weather mixed with a few teasingly warm days up north. Down south, it's a fine time to travel.

✤ New Orleans Jazz & Heritage Festival

The Big Easy hosts the country's best jazz jam (www.nojazzfest.com) for 10 days in late April with top-notch horn blowers and ivory ticklers. Almost better than the music is the food: soft-shell crab po'boys, Cajun rice with pork sausage and white-chocolate bread pudding.

🏃 Boston Marathon

At the country's oldest marathon (www.baa.org), tens of thousands of spectators watch runners cross the finish line at Copley Sq on Patriots' Day, a Massachusetts holiday held on the third Monday of April.

☆ Tribeca Film Festival

Robert De Niro co-organizes this NYC soiree (www.tribecafilm.com) showcasing documentaries and narrative features, held during 12 days in late April. It has quickly risen in stature since its 2002 inception.

May

May is true spring and one of the loveliest times to travel in the region, with blooming wildflowers and generally mild sunny weather. Summer crowds and high prices have yet to arrive.

☆ Kentucky Derby

On the first Saturday of the month, a who's who of upper-crust America put on their suits and most flamboyant hats and descend on Louisville for the horse race (www.kentuckyderby.com) known as the 'greatest two minutes in sports.'

☆ Movement

Billed as the world's largest electronic music festival (www.movement.us), Movement packs Detroit's Hart Plaza over Memorial Day weekend. You'll find both up-and-comers and the big names in the biz, such as Snoop Dog, Skrillex and Felix da Housecat, at the dance-loving extravaganza.

✤ Together Festival

Boston's burgeoning and aptly named week-long Together Festival (www.togetherboston.com) is all about how art and technology converge in this historic yet high-tech city, home to Harvard, Cambridge and cutting-edge MIT.

✤ North Charleston Arts Festival

Now in its fourth decade, this five-day South Carolina festival (www.northcharlestonartsfest.com) has grown from humble beginnings to be one of the most comprehensive arts festivals on the eastern seaboard.

June

Summer is here. Americans spend more time at outdoor cafes and restaurants, and head to the shore or to

national parks. School is out; vacationers fill the highways and resorts, bringing higher prices.

Bonnaroo

Set in Tennessee's heartland on a 700-acre farm, this sprawling music fest (www.bonnaroo.com) showcases big-name rock, soul, country and more over four days in mid-June.

☆ Chicago Blues Festival

It's the globe's biggest free blues fest (www.chicago bluesfestival.us), with three days of the electrified music that made Chicago famous. More than a half-million people unfurl blankets by the multiple stages that take over Grant Park in early June.

☆ CMA Music Festival

Legions of country-music fans don their cowboy boots and unite in Nashville for the chance to hear the genre's top crooners. Over 400 artists perform at stages in Riverfront Park and Nissan Stadium (www.cmafest.com).

Mermaid Parade

In Brooklyn, NYC, Coney Island celebrates summer's steamy arrival with a kitsch-loving parade (www.coneyisland.com), complete with skimpily attired mermaids and horn-blowing mermen.

Summerfest

Milwaukee lets loose with a heckuva music fest (www.summerfest.com) for 11 days in late June/early July, with hundreds of big-name rock, blues, jazz, country and alternative bands swarming 10 lakefront stages. Local beer, brats and cheese accompany the proceedings.

July

With summer in full swing, Americans break out the backyard barbecues or head for the beach. The prices are high and the crowds can be fierce, but it's one of the liveliest times to visit.

Independence Day

The nation celebrates its birthday with a fireworks-filled bang on the 4th. In Philadelphia, descendents of the Declaration of Independence signatories ring the Liberty Bell. Boston, New York and Washington, DC are also great spots to enjoy the fun.

National Black Arts Festival

Artists converge on Atlanta for this event (www.nbaf.org) celebrating African American music, theater, literature and film. Wynton Marsalis, Spike Lee and Youssou N'Dour are among those who've performed here.

Newport Folk Festival

Newport, Rhode Island, a summer haunt of the well-heeled, hosts this high-energy music fest (www.newportfolk.org) in late July. Top folk artists take to the storied stage, best remembered as the venue where Bob Dylan went electric.

Eastern Music Festival

For half a century, North Carolina's musical treasure (www.easternmusicfestival.org) has been educating and entertaining through its month-long series of workshops and performances.

August

Expect blasting heat in August, with temperatures and humidity less bearable the further south you go. You'll find people-packed beaches, high prices and empty cities on weekends, when residents escape to the nearest waterfront.

☆ Lollapalooza

This massive rock fest (www.lollapalooza.com) in Chicago is a raucous event, with 130 bands – including many A-listers – spilling off eight stages in Grant Park the first weekend in August.

Maine Lobster Festival

If you love lobster like Maine loves lobster, indulge in this feeding frenzy (www.mainelobsterfestival.com) held in Rockland in early August. King Neptune and the Sea Goddess oversee a week full of events and, of course, as much crustacean as you can eat.

September

With the end of summer, cooler days arrive, making for pleasant outings region-wide. The kids are back in school, and concert halls, gallery spaces and performing-arts venues kick off a new season.

☆ New York Film Festival

One of several big film fests in NYC, this one features world premieres from across the globe, plus Q&As with indie and mainstream directors alike. Lincoln Center (www.filmlinc.com) plays host.

✖ New Orleans Fried Chicken Festival

The inaugural Fried Chicken Festival in 2016 (www.friedchickenfestival. com) drew crowds of up to 40,000 and the future looks big, with an expanded program and even more golden deliciously fried bird.

October

Temperatures are falling as fall brings fiery colors to northern climes. It's high season where the leaves are most brilliant (New England); elsewhere expect lower prices and smaller crowds.

🏃 Halloween

It's not just for kids; adults celebrate Halloween at masquerade parties. In NYC, you can don a cos-

tume and join the Halloween parade up Sixth Ave. Chicago does a cultural take with skeleton-rich Day of the Dead events at the National Museum of Mexican Art.

✳ Fantasy Fest

Key West's answer to Mardi Gras brings more than 100,000 revelers to the subtropical enclave during the week leading up to Halloween. Expect parades, colorful floats, costume parties, the selecting of a conch king and queen and plenty of alcohol-fueled merriment (www.fantasyfest.com).

November

No matter where you go, this is generally low season, with cold winds discouraging visitors. Prices are lower (although airfares skyrocket around Thanksgiving). There's much happening culturally in the main cities.

🏃 Thanksgiving

On the fourth Thursday of November, Americans gather with family and friends over daylong feasts of roast turkey, sweet potatoes, cranberry sauce, wine, pumpkin pie and loads of

other dishes. New York City hosts a huge parade, and there's pro football on TV.

December

Winter arrives, though skiing conditions in eastern USA usually aren't ideal until January. Christmas lights and holiday fairs make the region come alive during the festive season.

✳ Art Basel

This massive arts fest (www.artbasel.com) has four days of cutting-edge art, film, architecture and design. More than 250 major galleries from across the globe come to the event, with works by some 2000 artists, plus much hobnobbing with a glitterati crowd in Miami Beach.

✳ New Year's Eve

Americans are of two minds when it comes to ringing in the New Year. Some join festive crowds to celebrate; others plot a getaway to escape the mayhem. Whichever you choose, plan well in advance. Expect high prices (especially in NYC).

Itineraries

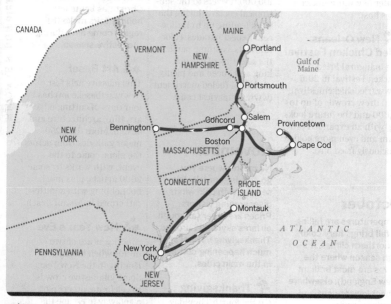

CANADA

MAINE

VERMONT

NEW HAMPSHIRE

Portland

Gulf of Maine

Portsmouth

Salem

Concord

Provincetown

Bennington

NEW YORK

Boston

MASSACHUSETTS

Cape Cod

CONNECTICUT

RHODE ISLAND

Montauk

PENNSYLVANIA

New York City

NEW JERSEY

ATLANTIC OCEAN

2 WEEKS Down the Coast

Get your big-city fill in the biggest city of all, then mosey into New England for small-town pleasures.

The great dynamo of art, fashion and culture, **New York City** is America at its most urbane. Spend three days blending touristy must-dos – Top of the Rock viewpoint, Upper East Side art museums, Central Park rambling – with vibrant nightlife and dining adventures, perhaps in the East Village. After big-city culture, catch your breath at the pretty beaches and enticing charms of **Montauk** on Long Island. Back in NYC, catch the train to **Boston**, for two days visiting historic sights, dining in the North End and pub-hopping in Cambridge. Rent a car and drive to **Cape Cod**, with its idyllic dunes, forests and pretty shores. Leave time for **Provincetown**, the Cape's liveliest settlement. Then set off for a three-day jaunt taking in New England's back roads, covered bridges, picturesque towns and beautiful scenery, staying at heritage B&Bs en route. Highlights include **Salem** and **Concord** in Massachusetts; **Bennington**, Vermont; and **Portsmouth**, New Hampshire. If time allows, head onward to Maine for lobster feasts amid beautifully rugged coastlines – **Portland** is a fine place to start.

Eastern Grand Tour

This road trip loops around the East through towns large and small, as blues joints, pie shops and civil rights sights flash by.

Start in **New York City** (but hire a car more cheaply in New Jersey) and hit the road for week one. Head west toward **Lancaster** to explore the idyllic back roads of Pennsylvania Dutch Country. Next is **Pittsburgh**, a surprising town of picturesque bridges and cutting-edge museums. Enter Ohio by interstate, but quickly step back in time amid the horses, buggies and byways of **Amish Country**. See the skyscrapers rising on the horizon? That's big-shouldered **Chicago**. Hang out for a few days to marvel at famous artworks and steely architecture, and chow through the city's celebrated restaurant scene.

For week two, motor south from Chicago on old Route 66, at least for a few time-warped, pie-filled miles. **Memphis** is the next destination, a mecca for Elvis fans, barbecue connoisseurs, civil rights students and blues-music buffs alike. Follow the Great River Rd south from here through juke-jointed **Clarksdale**, the Civil War battlegrounds of **Vicksburg** and the antebellum mansions of **Natchez**. It's not far now to **New Orleans**, where you can hear live jazz, consult with a voodoo priestess and spoon into thick, spicy-rich gumbo.

Begin journeying back east for week three. Wheel along the Gulf Coast to the azalea-lined boulevards of **Mobile**, then inland to **Montgomery**, where museums honor civil rights pioneers like Rosa Parks, who refused to give up her seat to a white man on a city bus. Fall under the spell of live oaks in **Savannah** and pastel architecture and decadent food in **Charleston**. Take your pick of **Durham** or **Chapel Hill**, side-by-side university towns offering groovy nightlife.

Begin week four brushing up on your history in Virginia. Visit **Jamestown**, where Pocahontas helped the New World's first English settlement survive, then wander through the 18th century at nearby **Williamsburg**. A pair of big cities completes the route: **Washington, DC** is a museum free-for-all, while **Philadelphia** fires up the Liberty Bell, Ben Franklin and the mighty, meaty cheesesteak.

Bright Lights, Big Cities

3 WEEKS

For big, brawny, bold metropolises, the East is your place. These are the cities that never sleep.

Begin with a few days in history-rich **Boston**. Walk the Freedom Trail past Paul Revere's house. Hang out in Harvard Sq's cafes and bookshops, and chow down in North End trattorias and oyster houses. Then catch the train to **New York City**. With four days, you can indulge in iconic Manhattan and beyond. Stroll Central Park, walk the canyons of Wall St, go bohemian in Greenwich Village and catch a ferry to the Statue of Liberty. For a more local scene, join residents on the High Line, in Nolita's stylish shops and in Queens' creative microbreweries and galleries.

Next hop onboard a train to **Philadelphia**, which is practically down the block from NYC. Philly was the birthplace of American independence, and has the Liberty Bell and Declaration of Independence artifacts to prove it. Spend a few days touring the historic sites and indulging in foodie neighborhoods like East Passyunk. Don't leave the Northeast without spending a few days in **Washington, DC**, a quick trip by bus or train. Beyond the staggering number of free museums and monuments – the Air and Space Museum and Lincoln Memorial among them – the US capital has rich dining and drinking scenes in Logan Circle, Shaw and along U St. Who knows what politico might be swirling a whisky next to you?

It's a long haul to **Miami** (flying is the easy way to go), so allocate four days to get your money's worth exploring the exotic museums and galleries, the art-deco district, Little Havana and sexy, sultry South Beach. For a change of pace, day-trip to the **Everglades** and commune with alligators. Keep the Southern thing going in jazz-loving **New Orleans**, with a soundtrack of smokin'-hot funk/brass bands and the sizzle of Cajun and Creole food. Three days of heavy eating with locals in Uptown, the Central Business District, Marigny and the Bywater should do it.

Last, but not least, **Chicago** leaps up; the *City of New Orleans* train is a scenic way to arrive. Bike to the beach, see mod art in Millennium Park and plug into the blues.

The Great Outdoors

This trip is for those who like their nature ancient and wild. Timbered mountains, raging rivers and sheltered islands are all on tap.

Shenandoah National Park rolls out the welcome mat: this sliver of gorgeousness straddles the Blue Ridge Mountains, so-named for their color when glimpsed in the hazy cerulean distance. Besides scenic drives, hiking is the big to-do here. Five hundred miles of paths – including 100 miles of the Appalachian Trail – wind by spring wildflowers, summer waterfalls and fiery autumn leaves. More activities await a few hours west at **Monongahela National Forest**, where you can strap on ropes for Seneca Rocks or a bicycle helmet for the Greenbrier River Trail. Adventure-sports enthusiasts will find their wet-and-wild bliss nearby at **New River Gorge National River**. Outfitters provide white-water rafting gear for the infamous Class V rapids.

Next up: **Great Smoky Mountains National Park**. Though it's the USA's most popular patch of parkland, you can leave most of the crowds behind if you're willing to hike or paddle (studies have shown that 95% of tourists here never venture more than 100 yards from their cars!). After a day spent in the wilderness surrounded by lush, heather-colored peaks, there's nothing quite like arriving in **Gatlinburg**, the park's kitschy base. Prepare for fudge shops, *Ripley's Believe It or Not* oddities and moonshine distilleries.

So goes the first week. Now it's time to fuel up for the twisty drive through the mountains and across to the coast, where the **Outer Banks** pay off big. Laid-back beach towns full of locally owned ice-cream shops and mom-and-pop motels dot the windswept barrier islands. Check out **Cape Hatteras**, with its unspoiled dunes, marshes and woodlands, or catch the ferry to remote **Ocracoke Island**, where the wild ponies run. Speaking of which: more wild horses roam **Assateague Island**, which floats to the north between Virginia and Maryland. It too offers brilliant, secluded beaches and a landscape ripe for birding, kayaking, crabbing and fishing.

Family-friendly, gay-friendly **Rehoboth Beach** bestows traditional gingerbread houses, kiddie amusements and a big ol' boardwalk along the oceanfront.

Top: Blues musician
Eddie Shaw at Kingston
Mines, Chicago (p537)

Bottom: Bodie Island
Lighthouse (p335),
North Carolina Coast

Plan Your Trip

Road Trips & Scenic Drives

There's no better way to experience the region than on a classic four-wheeled journey. Dawdle in diners along the Lincoln Hwy. Marvel at mansions on the Natchez Trace Parkway. Climb through the Appalachians on the Blue Ridge Parkway. Explore Hwy 1's beaches. Or swing into bluesy joints along the Great River Rd.

Blue Ridge Parkway

Snaking through the Appalachian Mountains of Virginia and North Carolina, the parkway immerses road trippers in glorious highlands scenery, with plenty of pull-offs for vista-gaping, hiking and Southern hospitality.

Why Go

Although it skirts dozens of small towns and a few metropolitan areas, the Blue Ridge Parkway feels far removed from modern-day America. Here, rustic log cabins with creaky rocking chairs on the front porches still dot the hillsides, while signs for folk-art shops and live-bluegrass-music joints entice travelers onto meandering side roads. Log-cabin diners dish up heaping piles of buckwheat pancakes with blackberry preserves and a side of country ham.

When you need to work off all that good Southern cooking, over 100 hiking trails can be accessed along the Blue Ridge Parkway, from gentle nature walks to rough-and-ready tramps along the legendary Appalachian Trail. Go canoeing, kayaking or inner-tubing along rushing rivers, or dangle a fishing line over the side of a rowboat on petite lakes.

Best Experiences

Best Beaches
See dazzling coastal scenery on Florida's Hwy 1.

Best Oddball Sights
Discover goofball roadside attractions on Route 66 and the Lincoln Hwy.

Best Scenery
Watch dramatic sunsets over the Appalachian Mountains on the Blue Ridge Parkway.

Best Music
Listen to blues at a Memphis juke joint on the Great River Rd, or crazy fiddling at a Galax mountain music hall on the Blue Ridge Parkway.

Best Food
Fork into Nashville's fried chicken and biscuits on the Natchez Trace, or New Orleans' famed Creole fare on the Great River Rd.

Best History
Explore the Civil War supersight of Gettysburg on the Lincoln Hwy, or 450-year-old St Augustine on Florida Hwy 1.

Road Trips & Scenic Drives

| 0 | 1000 km |
| 0 | 500 miles |

ATLANTIC OCEAN

1. Blue Ridge Parkway
2. Great River Road
3. Lincoln Highway
4. Natchez Trace Parkway
5. Florida Highway 1

The Route

The bucolic byway connects Virginia's Shenandoah National Park with Great Smoky Mountains National Park, straddling the North Carolina–Tennessee border. Towns along the way include Boone and Asheville in North Carolina and Galax and Roanoke in Virginia, with Charlottesville, VA, also a short drive away. Bigger cities within range of the parkway include Washington, DC (140 miles), and Richmond, VA (95 miles).

Many road trippers also add Skyline Drive (p317) onto their Blue Ridge route. The bendy, 105-mile Skyline connects to the parkway's northern end and ups the scenic ante by doling out mind-blowing mountain vistas on its ramble through Shenandoah National Park. One caveat: you will have to pay a $25 fee to travel the road – this is not a toll, but rather the park's admission charge.

When to Go

April through October, when visitor facilities are open (many close during winter) is best. May is best for wildflowers. Leaf-peepers pour in during October. Expect big crowds during the summer or early fall.

Resources

Blue Ridge Parkway (www.blueridgeparkway.org) Maps, activities and places to stay along the way. Also offers the free *Blue Ridge Parkway Travel Planner* to download.

Hiking the Blue Ridge Parkway (Randy Johnson; 2010) This book offers in-depth trail descriptions, topographic maps and other essential info for hikes both short and long.

Skyline Drive (www.visitskylinedrive.org) Lodging, hiking and wildlife along the picturesque addendum to the parkway.

Time & Mileage

Time At least two days, but allow five days to do it right. It's slow going on the steep, curvy roads, plus you'll want to pit-stop for hiking, eating and sightseeing.

Mileage 469 miles.

Start/End Front Royal, VA/Cherokee, NC.

Great River Road

The epic roadway edges the Mississippi River from its headwaters in northern Minnesota's pine forests all the way south to its endpoint in New Orleans. For a look at America across cultural divides – North/South, urban/rural, Baptist/bohemian – this is the road trip to make.

Why Go

The sweeping scenery awes as you meander alongside America's longest river, from the rolling plains of the north down to the sun-baked cotton fields of the Mississippi Delta. Wind-hewn bluffs, dense forests, flower-filled meadows and steamy swamps are all part of the backdrop – along with smokestacks, riverboat casinos and urban sprawl: this is the good, the bad and the ugly of life on the Mississippi.

The Route

Despite the name, the Great River Rd is not a single highway, but a series of linked federal, state and county roads that follow the Mississippi River as it flows through 10 different states. The one constant wherever you are is the green paddle-wheel sign that marks the way.

Small towns provide a glimpse into varying facets of American culture: there's Brainerd, MN, as seen in the Coen brothers' film Fargo; La Crosse, WI, where the world's largest six-pack pops its top; and Nauvoo, IL, a pilgrimage site for Mormons, complete with gleaming white temple.

The southern section of the route traces American musical history, from rock and roll in Memphis to blues in the Mississippi Delta to jazz in New Orleans. You won't go hungry either, with retro diners, Southern barbecue joints and smokehouses, and Cajun taverns and dance halls in Louisiana.

Major urban areas that provide easy access to the road include New Orleans, Memphis, St Louis and Minneapolis.

When to Go

May to October is best, for snow-free weather in the northern states.

Resources

Mississippi River Travel (www.experiencemississippiriver.com) Great resource for history, outdoor recreation and live music in all 10 Great River Rd states.

National Scenic Byways (www.fhwa.dot.gov/byways/byways/2279) Turn-by-turn directions.

Time & Mileage

Time Six days to drive the road from north to south; 10 days enables a more comfortable, realistic pace.

Mileage About 2000 miles.

Start/End Itasca State Park, MN/New Orleans, LA.

Lincoln Highway

America's first transcontinental roadway – begun in 1913 and paved to completion by 1925 – rambles from New York City to San Francisco. Its 1000-mile eastern portion traces a distinctive path through the nation's heartland, leaving giant coffee-pot statues, fried-chicken diners, jellybean murals and other Americana in its wake.

ADVANCE PLANNING

➡ Join an automobile club (p653) that provides 24-hour emergency roadside assistance and discounts on lodging and attractions.

➡ Some international automobile associations have reciprocal agreements with US clubs, so check first and bring your member card from home.

➡ International travelers might want to review the USA's road rules and common road hazards (p654).

➡ Make sure your vehicle has a spare tire, tool kit (eg jack, jumper cables, ice scraper, tire pressure gauge) and emergency equipment (eg flashers).

➡ Bring good maps, especially if you're touring off-road or away from highways. Don't rely solely on a GPS unit – it can malfunction, and in remote areas it may not even work.

➡ Always carry your driver's license (p653) and proof of insurance (p654).

Why Go

The Lincoln Hwy is authentic road tripping, sans much of the hype and commercialization of other famous byways. While the route navigates some of the East's prominent cities – NYC and Philadelphia among them – it also steers well off the tourist path in genuine back-road style. You'll tick off seven states along the way: New York, New Jersey, Pennsylvania, West Virginia, Ohio, Indiana and Illinois.

The Route

Between New York City and Fulton, IL, the roadway cuts across the middle Atlantic and Great Lakes regions. Note that the Lincoln Hwy doesn't appear on most maps, because it's no longer an official road, but rather a patchwork of federal and state highways.

The journey begins at Times Sq, where the bright lights of Broadway provide an epic send-off. From there it's on to New Jersey and Princeton, the natty Ivy League university town. Pennsylvania rolls up next, offering the Liberty Bell and Independence Hall in Philadelphia; quilts and clip-clopping horses in the Amish communities near Lancaster; the Civil War super-site of Gettysburg; and river-tastic, pop art–rich Pittsburgh. Cornfields and haunted prisons flash by in Ohio. Indiana's pit stops include more Amish areas and the town of South Bend, home to the foot-

DOWNLOADS: BLUEGRASS SOUNDS
....

➡ 'Blue Moon of Kentucky' – Bill Monroe and the Blue Grass Boys

➡ 'Foggy Mountain Breakdown' – Earl Scruggs

➡ 'Orange Blossom Special' – Rouse Brothers

➡ 'Rocky Top' – Osborne Brothers

➡ 'Windy Mountain' – Lonesome Pine Fiddlers

➡ 'Flame of Love' – Jim and Jesse

➡ 'I'm a Man of Constant Sorrow' – Stanley Brothers

➡ 'Every Time You Say Goodbye' – Alison Krauss and Union Station

➡ 'Like a Hurricane' – The Dillards

ball-crazed university of Notre Dame. In Illinois the route swipes Chicago's suburbs, then sets a course through small farming communities pressed flat against the horizon. After that the Lincoln Hwy heads over the Mississippi River and onward west to San Francisco.

Cities that provide easy access to the road include New York City, Philadelphia, Pittsburgh and Chicago.

When to Go

April through October is best, when the weather is snow-free and attractions are open (many shut down between November and March).

Resources

Lincoln Highway Association (www.lincolnhigh wayassoc.org) Lots of free info online. It also sells turn-by-turn directions that are the definitive source for navigating the road.

Greetings from the Lincoln Highway: A Road Trip Celebration of America's First Coast-to-Coast Highway (Brian Butko; 2013) Photos, maps and stories to keep you company along the way.

The Lincoln Highway (Michael Wallis; 2007) Coffee-table book filled with gorgeous photos and the lowdown on route hot spots.

Time & Mileage

Time Two and a half days without stopping much, but four or five days lets you soak up the highway's essence.

Mileage About 1000 miles for the eastern portion.

Start/End NYC/Fulton, IL (for eastern portion).

Natchez Trace Parkway

With emerald mounds, jade swamps, hiking trails, opulent mansions, riverside saloons and layer upon layer of American history, the Natchez Trace Parkway is the richest drive in the South.

Why Go

Think about this as you set out: you'll be following the same path as a who's who of historic figures, including Andrew Jackson (7th president of the USA and face of the $20 bill), Jefferson Davis (president of the Confederacy), James Audubon (naturalist

ROUTE 66

For a classic American road trip, nothing beats good ol' Route 66. Nicknamed the 'Mother Road' by novelist John Steinbeck, this string of small-town main streets and country byways first connected big-shouldered Chicago with the waving palm trees of Los Angeles in 1926.

Most of the Mother Road unfurls through the western part of the country, but Illinois' 300-mile portion offers classic, time-warped moseying. Fork into thick slabs of pie in neon-lit diners; snap photos of roadside attractions like the Gemini Giant, a sky-high fiberglass spaceman; and motor on past drive-in movie theaters, mom-and-pop motels and other Americana.

Road trippers with a couple of extra weeks to spare can keep on truckin' all the way to the Pacific. The route's remaining 2100 miles wind by singular sensations such as frozen custard stands in Missouri, a totem-pole park in Oklahoma, a barbed-wire museum in Texas, the Grand Canyon in Arizona, and wild and crazy Santa Monica Pier in California. For more detail, check out www.roadtripusa.com/route-66.

and painter), Meriwether Lewis (famous explorer who died on the Trace in 1809), Ulysses S Grant (18th president of the USA) and – wait for it – a young Elvis Presley. The drive meanders by various cultural and historic sites that let you learn more about each man.

The Route

Nashville is the easiest place to access the parkway, and for country-music fans and wannabe songwriters all over the world, a trip to the city is the ultimate pilgrimage, with boot-stomping honky-tonks, the Country Music Hall of Fame and a sweet historic district to explore. There's also good eatin' at local cafeterias, the ultimate way to indulge in everything from barbecue chicken and pig's feet to turnip greens and baked apples.

About 10 miles beyond Nashville, the road swings by one of the Civil War's bloodiest battlefields at Franklin, where 20,000 Confederates and 17,000 Union soldiers fought on November 30, 1864. Further along are Confederate grave sites for unknown soldiers. Several centuries-old indigenous burial mounds likewise rise up along the way. Emerald Mound, near Natchez, is one of the nation's largest, and the massive grassy pyramid still buzzes with ancient energy.

Other highlights en route include the town of Tupelo – where you can visit the humble house where Elvis grew up, learned to play the guitar and dreamed big – and tree-shaded, milky-green Cypress Swamp, filled with alligators. Natchez itself is a living antebellum museum, all sweeping spiral staircases, chandeliers and thick column houses.

When to Go

April to June and September to November are best. Summer can be hotter than hot.

Resources

Natchez Trace Parkway (www.nps.gov/natr) Park-service website that provides road construction updates, plus information on local activities and historic sites.

Natchez Trace Compact (www.scenictrace.com) State tourism bureaus of Tennessee, Alabama and Mississippi band together to offer route itineraries, maps and event info.

Time & Mileage

Time Three days, though you could do it in two. Travel times aren't exactly speedy on the two-lane road.

Mileage 444 miles.

Start/End Nashville, TN/Natchez, MS.

Florida Highway 1

The coast-hugging thoroughfare features miles and miles of beaches interspersed with fascinating historical sights, from the USA's oldest city to sobering slavery exhibits to NASA rockets. Glittering Miami provides the big finale.

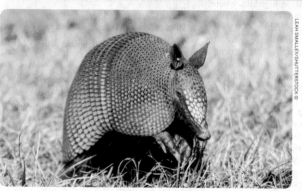

LEAH SMALLEY/SHUTTERSTOCK ©

Top: Florida Highway 1 (p39)

Bottom: An Armadillo on the Natchez Trace Parkway (p38)

Why Go

For quintessential Florida sights and experiences, Hwy 1 spanning the Atlantic shoreline is it: Palm Beach's mansions, Fort Lauderdale's yachts, Miami's domino-clacking Cuban enclave of Little Havana all pop up along the way. Pristine, windswept beaches harboring endangered birds and manatees? They're here (at Canaveral National Seashore). Beaches known for hard-partying nightlife and NASCAR racing? Also here (at Daytona). Delicious seafood shacks and pastel-hued waterfront hotels are everywhere.

The Route

Begin in Florida's northeastern tip at Amelia Island, an upper-class beach-resort town since the 1890s. From there the road drifts south, past cultural parks and plantations where you can see how slaves lived. Pull over in venerable St Augustine, founded in 1565, to seek out Ponce de León's fountain of youth and the Pirate Museum. Lighthouses, unspoiled strands of sand and surfing hot spots flash by. Moving on you'll come to the Kennedy Space Center, where shuttles used to launch into the stratosphere. After that, art-filled West Palm Beach appears among a slew of well-heeled towns. Hwy 1 then saves the best for last: Miami. The sexy city offers eye candy galore, from mural-splashed neigh-borhoods to the world's largest art-deco district to the young and glamorous locals preening around South Beach.

But let's back up a bit and cover a few basics. The road is actually called Hwy A1A (not to be confused with US 1, the larger, faster version that runs parallel). A1A is not continuous – there are a few towns where you have to detour onto other roads before picking up A1A again. Should you want more road-tripping after Miami, hop on US 1, which becomes the scenic Overseas Hwy at Key Largo and dips south to Key West – a fine way to keep the party going.

When to Go

March and April means Spring Break mayhem in Florida. Set out in temperate May or September if you can.

Resources

Florida Scenic Highways (www.floridascenic highways.com) Info for specially designated parts of the highway near St Augustine and Fort Lauderdale.

Highway A1A: Florida at the Edge (Herbert L Hiller; 2007) Part travel guide, part history about the cities and towns along the way.

Time & Mileage

Time Six days to take in the sights.

Mileage 475 miles.

Start/End Amelia Island/Miami.

OTHER GREAT ROAD TRIPS

ROUTE	STATE	START/END	SIGHTS & ACTIVITIES	BEST TIMES
Hwy 12	NC	Corolla/Sealevel	Beaches, lighthouses, Wright Brothers launching site; surfing, ferry rides	Apr-Oct
Hwy 13	WI	Bayfield/Superior	Lakeside beaches, forests, farmlands; nature walks	May-Sep
Hwy 61	MN	Duluth/Canadian Border	State parks, waterfalls, quaint towns; hiking	May-Sep
Kancamagus Hwy	VT	Conway/Lincoln	Craggy mountains, streams, waterfalls; camping, hiking, swimming	May-Sep
Old King's Hwy	MA	Sandwich/Orleans	Historic districts, period homes, coastal scenery	Apr-Oct
Overseas Hwy	FL	Key Largo/Key West	Beaches, protected coral reefs, plates of conch fritters, key lime pie; people-watching, diving	Dec-Apr
Rte 28	NY	Stony Hollow/Arkville	Catskills mountains, lakes, rivers; hiking, leaf-peeping, tubing	May-Sep
VT 100	VT	Stamford/Newport	Rolling pastures, green mountains; hiking, skiing	Jun-Sep

Plan Your Trip

Outdoor Activities

Smoky mountains, wave-bashed beaches, coral reefs, river-cut gorges: the eastern USA has no shortage of spectacular settings for a bit of adventure. No matter what your weakness – hiking, cycling, kayaking, rafting, surfing, diving or skiing – you'll find world-class places to commune with the great outdoors.

Best Outdoors

Best Hiking
Appalachian Trail, Shenandoah National Park (VA), Great Smoky Mountains National Park (NC and TN), Adirondack wilderness (NY)

Best Cycling
Chequamegon National Forest, WI (off-road); Cape Cod Rail Trail, MA (paved); Minneapolis, MN (city riding)

Best Paddling
Boundary Waters, MN (canoeing); New River Gorge National River, VA (white-water rafting); Apostle Islands, WI (kayaking); Pictured Rocks, MI (kayaking)

Best Surfing
Cocoa Beach, FL; Long Island, NY; Coast Guard Beach, MA

Best Diving
Florida Keys, FL (coral garden); Cape Hatteras, NC (Civil War shipwrecks); Dry Tortugas, FL (sea turtles); Crystal River, FL (manatees)

Best Wildlife-Watching
Baxter State Park, ME (moose); Provincetown, MA (whales); Florida Everglades, FL (alligators, manatees, sea turtles); Wabasha, MN (eagles)

Hiking & Trekking

Almost anywhere you go, great hiking and backpacking are within easy striking distance. National parks are ideal for short and long hikes. Beyond them, you'll find troves of state-maintained footpaths. There's no limit to the terrain you can explore, from the dogwood-choked **Wild Azalea Trail** (www.townofwoodworth.com/azalea-trail) in Louisiana to the multistate **North Country National Scenic Trail** (www.nps.gov/noco), winding across rugged landscapes from New York to Minnesota.

Resources

Survive Outdoors (www.surviveoutdoors.com) Dispenses safety and first-aid tips, plus helpful photos of dangerous critters.

Wilderness Survival (Gregory Davenport; 2006) Easily the best book on surviving nearly every contingency.

American Hiking Society (www.americanhiking. org) Links to 'volunteer vacations' building trails.

Backpacker (www.backpacker.com) Premier national magazine for backpackers, from novices to experts.

National Park Service (www.nps.gov) The federal government agency responsible for the management and conservancy of all national park resources, including hiking trails and campsites.

Cycling

Cycling's popularity increases by the day. The nation's biggest cities, led by New York and Chicago, are constantly adding more cycle lanes, and a growing number greenways have started striping the east's picturesque countryside. Minneapolis (MN), Cambridge (MA) and Washington (DC) also rate as among the most bike- (and therefore, eco-) friendly cities in the eastern USA.

Several abandoned rail lines across the region have been converted into paved cycling paths, offering gentle rides through quaint villages, over bridges and alongside verdant pastures. Massachusetts' Cape Cod Rail Trail (p194) is a popular one.

Mountain bikers should steer for Wisconsin's Chequamegon National Forest (p597), revered for its bad-ass trails and grueling Fat Tire Festival (www.cheqfattire.com) in September.

Resources

Bicycling (www.bicycling.com) This magazine has information on city rides, off-road trails and much in between.

Rails-to-Trails Conservancy (www.railstotrails.org) Publishes free trail reviews at www.traillink.com.

Kayaking & Canoeing

Paddlers will find their bliss in the eastern USA. Rentals and instruction are yours for the asking. Kayaking hot spots include Wisconsin's Apostle Islands National Lakeshore (p596), for gliding through arches and sea caves on Lake Superior; Michigan's Pictured Rocks National Lakeshore (p584), to paddle by wildly colored cliffs on Lake Superior; and Maine's Penobscot Bay (p245), to poke around the briny waters and spruce-fringed islets.

Canoeing is downright legendary here, including the 12,000 miles of wet and wild routes in Minnesota's Boundary Waters (p609) and Alabama's Bartram Canoe Trail (www.alabamacanoetrails.com), with 300,000 acres of marshy delta bayous, lakes and rivers.

Florida's Everglades National Park (p477), one of America's great natural treasures, is another legendary destination

THE APPALACHIAN TRAIL

Completed in 1937, the country's longest footpath is 2180 miles, crossing six national parks, traversing eight national forests and hitting 14 states from Georgia to Maine. Misty mountains, deep woods, flowery pastures and bear sightings are the rewards. Each year, roughly 2500 hardy souls attempt to hike the entire trail – only one in four makes it all the way through. But don't let that discourage you. It's estimated that two to three million people trek a portion of the Appalachian Trail annually, thanks to easy-to-access day hikes up and down its length. See www.appalachiantrail.org for more information.

for hitting the water – paddle past basking alligators and herons as you work your way through the vast network of mangrove canals and peaceful lakes that make up the park, which encompasses a whopping 1.5 million acres.

Resources

American Canoe Association (www.americancanoe.org) Has a water-trails database for canoeing and kayaking, as well as information on local paddling clubs and courses (including stand-up paddleboarding).

Whitewater Rafting

East of the Mississippi, West Virginia has an arsenal of famous white water. First, there's the New River Gorge National River (p326), which, despite its name, is one of the oldest rivers in the world. Slicing from North Carolina into West Virginia, it cuts a deep gorge, known as the Grand Canyon of the East, producing frothy rapids in its wake.

Then there's the Gauley (p326), arguably among the world's finest white water. Revered for its ultra-steep and turbulent chutes, the venerable Appalachian river is a watery roller coaster, dropping more than 668ft and churning up 100-plus rapids in a mere 28 miles. Six more rivers, all in the same neighborhood, offer training grounds for less-experienced river rats.

PLAN YOUR TRIP OUTDOOR ACTIVITIES

The Boundary Waters Canoe Area Wilderness (p609)

Resources

American Whitewater (www.americanwhite water.org) Works to preserve America's wild rivers; has links to local rafting clubs.

Surfing

The Atlantic states harbor some terrific and unexpected surfing spots – especially if you're after more moderate swells. The warmest waters are off Florida's Gulf Coast. Top spots to hang 10:

Cocoa Beach (p488) **and Melbourne Beach** (Ocean Park, Atlantic St), **Florida** Small crowds and mellow waves make it a paradise for beginners and longboarders. Just south is the Inlet, known for consistent surf and crowds to match.

Long Island, NY (p123) More than a dozen surfing areas dot the area, from Montauk's oft-packed Ditch Plains to Nassau County's Long Beach, with its 3-mile stretch of curling waves.

Coast Guard Beach (Ocean View Dr, off Doane Rd), **Eastham, MA** Part of the Cape Cod National Seashore, this family-friendly beach is known

for its consistent shortboard/longboard swell all summer long.

Resources

Surfer (www.surfermag.com) Has travel reports covering the eastern seaboard and just about every break in the USA.

Surfing America (www.surfingamerica.org) The national governing body for the sport of surfing.

Diving

Florida has the lion's share of great diving, with more than 1000 miles of coastline subdivided into 20 unique undersea areas. There are hundreds of sites and countless dive shops offering equipment and guided excursions. South of West Palm Beach, you'll find clear waters and fantastic year-round diving with ample reefs. In the Panhandle you can scuba in the calm and balmy waters of the Gulf of Mexico; off Pensacola (p509) and Destin are fabulous wreck dives (www.floridapanhandledive trail.com), and you can dive with manatees

TIPS FOR VISITING NATIONAL PARKS

➡ Park entrance fees vary, from nothing at all to $30 per vehicle.

➡ The 'America the Beautiful' annual pass ($80; https://store.usgs.gov/pass), which allows admission for four adults and all children under 16 years old to all federal recreational lands for 12 calendar months, is sold at park entrances and visitor centers.

➡ Lifetime senior-citizen passes ($10) are also available for US citizens over 62.

➡ Park lodges and campgrounds book up far in advance; for summer vacations, reserve six months to one year ahead.

➡ Some parks offer first-come, first-served campgrounds – for these, try to arrive between 10am and noon, when other campers may be checking out.

➡ For overnight backpacking and some day hikes, you'll need a wilderness permit; the number of permits is often subject to quotas, so apply far in advance (up to six months before your trip, depending on park regulations).

near **Crystal River** (☑352-563-2088; www. fws.gov/crystalriver; 1502 SE Kings Bay Dr; ◷8am-5:30pm Mon-Fri).

The Florida Keys are the crown jewel. Expect a brilliant mix of marine habitats, North America's only living coral garden and the occasional shipwreck. Key Largo is home to the John Pennekamp Coral Reef State Park (p482) and more than 200 miles of underwater idyll. The expansive reefs around **Dry Tortugas National Park** (☑305-242-7700; www.nps.gov/drto) swarm with barracuda, sea turtles and a couple of hundred sunken ships.

Other popular places to submerge in the eastern waters include North Carolina's Cape Hatteras National Seashore (p335), where you can explore Civil War wrecks and encounter tiger sand sharks, and **Lake Ouachita** (www.lakeouachita.org), Arkansas' largest lake, known for its pristine mountain waters and 16-mile water-based trail.

Resources

Scuba Diving (www.scubadiving.com) Provides the latest on diving destinations in the USA and abroad.

PADI (www.padi.com) Professional Association of Diving Instructors: the world's leading scuba diver training organization.

Skiing & Winter Sports

Vermont's first-rate **Stowe Mountain** (☑888-253-4849, 802-253-3000; www.stowe. com; 5781 Mountain Rd; lift tickest adult/child $124/104) offers sweet slopes – freeze your tail off on the lifts, but thaw out nicely après-ski in timbered bars with local brews. In Lake Placid (p138), New York, you can luge or bobsled at old Olympic facilities. Snowmobiles rev in northern Wisconsin, Michigan and Minnesota; in Minnesota, Voyageurs National Park (p610) hosts lots of wintry action on its frozen waterways.

Resources

SkiMag (www.skimag.com) Provides lodging info, downloadable trail maps and more.

Ski Central (www.skicentral.com) A one-stop shop for all things ski and snow in North America.

Plan Your Trip
Eat & Drink Like a Local

The East's cuisine mixes myriad cultures, and each region has evolved its own unique flavor palette. From seafood in Maine to slow-cooked brisket in Mississippi, you're in for a treat. Tipplers will find the East to be the country's most spirited side. A booming microbrewery industry has brought artful beers to every corner of the region, while New York and Virginia give wine drinkers vintages to appreciate, and Kentucky pours on the bourbon.

Lip-Smacking Festivals

Crawfish Festival
(www.bbcrawfest.com; Breaux Bridge, LA; ☺May) If you're in town during the first week of May, don't miss the gluttony of music, dancing and Cajun food at the Crawfish Festival.

Kentucky Bourbon Festival
(www.kybourbonfestival.com; Bardstown, KY ; ☺Sep) Historic downtown Bardstown, the 'Bourbon Capital of the World,' comes alive.

Maine Lobster Festival
(www.mainelobsterfestival.com; Rockland, ME; ☺early Aug) Lobster fanatics won't want to miss the five-day Maine Lobster Festival, there's plenty of live music, parades, an art show and a fun run.

World's Largest Brat Fest
(www.bratfest.com; Madison, WI; ☺late May) Bratwurst festival with a backdrop of carnival rides and bands.

Local Specialties
NYC: Foodie Heaven

They say that you could eat at a different restaurant every night of your life in New York City and not exhaust the possibilities. Considering that there are more than 20,000 restaurants in the five boroughs, with scores of new ones opening each year, it's true. Owing to its huge immigrant population and an influx of over 50 million tourists annually, New York captures the title of America's greatest restaurant city. Its diverse neighborhoods serve up authentic Italian food and thin-crust pizza, all manner of Asian food, French haute cuisine and classic Jewish deli food, from bagels to piled-high pastrami on rye. More exotic cuisines are found here as well, from Ethiopian to Scandinavian.

Don't let NYC's image as expensive get to you: you can eat well here without breaking the bank, especially if you limit your cocktail intake. There may be no free lunch in New York, but compared to other world cities, eating here can be a bargain.

New England: Clambakes & Lobster Boils

New England claims to have the nation's best seafood, and who's to argue? The North Atlantic Ocean offers up clams, mussels, oysters and huge lobsters, along with shad, bluefish and cod. The bounty gets stirred into a mighty fine chowder (soup), for which every seafood shack up the coast has its own secret recipe, put to the test during summertime chowder fests and cook-offs. The clambake is another tradition, where shellfish are buried in a pit fire with foil-wrapped corn, chicken and sausages. Fried clam fritters and lobster rolls (lobster meat with mayonnaise served in a bread bun) are served throughout the region.

Vermont makes excellent cheeses, Massachusetts harvests cranberries (a Thanksgiving staple), and New England's forests drip sweet maple syrup. Still hungry? Connecticut is famed for its thin-crust New Haven–style pizza (best topped with white clams); Boston specializes in baked beans and brown bread; and Rhode Islanders pour coffee syrup into milk and embrace traditional cornmeal johnnycakes.

Mid-Atlantic: Cheesesteaks, Crabcakes & Scrapple

From New York down through Virginia, the Mid-Atlantic states share a long coastline and a cornucopia of apple, pear and berry farms. New Jersey wins prizes for tomatoes and New York's Long Island for potatoes. Chesapeake Bay's blue crabs make diners swoon, as do Pennsylvania Dutch Country's heaped plates of chicken pot pie, noodles and meatloaf-like scrapple. In Philadelphia you can gorge on 'Philly cheesesteaks,' made with thin strips of sautéed beef, onions and melted cheese on a bun. Virginia serves its salt-cured 'country-style' ham with biscuits. New York's Finger Lakes, Hudson Valley and Long Island uncork highly regarded wines to accompany the region's well-set table.

The South: Barbecue, Biscuits and Gumbo

No region is prouder of its food culture than the South, which has a long history of mingling Anglo, French, African, Spanish and Native American foods. Slow-cooked barbecue is one of the top stokers of regional pride; there are as many meaty and saucy variations as there are towns in the South. Southern fried chicken and catfish pop out of the pan crisp on the outside and moist inside. Fluffy hot biscuits, corn bread, sweet potatoes, collard greens, and – most passionately – grits (ground corn cooked to a cereal-like consistency) accompany Southern plates, all butter-smothered. Treasured dessert recipes tend to produce big layer cakes or pies made with pecans, bananas and citrus. Sweet iced tea (nonalcoholic) or a cool mint-julep cocktail (with bourbon) help wash it down.

For the region's crème de la crème, pull up a chair at Louisiana's tables. The state stands out for its two main cuisines: Cajun

PLAN YOUR TRIP EAT & DRINK LIKE A LOCAL

MEALS OF A LIFETIME

Rose's Luxury (p270) Southern comfort food by candlelight in an industrial setting in Washington, DC.

Ulele (p497) Alligator beans, okra fries, pompano fish and guava pie in a former water-pumping station in Tampa, FL.

Alinea (p534) Book months in advance for multiple courses of three-Michelin-starred molecular gastronomy at this legendary Chicago restaurant.

Cochon Butcher (p440) The savory sandwiches of this 'swine bar and deli' encapsulate the best of New Orleans.

Eleven Madison Park (Map p70; ☎212-889-0905; www.elevenmadisonpark.com; 11 Madison Ave, btwn 24th & 25th Sts; tasting menu $295; ⏱5:30-10pm Mon-Thu & noon-1pm Fri-Sun; ⑤N/R, 6 to 23rd St) Inimitable poster-child for sustainable cooking – one of only six NYC three-Michelin-starred restaurants.

Pye Boat Noodle (p105) Top NYC Thai restaurant serves up fedora-wearing wait-staff, boat noodles, papaya salad and pink seafood soup!

WEIRD REGIONAL FOODS

Scrapple (rural Pennsylvania) Pork and cornmeal meatloaf

Lutefisk (Minnesota) Aged, gelatinous whitefish

Deep-fried cheese curds (Wisconsin)

Horseshoe sandwich (Illinois) Hamburger and fries on toast with cheese sauce

food is found in the bayou country and marries native spices like sassafras and chili peppers to provincial French cooking. Creole food is more urban and centered in New Orleans, where zippy dishes like shrimp rémoulade, crabmeat ravigote and gumbo (a soupy stew of chicken, shellfish and/or sausage, and okra) have eaters dabbing their brow.

The Great Lakes: Burgers, Bacon & Beer

Folks from the Great Lakes love their food. Portions are huge – this is farm country, after all, where people need sustenance to get their work done. The region is tops for serving American classics like pot roast, meatloaf, steak and pork chops; add walleye, perch and other freshwater fish to menus in towns near the Great Lakes. Count on a nice cold beer to complement the wares. Chicago stands tall as the region's best place to pile a plate, with hole-in-the-wall ethnic eateries

TOP VEGETARIAN NOSH

Green Elephant (p242), Portland, ME

Clover Food Lab (www.cloverfoodlab.com; 27 School St; mains $8-12; ⊙7am-11pm Mon-Fri, 8am-11pm Sat, 8am-8pm Sun; ⊠; Ⓣ State), Boston, MA

Moosewood Restaurant (p135), Ithaca, NY

Zenith (p164), Pittsburgh, PA

Butcher's Daughter (p96), New York City

Chef Allen's Farm-to-Table Dinner (p468), Miami, FL

cooking alongside many of the country's most acclaimed restaurants. Another great place to sample Midwestern foods is at a county fair, which offers everything from bratwurst to fried dough to grilled corn on the cob. Elsewhere at diners and family restaurants, you'll taste the varied influences of Eastern European, Scandinavian, Latino and Asian immigrants, especially in the cities.

Harvest Time

January The ice wine grape harvest takes place around the Finger Lakes, New York, and in northern Michigan. Sweet dessert drinks ensue.

March In Vermont and Maine, it's sugaring season, when fresh maple syrup flows. Down South, crawfish ramps up: Louisiana harvests around 110 million pounds of the critters between now and May.

May Georgia's peach harvest begins midmonth and goes until mid-August. To the north, Chesapeake Bay blue crabs hit the market through September.

July Early in the month Michigan goes wild, picking tart cherries and hosting fruity festivities like the International Cherry Pit Spitting Championship in Eau Claire.

August The action shifts to New England: the coast's lobster shacks and clambakes are in full swing, while Maine's wild blueberries get heaped into pies.

September & October It's prime time to pick apples in New York and Michigan (the nation's second- and third-largest producers). Cider houses pour their wares. Meanwhile it's cranberry season in Massachusetts and Wisconsin.

Habits and Customs

For breakfast Americans love their eggs and bacon, waffles and hash browns, and big glasses of orange juice. Most of all, they love a steaming cup of coffee. After a mid-morning snack break, the lunch hour of most American workers affords time enough for just a sandwich, quick burger or hearty salad. While you may spot (rarely)

Seafood clambake (p47)

diners drinking a glass of wine or beer with their noontime meal, the days of the 'three-martini lunch' are long gone. Early in the evening, people settle in to a more substantial weeknight dinner, which, given the workload of so many two-career families, might be takeout or prepackaged dishes.

Americans tend to eat dinner early, usually between 6pm and 8pm. In smaller towns, it may be hard to find anywhere to eat after 8:30pm or so. Dinner parties usually begin around 6:30pm or 7pm, with cocktails followed by a meal. If invited to dinner, it's polite to be prompt: ideally, you should plan to arrive within 15 minutes of the designated time. Americans are notoriously informal in their dining manners, although they will usually wait until everyone is served before eating.

Food Experiences

Many cooking schools offer courses for enthusiastic amateur chefs.

Chopping Block (☎312-644-6360; www. thechoppingblock.com; 222 Merchandise Mart Plaza, Ste 107; 2½hr class $50-95) Master knife skills or learn to make deep-dish pizza. Chicago's Chopping Block offers loads of cooking classes at its shop in Lincoln Sq, as well as downtown at its branch in the Merchandise Mart.

Zingerman's Bakehouse (☎734-761-7255; www. bakewithzing.com; 3723 Plaza Dr) Offers popular 'bake-cations,' making bread or pastries in Michigan's Ann Arbor.

League of Kitchens (www.leagueofkitchens.com; 2½/5½hr course $95/145) This unique service links you with new Americans who'll teach you the culinary arts of their home country (like shaping Uzbek dumplings, baking Argentinean *alfajores* or frying Trini roti), from the kitchens of their own homes.

Coke

In many parts of the South, a 'coke' means any kind of flavored, carbonated soft drink, so you may have to specify – if you say 'I'll have a Coke,' the waiter might ask, 'What kind?'. In the nation's heartland, the generic term is 'pop,' while the East Coast uses 'soda.'

Plan Your Trip
Travel with Children

From north to south, you'll find superb attractions for all ages: bucket-and-spade fun at the beach, amusement parks, zoos, eye-popping aquariums and natural-history exhibits, hands-on science museums, camping adventures, battlefields, leisurely bike rides through the countryside and plenty of other activities likely to wow young ones.

Best Regions for Kids

New York, New Jersey & Pennsylvania
New York City offers adventure such as row-boating in Central Park and kid-friendly museums. Head to the Jersey shore for boardwalk fun and to Pennsylvania for Amish Country horse-and-buggy rides.

New England
Boston's waterfront and green spaces entice with an aquarium, an 18th-century warship and pedal-powered swan boats. Plimoth Plantation, with its re-created Wampanoag and Pilgrim villages, is good family fun.

Washington, DC & the Capital Region
Washington has unrivaled allure for families with free museums, a panda-loving zoo and boundless green spaces. Virginia's Williamsburg is a slice of 18th-century America with costumed interpreters and fanciful activities.

Florida
Orlando's Walt Disney World® Resort is well worth planning a vacation around. Afterwards hit the state's beautiful beaches.

Eastern USA for Kids

Accommodations
Motels and hotels typically have rooms with two beds, which are ideal for families. Some also have roll-away beds or cribs that can be brought into the room for an extra charge – but keep in mind these are usually portable cribs, which not all children sleep well in. Some hotels offer 'kids stay free' programs for children up to 12 or sometimes 18 years old. Be wary of B&Bs, as many don't allow children; inquire before reserving.

Babysitting
Resort hotels may have on-call babysitting services; otherwise, ask the front-desk staff or concierge to help you make arrangements. Always ask if babysitters are licensed and insured, what they charge per hour per child, whether there's a minimum fee, and if they charge extra for transportation or meals. Most tourist bureaus list local resources for childcare and recreation facilities, medical services and so on.

Dining
The local restaurant industry seems built on family-style service: children are not

just accepted at most places, but are often encouraged by special children's menus with smaller portions and lower prices. In some restaurants children under a certain age even eat for free. Restaurants usually provide high chairs and booster seats. Some restaurants may also offer children crayons and puzzles, and occasionally live performances by cartoon-like characters.

Restaurants without children's menus don't necessarily discourage kids, though higher-end restaurants might. Even at the nicer places, however, if you show up early enough (right at dinnertime opening hours, often 5pm or 6pm), you can usually eat without too much stress – and you'll likely be joined by other foodies with kids. You can ask if the kitchen will make a smaller order of a dish, or if they will split a normal-size main dish between two plates for the kids. Chinese, Mexican and Italian restaurants seem to be the best bet for finicky young eaters.

Farmers markets are growing in popularity in the region, and every sizable town has at least one a week. This is a good place to assemble a first-rate picnic, sample local specialties and support independent growers in the process. After getting your stash, head to the nearest park or waterfront.

Discounts for Children

Child concessions often apply for tours, admission fees and transport, with some discounts as high as 50% off the adult rate. However, the definition of 'child' can vary from under 12 to under 16 years. Unlike in Europe, few popular sights have discount rates for families; those that do will help you save a few dollars compared to buying individual tickets. Most sights give free admission to children under two years.

Transportation

Every car-rental agency should be able to provide an appropriate child seat, since these are required in every state, but you need to request it when booking; expect to pay around $13 more per day.

Domestic airlines don't charge for children under two years of age. Those two years and up must have a seat, and discounts are unlikely. Rarely, some resort areas (like Disney) offer a 'kids fly free'

promotion. Amtrak and other train operators run similar deals (with kids up to age 15 riding free) on various routes.

Children's Highlights

Outdoor Adventure

Everglades, FL (p477) Kayak, canoe or join guided walks in the swamps.

New River Gorge National River, WV (p326) Go white-water rafting.

Provincetown, MA (p194) Spot humpbacks spouting on a whale-watch tour.

Mammoth Cave National Park, KY (p390) Take a jaunt through the underground chambers.

Theme Parks & Zoos

Walt Disney World® Resort, FL (p505) Immerse your children in the mightiest attraction of all, with four action-packed parks spread across 20,000 acres.

Bronx Zoo, NYC (p87) Hop the subway from Manhattan to one of the USA's biggest and best zoos.

Lion Country Safari, West Palm Beach, FL (561-793-1084; www.lioncountrysafari.com; 2003 Lion Country Safari Rd; adult/child $35/26; 9:30am-5:30pm;) Drive among 900 wild creatures roaming the landscape.

EASTERN LIT FOR KIDS

➡ *Little Women* (1868) Louisa May Alcott's wonderful book about girls growing up in 19th-century Concord, Massachusetts.

➡ *Paul Revere's Ride* (1861) Henry Wadsworth Longfellow combines history, poetry and suspense in his classic.

➡ *Eloise* (1955) Kay Thompson's six-year-old Eloise lives in the Plaza Hotel in NYC, a prime place to launch into all sorts of mischief.

➡ *The Wright 3* (2006) Tween sleuths solve a mystery involving ghosts, treasure and Frank Lloyd Wright's Robie House in Chicago in Blue Balliett's book.

Wisconsin Dells, **WI** (p593) Splash it up at 20-plus water parks and watch water-skiing thrill shows.

Cedar Point, **OH** (p558) Ride some of the planet's wildest roller coasters, then play at the mile-long beachfront and water park.

Six Flags, **DC** (www.sixflags.com/america) It's America's stalwart amusement-park chain, with nine coaster-rich locations in the eastern USA, including one in Washington, DC.

Traveling in Time

Williamsburg, **VA** (p308) Don 18th-century garb and mingle with costumed interpreters in the history-rich triangle where America began.

Fort Mackinac, **MI** (p583) Plug your ears as soldiers in 19th-century costumes fire muskets and cannons.

Freedom Trail, **Boston**, **MA** (p187) Go on a walking tour with Ben Franklin (or at least his 21st-century look-alike).

Lincoln Presidential Library & Museum, **Springfield**, **IL** (p543) Learn about America's favorite president via holograms, a replica log cabin and other interactive features.

St Augustine, **FL** (p490) Rattle along in a horse-drawn carriage through the historic streets of this 450-year-old city.

Planning

To find family-oriented accommodations and restaurants among our reviews, just look for the child-friendly icon.

When to Go

➡ Peak travel season is June to August, when schools are out and the weather is warmest. Expect high prices and abundant crowds – meaning long lines at amusement and water parks, fully booked resorts and heavy traffic on the roads; book well in advance for popular destinations.

➡ High season for winter resorts (in the Catskills and White Mountains) runs from January to March.

Need to Know

➡ Many public toilets have a baby-changing table (sometimes in men's toilets, too), and gender-neutral 'family' facilities appear in airports.

➡ Medical services and facilities in America are of a high standard.

➡ Items such as baby food, formula and disposable diapers (nappies) are widely available – including organic options – in supermarkets across the country.

➡ Single parents or guardians traveling with anyone under 18 should carry proof of legal custody or a notarized letter from the non-accompanying parent(s) authorizing the trip. This isn't required, but it can help avoid potential problems entering the USA.

Helpful Resources

For all-round information and advice, check out Lonely Planet's *Travel with Children*. To get the kids excited, check out *Not for Parents: USA* (also by Lonely Planet), filled with cool stories about candy bars, astronauts, heroic animals and more.

Baby's Away (www.babysaway.com) Rents cribs, high chairs, car seats, strollers and even toys at locations across the country.

Family Travel Files (www.thefamilytravelfiles.com) Ready-made vacation ideas, destination profiles and travel tips.

Kids.gov (www.kids.usa.gov) Enormous, eclectic national resource; download songs and activities or even link to the CIA Kids' Page.

Travel Babees (www.travelbabees.com) Another reputable baby-gear rental outfit, with locations nationwide.

Regions at a Glance

New York City is the East's hub. More than eight million inhabitants live in this megacity, a world center for fashion, food, arts and finance. The crowd thins out in neighboring New Jersey and Pennsylvania, where beaches, mountains and literal horse-and-buggy hamlets join the landscape. New England arches north to rocky shores, clapboard fishing villages and Ivy League universities.

The Mid-Atlantic begins the march south through voluptuous valleys and a slew of historic sites. By the time you reach the true South, the pace has slowed, pecan pie tempts on the table and bluesy tunes drift from juke joints. Surreal Florida brings on mermaids, manatees, Mickey Mouse and Miami, while the sensible Great Lakes region prefers burgers and beer with its natural attractions.

New York, New Jersey & Pennsylvania

Arts
History
Outdoors

Culture Spot

Home to the Met, MoMA and Broadway – and that's just New York City. Buffalo, Philadelphia and Pittsburgh have also world-renowned cultural institutions.

A Living Past

From preserved Gilded Age mansions in the Hudson Valley to Independence National Historic Park in Philadelphia and sites dedicated to formative moments in the nation's founding.

Wild Outdoors

The outdoors lurks just beyond the city's gaze, with hiking in the Adirondack wilderness and Catskill mountains, rafting down the Delaware River, and ocean frolics along the Jersey Shore and Hamptons.

p55

New England

Seafood
History
Outdoors

Land of Lobsters

New England is justifiably famous for its fresh seafood. Seaside eateries pepper the coast, where you can suck oysters, crack lobster claws and spoon into clam chowder while watching day-boats haul in the next meal's catch.

Legends of the Past

From the Pilgrims' landing in Plymouth and the witch hysteria in Salem to Paul Revere's revolutionary ride, New England has shaped American history.

Fall Foliage

The brilliance of fall in these parts is legendary. Changing leaves put on a fiery display all around New England, from the Litchfield Hills in Connecticut all the way up to the White Mountains in New Hampshire and Maine.

p166

Washington, DC & the Capital Region

Arts
History
Food

Museums & Music

Washington, DC has a superb collection of museums and galleries. Also mountain music on Virginia's Crooked Road and famous theaters and edgy art in Baltimore.

Times Past

For historical lore, Jamestown, Williamsburg and Yorktown offer windows into Colonial America, while Civil War battlefields litter the Virginia countryside.

Culinary Delights

Feasts await: Maryland blue crabs, oysters and seafood platters; international restaurants in DC; and farm-to-table dining rooms in Baltimore, Charlottesville, Staunton and Rehoboth.

p248

The South

Food
Music
Charm

Biscuits & Barbecue

Slow-cooked barbecue, fried chicken and catfish, butter-smothered biscuits, corn bread, grits and spicy Cajun-Creole dishes.

Country, Jazz & Blues

Nowhere on earth has a soundtrack as influential as the South. Head to music meccas for the authentic experience: country in Nashville, blues in Memphis and big-band jazz in New Orleans.

Southern Belles

Picture-book towns such as Charleston and Savannah have long captivated visitors with their historic tree-lined streets, antebellum architecture and friendly, down-home welcome. Other charmers include Chapel Hill, Oxford, Chattanooga and Natchez.

p330

Florida

Beaches
Outdoors
History

Shades of Sand

You'll find an array of sandy shores from steamy South Beach to upscale Palm Beach, island allure on Sanibel and Captiva, and panhandle rowdiness in Pensacola.

Outdoor Adventures

From the world-class theme parks of Orlando and Tampa, to getting swampy with egrets, eagles and alligators, or snorkeling with Florida manatees.

Historical Bounty

Florida has a complicated soul: it's the home of Miami's colorful art-deco district and Little Havana, plus a wealth of some of the nation's most historical but little-known attractions in St Augustine and the rich island heritage of Key West.

p452

Great Lakes

Food
Music
Culture

Heartland Cuisine

From James Beard Award–winning restaurants in Chicago and Minneapolis to fresh-from-the-dairy milkshakes, the region's farms, orchards and breweries satisfy the palate.

Rock & Roll

Home to the Rock and Roll Hall of Fame, blowout fests like Lollapalooza and a cacophony of thrashing clubs, Chicago knows how to turn up the volume.

Quirky Sights

A big ball of twine, a mustard museum, a cow-doo throwing contest: these gems of Americana appear along the region's back roads and in the backyards of passionate folks with imagination and maybe a little too much time on their hands.

p512

On the Road

New York, New Jersey & Pennsylvania

Best Places to Eat

➜ Totto Ramen (p100)

➜ Smorgasburg (p103)

➜ Morimoto (p158)

➜ Lobster House (p150)

➜ Bar Marco (p164)

Best Places to Sleep

➜ Yotel (p93)

➜ Scribner's Catskill Lodge (p132)

➜ White Pine Camp (p138)

➜ Priory Hotel (p164)

➜ Asbury Hotel (p146)

Why Go?

Where else could you visit an Amish family's farm, camp on a mountaintop, read the Declaration of Independence and view New York, New York from the 86th floor of an art-deco landmark – all in a few days? Even though this corner of the country is the most densely populated part of the USA, it's full of places where jaded city dwellers escape to seek simple lives, where artists retreat for inspiration, and where pretty houses line main streets in small towns set amid stunning scenery.

Urban adventures in NYC, historic and lively Philadelphia and river-rich Pittsburgh are a must. Miles and miles of glorious beaches are within reach, from glamorous Long Island to the Jersey Shore – the latter ranges from stately to kitsch, while the mountain wilderness of the Adirondacks reaches skyward just a day's drive north of NYC, a journey that perfectly encapsulates this region's heady character.

When to Go

New York City

Feb Winter-sports buffs head to the mountains of the Adirondacks, Catskills and Poconos.

31 May–5 Sep Memorial Day through Labor Day is for beaches from Montauk to Cape May.

Oct–Nov Fall in NYC brings cool temps, festivals, the marathon and gearing up for holiday season.

NEW YORK CITY

Epicenter of the arts. Dining and shopping capital. Trendsetter. New York City wears many crowns, and spreads an irresistible feast for all.

With its compact size and streets packed with eye-candy of all sorts – architectural treasures, Old World cafés, atmospheric booksellers and curio shops – NYC is an urban wanderer's delight. Crossing continents is as easy as walking over a few avenues in this jumbled city of 200-plus nationalities. You can lose yourself in the crowds of Chinatown amid brightly painted Buddhist temples, steaming noodle shops and fragrant fishmongers, then stroll up to Nolita for enticing boutiques and coffee-tasting among the craft-minded scenesters. Every neighborhood offers a dramatically different version of New York City – from the 100-year-old Jewish delis of the Upper West Side to the meandering cobblestone lanes of Greenwich Village. And the best way to experience this city is to walk its streets.

⊙ Sights

⊙ Financial District & Lower Manhattan

Gleaming with bold, architectural icons, eateries and a booming residential population, Manhattan's southern tip is no longer strictly business. It's in the Financial District (FiDi) that you'll find the National September 11 Memorial and Museum, One World Observatory and Wall Street, and seminal historic sites like Fraunces Tavern Museum, Federal Hall and, just offshore, Ellis Island and Lady Liberty herself. City Hall, the mayor's official seat of power, is a central landmark. North of FiDi are the warehouse conversions of Tribeca, a prosperous grown-up place where vibrant restaurants and bars schmooze with high-end galleries and idiosyncratic retail.

★**Brooklyn Bridge**   BRIDGE
(Map p62; ⑤ 4/5/6 to Brooklyn Bridge-City Hall; J/Z to Chambers St; R/W to City Hall) A New York icon, the Brooklyn Bridge, which connects Brooklyn and Manhattan, was the world's first steel suspension bridge. Indeed, when it opened in 1883, the 1596ft span between its two support towers was the longest in history. Although its construction was fraught with disaster, the bridge became a magnificent example of urban design, inspiring poets, writers and painters. Its pedestrian walkway delivers soul-stirring views of lower Manhattan, the East River and the rapidly developing Brooklyn waterfront.

★**National September 11 Memorial**   MONUMENT
(Map p62; www.911memorial.org; 180 Greenwich St; ⊙ 7:30am-9pm; ⑤ E to World Trade Center; R/W to Cortlandt St; 2/3 to Park Pl) **FREE** The focal point of the National September 11 Memorial is **Reflecting Absence**, two imposing reflecting pools that occupy the very footprints of the ill-fated twin towers. From their rim, a steady cascade of water pours 30ft down toward a central void. Bronze panels frame the pools, inscribed with the names of those who died in the terrorist attacks of September 11, 2001, and in the World Trade Center car bombing on February 26, 1993.

Just beyond the memorial is the site's **museum** (adult/child $24/15, 5-8pm Tue free; ⊙ 9am-8pm Sun-Thu, to 9pm Fri & Sat, last entry 2hr before close). Poignant and deeply affecting, it tells the story of that tragic day and its impact on America and the world.

★**One World Observatory**   VIEWPOINT
(Map p62; ☑ 844-696-1776; www.oneworldobserva tory.com; cnr West & Vesey Sts; adult/child $34/28; ⊙ 9am-8pm, last ticket sold at 7:15pm; ⑤ E to World Trade Center; 2/3 to Park Pl; A/C, J/Z, 4/5 to Fulton St; R/W to Cortlandt St) Spanning levels 100 to 102 of the tallest building in the Western Hemisphere, One World Observatory offers dazzling panoramic views from its sky-high perch. On a clear day you'll be able to see all five boroughs and some surrounding states. Not surprisingly, it's a hugely popular attraction. Purchase tickets online in advance.

National Museum of the American Indian   MUSEUM
(Map p62; ☑ 212-514-3700; www.nmai.si.edu; 1 Bowling Green; ⊙ 10am-5pm Fri-Wed, to 8pm Thu; ⑤ 4/5 to Bowling Green; R/W to Whitehall St) **FREE** An affiliate of the Smithsonian Institution, this elegant tribute to Native American culture is set in Cass Gilbert's spectacular 1907 **Custom House**, one of NYC's finest beaux-arts buildings. Beyond a vast elliptical rotunda, sleek galleries play host to changing exhibitions documenting Native American art, culture, life and beliefs. The museum's permanent collection includes stunning decorative arts, textiles and ceremonial objects that document the diverse native cultures across the Americas.

New York, New Jersey & Pennsylvania Highlights

1 New York City (p57)
Traveling around the world without ever leaving the city, with its kaleidoscope of neighborhoods and cultures.

2 Jersey Shore (p145)

Enjoying the kitsch, kettle corn, coastline and calm.

3 Independence National Historic Park (p151) Walking in the footsteps of the founding fathers in Philadelphia.

4 Catskills (p131) Hiking the densely forested paths.

5 Adirondacks (p136) Paddling a canoe in the shadow of majestic mountains.

6 Thousand Islands (p139)

Camping along the shores of the St Lawrence River.

7 Pittsburgh (p162) Admiring great modern art and old industry.

8 North Fork (p126) Tippling the whites and reds of Long Island.

9 Pennsylvania Dutch Country (p160) Touring the back roads.

10 Delaware Water Gap (p147) Floating gently past bucolic scenery (or white-water rafting after a wet spring).

★ **Statue of Liberty** MONUMENT
(Map p61; ☑ 212-363-3200, tickets 877-523-9849; www.nps.gov/stli; Liberty Island; adult/child incl Ellis Island $18.50/9, incl crown $21.50/12; ⊗ 8:30am-5:30pm, check website for seasonal changes; 🚢 to Liberty Island, 🚇 1 to South Ferry; 4/5 to Bowling Green) Reserve your tickets online well in advance (up to six months ahead) to access Lady Liberty's crown for breathtaking city and harbor views. If you miss out on crown tickets, you may have better luck with tickets for the pedestal, which also offers commanding views. If you don't score either, don't fret: all ferry tickets to Liberty Island offer basic access to the grounds, including **guided ranger tours** or self-guided audio tours. Book all tickets online (www.statue cruises.com) to avoid long queues.

Conceived as early as 1865 by French intellectual Edouard Laboulaye as a monument to the republican principles shared by France and the USA, the Statue of Liberty is still generally recognized as a symbol for at least the ideals of opportunity and freedom to many.

French sculptor Frédéric-Auguste Bartholdi traveled to New York in 1871 to select the site, then spent more than 10 years in Paris designing and making the 151ft-tall figure *Liberty Enlightening the World*. It was then shipped to New York, erected on a small island in the harbor and unveiled in 1886. Structurally, it consists of an iron skeleton (designed by Gustave Eiffel) with a copper skin attached to it by stiff but flexible metal bars. Access to the torch has been prohibited since 1916.

Liberty Island is usually visited in conjunction with nearby Ellis Island. **Ferries** (Map p62; ☑ 877-523-9849; www.statuecruises. com; adult/child from $18.50/9; ⊗ departures 8:30am-4pm; 🚇 4/5 to Bowling Green; R/W to Whitehall St; 1 to South Ferry) leave from Battery Park; South Ferry and Bowling Green are the closest subway stations. (Ferry tickets include admission to both sights.)

★ **Ellis Island** LANDMARK, MUSEUM
(☑ 212-363-3200, tickets 877-523-9849; www. nps.gov/elis; Ellis Island; ferry incl Statue of Liberty adult/child $18.50/9; ⊗ 9:30am-3:30pm; 🚢 to Ellis Island, 🚇 1 to South Ferry; 4/5 to Bowling Green) Ellis Island is America's most famous and historically important gateway. Between 1892 and 1924, over 12 million immigrants passed through this processing station, their dreams in tow. Today, its **Immigration Museum**

delivers a poignant tribute to the immigrant experience, featuring narratives from historians, the immigrants themselves and other sources; the tour brings to life the museum's hefty collection of personal objects, official documents, photographs and film footage. Always purchase your tickets online (www.statuecruises.com) to avoid the soul-crushingly long queues.

South Street Seaport AREA
(Map p62) The South Street Seaport is east of the financial district along the river, but a whole world away. This neighborhood of cobblestone and heritage buildings proudly carries on the traditions of its nautical past. Bars and restaurants have a funky, carefree vibe, and those looking to exercise their shopping muscle will be in heaven with the number of stores spread out across the neighborhood.

★ **Museum of Jewish Heritage** MUSEUM
(Map p62; ☑ 646-437-4202; www.mjhnyc.org; 36 Battery Pl; adult/child $12/free, 4-8pm Wed free; ⊗ 10am-6pm Sun-Tue, to 8pm Wed & Thu, to 5pm Fri mid-Mar–mid-Nov, to 3pm Fri rest of year, closed Sat; 🚻; 🚇 4/5 to Bowling Green; R/W to Whitehall St) An evocative waterfront museum exploring all aspects of modern Jewish identity and culture, from religious traditions to artistic accomplishments. The museum's core exhibition includes a detailed exploration of the Holocaust, with personal artifacts, photographs and documentary films providing a personal, moving experience. Outdoors is the **Garden of Stones** installation. Created by artist Andy Goldsworthy and dedicated to those who lost loved ones in the Holocaust, its 18 boulders form a narrow pathway for contemplating the fragility of life.

Skyscraper Museum MUSEUM
(Map p62; ☑ 212-968-1961; www.skyscraper.org; 39 Battery Pl; $5; ⊗ noon-6pm Wed-Sun; 🚇 4/5 to Bowling Green; R to Whitehall) Fans of phallic architecture will appreciate this compact, high-gloss gallery, examining skyscrapers as objects of design, engineering and urban renewal. Temporary exhibitions dominate the space, with past exhibitions exploring everything from New York's new generation of super-slim residential towers to the world's new breed of supertalls. Permanent fixtures include information on the design and construction of the Empire State Building and World Trade Center.

New York City

N

0   10 km
0   5 miles

22

9

BRONXVILLE

Cross County Pkwy

87

Boston Rd

1

4

ENGLEWOOD

Broadway

Hudson River

Woodlawn
Cemetery

95

Pelham Bay
Park

Long
Island
Sound

80

HACKENSACK

95

Overpeck
County
Park

Cloisters
Museum &
Gardens

INWOOD

New York
Botanical
Garden

BAYCHESTER

Bronx Zoo

Hart
Island

Pelham Bay
Park

City
Island

17

FAIRVIEW

63

HARLEM

BELMONT

Bronx
Park

Yankee
Stadium

**THROGS
NECK**

678

295

**GREAT
NECK**

KEARNY

9

See Central Park &
Uptown Map (p76)

MANHATTAN

Central
Park

**HUNTS
POINT**

Powells
Cove

Fort
Totten

BAYSIDE

New Jersey Turnpike

See Times Square, Midtown
Manhattan & Chelsea Map (p70)

The Kaufman
Arts District

ASTORIA

Museum of the
Moving Image

LaGuardia
Airport

FLUSHING

495

95

HOBOKEN

See East & West
Villages Map (p66)

**JACKSON
HEIGHTS**

Unisphere

New York Hall
of Science

Queens Museum

**JERSEY
CITY**

63

See Chinatown & Lower
Manhattan Map (p62)

MoMA PS1

Queens Blvd

QUEENS

HOLLISWOOD

Ellis
Island

78

GREENPOINT

Brooklyn Brewery

WILLIAMSBURG

GLENDALE

Statue of
Liberty

Governors
Island

**CLINTON
HILL**

Greater
Ridgewood
Historic Society

BUSHWICK

JAMAICA

678

New York
Transit Museum

Atlantic Ave

Brooklyn Children's Museum

Ferry to Staten Island

Brooklyn
Botanic Garden

Brooklyn Museum

**HOWARD
BEACH**

John F Kennedy
International Airport

27

Prospect
Park

Linden Blvd

**BAY
RIDGE**

Green-Wood
Cemetery

Spring
Creek Park

Elders
Point
Marsh

East High
Meadow

BROOKLYN

Gateway
National
Recreation Area

Jo Co
Marsh

Staten
Island

278

Lower
New York
Bay

Ave P

Bensonhurst
Park

Brooklyn
Marine
Park

Big
Channel

RICHMOND

**CONEY
ISLAND**

New York
Aquarium

Coney
Island

Rockaway
Inlet

Jacob
Riis
Park

Rockaway
Beach

*ATLANTIC
OCEAN*

NEW YORK

NEW JERSEY

Chinatown & Lower Manhattan

SOHO

LITTLE ITALY

Vestry St

Canal St

Sixth Ave (Avenue of the Americas)

Canal St

Canal St

Howard St

Canal St

Laight St

Varick St

Church St

Walker St

Cortlandt Al

Centre St

See East & West Villages Map (p66)

Hubert St

Beach St

White St

23

Bayard St

15

Hudson River Park

28

N Moore St

22

Franklin St

Franklin St

Franklin St

18

20

CHINATOWN

Columbus Park

Mosco St

West Side Hwy

Greenwich St

Franklin St

Hudson St

Leonard St

Leonard St

29

Harrison St

Duane St

Worth St

Thomas Paine Park

Pearl St

Washington Market Community Park

Reade St

Thomas St

Duane St

30

Federal Plaza

Foley Square

Nelson A Rockefeller Park

Chambers St

Chambers St

TRIBECA

Elk St

Park Row

Pearl St

River Tce

Warren St

W Broadway

Chambers St

Municipal Building

Murray St

LOWER MANHATTAN

Murray St

Broadway

City Hall

City Hall Park

Chambers St/ Brooklyn Bridge-City Hall

North End Ave

Park Place

Police Plaza

Barclay St

Park Pl

Park Pl

NYC Information Center

Beekman St

One World Observatory

Chambers St-WTC

Vesey St

Ann St

Pearl St

World Financial Center

7

World Trade Center Transportation Hub

Fulton St

Gold St

Cliff St

Guilbert Park

19

North Cove

5

6

Memorial Plaza

Fulton St

National September 11 Memorial

Cortlandt St

John St

Cortlandt St

10

National September 11 Memorial Museum

Liberty St

William St

Maiden La

Fletcher St

BATTERY PARK CITY

Thames St

New York Stock Exchange

Pine St

Water St

West Side Hwy

Carlisle St

Wall St

Washington St

Rector St

Broad St

Wall St

Wall St

Pearl St

South St

Franklin D Roosevelt Dr

W Thames St

FINANCIAL DISTRICT

New St

17

Old Slip

Hudson River

Battery Park City Esplanade

Bowling Green

Beaver St

Battery Pl

2nd Pl

Bowling Green

12

Vietnam Veterans Plaza

26

Museum of Jewish Heritage

4

13

Whitehall St

Broad St

South St

Pier 6

Robert F Wagner Jr Park

Battery Park

Pearl St

Whitehall St

Ferry to Hoboken (NJ)

Pier A

9

8

State St

Peter Minuit Plaza

Ferry to Statue of Liberty & Ellis Island

South St Viaduct

South Ferry

16

Ferry to Governors Island

Ferry to Ellis Island

Ferry to Statue of Liberty

Hugh L Carey Tunnel

Upper New York Bay

Ferry to Staten Island

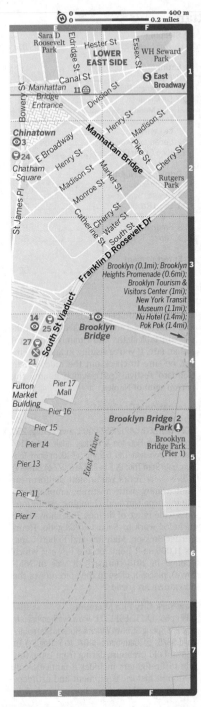

Battery Park
PARK

(Map p62; www.nycgovparks.org; Broadway, at Battery Pl; ☉ sunrise-1am; ⑤ 4/5 to Bowling Green; R to Whitehall St; 1 to South Ferry) Skirting the southern edge of Manhattan, this 12-acre oasis lures with public artworks, meandering walkways and perennial gardens. Its memorials include a Holocaust Memorial and the Irish Hunger Memorial. It was on this very part of the island that the Dutch settled in 1623. And it was right here that the first 'battery' of cannons was erected to defend the fledgling settlement of New Amsterdam. You'll also find historic Castle Clinton (Map p62; ☏ 212-344-7220; www.nps.gov/cacl/index.htm; ☉ 7:45am-5pm) and the ferry service to Ellis Island and the Statue of Liberty.

New York Stock
Exchange
NOTABLE BUILDING

(Map p62; www.nyse.com; 11 Wall St; ☉ closed to the public; ⑤ J/Z to Broad St; 2/3, 4/5 to Wall St) Home to the world's best-known stock exchange (the NYSE), Wall Street is an iconic symbol of US capitalism. Behind the portentous Romanesque facade, about one billion shares change hands daily, a sight no longer accessible to the public due to security concerns. Feel free to gawk outside the building, protected by barricades and the hawk-eyed NYPD (New York Police Department).

Federal Reserve Bank
of New York
NOTABLE BUILDING

(Map p62; ☏ 212-720-6130; www.newyorkfed.org; 33 Liberty St, at Nassau St, entrance at 44 Maiden Lane; reservation required; ☉ guided tours 1pm & 2pm Mon-Fri; ⑤ A/C, J/Z, 2/3, 4/5 to Fulton St) **FREE** The best reason to visit the Federal Reserve Bank is the chance to (briefly) ogle at its high-security vault – more than 10,000 tons of gold reserves reside here, 80ft below ground. You'll only see a small part of that fortune, but signing on to a free tour (the only way down; book several months ahead) is worth the effort.

☉ SoHo & Chinatown

SoHo (South of Houston), NoHo (North of Houston) and Nolita (North of Little Italy) represent three of Manhattan's trendiest neighborhoods, known for their intimidatingly hip boutiques, bars and eateries. Meanwhile, to the south, expanding and bustling Chinatown and a nostalgic sliver of Little Italy lure with idiosyncratic street life. Canal St, running from the Manhattan

Chinatown & Lower Manhattan

Bridge to the West Side Hwy, and one of the most traffic-clogged arteries in the city, is a world in itself. Taken together, these neighborhoods serve up a delicious, contradictory jumble of cast-iron architecture, strutting fashionistas, sacred temples and hook-hung ducks and salami.

★**Chinatown** AREA
(Map p62; www.explorechinatown.com; south of Broome St & east of Broadway; ⑤N/Q/R/W, J/Z, 6 to Canal St; B/D to Grand St; F to East Broadway) A walk through Manhattan's most colorful, cramped neighborhood is never the same, no matter how many times you hit the pavement. Catch the whiff of fresh fish and ripe persimmons, hear the clacking of mah-jongg tiles on makeshift tables, eye up dangling duck roasts swinging in store windows and shop for anything from rice-paper lanterns and 'faux-lex' watches to tire irons and a pound of pressed nutmeg. America's largest congregation of Chinese immigrants is your oyster – dipped in soy sauce, of course.

★**Little Italy** AREA
(Map p66; ⑤N/Q/R/W, J/Z, 6 to Canal St; B/D to Grand St) This once-strong Italian neighborhood (film director Martin Scorsese grew up on Elizabeth St) saw an exodus in the mid-20th century when many of its residents moved to more suburban neighborhoods in Brooklyn and beyond. Today it's mostly con-

centrated on Mulberry St between Broome and Canal Sts, a stretch packed with checkerboard tablecloths and (mainly mediocre) Italian fare. If you're visiting in late September, be sure to check out the raucous San Gennaro Festival (p91), which honors the patron saint of Naples.

International Center of Photography GALLERY
(ICP; Map p66; ☑212-857-0003; www.icp.org; 250 Bowery, btwn Houston & Prince; adult/child $14/ free, by donation Thu 6-9pm; ⊙10am-6pm Tue-Sun, until 9pm Thu; ⑤F to 2nd Ave; J/Z to Bowery) ICP is New York's paramount platform for photography, with a strong emphasis on photojournalism and changing exhibitions on a wide range of themes. Past shows have included work by Sebastião Salgado, Henri Cartier-Bresson, Man Ray and Robert Capa. Its 11,000-sq-ft home on the Bowery, which opened in 2016 (formerly it was in Midtown), places it close to the epicenter of the downtown art scene.

New York City Fire Museum MUSEUM
(Map p66; ☑212-691-1303; www.nycfiremuseum. org; 278 Spring St, btwn Varick & Hudson Sts; adult/ child $8/5; ⊙10am-5pm; ⑤C/E to Spring St) In a grand old firehouse dating from 1904, this ode to firefighters includes a fantastic collection of historic equipment and artifacts. Eye up everything from horse-drawn fire-

fighting carriages and early stovepipe firefighter hats, to Chief, a four-legged fire-fighting hero from Brooklyn. Exhibits trace the development of the NYC firefighting system, and the museum's heavy equipment and friendly staff make this a great spot for kids. The New York Fire Department (FDNY) lost half of its members in the collapse of the World Trade Center on September 11, 2001, and memorials and exhibits have become a permanent part of the collection. Fans can stock up on books about firefighting history and official FDNY clothing and patches in the gift shop.

Museum of Chinese in America   MUSEUM
(Map p66; ☑212-619-4785; www.mocanyc.org; 215 Centre St, btwn Grand & Howard Sts; adult/child $10/5, first Thu of month free; ◷11am-6pm Tue, Wed & Fri-Sun, to 9pm Thu; ⑤N/Q/R/W, J/Z, 6 to Canal St) In this space designed by architect Maya Lin (designer of the famed Vietnam Memorial in Washington, DC) is a multifaceted museum whose engaging permanent and temporary exhibitions shed light on Chinese American life, both past and present. Browse through interactive multimedia exhibits, maps, timelines, photos, letters, films and artifacts. The museum's anchor exhibit, *With a Single Step: Stories in the Making of America,* provides an intimate glimpse into topics that include immigration, cultural identity and racial stereotyping.

◉ East Village & Lower East Side

Shorthand for this duo's heady mix of old and new: the New Museum and the Tenement Museum. Continually evolving and simultaneously marked by waves of immigrants, the East Village and the Lower East Side are two of the city's hottest 'hoods for cramming into low-lit lounges; clubs for live music and cheap eats luring students, bankers and scruffier types alike. Luxury high-rise condominiums and hip boutique hotels coexist within blocks of tenement style buildings.

**★Lower East Side
Tenement Museum**   MUSEUM
(Map p66; ☑877-975-3786; www.tenement.org; 103 Orchard St, btwn Broome & Delancey Sts; tours adult/student & senior $25/20; ◷10am-6:30pm Fri-Wed, to 8:30pm Thu; ⑤B/D to Grand St; J/M/Z to Essex St; F to Delancey St) This museum puts the neighborhood's heartbreaking but inspiring heritage on full display in three re-created turn-of-the-20th-century tenement apartments, including the late-19th-century home and garment shop of the Levine family from Poland, and two immigrant dwellings from the Great Depressions of 1873 and 1929. Visits to the tenement building are available only as part of scheduled guided tours, with many departures each day.

NEW YORK, NEW JERSEY & PENNSYLVANIA IN...

One Week
Start off in Philadelphia (p151), birthplace of American independence. Visit Independence Hall (p151) and the new Museum of the American Revolution (p151), then spend an evening investigating the great restaurants and nightlife in up-and-coming neighborhoods such as Fishtown. Next, head to New Jersey for a bucolic night in Cape May (p149), a sleepy beach town full of Victorian charm. After a quick, scenic cruise along Ocean Dr, stop off overnight further up the Shore in Wildwood (p149), a treasure trove of iconic '50s kitsch. Land in New York City (p57) the following day and spend at least a couple of days blending touristy must-dos – such as the Top of the Rock (p74) and Central Park (p78) – with vibrant nightlife and eclectic dining.

Two Weeks
With NYC in your rear-view mirror, head north along the majestic Hudson and its palisades for a night or two in Beacon (p128), before reaching the Catskills (p131). After touring this beautiful region, head further north to the Adirondacks (p136) and its outdoor wonders, then loop back south through the Finger Lakes (p134) region with stops in wineries and waterfall-laden parks along the way. Spend a night in gorgeous college-town Ithaca (p134). From here you can head towards the Canadian border to Buffalo (p140) and Niagara Falls (p142), or southwest to Pittsburgh (p162).

East & West Villages

★ **New Museum of Contemporary Art**   MUSEUM

(Map p66; ☎212-219-1222; www.newmuseum.org; 235 Bowery, btwn Stanton & Rivington Sts; adult/child $18/free, 7-9pm Thu by donation; ⊙11am-6pm Tue & Wed & Fri-Sun, to 9pm Thu; ⓢR/W to Prince St; F to 2nd Ave; J/Z to Bowery; 6 to Spring St) Rising above the neighborhood, the New Museum of Contemporary Art is a sight to behold: a seven-story stack of off-kilter, white, ethereal boxes designed by Tokyo-based architects Kazuyo Sejima and Ryue Nishizawa of SANAA and the New York–based firm Gensler. It was a long-awaited breath of fresh air along what was a completely gritty Bowery strip when it arrived back in 2007 – though since its opening, many glossy new constructions have joined it, quickly transforming this once down-and-out avenue.

Tompkins Square Park   PARK

(Map p66; www.nycgovparks.org; E 7th & 10th Sts, btwn Aves A & B; ⊙6am-midnight; ⓢ6 to Astor Pl) This 10.5-acre park is like a friendly town square for locals, who gather for chess at concrete tables, for picnics on the lawn on warm days, and for spontaneous guitar or drum jams on various grassy knolls. It's also the site of basketball courts, a fun-to-watch dog run (a fenced-in area where humans can unleash their canines), a mini public swimming pool for kids, frequent summer concerts and an always-lively kids' playground.

Museum at Eldridge Street Synagogue   MUSEUM

(Map p62; ☎212-219-0302; www.eldridgestreet.org; 12 Eldridge St, btwn Canal & Division Sts; adult/child $14/8, Mon suggested donation; ⊙10am-5pm Sun-Thu, to 3pm Fri; ⓢF to East Broadway) This landmark house of worship, built in 1887, was once a center of Jewish life be-

See Times Square, Midtown Manhattan & Chelsea Map (p70)

fore falling into squalor in the 1920s. Left to rot, the synagogue was restored following a 20-year-long, $20-million restoration that was completed in 2007, and it now shines with original splendor. Museum admission includes a **guided tour** of the synagogue, which departs hourly, with the last one starting at 4pm.

Astor Place   SQUARE
(Map p66; 8th St, btwn Third & Fourth Aves; S N/R to 8th St-NYU; 6 to Astor Pl) Even with the *Alamo*, an iconic piece of public art more often referred to as 'the cube', restored after several years absence, this is not the Astor Place of old. No longer grungy and filled with gutter punks and squatters, this new iteration is also no longer a plaza. It's an orderly block between Broadway and Lafayette surrounded by sleek, glittery buildings and outfitted with well-designed benches and granite blocks good for people-watching.

West Village, Chelsea & Meatpacking District

Mellow and raucous, quaint and sleekly contemporary, this trio of downtown neighborhoods embodies contradictory vibes. The West Village's twisting streets and well-preserved townhouses offer intimate spaces for dining, drinking and being a *flaneur*. Washington Square Park and the surrounding blocks is dominated by New York University's booming student population. The Meatpacking District has evolved over the years into something of a meat market, with trendy nightlife. To the north is Chelsea, home to art galleries and a vibrant gay scene. And the High Line, the city's celebrated elevated park, ties things together, ending in the Hudson Yards, a new, massive development.

East & West Villages

★**High Line** PARK
(Map p66; ☎212-500-6035; www.thehighline.org; Gansevoort St; ⊗7am-11pm Jun-Sep, to 10pm Apr, May, Oct & Nov, to 7pm Dec-Mar; ⬚M11 to Washington St; M11, M14 to 9th Ave; M23, M34 to 10th Ave, ⑤A/C/E, L to 14th St-8th Ave; C/E to 23rd St-8th Ave) It's hard to believe that the High Line – a shining example of brilliant urban renewal – was once a dingy rail line that anchored a rather unsavory district of slaughterhouses. Today, this eye-catching attraction is one of New York's best-loved green spaces, drawing

visitors who come to stroll, sit and picnic 30ft above the city – while enjoying fabulous views of Manhattan's ever-changing urban landscape. Its final extension, which loops around the massive construction project at Hudson Yards, ends at 34th St.

★**Whitney Museum of
American Art** MUSEUM
(Map p66; ☎212-570-3600; www.whitney.org; 99 Gansevoort St, at Washington St; adult/child $22/ free; ⊗10:30am-6pm Mon, Wed, Thu & Sun, to

10pm Fri & Sat; [S] A/C/E, L to 14th St-8th Ave) After years of construction, the Whitney's new downtown location opened to much fanfare in 2015. Perched near the foot of the High Line, this architecturally stunning building – designed by Renzo Piano – makes a suitable introduction to the museum's superb collection. Inside the spacious galleries, you'll find works by all the great American artists, including Edward Hopper, Jasper Johns, Georgia O'Keeffe and Mark Rothko.

★ **Chelsea Market**   MARKET
(Map p70; [J] 212-652-2121; www.chelseamarket.com; 75 Ninth Ave, at W 15th St; ⊙7am-9pm Mon-Sat, 8am-8pm Sun; [S] A/C/E to 14th St; L to 8th Ave) In a shining example of redevelopment and preservation, the Chelsea Market has transformed a former factory into a shopping concourse that caters to foodies. More than two dozen food vendors ply their temptations including **Mokbar** (ramen with Korean accents), **Takumi Taco** (mixing Japanese and Mexican ingredients), **Tuck Shop** (Aussie-style savory pies), **Bar Suzette** (crepes), **Num Pang** (Cambodian sandwiches), **Ninth St Coffee** (perfect lattes), **Doughnuttery** (piping hot mini-doughnuts) and **L'Arte de Gelato** (rich ice cream).

★ **Hudson River Park**   PARK
(Map p66; www.hudsonriverpark.org; [⌖]) The High Line may be all the rage these days, but one block away from that famous elevated green space stretches a 5-mile-long ribbon of green that has dramatically transformed the city over the past decade. Covering 550 acres and running from Battery Park at Manhattan's southern tip to 59th St in Midtown, the Hudson River Park is Manhattan's wondrous backyard.

★ **Rubin Museum of Art**   GALLERY
(Map p70; [J] 212-620-5000; www.rmanyc.org; 150 W 17th St, btwn Sixth & Seventh Aves; adult/child $15/free, 6-10pm Fri free; ⊙11am-5pm Mon & Thu, to 9pm Wed, to 10pm Fri, to 6pm Sat & Sun; [S]1 to 18th St) The Rubin is the first museum in the Western world to dedicate itself to the art of the Himalayas and surrounding regions. Its impressive collections include embroidered textiles from China, metal sculptures from Tibet, Pakistani stone sculptures and intricate Bhutanese paintings, as well as ritual objects and dance masks from various Tibetan regions, spanning the 2nd to the 19th centuries.

★ **Washington Square Park**   PARK
(Map p66; Fifth Ave at Washington Sq N; [⌖]; [S] A/C/E, B/D/F/M to W 4th St-Washington Sq; R/W to 8th St-NYU) What was once a potter's field and a square for public executions is now the unofficial town square of Greenwich Village, and plays host to lounging NYU students, tuba-playing street performers, curious canines and their owners, speed-chess pros and bare-footed children who splash about in the fountain on warm days.

◉ Union Square, Flatiron District & Gramercy

The bustling, throbbing, frenzied heart of this trio of neighborhoods is Union Square. It's grungy past long in the rear-view mirror, it's a manicured meeting ground for New Yorkers of all types. The triangular Flatiron Building and the verdant respite of Madison Square Park mark the boundary with Midtown's canyons just to the north. Gramercy Park, a romantic private oasis, offers a more subdued, stately residential area to roam.

★ **Union Square**   SQUARE
(Map p70; www.unionsquarenyc.org; 17th St, btwn Broadway & Park Ave S; [S]4/5/6, N/Q/R, L to 14th St-Union Sq) Union Square is like the Noah's Ark of New York, rescuing at least two of every kind from the curling seas of concrete. In fact, one would be hard-pressed to find a more eclectic cross-section of locals gathered in one public place: suited businessfolk gulping fresh air during their lunch breaks, dreadlocked loiterers tapping beats on their tabla, skateboarders flipping tricks on the southeastern stairs, rowdy college kids guzzling student-priced eats, and throngs of protesting masses chanting fervently for various causes.

★ **Flatiron Building**   HISTORIC BUILDING
(Map p70; Broadway, cnr Fifth Ave & 23rd St; [S] N/R, F/M, 6 to 23rd St) Designed by Daniel Burnham and built in 1920, the 20-story Flatiron Building has a narrow triangular footprint that resembles the prow of a massive ship. It also features a traditional beaux-arts limestone and terra-cotta facade, built over a steel frame, that gets more complex and beautiful the longer you stare at it. Best viewed from the traffic island north of 23rd St between Broadway and Fifth Ave, this unusual structure dominated the plaza back in the dawning skyscraper era of the early 1900s.

Times Square, Midtown Manhattan & Chelsea

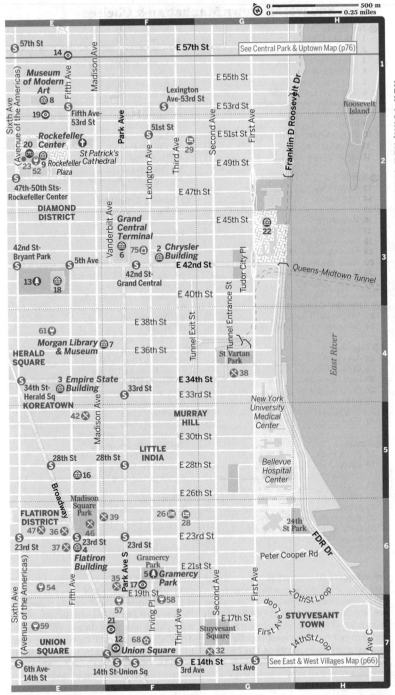

NEW YORK, NEW JERSEY & PENNSYLVANIA NEW YORK CITY

0 — 500 m
0 — 0.25 miles

E 57th St

57th St
14

See Central Park & Uptown Map (p76)

E 55th St

Museum of Modern Art
8

E 53rd St

19

Lexington Ave-53rd St

Fifth Ave-53rd St

51st St

E 51st St

29

Rockefeller Center
20
23 52
9 Rockefeller Plaza

St Patrick's Cathedral

E 49th St

47th-50th Sts-Rockefeller Center

E 47th St

DIAMOND DISTRICT

Grand Central Terminal
6   75

E 45th St

22

42nd St-Bryant Park

5th Ave

2 Chrysler Building
E 42nd St

42nd St-Grand Central

Queens-Midtown Tunnel

13
18

E 40th St

E 38th St

61

Morgan Library & Museum   7

E 36th St

HERALD SQUARE

St Vartan Park

East River

3 Empire State Building

33rd St

E 34th St

E 33rd St

34th St-Herald Sq

KOREATOWN

42

New York University Medical Center

LITTLE INDIA

E 30th St

28th St

28th St

E 28th St

16

Bellevue Hospital Center

E 26th St

FLATIRON DISTRICT

Madison Square Park

39

26   28

24th St Park

47   36

46

E 23rd St

FDR Dr

23rd St

37

23rd St

23rd St

Flatiron Building
4

Gramercy Park

E 21st St

Peter Cooper Rd

54

5 Gramercy Park

20thSt Loop

35

17
E 19th St

58

STUYVESANT TOWN

59

57

E 17th St

First Ave Loop

21

Stuyvesant Square

E 14thSt Loop

12
68 Union Square

32

Ave C

UNION SQUARE

6th Ave-14th St

14th St-Union Sq

E 14th St

3rd Ave

1st Ave

See East & West Villages Map (p66)

Times Square, Midtown Manhattan & Chelsea

Union Square Greenmarket MARKET
(Map p70; ☎212-788-7476; www.grownyc.org; E 17th St, btwn Broadway & Park Ave S; ☉8am-6pm Mon, Wed, Fri & Sat; ⑤4/5/6, N/Q/R/W, L to 14th St-Union Sq) ✎ On most days, Union Square's northern end hosts the most popular of the 53 greenmarkets throughout the five boroughs. Indeed, even celebrity chefs head here for just-picked rarities including fiddlehead ferns and heirloom tomatoes.

National Arts Club CULTURAL CENTER
(Map p70; ☎212-475-3424; www.nationalarts club.org; 15 Gramercy Park S; drawing classes $15-25; ⑤N/R, 6 to 23rd St) Founded in 1898 to promote public interest in the arts, the National Arts Club holds art exhibitions, usually open to the public from 10am to 5pm Monday to Friday (check the website for upcoming shows). Calvert Vaux – one of the creators of Central Park – designed the building itself,

its picture-lined front parlor adorned with a beautiful, vaulted, stained-glass ceiling. The place was once home to Samuel J Tilden, a former New York governor, and failed presidential candidate in 1876.

★ **Gramercy Park** PARK
(Map p70; E 20th St, btwn Park & Third Aves; ⑤ N/R, 6 to 23rd St) Romantic Gramercy Park was created by Samuel Ruggles in 1831 after he drained the area's swamp and laid out streets in an English style. You can't enter the private park (the only one in Manhattan), but peer through the gate and imagine tough guy James Cagney enjoying it – the Hollywood actor once resided at 34 Gramercy Park E. At 15 Gramercy Park S stands the National Arts Club, whose members include Martin Scorsese, Uma Thurman and Ethan Hawke.

◉ Midtown

The hub of the city, and according to boosters the crossroads of the world, Midtown *is* the NYC of postcards. More than 300,000 people a day jostle their way through its pedestrian-friendly streets. More sanitized and corporatized than in the past, it's nevertheless a heady part of town, home to icons including Times Square, Broadway theaters, Grand Central Terminal, the Empire State building and Tiffany & Co Fifth Ave. Cultural knockouts include MoMA, the New York Public Library and the Morgan Library & Museum, with the food-packed, gay-friendly streets of Hell's Kitchen nearby.

★ **Museum of Modern Art** MUSEUM
(MoMA; Map p70; ☑ 212-708-9400; www.moma.org; 11 W 53rd St, btwn Fifth & Sixth Aves; adult/child $25/free, 4-8pm Fri free; ◷ 10:30am-5:30pm Sat-Thu, to 8pm Fri; ▣; ⑤ E, M to 5th Ave-53rd St) Superstar of the modern-art scene, MoMA's galleries scintillate with heavyweights: Van Gogh, Matisse, Picasso, Warhol, Lichtenstein, Rothko, Pollock and Bourgeois. Since its founding in 1929, the museum has amassed almost 200,000 artworks, documenting the emerging creative ideas and movements of the late 19th century through to those that dominate today. For art buffs, it's Valhalla.

★ **Times Square** AREA
(Map p70; www.timessquarenyc.org; Broadway, at Seventh Ave; ⑤ N/Q/R/W, S, 1/2/3, 7 to Times Sq-42nd St) Love it or hate it, the intersection of Broadway and Seventh Ave (aka Times Square) pumps out the NYC of the global imagination – yellow cabs, golden arches, soaring skyscrapers and razzle-dazzle Broadway marquees. It's right here that Al Jolson 'made it' in the 1927 film *The Jazz Singer,* that photojournalist Alfred Eisenstaedt famously captured a lip-locked sailor and nurse on V-J Day in 1945, and that Alicia Keys and Jay-Z waxed lyrically about this 'concrete jungle where dreams are made'.

★ **Fifth Avenue** AREA
(Map p70; Fifth Ave, btwn 42nd & 59th Sts; ⑤ E, M to 5th Ave-53rd St; N/R/W to 5th Ave-59th St) Immortalized in film and song, Fifth Ave first developed its high-class reputation in the early 20th century, when it was known for its 'country' air and open spaces. The series of mansions called **Millionaire's Row** extended right up to 130th St, though most of those above 59th St faced subsequent demolition or conversion to the cultural institutions now constituting Museum Mile. Despite a proliferation of ubiquitous chains, the avenue's Midtown stretch still glitters with upmarket establishments, among them **Tiffany & Co** (Map p76; ☑ 212-755-8000; www.tiffany.com; 727 Fifth Ave, at E 57th St; ◷ 10am-7pm Mon-Sat, noon-6pm Sun; ⑤ F to 57th St; N/R/W to 5th Ave-59th St).

Home to President Donald Trump and family, the dark-glassed **Trump Tower**, at Fifth Ave and 56th St, has become a sight in and of itself, and a popular spot for protestors. Security around the building is extremely tight and traffic slow.

★ **Grand Central Terminal** HISTORIC BUILDING
(Map p70; www.grandcentralterminal.com; 89 E 42nd St, at Park Ave; ◷ 5:30am-2am; ⑤ S, 4/5/6, 7 to Grand Central-42nd St) Completed in 1913, Grand Central Terminal – more commonly, if technically incorrectly, called Grand Central Station – is one of New York's beaux-arts beauties. Adorned with Tennessee-marble floors and Italian-marble ticket counters, its glorious main concourse is capped by a vaulted ceiling depicting the constellations, designed by French painter Paul César Helleu.

★ **Rockefeller Center** HISTORIC BUILDING
(Map p70; www.rockefellercenter.com; Fifth to Sixth Aves, btwn W 48th & 51st Sts; ⑤ B/D/F/M to 47th-50th Sts-Rockefeller Center) This 22-acre 'city within a city' debuted at the height of the Great Depression, with developer John D

Rockefeller Jr footing the $100 million price tag. Taking nine years to build, it was America's first multi-use retail, entertainment and office space – a sprawl of 19 buildings (14 of which are the original Moderne structures). The center was declared a National Landmark in 1987. Highlights include the Top of the Rock observation deck and NBC Studio Tours (p90).

Top of the Rock VIEWPOINT
(Map p70; ✆212-698-2000; www.topoftherock nyc.com; 30 Rockefeller Plaza, entrance on W 50th St btwn Fifth & Sixth Aves; adult/child $39/33, sunrise/sunset combo $54/48; ⊙8am-midnight, last elevator at 11pm; ⑤B/D/F/M to 47th-50th Sts-Rockefeller Center) Designed in homage to ocean liners and opened in 1933, this 70th-floor open-air observation deck sits atop the **GE Building**, the tallest skyscraper at the Rockefeller Center. Top of the Rock beats the Empire State Building on several levels: it's less crowded, has wider observation decks (both outdoor and indoor) and offers a view of the Empire State Building itself.

★Chrysler Building HISTORIC BUILDING
(Map p70; 405 Lexington Ave, at E 42nd St; ⊙lobby 8am-6pm Mon-Fri; ⑤S, 4/5/6, 7 to Grand Central-42nd St) Designed by William Van Alen in 1930, the 77-floor Chrysler Building is prime-time architecture: a fusion of Moderne and Gothic aesthetics, adorned with steel eagles and topped by a spire that screams *Bride of Frankenstein*. The building was constructed as the headquarters for Walter P Chrysler and his automobile empire; unable to compete on the production line with bigger rivals Ford and General Motors, Chrysler trumped them on the skyline, and with one of Gotham's most beautiful lobbies.

★Empire State Building HISTORIC BUILDING
(Map p70; www.esbnyc.com; 350 Fifth Ave, at W 34th St; 86th-fl observation deck adult/child $34/27, incl 102nd-fl observation deck $54/47; ⊙8am-2am, last elevators up 1:15am; ⑤B/D/F/M, N/Q/R/W to 34th St-Herald Sq) This limestone classic was built in just 410 days – using seven million hours of labor during the Great Depression – and the view from its 86th-floor outdoor deck and 102nd-floor indoor deck are heavenly. Alas, the queues to the top are notorious. Getting here very early or very late will help you avoid delays – as will buying your tickets ahead of time online, where the extra $2 convenience fee is well worth the hassle it will save you.

★Morgan Library & Museum MUSEUM
(Map p70; ✆212-685-0008; www.themorgan.org; 225 Madison, at E 36th St, Midtown East; adult/child $20/free; ⊙10:30am-5pm Tue-Thu, to 9pm Fri, 10am-6pm Sat, 11am-6pm Sun; ⑤6 to 33rd St) Incorporating the mansion once owned by steel magnate JP Morgan, this sumptuous cultural center houses a phenomenal array of manuscripts, tapestries and books (with no fewer than three Gutenberg Bibles). Decorated with Italian and Dutch Renaissance artworks, Morgan's personal study is only trumped by his personal library (East Room), an extraordinary, vaulted space adorned with walnut bookcases, a 16th-century Dutch tapestry and zodiac-themed ceiling. The center's rotating exhibitions are often superb, as are its regular cultural events.

New York Public Library HISTORIC BUILDING
(Stephen A Schwarzman Building; Map p70; ✆917-275-6975; www.nypl.org; Fifth Ave, at W 42nd St; ⊙10am-6pm Mon & Thu-Sat, to 8pm Tue & Wed, 1-5pm Sun, guided tours 11am & 2pm Mon-Sat, 2pm Sun; ⑤B/D/F/M to 42nd St-Bryant Park; 7 to 5th Ave) **FREE** Loyally guarded by 'Patience' and 'Fortitude' (the marble lions overlooking Fifth Ave), this beaux-arts show-off is one of NYC's best free attractions. When dedicated in 1911, New York's flagship library ranked as the largest marble structure ever built in the USA, and to this day, its recently restored **Rose Main Reading Room** steals the breath away with its lavish coffered ceiling. It's only one of several glories inside, among them the **DeWitt Wallace Periodical Room**.

United Nations HISTORIC BUILDING
(Map p70; ✆212-963-4475; http://visit.un.org; visitors' gate First Ave at 46th St, Midtown East; guided tour adult/child $20/13, children under 5yr not admitted, grounds access Sat & Sun free; ⊙tours 9am-4:45pm Mon-Fri, visitor center also open 10am-4:45pm Sat & Sun; ⑤S, 4/5/6, 7 to Grand Central-42nd St) Welcome to the headquarters of the UN, a worldwide organization overseeing international law, international security and human rights. While the Le Corbusier–designed Secretariat building is off-limits, one-hour guided tours do cover the restored General Assembly Hall, Security Council Chamber, Trusteeship Council Chamber, and Economic and Social Council (ECOSOC) Chamber, as well as exhibitions about the UN's work and artworks donated by member states. Weekday tours must be

booked online and photo ID is required to enter the site.

St Patrick's Cathedral CATHEDRAL

(Map p70; www.saintpatrickscathedral.org; Fifth Ave, btwn E 50th & 51st Sts; ⊙6:30am-8:45pm; ⑤B/D/F/M to 47th-50th Sts-Rockefeller Center; E/M to 5th Ave-53rd St) Fresh from a $200 million restoration, America's largest Catholic cathedral graces Fifth Ave with Gothic Revival splendor. Built at a cost of nearly $2 million during the Civil War, the building did not originally include the two front spires; those were added in 1888. Step inside to appreciate the Louis Tiffany–designed altar and Charles Connick's stunning Rose Window, the latter gleaming above a 7000-pipe church organ. Walk-in guided tours are available several days a week; check website for details.

Museum of Arts & Design MUSEUM

(MAD; Map p76; ☏212-299-7777; www.mad museum.org; 2 Columbus Circle, btwn Eighth Ave & Broadway; adult/child $16/free, by donation 6-9pm Thu; ⊙10am-6pm Tue, Wed, Fri, Sat & Sun, to 9pm Thu; ☕; ⑤A/C, B/D, 1 to 59th St-Columbus Circle) MAD offers four floors of superlative design and handicrafts, from blown glass and carved wood to elaborate metal jewelry. Its temporary exhibitions are top-notch and innovative: one past show explored the art of scent. Usually on the first Sunday of the month, professional artists lead family-friendly explorations of the galleries, followed by hands-on workshops inspired by the current exhibitions. The museum gift shop sells some fantastic contemporary jewelry, while the 9th-floor restaurant/bar Robert (p110) is perfect for panoramic cocktails.

Paley Center for Media CULTURAL CENTER

(Map p70; ☏212-621-6800; www.paleycenter.org; 25 W 52nd St, btwn Fifth & Sixth Aves; suggested donation adult/child $10/5; ⊙noon-6pm Wed & Fri-Sun, to 8pm Thu; ⑤E, M to 5th Ave-53rd St) This pop-culture repository offers more than 160,000 TV and radio programs from around the world on its computer catalog. Reliving your favorite TV shows on one of the center's consoles is sheer bliss on a rainy day, as are the excellent, regular screenings, festivals, speakers and performers.

Bryant Park PARK

(Map p70; ☏212-768-4242; www.bryantpark. org; 42nd St, btwn Fifth & Sixth Aves; ⊙7am-midnight Mon-Fri, to 11pm Sat & Sun Jun-Sep, shorter hrs rest of year; ⑤B/D/F/M to 42nd St-Bryant Park, 7 to Fifth Ave) European coffee kiosks, alfresco chess games, summer film screenings and winter ice-skating: it's hard to believe that this leafy oasis was dubbed 'Needle Park' in the '80s. Nestled behind the beaux-arts New York Public Library building, it's a whimsical spot for a little time-out from the Midtown madness. Fancy taking a beginner Italian language, yoga or juggling class, joining a trivia contest, or signing up for a birding tour? The park offers a daily smorgasbord of quirky activities.

Intrepid Sea, Air & Space Museum MUSEUM

(Map p70; ☏877-957-7447; www.intrepidmuse um.org; Pier 86, Twelfth Ave at W 46th St; Intrepid & Growler submarine adult/child $26/19, incl Space Shuttle Pavilion adult/child $36/29; ⊙10am-5pm Mon-Fri, to 6pm Sat & Sun Apr-Oct, 10am-5pm Mon-Sun Nov-Mar; ☕; ☐westbound M42, M50 to 12th Ave, ⑤A/C/E to 42nd St-Port Authority Bus Terminal) In WWII, the USS *Intrepid* survived both a bomb and kamikaze attacks. Thankfully, this hulking aircraft carrier is now a lot less stressed, playing host to a multi-million-dollar interactive military museum that tells its tale through videos, historical artifacts and frozen-in-time living quarters. The flight deck features fighter planes and military helicopters, which might inspire you to try the museum's high-tech flight simulators.

Museum of Sex MUSEUM

(Map p70; ☏212-689-6337; www.museumofsex. com; 233 Fifth Ave, at 27th St; adult $17.50, $20.50 Sat & Sun; ⊙10am-9pm Sun-Thu, 11am-11pm Fri & Sat; ⑤N/R to 23rd St) Get the lowdown on anything from online fetishes to homosexual necrophilia in the mallard duck at this slick ode to all things hot and sweaty. The rotating program of temporary exhibitions has included explorations of cyber sex and retrospectives of controversial artists, while the permanent collection showcases the likes of erotic lithographs and awkward anti-onanism (masturbation) devices.

◉ Upper West Side & Central Park

For better or worse, banks and chain stores have homogenized the Upper West Side's formerly eclectic streetscape, yet somehow it still holds the power to make many a visitor feel like they've stepped into a Woody

Central Park & Uptown

0 — 0.5 miles
0 — 1 km

EDGEWATER

Hudson River

Riverbank State Park

Henry Hudson Pkwy
Riverside Dr

Riverside Dr E

Columbia University

116th St–Columbia University

W 140th St
W 137th St–City College
W 135th St
W 130th St
W 122nd St
W 112th St (Cathedral Pkwy)
W 110th St
W 106th St
W 104th St
W 102nd St
W 100th St

City College

St Nicholas Park
St Nicholas Ave
St Nicholas Tce
Convent Ave
Amsterdam Ave
Broadway

LaSalle St

MORNINGSIDE HEIGHTS

Cathedral Church of St John the Divine

W 125th St

W 138th St

W 135th St
W 130th St

Morningside Ave
Morningside Dr
Morningside Park

Cathedral Pkwy (110th St)

103rd St
Cathedral Pkwy (Duke Ellington Blvd)

UPPER WEST SIDE

Yankee Stadium (12hu)

Harlem River

Harlem River Dr

HARLEM

W 138th St
W 135th St
W 130th St
W 127th St
W 125th St
W 122nd St
W 120th St
W 118th St
W 116th St
W 112th St

Adam Clayton Powell Jr Blvd (Seventh Ave)
Malcolm X Blvd (Lenox Ave)
Fifth Ave
Frederick Douglass Blvd (Eighth Ave)
St Nicholas Ave

Apollo Theater

Studio Museum in Harlem

135th St
125th St
116th St
Central Park North (110th St)

Marcus Garvey Park
Madison Ave
Park Ave

Central Park North (110th St)

Great Hill
North Meadow
The Pool
The Loch
Harlem Meer
Conservatory Garden
East Meadow

MOTT HAVEN

E 138th St
E 127th St
E 122nd St
E 120th St
E 118th St
E 116th St
E 112th St
E 110th St
E 106th St
E 104th St
E 102nd St

Willis Ave
3rd Ave
138th St–3rd Ave
138th St–Grand Concourse

Major Deegan Expwy
Bruckner Blvd

Brook Ave
Cypress Ave

Bruckner Blvd

Robert F Kennedy Bridge (Triborough Bridge)

Franklin D Roosevelt Dr

Icahn Stadium
Ward's Island

Astoria Pool (0.7mi)

SPANISH HARLEM

First Ave
Second Ave
Third Ave (Luis Munoz Marin Blvd)
Park Ave
Madison Ave
Fifth Ave
Lexington Ave

La Marqueta
Jefferson Park

116th St (Luis Munoz Marin Blvd)
110th St
103rd St

Central Park North (110th St)

UPPER EAST SIDE

Martin Luther King Jr Blvd (W 125th St)

2 10 25 36 9 28 54 52 31 44 17 29 21 3

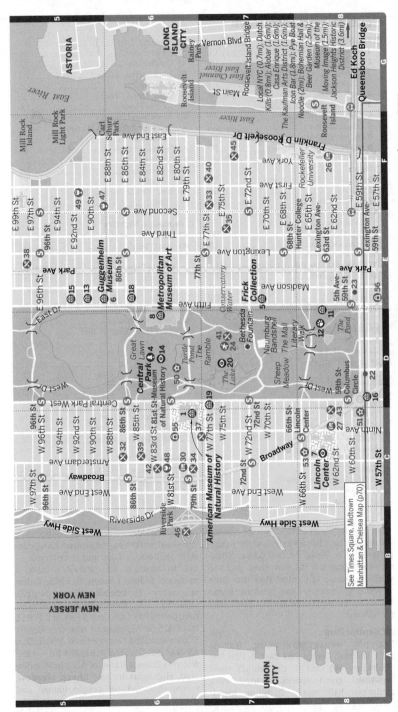

ASTORIA

LONG ISLAND CITY

Rainey Park

Vernon Blvd

Roosevelt Island Bridge

Local NYC (0.7mi); Dutch
Kills (0.8mi); Alobar (1.6mi);
Casa Enrique (1.6mi);
The Kaufman Arts District (1.6mi);
Icon Bar (1.8mi); Pye Boat
Noodle (2mi); Bohemian Hall &
Beer Garden (2.5mi);
Museum of the
Moving Image (1.5mi);
Jackson Heights Historic
District (3.6mi)

Ed Koch
Queensboro Bridge

Mill Rock Island

Mill Rock Light Park

East River

Carl Schurz Park

East River

East Channel

East River

Roosevelt Island

Main St

Roosevelt Island

Rockefeller University

Hunter College

Franklin D Roosevelt Dr

York Ave

First Ave

E 57th St

E 59th St

Lexington Ave

Park Ave

Madison Ave

5th Ave-59th St

See Times Square, Midtown
Manhattan & Chelsea Map (p70)

NEW YORK
NEW JERSEY

UNION CITY

Riverside Park

Riverside Dr

West Side Hwy

West End Ave

Broadway

Amsterdam Ave

Central Park West

American Museum of
Natural History

Central Park

Great Lawn

The Ramble

The Lake

Sheep Meadow

Bethesda Fountain

Naumburg Bandshell

The Mall

Literary Walk

Columbus Circle

59th St-
Columbus Circle

Lincoln
Center

Guggenheim Museum

Metropolitan Museum of Art

Frick Collection

Conservatory Water

The Pond

Central Park & Uptown

Allen movie. Several world-class cultural institutions have homes here, and the neighborhood is bordered by two parks: Riverside Park lines the Hudson River, and the verdant expanse of Central Park, the city's antidote to concrete and honking horns frames the eastern boundary like a backyard for millions.

★ **Central Park**   PARK
(Map p76; www.centralparknyc.org; 59th to 110th Sts, btwn Central Park West & Fifth Ave; ⊙6am-1am; ⊕) One of the world's most renowned green spaces, Central Park comprises 843 acres of rolling mead-

ows, boulder-studded outcroppings, elm-lined walkways, manicured European-style gardens, a lake and a reservoir — not to mention an outdoor theater, a memorial to John Lennon, an idyllic waterside eatery — the **Loeb Boathouse** (Map p76; ☑ 212-517-2233; www.thecentralparkboathouse. com; Central Park Lake, Central Park, at E 74th St; mains $25-36; ⊙restaurant noon-4pm Mon-Fri, 9:30am-4pm Sat & Sun year-round, 5:30-9:30pm Apr-Nov; ⑤B, C to 72nd St; 6 to 77th St) — and one very famous statue of Alice in Wonderland. Highlights include **Sheep Meadow**, where thousands of people lounge and play on warm days; precious animals at the

Central Park Zoo (Map p76; ☎212-439-6500; www.centralparkzoo.com; Central Park, 64th St, at Fifth Ave; adult/child $12/7; ☉10am-5pm Mon-Fri, to 5:30 Sat & Sun; ♿; ⒮N/Q/R to 5th Ave-59th St); and the forest-like paths of the **Ramble** (Map p76; Central Park, mid-park from 73rd to 79th Sts; ⒮B,C to 81st St), a wooded thicket that's popular with bird-watchers.

Like the city's subway system, the vast and majestic Central Park, a rectangle of open space in the middle of Manhattan, is a great class leveler – exactly what it was envisioned to be. Created in the 1860s and '70s by Frederick Law Olmsted and Calvert Vaux on the marshy northern fringe of the city, the immense park was designed as a leisure space for all New Yorkers regardless of color, class or creed. It's also an oasis from the insanity: the lush lawns, cool forests, flowering gardens, glassy bodies of water and meandering, wooded paths provide the dose of serene nature that New Yorkers crave.

Olmsted and Vaux — who also created Prospect Park (p85) in Brooklyn — were determined to keep foot and road traffic separated and cleverly designed the crosstown transverses under elevated roads to do so. That such a large expanse of prime real estate has survived intact for so long is proof that nothing eclipses the heart, soul and pride that forms the foundation of New York City's greatness.

Today this 'people's park' is still one of the city's most popular attractions, beckoning throngs of New Yorkers with free outdoor concerts on the **Great Lawn** (Map p76; www.centralparknyc.org; Central Park, btwn 79th & 86th Sts; ☉mid-Apr–mid-Nov; ⒮B, C to 86th St), and top-notch drama at the annual Shakespeare in the Park (p91) productions, held each summer at the open-air Delacorte Theater (p115). Other recommended stops include the ornate Bethesda Fountain, which edges the Lake and its Loeb Boathouse (p90), where you can rent rowboats or enjoy lunch at an outdoor cafe; the **Shakespeare Garden**, on the west side between 79th and 80th Sts, with its lush plantings and excellent skyline views. While parts of the park swarm with joggers, in-line skaters, musicians and tourists on warm weekends, it's quieter on weekday afternoons, especially in the less-trodden spots above 72nd St, such as the **Harlem Meer** and the **North Meadow** (north of 97th St).

Folks flock to the park even in winter, when snowstorms inspire cross-country skiing and sledding or just a simple stroll through the white wonderland, and crowds turn out every New Year's Eve for a midnight run. The Central Park Conservancy (p91) offers ever-changing **guided tours** of the park, including ones that focus on public art, wildlife and places of interest to kids.

Bethesda Fountain
FOUNTAIN

(Map p76; Central Park; ⒮B, C to 72nd St) This neoclassical fountain is one of New York's largest. It's capped by the *Angel of the Waters,* who is supported by four cherubim. The fountain, created by bohemian-feminist sculptor Emma Stebbins in 1868, makes a great meet-up and people-watching spot.

★Lincoln Center
CULTURAL CENTER

(Map p76; ☎212-875-5456, tours 212-875-5350; www.lincolncenter.org; Columbus Ave, btwn W 62nd & 66th Sts; tours adult/student $25/20; ♿; ⒮1 to 66th St-Lincoln Center) FREE This stark arrangement of gleaming Modernist temples houses some of Manhattan's most important performance companies: the New York Philharmonic, the New York City Ballet and the iconic Metropolitan Opera House, whose lobby's interior walls are dressed with brightly saturated murals by painter Marc Chagall. Various other venues are tucked in and around the 16-acre campus, including a theater and the renowned Juilliard School.

★American Museum of Natural History
MUSEUM

(Map p76; ☎212-769-5100; www.amnh.org; Central Park West, at W 79th St; suggested donation adult/child $22/12.50; ☉10am-5:45pm, Rose Center to 8:45pm Fri; ♿; ⒮B, C to 81st St-Museum of Natural History, 1 to 79th St) Founded in 1869, this classic museum contains a veritable wonderland of more than 30 million artifacts – including lots of menacing dinosaur skeletons – as well as the **Rose Center for Earth & Space**, with its cutting-edge planetarium. From September through May, the museum is home to the **Butterfly Conservatory**, a glasshouse featuring 500-plus butterflies from all over the world.

New-York Historical Society
MUSEUM

(Map p76; ☎212-873-3400; www.nyhistory.org; 170 Central Park West, at 77th St; adult/child $20/6, by donation 6-8pm Fri, library free; ☉10am-6pm Tue-Thu & Sat, to 8pm Fri, 11am-5pm Sun; ♿; ⒮B, C to 81st St-Museum of Natural History) As the antiquated hyphenated name implies, the

Central Park

THE LUNGS OF NEW YORK

The rectangular patch of green that occupies Manhattan's heart began life in the mid-19th century as a swampy piece of land that was carefully bulldozed into the idyllic nature-scape you see today. Since officially becoming Central Park, it has brought New Yorkers of all stripes together in interesting and unexpected ways. The park has served as a place for the rich to show off their fancy carriages (1860s), for the poor to enjoy free Sunday concerts (1880s) and for activists to hold be-ins against the Vietnam War (1960s).

Since then, legions of locals – not to mention travelers from all kinds of faraway places – have poured in to stroll, picnic, sunbathe, play ball and catch free concerts and performances of works by Shakespeare.

Loeb Boathouse
Perched on the shores of the Lake, the historic Loeb Boathouse is one of the city's best settings for an idyllic meal. You can also rent rowboats and bicycles and ride on a Venetian gondola.

Duke Ellington Circle

Harlem Meer

The Blockhouse   North Woods

97th St Transverse

Fifth Ave

86th St Transverse

The Great Lawn

Central Park West

Conservatory Garden
The only formal garden in Central Park is perhaps the most tranquil. On the northern end, chrysanthemums bloom in late October. To the south, the park's largest crab apple tree grows by the Burnett Fountain.

Jacqueline Kennedy Onassis Reservoir
This 106-acre body of water covers roughly an eighth of the park's territory. Its original purpose was to provide clean water for the city. Now it's a good spot to catch a glimpse of waterbirds.

Belvedere Castle
A so-called 'Victorian folly,' this Gothic-Romanesque castle serves no other purpose than to be a very dramatic lookout point. It was built by Central Park co-designer Calvert Vaux in 1869.

The park's varied terrain offers a wonderland of experiences. There are quiet, woodsy knolls in the north. To the south is the reservoir, crowded with joggers. There are European gardens, a zoo and various bodies of water. For maximum flamboyance, hit the Sheep Meadow on a sunny day, when all of New York shows up to lounge.

Central Park is more than just a green space. It is New York City's backyard.

FAST FACTS

➡ The landscape architects were Frederick Law Olmsted and Calvert Vaux.

➡ Construction commenced in 1858.

➡ The park covers 843 acres.

➡ Hundreds of movies have been shot on location, from Depression-era blockbuster *Gold Diggers* (1933) to monster-attack flick *Cloverfield* (2008).

Conservatory Water

This pond is popular in the warmer months, when children sail their model boats across its surface. Conservatory Water was inspired by 19th-century Parisian model-boat ponds and figured prominently in EB White's classic book, *Stuart Little*.

CHRISTOPHER PENLER/SHUTTERSTOCK ©

KRIDSADA KAMSOMBAT/SHUTTERSTOCK ©

Bethesda Fountain

This neoclassical fountain is one of New York's largest. It's capped by the *Angel of the Waters*, which is supported by four cherubim. The fountain was created by bohemian-feminist sculptor Emma Stebbins in 1868.

Metropolitan Museum of Art

Alice in Wonderland Statue

79th St Transverse

The Ramble

Delacorte Theater

The Lake

Fifth Ave

Central Park Zoo

65th St Transverse

Sheep Meadow

Strawberry Fields

A simple mosaic memorial pays tribute to musician John Lennon, who was killed across the street outside the Dakota Building. Funded by Yoko Ono, its name is inspired by the Beatles song 'Strawberry Fields Forever.'

The Mall/ Literary Walk

A Parisian-style promenade – the only straight line in the park – is flanked by statues of literati on the southern end, including Robert Burns and Shakespeare. It is lined with rare North American elms.

Columbus Center

Historical Society is the city's oldest museum, founded in 1804 to preserve the city's historical and cultural artifacts. Its collection of more than 60,000 objects is quirky and fascinating and includes everything from George Washington's inauguration chair to a 19th-century Tiffany ice-cream dish (gilded, of course), plus a remarkable collection of Hudson River School paintings. However, it's far from stodgy, having moved into the 21st century with renewed vigor and purpose.

Riverside Park   PARK
(Map p76; ☑212-870-3070; www.riverside parknyc.org; Riverside Dr, btwn 68th & 155th Sts; ⊙6am-1am; 🚇; Ⓢ1/2/3 to any stop btwn 66th & 157th Sts) A classic beauty designed by Central Park creators Frederick Law Olmsted and Calvert Vaux, this waterside spot, running north on the Upper West Side and banked by the Hudson River from 59th to 155th Sts, is lusciously leafy. Plenty of bike paths, playgrounds and dog runs make it a family favorite. Views from the park make the Jersey side of the Hudson look pretty.

Arsenal   HISTORIC BUILDING
(Map p76; ☑gallery 212-360-8163; www.nyc govparks.org; Central Park, at Fifth Ave & E 64th St; ⊙9am-5pm Mon-Fri; Ⓢ N/R/W to 5th Ave-59th St) **FREE** Built between 1847 and 1851 (its construction predates Central Park) as a munitions supply depot for the New York State National Guard, this landmark brick building was designed to look like a medieval castle. Today the building houses a small gallery, which often exhibits works with an historical or environmental focus, such as nature in the city, living landmarks or waterfalls of upstate New York.

◉ Upper East Side

Despite the storied mansions and outrageous per capita income, it's not all 'real housewives' up here. Post-collegiate bros share high-rise rentals east of the busy, commercial strip of Lexington Ave. You will find liveried doormen guarding marble lobbies in prewar condominiums lining Park Ave. And, yes, Botox is administered like vitamins. High-end boutiques line Madison Ave and Fifth Ave, which runs parallel to the leafy realms of Central Park and ends in an architectural flourish called Museum Mile – one of the most cultured strips in the city, if not the world.

★**Metropolitan Museum of Art**   MUSEUM
(Map p76; ☑212-535-7710; www.metmuseum. org; 1000 Fifth Ave, at 82nd St; suggested donation adult/student/child $25/12/free; ⊙10am-5:30pm Sun-Thu, to 9pm Fri & Sat; 🚇; Ⓢ4/5/6, Q to 86th St) This sprawling, encyclopedic museum founded in 1870 houses one of the largest art collections in the world. Its permanent collection has more than two million individual objects, from Egyptian temples to American paintings. Known colloquially as 'The Met,' the museum attracts over six million visitors a year to its 17 acres of galleries, making it the largest single-site attraction in New York City. In other words, plan on spending some time here – it is *B-I-G*.

★**Guggenheim Museum**   MUSEUM
(Map p76; ☑212-423-3500; www.guggenheim.org; 1071 Fifth Ave, at E 89th St; adult/child $25/free, by donation 5:45-7:45pm Sat; ⊙10am-5:45pm Sun-Wed & Fri, to 7:45pm Sat, closed Thu; 🚇; Ⓢ4/5/6 to 86th St) A sculpture in its own right, architect Frank Lloyd Wright's building almost overshadows the collection of 20th-century art it houses. The museum's holdings include works by Kandinsky, Picasso and Jackson Pollock. Over time, other key additions have been made, including paintings by Monet, Van Gogh and Degas, photographs by Robert Mapplethorpe, and key surrealist works. Temporary exhibitions are the real draw – the best of which are stunning site-specific installations by some of the great visionary artists of today.

★**Frick Collection**   GALLERY
(Map p76; ☑212-288-0700; www.frick.org; 1 E 70th St, cnr Fifth Ave; adult/student $22/12, pay-what-you-wish 2-6pm Wed; ⊙10am-6pm Tue-Sat, 11am-5pm Sun; Ⓢ6 to 68th St-Hunter College) This spectacular art collection sits in a mansion built by prickly steel magnate Henry Clay Frick, one of the many such residences lining the section of Fifth Ave that was once called 'Millionaires' Row.' The museum has over a dozen splendid rooms displaying masterpieces by Titian, Vermeer, Gilbert Stuart, El Greco, Joshua Reynolds, Goya and Rembrandt. Sculpture, ceramics and antique furniture and clocks are also on display.

**Cooper-Hewitt National
Design Museum**   MUSEUM
(Map p76; ☑212-849-8400; www.cooperhewitt. org; 2 E 91st St, at Fifth Ave; adult/child $18/free, pay-what-you-wish 6-9pm Sat; ⊙10am-6pm Sun-

Fri, to 9pm Sat; (S) 4/5/6 to 86th St) Part of the Smithsonian Institution in Washington, DC, this is the only US museum dedicated to both historic and contemporary design. Housed in the 64-room mansion built by billionaire Andrew Carnegie in 1901, the 210,000-piece collection offers artful displays spanning 3000 years over three floors of the building. An extensive renovation added exhibitions with interactive touch screens and a nifty electronic 'pen' that allows you to create your own designs and save them to a website for later retrieval.

Neue Galerie   MUSEUM
(Map p76; ☑ 212-628-6200; www.neuegalerie.org; 1048 Fifth Ave, cnr 86th St; adult/student $20/10, 6-8pm 1st Fri of the month free; ☉ 11am-6pm Thu-Mon; (S) 4/5/6 to 86th St) This restored Carrère and Hastings mansion from 1914 is a resplendent showcase for Austrian and German art, featuring works by Paul Klee, Ernst Ludwig Kirchner and Egon Schiele. In pride of place on the 2nd floor is Gustav Klimt's golden 1907 portrait of Adele Bloch-Bauer – acquired for the museum by cosmetics magnate Ronald Lauder for a whopping $135 million. The fascinating story of the painting's history is told in the 2015 film *Woman in Gold*.

Museum of the City of New York   MUSEUM
(Map p76; ☑ 212-534-1672; www.mcny.org; 1220 Fifth Ave, btwn E 103rd & 104th Sts; suggested admission adult/child $18/free; ☉ 10am-6pm; (S) 6 to 103rd St) Situated in a Georgian Colonial Revival-style building, this local museum focuses solely on New York City's past, present and future. Don't miss the 28-minute film *Timescapes* (on the 2nd floor), which charts NYC's growth from tiny native trading post to burgeoning metropolis.

Jewish Museum   MUSEUM
(Map p76; ☑ 212-423-3200; www.thejewish museum.org; 1109 Fifth Ave, btwn E 92nd & 93rd Sts; adult/child $15/free, Sat free, by donation 5-8pm Thu; ☉ 11am-6pm Sat-Tue, to 4pm Thu & Fri, closed Wed; ♿; (S) 6 to 96th St) This New York City gem occupies a French-Gothic mansion from 1908, housing 30,000 items of Judaica, as well as sculpture, painting and decorative arts. It hosts excellent temporary exhibits, featuring retrospectives on influential figures such as Art Spiegelman, as well as world-class shows on the likes of Marc Chagall, Édouard Vuillard and Man Ray, among other past luminaries.

☉ Harlem & Upper Manhattan

Originally settled by Dutch farmers in the 17th century, and later home to waves of Irish, Italian and Jewish immigrants, Harlem's identity is most inextricably connected to the African American experience. These days, despite ever-expanding gentrification, it remains packed with feverish preachers and choirs, soul-food menus and swinging jazz clubs. Franco African and French expat-owned restaurants add to the mix. Working-class East Harlem (known colloquially as Spanish Harlem or El Barrio) is a vibrant hub for Hispanic immigrants, while Columbia University is expanding into West Harlem. In the borough's north, leafy Inwood is home to unexpected medieval treasures.

★ **Cathedral Church of**
St John the Divine   CATHEDRAL
(Map p76; ☑ tours 212-316-7540; www.stjohn divine.org; 1047 Amsterdam Ave, at W 112th St, Morningside Heights; suggested donation $10, highlights tour $14, vertical tour $20; ☉ 7:30am-6pm, highlights tour 11am & 2pm Mon, 11am & 1pm Tue-Sat, 1pm selected Sun, vertical tour 10am Mon, noon Wed & Fri, noon & 2pm Sat; (S) B, C, 1 to 110th St-Cathedral Pkwy) The largest place of worship in the US has yet to be completed – and probably won't be any time soon. But this storied Episcopal cathedral nonetheless commands attention with its ornate Byzantine-style facade, booming vintage organ and extravagantly scaled nave – twice as wide as that of London's Westminster Abbey. Aside from a one-hour **highlights tour**, the cathedral also offers a one-hour **vertical tour**, taking you on a steep climb to the top of the cathedral (bring your own flashlight).

★ **Apollo Theater**   HISTORIC BUILDING
(Map p76; ☑ 212-531-5300, tours 212-531-5337; www.apollotheater.org; 253 W 125th St, btwn Frederick Douglass & Adam Clayton Powell Jr Blvds, Harlem; tickets from $16; (S) A/C, B/D to 125th St) The Apollo is an intrinsic part of Harlem history and culture. A leading space for concerts and political rallies since 1914, its venerable stage hosted virtually every major black artist in the 1930s and '40s, including Duke Ellington and Billie Holiday. Decades later, it would help launch the careers of countless stars, from Diana Ross and Aretha Franklin to Michael Jackson and Lauryn Hill. Today, its thriving program of music, dance, master classes and special events continues to draw crowds and applause.

Abyssinian Baptist Church   CHURCH
(Map p76; ☑212-862-7474; www.abyssinian.org;
132 Odell Clark Pl, btwn Adam Clayton Powell Jr &
Malcolm X Blvds, Harlem; ☺tourist gospel service
11:30am Sun early-Sep–Jul; Ⓢ2/3 to 135th St) A
raucous, soulful affair, the superb Sunday
gospel services here are the city's most famous. You'll need to arrive at least an hour
before the service to queue up, and ensure
you adhere to the strict entry rules: no tank
tops, flip-flops, shorts, leggings or back-
packs. The entry point for tourists is at the
southeast corner of West 138th Street and
Adam Clayton Powell Jr. Blvd.

★**Cloisters Museum & Gardens**   MUSEUM
(Map p61; ☑212-923-3700; www.metmuseum.org/
cloisters; 99 Margaret Corbin Dr, Fort Tryon Park;
suggested donation adult/child $25/free; ☺10am-
5:15pm; Ⓢ A to 190th St) On a hilltop overlooking the Hudson River, the Cloisters is a curious architectural jigsaw,
its many parts made up of various European monasteries and other historic
buildings. Built in the 1930s to house the
Metropolitan Museum's medieval treasures, its frescoes, tapestries and paintings are set in galleries that sit around a
romantic courtyard, connected by grand
archways and topped with Moorish
terra-cotta roofs. Among its many rare treasures is the beguiling 16th-century tapestry
series *The Hunt of the Unicorn*.

★**Studio Museum in Harlem**   MUSEUM
(Map p76; ☑212-864-4500; www.studio
museum.org; 144 W 125th St, at Adam Clayton Powell Jr Blvd, Harlem; suggested donation $7, Sun free;
☺noon-9pm Thu & Fri, 10am-6pm Sat, noon-6pm
Sun; Ⓢ2/3 to 125th St) This small, cultural
gem has been exhibiting the works of African American artists for more than four decades. While its rotating exhibition program
is always fascinating, the museum is not just
another art display center. It is an important
point of connection for Harlem cultural figures of all stripes, who arrive to check out
a rotating selection of shows, attend film
screenings or sign up for gallery talks.

⊙ Brooklyn

Brooklyn's sprawling checkerboard of distinct neighborhoods is more than three
times the size of Manhattan, not to mention
more diverse and far-reaching. For skyline
views and a pinch of history, try brownstone-
studded Brooklyn Heights, or Williamsburg
for vintage wares and late-night bar crawls.

★**Brooklyn Bridge Park**   PARK
(Map p62; ☑718-222-9939; www.brooklynbridge
park.org; East River Waterfront, btwn Atlantic Ave &
Adams St; ☺6am-1am; ⌖; Ⓢ A/C to High St; 2/3
to Clark St; F to York St) FREE This 85-acre park
is one of Brooklyn's best-loved new attractions. Wrapping around a bend on the East
River, it runs for 1.3 miles from the eastern
edge of the Manhattan Bridge in Dumbo to
the west end of Atlantic Ave in Cobble Hill.
It has revitalized a once-barren stretch of
shoreline, turning a series of abandoned
piers into beautifully landscaped parkland
with jaw-dropping views of Manhattan.
There's lots to see and do here, with playgrounds, walkways and lawns.

★**Coney Island**   AREA
(Map p61; www.coneyisland.com; Surf Ave & Boardwalk, btwn W 15th & W 8th Sts; Ⓢ D/F, N/Q to Coney Island-Stillwell Ave) About 50 minutes by
subway from Midtown, this popular beach
neighborhood makes for a great day trip.
The wide sandy beach of Coney Island has
retained its nostalgic, kitschy and slightly
sleazy charms, its wood-plank boardwalk
and its famous 1927 Cyclone roller coaster
amid a modern amusement-park area. Na-
than's Famous (p104) churns out hot dogs,
and the **New York Aquarium** (www.nyaquar-
ium.com) is a big hit with kids, as is taking
in an early evening baseball game at **MCU
Park** (☑718-372-5596; www.brooklyncyclones.
com; 1904 Surf Ave, at 17th St, Coney Island; tickets
$10-20, all tickets on Wed $10; Ⓢ D/F, N/Q to Coney
Island-Stillwell Ave), the waterfront stadium for
the minor league Brooklyn Cyclones.

The area traces its amusement-park roots
to the mid-1800s, when inhabitants of the increasingly industrialized city began to seek
relief from their sweltering tenements in
summer. By the late 19th century, the area
was a rough-and-tumble party spot dubbed
'Sodom by the Sea.' In the early 1900s, however, family amusements began to material-
ize. The most famous, Luna Park, opened in
1903 – a dream world with live camels and
elephants, illuminated by more than a million bulbs. Today, it is still possible to ride
the Wonder Wheel (opened in 1920) and the
clackety Cyclone roller coaster (1927). The
area was a bit of a ghost town in the '80s,
but it has experienced a resurgence in recent
years, drawing New Yorkers who come to
chow on hot dogs, catch a sideshow and dress
up like punk mermaids at the annual **Mer-
maid Parade** (☺late Jun). It ain't Disney –
but it isn't meant to be.

★**Brooklyn Museum**   MUSEUM
(Map p61; ☏ 718-638-5000; www.brooklynmuseum.
org; 200 Eastern Pkwy, Prospect Park; suggested
donation $16, 19yr & under free; ☉ 11am-6pm Wed
& Fri-Sun, to 10pm Thu; ☻; ⓢ 2/3 to Eastern Pkwy-
Brooklyn Museum) This encyclopedic museum
is housed in a five-story, 560,000-sq-ft beaux-
arts building designed by McKim, Mead
& White. Today, the building houses more
than 1.5 million objects, including ancient
artifacts, 19th-century period rooms, and
sculptures and painting from across several
centuries. It offers a great alternative to the
packed-to-the-gills institutions in Manhattan, and it often features thought-provoking
temporary exhibitions. The first Saturday
of the month (except September) features
special events (live music, performance art)
when the museum stays open until 11pm.

★**Prospect Park**   PARK
(☏ 718-965-8951; www.prospectpark.org; Grand
Army Plaza; ☉ 5am-1am; ⓢ 2/3 to Grand Army
Plaza; F to 15th St-Prospect Park) The creators of
the 585-acre Prospect Park – Frederick Law
Olmsted and Calvert Vaux – considered this
an improvement on their other New York
project, Central Park. Created in 1866, Prospect Park has many of the same features.
It's gorgeous, with a long meadow running
along the western half, filled with soccer,
football, cricket and baseball players (and
barbecuers), hilly forests and a lovely lake
and boathouse on the east side.

New York Transit Museum   MUSEUM
(Map p61; ☏ 718-694-1600; www.mta.info/mta/
museum; Schermerhorn St, at Boerum Pl; adult/
child $10/5; ☉ 10am-4pm Tue-Fri, 11am-5pm Sat
& Sun; ☻; ⓢ 2/3, 4/5 to Borough Hall; R to Court
St) Occupying an old subway station built
in 1936 (and out of service since 1946), this
kid-friendly museum takes on 100-plus years
of getting around town. The best part is the
downstairs area, on the platform, where you
can climb aboard 13 original subway and
elevated train cars dating from 1904. Temporary exhibitions highlight the subway's
fascinating history, including one dedicated
to the recently inaugurated Second Ave line.
The museum's gift shop sells popular sub-
way-map gifts.

Brooklyn Botanic Garden   GARDENS
(Map p61; www.bbg.org; 150 Eastern Pkwy, Prospect
Park; adult/child $12/free, Tue & 10am-noon Sat
free; ☉ 8am-6pm Tue-Fri, 10am-6pm Sat & Sun,
hours vary in winter; ☻; ⓢ 2/3 to Eastern Pkwy-
Brooklyn Museum) One of Brooklyn's most
picturesque attractions, this 52-acre garden
is home to thousands of plants and trees,
as well as a **Japanese garden** where river
turtles swim alongside a Shinto shrine. The
best time to visit is late April or early May,
when the blooming cherry trees (a gift from
Japan) are celebrated in **Sakura Matsuri**,
the Cherry Blossom Festival.

Brooklyn Children's Museum   MUSEUM
(Map p61; ☏ 718-735-4400; www.brooklynkids.org;
145 Brooklyn Ave, at St Marks Ave, Crown Heights;
11, free 2-6pm Thu; ☉ 10am-5pm Tue-Sun; ☻;
ⓢ C to Kingston-Throop Aves; 3 to Kingston Ave)
A bright-yellow, L-shaped structure houses this hands-on kids' favorite, which was
founded in 1899. The collection contains
almost 30,000 cultural objects (musical
instruments, masks and dolls) and natural history specimens (rocks, minerals and
a complete Asian elephant skeleton). But
Brooklyn is very much in the house, with a
re-created bodega, a pizza joint, and a Caribbean market that kids can play-act in. The
museum is located next to Brower Park and
is about a mile from the Grand Army Plaza.

Brooklyn Brewery   BREWERY
(Map p61; ☏ 718-486-7422; www.brooklynbrew
ery.com; 79 N 11th St, btwn Berry St & Wythe Ave,
Williamsburg; tours free Sat & Sun, $15 5pm Mon-
Thu; ☉ tours 5pm Mon-Thu, 1-5pm Sat, 1-4pm Sun;
tasting room 6-11pm Fri, noon-8pm Sat, noon-6pm
Sun; ⓢ L to Bedford Ave) Harking back to a time
when this area of New York was a beer brewing center, the Brooklyn Brewery not only
brews and serves tasty local suds, but also
offers tours of its facilities.

Brooklyn Heights Promenade   VIEWPOINT
(btwn Orange & Remsen Sts; ☉ 24hr; ☻; ⓢ 2/3 to
Clark St) All of the east–west lanes of Brooklyn Heights (such as Clark and Pineapple
Sts) lead to the neighborhood's number-one
attraction: a narrow park with breathtaking
views of Lower Manhattan and New York
Harbor, hanging over the busy Brooklyn–
Queens Expressway (BQE). This little slice of
urban beauty is a great spot for a sunset walk.

⊙ **The Bronx**

Home of hip-hop, known for its gritty South
Bronx street culture and its web of highways
carrying other New Yorkers further north,
the Bronx is actually as green as it is urban:
Wave Hill, Van Cortlandt Park, Pelham Bay
Park and the New York Botanical Gardens

City Walk
A Village Stroll

START COMMERCE ST
END WASHINGTON SQUARE PARK
LENGTH 1.2 MILES; ONE HOUR

Of all the neighborhoods in New York City, Greenwich Village is the most walkable, with its cobbled corners that stray from the signature gridiron that unfurls across the rest of the island. Start your walkabout at the ❶ **Cherry Lane Theater**. Established in 1924, the small theater is the city's longest continuously running off-Broadway establishment, and was the center of creative activity during the 1940s.

Make a left on Bedford and you'll find ❷ **90 Bedford** on the right-hand side at the corner of Grove St. You might recognize the apartment block as the fictitious home of the cast of *Friends*. For another iconic TV landmark, wander up Bleecker St and make a right on Perry St, stopping at ❸ **66 Perry St**, which was used as the facade and stoop of the city's turn-of-the-21st-century 'It Girl', Carrie Bradshaw, in *Sex and the City*.

Make a right on W 4th St until you reach ❹ **Christopher Park**, where two white, life-sized statues of same-sex couples stand guard. On the north side of the green space is the legendary Stonewall Inn, where a clutch of fed-up drag queens rioted for their civil rights in 1969, signaling the start of what would become the gay revolution.

Follow Christopher St to Sixth Ave to find the ❺ **Jefferson Market Library** straddling a triangular plot of land. The 'Ruskinian Gothic' spire was once a fire lookout tower. In the 1870s the building was used as a courthouse but today it houses a library.

Stroll down Sixth Ave, then make a left on Minetta Lane to swing by ❻ **Cafe Wha?**, the notorious institution where many young musicians and comedians – such as Bob Dylan and Richard Pryor – got their start.

End your wandering further along Mac-Dougal St in ❼ **Washington Square Park**, the Village's unofficial town square, which plays host to loitering NYU students, buskers and a regular crowd of protesters chanting about various global and municipal injustices.

are just a few of its leafy areas. Orchard Beach, the 'Bronx Riviera', draws crowds in summertime and America's oldest and largest zoo is here. Architectural gems line art-deco Grand Concourse, and Arthur Ave is the place to go for old school Italian red-sauce joints.

Yankee Stadium   STADIUM

(Map p61; ☑718-293-4300, tours 646-977-8687; www.newyork.yankees.mlb.com; E 161st St, at River Ave; tours $20; ⑤B/D, 4 to 161st St-Yankee Stadium) The Boston Red Sox like to talk about their record of eight World Series championships in the last 90 years...well, the Yankees have won a mere 27 in that period. The team's magic appeared to have moved with them across 161st St to the new Yankee Stadium, where they played their first season in 2009 – winning the World Series there in a six-game slugfest against the Phillies. The Yankees play from April to October.

Bronx Zoo   ZOO

(Map p61; ☑718-220-5100; www.bronxzoo.com; 2300 Southern Blvd; full experience tickets adult/child $37/27, suggested donation Wed; ☺10am-5pm Mon-Fri, to 5:30pm Sat & Sun Apr-Oct, to 4:30pm Nov-Mar; ⑤2, 5 to West Farms Sq-E Tremont Ave) This 265-acre zoo is the country's biggest and oldest, with over 6000 animals and re-created habitats from around the world, from African plains to Asian rainforests. It's deservedly popular, with especially large crowds on discounted Wednesdays and weekends, and any day in July or August (try to go Monday morning). If heading in on the subway, the southwest Asia Gate (a couple blocks north of the West Farms Sq–E Tremont Ave stop, up Boston Rd) is your easiest access point.

New York Botanical Garden   GARDENS

(Map p61; ☑718-817-8716; www.nybg.org; 2900 Southern Blvd; weekdays adult/child $23/10, weekends $28/12, Wed & 9-10am Sat grounds admission free; ☺10am-6pm Tue-Sun; ⚑; � Metro-North to Botanical Garden) First opened in 1891 and incorporating 50 acres of old-growth forest, the New York Botanical Garden is home to the restored **Enid A Haupt Conservatory**, a grand, Victorian iron-and-glass edifice that is now a New York landmark. See the website for a list of regular events, which include themed walking tours, children's book readings and film screenings.

City Island   ISLAND

(Map p61; ⌨Bx29) Although City Island is technically part of the Bronx, it has more in common with the small fishing villages that dot the north Atlantic seaboard. The approximately 1.5-mile-long island is home to a collection of alluring homes, teeming bars, some of the best seafood in the five boroughs and, of course, spectacular views of the Long Island Sound. This little slice of nautical heaven is for those interested in a truly unique New York City experience.

Woodlawn Cemetery   CEMETERY

(Map p61; ☑877-496-6352, 718-920-0500; www. thewoodlawncemetery.org; Webster Ave, at E 233rd St; ☺8:30am-4:30pm; ⑤4 to Woodlawn) As elegant as Brooklyn's Green-Wood is this 400-acre cemetery, the most prestigious resting place in the Bronx. Dating from the Civil War (1863), it claims more big names than Green-Wood – and yes, it is a contest – among its 300,000-plus headstones, including Herman Melville and jazz greats such as Miles Davis and Duke Ellington. Ask at the front for a photo pass if you want to snap pictures.

◉ Queens

The largest of the city's boroughs and with nearly half of its residents foreign-born, Queens is truly a world apart. But other than downtown Flushing and East River condominiums, it's mostly a low-rise sprawl, suburban (think of the TV show *King of Queens*) and a patchwork of diverse communities. *Terra incognita* to other New Yorkers and far from fashionable Brooklyn confines, pockets of Queens are as fascinating as anywhere in the city. Gorge at diners and delis from around the world, ride the surf in hip Rockaway Beach and visit contemporary art centers scattered throughout the borough.

★Museum of the Moving Image   MUSEUM

(Map p61; ☑718-777-6888; www.movingimage. us; 36-01 35th Ave, Astoria; adult/child $15/7, free 4-8pm Fri; ☺10:30am-2pm Wed & Thu, to 8pm Fri, 11:30am-7pm Sat & Sun; ⑤M, R to Steinway St) This super-cool complex is one of the world's top film, television and video museums. Galleries show a collection of 130,000-plus artifacts, including Elizabeth Taylor's wig from *Cleopatra,* nearly everything related to *Seinfeld* and a whole room of vintage arcade games. Interactive displays – such as a DIY flipbook station – show the science behind the art.

LOCAL KNOWLEDGE

THE SUBWAY IS YOUR FRIEND

A few tips for understanding the madness of the New York subway:

Numbers, letters, colors Color-coded subway lines are named by a letter or number, and most carry a collection of two to four trains on their tracks.

Express & local lines A common mistake is accidentally boarding an 'express train' and passing by a local stop you want. Know that each color-coded line is shared by local trains and express trains; the latter make only select stops in Manhattan (indicated by a white circle on subway maps). For example, on the red line, the 2 and 3 are express, while the slower 1 makes local stops. If you're covering a greater distance – say from the Upper West Side to Wall St – you're better off transferring to the express train (usually just across the platform from the local) to save time.

Getting in the right station Some stations – such as SoHo's Spring St station on the 6 line – have separate entrances for downtown or uptown lines (read the sign carefully). If you swipe in at the wrong one – as even locals do on occasion – you'll either need to ride the subway to a station where you can transfer for free, or just lose the $2.75 and re-enter the station (usually across the street). Also look for the green and red lamps above the stairs at each station entrance; green means that it's always open, while red means that particular entrance will be closed at certain hours, usually late at night.

Weekends All the rules switch on weekends, when some lines combine with others, some get suspended, some stations get passed, and others get reached. Locals and tourists alike stand on platforms confused, sometimes irate. Check www.mta.info for weekend schedules. Sometimes posted signs aren't visible until after you reach the platform.

★ **MoMA PS1** GALLERY
(Map p61; ☑ 718-784-2084; www.momaps1.org; 22-25 Jackson Ave, Long Island City; suggested donation adult/child $10/free, free with MoMA ticket, Warm Up party online/at venue $18/20; ☺ noon-6pm Thu-Mon, Warm Up parties 3-9pm Sat Jul-Aug; ⑤ E, M to Court Sq-23rd St; G, 7 to Court Sq) At MoMA's hip contemporary outpost, set in a converted former public school, you'll be peering at videos through floorboards, schmoozing at DJ parties and debating the meaning of nonstatic structures while staring through a hole in the wall.

Fort Totten HISTORIC SITE
(☑ 718-352-4793; https://www.nycgovparks.org/parks/fort-totten-park; Totten Ave & 15 Rd, Bayside; ☺ 7am-9pm; 🚌 Q16) FREE The remnants of a decommissioned Civil War-era fortress give this park its name, but that is hardly all Fort Totten has to offer. The grounds are full of historic buildings, rolling fields, and even a public pool. There are special tours – the Halloween-themed haunted lantern tour is a must – and events year-round. As the park is on the far edge of the city, it offers a slice of quiet that is rare in NYC.

New York Hall of Science MUSEUM
(Map p61; ☑ 718-699-0005; www.nysci.org; 47-01 111th St; adult/child $16/13; free 2-5pm Fri & 10-11am Sun; ☺ 9:30am-5pm Mon-Fri, 10am-6pm Sat & Sun; ⑤ 7 to 111th St) Occupying a weird 1965 building, rippling with stained glass, this science museum is unapologetically nerdy. An outdoor mini-golf course and playground don't require as much brain power.

Queens Museum MUSEUM
(Map p61; QMA; ☑ 718-592-9700; www.queensmuseum.org; Flushing Meadows Corona Park, Queens; suggested donation adult/child $8/free; ☺ 11am-5pm Wed-Sun; ⑤ 7 to 111th St or Mets-Willets Point) The Queens Museum is one of the city's unexpected pleasures. Its most famous installation is the Panorama of New York City, a gob-smacking 9335-sq-ft miniature New York City, with all buildings accounted for and a 15-minute dusk-to-dawn light simulation. The museum also hosts top exhibitions of global contemporary art, reflecting the diversity of Queens. A fascinating upcoming exhibit explores some of the interesting and avant-garde NYC designs that never came to fruition, realized through drawings and 3-D models.

Greater Ridgewood Historic Society HOUSE
(Map p61; www.onderdonkhouse.org; 1820 Flushing Ave, Ridgewood; suggested donation $3; ☺ 1-4pm Sat, noon-4pm Sun; ⑤ L to Jefferson St) On a mostly deserted block on the border

of Bushwick, Brooklyn and Ridgewood, Queens sits the oldest Dutch colonial stone house in New York City. The grounds and exterior are immaculately kept and the inside of the house features a permanent exhibit on the history of the house and NYC's history. Guided tours are given on Saturdays and Sundays for a suggested donation and there are special events year-round.

The Kaufman Arts District   ARTS CENTER
(http://www.kaufmanartsdistrict.com/; 34-12 36th St; Ⓢ M or R train to Steinway St, N or Q train to 36th St) Anchored by the legendary Kaufman studios in Long Island City, this up-and-coming arts district is a place you'll want to check out so you can say you knew it before it becomes the new Chelsea. In addition to institutions like the Noguchi Museum, the Kaufman Arts District also puts on events and public art pieces around the area. There are plenty of restaurants and bars to pop into between gallery visits.

Unisphere   MONUMENT
(Map p61; Flushing Meadows Park; Ⓢ 7 to 111th St or Mets-Willets Point) Designed for the 1964 World's Fair, this 12-story-high stainless-steel globe is the focal point of Flushing Meadows Park, and the de facto icon of Queens. (Nowadays, it's probably most recognizable as the backdrop for the Beastie Boys' *Licensed to Ill* album cover or scenes in the films *Men in Black* and *Iron Man 2*). In summer, it's ringed with fountains; at other times, it's crisscrossed by skateboarders.

◉ Staten Island

Staten Island feels a world away from Manhattan. This is the land of Shaolin (according to the Wu Tang Clan), of velour sweatsuits, pasta with gravy (red meat sauce), the starting point for the NYC marathon, homes of clapboard and aluminum siding and three cast members of MTV's *Jersey Shore*. If not for its namesake ferry that docks in downtown St George, on the island's northeastern tip, it would be mostly forgotten. Unfashionably suburban, it's not without its drawcards, especially cultural and gustatory ones, plus new developments in St George like a new 630 ft-high Ferris wheel, the world's tallest.

🏃 Activities

★ Staten Island Ferry   CRUISE
(Map p62; www.siferry.com; Whitehall Terminal, 4 South St, at Whitehall St; ⊙ 24hr; Ⓢ 1 to South Ferry; R/W to Whitehall St; 4/5 to Bowling Green) **FREE** Staten Islanders know these hulking, orange ferryboats as commuter vehicles, while Manhattanites like to think of them as their secret, romantic vessels for a spring-day escape. Yet many tourists (at last count, two million a year) are clued into the charms of the Staten Island Ferry, whose 25-minute, 5.2-mile journey across the harbor between lower Manhattan and the Staten Island neighborhood of St George is one of NYC's finest free adventures.

Central Park Bike Tours   CYCLING
(Map p76; ☑ 212-541-8759; www.centralpark biketours.com; 203 W 58th St, at Seventh Ave; rentals per 2hr/day $14/28, 2hr tours $49; ⊙ 9am-8pm; Ⓢ A/C, B/D, 1 to 59th St-Columbus Circle) This place rents out good bikes (helmets, locks and bike map included) and leads two-hour guided tours of Central Park and the Brooklyn Bridge area.

Russian & Turkish Baths   BATHHOUSE
(Map p66; ☑ 212-674-9250; www.russianturk ishbaths.com; 268 E 10th St, btwn First Ave & Ave A; per visit $45; ⊙ noon-10pm Mon-Tue & Thu-Fri, from 10am Wed, from 9am Sat, from 8am Sun; Ⓢ L to 1st Ave; 6 to Astor Pl) Since 1892, this cramped and grungy downtown spa has been drawing a polyglot and eclectic mix: actors, students, frisky couples, singles-on-the-make, Russian regulars and old-school locals, who strip down to their skivvies (or the roomy cotton shorts provided) and rotate between steam baths, an ice-cold plunge pool, a sauna and the sundeck. Most hours are co-ed (clothing required), but there are several blocks of men/women only hours (clothing optional). There are also massages, scrubs and Russian oak leaf treatments available.

Great Jones Spa   SPA
(Map p66; ☑ 212-505-3185; www.greatjonesspa. com; 29 Great Jones St, btwn Lafayette St & Bowery; ⊙ 9am-10pm; Ⓢ 6 to Bleecker St; B/D/F/M to Broadway-Lafayette St) Don't skimp on the services at this downtown feng shui–designed place, whose offerings include Moroccan rose sea-salt scrubs and stem-cell facials. If you spend over $100 per person (not difficult: hour-long massages start at $145; hour-long facials start at $135), you get access to the water lounge with thermal hot tub, sauna, steam room and cold plunge pool (swimwear required).

Downtown Boathouse KAYAKING

(Map p62; www.downtownboathouse.org; Pier 26, near N Moore St; ☺9am-5pm Sat & Sun mid-May–mid-Oct, plus 5-7:30pm Tue-Thu mid-Jun–mid-Sep; ⑤1 to Houston St) FREE New York's most active public boathouse offers free, walk-up 20-minute kayaking sessions (including equipment) in a protected embayment in the Hudson River on weekends and some weekday evenings. For more activities – kayaking trips, stand-up paddleboarding and classes – check out www.hudsonriverpark.org for the four other kayaking locations on the Hudson River. There's also a summer-only kayaking location on Governors Island (Map p61; ☎212-825-3045; www.govisland.com; ☺10am-6pm Mon-Fri, to 7pm Sat & Sun May-Oct; ⑤4/5 to Bowling Green; 1 to South Ferry) FREE.

Loeb Boathouse BOATING, CYCLING

(Map p76; ☎212-517-2233; www.thecentralpark boathouse.com; Central Park, btwn E 74th & 75th Sts; boating per $15, bike rental per $9-15; ☺10am-6pm Apr-Nov; ♿; ⑤B, C to 72nd St; 6 to 77th St) Central Park's boathouse has a fleet of 100 rowboats, as well as a Venetian-style gondola that seats up to six if you'd rather someone else do the paddling. Bicycles are also available (helmets included), weather permitting. Rentals require ID and a credit card.

Schooner Adirondack CRUISE

(Map p70; ☎212-627-1825; www.sail-nyc.com; Chelsea Piers Complex, Pier 62 at W 22nd St; tours $52-86; ⑤C, E to 23rd St) The two-masted *Dack* hits the New York Harbor with four two-hour sails daily from May to October. The 1920s-style, 80ft *Manhattan* and 100ft *Manhattan II* yachts offer tours throughout the week. Call or check the website for the latest times.

👉 Tours

NBC Studio Tours WALKING

(Map p70; ☎212-664-3700; www.thetouratnbc studios.com; 30 Rockefeller Plaza, entrance at 1250 Sixth Ave; tours adult/child $33/29, children under 6yr not admitted; ☺8:20am-2pm Mon-Fri, to 5pm Sat & Sun; ⑤B/D/F/M to 47th-50th Sts-Rockefeller Center) Peppered with interesting anecdotes, this revamped, one-hour tour takes TV fans through parts of the NBC Studios, home to iconic TV shows *Saturday Night Live* and *The Tonight Show Starring Jimmy Fallon*. Stops usually include the beautifully restored Art Deco Rotunda, two studios and the NBC Broadcast Operations Center. Things get interactive in the Tour Studio, where you get to 'star' or 'produce' your own talk show segment. Book online to avoid the queues.

On Location Tours BUS

(☎212-683-2027; www.onlocationtours.com; tours $49) Face it: you want to sit on Carrie Bradshaw's apartment stoop and check out the bar Michael Keaton frequents in *Birdman*. This company offers various tours – covering *Gossip Girl, Sex and the City, The Sopranos,* the *Real Housewives of NYC,*

NEW YORK FOR CHILDREN

The American Museum of Natural History (p79), with its dinosaurs, marine world, planetarium and IMAX films, should not be missed. Nearly every big museum – the Metropolitan Museum of Art (p82), the Museum of Modern Art (p73), Guggenheim Museum (p82), Museum of the City of New York (p83) and Cooper-Hewitt National Design Museum (p82) – all have kids' programs, but many smaller institutions are even more appealing for young visitors. Even the New-York Historical Society (p79) has its own children's history museum.

Toddler Time

For tots aged one to five, hit the **Children's Museum of the Arts** (Map p66; ☎212-274-0986; www.cmany.org; 103 Charlton St, btwn Greenwich & Hudson Sts; admission $12, 4-6pm Thu by donation; ☺noon-5pm Mon, noon-6pm Thu & Fri, 10am-5pm Sat & Sun; ♿; ⑤1 to Houston St; C/E to Spring St) in West SoHo and the Brooklyn Children's Museum (p85) in Crown Heights. Both have story times, art classes, craft hours and painting sessions.

Five & Over

Bigger kids can clamber on vintage subway cars at the New York Transit Museum (p85) or slide down a pole at the New York City Fire Museum (p64). Out in Astoria, the Museum of the Moving Image (p87) has hands-on exhibits for kids.

general TV and movie locations, and movie locations in Central Park – that let you live out your entertainment-obsessed fantasies.

Big Onion Walking Tours WALKING
(☑888-606-9255; www.bigonion.com; tours $25) Choose from nearly 30 tours, including Brooklyn Bridge and Brooklyn Heights, the 'Official' Gangs of New York Tour, a Gay and Lesbian History Tour – Before Stonewall, and Chelsea and the High Line.

Municipal Art Society WALKING
(☑212-935-3960; www.mas.org; tours from $25) The Municipal Art Society offers various scheduled tours focusing on architecture and history. Among them is a 75-minute tour of Grand Central Terminal (p73), departing daily at 12:30pm from the station's Main Concourse.

Central Park Conservancy WALKING
(Map p76; ☑212-310-6600; www.central parknyc.org/tours; 14 E 60th St, btwn Madison & Fifth Aves; ⑤N/R/W to 5th Ave-59th St) The non-profit organization that supports Central Park maintenance also offers a wide range of walking tours around the park. Some tours are free (such as the Heart of the Park tour, which takes in the park's highlights), while others cost $15 and require advance booking.

Big Apple Greeter (Accessible) TOURS
(☑212-669-8198; www.bigapplegreeter.org) FREE The Big Apple Greeter program has more than 50 volunteers with disabilities (visible or invisible) on staff, who are happy to show off their favorite corners of the city. The tours are free and the company has a no-tipping policy. It's best to contact them three to four weeks before your arrival.

Queens Historical Society WALKING
(☑718-939-0647; www.queenshistoricalsociety. org; 143-35 37th Ave, Flushing; admission $5, tours from $20; ⊙2:30-4:30pm Tue, Sat & Sun; ⑤7 to Flushing-Main St) Set in the 18th-century Kingsland Homestead, this group has a small museum and offers walking tours through various neighborhoods in Queens. These include nearby sites associated with early religious-freedom movements and later Underground Railroad efforts.

⭐ Festivals & Events

Shakespeare in the Park THEATER
(www.publictheater.org) The much-loved Shakespeare in the Park pays tribute to the Bard, with free performances in Central Park. It's a magical experience. The catch? You'll have to wait hours in line to score tickets, or win them in the online lottery.

Tribeca Film Festival FILM
(☑212-941-2400; www.tribecafilm.com; ⊙Apr) Founded in 2003 by Robert De Niro and Jane Rosenthal, the Tribeca Film Festival is now a major star of the indie movie circuit. Gaggles of celebs come to walk the red carpets each spring.

Restaurant Week FOOD & DRINK
(☑212-484-1222; www.nycgo.com/restaurant-week; ⊙Jan-Feb & Jul-Aug) Score big-time discounts at top-notch eateries during this biannual festival held in January and February, then again in July and August; three-course lunches go for around $29, and dinners are around $42.

San Gennaro Festival STREET CARNIVAL
(www.sangennaro.org; ⊙Sep) Rowdy, loyal crowds descend on the narrow streets of Little Italy for carnival games, sausage-and-fried-peppers sandwiches, deep-fried Oreos and more Italian treats than you can stomach in one evening. Held over 10 days in mid-September, it remains an old-world tradition; 2017 marked the festival's 90th year.

🛏 Sleeping

In general, expect high prices and small spaces. Room rates waver by availability, not by any high-season or low-season rules. Of course, you'll pay dearly during holidays. Accommodations fill up quickly – especially in summer – and range from boxy cookie-cutter chains to stylish boutiques. No Manhattan neighborhood has a monopoly on a single style and you'll find better value hotels in Brooklyn and Queens.

🛏 Financial District & Lower Manhattan

Wall Street Inn HOTEL $$
(Map p62; ☑212-747-1500; www.thewallstreet inn.com; 9 S William St; r $140-280; ❄ 🔊; ⑤2/3 to Wall St) The sedate stone exterior of this affordable, intimate inn belies its warm, colonial-style interior. Beds are big and plush, and rooms have glossy wood furnishings and long drapes. The bathrooms are full of appreciated touches, like Jacuzzis in the deluxe rooms and tubs in the others. Wi-fi and breakfast are included.

SoHo & Chinatown

Bowery House
HOSTEL **$**

(Map p66; ☑212-837-2373; www.thebowery house.com; 220 Bowery, btwn Prince & Spring Sts; s/d with shared bath from $80/130; ❄@☎; ⑤R/W to Prince St) Across the street from the New Museum, this former 1920s-era flophouse has been resurrected as an upmarket hostel, its rooms decked out with Bowery-themed film posters and custom-made mattresses (ie shorter and narrower), while communal bathrooms feature rain showers and heated floors. There's also a stylish lounge area with Chesterfield sofas and chandeliers, a buzzing bar and a roof terrace.

Light sleepers may wish to avoid this place, which attracts a nightlife-loving crowd; earplugs come standard with every room.

Soho Grand Hotel
BOUTIQUE HOTEL **$$**

(Map p66; ☑212-965-3000; www.sohogrand.com; 310 W Broadway; d $255-700; ❄@☎❄; ⑤A/C/E to Canal St) The original boutique hotel of the 'hood still reigns, with its striking glass-and-cast-iron lobby stairway, and 367 rooms with cool, clean lines plus Frette linens, plasma flat-screen TVs and Kiehl's grooming products. The lobby's Grand Lounge buzzes with scenesters and the occasional celebrity. Dogs are catered to, with amenities to match those of the human guests.

Solita SoHo
HOTEL **$$**

(Map p66; ☑212-925-3600; www.solitasoho hotel.com; 159 Grand St, at Lafayette St; d $185-285; ❄☎; ⑤N/Q/R, 6 to Canal St) Solita is good value for anyone wanting to soak up the flavor of Chinatown and (ever-shrinking) Little Italy. Part of the Ascend chain, the hotel has a clean, functional lobby and smallish, slightly octagonal rooms with wide beds and private baths with dual-massage shower heads. Low-season rates can see rooms go for less than $150.

East Village & Lower East Side

St Mark's Hotel
HOTEL **$**

(Map p66; ☑212-674-0100; www.stmarkshotel. net; 2 St Marks Pl, at Third Ave; d from $130; ❄☎; ⑤6 to Astor Pl) This East Village budget option draws a young, nightlife-loving crowd, who enjoy having one of the city's liveliest concentrations of bars and restaurants right outside the front door. With such low pric-

es, it's best to lower your expectations as the rooms are quite small and dated. Street noise is an issue for light sleepers and there's no elevator.

Bowery Hotel
BOUTIQUE HOTEL **$$$**

(Map p66; ☑212-505-9100; www.thebowery hotel.com; 335 Bowery, btwn 2nd & 3rd Sts; r $295-535; ❄@☎; ⑤F/V to Lower East Side-Second Ave; 6 to Bleecker St) Pick up your old-fashioned gold room key with its red tassel in the dark, hushed lobby filled with antique velvet chairs and faded Persian rugs. Then follow the mosaic-tiled floors to your room with huge factory windows and elegant four-poster beds. Settle in to watch a movie on your 42in plasma TV, or raid the luxury bathroom goodies.

The Bowery's zinc-topped bar, outside garden patio, and rustic Italian eatery, Gemma, are always packed.

West Village, Chelsea & Meatpacking District

Jane Hotel
HOTEL **$**

(Map p66; ☑212-924-6700; www.thejanenyc.com; 113 Jane St, btwn Washington St & West Side Hwy; r with shared/private bath from $115/295; [P]❄☎; ⑤L to Eighth Ave; A/C/E to 14th St; 1/2 to Christopher St-Sheridan Sq) The claustrophobic will want to avoid the Jane's tiny 50-sq-ft rooms, but if you want to live like a luxury sailor, check into this renovated red-brick gem, which was built for mariners in the early 20th century (*Titanic* survivors also stayed here in 1912). The gorgeous ballroom/bar looks like it belongs in a five-star hotel. More expensive captain's quarters come with private commodes.

Townhouse Inn of Chelsea
B&B **$$**

(Map p70; ☑212-414-2323; www.townhouseinn chelsea.com; 131 W 23rd St, btwn Sixth & Seventh Aves; d $150-300; ❄☎; ⑤F/V, 1 to 23rd St) Housed in a lone 19th-century, five-story townhouse with exposed brick and wood floors on busy 23rd St, this 14-room B&B is a Chelsea gem. Bought in 1998 and extensively renovated (with an elevator installed), the rooms are big and welcoming, with fanciful fabrics on big brass or poster beds and TVs held in huge armoires.

Standard
BOUTIQUE HOTEL **$$$**

(Map p66; ☑212-645-4646; www.standardhotels. com; 848 Washington St, at 13th St; d from $509; ❄☎; ⑤A/C/E to 14th St; L to Eighth Ave) Hipster hotelier André Balazs has built a wide, boxy, glass tower that straddles the High Line. Every room has sweeping Meatpacking District views and is filled with cascading sunlight, which makes the Standard's glossy, wood-framed beds and marbled bathrooms glow in a particularly homey way. There's also a hyper-modern Standard in the East Village.

The amenities are first-rate, with a buzzing German beer garden and a brasserie at street level (and ice rink in winter), and a plush nightclub on the top floor. The location is unbeatable, with the best of NYC right outside your door.

High Line Hotel HOTEL $$$
(Map p70; ☑212-929-3888; www.thehighline hotel.com; 180 Tenth Ave, btwn 20th & 21st Sts; d from $470) Serenity is assured during a stay inside this neo-Gothic building that was once part of the General Theological Seminary (still functioning in a building around the corner). The 60-room hotel has attractive guestrooms that blend contemporary and antique furnishings. The location is perfect for taking in the galleries of Chelsea or strolling the leafy High Line.

Union Square, Flatiron District & Gramercy

Carlton Arms HOTEL $
(Map p70; ☑212-679-0680; www.carltonarms. com; 160 E 25th St, at Third Ave; d with shared/private bath $120/150; ✷☎; ⑤6 to 23rd St or 28th St) The Carlton Arms channels the downtown edgy art world scene of yesteryear with the works of artists from all over the world adorning nearly every inch of the interiors. Murals follow the walls up five flights of stairs, and into each of the tiny guest rooms and shared bathrooms (there is a small sink in each guest room).

Marcel at Gramercy BOUTIQUE HOTEL $$
(Map p70; ☑212-696-3800; www.themarcelat gramercy.com; 201 E 24th St, at Third Ave; d from $300; ✷@☎; ⑤6 to 23rd St) The minimalist, 97-room Marcel is a poor-man's chic boutique, and that's not a bad thing. Rooms are simple yet modern (standard ones are walk-in closet size), their gray-and-beige color scheme shaken up by bold, canary-yellow Chesterfield bedheads. Bathrooms are uninspired but clean, while rooms on the avenue have decent views. Downstairs, the sleek lounge makes for a nifty place to unwind.

Midtown

★ **Yotel** HOTEL $$
(Map p70; ☑646-449-7700; www.yotel.com; 570 Tenth Ave, at 41st St, Midtown West; r from $250; ✷☎; ⑤A/C/E to 42nd St-Port Authority Bus Terminal; 1/2/3, N/Q/R, S, 7 to Times Sq-42nd St) Part futuristic spaceport, part *Austin Powers* set, this uber-cool 669-room option bases its rooms on airplane classes: premium cabin (economy), first cabins (business) and VIP suites (first); some first cabins and VIP suites include a private terrace with hot tub. Small but cleverly configured, premium cabins include automated adjustable beds, while all cabins feature floor-to-ceiling windows with killer views, slick bathrooms and iPod connectivity.

Pod 51 HOTEL $$
(Map p70; ☑212-355-0300; www.thepodhotel. com; 230 E 51st St, btwn Second & Third Aves, Midtown East; r with shared/private bathroom from $165/210; ✷☎; ⑤6 to 51st St; E/M to Lexington Ave-53rd St) A dream come true for folks who would like to live inside a cocoon – this affordable hot spot has a range of room types, most barely big enough for the bed. 'Pods' have bright bedding, tight workspaces, flat-screen TVs, iPod docking stations and 'raindrop' showerheads. In the warmer months, sip a drink on the perky rooftop deck.

414 Hotel HOTEL $$$
(Map p70; ☑212-399-0006; www.414hotel.com; 414 W 46th St, btwn Ninth & Tenth Aves, Midtown West; d from $256; ✷☎; ⑤C/E to 50th St) Set up like a guesthouse, with two combined brownstones, this friendly option offers 22 tidy rooms a couple of blocks west of Times Sq. Rooms are simply yet tastefully decorated, with cable TV, free wi-fi and private bathroom; those facing the leafy inner courtyard are the quietest. The courtyard itself is the perfect spot to enjoy the included breakfast during the warmer months.

Upper West Side & Central Park

Hostelling International New York HOSTEL $
(HI; Map p76; ☑212-932-2300; www.hinewyork. org; 891 Amsterdam Ave, at 103rd St; dm $54-75; ✷☎; ⑤1 to 103rd St) This red-brick mansion from the 1880s houses HI's 672 well-scrubbed and maintained bunks. It's rather 19th-century industrial, but benefits include good public areas, a backyard (that sees

barbecue action in the summer), a communal kitchen and a cafe. There are loads of activities on offer, from walking tours to club nights. There are attractive private rooms with private bathrooms too.

Lucerne
HOTEL $$

(Map p76; ☎212-875-1000; www.thelucerne hotel.com; 201 W 79th St, cnr Amsterdam Ave; d from $300; ❋☎; ⓢB, C to 81st St) This unusual 1903 structure breaks away from beaux arts in favor of the baroque with an ornately carved, terra-cotta-colored facade. Inside is a stately 200-room hotel, ideal for couples and families with children (Central Park and the American Museum of Natural History are a stone's throw away). Nine types of guest rooms evoke a contemporary Victorian look.

Empire Hotel
HOTEL $$$

(Map p76; ☎212-265-7400; www.empire hotelnyc.com; 44 W 63rd St, at Broadway; r from $370; ❋☎❋; ⓢ1 to 66th St-Lincoln Center) The bones are all that remain of the original Empire, just across the street from the Lincoln Center, with wholesale renovations dressing them in earthy tones and contemporary stylings complete with canopied pool deck, sexy rooftop bar and a dimly lit lobby lounge studded with zebra-print settees. Its 400-plus rooms come in various configurations, and feature brightly hued walls with plush dark leather furnishings.

🛏 Upper East Side

Bentley Hotel
BOUTIQUE HOTEL $$$

(Map p76; ☎212-644-6000; www.bentleyhotel nyc.com; 500 E 62nd St, at York Ave; d from $350; ❋☎; ⓢN/R to Lexington Ave/59th St, Q to Lexington Ave-63rd St) Featuring great East River views, the Bentley overlooks FDR Dr, as far east as you can go. Formerly an office building, the hotel has shed its utilitarian past in the form of chic boutique-hotel stylings, a swanky lobby and sleek rooms. The downside of staying here is the long walk to subway, restaurants and other essentials.

🛏 Harlem & Upper Manhattan

Harlem Flophouse
GUESTHOUSE $

(Map p76; ☎347-632-1960; www.harlemflop house.com; 242 W 123rd St, btwn Adam Clayton Powell Jr & Frederick Douglass Blvds, Harlem; d with shared bath $99-150; ☎; ⓢA/B/C/D, 2/3 to 124th St) Rekindle Harlem's Jazz Age in this atmospheric 1890s townhouse, its nostalgic rooms decked out in brass beds, polished

wood floors and vintage radios (set to a local jazz station). It feels like a delicious step back in time, which also means shared bathrooms, no air-con and no TVs. The owner is a great source of local information.

Allie's Inn
B&B $$

(Map p76; ☎646-283-3068, 212-690-3813; www. alliesinn.com; 313 W 136th St, btwn Frederick Douglass Blvd & Edgecombe Ave, Harlem; d $175-259, ste $310-340; ❋☎; ⓢB, C to 135th St) This Harlem charmer has just three guest rooms, all clean and comfortable, with oak floors, simple modern furnishings and small kitchen units. It's a refreshing alternative to the Midtown towers and ideal for those wanting to explore Harlem's rich culture, with notable eateries and bars nearby and the subway station just around the corner. Minimum two-night stay.

🛏 Brooklyn

Wythe Hotel
BOUTIQUE HOTEL $$

(☎718-460-8000; www.wythehotel.com; 80 Wythe Ave, at N 11th St, Williamsburg; d from $265; ❋☎; ⓢL to Bedford Ave; G to Nassau Ave) Set in a converted 1901 factory, the red-brick Wythe Hotel brings a serious dash of high design to Williamsburg. The industrial-chic rooms have beds made from reclaimed lumber, custom-made wallpaper (from Brooklyn's own Flavor Paper), exposed brick, polished concrete floors and original 13ft timber ceilings.

Nu Hotel
HOTEL $$

(☎718-852-8585; www.nuhotelbrooklyn.com; 85 Smith St; d from $220; ❋@☎; ⓢF, G to Bergen St) The 93 rooms in this downtown Brooklyn hotel are of the stripped-down variety, featuring lots of crisp whiteness (sheets, walls, duvets). Furnishings are made from recycled teak and the floors are cork. Groups can consider the bunk bed suite with a queen and twin bunks, or for something more daring, book a 'nu perspectives' room, adorned with colorful murals by Brooklyn artists.

🛏 Queens

Local NYC
HOSTEL $

(☎347-738-5251; www.thelocalny.com; 13-02 44th Ave, Long Island City; dm/d from $60/169; ❋☎; ⓢE, M to Court Sq-23rd St) This hostel has clean and small, simply designed rooms, with comfy mattresses and plenty of natural light. Guests have access to a fully stocked kitchen and the airy cafe-bar is a fine place to meet other travelers, with good coffee by day, and wine and beer by night. Throughout the week, there's a regular line-up of events (movie nights, live music, pub quizzes).

Eating

From inspired iterations of world cuisine where only corporate titans on expense accounts dare to dine to quintessentially local nibbles like hot dogs and pizza by the slice, New York City's dining scene is infinite, all-consuming and a testament to its kaleidoscopic citizenry. Even if you're not an obsessive foodie hitting ethnic enclaves or the newest cult-chef openings, an outstanding meal is always only a block away.

Financial District & Lower Manhattan

Hudson Eats   FAST FOOD $

(Map p62; ☑212-417-2445; www.brookfield placeny.com/directory/food; Brookfield Place, 230 Vesey St, at West St; dishes from $7; ⊙10am-9pm Mon-Sat, noon-7pm Sun; ☞; ⑤E to World Trade Center; 2/3 to Park Place; R/W to Cortlandt St; 4/5 to Fulton St; A/C to Chambers St) Renovated office and retail complex Brookfield Place is home to Hudson Eats, a sleek and upmarket food hall. It's decked out in terrazzo floors, marble counter tops and floor-to-ceiling windows with expansive views of Jersey City and the Hudson River.

Fish Market   SEAFOOD $

(Map p62; ☑917-363-8101; 111 South St, New York City; sandwiches from $9, mains $9-24; ⊙6pm-midnight Mon-Fri, noon-midnight Sat & Sun) This dive bar with a diverse seafood menu pays homage to the nautical South Street Seaport area of Manhattan that houses it. You will find cheap drinks any hour of the day and friendly bartenders and patrons. Throw in an order of popcorn shrimp or a seafood po'boy for the complete experience.

Brookfield Place   FOOD HALL, MARKET $$

(Map p62; ☑212-978-1698; www.brookfield placeny.com; 230 Vesey St, at West St; ☞; ⑤E to World Trade Center; 2/3 to Park Place; R/W to Cortlandt St; 4/5 to Fulton St; A/C to Chambers St) This polished, high-end office and retail complex offers two fabulous food halls. Francophile foodies should hit Le District, a charming and polished marketplace with several stand-alone restaurants and counters selling everything from stinky cheese to steak *frites*. One floor above is Hudson Eats, a

fashionable enclave of upmarket fast bites, from sushi and tacos to salads and burgers.

Da Mikele   PIZZA $$

(Map p62; ☑212-925-8800; www.luzzosgroup. com/about-us-damikele; 275 Church St, btwn White & Franklin Sts; pizzas $17-21; ⊙noon-10:30pm Sun-Wed, to 11:30pm Thu-Sat; ⑤1 to Franklin St; A/C/E, N/Q/R, J/Z, 6 to Canal St) An Italo-Tribeca hybrid where pressed tin and recycled wood meet retro Vespa, Da Mikele channels the *dolce vita* (sweet life) with its weeknight *aperitivo* (5pm to 7pm), where your drink includes a complimentary spread of lip-smacking bar bites. However, pizzas are the specialty. We're talking light, beautifully charred revelations, simultaneously crisp and chewy, and good enough to make a Neapolitan weep.

Le District   FRENCH $$

(Map p62; ☑212-981-8588; www.ledistrict.com; Brookfield Place, 225 Liberty St, at West St; market mains $16-24, Beauborg dinner mains $18-38; ⊙8:30am-11pm Mon-Sat, to 10pm Sun; ☞; ⑤E to World Trade Center; 2/3 to Park Place; R/W to Cortlandt St; 4/5 to Fulton St; A/C to Chambers St) Paris on the Hudson reigns at Le District, a sprawling French food emporium selling everything from high-gloss pastries and pretty *tartines* to smelly cheese and savory steak *frites*. Main restaurant **Beaubourg** has a large bistro menu, but for a quick sit-down feed, head to the **Market District** counter for a burger or the **Cafe District** for a savory crepe.

★ **Locanda Verde**   ITALIAN $$$

(Map p62; ☑212-925-3797; www.locandaverde nyc.com; 377 Greenwich St, at N Moore St; mains lunch $19-29, dinner $25-40; ⊙7am-11pm Mon-Thu, to 11:30pm Fri, 8am-11:30pm Sat, to 11pm Sun; ⑤A/C/E to Canal St; 1 to Franklin St) Step through the velvet curtains into a scene of loosened button-downs, black dresses and slick barmen behind a long, crowded bar. This celebrated brasserie showcases modern, Italo-inspired fare like housemade pappardelle with lamb Bolognese, mint-and-sheep's-milk ricotta and Sicilian-style halibut with heirloom squash and almonds. Weekend brunch is no less creative: try scampi and grits or lemon ricotta pancakes with blueberries. Bookings recommended.

Bâtard   MODERN AMERICAN $$$

(Map p62; ☑212-219-2777; www.batardtribeca.com; 239 W Broadway, btwn Walker & White Sts; 2/3/4 courses $58/75/85; ⊗5:30-10:30pm Mon-Sat, plus noon-2:30pm Fri; ⑤1 to Franklin St; A/C/E to Canal St) Austrian chef Markus Glocker heads this warm, Michelin-starred hot spot, where a pared-back interior puts the focus squarely on the food. Glocker's dishes are beautifully balanced and textured, whether it's a crispy branzino with cherry tomatoes, basil and asparagus; risotto with rabbit sausage, broccoli *spigarello* and preserved lemon; or scallop crudo with avocado mousse, lime, radish and black sesame.

SoHo & Chinatown

Bánh Mì Saigon Bakery VIETNAMESE $
(Map p66; ☑212-941-1541; www.banhmisaigon nyc.com; 198 Grand St, btwn Mulberry & Mott Sts; sandwiches $3.50-6; ⊗8am-6pm; ⑤N/Q/R, J/Z, 6 to Canal St) This no-frills storefront doles out some of the best *bánh mì* in town – we're talking crisp, toasted baguettes generously stuffed with hot peppers, pickled carrots, daikon, cucumber, cilantro and your choice of meat. Top billing goes to the classic barbeque pork version. Tip: head in by 3pm as the *bánh mì* sometimes sell out, upon which the place closes early. Cash only.

Café Gitane MEDITERRANEAN $
(Map p66; ☑212-334-9552; www.cafegitanenyc. com; 242 Mott St, at Prince St; salads $9.50-16, mains $14-17; ⊗8:30am-midnight Sun-Thu, to 12:30am Fri & Sat; ☑; ⑤N/R to Prince St; 6 to Spring St) Clear the Gauloise smoke from your eyes and blink twice if you think you're in Paris: bistro-esque Gitane has that kind of louche vibe. This is a classic see-and-be-seen haunt, popular with salad-picking models and the odd Hollywood regular. Join them for a nibble on the likes of blueberry and almond friands (small French cakes), heart-of-palm salad or Moroccan couscous with organic chicken. Cash only.

Grey Dog AMERICAN $
(Map p66; ☑212-966-1060; www.thegreydog. com; 244 Mulberry St; mains $8-15; ⊗7am-10pm Mon-Fri, 8am-10pm Sat & Sun; ⑤F/M/D/B train to Broadway-Lafayette) Whether you're looking to share a plate of cheese fries with your friends or indulge in a proper New York brunch, the Grey Dog won't disappoint. They do scrumptious takes on American classics that have full-on flavor without overdoing it. The order-at-the-counter system keeps this place bustling all day long.

Nice Green Bo CHINESE $
(New Green Bow; Map p62; ☑212-625-2359; www.nicegreenbo.com; 66 Bayard St, btwn Elizabeth & Mott Sts; mains $5.95-19.95; ⊗11am-midnight; ⑤N/Q/R, J/Z, 6 to Canal St; B/D to Grand St) Not a shred of effort – not even a new sign (you'll see!) – has been made to spruce up Nice Green Bo, and that's the way we like it. It's all about the food here: gorgeous *xiao long bao* served in steaming drums, heaping portions of noodles and gleaming plates of salubrious, sautéed spinach. Cash only.

Tacombi Fonda Nolita MEXICAN $
(Map p66; ☑917-727-0179; www.tacombi.com; 267 Elizabeth St, btwn E Houston & Prince Sts; tacos $4-7; ⊗11am-midnight Mon-Wed, to 1am Thu-Sat; ⑤F to 2nd Ave; 6 to Bleecker St) Festively strung lights, foldaway chairs and Mexican men flipping tacos in an old VW Kombi: if you can't make it to the Yucatan shore, here's your Plan B. Casual, convivial and ever-popular, Tacombi serves up fine, fresh tacos, including a fine *barbacoa* (roasted black Angus beef). Wash down the goodness with a pitcher of sangria and start plotting that south-of-the-border getaway.

★ Uncle Boons THAI $$
(Map p66; ☑646-370-6650; www.uncleboons. com; 7 Spring St, btwn Elizabeth St & Bowery; small plates $12-16, large plates $21-29; ⊗5:30-11pm Mon-Thu, to midnight Fri & Sat, to 10pm Sun; ☎; ⑤J/Z to Bowery; 6 to Spring St) Michelin-star Thai served up in a fun, tongue-in-cheek combo of retro wood-paneled dining room with Thai film posters and old family snaps. Spanning the old and the new, zesty, tangy dishes include fantastically crunchy *mieng kum* (betel-leaf wrap with ginger, lime, toasted coconut, dried shrimp, peanuts and chili), *kao pat puu* (crab fried rice) and banana blossom salad.

Butcher's Daughter VEGETARIAN $$
(Map p66; ☑212-219-3434; www.thebutchers daughter.com; 19 Kenmare St, at Elizabeth St; salads & sandwiches $12-14, dinner mains $16-18; ⊗8am-11pm; ☎☑; ⑤J to Bowery; 6 to Spring St) The butcher's daughter certainly has rebelled, peddling nothing but fresh herbivorous fare in her white-washed cafe. While healthy it is, boring it's not: everything from the soaked organic muesli to the spicy kale Caesar salad with almond Parmesan or the dinnertime Butcher's burger (vegetable and black-bean patty with cashew cheddar cheese) is devilishly delish.

La Esquina
MEXICAN $$

(Map p66; ☑646-613-7100; www.esquinanyc.com; 114 Kenmare St, at Petrosino Sq; tacos from $3.25, mains cafe $15-25, brasserie $18-34; ⊘taqueria 11am-1:45am daily, cafe noon-midnight Mon-Fri, from 11am Sat & Sun, brasserie 6pm-2am daily; ⑤6 to Spring St) This mega-popular and quirky little spot combines three places really: a stand-while-you-eat taco window, a casual Mexican cafe (entrance on Lafayette St) and a dim, slinky, cavernous brasserie downstairs requiring reservations. Standouts include the *elotes callejeros* (grilled corn with queso Cotija cheese, mayo and chili powder), pulled pork tacos and mango-jicama salad.

★Dutch
MODERN AMERICAN $$$

(Map p66; ☑212-677-6200; www.thedutchnyc.com; 131 Sullivan St, at Prince St; mains lunch $18-35, dinner $25-58; ⊘11:30am-11pm Mon-Thu, to 11:30pm Fri, 10am-11:30pm Sat, to 11pm Sun; ⑤C/E to Spring St; R/W to Prince St; 1 to Houston St) Whether perched at the bar or dining snugly in the back room, you can always expect smart, farm-to-table comfort grub at this see-and-be-seen stalwart. Flavors traverse the globe, from sweet potato tempura with Thai basil and fermented chili sauce to ricotta ravioli with Swiss chard and walnut pesto. Reservations are recommended, especially for dinner and all day on weekends.

★Estela
MODERN AMERICAN $$$

(Map p66; ☑212-219-7693; www.estelanyc.com; 47 E Houston St, btwn Mulberry & Mott Sts; dishes $15-38; ⊘5:30-11pm Sun-Thu, to 11:30pm Fri & Sat; ⑤B/D/F/M to Broadway-Lafayette St; 6 to Bleecker St) Estela might be hopeless at hide-and-seek (its location up some nondescript stairs hardly tricks savvy gourmands), but this busy, skinny wine-bar slays on the food and vino front. Graze from market-driven sharing plates, from phenomenal beef tartare (spiked with beef heart for added complexity) to moreish mussels *escabeche* on toast, or an impossibly sexy salad with walnuts and anchovy.

🍴 East Village & Lower East Side

Bait & Hook
SEAFOOD $

(Map p70; ☑212-260-8015; www.baitandhooknyc.com; 231 2nd Ave; specials start at $5, mains $12-18; ⊘noon-11pm Sun-Wed, noon-midnight Thu-Sat; ⑤L to 1st Ave) This Manhattan bar has happy hour specials worth celebrating and theme days that can't be missed. There's a good time any day of the week, be it Mussel Monday or Taco Tuesday. The interior is bright, airy and tastefully decorated with nautical kitsch.

El Rey
CAFE $

(Map p66; ☑212-260-3950; www.elreynyc.com; 100 Stanton St, btwn Orchard & Ludlow; small plates $8-15; ⊘7am-7pm Mon-Fri, from 8am Sat & Sun; ☑; ⑤F to 2nd Ave) This white, minimalist space on Stanton feels more SoCal than LES, and has a devoted following for its delectably inventive (and fairly priced) farm-to-table plates with a focus on hearty veggies. Microbrews, good coffees (from a Strada espresso machine) and wine round out the menu.

Meatball Shop
ITALIAN $

(Map p66; ☑212-982-8895; www.themeatballshop.com; 84 Stanton St, btwn Allen & Orchard Sts; sandwiches $13; ⊘11:30am-2am Sun-Thu, to 4am Fri-Sat; ⑤2nd Ave; F to Delancey St; J/M/Z to Essex St) Elevating the humble meatball to high art, the Meatball Shop serves up five varieties of juiciness (including a lentil vegetarian option and a mac 'n' cheese special). Order those balls on a hero (a long roll), add mozzarella and spicy tomato sauce, and voila: you have a tasty, if happily down-market, meal. This branch boasts a rock-and-roll vibe, with tattooed waitstaff and prominent beats. There are six other branches in NYC. Check the website for details.

Vanessa's Dumpling House
CHINESE $

(Map p66; ☑212-625-8008; www.vanessas.com; 118A Eldridge St, btwn Grand & Broome Sts; dumplings $1.50-6; ⊘10:30am-10:30pm Mon-Sat, to 10pm Sun; ⑤B/D to Grand St; J to Bowery; F to Delancey St) Tasty dumplings – served steamed, fried or in soup – are whipped together in iron skillets at lightning speed and tossed into hungry mouths at unbeatable prices.

Veselka
EASTERN EUROPEAN $

(Map p66; ☑212-228-9682; www.veselka.com; 144 Second Ave, at 9th St; mains $10-19; ⊘24hr; ⑤L to 3rd Ave; 6 to Astor Pl) A bustling tribute to the area's Ukrainian past, Veselka dishes out *varenyky* (handmade dumplings) and veal goulash amid the usual suspects of greasy comfort food. The cluttered spread of tables is available to loungers and carbo-loaders all night long, though it's a favorite any time of day, and a regular haunt for writers, actors and East Village characters.

★**Momofuku Noodle Bar** NOODLES $$
(Map p66; ☑212-777-7773; www.noodlebar-ny. momofuku.com; 171 First Ave, btwn E 10th & 11th Sts; mains $16; ☺noon-11pm Sun-Thu, to 1am Fri & Sat; ⓢL to 1st Ave; 6 to Astor Pl) With just 30 stools and a no-reservations policy, you'll always have to wait to cram into this bustling phenomenon. Queue up for the namesake special: homemade ramen noodles in broth, served with poached egg and pork belly, or some interesting combos. The menu changes daily and includes buns (such as brisket and horseradish), snacks (smoked chicken wings) and desserts.

★**Clinton Street Baking Company** AMERICAN $$
(Map p66; ☑646-602-6263; www.clintonstreet baking.com; 4 Clinton St, btwn Stanton & Houston Sts; mains $12-20; ☺8am-4pm & 5:30-11pm Mon-Sat, 9am-5pm Sun; ⓢJ/M/Z to Essex St; F to Delancey St; F to Second Ave) Mom-and-pop shop extraordinaire, Clinton Street Baking Company gets the blue ribbon in so many categories – best pancakes (blueberry!), best muffins, best po' boys (southern-style sandwiches), best biscuits etc – that you're pretty much guaranteed a stellar meal no matter what time you stop by. In the evenings, you can opt for 'breakfast for dinner' (pancakes, eggs Benedict, fish tacos or the excellent buttermilk fried chicken.

Katz's Delicatessen DELI $$
(Map p66; ☑212-254-2246; www.katzsdelica tessen.com; 205 E Houston St, at Ludlow St; sandwiches $15-22; ☺8am-10:45pm Mon-Wed, Sun to 2:45am Thu, from 8am Fri, 24hr Sat; ⓢF to 2nd Ave) Though visitors won't find many remnants of the classic, old-world Jewish LES dining scene, there are a few stellar holdouts, among them Katz's Delicatessen, where Meg Ryan faked her famous orgasm in the 1989 movie *When Harry Met Sally*. If you love classic deli grub like pastrami and salami on rye, it just might have the same effect on you. These days the lines are breathtakingly long, and the prices are high (Katz's signature hot pastrami sandwich costs a hefty $20).

Upstate SEAFOOD $$
(Map p66; ☑212-460-5293; www.upstatenyc.com; 95 First Ave, btwn E 5th & 6th Sts; mains $15-30; ☺5-11pm; ⓢF to 2nd Ave) Upstate serves outstanding seafood dishes and craft beers. The small, always-changing menu features the likes of beer-steamed mussels, seafood stew, scallops over mushroom risotto, softshell crab and wondrous oyster selections. There's no freezer – seafood comes from the market each day, so you know you'll be getting only the freshest ingredients. Lines can be long, so go early.

Degustation MODERN EUROPEAN $$$
(Map p66; ☑212-979-1012; www.degustation-nyc. com; 239 E 5th St, btwn Second & Third Aves; small plates $12-22, tasting menu $85; ☺6pm-11:30pm Mon-Sat, to 10pm Sun; ⓢ6 to Astor Pl) Blending Iberian, French and new-world recipes, Degustation does a beautiful array of tapas-style plates at this narrow, 19-seat eatery. It's an intimate setting, with guests seated around a long wooden counter while chef Oscar Islas Díaz and his team are center stage, firing up crisp octopus, lamb belly with soft poached egg, and paella with blue prawns and chorizo.

✗ West Village, Chelsea & Meatpacking District

★**Chelsea Market** MARKET $
(Map p70; www.chelseamarket.com; 75 9th Ave, btwn 15th & 16th Sts; ☺7am-9pm Mon-Sat, 8am-8pm Sun; ⓢA/C/E to 14th St) In a shining example of redevelopment and preservation, the Chelsea Market has taken a factory formerly owned by cookie giant Nabisco (creator of Oreo) and turned it into an 800ft-long shopping concourse that caters to foodies. Taking the place of the old factory ovens that churned out massive numbers of biscuits are eclectic eateries that fill the renovated hallways of this food haven.

Gansevoort Market MARKET $
(Map p70; www.gansmarket.com; 353 W 14th St, at Ninth Ave; mains $5-20; ☺8am-8pm; ⓢA/C/E, L to 14th St-8th Ave) Inside a brick building in the heart of the Meatpacking District, this sprawling market is the latest and greatest food emporium to land in NYC. A raw, industrial space lit by skylights, it features several dozen gourmet vendors slinging tapas, arepas, tacos, pizzas, meat pies, ice cream, pastries and more.

Red Bamboo CHINESE $
(Map p66; ☑212-260-7049; www.redbamboo-nyc. com/; 140 West 4th St; mains $8-13; ☺12:30pm-11pm Mon-Thu, 12:30pm-11:30pm Fri, noon-11:30pm Sat, noon-11pm Sun; ⓢD/B/F, M/A/C/E to West 4th Street) Flaky, hot bites of popcorn shrimp, ooey, gooey chicken Parmesan, chocolate cake so rich you can barely finish —

Red Bamboo offers all of that and more soul and Asian food options. The catch? Everything on their menu is vegan (some dishes do offer the option of real cheese). This is a must try for vegans, vegetarians or anyone looking to try something new.

Rosemary's   ITALIAN $$

(Map p66; ☑212-647-1818; www.rosemarysnyc. com; 18 Greenwich Ave, at W 10th St; mains $14-40; ⊗8am-4pm & 5-11pm Mon-Thu, until midnight Fri, opens 10am Sat-Sun, closes 11pm Sun; ⑤1 to Christopher St-Sheridan Sq) One of the West Village's hottest restaurants, Rosemary's serves high-end Italian fare that more than lives up to the hype. In a vaguely farmhouse-like setting, diners tuck into generous portions of housemade pastas, rich salads, and cheese and *salumi* (cured meat) boards. Everything from the simple walnut herb pesto to the succulent smoked lamb shoulder is incredible.

Cookshop   MODERN AMERICAN $$

(Map p70; ☑212-924-4440; www.cookshop ny.com; 156 Tenth Ave, btwn W 19th & 20th Sts; mains brunch $14-20, lunch $16-24, dinner $22-48; ⊗8am-11:30pm Mon-Fri, from 10am Sat, 10am-10pm Sun; ⑤L to 8th Ave; A/C/E to 23rd St) A brilliant brunching pit stop before (or after) tackling the verdant High Line across the street, Cookshop is a lively place that knows its niche and does it oh so well. Excellent service, eye-opening cocktails (good morning, bacon-infused BLT Mary!), a perfectly baked bread basket and a selection of inventive egg mains make this a Chelsea favorite on a Sunday afternoon.

★ Blue Hill   AMERICAN $$$

(Map p66; ☑212-539-1776; www.bluehillfarm. com; 75 Washington Pl, btwn Sixth Ave & Washington Sq W; prix-fixe menu $88-98; ⊗5-11pm Mon-Sat, to 10pm Sun; ⑤A/C/E, B/D/F/M to W 4th St-Washington Sq) A place for slow-food junkies with deep pockets, Blue Hill was an early crusader in the 'Local is Better' movement. Gifted chef Dan Barber, who hails from a farm family in the Berkshires, Massachusetts, uses harvests from that land and from farms in upstate New York to create his widely praised fare.

★ Foragers Table   MODERN AMERICAN $$$

(Map p70; ☑212-243-8888; www.foragers market.com/restaurant; 300 W 22nd St, at Eighth Ave; mains $17-32; ⊗5:30-10pm Mon-Fri, plus 9am-2:30pm Sat & Sun, to 9pm Sun; ☑; ⑤C/E, 1 to 23rd St) Owners of this outstanding restaurant run a 28-acre farm in the Hudson Valley, from which much of their seasonal menu is sourced. It changes frequently, but recent temptations include Long Island duck breast with roasted acorn squash, apples, chanterelle mushrooms and figs, grilled skate with red quinoa, creamed kale and *cippolini* onion and deviled farm eggs with Dijon mustard.

★ Jeffrey's Grocery   MODERN AMERICAN $$$

(Map p66; ☑646-398-7630; www.jeffreysgrocery. com; 172 Waverly Pl, at Christopher St; mains $25-39; ⊗8am-11pm Mon-Fri, from 9:30am Sat & Sun; ⑤1 to Christopher St-Sheridan Sq) This West Village classic is a lively eating and drinking spot that hits all the right notes. Seafood is the focus: there's an oyster bar and beautifully executed selections such as razor clams with caviar and dill, whole roasted dourade with curry, and sharing platters. Meat dishes include roasted chicken with Jerusalem artichoke and a humble but juicy pastrami burger.

★ RedFarm   FUSION $$$

(Map p66; ☑212-792-9700; www.redfarmnyc. com; 529 Hudson St, btwn W 10th & Charles Sts; mains $19-57, dumplings $14-20; ⊗5pm-11:45pm daily, plus 11am-2:30pm Sat & Sun, to 11pm Sun; ⑤A/C/E, B/D/F/M to W 4th St-Washington Sq; 1 to Christopher St-Sheridan Sq) RedFarm transforms Chinese cooking into pure, delectable artistry at this small, buzzing space on Hudson St. Fresh crab and eggplant bruschetta, juicy rib steak (marinated overnight in papaya, ginger and soy) and pastrami egg rolls are among the many creative dishes that brilliantly blend cuisines. Other hits include spicy crispy beef, pan-fried lamb dumplings and the grilled jumbo-shrimp red curry.

Waits can be long, so arrive early. Reservations are only made for parties of 8 or more. The bar downstairs, **Decoy**, is owned by the people behind RedFarm. Their specialty is a whole Peking duck. It's usually less crowded and serves a limited menu, but if you ask nicely you may be able to convince the bartender to bring down an order of soup dumplings for you.

✕ Union Square, Flatiron District & Gramercy

Tacombi Café El Presidente   MEXICAN $

(Map p70; ☑212-242-3491; www.tacombi.com; 30 W 24th St, btwn Fifth & Sixth Aves; tacos $4-5.50, quesadillas $6-9; ⊗11am-midnight Mon-Sat, to

10:30pm Sun; S F/M, R/W to 23rd St) Channeling the cafes of Mexico City, pink-and-green Tacombi covers numerous bases: from juice and liquor bar to taco joint. Score a table, order a margarita and hop your way around a menu of Mexican street-food deliciousness. Top choices include *esquites* (grilled corn with *cotija* cheese and chipotle mayonnaise, served in a paper cup) and succulent *carnitas michoacan* (beer-marinated pork) tacos.

Shake Shack
BURGERS $

(Map p70; ☑646-889-6600; www.shakeshack. com; Madison Square Park, cnr E 23rd St & Madison Ave; burgers $4.20-9.50; ⏲11am-10:30pm; S R/W, F/M, 6 to 23rd St) The flagship of chef Danny Meyer's gourmet burger chain, Shake Shack whips up hyper-fresh burgers, hand-cut fries and a rotating line-up of frozen custards. Veg-heads can dip into the crisp portobello burger. Lines are long – but worth it – and you can digest the filling meal while people-watching at tables and benches in the park.

Eisenberg's Sandwich Shop
SANDWICHES $

(Map p70; ☑212-675-5096; www.eisenbergs nyc.com; 174 Fifth Ave, btwn W 22nd & 23rd St; sandwiches $4-13; ⏲6:30am-8pm Mon-Fri, 9am-6pm Sat, to 5pm Sun; S R/W to 23rd St) This old-school diner – an anomaly on this mostly upscale stretch of real estate – is filled from morning to close with regulars in for traditional Jewish diner fare like chopped liver, pastrami and whitefish salad. Grab a stool at the long bar and rub elbows with an eclectic mix of customers who know meatloaf isn't a joke dish.

Eataly
FOOD HALL $$

(Map p70; ☑212-229-2560; www.eataly.com; 200 Fifth Ave, at W 23rd St; ⏲7am-11pm; ☑; S R/W, F/M, 6 to 23rd St) Mario Batali's sleek, sprawling temple to Italian gastronomy is a veritable wonderland. Feast on everything from vibrant *crudo* (raw fish) and *fritto misto* (tempura-style vegetables) to steamy pasta and pizza at the emporium's string of sit-down eateries. Alternatively, guzzle espresso at the bar and scour the countless counters and shelves for a DIY picnic hamper *nonna* would approve of.

★ Gramercy Tavern
MODERN AMERICAN $$$

(Map p70; ☑212-477-0777; www.gramercytavern. com; 42 E 20th St, btwn Broadway & Park Ave S; tavern mains $29-36, dining room 3-course menu $125, tasting menus $140-165; ⏲tavern noon-11pm Sun-Thu, to midnight Fri & Sat, dining room noon-2pm & 5:30-10pm Mon-Thu, to 11pm Fri, noon-1:30pm & 5:30-11pm Sat, 5:30-10pm Sun; ☑☑; S R/W, 6 to 23rd St) 🌿 Seasonal, local ingredients drive this perennial favorite, a vibrant, country-chic institution aglow with copper sconces, murals and dramatic floral arrangements. Choose from two spaces: the walk-in-only tavern and its à la carte menu, or the swankier dining room and its fancier prix-fixe and degustation feasts. Tavern highlights include a show-stopping duck meatloaf with mushrooms, chestnuts and brussels sprouts.

★ Craft
MODERN AMERICAN $$$

(Map p70; ☑212-780-0880; www.craftrestaurant. com; 43 E 19th St, btwn Broadway & Park Ave S; lunch $29-36, dinner mains $28-45; ⏲noon-10pm Mon-Thu, to 11pm Fri, 5:30pm-11pm Sat, to 10pm Sun; ☑; S 4/5/6, N/Q/R/W, L to 14th St-Union Sq) 🌿 Humming, high-end Craft flies the flag for small, family-owned farms and food producers, their bounty transformed into pure, polished dishes. Whether nibbling on flawlessly charred braised octopus, pillowy scallops or pumpkin mezzaluna pasta with sage, brown butter and Parmesan, expect every ingredient to sing with flavor. Book ahead Wednesday to Saturday or head in by 6pm or after 9:30pm.

🍴 Midtown

★ Totto Ramen
JAPANESE $

(Map p70; ☑212-582-0052; www.tottoramen.com; 366 W 52nd St, btwn Eighth & Ninth Aves; ramen from $11; ⏲noon-4:30pm & 5:30pm-midnight Mon-Sat, 4-11pm Sun; S C/E to 50th St) There might be another two branches in Midtown, but purists know that neither beats the tiny, 20-seat original. Write your name and number of guests on the clipboard and wait your turn. Your reward: extraordinary ramen. Go for the pork, which sings in dishes like miso ramen (with fermented soybean paste, egg, scallions, bean sprouts, onion and homemade chili paste).

Burger Joint
BURGERS $

(Map p70; ☑212-708-7414; www.burgerjointny. com; Le Parker Meridien, 119 W 56th St, btwn Sixth & Seventh Aves; burgers from $9.50; ⏲11am-11:30pm Sun-Thu, to midnight Fri & Sat; S F to 57th St) With only a small neon burger as your clue, this speakeasy-style burger hut lurks behind the lobby curtain in the Le Parker Meridien hotel. Though it might not be as 'hip' or as 'secret' as it once was, it still delivers the same winning formula of graffiti-strewn walls, retro booths and attitude-loaded staff slapping up beef 'n' patty brilliance.

Margon
CUBAN $

(Map p70; ☑ 212-354-5013; 136 W 46th St, btwn Sixth & Seventh Aves; sandwiches $4-8, mains from $9; ☺ 6am-5pm Mon-Fri, from 7am Sat; ⑤ B/D/F/M to 47th-50th Sts-Rockefeller Center) It's still 1973 at this ever-packed Cuban lunch counter, where orange Laminex and greasy goodness never went out of style. Go for gold with its legendary *cubano* sandwich (a pressed panino jammed with rich roast pork, salami, cheese, pickles, *mojo* sauce and mayo). It's obscenely good.

Hangawi
KOREAN, VEGAN $$

(Map p70; ☑ 212-213-0077; www.hangawirestaurant.com; 12 E 32nd St, btwn Fifth & Madison Aves; mains lunch $11-30, dinner $19-30; ☺ noon-2:30pm & 5:30-10:15pm Mon-Fri, 1-10:30pm Sat, 5-9:30pm Sun; ☑; ⑤ B/D/F/M, N/Q/R/W to 34th St-Herald Sq) Meat-free Korean is the draw at high-achieving Hangawi. Leave your shoes at the entrance and slip into a soothing, Zen-like space of meditative music, soft low seating and clean, complex dishes. Show-stoppers include the leek pancakes and a seductively smooth tofu claypot in ginger sauce.

Virgil's Real Barbecue
BARBECUE $$

(Map p70; ☑ 212-921-9494; www.virgilsbbq.com; 152 W 44th St, btwn Broadway & Sixth Ave, Midtown West; mains $14-38; ☺ 11:30am-11pm Mon, to midnight Tue-Fri, 11am-midnight Sat, 11am-11pm Sun; ☎; ⑤ N/Q/R, S, 1/2/3, 7 to Times Sq-42nd St) Rather than specializing in one specific style of American barbecue, Virgil's celebrates them all. Indeed, the menu covers the entire barbecue map, from Memphis-style pork spare ribs to Georgia chicken-fried steak and platters of sliced Texas beef brisket. Meats are smoked with a combo of hickory, oak and fruitwoods, keepin' fingers licked and clean.

Pio Pio
PERUVIAN $$

(Map p70; ☑ 212-459-2929; www.piopio.com; 604 Tenth Ave, btwn W 43rd & 44th Sts; mains $14-26; ☺ 11am-11pm Sun-Thu, to midnight Fri & Sat; ⑤ A/C/E to Port Authority-42nd St) This Peruvian restaurant is a favorite among New Yorkers for its delectable food, frothy pisco sours and breathtaking ambience. The specialty here is rotisserie-style chicken, seasoned and cooked to absolute perfection and served in a variety of ways (but always with plenty of

tangy, green *aji* sauce), along with classic Latin American sides such as plantains and avocado salad.

El Parador Cafe
MEXICAN $$

(Map p70; ☑ 212-679-6812; www.elparadorcafe.com; 325 E 34th St, btwn First & Second Aves, Midtown East; lunch $10-22, dinner mains $18-32; ☺ noon-10pm Mon, to 11pm Tue-Sat; ⑤ 6 to 33rd St) Back in the day, the far-flung location of this Mexican stalwart was much appreciated by philandering husbands. The shady regulars may have gone, but the old-school charm remains, from the beveled candleholders and dapper Latino waiters to the satisfying south-of-the-border standbys.

★ ViceVersa
ITALIAN $$$

(Map p70; ☑ 212-399-9291; www.viceversanyc.com; 325 W 51st St, btwn Eighth & Ninth Aves; 3-course lunch $29, dinner mains $24-33; ☺ noon-2:30pm & 4:30-11pm Mon-Fri, 4:30-11pm Sat, 11:30am-3pm & 4:30-10pm Sun; ⑤ C/E to 50th St) ViceVersa is quintessential Italian: suave and so-phisticated, affable and scrumptious. The menu features refined, cross-regional dishes like arancini with black truffle and fontina cheese. For a celebrated classic, order the *casoncelli alla bergamasca* (ravioli-like pasta filled with minced veal, raisins and amaretto cookies and seasoned with sage, butter, pancetta and Grana Padano), a nod to chef Stefano Terzi's Lombard heritage.

★ Le Bernardin
SEAFOOD $$$

(Map p70; ☑ 212-554-1515; www.le-bernardin.com; 155 W 51st St, btwn Sixth & Seventh Aves; prix-fixe lunch/dinner $87/150, tasting menus $180-270; ☺ noon-2:30pm & 5:15-10:30pm Mon-Thu, to 11pm Fri, 5:15-11pm Sat; ⑤ 1 to 50th St; B/D, E to 7th Ave) The interiors may have been subtly sexed-up for a 'younger clientele' (the stunning storm-themed triptych is by Brooklyn artist Ran Ortner), but triple-Michelin-starred Le Bernardin remains a luxe, fine-dining holy grail. At the helm is French-born celebrity chef Éric Ripert, whose deceptively simple-looking seafood often borders on the transcendental.

Grand Central Oyster Bar & Restaurant
SEAFOOD $$$

(Map p70; ☑ 212-490-6650; www.oysterbarny.com; Grand Central Terminal, 42nd St, at Park Ave; mains $15-39; ☺ 11:30am-9:30pm Mon-Sat; ⑤ S, 4/5/6, 7 to Grand Central-42nd St) This buzzing bar and restaurant within Grand Central is hugely atmospheric, with a vaulted tiled ceiling by Catalan-born engineer Rafael Guastavino.

While the extensive menu covers everything from clam chowder and seafood stews to pan-fried soft-shell crab, the real reason to head here is for the two-dozen oyster varieties. Get slurping.

Upper West Side & Central Park

Peacefood Cafe
VEGAN $

(Map p76; ☑212-362-2266; www.peacefoodcafe. com; 460 Amsterdam Ave, at 82nd St; mains $12-18; ☺10am-10pm; ☑; ⑤1 to 79th St) This bright and airy vegan haven dishes up a popular fried seitan panino (served on homemade focaccia and topped with cashew cheese, arugula, tomatoes and pesto), as well as pizzas, roasted vegetable plates and an excellent quinoa salad. There are daily raw specials, energy-fueling juices and rich desserts. Healthy and good – for you, the animals and the environment.

West 79th Street Boat Basin Café
CAFE $

(Map p76; ☑212-496-5542; www.boatbasincafe. com; W 79th St, at Henry Hudson Parkway; mains $14; ☺11am-11pm Apr-Oct, weather permitting; ⑤1 to 79th St) New ownership and an award-winning Culinary Institute of America chef are revitalizing this perennially popular waterside spot. The Robert Moses–era structure, with an elegant colonnade opening onto a outdoor rotunda, provides great marina and Hudson River views. Always deservedly popular for sunset drinks, the menu of salads, sandwiches, seafood and innovative NYC 'street food' is now another drawing card.

Jacob's Pickles
AMERICAN $$

(Map p76; ☑212-470-5566; www.jacobspickles. com; 509 Amsterdam Ave, btwn W 84th & 85th; mains $15-26; ☺10am-2am Mon-Thu, to 4am Fri, 9am-4am Sat, to 2am Sun; ⑤1 to 86th St) Jacob's elevates the humble pickle to exalted status at this inviting and warmly lit eatery. Aside from briny cukes and other preserves you'll find heaping portions of upscale comfort food, such as catfish tacos, wine-braised turkey-leg dinner, and mushroom mac 'n' cheese. The biscuits are top-notch.

Barney Greengrass
DELI $$

(Map p76; ☑212-724-4707; www.barneygreen grass.com; 541 Amsterdam Ave, at W 86th St; mains $12-22; ☺8:30am-4pm Tue-Fri, to 5pm Sat & Sun; ⑤1 to 86th St) The self-proclaimed 'King of Sturgeon' Barney Greengrass serves up the same heaping dishes of eggs and salty lox,

luxuriant caviar and melt-in-your-mouth chocolate babkas that first made it famous when it opened over a century ago. Pop in to fuel up in the morning or for a quick lunch (there are rickety tables set amid the crowded produce aisles).

PJ Clarke's
AMERICAN $$

(Map p76; ☑212-957-9700; www.pjclarkes.com; 44 W 63rd St, cnr Broadway; burgers $18-26, mains $21-26; ☺11:30am-2am; ⑤1 to 66th St-Lincoln Center) Across the street from Lincoln Center, this spot has red-checkered tablecloths, a buttoned-down crowd, friendly bartenders and a solid menu. If you're in a rush, sidle up to the bar for a Black Angus burger and a Brooklyn Lager. A raw bar offers fresh Long Island Little Neck and Cherry Stone clams, as well as jumbo shrimp cocktails.

Dovetail
MODERN AMERICAN $$$

(Map p76; ☑212-362-3800; www.dovetailnyc.com; 103 W 77th St, cnr Columbus Ave; prix fixe $68-88, tasting menu $145; ☺5:30-10pm Mon-Thu, to 11pm Fri & Sat, 5-10pm Sun; ☑; ⑤B, C to 81st St-Museum of Natural History; 1 to 79th St) This Michelin-starred restaurant showcases its Zen-like beauty in both its decor (exposed brick, bare tables) and its delectable, seasonal menus – think striped bass with sunchokes and burgundy truffle, and venison with bacon, golden beets and foraged greens. Each evening there are two seven-course tasting menus: one for omnivores ($145) and one for vegetarians ($125).

Burke & Wills
MODERN AUSTRALIAN $$$

(Map p76; ☑646-823-9251; www.burkeandwills ny.com; 226 W 79th St, btwn Broadway & Amsterdam Ave; mains lunch $19-30, dinner $19-39; ☺noon-3pm & 5:30pm-late Mon-Fri, from 11am Sat & Sun; ⑤1 to 79th St) This ruggedly attractive bistro and bar brings a touch of the outback to the Upper West Side. The menu leans toward Modern Australian pub grub: juicy kangaroo burgers with triple-fried chips, grilled prawns, kale Cobb salad, braised pork belly with apple-and-celery slaw, and seafood platters with oysters, clams and crab claws.

Upper East Side

★Earl's Beer & Cheese
AMERICAN $

(Map p76; ☑212-289-1581; www.earlsny.com; 1259 Park Ave, btwn W 97th & 98th Sts; grilled cheese $8; ☺11am-midnight Sun-Thu, to 2am Fri & Sat; ⑤6 to 96th St) This sibling-run, tiny, comfort-food outpost channels a hipster hunting vibe, complete with a giant deer-in-the-woods mural and a mounted buck's head. Basic grilled cheese is a paradigm shifter, served with pork belly, fried egg and kimchi. There is also mac 'n' cheese (with goat's cheese and crispy rosemary) and tacos (featuring braised pork shoulder and *queso fresco*).

Boqueria SPANISH $$
(Map p76; ☎212-343-2227; www.boquerianyc.com; 1460 Second Ave, btwn 76th & 77th Sts; tapas $6-18, paella for two $38-46; ☺noon-10:30pm Sun-Thu, 11am-11:30pm Fri & Sat; ☑; ⑤6 to 77th St; Q to 72nd St) This lively, much-loved tapas place brings a bit of downtown cool to the Upper East Side, with nicely spiced *patatas bravas*, tender slices of *jamon ibérico* and rich *pulpo a la plancha* (grilled octopus). Head chef Marc Vidal, who hails from Barcelona, also creates an exquisite seafood paella. Wash it all down with a pitcher of excellent sangria.

Jones Wood Foundry BRITISH $$
(Map p76; ☎212-249-2700; www.joneswood foundry.com; 401 E 76th St, btwn First & York Aves; mains lunch $16-28, dinner $17-34; ☺11am-11pm; ⑤Q to 72nd St-2nd Ave) Inside a narrow brick building that once housed an ironworks, the Jones Wood Foundry is a British-inspired gastropub serving first-rate beer-battered fish and chips, bangers and mash, lamb and rosemary pie and other hearty temptations. On warm days, grab a table on the enclosed courtyard patio.

Candle Cafe VEGAN $$
(Map p76; ☎212-472-0970; www.candlecafe.com; 1307 Third Ave, btwn 74th & 75th Sts; mains $15-22; ☺11:30am-10:30pm Mon-Sat, to 9:30pm Sun; ☑; ⑤Q to 72nd St-2nd Ave) The moneyed yoga set piles into this attractive vegan cafe serving a long list of sandwiches, salads, comfort food and market-driven specials. The specialty here is the housemade seitan. There is a juice bar and a gluten-free menu.

★**Tanoshi** SUSHI $$$
(Map p76; ☎917-265-8254; www.tanoshisushi nyc.com; 1372 York Ave, btwn E 73rd & 74th Sts; chef's sushi selection $80-100; ☺seatings 6pm, 7:30pm & 9pm Mon-Sat; ⑤Q to 72nd St) It's not easy to snag one of the 20 stools at Tanoshi, a wildly popular, pocket-sized sushi spot. The setting may be humble but the flavors are simply magnificent. Only sushi is on offer and only *omakase* (chef's selection) – which might include Hokkaido scallops,

king salmon or mouth-watering *uni* (sea urchin). BYO beer, sake or whatnot. Reserve well in advance.

Harlem & Upper Manhattan

★**Red Rooster** MODERN AMERICAN $$
(Map p76; ☎212-792-9001; www.redrooster harlem.com; 310 Malcolm X Blvd, btwn W 125th & 126th Sts, Harlem; mains $18-30; ☺11:30am-10:30pm Mon-Thu, to 11:30pm Fri, 10am-11:30pm Sat, 10am-10pm Sun; ⑤2/3 to 125th St) Transatlantic super-chef Marcus Samuelsson laces upscale comfort food with a world of flavors at his effortlessly cool, swinging brasserie. Like the work of the contemporary New York–based artists displayed on the walls, dishes are up to date: mac 'n' cheese joins forces with lobster, blackened catfish pairs with pickled mango, and spectacular Swedish meatballs salute Samuelsson's home country. The prix-fixe lunch is a bargain at $25.

Dinosaur Bar-B-Que BARBECUE $$
(Map p76; ☎212-694-1777; www.dinosaurbar bque.com; 700 W 125th St, at Twelfth Ave, Harlem; mains $12.50-25; ☺11:30am-11pm Mon-Thu, to midnight Fri & Sat, noon-10pm Sun; ⑤1 to 125th St) Jocks, hipsters, moms and pops: everyone dives into this honky-tonk rib bar for a rockin' feed. Get messy with dry-rubbed, slow-pit-smoked ribs, slabs of juicy steak and succulent burgers, or watch the waist with the lightly seasoned grilled-chicken options. The (very) few vegetarian options include a fantastic version of Creole-spiced deviled eggs.

Amy Ruth's Restaurant AMERICAN $$
(Map p76; ☎212-280-8779; www.amyruths.com; 113 W 116th St, btwn Malcolm X & Adam Clayton Powell Jr Blvds, Harlem; waffles $10-18, mains $14-25; ☺11am-11pm Mon, 8:30am-11pm Tue-Thu, 24hr Fri & Sat, to 11pm Sun; ⑤B/C 2/3 to 116th St) Perennially crowded Amy Ruth's serves up classic Southern American soul food, from fried catfish to mac 'n' cheese and fluffy biscuits. But it's the waffles that really merit a trip here – dished up 14 different ways, including with shrimp. Our all-time favorite is the 'Rev Al Sharpton,' a plate of waffles topped with succulent fried chicken.

Brooklyn

Smorgasburg MARKET
(www.smorgasburg.com; ☺11am-6pm Sat & Sun) The biggest foodie event in Brooklyn brings more than 100 vendors selling an incredible

array of goodness, along the lines of Italian street snacks, duck confit, Indian flatbread tacos, roasted-mushroom burgers, vegan Ethiopian comfort food, sea-salt caramel ice cream, passion-fruit doughnuts and more. Smorgasburg locations tend to change from season to season.

The market currently happens in Williamsburg – on the **waterfront** (☏718-782-2731; www.parks.ny.gov/parks/155; Kent Ave, btwn 8th & 9th Sts; ☉9am-dusk; ⑤L to Bedford Ave) – on Saturdays and Prospect Park – near **Lakeside** (☏718-462-0010; www.lakeside prospectpark.com; East Dr, Prospect Park, near Ocean & Parkside Aves; ice skating $6-9, skate rental $6; ☉9am-5:15pm Mon-Thu, to 9pm Fri, 11:30am-9pm Sat, to 5:15pm Sun; ♿; ⑤B/Q to Prospect Park) – on Sundays from April to October and a smaller version is held indoors at One Hanson Place in Fort Greene on weekends during the winter months.

★ Dough
BAKERY $

(☏347-533-7544; www.doughdoughnuts.com; 448 Lafayette Ave, cnr Franklin Ave, Clinton Hill; doughnuts around $3; ☉6am-9pm; ☎; ⑤G to Classon Ave) Situated on the border of Clinton Hill and Bed-Stuy, this tiny, out-of-the-way spot is a bit of a trek, but worth it if you're a pastry fan. Puffy raised doughnuts are dipped in a changing array of glazes, including pistachio, blood orange and hibiscus. Doughnut divinity for the tongue.

Chuko
JAPANESE $

(☏347-425-9570; www.chukobk.com; 565 Vanderbilt Ave, cnr Pacific St, Prospect Heights; ramen $15; ☉noon-3pm & 5:30-11pm; ✐; ⑤B/Q to 7th Ave; 2/3 to Bergen St) This contemporary, minimalist ramen shop brings a top-notch noodle game to Prospect Heights. Steaming bowls of al dente ramen are paired with one of several spectacularly silky broths, including an excellent roasted pork and a full-bodied vegetarian. The appetizers are *very* worthwhile, particularly the fragrant salt-and-pepper chicken wings.

Nathan's Famous
HOT DOGS $

(☏718-333-2202; www.nathansfamous.com; 1310 Surf Ave, cnr Stillwell Ave, Coney Island; hot dog from $4; ☉10am-midnight; ⑤D/F to Coney Island-Stillwell Ave) The hot dog was invented in Coney Island in 1867, which means that eating a frankfurter is practically obligatory here. The top choice: Nathan's Famous, which has been around since 1916. The hot dogs are the

real deal, but the menu runs the gamut from fried clams to fried chicken fingers.

Hungry Ghost
CAFE $

(☏718-797-3595; www.hungryghostbrooklyn.com/; 781 Fulton St; sandwiches from $7, breakfast from $3, coffees from $3; ☉7am-9pm; ⑤G to Fulton Street; C to Lafayette Ave) In a few short years Hungry Ghost has made a name for itself as one of the best places to grab coffee in North Brooklyn. The interior of every location boasts a striking, minimalist design that matches the unpretentious flavor of their strong brew. They also sell pastries, hand-made sandwiches, and other coffee shop fare if you're in the mood to eat.

Green Grape Annex
AMERICAN $

(www.greenegrape.com/annex; 753 Fulton St; mains $7-9; ☉7am-9pm Mon-Thu, 7am-10pm Fri, 8am-10pm Sat, 8am-9pm Sun; ⑤G to Fulton Ave or C to Lafayette Ave) Looking for a quick coffee – quality roasts that are perfectly brewed – or a hearty meal? The Green Grape Annex is well appointed cafe in Fort Greene that offers a wide array of food and beverage options in a large, airy space where it's rare to fight for space. In addition to coffee bar they also serve beer and wine.

67 Burger
BURGERS $

(☏718-797-7150; www.67burger.com; 67 Lafayette Ave, Brooklyn; specialty burgers from $8; ☉11:30am-10pm Mon-Thu, 11:30am-11pm Fri & Sat; ⑤G to Fulton Street) If there is a place that could give Shake Shack a run for its money, it is 67 Burger. Choose one of their custom burgers, such as the Parisian (sauteed onions and mushrooms with dijonaise) or the Oaxaca (avocado, cheddar cheese, and homemade chipotle mayo), or create your own big, beautiful, messy burger.

★ Pok Pok
THAI $$

(☏718-923-9322; www.pokpokny.com; 117 Columbia St, cnr Kane St, Columbia Street Waterfront District; sharing plates $12-20; ☉5:30-10pm Mon-Fri, from noon Sat & Sun; ⑤F to Bergen St) Andy Ricker's NYC outpost is a smashing success, wowing diners with a rich and complex menu inspired by Northern Thailand street food. Fiery, fish-sauce-slathered chicken wings; spicy green-papaya salad with salted black crab; smoky grilled eggplant salad and sweet pork belly with ginger, turmeric and tamarind are among the many unique dishes. The setting is fun and ramshackle. Reserve ahead.

Nick's Lobster House
SEAFOOD $$

(☑718-253-7117; www.nickslobsterhouse.com; 2777 Flatbush Ave, Brooklyn; mains starting at $18; ⊘2pm-10pm Tue-Thu, noon-11pm Fri, 11am-11pm Sat, 11am-10pm Sun) This charming eatery is located right on the water in the Mill Basin neighborhood of Brooklyn. The menu is simple, Northeast-style seafood, but the bisques, broils and, of course, lobster are all cooked to perfection. They have a full bar and gorgeous channel views from anywhere in the restaurant.

Sidecar
AMERICAN $$

(☑718-369-0077; http://sidecarbrooklyn.com/; 560 5th Ave, Brooklyn; mains $14-27; ⊘6pm-2am Mon-Wed, 6pm-4am Thu, 3pm-4am Fri, 11am-4am Sat, 11am-2am Sun; ⑤F/G/R to 4th Ave-9th St; R to Prospect Ave) Upscale classic American cuisine doesn't get any better than Sidecar. This atmospheric restaurant serves unfussy takes on classics that add a modern touch, such as fried chicken served with a savory root mash and sautéed kale on the side. Sidecar also specializes in cocktails that you can pair with your meal, or enjoy on their own at the bar.

Zenkichi
JAPANESE $$

(☑718-388-8985; www.zenkichi.com; 77 N 6th St, at Wythe Ave, Williamsburg; small plates $7-18, tasting menu $75; ⊘6pm-midnight Mon-Sat, 5:30-11:30pm Sun; ⑤L to Bedford Ave) A temple of refined Japanese cuisine, Zenkichi presents beautifully prepared dishes in an atmospheric setting that has wowed foodies from far and wide. The recommendation here is the *omakase*, a seasonal eight-course tasting menu featuring highlights like winter fruit with tofu sauce and deep-fried Suzuki striped bass, onion and carrot in a sweet, rich vinaigrette sauce topped with chili pepper.

Rabbit Hole
MODERN AMERICAN $$

(☑718-782-0910; www.rabbitholerestaurant.com; 352 Bedford Ave, btwn S 3rd & S 4th Sts, Williamsburg; mains breakfast $10-14, dinner $13-22; ⊘9am-11pm; ☑; ⑤L to Bedford Ave; J/M/Z to Marcy Ave) A warm and inviting spot in South Williamsburg, the very charming Rabbit Hole is a fine spot to disappear into, particularly if you're craving breakfast (served till 5pm). There's casual cafe-seating up front for good coffee and even better housemade pastries. Head to the back or the relaxing rear garden for creamy eggs Benedict or fresh fruit and granola.

Buttermilk Channel
AMERICAN $$

(☑917-832-8490; www.buttermilkchannelnyc.com; 524 Court St; brunch mains $8-18, dinner mains $16-28; ⊘11:30am-10pm Mon-Wed, 11:30am-11pm Thur, 11:30am-midnight Fri, 10am-midnight Sat, 10am-10pm Sun. Closed between 3-5pm daily; ⑤F/G train to Smith and 9th St station) There's nothing quite like a crispy fried chicken or a savory plate of eggs with lox and green onions. Buttermilk Channel offers dinner and brunch menus of simple, perfectly executed dishes. A comprehensive list of specialty cocktails – the brunch Bloody Mary menu alone is worth the visit – round out this yummy dining experience.

Olea
MEDITERRANEAN $$$

(☑718-643-7003; www.oleabrooklyn.com; 171 Lafayette Ave, Brooklyn; mains $24-32; ⊘10am-11pm Mon-Thu, to midnight Fri & Sat; ⑤G to Fulton Street; G/C to Clinton-Washington) Olea is a bustling Mediterranean restaurant with charming interior design and world class food. On the dinner menu they serve creamy paellas and light, delicious vegetarian pastas, while for brunch they specialize in Mediterranean spins on old standbys, such as lamb hash. There is also a tapas menu for those looking for a less substantial bite.

✖ The Bronx

Tony's Pier
SEAFOOD $

(☑718 885-1424; 1 City Island Ave, Bronx; seafood baskets from $16; ⊘11:30am-11:30pm Mon-Thu, 11:30am-1am Fri-Sun; ☐Bx29) Fried or broiled and served in a paper basket with your choice of dipping sauce – that is how Tony's Pier does seafood. This City Island spot is located right on the water, and as the name suggests there is a large pier with fantastic views of the Long Island Sound. Be sure to grab a beer or frothy mixed drink.

Getting to City Island can seem daunting if you don't have a car, but it can be done! Once you're in the Bronx the Bx29 bus goes to the island. This unique destination in the city is well worth the trip.

✖ Queens

★ Pye Boat Noodle
THAI $

(☑718-685-2329; 35-13 Broadway, Astoria; noodles $10-13; ⊘11:30am-10:30pm, to 11pm Fri & Sat; ☑; ⑤N/W to Broadway; M, R to Steinway) Young Thai waitresses in matching fedoras greet you at this cute place decked out like an old-fashioned country house. The specialty is rich, star-anise-scented boat noodles, topped with crispy pork cracklings. There's also delicate seafood *yen ta fo* (mild seafood soup, tinted pink), a rarity in NYC – good with a side of papaya salad (off-menu request: add funky fermented crab).

★ **Golden Shopping Mall** CHINESE $
(41-36 Main St, Flushing; meals from $3; ⊙10am-9:30pm; ⑤7 to Flushing-Main St) A chaotic jumble of hanging ducks, airborne noodles and greasy Laminex tables, Golden Mall's basement food court dishes up fantastic hawker-style grub. Don't be intimidated by the lack of English menus: most stalls have at least one English speaker, and the regulars are usually happy to point out their personal favorites, whether it's Lanzhou hand-pulled noodles or spicy pig ears.

Nan Xiang Xiao Long Bao DUMPLINGS $
(⊉718-321-3838; 38-12 Prince St, Queens; dumplings $5.50; ⊙8am-1am; ⑤7 to Main St.) Juicy, savory soup dumplings; thick, sticky noodles; spicy wontons – everything you'd want from a dumpling house you'll find at Nan Xiang Xiao Long Bao. This place is a no-frills affair and is usually very busy, but tables tend to open up quickly and the dishes come out fast. Bring some friends and order in excess.

Rockaway Surf Club TACOS $$
(www.rockawaybeachsurfclub.com; 302 Beach 87th St; $3.50, cocktails $9; ⊙noon-11pm) Down in the Rockaways are some of the best tacos in the five boroughs. The Rockaway Surf Club draws inspiration from beachside California taquerias, with a bar inside, and large outdoor dining area where the food is made to order. Whether you surf or just catch rays on the sand, it's the perfect post-beach hangout.

Casa Enrique MEXICAN $$
(⊉347-448-0640; www.henrinyc.com/casa-enrique.html; 5-48 49th Ave., Long Island City; mains $18-28; ⊙5-11:30pm Mon-Fri, 11am-3:45pm and 5-11pm Sat & Sun; ⑤7 to Vernon Blvd; G to 21st St/Van Alst) Don't let the unassuming facade of Casa Enrique fool you: this upscale eatery has a Michelin star and serves some of the best Mexican food in New York City. The menu is full of traditional Mexican favorites – chile relleno, carne asada and all manners of mole sauce – that are cooked to absolute perfection. Seating is limited, so a reservation is recommended.

Alobar AMERICAN $$
(⊉718-752-6000; http://www.alobarnyc.com/; 46-42 Vernon Blvd, Long Island City; dinner mains $22-29, brunch $12-16; ⊙5-9:30pm Tue & Wed, 5-10pm Thu, 5-11pm Fri, 11am-11pm Sat, 11am-9pm Sun; ⑤E, M to Court Square, 23rd St; 7 to Vernon Blvd-Jackson Ave, G to 21st St-Van Alst Station) Alobar is located right in the heart of the trendy Hunter's Point section of Long Island City, Queens, and this large, airy restaurant fits the neighborhood like a glove. Tuck into some classic American dishes like mussels and pork chops, or stop by for brunch for a mix of upgraded diner favorites and Brooklyn go-tos, like huevos rancheros.

■ Drinking & Nightlife

You'll find all species of thirst-quenching venues here, from terminally hip cocktail lounges and historic dive bars to specialty tap rooms and Third Wave coffee shops. Then there's the city's legendary club scene, spanning everything from celebrity staples to gritty, indie hangouts. The parts of the city that, apropos of its nickname, truly never sleep, tend to be downtown or in Brooklyn.

■ Financial District & Lower Manhattan

★ **Dead Rabbit** COCKTAIL BAR
(Map p62; ⊉646-422-7906; www.deadrabbitnyc.com; 30 Water St, btwn Broad St & Coenties Slip; ⊙taproom 11am-4am, parlor 5pm-2am Mon-Sat, to midnight Sun; ⑤R/W to Whitehall St; 1 to South Ferry) Named in honor of a dreaded Irish-American gang, this most-wanted rabbit is regularly voted one of the world's best bars. Hit the sawdust-sprinkled Taproom for specialty beers, historic punches and pop-inns (lightly hopped ale spiked with different flavors). Come evening, scurry upstairs to the cozy Parlor for meticulously researched cocktails.

Smith & Mills COCKTAIL BAR
(Map p62; ⊉212-226-2515; www.smithandmills.com; 71 N Moore St, btwn Hudson & Greenwich Sts; ⊙11am-2am Sun-Wed, to 3am Thu-Sat; ⑤1 to Franklin St) Petite Smith & Mills ticks all the cool boxes: unmarked exterior, design-conscious industrial interior, and expertly crafted cocktails with a penchant for the classics. Space is limited so head in early if you fancy kicking back on a plush banquette. A seasonal menu spans light snacks to a particularly notable burger pimped with caramelized onions.

Cowgirl Seahorse
BAR

(Map p62; ☎646-362-0981; http://cowgirlseahorse.com/; 259 Front St; ⊙11am-11pm Mon-Thu, 11am-midnight Fri, 10am-midnight Sat, 10am-11pm Sun; ⑤2/3/4/5/6 to Brooklyn Bridge-City Hall) In the sea of very serious bars and restaurants, Cowgirl Seahorse is a party bar. Its nautical theme and perfect bar fare – giant plates of nachos piled with steaming meat and frozen margaritas so sweet and tangy you won't be able to say no to a second round – make this dive a can't-miss for those looking to let loose.

Keg No 229
BEER HALL

(Map p62; ☎212-566-2337; www.kegno229.com; 229 Front St, btwn Beekman St & Peck Slip; ⊙11am-midnight Sun-Wed, to 1am Thu-Sat; ⑤A/C, J/Z, 2/3, 4/5 to Fulton St; R/W to Cortlandt St) From Butternuts Pork Slap to New Belgium Fat Tire, this bar's battalion of drafts, bottles and cans are a Who's Who of boutique American brews. One fun, potentially costly twist: if you lose count, some drafts are available for 'self-pour'.

Terroir Tribeca
WINE BAR

(Map p62; ☎212-625-9463; www.wineisterroir.com; 24 Harrison St, at Greenwich St; ⊙4pm-midnight Mon & Tue, to 1am Wed-Sat, to 11pm Sun; ⑤1 to Franklin St) Award-winning Terroir gratifies oenophiles with its well-versed, well-priced wine list (the offbeat, entertaining menu book is a must-read). Drops span the Old World and New, among them natural wines and inspired offerings from smaller producers. A generous selection of wines by the glass makes your global wine tour a whole lot easier. Offers early *and* late happy hours too.

SoHo & Chinatown

Pegu Club
COCKTAIL BAR

(Map p66; ☎212-473-7348; www.peguclub.com; 77 W Houston St, btwn W Broadway & Wooster St; ⊙5pm-2am Sun-Wed, to 4am Thu-Sat; ⑤B/D/F/M to Broadway-Lafayette St; C/E to Spring St) Dark, elegant Pegu Club (named after a legendary gentleman's club in colonial-era Rangoon) is an obligatory stop for cocktail connoisseurs. Sink into a velvet lounge and savor seamless libations such as the silky smooth Earl Grey MarTEAni (tea-infused gin, lemon juice and raw egg white). Grazing options are suitably Asianesque, among them duck wontons and Mandalay coconut shrimp.

Spring Lounge
BAR

(Map p66; ☎212-965-1774; www.thespringlounge.com; 48 Spring St, at Mulberry St; ⊙8am-4am Mon-Sat, from noon Sun; ⑤6 to Spring St; R/W to Prince St) This neon-red rebel has never let anything get in the way of a good time. In Prohibition days, it peddled buckets of beer. In the '60s its basement was a gambling den. These days, it's best known for its kooky stuffed sharks, early-start regulars and come-one, come-all late-night revelry. Perfect last stop on a bar-hopping tour of the neighborhood.

Genuine Liquorette
COCKTAIL BAR

(Map p66; ☎212-726-4633; www.genuine liquorette.com; 191 Grand St, at Mulberry St; ⊙6pm-midnight Tue & Wed, to 2am Thu-Sat; ⑤J/Z, N/Q/R/W, 6 to Canal St; B/D to Grand St) What's not to love about a jamming basement bar with canned cocktails and a Farah Fawcett-themed restroom? You're even free to grab bottles and mixers and make your own drinks (bottles are weighed before and after you're done). At the helm is prolific mixologist Eben Freeman, who regularly invites New York's finest barkeeps to create cocktails using less-celebrated hooch.

Mulberry Project
COCKTAIL BAR

(Map p66; ☎646-448-4536; www.mulberry project.com; 149 Mulberry St, btwn Hester & Grand Sts; ⊙6pm-2am Sun-Thu, to 4am Fri & Sat; ⑤N/Q/R, J/Z, 6 to Canal St) Lurking behind an unmarked door is this intimate, cavernous cocktail den, with its festive, 'garden-party' backyard – one of the best spots to chill in the 'hood. Bespoke, made-to-order cocktails are the specialty, so disclose your preferences and let the barkeep do the rest. If you're peckish, choose from a competent list of bites that might include peach salad with pecorino cheese.

Apothéke
COCKTAIL BAR

(Map p62; ☎212-406-0400; www.apothekenyc.com; 9 Doyers St; ⊙6:30pm-2am Mon-Sat, 8pm-2am Sun; ⑤J/Z to Chambers St; 4/5/6 to Brooklyn Bridge-City Hall) It takes a little effort to track down this former opium-den-turned-apothecary bar on Doyers St. Inside, skilled barkeeps work like careful chemists, using local, seasonal produce from greenmarkets to produce intense, flavorful 'prescriptions.' Their cocktail ingredient ratio is always on point, such as the pineapple-cilantro blend in the Sitting Buddha, one of the best drinks on the menu.

NEW YORK, NEW JERSEY & PENNSYLVANIA NEW YORK CITY

East Village & Lower East Side

Bar Goto
BAR

(Map p66; ☑212-475-4411; www.bargoto.com; 245 Eldridge St, btwn E Houston & Stanton Sts; ⏰5pm-midnight Tue-Thu & Sun, to 2am Fri & Sat; ⑤F to 2nd Ave) Maverick mixologist Kenta Goto has cocktail connoisseurs spellbound at his eponymous hot spot. Expect meticulous, elegant drinks that revel in Koto's Japanese heritage (the sake-spiked Sakura Martini is utterly smashing), paired with authentic, Japanese comfort bites such as *okonomiyaki* (savory pancakes).

Berlin
CLUB

(Map p66; ☑646-827-3689; 25 Ave A, btwn First & Second Aves; ⏰8pm-4am; ⑤F to 2nd Ave) Like a secret bunker hidden beneath the ever-gentrifying streets of the East Village, Berlin is a throwback to the neighborhood's more riotous days of wildness and dancing. Once you find the unmarked entrance, head downstairs to the grotto-like space with vaulted brick ceilings, a long bar and tiny dance floor, with funk and rare grooves.

Angel's Share
BAR

(Map p66; ☑212-777-5415; 2nd fl, 8 Stuyvesant St, near Third Ave & E 9th St; ⏰6pm-1:30am Sun-Wed, to 2:30am Thu-Sat; ⑤6 to Astor Pl) Show up early and snag a seat at this hidden gem, behind a Japanese restaurant on the same floor. It's quiet and elegant, with seriously talented mixologists serving up creative cocktails, plus a top flight collection of whiskeys. You can't stay if you don't have a table or a seat at the bar, and they tend to go fast.

LGBT NYC

....

From hand-locked married couples on the streets of Hell's Kitchen to a rainbow-hued Empire State Building at Pride, there's no doubt that New York City is one of the world's great gay cities. Indeed, few places come close to matching the breadth and depth of queer offerings here, from cabarets and clubs to festivals and readings.

Useful resources for travelers include the print and online versions of *Next Magazine* and *Get Out!*, both popular guides to all things gay in NYC; and Gay City News (www.gaycitynews.nyc) for news and current affairs with a queer bent, as well as arts and travel reviews.

Ten Bells
BAR

(Map p66; ☑212-228-4450; www.tenbellsnyc.com; 247 Broome St, btwn Ludlow & Orchard Sts; ⏰5pm-2am Mon-Fri, from 3pm Sat & Sun; ⑤F to Delancey St; J/M/Z to Essex St) This charmingly tucked-away tapas bar has a grotto-like design, with flickering candles, dark tin ceilings, brick walls and a U-shaped bar that's an ideal setting for a conversation with a new friend.

Wayland
BAR

(Map p66; ☑212-777-7022; www.thewaylandnyc.com; 700 E 9th St, cnr Ave C; ⏰5pm-4am; ⑤L to 1st Ave) Whitewashed walls, weathered floor-boards and salvaged lamps give this urban outpost a Mississippi flair, which goes well with the live music (bluegrass, jazz, folk) featured Monday to Wednesday nights. The drinks, though, are the real draw – try the 'I Hear Banjos', made of apple-pie moonshine, rye whiskey and applewood smoke, which tastes like a campfire (but slightly less burning).

Rue B
BAR

(Map p66; ☑212-358-1700; www.ruebnyc188.com; 188 Ave B, btwn E 11th & 12th Sts; ⏰noon-4am; ⑤L to 1st Ave) There's live jazz (and the odd rockabilly group) every night from about 8:30pm at this tiny, amber-lit drinking den on a bar-dappled stretch of Ave B. A young, celebratory crowd packs the small space – so mind the tight corners, lest the trombonist end up in your lap. B&W photos of jazz greats and other NYC icons enhance the ambience.

Webster Hall
CLUB

(Map p66; ☑212-353-1600; www.websterhall.com; 125 E 11th St, near Third Ave; ⏰10pm-4am Thu-Sat; ⑤L, N/Q/R/W, 4/5/6 to 14th St-Union Sq) The granddaddy of dance halls, Webster Hall has been around so long (performances have been underway since 1886) that it was granted landmark status in 2008. Following the old 'if it ain't broke, don't fix it' adage, what you'll get here is cheap drinks, pool tables, and enough room on the dance floor to work up a good sweat.

West Village, Chelsea & Meatpacking District

Employees Only
BAR

(Map p66; ☑212-242-3021; www.employeesonlynyc.com; 510 Hudson St, btwn W 10th & Christopher Sts; ⏰6pm-4am; ⑤1 to Christopher-Sheridan Sq) Duck behind the neon 'Psychic' sign to find this hidden hangout. Bartenders are ace mixologists, fizzing up crazy, addictive libations like the Ginger Smash and the Mata Hari. Great for late-night drinking and eating, courtesy of the on-site restaurant that serves till 3:30am – housemade chicken soup is ladled out to stragglers. The bar gets busier as the night wears on.

Happiest Hour
COCKTAIL BAR
(Map p66; ☑212-243-2827; www.happiesthournyc. com; 121 W 10th St, btwn Greenwich St & Sixth Ave; ☉5pm-late Mon-Fri, from 2pm Sat & Sun; ⓢA/C/E, B/D/F/M to W 4th St-Washington Sq; 1 to Christopher St-Sheridan Sq) A super-cool, tikilicious cocktail bar splashed with palm prints, '60s pop and playful mixed drinks. The crowd tends to be button-down afterwork types and online daters. Beneath sits its serious sibling, **Slowly Shirley**, an art deco-style subterranean temple to beautifully crafted, thoroughly researched libations.

Buvette
WINE BAR
(Map p66; ☑212-255-3590; www.ilovebuvette. com; 42 Grove St, btwn Bedford & Bleecker Sts; ☉7am-2am Mon-Fri, from 8am Sat & Sun; ⓢ1 to Christopher St-Sheridan Sq; A/C/E, B/D/F/M to W 4th St-Washington Sq) The rustic-chic decor here (think delicate tin tiles and a swooshing marble counter) makes it the perfect place for a glass of wine – no matter the time of day. For the full experience at this self-proclaimed *gastrotèque,* grab a seat at one of the surrounding tables and nibble on small plates while enjoying Old-World wines (mostly from France and Italy).

Le Bain
CLUB
(Map p70; ☑212-645-7600; www.standard hotels.com; 444 W 13th St, btwn Washington St & Tenth Ave; ☉10pm-4am Wed-Fri, from 2pm Sat, 2pm-midnight Sun; ⓢA/C/E, L to 14th St-8th Ave) The sweeping rooftop venue at the tragically hip Standard Hotel, Le Bain sees a garish parade of party promoters who do their thang on any day of the week. Brace yourself for skyline views, a dance floor with a giant Jacuzzi built right into it and an eclectic crowd getting wasted on pricey snifters.

Stonewall Inn
GAY
(Map p66; ☑212-488-2705; www.thestone wallinnnyc.com; 53 Christopher St; ☉2pm-4am; ⓢ1 to Christopher St-Sheridan Sq) Site of the Stonewall riots in 1969, this bar, considered almost a pilgrimage site because of its historic significance, pulls in varied crowds for nightly parties catering to everyone under the LGBT rainbow. It's far from trendy and more a welcoming, ordinary watering hole that otherwise might be overlooked.

Henrietta Hudson
LESBIAN
(Map p66; ☑212-924-3347; www.henrietta hudson.com; 438 Hudson St; ☉4pm-4am; ⓢ1 to Houston St) All sorts of young women, many from neighboring New Jersey and Long Island, storm this sleek lounge, where varying theme nights bring in spirited DJs who stick to particular genres (hip-hop, house, rock). The owner, Brooklyn native Lisa Canistraci, is a favorite promoter in the world of lesbian nightlife, and is often on hand to mix it up with her fans.

Marie's Crisis
BAR
(Map p66; ☑212-243-9323; 59 Grove St, btwn Seventh Ave & Bleecker St; ☉4pm-3am Mon-Thu, to 4am Fri & Sat, to midnight Sun; ⓢ1 to Christopher St-Sheridan Sq) Aging Broadway queens, wide-eyed out-of-town gay boys, giggly tourists and various other fans of musical theater assemble around the piano here and take turns belting out campy show tunes, often joined by the entire crowd – and the occasional celebrity. It's old-school fun, no matter how jaded you might be when you go in.

Union Square, Flatiron District & Gramercy

★Flatiron Lounge
COCKTAIL BAR
(Map p70; ☑212-727-7741; www.flatironlounge.com; 37 W 19th St, btwn Fifth & Sixth Aves; ☉4pm-2am Mon-Wed, to 3am Thu, to 4am Fri, 5pm-4am Sat; ⓢF/M, R/W, 6 to 23rd St) Head through a dramatic archway and into a dark, swinging, deco-inspired fantasy of lipstick-red booths, racy jazz tunes and sassy grown-ups downing seasonal drinks. The Lincoln Tunnel (dark rum, applejack, maple syrup and bitters) is scrumptious. Happy-hour cocktails go for $10 a pop (4pm to 6pm weekdays).

Birreria
BEER HALL
(Map p70; ☑212-937-8910; www.eataly.com; 200 Fifth Ave, at W 23rd St; ☉11:30am-11pm Sun-Thu, to midnight Fri & Sat; ⓢR/W, F/M, 6 to 23rd St) The crown jewel of Italian food emporium Eataly (p100) is this rooftop beer garden tucked betwixt the Flatiron's corporate towers. An encyclopedic beer menu offers drinkers some of the best suds on the planet. If you're hungry, the signature beer-braised pork shoulder will pair nicely, or check out the seasonally changing menu of the on-site pop-up restaurant (mains $17 to $37).

The sneaky access elevator is near the checkouts on the 23rd St side of the store.

Raines Law Room
COCKTAIL BAR

(Map p70; www.raineslawroom.com; 48 W 17th St, btwn Fifth & Sixth Aves; ⊗5pm-2am Mon-Wed, to 3am Thu-Sat, 7pm-1am Sun; ⑤F/M to 14th St, L to 6th Ave, 1 to 18th St) A sea of velvet drapes and overstuffed leather lounge chairs, the perfect amount of exposed brick, expertly crafted cocktails using meticulously aged spirits – these folks are as serious as a mortgage payment when it comes to amplified atmosphere. Reservations (recommended) are only accepted Sunday to Tuesday. Whatever the night, style up for a taste of a far more sumptuous era.

Pete's Tavern
BAR

(Map p70; ☎212-473-7676; www.petestavern. com; 129 E 18th St, at Irving Pl; ⊗11am-2:30am; ⑤4/5/6, N/Q/R/W, L to 14th St-Union Sq) With its original 19th-century mirrors, pressed-tin ceiling and rosewood bar, this dark, atmospheric watering hole has all the earmarks of a New York classic. You can get a respectable prime-rib burger here and choose from 17 draft beers, joined by everyone from post-theater couples and Irish expats to no-nonsense NYU students and the odd celebrity (see photos by the restrooms).

Old Town Bar & Restaurant
BAR

(Map p70; ☎212-529-6732; www.oldtownbar. com; 45 E 18th St, btwn Broadway & Park Ave S; ⊗11:30am-1am Mon-Fri, noon-2am Sat, 1pm-midnight Sun; ⑤4/5/6, N/Q/R/W, L to 14th St-Union Sq) It still looks like 1892 in here, with the mahogany bar, original tile floors and tin ceilings – the Old Town is an old-world drinking-man's classic (and -woman's: Madonna lit up at the bar here – when lighting up in bars was still legal – in her 'Bad Girl' video). There are cocktails around, but most come for beers and a burger (from $11.50).

Midtown

★ Bar SixtyFive
COCKTAIL BAR

(Map p70; ☎212-632-5000; www.rainbowroom. com; 30 Rockefeller Plaza, entrance on W 49th St; ⊗5pm-midnight Mon-Fri, 4-9pm Sun; ⑤B/D/F/M to 47th-50th Sts-Rockefeller Center) Not to be missed, sophisticated SixtyFive sits on level 65 of the GE Building at Rockefeller Center (p73). Dress well (no sportswear or guests under 21) and arrive by 5pm for a seat with a multi-million-dollar view. Even if you don't score a table on the balcony or by the window, head outside to soak up that sweeping New York panorama.

Flaming Saddles
GAY

(Map p70; ☎212-713-0481; www.flamingsaddles. com/nyc; 793 Ninth Ave, btwn 52nd & 53rd Sts, Midtown West; ⊗3pm-4am Mon-Fri, noon-4am Sat & Sun; ⑤C/E to 50th St) A country-and-western gay bar in Midtown! *Coyote Ugly* meets *Calamity Jane* at this Hell's Kitchen hangout, complete with studly bar-dancing barmen in skintight jeans, aspiring urban cowboys and a rough 'n' ready vibe. Slip on them Wranglers or chaps and hit the Saddle: you're in for a fun and boozy ride. There's Tex Mex bar food if you get hungry.

Therapy
GAY

(Map p70; ☎212-397-1700; www.therapy-nyc.com; 348 W 52nd St, btwn Eighth & Ninth Aves, Midtown West; ⊗5pm-2am Sun-Thu, to 4am Fri & Sat; ⑤C/E, 1 to 50th St) Multilevel Therapy was the first gay men's lounge/club to draw throngs to Hell's Kitchen, and it still pulls a crowd with its nightly shows (from live music to interviews with Broadway stars) and decent grub served Sunday to Friday (the quesadillas are especially popular). Drink monikers match the theme: 'oral fixation' and 'size queen', to name a few.

Robert
COCKTAIL BAR

(Map p76; ☎212-299-7730; www.robertnyc.com; Museum of Arts & Design, 2 Columbus Circle, btwn Eighth Ave & Broadway; ⊗11:30am-10pm Mon & Sun, to 11pm Tue, to midnight Wed-Sat; ⑤A/C, B/D, 1 to 59th St-Columbus Circle) Perched on the 9th floor of the Museum of Arts & Design (p75), '60s-inspired Robert is technically a high-end, Modern American restaurant. While the food is satisfactory, we say visit late afternoon or post-dinner, find a sofa and gaze out over Central Park with a MAD Manhattan (bourbon, blood orange vermouth and liquored cherries). Check the website for live jazz sessions.

Waylon
BAR

(Map p70; ☎212-265-0010; www.thewaylon.com; 736 Tenth Ave, at W 50th St; ⊗noon-4am; ⑤C/E to 50th St) Slip on your spurs, partner, there's a honky-tonk in Hell's! Celebrate Dixie at this saloon-style watering hole, where the jukebox keeps good folks dancing to Tim McGraw's broken heart, where the barkeeps pour American whiskeys and tequila, and where the grub includes Texan-style Frito pie and country-fried steak sandwiches.

Industry
GAY
(Map p70; ☏ 646-476-2747; www.industry-bar.com; 355 W 52nd St, btwn Eighth & Ninth Aves; ⊙ 4pm-4am; ⑤ C/E, 1 to 50th St) What was once a parking garage is now one of the hottest gay bars in Hell's Kitchen – a slick, 4000-sq-ft watering hole with handsome lounge areas, a pool table and a stage for top-notch drag divas. Head in between 4pm and 9pm for the two-for-one drinks special or squeeze in later to party with the eye-candy party hordes. Cash only.

Top of the Strand
COCKTAIL BAR
(Map p70; ☏ 646-368-6426; www.topofthe strand.com; Marriott Vacation Club Pulse, 33 W 37th St, btwn Fifth & Sixth Aves, Midtown East; ⊙ 5pm-midnight Mon & Sun, to 1am Tue-Sat; ⑤ B/D/F/M, N/Q/R to 34th St) For that 'Oh my God, I'm in New York' feeling, head to the Marriott Vacation Club Pulse (formerly the Strand Hotel) hotel's rooftop bar, order a martini (extra dirty) and drop your jaw (discreetly). Sporting comfy cabana-style seating, a refreshingly mixed-age crowd and a sliding glass roof, its view of the Empire State Building is simply unforgettable.

Upper West Side & Central Park

Manhattan Cricket Club
LOUNGE
(Map p76; ☏ 646-823-9252; www.mccnew york.com; 226 W 79th St, btwn Amsterdam Ave & Broadway; ⊙ 6pm-late; ⑤ 1 to 79th St) Above an Australian bistro (p102), this elegant drinking lounge is modeled on the classy Anglo-Aussie cricket clubs of the early 1900s. Sepia-toned photos of batsmen adorn the gold brocaded walls, while mahogany bookshelves and Chesterfield sofas create a fine setting for quaffing well-made (but pricey) cocktails. It's a guaranteed date-pleaser.

Dead Poet
BAR
(Map p76; ☏ 212-595-5670; www.thedeadpoet. com; 450 Amsterdam Ave, btwn W 81st & 82nd Sts; ⊙ noon-4am; ⑤ 1 to 79th St) This skinny, mahogany-paneled pub has been a neighborhood favorite since the turn of the millennium, with a mix of locals and students nursing pints of Guinness. Cocktails are named after dead poets, including a Walt Whitman Long Island Iced Tea ($12) and a Pablo Neruda spiced-rum sangria ($11). Funny – we always pegged Neruda as a pisco sour kind of guy.

Upper East Side

Drunken Munkey
LOUNGE
(Map p76; ☏ 646-998-4600; www.drunken munkeynyc.com; 338 E 92nd St, btwn First & Second Aves; ⊙ 4:30pm-2am Mon-Thu, to 3am Fri, 11am-3am Sat, to 2am Sun; ⑤ Q, 6 to 96th St) This playful lounge channels colonial-era Bombay with vintage wallpaper, cricket-ball door handles and jauntily attired waitstaff. The monkey chandeliers may be pure whimsy, but the craft cocktails and tasty curries (small, meant for sharing) are serious business. Gin, not surprisingly, is the drink of choice. Try the Bramble: Bombay gin, blackberry liqueur and fresh lemon juice and blackberries.

Auction House
BAR
(Map p76; ☏ 212-427-4458; www.theauction housenyc.com; 300 E 89th St, at Second Ave; ⊙ 7:30pm-2am Sun-Thu, to 4am Fri & Sat; ⑤ Q to 86th St) Dark maroon doors lead into a candlelit hangout that's perfect for a relaxing drink. Victorian-style couches and fat, overstuffed easy chairs are strewn about the wood-floored rooms. Take your well-mixed cocktail to a seat by the fireplace and admire the scene reflected in the gilt-edged mirrors propped up on the walls.

Harlem & Upper Manhattan

Ginny's Supper Club
COCKTAIL BAR
(Map p76; ☏ 212-421-3821, brunch reservations 212-792-9001; www.ginnyssupperclub.com; 310 Malcolm X Blvd, btwn W 125th & 126th Sts, Harlem; ⊙ 6pm-11pm Thu, to 3am Fri & Sat, brunch 10:30am-2pm Sun; ⑤ 2/3 to 125th St) Looking straight out of *Boardwalk Empire*, this roaring basement supper club is rarely short of styled-up regulars sipping cocktails, nibbling on soul and global bites (from the Red Rooster (p103) kitchen upstairs) and grooving to live jazz from 7:30pm Thursday to Saturday and DJ-spun beats from 11pm Friday and Saturday. Don't miss the weekly Sunday gospel brunch (reservations recommended).

Brooklyn

★ Maison Premiere
COCKTAIL BAR
(☏ 347-335-0446; www.maisonpremiere.com; 298 Bedford Ave, btwn S 1st & Grand Sts, Williamsburg; ⊙ 4pm-2am Mon-Thu, to 4am Fri, 11am-4am Sat, to 4pm Sun; ⑤ L to Bedford Ave) We kept expecting to see Dorothy Parker stagger into this

old-timey place, which features an elegant bar full of syrups and essences, suspendered bartenders and a jazzy soundtrack to further channel the French Quarter New Orleans vibe. The cocktails are serious business: the epic list includes more than a dozen absinthe drinks, various juleps and an array of specialty cocktails.

Excelsior
GAY & LESBIAN

(☑718-788-2710; www.excelsiorbrooklyn.com; 563 Fifth Ave, Brooklyn; ⊙6pm-4am Mon-Fri, 2pm-4am Sat & Sun; ⑤F/G/R to 4th Ave/ 9th St; R to Prospect Ave) This beloved neighborhood gay bar recently reopened in a new location with a chic remodel that includes a back patio and upstairs event area that hosts dance parties, drag shows and karaoke. Excelsior tends to cater to an older crowd (although everyone is welcome, of course), and is known for its congenial atmosphere and hilarious bartenders.

Union Hall
BAR

(☑718-638-4400; www.unionhallny.com; 702 Union St; drinks from $7; ⊙4pm-4am Mon-Fri, 1pm-4am Sat-Sun; ⑤R to Union St) Anyone looking for an authentically Brooklyn night out should look no further than Union Hall. This bar and event space is located in a converted warehouse and boasts a double-sided fireplace, towering bookshelves, leather couches and two full-size indoor bocce ball courts. Head to the basement for live music and comedy.

Spuyten Duyvil
BAR

(☑718-963-4140; www.spuytenduyvilnyc.com; 359 Metropolitan Ave, btwn Havemayer & Roebling Sts, Williamsburg; ⊙5pm-late Mon-Fri, from noon Sat & Sun; ⑤L to Lorimer St; G to Metropolitan Ave) This low-key Williamsburg bar looks like it was pieced together from a rummage sale. The ceilings are painted red, there are vintage maps on the walls and the furniture consists of tattered armchairs. But the beer selection is staggering, the locals from various eras are chatty and there's a decent-sized patio with leafy trees that's open in good weather.

Skinny Dennis
BAR

(www.skinnydennisbar.com; 152 Metropolitan Ave, btwn Wythe Ave & Berry St, Williamsburg; ⊙noon-4am; ⑤L to Bedford Ave) No need to fly to Austin – you can get your honky-tonk right here in Billyburg at this roadhouse saloon on bustling Metropolitan Ave. Aside from Kinky Friedman posters, a reverential painting of Willie Nelson, peanut shells on the floor and

a Patsy Cline–heavy jukebox in the corner, you'll find country crooners playing nightly to a garrulous, beer-swilling crowd.

Bossa Nova Civic Club
CLUB

(☑718-443-1271; 1271 Myrtle Ave, btwn Evergreen & Central Aves, Bushwick; ⊙5pm-4am; ⑤M to Central Ave) Yet another reason why you never need to leave Brooklyn, this smallish hole-in-the-wall club is a great place to get your groove on, with DJs spinning a wide mix of sounds in a somewhat tropical-themed interior. Great sound system, fairly priced drinks (at least as far as clubs are concerned) and snacks available when hunger strikes (empanadas, slow-cooked pork, arepas).

Radegast Hall & Biergarten
BEER HALL

(☑718-963-3973; www.radegasthall.com; 113 N 3rd St, at Berry St, Williamsburg; ⊙noon-2am Mon-Fri, from 11am Sat & Sun; ⑤L to Bedford Ave) An Austro-Hungarian beer hall in Williamsburg offers up a huge selection of Bavarian brews as well as a kitchen full of munchable meats. You can hover in the dark, woody bar area or sit in the adjacent hall, which has a retractable roof and communal tables to feast at – perfect for pretzels, sausages and burgers. Live music every night.

Queens

★Bohemian Hall & Beer Garden
BEER GARDEN

(☑718-274-4925; www.bohemianhall.com; 29-19 24th Ave, Astoria; ⊙5pm-1am Mon-Thu, to 3am Fri, noon-3am Sat, noon-midnight Sun; ⑤N/Q to Astoria Blvd) This Czech community center kicked off NYC's beer-garden craze, and nothing quite matches it for space and heaving drinking crowds, which pack every picnic table under the towering trees in summer. There's obligatory food (dumplings, sausages); the focus is on the cold Czech beers.

Dutch Kills
BAR

(☑718-383-2724; www.dutchkillsbar.com; 27-24 Jackson Ave, Long Island City; specialty cocktails from $13, beer and wine from $6; ⊙5pm-2am; ⑤E, M, or R to Queens Plaza; G to Court Square) When you step into Dutch Kills – through an unassuming door on an old industrial building in Long Island City – you are stepping back in time. This speakeasy-style bar is all about atmosphere and amazing craft cocktails. Their menu of specialty drinks is extensive, but if you're looking for an old standard, you can trust the expert bartenders to deliver.

Icon Bar GAY

(☑917-832-6364; 31-84 33rd St, Astoria; drinks from $7; ⊗5pm-4am; ⓢN/W to Broadway station) New York's famous gay nightlife scene doesn't end once you leave Manhattan. Icon Bar brings strong drinks and flirtatious ambiance to Astoria. They frequently host special DJ nights and drag shows, as well as a 2-for-1 happy hour on weekday evenings.

☆ Entertainment

Actors, musicians, dancers and artists flock to the bright lights of the Big Apple, hoping to forge careers in showbiz. As the saying goes: if you can make it here, you can make it anywhere. Whatever 'making it' means these days, audiences are spoiled by the continual influx of supremely talented, dedicated and boundary-pushing performers who maintain the city's status as one of the world's cultural capitals.

Live Music

Minton's JAZZ

(Map p76; ☑212-243-2222; www.mintonsharlem. com; 206 W 118th St, btwn St Nicholas Ave & Adam Clayton Powell Jr Blvd; ⊗6-11pm Wed-Sat, noon-3pm & 6-10pm Sun; ⓢB/C, 2/3 to 116th St) The birthplace of bebop, this Harlem jazz-and-dinner club is a musical holy grail. Everyone from Dizzy Gillespie to Louis Armstrong have jammed here, and dinner (mains $18 to $34) or Sunday brunch ($12 to $18) in its tinted-mirror dining room is an experience to behold. Book ahead, dress to impress and savor Southern flavors while toe-tapping to live, honey-sweet jazz.

★ Jazz at Lincoln Center JAZZ

(Map p76; ☑tickets to Dizzy's Club Coca-Cola 212-258-9595, tickets to Rose Theater & Appel Room 212-721-6500; www.jazz.org; Time Warner Center, Columbus Circle, Broadway at W 59th St; ⓢA/C, B/D, 1 to 59th St-Columbus Circle) Perched atop the Time Warner Center, Jazz at Lincoln Center consists of three state-of-the-art venues: the mid-sized **Rose Theater**; the panoramic, glass-backed **Appel Room**; and the intimate, atmospheric **Dizzy's Club Coca-Cola**. It's the last of these that you're most likely to visit, given its nightly shows. The talent is often exceptional, as are the dazzling Central Park views.

★ Carnegie Hall LIVE MUSIC

(Map p70; ☑212-247-7800; www.carnegiehall. org; 881 Seventh Ave, at W 57th St; ⊗tours 11:30am, 12:30pm, 2pm & 3pm Mon-Fri, 11:30am & 12:30pm Sat Oct-Jun; ⓢN/R/W to 57th St-7th Ave) This legendary music hall may not be the world's biggest, nor grandest, but it's definitely one of the most acoustically blessed venues around. Opera, jazz and folk greats feature in the Isaac Stern Auditorium, with edgier jazz, pop, classical and world music in the popular Zankel Hall. The intimate Weill Recital Hall hosts chamber-music concerts, debut performances and panel discussions.

New York Philharmonic CLASSICAL MUSIC

(Map p76; ☑212-875-5656; www.nyphil.org; Lincoln Center, Columbus Ave at W 65th St; ⚑; ⓢ1 to 66 St-Lincoln Center) The oldest professional orchestra in the USA (dating back to 1842) holds its season every year at **David Geffen Hall** (known as Avery Fisher until 2015); newly installed music director Jaap van Zweden took over from Alan Gilbert in 2017. The orchestra plays a mix of classics (Tchaikovsky, Mahler, Haydn) and contemporary works, as well as concerts geared toward children.

Blue Note JAZZ

(Map p66; ☑212-475-8592; www.bluenote.net; 131 W 3rd St, btwn Sixth Ave & MacDougal St; ⓢA/C/E, B/D/F/M to W 4th St-Washington Sq) This is by far the most famous (and expensive) of the city's jazz clubs. Most shows are $15 to $30 at the bar or $25 to $45 at a table, but can rise for the biggest stars. There's also jazz brunch on Sundays at 11:30am. Go on an off night, and don't talk – all attention is on the stage!

Joe's Pub LIVE MUSIC

(Map p66; ☑212-539-8778, tickets 212-967-7555; www.joespub.com; Public Theater, 425 Lafayette St, btwn Astor Pl & 4th St; ⓢ6 to Astor Pl; R/W to 8th St-NYU) Part bar, part cabaret and performance venue, intimate Joe's serves up both emerging acts and top-shelf performers. Past entertainers have included Patti LuPone, Amy Schumer, Leonard Cohen and British songstress Adele (in fact, it was right here that Adele gave her very first American performance, back in 2008).

Irving Plaza LIVE MUSIC

(Map p70; ☑212-777-6817; www.irvingplaza.com; 17 Irving Pl, at 15th St; ⓢ4/5/6, N/Q/R, L to 14th St-Union Sq) Rocking since 1978, Irving Plaza has seen them all: the Ramones, Bob Dylan, U2, Pearl Jam, you name it. These days it's a great in-between stage for quirkier rock and pop acts – from indie chicks Sleater-Kinney to hard rockers Disturbed. There's a cozy floor around the stage, and good views from the mezzanine.

Brooklyn Bowl
LIVE MUSIC

(☑718-963-3369; www.brooklynbowl.com; 61 Wythe Ave, btwn N 11th & N 12th Sts, Williamsburg; ⊙6pm-2am Mon-Fri, from 11am Sat & Sun; ⑤L to Bedford Ave; G to Nassau Ave) This 23,000-sq-ft venue inside the former Hecla Iron Works Company combines bowling (lane rental per 30min $25, shoe rental $5), microbrews, food and groovy live music. In addition to the live bands that regularly tear up the stage, there are NFL game days, karaoke and DJ nights. Aside from weekends (11am to 6pm), it's age 21 and up.

Bell House
LIVE MUSIC

(☑718-643-6510; www.thebellhouseny.com; 149 7th St, btwn Second & Third Aves, Gowanus; ⊙5pm-4am; ☎; ⑤F/G/R to 4th Ave-9th St) A big, old venue in the mostly barren neighborhood of Gowanus, the Bell House features high-profile live performances, indie rockers, DJ nights, comedy shows and burlesque parties. The handsomely converted warehouse has a spacious concert area, plus a friendly little bar in the front room with flickering candles, leather armchairs and 10 or so beers on tap.

Sports

Madison Square Garden
SPECTATOR SPORT, CONCERT VENUE

(MSG, 'the Garden'; Map p70; www.thegarden.com; 4 Pennsylvania Plaza, Seventh Ave, btwn 31st & 33rd Sts; ⑤A/C/E, 1/2/3 to 34th St-Penn Station) NYC's major performance venue – part of the massive complex housing Penn Station (p120) – hosts big-arena performers, from Kanye West to Madonna. It's also a sports arena, with **New York Knicks** (www.nba. com/knicks.com) and **New York Liberty** (www.liberty.wnba.com) basketball games and **New York Rangers** (www.nhl.com/rangers) hockey games, as well as boxing and events like the Annual Westminster Kennel Club Dog Show.

USTA Billie Jean King National Tennis Center
SPECTATOR SPORT

(☑718-760-6200; www.usta.com; Flushing Meadows Corona Park, Corona; ⊙6am-midnight; ⑤7 to Mets-Willets Pt) The US Open, one of the city's premier sporting events, takes place in late August. As of 2016, the Arthur Ashe Stadium (capacity 23,771) now has a retractable roof, there's a new stadium (the Grandstand, which replaced the Old Grandstand), and

outer courts have been renovated. Tickets usually go on sale at Ticketmaster in April or May, but are hard to get for marquee games. General admission to early rounds is easier.

Staten Island Yankees
BASEBALL

(☑718-720-9265; www.siyanks.com; Richmond County Bank Ballpark, 75 Richmond Tce; tickets $12; ⊙ticket office 9am-5pm Mon-Fri; ⑤Staten Island) These Yanks have been champions of the New York–Penn title four times since 2005 alone. If you don't catch a fly ball, you can at least catch some high-scoring Manhattan skyline views from the waterfront stadium. It's a 0.3-mile walk north of the ferry terminal and the construction site of a gigantic Ferris wheel scheduled to open in 2018.

Theater

★ Al Hirschfeld Theatre
THEATER

(Map p70; ☑tickets 877-250-2929; www.kinky bootsthemusical.com; 302 W 45th St, btwn Eighth & Ninth Aves; ⑤A/C/E to 42nd St-Port Authority Bus Terminal) Adapted from a 2005 British indie film, Harvey Fierstein and Cyndi Lauper's smash hit **Kinky Boots** tells the story of a doomed English shoe factory unexpectedly saved by Lola, a business-savvy drag queen. Its solid characters and electrifying energy have not been lost on critics: the musical won six Tony Awards, including Best Musical, in 2013.

★ Eugene O'Neill Theatre
THEATER

(Map p70; ☑tickets 212-239-6200; www.bookof mormonbroadway.com; 230 W 49th St, btwn Broadway & Eighth Ave; ⑤N/R/W to 49th St; 1 to 50th St; C/E to 50th St) Subversive, obscene and ridiculously hilarious, **Book of Mormon**, a cutting musical satire, is the work of *South Park* creators Trey Parker and Matt Stone and *Avenue Q* composer Robert Lopez. Winner of nine Tony Awards, it tells the story of two naive Mormons on a mission to 'save' a Ugandan village.

★ Richard Rodgers Theatre
THEATER

(Map p70; ☑tickets 877-250-2929; www.hamilton broadway.com; 226 W 46th St, btwn Seventh & Eighth Aves; ⑤N/R/W to 49th St) Broadway's hottest ticket, Lin-Manuel Miranda's acclaimed musical **Hamilton** uses contemporary hip-hop beats to recount the story of America's first Secretary of the Treasury, Alexander Hamilton. Inspired by Ron Chernow's biography *Alexander Hamilton,* the show has won a slew of awards, with 11 Tony Awards (including Best Musical), a Grammy for its triple-platinum cast album and the Pulitzer Prize for Drama.

Sleep No More THEATER
(Map p70; ☎ 866-811-4111; www.sleepnomore nyc.com; 530 W 27th St, btwn Tenth & Eleventh Aves; tickets from $105; ⊙ 7pm-midnight Mon-Sat; ⑤ C/E to 23rd St) One of the most immersive theater experiences ever conceived, *Sleep No More* is a loosely based retelling of *Macbeth* set inside a series of Chelsea warehouses that have been redesigned to look like the 1930s-era McKittrick Hotel and its hopping jazz bar.

It's a choose-your-own adventure kind of experience, where audience members are free to wander the elaborate rooms (ball-room, graveyard, taxidermy shop, lunatic asylum) and follow or interact with the ac-tors, who perform a variety of scenes that can run from the bizarre to the risqué. Be prepared: you must check in *everything* when you arrive (jackets, bag, cell phone), and you must wear a mask, à la *Eyes Wide Shut*.

Playwrights Horizons THEATER
(Map p70; ☎ 212-564-1235; www.playwrights horizons.org; 416 W 42nd St, btwn Ninth & Tenth Aves, Midtown West; ⑤ A/C/E to 42nd St-Port Authority Bus Terminal) An excellent place to catch what could be the next big thing, this veteran 'writers' theater' is dedicated to fostering contemporary American works. Notable past productions include Ken-neth Lonergan's *Lobby Hero,* Bruce Nor-ris' Tony Award–winning *Clybourne Park,* and Doug Wright's *I Am My Own Wife* and *Grey Gardens.*

BAM Harvey Theater THEATER
(Harvey Lichtenstein Theater; ☎ 718-636-4100; www.bam.org; 651 Fulton St, at Rockwell Pl, Fort Greene; ⑤ B, Q/R to DeKalb Ave; 2/3, 4/5 to Nevins St) This theater, an important cultural insti-tution in Brooklyn and New York City as a whole, has had long runs by important art-ists like Tony Kushner, Peter Brook and Lau-rie Anderson. The building itself is a striking combination of ornate and elegant with grit-ty and industrial – ideal for Brooklyn. (The balcony seats, narrow and elevated, aren't the most comfortable, though, and some have obstructed sight lines.)

★**Flea Theater** THEATER
(Map p62; ☎ tickets 212-226-0051; www.theflea. org; 20 Thomas St, btwn Church St & Broadway; ♿; ⑤ A/C, 1/2/3 to Chambers St; R/W to City Hall)

One of NYC's top off-off-Broadway compa-nies, Flea is famous for staging innovative and timely new works. A brand-new loca-tion offers three performance spaces, includ-ing one named for devoted alum Sigourney Weaver. The year-round program also in-cludes music and dance productions, as well as shows for young audiences (aged 5 and up) and a rollicking late-night competition series of 10-minute plays.

Delacorte Theater THEATER
(Map p76; www.publictheater.org; Central Park, en-ter at W 81st St; ⑤ B/C to 81st St) Every summer the Joseph Papp Public Theater presents its fabulous free productions of Shakespeare in the Park (p91) at Delacorte Theater, which Papp began back in 1954, before the lovely, leafy, open-air theater was even built. Pro-ductions are usually superb, and regardless of their quality, it's a magical experience and waiting in line for tickets is a rite of passage for newcomers to the city.

Ambassador Theatre THEATER
(Chicago; Map p70; ☎ tickets 212-239-6200; www. chicagothemusical.com; 219 W 49th St, btwn Broad-way & Eighth Ave; ⑤ N/R/W to 49th St; 1, C/E to 50th St) A New York landmark, the Ambas-sador Theatre, constructed in the 1920s, is curiously built kitty-corner on the lot, ena-bling the small space to have more seating. Like many of its peers it was sold in the '30s by the owners, the Schuberts, it became a mixed-use property for TV and movies, but was eventually repurchased by the family in 1956. Since then it has remained a theatre, and currently is the venue for Chicago, one of Broadway's most popular shows.

New York Theatre Workshop THEATER
(Map p66; ☎ 212-460-5475; www.nytw.org; 79 E 4th St, btwn Second & Third Aves; ⑤ F to 2nd Ave) For more than 30 years this innovative produc-tion house has been a treasure trove for those seeking cutting-edge, contemporary plays with purpose. It was the originator of two big Broadway hits, *Rent* and *Urinetown* – plus it's where the musical *Once* had its off-Broadway premiere – and offers a con-stant supply of high-quality drama.

La MaMa ETC THEATER
(Map p66; ☎ 212-352-3101; www.lamama.org; 74a E 4th St, btwn Bowery & Second Ave; tickets from $20; ⑤ F to Second Ave) A long-standing home for onstage experimentation (the ETC stands for Experimental Theater Club), La MaMa is now a three-theater complex with

a cafe, an art gallery and a separate studio building that features cutting-edge dramas, sketch comedy and readings of all kinds. Ten $10 tickets are available for each show. Book early to score a deal!

Comedy

★ Upright Citizens Brigade Theatre
COMEDY

(UCB; Map p70; ☑212-366-9176; www.ucb theatre.com; 307 W 26th St, btwn Eighth & Ninth Aves; free-$10; ☺7pm-midnight; ⓢC/E to 23rd St) Comedy sketch shows and improv reign at this below-ground 74-seat venue, which gets drop-ins from casting directors and often features well-known figures from TV. Getting in is cheap, and so is the beer and wine. You'll find quality shows happening nightly, from about 7:30pm, though the Sunday night Asssscat Improv session is always a riot.

Comedy Cellar
COMEDY

(Map p66; ☑212-254-3480; www.comedycellar. com; 117 MacDougal St, btwn W 3rd St & Minetta Lane; cover $12-24; ⓢA/C/E, B/D/F/M to W 4th St-Washington Sq) This long-established basement comedy club in Greenwich Village features mainstream material and a good list of regulars (Colin Quinn, Judah Friedlander, Wanda Sykes), plus occasional high-profile drop-ins like Dave Chappelle, Jerry Seinfeld and Amy Schumer. Its success continues: Comedy Cellar now boasts another location at the Village Underground around the corner on W 3rd St.

Caroline's on Broadway
COMEDY

(Map p70; ☑212-757-4100; www.carolines.com; 1626 Broadway, at 50th St, Midtown West; ⓢN/Q/R to 49th St; 1, C/E to 50th St) You may recognize this big, bright, mainstream classic from comedy specials filmed here on location. It's a top spot to catch US comedy big guns and sitcom stars.

Cinemas

Film Society of Lincoln Center
CINEMA

(Map p76; ☑212-875-5367; www.filmlinc.com; ⓢ1 to 66th St-Lincoln Center) The Film Society is one of New York's cinematic gems, providing an invaluable platform for a wide gamut of documentary, feature, independent, foreign and avant-garde art pictures. Films screen in one of two facilities at Lincoln Center: the Elinor Bunin Munroe Film Center (Map p76; ☑212-875-5232; Lincoln Center, 144 W 65th St), a more intimate, experimental venue, or

the Walter Reade Theater, with wonderfully wide, screening room–style seats.

Metrograph
CINEMA

(Map p66; ☑212-660-0312; www.metrograph.com; 7 Ludlow St, btwn Canal & Hester Sts; tickets $15; ⓢF to East Broadway; B/D to Grand St) The newest movie mecca for downtown cinephiles, this two-screen theater with red velvet seats shows curated art-house flicks. Most you'll never find at any multiplex, though the odd mainstream pic like *Magic Mike* is occasionally screened. In addition to movie geeks browsing the bookstore, you'll find a stylish and glamorous set at the bar or in the upstairs restaurant.

Film Forum
CINEMA

(Map p66; ☑212-727-8110; www.filmforum.com; 209 W Houston St, btwn Varick St & Sixth Ave; ⓢ1 to Houston St) This three-screen nonprofit cinema screens an astounding array of independent films, revivals and career retrospectives from greats such as Orson Welles. Theaters are small (as are the screens), so get there early for a good viewing spot. Showings are often combined with director talks or other film-themed discussions attended by hard-core cinephiles.

Walter Reade Theater
CINEMA

(Map p76; ☑212-875-5601; www.filmlinc.com; Lincoln Center, 165 W 65th St; ⓢ1 to 66th St-Lincoln Center) The Walter Reade boasts some wonderfully wide, screening-room–style seats. Every September it hosts the New York Film Festival, featuring plenty of New York and world premieres. At other times of the year you can catch independent films, career retrospectives and themed series.

Anthology Film Archives
CINEMA

(Map p66; ☑212-505-5181; www.anthology filmarchives.org; 32 Second Ave, at 2nd St; ⓢF to 2nd Ave) Opened in 1970, this theater is dedicated to the idea of film as an art form. It screens indie works by new filmmakers and revives classics and obscure oldies, from the surrealist works of Spanish director Luis Buñuel to Ken Brown's psychedelia.

Performing Arts

Metropolitan Opera House
OPERA

(Map p76; ☑tickets 212-362-6000, tours 212-769-7028; www.metopera.org; Lincoln Center, Columbus Ave at W 64th St; ⓢ1 to 66th St-Lincoln Center) New York's premier opera company is the place to see classics such as *Carmen, Madame Butterfly* and *Macbeth,* not to mention

Wagner's Ring Cycle. It also hosts premieres and revivals of more contemporary works, such as John Adams' *The Death of Klinghoffer*. The season runs from September to April.

New York City Ballet DANCE
(Map p76; ☑212-496-0600; www.nycballet.com; Lincoln Center, Columbus Ave at W 63rd St; ♿; Ⓢ1 to 66th St-Lincoln Center) This prestigious ballet company was first directed by renowned Russian-born choreographer George Balanchine back in the 1940s. Today, the company has 90 dancers and is the largest ballet organization in the USA, performing 23 weeks a year at Lincoln Center's David H Koch Theater. During the holidays the troupe is best known for its annual production of *The Nutcracker*.

Duplex CABARET
(Map p66; ☑212-255-5438; www.theduplex.com; 61 Christopher St, at Seventh Ave S; cover $10-25; ☺4pm-4am; Ⓢ1 to Christopher St-Sheridan Sq) Cabaret, karaoke and campy dance moves are par for the course at the legendary Duplex. Pictures of Joan Rivers line the walls, and the performers like to mimic her sassy form of self-deprecation while getting in a few jokes about audience members as well. It's a fun and unpretentious place, and certainly not for the bashful.

Joyce Theater DANCE
(Map p70; ☑212-691-9740; www.joyce.org; 175 Eighth Ave, at W 19th St; Ⓢ C/E to 23rd St; A, L to 14th St-8th Ave; 1 to 18th St) A favorite among dance junkies thanks to its excellent sight lines and offbeat offerings, this is an intimate venue, seating 472 in a renovated cinema. Its focus is on traditional modern companies such as Martha Graham, Stephen Petronio Company and Parsons Dance, as well as global stars such as Dance Brazil, Ballet Hispanico and MalPaso Dance Company.

🔒 Shopping

Not surprisingly for a capital of commercialism, creativity and fashion, New York City is quite simply one of the best shopping destinations on the planet. Every niche is filled. From indie designer-driven boutiques to landmark department stores, thrift shops to haute couture, record stores to the Apple store, antiques to edible gourmet groceries, it's quite easy to blow one's budget.

🔒 Brooklyn

Brooklyn Flea MARKET
(www.brooklynflea.com; 90 Kent Ave, btwn N 7th & N 10th Sts, Williamsburg; ☺10am-5pm Sat Apr-Oct; ♿; Ⓢ L to Bedford Ave) On the grounds of East River State Park (p104) in Williamsburg, every Saturday over 100 vendors sell their wares, ranging from antiques and records to vintage clothes and craft items. The Flea shares this space with the tasty treats of Smorgasburg (p103). On Sundays, the market moves to Dumbo near the archway at 80 Pearl St, under the Manhattan Bridge.

Beacon's Closet VINTAGE
(☑718-486-0816; www.beaconscloset.com; 74 Guernsey St, btwn Nassau & Norman Aves, Greenpoint; ☺11am-8pm; Ⓢ L to Bedford Ave; G to Nassau Ave) Twenty-something groovers find this massive 5500-sq-ft warehouse of vintage clothing part goldmine, part grit. Lots of coats, polyester tops and '90s-era T-shirts are handily displayed by color, but the sheer mass can take time to conquer. You'll also find shoes of all sorts, flannels, hats, handbags, chunky jewelry and brightly hued sunglasses.

Rough Trade MUSIC
(☑718-388-4111; www.roughtradenyc.com; 64 N 9th St, btwn Kent & Wythe Aves, Williamsburg; ☺11am-11pm Mon-Sat, to 9pm Sun; Ⓢ L to Bedford Ave) This sprawling, 10,000-sq-ft record store – a London import – stocks thousands of titles on vinyl and CD. It also has in-store DJs, listening stations, art exhibitions, and coffee and doughnuts from Brompton Bike Cafe. A small concert hall on site hosts live bands throughout the week (admission varies).

🔒 Downtown

★**Strand Book Store** BOOKS
(Map p66; ☑212-473-1452; www.strandbooks.com; 828 Broadway, at E 12th St; ☺9:30am-10:30pm Mon-Sat, from 11am Sun; Ⓢ L, N/Q/R/W, 4/5/6 to 14th St-Union Sq) Beloved and legendary, the iconic Strand embodies downtown NYC's intellectual *bona fides* – a bibliophile's Oz, where generations of book lovers carrying the store's trademark tote bags happily lose themselves for hours. In operation since 1927, the Strand sells new, used and rare titles, spreading an incredible 18 miles of books (over 2.5 million of them) among three labyrinthine floors.

Screaming Mimi's   VINTAGE
(Map p70; ☑212-677-6464; www.screaming
mimis.com; 240 W 14th St, btwn Seventh & Eighth
Aves; ◷noon-8pm Mon-Sat, 1-7pm Sun; ⓢA/
C/E/L to 8th Ave-14th St) If you dig vintage
threads, you may just scream too. This fun-
tastic shop carries an excellent selection of
yesteryear pieces, organized – ingeniously –
by decade, from the '50s to the '90s. (Ask
to see the small, stashed-away collection of
clothing from the 1920s through '40s.)

Evolution Nature Store   GIFTS & SOUVENIRS
(Map p66; ☑212-343-1114; www.theevolution
store.com; 687 Broadway; ◷11am-8pm; ⓢN/
Q/R/W to 8th Ave-NYU; 4/5/6 to Astor Place) In
the market for a shrunken head? Perhaps a
dried scarab beetle? This SoHo favorite has
display cases full of oddities from all over
the world. The store is cavernous and often
busy.

Obscura Antiques   ANTIQUES
(Map p66; ☑212-505-9251; www.obscura
antiques.com; 207 Ave A, btwn E 12th & 13th Sts;
◷noon-8pm Mon-Sat, to 7pm Sun; ⓢL to 1st Ave)
This small cabinet of curiosities pleases both
lovers of the macabre and inveterate antique
hunters. Here you'll find taxidermied animal heads, tiny rodent skulls and skeletons,
butterfly displays in glass boxes, photos of
dead people, disturbing little (dental?) instruments, German landmine flags (stack-
able so tanks could see them), old poison
bottles and glass eyes.

🅰 Midtown

Grand Central Market   MARKET
(Map p70; www.grandcentralterminal.com/market;
Grand Central Terminal, Lexington Ave, at 42nd St,
Midtown East; ◷7am-9pm Mon-Fri, 10am-7pm
Sat, 11am-6pm Sun; ⓢS, 4/5/6, 7 to Grand Cen-
tral-42nd St) It's not all arrivals and departures at Grand Central. The station also
harbors a 240ft corridor lined with perfectly coiffed fresh produce and artisan treats.
Stock up on anything from crusty bread and
fruit tarts to lobsters, chicken pot pies, Spanish quince paste, fruit and vegetables, and
roasted coffee beans. There's even a Murray's
Cheese stall, peddling milky wonders like
cave-aged Gruyère.

Hell's Kitchen Flea Market   MARKET
(Map p70; ☑212-220-0239; www.annexmarkets.
com; W 39th St, btwn Ninth & Tenth Aves; ◷9am-
5pm Sat & Sun; ⓢA/C/E to 42nd St-Port Authority
Bus Terminal) This weekend flea market lures

both collectors and the common curious
with its wonderful booty of vintage furnishings, accessories, clothing and unidentifia-
ble objects from past eras.

🅰 Uptown

**Flamekeepers
Hat Club**   FASHION & ACCESSORIES
(Map p76; ☑212-531-3542; 273 W 121st St, at
St Nicholas Ave; ◷noon-7pm Tue & Wed, to 8pm
Thu-Sat, to 6pm Sun; ⓢA/C, B/D to 125th St)
Sharpen your kudos at this sassy little hat
shop owned by affable Harlem local Marc
Williamson. His carefully curated stock is
a hat-lover's dream: buttery Barbisio fe-
doras from Italy, Selentino top hats from
the Czech Republic and woolen patchwork
caps from Ireland's Hanna Hats of Don-
egal. Prices range from $85 to $350, with
an optional customization service for true
individualists.

Flying Tiger Copenhagen   HOMEWARES
(Map p76; ☑646-998-4755; www.flyingtiger.
com; 424 Columbus Ave, btwn 80th & 81st Sts;
◷10am-8pm Mon-Sun; 🚻; ⓢB, C to 81st St-
Museum of Natural History) In the market for
well-designed, quirky and inexpensive doo-
dads and tchotchkes? This Danish import
will scratch that itch. Something of a miniature Ikea, with items grouped thematical-
ly (kitchen, kids, arts and crafts etc) – you
could never have imagined the things you
didn't know you needed. Remove the price
tag and friends will think you've spent too
much on a gift.

❶ Information

INTERNET ACCESS

Most public parks in the city now offer free
wi-fi. Some prominent ones include the High
Line, Bryant Park, Battery Park, Central Park,
City Hall Park, Madison Square Park, Tompkins
Square Park and Union Square Park (Brooklyn
and Queens are also well covered). For other
locations, check out www.nycgovparks.org/
facilities/wifi.

Now, even underground subway stations offer
free wi-fi, offering a way to pass time or get
work done while waiting for signal problems or
other delays to be resolved. LinkNYC (www.link.
nyc), a program rolled out in 2016 to replace
anachronistic pay phones (once iconic symbols
of the city and where Superman changed into
his skivvies) with free internet connected kiosks,
replete with charging stations and wi-fi access,
is experiencing some teething issues, with some
booths having become gathering spots for less

salubrious folk. Plans call for thousands of these small structures to be installed throughout the five boroughs.

It's rare to find accommodations in New York City that don't offer wi-fi, though it isn't always free. Of course, most cafes offer wi-fi for customers, as do the ubiquitous Starbucks around town.

MEDICAL SERVICES

Emergency services can be stress-inducing and slow (unless your medical condition is absolutely dire); a visit should be avoided if other medical services can be provided to mitigate the situation.

New York-Presbyterian Hospital (☑ 212-305-2500; www.nyp.org/locations/newyork-presbyterian-columbia-university-medical-center; 630 W 168th St, at Ft Washington Ave; ⑤ A/C, 1 to 168th St) Reputable hospital.

Bellevue Hospital Center (☑ 212-562-4141; www.nychealthandhospitals.org/bellevue; 462 First Ave, at 27th St, Midtown East; ⑤ 6 to 28th St) Major public hospital with emergency room and trauma center.

New York County Medical Society (☑ 212-684-4670; www.nycms.org) Provides doctor referrals over the phone, based on type of problem and language spoken.

Tisch Hospital (New York University Langone Medical Center; ☑ 212-263-5800; www.nyulangone.org/locations/tisch-hospital; 550 First Ave; ⊙ 24hr) Large, state-of-the-art facility with highly regarded departments in every critical care specialty.

Callen-Lorde Community Health Center (☑ 212-271-7200; www.callen-lorde.org; 356 W 18th St, btwn Eighth & Ninth Aves; ⊙ 8:15am-8:15pm Mon-Thu, to 4:45pm Fri, 8:30-3:15pm Sat; ⑤ A/C/E, L to 8th Ave-14th St) This medical center, dedicated to the LGBT community and people living with HIV/AIDS, serves people regardless of their ability to pay.

Lenox Hill Hospital (☑ 212-434-2000; www.northwell.edu/find-care/locations/lenox-hill-hospital; 100 E 77th St, at Lexington Ave; ⊙ 24hr; ⑤ 6 to 77th St) A good hospital with a 24-hour emergency room and multilingual translators in the Upper East Side.

Mount Sinai Hospital (☑ 212-241-6500; www.mountsinai.org/locations/mount-sinai; 1468 Madison Ave, at 101st St; ⊙ 24hr; ⑤ 6 to 103rd St) An excellent hospital in the Upper East Side.

Planned Parenthood (Margaret Sanger Center; ☑ 212-965-7000; www.plannedparenthood.org; 26 Bleecker St, btwn Mott & Elizabeth Sts; ⊙ 8am-6:30pm Mon, Tue, Thu & Fri, to 8:30pm Wed, to 4:30pm Sat; ⑤ B/D/F/V to Broadway-Lafayette St; 6 to Bleecker St) Provides birth control, STD screenings and gynecological care.

TOURIST INFORMATION

NYC Information Center (Map p70; ☑ 212-484-1222; www.nycgo.com; Broadway Plaza, btwn W 43rd & 44th Sts; ⊙ 9am-6pm; ⑤ N/Q/R/W, S, 1/2/3, 7 to Times Sq-42nd St) There are official NYC Visitor Information Centers throughout the city. The main office is in Midtown.

In this web-based world you'll find infinite online resources to get up-to-the-minute information about New York. In person, try one of the official branches of NYC & Company (www.nycgo.com) at **Times Square**, **Macy's Herald Square** (Map p70; ☑ 212-484-1222; www.nycgo.com; Macy's, 151 W 34th St, at Broadway; ⊙ 9am-7pm Mon-Fri, from 10am Sat, from 11am Sun; ⑤ B/D/F/M, N/Q/R/W to 34th St-Herald Sq), **City Hall** (Map p62; ☑ 212-484-1222; www.nycgo.com; City Hall Park, at Broadway; ⊙ 9am-6pm Mon-Sun; ⑤ 4/5/6 to Brooklyn Bridge-City Hall; R/W to City Hall; J/Z to Chambers St) and South Street Seaport.

The **Brooklyn Tourism & Visitors Center** (www.nycgo.com; 209 Joralemon St, btwn Court St & Brooklyn Bridge Blvd, Downtown; ⊙ 10am-6pm Mon-Fri; ⑤ 2/3, 4/5 to Borough Hall) has all sorts of info on this much-loved borough.

ⓘ Getting There & Away

With its three bustling airports, two main train stations and a monolithic bus terminal, New York City rolls out the welcome mat for millions of visitors who come to take a bite out of the Big Apple each year.

Direct flights are possible from most major American and international cities. Figure six hours from Los Angeles, seven hours from London and Amsterdam, and 14 hours from Tokyo. Consider getting here by train instead of car or plane to enjoy a mix of bucolic and urban scenery en route, without unnecessary traffic hassles, security checks and excess carbon emissions.

Flights, tours and rail tickets can be booked online at www.lonelyplanet.com/bookings.

AIR

John F Kennedy International Airport

John F Kennedy International Airport (JFK; ☑ 718-244-4444; www.kennedyairport.com; ⑤ A to Howard Beach or E, J/Z to Sutphin Blvd-Archer Ave then JFK Airtrain), 15 miles from Midtown in southeastern Queens, has six working terminals, serves nearly 50 million passengers annually and hosts flights coming and going from all corners of the globe. You can use the AirTrain (free within the airport) to move from one terminal to the another.

The timeline is uncertain, but a massive $10 billion overhaul of the airport was recently approved. Architectural and structural changes are the focus, but plans also call for a substantial upgrade of amenities and transportation alternatives.

LaGuardia

Used mainly for domestic flights, **LaGuardia** (LGA; ✆ 718-533-3400; www.panynj.gov; ▣ M60, Q70) is smaller than JFK but only 8 miles from midtown Manhattan; it sees nearly 30 million passengers per year.

Much maligned by politicians and ordinary travelers alike, the airport is set to receive a much-needed $4 billion overhaul of its terminal facilities. Scheduled in phases, from 2018 to 2021, plans call for a single, unified terminal to replace the four existing stand-alone ones, as well as an upgrade in amenities and transportation alternatives.

Newark Liberty International Airport

Don't write off New Jersey when looking for airfares to New York. About the same distance from Midtown as JFK (16 miles), **Newark** (EWR; ✆ 973-961-6000; www.panynj.gov) brings many New Yorkers out for flights (there's some 40 million passengers annually). It's a hub for United Airlines and offers the only nonstop flight to Havana, Cuba, in the New York City area. A $2.4 billion dollar redevelopment of Terminal A is scheduled to be completed in 2022.

BUS

For long-distance bus trips, you'll arrive and depart from the world's busiest bus station, the **Port Authority Bus Terminal** (Map p70; ✆ 212-502-2200; www.panynj.gov; 625 Eighth Ave, at W 42nd St; ⑤ A/C/E to 42nd St-Port Authority Bust Terminal), which sees more than 65 million passengers each year. Efforts to replace the aging and less than salubrious station are always on the agenda. Bus companies leaving from here include the following:

Greyhound (www.greyhound.com) Connects New York with major cities across the country.

Peter Pan Trailways (www.peterpanbus.com) Daily express services to Boston, Washington, DC, and Philadelphia.

Short Line Bus (www.shortlinebus.com) Serves northern New Jersey and upstate New York, focusing on college towns such as Ithaca and New Paltz; part of Coach USA.

Trailways (www.trailwaysny.com) Bus service to upstate New York, including Albany, Ithaca and Syracuse, as well as Montreal, Canada.

A number of budget bus lines operate from locations on the west side of Midtown:

BoltBus (Map p70; ✆ 877-265-8287; www.boltbus.com; W 33rd St, between Eleventh & Twelfth Aves; ⑥) Services from New York to Philadelphia, Boston, Baltimore and Washington, DC. The earlier you purchase tickets, the

better the deal. Notable for its free wi-fi, which occasionally actually works.

Megabus (Map p70; https://us.megabus.com; 34th St, btwn 11th & 12th Aves; ⑥ ; ⑤ 7 to 34th St-Hudson Yards) Travels from New York to Boston, Washington, DC, and Toronto, Canada among other destinations. Free (sometimes functioning) wi-fi. Departures leave from 34th St near the Jacob K Javits Convention Center and **arrivals** (Map p70; 7th Ave & 27th St) come to 27th and 7th.

Vamoose (Map p70; ✆ 212-695-6766; www.vamoosebus.com; ⑤ 1 to 28th St; A/C/E, 1/2/3 to 34th St-Penn Station) Buses head to Arlington, Virginia and Bethesda, Maryland, both not far outside Washington, DC.

BOAT

Seastreak (www.seastreak.com) has daily commuter services between Atlantic Highlands and Highlands, New Jersey and Pier 11 near Wall St and E 35th St; there's also summer services to Sandy Hook (return $46) in New Jersey. Martha's Vineyard (one way/round-trip $165/240, five hours) in Massachusetts is accessible on summer weekends from E 35th St.

Cruise ships dock at the Manhattan Cruise Terminal in Hell's Kitchen on the west side of Manhattan at several piers from W 46th to 54th Sts.

If you're arriving in NYC by yacht, there are ports at an exclusive boat slip at the World Financial Center, and at a long-term slip at the 79th St Boathouse on the Upper West Side.

TRAIN

Penn Station (W 33rd St, btwn Seventh & Eighth Aves; ⑤ 1/2/3, A/C/E to 34th St-Penn Station) The oft maligned departure point for all Amtrak (www.amtrak.com) trains, including the Acela Express services to Princeton, New Jersey, and Washington, DC (note that this express service costs twice as much as a normal fare). All fares vary, based on the day of the week and the time you want to travel. There's no baggage-storage facility at Penn Station. Derailments and maintenance issues plagued Amtrak lines out of Penn Station in the spring of 2017; repairs mean compromised service, with no certainty of when the issues will be resolved.

Long Island Rail Road (www.mta.info/lirr) The Long Island Rail Road serves more than 300,000 commuters each day, with services from Penn Station to points in Brooklyn and Queens, and on Long Island. Prices are broken down by zones. A peak-hour ride from Penn Station to Jamaica Station (en route to JFK via AirTrain) costs $10.25 if you buy it at the station (or a whopping $16 onboard!).

NJ Transit (www.njtransit.com) Also operates trains from Penn Station, with services to the suburbs and the Jersey Shore.

New Jersey PATH (www.panynj.gov/path) An option for getting into NJ's northern points, such as Hoboken and Newark. Trains ($2.75) run from Penn Station along the length of Sixth Ave, with stops at 33rd, 23rd, 14th, 9th and Christopher Sts, as well as at the reopened World Trade Center site.

Metro-North Railroad (www.mta.info/mnr) The last line departing from the magnificent Grand Central Terminal, the Metro-North Railroad serves Connecticut, Westchester County and the Hudson Valley.

ⓘ Getting Around

Check the Metropolitan Transportation Authority website (www.mta.info) for public transportation information (buses and subway), including a handy travel planner and regular notifications of delays and alternate travel routes during frequent maintenance. Unfortunately, the frequency and length of delays has only increased as ridership has expanded.

Subway Inexpensive, somewhat efficient and operates around the clock, though can be confusing to the uninitiated. Single ride is $2.75 with a MetroCard. A 7-Day Unlimited Pass costs $32.

Buses Convenient during off hours – especially when transferring between the city's eastern and western sides. Uses the MetroCard; same price as the subway.

Taxi Meters start at $2.50 and increase roughly $5 for every 20 blocks. See www.nyc.gov/taxi for more information.

Bicycle The city's popular bike share program Citi Bike provides excellent access to most parts of Manhattan, with growing service elsewhere.

Inter-borough ferries Spots along the East River in Manhattan, Brooklyn, Queens (and soon the Bronx), including the Rockaway beaches in Queens, are now connected by the new New York City Ferry (www.ferry.nyc); the New York Water Taxi (www.nywatertaxi.com) hits a few piers with regular services. Journey across New York Harbor on the free, commuter Staten Island Ferry (p89).

TO/FROM THE AIRPORT
John F Kennedy International Airport

Taxi A yellow taxi from Manhattan to the airport will use the meter; prices (often about $60) depend on traffic – it can take 45 to 60 minutes. From JFK, taxis charge a flat rate of $52 to any destination in Manhattan (not including tolls or tip); it can take 45 to 60 minutes for most destinations in Manhattan. To/from a destination in Brooklyn, the metered fare should be about $45 (Coney Island) to $62 (downtown Brooklyn). Note that the Williamsburg, Manhattan, Brooklyn and

Queensboro–59th St Bridges have no toll either way, while the Queens–Midtown Tunnel and the Hugh L Carey Tunnel (aka the Brooklyn–Battery Tunnel) cost $8.50 going into Manhattan.

Fares for ride hailing apps like Lyft and Uber change depending on the time of day.

Vans & car service Shared vans, like those offered by **Super Shuttle Manhattan** (www.supershuttle.com), cost around $20 to $26 per person, depending on the destination. If traveling to the airport from NYC, car services have set fares from $45.

Express bus The **NYC Airporter** (www.nycairporter.com) runs to Grand Central Station, Penn Station or the Port Authority Bus Terminal from JFK. The one-way fare is $18.

Subway The subway is the cheapest but slowest way of reaching Manhattan. From the airport, hop on the AirTrain ($5, payable as you exit) to Sutphin Blvd-Archer Ave (Jamaica Station) to reach the E, J or Z line (or the Long Island Rail Road). To take the A line instead, ride the AirTrain to Howard Beach station. The E train to Midtown has the fewest stops and takes a little over an hour.

Long Island Rail Road (LIRR) This is by far the most relaxing way to arrive in the city. From the airport, take the AirTrain ($5, as you exit) to Jamaica Station. From there, LIRR trains go frequently to Penn Station in Manhattan or to Atlantic Terminal in Brooklyn (near Fort Greene, Boerum Hill and the Barclay Center). It's about a 20-minute journey from station to station. One-way fares to either Penn Station or Atlantic Terminal cost $10.25 ($7.50 at off-peak times).

LaGuardia

Taxi A taxi to/from Manhattan costs about $42 for the approximately half-hour ride; it's metered with no set fare. Fares for ride-hailing apps like Lyft and Uber vary.

Car service A car service to LaGuardia costs around $35.

Express bus The **NYC Airporter** (www.nycairporter.com) costs $15 and goes to/from Grand Central, Penn Station and the Port Authority Bus Terminal.

Subway & bus It's less convenient to get to LaGuardia by public transportation than the other airports. The best subway link is the 74 St-Broadway station (7 line, or the E, F, M and R lines at the connecting Jackson Heights-Roosevelt Ave station) in Queens, where you can pick up the Q70 Express Bus to the airport (about 10 minutes to the airport). Or you can catch the M60 bus from several subway stops in upper Manhattan and Harlem or the N/Q stop at Hoyt Ave-32st St.

Newark Liberty International Airport

Car service A car service runs about $50 to $70 for the 45-minute ride from Midtown – a taxi is roughly the same. You'll have to pay a whopping $15 to get into NYC through the Lincoln (at 42nd St) and Holland (at Canal St) Tunnels and, further north, the George Washington Bridge, though there's no charge going back through to New Jersey. There are a couple of cheap tolls on New Jersey highways too, unless you ask your driver to take Hwy 1 or 9.

Subway/train NJ Transit (www.njtransit. com) runs a rail service (with a $5.50 AirTrain connection) between Newark airport (EWR) and New York's Penn Station for $13 each way. The trip takes 25 minutes and runs every 20 or 30 minutes from 4:20am to about 1:40am. Hold onto your ticket, which you must show upon exiting at the airport.

Express bus The Newark Liberty Airport Express (www.newarkairportexpress.com) has a bus service between the airport and Port Authority Bus Terminal, Bryant Park and Grand Central Terminal in Midtown ($16 one way). The 45-minute ride goes every 15 minutes from 6:45am to 11:15pm and every half-hour from 4:45am to 6:45am and 11:15pm to 1:15am.

BICYCLE

Hundreds of miles of designated bike lanes have been added over the past decade. Add to this the excellent bike-sharing network Citi Bike (www. citibikenyc.com), and you have the makings for a surprisingly bike-friendly city. Hundreds of Citi Bike kiosks in Manhattan and parts of Brooklyn house the iconic bright blue and very sturdy bicycles, which have reasonable rates for short-term users. Nearly 14 million City Bike 'trips' were taken in 2016 and there are there are an estimated 12,000 bikes in the system.

To use a Citi Bike, purchase a 24-hour or three-day access pass (around $12 or $24 including tax) at any Citi Bike kiosk. You will then be given a five-digit code to unlock a bike. Return the bike to any station within 30 minutes to avoid incurring extra fees. Reinsert your credit card (you won't be charged) and follow the prompts to check out a bike again. You can make an un-limited number of 30-minute check-outs during those 24 hours or three days.

Helmets aren't required by law, but strongly recommended. City parks like Central Park, the Brooklyn Waterfront Greenway and Prospect Park in Brooklyn are good places to test out your comfort level on wheels in less stressful environments than the chaotic city streets. And most importantly, for your safety and that of others, obey traffic laws.

You'll find routes and bike lanes for every borough on NYC Bike Maps (www.nycbikemaps. com). For downloadable maps and point-to-point route generator, visit NYC DOT (www.nyc.gov/html/dot/html/bicyclists/bikemaps.shtml). Free bike maps are also available at most bike shops.

PUBLIC TRANSPORTATION
Tickets and Passes

➜ The yellow-and-blue MetroCards (www.mta. info/metrocard) are the swipe cards used for all of NYC's public transportation. You can purchase or add value at one of several easy-to-use automated machines at any station. Each ride on the subway or bus (except for express buses) deducts $2.75 from the card.

➜ Purchase the MetroCard itself for $1 at kiosks in subway stations, and load it with credit ($20, which will give you eight rides and change, is a good start). If you plan to ride a lot, buy a 7-day Unlimited Pass ($32). These cards are handy for travelers – particularly if you're jumping around town to a few different places in one day.

➜ The subway kiosks take credit or ATM cards (larger machines also take cash). When you need to add more credit, just insert your card and follow the prompts (tip: when it asks for your ZIP, input '99999' if you're not from the USA).

➜ Transfers from subway to bus, or bus to subway, are free. Just swipe/insert your card, and no extra charge will be deducted.

NEW YORK STATE

For most, any trip to the Empire State starts or finishes in its iconic metropolis: New York City. However, if you were to confine your travels only to its five boroughs and a little beyond, you'd be missing out big time.

Upstate New York – ie anywhere outside NYC – is a dream destination for those who cherish the great outdoors as much as a bar crawl around the Lower East Side. The grand Hudson River heads straight north from NYC, like an escape route. From Albany, the 524-mile Erie Canal cuts due west to Lake Erie, by spectacular Niagara Falls and Buffalo, a fascinating, rust-belt city that's on the rebound.

The St Lawrence River forms the border with Canada in the beautiful Thousand Islands area. Sample fine wines in the Finger Lakes region, hike in the magnificent Adirondack and Catskills mountains, or simply kick back on the sandy beaches of Long Island.

ⓘ Resources

511 NY (www.511ny.org) Statewide traffic and transit info.

I Love NY (www.iloveny.com) Comprehensive state tourism bureau, with the iconic heart logo.

DVEIGHT (www.dveightmag.com) Online and print magazine focusing on upstate experiences for stylish urbanites.

New York State Office of Parks, Recreation and Historic Preservation (https://parks.ny.gov) Camping, lodging and general info on all state parks.

And North (http://andnorth.com) Curated online guide to upstate New York.

Escape Brooklyn (http://escapebrooklyn.com) Respected blog by clued-up Brooklynites on upstate getaways.

Lonely Planet (www.lonelyplanet.com/usa/new-york-state) Destination information, hotel bookings, traveler forum and more.

Long Island

Technically, the 118 miles of Long Island includes the boroughs of Brooklyn and Queens on the west edge, but in the popular imagination, 'Long Island' begins only where the city ends, in a mass of traffic-clogged expressways and suburbs that every teenager aspires to leave. (Levittown, the first planned 1950s subdivision, is in central Nassau County.) But there's plenty more out on 'Lawn-guy-land' (per the local accent). Push past the central belt of 'burbs to wind-swept dunes, glitzy summer resorts, fresh farms and wineries, and whaling and fishing ports established in the 17th century. Then you'll see why loyalists prefer the nickname 'Strong Island.'

ⓘ Getting There & Around

Thanks to Long Island Rail Road (LIRR; www.mta.info/lirr), which runs three lines from NYC's Penn Station to the farthest east ends of the island, it's possible to visit without a car. Additionally, the Hampton Jitney (www.hamptonjitney.com) and Hampton Luxury Liner (www.hamptonluxuryliner.com) buses connect Manhattan to various Hamptons villages and Montauk; the former also picks up in Brooklyn, and runs to the North Fork. With a car, however, it is easier to visit several spots on the island in one go. I-495, aka the Long Island Expwy (LIE), runs down the middle of the island – but avoid rush hour, when it's commuter hell.

South Shore

Easily accessible by public transit, these beaches can get crowded, but they're a fun day out. Not nearly as much of a schlep as the Hamptons, and far more egalitarian, the beach towns along these barrier islands each have their own vibe and audience – you can get lost in the crowds or go solo on the dunes. **Long Beach**, just over the border from Queens, and its main town strip is busy with ice-cream shops, bars and eateries.

⊙ Sights

Fire Island National Seashore ISLAND (☑631-687-4750; www.nps.gov/fiis) FREE Federally protected, this island offers sand dunes, forests, clean beaches, camping (dune-camping permits $20), hiking trails, inns, restaurants, 15 hamlets and two villages. Its scenery ranges from car-free areas of summer mansions and packed nightclubs to stretches of sand where you'll find nothing but pitched tents and deer.

Most of the island is accessible only by **ferry** (☑631-665-3600; www.fireislandferries.com; 99 Maple Ave, Bay Shore; one way adult/child $10/5, 1am ferry $19) and is free of cars – regulars haul their belongings on little wagons instead. You can drive to either end of the island (the lighthouse or the Wilderness Visitor Center) but there is no road in between. The island is edged with a dozen or so tiny hamlets, mostly residential. Party-center **Ocean Beach Village** and quieter **Ocean Bay Park** (take ferries from the Bayshore LIRR stop) have a few hotels; **Cherry Grove** and the **Pines** (ferries from Sayville) are gay enclaves, also with hotels.

Robert Moses State Park STATE PARK (☑631-669-0449; www.parks.ny.gov; 600 Robert Moses State Pkwy, Babylon, Fire Island; per car $10, lounge chairs $10, golf $11; ⊙dawn-dusk) Robert Moses State Park, one small part of Fire Island accessible by car, lies at the westernmost end and features wide, soft-sand beaches with mellower crowds than those at Jones Beach. It's also adjacent to the **Fire Island Lighthouse** (Fire Island National Seashore; ☑631-661-4876; www.nps.gov/fiis; Robert Moses Causeway; adult/child $7/4; ⊙9:30am-6pm Jul & Aug, 10am-4pm Mon-Fri, to 5pm Sat & Sun Sep-Jun), which you can walk to from here.

Sunken Forest FOREST (☑631-597-6183; www.nps.gov/fiis; Fire Island; ⊙visitor center mid-May–mid-Oct) FREE This 300-year-old forest, a surprisingly dense stretch of trees behind the dunes, is easily accessible via a 1.5-mile boardwalk trail looping through. It's pleasantly shady in summer, and vividly colored when the leaves change in fall. It's accessible by its own ferry stop (Sailors Haven, where there's also a visitor center), or a long walk in the winter season, after the ferry shuts down. Ranger-guided tours available.

Sleeping & Eating

Seashore Condo Motel HOTEL $$
(☑ 631-583-5860; www.seashorecondomotel.com; Bayview Ave, Ocean Bay Park, Fire Island; r from $240; ❄ 🤖) Small, wood-paneled rooms without many frills, despite the price.

Madison Fire Island Pines BOUTIQUE HOTEL $$$
(☑ 631-597-6061; www.themadisonfi.com; 22 Atlantic Walk, Fire Island Pines, Fire Island; r from $225; ❄ 🤖 🏊) Fire Island's first 'boutique' hotel, which rivals anything Manhattan has to offer in terms of amenities, but also has killer views from a rooftop deck.

Sand Castle SEAFOOD $$
(☑ 631-597-4174; www.fireislandsandcastle.com; 106 Lewis Walk, Cherry Grove, Fire Island; mains $15-30; ⏰ 11am-11pm Mon, Tue & Thu-Sat, 9:30am-11pm Sun May-Sep) One of Fire Island's only ocean-front (rather than bayfront) options, Sand Castle serves up satisfying appetizers (fried calamari, portobello fries) and lots of seafood temptations (mussels, crab cakes, seared sea scallops). Nice cocktails and people-watching.

Getting There & Away

You can drive to Fire Island by taking the Long Island Expwy to Exit 53 (Bayshore), 59 (Sayville) or 63 (Patchogue).

Using public transportation, take the LIRR to one of three stations with connections to the ferries: Patchogue (www.davisparkferry.com), Bayshore (www.fireislandferries.com) or Sayville (www.sayvilleferry.com). Patchogue is walking distance from the train to the boat. You can also purchase a train-taxi combination ticket for excursions to Sunken Forest and a train-bus combo for Jones Beach.

The LIRR (www.mtainfo.com/lirr) runs directly to Long Beach (55 minutes) from New York's Penn Station. You can buy special beach combination excursion tickets from the railroad.

The Hamptons

This string of villages is a summer escape for Manhattan's wealthiest, who zip to mansions by helicopter. Mere mortals take the Hampton Jitney bus and chip in on rowdy rental houses. Behind the glitz is a long cultural history, as noted artists and writers have lived here. Beneath the glamour, the gritty and life-risking tradition of fishing continues.

⊙ Sights

EAST HAMPTON

East Hampton Town Marine Museum MUSEUM
(www.easthamptonhistory.org; 301 Bluff Rd, Amagansett; $4; ⏰ 10am-5pm Sat, noon-5pm Sun Apr-Oct) One of your last outposts before you drive on to Montauk, this small museum dedicated to the fishing and whaling industries is as interesting as its counterpart in Sag Harbor, full of old harpoons, boats half the size of their prey, and a beautiful black-and-white photographic tribute to the local fishers and their families.

Osborn-Jackson House MUSEUM
(☑ 631-324-6850; www.easthamptonhistory.org; 101 Main St; donation $4; ⏰ 10am-4pm Tue-Sat) Check out East Hampton's colonial past with a visit to the East Hampton Historical Society. The Society tends to five historical attractions around East Hampton, including old colonial farms, mansions and a marine museum.

Pollock-Krasner House ARTS CENTER
(☑ 631-324-4929; www.stonybrook.edu/pkhouse; 830 Springs Fireplace Rd; $5, guided tours $10; ⏰ 1-5pm Thu-Sat May-Oct) Tour the home of husband-and-wife art stars Jackson Pollock and Lee Krasner – worth it just to see the paint-spattered floor of Pollock's studio. Reservations required for guided tour at noon.

SAG HARBOUR

Sag Harbor Whaling & Historical Museum MUSEUM
(☑ 631-725-0770; www.sagharborwhalingmuseum. org; 200 Main St; adult/child $6/2; ⏰ 10am-5pm Apr-Nov) The cool collection here includes actual artifacts from 19th-century whaling ships: sharp flensing knives, battered pots for rendering blubber, delicate scrimshaw and more. It's a bit surreal to see photos of the giant mammals in a village that's now a cute resort town.

SOUTHAMPTON

Parrish Art Museum MUSEUM
(☑ 631-283-2118; www.parrishart.org; 279 Montauk Hwy, Water Mill; adult/child $10/free, Wed free; ⏰ 10am-5pm Mon, Wed, Thu, Sat & Sun, to 8pm Fri) In a sleek long barn designed by Herzog & de Meuron, this institution spotlights local artists such as Jackson Pollock, Willem de Kooning and Chuck Close.

NEW YORK, NEW JERSEY & PENNSYLVANIA LONG ISLAND

Southampton Historical Museum   MUSEUM

(☑ 631-283-2494;   www.southamptonhistorical
museum.org; 17 Meeting House Lane; adult/child
$4/free; ☺ 11am-4pm Wed-Sat Mar-Dec) Before
the Hamptons was the Hamptons, there was
this clutch of buildings, now nicely maintained, and spread around Southampton.
The main museum is Rogers Mansion, once
owned by a whaling captain. Also visit a
former dry-goods store, now occupied by a
local jeweler, around the corner on Main St;
and a 17th-century homestead, the Halsey
House (Saturday only July to October).

St Andrew's Dune Church   CHURCH

(www.standrewsdunechurch.com; 12 Gin Lane;
☺ service 11am Sun Jun-Sep) The triple spires of
this 19th-century red wooden church glow
beautifully in the afternoon light. You can
come to Sunday service if so inclined, admiring the stained glass and quaint wooden
pews, or simply enjoy a stroll along the placid waterway across the street from the curious iron pot donated by an early congregant.
The building was the earliest life-saving station in New York, and is well worth the short
drive or walk from downtown.

🛏 Sleeping

★ Topping Rose House   BOUTIQUE HOTEL $$$

(☑ 631-537-0870; www.toppingrosehouse.com;
1 Bridgehampton-Sag Harbor Turnpike, Bridge-
hampton; r from $695; �P✻🅢🏊) In an 1842
home, this top-of-the-line modern boutique
hotel boasts 22 guest rooms, including six
suites decorated with local artists' work. A
Manhattan gallery curates the rotating art
collection (for sale, of course), and there's a
spa and heated pool in addition to the 75-
seat farm-to-table restaurant, some produce
for which is sourced from the 1-acre garden
adjoining the property.

1708 House   INN $$$

(☑ 631-287-1708; www.1708house.com; 126 Main
St; r from $250; ✻🅢) History buffs might
gravitate toward this local standout. It's in
central Southampton and prides itself on its
turn-of-the-century charm.

🍴 Eating

Candy Kitchen   DINER $

(☑ 631-537-9885; 2391 Montauk Hwy, Bridgehamp-
ton; mains $5-12; ☺ 7am-9pm; 🚸) An antidote
to glitz, this corner diner has been serving
good soups, homemade ice cream and other
staples since 1925. Its policy is similarly old-
school – cash only, please.

★ Fellingham's   PUB FOOD $$

(Restaurant Sports Bar; ☑ 631-283-9417; www.
fellinghamsrestaurant.com; 17 Cameron St; burgers $11, mains $19-21; ☺ 11am-11pm) Behind the
bank, in an alley off Main St, you'll get a dash
of local flavor at this favored sports bar, rich
with historical photos and memorabilia, and
boasting a hearty menu featuring a bacon-
cheeseburger named for baseball legend
Babe Ruth and a Sharapova burger with –
naturally – Russian dressing. There's so
much local flavor, this qualifies as the
'Cheers' of Southampton. Mains are heavy
on the steaks and chops.

★ Dockside Bar and Grill   SEAFOOD $$$

(☑ 631-725-7100; www.docksidesagharbor.com; 26
Bay St; mains $26-32; ☺ 11:30am-10pm) A local
favorite inside the American Legion Hall
(the original bar's still there), the seafood-
heavy menu features a prize-winning, stick-
to-the-spoon chowder and luscious lobster
spring rolls, among other mouth-watering
delights. The outdoor patio can be nice in
the summer.

🛈 Getting There & Away

Driving the Montauk Hwy (Rte 27) to and from
New York involves careful planning to avoid
major congestion, and it's often at a standstill
within the Hamptons itself on busy weekends.
It's better to take the ever-popular Hampton
Jitney out here from Manhattan or Brooklyn – it
serves the entire Hamptons with frequent comfortable buses. The LIRR is a second but often
more time-consuming option.

🛈 Getting Around

The app-driven, cool turquoise converted school
buses offered by Hampton Hopper (www.hamp
tonhopper.com) are an economical, hassle-free
way around the towns and run into the bar hours.

Montauk

Toward the east-pointing tip of Long Island's
South Fork, you'll find the mellow town of
Montauk, aka 'The End,' and the famous
surfing beach Ditch Plains. With the surfers
have come affluent hipsters and boho-chic
hotels, but the area is still far less of a scene
than the Hamptons, with proudly blue-
collar residents and casual seafood restaurants. Route 27, the Montauk Hwy, divides
east of Napeague State Park, with the
Montauk Hwy continuing down the center
of the peninsula while Old Montauk Hwy
hugs the water. The roads converge at the

edge of central Montauk and Fort Pond, a small lake. Two miles east is a large inlet called Lake Montauk, with marinas strung along its shore.

◉ Sights

Lost at Sea Memorial
MEMORIAL

(2000 Montauk Hwy, Montauk Lighthouse; Montauk State Park parking fee $8; ⊙10:30am-5:30pm Sun-Fri, to 7pm Sat mid-Jun–Aug, reduced hours mid-Apr–mid-Jun & Sep-Nov) Visitors to the Montauk Lighthouse may not immediately notice a smaller 15ft structure at the far east end of the park, where the 60ft cliffs fall off into the sea, but for local fishers it's a daily reminder of their struggle against the power of the sea. The 8ft, 2600lb bronze statue set on a 7ft slab of granite is inscribed with the names of local fishers lost to the waves, from the colonial days of New York to the present.

Montauk Point State Park
STATE PARK

(☑631-668-3781; www.parks.ny.gov; 2000 Montauk Hwy/Rte 27; per car $8; ⊙dawn-dusk) Covering the eastern tip of the South Fork is Montauk Point State Park, with its impressive **lighthouse** (☑631-668-2544; www.montauklighthouse.com; adult/child $11/4; ⊙10:30am-5:30pm Sun-Fri, to 7pm Sat mid-Jun–Aug, reduced hours mid-Apr–mid-Jun & Sep-Nov). A good place for windswept walks, surfing, surf fishing (with permit) and seal-spotting.

🛏 Sleeping

Hither Hills State Park
CAMPGROUND $

(☑631-668-2554; www.parks.ny.gov; 164 Old Montauk Hwy; campsites New York State residents/nonresidents $35/70, reservation fee $9) These wooded dunes form a natural barrier between Montauk and the Hamptons. The 189-site campground caters for tents and RVs, and there are spots for fishing (with a permit) and hiking through the dunes; online reservations are a must.

★Sunrise Guesthouse
GUESTHOUSE $$$

(☑631-668-7286; www.sunrisebnb.com; 681 Old Montauk Hwy; r/ste $395/495; 🅿❄🛜) A tasteful yet homey four-room B&B a mile from town, and just across the road from the beach. The breakfast is ample and delicious, served in a comfy dining area with a million-dollar view.

Surf Lodge
MOTEL $$$

(☑631-483-5037; www.thesurflodge.com; 183 Edgemere St; r $250-300; ❄🛜) Set on Fort Pond a half-mile north of the beach, this hipster haven has been at the forefront of Montauk's transformation. It has a casual-chic design scheme with private decks and cooking stoves, and Frette bedding.

🍴 Eating & Drinking

Lobster Roll
SEAFOOD $$

(☑631-267-3740; www.lobsterroll.com; 1980 Montauk Hwy, Amagansett; mains $14-28; ⊙11:30am-9:30pm Jun-Sep, 11:30am-4:30pm Mon, to 8pm Fri-Sun May) 'Lunch' is the sign to look for on the roadside west of Montauk, marking this clam-and-lobster shack that has been in operation since 1965.

★Clam Bar at Napeague
SEAFOOD $$

(☑631-267-6348; www.clambarhamptons.com; 2025 Montauk Hwy, Amagansett; items $15-30; ⊙11:30am-6pm Apr-Oct, 11:30am-6pm Sat & Sun Nov & Dec) You won't get fresher seafood or a saltier waitstaff, and holy mackerel, those lobster rolls are good, even if you choke a bit on the price. Three decades in business – the public has spoken – with cash only, of course. Locals favor this one. Find it on the road between Amagansett and Montauk.

Montauk Brewing Company
MICROBREWERY

(☑631-668-8471; www.montaukbrewingco.com; 62 S Erie Ave; ⊙2-7pm Mon-Fri, noon-7pm Sat & Sun) 'Come as you are,' preaches the small tasting room, and Cobain's family hasn't asked for their lyric back yet. There's a more-than-palatable rotating range of cervezas, from lagers to stouts, and an outdoor patio to enjoy them in the right weather.

Montauket
BAR

(☑631-668-5992; 88 Firestone Rd; ⊙noon-10pm) Experts agree: this is the best place to watch the sun go down on Long Island. An unassuming slate-blue-shingled building, full of local flavor (and local people).

ℹ Getting There & Away

Montauk is the last stop on the eastbound Jitney bus (www.hamptonjitney.com; $28) as well as the Long Island Railroad. The Suffolk County bus 10C runs out here from East Hampton – connect with the 94 to cover the rest of the distance to the lighthouse.

North Fork & Shelter Island

The North Fork of Long Island is known for its bucolic farmland and vineyards (though weekends can draw rowdy limo-loads on winery crawls). Rte 25, the main road through the towns of **Jamesport**, **Cutchogue** and **Southold**, is pretty and edged with farm stands.

The largest town on the North Fork is **Greenport**, a laid-back place with working fishing boats, a history in whaling, and an old carousel in its Harbor Front Park. It's compact and easily walkable from the LIRR station. Like a little pearl in Long Island's claw, Shelter Island rests between the North and South Forks. The island is a smaller, lower-key version of the Hamptons, with a touch of maritime New England. Parking is limited; long **Crescent Beach**, for instance, has spots only by permit. If you don't mind a few hills, it's a nice place to visit by bike.

◎ Sights

Mashomack Nature Preserve   NATURE RESERVE
(☑ 631-749-1001; www.shelter-island.org/mash omack.html; Rte 114, Shelter Island; donation adult/child $3/2; ◎ 9am-5pm Mar-Sep, to 4pm Oct-Feb) The 2000 acres of this Shelter Island reserve, shot through with creeks and marshes, are great for kayaking, birding and hiking (no cycling allowed). Take precautions against ticks, an ever-present problem on the island.

Orient Beach State Park   BEACH
(☑ 631-323-2440; www.parks.ny.gov; 40000 Main Rd, Orient; per car $10, kayaks per hour $25; ◎ 8am-dusk, swimming only Jul-Aug) A sandy slip of land at the end of the North Fork where you can swim in the calm ocean water (July and August) or rent kayaks to paddle in the small bay. True believers can view four different lighthouses, including the Orient Point Lighthouse, known to sailors as 'the coffee pot' for its stout bearing.

Horton Point Lighthouse   LIGHTHOUSE
(☑ 631-765-5500; www.southoldhistoricalsociety. org/lighthouse; 3575 Lighthouse Rd, Southold; $5; ◎ 11:30am-4pm Sat & Sun Jun-Sep) Perhaps a poorer sister to the famous Montauk lighthouse, Horton Point was also commissioned by President Washington, but finally built 60 years later by William Sinclair, a Scotsman, who was an engineer in Brooklyn's Navy Yard. There's a nice nature trail in the adjacent park that leads to two Long Island Sound overlooks and steps to the beach.

⊨ Sleeping & Eating

Greenporter Hotel   BOUTIQUE HOTEL $$$
(☑ 631-477-0066; www.greenporterhotel.com; 326 Front St, Greenport; r from $309; ✴ ☜ ☒) An older motel redone with white walls and

Ikea furniture, this place is good value for the area.

Love Lane Kitchen   MODERN AMERICAN $$
(☑ 631-298-8989; www.lovelanekitchen.com; 240 Love Lane, Mattituck; mains lunch $13-16, dinner $16-32; ◎ 7am-4pm Tue & Wed, 8am-9:30pm Thu-Mon) At this popular place on a cute street, local meat and vegetables drive the global-diner menu: burgers, of course, plus spicy chickpeas and duck tagine.

North Fork Table & Inn   AMERICAN $$$
(☑ 631-765-0177; www.nofoti.com; 57225 Main Rd, Southold; 3-course set menu $70; ◎ 5:30-8pm Mon, Thu & Sun, to 10pm Fri & Sat) A favorite foodies' escape, this four-room inn (rooms from $250) has an excellent farm-to-table restaurant, run by alums of the esteemed Manhattan restaurant Gramercy Tavern. Dinner is served Thursday to Monday, but if you're hankering for a gourmand-to-go lunch ($11 to $15), the inn's food truck is parked outside on those days from 11:30am to 3:30pm.

❶ Getting There & Away

The Hampton Jitney bus picks up passengers on Manhattan's East Side on 96th, 83rd, 77th, 69th, 59th and 40th Sts. It makes stops in 10 North Fork villages.

If you're driving, take the Midtown Tunnel out of Manhattan, which will take you onto I-495/Long Island Expwy. Take this until it ends at Riverhead and follow signs onto Rte 25. You can stay on Rte 25 for all points east, but note that the North Rd (Rte 48) is faster as it does not go through the town centers.

The Long Island Rail Road's line is the Ronkonkoma Branch, with trips leaving from Penn Station and Brooklyn and running all the way out to Greenport.

To get from the North Fork to the South Fork (or vice versa), take the North Ferry ($11, www.northferry.com) and the South Ferry ($15, www.southferry.com) services, crossing Shelter Island in between. There is no direct ferry – you must take one and then the other.

Hudson Valley

Winding roads along either side of the Hudson River take you by picturesque farms, Victorian cottages, apple orchards and old-money mansions built by New York's elite. Painters of the Hudson River School romanticized these landscapes, and fall is a particularly beautiful time for a trip.

The eastern side of the river is more populated thanks to the commuter train line between NYC and Albany. Several magnificent homes can be found near Tarrytown and Sleepy Hollow. The formerly industrial town of Beacon has been revived as an outpost of contemporary art, while historic Hudson attracts a wealthier set of weekenders with its restored Opera House, small galleries and antique shops.

In a car you can cross to the Hudson's west bank to explore several state parks, West Point military academy, and New Paltz with its access to superb rock climbing in the Minnewaska State Park Preserve and Mohonk Preserve.

❶ Getting There & Away

Metro-North Railroad (www.mta.info/mnr) runs as far north as Poughkeepsie from NYC's Grand Central; New Jersey Transit (www.njtransit.com) runs another line through New Jersey that gives access to Harriman. Amtrak (www.amtrak.com) also stops in Rhinecliff (for Rhinebeck), Poughkeepsie and Hudson. For New Paltz, you'll need the bus.

Lower Hudson Valley

Made famous by 19th-century author Washington Irving as the location of his headless horseman tale, *The Legend of Sleepy Hollow*, Sleepy Hollow and its larger neighbor Tarrytown are the jumping-off points for a trio of historic estates, as well as the gourmet and farm-activity destination of Stone Barn Center for Food & Agriculture.

Since the opening of the outstanding contemporary art museum Dia: Beacon in 2003, this blue-collar town beside the Hudson River has steadily evolved into a magnet for creatives, commuters and second-homers. Backed by Mt Beacon, the tallest summit in the Hudson Valley and a rewarding hike, Beacon also offers great shopping at the boutiques, galleries and craft shops strung along Main St as it runs down to picturesque Fishkill Falls. The town may be experiencing its moment of hipness, but it still proudly wears its working-class roots and is all the more attractive for it.

◉ Sights

★ **Dia: Beacon** GALLERY
(☑ 845-440-0100; www.diaart.org; 3 Beekman St; adult/child $15/free; ⊙ 11am-6pm Thu-Mon Apr-Oct, 11am-4pm Fri-Mon Nov-Mar) The 300,000 sq

ft of a former Nabisco box printing factory beside the Hudson River is now a storehouse for a series of stunning monumental works by the likes of Richard Serra, Dan Flavin, Louise Bourgeois and Gerhard Richter. The permanent collection is complemented by temporary shows of large-scale sculptures and installations, making this a must-see for contemporary art fans.

Boscobel House & Gardens HISTORIC BUILDING
(☑ 845-265 3638; www.boscobel.org; 1601 Rte 9D, Garrison; house & gardens adult/child $17/8, gardens only $11/5; ⊙ guided tours 10am-4pm Wed-Mon Apr-Oct, to 3pm Nov & Dec) The elegant backdrop for the summer season **Hudson Valley Shakespeare Festival** (☑ 845-265-9575; www.hvshakespeare.org; tickets from $45; ⊙ mid-May–early Sep), Boscobel dates from 1808 and is considered to be one of the finest examples of Federal-style architecture in the state. Entry to the house, which is 8 miles south of Beacon, is by guided tour (50 minutes), which run regularly through the day.

Stone Barn Center for Food & Agriculture FARM
(☑ 914-366-6200; http://story.stonebarnscenter.org; 630 Bedford Rd, Pocantico Hills; adult/child $20/10; ⊙ 10am-5pm Wed-Sun) Tours of the celebrated farm and the chance to take part in activities such as egg collecting, lettuce planting and meeting the flock of sheep are sure to entertain kids and land-loving adults. There's a good shop and a small take-out cafe.

Sunnyside HISTORIC BUILDING
(☑ 914-591-8763, Mon-Fri 914-631-8200; www.hudsonvalley.org; 3 W Sunnyside Lane, Tarrytown; adult/child $12/6; ⊙ tours 10:30am-3:30pm Wed-Sun May–mid-Nov) Washington Irving, famous for tales such as *The Legend of Sleepy Hollow*, built this imaginative home, which he said had more nooks and crannies than a cocked hat. Tour guides in 19th-century costume tell good stories, and the wisteria Irving planted a century ago still climbs the walls.

The closest train station to Sunnyside is Irvington, one stop before Tarrytown.

🛏 Sleeping & Eating

★ **Roundhouse** BOUTIQUE HOTEL $$
(☑ 845-765-8369; www.roundhousebeacon.com; 2 E Main St; r from $189; 🅿 😊 ❄ 🛜) Occupying a former blacksmiths and hat factory either side of the town's Fishkill Creek, Roundhouse

is a model of Beacon's renaissance as a tourist destination. Elements of the buildings' industrial past blend seamlessly with contemporary comforts in the spacious rooms, which feature designer lightbulbs, timber headboards and alpaca-wool blankets.

Two-Michelin-star-awarded chef Terrance Brennan heads up the hotel's excellent **restaurant and lounge** (ramen $16-21, mains $26-36, tasting menus from $85; ⊙3-9pm Mon & Tue, 11:30am-9pm Wed & Thu, to 10pm Fri & Sat, 11am-8pm Sun; ✈) grounded by a philosophy of sustainable 'whole-farm cuisine': do not miss the amazing ramen served in the lounge.

Homespun Foods CAFE $
(☑845-831-5096; www.homespunfoods.com; 232 Main St; mains $5-10; ⊙8am-5pm; ✈) A low-key gourmet legend in these parts, Homespun offers fresh everything, including creative salads, sandwiches and a veggie meatloaf made from nuts and cheese.

★**Blue Hill at Stone Barns** AMERICAN $$$
(☑914-366-9600; www.bluehillfarm.com; 630 Bedford Rd, Pocantico Hills; set menu $258; ⊙5-10pm Wed-Sat, 1-7:30pm Sun) ✈ Go maximum locavore at chef Dan Barber's farm (it also supplies his Manhattan restaurant). Settle in for an eye-popping multicourse feast based on the day's harvest lasting at least three hours, where the service is as theatrical as the presentation. Be sure to book around two months in advance and note the dress code: jackets and ties preferred for gentlemen; shorts not permitted.

❶ Getting There & Away

Metro-North (www.mta.info/mnr) commuter trains connect NYC with Beacon (one way off-peak/peak $23/28, 90 minutes).

Tarrytown Station (www.mta.info/mnr; 1 Depot Plaza, Tarrytown) has regular train connections with NYC ($17 to $20, 40 to 50 minutes). Irvington, one stop before Tarrytown, is the closest station to Sunnyside, while Philipse Manor, one stop after, is walkable to Philipsburg Manor.

For the most flexibility in getting around the area, hire a car.

New Paltz

The hippie vibe endures in New Paltz, a short drive from the west bank of the Hudson. You'll find a campus of the State University of New York here, and it's the gateway to

Shawangunk Ridge (aka 'The Gunks'), excellent for hiking and offering excellent options for rock climbing.

◉ Sights & Activities

Historic Huguenot Street HISTORIC SITE
(☑845-255-1660; www.huguenotstreet.org; 86 Huguenot St; guided tours $15) Step back in time on a stroll around this picturesque enclave of buildings remaining from a Huguenot settlement dating back to 1678.

The 10-acre National Historic Landmark District includes a visitor center (the departure point for guided tours of the area), seven historic stone houses, a reconstructed 1717 Huguenot church and a burial ground.

Mohonk Preserve PARK
(☑845-255-0919; www.mohonkpreserve.org; 3197 Rte 55, Gardiner; day pass hikers/climbers & cyclists $15/20; ⊙9am-5pm) Some 8000 acres of land held in private trust, with trails and other services maintained with visitor fees. This is home to some of the best rock climbing on the East Coast.

Rock & Snow ADVENTURE SPORTS
(☑845-255-1311; www.rockandsnow.com; 44 Main St; ⊙9am-6pm Mon-Thu, to 8pm Fri & Sat, 8am-7pm Sun) This long-running outfitters rents out tents, and rock-climbing, ice-climbing and other equipment. It can also team you up with guides for climbing and other outdoor adventures in the 'Gunks.'

⛏ Sleeping & Eating

New Paltz Hostel HOSTEL $
(☑845-255-6676; www.newpaltzhostel.com; 145 Main St; dm/r from $30/70; ❄🌐) Aligned with New Paltz's hippie vibe, this hostel in a big old house next to the bus station is popular with visiting rock climbers and hikers. Rooms have two bunk beds and a double bed with attached bathroom, and there's a good communal kitchen.

★**Mohonk Mountain House** RESORT $$$
(☑855-436-0832; www.mohonk.com; 1000 Mountain Rest Rd; r from $259; ❄@🌐❄) This giant faux 'Victorian castle' perches over a dark lake, offering guests all the luxuries, from lavish meals to golf to spa services, plus a full roster of outdoor excursions, including hiking and trail rides. Rates include all meals and most activities, and you can choose from rooms in the main building, cottages or the luxury Grove Lodge.

Huckleberry

AMERICAN $$

(☑ 845-633-8443; www.huckleberrynewpaltz.com; 21 Church St; mains $12-20; ☉ noon-2am Mon-Thu, to 4am Fri & Sat, 10am-2am Sun; ☎) This cute sea-green painted house hidden off the main road offers an appealing menu of gourmet items, including Wagyu burgers (with the option of gluten-free buns), fish tacos and stout mac 'n' cheese. There are also creative cocktails, craft beers and a lovely outdoor dining/drinking area in which to enjoy it all.

ⓘ Getting There & Away

Trailways (☑ 800-776-7548; www.trailwaysny. com; 139 Main St) connects New Paltz with NYC ($21.75, 1½ hours) and Woodstock ($6.25, one hour).

Poughkeepsie

The largest town in the Hudson Valley, Poughkeepsie (puh-*kip*-see) is home to the prestigious college Vassar, which was women-only until 1969, as well as an IBM office – once the 'Main Plant' where notable early computers were built. The main attraction here is the chance to walk across the Hudson River on the world's longest pedestrian bridge.

◉ Sights

Franklin D Roosevelt Home

HISTORIC BUILDING

(☑ 845-486-7770; www.nps.gov/hofr; 4097 Albany Post Rd; adult/child $18/free, museum only adult/ child $9/free; ☉ 9am-5pm) Rangers lead interesting hour-long tours around Springwood, the home of Franklin D Roosevelt (FDR) who won a record four presidential elections and led America from the Great Depression through WWII. Considering his family wealth, it's a modest abode, but can be unpleasantly crowded in summer. Intimate details have been preserved, including his desk – left as it was the day before he died – and the hand-pulled elevator he used to hoist his polio-stricken body to the 2nd floor.

The home is part of a 1520-acre estate, formerly a working farm, which also includes walking trails and the **FDR Presidential Library and Museum** (☑ 845-486-7770; www. fdrlibrary.org; adult/child $18/free; ☉ 9am-6pm Apr-Oct, to 5pm Nov-Mar), which details important achievements in FDR's presidency. Admission tickets last two days and include the Springwood tour and the presidential library.

Walkway Over the Hudson

PARK

(☑ 845-834-2867; www.walkway.org; 61 Parker Ave; ☉ 7am-sunset) This is the main eastern entrance (with parking) to what was once a railroad bridge crossing the Hudson. It's now the world's longest pedestrian bridge – 1.28 miles – and a state park. The span provides breathtaking views along the river.

🛏 Sleeping & Eating

★ Roosevelt Inn

MOTEL $

(☑ 845-229-2443; www.rooseveltinnofhydepark. com; 4360 Albany Post Rd; r $70-155; ☉ Mar-Dec; ❊ ☎) Family owned and run since 1971, this roadside motel offers a great deal, especially for its pine-paneled 'rustic' rooms. The upper-level deluxe rooms offer more space.

No breakfast is served, but there's a cafe on site.

Eveready Diner

AMERICAN $

(☑ 845-229-8100; www.theevereadydiner.com; 4184 Albany Post Rd/Rte 9; mains $10-13; ☉ 6am-midnight Sun-Thu, 24hr Fri & Sat) It's difficult to resist turning off the highway to visit this giant sparkling chrome diner. There's been a diner here since the 1950s and even though this building is from 1995 it's a classic, with an authentic interior and extensive menu to match.

ⓘ Getting There & Away

Amtrak has services to/from NYC ($27, 1½ hours) and up the Hudson to Albany ($27, 65 minutes) and beyond from **Poughkeepsie Station** (☑ 800-872-7245; www.amtrak.com; 41 Main St). Bus services by Short Line (https:// web.coachusa.com/shortline) to/from NYC ($22, 2½ hours) also stop at the train station.

Rhinebeck

Midway up the east side of the Hudson, Rhinebeck has a charming main street and an affluent air. The surrounding land has farms and wineries, as well as the holistic Omega Institute, and the super-liberal Bard College, 8 miles north, worth dropping by for its Frank Gehry–designed performing arts center.

◉ Sights

Staatsburg State Historic Site

HOUSE

(☑ 845-889-8851; https://parks.ny.gov/historic-sites/25/details.aspx; Old Post Rd, Staatsburg; adult/child $8/free; ☉ tours 11am-4pm Thu-Sun mid-Apr–Oct) FREE Take a tour around this beaux-arts mansion, the home of Ogden

Mills and his wife Ruth. It boasts 79 luxurious rooms filled with brocaded Flemish tapestries, gilded plasterwork, period paintings and Oriental art. Find it 6 miles south of Rhinebeck just off Rte 9.

Old Rhinebeck Aerodrome MUSEUM
(☑ 845-752-3200; www.oldrhinebeck.org; 9 Norton Rd, Red Hook; Mon-Fri adult/child $12/8, airshows adult/child $25/12, flights $75; ☉ 10am-5pm May-Oct, airshows from 2pm Sat & Sun) This museum, a short drive north of the center of Rhinebeck, has a collection of vintage planes and other related vehicles and artifacts that date back to 1900. On weekends you can watch an airshow or take a ride in an old biplane.

🛏 Sleeping & Eating

★ Olde Rhinebeck Inn B&B $$$
(☑ 845-871-1745; www.rhinebeckinn.com; 340 Wurtemberg Rd; r $250-325; ❀ 🕿) Built by German settlers between 1738 and 1745, this expertly restored oak-beamed inn oozes comfort and authenticity. It's run by a charming woman who has decorated the four cozy rooms beautifully.

Bread Alone Bakery & Cafe BAKERY $
(☑ 845-876-3108; www.breadalone.com/rhinebeck; 45 E Market St; sandwiches $8-10; ☉ 7am-5pm; 🕿) Superior quality baked goods, sandwiches and salads are served up at this popular bakery and cafe. If you prefer it has a full-service dining room, but the menu is exactly the same in both sections.

☆ Entertainment

Fisher Center for the Performing Arts ARTS CENTER
(☑ 845-758-7900; www.fishercenter.bard.edu; Robbins Rd, Bard College, Annandale-on-Hudson; tours 10am-5pm Mon-Fri) Architecture buffs will want to drop by to view this Frank Gehry–designed building, which looks like an alien spacecraft covered in stainless steel shingles that has landed on Bard College's manicured lawns. It contains two theaters and studio spaces and hosts a program of musical concerts, dance performances and theatrical events.

❶ Getting There & Away

Amtrak runs trains to/from NYC ($29, 1¾ hours). **Rhinecliff-Kingston Station** (☑ 800-872-7245; www.amtrak.com; 455 Rhinecliff Rd, Rhinecliff) is 3 miles west of the center of Rhinebeck.

Catskills

This beautiful mountainous region west of the Hudson Valley has been a popular getaway for New Yorkers since the 19th century. The romantic image of mossy gorges and rounded peaks, as popularized by Hudson Valley School painters, encouraged a preservation movement; in 1894 the state constitution was amended so that thousands of acres are 'forever kept as wild forest lands.'

In the early 20th century, the Catskills became synonymous with so-called 'borscht belt' hotels: summer escapes for middle-class NYC Jews. The vast majority of those hotels have closed, although Orthodox Jewish communities still thrive in many towns – as does a back-to-the-land, hippie ethos on numerous small farms.

❶ Getting There & Around

There is some bus service, the most useful being Trailways (www.trailwaysny.com) from NYC to Woodstock and Phoenicia. However, if you really want to tour the area, having a car is essential.

Phoenicia

This quirky hamlet sitting astride Esopus Creek is an ideal base for exploring the heart of the Catskills. Outdoor activities are easily arranged and include hiking, cycling, floating down the creek on an inner tube or swimming in mountain pools in summer and skiing at nearby Belleayre Mountain in winter. Fall is prime time to visit and also the best season for a jaunt in an open-air carriage on the Delaware & Ulster Railroad between nearby Arkville and Roxbury.

◉ Sights & Activities

Empire State Railway Museum MUSEUM
(☑ 845-688-7501; www.esrm.com; 70 Lower High St, Phoenicia; donations accepted; ☉ 11am-4pm Sat & Sun Jun-Oct) FREE Maintained by enthusiasts since 1960, this small museum occupies an old railway station on the largely decommissioned Delaware & Ulster line.

Delaware & Ulster Railroad RAIL
(☑ 800-225-4132; www.durr.org; 43510 Rte 28, Arkville; adult/child $18/12; ☉ Sat & Sun Jul-Oct) It takes around two hours to travel the 24 miles between Arkville and Roxbury in open-air carriages on this touristy rail journey; views are at their best during fall.

NEW YORK, NEW JERSEY & PENNSYLVANIA CATSKILLS

Belleayre Beach SWIMMING
(☑ 845-254-5202; www.belleayre.com/summer/
belleayre-beach; 33 Friendship Manor Rd, Pine Hill;
per person/car $3/10; ☺ 10am-6pm Mon-Fri, to
7pm Sat & Sun mid-Jun–Aug) Near the base of
Belleayre Mountain ski resort, this lake is
a popular and refreshing swimming spot.
Boats, kayaks and paddleboards can be rented, and there's also volleyball and basketball
courts and a climbing wall.

🛏 Sleeping & Eating

★ **Graham & Co** MOTEL $$
(☑ 845-688-7871; www.thegrahamandco.com; 80
Rte 214, Phoenicia; r $150-275; ❋ ☎ ☀) There's a
lot going for this hipster motel an easy walk
from the center of town. Rooms are white-
washed and minimalist, with the cheapest
ones in a 'bunkhouse' where bathrooms are
shared. Other pluses include a comfy den
with a fireplace, a provisions store, an out-
door pool, a wigwam and lawn games.

Foxfire Mountain House BOUTIQUE HOTEL $$
(www.foxfiremountainhouse.com; 72 Andrew Lane,
Mt Tremper; r $175-325; ☺ restaurant dinner
Fri-Sun; ℗ ⊖ ❋ ☎) Hidden away amid the
forest, this chic hotel effortlessly channels
Catskills cool in its 11 individually decorated
rooms and one three-bedroom cottage. The
cozy restaurant (offering dinner Friday to
Sunday) and bar, open to nonguests, serves
French-inspired cuisine such as steak au
poivre and *coq au cidre*.

★ **Phoenicia Diner** AMERICAN $
(☑ 845-688-9957; www.phoeniciadiner.com; 5681
Rte 28, Phoenicia; mains $9-12; ☺ 7am-5pm Thu-
Mon; ✍) New York hipsters and local families rub shoulders at this classic roadside
diner. The appealing menu offers all-day
breakfast, skillets, sandwiches and burgers.

★ **Peekamoose** AMERICAN $$$
(☑ 845-254-6500; www.peekamooserestaurant.
com; 8373 Rte 28, Big Indian; mains $20-36; ☺ 4-
10pm Thu-Mon) One of the finest restaurants in
the Catskills, this renovated farmhouse has
been promoting local farm-to-table dining
for more than a decade. The menu changes
daily, although the braised beef short ribs are
a permanent fixture.

❶ Getting There & Away

Trailways (www.trailwaysny.com) runs buses to
Phoenicia from NYC ($33.25, three hours, seven
daily).

Tannersville

The small town of Tannersville, which pri-
marily services the nearby ski resort of
Hunter Mountain, also offers access to the
gorgeous Kaaterskill Falls. There are su-
perb hikes and drives in the area, as well as
rustically charming hotels in which to stay
and enjoy the beautiful mountain scenery.
Tannersville itself sports a main street lined
with brightly painted shops and houses.

◉ Sights & Activities

Kaaterskill Falls WATERFALL
For the best view of New York State's highest
falls – 260ft, compared to Niagara's 167ft –
without a strenuous hike, head to the **view-
ing platform** (Laurel House Rd, Palenville). Pop-
ular paintings by the Hudson River Valley
School of painters in the mid-1800s elevated
this two-tier cascade to iconic status, making
it a draw for hikers, artists and nature lovers.

Hunter Mountain SKIING
(☑ 518-263-4223; www.huntermtn.com; 64 Klein
Ave, Hunter; 1-day lift pass weekday/weekend
$70/80; ☺ 9am-4pm Dec-Mar) Spectacular
views from the 56 trails (including some
challenging black runs that are a minefield
of moguls) draw crowds of snowhounds to
Hunter; avoid weekends and holidays if you
don't relish lines at the lifts. Snowmaking
ensures that skiing continues through the
season, whatever the weather.

Zipline New York ADVENTURE SPORTS
(☑ 518-263-4388; www.ziplinenewyork.com;
Hunter Mountain, Rte 23A; zip-line tours $89-129)
Throughout the year Hunter Mountain is
also the location of this zip-line course that's
not for the faint hearted.

🛏 Sleeping & Eating

★ **Scribner's Catskill Lodge** LODGE $$
(☑ 518-628-5130; www.scribnerslodge.com; 13
Scribner Hollow Rd; r from $110; ℗ ⊖ ❋ ☎ ☀ ❀)
Run by a super-cool staff, this 1960s motor
lodge has been given a stylish contemporary
makeover. Snow-white painted rooms, some
of which feature gas-fired stoves, contrast
with the warm tones of the long library
lounge with pool table and comfy nooks.

Deer Mountain Inn BOUTIQUE HOTEL $$$
(☑ 518-589-6268; www.deermountaininn.com;
790 Rte 25; r/cottage from $250/700; ☺ res-
taurant 5-9pm Mon, Thu & Sun, to 10pm Fri & Sat;
℗ ⊖ ❋ ☎) There are only six rooms and two

SAUGERTIES

Around 10 miles northeast of Woodstock, the town of Saugerties (www.discoversau gerties.com) dates back to the Dutch settling here in the mid-17th century. Today it's well worth making a day trip to a couple of local attractions. Opus 40 Sculpture Park & Museum (p133) is where artist Harvey Fite worked for nearly four decades to transform an abandoned quarry into a huge artwork. The picturesque 1869 **Saugerties Lighthouse** (☑845-247-0656; www.saugertieslighthouse.com; 168 Lighthouse Dr, Saugerties; tour suggested donation adult/child $5/3; ⊙trail dawn-dusk), on the point where Esopus Creek joins the Hudson, can be reached by a half-mile nature trail. Classic rock lovers may also want to search out **Big Pink** (www.bigpinkbasement.com; Parnassus Lane, West Saugerties; house $480; ❋ ☎), the house made famous by Bob Dylan and the Band, although note it's on a private road. It's possible to stay at both the Lighthouse and Big Pink, but you'll need to book well ahead.

cottages (sleeping up to nine guests) at this gorgeous arts-and-crafts-style property hidden within a vast mountainside estate. It's all been interior designed to the max.

Last Chance Cheese Antiques Cafe AMERICAN $$
(☑518-589-6424; www.lastchanceonline.com; 6009 Main St; mains $10-27; ⊙11am-10pm Fri & Sat, to 8pm Sun) A fixture on Main St since 1970, this is part roadhouse with live bands, part candy store and cheese shop, and part restaurant, serving hearty meals. Many of the antiques and whatnots that decorate the place are for sale too.

❶ Getting There & Away

The drive along Rte 23A to and from Tannersville is one of the most scenic in the Catskills, but take it slowly as there are several hairpin bends. It's possible to reach Tannersville from NYC by bus with Trailways (www.trailwaysny.com), but you'll have to change services in Kingston.

Woodstock

A minor technicality: the 1969 music festival was actually held in Bethel, an hour's drive west. Nonetheless, the town of Woodstock still attracts an arty, music-loving crowd and cultivates the free spirit of that era, with rainbow tie-dye style and local grassroots everything, from radio to a respected indie film festival and a farmers market.

◉ Sights

Center for Photography at Woodstock ARTS CENTER
(☑845-679-9957; www.cpw.org; 59 Tinker St; ⊙noon-5pm Thu-Sun) FREE Founded in 1977,

this creative space gives classes, hosts lectures and mounts exhibitions that expand the strict definition of the art form, thanks to a lively artist-in-residence program.

This was formerly the Café Espresso, and Bob Dylan once had a writing studio above it – that's where he typed up the liner notes for *Another Side of Bob Dylan* in 1964 – and Janis Joplin was a regular performer.

Opus 40 Sculpture Park & Museum PARK
(☑845-246-3400; www.opus40.org; 50 Fite Rd, Saugerties; adult/child $10/3; ⊙11am-5:30pm Thu-Sun May-Sep) Beginning in 1938, artist Harvey Fite worked for nearly four decades to coax an abandoned quarry into an immense work of land art, all sinuous walls, canyons and pools.

Karma Triyana Dharmachakra BUDDHIST MONASTERY
(☑845-679-5906; www.kagyu.org; 335 Meads Mountain Rd; ⊙8:30am-5:30pm) Join stressed-out New Yorkers and others needing a spiritual break and get your karma and chakras checked at this blissful Buddhist monastery about 3 miles from Woodstock. Soak up the serenity in the carefully tended grounds. Inside the shrine room is a giant golden Buddha statue; as long as you take off your shoes, you're welcome to meditate.

🛏 Sleeping & Eating

Woodstock Inn on the Millstream INN $$
(☑845-679-8211; www.woodstock-inn-ny.com; 48 Tannery Brook Rd; r/cottage from $159/375; ❋ ☎) Pleasantly decorated in quiet pastels, some of the rooms at this inn (surrounded by serene, flower-filled grounds) come with kitchenettes and electric fireplaces.

White Dove Rockotel INN $$
(☑ 845-306-5419; www.thewhitedoverockotel.com; 148 Tinker St; r/ste from $125/250; ☎☀) This purple-painted Victorian certainly stands out from the crowd – but its nothing compared to the rooms! The six units, split over two properties, are decorated with psychedelic colors, posters, record players and vintage vinyl. The suites feature kitchens.

★**Garden Cafe** VEGAN $
(☑ 845-679-3600; www.thegardencafewoodstock. com; 6 Old Forge Rd; mains $9-20; ⊙11:30am-9pm Mon & Wed-Fri, 10am-9pm Sat & Sun; ☑) All the ingredients used at this relaxed, charming cafe are organic. The food served is appealing, tasty and fresh, and includes salads, sandwiches, rice bowls and veggie lasagna.

Finger Lakes

Stretching across south-central New York, the rolling hills are cut through by 11 long narrow bodies of water – the eponymous Finger Lakes. The region is an outdoor paradise, as well as the state's premier wine-growing region, with more than 120 vineyards.

At the south of Cayuga Lake, Ithaca, home to Ivy League Cornell University, is the region's gateway and a good base. At the northern tip of Seneca Lake, Geneva is also a pretty and lively town, thanks to the student population at Hobart and William Smith Colleges. Here the restored 1894 Smith Opera House is a vibrant center for performing arts. To the west, Y-shaped Keuka Lake is edged by two small state parks that keep it relatively pristine; it's a favorite for trout fishing. Base yourself at sweet little Hammondsport, on the southwest end. Arts and crafts lovers should also schedule a stop in Corning to see the brilliant glass museum.

ⓘ Getting There & Around

Ithaca is the region's major hub with several daily bus connections to NYC ($53.50, five hours). **Ithaca Tompkins Regional Airport** has direct flights to Detroit, Newark and Philadelphia.

Ithaca

An idyllic home for college students and first-wave hippies, Ithaca, on the southern tip of Cayuga Lake, is the largest town around the Finger Lakes. With an art-house cinema, good eats and great hiking ('Ithaca is gorges' goes the slogan, for all the surrounding canyons and waterfalls), it's both a destination in itself and a convenient halfway point between NYC and Niagara Falls.

The center of Ithaca is a pedestrian street called the Commons. On a steep hill above is Ivy League Cornell University, founded in 1865, with a small business strip at the campus' front gates, called Collegetown. The drive from Ithaca up scenic Rte 89 (west side) or Rte 90 (east side) to Seneca Falls takes about an hour.

◉ Sights

★**Herbert F Johnson Museum of Art** MUSEUM
(☑ 607-255-6464; www.museum.cornell.edu; 114 Central Ave; ⊙10am-5pm Tue-Sun) FREE IM Pei's brutalist building looms like a giant concrete robot above the ornate neo-Gothic surrounds of Cornell's campus. Inside you'll find an eclectic collection ranging from medieval wood carvings to modern masters. Even if the art doesn't engage you, the panoramic views of Ithaca and Cayuga Lake from the top floor galleries will.

Cornell Botanic Gardens GARDENS
(☑ 607-255-2400; www.cornellbotanicgardens.org; 124 Comstock Knoll Dr; ⊙grounds dawn-dusk, visitor center 10am-4pm) FREE The verdant spaces in and around campus includes a 100-acre arboretum, a botanical garden and numerous trails. Stop at the Nevin Welcome Center for maps and to find out about tours.

A great way to reach here is by hiking up the dramatic **Cascadilla Gorge** (College Ave Bridge), which starts near the center of town.

Robert H Treman State Park STATE PARK
(☑ 607-273-3440; www.parks.ny.gov; 105 Enfield Falls Rd; per car Apr-Oct $8) Five and a half miles southwest of Ithaca, the biggest state park in the area offers extensive trails and a very popular **swimming hole** (late June to early September). Treman's gorge trail passes a stunning 12 waterfalls: don't miss Devil's Kitchen and **Lucifer Falls**, a multi-tiered wonder that spills Enfield Creek over rocks for about 100ft.

🛏 Sleeping

Firelight Camps TENTED CAMP $$
(☑ 607-229-1644; www.firelightcamps.com; 1150 Danby Rd; tent Sun-Thu/Fri & Sat $189/259; ⊙mid-May–Oct; ☎) Glamping comes to Ithaca at this attractive site attached to the La Tourelle Hotel and with quick access to the trails of nearby Buttermilk Falls State Park. The safari-style canvas tents rise over hard-

wood platforms and comfy beds. The bathhouse is separate.

★ **William Henry Miller Inn** B&B $$
(📞877-256-4553; www.millerinn.com; 303 N Aurora St; r from $195; 🅿️@🛜) Gracious and grand, and only a few steps from the Commons, this is a historic home with luxurious rooms (two with whirlpool tubs and two in a separate carriage house), gourmet breakfast and a dessert buffet.

★ **Inns of Aurora** HISTORIC HOTEL $$$
(📞315-364-8888; www.innsofaurora.com; 391 Main St, Aurora; r $200-400; 🅿️🅿️🛜) This beautiful historic hotel is composed of four properties: the main Aurora Inn, built in 1833 and little changed on the outside since, with 10 lovely rooms and a splendid dining room; Rowland House with 10 more rooms; E B Morgan House with seven rooms; and Wallcourt Hall, the most modern of the designs, but with no lake views.

🍴 Eating & Drinking

Ithaca Bakery CAFE $
(📞607-273-7110; www.ithacabakery.com; 400 N Meadow St; sandwiches $5-11; ⊙6am-8pm Sun-Thu, to 9pm Fri & Sat; 🚗) An epic selection of pastries, smoothies, sandwiches and prepared food, serving Ithacans of every stripe. Ideal for picnic goods and for vegetarians and vegans.

★ **Moosewood Restaurant** VEGETARIAN $$
(📞607-273-9610; www.moosewoodcooks.com; 215 N Cayuga St; mains $8-18; ⊙11:30am-8:30pm; 🚗) Established in 1973, this near-legendary veggie restaurant is run by a collective. It has a slightly upscale feel, with a full bar.

Sacred Root Kava Lounge & Tea Bar TEAHOUSE
(📞607-272-5282; www.sacredrootkava.com; 139 W State St; ⊙4pm-midnight) Pretty much as alternative as it gets for Ithaca is this chilled basement space serving the Polynesian non-alcoholic, psychoactive beverage kava. If that's not your bag, then there's a nice range of teas. Check online for events.

ℹ️ Getting There & Away

Ithaca Tompkins Regional Airport (ITH; 📞607-257-0456; www.flyithaca.com; 1 Culligan Dr) receives flights from Delta and United. Greyhound and Shortline buses ($50, five hours, daily) pull into **Ithaca Bus Station** (710 W State St).

AURORA

Around 28 miles north of Ithaca on the east side of Cayuga Lake is the picturesque village of Aurora. Established in 1795, the village has over 50 buildings on the National Register of Historic Places, including parts of the campus of Wells College, founded in 1868 for the higher education of women (it's now co-ed). The Inns of Aurora, which is composed of four grand properties – the Aurora Inn (1833), EB Morgan House (1858), Rowland House (1903) and Wallcourt Hall (1909) – is a wonderful place to stay. Alternatively stop by the Aurora Inn's lovely dining room for a meal with lakeside views and pick up a copy of the self-guided walking tour of the village.

Seneca Falls

The quiet, post-industrial town of Seneca Falls is said to have inspired visiting director Frank Capra to create Bedford Falls, the fictional small American town in his classic movie *It's a Wonderful Life*. Indeed, you can stand on a bridge crossing the town's river and just picture Jimmy Stewart doing the same. The town also has a special place in the history of democratization of the country as the location of the chapel where in 1848 Elizabeth Cady Stanton and friends declared that all men and women are created equal.

👁 Sights

Women's Rights National Historical Park MUSEUM
(📞315-568-0024; www.nps.gov/wori; 136 Fall St; ⊙9am-5pm Fri-Sun) **FREE** Visit the chapel where Elizabeth Cady Stanton and friends declared in 1848 that 'all men and women are created equal,' the first step toward women's suffrage. The adjacent museum tells the story, including the complicated relationship with abolition.

National Women's Hall of Fame MUSEUM
(📞315-568-8060; www.womenofthehall.org; 76 Fall St; adult/child $4/free; ⊙noon-4pm Wed-Fri, 10am-4pm Sat) The tiny National Women's Hall of Fame honors inspiring American women. Learn about some of the 256 inductees, including first lady Abigail Adams,

American Red Cross founder Clara Barton and civil-rights activist Rosa Parks.

🛏 Sleeping & Eating

Gould Hotel   BOUTIQUE HOTEL **$$**
(☑ 877-788-4010; www.thegouldhotel.com; 108 Fall St; r $169; ❋ ☎) Originally a 1920s-era hotel, the downtown building has undergone a stylish renovation with a nod to the past – the mahogany bar comes from an old Seneca Falls saloon. The standard rooms are small, but the decor, in metallic purple and gray, is quite flash. The hotel's upscale restaurant and tavern serves local food, wine and beer.

Mac's Drive In   BURGERS **$**
(☑ 315-539-3064; www.macsdrivein.net; 1166 US-20/Rte 5, Waterloo; mains $4-8; ⊘ 10:30am-10pm Fri-Sun Apr-Oct) Midway between Seneca Falls and Geneva, this classic drive-in restaurant established in 1961 (and little changed since) serves up burgers, fried chicken and fish dinners at bargain prices.

The Adirondacks

The Adirondack Mountains (www.visit adirondacks.com) may not compare in drama and height with mountains in the western USA, but they make up for it in area: the range covers 9375 sq miles, from the center of New York just north of the state capital Albany, up to the Canadian border. And with 46 peaks over 4000ft high, the Adirondacks provide some of the most wild-feeling terrain in the east. Like the Catskills to the south, much of the Adirondacks' dense forest and lake lands are protected by the state constitution, and it's a fabulous location to see the color show of fall leaves. Hiking, canoeing and backcountry camping are the most popular activities.

❶ Getting There & Around

The area's main airport is in Albany, although **Adirondack Regional Airport** (☑ 518-891-4600; www.adirondackairport.com; 96 Airport Rd) in Saranac Lake has connections via Cape Air (www.capeair.com) to Boston.

Both Greyhound (www.greyhound.com) and Trailways (www.trailwaysny.com) serve Albany and various towns in the Adirondacks, though a car is essential for exploring widely.

Amtrak (www.amtrak.com) runs from NYC to Albany (from $43, 2½ hours) and on to Ticonderoga ($68, five hours) and Westport ($68, six hours), on Lake Champlain, with a bus connection to Lake Placid ($93, seven hours).

Albany

Built between 1965 and 1976, the architectural ensemble of government buildings in Albany's central Empire State Plaza is a sight to behold and includes the excellent New York State Museum as well as a fine collection of modern public art. Downtown and around leafy Washington Park, stately buildings and gracious brownstones speak to the state capital's wealthy past.

Albany became state capital in 1797 because of its geographic centrality to local colonies and its strategic importance in the fur trade. These days its as much synonymous with legislative dysfunction as with legislative power. Its struggling economy is reflected in the number of derelict and abandoned buildings. The locals' friendliness and the city's usefulness as a gateway to the Adirondacks and Hudson Valley make it worth more than a casual look.

◉ Sights

★ **Empire State Plaza**   PUBLIC ART
(☑ 518-473-7521; www.empirestateplaza.org) **FREE**
While the plaza's ensemble of architecture surrounding a central pool is hugely impressive, it's the splendid collection of modern American art liberally sprinkled outside, inside and beneath the complex that is the true highlight here. The collection includes sculptures and massive paintings by Mark Rothko, Jackson Pollock, Alexander Calder and many other star artists.

★ **New York State Museum**   MUSEUM
(☑ 518-474 5877; www.nysm.nysed.gov; 222 Madison Ave; 9:30am-5pm Tue-Sun) **FREE** One of the quirks of Albany being the state capital means that a large chunk of this top-class museum is dedicated to the history and development of New York City. The section on 9/11, including a damaged fire truck and debris from the site, is very moving. For a complete contrast, don't miss a ride on the gorgeous antique carousel ($1) on the 4th floor.

New York State Capitol   HISTORIC BUILDING
(☑ 518-474-2418; www.hallofgovernors.ny.gov; Washington Ave; ⊘ guided tours 10am, noon, 2pm & 3pm Mon-Fri) **FREE** Completed in 1899, this grand building is the heart of the state government. The interior features detailed stone carving, carpentry, tile and mosaic work, with highlights being the Great Western Staircase, the Governor's Reception Room and the Senate Chamber.

🛏 Sleeping & Eating

⭐ Washington Park Inn
BOUTIQUE HOTEL **$$**

(☑ 518-225-4567; www.washingtonparkinn.com; 643 Madison Ave; r $119-139; ✿@🌐) Rocking chairs on the covered porch and tennis rackets for guests to use on the courts in the park across the road set the relaxed tone for this appealing hotel in one of Albany's heritage buildings. Rooms are big and stylishly decorated, and food and drink is available on a serve-yourself basis round the clock from the well-stocked kitchen.

Cafe Madison
BREAKFAST **$**

(☑ 518-935-1094; www.cafemadisonalbany.com; 1108 Madison Ave; mains $10-15; ⊙ 7:30am-2pm Mon-Thu, to 3pm Fri-Sun; 🥄) A highly popular breakfast spot, especially on the weekend, when 30-minute waits for one of the cozy booths or tables is not uncommon. The staff are friendly and the menu includes inventive omelets, hash browns, crepes, vegan options and a variety of cocktails.

⭐ Ginger Man
AMERICAN **$$$**

(☑ 518-427-5963; www.albanygingerman.com; 234 Western Ave; mains $22-30; ⊙ 11:30am-10:30pm Mon-Fri, 4:30-11pm Sat) Oenophiles will adore the Ginger Man with its stellar wine list, not to mention its strong showing of local beers and spirits. And the food is just as good, with generous cheese and charcuterie plates a great way to ease into delicious mains such as veal osso buco and paella.

❶ Getting There & Away

As state capital, Albany has the full range of transport connections. **Albany International Airport** (☑ 518-242-2200; www.albanyairport.com; Albany Shaker Rd, Colonie) is 10 miles north of downtown. The Amtrak **Albany-Rensselaer Station** (☑ 800-872 7245; www.amtrak.com; 525 East St, Rensselaer), on the east bank of the Hudson River, has services connecting with the rest of the state. Greyhound and Trailways bus services pull into and out of the centrally located **bus terminal** (☑ 518-427-7060; 34 Hamilton St).

Lake George

Lake George (www.visitlakegeorge.com), the southern gateway to the Adirondacks, is a majorly touristy town with arcades, fireworks every Thursday in July and August, and paddle-wheel-boat rides on the crystalline, 32-mile-long lake of the same name. It's a seasonal resort, so don't expect much

to be be going on between November and May. More upscale is the village of **Bolton Landing**, 11 miles north on the west bank of Lake George.

◉ Sights & Activities

Fort William Henry Museum
MUSEUM

(☑ 518-668-5471; www.fwhmuseum.com; 48 Canada St; adult/child $17/8, ghost tours $18/8; ⊙ 9:30am-6pm May-Oct; ⊕) Guides dressed as 18th-century British soldiers muster visitors along, with stops for battle re-enactments that include firing period muskets and cannons, at this replica of the 1755 wooden fort. Check online for details of the evening ghost tours.

Hyde Collection Art Museum
MUSEUM

(☑ 518-792-1761; www.hydecollection.org; 161 Warren St, Glens Falls; adult/child $12/free; ⊙ 10am-5pm Tue-Sat, noon-5pm Sun) This remarkable gathering of art was amassed by local newspaper heiress Charlotte Pryun Hyde. In her rambling Florentine Renaissance mansion, 12 miles south of Lake George, you'll stumble across Rembrandts, Rubens, Matisses and Eakins, as well as tapestries, sculptures and turn-of-the-century furnishings.

Lake George Steamboat Cruises
CRUISE

(☑ 518-668-5777; www.lakegeorgesteamboat.com; 57 Beach Rd; adult/child from $16/7.50; ⊙ May-Oct) In 2017 this company celebrated 200 years of running cruise boats on Lake George. In season take your pick between a variety of cruise options on its three vessels: the authentic steamboat *Minnie-Ha-Ha*, the 1907-vintage *Mohican*, and the flagship *Lac du Saint Sacrement*.

🛏 Eating

Saltwater Cowboy
SEAFOOD **$$**

(☑ 518-685-3116; 164 Canada St; mains $11-28; ⊙ 11am-9pm May-Oct) Never mind the super-casual, order-at-the-counter setup – this place has excellent fried clams and scallops, plus mammoth lobster rolls. Wash it down with fresh lemonade.

❶ Getting There & Away

Albany International Airport is 50 miles south of Lake George. Amtrak stops in Fort Edwards, about 20 minutes by car from Lake George. Greyhound and Trailways also have long-distance buses to the region. A rental car is the best way of getting around the lake area.

Lake Placid

The resort town of Lake Placid is synonymous with snow sports – it hosted the Winter Olympics in 1932 and 1980. Elite athletes continue to train here; the rest of us can ride real bobsleds, speed-skate and more. Mirror Lake (the main lake in town) freezes thick enough for ice-skating, tobogganing and dogsledding. The town is also pleasant in summer, as the unofficial center of the High Peaks region of the Adirondacks and a great base for striking out on a hike or going canoeing or kayaking on one of the area's many lakes.

⊙ Sights & Activities

A major draw at Lake Placid is the opportunity to play like an Olympian (or just watch athletes train). Most activities are managed by **Whiteface Mountain** (☑ 518-946-2223; www.whiteface.com; 5021 Rte 86, Wilmington; full-day lift ticket adult/child $92/58, gondola only $22/free; ⊙ 8:30am-4pm Dec-Apr), the ski area where the Olympic ski races were held, but located in other spots around the area. Among other activities, you can do a half-mile on the bobsled track ($95) or a modified biathlon (cross-country skiing and shooting; $55). A private group organizes **speed-skating** rental and tutorials ($20) at the Olympic Center. Many sports are modified for summer – bobsledding on wheels, for instance. The Olympic Sites Passport ($35), available at all Whiteface-managed venues, can be a good deal, covering admission at sites (such as the tower at the ski-jump complex and the gondola ride at Whiteface Mountain) and offering discounts on some activities.

Olympic Center STADIUM
(☑ 518-523-3330; www.whiteface.com; 2634 Main St; tours $10, adult/child skating $8/5, skating shows $10/8; ⊙ 10am-5pm, skating shows 4:30pm Fri; 🚗) This is the location of the 1980 'Miracle on Ice,' when the upstart US team trumped the unstoppable Soviets. In winter you can skate on the outside oval rink and year-round take a one-hour tour of the stadium. Also here is a small **museum** (☑ 518-523-3330; www.whiteface.com; 2634 Main St; adult/child $7/5; ⊙ 10am-5pm). There are usually figure-skating shows on Fridays, with an additional show Saturdays at 7:30pm July and August.

Whiteface Veteran's Memorial Highway SCENIC DRIVE
(www.whiteface.com; Rte 431; driver & vehicle $15, additional passengers $8; ⊙ 8:45am-5:15pm mid-Jun–mid-Oct) Whiteface, the state's 5th highest peak at 4867ft, is the only summit in the Adirondacks accessible by car, with a neat castle-style lookout and cafe at the top. It can be socked in with clouds, making for an unnerving drive up, but when the fog clears, the 360-degree view is awe-inspiring. Tolls are paid at Lake Steven.

🛏 Sleeping & Eating

★ **Adirondack Loj** LODGE $
(☑ 518-523-3441; www.adk.org; 1002 Adirondack Loj Rd; dm/r $60/169, lean-tos/cabins from $22.50/179; 🅿 🛜) The Adirondack Mountain

---

GREAT CAMPS

Far from big fields of canvas tents, the Adirondacks' 'great camps' were typically lake and mountainside compounds of grandiose log cabins built by the very wealthy, in the latter half of the 19th century, as rustic retreats. A prime example is **Great Camp Sagamore** (Sagamore Institute; ☑ 315-354-5311; www.greatcampsagamore.org; Sagamore Rd, Raquette Lake; tours adult/child $16/8; ⊙ hours vary mid-May–mid-Oct), a former Vanderbilt vacation estate on the west side of the Adirondacks, which is now open to the public for tours, workshops and overnight stays on occasional history-oriented weekends.

Less ostentatious is **White Pine Camp** (☑ 518-327-3030; www.whitepinecamp.com; 432 White Pine Rd, Paul Smiths; r/cabin from $165/315; 🛜), 12 miles northwest of Saranac Lake. This collection of rustically cozy cabins is set amid pine forests, wetlands and scenic Osgood Pond – a boardwalk leads out to an island on which sits a Japanese-style teahouse and an antique all-wood bowling alley. The fact that President Calvin Coolidge spent a few summer months here in 1926 is an interesting historical footnote, but the camp's charm comes through in its modest luxuries such as claw-footed tubs and wood-burning fireplaces. Naturalist walking tours are open to nonguests on select days from mid-June to September.

Club runs this rustic retreat on the shore of pretty Heart Lake. All rooms in the lodge share communal bathrooms. Rates include breakfast, and since it's 8 miles south of Lake Placid, you'll like want to arrange a trail lunch and dinner here too.

★ **Lake Placid Lodge** HERITAGE HOTEL $$$
(☑ 518-523-2700; www.lakeplacidlodge.com; 144 Lodge Way; r $500-1000; ◷ May-Mar; P ⊜ @ ☎) Overlooking Lake Placid and channeling the rustic glamor of classic Gilded Age Adirondack lodges, this luxury hotel offers 13 gorgeously decorated rooms and cabins. The cabins are 19th-century originals, but the main hotel is a remarkable reconstruction following a devastating 2008 fire.

Liquids & Solids at the Handlebar AMERICAN $$
(☑ 518-837-5012; www.liquidsandsolids.com; 6115 Sentinel Rd; mains $10-20; ◷ 4-10pm Tue-Sat, 5-9pm Sun) It's all about craft beers, creative cocktails and fresh, inventive dishes at this rustic bar and restaurant where the kielbasa sausages and other charcuterie are made in-house. Mains may include dishes such as fried trout or crispy pig head.

ⓘ Getting There & Away

Trailways (www.trailwaysny.com) serves Lake Placid. Amtrak (www.amtrak.com) runs once a day to Westport, with a bus connection to Lake Placid ($93, seven hours).

Adirondack Regional Airport (p136), 17 miles northwest near Saranac Lake, has connections via Cape Air (www.capeair.com) to Boston.

Thousand Islands

To downstate New Yorkers, this region is the source of the Thousand Islands salad dressing made of ketchup, mayonnaise and relish. In fact, it's a scenic wonderland along Lake Ontario and the St Lawrence River speckled with 1864 islands of all shapes and sizes either side of the US–Canada maritime border. The area was a Gilded Age playground for the rich; now it's more populist. Pros: beautiful sunsets, good-value lodging and Canada across the water. Cons: dead in winter and very large mosquitoes in summer (bring ample repellent).

The historic port of Oswego is the southern gateway to the region and makes a good base for exploring places such as Sackets Harbor, where re-enactors stage an annual War of 1812 Weekend. On the north side,

WORTH A TRIP

SARANAC LAKE

Saranac Lake is not as tourist-oriented as its neighbor Lake Placid and gives a better idea of regular Adirondacks life. The town, built up in the early 20th century as a retreat for tuberculosis patients, has an attractive old-fashioned main street leading toward the lake. Many other stretches of water pepper the surrounding forested hills, making this another great base for hiking, kayaking and canoeing; for full details of what's available in the area see www.saranaclake.com.

Clayton and Alexandria Bay both offer boat tours to the islands in the St Lawrence River, or you could camp amid glorious nature in the Wellesley Island State Park.

ⓘ Getting There & Around

The main airport for the region is **Syracuse Hancock International Airport** (☑ 315-454-4330; www.syrairport.org; 1000 Colonel Eileen Collins Blvd, Syracuse); connections here include NYC on JetBlue and Delta; Newark, Washington, DC and Chicago on United; and Toronto on Air Canada. Cars can be rented at the airport or in downtown Syracuse, which is connected to other parts of the state by bus and train.

Alexandria Bay

Alexandria Bay (A-Bay or Alex Bay), an early-20th-century resort town, is the center of tourism on the American side of the Thousand Islands region. While it's somewhat run-down and a bit tacky, there's enough around to keep you occupied, with Alex Bay and nearby Schermerhorn Harbor the bases for boat trips to the castle follies built by Gilded Age tycoons on Heart and Dark Islands.

◉ Sights & Activites

★ **Boldt Castle** CASTLE
(☑ 800-847-5263; www.boldtcastle.com; Heart Island; adult/child $9.50/6.50; ◷ 10am-6:30pm May–mid-Oct) This Gothic gem, a replica of a German castle, was (partly) built by tycoon hotelier George C Boldt in the late 19th century. In 1904, however, midway through construction, Boldt's wife died suddenly, and the project was abandoned. Since 1977 the Thousand Islands Bridge Authority has

WELLESLEY ISLAND STATE PARK

Midway between Clayton and Alexandria Bay, cross the Thousand Islands International Bridge (toll $2.75) to access Wellesley Island, the largest of the Thousand Islands on the US side of the border. Covering a 2636-acre chunk of the island's southern tip is the **state park** (☑315-482-2722; www. parks.ny.gov; Fineview; beach all day/after 4pm $7/4; ☉state park year-round, swimming 11am-7pm Jul & Aug) **FREE** packed with wildlife and offering a **nature center** (☑315-482-2479; www.parks.ny.gov; Nature Center Rd, Fineview; ☉8:30am-4pm) **FREE**, a beautiful swimming beach, and excellent **camping options** (☑315-482-2722; www.parks.ny.gov; 44927 Cross Island Rd, Fineview; campsites/cabins/cottages from $18/68/100), with riverfront tent sites, cabins and family cottages.

spent millions restoring the place to something of its planned grandeur.

Singer Castle
CASTLE

(☑877-327-5475; www.singercastle.com; Dark Island; adult/child $14.50/7.50; ☉10am-4pm mid-May–mid-Oct) This stone castle, on Dark Island in the middle of the St Lawrence River, was built in 1905 by American entrepreneur Frederick Bourne. It's full of secret passages and hidden doors and has a dungeon – all of which you'll see on a tour. Uncle Sam runs boats from Alex Bay; **Schermerhorn Harbor** (☑315-324-5966; www.schermerhornharbor. com; 71 Schermerhorn Landing, Hammond; shuttle to Singer Castle $31; ☉10:30am-2:30pm May-Sep) also visits.

Uncle Sam Boat Tour
BOATING

(☑315-482-2611; www.usboattours.com; 45 James St, Alexandria Bay; 2hr tour adult/child $23/11.50) The main offering from the largest boat-tour operator in the area is a two-hour ride that visits both the USA and Canada sides of the river and stops at Boldt Castle.

🛏 Sleeping & Eating

Bonnie Castle
RESORT $$

(☑800-955-4511; www.bonniecastle.com; 31 Holland St; r $100-250; ❄☎☲) This somewhat run-down resort, one of Alex Bay's largest and open year-round, offers a variety of rooms, some with nice views across the St Lawrence River toward Boldt Castle.

Dockside Pub
AMERICAN $$

(☑315-482-9849; www.thedocksidepub.com; 17 Market St; mains $8-18; ☉11am-midnight Sun-Thu, to 2am Fri & Sat; ☲) Unpretentious pub fare – burgers, fries, pizza and some specials. Despite the name its location is inland, with no dock view.

Western New York

Much activity in this region revolves around Buffalo, New York State's second-largest city. Nicknamed the Queen City, for being the largest and most prosperous metropolis along the Great Lakes at the turn of the 19th century, Buffalo fell on hard times in the 20th, but is bouncing back in the 21st. Its amazing stock of heritage architecture is being restored and reinvented into hotels, museums and other businesses.

The area first developed thanks to the hydroelectric power of Niagara Falls and the Erie Canal, which linked the Great Lakes to the Atlantic Ocean. The falls are now better known as a tourist destination, with millions of visitors flocking here annually. You can find out more about the canal in the town of Lockport. Also worth visiting are East Aurora, home to the arts and crafts Roycroft community, and Letchworth State Park with its magnificent waterfalls.

ℹ Getting There & Around

Buffalo Niagara International Airport (p142) is a regional hub with the widest range of flights, but you can also fly into and out of Niagara Falls International Airport (p144). Amtrak runs trains to both Buffalo and Niagara, with connections to and from NYC, Albany, Toronto, Canada and from Buffalo to/from Chicago. Greyhound has bus services to both Buffalo and Niagara. For other places in the region you are best getting there by rental car.

Buffalo

The winters may be long and cold, but Buffalo stays warm through a vibrant creative community and strong local pride. Settled by the French in 1758, the city is believed to derive its name from *beau fleuve* (beautiful river). With power from nearby Niagara Falls, it boomed in the early 1900s; Pierce-Arrow cars were made here, and it was the first American city to have electric streetlights. One of its nicknames – Queen City – was because it was the largest and most prosperous city along the Great Lakes.

Those rosy economic times are long over, leaving many abandoned industrial buildings in their wake. This said, revival is in Buffalo's air. Masterpieces of late-19th- and early-20th-century architecture, including designs by Frank Lloyd Wright and HH Richardson, have been magnificently restored. There's a gracious park system laid out by Frederick Law Olmsted, of NYC's Central Park fame, great museums, and a positive vibe that's impossible to ignore.

⊙ Sights & Activities

★ Buffalo City Hall   ARCHITECTURE
(☏716-852-3300; www.preservationbuffaloniagara. org; 65 Niagara Sq; ☺tours noon Mon-Fri) FREE This 32-story art-deco masterpiece, beautifully detailed inside and out and opened in 1931, towers over downtown. It's worth joining the free tour at noon that includes access to the mayor's office, the council chamber and the open-air observation deck.

★ Martin House Complex   ARCHITECTURE
(☏716-856-3858; www.darwinmartinhouse.org; 125 Jewett Pkwy; tour basic/extended $19/37; ☺tours hourly 10am-3pm Wed-Mon) This 15,000-sq-ft house, built between 1903 and 1905, was designed by Frank Lloyd Wright for his friend and patron Darwin D Martin. Representing Wright's Prairie House ideal, it consists of six interconnected buildings (some of which had to be rebuilt), each of which has been meticulously restored.

★ Albright-Knox Art Gallery   MUSEUM
(☏716-882-8700; www.albrightknox.org; 1285 Elmwood Ave; adult/child $12/6; ☺10am-5pm Tue-Sun) The gallery's superb collection, which ranges from Degas and Picasso to Ruscha, Rauschenberg and other abstract expressionists, occupies a neoclassical building planned for Buffalo's 1905 Pan American Expo. Its temporary exhibits are particularly creative and compelling.

Graycliff Estate   ARCHITECTURE
(☏716-947-9217; www.graycliffestate.org; 6472 Old Lake Shore Rd, Derby; tours 1/2hr $18/34) Occupying a dramatic cliff-top location on Lake Erie, 16 miles south of downtown Buffalo, is this 1920s vacation home designed by Frank Lloyd Wright for the wealthy Martin family. Having fallen into much disrepair, restora-

tion has been ongoing for the last 20 years, but you can learn a lot about Wright's overall plan on interesting tours (book in advance).

Guaranty Building   ARCHITECTURE
(Prudential Building; www.hodgsonruss.com/ Louis-Sullivans-Guaranty-Building.html; 140 Pearl St; ☺interpretive center 7:15am-9pm) FREE Completed in 1896 for the Guaranty Construction company, this gorgeous piece of architecture has a facade covered in detailed terra-cotta tiles and a superb stained-glass ceiling in its lobby. The interpretative center provides details of how groundbreaking this Adler & Sullivan–designed building was when it was built.

Explore Buffalo   TOURS
(☏716-245-3032; www.explorebuffalo.org; 1 Symphony Circle) Architectural and history tours around the Buffalo area by bus, on foot and by bicycle and kayak.

🛏 Sleeping

Hostel Buffalo Niagara   HOSTEL $
(☏716-852-5222; www.hostelbuffalo.com; 667 Main St; dm/r $30/85; ❄@☎) Conveniently located in Buffalo's downtown Theater District, this hostel occupies three floors of a former school, with a basement rec room, plenty of kitchen and lounge space, a small art gallery, and spotless if institutional bathrooms. Services include laundry facilities, free bikes, and lots of info on local music, food and arts happenings.

★ InnBuffalo off Elmwood   GUESTHOUSE $$
(☏716-867-7777; www.innbuffalo.com; 619 Lafayette Ave; ste $139-249; ❄☎) Ellen and Joe Lettieri have done a splendid job restoring this 1898 mansion, originally built for local brass and rubber magnate HH Hewitt. Preservation is ongoing, but the building has already recovered much of its grandeur and the nine suites are beautifully decorated, some with original features such as a Victorian needlespray shower.

Hotel Henry   HERITAGE HOTEL $$
(☏716-882-1970; www.hotelhenry.com; cnr Rockwell Rd & Cleveland Circle; r from $199; P❄☎) Occupying a grand late-19th-century lunatic asylum, Hotel Henry preserves much of the stately architecture of Henry Richardson's original building. Its 88 rooms, reached off super-broad corridors, have tall ceilings and contemporary decor.

Eating

Betty's AMERICAN **$$**
(☑ 716-362-0633; www.bettysbuffalo.com; 370 Virginia St; mains $16-24; ⊙ 8am-9pm Tue-Thu, to 10pm Fri, 9am-10pm Sat, to 2pm Sun; ☑) On a quiet Allentown corner, bohemian Betty's does flavorful, fresh interpretations of American comfort food such as meatloaf. Brunch is deservedly popular and there's a pleasant bar.

Plenty of vegetarian, gluten-free and dairy-free options are on the menu.

Cole's AMERICAN **$$**
(☑ 716-886-1449; www.colesonelmwood.com; 1104 Elmwood Ave; mains $11.50-15; ⊙ 11am-11pm Mon-Thu, to midnight Fri & Sat, to 10pm Sun; ☎) Since 1934 this atmospheric restaurant and bar has been dishing up local favorites such as beef on weck (roast beef on a caraway-seed roll) – try it with a side of spicy Buffalo chicken wings, or go for one of the juicy burgers. It's handy for lunch if you are visiting the Delaware Park area and its museums.

The spacious bar, decorated with all kinds of vintage stuff, offers scores of beers on tap.

Black Sheep INTERNATIONAL **$$$**
(☑ 716-884-1100; www.blacksheepbuffalo.com; 367 Connecticut St; mains $28-42; ⊙ 5-10pm Tue-Thu, to 11pm Fri & Sat, 11am-2pm Sun) Black Sheep likes to describe its style of western New York farm-to-table cuisine as 'global no-mad,' which means you might find pig-head stew alongside chef Steve Gedra's grandma's recipe for chicken paprikash (recommended!). You can also eat at the bar, which serves creative cocktails and local craft ales.

Drinking & Entertainment

⭐**Resurgence Brewing Company** MICROBREWERY
(☑ 716-381-9868; www.resurgencebrewing.com; 1250 Niagara St; ⊙ 4-10pm Tue-Thu, to 11:30pm Fri, noon-11:30pm Sat, to 5pm Sun) Housed in a former engine factory that was later to became the city's dog pound, Resurgence typifies Buffalo's skill at adaptive reuse of its infrastructure. The beers ($8 for a tasting flight) are excellent, with some 20 different ales on tap from fruity sweet Loganberry Wit to a porter with an amazing peanut-butter flavor.

Kleinhans Music Hall CLASSICAL MUSIC
(☑ 716-883-3560; www.kleinhansbuffalo.org; 3 Symphony Circle) This fine concert hall, home to the Buffalo Philharmonic Orchestra, has wonderful acoustics. The building is a National Historic Landmark and was partly designed by the famous Finnish father-and-son architecture team of Eliel and Eero Saarinen.

❶ Getting There & Away

Buffalo Niagara International Airport (BUF; ☑ 716-630-6000; www.buffaloairport.com; 4200 Genesee St), about 10 miles east of downtown, is a regional hub. JetBlue Airways offers affordable round-trip fares from NYC.

NFTA (www.nfta.com), the local transit service, runs express bus 204 to the **Buffalo Metropolitan Transportation Center** (☑ 716-855-7300; www.nfta.com; 181 Ellicott St) downtown. (Greyhound buses also pull in here.) NFTA local bus 40 goes to the American side of Niagara Falls ($2, one hour); express bus 60 also goes to the area, but requires a transfer.

From Amtrak's downtown **Exchange Street Station** (☑ 716-856-2075; www.amtrak.com; 75 Exchange St), you can catch trains to NYC ($66, 8¾ hours), Niagara Falls ($14, one hour), Albany ($52, six hours) and Toronto, Canada ($44, four hours). All services also stop at **Buffalo-Depew Station** (www.amtrak.com; 55 Dick Rd), 8 miles east, where you can also board trains to Chicago ($94, 11 hours).

Niagara Falls

It's a tale of two cities: Niagara Falls, New York (USA), and Niagara Falls, Ontario (Canada). Both overlook a natural wonder – 150,000 gallons of water per second, plunging more than 1000ft – and both provide a load of tourist kitsch surrounding it. The Canadian side offers somewhat better views and a much larger town. However, the view from the New York side is still impressive and the falls surroundings are far more pleasant as they are preserved within a beautifully landscaped national park. The town itself is also largely devoid of the commercial razzmatazz you'll find on the Canadian side; if that's what you want, it's easy to walk across the Rainbow Bridge between the two – just be sure to bring your passport.

◉ Sights & Activities

⭐**Cave of the Winds** VIEWPOINT
(☑ 716-278-1730; www.niagarafallsstatepark.com; Goat Island Rd; adult/child $17/14; ⊙ 9am-7:30pm mid-May–Oct) On the north corner of Goat Island, don a souvenir rain poncho and sandals (provided) and take an elevator down to walkways just 25ft from the crashing water at the base of Bridal Veil Falls.

NIAGARA FALLS, CANADA

The Canadian side of the falls is naturally blessed with superior views. Horseshoe Falls, on the west half of the river, are wider than Bridal Veil Falls on the eastern, American side, and they're especially photogenic from Queen Victoria Park.

The Canadian town is also livelier, in an over-the-top touristy way. Chain hotels and restaurants dominate, but there is an HI hostel, and some older motels have the classic honeymooners' heart-shaped tubs.

Crossing the Rainbow Bridge and returning costs US$3.75/50¢ per car/pedestrian. Walking takes about 10 minutes; car traffic can grind to a standstill in summer or if there's a major event on in Toronto. US citizens and overseas visitors must show a passport or an enhanced driver's license at immigration at either end. Driving a rental car from the USA over the border should not be a problem, but check with your rental company.

Old Fort Niagara MUSEUM
(☑716-745-7611; www.oldfortniagara.org; Youngstown; adult/child $12/8; ⊙9am-7pm Jul & Aug, to 5pm Sep-Jun) This 1726 French-built fortress, restored in the 1930s, defends the once very strategic point where the Niagara River flows into Lake Ontario. It has engaging displays of Native American artifacts, small weapons, furniture and clothing, as well as breathtaking views from its ramparts.

Whirlpool State Park STATE PARK
(☑716-284-4691; www.parks.ny.gov; Robert Moses State Pkwy) This park, 3 miles north of the falls, sits just above a sharp bend in the Niagara River – a bend that creates a giant whirlpool easily visible from your vantage point. Steps take you 300ft to the gorge below and mind you don't tumble into the vortex.

Rainbow Bridge BRIDGE
(www.niagarafallsbridges.com; ⊙pedestrians & cyclists 50¢, cars $3.75) Bring your passport for the walk or drive across this bridge linking the US and Canadian sides of the falls – there are good views along the way.

★ **Maid of the Mist** BOATING
(☑716-284-8897; www.maidofthemist.com; 1 Prospect St; adult/child $18.25/10.65; ⊙9am-7:30pm Jun-Aug, to 5pm Apr, May, Sep & Oct) The traditional way to see Niagara Falls is on this boat cruise, which has ferried visitors into the rapids right below the falls since 1846. Make sure you wear the blue poncho they give you, as the torrential spray from the falls will soak you.

🛏 Sleeping & Eating

**Seneca Niagara
Resort & Casino** RESORT $$
(☑877-873-6322; www.senecaniagaracasino.com; 310 4th St; r from $195; P❄⚛@🖥🐾) With some 600 spacious rooms and suites, and a lively casino, this purple-and-glass-covered tower is the American town's answer to the tourist glitz across on the Canadian side of the falls. There is a variety of music and comedy shows staged here too, headlined by relatively big names.

Giacomo BOUTIQUE HOTEL $$$
(☑716-299-0200; www.thegiacomo.com; 222 1st St; r $259; P❄@🖥) A rare bit of style among the bland chain hotels and motels of Niagara, the luxe Giacomo occupies part of a gorgeous art-deco office tower, with spacious, ornately decorated rooms. Even if you're not staying here, have a drink in the 19th-floor lounge (bar open from 5pm) for spectacular views, and music on Saturday.

**Third Street Retreat
Eatery & Pub** AMERICAN $
(☑716-371-0760; www.thirdstreetretreat.com; 250 Rainbow Blvd; mains $6-11; ⊙8am-9pm Tue-Thu, to 10pm Fri & Sat, 9am-4pm Sun) The walls are decorated with old LP covers at this popular local spot serving all-day breakfasts and other comforting pub-grub dishes. There's a good selection of beers on tap or in bottles, plus a pool table and darts in an upstairs section.

ℹ Getting There & Away

NFTA (www.nfta.com) bus 40 connects downtown Buffalo and Niagara Falls ($2, one hour); the stop in Niagara Falls is at 1st St and Rainbow Blvd. Express bus 60 goes to a terminal east of the town center; you'll have to transfer to bus 55 to reach the river. The **Amtrak train station** (☑716-285-4224; www.amtrak.com; 825 Depot Ave) is about 2 miles north of downtown; the station on the Canadian side is more central, but coming from NYC, you have to wait for Canadian customs. From Niagara Falls, daily trains go to Buffalo ($14, 35 minutes), Toronto, Canada ($33, three hours) and NYC ($66, nine hours).

Greyhound (www.greyhound.com; 240 1st St) buses stop at the Quality Inn.

Flights from Florida and South Carolina are offered by Allegiant Air and Spirit Airlines to **Niagara Falls International Airport** (☑ 716-297-4494; www.niagarafallsairport.com; 2035 Niagara Falls Blvd).

NEW JERSEY

Everything you've seen on TV, from the McMansions of *Real Housewives of New Jersey* to the thick accents of *The Sopranos*, is at least partially true. But Jersey (natives lose the 'New') is at least as well defined by its high-tech and banking headquarters, and a quarter of it is lush farmland (hence the Garden State nickname) and pine forests. And on the 127 miles of beautiful beaches, you'll find, yes, the guidos and guidettes of *Jersey Shore*, but also many oceanfront towns, each with a distinct character.

Stay east and you'll experience the Jersey (sub)urban jungle. Go west to find its opposite: the peaceful, refreshing landscape of the Delaware Water Gap.

ⓘ Getting There & Around

Though many NJ folks love their cars, there are other transportation options.

PATH Train (www.panynj.gov/path) Connects lower Manhattan to Hoboken, Jersey City and Newark.

NJ Transit (www.njtransit.com) Operates buses and trains around the state, including bus service to NYC's Port Authority and downtown Philadelphia, and trains to Penn Station, NYC. Train service has declined severely in the past decade – fair warning.

New York Waterway (www.nywaterway.com) New York Waterway ferries run up the Hudson River and from the NJ Transit train station in Hoboken to the World Financial Center.

Hoboken

The Square Mile City is among the trendiest of zip codes, with real-estate prices to match. On weekends the bars come alive, and loads of restaurants line Washington St. If you can step over the designer dogs, and navigate the mega-strollers and trolling black Uber cars with NY plates, it's a good walking town with amazing views of NYC.

◉ Sights

Hoboken Historical Museum　　MUSEUM
(☑ 201-656-2240; www.hobokenmuseum.org; 1301 Hudson St; adult/child $4/free; ☉ 2-7pm Tue-Thu, 1-5pm Fri-Sun) This small museum conveys a sense of Hoboken that's hard to imagine today – a city of blue-collar Irish and Italian Catholic immigrants, toiling in the shipyards and docks. It also offers self-guided walking tours of Frank Sinatra's Hoboken haunts, and *On the Waterfront* film locales.

✖ Eating

La Isla　　CUBAN $
(☑ 201-659-8197; www.laislarestaurant.com; 104 Washington St; breakfast $8-11, sandwiches $8-10, mains $18-21; ☉ 7am-10pm) The most authentic Cuban choice in town since 1970, the Formica counters ring with plates spilling over with grilled Cuban sandwiches, *maduros* (fried plantains) and rice with pigeon peas – all to the soundtrack of staccato Spanish chatter and salsa, under the watchful eye of Celia Cruz portraits. Forget the fancier 'uptown' branch – this is the real thing.

Amanda's　　GASTRONOMY $$$
(☑ 201-798-0101; www.amandasrestaurant.com; 908 Washington St; mains $24-36; ☉ 5-10pm Mon-Fri, 11am-3pm & 5-11pm Sat, 11am-3pm & 5-9pm Sun) For three decades the Flynn family has served first-rate fare in these conjoined, converted brownstones, each room with a different theme. An extensive wine list and monthly wine evenings make this a classy option. The bar dinner special (Sunday to Thursday) is great value.

ⓘ Getting There & Away

NY Waterway (www.nywaterway.com) runs the ferry between 39th St on Manhattan's West Side and Hoboken ($9, eight minutes). There is frequent, if crowded, NJ PATH train service from lower Manhattan to Hoboken terminal. Parking is atrocious – don't even think about driving here.

Princeton

Settled by an English Quaker missionary, this tiny town is filled with lovely architecture and several noteworthy sites, number one of which is its Ivy League university. Princeton is more upper-crust than collegiate, with preppie boutiques edging central Palmer Sq.

Like any good seat of learning, Princeton has a bookshop, record store, brew pub and indie cinema, all within blocks of the rabbit's warren of streets and alleys that crisscross Palmer Sq, as well as innumerable sweet shops, cafes and ice-cream specialty stores.

◎ Sights

★ Institute Woods
FOREST
(www.ias.edu; 1 Einstein Dr; ⊙dawn-dusk) Walk 1.5 miles down Mercer St to a bucolic slice of countryside seemingly completely removed from the jammed-up campus-area thoroughfares. Nearly 600 acres have been set aside here, and birders, joggers and dog-walkers luxuriate on the soft, loamy pathways. It's an avian paradise during the spring warbler migration.

Princeton University
UNIVERSITY
(☑609-258-3000; www.princeton.edu) Built in the mid-1700s, this institution soon became one of the largest structures in the early colonies. Now it's in the top-tier Ivy League. You can stroll around on your own, or take a student-led tour.

Morven Museum & Garden
MUSEUM
(☑609-924-8144; www.morven.org; 55 Stockton St; adult/child $10/8; ⊙10am-4pm Wed-Sun) Stop by for fine displays of decorative arts and fully furnished period rooms; other galleries change their exhibitions periodically. The gardens, and the house itself – a perfectly coiffed colonial revival mansion originally built by Richard Stockton, a prominent lawyer in the mid-18th century and signer of the Declaration of Independence – are worth a visit in and of themselves.

🛏 Sleeping & Eating

Inn at Glencairn
B&B $$
(☑609-497-1737; www.innatglencairn.com; 3301 Lawrenceville Rd; r from $199; 🕸) The best value in the Princeton area: five serene rooms in a renovated Georgian manor, 10 minutes' drive from campus.

Mediterra Restaurant & Taverna
MEDITERRANEAN $$
(☑609-252-9680; www.mediterrarestaurant.com; 29 Hulfish St; mains $19-30; ⊙11:30am-11pm Mon-Thu, to midnight Fri & Sat, to 10pm Sun) Centrally located in Palmer Sq, Mediterra is the sort of upscale, contemporary place designed for a college town, for visiting parents, flush students and locals craving menus that highlight locally sourced and organic ingredients, and that reflect the owners' mixed Chilean–Italian heritage.

★ Mistral
MEDITERRANEAN $$$
(☑609-688-8808; www.mistralprinceton.com; 66 Witherspoon St; sharing plates $13-36; ⊙5-9pm Mon & Tue, 11:30am-3pm & 5-9pm Wed-Sat, 10:30am-3pm & 4-9pm Sun) Princeton's most creative restaurant offers plates made to share, with flavors ranging from the Caribbean to Scandinavia. Sit at the chef's counter for a bird's-eye view of the controlled chaos in the open-plan kitchen.

❶ Getting There & Away

Coach USA (www.coachusa.com) express buses 100 and 600 run frequently between Manhattan and Princeton ($15, 1½ hours). NJ Transit (www.njtransit.com) trains run frequently from New York Penn Station to Princeton Junction railway station ($16, one to 1½ hours). The 'Dinky' shuttle will then run you to Princeton campus ($3, five minutes).

Jersey Shore

Perhaps the most famous and revered feature of New Jersey is its sparkling shore – and heading 'down the shore' (in local parlance, never 'to the beach') is an essential summer ritual. Stretching from Sandy Hook to Cape May, the coastline is dotted with resort towns both tacky and tony. In 2012 much of the shore was devastated by Hurricane Sandy – the roller coaster at Seaside Heights was even knocked into the ocean (and later demolished). But within three years the boardwalks were all rebuilt, and the area has largely returned to its vibrant state. It's mobbed on summer weekends (traffic is especially bad on the bridges to the barrier islands), and finding good-value accommodations is nearly as difficult as locating un-tattooed skin; campgrounds can be low-cost alternatives. By early fall, however, you could find yourself blissfully alone on the sand.

❶ Getting There & Around

Sitting in bumper-to-bumper traffic on the Garden State Pkwy may turn you lobster red, so driving early in the day to summer destinations is a must.

➡ New Jersey Transit (www.njtransit.com) runs twice-daily special Shore Express trains from June to September, stopping in Asbury Park, Bradley Beach, Belmar, Spring Lake, Manasquan, Point Pleasant Beach and Bay Head. You can buy a beach tag along with your train ticket, and there are two northbound express trains returning in the evening.

➡ NJ Transit buses from New York's Port Authority service Seaside Heights/Seaside Park, Island Beach State Park, Atlantic City, Wildwood and Cape May.

➡ Greyhound (www.greyhound.com) runs special buses to Atlantic City.

Asbury Park & Ocean Grove

During decades of economic stagnation, the town of Asbury Park had nothing more to its name than the fact that state troubadour Bruce Springsteen got his start at the Stone Pony nightclub here in the mid-1970s. But since 2000, blocks of previously abandoned Victorian homes have seen such a revival that Asbury is sometimes called 'Brooklyn on the Beach.' Thousands more units are projected over the next few years.

The downtown area – several blocks of Cookman and Bangs Aves – has antiques shops, hip restaurants (from vegan to French bistro) and an art-house cinema. Thirty-nine bars (and counting) lure trains full of young NY-based revelers to the convenient NJ transit depot, like moths to the vodka.

Immediately south of Asbury Park, Ocean Grove is a kind of time and culture warp. 'God's Square Mile at the Jersey Shore,' as it's still known, was founded by Methodists in the 19th century as a revival camp, and it's still a 'dry' town – no liquor is sold here – and the beach is closed Sunday mornings. Its Victorian architecture is so covered in gingerbread trim, you'll want to eat it. At the center, around a 6500-seat wooden auditorium with a huge pipe organ, the former revival camp is now **Tent City** – a historic site with more than a hundred quaint canvas tents used as summer homes.

☉ Sights & Activities

Historic Village at Allaire   MUSEUM
(☎ 732-919-3500; www.allairevillage.org; 4263 Atlantic Ave, Farmingdale; parking May-Sep $7; ⏰ bakery 10am-4pm Mon-Fri, historic village 11am-5pm Sat & Sun) **FREE** Just a 15 minute-drive from the 21st century and Asbury Park, this quirky museum is what remains of what was a thriving 19th-century village called Howell Works.

Silver Ball Museum Arcade   ARCADE
(Pinball Hall of Fame; ☎ 732-774-4994; www.silverballmuseum.com; 1000 Ocean Ave; per hour/half-day $10/15; ⏰ 11am-midnight Mon-Thu, to 1am Fri & Sat, 10am-10pm Sun) Dozens of pinball machines in mint condition, from mechanical

1950s games to modern classics such as Addams Family.

🛏 Sleeping

⭐ **Asbury Hotel**   BOUTIQUE HOTEL $$
(☎ 732-774-7100; www.theasburyhotel.com; 210 5th Ave; r $125-275; P ✳ ☎ ⧆) Wow. From the performance space/lobby stocked with LP records, old books and a solarium to the rooftop bar, this new hotel oozes cool. A 2016 addition to the AP scene, two blocks from Convention Hall and the boardwalk, you could stay inside all day, playing pool or lounging by the rooftop one.

Quaker Inn   INN $$
(☎ 732-775-7525; www.quakerinn.com; 39 Main Ave; r $90-200; ✳ ☎) A great old creaky Victorian with 28 rooms, some of which open onto wraparound porches or balconies. There's a nice common area/library to linger over your coffee, and the owners reflect the town's overall charm and hospitality.

🍴 Eating & Drinking

Moonstruck   ITALIAN $$$
(☎ 732-988-0123; www.moonstrucknj.com; 517 Lake Ave; mains $22-38; ⏰ 5-10pm Wed, Thu & Sun, to 11pm Fri & Sat) With views of Wesley Lake dividing Asbury and Ocean Grove and an extensive martini menu, it's hard to find fault. The menu is eclectic, though it leans toward Italian with a good selection of pastas; the meat and fish dishes have varied ethnic influences.

Asbury Festhalle and Biergarten   BEER GARDEN
(☎ 732-997-8767; www.asburybiergarten.com; 527 Lake Ave; ⏰ 4pm-1am Mon-Fri, 11am-1am Sat & Sun) Deutschland by the Sea: quaff from 41 draft ales in the rooftop beer garden or check out live music in a space as big as two barns, with classic long beer-hall tables. Snack on pretzels bigger than your face, fill up on plates of wurst (mains $13 to $20) or work your way through the 12 different schnapps on offer.

ℹ Getting There & Away

Driving along the S Main St (Rte 71) from the north or south, you'll see the impressive gates that mark the entranceway to Ocean Grove's Main Ave. If you're taking the NJ Transit's Shore Express, debark at neighboring Asbury Park and walk or taxi over to Ocean Grove. A $22 bus trip from the Port Authority requires a transfer at Lakewood.

DELAWARE WATER GAP

The beautiful spot where the Delaware River makes a tight S-curve through the ridge of the Kittatinny Mountains was, in the pre-air-conditioning days, a popular resort destination. In 1965 the **Delaware Water Gap National Recreation Area** (�570-426-2452; www.nps. gov/dewa; 1978 River Rd, Bushkill) was established, covering land in both NJ and Pennsylvania, and it's still an unspoiled recreational spot – just 70 miles east of New York City.

Old Mine Rd, one of the oldest continually operating commercial roads in the USA, meanders along the eastern side of the Delaware. A few miles inland, a 25-mile stretch of the Appalachian Trail runs along the Kittatinny Ridge. Day hikers can climb to the top of the 1547ft Mt Tammany in **Worthington State Forest** (⊙908-841-9575; www.state. nj.us/dep/parksandforests/parks/worthington.html; Old Mine Rd, Warren County; ⊙dawn-dusk) for great views (the 1.8-mile Blue Dot trail is the easiest route, though it's still strenuous) or walk to the serene-looking glacial Sunfish Pond. Hawks, bald eagles and ravens soar over the hemlock forest. It's about a two-hour bus ride from NYC to the area. Coach USA (www.coachusa.com) provides bus service from the Port Authority to Milford, PA ($25) and Martz Trailways (www.martztrailways.com) runs to Stroudsburg, PA ($37). NJ Transit has proposed a rail station in Smithfield Township, just outside the park, but it has yet to be built.

New Jersey Transit's Asbury Park Station is at the intersection of Cookman and Main Sts and is about 45 minutes from NYC. Some late-night trains run during the summer.

Barnegat Peninsula

Locals call this 22-mile stretch 'the barrier island,' though it's technically a peninsula, connected to the mainland at **Point Pleasant Beach**. Surfers should seek out **Inlet Beach** in Manasquan, immediately north (not on the peninsula), for the Shore's most reliable year-round waves.

South of **Mantoloking** and **Lavallette**, midway down the island, a bridge from the mainland (at Toms River) deposits the hordes in **Seaside Heights**, location of the MTV reality show *Jersey Shore,* and epitome of the deliciously tacky Shore culture. It's still a sticky pleasure to lick a Kohr's orange-vanilla twist cone and stroll through the boardwalk's raucous, deeply tanned, scantily clad crowds, refueling at an above-average number of bars. Look out for the 1910 Dentzel-Looff carousel, and the 310ft Ferris wheel and German-built roller-coaster added in 2017.

For a bit of quiet, escape south to residential **Seaside Park** and the wilderness of Island Beach State Park beyond.

◉ Sights

Island Beach State Park   PARK
(⊙732-793-0506; www.islandbeachnj.org; Seaside Park; weekday/weekend May-Sep $12/20, Oct-Apr

$5/10; ⊙8am-8pm Mon-Fri, 7am-8pm Sat & Sun May-Sep, 8am-dusk Oct-Apr) This beautiful tidal island offers fishing, a range of wildlife (from foxes to ospreys and other shorebirds), more than 40 trees and shrubs, including pepperbush and prickly pear cactus, and a killer view of Barnegat Lighthouse, seemingly only an arm's length across the water. Of the 10 miles of relatively untouched beach, one is open for swimming; the rest makes a nice bike ride. On the bay side, the lush tidal marshes are good for kayaking.

Casino Pier   AMUSEMENT PARK
(⊙732-793-6488; www.casinopiernj.com; 800 Ocean Tce, Seaside Heights; rides from $5, water park adult/child $35/29; ⊙noon-late Jun-Aug, hours vary Sep-May) The amusement pier at the north end of the Seaside boardwalk has a few kiddie rides and more extreme thrills for the 48in-and-taller set, plus a chairlift that runs above the boardwalk. Nearby is **Breakwater Beach**, a water park with tall slides.

🍽 Sleeping & Eating

Luna-Mar Motel   MOTEL $$
(⊙732-793-7955; www.lunamarmotel.com; 1201 N Ocean Ave, Seaside Park; r from $129; ❄ 🛜 🏊) Directly across the road from the beach, this tidy motel has tile floors (no sandy carpets). Rates include beach badges.

★Klee's   PUB FOOD $$
(⊙732-830-1996; www.kleesbarandgrill.com; 101 Boulevard, Seaside Heights; pizza from $12, mains

$14-28; ⊙10:30am-11pm Mon-Thu, to midnight Fri & Sat) Don't ask why an Irish bar has the best thin-crust pizza on the Shore – just enjoy.

ⓘ Getting There & Away

NJ Transit (www.njtransit.com) has a special Shore Express train (no transfer required) to Shore towns between Asbury Park and Bay Head; in the summer months it includes a beach pass. It also offers direct bus service to Seaside Heights from New York's Port Authority (bus 137; $27, 1½ hours) and Newark's Penn Station (bus 67; $17, one hour) from the end of June to Labor Day.

Atlantic City

Atlantic City (AC) may be the largest city on the Shore, but that currently doesn't mean much, as the vision of 'Vegas on the East Coast' has foundered, and casinos have gone bankrupt. But the hotels can be a bargain and the lovely beach is free and often empty because most visitors are indoors playing the slots. And in contrast with many homogeneous beach enclaves, the population here is more diverse.

As for the Prohibition-era glamour depicted in the HBO series *Boardwalk Empire*, there's little trace – though you can still ride along the boardwalk on a nifty wicker rolling chair (there's a price chart posted inside each chair). As you do, consider that the first boardwalk was built here, and if Baltic Ave rings a bell, it's because the game Monopoly uses AC's street names. A later contribution: the Miss America pageant, though it's now held in Vegas; the Miss'd America drag pageant (www.missdamerica.org) fills the gap.

⊙ Sights

Steel Pier AMUSEMENT PARK
(☑866-386-6659; www.steelpier.com; 1000 Boardwalk; ⊙3pm-midnight Mon-Fri, noon-1am Sat & Sun Jun-Aug, noon-midnight Sat & Sun Apr & May) The Steel Pier, directly in front of the

Taj Mahal casino, was the site of the famous high-diving horses that plunged into the Atlantic before crowds of spectators from the 1920s to the '70s. Today it's a collection of amusement rides, games of chance, candy stands and a Go-Kart track.

Ripley's Believe it or Not! MUSEUM
(Odditorium; ☑609-347-2001; www.ripleys.com; 1441 Boardwalk; adult/child $17/$11; ⊙11am-8pm Mon-Fri, 10am-8pm Sat & Sun) To call it a museum is a stretch, but Robert Ripley spent a lifetime collecting bizarre stuff, and a lot of it's here. Two-headed goat fetuses, a baling-wire Jimi Hendrix head, the world's smallest car, and a roulette wheel made of 14,000 jellybeans – you'll have fun, for about the cost of a movie.

Atlantic City Historical Museum MUSEUM
(☑609-347-5839; www.atlanticcityexperience.org; 1 N Tennessee Ave, Atlantic City Free Public Library; ⊙9:30am-5pm Mon, Fri & Sat, to 6pm Tue-Thu) **FREE** Small but informative – you'll learn all about AC's quirkiest details, such as the high-diving horses that once leaped off a 40ft tower at Steel Pier.

🛏 Sleeping & Eating

Tropicana Casino and Resort HOTEL $$
(☑609-340-4000; www.tropicana.net; 2831 Boardwalk; r from $105; ❷❋🐾🏊) The Trop is a sprawling city-within-a-city, including a casino, the Boogie Nights disco, a spa and high-end restaurants. We recommend the newer 'Havana' wing, and try to get up above the 40th floor for spectacular views.

★**Kelsey & Kim's Café** SOUTHERN US $
(Kelsey's Soul Food; ☑609-350-6800; www.kelseysac.com; 201 Melrose Ave; mains $9-12; ⊙7am-10pm) In the pretty residential Uptown area, this friendly cafe does excellent Southern comfort food, from morning grits and waffles to fried whiting and barbecue brisket. BYOB makes it a deal.

ⓘ Getting There & Away

The small **Atlantic City International Airport** (ACY; ☑609-573-4700; www.acairport.com; 101 Atlantic City International Airport, Egg Harbor Township) is a 20-minute drive from the town center. If you happen to be coming from Florida (where most of the flights come from), it's a great option for South Jersey or Philadelphia.

The only train service is NJ Transit (www.njtransit.com) from Philadelphia (one way $11, 1½ hours), arriving at the **train station** (☑973-

491-9400; 1 Atlantic City Expwy) next to the convention center. AC's **bus station** ([J]609-345-5403; www.njtransit.com; 1901 Atlantic Ave) receives NJ Transit and Greyhound service from NYC ($25 to $36, 2½ hours) and Philadelphia ($17, 1½ hours). A casino will often refund much of the fare (in chips, coins or coupons) if you get a bus, such as Greyhound's Lucky Streak service, directly to its door. When leaving AC, buses first stop at various casinos and only stop at the bus station if not already full.

Wildwood

Wildwood, and its neighboring towns of North Wildwood and Wildwood Crest, is a virtual outdoor museum of 1950s motel architecture and neon signs. The community has a relaxed atmosphere, somewhere between clean-cut fun and wild party. The beach is the widest in NJ, and there's no admission fee. Along the 2-mile boardwalk, several massive piers have roller coasters and rides best suited to aspiring astronauts.

⊙ Sights

Doo Wop Experience　MUSEUM
([J]609-523-1958; www.doowopusa.org; 4500 Ocean Ave; ⊙noon-9pm daily, trolley tours 8pm Tue & Thu Jun-Aug) FREE The Doo Wop Preservation League runs this small museum that tells the story of the Wildwoods' 1950s heyday. Its 'neon-sign garden' shows off relics from no-longer-standing buildings. Some summer nights, a trolley tour (adult/child $12/6) departs from here.

🛏 Sleeping & Eating

Heart of Wildwood　HOTEL **$$**
([J]609-522-4090; www.heartofwildwood.com; cnr Ocean & Spencer Aves; r $125-245; [P][❄][?][≋]) If you're here for water slides and roller coasters, book a room at Heart of Wildwood, facing the amusement piers. It's not fancy, but gets high marks for cleanliness (the tile floors help), and from the heated rooftop pool you can watch the big wheel go round and round.

Starlux　BOUTIQUE HOTEL **$$**
([J]609-522-7412; www.thestarlux.com; 305 E Rio Grande Ave; r from $205, trailer $240; [P][?][≋]) The sea-green-and-white Starlux has a soaring profile, lava lamps, boomerang-decorated bedspreads and sailboat-shaped mirrors, plus it's clean as a whistle. Even more authentically retro are its two chrome-sided Airstream trailers.

Key West Cafe　BREAKFAST **$**
([J]609-522-5006; 4701 Pacific Ave; mains $8-10; ⊙7am-2pm) Basically every permutation of pancakes and eggs imaginable, all freshly prepared – oh, and lunch too. Bonus: it's open year-round.

❶ Getting There & Away

New Jersey Transit (www.njtransit.com) runs bus service to Wildwood from NYC ($46, 4½ hours) and express bus service from Philadelphia's 30th St Station during summer ($30, 2½ hours). Driving from the Garden State Pkwy, take Rte 47 into Wildwood; from the south a more scenic route from Cape May is Rte 109, then Ocean Dr.

Cape May

Established in 1620, Cape May is a town with deep history and some 600 gorgeous Victorian buildings. Its sweeping beaches are a draw in summer, but its year-round population of about 4000 makes it a lively off-season destination, unlike most of the rest of the Jersey Shore. Whales can be spotted off the coast May to December, and migratory birds are plentiful in spring and fall: just check in at the Cape May Bird Observatory. The state's booming wine industry is represented by six different sites here, among them, trendy Willow Creek. And thanks to the location on New Jersey's southern tip (it's Exit 0 from the turnpike), you can watch the sun rise or set over the water.

⊙ Sights

Cape May Point State Park　STATE PARK
(www.state.nj.us/dep/parksandforests/parks/capemay.html; 707 E Lake Dr; ⊙8am-4pm) The 190-acre Cape May Point State Park, just off Lighthouse Ave, has 2 miles of trails, plus the famous **Cape May Lighthouse** ([J]609-884-5404; www.capemaymac.org; 215 Lighthouse Ave; adult/child $8/5; ⊙10am-5pm May-Sep, 11am-3pm Mar & Apr, 11am-3pm Sat Feb, Mar & Oct-Dec). Built in 1859, the 157ft lighthouse underwent a $2 million restoration in the 1990s, and its completely reconstructed light is visible as far as 25 miles out to sea. You can climb the 199 stairs to the top in the summer months. Lighthouse hours vary; phone ahead to confirm details.

Cape May Bird Observatory　BIRD SANCTUARY
([J]609-884-2736; www.birdcapemay.org; 701 East Lake Dr; ⊙9am-4:30pm Apr-Oct, Wed-Mon Nov-Mar) FREE Cape May is one of the country's

SANDY HOOK

The northernmost tip of the Jersey Shore is the **Sandy Hook Gateway National Recreation Area** (☑718-354-4606; www.nps.gov/gate; 128 S Hartshorne Dr, Highlands; parking May-Sep $15; ☺5am-9pm Apr-Oct) **FREE**, a 7-mile barrier island at the entrance to New York Harbor. From your beach blanket, you can see the NYC skyline. The wide beaches, including NJ's only legal nude beach (**Gunnison**), are edged by a system of bike trails, while the bay side is great for fishing or bird-watching.

Historic Fort Hancock and the nation's oldest operational **lighthouse** (☑732-872-5970; www.nps.gov/gate; 85 Mercer Road, Highlands; ☺visitor center 9am-5pm, tours half-hourly 1-4:30pm) **FREE** give a glimpse of Sandy Hook's prior importance as a military and navigational site.

top birding spots, with more than 400 species during migration season. The mile-long loop trail here is a good introduction, and there are plenty of books, binoculars and birding bric-a-brac in the bookstore here.

🛏 Sleeping & Eating

★ **Congress Hall** HOTEL **$$$**
(☑609-884-8421; www.caperesorts.com; 200 Congress Pl; r from $259; ▦ 🗢 ▨) Opened in 1816, the enormous Congress Hall is a local landmark, now suitably modernized without wringing out all the history. The same company manages several other excellent hotels in the area.

Mad Batter AMERICAN **$**
(☑609-884-5970; www.madbatter.com; Carroll Villa Hotel, 19 Jackson St; brunch $8-11; ☺8am-9pm May-Aug, hours vary Sep-Apr) Tucked in a white Victorian B&B, this restaurant is locally beloved for brunch – including fluffy oat pancakes and rich clam chowder. Dinner is fine, but pricier, with mains around $30.

The Chesapeake Bay Benedict, stuffed with crab, is to die for.

★ **Lobster House** SEAFOOD **$$**
(☑609-884-8296; www.thelobsterhouse.com; 906 Schellengers Landing Rd; mains $14-30; ☺11:30am-3pm & 4:30-10pm Apr-Dec, to 9pm Jan-Mar) This clubby-feeling classic on the wharf serves local oysters and scallops. No reservations means very long waits – go early or late, or have a drink on the boat-bar, the *Schooner American,* docked next to the restaurant.

🍷 Drinking & Nightlife

★ **Willow Creek Winery** WINERY
(☑609-770-8782; www.willowcreekwinerycapemay. com; 168 Stevens St; ☺11am-5pm Mon-Thu, to 9:30pm Fri, to 7pm Sat & Sun) The 'baby' of Cape May's six wineries, this former lima bean/dairy farm christened its first bottles in 2011, and produces a solid combo of reds and whites. The tapas menu and sangria bar on the weekend are pretty mind-blowing, and a tour around the 50 acres on an electric tram is a kick.

❶ Getting There & Away

NJ Transit (www.njtransit.com) buses serve Cape May from NYC ($48, three hours; may involve a transfer at Atlantic City) and a discounted round-trip express bus from Philadelphia during the summer months (return $33, three hours). For onward car travel, the **Cape May-Lewes Ferry** (☑800-643-3779; www.cmlf. com; 1200 Lincoln Blvd; car/passenger $47/10; ☺7am-6pm Apr-Oct) crosses the bay in 1½ hours to Lewes, Delaware, near Rehoboth Beach.

PENNSYLVANIA

More than 300 miles across, stretching from the East Coast to the edge of the Midwest, Pennsylvania contains multitudes. Philadelphia, once the heart of the British colonial empire, is very much a part of the east, a link on the Boston–Washington metro corridor. Outside the city, though, the terrain turns pastoral, emphasized by the Pennsylvania Dutch – that is, Mennonite, Amish and others – who tend their farms by hand, as if it were still the 18th century. West of here, the Appalachian mountains begin, as do the so-called Pennsylvania Wilds, a barely inhabited patch of deep forest. In the far west of the state, Pittsburgh, the state's only other large city and once a staggeringly wealthy steel manufacturing center, is fascinating in its combination of rust-belt decay and new energy.

❶ Getting There & Around

Pennsylvania is home to a number of airports, several of them with international connections, and it is near the giant hub of New Jersey's

Newark International, with connections across the world. Trains serve many of its major cities, while buses service most towns. That said, with so much of this state's beauty lying off the beaten path, renting a car and driving is highly recommended.

Philadelphia

Philadelphia, or 'Philly' as it's affectionately known, has all of the glamor of New York City and Washington, DC, while still retaining small-town charm. Because the city's oldest buildings are so well preserved, America's early history and role in building democracy are sometimes more accessible here than in the capital. Moreover, it's a beautiful place that is easy and rewarding to explore, its streets dotted with gracious squares and linked by cobbled alleys.

From the start of the Revolutionary War until 1790 (when Washington, DC, was founded), Philadelphia was the new nation's capital. Eventually, NYC rose as a cultural, commercial and industrial center, and Philly slipped into a decline, intensified by the loss of industrial jobs. Some areas of the city are still blighted, but its core, from the manicured campuses of the University of Pennsylvania to the redbrick buildings of the Old City, is solid.

◉ Sights & Activities

★Barnes Foundation   MUSEUM
(Map p152; ☑ 215-278-7200; www.barnesfoundation.org; 2025 Benjamin Franklin Pkwy; adult/child $25/10; ☺10am-5pm Wed-Mon) In the first half of the 20th century, collector and educator Albert C Barnes amassed a remarkable trove of artwork by Cézanne, Degas, Matisse, Renoir, Van Gogh and other European stars. Alongside, he set beautiful pieces of folk art from Africa and the Americas – an artistic desegregation that was shocking at the time. Today's Barnes Foundation is a modern shell, inside which is a faithful reproduction of Barnes' original mansion (still in the Philadelphia suburbs).

The art is hung according to Barnes' vision, a careful juxtaposition of colors, themes and materials. In one room, all the portraits appear to be staring at a central point. Even more remarkable: you've likely never seen any of these works before, because Barnes' will limits reproduction and lending.

★Independence Hall   HISTORIC BUILDING
(Map p156; ☑ 877-444-6777; www.nps.gov/inde; 520 Chestnut St; ☺9am-5pm, to 7pm late May-early Sep) **FREE** The 'birthplace of American government,' a modest Quaker building, is where delegates from the 13 colonies met to approve the Declaration of Independence on July 4, 1776. Entrance is at the corner of Chestnut and 5th Sts. Expect a line out the door, around the block, and perhaps even out of the city for this one – it's the prime attraction in a city full of history. Budget for at least an hour wait.

★Independence National
Historic Park   PARK
(Map p156; ☑ 215-965-2305; www.nps.gov/inde; 3rd & Chestnut Sts; ☺visitor center & most sites 9am-5pm; ☒9, 21, 38, 42, 47, Ⓤ SEPTA 5th St Station) This L-shaped park, along with Philly's Old City, has been dubbed 'America's most historic square mile.' Once the backbone of the US government, it has become the backbone of Philadelphia's tourist trade. Stroll around and you'll see storied buildings in which the seeds for the Revolutionary War were planted and the US government came into bloom. You'll also find beautiful, shaded urban lawns dotted with plenty of squirrels, pigeons and costumed actors.

★Museum of the
American Revolution   MUSEUM
(Map p156; ☑ 215-253-6731; www.amrevmuseum.org; 101 S 3rd St; adult/child $19/12; ☺10am-5pm Sep-late May, 9:30am-6pm late May-Aug) This massive, multimedia-rich new museum will have you virtually participating in the American Revolution, from interactive dioramas to 3-D experiences that take you all the way from contentment with British rule to the eventual rejection of it. Learn about the events, people, cultures and religions that participated in one of the world's most important revolutions. Lots of hands-on and video opportunities mean kids will have as much fun as adults. Note that all tickets are timed: reserve them early online.

★Philadelphia Museum of Art   MUSEUM
(Map p152; ☑ 215-763-8100; www.philamuseum.org; 2600 Benjamin Franklin Pkwy; adult/child $20/free; ☺10am-5pm Tue, Thu, Sat & Sun, to 8:45pm Wed & Fri) To many, this building is simply the steps Sylvester Stallone ran up in the 1976 flick *Rocky*. But well beyond that, this is one of the nation's finest treasure troves, featuring excellent collections

NEW YORK, NEW JERSEY & PENNSYLVANIA PHILADELPHIA

Philadelphia

of Asian art, Renaissance masterpieces, post-Impressionist works and modern pieces by Picasso, Duchamp and Matisse. Especially neat are the complete rooms: a medieval cloister, a Chinese temple, an Austrian country house.

There's so much to see that a ticket gives admission for two days, here and at the separate Perelman Building, two nearby historic homes and the Rodin Museum (p154). Wednesday and Friday nights are pay-what-you-wish (but note the Perelman is closed on both evenings).

Mütter Museum MUSEUM
(Map p152; ☎ 215-560-8564; www.muttermuse um.org; 19 S 22nd St; adult/child $15/10; ⊙ 10am-

5pm) Know what a bezoar is? If so, you're morbid enough to appreciate this trove of medical oddities. Maintained by the College of Physicians, this is definitely one of those unique, only-in-Philadelphia attractions, a

Philadelphia

museum dedicated to rare, odd or disturbing medical conditions.

★ **Benjamin Franklin Museum**   MUSEUM
(Map p156; ☑ 215-965-2305; www.nps.gov/inde; Market St, btwn 3rd & 4th Sts; adult/child $5/2; ⊙ 9am-5pm, to 7pm late May-early Sep) In a courtyard south of Market St is an underground museum dedicated to Benjamin Franklin's storied life as a printer (he started the nation's first newspaper), inventor (Bifocals! Lightning rods!) and political figure who signed the Declaration of Independence.

★ **Rodin Museum**   MUSEUM
(Map p152; ☑ 215-763-8100; www.rodinmuseum. org; 2151 Benjamin Franklin Pkwy; suggested admission $10; ⊙ 10am-5pm Wed-Mon) This newly renovated museum holds Rodin's great works *The Thinker* and *Burghers of Calais* among its 140 sculptures that span every part of the French sculptor's spectacular career.

Liberty Bell Center   HISTORIC SITE
(Map p156; ☑ 215-965-2305; www.nps.gov/inde; 526 Market St; ⊙ 9am-5pm, to 7pm late May-early Sep) FREE A glass-walled building protects this icon of Philadelphia history from the elements. You can peek from outside, or join the line to file past, reading about the

2080lb object's history along the way. The line starts on the building's north end, where the foundations of George Washington's house are marked. The gist of the story: the bell was made in 1751, to commemorate the 50th anniversary of Pennsylvania's constitution. Mounted in Independence Hall (p151), it tolled on the first public reading of the Declaration of Independence. The crack developed in the 19th century, and the bell was retired in 1846.

Philly from the Top   OBSERVATORY
(One Liberty Observation Deck; Map p152; ☑ 215-561-3325; http://phillyfromthetop.com; 1650 Market St; adult/child $14/9; ⊙ 10am-8pm) A lovely way to get a bird's-eye view of the city, and especially pretty after dark, this 883ft-high observation deck is on the 57th floor of One Liberty Place.

Shofuso Japanese House & Garden   GARDENS
(☑ 215-878-5097; www.japanesehouse.org; Horticultural Dr, Fairmount Park; adult/child $10/5; ⊙ 10am-4pm Wed-Fri, 11am-5pm Sat & Sun Apr-Oct) A picturesque home and teahouse, in the 16th-century style, set in 1.2 acres of traditional gardens. The cherry trees blooming in spring are not to be missed.

★ City Hall
NOTABLE BUILDING

(Map p152; ☑ 215-686-2840; www.phlvisitor center.com; cnr Broad & Market Sts; tower $6, tour & tower $12; ⊙ 9am-5pm Mon-Fri, also 11am-4pm one Sat per month, tour at 12:30pm, tower closes 4:15pm Mon-Fri) Completed in 1901, City Hall takes up a whole block, and, at 548ft, not counting the 27-ton bronze statue of William Penn, it's the world's tallest structure without a steel frame. The view from the observation deck near the top of the tower takes in most of the city (reserve tickets ahead). The daily interior tour is a treat too. In winter, there's ice-skating on the west-side plaza.

Eastern State Penitentiary
MUSEUM

(Map p152; ☑ 215-236-3300; www.easternstate. org; 2027 Fairmount Ave; adult/child $14/10; ⊙10am-5pm) The modern prison didn't just happen – it was invented, and Eastern State Penitentiary was the first one, opened in 1829 and finally closed in 1971. A self-guiding audio tour leads you through the eerie, echoing halls; one stop is Al Capone's famously luxurious cell. There's also info on America's current prison system, and art installations throughout. A popular stop, expect crowds at peak times.

Edgar Allen Poe National Historic Site
HISTORIC SITE

(Map p152; ☑ 215-597-8780; www.nps.gov/edal; 532 N 7th St; ⊙9am-noon, 1-5pm Fri-Sun) FREE Often called the creator of the horror story, Edgar Allen Poe lived for seven years in Philadelphia. This house, his only Philly home still remaining, has been turned into a small but interesting museum, with a lot of original items and restored rooms. Don't miss the creepy brick cellar (complete with cobwebs) thought to have inspired Poe's masterwork *The Black Cat*. A statue of a raven stands outside.

Mural Tours
TOURS

(☑ 215-925-3633; www.muralarts.org/tours; $22-32) Guided trolley, train and walking tours of the city's numerous outdoor murals. A free self-guided tour and map is available online.

Taste of Philly Food Tour
FOOD & DRINK

(Map p152; ☑ 800-838-3006; www.tasteofphilly foodtour.com; 51 N 12th St; adult/child $17/10; ⊙10am Wed & Sat) Snack and learn Philly food lore during this 75-minute tour with a local writer at the Reading Terminal Market. Reservations required.

✴ Festivals & Events

Feastival
FOOD & DRINK

(☑ 267-443-1886; http://phillyfeastival.com/; 140 N Columbus Blvd; $300) Eat, meet and greet at the city's highest-lauded food fest, held one evening every September to benefit FringeArts, the city cultural organization that puts on the Fringe Festival. Not for the budget-minded, but if you've got the cash to splash, it's a night you'll never forget.

Mummers Parade
CARNIVAL

(www.mummers.com; ⊙ Jan 1) Uniquely Philly: the closest parallel may be New Orleans' Mardi Gras krewes, with their elaborate costumes, music and deep lore – but in the bracing cold of winter. The parade often stretches more than a mile down Broad St in the center of the city.

Fringe Festival
PERFORMING ARTS

(www.fringearts.com; ⊙mid-Sep) Philly's performance fest has been running since 1996; it's a city-wide celebration of performance art for 17 days in mid-September, with events, productions and craziness.

🛏 Sleeping

★ Apple Hostels
HOSTEL $

(Map p156; ☑ 215-922-0222; www.applehostels. com; 33 Bank St; dm/d $20/95; ❄@🛜) This cheerful hostel is hidden down an Old City alley and spans both sides of the street. The apple-green color scheme fits the name, but the Hosteling International-affiliated place is strong on details: two spotless kitchens, lounges and a library, plus power outlets in lockers, USB ports and reading lights at every bed, free coffee and earplugs.

There are male, female and co-ed dorms, plus two private rooms. The friendly staff run nightly activities such as walking tours, pasta nights and a Thursday bar crawl.

Chamounix Mansion Hostel
HOSTEL $

(☑ 215-878-3676; www.philahostel.org; 3250 Chamounix Dr, West Fairmount Park; dm members/ non-members $22/25, private d $55; ⊙ closed 15 Dec-15 Jan; 🅿@; 🚌38 & 40) In a lovely wooded area on the north side of the city, this Hosteling International hostel is best for guests with a car, but it's worth the drive. In its public areas, set with 19th-century furnishings, the place looks more like a B&B than a hostel; the dorms themselves are basic, but the antiques, harp, oriental rugs and paintings make it feel like luxury.

NEW YORK, NEW JERSEY & PENNSYLVANIA PHILADELPHIA

Philadelphia – Old City

The building is in the Philadelphia register of historic places.

⭐ **Alexander Inn** BOUTIQUE HOTEL **$$**
(Map p152; ☎ 215-923-3535; www.alexanderinn.com; cnr 12th & Spruce Sts; s/d from $143/182; ❄ @ �🛜) Online photos undersell this place. The impeccably kept rooms have a subdued, slightly vintage style; some have old-fashioned half-size tubs. The continental breakfast is average – worth the convenience, but there are other breakfast options nearby if you have the time.

Independent BOUTIQUE HOTEL **$$**
(Map p152; ☎ 215-772-1440; www.theindependenthotel.com; 1234 Locust St; r from $175; ❄ ❄ @ 🛜) A good Center City option housed in a handsome brick Georgian-Revival building with a four-story atrium. The elevator is painted realistically to appear like a set of doors. The 24 wood-floored rooms are uncluttered and sunny, and the complimentary off-site gym pass and wine and cheese served Monday through Thursday sweeten the deal.

Philadelphia - Old City

Le Méridien HOTEL $$
(Map p152; ☎215-422-8200; www.starwood hotels.com; 1421 Arch St; d from $231; P❄❋@☎❀) Though part of a luxury chain, the location and tasteful appropriation of an old building to make a modern hotel sets Le Méridien apart. Proudly claiming to be entirely smoke-free, this hotel is pet-friendly as well, has a wide range of facilities – a workout room, business center, parking – and is central to all the City Hall fun.

Windsor Suites HOTEL $$
(Map p152; ☎215-981-5678; www.thewindsor suites.com; 1700 Benjamin Franklin Pkwy; ste from $229; P❄❋☎❀) Comfortable suite rooms with full kitchens, with options for extended stays or monthly rentals. Conveniently located two blocks from Logan Sq, the Windsor Suites have a unique pet-friendly take: pets stay free and even get their own amenities. Online booking can be substantially cheaper.

★**Rittenhouse Hotel** HOTEL $$$
(Map p152; ☎215-546-9000; www.rittenhouse hotel.com; 210 W Rittenhouse Sq; d $400; P❄❋@☎❀) A five-star – excuse me, make that five-*diamond* – hotel on Rittenhouse Square. Rooms have marble baths. Of the downtown options with a pool, this is one of the nicest. It proudly serves a top-notch brunch and a soothing afternoon tea service with music. Thursdays through Saturdays a live jazz band plays in the library bar.

✕ **Eating**

Big Gay Ice Cream ICE CREAM $
(Map p152; ☎267-886-8024; www.biggayice cream.com; 521 S Broad St; ice cream from $3; ⊙1-10pm Sun-Thu, to 11pm Fri & Sat; Ⓜ Lombard South) Ranked one of the best ice creameries in the *world,* Big Gay Ice Cream is not a Philly original (it's NYC-based), but who can resist the lure of its signature 'Salty Pimp' cone: vanil-

la, dulce de leche and a chocolate shell. The descriptions are as double-entendre-filled as the cones are good, so prepare for chuckles as you peruse the menu.

Luke's Lobster SEAFOOD $
(Map p152; ☎215-564-1415; www.lukeslobster. com; 130 S 17th St; lobster roll $16.50; ⊙11am-9pm Sun-Thu, to 10pm Fri & Sat) As one diner put it, 'Lobster roll. Drop mic.' Part of a casual East Coast mini-chain serving authentic tastes of Maine using sustainably sourced seafood. Wash down your buttered-bun lobster roll with a wild-blueberry soda.

Tom's Dim Sum CHINESE $
(Map p152; ☎215-923-8880; www.tomsdimsumpa. com; 59 N 11th St; mains $8-12; ⊙11am-10:30pm, to 11pm Fri-Sun) Tasty buns and soup dumplings in a casual spot near the bus station.

Zahav MIDDLE EASTERN $$
(Map p156; ☎215-625-8800; www.zahavrestau rant.com; 237 St James Pl, off Dock St; mains $15, tasting menus $45-54; ⊙5-10pm Sun-Thu, to 11pm Fri & Sat) Sophisticated 'modern Israeli' cuisine, drawing primarily from North African, Persian and Levantine kitchens. Pick your own mezze and grills, or go for the Mesibah ('Party Time') tasting menu. In a slightly incongruous building on Society Hill Towers grounds. No reservations accepted.

White Dog Cafe AMERICAN $$
(☎215-386-9224; www.whitedog.com; 3420 Sansom St; dinner mains $18-29; ⊙11:30am-9:30pm Mon-Fri, 10am-10pm Sat, 10am-9pm Sun) If the dozen Boston terriers on the wall seem incongruous with the food, don't worry: this place has been serving farm-to-table since 1983. Come here for your truffles and artisan cheeses, peak summer tomatoes and plenty more. Yes, the Greyhound is the signature drink. Need you have asked?

CLASSIC PHILLY FLAVOUR

Philadelphians argue over the nuances of cheesesteaks – hot sandwiches of thin-sliced, griddle-cooked beef on a chewy roll – like biblical scholars parsing Deuteronomy. What a visitor most needs to know is how to order. First say the kind of cheese – prov (provolone), American (melty yellow) or whiz (molten orange Cheez Whiz) then wit (with) or widdout (without), referring to fried onions: 'Prov wit,' for instance, or 'whiz widdout.'

Pat's King of Steaks (☎215-468-1546; www.patskingofsteaks.com; 1237 E Passyunk Ave; sandwiches $8; ⊙24hr) Pat's invented the cheesesteak, way back in 1930.

Jim's Steaks (Map p152; ☎215-928-1911; www.jimssouthstreet.com; 400 South St; sandwiches $10; ⊙10am-1am, to 3am Fri & Sat, from 11am Sun) 'Pizza steak' – topped with tomato sauce – is an option, as are hoagies (cold-cut sandwiches on long rolls). More comfortable than most, with indoor seats and beer.

Tony Luke's (☎215-551-5725; www.tonylukes.com; 39 E Oregon Ave; sandwiches $7-11; ⊙6am-midnight Mon-Thu, to 2am Fri & Sat, 11am-8pm Sun) Famous for its roast pork sandwich with provolone and broccoli rabe (a slightly bitter leafy, cruciferous vegetable also known as rapini). A veggie-only version is great too.

John's Roast Pork (☎215-463-1951; www.johnsroastpork.com; 14 E Snyder Ave; sandwiches $8-12; ⊙9am-7pm Mon-Sat) Located far south of the city next to a factory, this classic, cash-only joint has been on this corner since 1930.

★**Cuba Libre**　　　CARIBBEAN $$
(Map p156; ☎215-627-0666; www.cubalibrerestaurant.com; 10 S 2nd St; mains $15-24; ⊙11:30am-10pm Mon-Wed, 11:30am-11pm Thu, 11:30am-2am Fri, 10:30am-2am Sat, 10am-2am Sun) Colonial America couldn't feel further away at this festive, multistory Cuban eatery and rum bar. The creative and inspired menu includes shrimp ceviche, Cuban sandwiches, guava-spiced barbecue and excellent mojitos. A $43 tasting menu lets you get a variety of the specialties – it's not per person, so you can share. The check even comes in a cigar box.

Baril　　　FRENCH $$$
(Map p152; ☎267-687-2608; www.barilphilly.com; 267 S 19th St; mains from $25, prix fixe $35; ⊙4pm-2am Tue-Fri, from 10:30am Sat & Sun) This Rittenhouse Sq dining option has lovely *haute* French fare, creatively presented in a rustic, wood-heavy setting. Do not miss the chance to choose from the cheese cart, and the owner or staff will happily suggest a perfect wine. Handcrafted cocktails are sublime.

★**Morimoto**　　　JAPANESE $$$
(Map p152; ☎215-413-9070; www.morimotorestaurant.com; 723 Chestnut St; mains $30; ⊙11:30am-2pm, 5-10pm Mon-Thu, to midnight Fri & Sat, 5-10pm Sun) Morimoto is high-concept and heavily stylized, from a dining room that looks like a futuristic aquarium to a menu of globe-spanning influence and eclectic combinations. A meal at this *Iron Chef* regular's restaurant is a theatrical experience. If price isn't a problem, opt for the *omakase* – the chef's special.

★**Gran Caffè L'Aquila**　　　ITALIAN $$$
(Map p152; ☎215-568-5600; http://grancaffelaquila.com; 1716 Chestnut St; mains $18-30; ⊙7am-10pm Mon-Thu, 7am-11pm Fri, 8am-11pm Sat, 8am-10pm Sun, bar open 1 hr later) Mamma mia, this is impressive Italian food. Not only are the flavors everything you could ask for, one of the owners is an award-winning gelato maker and the 2nd floor has its own gelato factory. Some of the main courses even have savory gelato as a garnish. Coffee is house-roasted and the dapper waitstaff are eager to please.

The three co-owners came here after their village in Italy was destroyed by a 2014 earthquake. Reservations are highly recommended if you want to avoid a line..

☕ Drinking & Nightlife

1 Tippling Place　　　BAR
(Map p152; ☎215-665-0456; http://1tpl.com; 2006 Chestnut St; cocktails $8-15; ⊙5pm-2am Tue-Sun) Whether you pull up a seat at the bar or find a cozy couch to relax on, this spot has everything you could want in a craft cocktail bar. Extra points if you can spot more than

four typos on the menu. Note: be aware this place looks closed even when it isn't, with minimal (read: zero) outdoor signage.

★ Monk's Cafe
BAR
(Map p152; ☎ 215-545-7005; www.monkscafe. com; 264 S 16th St; ☺ 11:30am-2am, kitchen to 1am) Hop fans crowd this mellow, wood-paneled place for Belgian and American craft beers on tap. There's also a reasonably priced food menu, with typical mussels-and-fries as well as a daily vegan special. For those needing assistance with the selection, a 'Beer Bible' is available.

R2L Restaurant
LOUNGE
(Map p152; ☎ 215-564-5337; https://r2lrestaurant.com; 50 S 16th St; cocktails $15; ☺ lounge 4pm-1am Mon-Thu, 4pm-2am Fri-Sat, 4-11pm Sun) The view, the view, the view. And did we mention the view? This spot serves up the nightscape of Philly along with whatever is on the menu. Craft cocktails are smooth and balanced, but even tap water would seem ritzy when you're looking out at the cosmos of lights below you. Come here for that special event with that special someone.

★ Trestle Inn
BAR
(Map p152; ☎ 267-239-0290; www.thetrestleinn. com; 339 N 11th St; ☺ 5pm-1am Wed-Thu, 5pm-2am Fri & Sat) On a dark corner in the so-called 'Eraserhood' (the semi-industrial zone where director David Lynch found inspiration for his film *Eraserhead*), this classed-up old dive has craft cocktails and go-go dancers.

Double Knot
BAR
(Map p152; ☎ 215-631-3868; www.double knotphilly.com; 120 S 13th St; cocktails $10-15; ☺ 7am-midnight) Japanese-inspired, this is one of the few places in Philly that serves sake properly (poured into an overflowing cup inside a wooden *masu* container). Double Knot also makes great craft cocktails and has a delicious food menu as well. It's crowded, but the stylish modern decor and friendly service make it a fun spot to grab a bite and late-night drink or two.

Tavern on Camac
GAY & LESBIAN
(Map p152; ☎ 215-545-0900; www.tavernoncamac.com; 243 S Camac St; ☺ piano bar 4pm-2am, restaurant 6pm-1am Wed-Mon, club 9pm-2am Tue-Sun) One of the longest-established gay bars in Philly, with a piano bar and restaurant downstairs. Upstairs is a small club with a dance floor, called Ascend; Wednesday is

ladies' night, Friday and Saturday have DJs. And don't overlook Showtune Sunday.

Dirty Franks
BAR
(Map p152; ☎ 215-732-5010; www.dirtyfranksbar. com; 347 S 13th St; DF special $2.50; ☺ 11am-2am) The regulars at this place call it an 'institution' with some irony. Like many Philly dives, it offers the 'citywide special,' a shot of Jim Beam and a can of PBR for $2.50. Need cheaper? Try the 'DF Shelf of Shame' for just two bucks!

☆ Entertainment

PhilaMOCA
PERFORMING ARTS
(Philadelphia Mausoleum of Contemporary Art; Map p152; ☎ 267-519-9651; www.philamoca.org; 531 N 12th St) A former tombstone store, then producer Diplo's studios, this eclectic space now hosts movies, live shows, art, comedy and more.

Wanamaker Organ
LIVE MUSIC
(Macy's; Map p152; ☎ 484-684 7250; www.wan amakerorgan.com; 1300 Market St; ☺ concerts noon Mon-Sat, also 5:30pm Mon, Tue, Thu & Sat, 7pm Wed & Fri) Back when Macy's was Wanamaker's, owner John Wanamaker installed this enormous pipe organ in 1909, with free concerts to delight shoppers and make them linger. The tradition lives on, with classical and pop tunes filling the department store's central atrium a couple of times a day. The store staff are less than enthusiastic, but it's a treat for visitors.

Johnny Brenda's
LIVE MUSIC
(☎ 215-739-9684; www.johnnybrendas.com; 1201 N Frankford Ave; tickets $10-15; ☺ kitchen 11am-1am, showtimes vary; Ⓜ Girard) The hub of Fishtown/Northern Liberties' indie-rock scene, this is a great small venue with a balcony, plus a solid restaurant and bar with equally indie-minded beers.

🛍 Shopping

AIA Bookstore & Design Center
BOOKS
(Map p152; ☎ 215-569-3188; www.aiabookstore. com; 1218 Arch St; ☺ 10am-6pm Mon-Sat, noon-5pm Sun) Run by the American Institute of Architects, this bookstore has creative children's toys, such as building-related Lego sets and other unusual design-related gifts. Books about architecture, too as if that's not obvious.

Omoi Zakka Shop
FASHION & ACCESSORIES
(Map p152; ☎ 215-545-0963; http://omoionline. com; 1608 Pine St; ☺ noon-7pm Mon, 11am-7pm

Tue-Sat, noon-6pm Sun) Get your inner Japanophile on with this shop dedicated to all things Japanese. Fashion items, books, clothes, housewares, stationery and more, all with a Japan-inspired sense for cuteness or good design.

Shane Confectionery FOOD & DRINKS
(Map p156; ☑ 215-922-1048; www.shanecandies. com; 110 Market St; ⊗ 11am-8pm, to 10pm Fri & Sat) This wonderfully old-school candy shop makes beautiful treats from antique molds, and there's even a historic hot-chocolate operation in the back.

ⓘ Information

Independence Visitor Center (Map p156; ☑ 800-537-7676; www.phlvisitorcenter.com; 599 Market St; ⊗ 8:30am-6pm Sep-May, 8:30am-7pm Jun-Aug) Run by the Independence Visitor Center Corps and the National Park Service, the center covers the national park and all of the sights in Philadelphia.

Sister Cities Park Visitor Center (Map p152; ☑ 267-514-4760; www.phlvisitorcenter.com; 200 N 18th St; ⊗ 9:30am-5:30pm Mon-Sat, to 5pm Sun May-Sep) Near the fountain at Logan Sq, this seasonal visitor center sells tickets and gives info on city attractions.

ⓘ Getting There & Away

AIR

Philadelphia International Airport (PHL; ☑ 215-937-6937; www.phl.org; 8000 Essington Ave; ⓡ Airport Line), 10 miles southwest of Center City, is a hub for American Airlines, and served by direct international flights.

BUS

Greyhound (www.greyhound.com), Peter Pan Bus Lines (www.peterpanbus.com) and NJ Transit (www.njtransit.com) all depart from the **central bus station** (Map p152; 1001 Filbert St) downtown, near the convention center; Greyhound goes nationwide, Peter Pan focuses on the northeast and NJ Transit gets you to New Jersey. The former two offer cheaper online fares; Greyhound to Washington, DC, for example, can be $16 (3½ hours).

From near 30th St Station, **Megabus** (Map p152; http://us.megabus.com; JFK Blvd & N 30th St) serves major cities in the northeast, and Toronto. For NYC and Boston, Greyhound subsidiary **Bolt Bus** (Map p152; ☑ 877-265-8287; www.boltbus.com; JFK Blvd & N 30th St) has the roomiest buses; fares to NYC (2½ hours) can be as low as $9 when booked online.

CAR & MOTORCYCLE

From the north and south, I-95 (Delaware Expwy) follows the east edge of the city along the Delaware River, with several exits for Center City. In the north of the city, I-276 (Pennsylvania Turnpike) runs east over the river to connect with the New Jersey Turnpike.

TRAIN

Just west of downtown across the Schuylkill, beautiful neoclassical **30th St Station** (www. amtrak.com; 2955 Market St) is a major hub. From here, Amtrak provides service on its Northeast Corridor line to New York City ($56 to $190, one to 1½ hours) and Boston ($130 to $386, five to 5¾ hours), and Washington, DC ($56 to $216, two hours), as well as to Lancaster ($20 to $40, one hour) and Pittsburgh (from $64, 7½ hours).

A slower but cheaper way to get to NYC is on regional SEPTA (www.septa.org) to Trenton ($9, 50 minutes), then NJ Transit (www.njtransit. com) to NYC's Penn Station ($16.75, 1½ hours).

ⓘ Getting Around

SEPTA (www.septa.org) operates Philadelphia's transit system, including the Airport Line train ($8, 25 minutes, every 30 minutes), which stops in University City and Center City. A taxi to the center costs a flat fare of $28.50. There's also a one-day Independence Pass (individual/family $12/29) that offers unlimited rides on all buses, rail and subways, including the Airport Line.

Downtown, it's barely 2 miles between the Delaware and the Schuylkill, so you can walk most places. To rest your feet or travel further afield, choose from a web of SEPTA buses, two subway lines and a trolley (fare $2.25). Purchase the stored-value Key card for discounted fares. Market St is the main artery – hop on buses here to cross the center, or go underground to take the trolley to University City. In high tourist seasons, the purple Phlash (www.ridephillyphlash.com) bus makes a loop around major tourist sites. It's $2 a ride or $5 for a day pass; pay on board.

Philly's bike-share system is Indego (www. rideindego.com). Walk-up rates are $4 for 30 minutes; a 30-day membership is a steal at $15, but you must order the key ahead of time.

Cabs, especially around Center City, are easy to hail. The flag drop or fare upon entry is $2.70, then $2.30 per mile or portion thereof. All licensed taxis have GPS and most accept credit cards. Uber and Lyft also operate here.

Pennsylvania Dutch Country

Lancaster County and the broader area roughly between Reading and the Susquehanna River is the center of the so-called Pennsylvania Dutch community. These are myriad religious orders and cultures, with Germanic roots and established here since the 18th century. Amish, Mennonites and German Baptist (Brethren) are the best known. One common cultural thread: all are devoted to various degrees of low-tech plain living.

Somewhat paradoxically, this simple life, with its picturesque horse-drawn buggies, and ox teams tilling fields, attracts busloads of visitors and has spawned an astoundingly kitschy tourist industry. If you get onto the back roads, however, you can appreciate the quiet these religious orders have preserved.

Small settlements in the area include teeny Christiana and train-mad Strasburg. Lititz is home to Wilbur Chocolates (what locals prefer to Hershey's), and America's first pretzel factory, Sturgis. Ephrata is the headquarters of Ten Thousand Villages, a massive Mennonite-run fair-trade imports store with branches all over.

◎ Sights

★ Railroad Museum of Pennsylvania
MUSEUM

(☏717-687-8628; www.rrmuseumpa.org; 300 Gap Rd, Ronks; adult/child $10/8; ◷9am-5pm Mon-Sat, noon-5pm Sun Apr-Oct, closed Mon Nov-Mar; ♿) Set over nearly 18 acres, the Railroad Museum of Pennsylvania has 100 gigantic mechanical marvels to climb around and admire. Combo tickets are available for the Strasburg Railroad (☏866-725-9666; www.strasburgrailroad.com; 301 Gap Rd, Ronks; coach class adult/child $15/8; ◷times vary; ♿) across the road.

★ National Toy Train Museum
MUSEUM

(☏717-687-8976; www.nttmuseum.org; 300 Paradise Lane, Ronks; adult/child $7/4; ◷10am-5pm May-Oct, hours vary Nov-Apr; ♿) The push-button interactive dioramas are so up-to-date and clever (such as a 'drive-in movie' that's a live video of kids working the trains), and the walls are packed with so many gleaming railcars, that you can't help but feel a bit of that childlike Christmas-morning wonder.

Even if you're not a guest, you can stop at the Red Caboose Motel (☏717-687-5000; www.redcaboosemotel.com; 312 Paradise Lane, Ronks; s/d from $95/130; ❊✸) next door to the museum – you can climb the silo in back for wonderful views (50¢) and kids can enjoy a small petting zoo.

Landis Valley Museum
MUSEUM

(☏717-569-0401; www.landisvalleymuseum.org; 2451 Kissel Hill Rd; adult/child $12/8; ◷9am-5pm Tue-Sat, noon-5pm Sun Mar-Dec, reduced hours Jan & Feb) Based on an 18th-century village, this open-air museum is the best way to get an overview of early PA Dutch culture, and Mennonites in particular. Costumed staff are on hand to demonstrate tin-smithing, for instance, and there's a tavern, a gun shop and a beautiful crafts exhibit.

🛏 Sleeping & Eating

Cork Factory
BOUTIQUE HOTEL $$

(☏717-735-2075; www.corkfactoryhotel.com; 480 New Holland Ave, Suite 3000; r from $190; P❊✸❀) An abandoned brick behemoth now houses this stylish hotel, with 93 posh rooms. It's a short drive from downtown.

★ Maison
EUROPEAN $$$

(☏717-293-5060; www.maisonlancaster.com; 230 N Prince St; mains $26-30; ◷5-11pm Wed-Sat; ✐) A husband-and-wife team runs this homey but meticulous place downtown, giving local farm products a rustic Italian-French treatment: pork braised in milk, housemade rabbit sausage, fried squash blossoms or handmade gnocchi, depending on the season.

★ Lancaster Brewing Co
PUB FOOD $$

(☏717-391-6258; www.lancasterbrewing.com; 302 N Plum St; mains $16-24; ◷11:30am-9:30pm; ♿) This brewery, established in 1995, is a local favorite. The restaurant serves hearty but sophisticated food – lamb chops with tzatziki, say – and housemade sausages at tables with copper-clad tops and great views of the brewing tanks. You can't beat specials such as $5 all-you-can-eat wings and $6 beer-tasting flights.

❶ Getting There & Away

Lancaster lies at the heart of a squished 'H' shape made by Rte 30, Rte 283 and Rte 222. Buses head to Philly and Pittsburgh, but driving your own vehicle is the best option for sightseeing. Head east from Lancaster on Rte 30 to reach Strasburg.

Pennsylvania Wilds

North-central Pennsylvania, known as 'the Wilds,' is largely deep forest, with an occasional regal building or grand mansion, remnants of a time when lumber, coal and oil brought wealth to this now little-visited patch of the state. Several museums (in **Titusville**, **Bradford** and **Galeton**) tell the boom and bust story. Since the bust, this swath of 12 counties has reverted to its wild state; much of the area is national forest or state park land.

Scenic Rte 6 cuts through east–west, with the tiny college town of **Mansfield** as an eastern gateway. Just west of here, **Pine Creek Gorge** cuts south; its deeper end (1450ft) is down near Waterville, but it's more accessible, with good views and trails along the rim and down into the canyon, on the north end at **Colton Point State Park** (www.visitpaparks.com; 927 Colton Rd, Wellsboro; ⊙dawn-dusk). Follow signs outside the pretty, gas-lamp-lit town of **Wellsboro**.

⊙ Sights

★**Cherry Springs State Park** STATE PARK
(☑814-435-5011; http://dcnr.state.pa.us; 4639 Cherry Springs Rd, Coudersport; ⊙24hr) Considered one of the best places for stargazing east of the Mississippi, this mountaintop state park seems to have plenty of space, but be sure to book well ahead in July and August, when the Milky Way is almost directly overhead. First-timers will need to pay a one-time $5 additional fee (not per day).

Leonard Harrison State Park STATE PARK
(☑570-724-3061; www.visitpaparks.com; 4797 Rte 660, Wellsboro; ⊙park dawn-dusk, visitor center 10am-4:30pm Mon-Thu, to 6:30pm Fri-Sun) This park has full views of the Pine Creek Gorge, aka the Grand Canyon of PA, with trails that descend 800ft down to the creek below. A visitor center has modest displays of local fauna, there are toilets, and a viewing deck makes this side more accessible for people not planning to hike. For the undeveloped side go to Colton Point State Park instead.

★**Kinzua Bridge Skywalk** BRIDGE
(☑814-778-5467; www.visitpaparks.com; 1721 Lindholm Rd, Mt Jewett; ⊙skywalk 8am-dusk, visitor center 8am-6pm) **FREE** The world's tallest viaduct when it was built in 1882, this 301ft-high bridge was rebuilt in steel in 1900 – but then partially collapsed in 2003, when it was hit by an F-1 tornado. The remaining piece, jutting out into the air, is now an observation deck, with an impressive and perhaps unnerving view over the ruined steel piers into the valley below.

🛏 Sleeping & Eating

Mansfield Inn MOTEL **$**
(☑570-662-2136; www.mansfieldinn.com; 26 S Main St, Mansfield; r from $70; P🐾❄🛜) There may be more charming B&Bs deeper in the PA Wilds, but this well-maintained 24-room motel is hard to beat for straight-ahead value.

★**Night & Day Coffee Cafe** CAFE **$**
(☑570-662-1143; http://nightanddaycoffee.wixsite. com/cafe; 2 N Main St, Mansfield; sandwiches $7-10; ⊙7am-7pm Mon-Fri, to 5pm Sat, 8am-5pm Sun; 🐾) Well worth detouring for, the Night & Day Coffee Cafe proudly claims to be enriching the neighborhood one latte at a time, and it's doing a good job of it. Boutique coffees, great chai, and a wide selection of specialty salads and sandwiches make for a perfect breakfast or a great lunch.

Pittsburgh

Set between the Monongahela and Allegheny Rivers and a mountain ridge called Mt Washington, Pittsburgh has a unique character that is evident from the moment you arrive. Juxtaposed with the rumbling freight trains and the iconic bridges are the *Bladerunner*-esque self-driving Uber vehicles, scanning the roads with spinning Lidar scanners. Experiencing periods of boom and bust since its founding, the city is in a boom now (real estate that used to sell for $30,000 now goes for $300,000), and it's a fun place to visit, with top-notch museums, great gardens and parks, and amazing food, from humble to haute. Indeed, the once-struggling city has rediscovered itself as a food and brew mecca.

Carnegie is the biggest name in Pittsburgh – Scottish-born Andrew modernized steel production, and his legacy is still synonymous with the city and its many cultural and educational institutions. Second-biggest: Heinz, of ketchup fame, a company established here in 1869.

⊙ Sights & Activities

Points of interest in Pittsburgh are scattered in every neighborhood, and because of the hills, it's difficult to walk between them. Bike, taxi or bus (or light rail in some areas) are the best ways to span suburbs. You can also try your hand at e-reserving one of those futuristic, self-driving Ubers.

★ Andy Warhol Museum   MUSEUM

(☑412-237-8300; www.warhol.org; 117 Sandusky St; adult/child $20/10, 5-10pm Fri $10/5; ☺10am-5pm Tue-Thu, Sat & Sun, to 10pm Fri) This six-story museum celebrates Pittsburgh's coolest native son, who moved to NYC, got a nose job and made himself famous with pop art. The exhibits start with Warhol's earliest drawings and commercial illustrations, and include a simulated Velvet Underground happening, a DIY 'screen test' and pieces of Warhol's extensive knickknack collection. Cans of inflatable Campbell's soup are for sale.

★ Duquesne Incline   FUNICULAR

(☑412-381-1665; www.duquesneincline.org; one way adult/child $2.50/1.25; ☺5:30am-12:45am Mon-Sat, 7am-12:45am Sun) This nifty funicular, and its **Monongahela Incline** (5 Grandview Ave; one way adult/child $2.50/1.25; ☺5:30am-12:45am Mon-Sat, 7am-12:45am Sun) twin down the road, both built in the late 19th century, are Pittsburgh icons, zipping up the steep slope of Mt Washington every five to 10 minutes. They provide commuters a quick connection, and give visitors great city views, especially at night. You can make a loop, going up one, walking along aptly named Grandview Ave (about 1 mile, or take bus 40) and coming down the other.

If you ride just one, make it the Duquesne (du-*kane*). At the top, you can pay 50¢ to see the gears and cables at work.

Frick Art & Historical Center   MUSEUM

(☑412-371-0600; www.thefrickpittsburgh.org; 7227 Reynolds St; ☺10am-5pm Tue-Thu, Sat & Sun, to 9pm Fri) FREE Henry Clay Frick, of Manhattan's Frick Museum fame, built his steel fortune in Pittsburgh. This Frick shows a small art collection (including beautiful medieval icons), plus his cars. For more art and general splendor, join a tour (adult/child $12/6) of Clayton, the family mansion. The cafe here is excellent; reserve ahead.

Carnegie Museums   MUSEUM

(☑412-622-3131; www.carnegiemuseums.org; 4400 Forbes Ave; adult/child both museums $20/12; ☺10am-5pm Mon & Wed-Sat, noon-5pm Sun; ☺) Founded in 1895, these neighboring institutions are both tremendous troves of knowledge. The **Carnegie Museum of Art** has European treasures and an excellent architectural collection, while the **Carnegie Museum of Natural History** features a complete Tyrannosaurus Rex skeleton and beautiful old dioramas.

Cathedral of Learning   TOWER

(☑412-624-6001; www.tour.pitt.edu; 4200 Fifth Ave; ☺9am-4pm Mon-Sat, 11am-4pm Sun) FREE Soaring 42 stories, this Gothic tower at the center of the University of Pittsburgh is a city landmark. Visit to see the delightful Nationality Rooms, themed classrooms ranging from Russian to Syrian to African. Audio tours are available on Saturdays and Sundays (adult/child $4/2).

Center for PostNatural History   MUSEUM

(☑412-223-7698; www.postnatural.org; 4913 Penn Ave; admission by donation; ☺noon-4pm Sun) FREE 'Postnatural history,' according to the artist founder of this quirky museum, is the field of plants and animals designed by humankind. Learn all about spider-silk-making goats, selective breeding and more. Probably not your best first date spot, but definitely a fun and unconventional place to learn about all things *human*-ipulated.

Pittsburgh Glass Center   ART

(☑412-365-2145; www.pittsburghglasscenter.org; 5472 Penn Ave; ☺10am-7pm Mon-Thu, to 4pm Fri-Sun) See a variety of glass-making techniques and even try your hand at making something yourself in a demo. Or take an actual class; the PGC offers everything from newbie-level to advanced (prices vary).

'Burgh Bits & Bites   FOOD & DRINK

(☑412-901-7150; www.burghfoodtour.com; tours $42) These two-hour food tours through various neighborhoods are a fun way to discover the city's unique ethnic eats. The Strip District tour is the most popular, but Bits & Bites also visits Bloomfield, Brookline, Lawrenceville, South Side and more.

Pittsburgh History & Landmarks Foundation   WALKING

(☑412-471-5808; www.phlf.org; tours free-$20) This group runs a free walking tour from Market Sq on Fridays at noon, among other excursions.

🛏 Sleeping

Residence Inn by Marriott North Shore   HOTEL $$

(☑855-239-9485; www.marriott.com; 574 W General Robinson St; d/ste from $190/225; P☺ ✳@� ☺) This newly renovated chain-hotel option has a pool, a fitness center, free breakfasts, and rooms that feel like mansions. It's also well located: a quick zip over the bridges to the downtown, or within walking distance of some of the North Side areas and attractions. Note that it can be a zoo if there's a game at Heinz Field or the Pirates are playing.

★ **Priory Hotel** INN $$
(☑ 412-231-3338; www.thepriory.com; 614 Pressley St; s/d/ste from $115/210/270; P ❋ ✿) The monks had it good when this was still a Catholic monastery: spacious rooms, high ceilings, a fireplace in the parlor. Breakfast, with its pastries and cold cuts, is reminiscent of a European hostel. It's on the North Side, in the historic-but-scruffy Deutschtown area. The tiny **Monk's Bar** just off the lobby is open 5pm to 11pm daily, perfect for an evening tipple.

★ **Omni William Penn Hotel** HOTEL $$$
(☑ 412-281-7100; www.omnihotels.com; 530 William Penn Pl; r $215-540; P ❋ ⊖ ✿) Pittsburgh's stateliest old hotel, built by Henry Frick, has a cavernous lobby, with luxury suites that were remodeled in 2016. The great public spaces give it a sense of grandeur that some luxury hotels lack. Worth booking if you have the money...or can find it at a discount.

✗ Eating

E Carson St on the South Side has the highest concentration of restaurants, but the Strip District comes a close second. As in many categories, Lawrenceville has the most up-and-coming activity. Catering to a large Catholic population, many Pittsburgh restaurants serve fish on Fridays, and fried-fish sandwiches are especially popular – despite the city's lack of coastline, they're pretty tasty too!

Pittsburgh Public Market MARKET
(☑ 412-281-4505; www.pittsburghpublicmarket. org; 2401 Penn Ave; ⊙10am-4pm Wed-Fri & Sun, 9am-5pm Sat) This giant indoor market caters to the need for downtown to have easy access to fresh produce, meats, cheeses and other local products. Note that many vendors are also open on Monday and Tuesday as well.

Conflict Kitchen FAST FOOD $
(☑ 412-802-8417; www.conflictkitchen.org; 221 Schenley Dr; mains $8-14; ⊙11am-6pm Mon-Sat) This takeout stand near the Cathedral of Learning reinvents itself periodically, cooking food from a country the USA has issues

with. So far it has represented Afghani, Palestinian, Cuban and Native American cuisines, among other options.

★ **La Prima** CAFE $
(☑ 412-281-1922; www.laprima.com; 205 21st St; pastries $2-4; ⊙6am-4pm Mon-Wed, to 7pm Thu, to 5pm Fri & Sat, 7am-4pm Sun) Great Italian coffee and pastries have people lined up out the door at peak times. The 'Almond Mele' is the scrumptious signature sweet, but it has a range of other yummy treats (*sfogliatelle*, tarts, cookies etc). If you speak Italian you can enjoy the daily quote, written on the green chalkboard each morning.

Zenith VEGAN $
(☑ 412-481-4833; www.zenithpgh.com; 86 S 26th St; mains $7-10; ⊙11:30am-8:30pm Thu-Sat, 11am-2:30pm Sun; ✗) All meals are vegan here, though cheese is optional. Eating here is like eating in an antique shop, as everything, including the Formica tables, is for sale. The buffet Sunday brunch ($11.50) draws a great community of regulars.

★ **Bar Marco** ITALIAN $$
(☑ 412-471-1900; www.barmarcopgh.com; 2216 Penn Ave; mains $15-26; ⊙5-11pm Tue-Fri, 10am-3pm & 5-11pm Sat & Sun) A Strip District favorite, this is one of the city's more sophisticated kitchens, with an excellent brunch, too. Cocktails are unique, or try the bartender's suggestion based on what types of drinks you enjoy. The refreshing no-tipping policy means the staff are appropriately compensated in a fair and equitable way.

Legume FUSION $$$
(☑ 412-621-2700; www.legumebistro.com; mains $23-36, 3-course tasting menu $38; ⊙4:30pm-midnight Mon-Sat) Excellent meats and fish here, with a farm-to-table mindset and a menu that changes daily. If it's available, try the stinging-nettle soup – partly because where else can you try stinging nettles, but mostly because it's out of this world.

★ **Paris 66** FRENCH $$$
(☑ 412-404-8166; www.paris66bistro.com; 6018 Centre Ave; dinner mains $26-33; ⊙11am-10pm Mon-Thu, to 11pm Fri & Sat, 10am-3pm Sun) Don't think you can get away with saying *Merci* here and impressing the waitstaff; they all speak fluent *français*. This is top-end French at its best, in a cozy, bistro-style setting. Blink and you'll think you're in France.

Drinking & Entertainment

Church Brew Works
MICROBREWERY
(☑412-688-8200; www.churchbrew.com; 3525 Liberty Ave; ☺11:30am-9pm Sun-Thu, to 11pm Fri & Sat) There are some who put drunkenness next to godliness, and they probably invented Church Brew Works. Gleaming and shining, giant brewery vats sit in what was once the pulpit. If you think this is sacrilegious, you'll want to skip this place. Although, of course, many a great Belgian beer was proudly brewed by highly religious monks.

Wigle Whiskey
DISTILLERY
(☑412-224-2827; www.wiglewhiskey.com; 2401 Smallman St; tours from $25; ☺11am-6pm Mon, 10am-6pm Tue-Sat, to 4pm Sun) This family-owned craft distillery in a brick warehouse in the Strip gives tours on Saturdays (and some Fridays) and has inexpensive sample flights ($10) of the many libations. Whiskey is a top choice, but there's also gin, vodka, bitters and even a housemade absinthe.

Spice Island Tea House
TEAHOUSE
(☑412-687-8821; www.spiceislandteahouse.com; 253 Atwood St; ☺11:30am-8:45pm Mon-Thu, to 9:45pm Fri & Sat) If you fancy sipping a quiet cuppa (tea infusions $3.50 to $5.50) while your friend has a cocktail, this is the spot to come. Alongside a number of delectable teas it also serves Southeast Asian fusion food.

★Allegheny Wine Mixer
WINE BAR
(☑412-252-2337; www.alleghenywinemixer.com; 5326 Butler St; ☺5pm-midnight Tue-Thu, to 1am Fri-Sun) All the perks of a high-end wine bar – great list, smart staff, tasty nibbles – in the comfort of a neighborhood dive.

Rex Theater
LIVE MUSIC
(☑412-381-6811; www.rextheatre.com; 1602 E Carson St) A converted movie theater, this South Side favorite hosts touring jazz, rock and indie bands.

★Elks Lodge
LIVE MUSIC
(☑412-321-1834; www.elks.org; 400 Cedar Ave; cover $5; ☺bluegrass 8pm Wed, big band 7pm 1st & 3rd Thu) Find out why Pittsburgh is known as the Paris of Appalachia at the Elks' Banjo Night, when the stage is packed with players and the audience sings along to all the bluegrass classics. Also hosts a big-band night twice a month, with dance classes first. On the North Side in Deutschtown.

ℹ Information

VisitPITTSBURGH Main Branch (☑412-281-7711; www.visitpittsburgh.com; 120 Fifth Ave, Suite 2800; ☺8:30am-4:40pm Mon-Fri) Publishes the *Official Visitors Guide* and provides maps and tourist advice.

ℹ Getting There & Away

AIR
Pittsburgh International Airport (☑412-472-3525; www.flypittsburgh.com; 1000 Airport Blvd), 18 miles west of downtown, has direct connections to Europe, Canada and major US cities via a slew of airlines.

BUS
The **Greyhound bus station** (Grant Street Transportation Center; ☑412-392-6514; www.greyhound.com; 55 11th St), at the far edge of the Strip District, has frequent buses to Philadelphia (from $20, six to seven hours), NYC (from $30, 8½ to 11 hours) and Chicago, IL ($72, 11 to 14 hours).

CAR & MOTORCYCLE
Pittsburgh is accessible via I-76 or I-79 from the west and I-70 from the east. It's about a six-hour drive from NYC and about three hours from Buffalo.

TRAIN
Pittsburgh has a magnificent old train station – and **Amtrak** (☑800-872-7245; www.amtrak.com; 1100 Liberty Ave) drops you off in a dismal modern building behind it. Services run to Philadelphia (from $64, 7½ hours), NYC (from $97, 9½ hours), Chicago ($90, 10 hours) and Washington, DC ($52, eight hours).

ℹ Getting Around

PortAuthority (www.portauthority.org) provides public transport around Pittsburgh, including the 28X Airport Flyer ($2.75, 40 minutes, every 30 minutes 4:30am to midnight) from the airport to downtown and Oakland. A taxi from the airport costs about $40 (not including tip) to downtown. Various shuttles also make downtown runs for around $25 per person.

Driving in Pittsburgh can be frustrating – roads end with no warning or deposit you suddenly on bridges. Parking is scarce downtown. Where possible, use the extensive bus network, which includes a fast express busway (routes beginning with P). There is also a limited light-rail system, the T, useful for the South Side. Rides on the T downtown are free; other in-city fares are $2.50, and $1 for a transfer.

New England

Why Go?

The history of New England is the history of America. It's the Pilgrims who came ashore at Plymouth Rock and the minutemen who fought for American independence. It's the ponderings of Ralph Waldo Emerson and the protests of Harriet Beecher Stowe. It's hundreds of years of poets and philosophers, progressive thinkers who dared to dream and dared to do. It is generations of immigrants who have shaped New England into the dynamic region that it is today.

For outdoor adventure, the region undulates with the rolling hills and rocky peaks of the ancient Appalachian Mountains. Plus, nearly 5000 miles of coastline make for unlimited opportunities for fishing, swimming, surfing and sailing. Those are surefire ways to work up an appetite. Fortunately, New England is a bounty of epicurean delights: pancakes drenched in maple syrup; just-picked fruit and sharp cheddar cheese; and – most importantly – sublimely fresh seafood that is the hallmark of this region.

Best Places to Eat

➡ TJ Buckley's (p222)

➡ Simon Pearce Restaurant (p225)

➡ Captain Daniel Packer Inne (p216)

➡ Row 34 (p183)

➡ birch (p207)

Best Places to Sleep

➡ Liberty Hotel (p182)

➡ Carpe Diem (p195)

➡ Attwater (p210)

➡ Hopkins Inn (p215)

➡ Ale House Inn (p232)

When to Go
Boston

May–Jun Uncrowded sights and lightly trodden trails. Whale-watching begins.

Jul–Aug Top tourist season with summer festivals and warmer ocean weather.

Sep–Oct New England's blazing foliage peaks from mid-September to mid-October.

History

When the first European settlers arrived in the New World, they found about 100,000 Native American inhabitants, mostly Algonquians, organized into small regional tribes. The northern tribes were solely hunter-gatherers, while the southern tribes hunted and practiced slash-and-burn agriculture, growing corn, squash and beans.

In 1602 English Captain Bartholomew Gosnold landed at Cape Cod and sailed north to Maine; but it wasn't until 1614 that Captain John Smith, who charted the region's coastline for King James I, christened the land 'New England'. With the arrival of the Pilgrims at Plymouth in 1620, European settlement began in earnest. Over the next century the colonies expanded, often at the expense of the indigenous people.

Although subjects of the British Crown, New Englanders governed themselves with legislative councils and they came to view their affairs as separate from those of England. In the 1770s King George III imposed a series of taxes to pay for England's involvement in costly wars. The colonists, unrepresented in the British parliament, protested under the slogan 'no taxation without representation'. Attempts to squash the protests eventually led to battles at Lexington and Concord, setting off the War for Independence. The historic result was the birth of the USA in 1776.

Following independence, New England became an economic powerhouse, its harbors booming centers for shipbuilding and trade. New England's famed Yankee Clippers plied ports from China to South America. A thriving whaling industry brought unprecedented wealth to Nantucket and New Bedford. The USA's first water-powered cotton-spinning mill was established in Rhode Island in 1793. No boom lasts forever. By the early 20th century many of the mills had moved south. Today education, finance, biotechnology and tourism are linchpins of the regional economy.

ⓘ Resources

Visit New England (www.visitnewengland.com) Listings for events, sights, restaurants and hotels.

New England Guide (www.boston.com/travel/newengland) Travel tips and itineraries from the *Boston Globe*.

Lonely Planet (www.lonelyplanet.com/usa/new-england) Destination information, hotel bookings, traveler forum and more.

Appalachian Mountain Club (www.outdoors.org) Fantastic resource for hiking, biking, camping, climbing and paddling in New England's great outdoors.

New England Lighthouses (www.lighthouse.cc) A list of lighthouses by state.

MASSACHUSETTS

New England's most populous state, Massachusetts packs in appealing variety, from the sandy beaches of Cape Cod to college towns of the Pioneer Valley to the woodsy hills of the Berkshires. The state's rich history oozes from almost every quarter: discover the shoreline Plymouth, where the Pilgrims first settled in the New World; explore the battlefields in Lexington and Concord, where the first shots of the American Revolution rang out; and wander the cobbled streets and old ports of Salem, Nantucket and New Bedford, where whaling and merchant boats once docked. Modern-day Massachusetts is also diverse and dynamic. Boston is the state's undisputed cultural (and political) capital, but smaller towns like Provincetown and Northampton also offer lively art and music scenes, out and active queer populations and plenty of opportunities to enjoy the great outdoors.

ⓘ Information

Massachusetts Department of Conservation and Recreation (☑ 617-626-1250; www.mass.gov/dcr) Offers camping in 29 state parks.

Boston

Boston's history recalls revolution and transformation, and today it is still among the country's most forward-thinking and barrier-breaking cities.

The arts have thrived in Boston ever since the 19th century, when this cultural capital was dubbed the Athens of America. Certainly, the intellectual elite appreciated their fine paintings and classical music, but they were also dedicated to spreading the cultural wealth, establishing museums, libraries and symphony orchestras for all to enjoy. Today the lucky residents of (and visitors to) Boston benefit from their largesse. These venerable institutions play an integral role on Boston's cultural stage, which has significantly expanded to include dynamic contemporary art, music and theater scenes.

New England Highlights

1 Freedom Trail
(p181) Following the footsteps of Colonial rabble-rousers in Boston.

2 Cape Cod National Seashore
(p196) Romping across the dunes with the wind in your hair.

3 Nantucket Whaling Museum
(p197) Contemplating the history of this 19th-century whaling capital.

4 Tanglewood Music Festival
(p203) Listening to word-class music under the stars in Lenox.

5 Lincoln Woods Trail
(p234) Taking a relaxing hike among brilliant fall foliage in the White Mountains.

6 Mad River Glen
(p226) Anticipating

a black-diamond run from the last single chairlift in the Lower 48 in the Mad River Valley.

7 VINS Nature Center (p225) Catching your breath as raptors swoop past, outside Woodstock.

8 Acadia National Park (p245) Savoring the scenery of New England's only National Park on Mount Desert Island.

9 Lobster Dock (p244) Cracking open a freshly caught and steamed lobster in Boothbay Harbor.

Boston

Lizard Lounge
(0.1mi)

Bryant St

**HARVARD
SQUARE**

8 11

Kirkland St

Washington St

Chestnut St

15

Beacon St

Webster Ave

*Harvard
University* 5

*Harvard Art
4 Museums*

Broadway

Cambridge St

26

Harvard

Smith
20 Campus
Center

Fayette St

CAMBRIDGE

Fulkerson St

John F Kennedy St

*Cambridge Visitor
Information Kiosk*

The
Esplanade

Banks St

Massachusetts Ave

Harvard St

Prospect St

Norfolk St

Hampshire St

28

Franklin St

22

Central

Washington St

Soldiers Field Rd

Western Ave

River St

William St

Main St

Broadway

Perry St

10

Memorial Dr

Pleasant St

Magazine St

Pearl St

Brookline St

Albany St

Ames St

Charles River

Granite St

Waverly St

Vassar St

Memorial Dr

Massachusetts Ave

Babcock
Street

Pleasant
Street

St Paul
Street

Essex St

Commonwealth
Ave

BU Central

Beacon St

*John F Kennedy
National Historic Site
(0.1mi)*

BU West

Egmont St

BU East

Blandford

Kenmore

21

Commonwealth Ave

32

Babcock St

St Paul St

Ivy St

St Marys
Street

Lansdowne St

33

Hynes

30

Parkman St

Hawes Street

Beacon
St

Monmouth St

Fenway

**Fenway
Park** 3

Van Ness St

17
Boylston St

25

FENWAY

Westland Ave

9

13

St Paul Street

Kent Street

Back
Bay
Fens

Brookline Ave

Kilmarnock St

Jersey St

31

Symphony

Coolidge Corner

Longwood Ave

Stearns Rd

19

**Museum of
Fine Arts**
7

Northeastern

BROOKLINE

Longwood

Museum of
Fine Arts

Aspinwall Ave

**Isabella Stewart
Gardner Museum** 6

Huntington Ave

Riverway

Brookline
Village

Fenwood
Road

Mission Park

Brigham
Circle

Longwood
Medical Area

Ruggles

ROXBURY

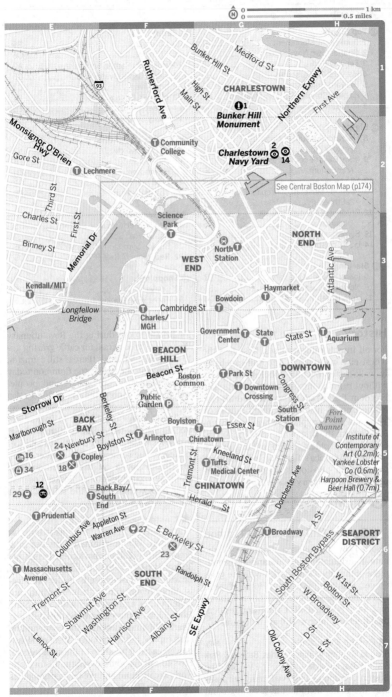

0   1 km
0   0.5 miles

E   **F**   **G**   **H**

Medford St
Bunker Hill St
CHARLESTOWN
Rutherford Ave
High St
Main St
Northern Expwy
First Ave
❶1
Bunker Hill Monument

Monsignor O'Brien Hwy
Gore St
🅣 Lechmere
Third St
🅣 Community College
2
Charlestown Navy Yard
◎ 14

See Central Boston Map (p174)

Charles St
First St
Memorial Dr
Binney St
🅣 Science Park
WEST END
🅣 North Station
NORTH END
Atlantic Ave

🅣 Kendall/MIT
Longfellow Bridge
Cambridge St
🅣 Bowdoin
🅣 Haymarket
Charles/ MGH
🅣 Government Center
🅣 State
State St
🅣 Aquarium

BEACON HILL
Beacon St
Boston Common
🅣 Park St
DOWNTOWN
🅣 Downtown Crossing
Congress St

Storrow Dr
Public Garden 🅿
Marlborough St
BACK BAY
Berkeley St
Newbury St
Boylston St
🅣 Arlington
🅣 Boylston
Essex St
🅣 South Station
Fort Point Channel

🅐16
🅐34
🅧24
🅣 Copley
18 🅧
Chinatown
Tremont St
Kneeland St
🅣 Tufts Medical Center
Dorchester Ave
Institute of Contemporary Art (0.2mi); Yankee Lobster Co (0.6mi); Harpoon Brewery & Beer Hall (0.7mi)

12
29 🅗 🅢
🅣 Back Bay/ South End
CHINATOWN
Herald St

🅣 Prudential
Columbus Ave
Appleton St
Warren Ave 🅧27
E Berkeley St
🅣 Broadway
A St
SEAPORT DISTRICT

🅣 Massachusetts Avenue
23
Randolph St
South Boston Bypass
W 1st St
Bolton St
W Broadway

Tremont St
Shawmut Ave
SOUTH END
Washington Ave
Harrison Ave
Albany St
SE Expwy
Old Colony Ave
D St
E St

Lenox St

E   **F**   **G**   **H**

1
2
3
4
5
6
7

Boston

History

For all intents and purposes, Boston is the oldest city in America. And you can hardly walk a step over its cobblestone streets without running into some historic site. The Freedom Trail winds its way around the city, connecting 16 historically significant sites. These are the very places where history unfolded: from the first public school in America to Boston's oldest church building to sites linked to America's fight for independence from Britain – Boston is, in effect, one enormous outdoor history museum.

◉ Sights

◉ Beacon Hill & Boston Common

Abutted by the Boston Common – the nation's original public park and the centerpiece of the city – and topped with the gold-domed Massachusetts State House, Beacon Hill is the neighborhood most often featured on Boston postcards. The retail and residential streets on Beacon Hill are delightful.

★ **Boston Common** PARK
(Map p174; btwn Tremont, Charles, Beacon & Park Sts; ⊙6am-midnight; ⓟ♿; ⓣPark St) The Boston Common has served many purposes over the years, including as a campground for British troops during the Revolutionary War and as green grass for cattle grazing until the 1830s. Although there is still a grazing ordinance on the books, the Common today serves picnickers, sunbathers and people-watchers. In winter, the **Frog Pond** (Map p174; www.bostonfrogpond.com; Boston Common; adult/child $6/free, rental $12/6; ⊙10am-3:45pm Mon, to 9pm Tue-Thu & Sun, to 10pm Fri & Sat mid-Nov–mid-Mar; ♿; ⓣPark St) attracts ice-skaters, while summer draws theater lovers for **Shakespeare on the Common** (Map p174; www.commshakes.org; Boston Common; ⊙Jul & Aug). This is also the starting point for the Freedom Trail.

★ **Massachusetts State House** NOTABLE BUILDING
(Map p174; www.sec.state.ma.us; cnr Beacon & Bowdoin Sts; ⊙8:45am-5pm Mon-Fri, tours 10am-3:30pm Mon-Fri; ⓣPark St) FREE High atop Beacon Hill, Massachusetts' leaders and legislators attempt to turn their ideas into concrete policies and practices within the State House. John Hancock provided the land; and Charles Bulfinch designed the commanding state capitol, but it was Oliver Wendell Holmes who called it 'the hub of the solar system'. Free 40-minute tours cover the history, artwork, architecture and political personalities of the State House.

BOSTON IN TWO DAYS...

Day One

Spend your first day in Boston following the Freedom Trail (p180), which starts on the Boston Common (p172) and continues through downtown. There isn't time to go inside every museum, but you can admire the architecture and learn the history. Highlights include the Old South Meeting House, the Old State House and Faneuil Hall (p176).

In the afternoon, the Freedom Trail continues into the North End, where you can visit the historic Paul Revere House (p177), Old North Church (p177) and Copp's Hill Burying Ground (p180). Move on to the exquisite Liberty Hotel (p182), former site of the Charles St Jail.

Day Two

Spend the morning admiring Boston's most architecturally significant collection of buildings, clustered around Copley Sq (p178). Admire the art and books at the Boston Public Library, ogle the magnificent stained-glass windows at Trinity Church and gaze at the clean lines on the John Hancock Tower.

Your afternoon is reserved for one of Boston's magnificent art museums. Unfortunately you'll have to choose between the excellent, encyclopedic collection at the Museum of Fine Arts (p179) or the smaller but no less extraordinary exhibits at the Isabella Stewart Gardner Museum (p179). Either way, you won't be disappointed.

In the evening, catch the Boston Symphony Orchestra at the acoustically magnificent Symphony Hall (p179), or for lower-brow entertainment, catch a baseball game at Fenway Park (p179) or go barhopping on Lansdowne St.

★ **Public Garden**   GARDENS
(Map p174; www.friendsofthepublicgarden.org; Arlington St; ☺dawn-dusk; ♿; Ⓣ Arlington) Adjoining Boston Common, the Public Garden is a 24-acre botanical oasis of Victorian flower beds, verdant grass and weeping willow trees shading a tranquil lagoon. The old-fashioned pedal-powered **Swan Boats** (Map p174; www.swanboats.com; Public Garden; adult/child $3.50/2; ☺10am-4pm mid-Apr–mid-Jun, to 5pm late Jun-Aug, noon-4pm 1st half of Sep) have been delighting children for generations. The most endearing spot in the Public Garden is the **Make Way for Ducklings Statue** (Map p174), depicting Mrs Mallard and her eight ducklings, the main characters in the beloved book by Robert McCloskey.

Granary Burying Ground   CEMETERY
(Map p174; Tremont St; ☺9am-5pm; Ⓣ Park St) Dating from 1660, this atmospheric atoll is crammed with historic headstones, many with evocative (and creepy) carvings. This is the final resting place of all your favorite revolutionary heroes, including Paul Revere, Samuel Adams, John Hancock and James Otis. Benjamin Franklin is buried in Philadelphia, but the Franklin family plot contains his parents.

⊙ Downtown & Waterfront

Much of Boston's business and tourist activity takes place in this central neighborhood. Downtown is a bustling district crammed with modern complexes and colonial buildings, including Faneuil Hall and Quincy Market.

★ **Old State House**   HISTORIC BUILDING
(Map p174; www.bostonhistory.org; 206 Washington St; adult/child $10/free; ☺9am-6pm Jun-Aug, to 5pm Sep-May; Ⓣ State) Dating from 1713, the Old State House is Boston's oldest surviving public building, where the Massachusetts Assembly used to debate the issues of the day before the Revolution. The building is best known for its balcony, where the Declaration of Independence was first read to Bostonians in 1776. Inside, the Old State House contains a small museum of revolutionary memorabilia, with videos and multimedia presentations about the Boston Massacre, which took place out front.

Old South Meeting House   HISTORIC BUILDING
(Map p174; www.osmh.org; 310 Washington St; adult/child $6/1; ☺9:30am-5pm Apr-Oct, 10am-4pm Nov-Mar; ♿; Ⓣ Downtown Crossing, State) 'No tax on tea!' That was the decision on December 16, 1773, when 5000 angry colonists gathered here to protest British taxes,

NEW ENGLAND

Central Boston

500 m
0.25 miles

EAST CAMBRIDGE

Monsignor O'Brien Hwy

Memorial Dr

Charles River Bridge

Museum of Science

51

3

10

North Point Blvd

Northpoint Park

Charles River

Charles River Bike Path

Longfellow Bridge

WEST END

Nashua St

Science Park

Martha Rd

Charlestown Bridge

Zakim Bridge

Paul Revere Park

US Coast Guard Piers

Constitution Wharf

Commercial St

NORTH END

Battery Wharf

Fire Boat Dock

Battery St

North St

Hanover St

Old North Church
4

12

Charter St

Snowhill St

Hull St

Sheafe St

Salem St

N Margin St

Cooper St

Endicott St

N Washington St

Lovejoy Pl

Lovejoy Wharf

Beverly St

North Station

Canal St

Valenti Way

Friend St

Portland St

Causeway St

Merrimac St

Stanford St

New Chardon St

New Sudbury St

Tileston St

N Bennet St

Prince St

Parmenter St

24

43

Cross St

North End Park

41

Haymarket

Creek

47

North Sq

32

13

National Park Service Visitors Center

Chatham St

State St

Richmond St

Fulton St

Commercial St

Atlantic Ave

Union Wharf

Sargents Wharf

Lewis Wharf

Commercial Wharf

Long Wharf

Ferry to Boston Harbor Islands

Boston Harbor Islands Pavilion

Aquarium

15

17

26

34

30

29

Boston Inner Harbor

Boston Harbor

Clark St

Fleet St

Congress St

City Hall Plaza

Cornhill St

Government Center

Somerset St

Bowdoin

New Chardon St

Bowdoin St

Temple St

Ridgeway La

Hancock St

Derne St

Cambridge St

S Russell St

Irving St

Garden St

Anderson St

Myrtle St

19

BEACON HILL

Phillips St

Revere St

Blossom St

Parkman St

Wm Cardinal O'Connell Way

Fruit St

36

Charles/MGH

Charles St

The Esplanade

10

Central Boston

leading to the Boston Tea Party. Download an audio of the historic pre–Tea Party meeting from the museum website, then visit the graceful meeting house to check out the exhibit on the history of the building and the protest.

Rose Kennedy Greenway PARK
(Map p174; www.rosekennedygreenway.org; [icon]; [T]Aquarium, Haymarket) The gateway to the newly revitalized waterfront is the Rose Kennedy Greenway. Where once was a hulking overhead highway, now winds a 27-acre strip of landscaped gardens, fountain-lined greens and public art installations, with the artist-driven **Greenway Open Market** (Map p174; www.newenglandopenmarkets.com; [icon]11am-5pm Sat, plus 1st & 3rd Sun May-Oct; [icon]; [T]Aquarium) for weekend shoppers, food trucks for weekday lunchers and a brand-new European-style beer garden, which made its debut in 2017. Cool off in the whimsical **Rings Fountain**, walk the calming

labyrinth, or take a ride on the custom-designed **Greenway Carousel**.

Faneuil Hall HISTORIC BUILDING
(Map p174; www.nps.gov/bost; Congress St; [icon]9am-5pm; [T]State, Haymarket, Government Center) **FREE** 'Those who cannot bear free speech had best go home,' said Wendell Phillips. 'Faneuil Hall is no place for slavish hearts.' Indeed, this public meeting place was the site of so much rabble-rousing that it earned the nickname the 'Cradle of Liberty.' After the revolution, Faneuil Hall was a forum for meetings about abolition, women's suffrage and war. On the 2nd floor, the historic hall is normally open to the public, who can hear about the building's history from National Park Service (NPS) rangers.

Design Museum Boston MUSEUM
(www.designmuseumboston.org; [icon]hours vary) Redefining what it means to be a 'museum', Design Museum Boston brings the goods to

you. This 'pop-up' museum launches exhibits in public spaces all around town, from shopping malls to public parks to airports.

West End & North End

Although the West End and North End are physically adjacent, they are atmospherically worlds apart. The West End is an institutional area without much zest. By contrast, the North End is delightfully spicy, thanks to the many Italian ristoranti and *salumerie* (delis) that line the streets.

★Museum of Science — MUSEUM

(Map p174; www.mos.org; Charles River Dam; adult/child $25/20; ⊙9am-7pm Sat-Thu Jul & Aug, to 5pm Sep-Jun, to 9pm Fri year-round; P ⊛; T Science Park/West End) This educational playground has more than 600 interactive exhibits. Favorites include the world's largest lightning-bolt generator, a full-scale space capsule, a world population meter and an impressive dinosaur exhibit. Kids and adults alike can go wild exploring computers and technology, maps and models, the birds and the bees, and human evolution. Recent additions include the Hall of Human Life, where visitors can witness the hatching of baby chicks, and the Yawkey Gallery, with dramatic floor-to-ceiling windows overlooking the Charles River.

The Discovery Center is a hands-on play area for kids under the age of eight. The museum also houses the **Charles Hayden Planetarium** (Map p174; www.mos.org; Museum of Science, Charles River Dam; adult/child $10/8; ⊙9am-5pm Sat-Thu, to 9pm Fri) and **Mugar Omni Theater** (Map p174; www.mos.org; Science Museum, Charles River Dam; adult/child $10/8; ⊛).

★Old North Church — CHURCH

(Map p174; www.oldnorth.com; 193 Salem St; requested donation $3, tour adult/child $6/4; ⊙9am-6pm Jun-Oct, 9am-5pm Mar-May, Nov & Dec, 10am-4pm Jan & Feb; T Haymarket; North Station) Longfellow's poem 'Paul Revere's Ride' has immortalized this graceful church. It was here, on the night of April 18, 1775, that the sexton hung two lanterns from the steeple, as a signal that the British would advance on Lexington and Concord via the sea route. Also called Christ Church, this 1723 Anglican place of worship is Boston's oldest church.

Paul Revere House — HISTORIC SITE

(Map p174; www.paulreverehouse.org; 19 North Sq; adult/child $5/1; ⊙9:30am-5:15pm mid-Apr–Oct, to 4:15pm Nov–mid-Apr, closed Mon Jan-Mar; T Haymarket) When silversmith Paul Revere rode to warn patriots of the British march to Lexington and Concord, he set out from this home on North Sq. This small clapboard house was built in 1680, making it the oldest house in Boston. A self-guided tour through the house and courtyard gives a glimpse of what life was like for the Revere family (which included 16 children!).

Seaport District

The Seaport District is a section of South Boston that is fast developing as an attractive waterside destination, thanks to the dynamic contemporary-art museum and the explosion of new dining options. Travel deeper into Southie for seaside breezes, a little history and a lot of beer.

★Institute of Contemporary Art — MUSEUM

(ICA; www.icaboston.org; 25 Harbor Shore Dr; adult/child $15/free; ⊙10am-5pm Tue, Wed, Sat & Sun, to 9pm Thu & Fri; ⊛; ⊡SL1, SL2, T South Station) Boston has become a focal point for contemporary art in the 21st century, with the Institute of Contemporary Art leading the way. The building is a work of art in itself: a glass structure cantilevered over a waterside plaza. The vast light-filled interior allows for multimedia presentations, educational programs and studio space, as well as the development of the permanent collection.

Boston Children's Museum — MUSEUM

(Map p174; www.bostonchildrensmuseum.org; 308 Congress St; $16, Fri 5-9pm $1; ⊙10am-5pm Sat-Thu, to 9pm Fri; ⊛; T South Station) ✈ The interactive, educational exhibits at the delightful Boston Children's Museum keep kids entertained for hours. Highlights include a bubble exhibit, rock-climbing walls, a hands-on construction site and intercultural immersion experiences. The light-filled atrium features an amazing three-story climbing maze. In nice weather kids can enjoy outdoor eating and playing in the waterside park. Look for the iconic Hood milk bottle on Fort Point Channel.

Boston Tea Party Ships & Museum — MUSEUM

(Map p174; www.bostonteapartyship.com; Congress St Bridge; adult/child $28/18; ⊙10am-5pm; ⊛; T South Station) 'Boston Harbor a teapot tonight!' To protest unfair taxes, a gang of rebellious colonists dumped 342 chests of tea into the water. The 1773 protest – the Boston Tea Party – set into motion the events leading to the Revolutionary War. Nowadays, replica Tea Party Ships are moored at Griffin's Wharf, alongside an excellent experiential museum dedicated to the catalytic event. Using re-enactments, multimedia and other exhibits, the museum addresses all aspects of the Boston Tea Party.

⊙ South End & Chinatown

Chinatown, the Theater District and the Leather District are overlapping areas, filled with glitzy theaters, Chinese restaurants and the remnants of Boston's shoe and leather industry (now converted lofts and clubs). Nearby, the Victorian manses in the South End have been reclaimed by artists and the like, who have created a vibrant restaurant and gallery scene.

Chinatown Gate   LANDMARK
(Map p174; Beach St; TChinatown) The official entrance to Chinatown is the decorative gate (paifong), a gift from the city of Taipei. It is symbolic – not only as an entryway for guests visiting Chinatown, but also as an entryway for immigrants who are still settling here, as they come to establish relationships and put down roots in their newly claimed home.

⊙ Back Bay

Back Bay includes the city's most fashionable window-shopping, latte-drinking and people-watching area, on Newbury St, as well as its most elegant architecture, around **Copley Sq** (Plaza).

Copley Sq represents the best of Back Bay architecture, as it gracefully blends dispa-

rate elements such as the Renaissance Revival **Boston Public Library** (www.bpl.org), the Richardsonian Romanesque **Trinity Church** (www.trinitychurchboston.org) and the modernist John Hancock Tower. Copley Sq should be your first stop in Back Bay, good for whiling away an hour or even a day.

Mary Baker Eddy Library & Mapparium   LIBRARY
(Map p170; www.marybakereddylibrary.org; 200 Massachusetts Ave; adult/child $6/4; ⊙10am-4pm Tue-Sun; ⚿; TSymphony) The Mary Baker Eddy Library houses one of Boston's hidden treasures. The intriguing Mapparium is a room-sized, stained-glass globe that visitors walk through on a glass bridge. It was created in 1935, which is reflected in the globe's geopolitical boundaries. The acoustics, which surprised even the designer, allow everyone in the room to hear even the tiniest whisper.

Prudential Center Skywalk Observatory   VIEWPOINT
(Map p170; www.skywalkboston.com; 800 Boylston St; adult/child $18/13; ⊙10am-10pm Mar-Oct, to 8pm Nov-Feb; P⚿; TPrudential) Technically called the Shops at Prudential Center, this landmark Boston building is not much more than a fancy shopping mall. But it does provide a bird's-eye view of Boston from its 50th-floor Skywalk. Completely enclosed by glass, the Skywalk offers spectacular 360-degree views of Boston and Cambridge, accompanied by an entertaining audiotour (with a special version catering to kids). Alternatively, enjoy the same view from **Top of the Hub** (Map p170; ☎617-536-1775; www.topofthehub.net; 800 Boylston St; ⊙11:30am-1am; ☎; TPrudential) for the price of a drink.

BOSTON FOR CHILDREN

Boston is one giant history museum, the setting for many lively and informative field trips. Cobblestone streets and costume-clad tour guides can bring to life the events that kids read about in history books, while hands-on experimentation and interactive exhibits fuse education and entertainment.

➡ Boston by Little Feet (p181) is the only Freedom Trail walking tour designed especially for children aged six to 12. Download a kid-friendly podcast or reading list for your child before setting out (www.thefreedomtrail.org)

➡ Kids of all ages are invited to drive the duck on the raging waters of the Charles River (p181) with Boston Duck Tours. Bonus: quacking loudly is encouraged.

➡ **Urban AdvenTours** (Map p174; ☎617-670-0637; www.urbanadventours.com; 103 Atlantic Ave; tours from $40, rentals per 24hr $40-75; ⊙9am-8pm Apr-Sep, shorter hours Oct-Mar; TAquarium) is great for all ages. Kids' bikes and helmets are available for rent, as are bike trailers for toddlers.

◉ Kenmore Square & Fenway

Kenmore Sq and Fenway attract club-goers and baseball fans to the streets surrounding Fenway Park, as well as art lovers and culture vultures to the artistic institutions along the Avenue of the Arts (Huntington Ave).

★**Fenway Park**   STADIUM
(Map p170; www.redsox.com; 4 Yawkey Way; tours adult/child $20/14, premium tour $35; ☉9am-5pm; T Kenmore) What is it that makes Fenway Park 'America's Most Beloved Ballpark'? It's not just that it's the home of the Boston Red Sox. Open since 1912, it is the oldest operating baseball park in the country. As such, the park has many quirks that make for a unique experience. See them all on a ballpark tour.

★**Museum of Fine Arts**   MUSEUM
(MFA; Map p170; www.mfa.org; 465 Huntington Ave; adult/child $25/free; ☉10am-5pm Sat-Tue, to 10pm Wed-Fri; T Museum of Fine Arts, Ruggles) Since 1876, the Museum of Fine Arts has been Boston's premier venue for showcasing art by local, national and international artists. Nowadays the museum's holdings encompass all eras, from the ancient world to contemporary times, and all areas of the globe, making it truly encyclopedic in scope. Most recently, the museum has added gorgeous new wings dedicated to the Art of the Americas and to contemporary art, contributing to Boston's emergence as an art center in the 21st century.

★**Isabella Stewart
Gardner Museum**   MUSEUM
(Map p170; www.gardnermuseum.org; 25 Evans Way; adult/child $15/free; ☉11am-5pm Wed-Mon, to 9pm Thu; T Museum of Fine Arts) The magnificent Venetian-style palazzo that houses this museum was home to 'Mrs Jack' Gardner herself until her death in 1924. A monument to one woman's taste for acquiring exquisite art, the Gardner is filled with some 2500 priceless objects, primarily European, including outstanding tapestries and Italian Renaissance and 17th-century Dutch paintings. The four-story greenhouse courtyard is a masterpiece and a tranquil oasis that alone is worth the price of admission.

Symphony Hall   HISTORIC BUILDING
(Map p170; www.bso.org; 301 Massachusetts Ave; ☉hrs vary; T Symphony) This majestic building has been the home of the Boston Symphony Orchestra since 1900, when it was built by McKim, Mead & White (of BPL fame). See the hall's public spaces and go behind the scenes on a free, one-hour tour. Tour dates vary and advance bookings are required.

◉ Cambridge

★**Harvard University**   UNIVERSITY
(Map p170; www.harvard.edu; Massachusetts Ave; tours free; T Harvard) Founded in 1636 to educate men for the ministry, Harvard is America's oldest college. The original Ivy League school has eight graduates who went on to be US presidents, not to mention dozens of Nobel laureates and Pulitzer Prize winners. The geographic heart of Harvard University – where red-brick buildings and leaf-covered paths exude academia – is Harvard Yard. Free historical tours of Harvard Yard depart from the Smith Campus Center (Map p170; www.harvard.edu/visitors; 30 Dunster St; ☉9am-5pm Mon-Sat; T Harvard); self-guided tours are also available.

★**Harvard Art Museums**   MUSEUM
(Map p170; www.harvardartmuseums.org; 32 Quincy St; adult/child/student $15/free/$10; ☉10am-5pm; T Harvard) The 2014 renovation and expansion of Harvard's art museums allowed the university's massive 250,000-piece collection to come together under one very stylish roof, designed by architect extraordinaire Renzo Piano. The artwork spans the globe, with separate collections devoted to Asian and Islamic cultures (formerly the Arthur M Sackler Museum), northern European and Germanic cultures (formerly the Busch-Reisinger Museum) and other Western art, especially European modernism.

MIT Museum   MUSEUM
(Map p170; http://mitmuseum.mit.edu; 265 Massachusetts Ave; adult/child $10/5; ☉10am-6pm Jul & Aug, to 5pm Sep-Jun; P ♿; T Central) Leave it to the mischievous brainiacs at Massachusetts Institute of Technology (MIT) to come up with the city's quirkiest museum. For example, an exhibit called Robots and Beyond demonstrates MIT's ongoing work on artificial intelligence. You can meet humanoid robots like observant Cog and personable Kismet and decide for yourself if they are smarter than humans.

**Harvard Museum
of Natural History**   MUSEUM
(Map p170; www.hmnh.harvard.edu; 26 Oxford St; adult/child/student $12/8/10; ☉9am-5pm; ♿;

City Walk
Freedom Trail

START BOSTON COMMON
END BUNKER HILL MONUMENT
LENGTH 2.5 MILES; THREE HOURS

Start at **1 Boston Common** (p172), America's oldest public park. On the northern side, you can't miss the gold-domed **2 Massachusetts State House** (p172) sitting atop Beacon Hill. Walk north on Tremont St, passing the soaring steeple of **3 Park St Church** and the Egyptian Revival gates of the **4 Granary Burying Ground** (p173).

At School St, the columned **5 King's Chapel** overlooks the adjacent burying ground. Turn east on School St, and take note of the plaque outside **6 Old City Hall** commemorating this spot as the site of the first public school.

Continue down School St past the **7 Old Corner Bookstore**. Diagonally opposite, the **8 Old South Meeting House** (p173) saw the beginnings of the Boston Tea Party. Further north on Washington St, the **9 Old State House** (p173) was the scene of the city's first public reading of the Declaration of Independence. Outside the Old State House a ring of cobblestones marks the **10 Boston Massacre site**, where yet another uprising fueled the revolution. Across the intersection, historic **11 Faneuil Hall** (p176) has served as a public meeting place and marketplace for over 250 years.

From Faneuil Hall, follow Hanover St across the Rose Kennedy Greenway. One block east, charming North Sq is the site of the **12 Paul Revere House** (p177). Back on Hanover St, the Paul Revere Mall offers a lovely vantage point to view the **13 Old North Church** (p177). From the church, head west on Hull St to **14 Copp's Hill Burying Ground**, with grand views across the river to Charlestown.

Across the Charlestown Bridge, Constitution Rd brings you to the Charlestown Navy Yard, home of the world's oldest commissioned warship, the **15 USS Constitution**. Finally, wind your way through the historic streets of Charlestown center to the **16 Bunker Hill Monument**, site of the devastating American Revolution battle.

📖86, Ⓣ Harvard) This institution is famed for its botanical galleries, featuring some 3000 pieces of handblown glass flowers and plants. At the intersection of art and science, the collection of intricately crafted flora is pretty amazing. There is a smaller, complementary exhibit of Sea Creatures in Glass by the same artists. Nearby, the zoological galleries house an enormous number of stuffed animals and reassembled skeletons, as well as an impressive fossil collection. Other cool exhibits feature climate change, sparkling gemstones and arthropods.

Peabody Museum of
Archaeology & Ethnology   MUSEUM
(Map p170; www.peabody.harvard.edu; 11 Divinity Ave; adult/child/student $12/8/10; ⊗9am-5pm; 📖86, Ⓣ Harvard) The centerpiece of the Peabody is the impressive Hall of the North American Indian, which traces how these peoples responded to the arrival of Europeans from the 15th to the 18th centuries. Other exhibits examine indigenous cultures throughout the Americas, including a fantastic comparison of cave paintings and murals of the Awatovi (New Mexico), the Maya (Guatemala) and the Moche (Peru).

🏃 Activities

Considering Boston's large student population and extensive green spaces, it's no surprise to see urban outdoorsy people running along the Esplanade and cycling the Emerald Necklace. For seafaring types, the Charles River and the Boston Harbor offer opportunities for kayaking, sailing and even swimming.

★ Freedom Trail   WALKING
(Map p174; www.thefreedomtrail.org; Ⓣ Park St) For a sampler of Boston's revolutionary sights, follow the red-brick road. It leads 2.5 miles through the center of Boston, from Boston Common to the Bunker Hill Monument, and traces the events leading up to and following the War of Independence. The Freedom Trail is well marked and easy to follow on your own. See opposite page for more information on walking this trail.

Codzilla   BOATING
(Map p174; www.bostonharborcruises.com/codzilla; 1 Long Wharf; adult/child $29/25; ⊗hours vary May-early Oct; Ⓣ Aquarium) 'Boating' may not be the proper word to describe this activity, which takes place on a 2800HP speedboat

that cruises through the waves at speeds of up to 40mph. Painted like a shark with a big toothy grin, the boat has a unique hull design that enables it to do the ocean version of doughnuts.

Boston Harbor Cruises   CRUISE
(BHC; Map p174; 📞617-227-4321; www.boston harborcruises.com; 1 Long Wharf; adult/child $29/25; Ⓣ Aquarium) With 50 vessels and over 300 daily departures in summer, BHC claims to be America's oldest and largest operator of passenger boats. The dizzying variety of options for those who want to get out on the water range from a basic Historic Sightseeing Tour around Boston's Inner Harbor to sunset cruises, weekend lighthouse cruises, whale-watching and more.

🏇 Tours

Boston by Foot   WALKING
(www.bostonbyfoot.com; adult/child $15/10; 🚶) This fantastic nonprofit organization offers 90-minute walking tours, with neighborhood-specific walks and specialty theme tours, like the Hub of Literary America, the Dark Side of Boston, and Boston by Little Feet – a kid-friendly version of the Freedom Trail.

Black Heritage Trail   WALKING
(Map p174; www.nps.gov/boaf; ⊗tours 10am, noon & 1pm Mon-Sat Jul & Aug; Ⓣ Park St) The NPS conducts excellent, informative 90-minute guided tours exploring the history of the abolitionist movement and African American settlement on Beacon Hill. Tours depart from the Robert Gould Shaw memorial on Boston Common. Alternatively, take a self-guided tour with the NPS Freedom Trail app (www.nps. gov/bost/planyourvisit/app.htm) or grab a route map from the **Museum of African American History** (Map p174; www.maah.org; 46 Joy St; adult/child $5/free; ⊗10am-4pm Mon-Sat; Ⓣ Park St, Bowdoin).

Boston Duck Tours   BOATING
(📞617-267-3825; www.bostonducktours.com; adult/child $39.50/27; 🚶; Ⓣ Aquarium, Science Park, Prudential) These ridiculously popular tours use WWII amphibious vehicles that cruise the downtown streets before splashing into the Charles River. The 80-minute tours depart from the Museum of Science, the Prudential Center or the New England Aquarium. Reserve in advance.

🎉 Festivals & Events

★ Boston Marathon
SPORTS

(www.baa.org; ⊘ 3rd Mon Apr) One of the country's most prestigious marathons takes runners on a 26.2-mile course ending at Copley Sq on Patriots' Day, a Massachusetts holiday on the third Monday in April.

Boston Pride Festival
LGBT

(☎ 617-262-9405; www.bostonpride.org; ⊘ Jun) During the first full week in June, Boston does its part for this now-national celebration, kicking off with the raising of a rainbow flag on City Hall Plaza. Events occur throughout the week. The highlight is the Pride Parade and Festival on the second Saturday in June.

Independence Day
CULTURAL

(www.bostonpopsjuly4th.org; ⊘ Jul 4) Boston hosts one of the biggest Independence Day bashes in the USA, with a free Boston Pops concert on the Esplanade and a fireworks display that's televised nationally.

🛏 Sleeping

Boston offers a wide range of accommodations, from inviting guesthouses in historic quarters to swanky hotels with all the amenities. Considering that Boston is a city filled with students, there are surprisingly few accommodations options targeting budget travelers and backpackers.

HI-Boston
HOSTEL $

(Map p174; ☎ 617-536-9455; www.bostonhostel.org; 19 Stuart St; dm from $40, d with bath from $170; ✱@🛜; Ⓣ Chinatown, Boylston) 🍃 HI-Boston sets the standard for urban hostels, with its modern, ecofriendly facility in the historic Dill Building. Purpose-built rooms are comfortable and clean, as are the shared bathrooms. Community spaces are numerous, from fully equipped kitchen to trendy ground-floor cafe, and there's a whole calendar of activities on offer.

Irving House at Harvard
GUESTHOUSE $$

(Map p170; ☎ 617-547-4600; www.irvinghouse.com; 24 Irving St; r with/without bath from $255/155; Ⓟ✱@🛜; Ⓣ Harvard) 🍃 Call it a big inn or a homey hotel, this property welcomes the world-weariest of travelers. The 44 rooms range in size, but every bed is covered with a quilt, and big windows let in plenty of light. There is a bistro-style atmosphere in the brick-lined basement, where you can browse its books, plan your travels or munch on a free continental breakfast.

★ Liberty Hotel
HOTEL $$$

(Map p174; ☎ 617-224-4000, 866-961-3778; www.libertyhotel.com; 215 Charles St; r from $515; Ⓟ🔄✱🛜; Ⓣ Charles/MGH) It is with intended irony that the notorious Charles Street Jail has been converted into the classy Liberty Hotel. Today the spectacular lobby soars under a 90ft ceiling. All 298 guest rooms come with luxurious linens and high-tech amenities, while the 18 in the original jail wing boast floor-to-ceiling windows with amazing views of the Charles River and Beacon Hill.

★ Verb Hotel
BOUTIQUE HOTEL $$$

(Map p170; ☎ 617-566-4500; www.theverbhotel.com; 1271 Boylston St; r $349-399; Ⓟ✱🛜🚭🐾; Ⓣ Kenmore) The Verb Hotel took a down-and-out HoJo property and turned it into Boston's most radical, retro, rock-and-roll hotel. The style is mid-Century Modern; the theme is music. Memorabilia is on display throughout the joint, with a jukebox cranking out tunes in the lobby. Classy, clean-lined rooms face the swimming pool or Fenway Park. A-plus for service and style.

Newbury Guest House
GUESTHOUSE $$$

(Map p170; ☎ 617-670-6000, 800-437-7668; www.newburyguesthouse.com; 261 Newbury St; d from $269; Ⓟ✱🛜; Ⓣ Hynes, Copley) Dating from 1882, these three interconnected brick and brownstone buildings offer a prime location in the heart of Newbury St. A recent renovation has preserved charming features like ceiling medallions and in-room fireplaces, but now the rooms feature clean lines, luxurious linens and modern amenities.

Omni Parker House
HISTORIC HOTEL $$$

(Map p174; ☎ 617-227-8600; www.omnihotels.com; 60 School St; r from $345; Ⓟ✱🛜🐾; Ⓣ Park St) History and the Parker House go hand in hand like JFK and Jackie (who got engaged here). Malcolm X was a busboy here; Ho Chi Minh was a pastry chef here; and Boston cream pie, the official state dessert, was created here. Rooms are comfortable, and the hotel's location, smack in the heart of the Freedom Trail, is incomparable.

🍴 Eating

🍴 Beacon Hill & Boston Common

★ Tatte
BAKERY $

(Map p174; www.tattebakery.com; 70 Charles St; pastries from $3; ⊘ 7am-8pm Mon-Fri, 8am-8pm Sat, 8am-7pm Sun; Ⓣ Charles/MGH) The aroma of buttery goodness – and the lines stretching out the door – signal your arrival at this fabulous bakery on the lower floor of the historic Charles St Meeting House. Swoonworthy pastries (divinely cinnamon-y morning buns, chocolate-hazelnut twists, avocado and mushroom tartines) taste even more amazing if you're lucky enough to score a table on the sunny front patio.

★**Paramount**   CAFETERIA **$$**
(Map p174; www.paramountboston.com; 44 Charles St; mains breakfast & lunch $8-15, dinner $17-24; ⊙7am-10pm Mon-Fri, 8am-10pm Sat & Sun; 🖉 ⊛; T Charles/MGH) This old-fashioned cafeteria is a neighborhood favorite. A-plus diner fare includes pancakes, home fries, burgers and sandwiches, and big, hearty salads. Banana and caramel French toast is an obvious go-to for the brunch crowd. Don't sit down until you get your food!

✕ Downtown & Waterfront

Gene's Chinese Flatbread   CHINESE **$**
(Map p174; 86 Bedford St; sandwiches $4.50, mains $6-11; ⊙11am-6:30am Mon-Sat; T Chinatown) It's not often that we recommend leaving Chinatown for Chinese food, but it's only a few blocks away. And it's worth the detour to this unassuming storefront for chewy Xi'an-style noodles. No 9 (cumin lamb hand-pulled noodles) and No 4 (pork flatbread sandwich) are perennial fan favorites.

James Hook & Co   SEAFOOD **$$**
(Map p174; www.jameshooklobster.com; 15-17 Northern Av; lobster rolls $20-24; ⊙10am-5pm Mon-Thu & Sat, to 6pm Fri, to 4pm Sat) For a superlative lobster roll close to downtown, look no further than this harborside seafood shack near the bridge to the Seaport district. Outdoor tables make it a perfect low-key lunch stop as you make your way between museums on a sunny afternoon.

Union Oyster House   SEAFOOD **$$$**
(Map p174; www.unionoysterhouse.com; 41 Union St; mains lunch $14-26, dinner $22-32; ⊙11am-9:30pm Sun-Thu, to 10pm Fri & Sat; T Haymarket) The oldest restaurant in Boston, ye olde Union Oyster House has been serving seafood in this historic redbrick building since 1826. Countless historymakers have propped themselves up at this bar, including Daniel Webster and John F Kennedy (apparently JFK used to order the lobster bisque). Overpriced but atmospheric.

✕ West End & North End

Maria's Pastry   BAKERY **$**
(Map p174; www.mariaspastry.com; 46 Cross St; pastries $2-5; ⊙7am-7pm Mon-Sat, to 5pm Sun; 🖉; T Haymarket) Three generations of Merola women are now working to bring you Boston's most authentic Italian pastries. Many claim that Maria makes the best cannoli in the North End, but you'll also find more elaborate concoctions like *sfogliatelle* (layered, shell-shaped pastry filled with ricotta) and *aragosta* (cream-filled 'lobster tail' pastry).

★**Pomodoro**   ITALIAN **$$**
(Map p174; 🖉 617-367-4348; 351 Hanover St; mains $23-24; ⊙5:30-11pm; T Haymarket) Seductive Pomodoro offers one of the North End's most romantic settings for delectable Italian. The food is simple but perfectly prepared: fresh pasta, spicy tomato sauce, grilled fish and meats, and wine by the glass. If you're lucky, you might be on the receiving end of a complimentary tiramisu for dessert.

✕ Seaport District

Yankee Lobster Co   SEAFOOD **$**
(www.yankeelobstercompany.com; 300 Northern Ave; mains $10-25; ⊙10am-9pm Mon-Sat, 11am-6pm Sun; 🚌 SL1, SL2, T South Station) The Zanti family has been fishing for three generations, so they definitely know their stuff. A relatively recent addition is this retail fish market, scattered with a few tables in case you want to dine in. And you do. Order something simple like clam chowder or a lobster roll, accompany it with a cold beer, and you will not be disappointed.

★**Row 34**   SEAFOOD **$$**
(Map p174; 🖉 617-553-5900; www.row34.com; 383 Congress St; oysters $2-3, mains $13-29; ⊙11:30am-10pm Sun-Thu, to 11pm Fri & Sat; T South Station) In the heart of the new Seaport District, set in a sharp, postindustrial space, this place offers a dozen types of raw oysters and clams, alongside an amazing selection of craft beers. There's also a full menu of cooked seafood, ranging from the traditional to the trendy.

✕ South End & Chinatown

Taiwan Cafe   TAIWANESE **$**
(Map p174; www.taiwancafeboston.com; 34 Oxford St; mains $6-16; ⊙11am-1am; 🖉; T Chinatown) Taiwan Cafe is a few steps off the main drag,

so you might not have to wait quite as long for the excellent soup dumplings and other Taiwanese specialties. Regulars rave about the roast beef scallion pancakes. Like most places in Chinatown, the decor is minimal and prices are cheap. Cash only.

Winsor Dim Sum Cafe
DIM SUM $

(Map p174; 10 Tyler St; dim sum from $3.50, other items $7-14; ⊙9am-10pm; ✐; ⊤Chinatown) The shrimp dumplings and steamed pork buns are highly recommended at this nononsense Chinatown favorite. The downside is that there are no pushcarts to choose your food from – the place is too small for them to fit! Instead you have to pre-order from a menu with photographs. The upside is that the food is freshly made to order and delicious.

★Myers & Chang
ASIAN $$

(Map p170; ✐617-542-5200; www.myersand chang.com; 1145 Washington St; small plates $9-19; ⊙11:30am-10pm Sun-Thu, to 11pm Fri & Sat; ✐; ⬚SL4, SL5, ⊤Tufts Medical Center) This superhip Asian spot blends Thai, Chinese and Vietnamese cuisines, which means delicious dumplings, spicy stir-fries and oodles of noodles. The kitchen staff do amazing things with a wok, and the menu of small plates allows you to sample a wide selection of dishes. Dim sum for dinner? This is your place.

🍴 Back Bay

Sweetgreen
VEGETARIAN $

(Map p170; ✐617-936-3464; www.sweetgreen. com; 659 Boylston St; mains $7-13; ⊙10:30am-10:30pm; ✐🛗; ⊤Copley) Vegetarians, gluten-free eaters, health nuts and all human beings will rejoice in the goodness that is served at Sweetgreen. Choose a salad or wrap, then custom-design your own; or choose one of the unexpected, delicious, fresh combos that have already been invented, including seasonal specialties. So healthy. So satisfying. So good.

★Courtyard
AMERICAN $$$

(Map p170; ✐617-859-2251; www.thecateredaf fair.com/bpl; 700 Boylston St; tea adult/child $39/19, with sparkling wine $49; ⊙11:30am-3pm Mon-Sat; ⊤Copley) The perfect destination for an elegant afternoon tea is – believe it or not – the Boston Public Library. Overlooking the beautiful Italianate courtyard, this grown-up restaurant serves an artfully prepared selection of sandwiches, scones and sweets, accompanied by a wide range of teas (black, green and herbal) and an optional glass of sparkling wine. Reserve ahead, especially on Saturdays.

🍴 Kenmore Square & Fenway

El Pelon
MEXICAN $

(Map p170; www.elpelon.com; 92 Peterborough St; tacos $4, burritos $6-8; ⊙11am-11pm; ✐; ⊤Fenway) If your budget is tight, don't miss this chance to fill up on Boston's best burritos, tacos and tortas, made with the freshest ingredients. The *tacos de la casa* are highly recommended, especially the *pescado,* made with Icelandic cod and topped with chili mayo. Plates are paper and cutlery is plastic.

Tasty Burger
BURGERS $

(Map p170; www.tastyburger.com; 1301 Boylston St; burgers $5-6; ⊙11am-2am; ⊤Fenway) Once a Mobil gas station, this place is now a retro burger joint, with picnic tables outside and a

---

LGBTQ BOSTON

Out and active gay communities are visible all around Boston, especially in the South End and Jamaica Plain.

There is no shortage of entertainment options catering to LGBTQ travelers. From drag shows to dyke nights, this sexually diverse community has something for everybody.

The biggest event of the year for the Boston gay and lesbian community is June's Boston Pride (p182), a week of parades, parties, festivals and flag-raisings.

There are excellent sources of information for the gay and lesbian community:

Bay Windows (www.baywindows.com) is a weekly newspaper for LGBTQ readers. The print edition is distributed throughout New England, but the website is also an excellent source of news and information.

Edge Boston (www.edgeboston.com) is the Boston branch of the nationwide network of publications offering news and entertainment for LGBTQ readers. Includes a nightlife section with culture and club reviews.

pool table inside. The name of the place is a nod to *Pulp Fiction,* as is the wall-mounted poster of Samuel L Jackson, whose character would agree that 'this is a tasty burger'.

Island Creek Oyster Bar SEAFOOD $$$
(Map p170; ☑617-532-5300; www.islandcreek oysterbar.com; 500 Commonwealth Ave; oysters $2.50-3.50, mains lunch $12-27, dinner $17-36; ⊘4-11pm Mon-Fri, 11:30am-11:30pm Sat, 10:30am-11pm Sun; ⊤Kenmore) Island Creek claims to unite farmer, chef and diner in one space – and what a space it is. ICOB serves up the region's finest oysters, along with other local seafood, in an ethereal new-age setting. The specialty – lobster-roe noodles topped with braised short ribs and grilled lobster – lives up to the hype.

✗ Cambridge

Hokkaido Ramen Santouka JAPANESE $
(Map p170; www.santouka.co.jp/en; 1 Bow St; mains $11-17; ⊘11am-9:30pm Mon-Thu, to 10:30pm Fri & Sat, to 9pm Sun; ⊤Harvard) This worldwide chain is bringing a bit of Japanese simplicity and subtlety to Harvard Sq. Service is pleasant and fast, while the noodles are perfectly satisfying. If you're wondering why the staff occasionally shout out, they are greeting and sending off their guests.

★**Life Alive** VEGETARIAN $
(Map p170; www.lifealive.com; 765 Massachusetts Ave; mains $6-10; ⊘8am-10pm Mon-Sat, 11am-7pm Sun; ; ⊤Central) 🍴 Life Alive offers a joyful, healthful, purposeful approach to fast food. The unusual combinations of animal-free ingredients yield delicious results, most of which come in a bowl (like a salad) or in a wrap.

🍷 Drinking & Nightlife

🍸 Downtown & Waterfront

Highball Lounge COCKTAIL BAR
(Map p174; www.highballboston.com; 90 Tremont St; ⊘5pm-midnight Mon & Tue, 2am Wed-Sat; ⊤Park St) Go out to play! Well stocked with board games, the Highball Lounge has yours, whether you're on a date (Connect Four) or in a group (Jenga). The Viewmaster is for looking at the menu, which features local beers, creative cocktails and intriguing snacks (tater-tot nachos, crispy brussels sprouts). This place will make you feel like a kid again. Except you can drink.

🍷 Seaport District

Harpoon Brewery & Beer Hall BREWERY
(www.harpoonbrewery.com; 306 Northern Ave; ⊘beer hall 11am-7pm Sun-Wed, to 11pm Thu-Sat, tours noon-5pm Mon-Wed, to 6pm Thu-Sat, 11:30am-5:30pm Sun; 🚌SL1, SL2, ⊤South Station) This brewery is the largest beer facility in the state of Massachusetts. Take an hour-long tour ($5) to see how the beer is made and to sample some of the goods. Or just take a seat at the bar in the beer hall.

🍸 South End & Chinatown

★**Beehive** COCKTAIL BAR
(Map p170; ☑617-423-0069; www.beehive boston.com; 541 Tremont St; ⊘5pm-midnight Mon-Wed, to 1am Thu, to 2am Fri, 9:30am-2am Sat, 9:30am-midnight Sun; ⊤Back Bay) The Beehive has transformed the basement of the Boston Center for the Arts into a 1920s Paris jazz club. This place is more about the scene than the music, which is often provided by students from Berklee College of Music. But the food is good and the vibe is definitely hip. Reservations required for a table.

🍷 Back Bay

Club Café GAY
(Map p174; www.clubcafe.com; 209 Columbus Ave; ⊘11am-2am; ⊤Back Bay) It's a club! It's a cafe! It's cabaret! Anything goes at this glossy, gay nightlife extravaganza. There is live cabaret in the Napoleon Room six nights a week, while the main dance and lounge area has tea parties, salsa dancing, trivia competitions, karaoke, bingo and good old-fashioned dance parties.

🍷 Kenmore Square & Fenway

Hawthorne COCKTAIL BAR
(Map p170; www.thehawthornebar.com; 500a Commonwealth Ave; ⊘5pm-1am; ⊤Kenmore) Located in the basement of the Hotel Commonwealth, this is a living-room-style cocktail lounge that attracts the city's sophisticates. Sink into the plush furniture and sip a custom cocktail.

🍷 Cambridge

★**Beat Brasserie** BAR
(Map p170; www.beatbrasserie.com; 13 Brattle St; ⊘4pm-late Mon-Fri, 10am-late Sat & Sun; ⊤Harvard) This vast, underground bistro packs in

good-looking patrons for international food, classy cocktails and live jazz and blues. It's inspired by the Beat Generation writers – and named for a run-down Parisian motel where they hung out – but there's nothing down-and-out about this hot spot.

★ **Lord Hobo** MICROBREWERY
(Map p170; www.lordhobo.com; 92 Hampshire St; ⏱4pm-1am Mon-Wed, 4pm-2am Thu & Fri, 11am-2am Sat, 11am-1am Sun; ⓣCentral, Kendall/MIT) If high-caliber craft IPAs are your idea of beer-drinking bliss, make a beeline for this unassuming corner brewpub north of Central Sq. What started as a local secret has exploded in popularity, with distribution of their trademark Hobo Life, Boom Sauce and Consolation Prize stretching clear to Colorado.

☆ Entertainment

Boston Red Sox BASEBALL
(Map p170; www.redsox.com; 4 Yawkey Way; bleachers $10-45, grandstand $23-87, box $38-189; ⓣKenmore) From April to September you can watch the Red Sox play at Fenway Park, the nation's oldest and most storied ballpark. Unfortunately it is also the most expensive – not that it stops the Fenway faithful from scooping up the tickets. There are sometimes game-day tickets on sale starting 90 minutes before the opening pitch.

★ **Boston Symphony Orchestra** CLASSICAL MUSIC
(BSO; Map p170; ☏617-266-1200; www.bso.org; 301 Massachusetts Ave; tickets $30-145; ⓣSymphony) Flawless acoustics match the ambitious programs of the world-renowned Boston Symphony Orchestra. From September to April, the BSO performs in the beauteous Symphony Hall (p179), featuring an ornamental high-relief ceiling and attracting a fancy-dress crowd.

★ **Red Room @ Café 939** LIVE MUSIC
(Map p170; www.cafe939.com; 939 Boylston St; ⓣHynes) Run by Berklee students, the Red

Room @ 939 has emerged as one of Boston's least predictable and most enjoyable music venues. It has an excellent sound system and a baby grand piano; most importantly, it books interesting, eclectic up-and-coming musicians. Buy tickets in advance at the **Berklee Performance Center** (Map p170; www.berklee.edu/bpc; 136 Massachusetts Ave; tickets $8-58; ⓣHynes).

Lizard Lounge LIVE MUSIC
(www.lizardloungeclub.com; 1667 Massachusetts Ave; cover $8-15; ⏱7:30pm-late Sun & Mon, 8:30pm-late Tue-Sat; ⓣHarvard) The underground Lizard Lounge doubles as a rock and jazz venue. The big drawcard is the Sunday-night poetry slam, featuring music by the jazzy Jeff Robinson Trio. Also popular are the Monday open-mike challenge and regular appearances by local favorite Club d'Elf. The bar stocks an excellent list of New England beers, which are complemented by the sweet-potato fries.

Located a quarter-mile north of Cambridge Common (the park), below Cambridge Common (the restaurant).

🛍 Shopping

Converse SHOES
(Map p170; www.converse.com; 348 Newbury St; ⏱10am-7pm Mon-Fri, to 8pm Sat, 11am-6pm Sun; ⓣHynes) Converse started making shoes right up the road in Malden, MA, way back in 1908. Chuck Taylor joined the 'team' in the 1920s and the rest is history. This retail store carries sneakers, denim and other gear. The iconic shoes come in all colors and patterns; better yet, make them uniquely your own at the 2nd-floor customization area.

Three Wise Donkeys CLOTHING
(Map p170; www.facebook.com/ThreeWiseDonkeys; 51 Gloucester St; ⏱11am-6pm Mon-Thu, 11am-8pm Fri & Sat, noon-5pm Sun; ⓣHynes Convention Center) Cool concept, awesome designs and quality product add up to a win. Three Wise Donkeys works directly with artists (some local) who have created the unique artwork that lines the walls. Find a design that you like and they'll print it on an organic cotton T-shirt in the color and style of your choosing. Made to order in 15 minutes.

Eugene Galleries ANTIQUES
(Map p174; www.eugenegalleries.com; 76 Charles St; ⏱11am-6pm Mon-Sat, noon-6pm Sun; ⓣCharles/MGH) This tiny shop has a remarkable selection of antique prints and maps, especially

---

ⓘ **CHEAP SEATS**

BosTix (www.bostix.org) offers discounted tickets to theater productions citywide (up to 25% off for advance purchases online). Discounts up to 50% are available for same-day, in-person purchase.

focusing on old Boston. Follow the history of the city's development by examining 18th- and 19th-century maps and witness the filling-in of Back Bay and the greening of the city. Historic prints highlight Boston landmarks, making for excellent old-fashioned gifts.

Information

Greater Boston Convention & Visitors Bureau (www.bostonusa.com) The website is packed with information on hotels, restaurants and special events, as well as LGBTQ, family travel and more.

Boston Harbor Islands Pavilion (Map p174; www.bostonharborislands.org; Rose Kennedy Greenway; ⊙9am-4:30pm mid-May–Jun & Sep-early Oct, to 6pm Jul & Aug; ⊛; ⓣ Aquarium) Ideally located on the Rose Kennedy Greenway, this information center will tell you everything you need to know to plan your visit to the Boston Harbor Islands. Don't miss the nearby *Harbor Fog* sculpture, which immerses passersby in the sounds and sensations of the harbor.

Cambridge Visitor Information Kiosk (Map p170; ☑617-441-2884; www.cambridge-usa.org; Harvard Sq; ⊙9am-5pm Mon-Fri, to 1pm Sat & Sun; ⓣHarvard) Detailed information on current Cambridge happenings and self-guided walking tours.

Massachusetts Office of Travel & Tourism (www.massvacation.com) Information about events and activities throughout the state, including an excellent guide to green tourism.

National Park Service Visitors Center (NPS; Map p174; www.nps.gov/bost/faneuil-hall-vc.htm; Faneuil Hall; ⊙9am-6pm; ⓣState) The NPS Visitors Center has loads of information about the Freedom Trail sights. This is also the starting point for the free **NPS Freedom Trail Tour** (Map p174; www.nps.gov/bost; Faneuil Hall; ⊙hourly 10am-3pm Jul-Sep; ⓣState). There is an additional NPS Visitors Center at the **Charlestown Navy Yard** (Map p170; www.nps.gov/bost; ⊙visitor center 9am-5pm Tue-Sun May-Sep, 1-5pm Thu-Sun Oct-Apr; ⓠ93 from Haymarket, ⬛Inner Harbor Ferry from Long Wharf, ⓣNorth Station).

Getting There & Away

Most travelers arrive in Boston by plane, with many national and international flights in and out of **Logan International Airport** (☑800-235-6426; www.massport.com/logan). Two smaller regional airports – Manchester Airport in New Hampshire and Green Airport near Providence, RI – offer alternatives that are also accessible to Boston and are sometimes less expensive.

Most trains operated by Amtrak (www.amtrak.com) go in and out of **South Station** (Map p174; www.south-station.net; 700 Atlantic Ave). Boston is the northern terminus of the Northeast Corridor, which sends frequent trains to New York (3½ to 4½ hours), Philadelphia, PA (five to six hours) and Washington, DC (6¾ to eight hours). The *Lake Shore Limited* goes daily to Buffalo, NY (11 hours) and Chicago (22 hours), while the *Downeaster* goes from North Station to Portland, ME (2½ hours).

Buses are most useful for regional destinations, although Greyhound (www.greyhound.com) operates services around the country. In recent years, there has been a spate of new companies offering cheap and efficient service to New York City (four to five hours).

Flights, cars and tours can be booked online at lonelyplanet.com/bookings.

Getting Around

Boston Logan International Airport Take the silver line bus (free) or blue line subway ($2.25 to $2.75) to central Boston from 5:30am to 12:30am, or catch a taxi for $25 to $30.

Manchester Airport Book in advance for the hourly Flight Line Inc shuttle bus to Logan International Airport, or catch the infrequent Greyhound bus to South Station, which is located in central boston on the red line.

Green Airport Take the commuter rail to South Station ($12).

PUBLIC TRANSPORTATION

T (Subway) The quickest and easiest way to get to most destinations. Runs from 5:30am or 6am until 12:30am.

Hubway Boston's bike-share program, with 1600 bikes available to borrow at 185 stations.

MBTA bus Supplements the subway system.

Northwest of Boston

Lexington

This upscale suburb, about 18 miles from Boston's center, is a bustling village of white churches and historic taverns, with tour buses surrounding the village green. Here, the skirmish between patriots and British troops jump-started the War of Independence. Each year on April 19, historians and patriots don their 18th-century costumes and grab their rifles for an elaborate re-enactment of the events of 1775.

While this history is celebrated and preserved, it is in stark contrast to the peaceful, even staid, community that is Lexington today. If you stray more than a few blocks from the green, you could be in Anywhere, USA, with few reminders that this is where it all started. Nonetheless, it is a pleasant enough Anywhere, USA, with restaurants and shops lining the main drag, and impressive Georgian architecture anchoring either end.

★ **Minute Man National Historic Park**   PARK
(www.nps.gov/mima; 3113 Marrett Rd; ⊙9am-5pm Apr-Oct; ⚑) FREE The route that British troops followed to Concord has been designated the Minute Man National Historic Park. The visitors' center at the eastern end of the park shows an informative multimedia presentation depicting Paul Revere's ride and the ensuing battles. Within the park, Battle Rd is a 5-mile wooded trail that connects the historic sites related to the battles – from Meriam's Corner, where gunfire erupted while British soldiers were retreating, to the Paul Revere capture site.

Minute Man National Historical Park is about 2 miles west of Lexington center on Rte 2A.

Concord

On April 18, 1775, British troops marched out of Boston, searching for arms that colonists had hidden west of the city. The following morning, they skirmished with Colonial minutemen in Lexington, then continued on to Concord, where the rivals faced off at North Bridge, in the first battle of the War of Independence.

Today tall white church steeples rise above ancient oaks, elms and maples, giving Concord a stateliness that belies the revolutionary drama that occurred centuries ago. Indeed, it's easy to see how writers such as Ralph Waldo Emerson, Nathaniel Hawthorne, Henry David Thoreau and Louisa May Alcott found their inspiration here. Concord was also the home of famed sculptor Daniel Chester French (who went on to create the Lincoln Memorial in Washington, DC).

These days travelers can relive history in Concord. Patriots' Day (www.lexingtonma.gov/patriotsday) is celebrated with gusto, and many significant literary sites are open for visitors.

◉ Sights & Activities

★ **Old North Bridge**   HISTORIC SITE
(www.nps.gov/mima; Monument St; ⊙dawn-dusk) FREE A half-mile north of Monument Sq in Concord center, the wooden span of Old North Bridge is the site of the 'shot heard around the world' (as Emerson wrote in his poem *Concord Hymn*). This is where enraged minutemen fired on British troops, forcing them to retreat to Boston. Daniel Chester French's first statue, *Minute Man*, presides over the park from the opposite side of the bridge.

★ **Sleepy Hollow Cemetery**   CEMETERY
(www.friendsofsleepyhollow.org; Bedford St) This is the final resting place for the most famous Concordians. Though the entrance is only a block east of Monument Sq, the most interesting part, **Authors' Ridge**, is a 15-minute walk along Bedford St. Henry David Thoreau and his family are buried here, as are the Alcotts and the Hawthornes. Ralph Waldo Emerson's tombstone is a large, uncarved rose-quartz boulder, an appropriate transcendentalist symbol.

❶ Getting There & Away

Concord is accessible by MBTA commuter rail (www.mbta.com) from Boston.

Lexington is accessible by bus (except on Sunday), but you'll need a car to see the Minute Man National Historic Park.

Around Boston

Salem

This town's very name conjures up images of diabolical witchcraft and people being burned at the stake. The famous Salem witch trials of 1692 are ingrained in the national memory. Indeed, Salem goes all out at Halloween, when the whole town dresses up for parades and parties, and shops sell all manner of Wiccan accessories.

These incidents obscure Salem's true claim to fame: its glory days as a center for clipper-ship trade with the Far East. Elias Hasket Derby, America's first millionaire, built Derby Wharf, which is now the center of the Salem Maritime National Historic Site.

Today Salem is a middle-class commuter suburb of Boston with an enviable location on the sea. Its rich history and culture, from witches to ships to art, continue to cast a spell of enchantment on all those who visit.

The Rockport/Newburyport line of the MBTA commuter rail (www.mbta.com) runs from Boston's North Station to Salem Depot ($7.50, 30 minutes). Trains run every 30 minutes during the morning and evening rush hours, hourly during the rest of day, and less frequently at weekends.

Plymouth

Plymouth calls itself 'America's Home Town.' It was here that the Pilgrims first settled in the winter of 1620, seeking a place where they could practice their religion as they wished, without interference from government. An innocuous, weathered ball of granite – the famous Plymouth Rock – marks the spot where they supposedly first stepped ashore in this foreign land, and many museums and historic houses in the surrounding streets recall their struggles, sacrifices and triumphs.

You can reach Plymouth from Boston by MBTA commuter rail trains (www.mbta.com), which depart from South Station three or four times a day ($11.50, 90 minutes). From the station at Cordage Park, PAL buses connect to Plymouth center.

Cape Cod

Quaint fishing villages, kitschy tourist traps and genteel towns – the Cape has many faces. Each attracts a different crowd. Families seeking calm waters perfect for little tykes favor Cape Cod Bay on the peninsula's quieter north side. College students looking to play hard in the day and let loose after the sun goes down set out for Falmouth or Wellfleet. Provincetown is a mecca for art lovers, whale-watchers, gay and lesbian travelers and...well, just about everyone.

🛈 Getting There & Around

Your own wheels (two or four) makes getting around easy, but there are also bus links; see the website of the Cape Cod Regional Transport Authority (www.capecodrta.org) for routes and schedules, including summertime shuttles in Falmouth, Hyannis and Provincetown.

Sandwich

The Cape's oldest town (founded in 1637) makes a perfect first impression as you cross over the canal from the mainland.

Head straight to the village center, where white-steepled churches, period homes and a working grist mill surround a picturesque swan pond.

⊙ Sights

★ Heritage Museums & Gardens   MUSEUM, GARDENS

(📞508-888-3300; www.heritagemuseumsandgardens.org; 67 Grove St; adult/child $18/8; ⊙10am-5pm mid-Apr–mid-Oct; 🖤) Fun for kids and adults alike, the 100-acre Heritage Museums & Gardens sports a superb vintage automobile collection in a Shaker-style round barn, an authentic 1908 carousel (rides free with admission) and unusual folk art collections. The grounds also contain one of the finest rhododendron gardens in America; from mid-May to mid-June thousands of 'rhodies' blaze with color. Here you'll also find ways to get your heart racing, via the new **Adventure Park** (📞508-866-0199; www.heritageadventurepark.org; 2hr ticket $34-45; ⊙8am-8pm Jun & Jul, to 7pm Aug, shorter hr mid-Apr–May & Sep–mid-Nov; 🖤).

Sandwich Boardwalk   WATERFRONT

(Boardwalk Rd) A local favorite that's missed by most visitors, this wooden-plank boardwalk extends a scenic 1350ft across an expansive marsh to **Town Neck Beach**. The beach itself is a bit rocky – so-so for swimming but perfect for walks and beachcombing. Once you reach the beach, turn right to make a 1.5-mile loop along the shoreline and then follow the creek back to the boardwalk. There's a $15 parking fee in July and August; at other times it's free.

🛏 Sleeping & Eating

Belfry Inn & Bistro   B&B $$$

(📞508-888-8550; www.belfryinn.com; 6 Jarves St; r $179-275; 🌢🛜) Ever fall asleep in church? Then you'll love the rooms, some with stained-glass windows, in this creatively restored former church, now an upmarket B&B. If, on the other hand, you're uneasy about the angel Gabriel watching over you in bed, Belfry also has two other nearby inns that are home to more conventional, high-quality rooms.

Seafood Sam's   SEAFOOD $$

(📞508-888-4629; www.seafoodsams.com; 6 Coast Guard Rd; mains $7-25; ⊙11am-9pm Mar-Oct; 🖤) Opposite the Cape Cod Canal Visitor Center, Sam's is a good, simple family choice for fish and chips, fried clams and lobster

NEW ENGLAND CAPE COD

rolls. The $7 kids' menu adds to the appeal, as do the outdoor picnic tables, placed perfectly for watching fishing boats sail by.

ⓘ Getting There & Away

If you arrive on the Cape via US 6, take exit 2 (MA 130). Water (MA 130), Main and Grove Sts converge in the village center at Shawme Pond. Tupper Rd, off MA 6A, leads to the Cape Cod Canal.

Falmouth

Crowd-pleasing beaches, a terrific bike trail and the quaint seaside village of Woods Hole are the highlights of the Cape's second-largest town. Falmouth puffs with pride over its most cherished daughter, Katharine Lee Bates, who wrote the words to the nation's favorite patriotic hymn, *America the Beautiful.*

🛏 Sleeping & Eating

Falmouth Heights Motor Lodge MOTEL $$
(☑508-548-3623; www.falmouthheightsresort. com; 146 Falmouth Heights Rd; r $149-269; ⊙May-Oct; ❇ 🛜 🐾) Don't be fooled by the name. This tidy operation is no drive-up motor lodge – it's not even on the highway. All eight styles of rooms (some small and economically priced; others larger, with kitchenettes) are a cut above the competition. And you can throw your own party: the extensive grounds harbor a picnic grove with gas barbecues.

Tides Motel of Falmouth MOTEL $$
(☑508-548-3126; www.tidesmotelcapecod.com; 267 Clinton Ave; r $120-260; ⊙mid-May–mid-Oct; ❇ 🛜) It's all about the water. This place is smack on its own private beach, and you could spit into the ocean from your deck. Otherwise, it's straightforward: the same rooms elsewhere would be a yawn (no-frills, many with kitchenette). Between the surf lullaby and million-dollar view, a steady stream of returnees keep the motel busy all summer, so book ahead.

Maison Villatte CAFE $
(☑774-255-1855; 267 Main St; snacks $3-10; ⊙7am-5pm Tue-Thu & Sun, to 7pm Fri & Sat) A pair of French bakers crowned in toques work the ovens at this buzzing bakery-cafe, creating crusty artisan breads, flaky croissants and sinful pastries. Hearty sandwiches and robust coffee make it an ideal lunch spot.

ⓘ Getting There & Away

Sitting at the southwest corner of the Cape, Falmouth is reached via MA 28, which becomes Main St in the center of town. Buses connect the town with Boston and other Cape destinations.

Ferries to Martha's Vineyard (p199) leave from Falmouth Harbor in summer, and year-round from Woods Hole, 4.5 miles southwest of downtown.

Hyannis

Ferries, buses and planes all converge on Hyannis, the Cape's commercial hub (and part of the larger Barnstable township). So there's a good chance you will too. The village center, especially the harborfront, has been rejuvenated, making it a pleasant place to break a journey.

In addition to being a jumping-off point for boats to Nantucket and Martha's Vineyard, Hyannis attracts Kennedy fans – JFK made his summer home here, and it was at the Kennedy compound that Teddy passed away in 2009. Hyannis Harbor, with its waterfront eateries and ferries, is a few minutes' walk from Main St.

⦿ Sights

★**John F Kennedy Hyannis Museum** MUSEUM
(☑508-790-3077; www.jfkhyannismuseum.org; 397 Main St; adult/child $10/5; ⊙9am-5pm Mon-Sat, noon-5pm Sun Jun-Oct, 10am-4pm Mon-Sat, noon-4pm Sun mid-Apr–May & Nov) Hyannis has been the summer home of the Kennedy clan for generations. Back in the day, JFK spent his summers here – times that are beautifully documented at this museum with photographs and video, from JFK's childhood to the Camelot years of his presidency. The exhibits are poignantly done, and present a theme that changes annually (previous years have covered matriarch Rose and explored the brotherly bond between Jack and Bobby).

Cape Cod Potato Chip Factory FACTORY
(☑888-881-2447; www.capecodchips.com; 100 Breed's Hill Rd; ⊙9am-5pm Mon-Fri) **FREE** These much-admired chips are of the potato, not the computer, variety, so although they won't work in your laptop, they'll taste good in your gateway. The factory has a self-guided tour; in effect, it's just observing the chips march across the production and

Cape Cod, Martha's Vineyard & Nantucket

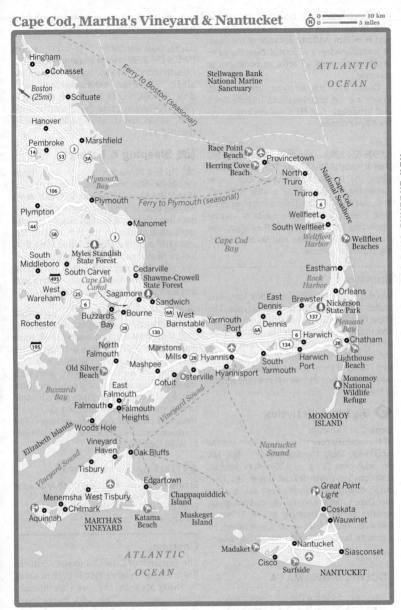

packaging lines through windows. The whole visit might take you 10 minutes, and you get free samples.

From MA 132 (just west of the airport), take Independence Rd a half-mile north to the factory.

🛏 Sleeping & Eating

HI Hyannis HOSTEL **$**

(☎508-775-7990; www.hiusa.org; 111 Ocean St; dm $35-40, d $79-99, q $99-129; ⏱ mid-May–mid-Oct; P@☎) For a million-dollar view on a backpacker's budget, book yourself a bed at this hostel overlooking the harbor. It was built in 2010 by adding new wings to a period home and is within walking distance of the Main St scene, beaches and ferries. Now the caveat: there are only 42 beds, so book well in advance.

Dorms and private rooms are available. Prices are for members and include linen and breakfast; non-HI members pay an extra $3 per person.

Tumi   SEAFOOD $$

(☑508-534-9289; www.tumiceviche.com; 592 Main St; ceviche $9-23, mains $19-31; ⊙11:30am-10pm; ✈) If you love seafood but you're hankering for something a little different, seek out this hidden Italian-Peruvian gem. Take your pick from nine kinds of ceviche (including vegetarian), as well as other raw shellfish, seafood pasta and some interesting Peruvian options.

Brewster

Woodsy Brewster, on the Cape's bay side, makes a good base for outdoorsy types. The Cape Cod Rail Trail cuts clear across town, and there's first-rate camping and water activities. Brewster also has fine restaurants, out of proportion to the town's small size. Everything of interest is on or just off MA 6A (also called Main St), which runs the length of the town.

👁 Sights & Activties

**Cape Cod Museum
of Natural History**   MUSEUM

(☑508-896-3867; www.ccmnh.org; 869 MA 6A; adult/child $15/6; ⊙9:30am-4pm Jun-Aug, 11am-3pm Sep, shorter hrs rest of year; ⚤) This family-friendly museum offers exhibits on the Cape's flora and fauna, including an aquarium and a butterfly house. It has a fine boardwalk trail across a salt marsh to a beach with tide pools. The muse-

---

SCENIC DRIVE: MA 6A

When exploring the Cape, eschew the speedy Mid-Cape Hwy (US 6) and follow instead the Old King's Hwy (MA 6A), which snakes along Cape Cod Bay. The longest continuous stretch of historic district in the USA, it's lined with gracious period homes, antique shops and art galleries, all of which make for good browsing en route.

---

um has a calendar rich with naturalist-led walks, talks and kids' programs.

Jack's Boat Rental   BOATING

(☑508-896-8556; www.jacksboatrental.com; Flax Pond, Nickerson State Park; boat rentals per 30min $11-31; ⊙10am-6pm mid-Jun–mid-Sep) Jack's Boat Rentals, found by Flax Pond within lovely Nickerson State Park, rents out canoes, kayaks and stand-up paddleboards by the half-hour.

🛏 Sleeping & Eating

⭐**Old Sea Pines Inn**   B&B $$

(☑508-896-6114; www.oldseapinesinn.com; 2553 Main St/MA 6A; r $125-170, ste $190-210; ⊛🖥) Staying here is a bit like staying at Grandma's house: antique fittings, sleigh beds and sepia photographs on the bureau. This former girls' boarding school dating from 1840 has 24 rooms: some small; others commodious, with fireplace; some suited to families. Mosey out to the rocking chairs on the porch and soak up the yesteryear atmosphere.

⭐**Brewster Fish House**   SEAFOOD $$$

(☑508-896-7867; www.brewsterfishhouse.com; 2208 Main St/MA 6A; lunch mains $12-20, dinner mains $21-39; ⊙11:30am-3pm & 5-9:30pm) It's not an eye-catcher from the outside, but it's heaven inside for seafood lovers. Start with the lobster bisque, naturally sweet and with chunks of fresh lobster. From there it's safe to cast your net in any direction; dishes are fresh and creative. Just a dozen tables, and no reservations, so try lunch or early dinner to avoid long waits.

ℹ Getting There & Away

Brewster stretches along Cape Cod Bay between Dennis and Orleans. Access is best via MA 6A. From the Cape's south, take MA 124 or MA 137 from Harwich.

Chatham

The patriarch of Cape Cod towns, Chatham has a genteel reserve that is evident along its shady Main St: the shops are upscale; the lodgings, tony. That said, there's something for everyone here – families flock to town for seal-watching, and birders migrate to the wildlife refuge. And then there are all those beaches. Sitting at the 'elbow' of the Cape, Chatham has an amazing 60 miles of shoreline along the ocean, the sound and countless coves and inlets.

MA 28 leads right to Main St, where the lion's share of shops and restaurants are lined up. Chatham is a town made for strolling. You'll find free parking along Main St and in the parking lot behind the Chatham Squire.

ⓘ Getting There & Away

Chatham sits at the 'elbow' of the Cape. MA 28 is the main route through it; it becomes Main St in the downtown area.

MA 137 connects Chatham with US 6.

Wellfleet

Art galleries, primo surfing beaches and those famous Wellfleet oysters lure visitors to this seaside village. Actually, there's not much Wellfleet doesn't have, other than crowds. It's a delightful throwback to an earlier era, from its drive-in movie theater to its unspoiled town center, which has barely changed in appearance since the 1950s.

During the **Wellfleet OysterFest** (www.wellfleetoysterfest.org), held on a weekend in mid-October, the entire town center becomes a food fair, with a beer garden, an oyster-shucking contest and, of course, belly-busters of the blessed bivalves. It's a wildly popular event and a great time to see Wellfleet at its most spirited.

◉ Sights & Activities

Wellfleet Bay
Wildlife Sanctuary   NATURE RESERVE
(☑508-349-2615; www.massaudubon.org; 291 US 6, South Wellfleet; adult/child $5/3; ☉trails 8am-dusk, nature center 8:30am-5pm late May–early Oct; 👪) Birders flock to Mass Audubon's 940-acre sanctuary, where 5 miles of trails cross tidal creeks, salt marshes and beaches. The most popular is the **Goose Pond Trail** (1.5-mile round-trip), which leads out to a salt marsh and offers abundant opportunities for spotting marine and bird life. The sanctuary also offers guided walks and kayaking tours, seal cruises and summer kids' programs.

SickDay Surf Shop   SURFING
(☑508-214-4158; www.sickday.cc; 361 Main St; surfboard rental per day/week $30/150; ☉9am-9pm Mon-Sat May-Oct) If you need surf gear, lessons or local advice, SickDay Surf Shop can help. They also rent wetsuits, stand-up paddleboards and body boards.

AT THE DRIVE-IN...

For an evening of nostalgia, park at **Wellfleet Drive-In** (☑508-349-7176; www.wellfleetcinemas.com; 51 US 6, South Wellfleet; tickets adult/child $11/8; ☉late May–mid-Sep; 👪), one of a dwindling number of drive-in theaters surviving in the USA. Built in the 1950s, before the word 'cineplex' became part of the vernacular, everything except the movie being shown on the giant screen is true to the era. Yep, they still have those original mono speakers that you hook over the car window, there's an old-fashioned snack bar and, of course, it's always a double feature. Plastic – what's that? It's cash-only at the gate.

OK, there are a few accommodations to modern times. So as to not block anyone's view, the lot is now divided into two sections: one for SUVs, the other for cars. And you don't need to use those boxy window speakers: you can also listen by tuning your stereo car radio to an FM station. But other things remain unchanged – bring bug spray and a blanket!

🍴 Sleeping & Eating

Even'Tide Motel   MOTEL $$
(☑508-349-3410; www.eventidemotel.com; 650 US 6, South Wellfleet; r $95-207, cottages per week $1400-2900; ☉May–mid-Oct; ❄🐾🏊) This highly regarded motel, set back from the highway in a grove of pine trees, has an assortment of options: regular motel rooms, plus 10 diverse cottages that can each accommodate two to 10 people (cottages are generally rented by the week). Pluses include a large, indoor heated pool and 5 acres of wooded grounds that harbor sports and picnic facilities.

★ PB Boulangerie & Bistro   BAKERY $
(☑508-349-1600; www.pbboulangeriebistro.com; 15 Lecount Hollow Rd, South Wellfleet; pastries $3-5; ☉bakery 7am-7pm Wed-Sun, bistro 5-9:30pm Wed-Sun) A Michelin-starred French baker setting up shop in tiny Wellfleet? You might think he'd gone crazy, if not for the line out the door. You can't miss PB: it's painted pink and set back from US 6. Scan the cabinets full of fruit tarts, chocolate-almond

DON'T MISS

CAPE COD RAIL TRAIL

The mother of all Cape bicycle trails, the Cape Cod Rail Trail (CCRT) runs 22 glorious paved miles through forest, past cranberry bogs and along sandy ponds ideal for a dip. This rural route, formerly used as a railroad line, is one of the finest bike trails in all of New England.

The path begins in Dennis on MA 134 and continues through **Nickerson State Park** (☑ 508-896-3491; www.mass.gov/dcr; 3488 MA 6A; parking $15; ☺ dawn-dusk; ⛺) in Brewster, into Orleans and across the Cape Cod National Seashore (p196), all the way to South Wellfleet.

There's a hefty dose of Ye Olde Cape Cod scenery en route and you'll have opportunities to detour into villages for lunch or sightseeing. If you have only enough time to do part of the trail, begin at Nickerson State Park and head for the National Seashore – the landscape is unbeatable.

Bicycle rentals are available at the trailheads in Dennis and Wellfleet, at Nickerson State Park and opposite the National Seashore's visitor center in Eastham. There's car parking at all four sites (free except for a small charge at Nickerson).

---

croissants and filled baguettes and you'll think you've died and gone to Paris.

Mac's on the Pier SEAFOOD $$
(☑ 508-349-9611; www.macsseafood.com; 265 Commercial St, Wellfleet Town Pier; mains $8-33; ☺ 11am-8:30pm late May-early Oct; ✍⛺) Head here for fish-market-fresh seafood at bargain prices. Fried-fish standards join the likes of oyster po'boys, sushi rolls and grilled striped-bass dinners. You order at a window and chow down at picnic tables overlooking Wellfleet Harbor.

❶ Getting There & Away

Most of Wellfleet east of US 6 is part of the Cape Cod National Seashore. To get to the town center, turn west off US 6 at either Main St or School St.

Provincetown

This is it: Provincetown is as far as you can go on the Cape, and more than just geographically. The draw is irresistible. Fringe writers and artists began making a summer haven in Provincetown a century ago. Today this sandy outpost has morphed into the hottest gay and lesbian destination in the Northeast. Flamboyant street scenes, brilliant art galleries and unbridled nightlife paint the town center. But that's only half the show. Provincetown's untamed coastline and vast beaches also beg exploring. Sail off on a whale-watch, cruise the night away, get lost in the dunes – but whatever you do, don't miss this unique, open-minded corner of New England.

◎ Sights

Start your exploration on Commercial St, the throbbing waterfront heart of Provincetown, where the lion's share of cafes, galleries and clubs vie for your attention. On any given day you may see cross-dressers, leather-clad motorcyclists, barely clad in-line skaters, same-sex couples strolling hand in hand and heterosexual tourists wondering what they've stumbled into on their way to a whale-watch.

★**Provincetown Art Association & Museum** MUSEUM
(PAAM; ☑ 508-487-1750; www.paam.org; 460 Commercial St; adult/child $10/free; ☺ 11am-8pm Mon-Thu, to 10pm Fri, to 6pm Sat, to 5pm Sun Jul & Aug, shorter hrs rest of year) Founded in 1914 to celebrate the town's thriving art community, this vibrant museum showcases the works of hundreds of artists who have found their inspiration on the Lower Cape. Chief among them are Charles Hawthorne, who led the early Provincetown art movement, and Edward Hopper, who had a home and gallery in the Truro dunes.

★**Pilgrim Monument & Provincetown Museum** MUSEUM
(☑ 508-487-1310; www.pilgrim-monument.org; 1 High Pole Hill Rd; adult/child $12/4; ☺ 9am-5pm Apr, May & Sep-Nov, to 7pm Jun-Aug) Climb to the top of the country's tallest all-granite structure (253ft) for a sweeping view of town, the beaches and the spine of the Lower Cape. The climb is 116 steps plus 60 ramps and takes about 10 minutes at a leisurely pace.

At the base of the c 1910 tower is an evocative museum depicting the landing of the *Mayflower* Pilgrims and other Provincetown history.

Provincetown Public Library
LIBRARY

(⏺508-487-7094; www.provincetownlibrary.org; 356 Commercial St; ⊘10am-5pm Mon & Fri, to 8pm Tue-Thu, 1-5pm Sat & Sun; ♿) Erected in 1860 as a church, this building was turned into a museum a century later, complete with a half-size replica of Provincetown's famed race-winning schooner *Rose Dorothea*. When the museum went bust, the town converted the building to a library. One catch: the boat, which occupies the building's upper deck, was too big to remove – so it's still there, with bookshelves built around it. Pop upstairs and take a look.

Race Point Beach
BEACH

(Race Point Rd) On the wild tip of the Cape, this Cape Cod National Seashore (p196) beach is a breathtaking stretch of sand, crashing surf and undulating dunes as far as the eye can see. Kick off your sandals, kids – the soft, grainy sand makes for a fun run. This is the kind of beach where you could walk for miles and see no one but the occasional angler casting for bluefish. Parking costs $20 in summer (the National Seashore fee).

🏃 Activities

Province Lands Bike Trail (www.nps.gov/caco), an exhilarating 7.5 miles of paved bike trails, crisscrosses the forest and undulating dunes of the Cape Cod National Seashore (p196). As a bonus, you can cool off with a swim: the main 5.5-mile loop trail has spur trails leading to both **Herring Cove Beach** (Province Lands Rd) and Race Point Beach.

★ Dolphin Fleet
Whale Watch
WILDLIFE

(⏺800-826-9300, 508-240-3636; www.whalewatch.com; 307 Commercial St; adult/child $47/31; ⊘mid-Apr–Oct; ♿) 🐾 Dolphin Fleet offers as many as 10 whale-watch tours daily in peak season, each lasting three to four hours. You can expect a lot of splashy fun. Humpback whales have a flair for acrobatic breaching and come surprisingly close to the boats, offering great photo ops. The naturalists on board not only have all the skinny on these mammoth leviathans but also play a vital role in monitoring the whale population.

🛏 Sleeping

Moffett House
GUESTHOUSE $$

(⏺508-487-6615; www.moffetthouse.com; 296a Commercial St; d without bathroom $75-164, with bathroom $115-184; P ❄ @ ⛶) Set back on an alleyway, this guesthouse is not only quiet but also has another bonus: every room comes with two bicycles for your stay. Rooms are basic – it's more like crashing with a friend than doing the B&B thing – but you get kitchen privileges, bagels and coffee in the morning (in summer), and lots of opportunities to meet fellow travelers.

★ Carpe Diem
BOUTIQUE HOTEL $$$

(⏺508-487-4242; www.carpediemguesthouse.com; 12-14 Johnson St; r $199-549; P ❄ ⛶) Sophisticated yet relaxed, this boutique inn blends a soothing mix of smiling Buddhas, orchid sprays and artistic decor. Each guest room is inspired by a different gay literary genius; the room themed on poet Raj Rao, for example, has sumptuous embroidered fabrics and hand-carved Indian furniture.

🍴 Eating

Cafe Heaven
CAFE $

(⏺508-487-9639; www.facebook.com/cafeheavenptown; 199 Commercial St; mains $8-17; ⊘8am-2pm & 6-10pm; ♿) Always bustling, this light and airy art-filled storefront is best known for its easy-on-the-wallet all-day breakfasts, with lunch and dinner sharing the bill as the day progresses. The menu ranges from sinfully good brioche French toast to healthy salads. Excellent sandwiches too, like croque monsieur and chicken pesto melt. Don't be deterred by the wait: the tables turn over quickly.

EAST END GALLERY DISTRICT

With the many artists who have worked here, it's no surprise that Provincetown hosts some of the finest art galleries in the region. For the best browsing, begin at **PAAM** and start walking southwest along Commercial St. Over the next few blocks every second storefront harbors a gallery worth a peek.

Pick up a copy of the *Provincetown Gallery Guide* (www.provincetowngalleryguide.com), or check out its website for gallery info, a map and details of events.

NEW ENGLAND CAPE COD

Lobster Pot
SEAFOOD $$$

(☑ 508-487-0842; www.ptownlobsterpot.com; 321 Commercial St; sandwiches $12-23, mains $25-34; ⊙ 11:30am-9pm Apr-Nov) True to its name, this busy fish house overlooking the harbor is *the* place for lobster, and many have been lured by its retro neon sign. Start with the lobster bisque, then put on a bib and crack open the perfect boiled lobster (there's a full gluten-free menu too). The best way to beat the crowd is to come mid-afternoon.

★ Mews Restaurant & Cafe
MODERN AMERICAN $$$

(☑ 508-487-1500; www.mews.com; 429 Commercial St; mains $22-44; ⊙ 5-10pm) A fantastic water view, the hottest martini bar in town and scrumptious food add up to Provincetown's finest dining scene. There are two sections. Opt to dine gourmet on lobster risotto and filet mignon downstairs, where you're right on the sand, or go casual with a juicy Angus burger from the bistro menu upstairs. Reservations recommended.

 ## Drinking

Aqua Bar
BAR

(☑ 774-593-5106; www.facebook.com/aquabarptown; 207 Commercial St; ⊙ 11am-8pm Mon-Thu, to 11pm Fri-Sun late Apr–Nov) Imagine a food court where the options include a raw bar, sushi, gelato and other international delights. Add a fully stocked bar with generous bartenders pouring the drinks. Now put the whole place in a gorgeous seaside setting, overlooking a little beach and beautiful harbor. Now imagine this whole scene at sunset. That's Aqua Bar.

Boatslip Beach Club
GAY

(☑ 508-487-1669; www.boatslipresort.com; 161 Commercial St; ⊙ tea dances daily from 4pm) Hosts wildly popular afternoon tea dances (4pm to 7pm), often packed with gorgeous guys. DJs fire things up: visit on Thursdays for dance classics from the '70s and '80s. There's accommodations too.

Crown & Anchor
GAY & LESBIAN

(☑ 508-487-1430; www.onlyatthecrown.com; 247 Commercial St; ⊙ hr vary) The queen of the scene, this multiwing complex has a nightclub, a video bar, a leather bar and a fun, steamy cabaret that takes it to the limit, plus loads of shows and events – from Broadway concerts to drag revues and burlesque troupes. Check the calendar (and buy tickets) online. Accommodations and restaurant on site too.

ⓘ Getting There & Away

From the Cape Cod Canal via US 6, it takes about 1½ hours to reach Provincetown (65 miles), depending on traffic. Commercial St is narrow and crowded with pedestrians, so you'll want to do most of your driving along the more car-friendly Bradford St.

BOAT

From around May to October, boats connect Provincetown's **MacMillan Pier** with Boston and Plymouth. Schedules are geared to day-trippers, with morning arrivals into Provincetown and late-afternoon departures. No ferries carry cars, but bikes can be transported for a fee (around $12 round-trip). Advance reservations are recommended, especially on weekends and in peak summer.

Bay State Cruise Co (www.boston-ptown.com) Fast ferry (1½ hours) operates three times daily from Boston's World Trade Center Pier.

Boston Harbor Cruises (www.bostonharborcruises.com) Fast-ferry service (1½ hours) from Long Wharf in Boston up to three times daily.

Plymouth-to-Provincetown Express Ferry (www.captjohn.com) Ferry from Plymouth (1½ hours, once daily) to Provincetown's MacMillan Pier.

BUS

The Plymouth & Brockton bus (www.p-b.com), which terminates at **MacMillan Pier**, runs several times a day from Boston (one way $32 to $38, three to 3½ hours), stopping at other Cape towns along the way. In Boston, it stops at Logan airport and South Station.

CAPE COD NATIONAL SEASHORE

Extending some 40 miles around the curve of the Outer Cape **Cape Cod National Seashore** (☑ 508-255-3421; www.nps.gov/caco; pedestrian/cyclist/motorcycle/car per day $3/3/10/20) encompasses the Atlantic shoreline from Orleans all the way to Provincetown. Under the auspices of the National Park Service, it's a treasure trove of unspoiled beaches, dunes, salt marshes, nature trails and forests. Thanks to the backing of President John F Kennedy, this vast area was set aside for preservation in the 1960s, just before a building boom hit the rest of his native Cape Cod.

Nantucket

One need not be a millionaire to visit Nantucket, but it couldn't hurt. This compact island, 30 miles south of Cape Cod, grew rich from whaling in the 19th century. In recent decades it's seen a rebirth as a summer getaway for CEOs, society types and other well-heeled visitors from Boston and New York.

It's easy to see why. Nantucket is New England at its most rose-covered, cobble-stoned, picture-postcard perfect, and even in the peak of summer there's always an empty stretch of sandy beach to be found. Outdoor activities abound, and there are fine museums, smart restaurants and fun bars.

The town of Nantucket (called 'Town' by the locals) is the island's only real population center. Once home port to the world's largest whaling fleet, the town's storied past is reflected in the gracious period buildings lining its leafy streets. It boasts the nation's largest concentration of houses built prior to 1850 and is the only place in the USA where the entire town is a National Historic Landmark. It's a thoroughly enjoyable place to just amble about and soak up the atmosphere.

◉ Sights

★ Nantucket Whaling Museum   MUSEUM
(☑ 508-228-1894; www.nha.org; 13 Broad St; adult/child $20/5; ⊗ 11am-4pm Apr & May, 10am-5pm Jun-Oct, reduced hr Nov, Dec & mid-Feb–Mar, closed Jan–mid-Feb) One of the island's highlights, this evocative museum occupies an 1847 spermaceti (whale oil) candle factory and the excellent exhibits relive Nantucket's 19th-century heyday as the whaling center of the world. There's a worthwhile, albeit long (54 minutes), documentary on the island, incredible scrimshaw exhibits (engravings and carvings done by sailors on ivory, whalebone or baleen), and a 46ft sperm whale skeleton rising above it all. Be sure to head to the rooftop deck for lovely views.

⌷ Sleeping

Unless you've got island friends with a spare room, a summer stay on Nantucket won't be cheap. Don't even look for a motel or campground – tony Nantucket is all about inns, and many of those are receiving dramatic makeovers to bring them to design-magazine standard.

GO LANING

Go local, go laning. That's the 1930s term Nantucketers coined for wandering about the narrow streets of the town's historic district, especially in the early evening. For the finest stroll, walk up cobbled Main St, just past the c 1818 Pacific National Bank. There you'll find the grandest whaling-era mansions lined up in a row. Other laning favorites: Gardner and Liberty Sts and the honey-combed lanes between Federal and S Water Sts.

★ HI Nantucket   HOSTEL $
(Star of the Sea; ☑ 508-228-0433; www.hiusa.org; 31 Western Ave; dm $39-45; ⊗ mid-May–mid-Oct; @ ☎) Known locally as Star of the Sea, this cool hostel has a million-dollar setting just minutes from Surfside Beach. It's housed in a former lifesaving station that dates from 1873 and is listed on the National Register of Historic Places. As Nantucket's sole budget option, its 49 beds are in high demand, so book as far in advance as possible.

Prices include breakfast and linen; non-HI members pay an additional $3.

Barnacle Inn   B&B $$
(☑ 508-228-0332; www.thebarnacleinn.com; 11 Fair St; r without bathroom $125-300, with bathroom $155-420, ste $180-550; ⊗ late Apr-early Nov; ❄ ☎) This is what old Nantucket is all about: folksy owners and simple, quaint accommodations that hearken to earlier times. Rooms in this turn-of-the-19th-century inn don't have phones or TVs, but they do have good rates, particularly if you opt for a shared bath.

✖ Eating & Drinking

Downyflake   DINER, BAKERY $
(☑ 508-228-4533; www.thedownyflake.com; 18 Sparks Ave; mains $5-13; ⊗ 6am-2pm Mon-Sat, to 1pm Sun Apr–mid-Jan) A popular stop for the island's working-class folks, this no-frills eatery on the edge of town is known for its all-day breakfasts (blueberry pancakes, big omelets) and simple comfort fare. It also doubles as a bakery with homemade doughnuts.

UP-ISLAND

Known as Up Island, the rural western half of Martha's Vineyard is a patchwork of rolling hills, small farms and open fields frequented by wild turkeys and deer. Feast your eyes and your belly at the picturesque fishing village of **Menemsha**, where you'll find seafood shacks with food so fresh the boats unload their catch at the back door. They'll shuck you an oyster and steam you a lobster while you watch and you can eat alfresco on a harborside bench.

The coastal **Aquinnah Cliffs**, also known as the Gay Head Cliffs, are so special they're a National Natural Landmark. These 150ft-high cliffs glow with an amazing array of colors that can be best appreciated in the late afternoon light. You can hang out at **Aquinnah Public Beach**, just below the multihued cliffs, or walk a mile north along the shore to an area that's popular with nude sunbathers.

Cedar Tree Neck Sanctuary (☑508-693-5207; www.sheriffsmeadow.org; Obed Daggett Rd, off Indian Hill Rd; ☺8:30am-5:30pm) **FREE**, off State Rd, has an inviting 2.5-mile hike across native bogs and forest to a coastal bluff with views of Cape Cod. The Massachusetts Audubon Society's **Felix Neck Wildlife Sanctuary** (☑508-627-4850; www.massaudubon.org; 100 Felix Neck Dr; adult/child $4/3; ☺trails dawn-dusk, visitor center 9am-4pm Mon-Fri, 10am-3pm Sat & Sun Jun-Sep; ♿) is a birder's paradise with 4 miles of trails skirting marshes and ponds.

Black-Eyed Susan's MODERN AMERICAN **$$$**
(☑508-325-0308; www.black-eyedsusans.com; 10 India St; breakfast mains $8-13, dinner $26-29; ☺7am-1pm daily & 6-10pm Mon-Sat Apr-Oct; ☑) It's hard to find anyone who doesn't adore this petite, long-running, quietly gourmet place. At breakfast, try the sourdough French toast topped with cinnamon pecans and orange butter; at dinner, sit at the bar to watch chefs perform magic in a *tiny* space. The fish of the day often takes top honors (with strong competition). BYOB.

★**Cisco Brewers** BREWERY
(☑508-325-5929; www.ciscobrewers.com; 5 Bartlett Farm Rd; tours $20; ☺11am-7pm Mon-Sat, noon-6pm Sun year-round, tours mid-May–Dec) Enjoy a hoppy pint of Whale's Tale pale ale at the friendliest brewery you'll likely ever see. Cisco Brewers is the 'other' Nantucket, a laid-back place where fun banter loosens those stiff upper lips found in primmer quarters. In addition to the brewery, there's a small **distillery**, casual indoor and outdoor bars, regular food trucks and live music.

ℹ Information

Visitor Services & Information Bureau
(☑508-228-0925; www.nantucket-ma.gov; 25 Federal St; ☺9am-5pm daily mid-Apr–mid-Oct, Mon-Sat rest of year) Tourist office in Nantucket town.

Nantucket.net (www.nantucket.net) Has private listings of restaurants, housing, arts and recreation.

Inquirer and Mirror (www.ack.net) Local newspaper, with a decent visitors' guide.

ℹ Getting There & Away

AIR

Nantucket Memorial Airport (☑508-325-5300; www.nantucketairport.com; 14 Airport Rd) is 3 miles southeast of Nantucket town. Cape Air (www.capeair.com) offers year-round service to Boston, Hyannis, New Bedford and Martha's Vineyard, and seasonal service to New York. Delta, American, United and JetBlue also offer seasonal services to/from New York, Newark and Washington, DC.

The airport is connected by local bus to town ($2) from mid-June to early September.

BOAT

The most common way to reach Nantucket is by the Steamship Authority and Hy-Line Cruises ferries from Hyannis.

The Steamship Authority (www.steamshipauthority.com) runs frequent, year-round ferries between Hyannis and Nantucket from Steamboat Wharf.

Hy-Line Cruises (www.hylinecruises.com) operates a fast passenger ferry from Hyannis to Nantucket from Straight Wharf year-round and a daily summer ferry between Nantucket and Oak Bluffs on Martha's Vineyard.

Seastreak (www.seastreak.com) operates high-speed passenger ferries in the summer (mid-May to early September) to Nantucket daily from New Bedford, MA, and with weekend services from New Jersey and New York City.

Martha's Vineyard

Bathed in scenic beauty, Martha's Vineyard attracts wide-eyed day-trippers, celebrity second-home owners, and urbanites seeking a restful getaway; its 15,000 year-round residents include many artists, musicians and back-to-nature types. The Vineyard remains untouched by the kind of rampant commercialism found on the mainland – there's not a single chain restaurant or cookie-cutter motel in sight. Instead you'll find cozy inns, chef-driven restaurants and a bounty of green farms and grand beaches. And there's something for every mood here – fine dining in gentrified Edgartown one day and hitting the cotton candy and carousel scene in Oak Bluffs the next.

Martha's Vineyard is the largest island in New England, extending some 23 miles at its widest. Although it sits just 7 miles off the coast of Cape Cod, Vineyarders feel themselves such a world apart that they often refer to the mainland as 'America.'

◉ Sights & Activities

★ **Campgrounds & Tabernacle**　HISTORIC SITE
(🔌508-693-0525; www.mvcma.org) Oak Bluffs started out in the mid-19th century as a summer retreat by a revivalist church, whose members enjoyed a day at the beach as much as a gospel service. They first camped out in tents, then built some 300 wooden cottages, each adorned with whimsical filigree trim.

Flying Horses Carousel　HISTORIC SITE
(🔌508-693-9481; www.mvpreservation.org; Oak Bluffs Ave; per ride/10 rides $3/25; ⊙10am-10pm mid-Jun–mid-Sep; ♿) Take a nostalgic ride on

this National Historic Landmark, which has been captivating kids of all ages since 1876. It's the USA's oldest continuously operating merry-go-round, and these antique horses have manes of real horse hair.

Anderson's Bike Rentals　CYCLING
(🔌508-693-9346;　www.andersonsbikerentals. com; Circuit Ave Extension; bike rental per day/ week $22/95; ⊙9am-6pm May-Oct) Step off the ferry and you'll find a slew of wheelers and dealers renting out bicycles. Keep walking until you reach Anderson's Bike Rentals, an established, family-run operation with well-maintained bikes offered at honest prices. Can also deliver bikes to you.

🛏 Sleeping

HI Martha's Vineyard　HOSTEL $
(🔌508-693-2665; www.hiusa.org; 525 Edgartown–West Tisbury Rd; dm $36-42, tw $99, q $125-149; ⊙mid-May–early Oct; 🅿@🛜) Reserve early for a bed at this popular, purpose-built hostel in the center of the island. It has everything you'd expect: a solid kitchen, games room, bike delivery, no curfew and friendly staff. The public bus stops out front and it's right on the bike path. Dorms and private rooms are available.

Nashua House　INN $$
(🔌508-693-0043; www.nashuahouse.com; 9 Healy Way; r $119-219; ❄🛜) The Vineyard the way it used to be...but with some concessions to modernity (some rooms have TV, some have private bathroom). You'll find simple, spotless, characterful accommodations at this quaint 1873 inn with restaurants and pubs just beyond the front door. It's good value in the summer; in the off-season, when rates drop by nearly half, it's a steal.

LIGHTHOUSES OF MARTHA'S VINEYARD

What's more New England than a lighthouse? And which island has the greatest diversity of lighthouses in America? One guess.

West Chop The island's last staffed lighthouse dates from 1838 and sits on the west side of Vineyard Haven Harbor.

East Chop This cast-iron structure built in 1875 is an Oak Bluffs landmark.

Edgartown It was erected on an island in 1828, but shifting sands have since filled in the inlet and it's now connected to Edgartown by land.

Cape Poge Harsh storm erosion has forced the relocation of this Chappaquiddick Island lighthouse four times since 1801.

Gay Head Built in 1844, this red-brick structure on the Aquinnah Cliffs is arguably the most scenic lighthouse on the Vineyard.

✕ Eating & Drinking

★ ArtCliff Diner
CAFE $

(☑508-693-1224; 39 Beach Rd; mains $8-20; ⊘7am-2pm Thu-Tue) 🍴 Hands-down the best place in town for breakfast and lunch. Chef-owner Gina Stanley, a grad of the prestigious Culinary Institute of America, adds flair to everything she touches, from the almond-encrusted French toast to the fresh fish tacos. The eclectic menu utilizes farm-fresh island ingredients. Expect a line, but it's worth the wait.

Among the Flowers Café
CAFE $$

(☑508-627-3233; 17 Mayhew Lane; lunch $8-20, dinner mains $22-35; ⊘8am-4pm mid-Apr–Oct, to 10pm Jun-Aug; 🍴) Join the in-the-know crowd on the garden patio (under cute striped awnings and – yes – among the flowering plants) for homemade soups, waffles, sandwiches, crepes and even lobster rolls. Although everything's served on paper or plastic, it's still kinda chichi. In summer, it serves dinner as well, and the kitchen kicks it up a notch.

★ Offshore Ale Co
MICROBREWERY

(☑508-693-2626; www.offshoreale.com; 30 Kennebec Ave; ⊘11:30am-9pm Sun-Thu, to 10pm Fri & Sat) Join the throngs of locals and visitors at this popular microbrewery – enjoy a pint of Hop Goddess ale, some superior pub grub (including a knockout lobster roll) and the kind of laid-back atmosphere where boats are suspended from the ceiling and peanut shells are thrown on the floor.

❶ Getting There & Away

AIR

Martha's Vineyard Airport (MVY; www.mvyairport.com) is in the center of the island, about 6 miles south of Vineyard Haven, and is served by buses. It has year-round service to Boston and Nantucket and seasonal services to Hyannis, New Bedford, MA, and New York. Check Cape Air (www.capeair.com) for schedules. Delta and JetBlue also offer seasonal services from New York's JFK Airport.

BOAT

Steamship Authority (www.steamshipauthority.com) operates a frequent, year-round ferry service to Martha's Vineyard. It connects Vineyard Haven with Woods Hole, south of Falmouth on the Cape (a 45-minute voyage). This is the only ferry that carries vehicles – if you're bringing a car, book well in advance . There are up to 14 services daily in each direction.

❶ Getting Around

Getting around is easy by car, though roads are narrow and summertime traffic jams in the main towns are the norm. If you don't have your own wheels, no problem – the extensive public bus system connects every village on the island.

Cycling is another great option; you can rent bikes in Edgartown, Oak Bluffs and Vineyard Haven.

Central Massachusetts

Artfully blending the cultural and cosmopolitan with the rural and rustic, the Pioneer Valley and the Berkshires offer a tantalizing mix of artistic offerings, verdant hills and sweet farmland.

Stretch your quads on hiking trails up Massachusetts' highest mountain and through nature preserves that blanket the surrounding hills. Alternatively, ramble through estate homes of the once famous, listen to world-class musicians from a picnic blanket on a well-manicured lawn, and feast on farm-to-table cuisine at chef-driven restaurants. You could easily spend an entire summer hopscotching the patchwork of wilderness areas, while taking in a dance festival here, an illustrious music series there and summer theater all over the place.

At every turn, you'll come across peppy college towns with shady campuses, bohemian cafes and exceptional art museums. And those lucky enough to be here in autumn will find apples ripe for the picking and hillsides ablaze in brilliant fall foliage.

Northampton

In a region famous for its charming college towns, you'd be hard-pressed to find anything more appealing than the crooked streets of downtown Northampton. Old redbrick buildings and lots of pedestrian traffic provide a lively backdrop for your wanderings, which will likely include cafes, rock clubs and bookstores (which explains why locals call their town 'NoHo'). Move a few steps outside of the picturesque commercial center and you'll stumble onto the bucolic grounds of Smith College. Northampton is a well-known liberal enclave in these parts. The lesbian community is famously outspoken, and rainbow flags wave wildly all over this town.

⊙ Sights

Smith College   COLLEGE
(☑413-584-2700; www.smith.edu; Elm St) Found-
ed 'for the education of the intelligent gen-
tlewoman' in 1875, Smith College is one of
the largest women's colleges in the country,
with 2600 students. The verdant 125-acre
campus holds an eclectic architectural mix
of nearly 100 buildings, set on a pretty pond.
Notable alumnae of the college include Sylvia
Plath, Julia Child and Gloria Steinem. After
exploring the campus, take a stroll around
Paradise Pond and snap a photo at the Japanese tea hut.

Smith College Museum of Art   MUSEUM
(☑413-585-2760; www.smith.edu/artmuseum; 20
Elm St; adult/child $5/free; ⊙10am-4pm Tue-Sat,
noon-4pm Sun) This impressive campus museum boasts a 25,000-piece collection. The
collection is particularly strong in 19th- and
20th-century European and North American paintings, including works by Degas,
Winslow Homer, Picasso and James Abbott
McNeill Whistler. Another highlight is the
so-called 'functional art': the remarkable
restrooms and the eclectic collection of
benches (that you can actually sit on) – all
designed and created by contemporary
American artists.

🏃 Activities

The **Norwottuck Rail Trail** (nor-wah-tuk;
www.mass.gov/eea/agencies/dcr/massparks/
region-west/norwottuck-rail-trail.html) is a walking and cycling path that follows the former
Boston & Maine Railroad right-of-way from
Amherst to Hadley to Northampton, a total
distance of 11 miles. For much of its length,
the trail parallels MA 9, passing through
open farms and crossing the broad Connecticut River on a historic 1500ft-long bridge.

Parking and access to the trail can be
found on Station Rd in Amherst, at the
Mountain Farms Mall on MA 9 in Hadley and at Elwell State Park on Damon Rd
in Northampton. You can rent bikes from
Northampton Bicycle (www.nohobike.com;
319 Pleasant St; per day from $25; ⊙9:30am-7pm
Mon-Fri, to 5pm Sat, noon-5pm Sun).

🛏 Sleeping & Eating

Hotel Northampton   HISTORIC HOTEL $$
(☑413-584-3100;   www.hotelnorthampton.com;
36 King St; r $186-286; P🅿🛜) This old-timer
is perfectly situated smack in the center of
Northampton and has been the town's best

bet since 1927. The 100 rooms are airy and
well fitted, with traditional furnishings and
floral quilts and curtains. There's a quiet
grandeur to the place. And mailing a post-
card via an antiquated letterbox system al-
ways feels good.

Bela   VEGETARIAN $
(☑413-586-8011; www.belaveg.com; 68 Masonic
St; mains $8-13; ⊙noon-8:30pm Tue-Sat; 🛒🪑)
🍃 This cozy vegetarian restaurant puts such
an emphasis on fresh ingredients that the
chalkboard menu changes daily depending
on what local farmers are harvesting. Think
home-cooked comfort food and a setting
that welcomes families – there's even a col-
lection of toys for the kids! Cash only.

Paul & Elizabeth's   SEAFOOD $$
(☑413-584-4832;   www.paulandelizabeths.com;
150 Main St; mains $8-21; ⊙11:30am-9pm Sun-Thu,
to 9:45pm Fri & Sat; 🛜🛒🪑) 🍃 This airy, plant-
adorned restaurant, known locally as P&E's,
sits on the top floor of Thornes Marketplace
and is the town's premier natural-foods restaurant. It serves vegetarian cuisine and
seafood, often with an Asian bent. From fall
to early spring, don't miss the rare opportunity to sample their old-fashioned Indian
pudding.

ℹ Getting There & Away

Northampton is 18 miles north of Springfield on
I-91. If you don't score a parking spot on Main
St, you'll find public parking at **Thornes Market-
place** (www.thornesmarketplace.com; 150 Main
St; ⊙10am-6pm Mon-Wed, to 8pm Thu-Sat,
noon-5pm Sun) in the town center.

Pioneer Valley Transit Authority (www.pvta.
com) provides bus services (with bike racks)
throughout the Five College area, with the
Northampton–Amherst route having the most
frequent service.

Amherst

This quintessential college town is home to
the prestigious Amherst College, a pretty
'junior ivy' that borders the town green, as
well as the hulking University of Massachusetts and the cozy liberal-arts Hampshire
College. Start your explorations at the town
green, at the intersection of MA 116 and MA
9. In the surrounding streets, you'll find a
few funky galleries, a bookshop or two,
countless coffeehouses, and a few small but
worthwhile museums (several of which are
associated with the colleges).

Emily Dickinson Museum MUSEUM
(☑413-542-8161; www.emilydickinsonmuseum.
org; 280 Main St; guided tour adult/child $15/free;
☺10am-5pm Wed-Mon Jun-Aug, 11am-4pm Wed-
Sun Apr, May & Sep-Dec, 11am-4pm Sat & Sun Mar)
During her lifetime, Emily Dickinson (1830–
86) published only seven poems, but more
than 1000 of her poems were discovered
and published posthumously, and her verses
on love, nature and immortality have made
her one of the USA's most important poets.
Dickinson spent most of her life in near se-
clusion in this stately home near the center
of Amherst. Guided tours (60 minutes) focus on the poet and her works, visiting both
the Dickinson Homestead and the adjacent
Evergreens.

You can also explore the grounds using a
self-guided audio tour. Check the website for
the tour schedules.

**Eric Carle Museum of
Picture Book Art** MUSEUM
(☑413-559-6300; www.carlemuseum.org; 125 W
Bay Rd; adult/child $9/6; ☺10am-4pm Tue-Fri, to
5pm Sat, noon-5pm Sun; 🚸) Co-founded by the
author and illustrator of *The Very Hungry
Caterpillar,* this superb museum celebrates
book illustrations from around the world
with rotating exhibits in three galleries, as
well as a permanent collection. All visitors
(grown-ups included) are encouraged to
express their own artistic sentiments in the
hands-on art studio.

The Berkshires

Few places in America combine culture and
country living as deftly as the Berkshire
hills, home to world-class music, dance and
theater festivals – the likes of Tanglewood
and Jacob's Pillow – as well as miles of hiking trails and acres of farmland.

Extending from the highest point in the
state – Mt Greylock – southward to the Connecticut state line, the Berkshires have been
a summer refuge for more than a century,
when the rich and famous arrived to build
summer 'cottages' of grand proportions.
Many of these mansions survive as inns
or performance venues. And still today, on
summer weekends when the sidewalks are
scorching in Boston and New York, crowds
of city dwellers jump in their cars and head
for the Berkshire breezes.

❶ Getting There & Around

Most travelers are likely to reach this region by
driving from Boston, Hartford or New York. It
is possible to arrive by bus or train, but you'll
want your own vehicle if you intend to visit the
more rural areas. If not, the Berkshire Regional
Transit Authority (www.berkshirerta.com) runs
buses between major Berkshire towns. A ride
costs $1.75.

Great Barrington

Great Barrington's Main St used to consist of
Woolworth's, hardware stores, thrift shops
and a run-down diner. These have given way
to artsy boutiques, antique shops, coffeehouses and restaurants. Nowadays the town
boasts the best dining scene in the region,
with easy access to hiking trails and magnificent scenery in the surrounding hills.

The Housatonic River flows through the
center of town just east of Main St/US 7, the
central thoroughfare.

❍ Sights & Activities

Beartown State Forest FOREST
(☑413-528-0904; www.mass.gov/dcr; 69 Blue
Hill Rd, Monterey; parking $15) This lovely state
park is centered on Benedict Pond, a perfect
spot for swimming, fishing, canoeing and
kayaking. There are miles of hiking trails,
including a piece of the Appalachian Trail.
The furthest reaches of this forest are home
to deer, bears, bobcats and fishers. Less ambitious hikers can stroll the 1.5-mile Benedict Pond Loop.

Housatonic River Walk WALKING
(www.gbriverwalk.org; ☺sunrise-sunset Apr-Nov)
FREE The picturesque Housatonic River
flows through the center of Great Barrington, with the River Walk offering a perfect
perch from which to admire it. Access the
walking path from Main St (behind Rite-
Aid) or from Bridge St.

✖ Eating & Drinking

Baba Louie's PIZZA $$
(☑413-528-8100; www.babalouiespizza.com; 286
Main St; pizzas $10-20; ☺11:30am-3pm & 5-9:30pm;
🚰🚸) Baba's is known for its organic sour-
dough crust and for the guys with dreadlocks.
There's a pizza for every taste, running the
gamut from the fan-favorite Dolce Vita with
figs, gorgonzola and prosciutto to the gluten-
free Vegetazione with artichoke hearts, broc-
coli, tofu and soy mozzarella.

Barrington Brewery
MICROBREWERY
(☑413-528-8282; www.barringtonbrewery.net; 420 Stockbridge Rd; ⊙11:30am-9:30pm; 🛜) 🖋
You can rest easy, knowing your beer was brewed with solar power. The frothy, hoppy brews are the star of the show here, but the grass-fed beef burgers make a decent complement and the outdoor seating takes it up a notch on a balmy summer night.

Stockbridge

Take a good look down Stockbridge's wide Main St. Notice anything? More specifically, notice anything missing? Not one stoplight stutters the view, not one telephone pole blights the picture-perfect scene – it looks very much the way Norman Rockwell might have seen it.

In fact, Rockwell did see it – he lived and worked in Stockbridge during the last 25 years of his life. Nowadays Stockbridge attracts summer and fall visitors en masse, who come to stroll the streets, inspect the shops and sit in the rockers on the porch of the historic Red Lion Inn. And they come by the busload to visit the Norman Rockwell Museum on the town's outskirts.

All that fossilized picturesqueness bears a price. Noticeably absent from the village center is the kind of vitality that you find in the neighboring towns.

Norman Rockwell Museum
MUSEUM
(☑413-298-4100; www.nrm.org; 9 Glendale Rd/MA 183; adult/child $20/free; ⊙10am-5pm May-Oct, to 4pm Nov-Apr) Born in New York City, Norman Rockwell (1894–1978) sold his first magazine cover illustration to the *Saturday Evening Post* in 1916. In the following half-century he did another 321 covers for the *Post*, as well as illustrations for books, posters and many other magazines on his way to becoming the most popular illustrator in US history. This excellent little museum has the largest collection of Rockwell's original art, as well as Rockwell's studio, which was moved here from his Stockbridge home.

To find the museum follow MA 102 west from Stockbridge and turn left (south) on MA 183.

Lenox

This gracious, wealthy town is a historical anomaly: firstly, its charm was not destroyed by the Industrial Revolution; and then, prized for its bucolic peace, the town became a summer retreat for wealthy families with surnames like Carnegie, Vanderbilt and Westinghouse, who had made their fortunes by building factories in other towns.

As the cultural heart of the Berkshires, Lenox's illustrious past remains tangibly present today. The superstar among its attractions is the Tanglewood Music Festival, an incredibly popular summer event drawing scores of visitors from New York City, Boston and beyond.

Tanglewood Music Festival
MUSIC
(☑888-266-1200; www.tanglewood.org; 297 West St/MA 183, Lenox; lawn tickets from $12, kids free; ⊙late Jun-early Sep) Dating from 1934, the Tanglewood Music Festival is among the most esteemed summertime music events in the world. Symphony, pops, chamber music, jazz and blues are performed from late June through early September. You can count on renowned cellist Yo-Yo Ma, violinist Joshua Bell and singer James Taylor to perform each summer, along with a run of world-class guest artists and famed conductors.

🛏 Sleeping & Eating

Birchwood Inn
INN $$$
(☑413-637-2600; www.birchwood-inn.com; 7 Hubbard St; r $199-289, deluxe r $359-394; 🌸🛜🐾) A pretty hilltop inn a couple of blocks from the town center, Birchwood occupies the oldest (1767) home in Lenox. The 11 spacious rooms vary in decor; some swing with a vintage floral design, others are more country classic, but all are romantic and luxurious. Deluxe rooms feature king-size beds and wood-burning fireplaces.

Home-cooked breakfasts, perhaps fondue Florentine soufflé or blueberry cheese blintzes, are served in a fireside dining room.

Haven Cafe & Bakery
CAFE $
(☑413-637-8948; www.havencafebakery.com; 8 Franklin St; mains $8-16; ⊙7:30am-3pm Mon-Fri, from 8am Sat & Sun; 🛜🖋) It looks like a cafe, but the sophisticated food evokes a more upscale experience. For breakfast, try croissant French toast or inventive egg dishes like salmon scramble; for lunch there are fancy salads and sandwiches – all highlighting local organic ingredients. Definitely save room for something sweet from the bakery counter.

★ Nudel
AMERICAN $$$
(☑413-551-7183; www.nudelrestaurant.com; 37 Church St; mains $26, 3-/4-course prix fixe menu

$45/55; ⊙ 5-9:30pm Tue-Sat, to 9pm Sun) Nudel is a driving force in the area's sustainable-food movement, with just about everything on the menu seasonally inspired and locally sourced. The back-to-basics approach rings through in inventive dishes, which change daily but never disappoint. Incredible flavors. Nudel has a loyal following, so reservations are recommended in season.

Williamstown

Small but gracious Williamstown is nestled within the heart of the Purple Valley, so named because the surrounding mountains often seem shrouded in a lavender veil at dusk. Folks congregate in the friendly town center, which is only two blocks long, while dogs and kids frolic in the green spaces.

Williamstown is a quintessential New England college town, its charming streets and greens dotted with the stately brick and marble buildings of Williams College. Cultural life is rich, with a pair of exceptional art museums and one of the region's most respected summer theater festivals.

⊙ Sights

★**Clark Art Institute** MUSEUM
(☑ 413-458-2303; www.clarkart.edu; 225 South St; adult/child $20/free; ⊙ 10am-5pm Tue-Sun Sep-Jun, daily Jul & Aug) Even if you're not an avid art lover, don't miss this gem, set on 140 gorgeous acres of expansive lawns, flower-filled meadows and rolling hills. The building – with its triple-tiered reflecting pool – is a stunner. The collections are particularly strong in the Impressionists, with significant works by Monet, Pissarro and Renoir. Mary Cassatt, Winslow Homer and John Singer Sargent represent contemporary American painting.

Williams College Museum of Art MUSEUM
(☑ 413-597-2429; https://wcma.williams.edu; 15 Lawrence Hall Dr; ⊙ 10am-5pm, to 8pm Thu, closed Wed Sep-May) FREE This sister museum of the Clark Art Institute graces the center of town and has an incredible (free!) collection of its own. Around half of its 13,000 pieces comprise the American Collection, with substantial works by notables such as Edward Hopper (*Morning in a City*), Winslow Homer and Grant Wood, to name only a few. The photography collection is also noteworthy, with representation by Man Ray and Alfred Stieglitz. Did we mention it's free?

★ Festivals

Williamstown Theatre Festival THEATER
(☑ box office 413-458-3253; www.wtfestival.org; 1000 Main St; ⊙ Jun-Aug; ⊞) Stars of the theater world descend upon Williamstown every year from the third week in June to the third week in August. Widely considered the best summer theater in the area, the Williamstown Theatre Festival was the first to win the Regional Theatre Tony Award.

⊨ Sleeping & Eating

Maple Terrace Motel MOTEL $$
(☑ 413-458-9677; www.mapleterrace.com; 555 Main St; d $119-178; ☞⊠⊛) The Maple Terrace is a simple yet cozy 15-room place on the eastern outskirts of town. The Swedish innkeepers have snazzed up the grounds with gardens that make you want to linger. There's nothing fancy going on here, but the place is comfortable and service is warmly attentive.

River Bend Farm B&B B&B $$
(☑ 413-458-3121; www.riverbendfarmbb.com; 643 Simonds Rd/US 7; r $120; ⊙ Apr-Oct; ⊛☞) Step back in time to 1770, when this Georgian Colonial was a local tavern owned by Benjamin Simonds. The house owes its painstaking restoration to hosts Judy and Dave Loomis. Four simple, comfortable doubles share two bathrooms with claw-foot tubs. Breakfast is served in the wood-paneled tap room, next to the wide stone fireplace.

Despite the name, it's not on a farm but along US 7 on the north side of the little bridge over the Hoosic River.

Pappa Charlie's Deli DELI $
(☑ 413-458-5969; 28 Spring St; mains $5-8; ⊙ 8am-8pm Mon-Sat, to 7pm Sun; ☞) Here's a welcoming breakfast spot where locals really do ask for 'the usual.' The stars themselves created the lunch sandwiches that bear their names. The Mary Tyler Moore is a favorite (bacon, lettuce, tomato and avocado), though the actress later went vegetarian, so you can also get a version with soy bacon instead. Or order a Politician and get anything you want on it.

★**Mezze Bistro & Bar** FUSION $$
(☑ 413-458-0123; www.mezzerestaurant.com; 777 Cold Spring Rd/US 7; mains $18-28; ⊙ 5-9pm Sun-Thu, to 10pm Fri & Sat) You don't know exactly what you're going to get at this contemporary chic restaurant – the menu changes frequently – but you know it's going to be good. Situated on 3 spectacular acres, Mez-

NORTH ADAMS: MASS MOCA

At first glance, North Adams' beautiful and bleak 19th-century downtown seems out of sync with the rest of the Berkshires. It's not so lively and the amenities are limited. But it doesn't take long to discover the appeal – mainly, Mass MoCA, an exemplary contemporary-art museum of staggering proportions. Indeed, the place is big enough to be its own village, and its grounds do in fact contain some of the city's best dining, drinking and shopping.

MASS MoCA (Massachusetts Museum of Contemporary Art; ☑ 413-662-2111; www.mass moca.org; 1040 MASS MoCA Way; adult/child $20/8; ☺ 10am-6pm Sun-Wed, to 7pm Thu-Sat Jul & Aug, 11am-5pm Wed-Mon Sep-Jun; ☼) sprawls over 13 acres of downtown North Adams – one-third of the entire business district. After the Sprague Electric Company closed in 1985, some $31 million was spent to modernize the property into 'the largest gallery in the United States.' The museum encompasses 222,000 sq ft in 25 buildings, including art construction areas, performance centers and 19 galleries. One gallery is the size of a football field, giving installation artists the opportunity to explore a whole new dimension. Bring your walking shoes!

ze's farm-to-table approach begins with an edible garden right on site. Much of the rest of the seasonal menu, from small-batch microbrews to organic meats, is locally sourced as well.

RHODE ISLAND

Rhode Island, the smallest of the US states, isn't actually an island. Although it takes only 45 minutes to traverse, this little wonder packs in over 400 miles of coastline with some of the finest white-sand swimming beaches in the Northeast, deserted coves, rugged cliffs and isolated lighthouses.

Hugging the shoreline before heading inland, delightful resorts, quaint Colonial villages and extravagant mansions give way to lush fields of berry farms, vineyards, and the horse studs of Middletown and Portsmouth. Rhode Island's two cities – Providence, of working-class roots, and Newport, born of old money the likes of which most cannot conceive – are each among New England's finest, brimming with fantastic museums, neighborhoods boasting utterly gorgeous historic homes, and an urban fabric of top-notch restaurants and seriously cool bars. It's no wonder the nouveau riche continue to flock here for summer shenanigans.

History

Ever since it was founded in 1636 by Roger Williams, a religious outcast from Boston, Providence has enjoyed an independent frame of mind. Williams' guiding principle, the one that got him ostracized from Massachusetts, was that all people should have

freedom of conscience. He put his liberal beliefs into practice when settling Providence, remaining on friendly terms with the local Narragansett Native Americans after purchasing from them the land for a bold experiment in tolerance and peaceful coexistence.

Williams' principles would not last long. As Providence and Newport grew and merged into a single colony, competition and conflict with area tribes sparked several wars, leading to the decimation of the Wampanoag, Pequot, Narragansett and Nipmuck peoples. Rhode Island was also a prolific slave trader and its merchants would control much of that industry in the years after the Revolutionary War.

The city of Pawtucket birthed the American Industrial Revolution with the establishment of the water-powered Slater Mill in 1790. Industrialism impacted the character of Providence and surrounds, particularly along the Blackstone River, creating urban density. As with many small East Coast cities, these urban areas went into a precipitous decline in the 1940s and '50s as manufacturing industries (textiles and costume jewelry) faltered. In the 1960s, preservation efforts salvaged the historic architectural framework of Providence and Newport. Today Newport has flourished into one of the nation's most attractive historical centers.

Providence also rerouted its destiny to emerge as a lively and stylish city with a dynamic economy and vibrant downtown core, largely due to the work of Buddy Cianci, twice-convicted felon and twice-elected mayor (1975–84, 1991–2002). Cianci is credited with saving the city from industrial and urban decline with a large-scale revitalization project that uncovered and rerouted previously subterranean river tributaries into a central artificial pond. The spectacle of today's wildly popular WaterFire festival (p207) is a powerful symbol of the city's phoenixlike rebirth along the confluence of the three rivers that gave it life. Cianci died in 2016, aged 74.

❶ Information

Rhode Island Division of Parks & Recreation (www.riparks.com) For a listing of all of Rhode Island's state beaches.

Rhode Island Tourism Division (www.visitrhodeisland.com) The official state provider of tourist information on Rhode Island.

Providence

Atop the confluence of the Providence, Moshassuck and Woonasquatucket Rivers, Rhode Island's capital city offers some of the finest urban strolling in New England: around Brown University's historic campus on 18th-century College Hill, along the landscaped Riverwalk trail, and among downtown's handsome streets and lanes with their hipster-y cafes, art-house theaters, fusion restaurants and trendsetting bars.

Once destined to become an industrial relic, Providence's fate was spared when Buddy Cianci, its then controversial two-time mayor, rolled out a plan to revitalize the downtown core by rerouting subterranean rivers, reclaiming land and restoring historic facades. It created a city where history's treasures are integrated into a creative present, not simply memorialized; where three centuries of architectural styles are unified in colorful urban streetscapes that are at once bold, beautiful and cooler than cool. A large student population here helps keep the city's social and arts scenes lively and current.

◉ Sights

★**Providence Athenaeum**   LIBRARY
(☑401-421-6970;   www.providenceathenaeum.org; 251 Benefit St; ⊙10am-6pm Mon-Thu, 9am-5pm Fri, 10am-2pm Sat) **FREE** One of the most prominent buildings on Benefit St, the Greek Revival Providence Athenaeum was designed by William Strickland and completed in 1838. This is a library of the old school, with plaster busts and oil paintings filling in spaces not occupied by books. Edgar Allen Poe used to court ladies here. Pick up a brochure for a self-guided **Raven Tour** of the building's artwork and architecture.

★**Rhode Island State House**   NOTABLE BUILDING
(☑401-222-3983; www.sos.ri.gov; 82 Smith St; ⊙self-guided tours 8:30am-4:30pm Mon-Fri, guided tours 9am, 10am, 11am, 1pm, 2pm Mon-Fri) **FREE** Designed by McKim, Mead and White in 1904, the Rhode Island State House rises above the Providence skyline, easily visible from miles around. Modeled in part on St Peter's Basilica in Vatican City, it has the world's fourth-largest self-supporting marble dome and houses one of Gilbert Stuart's portraits of George Washington.

★**John Brown House**   MUSEUM
(☑401-331-8575 ext 362; www.rihs.org; 52 Power St; adult/child $10/6; ⊙tours 1:30pm & 3pm Tue-Fri, 10:30am, noon, 1:30pm & 3pm Sat Apr-Nov) On College Hill, the brick John Brown House, called the 'most magnificent and elegant mansion' that I have ever seen on this continent' by John Quincy Adams, was built in 1786.

★**Brown University**   UNIVERSITY
(☑401-863-1000; www.brown.edu) Dominating the crest of the College Hill neighborhood on the East Side, the campus of Brown University exudes Ivy League charm. **University Hall**, a 1770 brick edifice used as a barracks during the Revolutionary War, sits at its center. To explore the campus, start at the wrought-iron gates opening from the top of College St and make your way across the green toward Thayer St.

Benefit Street   ARCHITECTURE
Immediately east of Providence's downtown, you'll find College Hill, where you can see the city's Colonial history reflected in the 18th-century houses that line Benefit St on the East Side. These are, for the most part, private homes, but many are open for tours one weekend in June during the annual **Festival of Historic Homes**. Benefit St is a fitting symbol of the Providence renaissance, rescued by local preservationists in the 1960s from misguided urban-renewal efforts that would have destroyed it.

RISD Museum of Art   MUSEUM
(☑401-454-6500; www.risdmuseum.org; 224 Benefit St; adult/child $12/3; ⊙10am-5pm Tue-Sun, to 9pm 3rd Thu of month; ♿) Wonderfully eclectic, the Rhode Island School of Design's art

museum showcases everything from ancient Greek art to 20th-century American paintings and decorative arts. Pop in before 1pm Sunday and admission is free.

Roger Williams Park
PARK

(1000 Elmwood Ave) FREE In 1871 Betsey Williams, great-great-great-granddaughter of the founder of Providence, donated her farm to the city as a public park. Today this 430-acre expanse of greenery, only a short drive south of Providence, includes lakes and ponds, forest copses and broad lawns, picnic grounds, the **Planetarium and Museum of Natural History** (401-680-7221; www.providenceri.com/museum; museum/planetarium $2/3; 10am-4pm;), an operating Victorian carousel, greenhouses and Williams' cottage.

Festivals

WaterFire
STREET CARNIVAL

(401-273-1155; www.waterfire.org; dates vary) Particularly during summer, much of downtown Providence transforms into a carnivalesque festival thanks to the exceedingly popular WaterFire art installation created by Barnaby Evans in 1994. Marking the convergence of the Providence, Moshassuck and Woonasquatucket Rivers, 100 anchored, flaming braziers illuminate the water, overlooked by crowds of pedestrians strolling over the bridges and along the riverside.

Sleeping

Christopher Dodge House
B&B $$

(401-351-6111; www.providence-hotel.com; 11 W Park St; r $149-189;) This 1858 Federal-style house is furnished with early American reproduction furniture and marble fireplaces. Austere on the outside, it has elegant proportions, large, shuttered windows and wooden floors.

Old Court B&B
INN $$

(401-751-2002; www.oldcourt.com; 144 Benefit St; r weekday $155-195, weekend $185-225) Well positioned among the historic buildings of College Hill, this three-story, 1863 Italianate home has stacks of charm. Enjoy eccentric wallpaper, good jam at breakfast and occasional winter discounts.

Providence Biltmore
HISTORIC HOTEL $$

(401-421-0700; www.providencebiltmore.com; 11 Dorrance St; r $165-379;) The granddaddy of Providence's hotels, the Biltmore dates from the 1920s. The lobby, both intimate

and regal, nicely combines dark wood, twisting staircases and chandeliers, while well-appointed rooms stretch many stories above the old city. Ask for one of the 292 rooms that are on a high floor.

Eating

Louis Family Restaurant
DINER $

(401-861-5225; www.louisrestaurant.org; 286 Brook St; mains $4-9; 5am-3pm;) Wake up early to watch bleary-eyed students and carpenters eat strawberry-banana pancakes and drink drip coffee at their favorite greasy spoon long before the rest of College Hill shows signs of life.

Haven Brothers Diner
DINER $

(401-603-8124; www.havenbrothersmobile.com; cnr Dorrance & Fulton Sts; meals $5-12; 5pm-3am) Parked next to City Hall, this diner sits on the back of a truck that has rolled into the same spot every evening for decades. Climb up a rickety ladder to get basic diner fare alongside everyone, from prominent politicians to college kids pulling an all-nighter to drunks. The murder burger comes highly recommended.

Local 121
MODERN AMERICAN $$

(401-274-2121; www.local121.com; 121 Washington St; mains $17-30; 5-10pm Wed & Thu, 5-11pm Fri, 10am-3pm & 5-11pm Sat, 10am-3pm & 5-9pm Sun) Locavore mania comes to Providence with this opulent, old-school restaurant with contemporary aspirations. Housed in the old Dreyfus hotel (built in the 1890s), a building owned by the arts organization AS220, Local 121 has an easy, unpretentious grandeur – and some damn fine food. The menu is seasonal, but recent options include a perfect (local) scallop po'boy and (local) duck-ham pizza.

birch
MODERN AMERICAN $$$

(401-272-3105; www.birchrestaurant.com; 200 Washington St; 4-course dinner $49, beverage pairings $35; 5-10pm Thu-Mon) With a background at Noma in Copenhagen and the fabulous Dorrance at the Biltmore, chef Benjamin Sukle and his wife, Heidi, have their own place: the understated, but fabulously good, birch. Its intimate size and style (seating is around a U-shaped bar) means attention to detail is exacting in both the decor and the food, which focuses on underutilized, small-batch and hyper-seasonal produce.

🍷 Drinking

AS220

CLUB

(☑ 401-831-9327; www.as220.org; 115 Empire St; ☺ bar 5pm-1am Tue-Sat, cafe noon-10pm Tue-Sat) A long-standing outlet for all forms of Rhode Island art, AS220 (say 'A-S-two-twenty') books experimental bands, hosts readings and provides gallery space for a very active community. If you need a cup of coffee, vegan cookie or spinach pie, it also operates a cafe and bar: hours vary.

Salon

BAR, CLUB

(☑ 401-865-6330; www.thesalonpvd.com; 57 Eddy St; ☺ 7pm-1am Tue-Thu, to 2am Fri & Sat) The Salon mixes ping-pong tables and pinball machines with 1980s pop and pickleback shots (whiskey with a pickle juice chaser) upstairs, with live shows, open mike, DJs and dance parties downstairs. If you get hungry, there are PB&J sandwiches.

❶ Getting There & Around

With hills, two interstates and two rivers defining its downtown topography, Providence can be a confusing city to find your way around. Parking can be difficult downtown and near the train station. For a central lot, try the huge garage of the Providence Place mall and get a merchant to validate your ticket. On the East Side, you can usually find street parking easily.

Major car-rental companies have airport and downtown locations.

Providence is small, pretty and walkable, so once you arrive you'll probably want to get around on foot.

Rhode Island Public Transit Authority (www.ripta.com) operates two 'trolley' routes. The Green Line runs from the East Side through downtown to Federal Hill. The Gold Line runs from the Marriott hotel south to the hospital via Kennedy Plaza, and stops at the Point St Ferry Dock.

BUS

➡ All long-distance buses and most local routes stop at the central **Intermodal Transportation Center** (Kennedy Plaza; ☺ 6am-7pm). Greyhound (www.greyhound.com) and Peter Pan Bus Lines (www.peterpanbus.com) have ticket counters inside, and there are maps outlining local services.

➡ Peter Pan connects Providence and Green Airport with Boston's South Station (from $9, one hour, 12 daily) and Logan International Airport (from $18, 70 minutes, 10 daily).

➡ Greyhound (www.greyhound.com) buses depart for Boston (from $9, 65 minutes), New York City (from $15, 5½ to six hours) and elsewhere.

TRAIN

➡ Amtrak (www.amtrak.com) trains, including high-speed Acela trains, connect Providence with Boston (from $12, 50 minutes) and New York (from $50, three to 3½ hours).

➡ MBTA commuter rail (www.mbta.com) connects to Boston ($11.50, 60 to 75 minutes).

Newport

Established by religious moderates, 'new port' flourished in the independent colony of Rhode Island, which declared itself a state here in 1776. Downtown, shutterbugs snap excitedly at immaculately preserved Colonial-era architecture and landmarks at seemingly every turn.

Fascinating as Newport's early history is, the real intrigue began in the late 1850s, when wealthy industrialists began building opulent summer residences along cliff-top Bellevue Ave. Impeccably styled on Italianate palazzi, French châteaus and Elizabethan manor houses, these gloriously restored mansions filled with priceless antiques and their breathtaking location must be seen to be believed. The curiosity, variety, extravagance and uniqueness of this spectacle is unrivaled.

Honoring its maritime roots, Newport remains a global center for yachting. Put simply, summers here sparkle: locals have excellent taste and know how to throw a shindig. There's always something going on, including a series of cross-genre festivals that are among the best in the USA.

◎ Sights & Activities

During the 19th century, the wealthiest New York bankers and business families chose Newport as their summer playground, building their fabulous mansions along Bellevue Ave. Ten of the mansions (not including Rough Point or Ochre Court) are under the management of the **Preservation Society** (☑ 401-847-1000; www.newportmansions.org; 424 Bellevue Ave; 5-site tickets adult/child $35/12), and are open seasonally between June and November. Some are open year-round. Combination tickets are better value if you intend visiting several of the properties, and some tours require advance booking, which is advisable during high season. Tickets can be purchased online or on site. The society also offers a range of food- and wine-themed events.

Alternatively, hire a bike and cruise along Bellevue Ave enjoying the view of the mansions and their grounds or saunter along the famed Cliff Walk, a pedestrian path that runs along the headland between the mansions and their sea view.

★ **The Breakers** HISTORIC BUILDING
(☑ 401-847-1000; www.newportmansions.org; 44 Ochre Point Ave; adult/child $24/8; ☉ 9am-5pm Apr–mid-Oct, hours vary mid-Oct–Mar; ℗) A 70-room Italian Renaissance megapalace inspired by 16th-century Genoese palazzi, the Breakers is the most magnificent Newport mansion. At the behest of Cornelius Vanderbilt II, Richard Morris Hunt did most of the design (though craftspeople from around the world perfected the decorative program). The building was completed in 1895 and sits at Ochre Point, on a grand oceanside site. The furnishings, most made expressly for the Breakers, are all original. Don't miss the **Children's Cottage** on the grounds.

★ **The Elms** HISTORIC BUILDING
(☑ 401-847-1000; www.newportmansions.org; 367 Bellevue Ave; adult/child $17.50/8, servant life tours adult/child $18/7.50; ☉ 10am-5pm Apr–mid-Oct, hours vary mid-Oct–Mar; ℗ ♿) Designed by Horace Trumbauer in 1901, the Elms is a replica of Château d'Asnières, built near Paris in 1750. Here you can take a 'behind-the-scenes' tour that will have you snaking through the servants' quarters and up onto the roof. Along the way you'll learn about the activities of the army of servants and the architectural devices that kept them hidden from the view of those drinking port in the formal rooms.

★ **Rough Point** HISTORIC BUILDING
(☑ 401-849-7300; www.newportrestoration.com; 680 Bellevue Ave; adult/child $25/free; ☉ 9:30am-2pm Thu-Sun Apr-early May, 9:30am-3:30pm Tue-Sun early May-early Nov; ℗) While the peerless position and splendor of the grounds alone are worth the price of admission, this faux-English manor house also contains heiress and philanthropist Doris Duke's impressive art holdings, including medieval tapestries, furniture owned by French emperors, Ming dynasty ceramics, and paintings by Renoir and Van Dyck.

★ **Fort Adams State Park** STATE PARK
(www.fortadams.org; Harrison Ave; ☉ sunrise-sunset) The centerpiece of this gorgeous state park, which juts out into Narragansett Bay, **Fort Adams** (☑ 401-841-0707; 90 Fort Adams Dr; tours adult/child $12/6; ☉ 10am-4pm late May–Oct, reduced hours Nov & Dec) is America's largest coastal fortification. It's the venue for the Newport jazz (www.newportjazz.org; tickets $65-89, 3 days $170; ☉ Jul/Aug) and folk festivals (p210) and numerous special events. A beach, picnic and fishing areas and a boat ramp are open daily.

Museum of Newport History MUSEUM
(☑ 401-841-8770; www.newporthistory.org; 127 Thames St; suggested donation adult/child $4/2; ☉ 10am-5pm) Newport's excellent local history museum brings the city's past to life.

International Tennis Hall of Fame MUSEUM
(☑ 401-849-3990; www.tennisfame.com; 194 Bellevue Ave; adult/child $15/free; ☉ 10am-5pm Sep-Jun, to 6pm Jul & Aug, closed Tue Jan-Mar) To experience something of the American aristocracy's approach to 19th-century

---

NEWPORT'S BEST BEACHES

Newport's public beaches are on the eastern side of the peninsula along Memorial Blvd. All are open 9am to 6pm in summer and charge a parking fee of $10/20 on weekdays/ weekends (except for Gooseberry Beach, which charges $20 all week for parking).

Easton Beach (First Beach; Memorial Blvd) This is the largest beach with a pseudo-Victorian pavilion containing bathhouses and showers, a snack bar and a large carousel. You can rent umbrellas, chairs and surf boards at the pavilion.

Sachuest Beach (Second Beach; ☑ 401-846-6273; http://parks.middletownri.com; Sachuest Point Rd, Middletown) The most beautiful beach on Aquidneck Island curves around Sachuest Bay and is backed by the 450-acre Norman Bird Sanctuary.

Third Beach (Third Beach Rd, Middleton) Popular with families because it is protected from the open ocean, Third Beach also appeals to windsurfers because the water is calm and the winds steady.

Gooseberry Beach (130 Ocean Ave) Calm waters, white sand and a restaurant.

leisure, visit this museum. It lies inside the historic Newport Casino building (1880), which served as a summer club for Newport's wealthiest residents. The US National Lawn Tennis Championships (forerunner of today's US Open tennis tournament) were held here in 1881. A scavenger hunt, available at reception, gets kids engaged with eight centuries of tennis.

✹ Festivals

Newport Folk Festival   MUSIC
(www.newportfolk.org; Fort Adams State Park; 1-/3-day passes $85/199, parking per day $15; ⊙late Jul) Big-name stars and up-and-coming groups perform at Fort Adams State Park (p209) and other venues around town. Bring sunscreen.

Newport Music Festival   MUSIC
(www.newportmusic.org; tickets $25-50; ⊙mid-Jul) This internationally regarded festival offers classical music concerts in many of the great mansions.

🛏 Sleeping

Newport International Hostel   HOSTEL $
(William Gyles Guesthouse; ☑401-369-0243; www.newporthostel.com; 16 Howard St; dm $29-99, d $59-200; ⊙May-Nov; 🛜) Book as early as you can to get into Rhode Island's only hostel, run by an informal and knowledgeable host. The tiny guesthouse contains fixings for a simple breakfast, a laundry machine and spare, clean digs in a dormitory room.

Sea Whale Motel   MOTEL $$
(☑888-257-4096; www.seawhale.com; 150 Aquidneck Ave, Middletown; d midweek $139-149, weekend $209-239; 🅿🛜) This owner-occupied motel is a lovely place to stay with rooms facing Easton's Pond and flowers hung about the place everywhere. Rooms have little style, but are comfortable and neat, with fridges, microwaves, and tea and coffee provided.

★ Attwater   BOUTIQUE HOTEL $$$
(☑401-846-7444; www.theattwater.com; 22 Liberty St; r $259-599; 🅿❄🛜) Newport's newest hotel has the bold attire of a midsummer beach party with turquoise, lime-green and coral prints, ikat headboards and snazzily patterned geometric rugs. Picture windows and porches capture the summer light and rooms come furnished with thoughtful luxuries, like iPads, Apple TV and beach bags.

✗ Eating

★ Rosemary & Thyme Cafe   BAKERY, CAFE $
(☑401-619-3338; www.rosemaryandthymecafe.com; 382 Spring St; baked goods $2.50-5, sandwiches $8-11; ⊙7am-2pm Tue-Sat, to 11:30am Sun; 🖐) With a German baker in the kitchen it's hardly surprising that the counter at Rosemary & Thyme is piled high with buttery croissants, apple and cherry tarts and plump muffins. At lunchtime gourmet sandwiches feature herbed goat's cheese and Tuscan dried tomatoes, Havana Cuban pork loin and an Alsatian cheese mix. A children's menu is also thoughtfully provided.

Flo's Clam Shack   SEAFOOD $$
(☑401-847-8141; www.flosclamshacks.com; 4 Wave Ave, Middletown; mains $11-22; ⊙11am-9pm Sun-Thu, to 10pm Fri & Sat mid-May–mid-Sep, reduced hours mid-Sep–mid-May) This unfancy local institution has been the go-to for chip shop–style fish and chips, chowder, fried clams and quahog stuffies since the 1930s, only this one has a raw bar too.

★ Fluke Wine Bar   SEAFOOD $$$
(☑401-849-7778; www.flukenewport.com; 41 Bowens Wharf; mains $26-36; ⊙5-11pm daily May-Oct, Wed-Sat Nov-Apr) Fluke's Scandinavian-inspired dining room, with its blond wood and picture windows, offers an accomplished seafood menu featuring roasted monkfish, seasonal striped sea bass and plump scallops.

☆ Entertainment

Newport Blues Café   LIVE MUSIC
(☑401-841-5510; www.newportblues.com; 286 Thames St; ⊙7pm-1am Tue-Sun) This popular rhythm and blues bar and restaurant draws top acts to an old brownstone that was once a bank. It's an intimate space with many enjoying quahogs, house-smoked ribs or pork loins at tables adjoining the small stage. Dinner is offered from 7pm to 10pm; the music starts at 9:30pm.

Newport Polo Club   SPECTATOR SPORT
(☑401-846-0200; www.nptpolo.com; 250 Linden Lane, Portsmouth; lawn seats adult/child $12/free; ⊙gates open 1pm) In summer, come to watch the club's polo matches (check the website for dates) to get an authentic taste of Newport high life.

❶ Information

Newport Visitor Center (☑401-845-9131; www.discovernewport.org; 23 America's Cup Ave; ⊙9am-5pm) Offers maps, brochures,

BLOCK ISLAND

From the deck of the ferry, a cluster of mansard roofs and gingerbread houses rises picturesquely from the commercial village of Old Harbor, where little has changed since 1895, short of adding electricity and flush toilets! If you remain after the departure of the masses on the last ferry, the scale and pace of the island will delight or derange you: some find it blissfully quiet, others get island fever fast.

Block Island's simple pleasures center upon strolling the beach, which stretches for miles to the north of Old Harbor, biking around the island's rolling farmland and getting to know the calls of the many bird species that make the island home. During off-season, when the population dwindles to a few hundred, the landscape has the spare, haunted feeling of an Andrew Wyeth painting, with stone walls demarcating centuries-old property lines and few trees interrupting the spectacular ocean vistas.

Many places have a two- or three-day minimum stay in summer and close between November and April. Advance reservations are essential. Peak season runs roughly from mid-June to Labor Day. Off-season prices can be far cheaper than those listed here. Camping is not allowed on the island.

The **Visitor Center** (☎401-466-2982; www.blockislandchamber.com; Water St, Old Harbor Ferry Landing; ☉9am-5pm late May–early Sep, 10am-4pm rest of year) near the ferry dock keeps track of vacancies, and will try to help should you arrive sans reservation.

The island can only be reached by sea or air:

Block Island Ferry (☎401-783-7996; www.blockislandferry.com) runs a year-round traditional car ferry and a high-speed ferry from Point Judith in Narragansett from Memorial Day to mid-October. There are additional high-speed passenger-only ferries from Newport and Fall River, MA.

Block Island Express (www.goblockisland.com) operates services from New London, CT, to Old Harbor, Block Island between May and September.

New England Airlines (☎800-243-2460; www.block-island.com/nea; 56 Airport Rd; one way/round-trip $54/99) flies between Westerly State Airport, on Airport Rd off RI 78, and Block Island State Airport (12 minutes).

---

local bus information, tickets to major attractions, public restrooms and an ATM.

❶ Getting There & Away

Parking can be tough in Newport. Free street parking spaces do pop up, but check to make sure any non-metered spots aren't reserved for Newport residents.

Bonanza Bus Lines operates buses to Boston (from $22, 1¾ to two hours, four to five daily) from the Newport Visitor Center.

RIPTA (www.ripta.com) bus 60 serves Providence ($2, one hour) almost every hour. For the West Kingston Amtrak station, take bus 64 ($2, one hour, five buses Monday to Friday, three on Saturday). Bus 14 serves TF Green airport ($2, one hour) in Warwick. Most RIPTA buses arrive and depart from the **Newport Visitor Center**.

East Bay

Rhode Island's jagged East Bay captures the early American story in microcosm, from the graves of early settlers in Little Compton to the farmsteads and merchant homes of whalers and farmers in Warren and Barrington, and the mansions of slave traders in Bristol.

Aside from Barrington's historic and picturesque **Tyler Point Cemetery**, set between the Warren and Barrington Rivers, and Warren's clutch of early stone and clapboard churches (built in the 18th and 19th centuries), the most interesting of the three communities is Bristol. Further south is Sakonnet, the Wampanoag's 'Place of Black Geese,' a rural landscape of pastures and woods centered on the two tiny communities of Tiverton and Little Compton.

◉ Sights

Colt State Park   STATE PARK

(☎401-253-7482; www.riparks.com; RI 114; ☉sunrise-sunset; [P]) FREE Bristol's Colt State Park is Rhode Island's most scenic park, with its entire western border fronting Narragansett Bay, fringed by 4 miles of cycling trails and shaded picnic tables.

Blithewold Mansion
HISTORIC BUILDING

(☑ 401-253-2707; www.blithewold.org; 101 Ferry Rd; adult/child $14/5; ⊙10am-4pm Tue-Sat, to 3pm Sun Apr–mid-Oct; P) Local resident Augustus Van Wickle bought a 72ft Herreshoff yacht for his wife Bessie in 1895, but having nowhere suitable to moor it, he then had to build Blithewold Mansion. The arts-and-crafts mansion sits in a peerless position on Narragansett Bay and is particularly lovely in spring, when the daffodils line the shore.

Wilbor House
HISTORIC SITE

(☑ 401-635-4035; www.littlecompton.org; 548 West Main Rd; adult/child $6/3; ⊙1-5pm Thu-Sun Apr-Oct, 9am-3pm Tue-Fri Nov-Mar) Seventeenth-century Wilbor House belonged to early settler Samuel Wilbor, who crossed the Sakonnet River from Portsmouth in 1690 and built this big square home, which served his family for eight generations.

🛏 Sleeping & Eating

Stone House Inn
HISTORIC HOTEL $$$

(☑ 401-635-2222; www.newportexperience.com/stonehouse; 122 Sakonnet Point Rd; d $229-544; P 🖘) When this unashamedly upmarket inn opened its doors in 2016, Little Compton's notoriously private elite feared it meant the out-of-towners were coming. With only 13 rooms (lavish as they may be), it's hardly cause for an invasion. If you have cash and the inclination, this is your chance to take a peek at how the other half live.

Listed on the National Register of Historic Places, the building once housed an inn and speakeasy before it fell by the wayside. Today, with its own private yacht, luxurious spa, taproom and service from the good-ole-days, the unique inn is a destination in itself, within a very special, very sheltered and beautiful historic New England cloister.

Provender Fine Foods
DELI $

(☑ 401-624-8084; www.provenderfinefoods.com; 3883 Main Rd; items $4-18; ⊙9am-5pm Tue-Sun) At Tiverton's 'Four Corners,' you can drop in at the Provender for a hearty sandwich on fresh bread or some cookies.

Gray's Ice Cream
ICE CREAM $

(☑ 401-624-4500; www.graysicecream.com; 16 East Rd; scoops from $3; ⊙6:30am-9pm) In business since 1923, Gray's Ice Cream makes over 40 flavors of fresh dairy ice cream on-site daily. Stop by for a coffee cabinet (milkshake with ice cream), as beachgoers have been doing for decades.

CONNECTICUT

Known for its commuter cities, New York's neighbor is synonymous with the affluent lanes and mansions of *The Stepford Wives* and TV's *Gilmore Girls*. In old-moneyed Greenwich, the Litchfield Hills and the Quiet Corner, these representations ring true.

Many regard the state as a mere stepping stone to the 'real' New England, from whose tourist boom Connecticut has been spared. The upside is that Connecticut retains a more 'authentic' feel. The downside is a slow decaying of former heavyweights like Hartford and New London, where visitors can ponder the price of progress and get enthused about urban renewal. New Haven, home of Yale University, is one such place rewiring itself as a vibrant cultural hub.

Dense with historical attractions and the kind of bucolic nature that continues to inspire artists as it has for over a century, Connecticut begs for your attention and a well-deserved spot on your New England itinerary.

History

A number of Native American tribes (notably the Pequot and the Mohegan, whose name for the river became the name of the state) were here when the first European explorers, primarily Dutch, appeared in the early 17th century. The first English settlement was at Old Saybrook in 1635, followed a year later by the Connecticut Colony, built by Massachusetts Puritans under Thomas Hooker. A third colony was founded in 1638 in New Haven. After the Pequot War (1637), the Native Americans were no longer a check to colonial expansion in New England, and Connecticut's English population grew. In 1686 Connecticut was brought into the Dominion of New England.

The American Revolution swept through Connecticut, leaving scars with major battles at Stonington (1775), Danbury (1777), New Haven (1779) and Groton (1781). Connecticut became the fifth state in 1788. It embarked on a period of prosperity, propelled by its whaling, shipbuilding, farming and manufacturing industries (from firearms to bicycles to household tools), which lasted well into the 19th century.

The 20th century brought world wars and the Depression but, thanks in no small part to Connecticut's munitions industries, the state was able to fight back. Everything from planes to submarines were made in the state, and when the defense industry began to decline in the 1990s, the growth of other businesses (such as insurance) helped pick up the slack.

ℹ Resources

Connecticut Office of Tourism (www.ctvisit. com) The official site for tourism in Connecticut.

CTNow (www.ctnow.com) Regularly updated listings and information on what's hot, where and when.

Connecticut River Valley and Shoreline Travel Information (www.ctrivervalley.com) A privately maintained resource of tourist information relating to the Connecticut River Valley.

Lonely Planet (www.lonelyplanet.com/usa/new-england/connecticut) Destination information, hotel bookings, traveller forum and more.

Hartford

Connecticut's capital, one of America's oldest cities, is famed for the 1794 birth of the lucrative insurance industry, conceived when a local landowner sought fire insurance. Policy documents necessitated printing presses, which spurred a boom in publishing that lured the likes of Mark Twain, Harriet Beecher Stowe and Wallace Stevens. In 1855 Samuel Colt made the mass production of the revolver commercially viable. Big business boomed in Hartford.

It's ironic that the industries responsible for the city's wealth (insurance and guns) have contributed to its slow decline: Hartford has a gritty track record for crime. Although things are improving, keep this in mind. Old money has left a truly impressive legacy of fine historic attractions worthy of any New England itinerary. Visit during spring when the darling buds burst to life or in summer when trees are green and skies are blue and you're likely to be pleasantly surprised.

◉ Sights

★**Mark Twain House & Museum** MUSEUM (☑ 860-247-0998; www.marktwainhouse.org; 351 Farmington Ave, parking at 385 Farmington Ave; adult/child $20/11; ☺ 9:30am-5:30pm, closed Tue Jan & Feb; **P**) For 17 years, encompassing the most productive period of his life, Samuel Langhorne Clemens (1835–1910) and his family lived in this striking orange-and-black brick Victorian house, which then stood in the pastoral area of the city called Nook Farm. Architect Edward Tuckerman

Potter lavishly embellished it with turrets, gables and verandahs, and some of the interiors were done by Louis Comfort Tiffany. Admission to the house and museum is by guided tour only. Advance purchase is recommended.

★**Wadsworth Atheneum** MUSEUM (☑ 860-278-2670; https://thewadsworth.org; 600 Main St; adult/child $15/free; ☺ 11am-5pm Wed-Fri, from 10am Sat & Sun) The nation's oldest public art museum completed a five-year, $33-million renovation, renewing 32 galleries and 15 public spaces in 2015. The Wadsworth houses nearly 50,000 pieces of art in a castle-like Gothic Revival building. On display are paintings by members of the Hudson River School, including some by Hartford native Frederic Church; 19th-century Impressionist works; 18th-century New England furniture; sculptures by Connecticut artist Alexander Calder; and an outstanding array of surrealist, postwar and contemporary works.

Old State House HISTORIC BUILDING (☑ 860-522-6766; www.ctoldstatehouse.org; 800 Main St; adult/child $6/3; ☺ 10am-5pm Tue-Sat Jul–mid-Oct, Mon-Fri mid-Oct–Jun; ♿) Connecticut's original capitol building (from 1797 to 1873) was designed by Charles Bulfinch, who also designed the Massachusetts State House in Boston, and was the site of the trial of the *Amistad* prisoners. Gilbert Stuart's famous 1801 portrait of George Washington hangs in the senate chamber. The newly expanded space houses interactive exhibits aimed at kids, as well as a **Museum of Curiosities** that features a two-headed calf, a narwhal's horn and a variety of mechanical devices.

Harriet Beecher-Stowe Center MUSEUM (☑ 860-522-9258; www.harrietbeecherstowe.org; 77 Forest St; adult/child $14/8; ☺ 9:30am-5pm Mon-Sat, noon-5pm Sun; **P**) Along with literary titan Mark Twain, Hartford was also home to Harriet Beecher Stowe, author of the antislavery book *Uncle Tom's Cabin*. Upon meeting Stowe, Abraham Lincoln reputedly said, 'So this is the little lady who made this big war.' The facility centers on the Stowe House, built in 1871 and newly restored in 2017, which reflects the author's strong ideas about decorating and domestic efficiency, as expressed in her bestseller *American Woman's Home* (nearly as popular as her famous novel).

🛏 Sleeping

Sadly it's slim pickings for decent hotels in Hartford's downtown core and prices can be steep for what you get. Better value may be found in chain offerings outside the city center.

Daniel Rust House B&B $$
(☑ 860-742-0032; www.thedanielrusthouse.com; 2011 Main St, Coventry; d $120-185; ⓟ☺☎) Serving travelers since 1800, the four period rooms brim with history. The finest is the Anna White room with its antique canopy bed, although the Mary Rose has a secret closet that was used to hide slaves traveling to freedom on the Underground Railroad.

✕ Eating & Drinking

Salute ITALIAN $$
(☑ 860-899-1350; www.salutehartford.com; 100 Trumbull St; lunch mains $8-18, dinner $16-36; ☺11:30am-11pm Mon-Thu, to midnight Fri & Sat, 3-10pm Sun; ☑) Charming service is the hallmark of this urban gem, which offers a contemporary take on Italian flavors. Regulars rave about the cheesy garlic bread, but other offerings are a tad more sophisticated. The pleasant patio overlooks Bushnell Park.

★ City Steam Brewery Café BREWERY
(☑ 860-525-1600; www.citysteam.biz; 942 Main St; ☺11:30am-midnight Mon-Thu, to 1am Fri & Sat, 11am-10pm Sun) This big and boisterous place has housemade beers on tap. The Naughty Nurse Pale Ale is a bestseller, but the seasonals are also worth a try. The brewery's basement is home to the **Brew Ha Ha Comedy Club** (☑ 860-525-1600; www.citysteam.biz; 942 Main St; ticket prices vary; ☺ show times vary), where you can yuk it up with visiting comedians from New York and Boston. There's plenty of great food to soak up the ale too.

❶ Getting There & Away

Centrally located **Union Station** (www.amtrak. com; 1 Union Pl) is the city's transportation hub. Catch trains, airport shuttles, intercity buses and taxis from here.

Litchfield Hills

The rolling hills in the northwestern corner of Connecticut are sprinkled with lakes and dotted with forests and state parks. Historic Litchfield is the hub of the region, but lesser-known Bethlehem, Kent and Norfolk

boast similarly illustrious lineages and are just as photogenic.

An intentional curb on development continues to preserve the area's rural character. Accommodations are limited. Volunteers staff a useful information booth on Litchfield's town green from June to November.

If you have your own car, there's no shortage of postcard-perfect country roads to explore in the Litchfield Hills. One particularly delightful stretch is from Cornwall Bridge taking CT 4 west and then CT 41 north to Salisbury.

❶ Getting There & Around

The Litchfield Hills run north from Danbury and cover the northwest portion of the state, as far as the Massachusetts and New York borders, to the north and west, respectively.

Highways US 7 and CT 8 are the main north–south trunk roads. You'll need a car.

Litchfield

Litchfield is Connecticut's best-preserved late 18th-century town and the site of the nation's first law school. The town itself converges on a long oval green, and is surrounded by lush swaths of protected land just asking to be hiked through and picnicked on.

Founded in 1719, Litchfield prospered from 1780 to 1840 on the commerce brought by stagecoaches en route between Hartford and Albany, NY. In the mid-19th century, railroads did away with the coach routes, and industrial water-powered machinery drove Litchfield's artisans out of the markets, leaving the town to languish in faded gentility. Today farming and tourism rule the roost.

⊙ Sights & Activities

Litchfield History Museum MUSEUM
(☑ 860-567-4501; www.litchfieldhistoricalsociety. org; 7 South St; ☺11am-5pm Tue-Sat, 1-5pm Sun mid-Apr–Nov) **FREE** This museum features a small permanent collection, including a modest photographic chronicle of the town and a dress-up box with Colonial clothes for children to try on, plus some local-interest rotating exhibits.

Reeve House & Litchfield Law School HISTORIC SITE
(☑ 860-567-4501; www.litchfieldhistoricalsociety. org; 82 South St; ☺11am-5pm Tue-Sat, 1-5pm Sun mid-Apr–Nov) **FREE** In 1775 Tapping Reeve established the English-speaking world's first

law school at his home. When attendance overwhelmed his own house, he built the meticulously preserved one-room schoolhouse in his side yard. John C Calhoun and 130 members of Congress studied here.

White Memorial
Conservation Center   WALKING
(☑ 860-567-0857; www.whitememorialcc.org; 80 Whitehall Rd, off US 202; park free, museum adult/child $6/3; ☺ park dawn-dusk, museum 9am-5pm Mon-Sat, noon-5pm Sun) **FREE** Made up of 4000 supremely serene acres, this park has two dozen trails (0.2 miles to 6 miles long) that crisscross the center, including swamp paths on a raised boardwalk. The center also manages three campgrounds and there's a small nature museum. The center is 2 miles west on US 202 from Litchfield.

Lake Waramaug

Among the plentiful lakes and ponds in the Litchfield Hills, Lake Waramaug, north of New Preston, stands out. Gracious inns dot its shoreline, parts of which are a state park.

★**Hopkins Inn**   INN $$
(☑ 860-868-7295; www.thehopkinsinn.com; 22 Hopkins Rd, Warren; r $135-145, without bath $125, apt $160-250; P ❄ ☷) The 19th-century Hopkins Inn boasts a well-regarded restaurant with Austrian-influenced country fare and a variety of lodging options, from simple rooms with shared bathrooms to lake-view apartments. Whatever the season, there's something magical about sitting on the porch gazing upon Lake Waramaug and the hills beyond.

Connecticut Coast

The southeastern corner of Connecticut is home to the state's number-one tourist attraction and the country's largest maritime museum, Mystic Seaport. Built on the site of a former shipbuilding yard in 1929, the museum celebrates the area's seafaring heritage when fishermen, whalers and clipper-ship engineers broke world speed records and manufactured gunboats and warships for the Civil War.

To the west of Mystic, you'll find the submarine capital of the USA, Groton, where General Dynamics built WWII subs, and across the Thames River, New London. To the east is the historic fishing village of Stonington, extending along a narrow mile-long peninsula into the sea. It's one of the most charming seaside villages in New England, where Connecticut's only remaining commercial fleet operates and yachties come ashore in summer to enjoy the charming restaurants on Water St.

❶ Getting There & Around

The area is served well by road, with the I-95 plowing through the middle of New London and around the outskirts of Mystic. I-395 runs northeast to Norwich and beyond.

Many Amtrak trains from New York City stop in New London (from $39, three hours) and Mystic (from $41, 3¼ hours). The return run from Boston also stops in Mystic (from $26, 80 minutes), then New London (from $29, 1½ hours).

SEAT (www.seatbus.com) operates local buses services linking the communities of Norwich, New London, Groton and Mystic.

Mystic

A skyline of masts greets you as you arrive in town on US 1. They belong to the vessels bobbing ever so slightly in the postcard-perfect harbor. There's a sense of self-satisfied calm and composure in the air – until suddenly a heart-stopping steamer whistle blows, followed by the cheerful cling of a drawbridge bell. You know you've arrived in Mystic.

From simple beginnings in the 17th century, the village of Mystic grew to become a prosperous whaling center and one of the great shipbuilding ports of the East Coast. In the mid-19th century, Mystic's shipyards launched clipper ships, gunboats and naval transport vessels, many from the George Greenman & Co Shipyard, now the site of Mystic Seaport Museum.

◉ Sights & Activities

★**Mystic Seaport Museum**   MUSEUM
(☑ 860-572-0711; www.mysticseaport.org; 75 Greenmanville Ave; adult/child $29/19; ☺ 9am-5pm Apr-Oct, 10am-4pm Thu-Sun Nov-Mar; P ♿) More than a museum, Mystic Seaport is the re-creation of an entire New England whaling village spread over 17 acres of the former George Greenman & Co Shipyard. To re-create the past, 60 historic buildings, four tall ships and almost 500 smaller vessels are gathered along the Mystic River. Interpreters staff the site and are glad to discuss traditional crafts and trades. Most illuminating are the demonstrations on such topics as ship rescue, oystering and whaleboat launching.

Mystic Aquarium
& Institute for Exploration　　AQUARIUM
(🏛 860-572-5955; www.mysticaquarium.org; 55 Coogan Blvd; adult/teen/child $36/30/26; ⊙ 9am-5:50pm Apr-Aug, 9am-4:50pm Mar & Sep-Nov, 10am-4:50pm Dec-Feb; 🅰) This state-of-the-art aquarium boasts more than 6000 species of sea creatures, as well as an outdoor viewing area for watching seals and sea lions below the waterline and a penguin pavilion. The aquarium's most famous (and controversial) residents are the three beluga whales, who reside in the Arctic Coast exhibit. Animal-welfare groups claim it is debilitating to keep whales in enclosed containers.

Argia Mystic Cruises　　CRUISE
(🏛 860-536-0416; www.argiamystic.com; 12 Steamboat Wharf; adult/child $50/40) This outfit offers two- to three-hour daytime or sunset cruises down the Mystic River to Fishers' Island Sound on the authentic 19th-century replica schooner *Argia*.

🛏 Sleeping & Eating

Whaler's Inn　　INN $$
(🏛 860-536-1506; www.whalersinnmystic.com; 20 E Main St; d $159-299; 🅿@🛜) In downtown Mystic, beside its historic drawbridge, this hotel combines an 1865 Victorian house with a reconstructed luxury hotel from the same era (the original landmark 'Hoxie House' burned down in the 1970s) and a modern motel known as Stonington House. Seasonal packages available; these include the price of dinners and area attractions. Rates include continental breakfast, a small gym and complimentary bicycles.

★**Steamboat Inn**　　INN $$$
(🏛 860-536-8300; www.steamboatinnmystic.com; 73 Steamboat Wharf; d $220-350; 🅿❄🛜) Located right in the heart of downtown Mystic, the rooms of this historic inn have wrap-around water views and luxurious amenities, including two-person whirlpool tubs, cable TV, free local calls and fireplaces. Antiques lend the interior a romantic, period feel, and service is top-notch with baked goods for breakfast, complimentary bikes and boat docks.

★**Captain Daniel**
Packer Inne　　AMERICAN $$$
(🏛 860-536-3555; www.danielpacker.com; 32 Water St; mains $14-34; ⊙ 11am-4pm & 5-10pm) This 1754 historic house has a low-beam ceiling and creaky floorboards. On the lower pub level, you'll find regulars at the bar, a good selection of beer on tap and excellent pub grub: try the fish and chips. Upstairs, the dining room has river views and an imaginative American menu, including petite filet mignon with Gorgonzola sauce and walnut demi-glace. Reservations recommended.

★**Oyster Club**　　SEAFOOD $$$
(🏛 860-415-9266; www.oysterclubct.com; 13 Water St; oysters $2-2.50, lunch mains $13-20, dinner mains $18-40; ⊙ noon-3pm & 5-10pm Fri & Sat, 10am-3pm & 5-9pm Sun, 5-9pm Mon-Thu; 🅿🛎) Offering casual fine dining at its best, this is the place locals come to knock down oysters on the deck out back. Grilled lobster and pan-roasted monkfish or flounder feature alongside veal, steak and a drool-worthy burger. If oysters are an aphrodisiac, anything could happen at the bar after the daily happy hour (4pm to 6pm), when shucked oysters are a buck each.

New London

During its golden age in the mid-19th century, New London, then home to some 200 whaling vessels, was one of the largest whaling centers in the USA and one of the wealthiest port cities. In 1858 the discovery of crude oil in Pennsylvania sent the value of whale oil plummeting and began a long period of decline for the city, from which it has never fully recovered. Even so, New London retains strong links with its seafaring past (the US Coast Guard Academy and US Naval Submarine Base are here) and its downtown is listed on the National Register of Historic Places. Despite lacking the sanitized tourism push of nearby Mystic and Stonington, remnants of New London's glorious and opulent times are still evident throughout the city, making it one of Connecticut's most surprising destinations for those interested in history, architecture and urban sociology.

Lower Connecticut River Valley

The Connecticut River, New England's longest, flows southwards 410 miles from its humble source at Fourth Connecticut Lake, just 300 yards from the Canadian border in New Hampshire. It forms the state boundary between Vermont and New Hampshire, before snaking its way through Massachusetts and Connecticut until it meets the Atlantic at Long Island Sound. Mercifully, it escaped

GILLETTE CASTLE

Built in 1919 by actor William Hooker Gillette, who made his fortune playing Sherlock Holmes, the gaudy, medieval-style **Gillette Castle** (☑ 860-526-2336; www.ct.gov/deep/gillettecastle; 67 River Rd; adult/child $6/2; ☺ castle 11am-5pm Thu-Sun late May–early Sep, grounds 8am-dusk year-round; ℙ) is an eccentric turreted mansion made of fieldstone. Looming on one of the Seven Sisters hills above East Haddam, the folly is modeled on the medieval castles of Germany's Rhineland and the views from its terraces are spectacular. The surrounding 125 acres are a designated state park.

In summer, you can cross the Connecticut River on the Chester–Hadlyme Ferry (www.ctvisit.com/listings/chesterhadlyme-ferry). The short, five-minute river crossing affords great views, and deposits passengers at the foot of Gillette Castle.

the bustle of industry and commerce that marred many of the Northeast's rivers.

Today well-preserved historic towns grace the river's banks, notably Old Lyme, Essex, Ivoryton, Chester and East Haddam. Together, they enchant visitors with gracious country inns, fine dining, train rides and river excursions that allow authentic glimpses into provincial life on the Connecticut.

Old Lyme

Near the mouth of the Connecticut River and perched on the smaller Lieutenant River, Old Lyme was home to some 60 sea captains in the 19th century. Since the early 20th century, however, Old Lyme has been known as the center of the Lyme Art Colony, which cultivated the nascent American Impressionist movement. Numerous artists, including William Chadwick, Childe Hassam, Willard Metcalfe and Henry Ward Ranger, came here to paint, staying in the mansion of local art patron Florence Griswold.

◉ Sights

Florence Griswold Museum   MUSEUM
(☑ 860-434-5542; http://florencegriswoldmuseum.org; 96 Lyme St; adult/child $10/free; ☺ 10am-5pm Tue-Sat, 1-5pm Sun; ℙ) The 'home of American Impressionism,' the Florence Griswold Museum exhibits 6000 works with solid collections of American Impressionist and Barbizon paintings, as well as sculpture and decorative arts. Her house, which her artist friends decorated with murals (often in lieu of paying rent), is now the Florence Griswold Museum. The estate consists of her Georgian-style house, the Krieble Gallery, the Chadwick studio and Griswold's beloved gardens.

Lyme Academy of Fine Arts   GALLERY
(☑ 860-434-5232; www.lymeacademy.edu; 84 Lyme St; ☺ 10am-4pm Mon-Sat) **FREE** A neigh-

bor of the Florence Griswold Museum, Lyme Academy of Fine Arts, a college of the University of New Haven, features rotating drawing, painting and sculpture exhibits by students.

🛏 Sleeping

★ **Bee & Thistle Inn**   INN $$
(☑ 860-434-1667; www.beeandthistleinn.com; 100 Lyme St; r $129-289; ℙ🛜) Occupying a handsome, Dutch Colonial farmhouse dating to 1756, this classy establishment has beautiful, well-tended gardens that stretch down to the Lieutenant River. Most of its 11 plush, well-appointed rooms feature abundant antiques and a canopy or four-poster bed.

The Inn's romantic dining room is the perfect setting for superlative New American cuisine. Lunch and dinner (meals $30 to $60) are served Wednesday to Sunday, often enhanced by a harpist. Reservations essential.

Essex

Tree-lined Essex, established in 1635, stands as the chief town of the Connecticut River Valley region. It's worth a visit if only to gawk at the beautiful, well-preserved Federal-period houses, legacies of rum and tobacco fortunes made in the 19th century. The town also has a strong following with steam train and riverboat enthusiasts.

◉ Sights & Activities

**Hammonasset Beach
State Park**   STATE PARK
(☑ 203-245-2785; www.ct.gov/deep/hammonasset; 1288 Boston Post Rd; weekdays/weekends $15/22; ☺ 8am-sunset; ℙ) Though not off the beaten path by any means, the two full miles of flat, sandy beach at Hammonasset Beach State Park handily accommodate summer crowds. This is the ideal beach at which to

set up an umbrella chair, crack open a book and forget about the world. The surf is tame, making swimming superb. Restrooms and showering facilities are clean and ample, and a wooden boardwalk runs the length of the park.

Connecticut River Museum MUSEUM
(☎ 860-767-8269; www.ctrivermuseum.org; 67 Main St; adult/child $10/6; ⊙10am-5pm, closed Mon Oct-May; 🅿🐾) Adjacent to Essex's Steamboat Dock, this museum's meticulously presented exhibits recount regional history and include a reproduction of the world's first submarine, the *American Turtle*: a hand-propelled, barrel-like vessel built by Yale student David Bushnell in 1776 and launched at nearby Old Saybrook. The museum also hosts visiting exhibitions, runs summer workshops and organizes river paddles – dates and prices vary.

⭐ **Essex Steam Train & Riverboat Ride** TOURS
(☎ 860-767-0103; www.essexsteamtrain.com; 1 Railroad Ave; adult/child $19/10, incl cruise $29/19; ⊙May-Oct; 🐾) This wildly popular attraction features a steam locomotive and antique carriages. The journey travels six scenic miles to Deep River, where you can cruise to the Goodspeed Opera House (☎ 860-873-8668; www.goodspeed.org; 6 Main St; tickets $45-85) in East Haddam, before returning to Essex via train. The round-trip train ride takes about an hour; with the riverboat ride it's 2½ hours.

A variety of themed excursions are available – consult the website for fares, times and details. If you're staying in Essex where nightly dining options are limited, you might elect to take the Essex Clipper Dinner Train, whose $80 (tax included) round-trip fare includes a 2½-hour train ride and four-course meal with a cash bar.

🛌 Sleeping

Griswold Inn INN $$
(☎ 860-767-1776; www.griswoldinn.com; 36 Main St; d/ste from $195/240; 🅿🛜) The landmark Griswold Inn is one of the oldest continually operating inns in the country and has been Essex's physical and social centerpiece since 1776. The inn's buffet-style Hunt Breakfast (served 11am to 1pm Sunday) is a tradition dating from the War of 1812, when British soldiers occupying Essex demanded to be fed.

At other times, the dining room remains a favorite place to enjoy traditional New England cuisine in a historic setting.

New Haven

As you wander around Yale University's venerable campus, admiring the gorgeous faux-Gothic and Victorian architecture, it's hard to fathom New Haven's struggle to shake its reputation as a dangerous, decaying seaport.

Connecticut's second-largest city radiates out from pretty New Haven Green, laid by Puritan settlers in the 1600s. Around it, Yale's over-300-year-old accessible campus offers visitors a wealth of world-class attractions, from museums and galleries to a lively concert program and walking-tour tales of secret societies. As New Haven repositions itself as a thriving home for the arts, architecture and the human mind, the good news is tourism is on the up and crime is in decline.

While Yale may have put New Haven on the map, there's much to savor beyond campus. Well-aged dive bars, ethnic restaurants, barbecue shacks and cocktail lounges make the area almost as lively as Cambridge's Harvard Sq – but with better pizza and less ego.

⊙ Sights

⭐ **Yale University** UNIVERSITY
(☎ 203-432-2300; www.yale.edu/visitor; 149 Elm St; ⊙visitor center 9am-4:30pm Mon-Fri, 11am-4pm Sat & Sun) FREE Each year, thousands of high-school students make pilgrimages to Yale, nursing dreams of attending the country's third-oldest university, which boasts such notable alums as Noah Webster, Eli Whitney, Samuel Morse, and Presidents William H Taft, George HW Bush, Bill Clinton and George W Bush. You don't need to share the students' ambitions in order to take a stroll around the campus, just pick up a map at the visitor center or join a free, one-hour guided tour.

⭐ **Yale Center for British Art** MUSEUM
(☎ 203-432-2800; www.ycba.yale.edu; 1080 Chapel St; ⊙10am-5pm Tue-Sat, noon-5pm Sun) FREE Reopened in 2016 after extensive restoration, this fabulous gallery was architect Louis Kahn's last commission and is the setting for the largest collection of British art outside the UK. Spanning three centuries from the Elizabethan era to the 19th century, and arranged thematically as well as chronologically, the

collection gives an unparalleled insight into British art, life and culture. A visit is an absolute must for anyone interested in beautiful things. And yes, it's free. Public and private group tours are available.

★**Yale University Art Gallery** MUSEUM
(☑203-432-0600; http://artgallery.yale.edu; 1111 Chapel St; ☺10am-5pm Tue-Fri, to 8pm Thu, 11am-5pm Sat & Sun) **FREE** This outstanding museum was architect Louis Kahn's first commission and houses the oldest university art collection in the country, including Vincent van Gogh's *The Night Café* and European masterpieces by Frans Hals, Peter Paul Rubens, Manet and Picasso. In addition there are displays of American masterworks by Winslow Homer, Edward Hopper and Jackson Pollock, silver from the 18th century, and art from Africa, Asia, the pre- and post-Columbian Americas. Best of all, it won't cost you a penny to take a peek.

★**Shore Line
Trolley Museum** MUSEUM, TROLLEY
(☑203-467-6927; www.shorelinetrolley.org; 17 River St, East Haven; adult/child $10/7; ☺10:30am-4:30pm daily Jul & Aug, Sat & Sun May, Jun, Sep & Oct; ➍) For a unique take on East Haven's shoreline, take a ride on this open-sided antique trolley – the oldest continuously running suburban trolley line in the country – along 3 miles of track that takes you from River St in East Haven to Short Beach in Branford. Enjoy the museum and its beautifully maintained carriages when you're done. Bring a picnic lunch.

New Haven Green PARK
New Haven's spacious green has been the spiritual center of the city since its Puritan fathers designed it in 1638 as the prospective site for Christ's second coming. Since then it has held the municipal burial grounds (graves were later moved to Grove St Cemetery), several statehouses and an array of churches, three of which still stand.

🛏 **Sleeping**

Hotel Duncan HISTORIC HOTEL $
(☑203-787-1273; 1151 Chapel St; s $65-80, d $85-100; ❄�🛜) Though the shine has rubbed off this antique New Haven gem – with stained carpets, unstable water pressure and exfoliating towels – it's the enduring features that some will enjoy, like the handsome lobby and the hand-operated elevator with uniformed attendant. Rooms are rented on both a long-term and overnight basis. Don't expect the earth and you might be surprised.

Farnam Guest House B&B $$
(☑203-562-7121; www.farnamguesthouse.com; 616 Prospect St; r $149-199, with shared bath $89-139; ℗❄🛜) The Farnams have a long association with Yale as alums, donors and professors, and you can stay in their grand Georgian Colonial mansion in the best neighborhood in town. Expect old-world ambience, with Chippendale sofas, wing-back chairs, Victorian antiques and plush oriental carpets. There's a Steinway grand piano in the parlor.

The Study at Yale HOTEL $$$
(☑203-503-3900; www.thestudyatyale.com; 1157 Chapel St; r $219-389; ℗🛜) The Study at Yale manages to evoke a mid-Century Modern sense of sophistication (call it '*Mad Men* chic') without being over the top or intimidating. Ultra-contemporary touches include in-room iPod docking stations and cardio machines with built-in TV. There's also an in-house restaurant and cafe, where you can stumble for morning snacks.

✖ **Eating**

Frank Pepe PIZZA $
(☑203-865-5762; www.pepespizzeria.com; 157 Wooster St; pizzas $7-29; ☺10:30am-10pm Sun-Thu, to 11pm Fri & Sat; 🅿➍) Pepe's lays claim to baking the 'best pizza in America,' a title it's won three times running. We'll let you be the judge, but can confirm this joint cranks out tasty pies fired in a coal oven, just as it has since 1925; only now it has a bunch of other locations across Connecticut, making consistency harder to master. Cash only.

The white-clam pizza is the pie the people praise.

★**Caseus Fromagerie & Bistro** BISTRO $$
(☑203-624-3373; http://caseusnewhaven.com; 93 Whitney Ave; mains $12-30; ☺11:30am-2:30pm Mon-Sat plus 5:30-9pm Wed-Sat; 🅿) With a boutique cheese counter piled with locally sourced labels and a concept menu devoted to *le grand fromage*, Caseus has hit upon a winning combination. After all, what's not to like about a perfectly executed mac-and-cheese or the dangerously delicious poutine (*pommes frites*, cheese curds and velouté).

Miya's Sushi SUSHI $$$
(☑203-777-9760; www.miyassushi.com; 68 Howe St; mains $11-35; ☺5-11pm Wed, to midnight

NEW ENGLAND NEW HAVEN

Thu-Sat;) Two-time winner of the Taste of the Nation Award, Chef Bun Lai's immaculately presented, sustainable sushi and sashimi concoctions sport fantastic names. Even more fantastic are the freshness and flavors of the raw ingredients. Strip it back and keep it natural (sashimi), or go with Bun's adventurous combinations of ingredients: if you're a fan of modern American sushi, you will be impressed.

▼ Drinking & Entertainment

Whether you're in the mood for an artisanal cocktail in a chic setting or a local beer in an old-school dive bar, New Haven has no shortage of nightspots, and plenty of funky arts-and-drama kids, divorced professors and tomorrow's millionaires to have a drink with.

Toad's Place   LIVE MUSIC
(☑ 203-624-8623; www.toadsplace.com; 300 York St) Toad's is arguably New England's premier music hall, having earned its rep hosting the likes of the Rolling Stones, U2 and Bob Dylan. These days, an eclectic range of performers work the intimate stage, including They Might Be Giants and Martin & Wood.

Shubert Theater   THEATER
(☑ 203-562-5666; www.shubert.com; 247 College St) Dubbed 'Birthplace of the Nation's Greatest Hits,' the Shubert has, since 1914, been hosting ballet and Broadway musicals on their trial runs before heading off to New York City. In recent years it has expanded its repertoire to include a broader range of events, including a series of interviews and musical performances.

ℹ Information

INFO New Haven (☑ 203-773-9494; www. infonewhaven.com; 1000 Chapel St; ☺10am-9pm Mon-Sat, noon-5pm Sun) This downtown bureau offers maps and helpful advice.

ℹ Getting There & Away

New Haven is 141 miles southwest of Boston, 36 miles south of Hartford, 75 miles from New York and 101 miles from Providence via interstate highways.

Metro-North (www.mta.info/mnr) trains make the run between Union Station and New York City's Grand Central Terminal almost every hour from 7am to midnight.

Shore Line East (www.shorelineeast.com) runs regional trains up the shore of Long Island Sound to Old Saybrook (45 minutes) and New London (70 minutes), as well as Commuter Connection buses that shuttle passengers from Union Station (in the evenings) and from State St Station (in the mornings) to New Haven Green.

Amtrak (www.amtrak.com) trains run express from New York City's Penn Station to New Haven (from $32, 1¾ hours).

Peter Pan Bus Lines (www.peterpanbus.com) connects New Haven with New York City (from $12, two hours, eight daily), Hartford (from $12, one hour, six daily) and Boston (from $11, four to five hours, seven daily), as does Greyhound (www.greyhound.com). Buses depart from inside New Haven's Union Station.

Connecticut Limousine (www.ctlimo.com) is an airport shuttle servicing Hartford's Bradley airport, New York's JFK and LaGuardia airports and New Jersey's Newark airport. Pick-up and drop-off is at Union Station and select downtown New Haven hotels. Services to Newark attract a higher rate.

VERMONT

Whether seen under blankets of snow, patchworks of blazing fall leaves or the exuberant greens of spring and summer, Vermont's blend of bucolic farmland, mountains and picturesque small villages make it one of America's most uniformly appealing states. Hikers, bikers, skiers and kayakers will find four-season bliss here, on the expansive waters of Lake Champlain, the award-winning Kingdom Trails Network, the 300-mile Long and Catamount Trails, and the fabled slopes of Killington, Stowe and Sugarbush.

Foodies will love it here: small farmers have made Vermont a locavore paradise, complemented by America's densest collection of craft brewers. But most of all, what sets Vermont apart is its independent spirit: the only state with a socialist senator and the only one without a McDonald's in its capital city, Vermont remains a haven for quirky creativity, a champion of grassroots government and a bastion of 'small is beautiful' thinking, unlike anyplace else in America.

History

Frenchman Samuel de Champlain explored Vermont in 1609, becoming the first European to visit these lands long inhabited by the native Abenaki.

Vermont played a key role in the American Revolution in 1775 when Ethan Allen led a local militia, the Green Mountain Boys, to Fort Ticonderoga, capturing it from the Brit-

Vermont & New Hampshire

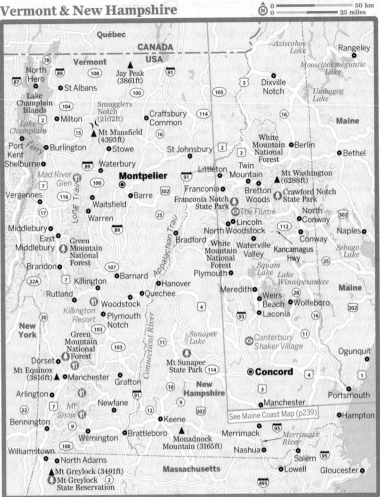

ish. In 1777 Vermont declared independence as the Vermont Republic, adopting the first New World constitution to abolish slavery and establish a public school system. In 1791 Vermont was admitted to the USA as the 14th state.

ⓘ Information

Vermont Chamber of Commerce (www.visitvt. com) Distributes a wealth of information about the state.

Vermont Division of Tourism (www.vermont vacation.com) Maintains a fabulous Welcome Center on I-91 near the Massachusetts state line, one on VT 4A near the New York state line, and three others along I-89 between White River Junction and the Canadian border. Produces a free, detailed road map and camping guide.

Vermont Public Radio (www.vpr.net) Vermont's statewide public radio station features superb local programming, including 'Vermont Edition' (weekdays at noon) for coverage of Vermont current events, and the quirky, information-packed 'Eye on the Sky' weather forecast.

Vermont Ski Areas Association (www.skiver mont.com) Helpful information for planning ski trips, as well as summer adventures at Vermont ski resorts.

Southern Vermont

White churches and inns surround village greens throughout historic southern Vermont, a region that's home to several towns that predate the American Revolution. In summer the roads between the three 'cities' of Brattleboro, Bennington and Manchester roll over green hills; in winter, they wind their way toward the ski slopes of Mt Snow, southern Vermont's cold-weather playground. For hikers, the Appalachian and Long Trails pass through the Green Mountain National Forest here, offering a colorful hiking experience during the fall foliage season.

❶ Getting There & Around

Drivers coming from Massachusetts, Connecticut and Rhode Island will most likely enter southern Vermont via one of two routes: I-91 in the east, or US 7 in the west. Public transit here is limited to once-daily buses and trains plying the Connecticut River valley. While southern Vermont has no commercial airport of its own, the airports at Albany, NY, Hartford, CT, and Manchester, NH, are all within one to two hours of the Vermont state line.

Brattleboro

Perched at the confluence of the Connecticut and West Rivers, Brattleboro is a little gem that reveals its facets to those who stroll the streets and prowl its dozens of independent shops and eateries. An energetic mix of aging hippies and the latest crop of pierced and tattooed hipsters fuels the town's sophisticated eclecticism, keeping the downtown scene percolating and skewing its politics decidedly leftward.

Whetstone Brook runs through the south end of town, where a wooden stockade dubbed Fort Dummer was built in 1724, becoming the first European settlement in Vermont (theretofore largely a wilderness populated exclusively by Native Americans).

At the Old Town Hall (location of the current Main Street Gallery), celebrated thinkers and entertainers, including Oliver Wendell Holmes, Horace Greeley and Will Rogers, held forth on civic and political matters. Rudyard Kipling married a Brattleboro woman in 1892, and while living here he wrote *The Jungle Book*.

◉ Sights

While most of Brattleboro's action is easily found in the downtown commercial district, the surrounding hillsides are well salted with farms, cheese makers and artisans, all awaiting discovery on a pleasant back-road ramble.

Brattleboro Museum & Art Center   MUSEUM
(☑ 802-257-0124; www.brattleboromuseum.org; 10 Vernon St; adult/child $8/free; ◷ 11am-5pm Wed-Mon) Located in a 1915 railway station, this museum hosts a wealth of inventive exhibits by local artists in a variety of media. It also has a rotating multimedia exhibition program of contemporary art.

🛏 Sleeping & Eating

Latchis Hotel   HOTEL $$
(☑ 802-348-4070, 800-798-6301; www.latchishotel.com; 50 Main St; r $100-200, ste $180-240; ☎) You can't beat the location of these 30 reasonably priced rooms and suites, in the epicenter of downtown and adjacent to the historic theater of the same name. The hotel's art-deco overtones are refreshing, and wonderfully surprising for New England.

⭐**Inn on Putney Road**   B&B $$$
(☑ 802-254-6268; www.vermontbandbinn.com; 192 Putney Rd; r $179-299; @☎) Under new ownership as of 2016, this sweet 1930s-vintage B&B north of town has a glorious yard, five rooms and one luxurious suite with fireplace. Overlooking the West River estuary, it offers opportunities for walking, biking and boating right on its doorstep, and plenty of rainy-day activities, including billiards, board games, DVDs, a guest library and an indoor hot tub.

⭐**TJ Buckley's**   AMERICAN $$$
(☑ 802-257-4922; www.tjbuckleysuptowndining.com; 132 Elliot St; mains $45; ◷ 5:30-9pm Thu-Sun year-round, plus Wed mid-Jun–early Oct) 🍃 Chef-owner Michael Fuller founded this exceptional, upscale little eatery in an authentic 1927 diner over 30 years ago. Ever since, he's been offering a verbal menu of four seasonally changing items, sourced largely from local farms. Locals rave that the food here is Brattleboro's best. The diner seats just 18 souls, so reserve ahead. No credit cards.

❶ Information

Brattleboro Chamber of Commerce (☑ 802-254-4565, 877-254-4565; www.brattleboro

chamber.org; 180 Main St; ⊙9am-5pm Mon-Fri)
Dependable year-round source of tourist info.

Brattleboro Chamber of Commerce Information Booth (80 Putney Rd; ⊙Sat & Sun late May–mid-Oct) On the green just north of downtown.

Bennington

Bennington is a mix of historic Vermont village (Old Bennington), workaday town (Bennington proper) and college town (North Bennington). It is also home to the famous **Bennington Battle Monument** (☑802-447-0550; www.benningtonbattlemonument.com; 15 Monument Circle, Old Bennington; adult/child $5/1; ⊙9am-5pm mid-Apr–Oct), which commemorates the crucial Battle of Bennington during the American Revolution. Had Colonel Seth Warner and the local 'Green Mountain Boys' not helped weaken British defenses during this battle, the colonies might well have been split.

The charming hilltop site of Colonial Old Bennington is studded with 80 Georgian and Federal houses (dating from 1761 – the year Bennington was founded – to 1830). The poet Robert Frost is buried here and a museum in his old homestead pays eloquent tribute. As Bennington is within the bounds of the Green Mountain National Forest, there are many hiking trails nearby, including the granddaddies of them all: the Appalachian and Long Trails.

◉ Sights

Bennington Museum MUSEUM
(☑802-447-1571; www.benningtonmuseum.org; 75 Main St; adult/child $10/free; ⊙10am-5pm daily Jun-Oct, Thu-Tue Nov-May, closed Jan) Between downtown and Old Bennington, this ever-expanding museum offers 14 galleries of ongoing and changing exhibits. It features the world's largest collections of Grandma Moses paintings and Bennington pottery, along with a rich array of Vermont paintings, decorative arts and folk art from the 18th century to the present, encompassing everything from Vermont's Gilded Age to Bennington Modernism to 'Outsider' Art. New in 2015, the Works on Paper Gallery displays prints, lithographs, photography and more by nationally recognized artists.

Old First Church HISTORIC SITE
(☑802-447-1223; www.oldfirstchurchbenn.org; cnr Monument Ave & VT 9; ⊙10am-4pm Mon-Sat, 1-4pm Sun Jul–mid-Oct, weekends only late May–Jun) **FREE** Gracing the center of Old Bennington, this historic church was built in 1805 in Palladian style. Its churchyard holds the remains of five Vermont governors, numerous American Revolution soldiers and poet Robert Frost (1874–1963) – the best-known, and perhaps best-loved, American poet of the 20th century – buried beneath the inscription 'I Had a Lover's Quarrel with the World.'

🛏 Sleeping & Eating

Greenwood Lodge & Campsites HOSTEL, CAMPGROUND $
(☑802-442-2547; www.campvermont.com; VT 9, Prospect Mountain; 2-person tent/RV sites $30/39, dm $35-38, r $79; ⊙mid-May–late Oct; ☎) Nestled in the Green Mountains in Woodford, this 120-acre space with three ponds is home to one of Vermont's best-sited hostels. Accommodations include 17 budget beds and 40 campsites. You'll find it easily, 8 miles east of Bennington on VT 9 at the Prospect Mountain ski area. Facilities include hot showers and a games room.

Blue Benn Diner DINER $
(☑802-442-5140; 314 North St; mains $6-14; ⊙6am-5pm Mon & Tue, to 8pm Wed-Fri, to 4pm Sat, 7am-4pm Sun; ☑) This classic 1950s-era diner serves breakfast all day and a healthy mix of American, Asian and Mexican fare, including vegetarian options. Enhancing the retro experience are little tabletop jukeboxes where you can you play Willie Nelson's 'Moonlight in Vermont' or Cher's 'Gypsies, Tramps and Thieves' till your neighbors scream for mercy.

★Pangaea INTERNATIONAL $$
(☑802-442-7171; www.vermontfinedining.com; 1 Prospect St, North Bennington; mains lounge $10-24, restaurant $31; ⊙lounge 5-10pm daily, restaurant 5-9pm Tue-Sat) Whether you opt for the tastefully decorated dining room, the intimate lounge or the small riverside terrace, you'll be served exceptional food here. The menu is full of fresh ingredients and international influences; try the Thai shrimp on organic udon noodles in a curry peanut sauce or the herbes de Provence–rubbed Delmonico steak topped with Gorgonzola. One of Vermont's finest restaurants.

ⓘ Information

Bennington Welcome Center (☑802-447-2456; www.informationcenter.vermont.gov; 100 VT 279; ⊙7am-9pm) Bennington's spiffy new tourist office has loads of information, long hours, and free coffee and tea for motorists; it's at the highway interchange where VT 279 and US 7 meet.

Manchester

Manchester has been a fashionable resort town for almost two centuries. These days, the draw is mostly winter skiing and upscale outlet shopping (there are more than 100 shops, from Armani to Banana Republic).

Two families put Manchester on the map. The first was native son Franklin Orvis (1824–1900), who became a New York businessperson but returned to Manchester to establish the Equinox House Hotel (1849). Franklin's brother, Charles, founded the Orvis Company, makers of fly-fishing equipment, in 1856. The Manchester-based company now has a worldwide following.

The second family was that of Abraham Lincoln (1809–65). His wife, Mary Todd Lincoln (1818–82), and their son Robert Todd Lincoln (1843–1926), came here during the Civil War, and Robert returned to build a mansion – Hildene – a number of years later.

◉ Sights & Activites

★ **Hildene** HISTORIC SITE
(☑ 802-362-1788; www.hildene.org; 1005 Hildene Rd/VT 7A; adult/child $20/5, guided tours $7.50/2; ☉ 9:30am-4:30pm) Outside Manchester, the 24-room Georgian Revival mansion of Robert Todd Lincoln, son of Abraham and Mary Lincoln, is a national treasure. Lincoln family members lived here until 1975, when it was converted into a museum and filled with many of the family's personal effects and furnishings. These include the hat Abraham Lincoln probably wore when he delivered the Gettysburg Address, and remarkable brass casts of his hands, the right one swollen from shaking hands while campaigning for the presidency.

Mt Equinox Skyline Drive SCENIC DRIVE
(☑ 802-362-1114; www.equinoxmountain.com; VT 7A, btwn Manchester & Arlington; car & driver $15, each additional passenger $5, under 13yr free; ☉ 9am-4pm late May-Oct) For exceptional views, climb the insanely steep 5-mile Skyline Dr, a private toll road that leads to the summit of 3848ft Mt Equinox, highest mountain in the Taconic Range; it's just off VT 7A, south of Manchester.

🛏 Sleeping & Eating

Aspen Motel MOTEL $$
(☑ 802-362-2450; www.theaspenatmanchester.com; 5669 Main St/VT 7A; r $95-160; ✻ 🛜 🌊) An affordable standout, this family-run hotel set back serenely from the road has 25 comfortable rooms, a swimming pool and a convenient location within walking distance of Manchester Center.

Ye Olde Tavern AMERICAN $$$
(☑ 802-362-0611; www.yeoldetavern.net; 5183 Main St; mains $19-34; ☉ 5-9pm) Hearthside dining at candlelit tables enhances the experience at this gracious roadside 1790s inn. The menu is wide-ranging: 'Yankee favorites' like traditional pot roast cooked in the tavern's own ale; New England scrod baked with Vermont cheddar, bread crumbs, sherry and lemon; and local venison (a regular Friday special) seal the deal.

ℹ Information

Green Mountain National Forest Ranger Station (☑ 802-362-2307; www.fs.usda.gov/gmfl; 2538 Depot St, Manchester Center; ☉ 8am-4:30pm Mon-Fri) Stop by for info about the Appalachian and Long Trails, trail maps and details about shorter day hikes.

Central Vermont

Vermont's heart features some of New England's most bucolic countryside. Cows begin to outnumber people just north of Rutland (Vermont's second-largest city, with a whopping 16,500 residents). Lovers of the outdoors make frequent pilgrimages to central Vermont, especially to the resort areas of Killington, Sugarbush and Mad River Glen, which attract countless skiers and summer hikers. For those interested in indoor pleasures, antique shops and art galleries dot the back roads between picturesque covered bridges.

ℹ Getting There & Around

The best way to get around central Vermont is with your own wheels, whether that means car or bicycle. The major driving thoroughfares are US 4, running east–west, and VT 100, running north–south – with the two crossing paths in Killington. Public transit here is limited to Vermont Translines' once-daily east–west bus service between Rutland, VT, and Hanover, NH, and Amtrak's once-daily *Vermonter* train, which runs up the Connecticut and White River valleys between Brattleboro and Burlington. There is a small airport in Rutland, but service is limited to commuter flights to/from Boston.

Woodstock & Quechee

Chartered in 1761, Woodstock has been the highly dignified seat of scenic Windsor County since 1766. Many grand houses surround the oval village green, and four of Woodstock's churches can claim bells cast by Paul Revere. Senator Jacob Collamer, a friend of Abraham Lincoln's, once observed, 'The good people of Woodstock have less incentive than others to yearn for heaven.'

Today Woodstock is still very beautiful and very wealthy. Spend some time walking around the green, surrounded by Federal and Greek Revival homes and public buildings, or along the Ottauquechee River, spanned by three covered bridges. The Rockefellers and the Rothschilds own estates in the surrounding countryside, and the well-to-do come to stay at the grand Woodstock Inn & Resort.

About five minutes' drive east of Woodstock, small, twee Quechee Village is home to Quechee Gorge – Vermont's diminutive answer to the Grand Canyon – as well as some outstanding restaurants.

◉ Sights

★ Quechee Gorge   CANYON
(US 4, Quechee) **FREE** Lurking beneath US 4, less than a mile east of Quechee Village, the gorge is a 163ft-deep scar that cuts about 3000ft along a stream that you can view from a bridge or easily access by footpaths from the road. A series of well-marked, undemanding trails, none of which should take more than an hour to cover, lead down into the gorge.

Billings Farm & Museum   FARM
(☑ 802-457-2355; www.billingsfarm.org; 69 Old River Rd, Woodstock; adult/child $15/8; ☉ 10am-5pm daily Apr-Oct, to 4pm Sat, Sun & holidays Nov-Feb, closed Mar; ⊛) A mile north of Woodstock's village green, this historic farm founded by 19th-century railroad magnate Frederick Billings delights children with hands-on activities related to old-fashioned farm life. Farm animals, including pretty cows descended from Britain's Jersey island, are abundant. Family-friendly seasonal events include wagon and sleigh rides, pumpkin and apple festivals, and old-fashioned Halloween, Thanksgiving and Christmas celebrations.

Marsh-Billings-Rockefeller National Historical Park   PARK
(☑ 802-457-3368; www.nps.gov/mabi; 54 Elm St, Woodstock; mansion tours adult/child $8/free, trails & carriage roads free; ☉ visitor center & tours 10am-5pm late May-Oct, trails & carriage roads year-round) Built around the historic home of early American conservationist George Perkins Marsh, Vermont's only national park examines the relationship between land stewardship and environmental conservation. The estate's 20 miles of trails and carriage roads are free for exploring on foot, cross-country skis or snowshoes.

VINS Nature Center   WILDLIFE RESERVE
(Vermont Institute of Natural Science; ☑ 802-359-5000; www.vinsweb.org; 6565 Woodstock Rd, Quechee; adult/child $15/13; ☉ 10am-5pm mid-Apr–Oct, to 4pm Nov–mid-Apr; ⊛) This science center near Quechee houses two dozen species of raptors, ranging from the tiny, 3oz saw-whet owl to the mighty bald eagle. The birds that end up here have sustained permanent injuries that prevent them from returning to the wild. On offer are regular educational presentations and three self-guided nature trails, delightful for summer hiking and winter snowshoeing.

⊨ Sleeping & Eating

Shire   HOTEL $$
(☑ 802-457-2211; www.shiremotel.com; 46 Pleasant St/US 4, Woodstock; r $159-269; ⊛ ⊚ ⊛) Set within walking distance of Woodstock's town center on US 4, this recently remodeled hotel has 44 comfortable rooms, the best of which come with fireplaces, Jacuzzis and/or decks with rockers looking out over the Ottauquechee River. Many units received new beds in 2015, all have brand-new linens, and rooms 218 and 405 have especially nice river views.

Ardmore Inn   B&B $$$
(☑ 802-457-3887; www.ardmoreinn.com; 23 Pleasant St, Woodstock; r incl breakfast $189-299; ⊛ ⊚) This congenial, centrally located inn in a stately 1867 Victorian–Greek Revival building has four antique-laden rooms with oriental rugs and private marble bathrooms. The owners are especially helpful, and the breakfasts are seemingly never-ending.

★ Simon Pearce Restaurant   MODERN AMERICAN $$$
(☑ 802-295-1470; www.simonpearce.com; 1760 Quechee Main St, Quechee; mains lunch $14-19,

dinner $22-40; ⊘11:30am-2:45pm & 5:30-9pm Mon-Sat, from 10:30am Sun) Be sure to reserve a window table overlooking the falls in Simon Pearce's dining room, which is suspended over the river in this converted brick mill. Local ingredients are used to inventive effect in such delicacies as crab and cod melt or seared chicken with roasted-corn mascarpone polenta. The restaurant's stemware is blown by hand in the adjacent glass workshop.

ⓘ Information

Woodstock Area Chamber of Commerce Welcome Center (☑ 888-496-6378, 802-457-3555; www.woodstockvt.com; 3 Mechanic St, Woodstock; ⊘9am-5pm late May–mid-Oct, 10am-5pm rest of year) Woodstock's welcome center is housed in a lovely red building on a riverside backstreet, two blocks from the village green. There's also a small information booth on the village green itself. Both places can help with accommodations.

Killington

The largest ski resort in the East, Killington spans seven mountains, dominated by 4241ft Killington Peak, the second highest in Vermont. Although upwards of 20,000 people can find lodging within 20 miles, its numerous outdoor activities are centrally located on the mountain. Officially the mountain town is Killington Village, but all the action can be found along Killington Rd on the way up the mountain.

Virtually everyone is here to ski, which means that Killington Resort's mountainside lodges and condos are the accommodations of choice for many. However, you'll find plenty of other options in the surrounding 'lowlands' along US 4 and VT 100, from motels to campgrounds to a historic trailside inn that has welcomed many a weary Long Trail hiker.

Killington Resort   SKIING
(☑ info 800-734-9435, reservations 800-621-6867; www.killington.com; 4763 Killington Rd; lift tickets adult/teen/senior $105/89/81) Known as the 'Beast of the East,' Vermont's prime ski resort is enormous, yet runs efficiently enough to avoid overcrowding; it has five separate lodges, each with a different emphasis, as well as 29 lifts and 92 miles of trails. The ski season runs from November through early May, enhanced by America's largest snowmaking system.

ⓘ Information

Killington Welcome Center (☑ 802-773-4181; http://killingtonpico.org; 2319 US 4; ⊘9am-4pm Mon-Fri, 10am-2pm Sat & Sun) General tourist information, conveniently located on US 4.

Killington/Pico Central Reservations (☑ 800-621-6867; www.killington.com; 4763 Killington Rd; ⊘8am-9pm Nov-Apr, to 4pm May-Oct) Advice on accommodations, including package deals.

Mad River Valley

North of Killington, VT 100 is one of the finest stretches of road in the country: a bucolic mix of rolling hills, covered bridges, white steeples and fertile farmland. Here you'll find the Mad River Valley, where the pretty villages of Waitsfield and Warren nestle in the shadow of two major ski areas, Sugarbush and Mad River Glen.

For tantalizing valley perspectives, go exploring the glorious back roads on either side of VT 100. Leave the pavement behind and meander up the valley's eastern side, following Brook, E Warren, Common, North and Pony Farm Rds from Warren north to Moretown; or head west from Warren over Lincoln Gap Rd, the highest, steepest and perhaps prettiest of all the 'gap roads' that run east to west over the Green Mountains. Stop at Lincoln Gap (2424ft) for the scenic 3-mile hike up the **Long Trail** to Mt Abraham (4017ft), Vermont's fifth-highest peak.

🏃 Activities

★ Mad River Glen   SKIING
(☑ 802-496-3551; www.madriverglen.com; VT 17, Waitsfield; lift tickets adult/child weekend $79/63, midweek $65/60) The most rugged lift-served ski area in the East, Mad River is also one of the quirkiest. Managed by an owner cooperative, not a major ski corporation, it largely eschews artificial snowmaking, prohibits snowboarding, and proudly continues to use America's last operating single chairlift, a vintage 1948 model!

Vermont Icelandic Horse Farm   HORSEBACK RIDING
(☑ 802-496-7141; www.icelandichorses.com; 3061 N Fayston Rd, Waitsfield; 1-3hr rides $60-120, full day incl lunch $220, multiday treks $675-1695; ⊘by appointment; ♿) Explore the scenic hills above Waitsfield on beautiful, gentle and easy-to-ride Icelandic horses. Rides range from hour-long jaunts to multiday inn-to-inn treks.

🛏 Sleeping & Eating

★ **Inn at Round Barn Farm** INN $$$

(☎802-496-2276; www.roundbarninn.com; 1661 E Warren Rd, Waitsfield; r incl breakfast $179-359; 🖥🛏) This place gets its name from the adjacent 1910 round barn – among the few authentic examples remaining in Vermont. The decidedly upscale inn has antique-furnished rooms with mountain views, gas fireplaces, canopy beds and antiques. All overlook the meadows and mountains. In winter guests leave their shoes at the door to preserve the hardwood floors. The country-style breakfast is huge.

★ **Warren Store** SANDWICHES $

(☎802-496-3864; www.warrenstore.com; 284 Main St, Warren; sandwiches & light meals $5-9; ☉7:45am-7pm Mon-Sat, to 6pm Sun) This atmospheric country store serves the area's best sandwiches along with delicious pastries and breakfasts. In summer, linger over coffee and the *New York Times* on the front porch, or eat on the deck overlooking the waterfall, then descend for a cool dip among river-sculpted rocks. Browsers will love the store's eclectic upstairs collection of clothing, toys and jewelry.

ⓘ Information

Mad River Valley Chamber of Commerce (☎800-828-4748, 802-496-3409; www. madrivervalley.com; 4061 Main St/VT 100, Waitsfield; ☉8am-5pm Mon-Fri) Staff here can assist with lodging and the latest skiing info. The chamber also provides a 24-hour information kiosk and public restrooms for visitors.

Northern Vermont

Northern Vermont is home to the state's largest city, Burlington, and the state capital, Montpelier. Never fear, however: this area still has all of the rural charms found elsewhere. Even within Burlington, cafe-lined streets coexist with scenic paths along Lake Champlain and the Winooski River. Further north, the pastoral Northeast Kingdom offers a full range of outdoor activities, from skiing to biking, in the heart of the mountains.

ⓘ Getting There & Around

Burlington has Vermont's only international airport and its best bus connections, making this the logical starting point for visitors arriving by plane or public transportation. Car travel in northern Vermont is also faster and more efficient than elsewhere in the state, thanks to two interstate highways, I-89 serving the Montpelier–Burlington corridor and I-91 serving St Johnsbury and the Northeast Kingdom. Even so, the going gets slower once you stray onto scenic back roads like VT 108 over beautiful Smugglers Notch.

Montpelier

Montpelier (mont-*peel*-yer) would qualify as nothing more than a large village in most places. But in sparsely populated Vermont it's the state capital – the smallest in the country (and the only one without a McDonald's, in case you were wondering). Surprisingly cosmopolitan for a town of 8000 residents, its two main thoroughfares – State St and Main St – make for a pleasant wander, with some nice bookstores, boutiques and eateries.

Montpelier's smaller, distinctly working-class neighbor Barre (*bear*-ee), which touts itself as the 'granite capital of the world,' is a 15-minute drive southeast of the capital.

State House HISTORIC BUILDING

(☎802-828-1411; www.vtstatehousefriends.org; 115 State St; ☉ guided tours 10am-3:30pm Mon-Fri, 11am-2:30pm Sat Jul–mid-Oct, 9am-3pm Mon-Fri mid-Oct–Jun) **FREE** Montpelier's main landmark, the gold-domed capitol building, is open year-round for guided tours by volunteer guides; there are also self-guided audio tours in English, French, Spanish and German. The front doors are guarded by a massive statue of American Revolutionary hero Ethan Allen, and the base supporting the gold dome was built of granite quarried in nearby Barre in 1836.

La Brioche CAFE, BAKERY $

(☎802-229-0443; www.neci.edu/labrioche; 89 Main St; pastries $1-5, sandwiches $5-8; ☉7am-6pm Mon-Fri, to 3pm Sat) The New England Culinary Institute's first restaurant, this casual bakery and cafe serves delicious pastries and coffee drinks for breakfast, followed by soups, salads and sandwiches on homemade bread at lunchtime.

ⓘ Information

Capitol Region Visitors Center (☎802-828-5981; www.informationcenter.vermont.gov; 134 State St; ☉6am-5pm Mon-Fri, 9am-5pm Sat & Sun) Opposite the Vermont state capitol building.

Stowe

In a cozy valley where the West Branch River flows into Little River and mountains rise in all directions, the quintessential Vermont village of Stowe (founded in 1794) bustles quietly. The town's long-standing reputation as one of the east's classiest mountain resorts draws well-heeled urbanites from Boston, New York and beyond. A bounty of inns and eateries lines the thoroughfares leading up to Smuggler's Notch, an enchantingly narrow rock-walled pass through the Green Mountains just below Mt Mansfield (4393ft), the highest point in Vermont. More than 200 miles of cross-country ski trails, some of the finest mountain biking and downhill skiing in the east, and world-class rock- and ice-climbing make this a natural mecca for adrenaline junkies.

Waterbury, on the interstate highway 10 miles south, is Stowe's gateway. Its attractions include a pair of standout restaurants, a beloved brewery and the famous Ben & Jerry's Ice Cream Factory.

◎ Sights & Activities

★ Ben & Jerry's
Ice Cream Factory   FACTORY
(✆802-882-2047; www.benjerrys.com; 1281 VT 100, Waterbury; adult/child under 13yr $4/free; ☺9am-9pm Jul–mid-Aug, to 7pm mid-Aug–mid-Oct, 10am-6pm mid-Oct–Jun; ♠) In 1978 Ben Cohen and Jerry Greenfield took over an abandoned gas station in Burlington and, with a modicum of training, launched the outlandish flavors that forever changed the way ice cream would be made. While a tour of Ben & Jerry's Ice Cream Factory is no over-the-top Willy Wonka experience, there is a campy video that follows the company's long, strange trip to corporate giant – albeit a very nice giant with an inspiring presence of community building and leadership.

★ Stowe Recreation Path   OUTDOORS
(☺year-round; ♠♥) The flat to gently rolling 5.5-mile Stowe Recreation Path, which starts from the pointy-steepled Stowe Community Church in the village center, offers a fabulous four-season escape for all ages. It rambles through woods, meadows and outdoor sculpture gardens along the West Branch of Little River, with sweeping views of Mt Mansfield unfolding in the distance.

Bike, walk, skate or ski – and swim in one of the swimming holes along the way.

🛏 Sleeping & Eating

Stowe Motel &
Snowdrift   MOTEL, APARTMENT $$
(✆802-253-7629, 800-829-7629; www.stowe motel.com; 2043 Mountain Rd; r $99-210, ste $190-250, apt $169-275; @ �🖥 ⚞) In addition to the efficiency rooms (with kitchenettes), suites, apartment and two- to six-bedroom houses (rates highly variable; call to inquire), this motel set on a generous 16 acres offers such amenities as a tennis court, hot tubs, badminton and lawn games.

Pie-casso   PIZZA $$
(✆802-253-4411; www.piecasso.com; 1899 Mountain Rd; mains $8-22; ☺11am-9pm Sun-Thu, to 10pm Fri & Sat) Best known for its ample pizzas, from the sausage-and-pepperoni-laden Heart Stopper to the veggie-friendly Vienna with spinach, olives, sun-dried tomatoes and mozzarella, Pie-casso also serves everything from eggplant Parmesan subs to fettuccine Alfredo and penne with pesto. Gluten-free crusts using flour from nearby West Meadow Farm are also available.

Bistro at Ten Acres   FUSION $$$
(✆802-253-6838; www.tenacreslodge.com; 14 Barrows Rd; mains $19-32; ☺5-10pm Wed-Sun) This immensely popular eatery in a plank-floored 1820s farmhouse blends cozy atmosphere with delicious food from New York–trained chef Gary Jacobson (think *steak frites*, slow-roasted duck, or lobster with bourbon-tarragon sauce and polenta). The attached bar serves a good selection of cocktails and draft beers, plus a cheaper burger-centric menu.

❶ Information

Green Mountain Club Visitors Center (✆802-244-7037; www.greenmountainclub.org; 4711 Waterbury-Stowe Rd/VT 100, Waterbury Center; ☺9am-5pm daily mid-May–mid-Oct, 10am-5pm Mon-Fri mid-Oct–mid-May) Stop by this office (5 miles south of Stowe) or check the website for details about the Long Trail and shorter day hikes in the region.

Stowe Area Association (✆802-253-7321, 800-467-8693; www.gostowe.com; 51 Main St; ☺9am-5pm Mon-Sat, 11am-5pm Sun; ♠) This well-organized association can help you plan your trip, including making reservations for rental cars and local accommodations.

Burlington

Perched on the shore of Lake Champlain, Vermont's largest city would be considered tiny in most other states, but its relatively diminutive size is one of Burlington's charms. With the University of Vermont (UVM) swelling the city by 13,400 students, and a vibrant cultural and social life, Burlington has a spirited, youthful character. And when it comes to nightlife, this is Vermont's epicenter.

Due south of Burlington is Shelburne, an upscale village that's home to the one of Vermont's crown jewels, the Shelburne Museum. The village is considered more of an extension of Burlington rather than a separate suburb – people think nothing of popping down for an evening meal to one of its fine restaurants.

Burlington is less than an hour's drive from Stowe and other Green Mountain towns. The city can be used as a base for exploring much of northwestern Vermont.

⊙ Sights & Activities

★ Shelburne Museum   MUSEUM
(☑ 802-985-3346; www.shelburnemuseum.org; 6000 Shelburne Rd/US 7, Shelburne; adult/child/teen $24/12/14; ⊙10am-5pm daily May-Dec, Wed-Sun Jan-Apr; ☀) This extraordinary 45-acre museum, 9 miles south of Burlington, showcases the priceless Americana collections of Electra Havemeyer Webb (1888–1960) and her parents – 150,000 objects in all. The mix of folk art, decorative arts and more is housed in 39 historic buildings, most of them moved here from other parts of New England to ensure their preservation.

★ Intervale Center   FARM
(☑ 802-660-0440; www.intervale.org; 180 Intervale Rd) **FREE** You'd never guess it standing on a busy Burlington street corner, but one of Vermont's most idyllic green spaces is less than 2 miles from downtown. Tucked among the lazy curves of the Winooski River, Burlington's Intervale Center encompasses a dozen organic farms and a delightful trail network, open 365 days a year for hiking, biking, skiing, berry picking and more.

Echo Leahy Center for Lake Champlain   AQUARIUM
(☑ 802-864-1848; www.echovermont.org; 1 College St; adult/child $16.50/13.50; ⊙10am-5pm; ☀) This kid-friendly lakeside museum examines the colorful past, present and future of Lake Champlain. A multitude of aquariums wriggle with life, and nature-oriented displays invite inquisitive minds and hands to splash, poke, listen and crawl. Regular ro-

tating exhibits focus on scientific themes – from wind power to giant insects, and dinosaurs to cadavers – with plenty of hands-on activities.

Whistling Man Schooner Company   BOATING
(☑ 802-825-7245; www.whistlingman.com; Burlington Community Boathouse, 1 College St, at Lake Champlain; 2hr cruises adult/child $50/35; ⊙3-4 trips daily, late May-early Oct) Sail around Lake Champlain with the breeze in your hair and a Vermont microbrew in your hand on the *Friend Ship,* a classic 43ft New England beauty that holds up to 17 passengers. Captains are knowledgeable about the area, and encourage passengers to bring food and drink on board. Private charters are also available (from $450 for two hours).

🛏 Sleeping

Burlington Hostel   HOSTEL $
(☑ 802-540-3043; www.theburlingtonhostel.com; 53 Main St, 2nd floor; dm incl breakfast weekday/weekend $39/49; ⊙May-Oct; ❄@☎) Just minutes from the action centers of Church St and Lake Champlain, Burlington's hostel accommodates up to 48 guests and offers both mixed and women-only dorms.

★ Willard Street Inn   INN $$
(☑ 802-651-8710; www.willardstreetinn.com; 349 S Willard St; r incl breakfast $169-269; ☎) Perched on a hill within easy walking distance of UVM and the Church St Marketplace, this mansion, fusing Queen Anne and Georgian Revival styles, was built in the late 1880s. It has a fine-wood and cut-glass elegance, yet radiates a welcoming warmth. Many of the guest rooms overlook Lake Champlain.

★ Inn at Shelburne Farms   INN $$$
(☑ 802-985-8498; www.shelburnefarms.org/staydine; 1611 Harbor Rd, Shelburne; r $270-525, without bath $160-230, cottages & houses $270-850; ⊙early May-late Oct; ☎) One of New England's top 10 places to stay, this inn, 7 miles south of Burlington off US 7, was once the summer mansion of the wealthy Webb family. It now welcomes guests, with rooms in the gracious country manor house by the lakefront, as well as four independent, kitchen-equipped cottages and guesthouses scattered across the property, which can be visited without staying (adult/child $8/5). From Mid-May to mid-October you can hike miles of walking trails, visit the animals in the children's farmyard or take a guided tour.

✖ Eating

★ Penny Cluse Cafe
CAFE **$**

(☑ 802-651-8834; www.pennycluse.com; 169 Cherry St; mains $6-14; ⊙ 6:45am-3pm Mon-Fri, 8am-3pm Sat & Sun) In the heart of downtown, one of Burlington's most popular breakfast spots serves pancakes, biscuits and gravy, breakfast burritos, omelets and tofu scrambles, along with sandwiches, fish tacos, salads and the best chile relleno you'll find east of the Mississippi. Expect an hour's wait on weekends.

Stone Soup
VEGETARIAN **$**

(☑ 802-862-7616; www.stonesoupvt.com; 211 College St; buffet per lb $11.25, sandwiches $9.50-12; ⊙ 7am-9pm Mon-Fri, 9am-9pm Sat; 🐾🖫) Best known for its excellent vegetarian- and vegan-friendly buffet, this longtime local favorite also has homemade soups, sandwiches on home-baked bread, a salad bar, pastries and locally raised meats.

★ American Flatbread
PIZZA **$$**

(☑ 802-861-2999; www.americanflatbread.com; 115 St Paul St; flatbreads $14-23; ⊙ 11:30am-3pm & 5-11:30pm Mon-Fri, 11:30am-11:30pm Sat & Sun) 🐾 Central downtown location, bustling atmosphere, great beers on tap from the in-house Zero Gravity microbrewery, and superb flatbread (thin-crust pizza) with locally sourced ingredients are reason enough to make this one of your first lunch or dinner stops in Burlington.

Revolution Kitchen
VEGAN, VEGETARIAN **$$**

(☑ 802-448-3657; http://revolutionkitchen.com; 9 Center St; mains $14-18; ⊙ 5-10pm Tue-Sat; 🖫) Vegetarian fine dining? And romantic atmosphere to boot? Yep, they all come together at this cozy brick-walled restaurant that makes ample and creative use of Vermont's abundant organic produce. Asian, Mediterranean and Latin American influences abound in house favorites like Revolution tacos, crispy seitan piccata and the Laksa noodle pot. Most items are vegan.

🍷 Drinking & Entertainment

Citizen Cider
MICROBREWERY

(☑ 802-497-1987; www.citizencider.com; 316 Pine St; ⊙ 11am-10pm Mon-Sat, to 7pm Sun) Tucked into an industrial-chic building with painted concrete floors and long wooden tables, this animated cidery is a homegrown success story, using only Vermont apples to make its ever-growing line of hard ciders. Taste test a flight of five for $7, including perennial favorites such as the crisp, classic Unified Press, or the Dirty Mayor, infused with ginger and lemon peel.

★ Light Club Lamp Shop
LIVE MUSIC

(☑ 802-660-9346; www.facebook.com/LightClubLampShop; 12 N Winooski Ave; ⊙ 7pm-2am Mon-Thu, 5pm-2am Fri-Sun) One of Burlington's coolest and quirkiest venues, this place doubles – well, OK, *triples* – as a lamp shop (witness the amazing collection hanging from the walls and ceiling), a wine bar and a performance space. Shows (generally free) run the gamut from indie singer-songwriter to poetry and comedy.

Nectar's
LIVE MUSIC

(☑ 802-658-4771; www.liveatnectars.com; 188 Main St; ⊙ 7pm-2am Mon & Tue, 5pm-2am Wed-Sun) Indie darlings Phish got their start here and the joint still rocks out with the help of aspiring acts. Grab a vinyl booth, chill at the bar or dance upstairs at Club Metronome (http://clubmetronome.com), which hosts a slew of theme nights (every Friday is '90s night) along with larger live acts.

ℹ Information

BTV Information Center (☑ 802-863-1889; www.vermont.org; Burlington International Airport; ⊙ 4pm-midnight) This helpful office in Burlington's airport is staffed by the Lake Champlain Regional Chamber of Commerce.

Lake Champlain Regional Chamber of Commerce (☑ 877-686-5253, 802-863-3489; www.vermont.org; 60 Main St; ⊙ 8am-5pm Mon-Fri) Staffed tourist office in the heart of downtown.

Waterfront Tourism Center (College St; ⊙ 10am-8pm daily late May–Aug, to 6pm Sep–mid-Oct) Opens seasonally down near the lakefront.

ℹ Getting There & Away

To get here by car from Boston (3½ hours, 216 miles), take I-93 to I-89. It's another 1¾ hours (95 miles) north from Burlington to Montreal, Canada.

AIR

A number of national carriers, including JetBlue, serve **Burlington International Airport** (BTV; ☑ 802-863-2874; www.btv.aero; 1200 Airport Dr, South Burlington), 3 miles east of the city center. You'll find all the major car-rental companies at the airport.

BUS

Greyhound (www.greyhound.com) runs multiple buses daily from Burlington International Airport to Montreal, Canada (from $16, 2½ hours) and Boston (from $29, 4½ to 5½ hours).

231

Megabus (☑877-462-6342; www.megabus.
com; 119 Pearl St) offers a once-daily bus
service to Boston (from $10, four hours) and
occasional services to New York City from Burlington's brand-new **GMT Downtown Transit
Center** (Green Mountain Transit; ☑802-864-
2282; www.ridegmt.com; cnr St Paul & Cherry
Sts). GMT also operates a few long-distance
buses to other cities in northwestern Vermont.
See the website (www.ridegmt.com) for fares
and schedules.
Middlebury Routes 46 and 76
Montpelier Route 86

TRAIN

Amtrak's daily *Vermonter* train (www.amtrak.
com/vermonter-train), which provides service as
far south as New York City and Washington, DC,
stops in Essex Junction, 5 miles from Burlington.

NEW HAMPSHIRE

New Hampshire woos visitors with jagged
mountains, scenic valleys and forest-lined
lakes – they lurk in every corner of this
rugged state. It all begs you to embrace the
outdoors, from kayaking the hidden coves
of the Lakes Region to trekking the upper
peaks surrounding Mt Washington. Each
season yields a bounty of adrenaline and
activity: skiing and snowshoeing in winter;
magnificent walks and drives through fall's
fiery colors; and swimming in crisp mountain streams and berry-picking in summer.

Jewel-box colonial settlements like Portsmouth set a sophisticated tone, while historical allure and small-town culture live
on in pristine villages like Keene and Peterborough. But there's a relaxing whiff in the
air too – you're encouraged to gaze out at a
loon-filled lake, recline on a scenic railway
trip or chug across a waterway on a sunset
cruise – all while digging into a fried-clam
platter or a lobster roll, of course.

History

Named in 1629 after the English county of
Hampshire, New Hampshire was one of the
first American colonies to declare its independence from England in 1776. During the
19th-century industrialization boom, Manchester became such a powerhouse that its
textile mills were the world's largest.

New Hampshire played a high-profile
role in 1944 when President Franklin D
Roosevelt gathered leaders from 44 Allied
nations to remote Bretton Woods for a conference to rebuild global capitalism. It was

from the Bretton Woods Conference that the
World Bank and the International Monetary
Fund emerged.

In 1963 New Hampshire, long famed for
its anti-tax sentiments, found another way
to raise revenue – by becoming the first state
in the USA to have a legal lottery.

ⓘ Information

**New Hampshire Division of Parks & Recrea-
tion** (www.nhstateparks.org) Offers information on a statewide bicycle route system and a
very complete camping guide.
**New Hampshire Division of Travel & Tourism
Development** (www.visitnh.gov) Ski conditions
and fall foliage reports, among other things.

Portsmouth

Perched on the edge of the Piscataqua River, Portsmouth is one of New Hampshire's
most elegant towns, with a historical center
set with tree-lined streets and 18th-century
Colonial buildings. Despite its venerable history as an early hub of America's maritime
industry, the town exudes a youthful energy, with tourists and locals filling its many
restaurants and cafes. Numerous museums
and historic houses allow visitors a glimpse
into the town's multilayered past, while its
proximity to the coast brings both lobster
feasts and periodic days of fog that blanket
the waterfront.

Still true to its name, Portsmouth remains
a working port town, and its economic vitality has been boosted by the naval shipyard
(actually located across the river in Maine)
and by the influx of high-tech companies.

⊙ Sights & Activities

★**Strawbery Banke Museum**   MUSEUM
(☑603-433-1100; www.strawberybanke.org; 14
Hancock St; adult/child $19.50/9; ⊙10am-5pm
May-Oct, special events only Nov-Apr) Spread
across a 10-acre site, the Strawbery Banke
Museum is an eclectic blend of period homes
that date back to the 1690s. Costumed
guides recount tales that took place among
the 40 buildings (10 furnished). Strawbery
Banke includes **Pitt Tavern** (1766), a hotbed of American revolutionary sentiment,
Goodwin Mansion, a grand 19th-century
house from Portsmouth's most prosperous
time, and **Abbott's Little Corner Store**
(1943). The admission ticket is good for two
consecutive days.

NEW ENGLAND PORTSMOUTH

USS Albacore
MUSEUM

(☑ 603-436-3680; www.ussalbacore.org; 600 Market St; adult/child $7/3; ◑ 9:30am-5pm late May–mid-Oct, reduced hours rest of year) Like a fish out of water, this 205ft-long submarine is now a beached museum on a grassy lawn. Launched from Portsmouth Naval Shipyard in 1953, the *Albacore* was once the world's fastest submarine.

Isles of Shoals Steamship Co
CRUISE

(☑ 603-431-5500; www.islesofshoals.com; 315 Market St; adult/child from $28/18; ◉) From mid-June to October this company runs an excellent tour of the harbor and the historic Isles of Shoals aboard a replica 1900s ferry. It also offers walking tours of Star Island and party cruises featuring DJs or live bands.

🛏 Sleeping & Eating

Portsmouth is a terrific foodie destination, serving up everything from lobster rolls to international street food, from quality vegetarian fare to nouvelle New England cuisine.

Port Inn
MOTEL $$

(☑ 603-436-4378; www.portinnportsmouth.com; 505 US 1 Bypass; r $189-339; ❄@🔊🐾❄) Wrapped neatly around a small courtyard, this welcoming motel is conveniently located off I-95, about 1.5 miles southwest of downtown. In the rooms, monochromatic pillows and throws add a dash of color to classic furnishings. Pets are $20 per night.

★ Ale House Inn
INN $$$

(☑ 603-431-7760; www.alehouseinn.com; 121 Bow St; r $209-379; 🅿❄🔊) This former brick warehouse for the Portsmouth Brewing Company is now Portsmouth's snazziest boutique inn, fusing contemporary design with comfort. Rooms are modern, with clean lines of white, flat-screen TVs and, in the suites, plush tan sofas. Deluxe rooms feature an in-room iPad. Rates include use of vintage cruising bikes.

Surf
SEAFOOD $$

(☑ 603-334-9855; www.surfseafood.com; 99 Bow St; lunch $10-24, dinner $12-42; ◑ 4-9pm Tue & Wed, 11am-9pm Thu & Sun, 11am-10pm Fri & Sat) We're not sure if the view of the Piscataqua River complements the food or the food complements the view at this airy restaurant, especially at sunset. Either way, it's a satisfying way to close out the day. The seafood offerings sport some global flair, with haddock tacos, Portuguese seafood stew and shrimp vindaloo.

★ Black Trumpet Bistro
INTERNATIONAL $$$

(☑ 603-431-0887; www.blacktrumpetbistro.com; 29 Ceres St; mains $17-32; ◑ 5-9pm) With brick walls and a sophisticated ambience, this bistro serves unique combinations – anything from housemade sausages infused with cocoa beans to seared haddock with yuzu (an Asian citrus fruit) and miso. The full menu is also available at its wine bar upstairs, which whips up equally inventive cocktails.

❶ Information

Greater Portsmouth Chamber of Commerce
(☑ 603-610-5510; www.portsmouthchamber.org; 500 Market St; ◑ 9am-5pm Mon-Fri year-round, plus 10am-5pm Sat & Sun late May–mid-Oct) also operates a seasonal **information kiosk** (Market Sq) in the city center.

❶ Getting There & Away

Portsmouth is equidistant (57 miles) from Boston and Portland, ME. It takes roughly 1¼ hours to reach Portland and 1½ hours to Boston, both via I-95. Rush-hour and high-season traffic can easily double or triple this, however.

Lakes Region

The Lakes Region, with an odd mix of natural beauty and commercial tawdriness, is one of New Hampshire's most popular holiday destinations. Vast Lake Winnipesaukee, the region's centerpiece, has 183 miles of coastline, more than 300 islands and excellent salmon fishing. Catch the early-morning mists off the lake and you'll understand why the Native Americans named it 'Smile of the Great Spirit.' The prettiest stretches are in the southwest corner between Glendale and Alton (on the shoreline Belknap Point Rd), and in the northeast corner between Wolfeboro and Moultonborough (on NH 109). Just to the north lie the smaller Squam Lake and Little Squam Lake.

The roads skirting the shores and connecting the lakeside towns are a riotous spread of small-town Americana: amusement arcades, go-kart tracks, clam shacks, junk-food outlets and boat docks.

❶ Getting There & Around

The fastest way to reach the Lakes Region is via I-93. Coming from Boston and other points south, take exit 15E for Wolfeboro, exit 20 for Weirs Beach, exit 23 for Meredith or exit 24 for Holderness (Squam Lake).

Weirs Beach

Called 'Aquedoctan' by its Native American settlers, Weirs Beach takes its English name from the weirs (enclosures for catching fish) that the first European settlers found along the small sand beach. Today Weirs Beach is the honky-tonk heart of Lake Winnipesaukee's childhood amusements, famous for video-game arcades and fried dough. The vacation scene is completed by a lakefront promenade, a public beach and a dock for small cruising ships. A water park and drive-in theater are also in the vicinity. Away from the din on the waterfront, you will notice evocative Victorian-era architecture – somewhat out of place in this capital of kitsch.

South of Weirs Beach lie Laconia, the largest town in the region but devoid of any real sights, and lake-hugging Gilford. Note that this side of the lake gets mobbed with bikers for nine days each June during Laconia Motorcycle Week (www.laconiamcweek.com), the world's oldest motorcycle rally.

MS Mount Washington CRUISE
(☑ 603-366-5531; www.cruisenh.com; 211 Lakeside Ave; adult/child regular cruises $32/16, Sunday brunch cruises $50/25) The classic MS *Mount Washington* steams out of Weirs Beach daily from mid-May to mid-October, making a relaxing 2½-hour scenic circuit around Lake Winnipesaukee, with regular stops in Wolfeboro and occasional visits to Alton Bay, Center Harbor and/or Meredith. Special events include the weekly champagne brunch cruise on Sundays and themed cruises throughout summer.

Winnipesaukee Scenic Railroad RAIL
(☑ 603-745-2135; www.hoborr.com; 211 Lakeside Ave; adult/child 1hr $18/14, 2hr $20/16) The touristy Scenic Railroad offers one- or two-hour lakeside rides aboard 1920s and '30s train cars departing from Weirs Beach and Meredith (154 Main St). The train travels to Lake Winnipesaukee's southern tip at Alton Bay before making a U-turn.

❶ Information

Lakes Region Chamber of Commerce
(☑ 603-524-5531; www.lakesregionchamber.org; 383 S Main St, Laconia; ☺9am-3pm Mon-Fri) Supplies information about the greater Laconia/Weirs Beach area.

Weirs Beach Information Booth (513 Weirs Blvd; ☺24hr late May-early Sep) Useful for same-day accommodations.

Wolfeboro

On the eastern shore of Lake Winnipesaukee, Wolfeboro is an idyllic town where children still gather around the ice-cream stand on warm summer nights and a grassy lakeside park draws young and old to weekly concerts. Named for General Wolfe, who died vanquishing Montcalm on the Plains of Abraham in Quebec, Wolfeboro (founded in 1770) claims to be 'the oldest summer resort in America.' Whether that's true or not, it's certainly one of the most charming, with pretty lake beaches, intriguing museums, beautiful New England architecture (from Georgian through Federal, Greek Revival and Second Empire), cozy B&Bs and a worthwhile walking trail that runs along several lakes as it leads out of town.

🛏 Sleeping & Eating

Wolfeboro Campground CAMPGROUND $
(☑ 603-569-9881; www.wolfeborocampground.com; 61 Haines Hill Rd; tent/RV sites $29/33; ☺late May–mid-Oct; 🐾) Off NH 28, and about 4.5 miles north of Wolfeboro's town center, this campground has 50 private, wooded sites.

Wolfe's Tavern AMERICAN $$
(☑ 603-569-3016; www.wolfestavern.com; 90 N Main St; dinner mains $15-34; ☺7am-9pm Sun-Thu, to 10pm Fri & Sat) The ample menu at the rustically colonial Wolfeboro Inn ranges from pizza to burgers, seafood to steaks, with vegetarian and gluten-free options thrown in for good measure. Terrace tables are set outside in good weather.

❶ Information

Wolfeboro Chamber of Commerce Information Booth (☑ 603-569-2200; www.wolfeborochamber.com; 32 Central Ave; ☺10am-3pm Mon-Sat, to noon Sun late May–mid-Oct, reduced hours rest of year) Located inside the old train station, this small office has the scoop on local activities.

White Mountains

Covering one-quarter of New Hampshire (and part of Maine), the vast White Mountains area is a spectacular region of soaring peaks and lush valleys, and contains New England's most rugged mountains. There are numerous activities on offer, including hiking, camping, skiing and canoeing. Much of the area – 780,000 acres – is designated as the White Mountain National Forest (WMNF), thus protecting it from overdevelopment and guaranteeing its wondrous natural beauty for years to come. Keep in mind, however, that this place is popular: six million visitors flock here every year, making it the nation's second-most-visited park after the Great Smoky Mountains.

Certain National Forest trails and parking areas require you to have a recreation pass ($5/30 per day/year). Purchase passes at any of the visitor centers in the area or at self-serve pay stations at the trailhead.

ℹ Information

Ranger stations with information about trails and sites are scattered along major roadways throughout the national forest. Check the website (www.fs.usda.gov/whitemountain) for locations.

ℹ Getting There & Around

I-93, running north from Boston to St Johnsbury, VT, offers the most efficient access to the White Mountains. Take any of the exits between Waterville Valley in the south and Littleton in the north to explore smaller east–west roads that lead deeper into the mountains.

Kancamagus Highway

One of New Hampshire's prettiest driving routes, the winding 35-mile Kancamagus Hwy (NH 112) between Lincoln and Conway runs right through the White Mountain National Forest (WMNF) and over Kancamagus Pass (2868ft). Paved only in 1964, and still unspoiled by commercial development, the 'Kanc' offers easy access to US Forest Service (USFS) campgrounds, hiking trails and fantastic scenery.

The route is named for Chief Kancamagus (The Fearless One), who assumed the powers of *sagamore* (leader) of the Penacook Native American tribe around 1684. He was the final *sagamore,* succeeding his grandfather, the great Passaconaway, and his uncle Wonalancet. Kancamagus tried to maintain peace between the indigenous peoples and European explorers and settlers, but the newcomers pushed his patience past breaking point. He finally resorted to battle to rid the region of Europeans, but in 1691 he and his followers were forced to escape northward.

★ Lincoln Woods Trail　　HIKING
(NH 112/Kancamagus Hwy, 5 miles east of I-93) Among the easiest and most popular trails in White Mountain National Forest, the 2.9-mile, 1157ft-elevation Lincoln Woods Trail follows an abandoned railway bed to the Pemigewasset Wilderness boundary (elevation 1450ft). To reach the trailhead, follow the Kancamagus Hwy 5 miles east of I-93 and park in the Lincoln Woods Visitor Center parking lot.

Upon arrival at the Pemigewasset Wilderness boundary, you can either retrace your steps, or continue 6 miles on the easy Wilderness Trail to Stillwater Junction (elevation 2060ft), where you can pick up the Cedar Brook and Hancock Notch Trails and loop back to the Kancamagus Hwy (5.5 miles east of the Lincoln Woods trailhead parking lot).

Saco Ranger District Office　　TOURIST INFORMATION
(☑603-447-5448; 33 Kancamagus Hwy, Conway; ⊗8am-4:30pm Tue-Sun, 9am-4:30pm Mon) You can pick up WMNF brochures and hiking maps at the Saco Ranger District Office at the eastern end of the Kancamagus Hwy near Conway.

North Woodstock & Lincoln

North Woodstock and its neighboring settlement Lincoln gather a mix of adventure seekers and drive-by sightseers en route to the Kancamagus Hwy (NH 112). North Woodstock has a busy but small-town feel with battered motels and diners lining the main street and a gurgling river running parallel to it. Nearby Lincoln has less charm, but serves as the starting point for the entertaining Hobo Railroad and other family-friendly activities such as zipline tours and an aerial adventure park.

🛏 Sleeping & Eating

Woodstock Inn Station & Brewery　INN $$
(☑603-745-3951; www.woodstockinnnh.com; 135 Main St/US 3, North Woodstock; r incl breakfast $102-257; ❄🐾) This Victorian country inn is North Woodstock's centerpiece. It has 33 individually appointed rooms across five separate buildings (three in a cluster, two across the street), each with modern amenities but in an old-fashioned style. The on-site upscale restaurant, Woodstock Inn Station & Microbrewery, has outdoor seating on the lovely flower-filled patio.

Woodstock Inn
Station & Brewery
PUB FOOD $$

(📞603-745-3951; www.woodstockinnnh.com; 135 Main St/US 3, North Woodstock; mains $9-27; ⏲11:30am-1am) Formerly a railroad station, this eatery tries to be everything to everyone. In the end, with more than 150 items, it can probably satisfy just about any food craving, but the pastas, sandwiches and burgers are the most interesting.

ℹ Information

Western White Mountains Chamber of Commerce (📞603-745-6621; www.lincoln woodstock.com; 126 Main St/US 3, North Woodstock; ⏲8am-4pm Mon-Fri) General visitor info.

White Mountains Visitor Center (📞National Forest info 603-745-3816, visitor info 603-745-8720; www.visitwhitemountains.com; 200 Kancamagus Hwy, off I-93, exit 32, North Woodstock; ⏲visitor info 8:30am-5pm daily year-round, National Forest desk 9am-3:30pm daily mid-May–Oct, Fri-Sun rest of year) Trail info and National Forest recreation passes.

Franconia Notch State Park

Franconia Notch, a narrow gorge shaped over the eons by a wild stream cutting through craggy granite, is a dramatic mountain pass. This was long the residence of the beloved Old Man of the Mountain, a natural rock formation that became the symbol of the Granite State. Sadly the Old Man collapsed in 2003, which does not stop tourists from coming to see the featureless cliff that remains. Despite the Old Man's absence, the attractions of Franconia Notch are many, from the dramatic hike down the Flume Gorge to the fantastic views of the Presidential Range.

The most scenic parts of the notch are protected by the narrow Franconia Notch State Park. Reduced to two lanes, I-93 squeezes through the gorge. Services are available in Lincoln and North Woodstock to the south and in Franconia and Littleton to the north.

⦿ Sights & Activities

Cannon Mountain
Aerial Tramway
CABLE CAR

(📞603-823-8800; www.cannonmt.com; 260 Tramway Dr, off I-93, exit 34B; round-trip adult/child $18/16; ⏲8:30am-5pm Jun–mid-Oct; 👪) This tram shoots up the side of Cannon Mountain, offering a breathtaking view of Franco-

WORTH A TRIP

MONADNOCK STATE PARK

Majestic 3165ft **Mt Monadnock** (📞603-532-8862; www.nhstateparks.org; 169 Poole Rd, Jaffrey; day use adult/child $5/2) is the centerpiece of this popular state park between Keene and Jaffrey. Stop at the visitor center for hiking information, then set off on a scenic loop to the bare-topped summit via the White Dot and White Cross Trails (about 3½ hours round-trip). If you want to stay overnight, there's camping on site at **Gilson Pond Campground** (📞info 603-532-2416, reservations 877-647-2757; 585 Dublin Rd/NH 124, Jaffrey; tent sites $25; ⏲May-Oct).

nia Notch. In 1938 the first passenger aerial tramway in North America was installed on this slope. It was replaced in 1980 by the current, larger cable car, capable of carrying 80 passengers up to the summit of Cannon Mountain – a 1-mile ride with 2022ft vertical gain – in less than 10 minutes. You can also hike up the mountain and take the tramway down (adult/child $13/10).

Echo Lake Beach
BEACH

(📞603-745-8391; www.nhstateparks.org; I-93, exit 34C; adult/child $4/2; ⏲9am-5pm late May-early Oct) Despite its proximity to the highway, this little lake at the foot of Cannon Mountain is a pleasant place to pass an afternoon swimming, kayaking or canoeing (from $11 per hour) in the crystal-clear waters.

★ Flume Gorge & the Basin
HIKING

(📞603-745-8391; www.flumegorge.com; I-93, exit 34A; adult/child $16/14; ⏲8:30am-5pm early May–late Oct) To see this natural wonder, take the 2-mile self-guided nature walk that includes the 800ft boardwalk through the Flume, a natural 12ft- to 20ft-wide cleft in the granite bedrock. The granite walls tower 70ft to 90ft above you, with moss and plants growing from precarious niches and crevices. Signs along the way explain how nature formed this natural phenomenon.

ℹ Information

Franconia Notch State Park Visitor Center (📞603-745-8391; www.nhstateparks.org; I-93, exit 34A; ⏲8:30am-5pm early May–late Oct) Open seasonally, the state park visitor center at Flume Gorge has information about the park and surrounding area. There's also a cafeteria and gift shop.

Mt Washington Valley

Dramatic mountain scenery surrounds the tiny villages of this popular alpine destination, providing an abundance of outdoor adventures. There's great hiking, skiing, kayaking and rafting, along with idyllic activities like swimming in local creeks, overnighting in country farmhouses and simply exploring the countryside.

Mt Washington Valley stretches north from Conway, at the eastern end of the Kancamagus Hwy, and forms the eastern edge of the White Mountain range. The valley's hub is North Conway, though any of the towns along NH 16/US 302 (also called the White Mountain Hwy) can serve as a White Mountain gateway. The valley's namesake is, of course, Mt Washington, New England's highest peak (6288ft), which towers over the valley in the northwest.

MT WASHINGTON

Mt Washington's summit is at 6288ft, making it the tallest mountain in New England. The mountain is renowned for its frighteningly bad weather – the average temperature on the summit is 26.5°F(-3°C). The mercury has fallen as low as -47°F (-43°C), but only risen as high as 72°F (22°C). About 256in (more than 21ft) of snow falls each year. (One year, it was 47ft.) At times the climate can mimic Antarctica's, and hurricane-force winds blow every three days or so, on average. In fact, the second-highest wind speed ever recorded was here during a storm in 1934, when gusts reached 231mph.

If you attempt the summit, pack warm, windproof clothes and shoes, even in high summer, and always consult with Appalachian Mountain Club (AMC) hut personnel. Don't be reluctant to turn back if the weather changes for the worse. Dozens of hikers who ignored such warnings and died are commemorated by trailside monuments and crosses.

In good weather, the hike is exhilarating. The only disappointment is exerting hours of effort, exploring remote paths and finally reaching the summit, only to discover a parking lot full of cars that motored up. Don't feel bad – just treat yourself to a 'This car climbed Mt Washington' bumper sticker.

BRETTON WOODS & CRAWFORD NOTCH

This beautiful 1773ft mountain pass on the western slopes of Mt Washington is deeply rooted in New Hampshire lore. In 1826 torrential rains here triggered massive mudslides, killing the Willey family in the valley below. The dramatic incident made the newspapers and fired the imaginations of painter Thomas Cole and author Nathaniel Hawthorne. Both men used the incident for inspiration, thus unwittingly putting Crawford Notch on the tourist maps.

Even so, the area remained known mainly to locals and wealthy summer visitors who patronized the grand Mt Washington Hotel in Bretton Woods – until 1944, when President Roosevelt chose the hotel as the site of a conference to establish a post-WWII global economic order.

Today the hotel is as grand as ever, while a steady flow of visitors comes to climb Mt Washington – on foot, or aboard a steam-powered locomotive on the dramatic Mount Washington Cog Railway.

◉ Sights & Activities

★ **Crawford Notch State Park**   STATE PARK
(☑ 603-374-2272; www.nhstateparks.org; 1464 US 302, Harts Location; ☺ visitor center 9:30am-5pm late May–mid-Oct, park year-round unless posted otherwise) FREE This pretty park maintains an extensive system of hiking trails. From the Willey House visitor center, you can walk the easy 0.5-mile Pond Loop Trail, the 1-mile Sam Willey Trail and the Ripley Falls Trail, a 1-mile hike from US 302 via the Ethan Pond Trail. The trailhead for Arethusa Falls, a 1.3-mile hike, is 0.5 miles south of the Dry River Campground on US 302. Serious hikers can also tackle the much longer trek up Mt Washington.

★ **Mount Washington Cog Railway**   RAIL
(☑ 603-278-5404; www.thecog.com; 3168 Base Station Rd; adult $69-75, child $39; ☺ daily Jun-Oct, Sat & Sun late Apr, May & Nov) Purists walk and the lazy drive, but the quaintest way to reach Mt Washington summit is via this cog railway. Since 1869 coal-fired, steam-powered locomotives have climbed this scenic 3.5-mile track up a steep mountainside trestle (three hours round-trip). Two old-fashioned steam trains run daily late May to October, supplemented by biodiesel-fueled trains late April to November.

Bretton Woods Canopy Tour   ADVENTURE

(☑ 603-278-4947; www.brettonwoods.com; US 302; per person $89-110; ⊙ tours twice daily year-round, additional times during peak periods) This four-season canopy tour sends you hiking through the woods, strolling over sky bridges and swooshing down ziplines that drop 1000ft at 30mph to tree platforms.

🛏 Sleeping

AMC Highland Lodge   LODGE $$

(☑ front desk 603-278-4453, reservations 603-466-2727; www.outdoors.org; NH 302, Bretton Woods; incl breakfast & dinner per adult/child/teen r from $163/50/95, without bath from $113/50/95; 🖥) This cozy Appalachian Mountain Club (AMC) lodge is set amid the splendor of Crawford Notch, an ideal base for hiking the trails crisscrossing the Presidential Range. The grounds are beautiful, rooms are basic but comfortable, meals are hearty and guests are outdoor enthusiasts. Discounts available for AMC members.

★ Omni Mt Washington
Hotel & Resort   HOTEL $$$

(☑ 603-278-1000; www.omnihotels.com; 310 Mt Washington Hotel Rd, Bretton Woods; r $259-849; ✴ @ 🖥 🖥) Open since 1902, this grand hotel maintains a sense of fun – note the moose's head overlooking the lobby and the framed local wildflowers in many of the guest rooms. Also offers 27 holes of golf, red-clay tennis courts, an equestrian center and a spa. There's a $25 daily resort fee.

ℹ Information

Twin Mountain-Bretton Woods Chamber of Commerce (☑ 800-245-8946; www.twin mountain.org; cnr US 302 & US 3; ⊙ info booth staffed 9am-5pm Fri-Sun late May–mid-Oct, daily Jul & Aug, self-serve rest of year) Year-round info board and seasonally staffed kiosk providing tourist info. Look for the brightly colored train cars on the hillside at the US 3–US 302 intersection.

Hanover

Hanover is the quintessential New England college town. On warm days, students toss Frisbees on the wide college green fronting Georgian ivy-covered buildings, while locals and academics mingle at the laid-back cafes, restaurants and shops lining Main St. Dartmouth College has long been the town's focal point, giving the area a vibrant connection to the arts.

Dartmouth was chartered in 1769 primarily 'for the education and instruction of Youth of the Indian Tribes.' Back then, the school was located in the forests where its prospective students lived. Although teaching 'English Youth and others' was its secondary purpose, in fact, Dartmouth College graduated few Native Americans and was soon attended almost exclusively by colonists. The college's most illustrious alumnus is Daniel Webster (1782–1852), who graduated in 1801 and went on to be a prominent lawyer, US senator, secretary of state and perhaps the USA's most esteemed orator.

⊙ Sights & Activities

Dartmouth College   UNIVERSITY

(☑ 603-646-1110; www.dartmouth.edu) Hanover is all about Dartmouth College, so hit the campus. Join a free student-guided **campus walking tour** (☑ 603-646-2875; http://dartmouth.edu; 6016 McNutt Hall, 10 N Main St) or just pick up a map at the admissions office and head off on your own. Don't miss the **Baker Berry Library** (☑ 603-646-2560; http://dartmouth.edu; 25 N Main St; ⊙ 8am-2am Mon-Fri, 10am-2am Sat & Sun), splashed with the grand *Epic of American Civilization*, painted by the outspoken Mexican muralist José Clemente Orozco (1883–1949), who taught at Dartmouth in the 1930s.

Sanborn Library   NOTABLE BUILDING

(Dartmouth College; ⊙ 8am-midnight daily, teatime 4pm Mon-Fri) Named for Professor Edwin Sanborn, who taught for almost 50 years in Dartmouth's English department, the Sanborn Library features ornate woodwork, plush leather chairs, and books lining the walls floor to ceiling on two levels. One of Dartmouth's most endearing traditions is the afternoon tea served here on weekdays between 4pm and 5pm – tea costs 10¢ and cookies 15¢; visitors are welcome but expected to maintain a respectful silence for the benefit of the diligently toiling students.

Gile Mountain   HIKING

Just over the river in Norwich, VT, about 7 miles from Hanover, the mountain is a popular destination for Dartmouth students looking for a quick escape from the grind. A half-hour hike – and a quick climb up the **fire tower** – rewards adventurers with an incredible view of the Connecticut River Valley.

🛏 Sleeping & Eating

Hanover Inn
INN $$$

(☎603-643-4300; www.hanoverinn.com; 2 E Wheelock St; r $259-619; @🅰🐾🅰) Owned by Dartmouth and situated directly opposite the college green, Hanover's loveliest guesthouse has nicely appointed rooms with elegant wood furnishings. It has a wine bar and an award-winning restaurant on site.

Lou's
DINER $

(☎603-643-3321; www.lousrestaurant.net; 30 S Main St; mains $9-15; ⊗6am-3pm Mon-Fri, 7am-3pm Sat & Sun) A Dartmouth institution since 1947, this is Hanover's oldest establishment, always packed with students meeting for a coffee or perusing their books. From the retro tables or the Formica-topped counter, order typical diner food like eggs, sandwiches and burgers.

🍷 Drinking & Entertainment

Murphy's on the Green
PUB

(☎603-643-4075; www.murphysonthegreen.com; 11 S Main St; ⊗4pm-12:30am Mon-Thu, 11-12:30am Fri-Sun) This classic collegiate tavern is where students and faculty meet over pints (it carries more than 10 beers on tap, including local microbrews like Long Trail Ale) and satisfying pub fare.

Hopkins Center for the Arts
PERFORMING ARTS

(☎603-646-2422; http://hop.dartmouth.edu; 4 E Wheelock St) A long way from the big-city lights of New York and Boston, Dartmouth hosts its own entertainment at this outstanding performing-arts venue. The season brings everything from movies to live performances by international companies.

ℹ Information

Hanover Area Chamber of Commerce

(☎603-643-3115; www.hanoverchamber.org; 53 S Main St, Suite 208; ⊗9am-noon & 1-4pm Mon-Fri) also maintains an **information booth** (Dartmouth Green; ⊗mid-Jun–mid-Sep) on the village green.

ℹ Getting There & Around

From Boston to Hanover, it's a two- to three-hour drive depending on traffic; take I-93 to I-89 to I-91. From Hanover to Burlington, VT, it's an additional 1½ hours north via I-89.

Advance Transit (www.advancetransit.com) provides a free service to White River Junction, Lebanon, West Lebanon and Norwich. Bus stops are indicated by a blue-and-yellow AT symbol.

MAINE

With more lobsters, lighthouses and charming resort villages than you can shake a selfie stick at, Maine is New England at its most iconic. The sea looms large here, with mile upon mile of jagged sea cliffs, peaceful harbors and pebbly beaches. Eat and drink your way through food- and beer-crazed Portland, one of America's coolest small cities. Explore the historic shipbuilding villages of the Midcoast. Hike through Acadia National Park, a spectacular island of mountains and fjord-like estuaries. Let the coastal wind whip through those cobwebs and inhale the salty air. Venture into the state's inland region, a vast wilderness of pine forest and snowy peaks.

History

Maine's first inhabitants were descendants of ice-age hunters, collectively known as the Wabanaki ('people of the dawn'). They numbered perhaps 20,000 when the first English settlers descended in the early 1600s.

Over the 17th century, a number of English settlements sprang up in the Province of Maine, though settlers there suffered enormous hardship from harsh winters and tensions with local Native American tribes, who were (rightly) suspicious of the European newcomers – the latter were known to kidnap natives to put on display back in England. Adding insult to injury, Maine lost its sovereignty when Massachusetts took over the failing colony in 1692.

Bloody battles raged for many generations, destroying entire villages in Maine, with settlers warring over land with Native Americans, the French and later the British. This didn't end until after the War of 1812, when the British finally withdrew from Maine. In 1820 Maine became the 23rd state in the Union.

The 19th century was one of tremendous growth for the new state, with the emergence of new industries. Timber brought wealth to the interior, with Bangor becoming the lumber capital of the world in the 1830s. Fishing, shipbuilding, granite quarrying and farming were also boom industries, alongside manufacturing, with textile and paper mills employing large swaths of the population.

Unfortunately the boom days were short-lived, as sawmills collapsed and the seas became devastatingly overfished. By the turn of the 20th century, population growth

Maine Coast

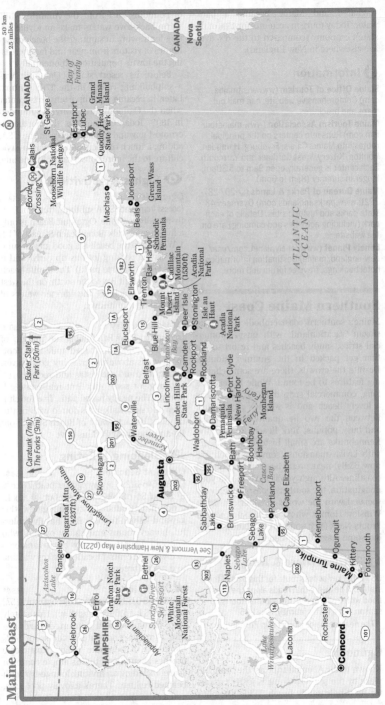

See Vermont & New Hampshire Map (p221)

stagnated and Maine became a backwater. Today tourism accounts for 15% of the state's economy (compared to the 6% average elsewhere in New England).

ⓘ Information

Maine Office of Tourism (www.visitmaine.com) Comprehensive website; can mail out maps and brochures.

Maine Tourism Association (www.mainetourism.com) Runs info centers on the principal routes into Maine: Calais, Fryeburg, Hampden, Houlton, Kittery, West Gardiner and Yarmouth. Each center is generally open 9am to 5:30pm; longer in summer (8am to 6pm).

Maine Bureau of Parks & Lands (☑207-287-3821; www.parksandlands.com) Oversees 48 state parks and historic sites. Details of each park (including activities and camping) are on the website.

Lonely Planet (www.lonelyplanet.com/usa/new-england/maine) Destination information, hotel bookings, traveler forum and more.

Southern Maine Coast

Maine's southern coast embodies the state slogan 'Vacationland,' with busy commercial strips, sandy beaches and resort towns that get packed in the summer months. Despite the crowds, there are some charming features to be found. While Kittery is a long, commercial strip mall, Ogunquit has a lovely beach and is Maine's gay mecca. Between the two lie quaint York Village and busy, populist York Beach. Beyond, the Kennebunks are small historic settlements with lavish mansions (some of which are now B&Bs) near pretty beaches and rugged coastline. Although you'll have to use your imagination, the southern coast is deeply associated with the works of American artist Winslow Homer, who spent his summers in Prouts Neck (just south of Portland), which has some magnificent scenery.

ⓘ Getting There & Away

US 1 is the key access route for this part of the state, but be aware that roads along the coast flood with traffic during the summer tourist season. For a faster journey, take I-95.

The nearest major airport is in Portland.

Ogunquit

Known to the Abenaki tribe as 'the beautiful place by the sea,' Ogunquit is justly famous for its 3-mile sandy beach. Wide stretches of pounding surf front the Atlantic, while warm back-cove waters make an idyllic setting for a swim. In summer the beach draws hordes of visitors from near and far, increasing the town's population exponentially.

Before its resort status, Ogunquit was a shipbuilding center in the 17th century. Later it became an important arts center when the Ogunquit art colony was founded in 1898. Today Ogunquit is the northeasternmost gay and lesbian mecca in the USA, adding a touch of open, San Francisco–style culture to the more conservative Maine one.

◉ Sights & Activities

Ogunquit Beach   BEACH
(access from Beach St) A sublime stretch of family-friendly coastline, Ogunquit Beach is only a five-minute walk along Beach St, east of US 1. Walking to the beach is a good idea in summer as the parking lot fills up early (and it costs $4 per hour to park!). The 3-mile beach fronts Ogunquit Bay to the south; on the west side of the beach are the warmer waters of the tidal Ogunquit River.

★ Marginal Way   WALKING
(access from Shore Rd) Tracing the 'margin' of the sea, Ogunquit's famed mile-long footpath winds above the crashing gray waves, taking in grand sea vistas and rocky coves, allowing for some excellent real-estate admiring. The neatly paved path, fine for children and slow walkers, is dotted with restful benches. It starts south of Beach St at Shore Rd and ends near Perkins Cove.

🛏 Sleeping & Eating

Ogunquit Beach Inn   B&B $$
(☑207-646-1112;   www.ogunquitbeachinn.com; 67 School St; r $169-249; ☺May-Oct; ❋🐾🛜) In a tidy little Craftsman-style bungalow, this gay-and-lesbian-friendly B&B has five colorful, homey rooms and chatty owners who know all about the best new bistros and bars in town. The central location makes walking to dinner a breeze.

★ Gazebo Inn   B&B $$
(☑207-646-3733;   www.gazeboinnogt.com;   572 Main St/US 1; r $169-369; ❋🛜🏊) This stately 1847 farmhouse and converted barn feature 14 rooms and suites – the space feels more like a boutique lodge. Rustic-chic touches abound and there's ample common space, including an inviting lounge-bar with beamed ceilings. There's a lovely pool area, and a calm, mature feel (it's kid-free).

Lobster Shack

SEAFOOD $$

(☑ 207-646-2941; www.lobster-shack.com; 110 Perkins Cove Rd; mains $5-28; ⊗ 11am-9pm Apr-Oct) If you want good seafood and aren't particular about the view, this friendly, reliable joint serves lobster in all its various incarnations, from lobster rolls to lobster in the shell, by way of chowder, steamed clams, fish tacos and even cheeseburgers.

❶ Getting There & Away

There's no direct bus service to Ogunquit; the nearest Greyhound (www.greyhound.com) stop is in Portsmouth, NH, 16 miles south.

Amtrak's *Downeaster* (www.amtrakdowneaster.com) train service stops in Wells on its Portland–Boston loop.

❶ Getting Around

From late June through to Labor Day (early October), red trolleys (adult/child $2/1.50 per trip) circulate through Ogunquit (every 20 to 30 minutes, 8am to 11pm). From Labor Day to Columbus Day (mid-October), they run from 9am to 5pm. Leave the driving to them in this horribly congested town; they'll take you from the center to the beach or Perkins Cove, and all the way north through Wells.

The Kennebunks

A longtime destination of moneyed East Coasters, the Kennebunks comprise the towns of Kennebunk and Kennebunkport.

Kennebunk is a modest town largely centered on US 1, with few tourist attractions beyond its lovely beaches. Just across the river, proudly waspy Kennebunkport crawls with tourists year-round. The epicenter of activity is Dock Sq, lined with cafes, art galleries and upscale boutiques selling preppy essentials (whale-print shorts, anyone?). Drive down Ocean Ave to gawk at the grand mansions and hotels overlooking the surf, including the massive compound belonging to George HW Bush, set on a protected spit of land called Walker's Point.

At the eastern terminus of School St is the charming hamlet of Cape Porpoise, home to affordable hotels and restaurants.

🛏 Sleeping & Eating

Franciscan Guest House

GUESTHOUSE $$

(☑ 207-967-4865; www.franciscanguesthouse.com; 26 Beach Ave, Kennebunk; d $89-189, f $135-259; ❄ @ 🛜 🏊) You can almost smell the blackboard chalk inside this high-school-turned-guesthouse on the peaceful grounds of the St Anthony Monastery. Guest rooms – once classrooms – are basic and unstylish: acoustic tile, faux wood paneling, motel beds.

Bandaloop

INTERNATIONAL $$

(☑ 207-967-4994; www.bandaloop.biz; Cross St, Kennebunkport; small plates $9-21, mains $18-31; ⊗ 5-9pm Tue-Sun, to 10pm Fri & Sat; 🍴) 🌿 Local, organic and deliciously innovative, Bandaloop mains run the gamut from grilled rib-eye steak to baked tofu with hemp-seed crust. For the perfect starter order the skillet steamed mussels and a Peak organic ale. Salads are truly flavorful, and the cocktails creative. Vegans and vegetarians will find joy here.

❶ Getting There & Away

The Kennebunks lie halfway (28 miles from each city) between Portsmouth, NH, and Portland, ME, just off I-95 on ME 9.

There's no direct bus service to Kennebunkport; Greyhound (www.greyhound.com) stops in both Portland and Portsmouth.

Amtrak's *Downeaster* (www.amtrakdowneaster.com) train service stops in Wells, about 9 miles to the south, on its Boston–Portland loop.

Portland

Maine's largest city has capitalized on the gifts of its port history – the redbrick warehouse buildings, the Victorian shipbuilders' mansions, the narrow cobblestone streets – to become one of the hippest, most vibrant small cities in America. With a lively waterfront, excellent museums and galleries, abundant green space, and both a food culture and a brewing scene worthy of a town many times its size, it's worth much more than a quick stopover.

Set on a peninsula jutting into the gray waters of Casco Bay, Portland's always been a city of the sea. Established in 1633 as a fishing village, it grew to become New England's largest port. Today the Old Port district is the town's historic heart, with handsomely restored brick buildings filled with cafes, shops and bars. The working wharves keep things from getting too precious or museum-like, though, as fishmongers in rubber boots mingle with well-heeled Yankee matrons.

◉ Sights & Activities

⭐ **Fort Williams Park**

PARK

(☑ 207-767-3707; www.fortwilliams.org; 1000 Shore Rd, Cape Elizabeth; ⊗ sunrise-sunset) 🌿 **FREE**

Four miles southeast of Portland on Cape Elizabeth, 90-acre Fort Williams Park is worth visiting simply for the panoramas and picnic possibilities. Stroll around the ruins of the fort, a late-19th-century artillery base, checking out the WWII bunkers and gun emplacements that still dot the rolling lawns.

Portland Head Light
LIGHTHOUSE

(207-799-2661; https://portlandheadlight.com; 1000 Shore Rd, Cape Elizabeth; museum adult/child $2/1; museum 10am-4pm Jun-Oct, Sat & Sun only Apr, May & Nov) Portland Head Light is the oldest of Maine's 52 functioning lighthouses. It was commissioned by President George Washington in 1791 and staffed until 1989, when machines took over. The keeper's house is now a museum, which traces the maritime and military history of the region.

Portland Museum of Art
MUSEUM

(207-775-6148; www.portlandmuseum.org; 7 Congress Sq; adult/child $15/free, 4-8pm Fri free; 10am-6pm Sat-Wed, to 8pm Thu & Fri, shorter hours Oct-May) Founded in 1882, this well-respected museum houses an outstanding collection of American artists. Maine artists, including Winslow Homer, Edward Hopper, Louise Nevelson and Andrew Wyeth, are particularly well represented. You'll also find a few works by European masters, including Monet, Degas, Picasso and Renoir.

★ Maine Brew Bus
BUS

(207-200-9111; https://themainebrewbus.com; 79 Commercial St; tours $55-80) Want to drink your way around Portland? We know the feeling. Hop aboard the green bus for tours and tastings at some of Portland's most beloved breweries, brewpubs and distilleries, from established to up-and-coming.

Casco Bay Lines
CRUISE

(207-774-7871; www.cascobaylines.com; Maine State Pier, 56 Commercial St; mailboat run adult/child $16/8) This outfit cruises the Casco Bay islands year-round, delivering mail, freight and visitors. Peaks Island, just 17 minutes from Portland, is a popular day-trip destination (round-trip $7.70) for walks or cycling; bikes can be hired on the island.

🛏 Sleeping & Eating

Morrill Mansion
B&B $$

(207-774-6900; www.morrillmansion.com; 249 Vaughan St; r $179-259; P❄🤖) Charles Morrill, the original owner of this 19th-century West End town house, made his fortune by founding B&M baked beans, still a staple of Maine pantries. His home has been transformed into a handsome B&B, with eight guest rooms furnished in a trim, classic style.

Portland Harbor Hotel
HOTEL $$$

(207-775-9090; www.portlandharborhotel.com; 468 Fore St; r $299-519; P❄@🤖🐾) This handsome independent hotel has a classically coiffed lobby, where guests relax on upholstered leather chairs surrounding the glowing fireplace.

Green Elephant
VEGETARIAN, ASIAN $

(207-347-3111; http://greenelephantmaine.com; 608 Congress St; mains $12-15; 11:30am-2:30pm & 5-9:30pm Mon-Sat, 5-9pm Sun; 🥄) Even carnivores shouldn't miss the vegetarian fare at this Zen-chic, Thai-inspired cafe (with lots of vegan and gluten-free options too). Start with the crispy spinach wontons, then move on to one of the stir-fry, noodle or curry favorites like tofu tikka masala or Malaysian *char kway teow* (fried flat rice noodles).

★ Fore Street
MODERN AMERICAN $$$

(207-775-2717; www.forestreet.biz; 288 Fore St; small plates $12-15, mains $26-38; 5:30-10pm Sun-Thu, to 10:30pm Fri & Sat) Fore Street is the lauded, long-running restaurant many consider to be the originator of today's food obsession in Portland. Chef-owner Sam Hayward has turned roasting into a high art: chickens turn on spits in the open kitchen as chefs slide iron kettles of mussels into the wood-burning oven.

🍷 Drinking & Entertainment

Allagash Brewing Company
BREWERY

(207-878-5385; www.allagash.com; 50 Industrial Way; tastings 11am-6pm) Nationally known for its Belgian-style beers, Allagash opens its doors for free tours and tastings every day (book a tour online; weekend tours are super-popular). The brewery is 3.5 miles northwest of Portland's Old Port, off Forest Ave.

Port City Music Hall
CONCERT VENUE

(207-956-6000; www.portcitymusichall.com; 504 Congress St) This three-story performance space hosts big-name touring bands and smaller-scale performances.

ℹ Information

Ocean Gateway Information Center (207-772-5800; www.visitportland.com; 14 Ocean Gateway Pier; 9am-5pm Mon-Fri, to 4pm Sat & Sun Jun-Oct, shorter hours rest of year) Visitor information, down at the waterfront.

Visitor Information Booth (☑207-772-6828; www.portlandmaine.com; Tommy's Park, Exchange St; 10am-5pm Jun-Oct) Summertime info kiosk in the Old Port.

❶ Getting There & Away

AIR

Portland International Jetport (PWM; ☑207-874-8877; www.portlandjetport.org; 1001 Westbrook St) Is Maine's largest and most chaotic air terminal. It's served by domestic airlines, with nonstop flights to cities in the eastern USA. Metro bus 5 takes you to the center of town for $1.50. Taxis are about $20 to downtown.

BUS

Greyhound (☑800-231-2222, 207-772-6588; www.greyhound.com; 950 Congress St) offers direct daily trips to Bangor and Boston, with connections on to the rest of the USA.

Concord Coach Lines (www.concordcoach lines.com) operates daily buses between Boston (including Logan Airport) and Portland, continuing on to Midcoast Maine towns. There are also services connecting Boston, Portland and the towns of Augusta, Waterville and Bangor. Two services a day link Portland with New York City.

TRAIN

The *Downeaster*, run by Amtrak (www.amtrak. com), makes five trips daily between Boston and Portland (2½ hours) from **Portland Transportation Center** (100 Thompson's Point Rd). A couple of these services extend to Freeport and Brunswick too.

Midcoast Maine

Carved by ancient glaciers, the coastline of Midcoast Maine is jagged and dramatic. With its wild natural beauty and down-to-earth residents, this is what many people imagine when they think of Maine – riding bikes and shopping for antiques in postcard-pretty seaside villages, taking leisurely scenic drives down the rural peninsulas, and riding the deep blue seas aboard one of the Midcoast's famous windjammers. It's a landscape that rewards slow, aimless exploration: you never know when you're going to stumble upon the next great lobster shack, lost-in-time fishing village or you-pick blueberry patch.

The English first settled this region in 1607, which coincided with the Jamestown settlement in Virginia. Unlike their southerly compatriots, though, these early settlers returned to England within a year. British colonization resumed in 1620. After suffering through the long years of the French and Indian War, the area became home to a thriving shipbuilding industry, which continues today.

❶ Getting There & Around

US 1 is the key access route for this part of the state, but note that roads along the coast flood with traffic during the summer tourist season.

Concord Coach Lines (www.concordcoach lines.com) operates daily buses between Boston (including Logan Airport) and Portland, continuing on to midcoast Maine towns (Bath, Belfast, Brunswick, Camden, Damariscotta, Lincolnville, Rockland, Searsport and Waldoboro). Greyhound (www.greyhound.com) stops in Bangor, Portland, Bath, Rockland and various other towns.

Freeport

Nestled amid the natural beauty of Maine's rockbound coast is a town devoted almost entirely to shopping. Nearly 200 stores line the town's mile-long stretch of US 1, leading to long traffic jams during the summer. Strict zoning codes forbid the destruction of historic buildings, which is why you'll find a McDonald's housed in an 1850s Greek Revival home and an Abercrombie & Fitch outlet in a turn-of-the-20th-century library. It all adds up to a slightly eerie 'Main Street, USA' vibe.

Freeport's fame and fortune began a century ago when Leon Leonwood Bean opened a shop to sell equipment and provisions to hunters and fishermen heading north into the Maine woods. His success later brought other retailers to the area, making Freeport what it is today.

Bath

Known as the 'City of Ships,' this quaint Kennebec River town was once home to more than 20 shipyards producing more than a quarter of early America's wooden sailing vessels. In Bath's 19th-century heyday, it was one of Maine's largest cities, with a bustling downtown lined with banks and grand municipal buildings. Bath-built schooners and clipper ships sailed the seven seas and the city's name was known far and wide.

Downtown, redbrick sidewalks and solid 19th-century buildings line quaint Front St, while just downhill lies a small grassy park overlooking the water. South of Bath stretch two scenic peninsulas well worth a detour: ME 209 takes you to **Phippsburg**, home to excellent beaches and a historic fort, while ME 127 runs south to **Georgetown**, terminating at a great lobster shack overlooking an island-dotted cove.

★ **Maine Maritime Museum**   MUSEUM
(207-443-1316; www.mainemaritimemuseum. org; 243 Washington St; adult/child $16/10; ⊙9:30am-5pm) On the western bank of the Kennebec River, this wonderful museum preserves the Kennebec's long shipbuilding tradition with paintings, models and hands-on exhibits that tell the tale of the past 400 years of seafaring. One highlight is the remains of the *Snow Squall,* a three-mast 1851 clipper ship. The on-site 19th-century Percy & Small Shipyard, preserved by the museum, is America's only remaining wooden-boat shipyard. There's also a life-size sculpture of the *Wyoming,* the largest wooden sailing vessel ever built.

Boothbay Harbor

Once a beautiful little seafarers' village on a wide blue harbor, Boothbay Harbor is now an extremely popular tourist resort in the summer, when its narrow and winding streets are packed with visitors. Still, there's good reason to join the holiday masses in this picturesque place. Overlooking a pretty waterfront, large, well-kept Victorian houses crown the town's many knolls, and a wooden footbridge ambles across the harbor. From May to October, whale-watching is a major draw.

After you've strolled the waterfront along Commercial St and the business district along Todd and Townsend Aves, walk along McKown St to the top of **McKown Hill** for a fine view.

🛏 Sleeping & Eating

Topside Inn   B&B $$$
(207-633-5404; www.topsideinn.com; 60 McKown St; r $219-369; ⊙May–mid-Oct; ❄🐾) Atop McKown Hill, this grand gray mansion has Boothbay's best harbor views. Rooms are elegantly turned out in crisp nautical prints and beachy shades. Main-house rooms have more historic charm, but rooms in the two adjacent modern guesthouses are sunny and lovely too.

Lobster Dock   SEAFOOD $$
(207-633-7120; www.thelobsterdock.com; 49 Atlantic Ave; mains $15-29; ⊙11:30am-8:30pm late May–mid-Oct) Of all the lobster joints in Boothbay Harbor, this sprawling, wooden waterfront shack is one of the best and cheapest. It serves traditional fried seafood platters, sandwiches and steamers, but whole, butter-dripping lobster is definitely the main event. Get your lobster roll ($17) warm with butter, or cold with mayo.

❶ Information

Boothbay Harbor Region Chamber of Commerce (207-633-2353; www.boothbay harbor.com; 192 Townsend Ave; ⊙8am-5pm Mon-Fri year-round, plus 10am-4pm Sat late May–early Oct) Offers good info on its website; also operates a downtown **information center** (17 Commercial St; ⊙9am-6pm late May–early Oct) in summer.

Rockland

This thriving commercial port boasts a large fishing fleet and a proud year-round population that gives Rockland a vibrancy lacking in some other Midcoast towns. Main St is a window into the city's sociocultural diversity, with a jumble of working-class diners, bohemian cafes and high-end restaurants alongside galleries, old-fashioned storefronts and one of the state's best art museums, the **Center for Maine Contemporary Art** (CMCA; www.cmcanow.org). Rockland is developing a reputation as an art center, partly thanks to the CMCA's relocation here in 2016, and the **Farnworth Art Museum** (www.farnsworthmuseum.org).

Settled in 1769, Rockland was once an important shipbuilding center and a transportation hub for goods moving up and down the coast. Today tall-masted sailing ships still fill the harbor, as Rockland is a center for Maine's busy windjammer cruises (along with Camden).

★ **Rockland Breakwater Lighthouse**   LIGHTHOUSE
(207-542-7574; www.rocklandharborlights.org; Samoset Rd; ⊙10am-5pm Sat & Sun late May–mid-Oct) **FREE** Tackle the rugged stone breakwater that stretches almost 1 mile into Rockland Harbor from Jameson Point at the harbor's northern shore. Made of granite blocks, this 'walkway' – which took 18 years to build – ends at the Rockland Breakwater

Lighthouse, a sweet light sitting atop a brick house, with a sweeping view of town.

Maine Windjammer Association CRUISE
(☑800-807-9463; www.sailmainecoast.com; ☺cruises late May–mid-Oct) Although traveling by schooner largely went out of style at the dawn of the 20th century, adventurers can still explore the rugged Maine coast the old-fashioned way: aboard fast sailing ships known as windjammers. Nine of these multi-masted vessels anchor at Rockland and Camden and offer trips ranging from overnight to 11 days around Penobscot Bay.

Camden

Camden, with its picture-perfect harbor, framed against the mountains of Camden Hills State Park, is one of the prettiest sites in Maine. Home to the state's large and justly famed fleet of windjammers, Camden continues its historical intimacy with the sea. Most vacationers come to sail, but Camden also has galleries, fine restaurants and backstreets ideal for exploring. Pick up a walking-tour guide to the town's historic buildings at the chamber of commerce. The adjoining state park offers hiking, picnicking and camping.

Like many communities along the Maine coast, Camden has a long history of shipbuilding. The mammoth six-masted schooner *George W Wells* was built here in 1900, setting the world record for the most masts on a sailing ship.

Like nearby Rockland, Camden offers many windjammer cruises, from two-hour trips to multiday journeys up the coast. A number of boats depart from Camden's Town Landing or adjoining Bayview Landing, offering two-hour cruises (including sunset sails) for a similar price – check out the schedules online for **Appledore II** (☑207-236-8353; https://appledore2.com; Bayview Landing; adult/child $45/25; ☺Jun-Oct), **Olad** (☑207-236-2323; www.maineschooners.com; Public Landing; adult/child $43/33; ☺late May–mid-Oct) and **Surprise** (☑207-236-4687; http://schoonersurprise.com; Public Landing; adult/child $43/33; ☺late May–mid-Oct). This is the quintessential Midcoast sightseeing experience.

Penobscot Bay Regional Chamber of Commerce (☑207-236-4404; www.camdenrockland.com; 2 Public Landing; ☺9am-5pm Mon-Fri, 10am-4pm Sat & Sun late May–mid-Oct, 9am-4pm Mon-Fri rest of year) has an information office on the waterfront at the public landing in Camden.

PARK LOOP ROAD

For some visitors, driving the 27-mile Park Loop Rd is the extent of their trip to Acadia National Park. On the portion called Ocean Dr, stop at lovely **Sand Beach**, and at **Thunder Hole** for a look at the surf crashing into a cleft in the granite. The effect is most dramatic with a strong incoming tide.

Otter Cliff, not far south of Thunder Hole, is basically a wall of pink granite rising right out from the sea. This area is popular with rock climbers.

The road is largely one-way; in summer you can cover the route on the Island Explorer bus system (shuttle route 4; www.exploreacadia.com). Note that the loop road is closed in winter, and its opening may be delayed by heavy snow.

Acadia National Park

New England's only national park Acadia National Park (☑207-288-3338; www.nps.gov/acad; 7-day admission per car/motorcycle $25/20, walk-ins & cyclists $12) turned 100 in 2016 – it's a fine-looking centenarian. Within its borders are impressive coastal landmarks and visitor activities.

Drivers and hikers alike can thank John D Rockefeller and other wealthy landowners for the aesthetically pleasing bridges, overlooks and stone steps that give the park its artistic merit. Rockefeller in particular worked diligently with architects and masons to ensure that the infrastructure would complement the surrounding landscapes.

Stop by the Acadia Welcome Center (☑207-288-5103, 800-345-4617; www.acadiainfo.com; 1201 Bar Harbor Rd/ME 3, Trenton; ☺9am-5pm Mon-Sat, 10am-4pm Sun late May–mid-Oct, 9am-5pm Mon-Fri mid-Apr–May & mid-Oct–Nov) in Trenton for brochures, maps and local information. It's located north of the bridge crossing to Mt Desert Island (about 11 miles before reaching Bar Harbor).

Downeast Maine

Without question, this is quintessential Maine: as you head further and further up the coast toward Canada, the peninsulas seem to become more and more narrow, jutting further into the sea. The fishing villages seem to get smaller; the lobster pounds, closer to the water. If you make time to drive to the edge of the shore, south off US 1, let it be here. 'Down East' starts at the Penobscot River, where a bridge observatory unofficially marks the boundary. The region continues 'further Down East,' from Acadia all the way to the border with New Brunswick, Canada.

Information on the region is online at www.downeastacadia.com.

Bar Harbor

The agreeable hub for Acadia visits, Bar Harbor is crowded for most of the year with vacationers and visiting cruise-ship passengers. Downtown is packed with souvenir stores, ice-cream shops, cafes and bars, each advertising bigger and better happy hours, early-bird specials or two-for-one deals. The quieter residential backstreets seem to have almost as many B&Bs as private homes.

Although Bar Harbor's hustle and bustle is not for everybody, it has by far the most amenities of any town around here. Even if you stay somewhere else, you'll probably wind up here to eat dinner, grab a drink or schedule a kayaking, sailing or rock-climbing tour. Bar Harbor's busiest season is late June through August. There's a short lull just after Labor Day (early September); it gets busy again during foliage season, which lasts through mid-October. The season ends with the Mount Desert Island Marathon (www.runmdi.org).

☉ Sights & Activities

Abbe Museum   MUSEUM
(☑207-288-3519; www.abbemuseum.org; 26 Mount Desert St; adult/child $8/4; ☉10am-5pm May-Oct, 10am-4pm Thu-Sat Nov-Apr) This downtown museum contains a fascinating collection of cultural artifacts related to Maine's Native American heritage. More than 50,000 objects are in the collection, including pottery, tools, combs and fishing implements spanning the last 2000 years. Contemporary pieces include finely wrought wood carvings, birch-bark containers and baskets. The museum also has a smaller, summer-only **branch** (☑207-288-3519; www.abbemuseum.org; ME 3 & Park Loop Rd; adult/child $3/1; ☉10am-5pm late May-Oct) in a lush park-like setting at Sieur de Monts Spring, inside Acadia National Park.

National Park Sea Kayak Tours   KAYAKING
(☑800-347-0940; www.acadiakayak.com; 39 Cottage St; half-day tour $52; ☉late May–mid-Oct) Four-hour kayak tours leave at various times (morning, afternoon, sunset) and explore Mount Desert Island's 'Quietside' – ie the remote west coast. Small groups of kayakers spend about 2½ to three hours on the water; transport is provided from Bar Harbor to the put-in point.

🛏 Sleeping & Eating

**Moseley Cottage Inn
& Town Motel**   B&B, MOTEL $$
(☑207-288-5548; http://moseleycottage.net; 12 Atlantic Ave; r $175-305; ❇🐾) This two-faced option is down a quiet street just steps from Main St, and covers its bases very well. There are nine large, charming, antique-filled B&B rooms in a traditional 1884 inn (options with fireplace and private porch), plus a small collection of cheaper motel-style units next door. All are of a consistently high standard.

★Bass Cottage Inn   INN $$$
(☑207-288-1234; www.basscottage.com; 14 The Field; r $230-440; ☉mid-May–Oct; ❇🐾) If most Bar Harbor B&Bs rate about a '5' in terms of stylishness, this Gilded Age mansion deserves an '11.' The 10 light-drenched guest rooms have an elegant summer-cottage chic, all crisp white linens and understated botanical prints.

2 Cats   BREAKFAST $
(☑207-288-2808; http://twocatsbarharbor.com; 130 Cottage St; mains $9-15; ☉7am-1pm; 🍴) It's the most important meal of the day, so 2 Cats channels all its attention to breakfast. On weekends, crowds line up for banana pecan pancakes, smoked-trout omelets, tofu scrambles and homemade muffins at this sunny, arty little cafe. Pick up a kitty-themed souvenir in the gift shop.

★Havana   LATIN AMERICAN $$$
(☑207-288-2822; www.havanamaine.com; 318 Main St; mains $27-39; ☉5-9pm May-Oct) First things first: order a rockin' Cuba libre or mojito. Once that's done, you can take your time with the menu and the epic global wine list. Havana puts a Latin spin on dishes that highlight local produce, and the kitchen output is accomplished. Signature dishes include crab cakes, paella and a deliciously light lobster *moqueca* (stew). Reservations recommended.

❶ Information

There are a number of options for visitor info. First for motorists is the **Acadia Welcome Center** (p245) as you reach Mt Desert Island (about 11 miles northwest of Bar Harbor), then the NPS-run **Hulls Cove Visitor Center** (📞207-288-8832; www.nps.gov/acad; ME 3; ⊘8:30am-4:30pm mid-Apr–Jun, Sep & Oct, 8am-6pm Jul & Aug) inside Acadia National Park.

The **Bar Harbor Chamber of Commerce** (Acadia Welcome Center; 📞207-801-2558, 800-345-4617; www.barharborinfo.com; cnr Main & Cottage Sts; ⊘8am-8pm mid-Jun–Sep, 9am-5pm Sep–mid-Jun) maintains a central year-round information office in downtown Bar Harbor.

Inland Maine

Interstate 95 (I-95), the East Coast's major north–south superhighway, runs through Maine for 303 miles, from the New Hampshire border near Kittery to the Canadian border near Houlton. En route it passes by Maine's major cities: Portland; Augusta, the state capital; and Bangor. Augusta and Bangor (as well as nearby Waterville) are home to colleges, a handful of decent museums and some good eateries, but they are not especially tourism-focused destinations.

North of Bangor, traffic levels drop considerably. This is your gateway to the North Woods and to the large, sparsely populated Aroostook County.

Bethel

A 90-minute drive northwest of Portland, Bethel is surprisingly lively and refined for a town surrounded on all sides by deep, dark woods. Summer visitors have been coming here to escape the coastal humidity since the 1800s, and many of its fine old cottages are still operating. It's a prime spot to be during Maine's colorful fall-foliage months and during the winter ski season.

❷ Sights & Activities

Grafton Notch State Park   STATE PARK
(📞207-824-2912; www.maine.gov/graftonnotch; 1941 Bear River Rd/ME 26; adult/child $4/1; ⊘9am-sunset mid-May–mid-Oct) Sitting astride the Grafton Notch Scenic Byway within the Mahoosuc Range, this rugged park is a stunner. Carved by a glacier that retreated 12,000 years ago, the notch is a four-season playground, chock-full of waterfalls, gorges, lofty viewpoints and hiking trails, including 12 strenuous miles of the **Appalachian Trail** (www.appalachiantrail.org).

Bethel Outdoor Adventure & Campground   KAYAKING
(📞207-824-4224; www.betheloutdooradventure. com; 121 Mayville Rd/US 2; kayak per day with/ without shuttle $45/32; ⊘8am-6pm mid-May–late Oct) Based at a bucolic riverside campground, this outfitter rents out canoes, kayaks and stand-up paddleboards. It can shuttle you upriver to the drop-off point, and you paddle back downstream.

🛏 Sleeping

Chapman Inn   B&B $
(📞207-824-2657; www.chapmaninn.com; 2 Church St; dm $35, r $59-139; 🅿🛜) Run by a friendly, globe-trotting retiree, this roomy downtown guesthouse has character in spades. The 10 private rooms are done up in florals and antiques, with slightly sloping floors attesting to the house's age.

❶ Information

Bethel Area Chamber of Commerce (📞800-442-5826, 207-824-2282; www.bethelmaine. com; 8 Station Pl; ⊘9am-5pm Mon-Fri year-round, weekend hours vary in peak season) This helpful organization maintains an information office in the Bethel Station building, with loads of handouts on various sights, trails and activities.

Baxter State Park

Baxter State Park is Maine at its most primeval: the wind whips around dozens of mountain peaks, black bears root through the underbrush and hikers go for miles without seeing another soul. Visitors can hike hundreds of miles of trails through the park, climb the sheer cliffs (this is a rock-climber's paradise), fly-fish the ponds and rivers, and spot wild animals, such as bald eagles, moose and fox-like martens. The park is most popular in the warmer months, but it's also open for winter sports like snowmobiling. Baxter's 5267ft **Mt Katahdin** – the park's crowning glory – is Maine's tallest mountain and the northern end of the 2190-mile-long Appalachian Trail.

Katahdin Area Chamber of Commerce   TOURIST INFORMATION
(📞207-723-4443; www.katahdinmaine.com; 1029 Central St, Millinocket; ⊘9am-3pm Mon-Fri) Info on the area, including accommodations.

Washington, DC & the Capital Region

Includes →

Why Go?

No matter your politics, it's hard not to fall for the nation's capital. Iconic monuments, vast (and free) museums and venerable restaurants serving global cuisines are just the beginning of the great DC experience. There's much to discover: leafy, cobblestoned neighborhoods, sprawling markets, heady multicultural nightspots and verdant parks, and, of course, the corridors of power. Beyond the Beltway, the diverse landscapes of Maryland, Virginia, West Virginia and Delaware offer potent enticement to travel beyond the marble city. Craggy mountains, rushing rivers, vast nature reserves (including islands where wild horses run), sparkling beaches, historic villages and the magnificent Chesapeake Bay form the backdrop to memorable adventures: sailing, hiking, rafting, camping or just sitting on a pretty stretch of shoreline, planning the next seafood feast. It's a place where traditions run deep, from the nation's birthplace to Virginia's bluegrass scene.

Best Places to Eat

→ Rose's Luxury (p270)

→ Woodberry Kitchen (p284)

→ L'Opossum (p307)

→ Public Fish & Oyster (p314)

→ Faidley's (p284)

Best Places to Sleep

→ Hotel Lombardy (p268)

→ Inn at 2920 (p283)

→ Georges (p318)

→ HI Richmond (p306)

When to Go
Washington DC

May–Apr Cherry blossoms bring crowds to the city during DC's most popular festival.

Jun–Aug Beaches and resorts heave; prices are high and accommodations scarce.

Sep–Oct Smaller crowds and lower prices, but with pleasant temperatures and fiery fall scenery.

History

Native Americans populated this region long before European settlers arrived. Many of the area's geographic landmarks are still known by their Native American names, such as Chesapeake, Shenandoah, Appalachian and Potomac. In 1607 a group of 108 English colonists established the first permanent European settlement in the New World: Jamestown. During the early years, colonists battled harsh winters, starvation, disease and, occasionally, hostile Native Americans.

Jamestown survived, and the Royal Colony of Virginia came into being in 1624. Ten years later, fleeing the English Civil War, Lord Baltimore established the Catholic colony of Maryland at St Mary's City, where a Spanish Jewish doctor treated a town council that included a black Portuguese sailor and Margaret Brent, the first woman to vote in North American politics. Delaware was settled as a Dutch whaling colony in 1631, practically wiped out by Native Americans, and later resettled by the British. Celts displaced from Britain filtered into the Appalachians, where they created a fiercely independent culture that persists today. Border disputes between Maryland, Delaware and Pennsylvania led to the creation of the Mason-Dixon line, which eventually separated the industrial North from the agrarian, slave-holding South.

The fighting part of the Revolutionary War finished here with the British surrender at Yorktown in 1781. Then – to diffuse regional tension – central, swampy Washington, District of Columbia (DC), was made the new nation's capital. But divisions of class, race and economy were strong, and this area in particular split along its seams during the Civil War (1861–65): Virginia seceded from the Union, while its impoverished western farmers, long resentful of genteel plantation owners, seceded from Virginia. Maryland stayed in the Union, but its white slave-owners rioted against Northern troops, while thousands of black Marylanders joined the Union Army.

WASHINGTON, DC

The USA's capital teems with iconic monuments, vast museums and the corridors ofpower where visionaries and demagogues roam. But it's more than that. It's also home to tree-lined neighborhoods and groovy markets, with ethnically diverse restaurants, large numbers of immigrants and a dynamism percolating just beneath the surface. There's always a buzz here – no surprise, as DC gathers more overachieving and talented types than any city of this size deserves. Plan on jam-packed days sightseeing in the countless museums (most of them free). At night, join the locals sipping DC-made brews and chowing in cozy restaurants in buzzy quarters such as U St and Logan Circle.

History

Following the Revolutionary War, a balance was struck between Northern and Southern politicians, who wanted to plant a federal city somewhere between their power bases. Potential capitals such as Boston, Philadelphia and Baltimore were rejected by Southern plantation owners, as too urban-industrial so it was decided a new city would be carved at midway point of the 13 colonies, along the banks of the Potomac River. Maryland and Virginia donated the land.

DC was torched by the British during the War of 1812, and ceded the south-bank slave port of Alexandria to Virginia in 1846 (when abolition talk was buzzing in the capital). Over the years, DC evolved along diverging tracks: as a marbled temple to the federal government on one hand, and as an urban ghetto for northbound African Americans and overseas immigrants on the other. The city finally got its own mayor in 1973 (Walter Washington, among the first African American mayors of a major American city); Congress governed it prior to that.

Today, DC residents are taxed just as other American citizens are, yet lack a voting seat in Congress. DC has undergone extensive gentrification since the late 1990s. With the election of Barack Obama in 2008, the city gained a bit of cool cachet – New Yorkers are coming here now, instead of the other way around. Unfortunately they've jacked up the cost of living. DC's costs are among the highest in the nation, and as the city's economy keeps on booming, it's likely to stay that way.

◉ Sights

◉ National Mall

The Mall – aka 'America's front yard' – holds most of the Smithsonian museums and major monuments. The Lincoln Memorial,

Washington, DC & the Capital Region Highlights

1 National Air and Space Museum (p252) Visiting Washington, DC's museums.

2 Lincoln Memorial (p252) Watching the sun set over the monument.

3 Colonial Williamsburg (p308) Tracing America's roots at this living-history museum.

4 Annapolis (p285) Exploring the city's historic

and nautical past with a stroll through the capitol, the Naval Academy and along Main St to Ego Alley.

5 Shenandoah National Park (p317) Taking a Sunday

drive on Skyline Drive, followed by hiking and camping under the stars.

6 **Monticello** (p313) Marveling at Thomas Jefferson's masterpiece.

7 **Rehoboth Beach** (p294) Strolling the boardwalk in this family- and gay-friendly resort.

8 **New River Gorge National River** (p326) Tackling the Gauley River rapids.

9 **Faidley's** (p284) Savoring one of the world's best crab cakes in Baltimore.

10 **Floyd** (p322) Feeling the beat of the old-time music at a jamboree.

Washington Monument, Air and Space Museum, National Gallery of Art and much more crowd around a 2-mile-long strip of scrubby grass.

★ Lincoln Memorial   MONUMENT

(www.nps.gov/linc; 2 Lincoln Memorial Circle NW; ⏰24hr; 🚌Circulator, Ⓜ Orange, Silver, Blue Lines to Foggy Bottom-GWU) FREE Anchoring the Mall's west end is the hallowed shrine to Abraham Lincoln, who gazes peacefully across the Reflecting Pool beneath his neoclassical, Doric-columned abode. The words of his Gettysburg Address and Second Inaugural speech flank the statue on the north and south walls. On the steps, Martin Luther King Jr delivered his famed 'I Have a Dream' speech; look for the engraving that marks the spot.

★ National Air and
Space Museum   MUSEUM

(☎202-633-2214;   www.airandspace.si.edu;   cnr 6th St & Independence Ave SW; ⏰10am-5:30pm, to 7:30pm some days; 👶; 🚌Circulator, Ⓜ Orange, Silver, Blue, Green, Yellow Lines to L'Enfant Plaza) FREE The Air and Space Museum is one of the most popular Smithsonian museums. Everyone flocks to see the Wright brothers' flyer, Chuck Yeager's *Bell X-1*, Charles Lindbergh's *Spirit of St Louis*, Amelia Earhart's natty red plane and the Apollo Lunar Module. An Imax theater, a planetarium and flight simulators are all here ($8 to $10

WASHINGTON, DC IN TWO DAYS...

Day One

You might as well dive right into the good stuff, and the Lincoln Memorial is about as iconically DC as it gets. It's also a convenient starting point, since Abe sits at the far end of the Mall. Next up as you walk east is the powerful Vietnam Veterans Memorial. Then comes the Washington Monument (p253), which is pretty hard to miss, being DC's tallest structure and all.

For lunch you can munch sandwiches by an artsy waterfall at Cascade Cafe in the National Gallery of Art before exploring the gallery.

Then it's time to explore the National Museum of African American History and Culture, assuming you've procured a ticket. Pick a side: East, for modern; or West, for Impressionists and other classics. Afterward, mosey across the lawn to the National Air and Space Museum (p252) and gape at the stuff hanging from the ceiling. The missiles and Wright Brothers' original plane are incomparably cool.

Have a hearty, low-key dinner at Duke's Grocery (☎202-733-5623; www.dukesgrocery. com; 1513 17th St NW; mains $12-16; ⏰11am-10pm Mon & Tue, 11am-1am Wed & Thu, 11am-2am Fri, 10am-2am Sat, 10am-10pm Sun; 🛜; Ⓜ Red Line to Dupont Circle) then linger over luscious libations at Bar Charley (p276) – the night is young! But if you prefer a quiet night settle in for some table games at Board Room (p276).

Day Two

Do the government thing today. Start in the Capitol (p260) and tour the statue-cluttered halls. Then walk across the street and up the grand steps to the Supreme Court (p261); hopefully you'll get to hear a case argument. The Library of Congress (p261) and its 500 miles of books blow minds next door.

For lunch have a burger amid politicos at Old Ebbitt Grill (☎202-347-4800; www.ebbitt.com; 675 15th St NW; mains $18-28; ⏰7:30am-1am Mon-Fri, from 8:30am Sat & Sun; Ⓜ Red, Orange, Silver, Blue Lines to Metro Center).

Hopefully you planned ahead and booked a White House (p261) tour. If not, make do at the White House Visitor Center. Pop into the Round Robin to see if any big wigs and lobbyists are clinking glasses. Zip over to the Kennedy Center (p277) to watch the free 6pm show.

Afterwards go for French in laid-back elegance at Chez Billy Sud (p274) in Georgetown, then sink a pint in a friendly pub like the Tombs (p277). On warm nights the outdoor cafes and boating action make Georgetown Waterfront Park (p264) a hot spot. And check if anyone groovy is playing at iconic jazz club Blues Alley (www.bluesalley.com).

each). More avionic pieces reside in Virginia at the **Steven F Udvar-Hazy Center** (☏703-572-4118; www.airandspace.si.edu/visit/udvar-hazy-center; 14390 Air & Space Museum Pkwy, Chantilly; ⊙10am-5:30pm; 🛗; Ⓜ Wiehle-Reston East for bus 983) **FREE**, an annex to hold this museum's leftovers.

★**Vietnam Veterans Memorial** MONUMENT (www.nps.gov/vive; 5 Henry Bacon Dr NW; ⊙24hr; 🚌Circulator, Ⓜ Orange, Silver, Blue Lines to Foggy Bottom-GWU) **FREE** The opposite of DC's white, gleaming marble is this black, low-lying 'V,' an expression of the psychic scar wrought by the Vietnam War. The monument descends into the earth, with the names of the war's 58,300-plus casualties – listed in the order they died – chiseled into the dark, reflective wall. It's a subtle but profound monument – and all the more surprising as it was designed by 21-year-old undergraduate student Maya Lin in 1981.

★**National Gallery of Art** MUSEUM (☏202-737-4215; www.nga.gov; Constitution Ave NW, btwn 3rd & 7th Sts; ⊙10am-5pm Mon-Sat, 11am-6pm Sun; 🚌Circulator, Ⓜ Green, Yellow Lines to Archives) **FREE** The staggering collection spans the Middle Ages to the present. The neoclassical west building showcases European art through the early 1900s; highlights include the Western Hemisphere's only da Vinci painting and a slew of Impressionist and post-Impressionist works. The IM Pei–designed east building displays modern art, with works by Picasso, Matisse and Pollock and a massive Calder mobile over the entrance lobby. Recently renovated and expanded, this new wing really dazzles. A trippy underground walkway connects the two buildings.

★**Washington Monument** MONUMENT (www.nps.gov/wamo; 2 15th St NW; ⊙9am-5pm, to 10pm Jun-Aug; 🚌Circulator, Ⓜ Orange, Silver, Blue Lines to Smithsonian) **FREE** Peaking at 555ft (and 5in) and comprised of 36,000 blocks of stone, the Washington Monument is the tallest building in the district. It took so long to build that the original quarry ran out; note the delineation in color where the old and new marble meet about a third of the way up. Alas, the monument is closed until spring 2019 for repairs, so you'll have to wait until then for stellar views from the observation deck.

★**Martin Luther King Jr Memorial** MONUMENT (www.nps.gov/mlkm; 1850 W Basin Dr SW; ⊙24hr; 🚌Circulator, Ⓜ Orange, Silver, Blue Lines to Smithsonian) **FREE** Opened in 2011, this is the Mall's newest memorial and the first one to honor an African American. Sculptor Lei Yixin carved the piece. Besides Dr King's striking, 30ft-tall image, known as the Stone of Hope, there are two blocks of granite behind him that represent the Mountain of Despair. A wall inscribed with King's moving quotes about democracy, justice and peace flanks the piece. It sits in a lovely spot on the banks of the Tidal Basin.

★**National Museum of African American History and Culture** MUSEUM (☏844-750-3012; www.nmaahc.si.edu; 1400 Constitution Ave NW; ⊙10am-5:30pm; 🛗; 🚌Circulator, Ⓜ Orange, Silver, Blue Lines to Smithsonian or Federal Triangle) **FREE** Opened in 2016, the Smithsonian's newest museum covers the diverse African American experience and how it helped shape the nation. The collection includes everything from Harriet Tubman's hymnal to Emmett Till's casket and Louis Armstrong's trumpet. The museum is so wildly popular you need a timed entry pass to get in. Your best bet to obtain one is via the same-day online release, when tickets are made available at 6:30am on the museum's website. Be ready, because they're snapped up within minutes.

National Sculpture Garden GARDENS (cnr Constitution Ave NW & 7th St NW; ⊙10am-6pm Mon-Thu & Sat, 10am-8:30pm Fri, 11am-6pm Sun; 🚌Circulator, Ⓜ Green, Yellow Lines to Archives) **FREE** The National Gallery of Art's 6-acre garden is studded with whimsical sculptures such as Roy Lichtenstein's *House,* a giant Claes Oldenburg typewriter eraser and Louise Bourgeois' leggy *Spider.* They are scattered around a fountain – a great place to dip your feet in summer. From mid-November to mid-March the fountain becomes a festive **ice rink** (adult/child $8.50/7.50, skate rental $3; ⊙10am-9pm Mon-Thu, 10am-11pm Fri, 11am-11pm Sat, 11am-9pm Sun mid-Nov–mid-Mar; 🚌Circulator, Ⓜ Green, Yellow Lines to Archives), and the garden stays open a bit later.

Tail Up Goat (50yds);
Adam's Inn
(0.1mi)

Washington National
Cathedral (0.7mi);

Woodley Park
Guesthouse (0.25mi);
National Zoo (0.5mi)

WOODLEY PARK

United
States Naval
Observatory

80 99
18 76

Mexican
Cultural
Institute
(0.2mi)

Kalorama
Park

55

97

**ADAMS
MORGAN**

Whitehaven St NW

Columbia Rd NW

Rock Creek and Potomac Pkwy NW

Rock Creek

Belmont Rd NW

Connecticut Ave NW

Massachusetts Ave NW

Kalorama
Circle

California St NW

Vernon St NW

16 St NW

Dumbarton
Oaks Park

Wyoming Ave NW

Wyoming
Ave NW

KALORAMA

Willard Pl NW

T St NW

92

Swann
St NW

S St NW
R St NW

Montrose Park

19

37

Waterside Dr NW

California St NW

Florida Ave NW

S St NW

94

Avon Pl NW

Oak Hill
Cemetery

Decatur Pl NW

New Hampshire Ave NW

Corcoran St NW

89

45

28

Sheridan
Circle

52

69

93

Washington
Deluxe

39

91

Q St NW

79

32nd St NW

Q St NW

**Embassy
Row** 2

64

82

Wisconsin Ave NW

P St NW

GEORGETOWN

BestBus

Dupont Circle

O St NW

O St NW

30th St NW

29th St NW

28th St NW

Rock Creek

Scott
Circle

85

Dumbarton
St NW

N St NW

**DUPONT
CIRCLE**

62

N St NW

33rd St NW

31st St NW

27th St NW

Thomas
Jefferson St NW

Rock Creek

22nd St NW

21st St NW

Connecticut Ave NW

29

16th St NW

53

M St NW

M St NW

Pennsylvania Ave NW

L St NW

17th St NW

72
65

Whitehurst Fwy

23rd St NW

New Hampshire Ave NW

20th St NW

19th St NW

18th St NW

K St NW

**Farragut
North**

51

54

61

Capital Crescent
Trail (0.2mi);
Key Bridge Boathouse
(0.2mi);
Exorcist Stairs (0.25mi);
Tombs (0.25mi);
Georgetown University
(0.5mi); Dalhgren
Chapel (0.5mi);
Healy Hall (0.5mi)

24

Washington
Harbour
Complex

Foggy
Bottom-GWU

57

I St NW

Pennsylvania Ave NW

**Farragut
West**

H St NW

25th St NW

78

44

H St NW

G St NW

41

Theodore
Roosevelt
Island

104

F St NW

E St NW

24th St NW

23rd St NW

22nd St NW

20th St NW

19th St NW

18th St NW

15

17th St NW

White House

Lafayette Sq

South Lawn

E St NW

FOGGY BOTTOM

Rawlins Park

Theodore
Roosevelt
Memorial Bridge

Virginia Ave NW

D St NW

C St NW

C St NW

The
Ellipse

Mount Vernon Trail

Constitution Ave NW

Iwo Jima
Memorial (0.4mi);
Continental
(0.6mi)

George Washington Memorial Pkwy NW

Rock Creek and Potomac Pkwy NW

**Vietnam
Veterans
Memorial** 13

Constitution
Gardens

35

**Washington
Monument**

14

Arlington
House (0.4mi);
Challenger
Memorial
(0.8mi)

Arlington
Cemetery

4

Reflecting
Pool

40

**Lincoln
Memorial**

West
Potomac
Park

NATIONAL MALL

Independence Ave SW

1

**Arlington
National
Cemetery**

Arlington
Boundary Dr

Lady Bird
Johnson
Park

23

Potomac River

5

**Martin Luther
King Jr Memorial**

21

W Basin Dr SW

Ohio Dr SW

Tidal Basin

Memorial
Park

Pentagon Memorial (0.75mi);
Pentagon (0.9mi);
Air Force Memorial (1.2mi)

(2mi)

27

East Potomac Park

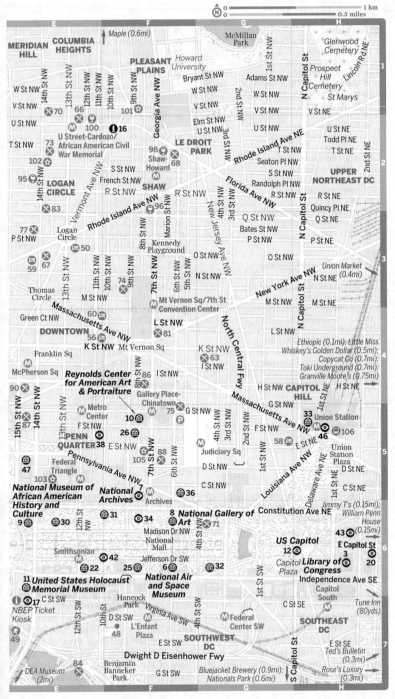

Washington, DC

National Museum of Natural History MUSEUM
(☎202-663-1000; www.naturalhistory.si.edu; cnr 10th St & Constitution Ave NW; ⊙10am-5:30pm, to 7:30pm some days; ⊕; ☐Circulator, Ⓜ Orange, Silver, Blue Lines to Smithsonian or Federal Triangle) FREE Smithsonian museums don't get more popular than this one, so crowds are pretty much guaranteed. Wave to Henry, the elephant who guards the rotunda, then zip to the 2nd floor's Hope Diamond. The 45.52-carat bauble has cursed its owners, including Marie Antoinette, or so the story goes. The beloved dinosaur hall is under renovation until 2019, but the giant squid (1st floor, Ocean Hall) and tarantula feedings (2nd floor, Insect Zoo) fill in the thrills at this kid-packed venue.

National Museum of American History MUSEUM
(☎202-663-1000; www.americanhistory.si.edu; cnr 14th St & Constitution Ave NW; ⊙10am-5:30pm, to 7:30pm some days; ⊕; ☐Circulator, Ⓜ Orange, Silver, Blue Lines to Smithsonian or Federal Triangle) FREE The museum collects all kinds of artifacts of the American experience. The centerpiece is the flag that flew over Fort McHenry in Baltimore during the War of 1812 – the same flag that inspired Francis Scott Key to pen 'The Star-Spangled Banner.' Other highlights include Julia Child's kitchen (1st floor, Food exhibition), George Washington's sword (3rd floor, Price of Freedom exhibition), Dorothy's ruby slippers and a piece of Plymouth Rock (both on the 2nd floor, American Stories exhibition).

Jefferson Memorial MONUMENT
(www.nps.gov/thje; 900 Ohio Dr SW; ⊙24hr; 🚌 Circulator, Ⓜ Orange, Silver, Blue Lines to Smithsonian) FREE Set on the south bank of the Tidal Basin amid the cherry trees, this memorial honors the third US president, political philosopher, drafter of the Declaration of Independence and founder of the University of Virginia. Designed by John Russell Pope to resemble Jefferson's library at the university, the rounded monument was initially derided by critics as 'the Jefferson Muffin.'

National WWII Memorial MONUMENT
(www.nps.gov/wwii; 17th St; ⊙24hr; 🚌 Circulator, Ⓜ Orange, Silver, Blue Lines to Smithsonian) FREE Dedicated in 2004, the WWII memorial honors the 400,000 Americans who died in the conflict, along with the 16 million US soldiers who served between 1941 and 1945. The plaza's dual arches symbolize victory in the Atlantic and Pacific theaters. The 56 surrounding pillars represent each US state and territory.

Hirshhorn Museum MUSEUM
(📞202-633-1000; www.hirshhorn.si.edu; cnr 7th St & Independence Ave SW; ⊙10am-5:30pm; 👶; 🚌 Circulator, Ⓜ Orange, Silver, Blue, Green, Yellow Lines to L'Enfant Plaza) FREE The Smithsonian's cylindrical modern art museum stockpiles sculptures and canvases from modernism's early days to pop art to contemporary art. Special exhibits ring the 2nd floor. Rotating pieces from the permanent collection circle the 3rd floor, where there's also a swell sitting area with couches, floor-to-ceiling windows and a balcony offering Mall views.

National Mall

A DAY TOUR

Folks often call the Mall 'America's Front Yard,' and that's a pretty good analogy. It is indeed a lawn, unfurling scrubby green grass from the Capitol west to the Lincoln Memorial. It's also America's great public space, where citizens come to protest their government, go for scenic runs and connect with the nation's most cherished ideals writ large in stone, landscaping, monuments and memorials.

You can sample quite a bit in a day, but it'll be a full one that requires roughly 4 miles of walking

Start at the ❶ **Vietnam Veterans Memorial**, then head counterclockwise around the Mall, swooping in on the ❷ **Lincoln Memorial**, ❸ **Martin Luther King Jr Memorial** and ❹ **Washington Monument**. You can also pause for the cause of the Korean War and WWII, among other monuments that dot the Mall's western portion.

Martin Luther King Jr Memorial

Walk all the way around the towering statue of Dr King by Lei Yixin and read the quotes. His likeness, incidentally, is 11ft taller than Lincoln and Jefferson in their memorials.

Tidal Basin

Smithsonian Castle

Seek out the tomb of James Smithson, the eccentric Englishman whose 1826 financial gift launched the Smithsonian Institution. His crypt is in a room by the Mall entrance.

Department of Agriculture

West Building

East Building

National Air & Space Museum

Simply step inside and look up, and you'll be impressed. Lindbergh's *Spirit of St Louis* and Chuck Yeager's sound barrier–breaking Bell X-1 are among the machines hanging from the ceiling.

National Museum of the American Indian

US Capitol

Then it's onward to the museums, all fabulous and all free. Begin at the ❺ **Smithsonian Castle** to get your bearings – and to say thanks to the guy making all this awesomeness possible – and commence browsing through the ❻ **National Air & Space Museum**, ❼ **National Gallery of Art & National Sculpture Garden** and ❽ **National Museum of Natural History**.

TOP TIPS

Start early, especially in summer. You'll avoid the crowds, but more importantly you'll avoid the blazing heat. Try to finish with the monuments and be in the air-conditioned museums by 10:30am. Also, consider bringing snacks, since the only food available is from scattered cart vendors and museum cafes.

Lincoln Memorial

Commune with Abe in his chair, then head down the steps to the marker where Martin Luther King Jr gave his 'Dream' speech. The view of the Reflecting Pool and Washington Monument is one of DC's best.

Korean War Veterans Memorial

National WWII Memorial

Vietnam Veterans Memorial

Check the symbol that's beside each name. A diamond indicates 'killed, body recovered.' A plus sign indicates 'missing and unaccounted for.' There are approximately 1200 of the latter.

National Museum of African American History & Culture

National Museum of American History

Washington Monument

As you approach the obelisk, look a third of the way up. See how it's slightly lighter in color at the bottom? Builders had to use different marble after the first source dried up.

National Sculpture Garden

National Museum of Natural History

Wave to Henry, the elephant who guards the rotunda, then zip to the 2nd floor's Hope Diamond. The 45.52-carat bauble has cursed its owners, including Marie Antoinette, or so the story goes.

National Gallery of Art & National Sculpture Garden

Beeline to Gallery 6 (West Building) and ogle the Western Hemisphere's only Leonardo da Vinci painting. Outdoors, amble amid whimsical sculptures by Miró, Calder and Lichtenstein. Also check out IM Pei's design of the East Building.

Smithsonian Castle
NOTABLE BUILDING

(☑ 202-633-1000; www.si.edu; 1000 Jefferson Dr SW; ⊗ 8:30am-5:30pm; ☒ Circulator, Ⓜ Orange, Silver, Blue Lines to Smithsonian) James Renwick designed this turreted, red-sandstone fairy-tale in 1855. Today the castle houses the **Smithsonian Visitors Center**, which makes a good first stop on the Mall. Inside you'll find history exhibits, multilingual touch-screen displays, a staffed information desk, free maps, a cafe – and the tomb of James Smithson, the institution's founder. His crypt lies inside a little room by the main entrance off the Mall.

Freer-Sackler Museums of Asian Art
MUSEUM

(☑ 202-633-1000; www.asia.si.edu; cnr Independence Ave & 12th St SW; ⊗ 10am-5:30pm; ☒ Circulator, Ⓜ Orange, Silver, Blue Lines to Smithsonian) **FREE** This is a lovely spot in which to while away a Washington afternoon. Japanese silk scrolls, smiling Buddhas, rare Islamic manuscripts and Chinese jades spread through cool, quiet galleries. The Freer and Sackler are actually separate venues, connected by an underground tunnel. The Sackler focuses more on changing exhibits, while the Freer, rather incongruously, also houses works by American painter James Whistler. Don't miss the blue-and-gold, ceramics-crammed Peacock Room.

National Museum of the American Indian
MUSEUM

(☑ 202-663-1000; www.nmai.si.edu; cnr 4th St & Independence Ave SW; ⊗ 10am-5:30pm; 👫; ☒ Circulator, Ⓜ Orange, Silver, Blue, Green, Yellow Lines to L'Enfant Plaza) **FREE** Ensconced in honey-colored, undulating limestone, this museum makes a striking architectural impression. Inside it offers cultural artifacts, costumes, video and audio recordings related to the indigenous people of the Americas. Exhibits are largely organized and presented by individual tribes, which provides an intimate, if sometimes disjointed, overall narrative. The 'Our Universes' gallery (on Level 4) about Native American beliefs and creation stories is intriguing.

Franklin Delano Roosevelt Memorial
MONUMENT

(www.nps.gov/frde; 400 W Basin Dr SW; ⊗ 24hr; ☒ Circulator, Ⓜ Orange, Silver, Blue Lines to Smithsonian) **FREE** The 7.5-acre memorial pays tribute to the longest-serving president in US history and the era he governed. Visitors are taken through four red-granite 'rooms' that narrate FDR's time in office, from the Depression to the New Deal to WWII. The story is told through statuary and inscriptions, punctuated with fountains and peaceful alcoves. It's especially pretty at night, when the marble shimmers in the glossy stillness of the Tidal Basin.

◉ Capitol Hill

The city's geographic and legislative heart surprises by being mostly a row house–lined residential neighborhood. The vast area holds top sights such as the Capitol, Library of Congress and Holocaust Memorial Museum. The areas around Eastern Market and H St NE are locals' hubs, with good-time restaurants and nightlife.

★ US Capitol
LANDMARK

(☑ 202-226-8000; www.visitthecapitol.gov; 1st St NE & E Capitol St; ⊗ 8:30am-4:30pm Mon-Sat; Ⓜ Orange, Silver, Blue Lines to Capitol South) **FREE** Since 1800, this is where the legislative branch of American government – ie Congress – has met to write the country's laws. The lower House of Representatives (435 members) and upper Senate (100) meet respectively in the south and north wings of the building. Enter via the underground visitor center below the East Plaza. Guided tours of the building are free, but tickets are limited and there's often a long wait. It's best to reserve online in advance (there's no fee).

The hour-long jaunt showcases the exhaustive background of a building that fairly sweats history. You'll watch a cheesy film first, then staff members lead you into the ornate halls and whispery chambers cluttered with the busts, statues and personal mementos of generations of Congress members.

To watch Congress in session, you need a separate pass. US citizens must get one from their representative or senator; foreign visitors should take their passports to the House and Senate Appointment Desks on the upper level. Congressional committee hearings are actually more interesting (and substantive) if you care about what's being debated; check for a schedule, locations and to see if they're open to the public (they often are) at www.house.gov and www.senate.gov.

★ United States Holocaust Memorial Museum
MUSEUM

(☑ 202-488-0400; www.ushmm.org; 100 Raoul Wallenberg Pl SW; ⊗ 10am-5:20pm, extended hours Apr–mid-Jun; ☒ Circulator, Ⓜ Orange, Silver, Blue

Lines to Smithsonian) **FREE** For a deep understanding of the Holocaust – its victims, perpetrators and bystanders – this harrowing museum is a must-see. The main exhibit gives visitors the identity card of a single Holocaust victim, whose story is revealed as you take a winding route into a hellish past marked by ghettos, rail cars and death camps. It also shows the flip side of human nature, documenting the risks many citizens took to help the persecuted.

★**Library of Congress** LIBRARY
(☑202-707-8000; www.loc.gov; 1st St SE; ☺8:30am-4:30pm Mon-Sat; Ⓜ Orange, Silver, Blue Lines to Capitol South) **FREE** The world's largest library – with 164 million books, manuscripts, maps, photos, films and other items – awes in both scope and design. The centerpiece is the 1897 Jefferson Building. Gawk at the Great Hall, done up in stained glass, marble and mosaics of mythical characters, then seek out the Gutenberg Bible (c 1455), Thomas Jefferson's round library and the reading room viewing area. Free tours of the building take place between 10:30am and 3:30pm on the half-hour.

Supreme Court LANDMARK
(☑202-479-3030; www.supremecourt.gov; 1 1st St NE; ☺9am-4:30pm Mon-Fri; Ⓜ Orange, Silver, Blue Lines to Capitol South) **FREE** The highest court in the USA sits in a pseudo-Greek temple protected by 13,000lb bronze doors. Arrive early to watch arguments (periodic Monday through Wednesday October to April). You can visit the permanent exhibits and the building's five-story, marble-and-bronze, spiral staircase year-round. On days when court is not in session you also can hear lectures (every hour on the half-hour) in the courtroom. When departing, be sure to exit via the doors that lead to the regal front steps.

National Postal Museum MUSEUM
(☑202-633-5555; www.postalmuseum.si.edu; 2 Massachusetts Ave NE; ☺10am-5:30pm; ♿; Ⓜ Red Line to Union Station) **FREE** The Smithsonian-run Postal Museum is way cooler than you might think. Level 1 has exhibits on postal history from the Pony Express to modern times, where you'll see antique mail planes and touching old letters from soldiers and pioneers. Level 2 holds the world's largest stamp collection. Join the stamp geeks pulling out drawers and snapping photos of the world's rarest stamps (the Ben Franklin Z Grill!), or start your own collection, choosing from among thousands of free international stamps (Guyana, Congo, Cambodia...).

Folger Shakespeare Library LIBRARY
(☑202-544-4600; www.folger.edu; 201 E Capitol St SE; ☺10am-5pm Mon-Sat, noon-5pm Sun; Ⓜ Orange, Silver, Blue Lines to Capitol South) **FREE** Bard-o-philes will be all aflutter here, as the library holds the largest collection of old Billy's works in the world. Stroll through the Great Hall to see Elizabethan artifacts, paintings, etchings and manuscripts. The highlight is a rare First Folio that you can leaf through digitally. Pop into the evocative on-site **theater** (www.folger.edu/theatre; tickets from $30), a replica of the Elizabethan Globe Theatre; return in the evening to catch a show.

Bureau of Engraving & Printing LANDMARK
(☑202-874-2330; www.moneyfactory.gov; cnr 14th & C Sts SW; ☺9-10:45am, 12:30-3:45pm & 5-6pm Mon-Fri Mar-Aug, reduced hours Sep-Feb; 🖥 Circulator, Ⓜ Orange, Silver, Blue Lines to Smithsonian) **FREE** Cha-ching! The nation's paper currency is designed and printed here. Guides lead 40-minute tours during which you peer down onto the work floor where millions of dollars roll off the presses and get cut (by guillotine!). It's actually a pretty dry jaunt; don't expect exciting visuals or snappy dialogue. In peak season (March to August), timed entry tickets are required. Get in line early at the **ticket kiosk** (Raoul Wallenberg Pl, aka 15th St; ☺8am-whenever tickets run out; Ⓜ Orange, Silver, Blue Lines to Smithsonian). It opens at 8am. Tickets are often gone by 10am.

◉ White House & Foggy Bottom

The president lives at the center of the 'hood. The State Department, World Bank and other institutions hover nearby in Foggy Bottom. It's mostly a business district by day, and not terribly active by night, with the exception of the Kennedy Center for performing arts.

★**White House** LANDMARK
(☑202-456-7041; www.whitehouse.gov; 1600 Pennsylvania Ave NW; ☺tours 7:30-11:30am Tue-Thu, to 1:30pm Fri & Sat; Ⓜ Orange, Silver, Blue Lines to Federal Triangle or McPherson Sq) **FREE** The 'President's House' was built between 1792 and 1800. If you're lucky enough to get inside on a public tour, you'll see several rooms in the main residence, each rich in presidential lore. Tours must be arranged in advance. Americans must apply via one

of their state's members of Congress, and non-Americans must apply through their country's embassy in DC. Applications are taken from 21 days to three months in advance; the earlier you request during this time frame the better.

White House Visitor Center MUSEUM
(☑202-208-1631; www.nps.gov/whho; 1450 Pennsylvania Ave NW; ⊙7:30am-4pm; Ⓜ Orange, Silver, Blue Lines to Federal Triangle) **FREE** Getting inside the White House can be tough, so here is your back-up plan. Browse artifacts such as Roosevelt's desk for his fireside chats and Lincoln's cabinet chair. Multimedia exhibits give a 360-degree view into the White House's rooms. It's obviously not the same as seeing the real deal first-hand, but the center does do its job very well, giving good history sprinkled with great anecdotes on presidential spouses, kids, pets and dinner preferences.

Textile Museum MUSEUM
(☑202-994-5200; www.museum.gwu.edu; 701 21st St NW; suggested donation $8; ⊙11am-5pm Mon & Fri, 11am-7pm Wed & Thu, 10am-5pm Sat, 1-5pm Sun; Ⓜ Orange, Silver, Blue Lines to Foggy Bottom-GWU) This gem is the country's only textile museum. Galleries spread over two floors hold exquisite fabrics and carpets. Exhibits revolve around a theme – say Asian textiles depicting dragons or Kuba cloth from the Democratic Republic of Congo – and rotate a few times a year. Bonus: the museum shares space with George Washington University's Washingtonia trove of historic maps, drawings and ephemera.

Renwick Gallery MUSEUM
(☑202-633-7970; http://renwick.americanart.si.edu; 1661 Pennsylvania Ave NW; ⊙10am-5:30pm; Ⓜ Orange, Silver, Blue Lines to Farragut West) **FREE** Part of the Smithsonian diaspora, the Renwick Gallery is set in a stately 1859 mansion and exhibits a playful collection of contemporary American crafts and art pieces.

◎ Downtown & Penn Quarter

Penn Quarter forms around Pennsylvania Ave as it runs between the White House and the Capitol. Downtown extends west beyond it. Major sights include the National Archives, Reynolds Center for American Art & Portraiture and Ford's Theatre. It's also DC's theater district and home to the basketball/ hockey sports arena.

★**National Archives** LANDMARK
(☑866-272-6272; www.archives.gov/museum; 700 Pennsylvania Ave NW; ⊙10am-5:30pm; Ⓜ Green, Yellow Lines to Archives) **FREE** It's hard not to feel a little in awe of the big three documents in the National Archives: the Declaration of Independence, the Constitution and the Bill of Rights, plus one of four copies of the Magna Carta. Taken together, it becomes clear just how radical the American experiment was for its time. The Public Vaults, a bare scratching of archival bric-a-brac, make a flashy rejoinder to the main exhibit.

Newseum MUSEUM
(☑202-292-6100; www.newseum.org; 555 Pennsylvania Ave NW; adult/child $25/15; ⊙9am-5pm; ⦿; Ⓜ Green, Yellow Lines to Archives) This six-story, highly interactive news museum is worth the admission price. You can delve into the major events of recent years (the fall of the Berlin Wall, September 11, Hurricane Katrina), and spend hours watching moving film footage and perusing Pulitzer Prize–winning photographs. The concourse level displays FBI artifacts from prominent news stories, such as the Unabomber's cabin and gangster Whitey Bulger's fishing hat.

Ford's Theatre Center for Education and Leadership MUSEUM
(☑202-347-4833; www.fords.org; 514 10th St NW; ⊙9am-5pm; Ⓜ Red, Orange, Silver, Blue Lines to Metro Center) **FREE** More exhibits for Lincolnphiles. Across the street from the famous theater where Lincoln was shot, you're funneled through the **Petersen House** (www.nps.gov/foth), where he died, and work your way down from the 4th floor of this museum, which showcases permanent displays examining how Lincoln's legacy lives on in current politics and pop culture. The 2nd floor takes a look at leaders inspired by Lincoln. Visitors use the same ticket they used to tour Ford's Theatre and Petersen House.

★**Reynolds Center for American Art & Portraiture** MUSEUM
(☑202-633-1000; www.americanart.si.edu; cnr 8th & F Sts NW; ⊙11:30am-7pm; Ⓜ Red, Yellow, Green Lines to Gallery Pl-Chinatown) **FREE** If you only visit one art museum in DC, make it the Reynolds Center, which combines the National Portrait Gallery and the American Art Museum. There is simply no better collection of American art in the world than at these two Smithsonian museums. Famed works by Edward Hopper, Georgia O'Keef-

fe, Andy Warhol, Winslow Homer and loads more celebrated artists fill the galleries.

International Spy Museum   MUSEUM
(📞 202-393-7798; www.spymuseum.org; 800 F St NW; adult/child $22/15; ⊙ 9am-7pm mid-Apr–mid-Aug, 10am-6pm rest of year; 👪; Ⓜ Red, Yellow, Green Lines to Gallery Pl-Chinatown) One of DC's most popular museums, it's flashy, over the top and probably guilty of overtly glamming up a life of intelligence-gathering. But who cares? You basically want to see Q's lab, and that's what the Spy Museum feels like. Check out James Bond's tricked-out Aston Martin, the KGB's lipstick-concealed pistol and more. Kids go crazy for this spot, but be warned: lines form long and early. Ease the wait somewhat by reserving online.

⊙ Logan Circle, U Street & Columbia Heights

These neighborhoods have changed more in recent years than almost anywhere else in DC. The U St Corridor – DC's richest nightlife zone – has quite a history. It was once the 'Black Broadway' where Duke Ellington and Ella Fitzgerald hit their notes in the 1920s to 1950s. It was the smoldering epicenter of the 1968 race riots. There was a troubled descent, and then a vibrant rebirth in recent years. A stroll here is a must and rewards with mural-splashed alleys, red-hot music clubs and antique-crammed shops.

U St becomes part of the larger Shaw district, which is DC's current 'it' 'hood. But it's not annoyingly trendy. Instead, the breweries, bars and cafes that seem to pop up weekly are local places, where neighbors come to sip among neighbors (and students among students, as Howard University is here). Logan Circle is next door and also booming. Walk down 14th St NW and hot-chef wine bars, beer bars, tapas bars and oyster bars flash by. The side streets hold stately old manors that give the area its class.

To the north, Columbia Heights has a reputation as an enclave for Latino immigrants and hipsters. There are no real sights, but the cheap ethnic food and unassuming punk dive bars can occupy many an evening.

Northeast DC is a vast stretch of leafy residential blocks holding several far-flung sights (and breweries). Nature lovers have a couple of groovy, free landscapes to explore, as long as you have a car or don't mind lengthy public-transportation trips.

African American Civil War Memorial   MONUMENT
(www.afroamcivilwar.org; cnr U St & Vermont Ave NW; Ⓜ Green, Yellow Lines to U St) Standing at the center of a granite plaza, this bronze memorial depicting rifle-bearing troops is DC's first major art piece by black sculptor Ed Hamilton. The statue is surrounded on three sides by the Wall of Honor, listing the names of 209,145 black troops who fought in the Union Army, as well as the 7000 white soldiers who served alongside them. You can use the directory to locate individual names within each of the regiments.

To get there, depart the Metro station via the 10th St exit (follow the 'memorial' signs as you leave the train).

Mexican Cultural Institute   NOTABLE BUILDING
(📞 202-728-1628; www.instituteofmexicodc.org; 2829 16th St NW; ⊙ 10am-6pm Mon-Fri, noon-4pm Sat; Ⓜ Green, Yellow Lines to Columbia Heights) **FREE** The Mexican Cultural Institute looks locked up and imposing, but don't be deterred. The gilded beaux-arts mansion is open to the public and hosts excellent art and cultural exhibitions related to Mexico. You might see a show on Diego Rivera's art or Mayan religious artifacts or Octavio Paz's writings. Ring the doorbell for entry.

⊙ Dupont Circle & Kalorama

Dupont offers flashy new restaurants, hip bars, cafe society and cool bookstores. It's also the heart of the city's LGBT community. It used to be where turn-of-the-century millionaires lived. Today those mansions hold DC's greatest concentration of embassies. Kalorama sits in the northwest corner and ups the regal reserve.

★ Embassy Row   ARCHITECTURE
(www.embassy.org; Massachusetts Ave NW, btwn Observatory & Dupont Circles NW; Ⓜ Red Line to Dupont Circle) Want to take a trip around the world? Stroll northwest along Massachusetts Ave from Dupont Circle (the actual traffic circle) and you pass more than 40 embassies housed in mansions that range from elegant to imposing to discreet. Tunisia, Chile, Turkmenistan, Togo, Haiti – flags flutter above heavy doors and mark the nations inside, while dark-windowed sedans ease out of driveways ferrying diplomats to and fro. The district has another 130 embassies sprinkled throughout, but this is the main vein.

National Geographic Museum   MUSEUM

(☑ 202-857-7700;   www.nationalgeographic.org/dc; 1145 17th St NW; adult/child $15/10; ⊙ 10am-6pm; Ⓜ Red Line to Farragut North) The museum at National Geographic Society headquarters can't compete with the Smithsonian's more extensive offerings, but it can be worth a stop, depending on what's showing. Exhibits are drawn from the society's well-documented expeditions to the far corners of the Earth, and they change periodically.

Phillips Collection   MUSEUM

(☑ 202-387-2151; www.phillipscollection.org; 1600 21st St NW; Tue-Fri free, Sat & Sun $10, ticketed exhibitions per day $12; ⊙ 10am-5pm Tue, Wed, Fri & Sat, to 8:30pm Thu, noon-7pm Sun; Ⓜ Red Line to Dupont Circle) The first modern-art museum in the country (opened in 1921) houses a small but exquisite collection of European and American works. Renoir's *Luncheon of the Boating Party* is a highlight, along with pieces by Gauguin, Van Gogh, Matisse, Picasso and many other greats. The intimate rooms, set in a restored mansion, put you unusually close to the artworks. The permanent collection is free on weekdays. Download the free app or dial ☑ 202-595-1839 for audio tours through the works.

⊙ Adams Morgan

Adams Morgan has long been Washington's fun, nightlife-driven neighborhood. It's also a global village of sorts. The result today is a raucous mash-up centered on 18th St NW. Vintage boutiques, record shops and ethnic eats poke up between thumping bars and a growing number of stylish spots for gastronomes.

District of Columbia Arts Center   ARTS CENTER

(DCAC; ☑ 202-462-7833; www.dcartscenter.org; 2438 18th St NW; ⊙ 2-7pm Wed-Sun; Ⓜ Red Line to Woodley Park-Zoo/Adams Morgan) FREE The grassroots DCAC offers emerging artists a space to showcase their work. The 800-sq-ft gallery features rotating visual-arts exhibits, while plays, improv, avant-garde musicals and other theatrical productions take place in the 50-seat theater. The gallery is free and worth popping into to see what's showing.

⊙ Georgetown

Georgetown is DC's most aristocratic neighborhood, home to elite university students, ivory-tower academics and diplomats. Chi brand-name shops, dark-wood pubs and upscale restaurants line the streets. Lovely parks and gardens color the edges.

Dumbarton Oaks   GARDENS, MUSEUM

(☑ 202-339-6401; www.doaks.org; 1703 32nd St NW; museum free, gardens adult/child $10/5; ⊙ museum 11:30am-5:30pm Tue-Sun, gardens 2-6pm; ☐ Circulator) The mansion's 10 acres of enchanting formal gardens are straight out of a storybook. In springtime, the blooms – including heaps of cherry blossoms – are stunning. The mansion itself is worth a walk-through to see exquisite Byzantine and pre-Columbian art (including El Greco's *The Visitation*) and the fascinating library of rare books.

Georgetown Waterfront Park   PARK

(www.georgetownwaterfrontpark.org; Water St NW, btwn 30th St & Key Bridge; ⊛ ; ☐ Circulator) The park is a favorite with couples on first dates, families on an evening stroll and power players showing off their big yachts. Benches dot the way, where you can sit and watch the rowing teams out on the Potomac River. Alfresco restaurants cluster near the harbor at 31st St NW. They ring a terraced plaza filled with fountains (which become an ice rink in winter). The docks are also here for sightseeing boats that ply the Potomac to Alexandria, VA.

Georgetown University   UNIVERSITY

(☑ 202-687-0100; www.georgetown.edu; cnr 37th & O Sts NW; ☐ Circulator) Georgetown is one of the nation's top universities, with a student body that's equally hard-working and hard-partying. Founded in 1789, it was America's first Roman Catholic university. Notable Hoya (derived from the Latin *hoya saxa,* 'what rocks') alumni include Bill Clinton, as well as many international royals and heads of state. Near the campus' east gate, medieval-looking **Healy Hall** impresses with its tall, Hogwarts-esque clock tower. Pretty **Dalghren Chapel** and its quiet courtyard hide behind it.

Exorcist Stairs   FILM LOCATION

(3600 Prospect St NW; ☐ Circulator) The steep set of stairs dropping down to M St is a popular track for joggers, but more famously it's the spot where demonically possessed Father Karras tumbles to his death in horror-film classic *The Exorcist* (1973). Come on foggy nights, when the stone steps really are creepy as hell.

Tudor Place
MUSEUM

(☑202-965-0400; www.tudorplace.org; 1644 31st St NW; 1hr house tour adult/child $10/3, self-guided garden tour $3; ☺10am-4pm Tue-Sat, from noon Sun, closed Jan; ☐Circulator) This 1816 neoclassical mansion was owned by Thomas Peter and Martha Custis Peter, the step-granddaughter of Martha Washington. Today the mansion functions as a small museum, featuring furnishings and artwork from Mount Vernon, which give good insight into American decorative arts. The grand, 5-acre gardens bloom with roses, lilies, poplar trees and palms.

◉ Upper Northwest DC

★ Washington National Cathedral
CHURCH

(☑202-537-6200; https://cathedral.org; 3101 Wisconsin Ave NW; adult/child $12/8, Sun free; ☺10am-5:30pm Mon-Fri, 10am-4pm Sat, 8am-4pm Sun; Ⓜ Red Line to Tenleytown-AU then southbound bus 30, 31, 33 or 37) This Gothic cathedral, as dramatic as its European counterparts, blends both the spiritual and the profane in its architectural treasures. The stained-glass windows are stunning (check out the 'Space Window' with an embedded lunar rock); you'll need binoculars to spy the Darth Vader gargoyle on the exterior. Specialized tours delve deeper into the esoteric; call or go online for the schedule.

National Zoo
ZOO

(☑202-633-4888; www.nationalzoo.si.edu; 3001 Connecticut Ave NW; ☺9am-6pm mid-Mar–Sep, to 4pm Oct–mid-Mar, grounds 8am-7pm mid-Mar–Sep, to 5pm Oct–mid-Mar; Ⓜ Red Line to Cleveland Park or Woodley Park-Zoo/Adams Morgan) FREE Home to more than 1800 individual animals (300-plus different species) in natural habitats, the National Zoo is famed for its giant pandas Mei Xiang and Tian Tian. Other highlights include the African lion pride, Asian elephants, and dangling orangutans swinging 50ft overhead from steel cables and interconnected towers.

🏃 Activities

Hiking & Cycling

Capital Bikeshare
CYCLING

(☑877-430-2453; www.capitalbikeshare.com; per 1/3 days $8/17) It has a network of 3700-plus bicycles scattered at 440-odd stations around the region. Kiosks issue passes (one day or three days) on the spot. Insert a credit card, get your ride code, then unlock a bike. The first 30 minutes are free; after that, rates rise fast if you don't dock the bike.

Capital Crescent Trail
CYCLING

(www.cctrail.org; Water St; ☐Circulator) Stretching between Georgetown and Bethesda, MD, the constantly evolving Capital Crescent Trail is a fabulous (and very popular) jogging and biking route. Built on an abandoned railroad bed, the 11-mile trail is paved and is a great leisurely day trip. It has beautiful lookouts over the Potomac River, and winds through woodsy areas and upscale neighborhoods.

Boating

Tidal Basin Boathouse
BOATING

(☑202-479-2426; www.boatingindc.com/boathouses/tidal-basin; 1501 Maine Ave SW; 2-/4-person boat rental $18/30; ☺10am-6pm mid-Mar–mid-Oct; ☐Circulator, Ⓜ Orange, Silver, Blue Lines to Smithsonian) It rents paddleboats to take out on the Tidal Basin. Make sure you bring a camera. There are great views, of the Jefferson Memorial in particular, from the water.

Key Bridge Boathouse
KAYAKING

(☑202-337-9642; www.boatingindc.com/boathouses/key-bridge-boathouse; 3500 Water St NW; ☺hours vary mid-Apr–Oct; ☐Circulator) Located beneath the Key Bridge, the boathouse rents canoes, kayaks and stand-up paddleboards (prices start at $16 per hour). In summer, it also offers guided, 90-minute kayak trips ($45 per person) that glide past the Lincoln Memorial as the sun sets. If you have a bike, the boathouse is a mere few steps from the Capital Crescent Trail.

🚩 Tours

DC by Foot
WALKING

(☑202-370-1830; www.freetoursbyfoot.com/washington-dc-tours) Guides for this pay-what-you-want walking tour offer engaging stories and historical details on different jaunts covering the National Mall, Lincoln's assassination, Dupont Circle's ghosts and many more. Most takers pay around $10 per person. Reserve in advance to guarantee a spot.

DC Metro Food Tours
WALKING

(☑202-851-2268; www.dcmetrofoodtours.com; per person $30-65) These walkabouts explore the culinary riches of various neighborhoods, stopping for multiple bites along the way. Offerings include Eastern Market, U St, Little Ethiopia, Georgetown and Alexandria, VA. Most last from 1½ to 3½ hours. Departure points vary.

City Walk
Genteel Georgetown

START MT ZION CEMETERY
END GEORGETOWN WATERFRONT PARK
LENGTH 3 MILES; THREE HOURS

African American ❶ **Mt Zion Cemetery**, near the intersection of 27th and Q Sts, dates from the early 1800s. A nearby church was a stop on the Underground Railroad, and it hid escaping slaves in a vault in the cemetery.

The entrance to ❷ **Oak Hill Cemetery** (9am-4:30pm Mon-Fri, 11am-4pm Sat, 1-4pm Sun) is a few blocks away at 30th and R Sts NW. Stroll the obelisk-studded grounds and look for gravesites of prominent Washingtonians such as Edwin Stanton (Lincoln's war secretary). Up the road, ❸ **Dumbarton Oaks** (p264) offers exquisite Byzantine art inside and sprawling, fountain-dotted gardens outside. The blooms in springtime are stunning.

George Washington's step-granddaughter Martha Custis Peter owned ❹ **Tudor Place** (p265), the neoclassical mansion at 1644 31st St NW. It has some of George's furnishings from Mount Vernon on show and pretty landscaped grounds.

Head over to Wisconsin Ave NW, and stop in at ❺ **Martin's Tavern** (www.martinstavern.com), where John F Kennedy proposed to Jackie. Walk west along N St and you'll pass several Federal-style townhouses in the 3300 block. JFK and Jackie lived at ❻ **3307 N St** between 1958 and 1961, when they left for the White House. At the corner of 36th NW and Prospect Sts, stare down the ❼ **Exorcist Stairs** (p264). This is the spot where demonically possessed Father Karras tumbles to his death in the 1973 horror film *The Exorcist*. Joggers use the steep steps by day, but at night they're legitimately creepy as hell.

Go down to M St NW, with its boutiques and high-end stores. At Thomas Jefferson St turn right and sniff your way to ❽ **Baked & Wired** (p274) to replenish with a monster cupcake and cappuccino. From there you can stroll down to ❾ **Georgetown Waterfront Park** (p264) to watch the boats and other action along the Potomac River.

DC Brew Tours
BUS

(☑ 202-759-8687; www.dcbrewtours.com; 801 F ST NW; tours $65-90; Ⓜ Red, Yellow, Green Lines to Gallery Pl-Chinatown) Visit three to four breweries by van. Routes vary but could include DC Brau, Bardo, Capital City and Port City, among others. Five-hour jaunts feature tastings of 15-plus beers and a beer-focused meal. The 3½-hour Sips and Sights tour forgoes the meal and adds stops at the Lincoln Memorial, Pentagon and more. Departure is from downtown by the Reynolds Center.

Bike & Roll – L'Enfant Plaza
CYCLING

(☑ 202-842-2453; www.bikeandrolldc.com; 955 L'Enfant Plaza SW; tours adult/child $45/35; ⊙ mid-Mar–early Dec; Ⓜ Orange, Silver, Blue, Yellow, Green Lines to L'Enfant Plaza) This branch of the bike-rental company (from $16 per two hours) is the one closest to the Mall. In addition to bike rental, it also provides tours. Three-hour jaunts wheel by the main sights of Capitol Hill and the National Mall.

Old Town Trolley Tours
BUS

(☑ 202-832-9800; www.trolleytours.com; 1001 E St NW; adult/child $40/30; Ⓜ Red, Orange, Silver, Blue Lines to Metro Center) This open-sided bus offers hop-on, hop-off exploring of some 25 major sights around the Mall, Arlington and downtown. The company also offers a 'monuments by moonlight' tour and the DC Ducks tour, via an amphibious vehicle that plunges into the Potomac. Buy tickets at the Washington Welcome Center (1001 E St NW), at Union Station or online.

★☆ Festivals & Events

Independence Day
CULTURAL

(⊙ Jul 4) On July 4, huge crowds gather on the Mall to watch marching bands parade and hear the Declaration of Independence read from the National Archives steps. Later, the National Symphony Orchestra plays a concert on the Capitol's steps, followed by mega-fireworks.

National Cherry Blossom Festival
CULTURAL

(www.nationalcherryblossomfestival.org; ⊙ late Mar–mid-Apr) The star of DC's annual calendar celebrates spring's arrival with boat rides in the Tidal Basin, evening walks by lantern light, cultural fairs and a parade. The three-week event, from late March to mid-April, also commemorates Japan's gift of 3000 cherry trees in 1912. It's DC at its prettiest.

Smithsonian Folklife Festival
CULTURAL

(www.festival.si.edu; ⊙ late Jun–early Jul; 🏃; 🚻 Circulator, Ⓜ Orange, Silver, Blue, Green, Yellow Lines to L'Enfant Plaza) This fun family event, held over 10 days in late June and early July, celebrates international and US cultures. The fest features folk music, dance, crafts, storytelling and ethnic fare, and it highlights a diverse mix of countries and regions. It takes place on the Mall's east end.

🛏 Sleeping

Capitol Hill

William Penn House
HOSTEL $

(☑ 202-543-5560; www.williampennhouse.org; 515 E Capitol St SE; dm $45-55; ⊛ ❋ @; Ⓜ Orange, Silver, Blue Lines to Capitol South or Eastern Market) This friendly Quaker-run guesthouse with garden offers clean, well-maintained dorms, though it could use more bathrooms. There are 30 beds in total, including a four-bed room for families ($150 per night). The facility doesn't require religious observance, but there is a religious theme throughout, and it prefers guests be active in progressive causes.

Kimpton George Hotel
BOUTIQUE HOTEL $$

(☑ 202-347-4200; www.hotelgeorge.com; 15 E St NW; r $269-389; P ⊛ ❋ @ 🛜 🐾; Ⓜ Red Line to Union Station) DC's first chic boutique hotel is still one of its best. Chrome-and-glass furniture and modern art frame the bold interior. Rooms exude a cool, creamy-white Zen. The pop-art presidential accents (paintings of American currency, artfully rearranged and diced up) are a little overdone, but that's a minor complaint about what is otherwise the hippest lodging on the Hill.

White House & Foggy Bottom

Club Quarters
HOTEL $$

(☑ 202-463-6400; www.clubquarters.com/washington-dc; 839 17th St NW; r $179-259; P ⊛ ❋ @ 🛜; Ⓜ Orange, Silver, Blue Lines to Farragut West) Club Quarters is a no-muss, no-fuss kind of place often used by business travelers on the go. Room are small and without views, and lack charm or quirk, but the bed is restful, the desk workable, the wi-fi fast enough and the coffee maker well stocked. Oh, and the prices are reasonable in an area where they're usually sky-high.

★ **Hotel Lombardy**   HISTORIC HOTEL **$$**
(☎202-828-2600; www.hotellombardy.com; 2019 Pennsylvania Ave NW; r $180-330; P❖✆@🛜; M Orange, Silver, Blue Lines to Foggy Bottom-GWU) Done up in Venetian decor (shuttered doors, warm gold walls) and beloved by World Bank and State Department types, this European boutique hotel has multilingual staff and an international vibe – you hear French and Spanish as often as English in its halls. The attitude carries into rooms decorated with original artwork, and Chinese and European antiques.

★ **Hay-Adams Hotel**   HERITAGE HOTEL **$$$**
(☎202-638-6600; www.hayadams.com; 800 16th St NW; r from $400; P✳@🛜❖; M Orange, Silver, Blue Lines to McPherson Sq) One of the city's great heritage hotels, the Hay is a beautiful old building where 'nothing is overlooked but the White House.' The property has a palazzo-style lobby and probably the best rooms of the old-school luxury genre, all puffy mattresses like clouds shaded by four-poster canopies and gold-braid tassels.

St Regis Washington   HOTEL **$$$**
(☎202-638-2626; www.stregiswashingtondc.com; 923 16th St NW; r from $500; P✳@🛜❖; M Orange, Silver, Blue Lines to McPherson Sq) The neo-renaissance St Regis is one of the grandest hotels in the city. What else can you say about a building designed to resemble nothing less than an Italian palace? Rooms are as gilded as you'd expect, with hand-carved armoires, double-basin marble sinks and TVs embedded in the bathroom mirrors. Wifi costs $7 per day.

🛏 Downtown & Penn Quarter

Hostelling International – Washington DC   HOSTEL **$**
(☎202-737-2333; www.hiwashingtondc.org; 1009 11th St NW; dm $33-55, r $110-150; ❖✳@🛜; M Red, Orange, Silver, Blue Lines to Metro Center) Top of the budget picks, this large, friendly hostel attracts a laid-back international crowd and has loads of amenities: lounge rooms, a pool table, a 60in TV for movie nights, free tours, free continental breakfast and free wi-fi.

Morrison-Clark Inn   HISTORIC HOTEL **$$**
(☎202-898-1200; www.morrisonclark.com; 1011 L St NW; r $180-310; P❖✳@🛜; M Green, Yellow Lines to Mt Vernon Sq/7th St-Convention Center) Listed on the Register of Historic Places and helmed by a doting staff, the elegant, 114-room Morrison-Clark comprises two 1864 Victorian residences filled with fine antiques, tear-drop chandeliers and gilded mirrors, and a newer wing with Asian-influenced decor set in the repurposed Chinese church next door. It may sound odd, but the overall effect is lovely and dignified.

🛏 Logan Circle, U Street & Columbia Heights

★ **Chester Arthur House**   B&B **$$**
(☎877-893-3233; www.chesterarthurhouse.com; 23 Logan Circle NW; r $180-215; ❖✳🛜; M Green, Yellow Lines to U St) Snooze in one of four rooms in this beautiful Logan Circle row house, located a stumble from the restaurant boom along P and 14th Sts. The 1883 abode is stuffed with crystal chandeliers, antique oil paintings, oriental rugs and a mahogany paneled staircase, plus ephemera from the hosts' global expeditions.

Kimpton Mason & Rook Hotel   HOTEL **$$**
(☎202-742-3100; www.masonandrookhotel.com; 1430 Rhode Island Ave NW; r $189-399; P❖✳@🛜❖; M Orange, Silver, Blue Lines to McPherson Sq) 🐾 Snuggled into a tree-lined neighborhood near trendy 14th St, Mason & Rook feels like your urbane friend's chic apartment. The lobby resembles a handsome living room, with comfy seating, bookshelves and eclectic art. The large guest rooms invite lingering with plush fabrics, rich dark wood and leather decor, and marble bathrooms with walk-in rain showers. The free bicycles are handy for cruising around town.

🛏 Dupont Circle & Kalorama

Embassy Circle Guest House   B&B **$$**
(☎202-232-7744; www.dcinns.com; 2224 R St NW; r $200-310; ❖✳🛜; M Red Line to Dupont Circle) Embassies surround this 1902 French country–style home, which sits a few blocks from Dupont's nightlife hubbub. The 11 big-windowed rooms are decked out with Persian carpets and original art on the walls; they don't have TVs, though they do each have wi-fi. Staff feed you well throughout the day, with a hot organic breakfast, afternoon cookies, and an evening wine and beer soirée.

★ **Tabard Inn**   BOUTIQUE HOTEL **$$**
(☎202-785-1277; www.tabardinn.com; 1739 N St NW; r $200-270, without bathroom $115-170; ❖✳@🛜; M Red Line to Dupont Circle) Named

for the inn in *The Canterbury Tales*, the Tabard spreads through a trio of Victorian-era row houses. The 40 rooms are hard to generalize: all come with vintage quirks such as iron bed frames and wing-backed chairs, though little accents distinguish them – a Matisse-like painted headboard here, Amish-looking quilts there. There are no TVs, and wi-fi can be dodgy, but the of-yore atmospherics prevail.

Adams Morgan

Adam's Inn
B&B $

(☎202-745-3600; www.adamsinn.com; 1746 Lanier Pl NW; r $109-204, without bathroom $89-110; P❂❀@☎; Ⓜ️Red Line to Woodley Park-Zoo/Adams Morgan) Tucked on a shady residential street, this 27-room inn is known for its personalized service, fluffy linens and handy location just a few blocks from 18th St's global smorgasbord. Inviting, homey rooms sprawl through two adjacent townhouses and a carriage house. The common areas have a nice garden patio, and there's a general sense of sherry-scented chintz.

HighRoad Hostel
HOSTEL $

(☎202-735-3622; www.highroadhostels.com; 1804 Belmont Rd NW; dm $42-60; ❂☎; Ⓜ️Red Line to Woodley Park-Zoo/Adams Morgan) HighRoad's Victorian row house exterior belies its brand spankin' new interior. The mod dorms come in various configurations: from four to 14 beds – some co-ed, others gender-specific. All have stark white walls, gray metal bunks and black lockers. There's a fancy (though small) community kitchen and common room with a fireplace and a jumbo, Netflix-wired TV. Nighthawks will gorge on nearby 18th St's bounty.

Georgetown

Graham Georgetown
BOUTIQUE HOTEL $$

(☎202-337-0900; www.thegrahamgeorgetown.com; 1075 Thomas Jefferson St NW; r $300-375; P❂❀@☎; ☐Circulator) Set smack in the heart of Georgetown, the Graham occupies the intersection between stately tradition and modernist hip. Good-sized rooms have tasteful silver, cream and black furnishings with pops of ruby and geometric accents. Even the most basic rooms have linens by Liddell Ireland and L'Occitane bath amenities, which means you'll be as fresh, clean and beautiful as the surrounding Georgetown glitterati.

Eating

A homegrown foodie revolution has transformed the once buttoned-up DC dining scene. Driving it is the bounty of farms at the city's doorstep, along with the booming local economy and influx of worldly younger residents. Small, independent, local-chef-helmed spots now lead the way. And they're doing such a fine job that Michelin deemed the city worthy of its stars.

Capitol Hill

Capitol Hill has long been an outpost for the DC burger bar, the type of unpretentious spot where you roll up your sleeves, slather on ketchup and knock back a side of beer with your patty. Hip, upscale eateries have colonized the neighborhood, especially along Pennsylvania Ave, Barracks Row (ie 8th St SE, near the Marine Barracks) and around the Navy Yard (near the baseball park). H St NE, east of Union Station, has seen lots of action. The formerly beat-up area continues to transform with scads of fun, offbeat restaurants and bars stretching from 4th to 14th Sts NE.

Toki Underground
ASIAN $

(☎202-388-3086; www.tokiunderground.com; 1234 H St NE; mains $13-15; ☺11:30am-2:30pm & 5-10pm Mon-Thu, to midnight Fri & Sat; Ⓜ️Red Line to Union Station then streetcar) Spicy ramen noodles and dumplings sum up wee Toki's menu. Steaming pots obscure the busy chefs, while diners slurp and sigh contentedly. The eatery takes limited reservations, so there's typically a wait. Use the opportunity to explore the surrounding bars; Toki will text when your table is ready. The restaurant isn't signposted; look for the Pug bar, and Toki is above it.

Maine Avenue Fish Market
SEAFOOD $

(1100 Maine Ave SW; mains $7-13; ☺8am-9pm; Ⓜ️Orange, Silver, Blue, Yellow, Green Lines to L'Enfant Plaza) The pungent, open-air Maine Avenue Fish Market is a local landmark. No-nonsense vendors sell fish, crabs, oysters and other seafood so fresh it's almost still flopping. They'll kill, strip, shell, gut, fry or broil your selection, which you can take to the waterfront benches and eat blissfully (mind the seagulls!).

Jimmy T's
DINER $

(☎202-546-3646; 501 E Capitol St SE; mains $6-10; ☺6:30am-3pm Tue-Fri, from 8am Sat & Sun; ♿; Ⓜ️Orange, Silver, Blue Lines to Eastern Market)

WASHINGTON, DC & THE CAPITAL REGION WASHINGTON, DC

EAT STREETS

14th St NW (Logan Circle) DC's most happening road: an explosion of hot-chef bites and bars.

18th St NW (Adams Morgan) Korean, West African, Japanese and Latin mash-up, plus late-night snacks.

11th St NW (Columbia Heights) Ever-growing scene of hipster cafes and edgy gastropubs.

8th St SE (Capitol Hill) Known as Barracks Row, it's the locals' favorite for welcoming comfort food–type spots.

H St NE (Capitol Hill) Hip strip of pie cafes, noodle shops and foodie pubs.

Jimmy's is a neighborhood joint of the old school, where folks come in with their dogs, cram in to read the *Post,* have a burger or a coffee or an omelet (breakfast all day, by the way) and basically be themselves. If you're hungover on Sunday and in Cap Hill, come here for a greasy cure. Cash only.

Ted's Bulletin   AMERICAN **$$**
(☑202-544-8337; www.tedsbulletincapitolhill. com; 505 8th St SE; mains $11-19; ⊙7am-10:30pm Sun-Thu, to 11:30pm Fri & Sat; 🖾; Ⓜ Orange, Silver, Blue Lines to Eastern Market) Plop into a booth in the art-deco-meets-diner ambience, and loosen the belt. Beer biscuits and sausage gravy for breakfast, meatloaf with ketchup glaze for dinner and other hipster spins on comfort foods hit the table. You've got to admire a place that lets you substitute pop tarts for toast. Breakfast is available all day.

Ethiopic   ETHIOPIAN **$$**
(☑202-675-2066; www.ethiopicrestaurant.com; 401 H St NE; mains $13-19; ⊙5-10pm Tue-Thu, from noon Fri-Sun; 🖋; Ⓜ Red Line to Union Station) In a city with no shortage of Ethiopian joints, Ethiopic stands above the rest. Top marks go to the various *wats* (stews) and the signature *tibs* (sauteed meat and veg), derived from tender lamb that has sat in a bath of herbs and hot spices. Vegans get lots of love here too.

★**Rose's Luxury**   AMERICAN **$$$**
(☑202-580-8889; www.rosesluxury.com; 717 8th St SE; small plates $13-16, family-style plates $28-33; ⊙5-10pm Mon-Sat; Ⓜ Orange, Silver, Blue Lines to Eastern Market) Michelin-starred Rose's is one of DC's most buzzed-about eateries. Crowds fork into worldly Southern comfort food as twinkling lights glow overhead and candles flicker around the industrial, half-finished room. Rose's doesn't take reservations, but ordering your meal at the upstairs bar can save time (and the cocktails are delicious).

White House & Foggy Bottom

Woodward Takeout Food   AMERICAN **$**
(☑202-347-5355; http://woodwardtable.com; 1426 H St NW; mains $7-11; ⊙7:30am-4:30pm Mon-Fri; Ⓜ Orange, Silver, Blue Lines to McPherson Sq) Woodward Takeout is the small, mostly carryout adjunct to Woodward Table, a sharp, sit-down restaurant. Go ahead: jump in the line with all the office workers angling for the duck Reuben sandwich, housemade pastrami on sourdough rye or butternut squash flatbread. It'll move fast. Breakfast is busy too, with egg-laden sandwiches on crumbly biscuits and salted chocolate croissants flying from the kitchen.

A smattering of close-set tables provides seating. You can pre-order via the website and save some waiting time.

Founding Farmers   AMERICAN **$$**
(☑202-822-8783; www.wearefoundingfarmers. com; 1924 Pennsylvania Ave NW; mains $15-28; ⊙7am-10pm Mon, 7am-11pm Tue-Thu, 7am-midnight Fri, 9am-midnight Sat, 9am-10pm Sun; 🖋; Ⓜ Orange, Silver, Blue Lines to Foggy Bottom-GWU or Farragut West) 🍃 A frosty decor of pickled goods in jars adorns this buzzy dining space. The look is a combination of rustic-cool and modern art that reflects the nature of the food: locally sourced, New American fare. Buttermilk fried chicken and waffles, and butternut squash mascarpone ravioli, are a few of the favorites that hit the wood tables. The restaurant is located in the IMF building.

Downtown & Penn Quarter

★**A Baked Joint**   CAFE **$**
(☑202-408-6985; www.abakedjoint.com; 440 K St NW; mains $5-11; ⊙7am-8pm Mon-Thu, 7am-9pm Fri, 8am-8pm Sat & Sun; Ⓜ Red, Yellow, Green Lines to Gallery Pl-Chinatown) Order at the counter then take your luscious, heaped-on-housemade-bread sandwich – perhaps the roasted sweet potato and goat cheese on focaccia, or the Nutella and banana on whole-wheat sourdough – to a bench or table in the big,

open room. Natural light streams in the floor-to-ceiling windows. Not hungry? It's also a great place for a well-made latte.

Daikaya JAPANESE $
(☏ 202-589-1600; www.daikaya.com; 705 6th St NW; mains $12-14; ⏰ 11am-10pm Sun & Mon, to 10:30pm Tue & Wed, to 11pm Thu-Sat; Ⓜ Red, Yellow, Green Lines to Gallery Pl-Chinatown) Daikaya offers two options. Downstairs it's a casual ramen-noodle shop, where locals swarm in and slurp with friends in the slick wooden booths. Upstairs it's a sake-pouring Japanese *izakaya* (tavern), with rice-bowl lunches and fishy small plates for dinner. Note the upstairs closes between lunch and dinner (ie between 2pm and 5pm).

Rasika INDIAN $$
(☏ 202-637-1222; www.rasikarestaurant.com; 633 D St NW; mains $14-28; ⏰ 11:30am-2:30pm Mon-Fri, 5:30-10:30pm Mon-Thu, 5-11pm Fri & Sat; ☏; Ⓜ Green, Yellow Lines to Archives) Rasika is as cutting-edge as Indian food gets. The room resembles a Jaipur palace decorated by a flock of modernist art-gallery curators. Top marks go to the *murgh mussalam*, a plate of juicy tandoori chicken with cashews and quail eggs; and to the deceptively simple *dal* (lentils), which have just the right kiss of sharp fenugreek. Vegetarians will feel a lot of love here.

Matchbox Pizza PIZZA $$
(☏ 202-289-4441; www.matchboxrestaurants.com; 713 H St NW; 10in pizzas $13-15; ⏰ 11am-10:30pm Mon-Thu, 11am-11:30pm Fri, 10am-11:30pm Sat, 10am-10:30pm Sun; ☏; Ⓜ Red, Yellow, Green Lines to Gallery Pl-Chinatown) The pizza here has a devout following of gastronomes and the restaurant's warm, exposed-brick interior typically is packed. What's so good about it? Fresh ingredients, a thin, blistered crust baked by angels, and more fresh ingredients. Oh, and the beer list rocks, with Belgian ales and hopped-up craft brews flowing from the taps. Reserve ahead to avoid a wait.

Kinship AMERICAN $$
(☏ 202-737-7700; http://kinshipdc.com; 1015 7th St NW; mains $16-28; ⏰ 5:30-10pm Sat-Friday; Ⓜ Yellow, Green Lines to Mount Vernon Square 7th Street-Convention Center) Round up your friends and enjoy a convivial night at this Michelin-starred restaurant by Eric Ziebold. Pick and choose across the menu's five categories echoing the chef's passions: ingredients (surf clams, Rohan duck), history (classics), craft (using culinary techniques),

indulgence (caviar, white truffles), and 'For the Table.'

★ Dabney AMERICAN $$$
(☏ 202-450-1015; www.thedabney.com; 122 Blagden Alley NW; small plates $14-22; ⏰ 5:30-10pm Tue-Thu, 5:30-11pm Fri & Sat, 5-10pm Sun; Ⓜ Green, Yellow Line to Mount Vernon Square/7th St-Convention Center) Chef Jeremiah Langhorne studied historic cookbooks, discovering recipes that used local ingredients and lesser-explored flavors in his quest to resuscitate mid-Atlantic cuisine lost to the ages. Most of the dishes are even cooked over a wood-burning hearth. But this isn't George Washington's resto. Chef Langhorne has given it all a modern twist – enough to earn him a Michelin star.

🍴 Logan Circle, U Street & Columbia Heights

★ Ben's Chili Bowl AMERICAN $
(☏ 202-667-0909; www.benschilibowl.com; 1213 U St; mains $6-10; ⏰ 6am-2am Mon-Thu, 6am-4am Fri, 7am-4am Sat, 11am-midnight Sun; Ⓜ Green, Yellow Lines to U St) Ben's is a DC institution. The main stock in trade is half-smokes, DC's meatier, smokier version of the hot dog, usually slathered with mustard, onions and the namesake chili. For nearly 60 years presidents, rock stars and Supreme Court justices have come in to indulge in the humble diner, but despite the hype, Ben's remains a true neighborhood establishment. Cash only.

★ Compass Rose INTERNATIONAL $$
(☏ 202-506-4765; www.compassrosedc.com; 1346 T St NW; small plates $10-15; ⏰ 5pm-2am Mon-Thu, 5pm-3am Fri & Sat, 11am-2am Sun; Ⓜ Green, Yellow Lines to U St) Compass Rose feels like a secret garden, set in a discreet townhouse a whisker from 14th St's buzz. The exposed brick walls, rustic wood decor and sky-blue ceiling give it a casually romantic air. The menu is a mash-up of global comfort foods, so dinner might entail, say, a Chilean *lomito* (pork sandwich), Lebanese *kefta* (ground lamb and spices) and Georgian *khachapuri* (buttery, cheese-filled bread).

Estadio SPANISH $$
(☏ 202-319-1404; www.estadio-dc.com; 1520 14th St NW; tapas $6-17; ⏰ 5-10pm Mon-Thu, to 11pm Fri & Sat, to 9pm Sun, 11:30am-2pm Fri-Sun; Ⓜ Green, Yellow Lines to U St) Estadio buzzes with a low-lit, date-night vibe. The tapas menu (which

is the focus) is as deep as an ocean trench. There are three variations of *Iberico* ham and a delicious foie gras, scrambled egg and truffle open-faced sandwich. Wash it down with some traditional *calimocho* (red wine and Coke). No reservations after 6pm, which usually means a wait at the bar.

Busboys & Poets
CAFE **$$**

(☎ 202-387-7638; www.busboysandpoets.com; 2021 14th St NW; mains $11-21; � 8am-midnight Mon-Thu, 8am-2am Fri, from 9am Sat & Sun; ☎; Ⓜ Green, Yellow Lines to U St) Busboys & Poets is one of U St's linchpins. Locals pack the place for coffee, wi-fi and a progressive vibe (and attached bookstore) that make San Francisco feel conservative. The hearty menu spans sandwiches, pizzas and Southern fare like shrimp and grits. Tuesday night's open-mike poetry reading ($5 admission, from 9pm to 11pm) draws big crowds.

Maple
ITALIAN **$$**

(☎ 202-588-7442; www.dc-maple.com; 3418 11th St NW; mains $16-23; � 5:30-11:30pm Mon-Thu, 5pm-1am Fri, 10:30am-1am Sat, 10:30am-11pm Sun; Ⓜ Green, Yellow Lines to Columbia Heights) At snug Maple, ladies in thrifty dresses and black tights fork into rich pasta dishes next to guys clad in T-shirts and tattoo sleeves on a reclaimed wood bar. Housemade *limoncello*, Italian and craft beers, and unusual wine varietals also move across the lengthy slab.

Bistro Bohem
EASTERN EUROPEAN **$$**

(☎ 202-735-5895; www.bistrobohem.com; 600 Florida Ave NW; mains $14-22; �) 11am-10pm Mon, 11am-11pm Tue-Thu, 5pm-midnight Fri, 10am-midnight Sat, 10am-10pm Sun; ☎; Ⓜ Green, Yellow Lines to Shaw-Howard U) Cozy Bistro Bohem is a community favorite for its rib-sticking Czech schnitzels, goulash and pilsners, served with a side of local art on the walls and occasional Czech film screenings. The warm, bohemian environs make you swear you're in Prague.

Le Diplomate
FRENCH **$$$**

(☎ 202-332-3333; www.lediplomatedc.com; 1601 14th St NW; mains $23-35; �)during 5-11pm Mon-Thu, 5pm-midnight Fri, 9:30am-midnight Sat, 9:30am-11pm Sun; Ⓜ Green, Yellow Lines to U St) This charming French bistro is one of the hottest tables in town. DC celebrities galore cozy up in the leather banquettes and at the sidewalk tables. They come for an authentic slice of Paris, from the *coq au vin* (wine-braised chicken) and aromatic baguettes to the vintage curios and nudie photos decorating the bathrooms. Make reservations.

✖ Dupont Circle & Kalorama

Zorba's Cafe
GREEK **$**

(☎ 202-387-8555; www.zorbascafe.com; 1612 20th St NW; mains $13-16; �(·)11am-11:30pm Mon-Sat, to 10:30pm Sun; ☎; Ⓜ Red Line to Dupont Circle) Generous portions of moussaka and souvlaki, as well as pitchers of Rolling Rock beer, make family-run Zorba's Cafe one of DC's best bargain haunts. On warm days the outdoor patio packs with locals. With the bouzouki music playing, you can almost imagine you're in the Greek islands.

Afterwords Cafe
AMERICAN **$$**

(☎ 202-387-3825; www.kramers.com; 1517 Connecticut Ave NW; mains $17-21; �(·)7:30am-1am Sun-Thu, to 3am Fri & Sat; Ⓜ Red Line to Dupont Circle) Attached to Kramerbooks, this buzzing spot is not your average bookstore cafe. The packed indoor tables, wee bar and outdoor patio overflow with good cheer. The menu features tasty bistro fare and an ample beer selection, making it a prime spot for happy hour, for brunch and at all hours on weekends (open until 3am, baby!).

Browsing the stacks before stuffing the gut is many locals' favorite way to spend a Washington weekend.

★ Bistrot du Coin
FRENCH **$$**

(☎ 202-234-6969; www.bistrotducoin.com; 1738 Connecticut Ave NW; mains $16-29; �(·)11:30am-midnight Mon-Wed, 11:30am-1am Thu & Fri, noon-1am Sat, noon-midnight Sun; Ⓜ Red Line to Dupont Circle) The lively and much-loved Bistrot du Coin is a neighborhood favorite for roll-up-your sleeves, working-class French fare. The kitchen sends out consistently good onion soup, classic *steak-frites* (grilled steak and French fries), cassoulet, open-face sandwiches and nine varieties of its famous *moules* (mussels). Regional wines from around the motherland accompany the food by the glass, carafe and bottle.

★ Little Serow
THAI **$$$**

(www.littleserow.com; 1511 17th St NW; set menu $49; �(·)5:30-10pm Tue-Thu, to 10:30pm Fri & Sat; Ⓜ Red Line to Dupont Circle) Little Serow has no phone, no reservations and no sign on the door. It only seats groups of four or fewer (larger parties will be separated), but despite all this, people line up around the block. And what for? Superlative Northern Thai cuisine. The single-option menu – which consists of six or so hot-spiced courses – changes by the week.

FOOD TRUCKIN'

More than 150 food trucks roll in DC, and the White House neighborhood welcomes the mother lode. They congregate at Farragut Sq, Franklin Sq, the State Department and George Washington University on weekdays between 11:30am and 1:30pm. Follow the locals' lead, and stuff your face with a delicious meal for under $15 – maybe a lobster roll poached in butter or a bowl of Lao drunken noodles. Food Truck Fiesta (www.foodtruck fiesta.com) tracks the ever-evolving fleet via Twitter. Here are some favorites:

Lilypad on the Run (twitter.com/LilypadontheRun) Ethiopian meat and veggie combos that make you want to lick the styrofoam container.

Far East Taco Grille (twitter.com/fareasttg) Asian-flavored tacos using meats or tofu, corn or flour tortillas.

DC Pie Truck (twitter.com/ThePieTruckDC) The Dangerously Delicious piemakers swing out in two big red trucks. Sweet and savory slices emerge from the windows. Pies range from spinach with goat cheese, to chocolate cream, and coconut chess.

Red Hook Lobster Truck (twitter.com/LobsterTruckDC) Take your pick: mayo-based, Maine-style lobster rolls or butter-slathered Connecticut-style rolls.

Komi
FUSION $$$

(202-332-9200; www.komirestaurant.com; 1509 17th St NW; set menu $150; 5:30-10pm Tue-Sat; Red Line to Dupont Circle) There is an admirable simplicity to Komi's changing menu, which is rooted in Greece and influenced by everything – primarily genius. Dinner comprises 12 or so dishes; say suckling pig, scallops and truffles, or roasted baby goat. Komi's fairy-tale of a dining space doesn't take groups larger than four, and you need to reserve in advance. Call a month before your desired dining date.

Hank's Oyster Bar
SEAFOOD $$$

(202-462 4265; www.hanksoysterbar.com; 1624 Q St NW; mains $22-30; 11:30am-1am Mon & Tue, 11:30am-2am Wed-Fri, 11am-2am Sat, 11am-1am Sun; Red Line to Dupont Circle) DC has several oyster bars, but mini-chain Hank's is our favorite, mixing power-player muscle with good-old-boy ambience. As you'd expect, the oyster menu is extensive and excellent; there are always at least four varieties on hand. Quarters are cramped, and you often have to wait for a table – nothing a sake oyster bomb won't fix.

✖ Adams Morgan

Diner
AMERICAN $

(202-232-8800; www.dinerdc.com; 2453 18th St NW; mains $9-18; 24hr; Red Line to Woodley Park-Zoo/Adams Morgan) The Diner serves hearty comfort food, any time of the day or night. It's ideal for wee-hour breakfast scarf-downs, weekend Bloody Mary brunches (if you don't mind crowds) or any time you want unfussy, well-prepared American fare. Omelets, fat pancakes, mac 'n' cheese, grilled tofu tacos and burgers hit the tables with aplomb. It's a good spot for kids, too.

★ Donburi
JAPANESE $

(202-629-1047; www.facebook.com/donburidc; 2438 18th St NW; mains $10-15; 11am-10pm; Red Line to Woodley Park-Zoo/Adams Morgan) Hole-in-the-wall Donburi has 15 seats at a wooden counter where you get a front-row view of the slicing, dicing chefs. *Donburi* means 'bowl' in Japanese, and that's what arrives steaming hot and filled with, say, panko-coated shrimp atop rice and blended with the house's sweet-and-savory sauce. It's a simple, authentic meal. There's often a line, but it moves quickly. No reservations.

Julia's Empanadas
LATIN AMERICAN $

(202-328-6232; www.juliasempanadas.com; 2452 18th St NW; empanadas from $5; 10am-midnight Mon-Thu, to 4am Fri & Sat, to 8pm Sun; Red Line to Woodley Park-Zoo/Adams Morgan) A frequent winner in DC's 'best late-night eats' polls, Julia's stuffs its dough bombs with chorizo, Jamaican beef curry, spinach and more. Flavors peak if you've been drinking. The little chain has a handful of takeaway shops around town. Cash only.

★ Tail Up Goat
MEDITERRANEAN $$

(202-986-9600; www.tailupgoat.com; 1827 Adams Mill Rd NW; mains $18-27; 5:30-10pm Mon-Thu, 5-10pm Fri-Sun; Red Line to Woodley Park-Zoo/Adams Morgan) With its pale blue walls, light wood decor and lantern-like lights dangling overhead, Tail Up Goat wafts a warm, island-y vibe. The lamb ribs are the specialty – crispy and lusciously fatty, with grilled lemon, figs and spices. The house-made breads and spreads star on the menu too – say, flaxseed sourdough with beets. No wonder Michelin gave it a star.

Georgetown

★ Simply Banh Mi VIETNAMESE $
(☎202-333-5726; www.simplybanhmidc.com; 1624 Wisconsin Ave NW; ⊙11am-7pm Tue-Sun; ⚑; ⧉Circulator) There's nothing fancy about the small, below-street-level space, and the compact menu sticks mostly to sandwiches and bubble tea. But the owners know how to take a crusty baguette, stuff it with delicious lemongrass pork or other meat (or tofu), and make your day.

Baked & Wired BAKERY $
(☎202-333-2500; www.bakedandwired.com; 1052 Thomas Jefferson St NW; baked goods $3-6; ⊙7am-8pm Mon-Thu, 7am-9pm Fri, 8am-9pm Sat, 8am-8pm Sun; ⧉Circulator) Sniff out Baked & Wired, a cheery cafe that whips up beautifully made coffees, bacon cheddar buttermilk biscuits and enormous cupcakes (like the banana and peanut-butter-frosted Elvis). It's a fine spot to join university students and cyclists coming off the nearby trails.

Chez Billy Sud FRENCH $$$
(☎202-965-2606; www.chezbillysud.com; 1039 31st St NW; mains $26-37; ⊙11:30am-2pm Tue-Fri, 11am-2pm Sat & Sun, plus 5-10pm Tue-Thu & Sun, 5-11pm Fri & Sat; ⧉Circulator) An endearing little bistro tucked away on a residential block, Billy's mint-green walls, gilt mirrors and wee marble bar exude laid-back elegance. Mustachioed servers bring baskets of warm bread to the white linen–clothed tables, along with crackling pork and pistachio sausage, golden trout, tuna niçoise salad and plump cream puffs.

Drinking & Nightlife

When Andrew Jackson swore the oath of office in 1800, the self-proclaimed populist dispensed with pomp and circumstance and, quite literally, threw a raging kegger. Folks got so gone they started looting art from the White House. The historical lesson: DC loves a drink, and these days it enjoys said tipples in many incarnations besides executive-mansion-trashing throwdowns.

Capitol Hill

Copycat Co COCKTAIL BAR
(☎202-241-1952; www.copycatcompany.com; 1110 H St NE; ⊙5pm-2am Sun-Thu, to 3am Fri & Sat; ⧆Red Line to Union Station then streetcar) When you walk into Copycat it feels like a Chinese fast-food restaurant. That's because it is (sort of) on the 1st floor, where Chinese street-food nibbles are available. The fizzy drinks and egg-white-topped cocktails fill glasses upstairs, in the dimly lit, speakeasy-meets-opium-den-vibed bar. Staff are unassuming and gracious in helping newbies with the lengthy menu.

Little Miss Whiskey's Golden Dollar BAR
(www.littlemisswhiskeys.com; 1104 H St NE; ⊙5pm-2am Sun-Thu, to 3am Fri & Sat; ⧆Red Line to Union Station then streetcar) If Alice had returned from Wonderland so traumatized by her near beheading that she needed a stiff drink, we imagine she'd pop down to Little Miss Whiskey's. She'd love the whimsical-meets-dark-nightmares decor. And she'd probably have fun with the club kids partying on the upstairs dance floor on weekends.

Bluejacket Brewery BREWERY
(☎202-524-4862; www.bluejacketdc.com; 300 Tingey St SE; ⊙11am-1am Sun-Thu, to 2am Fri & Sat; ⧆Green Line to Navy Yard) Beer-lovers' heads will explode in Bluejacket. Pull up a stool at the mod-industrial bar, gaze at the silvery tanks bubbling up the ambitious brews, then make the hard decision about which of the 25 tap beers you want to try. A dry-hopped kolsch? Sweet-spiced stout? A cask-aged farmhouse ale? Four-ounce tasting pours help with decision-making.

Granville Moore's PUB
(☎202-399-2546; www.granvillemoores.com; 1238 H St NE; ⊙5pm-midnight Mon-Thu, 5pm-3am Fri, 11am-3am Sat, 11am-midnight Sun; ⧆Red Line to Union Station then streetcar) Besides being one of DC's best places to grab frites and a steak sandwich, Granville Moore's has an extensive Belgian beer menu that should satisfy any fan of low-country boozing. With its raw, wooden fixtures and walls that look as if they were made from daub and mud, the interior resembles a medieval barracks. The fireside setting is ideal on a winter's eve.

Tune Inn BAR
(☎202-543-2725; 331 Pennsylvania Ave SE; ⊙8am-2am Sun-Thu, to 3am Fri & Sat; ⧆Orange, Silver, Blue Lines to Capitol South or Eastern Market)

Dive bar Tune Inn has been around for decades and is where the neighborhood's older residents come to knock back Budweisers. The mounted deer heads and antler chandelier set the mood, as greasy-spoon grub and all-day breakfasts get scarfed in the vinyl-backed booths.

White House & Foggy Bottom

★ Off The Record   BAR
(📞 202-638-6600; 800 16th St NW, Hay-Adams Hotel; ⊗ 11:30am-midnight Sun-Thu, to 12:30am Fri & Sat; Ⓜ Orange, Silver, Blue Lines to McPherson Sq) Intimate red booths and a hidden basement location in one of the city's most prestigious hotels, right across from the White House – no wonder DC's important people submerge to be seen and not heard (as the tagline goes) at Off The Record. Experienced bartenders swirl martinis and Manhattans for the suit-wearing crowd. Groovy framed political caricatures hang on the walls.

Downtown & Penn Quarter

★ Columbia Room   COCKTAIL BAR
(📞 202-316-9396; www.columbiaroomdc.com; 124 Blagden Alley NW; ⊗ 5pm-12:30am Tue-Thu, to 1:30am Fri & Sat; Ⓜ Green, Yellow Lines to Mt Vernon Sq/7th St-Convention Center) Serious mixology goes on at Columbia Room, the kind of place that sources spring water from Kentucky to Scotland, and uses pickled cherry blossom and barley tea among its ingredients. But it's done in a refreshingly non-snooty environment. Choose from three distinct areas: the festive Punch Garden on the outdoor roof deck, the comfy, leather-chair-dotted Spirits Library or the 14-seat, prix-fixe Tasting Room.

Logan Circle, U Street & Columbia Heights

★ Right Proper Brewing Co   BREWERY
(📞 202-607-2337; www.rightproperbrewery.com; 624 T St NW; ⊗ 5pm-midnight Mon-Thu, 11:30am-1am Fri & Sat, 11:30am-11pm Sun; Ⓜ Green, Yellow Lines to Shaw-Howard U) As if the artwork – a chalked mural of the National Zoo's giant pandas with laser eyes destroying downtown DC – wasn't enough, Right Proper Brewing Co makes sublime ales in a building where Duke Ellington used to play pool. It's the Shaw district's neighborhood clubhouse, a big, sunny space filled with folks gabbing at reclaimed wood tables.

BEER
....
The city is serious about beer. It even brews much of its own delicious stuff. That trend started in 2009, when DC Brau became the District's first brewery to launch in more than 50 years. Several more beer makers followed. As you drink around town, keep an eye out for local concoctions from 3 Stars, Atlas Brew Works, Hellbender and Lost Rhino (from northern Virginia).

★ Dacha Beer Garden   BEER GARDEN
(📞 202-350-9888; www.dachadc.com; 1600 7th St NW; ⊗ 4-10:30pm Mon-Thu, noon-midnight Fri & Sat, 11am-10:30pm Sun; Ⓜ Green, Yellow Lines to Shaw-Howard U) Happiness reigns in Dacha's freewheeling beer garden. Kids and dogs bound around the picnic tables, while adults hoist glass boots filled with German brews. When the weather gets nippy, staff bring heaters and blankets and stoke the fire pit. And it all takes place under the sultry gaze of Elizabeth Taylor (or a mural of her, which sprawls across the back wall).

Churchkey   BAR
(📞 202-567-2576; www.churchkeydc.com; 1337 14th St NW; ⊗ 4pm-1am Mon-Thu, 4pm-2am Fri, 11:30am-2am Sat, 11:30am-1am Sun; Ⓜ Orange, Silver, Blue Lines to McPherson Sq) Coppery, mod-industrial Churchkey glows with hipness. Fifty beers flow from the taps, including five brain-walloping, cask-aged ales. If none of those please you, another 500 types of brew are available by bottle (including gluten-free suds). Churchkey is the upstairs counterpart to Birch & Barley (📞 202-567-2576; www.birchandbarley.com; mains $16-29; ⊗ 5:30-10pm Tue-Thu, 5:30-11pm Fri & Sat, 11am-8pm Sun), a popular nouveau comfort-food restaurant, and you can order much of its menu at the bar.

Cork Wine Bar   WINE BAR
(📞 202-265-2675; www.corkdc.com; 1720 14th St NW; ⊗ 5pm-midnight Tue & Wed, 5pm-1am Thu-Sat, 11am-3pm & 5-10pm Sun; Ⓜ Green, Yellow Lines to U St) This dark 'n' cozy wine bar manages to come off as foodie magnet and friendly neighborhood hangout all at once, which is a feat. Around 50 smart wines are available by the glass and 160 types by the bottle. Accompanying nibbles include cheese and charcuterie platters.

U Street Music Hall
CLUB

(☑202-588-1889; www.ustreetmusichall.com; 1115 U St NW; ⊙hours vary; Ⓜ Green, Yellow Lines to U St) This is the spot to get your groove on sans the VIP/bottle service crowd. Two local DJs own and operate the basement club. It looks like a no-frills rock bar, but it has a pro sound system, a cork-cushioned dance floor and other accoutrements of a serious dance club. Alternative bands also thrash a couple of nights per week to keep it fresh.

🍸 Dupont Circle & Kalorama

Bar Charley
BAR

(☑202-627-2183; www.barcharley.com; 1825 18th St NW; ⊙5pm-12:30am Mon-Thu, 4pm-1:30am Fri, 10am-1:30am Sat, 10am-12:30am Sun; Ⓜ Red Line to Dupont Circle) Bar Charley draws a mixed crowd from the neighborhood – young, old, gay and straight. They come for groovy cocktails sloshing in vintage glassware and ceramic tiki mugs, served at very reasonable prices by DC standards. Try the gin and gingery Suffering Bastard. The beer list isn't huge, but it is thoughtfully chosen with some wild ales. Around 60 wines are available too.

Board Room
BAR

(☑202-518-7666; www.boardroomdc.com; 1737 Connecticut Ave NW; ⊙4pm-2am Mon-Thu, 4pm-3am Fri, noon-3am Sat, noon-2am Sun; Ⓜ Red Line to Dupont Circle) Grab a table, pull up a stool and crush your opponent at Hungry Hungry Hippos. Or summon spirits with a Ouija board. Board Room lets you flash back to childhood via its stacks of board games. Battleship, Risk, Operation – name it, and it's available to rent for $2.

JR's
GAY

(☑202-328-0090; www.jrsbar-dc.com; 1519 17th St NW; ⊙4pm-2am Mon-Thu, 4pm-3am Fri, 1pm-3am Sat, 1pm-2am Sun; Ⓜ Red Line to Dupont Circle) Button-down shirts are de rigueur at this popular gay hangout frequented by the 20- and 30-something, work-hard-and-play-hard set. Some DC residents claim that the crowd at JR's epitomizes the conservative nature of the capital's gay scene, but even if you love to hate it, as many do, JR's knows how to rock a happy hour and is teeming more often than not.

Cobalt
GAY

(☑202-232-4416; www.cobaltdc.com; 1639 R St NW; ⊙4pm-2am Sun-Thu, to 3am Fri & Sat; Ⓜ Red Line to Dupont Circle) Featuring lots of hair product and buff gym bodies, Cobalt tends to gather a well-dressed late-20s to 30-something crowd who come for fun (but loud!) dance parties throughout the week. The time-hallowed dance club is on the 3rd floor; the venue also has a restaurant on the 1st floor and a lounge on the 2nd.

🍸 Adams Morgan

★ Dan's Cafe
BAR

(☑202-265-0299; 2315 18th St NW; ⊙7pm-2am Tue-Thu, to 3am Fri & Sat; Ⓜ Red Line to Woodley Park-Zoo/Adams Morgan) This is one of DC's great dive bars. The interior looks sort of like an evil Elks Club, all unironically old-school 'art,' cheap paneling and dim lights barely illuminating the unapologetic slumminess. It's famed for its whopping, mix-it-yourself drinks, where you get a ketchup-type squirt bottle of booze, a can of soda and bucket of ice for barely $20. Cash only.

LGBT DC

DC is one of the most gay-friendly cities in the USA. It has an admirable track record of progressivism and a fair bit of scene to boot. The rainbow stereotype here consists of well-dressed professionals and activists working in politics on LGBT issues such as gay marriage (legal in DC since 2010). The community concentrates in Dupont Circle, but U Street, Shaw, Capitol Hill and Logan Circle also have lots of gay-friendly businesses.

Capital Area Gay & Lesbian Chamber of Commerce (www.caglcc.org) Sponsors lots of networking events around town.

LGBT DC (https://washington.org/lgbtq) The DC tourism office's portal with events, neighborhood breakdowns and a travel resource guide.

Metro Weekly (www.metroweekly.com) Free weekly news magazine. Aimed at a younger demographic than its rival, the *Washington Blade*.

Washington Blade (www.washingtonblade.com) Free weekly gay newspaper. Covers politics and has lots of business and nightlife listings.

Songbyrd Record Cafe & Music House
CAFE

(☑202-450-2917; www.songbyrddc.com; 2477 18th St NW; ⊙8am-2am Sun-Thu, to 3am Fri & Sat; 🛜; Ⓜ Red Line to Woodley Park-Zoo/Adams Morgan) By day hang out in the retro cafe, drinking excellent coffee, munching delicious sandwiches and browsing the small selection of soul and indie LPs for sale. You can even cut your own record in the vintage recording booth ($15). By night the party moves to the bar, where beer and cocktails flow alongside burgers and tacos, and indie bands rock the basement club.

🏛 Georgetown

Tombs
PUB

(☑202-337-6668; www.tombs.com; 1226 36th St NW; ⊙11:30am-1:30am Mon-Thu, to 2:30am Fri & Sat, 9:30am-1:30am Sun; 🚐Circulator) Every college of a certain pedigree has 'that' bar – the one where faculty and students alike sip pints under athletic regalia of the old school. The Tombs is Georgetown's contribution to the genre. If it looks familiar, think back to the '80s: the subterranean pub was one of the settings for the film *St Elmo's Fire.*

☆ Entertainment

Live Music

★Black Cat
LIVE MUSIC

(☑202-667-4490; www.blackcatdc.com; 1811 14th St NW; Ⓜ Green, Yellow Lines to U St) A pillar of DC's rock and indie scene since the 1990s, the battered Black Cat has hosted all the greats of years past (White Stripes, the Strokes, and Arcade Fire among others). If you don't want to pony up for $20-a-ticket bands on the upstairs main stage (or the smaller Backstage below), head to the Red Room for the jukebox, billiards, pinball and strong cocktails.

9:30 Club
LIVE MUSIC

(☑202-265-0930; www.930.com; 815 V St NW; Ⓜ Green, Yellow Lines to U St) The 9:30, which can pack 1200 people into a surprisingly compact venue, is the granddaddy of the live-music scene in DC. Pretty much every big name that comes through town ends up on this stage, and a concert here is the first-gig memory of many a DC-area teenager. Headliners usually take the stage between 10:30pm and 11:30pm. Tickets range from $20 to $35.

Performing Arts

★Kennedy Center
PERFORMING ARTS

(☑202-467-4600; www.kennedy-center.org; 2700 F St NW; Ⓜ Orange, Silver, Blue Lines to Foggy Bottom-GWU) Sprawled on 17 acres along the Potomac River, the magnificent Kennedy Center hosts a staggering array of performances – more than 2000 each year among its multiple venues including the Concert Hall (home to the National Symphony) and Opera House (home to the National Opera). A free shuttle bus runs to and from the Metro station every 15 minutes from 9:45am (noon on Sunday) to midnight.

Shakespeare Theatre Company
THEATER

(☑202-547-1122; www.shakespearetheatre.org; 450 7th St NW; Ⓜ Green, Yellow Lines to Archives) The nation's foremost Shakespeare company presents masterful works by the bard, as well as plays by George Bernard Shaw, Oscar Wilde, Eugene O'Neill and other greats. The season spans about a half-dozen productions annually, plus a free summer Shakespeare series on site for two weeks in late August.

Woolly Mammoth Theatre Company
THEATER

(☑202-393-3939; www.woollymammoth.net; 641 D St NW; Ⓜ Green, Yellow Lines to Archives) Woolly Mammoth is the edgiest of DC's experimental groups. For most shows, $20 'stampede' seats are available at the box office two hours before performances. They're limited in number, and sold first-come, first-served, so get there early.

Capitol Steps
COMEDY

(☑202-397-7328; www.capsteps.com; Ronald Reagan Bldg, 1300 Pennsylvania Ave NW; tickets $40.50; ⊙shows 7:30pm Fri & Sat; Ⓜ Orange, Silver, Blue Lines to Federal Triangle) This singing troupe claims to be the only group in America that tries to be funnier than Congress. It's composed of current and former congressional staffers, so they know their political stuff, although sometimes it can be overtly corny. The satirical, bipartisan jokes poke fun at both sides of the spectrum.

Sports

★Nationals Park
STADIUM

(☑202-675-6287; www.mlb.com/nationals; 1500 S Capitol St SE; 🛜; Ⓜ Green Line to Navy Yard) The major-league Washington Nationals play baseball at this spiffy stadium beside the Anacostia River. Don't miss the mid-fourth-inning 'Racing Presidents' – an odd foot race between giant-headed caricatures of George Washington, Abraham Lincoln, Thomas Jefferson, Teddy Roosevelt and William Taft. Hip bars and eateries and playful green spaces surround the ballpark, and more keep coming as the area gentrifies.

ℹ Information

Cultural Tourism DC (www.culturaltourismdc.org) Neighborhood-oriented events and tours.

Destination DC (www.washington.org) Official tourism site packed with sightseeing and event info.

Lonely Planet (www.lonelyplanet.com/usa/washington-dc) Destination information, hotel bookings, traveler forum and more.

Washingtonian (www.washingtonian.com) Features on dining, entertainment and local luminaries.

ℹ Getting There & Away

AIR

Washington Dulles International Airport (IAD; www.flydulles.com) is in the Virginia suburbs 26 miles west of DC. It has free wi-fi, several currency exchanges and restaurants throughout the terminals. Famed architect Eero Saarinen designed the swooping main building. The Metro Silver Line is slated to reach Dulles in late 2019, providing a transfer-free ride at long last.

Ronald Reagan Washington National Airport (DCA; www.flyreagan.com) is 4.5 miles south of downtown in Arlington, VA. There's free wi-fi, several eateries and a currency exchange (National Hall, Concourse Level).

Baltimore/Washington International Thurgood Marshall Airport (BWI; ☎ 410-859-7111; www.bwiairport.com) is 30 miles northeast of DC in Maryland.

BUS

Cheap bus services to and from Washington abound. Most charge $25 to $30 for a one-way trip to NYC (it takes four to five hours). Many companies use Union Station as their hub; other pick-up locations are scattered around town, but are always Metro-accessible. Tickets usually need to be bought online, but can sometimes be purchased on the bus itself if there are still seats available.

BestBus (☎ 202-332-2691; www.bestbus.com; 20th St & Massachusetts Ave NW; 🖥; Ⓜ Red Line to Dupont Circle) Several trips to/from NYC daily. The main bus stop is by Dupont Circle; there's another at Union Station.

BoltBus (☎ 877-265-8287; www.boltbus.com; 50 Massachusetts Ave NE; 🖥; Ⓜ Red

Line to Union Station) It goes to NYC multiple times each day, and to other east-coast cities. Lateness and spotty wi-fi can be issues. It uses Union Station as its terminal.

Greyhound (☎ 202-589-5141; www.greyhound.com; 50 Massachusetts Ave NE; Ⓜ Red Line to Union Station) Provides nationwide service. The terminal is at Union Station.

Megabus (☎ 877-462-6342; http://us.megabus.com; 50 Massachusetts Ave NE; 🖥; Ⓜ Red Line to Union Station) Offers the most trips to NYC (around 20 per day), as well as other east-coast cities; arrives at/departs from Union Station. Buses run behind schedule fairly often.

Peter Pan Bus Lines (☎ 800-343-9999; www.peterpanbus.com; 50 Massachusetts Ave NE; Ⓜ Red Line to Union Station) Travels throughout the northeastern USA; has its terminal at Union Station.

Vamoose Bus (☎ 212-695-6766; www.vamoosebus.com; 1801 N Lynn St) Service between NYC and Arlington, VA (the stop is near the Rosslyn Metro station).

Washington Deluxe (☎ 866-287-6932; www.washny.com; 1610 Connecticut St NW; 🖥; Ⓜ Red Line to Dupont Circle) Good express service to/from NYC. It has stops at both Dupont Circle and Union Station.

TRAIN

Magnificent, beaux-arts **Union Station** (www.unionstationdc.com; 50 Massachusetts Ave NE; Ⓜ Union Station) is the city's rail hub. There's a handy Metro station (Red Line) here for transport onward in the city.

Amtrak (www.amtrak.com) arrives at least once per hour from major east-coast cities. Northeast Regional trains are cheaper but slower (about 3½ hours between NYC and DC).

Acela Express trains are more expensive but faster (two hours and 45 minutes between NYC and DC; 6½ hours between Boston and DC). The express trains also have bigger seats and other business class amenities.

MARC trains (www.mta.maryland.gov) arrive frequently from downtown Baltimore (one hour) and other Maryland towns, as well as Harpers Ferry, WV.

ℹ Getting Around

The Metro is the main way to move around the city. Buy a rechargeable SmarTrip card at any Metro station. You must use the card to enter *and* exit station turnstiles.

Metro Fast, frequent, ubiquitous (except during weekend track maintenance). It operates between 5am and midnight (3am on Friday and Saturday). Fares from $1.85 to $6 depending on distance traveled. A day pass costs $14.50.

DC Circulator bus Useful for the Mall, Georgetown, Adams Morgan and other areas with limited Metro service. Fare is $1.

Bicycle Capital Bikeshare stations are everywhere; a day pass costs $8.

Taxi Relatively easy to find (less so at night), but costly. The ride-hailing companies Uber, Lyft and Via are used more in the District.

TO/FROM THE AIRPORT

Washington Dulles International Airport

Washington Flyer's (www.washfly.com) Silver Line Express bus runs every 15 to 20 minutes from Dulles (main terminal, arrivals level door 4) to the Wiehle-Reston East Metro station between 6am and 10:40pm (from 7:45am weekends). Total time to DC's center is 60 to 75 minutes; total bus-Metro cost around $11.

Metrobus 5A (www.wmata.com) runs every 30 to 40 minutes from Dulles to Rosslyn Metro (Blue, Orange and Silver Lines) and on to central DC (L'Enfant Plaza) between 5:50am (6:30am weekends) and 11:35pm. Total time to the center is around 60 minutes; total fare is $7.

The Supershuttle (www.supershuttle.com) door-to-door shared van service goes downtown for $30. It takes 30 to 60 minutes and runs from 5:30am to 12:30am.

Taxi rides to the city center take 30 to 60 minutes (depending on traffic) and cost $62 to $73. Follow the 'Ground Transportation' or 'Taxi' signs to where they queue.

Ronald Reagan Washington National Airport

The airport has its own Metro (www.wmata.com) station on the Blue and Yellow Lines. Trains (around $2.60) depart every 10 minutes or so between 5am and midnight (to 3am Friday and Saturday); they reach the city center in 20 minutes. It connects to the concourse level of terminals B and C.

The Supershuttle (www.supershuttle.com) door-to-door shared van service goes downtown for $16. It takes 10 to 30 minutes and runs from 5:30am to 12:30am.

Rides to the city center take 10 to 30 minutes (depending on traffic) and cost $15 to $22. Taxis queue outside the baggage-claim area at each terminal.

Baltimore-Washington International Thurgood Marshall Airport

Metrobus B30 (www.wmata.com) runs from BWI to the Greenbelt Metro station (last stop on the Green Line); it departs every 40 minutes from bus stops on the lower level of the international concourse and concourse A/B. The total bus-Metro fare is about $11. Total trip time is around 75 minutes.

The Supershuttle (www.supershuttle.com) door-to-door shared-van service goes to downtown DC for $37. The ride takes 45 minutes to an hour and runs from 5:30am to 12:30am.

A taxi to DC takes 45 minutes or so and costs $90. Taxis queue outside the baggage claim area of the Marshall terminal.

Both MARC (Maryland Rail Commuter; www.mta.maryland.gov) and Amtrak (www.amtrak.com) trains travel to DC's Union Station. They depart from a terminal 1 mile from BWI; a free bus shuttles passengers there. Trains leave once or twice per hour, but there's no service after 9:30pm (and limited service on weekends). It takes 30 to 40 minutes; fares start at $7.

MARYLAND

The nickname 'America in Miniature' perfectly captures Maryland: this small state possesses all of the best bits of the country, from the Appalachian Mountains in the west to sandy white beaches in the east. A blend of Northern streetsmarts and Southern down-home appeal gives this osmotic border state an appealing identity crisis. Its main city, Baltimore, is a sharp, demanding port town; the Eastern Shore jumbles art-and-antique-minded city refugees and working fishermen; while the DC suburbs are packed with government and office workers seeking green space, and the poor seeking lower rents. Yet it all somehow works – scrumptious blue crabs, Natty Boh beer and lovely Chesapeake country being the glue that binds it all. This is also an extremely diverse and progressive state, and was one of the first in the country to legalize gay marriage.

History

George Calvert established Maryland as a refuge for persecuted English Catholics in 1634 when he purchased St Mary's City from the local Piscataway tribe, with whom he initially tried to coexist. Puritan refugees drove both Piscataway and Catholics from control and shifted power to Annapolis; their harassment of Catholics produced the Tolerance Act, a flawed but progressive law that allowed freedom of any (Christian) worship in Maryland – a North American first.

A commitment to diversity has always characterized this state, despite a mixed record on slavery. Although state loyalties were split during the Civil War, a Confederate invasion was halted here in 1862 at Antietam. Following the war, Maryland harnessed its black, white and immigrant work

SCENIC DRIVE: MARITIME MARYLAND

Maryland and Chesapeake Bay have always been inextricable, but there are some places where the old-fashioned way of life on the bay seems to have changed little over the passing centuries.

About 150 miles south of Baltimore, at the edge of the Eastern Shore, is **Crisfield**, the top working water town in Maryland. Get visiting details at the **J Millard Tawes Historical Museum** (☑ 410-968-2501; www.crisfieldheritagefoundation.org/museum; 3 9th St, Crisfield; adult/child $3/1; ⊕ 11am-5pm Wed-Sat & 11am-3pm Sun Jun-Aug, closed rest of the year), which doubles as a visitor center. Any seafood you eat will be first-rate, but for a true Shore experience, **Watermen's Inn** (☑ 410-968-2119; www.crisfield.com/watermens; 901 W Main St, Crisfield; mains $8-27; ⊕ 3-8pm Thu, to 9pm Fri & Sat, noon-8pm Sun) is legendary; in an unpretentious setting you can feast on local catch from an ever-changing menu. You can find local waterfolk at their favorite hangout – **Gordon's Confectionery** (☑ 410-968-0566; 831 W Main St, Crisfield; mains $2-7; ⊕ 4am-8:30pm) – having 4am coffee before shipping off to check and set traps.

From here you can leave your car and take a boat to **Smith Island** (www.smithisland. org), the only offshore settlement in the state. Settled by fisherfolk from the English West Country some 400 years ago, the island's tiny population still speak with what linguists reckon is the closest thing to a 17th-century Cornish accent.

We'll be frank: this is more of a dying fishing town than charming tourist attraction, although there are B&Bs and restaurants (check the website for details). But it's also a last link to the state's past, so if you approach Smith Island as such, you may appreciate the limited amenities on offer. These notably include paddling through miles of some of the most pristine marshland on the eastern seaboard. Ferries will take you back to the mainland (and the present day) at 3:30pm.

force, splitting the economy between Baltimore's industry and shipping, and the later need for services in Washington, DC. Today the answer to 'What makes a Marylander?' is 'all of the above': the state mixes rich, poor, foreign-born, urban sophisticates and rural villages like few other states do.

Baltimore

Once among the most important port towns in America, Baltimore – or 'Bawlmer' to locals – is a city of contradictions. It remains a defiant, working-class city tied to its nautical past, but in recent years has earned acclaim for up-to-the-minute entrepreneurial ventures that are impressing visitors and locals alike, from new boutique hotels to edgy exhibits at world-class museums to forgotten neighborhoods now bustling with trendy food courts and farm-to-table restaurants. But don't worry, traditionalists – local culture and hometown sports, from lacrosse to baseball, remain part of the appeal.

For travelers, a visit to B'more (another nickname) should include one trip to the waterfront, whether its the Disney-fied Inner Harbor, the cobblestoned streets of port-

side Fell's Point or the shores of Fort McHenry, birthplace of America's national anthem, 'The Star-Spangled Banner.' As you'll discover, there's an intense, sincere friendliness here, which is why Baltimore lives up to its final, most accurate nickname: 'Charm City.'

◉ Sights

◉ Harborplace & Inner Harbor

This is where most tourists start and, unfortunately, end their Baltimore sightseeing. The Inner Harbor is a big, gleaming waterfront-renewal project of shiny glass, air-conditioned malls and flashy bars that manages to capture the maritime heart of this city, albeit in a safe-for-the-family kinda way. The neighborhood is home to an amazing aquarium and several impressive historic ships, but these worthy sights are just the tip of Baltimore's iceberg.

National Aquarium   AQUARIUM
(☑ 410-576-3800; www.aqua.org; 501 E Pratt St, Piers 3 & 4; adult/child 3-11yr $40/25; ⊕ 9am-5pm Sun-Thu, to 8pm Fri, to 6pm Sat) Standing seven stories high and capped by a glass pyramid, this is widely considered to be the best aquarium in America, with almost 20,000

creatures and more than 700 species, a roof-top rainforest, a multistory shark tank and a vast re-creation of an Indo-Pacific reef that is home to blacktip reef sharks, a green sea turtle and stingrays. There's also a reconstruction of the Umbrawarra Gorge in Australia's Northern Territory, complete with 35ft waterfall, rocky cliffs and free-roaming birds and lizards.

⊙ Downtown & Little Italy

You can easily walk from downtown Baltimore to Little Italy, but follow the delineated path: there's a rough housing project along the way.

National Great Blacks in Wax Museum   MUSEUM

(☑410-563-3404; www.greatblacksinwax.org; 1601 E North Ave; adult/student/child 3-11yr $15/14/12; ⊙9am-5pm Tue-Sat, noon-5pm Sun, also Mon & to 6pm Sun Jul & Aug) This simple but thought-provoking African American history museum has exhibits on Frederick Douglass, Jackie Robinson, Martin Luther King Jr and Barack Obama, as well as lesser-known figures such as explorer Matthew Henson. The museum also covers slavery, the Jim Crow era and African leaders – all told in surreal but informative fashion through Madame Tussaud–style wax figures. Unflinching and graphic exhibits about the horrors of slave ships and lynchings may not be well suited to younger children.

Star-Spangled Banner Flag House & 1812 Museum   MUSEUM

(☑410-837-1793; www.flaghouse.org; 844 E Pratt St; adult/child $8/6; ⊙10am-4pm Tue-Sat; 👪) This historic home, built in 1793, is where Mary Pickersgill sewed the gigantic flag that inspired America's national anthem. Costumed interpreters and 19th-century artifacts transport visitors back in time to dark days during the War of 1812; there's also a hands-on discovery gallery for kids.

Jewish Museum of Maryland   MUSEUM

(☑410-732-6400; www.jewishmuseummd.org; 15 Lloyd St; adult/student/child 4-12yr $10/6/4; ⊙10am-5pm Sun-Thu) Maryland has traditionally been home to one of the largest, most active Jewish communities in the country, and this is a fine place to explore their experience in America. It also houses two wonderfully preserved historical synagogues. Call or go online for the scheduled hours of synagogue tours.

Edgar Allan Poe House & Museum   MUSEUM

(☑410-462-1763; www.poeinbaltimore.org; 203 N Amity St; adult/student/child $5/4/free; ⊙11am-4pm Thu-Sun) Home to Baltimore's most famous adopted son from 1832 to 1835, it was here that the macabre poet and writer first found fame after winning a $50 short-story contest. After moving around, Poe later returned to Baltimore in 1849, where he died under mysterious circumstances. His grave can be found in Westminster Cemetery.

⊙ Mt Vernon

★Walters Art Museum   MUSEUM

(☑410-547-9000; www.thewalters.org; 600 N Charles St; ⊙10am-5pm Wed-Sun, to 9pm Thu) FREE The magnificent Chamber of Wonders looks like the study of a world-traveling scholar, one with a taste for adventure. The abutting Arms and Armor gallery is the most impressive collection of medieval weaponry you'll see this side of *Game of Thrones*. In sum, don't pass up this excellent, eclectic museum. It spans more than 55 centuries, from ancient to contemporary, with excellent displays of Asian treasures, rare and ornate manuscripts and books, and a comprehensive French paintings collection.

Washington Monument   MONUMENT

(www.mvpconservancy.org; 699 Washington Pl; suggested donation $5; ⊙11am-3pm Wed-Fri, 10am-5pm Sat & Sun) For the best views of Baltimore, climb the 228 steps of the 178ft-tall Doric column dedicated to America's Founding Father, George Washington. It was designed by Robert Mills, who also created DC's Washington Monument, and is looking better than ever following a $6 million restoration project. The ground floor contains a museum about Washington's life. To climb the monument, buy a ticket on site or reserve online (adult/child under 14 years $6/4).

Maryland Historical Society   MUSEUM

(☑410-685-3650; www.mdhs.org; 201 W Monument St; adult/child 3-18yr $9/6; ⊙10am-5pm Wed-Sat, noon-5pm Sun) With more than 350,000 objects and seven million books and documents, this is one of the largest collections of Americana in the world. Highlights include one of two surviving Revolutionary War officer's uniforms, photographs from the 1930s Civil Rights movement in Baltimore and Francis Scott Key's original manuscript of 'The Star-Spangled Banner' (displayed at the top of the hour). The 10ft-tall replica mastodon – the original was preserved by artist and Maryland native Charles Wilson Peale – is impressive. A few original bones are displayed.

Federal Hill & Around

On a bluff overlooking the harbor, Federal Hill Park lends its name to the comfortable neighborhood that's set around Cross Street Market and comes alive after sundown.

★ American Visionary Art Museum
MUSEUM

(AVAM; ☑ 410-244-1900; www.avam.org; 800 Key Hwy; adult/child $16/10; ⊘10am-6pm Tue-Sun) Housing a jaw-dropping collection of self-taught (or 'outsider' art), AVAM is a celebration of unbridled creativity utterly free of arts-scene pretension. Across two buildings and two sculpture parks, you'll find broken-mirror collages, homemade robots and flying apparatuses, elaborate sculptural works made of needlepoint, and gigantic model ships painstakingly created from matchsticks. Don't miss the whimsical automata in the Cabaret Mechanical Theater.

Fort McHenry National Monument & Historic Shrine
HISTORIC SITE

(☑ 410-962-4290; www.nps.gov/fomc; 2400 E Fort Ave; adult/child under 16yr $10/free; ⊘9am-5pm) On September 13 and 14, 1814, this star-shaped fort successfully repelled a British navy attack during the Battle of Baltimore. After a long night of bombs bursting in the air, ship-bound prisoner Francis Scott Key saw, 'by dawn's early light,' the tattered flag still waving. Inspired, he penned 'The Star-Spangled Banner,' which was set to the tune of a popular drinking song.

Fell's Point & Canton

Once the center of Baltimore's shipbuilding industry, the historic cobblestoned neighborhood of Fell's Point is now a gentrified mix of 18th-century homes and restaurants, bars and shops. The neighborhood has been the setting for several films and TV series, most notably *Homicide: Life on the Street*. Further east, the slightly more sophisticated streets of Canton fan out, with its grassy square surrounded by restaurants and bars.

North Baltimore

The 'Hon' expression of affection – an oft-imitated, never-quite-duplicated 'Bawlmerese' peculiarity – originated in Hampden, an area straddling the line between working class and hipster-creative class. Spend a lazy afternoon browsing kitsch, antiques and vintage clothing along the Avenue (aka W 36th St). To get to Hampden, take the I-83 N, merge onto Falls Rd (northbound) and take a right onto the Avenue. The prestigious Johns Hopkins University (☑ 410-516-8000; www.jhu.edu; 3400 N Charles St) is nearby. South of Johns Hopkins, just east of I-83, new restaurants and housing developments mark rapidly gentrifying Remington, a walkable neighborhood with a demographic similar to that of Hampden.

★ Evergreen Museum
MUSEUM

(☑ 410-516-0341; http://museums.jhu.edu; 4545 N Charles St; adult/child $8/5; ⊘11am-4pm Tue-Fri, noon-4pm Sat & Sun) Well worth the drive out, this grand 19th-century mansion provides a fascinating glimpse into upper-class Baltimore life of the 1800s. The house is packed with fine art and masterpieces of the decorative arts – including paintings by Modigliani, glass by Louis Comfort Tiffany and exquisite Asian porcelain – not to mention the astounding rare book collection, numbering some 32,000 volumes.

☞ Tours

Baltimore Ghost Tours
WALKING

(☑ 410-357-1186; www.baltimoreghosttours.com; adult/child $15/10; ⊘7pm Fri & Sat Mar-Nov) Offers several walking tours exploring the spooky and bizarre side of Baltimore. The popular Fell's Point ghost walk departs from Max's on Broadway (731 S Broadway). Book online to save $2 per ticket.

★★ Festivals & Events

Artscape
ART

(www.artscape.org; 140 W Mt Royal Ave, Patricia & Arthur Modell Performing Arts Center; ⊘mid-Jul) America's largest free arts festival features art displays, live music, theater and dance.

Honfest
CULTURAL

(www.honfest.net; ⊘Jun) Put on your best 'Bawlmerese' accent and head to Hampden for this celebration of kitsch, beehive hair-dos, rhinestone glasses and other Baltimore eccentricities.

BALTIMORE FOR CHILDREN

Most attractions are centered on the Inner Harbor, including the National Aquarium (p280), perfect for pint-sized visitors. Kids can run wild o'er the ramparts of historic **Fort McHenry National Monument & Historic Shrine**.

Maryland Science Center (☎410-685-2370; www.mdsci.org; 601 Light St; adult/child 3-12yr $25/19; ☯10am-5pm Mon-Fri, to 6pm Sat, 11am-5pm Sun, longer hours in summer) is an awesome center featuring a three-story atrium, tons of interactive exhibits on dinosaurs, outer space and the human body, and the requisite IMAX theater ($4 extra).

Two blocks north is the converted fish market of **Port Discovery** (☎410-727-8120; www.portdiscovery.org; 35 Market Pl; $15; ☯10am-5pm Mon-Sat & noon-5pm Sun Jun-Aug, closes earlier Sep-May), which has a tree house, a laboratory and an artist's studio. Wear your kids out here. At **Maryland Zoo in Baltimore** (www.marylandzoo.org; 1 Safari Place, Druid Hill Park; adult/child 2-11yr $18/14; ☯10am-4pm daily Mar-Dec, 10am-4pm Fri-Mon Jan & Feb), lily-pad hopping adventures with Billy the Bog Turtle and grooming live animals are all in a day's play.

🛏 Sleeping

Stylish and affordable B&Bs are mostly found in the downtown 'burbs of Canton, Fell's Point and Federal Hill. New boutique hotels are bringing some fresh and hip style to downtown and Mt Vernon.

HI-Baltimore Hostel
HOSTEL $

(☎410-576-8880; www.hiusa.org/baltimore; 17 W Mulberry St, Mt Vernon; dm $29-30; ✱@🗐) Located in a beautifully restored 1857 mansion, the HI-Baltimore has four-, eight- and 12-bed dorms. Helpful management, a nice location and a filigreed classical chic look make this one of the region's best hostels.

Hotel Brexton
HOTEL $$

(☎443-478-2100; www.hotelbrexton.com; 868 Park Ave, Mt Vernon; r $159-219; P✱🗐✱) This red-brick 19th-century landmark building has recently been reborn as an appealing, if not overly lavish, hotel. Rooms offer a mix of wood floors or carpeting, comfy mattresses, mirrored armoires and framed art prints on the walls. Curious historical footnote: Wallis Simpson, the woman whom Britain's King Edward VIII abdicated the throne for, lived in this building as a young girl.

★ Inn at 2920
B&B $$

(☎410-342-4450; www.theinnat2920.com; 2920 Elliott St, Canton; r $195-235; ✱@🗐) Housed in a former bordello, this boutique B&B offers five individual rooms; high-thread-count sheets; sleek, avant-garde decor; and the nightlife-charged neighborhood of Canton right outside your door.

🍴 Eating

Baltimore is an ethnically rich town that sits on top of the greatest seafood repository in the world, not to mention the fault line between the down-home South and cutting-edge innovation of the Northeast.

Papermoon Diner
DINER $

(www.papermoondiner24.com; 227 W 29th St, Harwood; mains $10-18; ☯7am-9pm Sun, Mon, Wed & Thu, to 10pm Fri & Sat) This brightly colored, quintessential Baltimore diner is decorated with thousands of old toys, creepy mannequins and other quirky knickknacks. The real draw here is the anytime breakfast – fluffy buttermilk pancakes, crispy bacon and crab and artichoke heart omelets. Wash it down with a caramel and sea-salt milkshake.

Artifact
CAFE $

(www.artifactcoffee.com; 1500 Union Ave, Woodberry; mains $7-14; ☯7am-7pm Mon-Fri, 8am-7pm Sat & Sun; 🗐) Artifact serves the city's best coffee, along with tasty light meals, such as egg muffins, spinach salad, vegetarian *banh mi* and pastrami sandwiches. It's inside a former mill space, handsomely repurposed from its industrial past. It's a two-minute stroll from the Woodberry light-rail station.

Vaccaro's Pastry
ITALIAN $

(www.vaccarospastry.com; 222 Albemarle St, Little Italy; desserts $3-7; ☯9am-10pm Sun-Thu, to midnight Fri & Sat) Open more than 60 years, Vaccaro's serves some of the best desserts and coffee in town. The cannolis are legendary.

Lexington Market
FAST FOOD $

(www.lexingtonmarket.com; 400 W Lexington St, Mt Vernon; ☯6:30am-6pm) Around since 1782,

Mt Vernon's Lexington Market is one of Baltimore's true old-school food markets. It's a bit shabby on the outside, but the food is great.

Faidley's
SEAFOOD $$

(☑ 410-727-4898; www.faidleyscrabcakes.com; 203 N Paca St, Lexington Market; mains $10-20; ⊙ 9am-5pm Mon-Wed, to 5:30pm Thu-Sat) Here's a fine example of a place that the press and the tourists found out about long ago, yet whose brilliance hasn't been dimmed by the publicity. Faidley's is best known for its crab cakes, in-claw meat, backfin (body meat) or all lump (the biggest chunks of body meat). Tuck in at a stand-up counter with a cold beer and know happiness.

★ Thames St Oyster House
SEAFOOD $$

(☑ 443-449-7726; www.thamesstreetoysterhouse.com; 1728 Thames St, Fell's Point; mains $12-29; ⊙ 11:30am-2:30pm Wed-Sun & 5-9:30pm Sun-Thu, to 10:30pm Fri & Sat) An icon of Fell's Point, this vintage dining and drinking hall serves some of Baltimore's best seafood. Dine in the polished upstairs dining room with views of the waterfront, take a seat in the backyard, or plunk down at the bar in front (which stays open till midnight) and watch the drink-makers and oyster-shuckers in action. The lobster rolls are recommended too.

Birroteca
PIZZA $$

(☑ 443-708-1934; www.bmorebirroteca.com; 1520 Clipper Rd, Roosevelt Park; pizzas $18-22; ⊙ 5-11pm Mon-Fri, noon-11pm Sat, noon-10pm Sun) Amid stone walls and indie rock, Birroteca fires up delicious thin-crust pizzas in imaginative combos (like duck confit with fig-onion jam). There's craft beer, good wines, fancy cocktails and impressively bearded bartenders. It's about a half-mile from either Hampden's 36th St or the Woodberry light-rail station.

Helmand
AFGHANI $$

(☑ 410-752-0311; www.helmand.com; 806 N Charles St, Mt Vernon; mains $14-19; ⊙ 5-10pm Sun-Thu, to 11pm Fri & Sat) The Helmand is a longtime favorite for its *kaddo borawni* (pumpkin in yogurt-garlic sauce), vegetable platters and flavorful beef-and-lamb meatballs, followed by cardamom ice cream. If you've never tried Afghan cuisine, this is a great place to do so.

LP Steamers
SEAFOOD $$

(☑ 410-576-9294; www.locustpointsteamers.com; 1100 E Fort Ave, South Baltimore; mains $8-27; ⊙ 11:30am-9:30pm Sun-Thu, to 10pm Fri & Sat) LP is the best in Baltimore's seafood stakes: working class, teasing smiles and the freshest crabs on the southside.

★ Woodberry Kitchen
AMERICAN $$$

(☑ 410-464-8000; www.woodberrykitchen.com; 2010 Clipper Park Rd, Woodberry; mains $20-35; ⊙ dinner 5-10pm Mon-Thu, to 11pm Fri & Sat, to 9pm Sun, brunch 10am-2pm Sat & Sun) The Woodberry takes everything the Chesapeake region has to offer, plops it into an industrial barn and creates culinary magic. The entire menu is like a playful romp through the best of local produce, seafood and meats, from Maryland rockfish with Carolina Gold grits to Shenandoah Valley lamb with collard greens, and hearty vegetable dishes plucked from nearby farms. Reserve ahead.

Food Market
MODERN AMERICAN $$$

(☑ 410-366-0606; www.thefoodmarketbaltimore.com; 1017 W 36th St, Hampden; mains $18-36; ⊙ 5-11pm Sun-Thu, to midnight Fri & Sat, plus 9am-3pm Fri-Sun) On Hampden's lively restaurant- and shop-lined main drag, the Food Market was an instant success when it opened back in 2012. Award-winning local chef Chad Gauss elevates American comfort fare to high art in dishes like bread-and-butter-crusted sea bass with black-truffle vinaigrette, and crab cakes with lobster mac 'n' cheese.

🍷 Drinking & Nightlife

On weekends, Fell's Point and Canton turn into temples of alcoholic excess that would make a Roman emperor blush. Mt Vernon and North Baltimore are a little more civilized, but any one of Baltimore's neighborhoods houses a cozy local pub. Closing time is generally 2am.

Brewer's Art
PUB

(☑ 410-547-6925; www.thebrewersart.com; 1106 N Charles St, Mt Vernon; ⊙ 4pm-1:45am Mon-Fri, noon-1:45am Sat & Sun) In a vintage early-20th-century mansion, Brewer's Art serves well-crafted Belgian-style microbrews to a laid-back Mt Vernon crowd. There's tasty pub fare (mac 'n' cheese, portobello wraps) in the bar, and upscale American cuisine in the elegant back dining room. Head to the subterranean drinking den downstairs for a more raucous crowd. During happy hour (4pm to 7pm) house drafts are just $3.75.

Ale Mary's
BAR

(☑ 410-276-2044; www.alemarys.com; 1939 Fleet St, Fell's Point; ⊙ 4pm-2am Mon-Thu, 2pm-2am

Fri, 10am-2am Sat & Sun) Its name and decor pay homage to Maryland's Catholic roots, with crosses and rosaries scattered about. It draws a buzzing neighborhood crowd, who come for strong drinks and good, greasy bar food (tater tots, cheesesteak subs) as well as mussels and Sunday brunch.

Little Havana BAR
(☑ 410-837-9903; www.litlehavanas.com; 1325 Key Hwy, Federal Hill; ⊙11:30am-midnight Mon-Thu, 11:30am-2am Fri & Sat, 11am-midnight Sun) A good after-work spot and a great place to sip mojitos on the waterfront deck, this converted brick warehouse is a major draw on warm, sunny days (especially around weekend brunch time).

Club Charles BAR
(☑410-727-8815; www.clubcharles.us; 1724 N Charles St, Mt Vernon; ⊙6pm-2am) Hipsters adorned in the usual skinny jeans/vintage T-shirt uniform, as well as characters from other walks of life, flock to this 1940s art-deco cocktail lounge to enjoy good tunes and cheap drinks.

☆ Entertainment

Baltimoreans *love* sports. The town plays hard and parties even harder, with tailgating parties in parking lots and games showing on numerous televisions.

★ Oriole Park at Camden Yards STADIUM
(☑888-848-2473; www.orioles.com; 333 W Camden St, Downtown) The **Baltimore Orioles** play here, arguably the best ballpark in America. Daily tours (adult/child under 15 years $9/6) of the stadium are offered during regular season (April through September).

M&T Bank Stadium STADIUM
(☑410-261-7283; www.baltimoreravens.com; 1101 Russell St, Downtown) The **Baltimore Ravens** play football here from September to January.

❶ Information

Baltimore Area Visitor Center (☑877-225-8466; www.baltimore.org; 401 Light St, Inner Harbor; ⊙10am-5pm Oct-Apr, 9am-6pm May-Sep, closed Mon Jan & Feb) Located on the Inner Harbor. Sells the Harbor Pass (adult/child $52/38), which gives admission to five major area attractions.

University of Maryland Medical Center (☑410-328-8667; www.umm.edu; 22 S Greene St, University of Maryland-Baltimore) Has a 24-hour emergency room.

❶ Getting There & Away

The **Baltimore/Washington International Thurgood Marshall Airport** (p278) is 10 miles south of downtown via I-295.

Departing from a terminal 2 miles southwest of Inner Harbor, Greyhound (www.greyhound.com) and **Peter Pan Bus Lines** (☑800-343-9999; www.peterpanbus.com; 2110 Haines St, Carroll-Camden) have numerous buses from Washington, DC ($8 to $12, roughly every 45 minutes, one hour) and from New York ($15 to $42, 14 to 17 per day, 4½ hours). The **BoltBus** (☑877-265-8287; www.boltbus.com; 1578 Maryland Ave; ☎) ($15 to $34) has six to 10 buses a day to/from NYC; it departs from a street-side location outside of Baltimore's Penn Station.

Penn Station (https://mta.maryland.gov/marc-train; 1500 N Charles St, Charles North) is in north Baltimore. MARC operates weekday commuter trains to/from Washington, DC ($8, about one hour). Amtrak (www.amtrak.com) trains serve the East Coast and beyond.

❶ Getting Around

Light rail (http://mta.maryland.gov/light-rail) runs from BWI airport to Lexington Market and Penn Station. Train frequency is every five to 10 minutes. MARC trains run hourly on weekdays (and six to nine times daily on weekends) between Penn Station and BWI airport for $5. Check Maryland Transit Administration (www.mtamaryland.gov) for all local transportation schedules.

Supershuttle (www.supershuttle.com) provides a BWI-van service to the Inner Harbor for $23.

Baltimore Water Taxi (☑410-563-3900; www.baltimorewatertaxi.com; Inner Harbor; daily pass adult/child 3-12yr $14/6; ⊙10am-midnight May-Aug, shorter hours rest of year) docks at all harborside attractions.

Annapolis

Annapolis is as charming as state capitals get. The Colonial architecture, cobblestones, flickering lamps and brick row houses are worthy of Dickens, but the effect isn't artificial: this city has preserved, rather than created, its heritage.

Perched on Chesapeake Bay, Annapolis revolves around the city's rich maritime traditions. It's home to the US Naval Academy, whose 'middies' (midshipmen students) stroll through town in their starched white uniforms. Sailing is not just a hobby here but a way of life, and the city docks are crammed with vessels of all shapes and sizes. With its historic sights, water adventures and great dining and shopping, Annapolis is worthy of more than a day trip.

◉ Sights

US Naval Academy UNIVERSITY
(🗹visitor center 410-293-8687; www.usnabsd.com/for-visitors; Randall St, btwn Prince George and King George Sts) The undergraduate college of the US Navy is one of the most selective universities in America. The Armel-Leftwich visitor center is the place to book tours and immerse yourself in all things Academy-related. Come for the formation weekdays at 12:05pm sharp, when the 4000 midshipmen and -women conduct a 20-minute military marching display in the yard. Photo ID is required for entry. If you've got a thing for American naval history, revel in the Naval Academy Museum (🗹410-293-2108; www.usna.edu/museum; 118 Maryland Ave; ⊙9am-5pm Mon-Sat, 11am-5pm Sun) FREE.

Maryland State House HISTORIC BUILDING
(🗹410-946-5400; http://msa.maryland.gov/msa/mdstatehouse/html/home.html; 91 State Circle; ⊙9am-5pm) FREE The country's oldest state capitol in continuous legislative use, the grand 1772 State House also served as national capital from 1733 to 1734. Notably, Gen George Washington returned his commission here as Commander in Chief of the Continental Army in 1783 after the Revolutionary War, ensuring that power would be shared with Congress. The Maryland Senate is in action from January to April. The giant acorn atop the dome stands for wisdom.

Hammond Harwood House MUSEUM
(🗹410-263-4683; www.hammondharwoodhouse.org; 19 Maryland Ave; adult/child $10/5; ⊙noon-5pm Tue-Sun Apr-Dec) Of the many historical homes in town, the 1774 HHH is the one to visit. It has a superb collection of decorative arts, including furniture, paintings and ephemera dating from the 18th century, and is one of the finest existing British Colonial homes in America. Knowledgeable guides help bring the past to life on 50-minute house tours (held at the top of the hour).

William Paca House & Garden HISTORIC BUILDING
(🗹410-990-4543; www.annapolis.org; 186 Prince George St; full house & garden tour $10, 1st floor house & garden tour $8, garden tour only $5; ⊙10am-5pm Mon-Sat, noon-5pm Sun late Mar-Dec) Take a tour (offered hourly on the half-hour) through this Georgian mansion for insight into 18th-century life for the upper class in Maryland. Don't miss the blooming garden in spring.

Kunta Kinte–Alex Haley Memorial MONUMENT
Beside City Dock, the Kunta Kinte–Alex Haley Memorial marks the spot where Kunta Kinte – ancestor of *Roots* author Alex Haley – was brought in chains from Africa. The statues here depict Haley sharing the story of his ancestor with three children.

☞ Tours

Four Centuries Walking Tour WALKING
(🗹410-268-7601; www.annapolistours.com; 2¼ hr tour adult/child 3-11yr $18/10) A costumed docent will lead you on this great introduction to all things Annapolis. The 10:30am tour leaves from the visitor center and the 1:30pm tour leaves from the information booth at City Dock. There's a slight variation in sights visited by each, but both cover the country's largest concentration of 18th-century buildings, influential African Americans and colonial spirits who don't want to leave. The associated one-hour Pirates of the Chesapeake Cruise (🗹410-263-0002; www.chesapeakepirates.com; 311 3rd St; $22; ⊙mid-Apr–Sep; ♠) is good 'yar'-worthy fun

Woodwind CRUISE
(🗹410-263-7837; www.schoonerwoodwind.com; 80 Compromise St; sunset cruise adult/child under 12yr $46/29; ⊙mid-Apr–Oct) This beautiful 74ft schooner offers two-hour day and sunset cruises. Or splurge for the Woodwind 'boat & breakfast' package, one of the more unique lodging options in town.

⌨ Sleeping

Inns and B&Bs fills the historic downtown. Several hotels line West St, which runs west from Church Circle. National hotel chains cluster near exits 22 and 23 off USA 50/301.

Historic Inns of Annapolis HOTEL $$
(🗹410-263-2641; www.historicinnsofannapolis.com; 58 State Circle; r from $189; P❋🐾) The Historic Inns comprise three different boutique guesthouses, each set in a heritage building in the heart of old Annapolis: the Maryland Inn, the Governor Calvert House and the Robert Johnson House. Common areas are packed with period details, and the best rooms boast antiques, a fireplace and attractive views (while the cheapest can be small). Check in at Governor Calvert House.

ScotLaur Inn GUESTHOUSE $$
(🗹410-268-5665; www.scotlaurinn.com; 165 Main St; r $119-149; P❋🐾) The folks from Chick

& Ruth's Delly offer 10 rooms, each with wrought-iron beds, floral wallpaper and private bath. The quarters are small but have a familial atmosphere (the guesthouse is named after the owners' children Scott and Lauren).

O'Callaghan Hotel
HOTEL $$

(☑ 410-263-7700; www.ocallaghanhotels-us.com; 174 West St; r from $180; [P][✳][☎]) This Irish chain offers attractively furnished rooms that are nicely equipped, with big windows, a writing desk, brass fixtures and comfy mattresses. It's on West St, just a short stroll to a good selection of bars and restaurants, and about a 12-minute walk to the old quarter.

✗ Eating & Drinking

With the Chesapeake at its doorstep, Annapolis has superb seafood. The recent openings of several farm-to-table-minded restaurants have added some depth to the dining scene along Main St and near the dock.

The historic downtown is festive on Friday and Saturday nights on Main St and along the waterfront, with many folks kicking back and sipping beers – many beers – on patios near the dock, watching the boats parade past. Plenty of cozy pubs downtown.

49 West
CAFE $

(☑ 410-626-9796; www.49westcoffeehouse.com; 49 West St; breakfast mains $6-14, lunch mains $9-15, dinner mains $9-24; ⊗ 7:30am-midnight Sun-Thu, to 2am Fri & Sat; [☎]) This comfy, art-filled coffeehouse is a good spot for coffee and light bites during the day (sandwiches, soups, salads) and heartier bistro fare by night, along with wines and cocktails. There's live music some nights.

Chick & Ruth's Delly
DINER $

(☑ 410-269-6737; www.chickandruths.com; 165 Main St; mains $8-15; ⊗ 6:30am-11:30pm Sun-Thu, to 12:30am Fri & Sat; [♿]) A cornerstone of Annapolis, the Delly is bursting with affable quirkiness and a big menu, heavy on sandwiches and breakfast fare. Patriots can relive grade-school days reciting the Pledge of Allegiance weekdays at 8:30am and Saturdays and Sundays at 9:30am.

★ Vin 909
AMERICAN $$

(☑ 410-990-1846; www.vin909.com; 909 Bay Ridge Ave; small plates $12-20; ⊗ 5:30-10pm Tue-Sun & noon-3pm Wed-Sat, closes at 9pm Tue & Sun in winter) Perched on a little wooded hill and boasting intimate but enjoyably casual ambience, Vin is the best thing happening in Annapolis for food. Farm-sourced goodness features in the form of duck confit, barbecue sliders and homemade pizzas with toppings like wild mushrooms, foie gras and Spanish chorizo. There's a great wine selection, including over three dozen wines by the glass.

★ Jimmy Cantler's Riverside Inn
SEAFOOD $$

(☑ 410-757-1311; www.cantlers.com; 458 Forest Beach Rd, Annapolis; mains $10-34; ⊗ 11am-11pm Sun-Thu, to midnight Fri & Sat) This is one of the best crab shacks in the state, and eating a steamed crab has been elevated to an art form – a hands-on, messy endeavor, normally accompanied by corn on the cob and ice-cold beer. Cantler's is a little ways outside of Annapolis, but like many crab houses, it can be approached by road or boat (a waterfront location is crab-eating industry standard).

Boatyard Bar & Grill
SEAFOOD $$

(☑ 410-216-6206; www.boatyardbarandgrill.com; 400 4th St; mains $10-27; ⊗ 7:30am-midnight Mon-Fri, 8am-midnight Sat & Sun; [♿]) This bright, nautically themed restaurant is an inviting spot for crab cakes, fish and chips, fish tacos and other seafood. Happy hour (3pm to 7pm Monday to Friday) draws in the crowds with 99¢ oysters and $3 drafts. It's a short drive (or 10-minute walk) from the City Dock, across the Spa Creek Bridge.

Rams Head Tavern
PUB FOOD $$$

(☑ 410-268-4545; www.ramsheadtavern.com; 33 West St; mains $10-30; ⊗ 11am-2am Mon-Sat, from 10am Sun) Serves pub fare and refreshing microbrews in an attractive exposed-brick and oak-paneled setting. Well-known bands perform next door at the Rams Head On Stage (tickets $23 to $115).

Fox's Den
PUB

(☑ 443-808-8991; www.foxsden.com; 179 Main St; ⊗ 5-11pm Mon, Wed & Thu, 5pm-midnight Fri, 4pm-midnight Sat, 4-11pm Sun) Head underground for microbrews and craft cocktails, all served in a snug gastropub in the thick of the Main St action.

ℹ Information

There's a **visitor center** (☑ 410-280-0445; www.visitannapolis.org; 26 West St; ⊗ 9am-5pm) on West St and a seasonal information booth at City Dock (open 9am to 5pm March to October). For information about tours and sights at the Naval Academy, stop by the expansive **Armel-Leftwich Visitor Center** (☑ 410-293-8687; www.usnabsd.com/for-visitors; 52 King

George St, Gate 1, City Dock entrance; tours adult/child $11/9; ⊘9am-5pm Mar-Dec, 9am-4pm Jan & Feb) on the Yard near the waterfront.

ⓘ Getting There & Away

Greyhound (☑800-231-2222; www.greyhound.com; 275 Harry S Truman Pkwy) (www.greyhound.com) runs buses to Washington, DC ($12 to $15, daily) from a pick-up and drop-off stop five miles west of the historic downtown.

Eastern Shore

Just across the Chesapeake Bay Bridge, nondescript suburbs give way to unbroken miles of bird-dotted wetlands, serene waterscapes, endless cornfields, sandy beaches and friendly villages. The Eastern Shore retains its charm despite the growing influx of city-dwelling yuppies and day-trippers. This area revolves around the water: working waterfront communities still survive off Chesapeake Bay and its tributaries, and boating, fishing, crabbing and hunting are integral to local life. Come here to explore nature by trail, boat or bicycle, to read on the beach, delve into regional history and, of course, enjoy the delicious seafood.

ⓘ Getting There & Around

The region is best explored by car. Baltimore is 70 miles from Easton and 150 miles from Ocean City.

St Michaels & Tilghman Island

The prettiest little village on the Eastern Shore, St Michaels lives up to its motto as the 'Heart and Soul of Chesapeake Bay.' Hugging US 33, it's a mix of old Victorian homes, quaint B&Bs, boutique shops and working docks, where escape artists from Washington mix with salty-dog watermen. During the War of 1812, inhabitants rigged up lanterns in a nearby forest and blacked out the town. British naval gunners shelled the trees, allowing St Michaels to escape destruction. The building now known as the **Cannonball House** (Mulberry St, St Michaels) was the only structure to have been hit.

At the end of the road at the end of the peninsula, and over the US 33 drawbridge, tiny **Tilghman Island** still runs a working waterfront, where local captains take visitors out on graceful sailing vessels.

◉ Sights & Activities

Chesapeake Bay Maritime Museum   MUSEUM

(☑410-745-2916; www.cbmm.org; 213 N Talbot St, St Michaels; adult/child 6-17yr $15/6; ⊘9am-5pm May-Oct, 10am-4pm Nov-Apr; ⚑) Throughout its indoor-outdoor exhibits, the Chesapeake Bay Maritime Museum delves into the deep ties between Shore folk and America's largest estuary. Learn about a lighthouse keeper's life in the 1800s inside the relocated 1879 lighthouse.

Lady Patty Classic Yacht Charters   BOATING

(☑410-886-1127; www.ladypatty.com; 6176 Tilghman Island Rd, Tilghman Island; cruise adult/child under 13yr from $40/25; ⊘tours Wed-Mon May-Oct) Runs memorable two-hour sails on the Chesapeake on a 1935 racing yacht.

🛏 Sleeping & Eating

Parsonage Inn   INN $$

(☑410-745-8383; www.parsonage-inn.com; 210 N Talbot St, St Michaels; r $210-290; P❄🤶) Classic Victorian-era decor is brightened here and there with unexpected splashes of color – is that a Hawaiian quilt? – inside the red-brick Parsonage Inn, which is under new ownership. Breakfast is a focus, and you might find deconstructed scotch eggs on the menu. Close to the maritime museum.

Crab Claw   SEAFOOD $$

(☑410-745-2900; www.thecrabclaw.com; 304 Burns St, St Michaels; mains $11-30; ⊘11am-10pm mid-Mar–Oct) Next door to the Chesapeake Bay Maritime Museum, the Crab Claw serves up tasty Maryland blue crabs to splendid views over the harbor. Avoid the seafood sampler, unless you're a fan of deep-fried seafood.

ⓘ Getting There & Away

St Michaels and Tilghman Island border US 33 on a narrow, zigzagging peninsula. US 33 leads west toward the towns from Easton. If you have a friend with a boat docked on the Chesapeake Bay, this is the time to ask for a ride – both towns have docks. They are also in Talbot County, which has more than 600 miles of shoreline.

Berlin

Imagine a typical small-town-America main street, cute that vision up by a few points, and you've come close to the Eastern Shore village of Berlin. Most of the buildings here are handsomely preserved, and antique shops litter the area. Several great restaurants dot the easily walkable downtown. The city is a convenient and appealing launchpad for exploring Assateague Island (p290) and the surrounding Eastern Shore.

For such a small town, Berlin has an impressive number of restaurants serving great seafood and American dishes. Most are within walking distance of the historic inn downtown.

✖ Eating

Drummer's Cafe   AMERICAN $$
(https://atlantichotel.com/drummers-cafe-atlantic-hotel; 2 N Main St; lunch mains $10-16, dinner mains $18-34; ⊙11am-9pm) The dining room of the Atlantic Hotel is as grand as the hotel itself, all big windows, natural sunshine and – come evening – flickering candlelight. The food references the best of the Chesapeake; filet mignon gets even more decadent with a crab cake. In the evening it's also fun to watch the small town roll by while enjoying a drink on the front porch of the hotel.

Fins Ale House & Raw Bar   SEAFOOD $$
(☑410-641-3000; www.facebook.com/FinsAleHouseBerlin; 119 N Main St; mains $12-30; ⊙11am-9:15pm Sun-Thu, to 10pm Fri & Sat) The lump crab cake is so darn good you might just consider packing up and moving to Berlin. And from the happy crowds filling the place, others may have the same idea. It's not on the water, but considerate service, big windows, a cozy patio and enticing seafood dishes in every direction make Fins the next best thing to a seafood shack by the ocean.

❶ Getting There & Away

Berlin sits near the junction of Hwy 113 and US 50, about 8 miles southwest of Ocean City.

Ocean City

Two words describe 'The OC' from June through August: party central. This is where you'll experience the American seaside resort in its wildest glory. Some might call it tacky. Others might call it, well, fun. Here you can take a spin on nausea-inducing thrill rides, buy a T-shirt with obscene slogans and drink to excess at cheesy theme bars. The center of action is the 2.5-mile-long boardwalk, which stretches from the inlet to 27th St. The beach is attractive, but you'll have to contend with horny teenagers, heavy traffic and noisy crowds; the beaches north of the boardwalk are much quieter. How busy is it? They say Ocean City welcomes 3.4 million visitors in summer – in a town with a year-round population just over 7000!

◎ Sights

Ocean City Life-Saving
Station Museum   MUSEUM
(☑410-289-4991; www.ocmuseum.org; 813 S Atlantic Ave; adult/child 6-17yr $3/1; ⊙10am-4pm May & Oct, to 6pm Jun-Sep, 10am-4pm Wed-Sun Apr & Nov) At the southern end of the boardwalk, this small but engaging museum sits inside an 1891 life-saving station. Here, the keeper and six to eight 'surfmen' lived and responded to emergency calls for ships in distress. Exhibits include stories about nearby shipwrecks and a display spotlighting rescue gear, including a 26ft-long rescue boat, which would look rather small and fragile in a storm!

Trimpers Rides   AMUSEMENT PARK
(☑410-289-8617; www.trimpersrides.com; S 1st St & Boardwalk; unlimited afternoon rides $26; ⊙3pm-midnight Mon-Fri, noon-midnight Sat & Sun, hours vary seasonally) If you really want

WASHINGTON, DC & THE CAPITAL REGION OCEAN CITY

MARYLAND BLUE CRABS

Eating at a crab shack, where the dress code stops at shorts and flip-flops, is the quintessential Chesapeake Bay experience. Folks in these parts take their crabs seriously, and can spend hours debating the intricacies of how to crack a crab, the proper way to prepare crabs and where to find the best ones. There is one thing Marylanders can agree on: they must be blue crabs (scientific name: *Callinectes sapidus*, or 'beautiful swimmers'). Sadly, blue crab numbers have suffered with the continuing pollution of the Chesapeake Bay, and many crabs you eat here are imported from elsewhere.

Steamed crabs are prepared very simply, using beer and Old Bay seasoning. One of the best crab shacks in the state is near Annapolis at Jimmy Cantler's Riverside Inn (p287), located 4 miles northeast of the Maryland State House, across the Severn River Bridge. Another fine spot is across the bay at the Crab Claw.

ASSATEAGUE ISLAND

Just 8 miles south but a world away from Ocean City is Assateague Island seashore, a perfectly barren landscape of sand dunes and beautiful, secluded beaches. This undeveloped barrier island is populated by a herd of wild horses, made famous in the book *Misty of Chincoteague*.

The island is divided into three sections. In Maryland there's **Assateague State Park** (410-641-2918; Rte 611; admission $6; campsites $28-39; day-use areas 7am-sunset, campground late Apr-Oct) and federally administered **Assateague Island National Seashore** (410-641-1441; www.nps.gov/asis; Rte 611; per pedestrian/vehicle per week $5/20; visitor center 9am-5pm Mar-Dec, closed Tue & Wed Jan & Feb). **Chincoteague National Wildlife Refuge** (www.fws.gov/refuge/chincoteague; 8231 Beach Rd, Chincoteague Island; daily/weekly vehicle pass $8/15; 5am-10pm May-Sep, 6am-6pm Nov-Mar, to 8pm Apr & Oct; P) is in Virginia. For an overview of the three sections, check out the Plan your Visit section of the national park website (www.nps.gov/asis) or pick up the *Assateague Island National Seashore* pamphlet, which has a helpful map.

As well as swimming and sunbathing, recreational activities include birding, kayaking, canoeing, crabbing and fishing. There are no services on the Maryland side of the island, so you must bring all your own food and drink. Don't forget insect repellent: the mosquitoes and biting horseflies can be ferocious!

to engage in tacky seaside fun to the fullest extent possible, hit up Trimpers Rides, one of the oldest of old-school amusement parks. Have some fries with vinegar, play the games and enjoy watching the teenage staff dance the ballet of summer hormonal overload. Tickets are 60¢ each, with a varying number required per ride.

🛏 Sleeping

Hotels and motels line the boardwalk and the streets running parallel to the ocean. These lodgings are a mix of national chains and independently owned accommodations. From June through August they're ready to pack in guests. For a quieter stay, try a B&B or spend the night in Berlin, 8 miles south.

King Charles Hotel   GUESTHOUSE **$$**
(410-289-6141; www.kingcharleshotel.com; 1209 N Baltimore Ave, cnr N Baltimore Ave & 12th St; r $169-189; P) This place could be a quaint summer cottage, except it happens to be a short stroll to the heart of the boardwalk action. It has aging but clean rooms with small porches attached, and it's quiet (ie it's not a party hotel).

🍴 Eating & Drinking

Surf 'n' turf and all-you-can-eat deals are the order of the day.

Beer. Wine. Booze. Sugary cocktails. You'll find it all here in excess. And often at ridiculously low prices, especially during happy

hour late in the afternoon. The boardwalk is a lively spot well into the evening, with a theme park, wacky museums and street performers keeping things interesting.

Liquid Assets   MODERN AMERICAN **$$**
(410-524-7037; https://la94.com/; 9301 Coastal Hwy, cnr 94th St & Coastal Hwy; mains $13-34; 11:30am-11pm Sun-Thu, to midnight Fri & Sat) Like a diamond in the rough, this bistro and wine shop is hidden in a strip mall in north OC. The menu is a refreshing mix of innovative seafood, grilled meats and regional classics.

Seacrets   BAR
(410-524-4900; www.seacrets.com; 117 49th St, cnr W 49th St & the Bay; 11am-midnight) A Jamaican-themed, rum-soaked bar straight out of MTV's *Spring Break*. You can drift around in an inner tube while sipping a drink and people-watching at OC's most famous meat-market. When it comes to the wildest beach party bar, this is the one against which all other claimants must be judged. The distillery, which opened in 2016, seems a bit superfluous.

ℹ Getting There & Around

Ocean City is 140 miles southeast of Baltimore via Hwy 10 and US 50. Greyhound no longer runs to Ocean City.

The **Coastal Highway Beach Bus** (410-723-2174; http://ococean.com/explore-oc/getting-around-oc; day pass $3; 24hr) travels up and down the length of the beach around the clock year-round. There's also a **tram** (📞 410-289-5311; http://ococean.com/explore-oc/getting-around-oc; per ride $3, day pass $6; ⊙11am-midnight Jun-Aug) that runs along the boardwalk (https://oceancitymd.gov/oc) from June through September. For details about off-season transit and schedules, visit www.shoretransit.org.

Western Maryland

The western spine of Maryland is mountain country. The Appalachian peaks soar to 3000ft above sea level, and the surrounding valleys are packed with rugged scenery and Civil War battlefields. This is Maryland's playground, where hiking, skiing, rock climbing and white-water rafting draw the outdoors-loving crowd.

When trip planning, remember that the narrow Maryland panhandle is bordered by Virginia, West Virginia and Pennsylvania. If you're exploring Civil War battlefields or looking for larger towns for an overnight stay, check our regional map for options that may be just a few miles over state lines.

ⓘ Getting There & Around

Towns in western Maryland may look close to each other on a map, but narrow and twisting mountain roads can extend driving times. The main interstates running east–west are the I-70 and I-68, with I-81 traveling north–south through the region. MARC trains stop in **Frederick** (📞 301-682-9716; https://mta.maryland.gov/marc-train; 100 S East St, Frederick) while Amtrak services Cumberland (p293). Greyhound stops in both Cumberland and Frederick. For flights, consider Dulles (p298) or Baltimore/Washington International Thurgood Marshall Airport (p278).

Frederick & Mt Airy

Central Frederick is, well, perfect. Its historic, pedestrian-friendly center of red-brick row houses is filled with a diverse array of restaurants. You'll also find an engaged, cultured arts community anchored by the excellent Weinberg Center for the Arts. The meandering Carroll Creek runs through it all, flanked by a lovely park with a mural-painted bridge, found at Carroll St. Unlike other communities in the region with historic districts, this is a mid-sized city, an important commuter base for thousands of federal government employees and a biotechnology hub in its own right.

The town of Mt Airy is 7 miles east of Frederick. Its compact downtown historic district is lined with 19th- and 20th-century buildings. Once a busy commercial stop along the B&O Railroad, today the downtown is a nice place to stretch your legs on a drive along the National Historic Road scenic byway (www.visitmaryland.org), which links Baltimore to western Maryland. Vineyards dot the region.

◉ Sights

Brunswick Visitor Center MUSEUM
(📞 301-834-7100; www.nps.gov/choh; 40 W Potomac St, Brunswick; rail museum adult/child $7/4; ⊙10am-2pm Thu & Fri, to 4pm Sat, 1-4pm Sun) The C&O Canal's little Brunswick Visitor Center doubles as the Brunswick Rail Museum. As quiet as this town is, it was once home to the largest rail yard (7 miles long) owned by a single company in the world. Those days are long past, but the museum will appeal to trainspotters, and you have to have a heart of stone not to be charmed by the 1700-square-foot model railroad that depicts the old Baltimore and Ohio railway.

Elk Run Vineyards WINERY
(📞 410-775-2513; www.elkrun.com; 15113 Liberty Rd, Mt Airy; tastings from $6, tours free; ⊙10am-6pm Tue, Wed & Sat, to 9pm Fri & 1-5pm Sun May-Sep, 10am-5pm Wed-Sat & noon-5pm Sun Oct-Apr) It's tough to go wrong with Elk Run Vineyards, almost exactly halfway between Mt Airy and New Market. Stop by for live music on Wine Down Fridays ($5, 3pm to 5pm).

National Museum of Civil War Medicine MUSEUM
(📞 301-695-1864; www.civilwarmed.org; 48 E Patrick St; adult/student/child $9.50/7/free; ⊙10am-5pm Mon-Sat, from 11am Sun) The National Museum of Civil War Medicine gives a fascinating, and sometimes gruesome, look at the health conditions soldiers and doctors faced during the war, as well as important medical advances that resulted from the conflict.

Antietam National Battlefield HISTORIC SITE
(📞 301-432-5124; www.nps.gov/anti; 5831 Dunker Church Rd, Sharpsburg, MD; 3-day pass per person/vehicle $5/10; ⊙grounds sunrise-sunset, visitor center 9am-5pm) The site of the bloodiest day in American history is now, ironically, supremely peaceful, quiet and haunting –

and uncluttered, save for plaques and statues. On September 17, 1862, General Robert E Lee's first invasion of the North was stalled here in a tactical stalemate that left more than 23,000 dead, wounded or missing – more casualties than America had suffered in all its previous wars combined. Check out the exhibits in the visitor center then walk or drive the grounds.

🛏 Sleeping & Eating

Hollerstown Hill B&B
B&B $$

(☑ 301-228-3630; www.hollerstownhill.com; 4 Clarke Pl, Frederick; r $149; 🅿 ✳ 🛜) The elegant, friendly Hollerstown has four pattern-heavy rooms, two resident terriers and an elegant billiards room. This lovely Victorian sits right in the middle of the historic downtown area of Frederick, so you're within easy walking distance of all the goodness.

Brewer's Alley
PUB FOOD $$

(☑ 301-631-0089; www.brewers-alley.com; 124 N Market St, Frederick; mains $9-22; ☉ noon-11:30pm; 🛜) This bouncy brewpub is one of our favorite places in Frederick for several reasons. First, the beer: house-brewed, plenty of variety, delicious. Second, the burgers: enormous, half-pound monstrosities of staggeringly yummy proportions. Third, the rest of the menu: excellent Chesapeake seafood (including a wood-fired pizza topped with crab) and Frederick county farm produce and meats. The small patio is pleasant on sunny days.

❶ Getting There & Away

Frederick is accessible via Greyhound (www.greyhound.com) and MARC (p291) trains at the station located across from the **visitor center** (☑ 301-600-4047; www.visitfrederick.org/visit/visitor-center; 151 S East St; ☉ 9am-5:30pm). The MARC train Brunswick Line connects Frederick with Harpers Ferry, WV, Silver Spring, MD and Washington, DC.

Cumberland

At the Potomac River, the frontier outpost of Fort Cumberland (not to be confused with the Cumberland Gap between Virginia and Kentucky) was the pioneer gateway across the Alleghenies to Pittsburgh and the Ohio River. Today Cumberland has expanded into the outdoor recreation trade to guide visitors to the region's rivers, forests and mountains. Sights are a short stroll from the pedestrian-friendly streets of downtown.

◉ Sights & Activities

C&O Canal National Historic Park
NATIONAL PARK

(☑ 301-739-4200; www.nps.gov/choh; ☉ sunrise-sunset) FREE A marvel of engineering, the C&O Canal was designed to stretch alongside the Potomac River from Chesapeake Bay to the Ohio River. Construction on the canal began in 1828 but was halted here in 1850 by the Appalachian Mountains. The park's protected 185-mile corridor includes a 12ft-wide towpath, hiking and bicycling trail, which goes all the way from here to Georgetown in DC. The **Cumberland Visitor Center** (☑ 301-722-8226; www.nps.gov/choh; 13 Canal St; ☉ 9am-5pm; 🅿) has displays chronicling the importance of river trade in eastern seaboard history.

Allegany Museum
MUSEUM

(☑ 301-777-7200; www.alleganymuseum.org; 3 Pershing St; ☉ 10am-4pm Tue-Sat, from 1pm Sun) FREE Set in the old courthouse, this is an intriguing place to delve into Cumberland's past, with exhibits by local folk artist and woodcarver Claude Yoder; a model of the old shanty town that sprang up along the canal; 1920s firefighting gear; and beautifully garbed puppets and other curiosities.

Western Maryland Scenic Railroad
TOURS

(☑ 800-872-4650; www.wmsr.com; 13 Canal St; adult/child $46/31; ☉ generally 11:30am Fri & Sat, 1pm Sun mid-Apr–Oct, hours & trips vary seasonally) Outside the Cumberland Visitor Center, near the start of the C&O Canal, passengers can catch steam-locomotive rides, traversing forests and steep ravines, to the Frostburg depot, a 3½-hour round-trip.

Cumberland Trail Connection
CYCLING

(☑ 301-777-8724; www.ctcbikes.com; 14 Howard St, Canal Pl; per half-day/day/week from $20/30/150; ☉ 8am-7pm Apr-Oct, 10:30am-6pm Nov-Mar) Conveniently located near the start of the C&O Canal, this outfit rents out bicycles (cruisers, touring bikes and mountain bikes), and also arranges shuttle service anywhere from Pittsburgh to DC.

🛏 Sleeping & Eating

Inn on Decatur
GUESTHOUSE $$

(☑ 301-722-4887; www.theinnondecatur.net; 108 Decatur St; r $142; ✳ 🛜) Offers comfy guestrooms just a short stroll to pedestrianized Baltimore St in downtown Cumberland. The friendly owners have a wealth of knowledge on the area, and offer a bike shuttle package.

Queen City Creamery & Deli   DINER $

([☎] 301-777-0011; www.queencitycreamery.com; 108 W Harrison St; mains $4-9; ⊗ 7am-9pm Mon-Thu, 7am-10pm Fri, 8am-10pm Sat, 8am-9pm Sun) This retro soda fountain is like a 1940s time warp, with creamy shakes and homemade frozen custard, thick sandwiches and belly-filling breakfasts.

ⓘ Getting There & Away

The **Amtrak station** (www.amtrak.com; 201 E Harrison St) is close to downtown. Cumberland is on the daily Capitol Limited route that links Washington, DC and Chicago. Pittsburgh is 100 miles northwest of the city. Greyhound buses also stop here. From the eastern part of the Maryland, Cumberland can be reached via I-70 and I-68.

DELAWARE

Tiny Delaware, the nation's second-smallest state (96 miles long and less than 35 miles across at its widest point) is overshadowed by its neighbors – and often overlooked by visitors to the region. And that's too bad, because Delaware has a lot more on offer than just tax-free shopping and chicken farms.

Long, white sandy beaches, cute colonial villages, a cozy countryside and small-town charm characterize the state that happily calls itself the 'Small Wonder.' It's also the home state of former vice president and US senator Joe Biden, a resident of Wilmington.

History

In colonial days, Delaware was the subject of an aggressive land feud between Dutch, Swedish and British settlers. The first two imported classically northern European middle-class concepts; the last a plantation-based aristocracy – which is partly why Delaware remains a typically mid-Atlantic cultural hybrid today.

The little state's big moment came on December 7, 1787, when Delaware became the first colony to ratify the US Constitution, thus becoming the first state in the Union. It remained in that union throughout the Civil War, despite supporting slavery. During this period, as throughout much of the state's history, the economy drew on its chemical industry. DuPont, the world's second-largest chemical company, was founded here in 1802 as a gunpowder factory by French immigrant Eleuthère Irénée du Pont. Low taxes drew other firms in the 20th century, boosting the state's prosperity.

ⓘ Getting There & Around

The coastal cities are 120 miles from both Washington, DC and Baltimore. Wilmington is in the northern reaches of the state, 75 miles northeast of Baltimore via I-95 and 30 miles south of Philadelphia via I-95 – and just a few miles from the Pennsylvania state line. Amtrak run seven routes through Wilmington. The closest major airport to Wilmington is Philadelphia International Airport.

Delaware Beaches

With beach towns for every personality along with gorgeous coastal views, Delaware's 28 miles of sandy Atlantic beaches are the best reason to linger here. They're also quick and easy to reach for city folk from Washington, DC, Baltimore and NYC looking to escape the grind. Most businesses and services are open year-round. Outside of June to August, bargains abound.

Lewes

In 1631 the Dutch gave this whaling settlement the pretty name of Zwaanendael, or Valley of the Swans, before promptly getting massacred by local Nanticokes. The name was changed to Lewes (*loo*-iss) when William Penn gained control of the area. Today it's an attractive gem with a mix of English and Dutch architecture. Pretty Cape Henlopen State Park is 2½ miles from downtown.

⊙ Sights & Activities

Cape Henlopen State Park   STATE PARK
([☎] 302-645-8983; www.destateparks.com/park/cape-henlopen; 15099 Cape Henlopen Dr; per car out-of-state/in-state $10/5; ⊗ 8am-sunset) One mile east of Lewes, more than 4000 acres of dune bluffs, pine forests and wetlands are preserved at this lovely state park that's popular with bird-watchers, beachgoers and campers. You can see clear to Cape May from the observation tower. **North Shores beach** draws many gay and lesbian couples. Campsites ($30 to $54) and cabins ($120) are also available. The admission fee is cash only.

Zwaanendael Museum   MUSEUM
([☎] 302-645-1148; www.http://history.delaware.gov/museums/zm/zm_main.shtml; 102 Kings Hwy; ⊗ 10am-5pm Tue, to 4:30pm Wed-Sat, 1:30-4:30pm Sun, open Wed-Sat only Mar-Oct) **FREE** This small, appealing museum is a good place to learn about the Dutch roots of Lewes.

Quest Fitness Kayak
KAYAKING

(☑ 302-745-2925; www.questkayak.com; 514 E Savannah Rd; kayak hire per 2-/8-hr $25/50; ☺ from 8am, close hours vary May-Sep, reservation only Oct-Apr) For aquatic action, Quest Fitness Kayak operates a kayak rental stand next to the Beacon Motel. It also runs scenic paddle tours around the Cape ($65).

🛏 Sleeping & Eating

Hotel Rodney
HOTEL $$

(☑ 302-645-6466; www.hotelrodneydelaware.com; 142 2nd St; r $179-259, ste $329; P ❄ @ 🛜 ☒) This charming boutique hotel features exquisite bedding and restored antique furniture, but it also has plenty of modern touches that keep it all feeling very fresh.

Wharf
SEAFOOD $$

(☑ 302-645-7846; www.thewharflewes.com; 7 Anglers Rd; mains $13-30; ☺ 11:30am-1am mid-May-early Oct; P 🖐) Across the drawbridge, the Wharf has a relaxing waterfront location, and serves a big selection of seafood and pub grub. Live music on weekends.

ℹ Getting There & Away

Cape May–Lewes Ferry (☑ 800-643-3779; www.capemaylewesferry.com; 43 Cape Henlopen Dr; per motorcycle/car $39/47, per adult/child 6-13yr $10/5) runs daily 90-minute ferries across Delaware Bay to New Jersey from the terminal, 1 mile from downtown Lewes. For foot passengers, a seasonal shuttle bus ($5) operates between the ferry terminal and Lewes. Reservations recommended. The town sits on the coast just off the Coastal Hwy/Rte 1.

Rehoboth Beach

As the closest stretch of sand to Washington, DC (121 miles), Rehoboth Beach is often dubbed 'the Nation's Summer Capital.' It is both a family-friendly and gay-friendly destination. To escape the chaos of busy Rehoboth Ave (and the heavily built-up outskirts), wander into the side streets downtown. There you'll find a mix of gingerbread houses, tree-lined streets, posh restaurants and kiddie amusements, plus a wide beach fronted by a mile-long boardwalk.

🛏 Sleeping

★ Cottages at Indian River Marina
COTTAGE $$$

(☑ 302-227-3071; www.destateparks.com/camping/cottages; 39415 Inlet Rd; weekly peak/shoulder/off-season $1900/1250/850, 2 days off-season $300; P ❄) These cottages, located in Delaware Seashore State Park five miles south of town, are some of our favorite local vacation rentals. Not for the decor per se, but for the patios and unadulterated views across the pristine beach to the ocean. Each cottage has two bedrooms and a loft.

Crosswinds Motel
MOTEL $$$

(☑ 302-227-7997; www.crosswindsmotel.com; 312 Rehoboth Ave; r $269-299; P ❄ 🛜) Rooms pop with a bit of fresh modern style at this simple but nicely designed motel in the heart of Rehoboth, with welcome amenities (mini fridge, coffeemaker, flat-screen TV) and friendly service. Walk to the beach in 12 minutes. Note that rates drop significantly during the week and in the off-season.

Hotel Rehoboth
BOUTIQUE HOTEL $$$

(☑ 302-227-4300; www.hotelrehoboth.com; 247 Rehoboth Ave; r $359; P ❄ @ 🛜 ☒) This boutique hotel has gained a reputation for great service and luxurious amenities, including a free shuttle to the beach.

🍴 Eating & Drinking

Henlopen City Oyster House
SEAFOOD $$$

(☑ 302-260-9193; www.hcoysterhouse.com; 50 Wilmington Ave; mains $10-36; ☺ 3-5pm happy hour only, dinner from 5pm, lunch served in the off-season) Seafood lovers won't want to miss this elegant but inviting spot, where an enticing raw bar and mouth-watering seafood dishes draw crowds (arrive early; no reservations). Good microbrews, cocktails and wine selections.

★ Dogfish Head Brewings & Eats
MICROBREWERY

(☑ 302-226-2739; www.dogfish.com; 320 Rehoboth Ave; mains $12-25; ☺ 11am-1am) Check the chalkboard to see the long list of brews available at this iconic brewery, which also serves up tasty pizzas, burgers, crab cakes and other pub fare. It all goes perfectly with the award-winning IPAs. Kids menu available with $6 meals. Dogfish, in its current location for 22 years, was preparing to open a $4 million brewpub next door at the time of research, with space for live music.

ℹ Getting There & Away

BestBus (www.bestbus.com) offers bus service from DC ($40, 2¼ hours) and NYC ($49, 4½ hours) to Rehoboth; runs summertime only (late May through early September).

The Jolly Trolley (www.jollytrolly.com) connects Rehoboth and Dewey beaches, and makes frequent stops along the way. A round-trip costs $5, and the trolley runs from 8am to 2am June to August. Cash only.

Wilmington

A unique cultural milieu (African Americans, Jews and Caribbeans) and an energetic arts scene make this city worth a visit. Wilmington is also a good launchpad for exploring the scenic Brandywine Valley, 6 miles north. And no description of Wilmington is complete without mentioning hometown politician Joe Biden, former vice-president and US senator, who regularly rode Amtrak between Wilmington and Washington, DC. After his tenure as vice-president ended in 2017, he rode Amtrak home.

⊙ Sights

Delaware Art Museum MUSEUM
(☑ 302-571-9590; www.delart.org; 2301 Kentmere Pkwy; adult/child 7-18yr $12/6, admission free Thu evenings & Sun; ☉ 10am-4pm Wed & Fri-Sun, to 8pm Thu) Exhibits work of the local Brandywine School, including Edward Hopper, John Sloan and three generations of Wyeths.

**Delaware Center for
the Contemporary Arts** MUSEUM
(☑ 302-656-6466; www.thedcca.org; 200 S Madison St; ☉ noon-5pm Tue & Sun, noon-7pm Wed, 10am-5pm Thu-Sat) FREE Consistently displays innovative exhibitions.

Delaware History Museum MUSEUM
(☑ 302-656-0637; www.dehistory.org; 504 N Market St; adult/child 3-18yr $6/4; ☉ 11am-4pm Wed-Sat) An art-deco Woolworth's building, this museum run by the Delaware Historical society proves the First State has done much more than earn its nickname, with historic documents, apparel and a range of artifacts.

🛏 Sleeping & Eating

Inn at Wilmington HOTEL $$
(☑ 855-532-2216; www.innatwilmington.com; 300 Rocky Run Pkwy; r/ste $129/159; P ❄ 🛜) This is a charming, good-value option 5 miles north of downtown.

Hotel du Pont HOTEL $$$
(☑ 302-594-3100; www.hoteldupont.com; cnr Market & 11th Sts; r from $199; P ❄ 🛜) The premier hotel in the state, the du Pont is luxurious and classy enough to satisfy its namesake (one of America's most successful industrialist families). The spot exudes an art-deco majesty that Jay Gatsby would have been proud of, but the goodness goes beyond the impressive lobby to well-appointed rooms and proximity to a handsome shopping arcade.

Iron Hill Brewery PUB FOOD $$
(☑ 302-472-2739; www.ironhillbrewery.com; 620 Justison St; mains $12-30; ☉ 11:30am-11pm Mon-Fri, from 11am Sat & Sun) The spacious and airy multilevel Iron Hill Brewery is set in a converted brick warehouse on the riverfront. Satisfying microbrews go nicely with hearty pub grub.

❶ Getting There & Away

Just off I-95, Wilmington is midway between Washington, DC and New York City, about two hours from either city. **Greyhound** (101 N French St) stops downtown. Amtrak (www.amtrak.com) trains leave from the **Joseph R. Biden Jr Railroad Station** (☑ 800-872-7245; www.amtrak.com; 100 S French St) and connect Wilmington with DC (1½ hours), Baltimore (45 minutes) and New York (two hours).

Brandywine Valley

After making their fortune, the French-descended Du Ponts turned the Brandywine Valley into a sort of American Loire Valley. It remains a nesting ground for the wealthy and ostentatious to this day. A few miles north of downtown Wilmington, the Delaware section is just one part of the 350-square-mile valley, which straddles the Brandywine River into Pennsylvania.

⊙ Sights & Activities

Winterthur HISTORIC SITE
(☑ 302-888-4600; www.winterthur.org; 5105 Kennett Pike (Rte 52); adult/child 2-11yr $20/5; ☉ 10am-5pm Tue-Sun) Six miles northwest of Wilmington is the 175-room country estate of industrialist Henry Francis du Pont and his collection of antiques and American arts, one of the world's largest. Nice gardens too.

Brandywine Creek State Park STATE PARK
(☑ 302-577-3534; www.destateparks.com/park/brandywine-creek; 41 Adams Dam Rd; per vehicle $8; ☉ 8am-sunset) This state park is the gem of the area. This green space would be impressive anywhere, but is doubly so considering how close it is to prodigious urban development. Nature trails and shallow streams wend through the park.

Wilderness Canoe Trips
CANOEING

(☑302-654-2227; www.wildernesscanoetrips.com; 2111 Concord Pike; solo kayak $53, tandem kayak or canoe trip from $63, tube $23) Call this outfit for for information on paddling or tubing down the dark-green Brandywine Creek.

🍽 Sleeping & Eating

You'll find chain hotels in downtown Wilmington. B&Bs and inns dot the landscape around the Brandywine River just north of downtown and in nearby southern Pennsylvania.

For a wide range of choices, head into Wilmington, while fine dining and tavern and pub fare are highlights in Chadd's Ford and Kennett Sq just over the state line in Pennsylvania.

ℹ Getting There & Away

Greyhound stops at the Wilmington Transportation Center (p295). Amtrak (www.amtrak.com) trains also leave from here and connect Wilmington with DC (1½ hours), Baltimore (45 minutes) and New York (two hours).

New Castle

As cute as a colonial kitten, New Castle is a web of cobblestoned streets and beautifully preserved 18th-century buildings lying near a riverfront (that said, however, the surrounding area is unfortunately a bit of an urban wasteland). Sights include the Old Court House, the arsenal on the Green, churches and cemeteries dating back to the 17th century, and historic houses.

👁 Sights

Amstel House
MUSEUM

(☑302-322-2794; www.newcastlehistory.org; 2 E 4th St; adult/child 6-12yr $6/2, with Dutch House $10/3; ⊙10am-4pm Wed-Sat, from noon Sun Apr-Dec) One of three museums overseen by the New Castle Historical Society, this house is a surviving remnant of 1730s colonial opulence. Guided tours available April through December.

Dutch House
MUSEUM

(☑302-322-2794; www.newcastlehistory.org; 32 E 3rd St; adult/child 6-12yr $6/2, with Amstel House $10/3; ⊙10am-4pm Wed-Sat, from noon Sun Apr-Dec) A small example of a working residence dating from the late 1600s. Tours offered at 1pm and 3pm.

Old Court House
MUSEUM

(☑302-323-4453; http://history.delaware.gov; 211 Delaware St; ⊙10am-4:30pm Tue-Sat, 1:30-4:30pm Sun) FREE Dates back to the 17th century and is now operated as a museum by the state.

🍽 Sleeping & Eating

Terry House B&B
B&B $$

(☑302-322-2505; www.terryhouse.com; 130 Delaware St; r $90-110; P 🛜) The owner of the five-room Terry House B&B will sometimes play the piano for guests while they enjoy a full breakfast. That's a treat for sure, but we're more impressed by the historical grounds and the supremely cozy rooms; there's nothing like stepping from a historical village into historical accommodations.

Dog House
AMERICAN $

(☑302-328-5380; 1200 N Dupont Hwy; mains under $10; ⊙10:30am-midnight) This unassuming countertop diner on the outskirts of New Castle might be the best dining option in town. Don't be fooled by the name; while this place does hot dogs and does them exceedingly well (the chili dogs are a treat), it also whips out mean subs and cheesesteaks that could pass muster in Philly.

Jessop's Tavern
AMERICAN $$

(☑302-322-6111; www.jessops-tavern; 114 Delaware St; mains $12-24; ⊙11:30am-10pm Mon-Thu, to 11pm Fri & Sat, to 9pm Sun) Tonight we're going to party like its 1679. Serves up Dutch pot roast, 'Pilgrim's Feast' (oven-roasted turkey with all the fixings) and Belgian beers in a colonial atmosphere. Offers 21 beers on draft – 11 Belgian and 10 craft. The building dates from 1674.

ℹ Getting There & Away

New Castle borders the Delaware River. Hwy 9 connects New Castle with Wilmington, which is 7 miles north.

Dover

Dover's city center is quite attractive; the row house–lined streets are peppered with restaurants and shops, while broadleaf trees spread their branches over pretty little lanes. Most museums and historic sites are downtown near the capitol, with a couple just south of downtown off Rte 1.

⊙ Sights

Old State House
MUSEUM

(☎302-744-5055; http://history.delaware.gov/museums; 25 The Green; ⊙9am-4:30pm Mon-Sat, plus 1:30-4:30pm Sun Apr-Sep) **FREE** Take a moment to enjoy the short docent tour for this small but interesting site. Built in 1791 and since restored, the Old State House contains art galleries and in-depth exhibits about the First State's history and politics. We learned here that every state house in the USA has a portrait of George Washington!

First State Heritage Park Welcome Center & Galleries
MUSEUM

(☎302-739-9194; www.destateparks.com/park/first-state-heritage; 121 Martin Luther King Blvd N; ⊙8am-4:30pm Mon-Fri, 9am-4:30pm Sat, 1:30-4:30pm Sun) **FREE** Delve into the history of Delaware at the First State Heritage Park, which serves as a welcome center for the city of Dover, the state of Delaware and the adjacent state house. This so-called 'park without boundaries' includes some two dozen historic sites within a few blocks of one another. Start out at the Welcome Center & Galleries, which has exhibitions exploring Delaware's history. You can pick up more info here on other key sites nearby.

John Dickinson Plantation
MUSEUM

(☎302-739-3277; http://history.delaware.gov/museums; 340 Kitts Hummock Rd; ⊙10am-4:30pm Tue-Sat, plus Sun 1:30-4:30pm Apr-Sep; P) **FREE** A restored 18th-century home of the founding father of the same name, also known as the Penman of the Revolution for his eloquent arguments for independence.

Air Mobility Command Museum
MUSEUM

(☎302-677-5938; www.amcmuseum.org; 1301 Heritage Rd; ⊙9am-4pm Tue-Sun) **FREE** If you're into aviation, you'll enjoy this museum; the nearby airfield holds more than 30 restored vintage cargo and freight planes, including C-130s, a Vietnam War–era C-7 and a World War 2–era 'Flying Boxcar.'

Dover Air Force Base (AFB) is a visible symbol of American military muscle and a poignant reminder of the cost of war. This is the location of the Department of Defense's largest mortuary, and traditionally the first stop on native soil for the remains of American service members killed overseas.

Bombay Hook National Wildlife Refuge
WILDLIFE RESERVE

(☎302-653-9345; www.fws.gov/refuge/Bombay_Hook; 2591 Whitehall Neck Rd, Smyrna; per vehicle/pedestrian $4/2; ⊙sunrise-sunset) Hundreds of thousands of waterfowl use this protected wetland as a stopping point along their migration routes. A 12-mile wildlife driving trail, running through 16,251 acres of saltwater marsh, cordgrass and tidal mud flats, manages to encapsulate all of the soft beauty of the DelMarVa peninsula in one perfectly preserved ecosystem. There are also short walking trails and observation towers.

🛏 Sleeping

Dover may be somewhat small but it's the state capital, so there are plenty of options.

State Street Inn
B&B $$

(☎302-734-2294; www.statestreetinn.com; 228 N State St; r $100-135; ❄) The inn was switching ownership at the time of research, so there may be a few changes in the works, but the current incarnation has cute rooms with flower-patterned wallpapers. It offers an unbeatable central location.

✗ Eating & Drinking

Flavors of India
INDIAN $$

(☎302-677-0121; www.flavorofindia.com; 348 N Dupont Hwy; mains $12-19; ⊙11am-10pm; P🖋♿) To say this place is an unexpected delight would be an understatement. First: it's in a Super 8 Motel off the highway. Second: *it's great.* The standards – vindaloos and kormas and tikka masalas – are all wonderful. Goat palakwala (goat curry with a spinach base)? Amazing. Also by far the best vegetarian option in the area.

Golden Fleece
PUB

(☎302-674-1776; www.goldenfleecetavern.com; 132 W Loockerman St; mains $4-11; ⊙6pm-1am Sat-Thu, from 4pm Fri) The best bar in Dover also serves up some good food – that you can order from the local pizza joint. First priority is maintaining the atmosphere of an old English pub, which meshes well with the surrounding red-brick Dover historical center. Has an outdoor patio for summer nights.

❶ Getting There & Away

Dover is 50 miles south of Wilmington via Rte 1. US 301 connects Dover and Baltimore, which is 85 miles west. DART Bus 301 runs between Wilmington and the **Dover Transit Center** (www.dartfirststae.com), which is a half-mile from downtown Dover. One-way fare is $6. **Greyhound** (☎800-231-2222; www.greyhound.com; 654 N Dupont Hwy) buses stop 2 miles north of downtown.

VIRGINIA

The Commonwealth of Virginia is steeped in history and tradition. It's the birthplace of America, where English settlers established the first permanent colony in the New World in 1607. From then on, Virginia has played a lead role in nearly every major American drama, from the Revolutionary and Civil Wars to the Civil Rights movement and the attacks of September 11, 2001.

Virginia's natural beauty is as diverse as its history and people. Chesapeake Bay and the wide sandy beaches kiss the Atlantic Ocean. Pine forests, marshes and rolling green hills form the soft curves of the central Piedmont region, while the rolling Blue Ridge mountains and stunning Shenandoah Valley line its back.

Beyond northern Virginia, the state is shaking off cobwebs and outdated traditions. As the old joke goes: How many Virginians does it take to change a lightbulb? Two. One to change the bulb and the other to talk about how much better the old one was. While this is still marginally true, slow-to-change cities like Richmond and Roanoke are recently energized. The markers of change include vibrant art scenes, a slew of buzzy new restaurants and microbreweries, and marketing campaigns spotlighting outdoor adventures – like new cycling and paddling trails – and not just stodgy history.

History

Humans have occupied Virginia for at least 5000 years. Several thousand Native Americans were already here in May 1607 when Captain James Smith and his crew sailed up Chesapeake Bay and founded Jamestown, the first permanent English colony in the New World. Named for Queen Elizabeth I – aka the 'Virgin Queen' – the territory originally occupied most of America's eastern seaboard. By 1610 most of the colonists had died from starvation in their quest for gold, until colonist John Rolfe (husband of Pocahontas) discovered Virginia's real riches: tobacco.

A feudal aristocracy grew out of tobacco farming, and many gentry scions became Founding Fathers, including native son George Washington. In the 19th century the slave-based plantation system grew both in size and incompatibility with the industrializing North; Virginia seceded in 1861 and became the epicenter of the Civil War. Following its defeat, the state walked a tense cultural tightrope, accruing a layered identity

that included older aristocrats, a rural and urban working class, waves of immigrants and, today, the burgeoning tech-heavy suburbs of DC. The state revels in its history, yet still wants to pioneer the American experiment; thus, while Virginia only reluctantly desegregated in the 1960s, today it houses one of the most ethnically diverse populations of the New South.

❶ Getting There & Around

The largest regional airports include **Washington Dulles International Airport** (IAD; www.metwashairports.com; 🖥) in Northern Virginia, Richmond International Airport (p307) in Richmond, **Norfolk International Airport** (NIA; ☑757-857-3351; www.norfolkairport.com; 2200 Norview Ave; 🖥) in Norfolk, and **Roanoke-Blacksburg Regional Airport** (☑540-362-1999; www.roanokeairport.com; 5202 Aviation Dr NW) in Southwest Virginia. American and Delta serve Charlottesville Albemarle Airport (p314) in the Piedmont region.

Amtrak stops in Richmond at Main St Station (p307) and Staples Mill Rd Station (p307). There are also trains stations in Charlottesville (p314) and in Staunton (p315). In and around Northern Virginia, Amtrak stops in Fredericksburg (p304) and near Manassas National Battlefield Park (p299).

Northern Virginia

Safe, green-conscious, well trimmed and full of surprises, Northern Virginia (NoVa) is DC's perfect neighbor, just across from the picket fence of the Potomac River. NoVa communities are basically suburbs of Washington, attached via the Metro. We concentrate on the towns of Arlington and Alexandria, which combine crucial capital sites with historic sites, cozy pubs and a buzzing food scene.

Start with Arlington. It's quite close, just a Metro stop from DC, and it holds the two main reasons to cross the border: Arlington National Cemetery and the Pentagon. Plan on a half-day for these two sights alone. Beyond Arlington you'll find the jaw-dropping Steven F Udvar-Hazy Center, aka the annex of the National Air and Space Museum, which holds three times as many jets and rockets as the Mall building. Also out this way are the Eden Center, a Saigon-style foodie emporium where the Vietnamese community clusters, and Annandale, the Korean community's hub. Unfortunately you'll be hard-pressed to reach these places without a car.

The charming village of Alexandria is 5 miles and 250 years away from Washington. Once a salty port, Alexandria – known as 'Old Town' to locals – is today a posh collection of red-brick homes, cobblestone streets, gas lamps and a waterfront promenade. Boutiques, outdoor cafes and bars pack the main thoroughfare, making the town a fine afternoon or evening jaunt. It's also a jumping-off spot for excursions to Mount Vernon.

Arlington

◉ Sights

★ **Pentagon**   NOTABLE BUILDING
(☑ 703-697-1776; www.pentagontours.osd.mil; Arlington; ⊙ memorial 24hr, tours by appointment 10am-4pm Mon-Thu, noon-4pm Fri; Ⓜ Blue, Yellow Lines to Pentagon) South of Arlington Cemetery is the Pentagon, the largest office building in the world. Outside you may visit the **Pentagon Memorial** (www.pentagonmemorial. org; ⊙ 24hr) FREE; 184 illuminated benches honor each person killed in the September 11, 2001, terrorist attack on the Pentagon. To get inside the building, you'll have to book a free guided one-hour tour on the website and provide appropriate photo ID. Make reservations 14 to 90 days in advance.

Nearby, the Pentagon, you can spot three soaring arcs of the **Air Force Memorial** (☑ 703-247-5805; www.airforcememorial.org; 1 Air Force Memorial Dr; ⊙ 9am-9pm Apr-Sep, 8am-8pm Oct-Mar) FREE, which invokes the contrails of jets.

★ **Arlington National Cemetery**   CEMETERY
(☑ 877-907-8585; www.arlingtoncemetery.mil; ⊙ 8am-7pm Apr-Sep, to 5pm Oct-Mar; Ⓜ Blue Line to Arlington Cemetery) FREE Arlington is the somber final resting place for more than 400,000 military personnel and their dependents. The 624-acre grounds contain the dead of every war the USA has fought since the Revolution. Highlights include the Tomb of the Unknown Soldier, with its elaborate changing of the guard ceremony (every hour on the hour October through March; every half-hour April through September), and the grave of John F Kennedy and his family, marked by an eternal flame.

Departing from the visitor center, hop-on, hop-off bus tours are an easy way to visit the cemetery's main sights. Other points of interest include the Space **Shuttle Challenger Memorial**; the **USS Maine Memo-**

OFF THE BEATEN TRACK

MANASSAS NATIONAL BATTLEFIELD PARK

The site of two major Confederate victories early in the Civil War, **Manassas National Battlefield Park** (☑ 703-361-1339; www.nps.gov/mana; 12521 Lee Hwy; ⊙ park dawn-dusk, visitor center 8:30am-5pm, tours 11:15am, 12:15pm & 2:15pm Jun-Aug) today is a curving green hillscape, sectioned into fuzzy fields of tall grass and wildflowers by split-rail wood fences. Start your tour at the **Henry Hill Visitor Center** (☑ 703-361-1339; www.nps. gov/mana; ⊙ 8:30am-5pm) FREE to watch the orientation film and pick up park and trail maps. Guided tours also offered.

rial, marked by the battleship's huge mast; the controversial **Confederate Memorial** that honors war dead from the Civil War's breakaway states; and the tomb of DC city planner **Pierre L'Enfant**. The **Iwo Jima Memorial** (Ⓜ Blue Line to Arlington Cemetery), displaying the famous raising of the flag over Mt Suribachi, is on the cemetery's fringes.

Much of the cemetery was built on the grounds of **Arlington House** (☑ 703-235-1530; www.nps.gov/arho; ⊙ 9:30am-4:30pm) FREE, the former home of Robert E Lee and his wife Mary Anna Custis Lee, a descendant of Martha Washington. When Lee left to lead Virginia's army in the Civil War, Union troops confiscated the property to bury their dead.

George Washington Memorial Parkway   PARKWAY
(☑ 703-289-2500; www.nps.gov/gwmp; Ⓜ Blue Line to Arlington Cemetery) The 25-mile Virginia portion of the highway honors its namesake with recreation areas and memorials all the way south to his old estate at Mount Vernon. It's lined with remnants of George Washington's life and works, such as his old Patowmack Company canal (in Great Falls National Park) and parks that were once part of his farmlands (Riverside Park, Fort Hunt Park). The 18.5-mile-long **Mount Vernon Trail** parallels the parkway.

Kennedy Gravesites   TOMB
(Ⓜ Blue Line to Arlington Cemetery) An eternal flame flickers beside this simple but moving gravesite – the final resting place for President John F Kennedy and Jacqueline Kennedy Onassis.

DEA Museum

MUSEUM

(United States Drug Enforcement Agency Museum; ☑ 202-307-3463; www.deamuseum.org; 700 Army Navy Dr, entrance on S Hayes St; ⊙10am-4pm Tue-Fri; Ⓜ Blue, Yellow Lines to Pentagon City) FREE The propaganda is served up with nary a chuckle at this heavy-handed museum brought to you by the Drug Enforcement Agency (DEA). Exhibits cover the last century-and-a-half of drug use, from the opium parlors of the 19th century to 1920s cocaine-dispensing apothecaries, on to the trippy days of the 1960s, the crack epidemic of the 1980s, and more recent days of crystal-meth labs and the powder drugs favored by the 24-hour party people of today.

🛏 Sleeping & Eating

In addition to hotels, there are dozens of chic restaurants and bars located along Clarendon and Wilson Blvds, clustered near the Rosslyn and Clarendon Metro stations.

El Pollo Rico

LATIN AMERICAN $

(☑ 703-522-3220; www.elpolloricorestaurant. com; 932 N Kenmore St; chicken with sides $7-18; ⊙11:30am-8:30pm; Ⓜ Orange, Silver Lines to Clarendon or Virginia Sq-GMU) Drooling locals have flocked to this Peruvian chicken joint for decades, in search of tender, juicy, flavor-packed birds served with succulent (highly addictive) dipping sauces, crunchy fries and sloppy 'slaw. Lines form outside the door come dinnertime.

Myanmar

BURMESE $

(☑ 703-289-0013; 7810 Lee Hwy, Falls Church; mains $10-14; ⊙noon-10pm; Ⓜ Orange Line to Dunn Loring Merrifield) Myanmar's decor is barebones; the service is slow; the portions are small; and the food is delicious. This is home-cooked Burmese: curries prepared with lots of garlic, turmeric and oil, chili fish, mango salads and chicken swimming in rich gravies.

Yechon

KOREAN $$

(☑ 703-914-4646; www.yechon.com; 4121 Hummer Rd, Annandale; mains $7-40; ⊙24hr; Ⓜ Blue, Yellow Lines to King St) Debates over who does the best Korean in the DC area have been the source of much gastronomic bickering, but Yechon is always among the frontrunners. The *kalbi* (barbecue ribs) is rich, smoky and packed with flavor, and goes nicely with the complex seaweed and searing kimchi.

🍷 Drinking & Entertainment

Continental

LOUNGE

(www.continentalpoollounge.com; 1911 N Fort Myer Dr; ⊙11:30am-2am Mon-Fri, 6pm-2am Sat & Sun; Ⓜ Rosslyn) A stone's throw from many Rosslyn hotels, this buzzing pool lounge evokes a trippy, tropical vibe with its murals of palm trees, oversized tiki heads and color-saturated bar stools. All of which sets the stage for an alternating night of shooting pool, playing ping pong or trying shuffleboard.

Whitlow's on Wilson

BAR

(☑ 703-276-9693; www.whitlows.com; 2854 Wilson Blvd; ⊙11am-2am Mon-Fri, 9am-2am Sat & Sun; Ⓜ Clarendon) Occupying almost an entire block just east of Clarendon Metro, Whitlow's on Wilson has something for everyone: burgers, brunch and comfort food on the menu; happening happy hours and positive pick-up potential; plus 12 brews on tap, a pool table, jukebox, live music and an easygoing atmosphere. Head to the rooftop tiki bar in warmer months.

⭐ Iota

LIVE MUSIC

(☑ 703-522-8340; www.iotaclubandcafe.com; 2832 Wilson Blvd; tickets $10-15; ⊙4pm-2am Mon-Thu, from 10am Fri-Sun; 🎤; Ⓜ Clarendon) With shows almost every night of the week, Iota is the best venue for live music in Clarendon's music strip. Bands span genres: folk, reggae, traditional Irish and Southern rock are all distinct possibilities. Tickets are available at the door only (no advance sales) and this place packs 'em in.

🛈 Getting There & Away

Arlington borders I-66 and is partially encircled by I-495, which loops around DC.

Massive **Washington Dulles International Airport** (p298) is 26 miles west of DC.

From DC, use the Arlington Cemetery (Blue Line) to get to the cemetery and the Pentagon (Blue and Yellow Lines) stations to visit Pentagon sites.

Alexandria

◉ Sights

⭐ Mount Vernon

HISTORIC SITE

(☑ 800-429-1520, 703-780-2000; www.mount vernon.org; 3200 Mount Vernon Memorial Hwy; adult/child 6-11yr $20/10; ⊙8am-5pm Apr-Aug, 9am-4pm Nov-Feb, to 5pm Mar, Sep & Oct, gristmill & distillery 10am-5pm Apr-Oct) One of the most visited historic shrines in the nation, Mount

Vernon was the beloved home of George and Martha Washington, who lived here from the time of their marriage in 1759 until George's death in 1799. Now owned and operated by the Mount Vernon Ladies Association, the estate offers glimpses of 18th-century farm life and the first president's life as a country planter. Mount Vernon does not gloss over the Founding Father's slave ownership: visitors can tour the slave quarters and burial ground.

★ **Carlyle House** HISTORIC BUILDING
(☑703-549-2997; www.novaparks.com; 121 N Fairfax St; adult/child 6-12yr $5/3; ☺10am-4pm Tue-Sat, noon-4pm Sun; Ⓜ King St, Old Town) If you have time for just one historic house tour in Alexandria, make it this one. The house dates from 1753 when merchant and city founder, John Carlyle, built the most lavish mansion in town (which in those days was little more than log cabins and muddy lanes). The Georgian Palladian-style house is packed with paintings, historic relics and period furnishings that help bring the past to life.

Freedom House Museum MUSEUM
(☑708-836-2858; www.visitalexandriava.com/listings/freedom-house/4676; 1315 Duke St; ☺10:30am-2:30pm Mon-Fri, guided tours & weekends by appointment only; Ⓜ King St, Old Town) FREE This demure Federal-style row house holds a tragic story. At a time when Alexandria was the nation's second-largest slave center (after New Orleans), a flourishing slave-trading business occupied this building and adjoining space. A well-presented basement museum, developed by the Northern Virginia Urban League, powerfully tells the stories of the thousands of enslaved people who passed through. Personal video narratives and artifacts are on view in a heartbreaking setting.

George Washington Masonic National Memorial MONUMENT
(☑703-683-2007; www.gwmemorial.org; 101 Callahan Dr at King St; adult/child under 13yr $15/free; ☺9am-5pm; Ⓜ Blue, Yellow Lines to King St, Old Town) Alexandria's most prominent landmark features a fine view from its 333ft tower, where you can see the Capitol, Mount Vernon and the Potomac River. It is modeled after Egypt's Lighthouse of Alexandria, and honors the first president (who was initiated into the Masons in Fredericksburg in 1752 and later became Worshipful Master of Alexandria Lodge No 22). There's a commanding

17ft-high statue of Washington in the portico. On the tour you'll see artifacts donated by Washington's family, including the 1792 family bible.

Torpedo Factory Art Center ARTS CENTER
(☑703-746-4570; www.torpedofactory.org; 105 N Union St; ☺10am-6pm Fri-Wed, to 9pm Thu; Ⓜ King St) FREE What do you do with a former munitions dump and arms factory? How about turning it into one of the best art spaces in the region? Three floors of artist studios and free creativity are on offer in Old Town Alexandria, as well as the opportunity to buy paintings, sculptures, glass works, textiles and jewelry direct from their creators. The Torpedo Factory anchors Alexandria's revamped waterfront with a marina, parks, walkways, residences and restaurants.

National Inventors Hall of Fame & Museum MUSEUM
(☑571-272-0095; www.invent.org/honor/hall-of-fame-museum/; 600 Dulany St, Madison Bldg; ☺10am-5pm Mon-Fri, 11am-3pm Sat; Ⓜ Blue, Yellow Lines to King St) FREE This museum, in the atrium of the US Patent and Trademark Office, tells the history of the US patent. Step inside to see where the story started in 1917 in Memphis, Tennessee, when a wholesale grocer named Clarence Saunders invented and patented what he called 'self-servicing' stores, now commonly known as supermarkets.

🛏 Sleeping

Expensive boutique hotels cluster in and around Old Town. You'll have to travel outside the neighborhood to find cheaper options.

Alexandrian HISTORIC HOTEL $$
(☑703-549-6080; www.thealexandrian.com; 480 King St; r $209-259; ❄✦🐾; Ⓜ Blue, Yellow Lines to King St-Old Town) Bold colors and fun details (mod throw pillows, geometric carpets) add a dash of bohemian whimsy to the 241 guestrooms and suites of this sophisticated, one-of-a-kind hotel. Occupying a historic six-story red-brick structure, it's ideally located on King St just four blocks from the waterfront. Guests applaud its friendly staff, proximity to restaurants and shops, and indoor heated pool.

Morrison House BOUTIQUE HOTEL $$
(☑703-838-8000; www.morrisonhouse.com; 116 S Alfred St; r $199-259, ste $329; ℗✦❄@ ❄✦🐾; Ⓜ Blue Line to King St) 🌱 A romantic Old Town mainstay, this chic boutique hotel

is now managed by Marriott as a member of the Autograph Collection family of hotels. The Federal-style beauty combines modern takes on tradition: four-poster beds, orange-plaid carpeting, bright blue artwork, Italian marble bathrooms and natural light everywhere.

✖ Eating

Busy restaurants and bars line King St and its offshoots in Old Town. Along Mt Vernon Ave in the Del Ray neighborhood, a short drive from Old Town, you'll find a growing line-up of coffee shops and restaurants, many with inviting patios. The free trolley from the King St metro station will get you to Alexandria's Old Town's eateries.

Stomping Ground   BREAKFAST $
(☑703-364-8912; www.stompdelray.com; 309 Mt Vernon Ave; mains $9-12; ☻7am-3pm Tue-Sat, 9am-3pm Sun) Did somebody say biscuit? Oh yes they did. And make that a scratch-made buttermilk biscuit piled with fillings of your choice, from fried chicken and Benton's bacon to poached eggs, pimiento cheese and avocado. Or just stop by this Del Ray spot for coffee and to work on your laptop. Order at the counter then settle into the rustically chic digs.

Caphe Banh Mi   VIETNAMESE $
(☑703-549-0800; www.caphebahnmi.com; 407 Cameron St; mains $6-12; ☻11am-3pm & 5-9pm Mon-Fri, 11am-9pm Sat, 11am-8pm Sun; Ⓜ King St) Stop in this neighborhood favorite for delicious *banh mi* sandwiches, big bowls of pho, pork-belly steamed buns and other simple but well-executed Vietnamese dishes. The small but cozy space always draws a crowd, so go early to beat the dinner rush.

Hank's Oyster Bar   SEAFOOD $$
(☑703-739-4265; www.hanksoysterbar.com; 1026 King St; lunch mains $13-25, dinner mains $14-32; ☻11:30am-midnight Mon-Fri, from 11am Sat & Sun) Get your oyster fix during happy hour (3pm to 7pm Monday to Friday) when the briny critters are only $2.50 apiece at this new outpost of the popular Dupont Circle flagship. If you're not sure which oysters to pick from the long list, they'll do a sampler for ya. The seafood dishes and varied small plates are also strong. The bar is the place to be.

Brabo Tasting Room   BELGIAN $$
(☑703-894-5252; www.braborestaurant.com; 1600 King St; breakfast mains $14-16, lunch & dinner mains $14-22; ☻7:30-10:30am & 11:30am-11pm

Mon-Thu, 7:30am-10:30am & 11:30am-midnight Fri, 8-11am & 11:30am-midnight Sat, 8-11am & 11:30am-10pm Sun; Ⓜ King St) The inviting and sunlit Brabo Tasting Room serves its signature mussels, tasty wood-fired tarts and gourmet sandwiches with a good beer and wine selection. In the morning, stop by for brioche French toast and Bloody Marys. Brabo restaurant, next door, is the high-end counterpart serving seasonal fare.

Restaurant Eve   AMERICAN $$$
(☑703-706-0450; www.restauranteve.com; 110 S Pitt St; lunch mains $17-26, dinner mains $27-42, 5-course tasting menu $105; ☻11:30am-2pm Mon-Fri, 5:30-10pm Mon-Sat; ✐; Ⓜ King St) One of Alexandria's best (and priciest) dining rooms, Eve blends great American ingredients, precise French technique and first-rate service. Splurge here on the tasting menus, which are simply on another level of gastronomic experience. The Lickety Split menu ($15; two choices from limited menu) draws a crowd to the bar at lunch.

▼ Drinking & Entertainment

Head to King St for good bar-hopping with a crowd of folks who seem to be perpetually enrolled in the University of Virginia, Virginia Tech or George Mason University.

Captain Gregory's   COCKTAIL BAR
(www.captaingregorys.com; 804 N Henry St; ☻6pm-midnight Wed & Thu, 5:30pm-2am Fri & Sat, 5:30pm-11pm Sun) This nautical-themed speakeasy is hidden inside a Sugar Shack doughnut shop, which explains the decadent gourmet doughnut on the menu. As for drinks, from Anais Needs a Vacay to Moaning Myrtles Morning Tea, the names are as diverse as the ingredients. Think flavored liqueurs, infused spirits and a range of fruit and spices. Cocktails run $14 to $16, and the menu changes frequently. Reservations required.

Union Street Public House   PUB
(☑703-548-1785; www.unionstreetpublichouse. com; 121 S Union St; ☻11:30am-10pm Mon-Thu, 11:30am-11pm Fri, 10am-11pm Sat, 10am-9pm Sun; Ⓜ King St) Gas lamps out front welcome tourists and locals into this spacious taproom for frosty brews, raw-bar delights and nightly dinner specials.

Birchmere   LIVE MUSIC
(www.birchmere.com; 3701 Mt Vernon Ave; tickets $25-70; ☻box office 5-9pm, shows 7:30pm; Ⓜ Pentagon City) This 50-year-old place, hailing

itself as 'America's Legendary Music Hall,' hosts a wide range of fare, from old-time folk musicians to country, blues and R&B stars. The line-up also features the odd burlesque show, indie rock bands and the occasional one-person comedy show.

ℹ Getting There & Away

To get to Alexandria from downtown DC, take the metro to the King St station. A free **trolley** (www.dashbus.com/trolley; ⊙10am-10:15pm Sun-Wed, to midnight Thu-Sat) makes the 1-mile journey between the metro station and the waterfront. **Capitol Bikeshare** (☑877-430-2453; www.capitalbikeshare.com) has 31 stations across Alexandria.

Fredericksburg

Fredericksburg is a pretty town with a historic district that's almost a cliché of small-town Americana. George Washington grew up here, and the Civil War exploded in the streets and surrounding fields. Today the main street is a pleasant amble of bookstores, gastropubs and cafes.

◉ Sights

Ellwood Manor   HISTORIC SITE
(☑540-786-2880; www.nps.gov/frsp; Rte 20, just west of Rte 3; ⊙10am-5pm Sat & Sun) This fascinating home sits on the grounds of the Wilderness Battlefield. Perhaps best known as the burial site for Confederate Gen Stonewall Jackson's amputated arm – there is a marker – the circa 1790 manor here once anchored a 5000-acre estate. Step inside to learn the interesting history of the house; the Marquis de Lafayette once dined here.

Fredericksburg & Spotsylvania
National Military Park   HISTORIC SITE
(☑540-693-3200; www.nps.gov/frsp; 1013 Lafayette Blvd; ⊙Fredericksburg & Chancellorsville visitor centers 9am-5pm, hours vary at other exhibit areas) FREE More than 13,000 Americans were killed during the Civil War in four battles fought in a 17-mile radius covered by this park: Fredericksburg, Chancellorsville, the Wilderness and Spotsylvania Courthouse. Today, they are maintained by the National Park Service. Check the park website for the locations of various visitor centers and exhibit shelters, and for staffing, which may be seasonal at some locations. Audio tours of the battlefields are available for rent ($20 deposit).

James Monroe Museum
& Memorial Library   HISTORIC SITE
(☑540-654-1043; http://jamesmonroemuseum.umw.edu; 908 Charles St; adult/child 6-17yr $6/2; ⊙10am-5pm Mon-Sat, from 1pm Sun, closes at 4pm Dec-Feb) The museum's namesake was the nation's fifth president. US history buffs will delight in the small and eclectic collection of Monroe memorabilia, including the desk on which he wrote the famous Monroe Doctrine. His diplomatic court suit, worn at the coronation of Napoleon and dating from 1785 or so, is also on display.

Mary Washington House   HISTORIC BUILDING
(☑540-373-1569; www.washingonheritagemuseums.org; 1200 Charles St; adult/child 6-18yr $7/3; ⊙10am-4pm Mon-Sat & noon-4pm Sun Mar-Oct, 11am-4pm Mon-Sat & noon-4pm Sun Nov-Feb) At the 18th-century home of George Washington's mother, knowledgeable tour guides in period costume shed light on Mary and what life was like in her time. The lovely garden is an excellent re-creation from the era.

🍴 Sleeping & Eating

Richard Johnston Inn   B&B $$
(☑540-899-7606; www.therichardjohstoninn.com; 711 Caroline St; r $165-300; [P][❄][🐾][🛜]) In an 18th-century brick mansion, this cozy B&B scores points for its downtown location, comfort and friendliness. The cookies offered in the afternoon are delicious.

Sammy T's   AMERICAN $
(☑540-371-2008; www.sammyts.com; 801 Caroline St; ⊙11:30am-9pm Mon, Wed & Thu, 1:30am-10pm Fri & Sat, 9:30am-7pm Sun; 🛜🐾) Located in a circa 1805 building in the heart of historic Fredericksburg, Sammy T's serves soups and sandwiches and pub-y fare, with an admirable mix of vegetarian options including a local take on lasagna and blackbean quesadillas.

Foode   AMERICAN $$
(☑540-479-1370; www.facebook.com/foodeonline; 900 Princess Anne St; lunch mains $10-12, dinner mains $15-26; ⊙11am-9pm Tue-Thu, 11am-10pm Fri, 9am-10pm Sat, 9am-3pm Sun; 🐾) Foode serves up tasty farm-to-table fare in a rustic but artsy setting. Lots of intriguing small plates for sharing at dinner. Attentive service too.

Bistro Bethem   AMERICAN $$$
(☑540-371-9999; www.bistrobethem.com; 309 William St; lunch mains $9-22, dinner mains $17-32; ⊙11:30am-2:30pm & 5-10pm Tues-Sat, to 9pm Sun) The New American menu, seasonal

ingredients and down-to-earth but dedicated foodie vibe here all equal gastronomic bliss. On any given day duck confit and quinoa may share the table with a roasted beet salad and local clams.

ℹ️ Getting There & Away

Virginia Railway Express (www.vre.org; $11.90, 1½ hours) and Amtrak ($20 to $67, 1¼ hours) trains depart from the **Fredericksburg train station** (www.amtrak.com; 200 Lafayette Blvd) with service to DC. Greyhound has buses to/ from DC ($10 to $24, four or five per day, 1½ hours) and Richmond ($10 to $30, two or three per day, one hour). The **Greyhound station** (🚍 540-373-2103; www.greyhound.com; 1400 Jefferson Davis Hwy) is roughly 2 miles west of the historic district. Fredericksburg borders I-95 midway between Washington, DC and Richmond, VA. It's about 55 miles north to DC and 60 miles south to Richmond.

Richmond

Richmond has woken up from a very long nap – and we like it. The capital of the Commonwealth of Virginia since 1780, and the capital of the Confederacy during the Civil War, it's long been an old-fashioned city clinging too tightly to its Southern roots. For decades, Civil War–era sights were the primary attraction, and residents didn't give much social thought to its streets and schools named for Confederate generals.

But an influx of new and creative young residents is energizing and modernizing the community. Today the 'River City' shares a buzzing food-and-drink scene and an active arts community. The rough-and-tumble James River has also grabbed more of the spotlight, drawing outdoor adventurers to its rapids and trails. Richmond is also an undeniably handsome town and easy to stroll, full of red-brick row houses, stately drives and leafy parks.

⦿ Sights & Activities

Virginia State Capitol NOTABLE BUILDING
(🚍 804-698-1788; www.virginiacapitol.gov; cnr 9th & Grace Sts, Capitol Sq; ⊙ 9am-5pm Mon-Sat, 1-5pm Sun) FREE Designed by Thomas Jefferson, the capitol building was completed in 1788 and houses the oldest legislative body in the Western Hemisphere – the Virginia General Assembly, established in 1619. Free guided tours available and there is a self-guided tour brochure on the website.

Virginia Museum of Fine Arts MUSEUM
(VMFA; 🚍 804-340-1400; www.vmfa.museum; 200 N Blvd; ⊙ 10am-5pm Sun-Wed, to 9pm Thu & Fri) FREE Has a remarkable collection of European works, sacred Himalayan art and one of the largest Fabergé egg collections on display outside Russia. Don't miss Andy Warhol's *Triple Elvis* or the striking new *Chloe* sculpture by Jaume Plensa in the outdoor sculpture garden. Also hosts excellent temporary exhibitions (admission ranges from free to $22). After a morning exploring the collection, the museum's big-windowed Amuse restaurant is a pretty spot for lunch.

Virginia Historical Society MUSEUM
(www.vahistorical.org; 428 North Blvd; ⊙ 10am-5pm Mon-Sat) FREE Virginia's attic is looking pretty darn impressive after a multi-million-dollar renovation. With easy-to-digest changing and permanent exhibits tracing the story of the Commonwealth from its prehistoric beginnings to today, this is a great place for a quick history primer before setting out to explore the state's many sites.

St John's Episcopal Church CHURCH
(🚍 804-648-5015; www.historicstjohnschurch. org; 2401 E Broad St; tours adult/child 7-18yr $8/6; ⊙ 10am-4pm Mon-Sat, from 1pm Sun) It was here that firebrand Patrick Henry uttered his famous battle cry – 'Give me Liberty, or give me Death!' – during the rebellious 1775 Second Virginia Convention. The short but informative tour traces the history of the church and of the famous speech. Above the pulpit, the rare 1741 sounding board and its sunburst are worth a closer look. Henry's speech is re-enacted at 1pm on Sundays in summer.

Monument Avenue Statues STATUE
(btwn N Lombardy St & Roseneath Rd) Monument Ave, a beautiful tree-lined boulevard in northeast Richmond, holds statues of such revered Southern heroes as JEB Stuart, Robert E Lee, Matthew Fontaine Maury, Jefferson Davis, Stonewall Jackson and – in a nod to diversity – African American tennis champion Arthur Ashe. Snarky students at the nearby University of Richmond have been known to refer to the avenue as the 'largest collection of second place trophies in America.'

American Civil War Museum: Historic Tredegar MUSEUM
(🚍 804-649-1861; www.acwm.org; 500 Tredegar St; adult/child 6-17yr $10/5; ⊙ 9am-5pm) Now a

VINEYARDS OF VIRGINIA

Home to some 230 vineyards, Virginia has a rising presence in the wine world. Good places to begin the foray lie just outside of DC in Loudon County. For maps, wine routes and loads of other viticultural info, visit www.virginiawine.org.

King Family Vineyards (☑434-823-7800; www.kingfamilyvineyards.com; 6550 Roseland Farm, Crozet; tastings $10; ◷10am-5:30pm Thu-Tue, to 8:30pm Wed; 🐾) Consistently ranks as one of Virginia's best wineries. Bring a picnic (the winery also sells gourmet goodies) and enjoy the expansive scenery. At 1pm on summer Sundays (late May to mid-October), you can also catch a free polo match. It's 18 miles east of Charlottesville.

Jefferson Vineyards (☑434-977-3042; www.jeffersonvineyards.com; 1353 Thomas Jefferson Pkwy; tastings $12; ◷11am-6pm; 🐾) Near Charlottesville, this winery harvests from its namesake's original 1774 vineyard site. It also hosts twice-monthly free outdoor concerts in summer.

Bluemont Vineyard (☑540-554-8439; www.bluemontvineyard.com; 18755 Foggy Bottom Rd, Bluemont; tastings $10; ◷11am-6pm Sat-Thu, to 8pm Fri; 🐾) Bluemont produces ruby-red Nortons and crisp Viogniers, though it's equally famous for its spectacular location – at a 950ft elevation with sweeping views over the countryside.

Chrysalis Vineyards (☑540-687-8222; www.chrysaliswine.com; 39025 John Mosby Hwy; tastings $7-10; ◷10am-6pm; 🐾) Proudly using the native Norton grape (which dates back to 1820), Chrysalis produces highly drinkable reds and whites – including a refreshing Viognier. The pretty estate hosts a bluegrass fest in October.

Tarara Vineyard (☑703-771-7100; www.tarara.com; 13648 Tarara Lane; tastings $6-10; ◷11am-5pm Mon-Thu, to 6pm Fri-Sun) On a bluff overlooking the Potomac, this 475-acre estate provides guided tours showing the grape's journey from vine to glass. The winery has a 6000-sq-ft cave/cellar, and visitors can pick fruit in the orchard or hike the 6 miles of trails through rolling countryside. Tarara also hosts summertime Saturday-evening concerts and three major wine festivals.

stop within the multisite American Civil War Museum, this fascinating museum – inside an 1861 gun foundry – explores the causes and course of the Civil War from the perspectives of Union, Confederate and African American experiences. Next door is a free site run by the National Park Service that delves into Richmond's role during the war. This is also one of 13 protected area sites that make up **Richmond National Battlefield Park** (☑804-771-2145; www.nps.gov/rich; 470 Tredegar St; ◷battlefield sunrise-sunset, Tredegar Visitor Center 9am-5pm) **FREE**.

Belle Isle PARK
(www.jamesriverpark.org; 300 Tredegar St) A long pedestrian bridge leads from Tredegar St (just past the national park site) out to this car-free island. Once a quarry, power plant and POW camp during the Civil War (though never all at once), today this is one of Richmond's finest city parks. Big flat rocks are lovely for sunbathing, and hiking and biking trails abound – but don't swim in the James River. The currents are treacherous.

Canal Walk WATERFRONT
(www.rvariverfront.com; btwn 5th & 17th Sts) The 1.25-mile waterfront Canal Walk between the James River and the Kanawha (ka-*naw*-wha) and Haxall Canals is a lovely way of seeing a dozen highlights of Richmond history in one go. There's also a pedestrian bridge across to Belle Isle, a scruffy but intriguing island in the James.

Poe Museum MUSEUM
(☑804-648-5523; www.poemuseum.org; 1914-16 E Main St; adult/child 7-17yr $8/6; ◷10am-5pm Tue-Sat, from 11am Sun) Contains the world's largest collection of manuscripts and memorabilia of poet and horror writer Edgar Allan Poe, who lived and worked in Richmond. Exhibits include the first printing of 'The Raven', Poe's vest, his pen knife and a work chair with the back cut off – they say his boss at the *Southern Literary Messenger* wanted Poe to sit up straight. Pesky know-it-all. Stop by on the 4th Thursday of the month for the Poe-themed Unhappy Hour (6pm to 9pm April to October; $8).

Hollywood Cemetery
CEMETERY

(☑ 804-648-8501; www.hollywoodcemetery.org; 412 S Cherry St, entrance cnr Albemarle & Cherry Sts; ☺ 8am-6pm) **FREE** This tranquil cemetery, perched above the James River rapids, contains the gravesites of two US presidents (James Monroe and John Tyler), the only Confederate president (Jefferson Davis) and 18,000 Confederate soldiers. Guided walking tours are given at 10am Monday through Saturday April to October, and Saturday only in November ($15 per person). For a self-guided walk, check the virtual tour offered on the website.

Riverside Outfitters
CANOEING

(☑ 804-560-0068; www.riversideoutfitters.net; Brown's Island, Downtown; per hour kayak/SUP boards/bike rental $15/15/10; ☺ 11am-6pm Jun-Aug) Rent a kayak, stand-up paddle board or bike. The shop is on Brown's Island across the street from Historic Tredegar at 500 Tredegar St. These folks also offer guided rafting trips, which launch from various locations.

Virginia Capital Trail
CYCLING

(www.virginiacapitaltrail.org) Open to cyclists and pedestrians, this new 52-mile paved trail links Richmond with Jamestown and outer Williamsburg, passing several plantations along the way. Check the helpful website for a map showing parking areas, restrooms, bike shops, restaurants and lodging. There are loads of historic sights and markers along the way. Starts at the junction of S 17th and Dock Sts.

🛏 Sleeping

HI Richmond
HOSTEL $

(☑ 804-729-5410; www.hiusa.org; 7 N 2nd St; dm $30-34, r $90-135, non-members add $3; ❄ 🛜) 🧼 Inside a historic 1924 building, this spiffy and eco-friendly hostel has a great central location and bright rooms (both dorms and private rooms), with high ceilings and loads of original details. There's a kitchen for guests, inviting common areas, and it's completely accessible for travelers with disabilities.

Linden Row Inn
BOUTIQUE HOTEL $$

(☑ 804-783-7000; www.lindenrowinn.com; 100 E Franklin St; r from $139, ste $289; P ❄ @ 🛜) This antebellum gem has 70 attractive rooms (with period Victorian furnishings) spread among neighboring Greek Revival town houses in an excellent downtown location. Friendly southern hospitality, reasonable prices and thoughtful extras (free passes to

the YMCA, free around-town shuttle service, included breakfast) sweeten the deal.

★ Jefferson Hotel
LUXURY HOTEL $$$

(☑ 804-649-4750; www.jeffersonhotel.com; 101 W Franklin St; r from $355; P ❄ 🛜 🏊) The Jefferson is Richmond's grandest hotel and one of the finest in America. The vision of tobacco tycoon and Confederate major Lewis Ginter, the beaux arts–style hotel was completed in 1895. Rooms are plush but inviting – you will sleep well. According to rumor (probably untrue), the magnificent grand staircase in the lobby served as the model for the famed stairs in *Gone with the Wind*.

✕ Eating

Kuba Kuba
CUBAN $

(☑ 804-355-8817; www.kubakuba.info; 1601 Park Ave; mains $5-20; ☺ 9am-9:30pm Mon-Thu, to 10pm Fri & Sat, to 8pm Sun) In the Fan district, this tiny hole in the wall feels like a bodega straight out of Old Havana, with mouthwatering roast pork dishes, Spanish-style omelets and panini at rock-bottom prices.

Mama J's
AMERICAN $

(☑ 804-225-7449; www.mamajskitchen.com; 415 N 1st St; mains $7-10; ☺ 11am-9pm Sun-Thu, to 10pm Fri & Sat) The fried catfish may not look fancy, but it sure tastes like heaven. Set in the historic African American neighborhood of Jackson Ward, Mama J's serves delicious fried chicken and legendary fried catfish, along with collard greens, mac 'n' cheese, candied yams and other fixings. The service is friendly and the lines are long. Go early to beat the crowds.

Sidewalk Cafe
AMERICAN, GREEK $

(☑ 804-358-0645; www.sidewalkinthefan.com; 2101 W Main St; mains $9-18; ☺ 11am-2am Mon-Fri, from 9:30am Sat & Sun) A much-loved local haunt, Sidewalk Cafe feels like a dive bar (year-round Christmas lights, wood-paneled walls, kitschy artwork), but the food is first-rate. There's outdoor seating on the sidewalk, daily specials and weekend brunches.

Burger Bach
PUB FOOD $

(☑ 804-359-1305; www.theburgerbach.com; 10 S Thompson St; mains $9-13; ☺ 11am-10pm Sun-Thu, to 11pm Fri & Sat; ❄ 🖊 🚼) 🧼 We give Burger Bach credit for being the only restaurant found in the area that self-classifies as a New Zealand–inspired burger joint. And that said, why yes, they do serve excellent lamb burgers here, although the locally sourced beef (and vegetarian) options are awesome as well. You should go crazy with the 14 different sauces available for the thick-cut fries.

Daily Kitchen & Bar   MODERN AMERICAN $$

(☑804-342-8990; www.thedailykitchenandbar.com; 2934 W Cary St; lunch mains $9-20, dinner mains $9-26; ☺7am-11pm Sun-Thu, to 1am Fri & Sat; 🅿) ✐ In the heart of Carytown, the Daily is a great dining and drinking choice no matter the time of day. Stop by for lump crab omelets at breakfast, blackened mahi-mahi BLT at lunch and seared scallops by night. Extensive vegan options, first-rate cocktails and a buzzing, artfully designed space seals the deal.

Millie's Diner   MODERN AMERICAN $$

(☑804-643-5512; www.milliesdiner.com; 2603 E Main St; lunch mains $9-14, dinner mains $16-29; ☺11am-2:30pm & 5:30-10:30pm Tue-Fri, 9am-3pm & 5:30-10:30pm Sat & Sun) Lunch, dinner or weekend brunch – Richmond icon Millie's does it all, and does it well. It's a small, but handsomely designed space with creative seasonal fare. The Devil's Mess – an open-faced omelet with spicy sausage, curry, veg, cheese and avocado – is legendary.

Croaker's Spot   SEAFOOD $$

(☑804-269-0464; www.croakersspot.com; 1020 Hull St; mains $10-26; ☺11am-9pm Mon-Wed, to 10pm Thu, to 11pm Fri, noon-11pm Sat, noon-9pm Sun; 🅿) Croaker's is an institution in these parts, and a backbone of the African American dining scene. Richmond's most famous rendition of refined soul food is comforting, delicious and sits in your stomach like a brick. Beware the intimidating Fish Boat: fried catfish, cornbread and mac 'n' cheese.

★L'Opossum   AMERICAN, FRENCH $$$

(☑804-918-6028; www.lopossum.com; 626 China St; mains $18-32; ☺5pm-midnight Tue-Sat) We're not exactly sure what's going on here, but it works. The name of the place is terrible. Statues of Michelangelo's David pose here and there. And dishes come with names that are almost too hip, like the Darth Grouper Held at Bay by a Rebellious Coalition.

🍷 Drinking & Entertainment

Saison   COCKTAIL BAR

(☑804-269-3689; www.saisonrva.com; 23 W Marshall St; ☺5pm-2am) This classy drinking den attracts serious cocktail lovers, who clink glasses over creative libations, craft beer and farm-to-table fare. It's in Jackson Ward, near downtown.

Veil Brewing   MICROBREWERY

(www.theveilbrewing.com; 1301 Roseneath Rd; ☺4-9pm Tue-Thu, to 10pm Fri, noon-10pm Sat, noon-6pm Sun) If you see a queue of businessmen standing beside a nondescript brick building on Roseneath Rd just west of Broad St, it's probably Tuesday. That's when this much-praised new brewery sells its limited release brews, which do sell out. One of the most popular craft breweries in the emerging Scott's Addition neighborhood.

Byrd Theater   CINEMA

(☑804-353-9911; www.byrdtheatre.com; 2908 W Cary St; tickets from $4) You can't beat the price at this classic 1928 cinema, which shows second-run films and longtime favorites. Wurlitzer-organ concerts precede the Saturday-night shows.

ℹ Getting There & Around

Amtrak (www.amtrak.com) trains stop at the **Staples Mill Rd station** (www.amtrak.com; 7519 Staples Mill Rd), 7 miles north of town (accessible to downtown via bus 27). More-convenient but less-frequent trains stop downtown at the **Main St Station** (www.amtrak.com; 1500 E Main St).

The **Greyhound/Trailways Bus Station** (☑804-254-5910; www.greyhound.com) is at 2910 North Blvd.

The cab fare from **Richmond International Airport** (RIC; ☑804-226-3000; www.flyrichmond.com; 1 Richard E Byrd Terminal Dr), 10 miles east of town, costs $30 to $35.

A new **Bikeshare** program is slated to launch by the fall of 2017.

➡ Greater Richmond Transit Company (www.ridegrtc.com) runs local buses. Exact change only.

Historic Triangle

This is America's birthplace. Nowhere else in the country has such a small area played such a pivotal role in the course of the nation's history. The nation's roots were planted in Jamestown, the first permanent English settlement in the New World; the flames of the American Revolution were fanned at the colonial capital of Williamsburg; and America finally won its independence from Britain at Yorktown. You'll need at least two days to do the Triangle any justice.

ℹ Getting There & Around

The Historic Triangle surrounds I-64. The largest regional airport is Norfolk International Airport (p298) followed by Newport News/Williamsburg International Airport (PHF; www.flyphf.com).

Williamsburg

If you visit only one historic town in Virginia, make it Williamsburg – home to Colonial Williamsburg, one of the largest, most comprehensive living-history museums in the world. If any place is going to get kids into history, this is it, but it's plenty of fun for adults too.

The actual town of Williamsburg, Virginia's capital from 1699 to 1780, is a stately place. The campus of the College of William & Mary adds a decent dash of youth culture, with coffee shops, cheap pubs and fashion boutiques.

◎ Sights

★ **Colonial Williamsburg** HISTORIC SITE
(☑888-974-7926; www.colonialwilliamsburg.org; adult/child 6-12yr one day $41/21, multi-day $51/26; ☺9am-5pm) The restored capital of England's largest colony in the New World is a must-see attraction for visitors of all ages. This is not some phony, fenced-in theme park: Colonial Williamsburg is a living, breathing, working history museum with a painstakingly researched environment that brilliantly captures America of the 1700s.

The 301-acre historic area contains 88 original 18th-century buildings and several hundred faithful reproductions. Costumed townsfolk and 'interpreters' in period dress go about their colonial jobs as blacksmiths, apothecaries, printers, barmaids, soldiers and patriots, breaking character only long enough to pose for a snapshot.

Costumed patriots like Patrick Henry and Thomas Jefferson still deliver impassioned speeches for freedom, but the park doesn't gloss over America's less glorious moments. Today's re-enactors debate and question slavery, women's suffrage, the rights of indigenous Americans and whether or not it is even moral to engage in revolution.

Walking around the historic district and patronizing the shops and taverns is free, but entry to building tours and most exhibits is restricted to ticketholders. Expect crowds, lines and petulant children, especially in summer.

To park and to purchase tickets, follow signs to the **visitor center** (☑757-220-7645, 888-965-7254; www.colonialwilliamsburg.com; 101 Visitor Center Dr; ☺8:45am-9pm), found north of the historic district between Hwy 132 and Colonial Pkwy; kids can also hire out period costumes here for $25 per day. Start off with a 30-minute film about Williamsburg, and ask about the day's programs and events.

Parking is free; shuttle buses run frequently to and from the historic district, or you can walk along the tree-lined footpath. You can also buy tickets at the **Merchants Square information booth** (W Duke of Gloucester St; ☺9am-5pm).

College of William & Mary HISTORIC BUILDING
(☑757-221-4000; www.wm.edu; 200 Stadium Dr) Chartered in 1693, the College of William & Mary is the second-oldest college in the country and retains the oldest academic building in continued use in the USA, the **Sir Christopher Wren Building**. The school's alumni include Thomas Jefferson, James Monroe and comedian Jon Stewart. A free campus audio tour is available online.

JAMES RIVER PLANTATIONS

The grand homes of Virginia's slave-holding aristocracy were a clear sign of the era's class divisions. A string of them line scenic Hwy 5 on the north side of the river, though only a few are open to the public. For cyclists, the Virginia Capital Trail (p306) linking Richmond and Williamsburg travels beside Rte 5.

Berkeley Plantation (☑804-829-6018; www.berkeleyplantation.com; 12602 Harrison Landing Rd, Charles City; adult/child 6-16yr $12/7; ☺9:30am-4:30pm) Berkeley was the site of the first official Thanksgiving in 1619. It was the birthplace and home of Benjamin Harrison V, a signatory of the Declaration of Independence, and his son William Henry Harrison, the 9th US president.

Shirley Plantation (☑800-829-5121; www.shirleyplantation.com; 501 Shirley Plantation Rd, Charles City; adult/child 7-16yr $12.50/8.50; ☺9:30am-4pm) Shirley, situated picturesquely on the river, is Virginia's oldest plantation (1613) and is perhaps the best example of how a British-model plantation actually appeared, with its tidy row of brick service and trade houses – tool barn, ice house, laundry etc – leading up to the big house.

🛏 Sleeping & Eating

Governor's Inn
HOTEL $

(📞 757-220-7940; www.colonialwilliamsburg.com; 506 N Henry St; r incl breakfast $74-89; 🅿 ❄ 🐾) Williamsburg's official 'economy' choice is a big box by any other name, but rooms are clean, and guests can use the pool and facilities of the Woodlands Hotel. It's in a great location near the visitor center, three blocks from the historic district.

Williamsburg Woodlands
Hotel & Suites
HOTEL $$

(📞 757-220-7960; www.colonialwilliamsburg.com; 105 Visitor Center Dr; r/ste $179/209; 🅿 ❄ ❄ 🐾) This good-value option has comfy, carpeted rooms (some of which go a bit heavy on the patterned wallpaper) near the main Visitor Center in Colonial Williamsburg. The splash park, games (minigolf, volleyball court) and complimentary breakfast make it a hit with families. Can feel a little more impersonal than other local lodging options.

Colonial Williamsburg Historic
Lodging – Colonial Houses
GUESTHOUSE $$$

(📞 888-965-7254, 757-565-8440; www.colonialwilliamsburg.com; 136 E Francis St; r $199) For true 18th-century immersion, guests can stay in one of 26 original colonial houses inside the historic district. Accommodations range in size and style, though the best have period furnishings, canopy beds and wood-burning fireplaces.

Cheese Shop
DELI $

(📞 757-220-0298; www.cheeseshopwilliamsburg.com; 410 W Duke of Gloucester St, Merchants Sq; mains $6-8; ⏱ 10am-8pm Mon-Sat, 11am-6pm Sun) This gourmet deli showcases some flavorful sandwiches and antipasti, plus baguettes, pastries, wine, beer and wonderful cheeses. Order a sandwich and a glass of wine – at different counters – then enjoy your meal and the people-watching from the patio.

Aromas
CAFE $

(📞 757-221-6676; www.aromasworld.com; 431 Prince George St; lunch mains $7-9, dinner mains $7-15; ⏱ 7am-10pm Mon-Thu, to 1pm Fri & Sat, 8am-8pm Sun; ❄) One block north of Merchants Sq, Aromas is an inviting coffeehouse serving salads, sandwiches and a few dinner mains including blackened salmon and barbecue chicken over mac 'n' cheese, plus wine and beer. There's outdoor seating and live music (jazz on Tuesdays; wide-ranging sounds on weekends).

King's Arms Tavern
MODERN AMERICAN $$$

(📞 866-348-9022; www.colonialwilliamsburg.com; 416 E Duke of Gloucester St; lunch mains $14-16, dinner mains $25-40; ⏱ 11:30am-2:30pm & 5-8pm) This traditional tavern serves early-American cuisine such as game pie – venison, rabbit and duck braised in port-wine sauce. Of the four restaurants within Colonial Williamsburg, this is the most elegant. You might hear live flute music with your meal, and staff will share history about Colonial dining habits.

ℹ Getting There & Away

Amtrak (www.amtrak.com) trains run from the **Williamsburg Transportation Center** (📞 757-229-8750; www.williamsburgva.gov; 468 N Boundary St, cnr Boundary & Lafayette Sts; ⏱ 7:30am-10pm) twice a day to Washington, DC ($46, four hours) and Richmond ($22, 90 minutes), both on the Northeast Regional route.

Jamestown

On May 14, 1607, a group of 104 English men and boys settled on this swampy island, bearing a charter from the Virginia Company of London to search for gold and other riches. Instead they found starvation and disease. By January 1608, only about 40 colonists were still alive, and these had resorted to cannibalism to survive. The colony survived the 'Starving Time' with the leadership of Captain James Smith and help from Powhatan, a local Native American leader. In 1619 the elected House of Burgesses convened, forming the first democratic government in the Americas.

👁 Sights

Historic Jamestowne
HISTORIC SITE

(📞 757-856-1250; www.historicjamestowne.org; 1368 Colonial Pkwy; adult/child under 16yr $14/free; ⏱ 9am-5pm) Run by the NPS, this fascinating place is the original Jamestown site, established in 1607 and home of the first permanent English settlement in North America. Start at the museum then check out the statues of Pocahontas and John Smith. The original Jamestown ruins were rediscovered in 1994; visitors can watch ongoing archaeological work at the site. Don't miss the Archaearium, which displays more than 4000 artifacts, including the skull of a young settler who was likely the victim of cannibalism!

Jamestown Settlement HISTORIC SITE

(☑ 757-253-4838; www.historyisfun.org; 2110 Jamestown Rd; adult/child 6-12yr $17/8, incl American Revolutionary Museum at Yorktown $23/12; ⊙ 9am-5pm, to 6pm mid-Jun–mid-Aug; P 🚻) Popular with kids, the state-run Jamestown Settlement reconstructs the 1607 James Fort; a Native American village; and full-scale replicas of the first ships that brought the settlers to Jamestown, along with living-history fun. Multimedia exhibits and costumed interpreters bring the 17th century to life. This one can get uncomfortably busy with elementary school field trips, so arrive early during the school year.

❶ Getting There & Away

The best way to get to Jamestown is by car. Amtrak (www.amtrak.com) stops in nearby Williamsburg, with trains running from the Williamsburg Transportation Center twice a day to Washington, DC ($46, four hours) and Richmond ($22, 90 minutes), both on the Northeast Regional route.

Yorktown

On October 19, 1781, British General Cornwallis surrendered to George Washington here, effectively ending the American Revolution. Overpowered by massive American guns on land and cut off from the sea by the French, the British were in a hopeless position. Although Washington anticipated a much longer siege, the devastating barrage quickly overwhelmed Cornwallis, who surrendered within days. The actual town of Yorktown is a pleasant waterfront village overlooking the York River, with a nice range of shops, galleries, restaurants and pubs.

❍ Sights

American Revolution Museum at Yorktown MUSEUM

(☑ 757-887-1776; www.historyisfun.org; 200 Water St; adult/child 6-12yr $12/7; combo with Jamestown Settlement adult/child $23/12; ⊙ 9am-5pm, to 6pm mid-July–mid-Aug; P 🚻) Formerly the Yorktown Victory Center, this new and expanded exhibit space and living history museum vividly describes the build-up to the Revolutionary War, the war itself and daily life on the home front. The thrilling *Siege* is a nine-minute 4D movie spotlighting the war-ending Battle of of Yorktown. Lots of significant artifacts are here too, including an early printing of the Declaration of Independence. At the re-created military en-campment outside, costumed Continental soldiers share details about daily life in a Revolutionary War camp.

Yorktown Battlefield HISTORIC SITE

(☑ 757-898-2410; www.nps.gov/york; 1000 Colonial Pkwy; adult/child under 16yr $7/free; ⊙ 9am-5pm; P 🚻) Yorktown Battlefield, run by the NPS, is the site of the last major battle of the American Revolution. Start your tour at the visitor center and check out the orientation film and the display of Washington's original tent. The 7-mile Battlefield Rd Tour takes you past the major highlights. Don't miss a walk through the last British defensive sites, Redoubts 9 and 10, reached via Ballard St.

❶ Getting There & Away

The best way to get to Yorktown is by car. A free trolley loops between historic sites and the village every 20 to 35 minutes(11am to 5pm April to mid-November; extended hours June to August).

Hampton Roads

Hampton Roads (named not for asphalt, but for the confluence of the James, Nansemond and Elizabeth Rivers and Chesapeake Bay) has always been prime real estate. The Powhatan Confederacy fished these waters and hunted this part of the Virginia coast for thousands of years before John Smith arrived in 1607. Today Hampton Roads is known for congestion – particularly around the Chesapeake Bay Bridge Tunnel – and a cultural mishmash of history, the military and the arts. Norfolk is hoping a brand-new waterfront dining and entertainment district will re-energize downtown.

❶ Getting There & Around

Norfolk International Airport (p298) is the primary airport for the region. I-64 is the main interstate. Expect slowdowns around the Hampton Roads-Bridge Tunnel, which links Newport News and Norfolk. If the electronic traffic signs suggest using the I-664 detour, take it.

Norfolk

Home to the world's largest naval base, it's not surprising that Norfolk has had a reputation as a rowdy port town filled with drunken sailors. In recent years, the city has worked hard to clean up its image through development, gentrification and focusing on its burgeoning arts scene. The Waterside

District, a new dining and entertainment complex on the Elizabeth River downtown, opened in the spring of 2017.

◉ Sights

Chrysler Museum of Art
MUSEUM

(☑757-664-6200; www.chrysler.org; 1 Memorial Pl; ⊙10am-5pm Tue-Sat, noon-5pm Sun) FREE A glorious setting for an eclectic collection of artifacts from ancient Egypt to the present day, including works by Henri Matisse, Albert Bierstadt, Georgia O'Keeffe Jackson Pollock, Andy Warhol and an expansive collection of glass objects spanning 3000 years. Don't miss the collection of Tiffany blown glass. Gallery talks daily at 2pm.

Naval Station Norfolk
MUSEUM

(☑757-444-7955; www.cnic.navy.mil/norfolksta; 9079 Hampton Blvd, near Gate 5; adult/child 3-11yr $10/5; ⊙tour times vary) The world's largest navy base, and one of the busiest airfields in the country, this is a must-see. The 45-minute bus tours are conducted by naval personnel and must be booked in advance (hours vary). Photo ID is required for adults.

Nauticus
MUSEUM

(☑757-664-1000; www.nauticus.org; 1 Waterside Dr; adult/child 4-12yr $16/11.50; ⊙10am-5pm daily Jun-Aug, 10am-5pm Tue-Sat & noon-5pm Sun Sep-May) This massive, interactive, maritime-themed museum has exhibits on undersea exploration, aquatic life of the Chesapeake Bay and US Naval lore. The museum's highlight is clambering around the decks and inner corridors of the USS Wisconsin. Built in 1943, it was the largest (887ft long) and last battleship built by the US Navy.

⊨ Sleeping

Residence Inn
HOTEL $$

(☑757-842-6216; www.marriott.com; 227 W Brambleton Ave; r/ste $164/174; P@🏠🏊) A short stroll to the Granby St eating strip, this friendly chain hotel has a boutique feel, with stylish, spacious rooms featuring small kitchenettes and excellent amenities.

Main Hotel
HOTEL $$$

(☑757-763-6200; www.3hilton.com; 100 E Main St; r $239-329, ste $369; P❄🏠🏊) The rooms are spare but swanky at this new member of the Hilton family, which had just opened at research time. You'll pay more for a view of the Elizabeth River, but you may not need it – just settle in for a drink and river view at the rooftop lounge Grain, one of three dining-drinking establishments within the property.

✖ Eating & Drinking

Luna Maya
MEXICAN $$

(☑757-622-6986; www.lunamayarestaurant.com; 2010 Colley Ave; mains $13-19; ⊙4:30-10pm Tue-Sat) With exposed brick, a pressed-tin ceiling and a big-windowed but spare dining room, this buzzy place is certainly hip, but the friendly service and awesome burritos set it apart from the competition on busy Colley Ave. Not to mention the tasty margaritas and the extensive selection of vegetarian dishes for the non-carnivores in your group.

Press 626 Cafe & Wine Bar
MODERN AMERICAN $$

(☑757-282-6234; www.press26.com; 626 W Olney Rd; lunch mains $10-13, dinner mains $10-24; ⊙11am-11pm Mon-Fri, 5-11pm Sat, 10:30am-2:30pm Sun; ⚲) Embracing the Slow Food movement, the very charming Press 626 has a wide-ranging menu, with pressed gourmet sandwiches (at lunch), seared scallops, bouillabaisse and a great wine selection.

Smartmouth Brewing
BREWERY

(☑757-624-3939; www.smartmouthbrewing.com; 1309 Raleigh Ave; ⊙4:30-9pm Wed-Fri, noon-7pm Sat, 1-5pm Sun) In the burgeoning Chelsea arts district, this indoor-outdoor tasting room and brewery has an inviting neighborhood feel, plus there's a barbecue food truck for sustenance. If you like hefeweizens, give the seasonal Sommer Fling a try (April to December).

ⓘ Getting There & Away

The region is served by Norfolk International Airport (p298), 7 miles northeast of downtown Norfolk. **Greyhound** (☑757-625-7500; www.greyhound.com; 701 Monticello Ave) runs buses to Virginia Beach ($16, 35 minutes), Richmond ($32, 2¾ hours) and Washington, DC ($50, 6½ hours). Hampton Roads Transit (www.gohrt.com) buses ($1.75) run from downtown throughout the city and to Newport News and Virginia Beach.

Virginia Beach

With 35 miles of sandy beaches, a 3-mile concrete oceanfront boardwalk and nearby outdoor activities, it's no surprise that Virginia Beach is a prime tourist destination. The city has worked hard to shed its reputation as a rowdy 'Redneck Riviera,' and hey, the beach *is* wider and cleaner now and there are fewer louts. Beach aside, you'll find some lovely parks and nature sites beyond the crowded high-rises lining the shore. Expect thick crowds, heavy traffic and high prices if visiting in the summer.

◉ Sights

Virginia Aquarium
& Marine Science Center   AQUARIUM
(☑757-385-3474; www.virginiaaquarium.com; 717 General Booth Blvd; adult/child 3-11yr $25/20; ☺9am-5pm) If you want to see an aquarium done right, come here. In various habitats, you can see a great array of aquatic life, including sea turtles, river otters and Komodo dragons. If the kids have more energy to burn, try the ropes course and zipline in the new Adventure Park (adult/child aged seven to 11 years $52/44), tucked in the woods between aquarium buildings.

Virginia Museum
of Contemporary Art   MUSEUM
(☑757-425-0000; www.virginiamoca.org; 2200 Parks Ave; adult/child $7.70/5.50; ☺10am-9pm Tue, to 5pm Wed-Fri, to 4pm Sat & Sun) Has excellent rotating exhibitions housed in a fresh, ultramodern building.

Back Bay National
Wildlife Refuge   NATURE RESERVE
(☑757-301-7329; www.fws.gov/refuge/back_bay; 4005 Sandpiper Rd; per vehicle/pedestrian Apr-Oct $5/2, free admission Nov-Mar; ☺sunrise-sunset) This 9250-acre wildlife and migratory-bird marshland habitat is most stunning during the December migration season.

First Landing State Park   NATURE RESERVE
(☑757-412-2300; www.dcr.virginia.gov; 2500 Shore Dr; per vehicle $7-9; ☺8am-dusk) Shake off the Virginia Beach flash at this lower key 2888-acre woodland, which has 20 miles of **hiking trails**, plus opportunities for camping, cycling, fishing, kayaking and swimming.

🛏 Sleeping & Eating

First Landing State Park   CAMPGROUND $
(☑800-933-7275; http://dcr.virginia.gov; Cape Henry; campsites $28-41, cabins from $83; ℗) You couldn't ask for a prettier campground than the one at this bay-front state park, though the cabins have no water view.

Hilton Virginia
Beach Oceanfront   HOTEL $$$
(☑757-213-3000; www.hiltonvb.com; 3001 Atlantic Ave; r from $417; ℗🛜🏊) The premier place to

stay on the beach, this 21-story hotel is super luxurious. The oceanfront rooms are spacious, comfortable and packed with amenities including huge flat-screen TVs, dreamy bedding and large balconies that open out to the beach and Neptune Park below. Rates drop $100 during the week in summer.

Blue Pete's   SEAFOOD $$
(☑757-426-2278; www.bluepetespungo.com; 1400 N Muddy Creek Rd; mains $11-32; ☺5-10pm Mon-Fri, noon-11:45pm Sat, noon-10pm Sun) Perched over a peaceful creek near Back Bay, Blue Pete's has an enchanting woodland setting and a wide-ranging menu: crab cakes, brisket sandwiches, pastas and coconut-breaded shrimp.

Esoteric   AMERICAN $$$
(☑757-822-6008; www.esotericvb.com; 501 Virginia Beach Blvd; mains $10-30; ☺4-10pm Mon-Wed, to 11pm Thu, to midnight Fri, noon-midnight Sat) Gourmet sandwiches and an eclectic array of innovative American dishes keep locals happy, as does the craft beer. The husband-and-wife team behind this stylish spot embrace local food producers and collaborators.

❶ Getting There & Away

Greyhound (☑757-422-2998; www.greyhound.com; 971 Virginia Beach Blvd) runs buses daily to Richmond (from $14, 3½ hours), which also stop in Norfolk and Hampton; transfer in Richmond for services to Washington, DC, Wilmington; NYC and beyond. Buses depart from Circle D Food Mart, 1 mile west of the boardwalk.

Hampton Roads Transit runs the Virginia Beach Wave trolley (tickets $2), which plies Atlantic Ave in summer.

The Piedmont

Central Virginia's rolling central hills and plateaus separate the coastal lowlands from the mountainous frontier. The fertile valley gives way to dozens of wineries, country villages and grand colonial estates. New microbreweries, cideries and distilleries are garnering lots of well-deserved attention.

❶ Getting There & Around

The Piedmont region is flanked by Interstates I-81 and I-64. The area is best explored by car. Charlottesville anchors the region and has an **airport** and an **Amtrak** station. On Fridays you'll likely join a few UVA students hopping the train to Washington, DC.

Charlottesville

Set in the shadow of the Blue Ridge Mountains, Charlottesville is regularly ranked as one of the country's best places to live. This culturally rich town is home to the University of Virginia (UVA), which attracts Southern aristocracy and artsy lefties in equal proportions. With the UVA grounds and pedestrian downtown mall area overflowing with students, couples, professors and the occasional celebrity under a blanket of blue skies, 'C-ville' is practically perfect.

⊙ Sights

Monticello   HISTORIC SITE
(☑ 434-984-9800; www.monticello.org; 931 Thomas Jefferson Pkwy; adult/child 5-11yr $28/9; ⊙ 8:30am-6pm Mon-Fri, to 7pm Sat & Sun, hours vary seasonally) Monticello is an architectural masterpiece designed and inhabited by Thomas Jefferson, founding father and third US president, who spent 40 years building his dream home, finally completed in 1809. Today it is the only home in America designated a UN World Heritage site. 'I am as happy nowhere else and in no other society, and all my wishes end, where I hope my days will end, at Monticello,' wrote Jefferson.

University of Virginia   UNIVERSITY
(☑ 434-924-0311; www.virginia.edu; Charlottesville) Thomas Jefferson founded the University of Virginia, whose classically designed buildings and grounds embody the spirit of communal living and learning that Jefferson envisioned. Free, student-led guided tours of the campus depart daily from the Rotunda at 10am, 11am and 2pm during the school year (www.uvaguides.org; September to April). You can also tour the Jefferson-designed **Rotunda** (☑ 434-924-7969; www.rotunda.virginia.edu; 1826 University Ave; ⊙ 9am-5pm), a scale replica of Rome's Pantheon. UVA's **Fralin Art Museum** (☑ 434-924-3592; http://uvafralinartmuseum.virginia.edu/; 155 Rugby Rd; ⊙ 10am-5pm Tue, Wed, Fri & Sat, to 7pm Thu, noon-5pm Sun) **FREE** has an eclectic collection of American, European and Asian arts.

Ash Lawn-Highland   HISTORIC BUILDING
(☑ 434-293-8000; www.ashlawnhighland.org; 2050 James Monroe Pkwy; adult/child 6-11yr $14/8; ⊙ 9am-6pm Apr-Oct, 11am-5pm Nov-Mar) This historic site was the home of James Monroe (the fifth US president) and his wife Elizabeth from 1799 to 1823.

WORTH A TRIP

MONTPELIER

Thomas Jefferson gets all the attention in these parts, but it's well worth branching out and visiting James Madison's **Montpelier** (www.montpelier.org; 11350 Constitution Hwy; adult/child $20/7; ⊙ 9am-5pm Apr-Oct, 10am-4pm Nov-Mar), a spectacular estate 25 miles northeast of Charlottesville (off Hwy 20). Madison was a brilliant but shy man, who devoted himself to his books; he was almost single-handedly responsible for developing and writing the US Constitution. **Guided tours** shed a light on the life and times of James as well as his gifted and charismatic wife Dolley, plus other residents of the estate.

🛏 Sleeping

Fairhaven   GUESTHOUSE $
(☑ 434-933-2471; www.fairhavencville.com; 413 Fairway Ave; r $80; ⏸✳🕸) This friendly and welcoming guesthouse is a great deal if you don't mind sharing facilities (there's just one bathroom for the three rooms). Each room has wood floors, with comfy beds and a cheerful color scheme, and guests can use the kitchen, living room or backyard. It's about a 1-mile walk to the pedestrian mall.

South Street Inn   B&B $$
(☑ 434-979-0200; www.southstreetinn.com; 200 South St; r $169-219, ste $249-259; ⏸✳🕸) In the heart of downtown Charlottesville, this elegant 1856 building has gone through previous incarnations as a girls' finishing school, a boarding house and a brothel. Now it houses heritage-style rooms – a total of two dozen, which gives this place more depth and diversity than your average B&B.

Hyatt Place   HOTEL $$
(☑ 434-995-5200; https://charlottesville.place.hyatt.com; 2100 Bond Pl; r from $209; ⏸@🕸✳) Sometimes you just don't want a historic inn or a chatty B&B. You want hip furnishings, strong wi-fi and a good free breakfast that doesn't come with a side of conversation about your plans for the day. In those situations, the new Hyatt Place has your back. Pet fee is $75 per stay.

✕ Eating & Drinking

Citizen Burger AMERICAN $
(☑434-979-9944; www.citizenburgerbar.com; 212 E Main St; mains $12-15; ☉noon-midnight Sun-Thu, to 2am Fri & Sat) On the pedestrian mall, Citizen Burger serves up delicious burgers and microbrews in a buzzing, brick-lined dining room. The ethos is local and sustainable (organically raised, grass-fed cows, Virginia-made cheeses and beers). Don't miss the truffle fries.

Oakhart Social MODERN AMERICAN $$
(☑434-995-5449; www.oakhartsocial.com; 511 W Main St; small plates $10-23; ☉5pm-midnight Tue-Sun, to 2am Fri & Sat) The stylish place serves creative seasonally inspired small plates (grilled octopus with garbanzo puree, sweet and crispy pork-belly salad) as well as wood-fired pizzas in a handsomely laid-back setting. The front patio is a festive spot to sit and sip a refreshing 'Corpse Reviver #2' and other well-made cocktails.

★ Public Fish & Oyster SEAFOOD $$$
(☑434-995-5542; www.publicfo.com; 513 W Main St; mains $19-29; ☉4-9:30pm Mon-Thu, to 10pm Fri & Sat, to 9pm Sun) This bright and inviting brick box will catch your eye, but it's the skillfully seasoned seafood dishes that will keep you inside ordering plate after plate of oysters, mussels and other maritime delights. If you're a raw oyster virgin, this is the place change that story. The twice-cooked Belgian fries with sea salt are fantastic.

Whiskey Jar COCKTAIL BAR
(☑434-202-1549; http://thewhiskeyjarcville.com; 227 W Main St; lunch mains $10-15, dinner mains

---

VIRGINIA'S BREW RIDGE TRAIL

A string of fantastic craft breweries stretches west from Charlottesville to Crozet and along Hwy 151, which ribbons along the base of the Blue Ridge Mountains below the Blue Ridge Pkwy. Part of the Brew Ridge Trail (www.brewridgetrail.com), many of the breweries offer fine craft beer, mountain views and great food. On pretty days you'll find the patios loaded with beer connoisseurs and outdoor adventurers. Charlottesville Hop on Tours (www.cvillehopontours.com) shuttles between many of the breweries.

$12-32; ☉11am-midnight Mon-Thu, to 2am Fri & Sat, 10am-2:30pm Sun) On the pedestrian mall, the Whiskey Jar offers a huge (more than 125 varieties!) whiskey selection in a hiply rustic setting – wooden furniture with waitstaff wearing plaid and drinks in Mason jars. And note, if you like your Bloody Mary's spicy – it will be spicy. Also serves neo-Southern comfort food, including great barbecue.

ℹ Getting There & Around

Amtrak (www.amtrak.com; 810 W Main St) Two daily trains to Washington, DC (from $30, three hours).

Charlottesville Albemarle Airport (CHO; ☑434-973-8342; www.gocho.com) Ten miles north of downtown; offers non-stop flights along the east coast and to Chicago.

Greyhound/Trailways Terminal (☑434-295-5131; www.greyhound.com; 310 W Main St) Runs three daily buses to Richmond (from $18, 1¼ hours) and one to Washington, DC (from $21, three hours).

A free trolley connects W Main St with UVA.

Appomattox

At the McLean House in the town of Appomattox Court House, General Robert E Lee surrendered the Army of Northern Virginia to General Ulysses S Grant, in effect ending the Civil War.

Today, the town of Appomatox (3 miles southwest of the national park) is small but charming, with a main street dotted with antique shops (a goldmine for hunters of Civil War memorabilia).

◉ Sights

Appomattox Court House National Historic Park PARK
(☑434-352-8987; www.nps.gov/apco; 111 National Park Dr; ☉9am-5pm) FREE On April 9, 1865, the surrender of the Army of Northern Virginia occurred here at McLean House. The park comprises over two dozen restored buildings; a number are open to visitors, and set with original and period furnishings from 1865.

Highlights include the parlor of the **McLean House**, where Lee and Grant met; the **Clover Hill Tavern**, used by Union soldiers to print 30,000 parole passes for Confederate soldiers; and the dry-goods-filled **Meeks General Store**.

🛏 Sleeping & Eating

Longacre
B&B $$

(☑434-352-9251; www.longacreva.com; 1670 Church St; r from $115; P❀) Longacre looks like it got lost somewhere in the English countryside and decided to set up shop in Virginia. Its elegant rooms are decorated with antiques, and lush grounds surround the sprawling Tudor house.

Baine's Books and Coffee
CAFE $

(☑434-432-3711; www.bainesbooks.com; 205 Main St; snacks $2-6; ⊙7am-8pm Mon-Wed, to 9:30pm Thu & Fri, 8:30am-9:30pm Sat, 9am-5pm Sun) Stop in for sandwiches, quiche and scones (plus live music several nights a week).

Shenandoah Valley

Local lore says Shenandoah was named for a Native American word meaning 'Daughter of the Stars.' True or not, there's no question this is God's country, and one of the most beautiful places in America. The 200-mile-long valley and its Blue Ridge Mountains are packed with picturesque small towns, wineries, microbreweries, preserved battlefields and caverns. This was once the western border of colonial America, settled by Scots–Irish frontiersmen who were Highland Clearance refugees. Outdoor activities – hiking, cycling, camping, fishing, horseback riding and canoeing – abound.

ℹ Getting There & Around

The I-81 and I-64 are the primary interstates here. The largest airport is Roanoke-Blacksburg Regional Airport (p298). Amtrak stops at the train station (www.amtrak.com; 1 Middlebrook Ave) in Staunton.

Front Royal & Luray

The northernmost tip of Skyline Dr at Front Royal looks like a drab strip of gas stations, but there's a friendly main street and some cool caverns nearby. Stop at the visitor center (☑800-338-2576; https://frontroyalva.com/101/Visiting; 414 E Main St; ⊙9am-5pm) before heading 'up' the valley. Luray may be best known for its caverns, but the downtown is a charming place to stroll.

◉ Sights

Luray Caverns
CAVE

(☑540-743-6551; www.luraycaverns.com; 970 US Hwy 211 W, Luray; adult/child 6-12yr $27/14; ⊙9am-

7pm daily mid-Jun–Aug, to 6pm Sep-Nov & Apr–mid-Jun, to 4pm Mon-Fri & to 5pm Sat & Sun Dec-Mar) If you can only fit one cavern into your itinerary, head 25 miles south from Front Royal to the world-class Luray Caverns and hear the 'Stalacpipe Organ' – hyped as the largest musical instrument on earth. Tours can feel like a cattle call on busy weekends, but the stunning underground formations make up for all the elbow-bumping. To save time at the entrance, buy your ticket online ahead of time, then join the entry line.

Museum of the Shenandoah Valley
MUSEUM

(☑540-662-1473, 888-556-5799; www.themsv.org; 901 Amherst St, Winchester; adult/student 13-18yr/child $10/8/free, Wed free; ⊙10am-5pm Tue-Sun Apr-Dec, 11am-4pm Jan-Mar) Located in the town of Winchester, some 25 miles north of Front Royal, this museum comprises an 18th-century house museum filled with period furnishings, a 6-acre garden and a multimedia museum that delves into the valley's history.

Skyline Caverns
CAVE

(☑800-296-4545; www.skylinecaverns.com; 10344 Stonewall Jackson Hwy, near entrance to Skyline Dr, Front Royal; adult/child 7-13yr $22/11; ⊙9am-5pm, hours vary seasonally) Front Royal's claim to fame is Skyline Caverns, which boasts rare, white-spiked anthodites – mineral formations that look like sea urchins.

🛏 Sleeping & Eating

Yogi Bear's Jellystone Park Campsite
CAMPGROUND $

(☑540-743-4002; www.campluray.com; 2250 Hwy 211 E, Luray; campsites/cabins from $45/116) Miniature-golf courses, waterslides and paddleboats all await inside this fanciful campus. Bargain-basement campsite and cabin prices don't reflect the possibility you might strike it rich while panning for gold at Old Faceful Mining Company.

Woodward House on Manor Grade
B&B $$

(☑540-635-7010, 800-635-7011; www.acountryhome.com; 413 S Royal Ave/US 320, Front Royal; r $110-155, cottage $225; P❀) Offers seven cheerful rooms and a separate cottage. Sip your coffee from the deck and don't let the busy street below distract from the Blue Ridge Mountain vista.

Element
FUSION $$

(☑540-636-9293; www.jsgourmet.com; 317 E Main St, Front Royal; lunch mains $8-10, dinner mains $14-28; ⊙11am-3pm & 5-9pm Tue-Sat; ❀) Element is a foodie favorite for quality bistro

WASHINGTON, DC & THE CAPITAL REGION SHENANDOAH VALLEY

fare. The small dinner menu features changing specials such as roasted quail with Mexican corn salad and sweet potatoes.

🛈 Getting There & Away

The best way to explore the region is by car. Washington, DC is 70 miles east of Front Royal. Luray borders US 211 between I-81 and the Thornton Gap entrance to the national park.

Staunton

This small-town beauty has much going for it, including a historic and walkable town center, a fantastic foodie scene, great microbreweries, some intriguing museums, regular live music downtown and a first-rate theater. Add to this an abundance of outdoor activities nearby and you may find yourself looking into local real estate when you get here.

⊙ Sights

The pedestrian-friendly, handsome center boasts more than 200 buildings designed by noted Victorian architect TJ Collins. There's an artsy yet unpretentious bohemian vibe thanks to the presence of Mary Baldwin, a small liberal arts university.

Frontier Culture Museum   MUSEUM
(☑ 540-332-7850; www.frontiermuseum.org; 1290 Richmond Rd; adult/student/child 6-12yr $12/11/7; ⊙ 9am-5pm mid-Mar–Nov, 10am-4pm Dec–mid-Mar) The excellent Frontier Culture Museum is cooler than its name might suggest. On the 100-plus acre grounds you'll find authentic historic buildings from Germany, Ireland and England, plus re-created West African dwellings and a separate area of American frontier dwellings.

Woodrow Wilson Presidential Library   HISTORIC SITE
(www.woodrowwilson.org; 20 N Coalter St; adult/student/child 6-12yr $14/7/5; ⊙ 9am-5pm Mon-Sat, from noon Sun) History buffs should check out the Woodrow Wilson Presidential Library near downtown. Stop by and tour the hilltop Greek Revival house where Wilson grew up, which has been faithfully restored to its original 1856 appearance.

🛏 Sleeping & Eating

Frederick House   B&B $$
(☑ 540-885-4220; www.frederickhouse.com; 28 N New St; r $145-208; 🅿 ❄ 🛜) Stay right downtown in the thoroughly mauve and immensely welcoming Frederick House, which consists of five historical residences with 25 varied rooms and suites – all with private bathrooms and some with antique furnishings and decks.

Stonewall Jackson Hotel   HOTEL $$
(☑ 540-885-4848; www.stonewalljacksonhotel.com; 24 S Market St; r/ste $179/385; 🅿 ❄ 🛜 ♨ 🐾) A restored and renovated Staunton classic, the Stonewall oozes class and the restrained Southern style of the classical Commonwealth. The central lobby could be plucked from a chapter of *The Great Gatsby* (if *Gatsby* was set in old Virginia). Rooms are comfortable and retain the classic atmosphere promised by the entrance, and amenities are extensive.

Byers Street Bistro   MODERN AMERICAN $$
(☑ 540-887-6100; www.byersstreetbistro.com; 18 Byers St; lunch mains $10-19, dinner mains $10-28; ⊙ 11am-midnight) By the train station, Byers Street Bistro cooks up high-end pub grub (applewood bacon and caramelized onion pizzas, mahimahi tacos, Angus burgers, slow-roasted baby back ribs) that's best enjoyed at the outdoor tables on warm days. Come on Friday and Saturday nights for live bands (bluegrass, blues and folk).

Zynodoa   SOUTHERN US $$$
(☑ 540-885-7775; www.zynodoa.com; 115 E Beverley St; mains $19-32; ⊙ 5-9:30pm Sun-Tue, to 10:30pm Wed-Sat; 🍷) 🍽 Classy Zynodoa puts together some fine dishes in the vein of Virginia artisan cheeses, Shenandoah-sourced roasted chicken and rainbow trout from Casta Line (raised nearby). Local farms and wineries are the backbone of Zynodoa's larder.

🍸 Drinking & Entertainment

Yelping Dog   WINE BAR
(☑ 540-885-2275; www.yelpingdogwine.com; 9 E Beverly St; ⊙ 11am-9pm Tue-Thu, to 10pm Fri & Sat, noon-6pm Sun) Catch up with friends over a glass of wine and a scrumptious cheese plate at this inviting wine bar in the thick of the downtown action. And if you're on the fence about ordering one of the gourmet grilled cheese sandwiches ($9 to $10), go ahead.

Redbeard Brewery   MICROBREWERY
(www.redbeardbrews.com; 102 S Lewis St; ⊙ 4-11pm Tue-Thu, 1-11pm Fri-Sun) A small-batch brewery that serves up tasty IPAs, saisons, ambers and other seasonal selections.

SHENANDOAH NATIONAL PARK

One of the most spectacular national parks in the country, **Shenandoah National Park** (☑540-999-3500; www.nps.gov/shen; Skyline Dr; one-week pass per car $25) is like a new smile from nature: in spring and summer the wildflowers explode, in fall the leaves burn bright red and orange, and in winter a cold, starkly beautiful hibernation period sets in. White-tailed deer are a common sight and, if you're lucky, you might spot a black bear, bobcat or wild turkey. The park lies just 75 miles west of Washington, DC.

Your first stop should be the **Dickey Ridge Visitors Center** (☑540-635-3566; www.nps.gov/shen; Mile 4.6, Skyline Dr; ⊙9am-5pm mid-Apr–Nov), close to the northern end of Skyline Dr, or the **Byrd Visitors Center** (☑540-999-3283; www.nps.gov/shen; Mile 51, Skyline Dr; ⊙9am-5pm late Mar-Nov). Both places have exhibits on flora and fauna, as well as maps and information about hiking trails and activities.

Shenandoah National Park is easy on the eyes, set against a backdrop of the dreamy Blue Ridge Mountains, ancient granite and metamorphic formations that are more than one billion years old. The park itself was founded in 1935 as a retreat for East Coast urban populations. It is an accessible day-trip destination from DC, but stay longer if you can. The 500 miles of hiking trails, 75 scenic overlooks, 30 fishing streams, seven picnic areas and four campgrounds are sure to keep you entertained.

Skyline Drive is the breathtaking road that follows the main ridge of the Blue Ridge Mountains and winds 105 miles through the center of the park. It begins in Front Royal near the western end of I-66, and ends in the southern part of the range near Rockfish Gap near I-64. Mile markers at the side of the road provide a reference. Miles and miles of blazed trails wander through the park.

The most famous trail in the park is the stretch of **Appalachian Trail** (AT), which travels 101 miles through Shenandoah from south to north, and is part of the 2175-mile Appalachian Trail crossing through 14 states. Access the trail from Skyline Dr, which roughly runs parallel. Aside from the AT, Shenandoah has over 400 miles of hiking trails in the park. Options for shorter hikes include **Compton Peak** (Mile 10.4; 2.4 miles; easy to moderate), **Traces** (Mile 22.2; 1.7 miles; easy), **Overall Run** (Mile 22.2; 6 miles; moderate) and **White Oak Canyon** (Mile 42.6; 4.6 miles; strenuous). **Hawksbill Mountain Summit** (Mile 46.7; 2.1 miles; moderate) is the park's highest peak.

Amtrak (www.amtrak.com) trains runs daily to Charlottesville (from $35, two hours 45 minutes), and Wednesdays, Fridays and Sundays to Staunton (from $55, four hours), from Washington, DC . You'll really need your own wheels to explore the length and breadth of the park, which can be easily accessed from several exits off I-81.

There is a **gas station** (Mile 51.2, Skyline Dr) at Big Meadows Wayside.

★**Blackfriars
Playhouse**   THEATER

(☑540-851-1733; www.americanshakespearecenter.com; 10 S Market St; tickets $29-49) Don't leave Staunton without catching a show at the Blackfriars Playhouse, where the American Shakespeare Center company performs in this re-creation of Shakespeare's original indoor theater. The acting is up-close and engaged, and brave guests can grab a seat on the side of the stage.

ⓘ Getting There & Away

Staunton sits beside I-81, not far from its junction with I-64 E. Amtrak (p315) stops here three times per week.

Lexington & Rockbridge County

This is the place to see Southern gentry at their stately best, as cadets from the Virginia Military Institute jog past the prestigious academics of Washington & Lee University. Two Civil War generals, Robert E Lee and Stonewall Jackson, are buried here, and Lexington has long been a favorite stop for Civil War enthusiasts. Today you're as likely to see hikers, cyclists and paddlers using Lexington as a launchpad for adventures in the nearby Blue Ridge Mountains, where the Blue Ridge Pkwy and the Appalachian Trail overlook the valley, as well as on the James River. The opening of new hotels, bars and restaurants have re-energized the city.

◉ Sights & Activities

Virginia Military Institute UNIVERSITY
(VMI; www.vmi.edu; Letcher Ave) You'll either be impressed or put off by the extreme discipline of the cadets at Virginia Military Institute, the only university to have sent its entire graduating class into combat (plaques to student war dead are touching and ubiquitous). The **VMI Museum** (📞 540-464-7334; ⊙ 9am-5pm) FREE houses the stuffed carcass of Stonewall Jackson's horse, a homemade American flag made by an alumnus prisoner of war in Vietnam, and a tribute to VMI students killed in the 'War on Terror'.

Contact the museum for a free guided tour of the campus, offered at noon. A full-dress parade takes place most Fridays at 4:30pm during the school year. The school's **George C Marshall Museum** (📞 540-463-2083; www.marshallfoundation.org/museum/; adult/student $5/2; ⊙ 11am-4pm Tue-Sat) honors the creator of the Marshall Plan for post-WWII European reconstruction.

Washington & Lee University UNIVERSITY
(📞 540-458-8400; www.wlu.edu) Named for George Washington and Robert E Lee, this pretty and preppy liberal arts college was founded in 1749. George Washington saved the young school in 1796 with a gift of $20,000. Confederate Gen Robert E Lee served as president after the Civil War in the hopes of unifying the country through education. Visitors today can stroll along the striking red-brick Colonnade and visit **Lee Chapel & Museum** (📞 540-458-8768; http://leechapel.wlu.edu; ⊙ 9am-4pm Mon-Sat & 1-4pm Sun Nov-Mar, to 5pm Apr-Oct).

Natural Bridge State Park BRIDGE
(📞 540-291-1326; www.dcr.virginia.gov; 6477 S Lee Hwy; adult/child 6-12yr $8/6; ⊙ 8am-dusk) We're going to let Thomas Jefferson write the review of this new state park, which he once owned and described in his book *Notes on Virginia*: 'It is impossible for the emotions arising from the sublime, to be felt beyond what they are here: so beautiful an arch, so elevated, so light, and springing as it were up to heaven, the rapture of the spectator is really indescribable!' Yep, no longer a kitschy tourist trap, this park spotlights a very photogenic 215ft-high limestone bridge.

Dinosaur Kingdom II AMUSEMENT PARK
(📞 540-464-2253; www.facebook.com/dinosaur kingdom; 5781 S Lee Hwy, Lexington; adult/child 3-12yr $10/3; ⊙ 10am-6pm; 🚼) One of the wackiest attractions yet from artist and creative wunderkind Mark Cline, this kitschy theme park transports visitors to an alternate reality: a forested kingdom where Union soldiers are attempting to use life-size dinosaurs as weapons of mass destruction against Confederate forces during the Civil War. Even President Lincoln is here, trying to lasso a flying pteranodon. The Styrofoam and fiberglass creations are lifelike enough to amaze younger kids, and the offbeat historic juxtapositions will entertain even the grouchiest of adults.

Twin River Outfitters CANOEING; TUBING
(📞 540-261-7334; https://canoevirginia.net/; 653 Lowe St, Buchanan; 2hr paddling trip from $34; ⊙ 9am-5pm Apr-Oct) Scan for eagles and deer as you paddle or tube down the James River on the new Upper James River Paddling Trail with this popular outfitter, owned by twin brothers. Mileage and travel times vary, as does difficulty. A shuttle ride is included in the price.

Upper James River Water Trail CANOEING
(www.upperjamesriverwatertrail.com; Botetourt) This new paddling trail follows the James River as it flows through the foothills of the Blue Ridge Mountains toward Richmond and the coast.

🛏 Sleeping & Eating

Georges BOUTIQUE HOTEL $$
(📞 540-463-2500; www.thegeorges.com; 11 N Main St; r from $205; 🅿 ❄ 🛜) Set in two historic buildings on opposite sides of Main St, the Georges has beautifully set rooms, each custom-designed with high-end furnishings. The great location, friendly service and on-site eateries add to the appeal.

Applewood Inn & Llama Trekking INN $$
(📞 540-463-1962; www.applewoodbb.com; 242 Tarn Beck Lane; r $169-175, cottage from $235; 🅿 ❄) The charming, ecominded Applewood Inn & Llama Trekking offers accommodations and a slew of outdoorsy activities (including, yes, llama trekking) on a farm in a bucolic valley just a 10-minute drive away from downtown Lexington. And note that you don't ride a llama when trekking – you just walk side by side like old friends. Who sometimes spit at you.

Blue Sky Bakery SANDWICHES $
(📞 540-463-6546; 125 W Nelson St; sandwiches $8; ⊙ 10:30am-4pm Mon-Fri) This local favorite

SCENIC DRIVE: VIRGINIA'S HORSE COUNTRY

About 40 miles west of Washington, DC, suburban sprawl gives way to endless green farms, vineyards, quaint villages and palatial estates and ponies. This is 'Horse Country,' where wealthy Washingtonians pursue their equestrian pastimes.

The following route is the most scenic drive to Shenandoah National Park (p317). From DC, take Rte 50 West to **Middleburg**, a too-cute-for-words town of B&Bs, taverns, wine shops and boutiques. The **National Sporting Library** (☑540-687-6542; www.nationalsporting.org; 102 The Plains Rd; museum adult/child 13-18yr $10/8, library free; ☉10am-5pm Wed-Sun) is a museum and research center devoted to horse and field sports such as foxhunting, dressage, steeplechase and polo. About 20 miles northeast of Middleburg is **Leesburg**, another charming town with a colonial feel and historic sites. Stop in **Morven Park** (☑703-777-2414; www.morvenpark.org; 17263 Southern Planter Lane; grounds free, mansion tours adult/child $10/5; ☉grounds 8am-5:45pm daily, mansion tours hourly noon-5pm Sat & Sun, last tour 4pm) for a tour of a staggering Virginia home on 1000 acres. For more Greek Revival grandeur, visit **Oatlands Plantation** (☑703-777-3174; www.oatlands.org; 20850 Oatlands Plantation Lane; adult/child 6-16yr $15/8, grounds only $10; ☉10am-5pm Mon-Sat & 1-5pm Sun Apr-Dec, closed Jan-Mar), outside of town.

The area has a wealth of appealing dining options. Stop in the **Shoes Cup & Cork** (☑703-771-7463; www.shoescupandcork.com; 17 N King St; lunch mains $10-18, dinner mains $11-25; ☉7am-9pm Mon-Thu, to 10pm Fri, 9am-10pm Sat, 9am-9pm Sun) in Leesburg for creative American fare or **Chimole** (☑703-777-7011; www.facebook.com/CH1MOLE; 10 S King St; tapas $8-18; ☉11am-2pm Mon-Fri, 5-10pm Wed & Thu, 5pm-1am Fri & Sat) for wine and Latin American tapas. In Middleburg, the **Red Fox Inn & Tavern** (☑540-687-6801; www.redfox.com; 2 E Washington St; breakfast mains $12-15, dinner mains $26-58; ☉8-10am & 5-9pm Mon-Fri, 11:30am-2:30pm & 5-9pm Sat, 11:30am-2:30pm & 5-8pm Sun) has first-rate American cooking served in a beautifully preserved 1728 dining room.

Located 6 miles west of Middleburg, the **Welbourne B&B** (☑540-687-3201; www.welbourneinn.com; 22314 Welbourne Farm Lane; r $147; ❉ 🛜 🐾 🎿) has five heritage rooms set in a historic landmark house (c 1770) surrounded by 520 acres. The **Leesburg Colonial Inn** (☑703-777-5000; www.theleesburgcolonialinn.com; 19 S King St; r $129-179) has a great central location and unbeatable prices.

Further down the road at the foothills of the Blue Ridge Mountains is **Sperryville**. Its many galleries and shops are a must-stop for antique-lovers. Continue 9 miles west to reach the Thornton Gap entrance of Skyline Dr in Shenandoah National Park.

has tasty focaccia sandwiches, hearty soups and fresh salads.

Red Hen SOUTHERN US $$$
(☑540-464-4401; www.redhenlex.com; 11 E Washington St; mains $24-28; ☉5-9:30pm Tue-Sat; 🍴) 🌿 Reserve well ahead for a memorable meal at Red Hen, which features a creative menu showcasing fine local produce. Great cocktails and desserts too.

🍸 Drinking & Entertainment

Taps BAR
(☑540-463-2500; www.thegeorges.com; 11 N Main St, Georges; ☉3-11pm Mon-Thu, from 11am Fri & Sat) This cozy place in Georges doubles as Lexington's living room, with students, professors and other locals hanging out on the fancy couches or at the small bar. Come here

for craft beer, fine cocktails and local gossip. The short pub grub menu is strong.

Hull's Drive-in CINEMA
(☑540-463-2621; www.hullsdrivein.com; 2367 N Lee Hwy/US 11; adult/child 5-11yr $7/3; ☉gates open 7pm Fri & Sat May-Oct; ♿) For old-fashioned amusement, catch a movie at this drive-in movie theater, set 5.5 miles north of Lexington. Movies start 20 minutes after sunset.

ℹ️ Getting There & Away

Lexington sits at the junction of I-81 and I-64. The closest airport is Roanoke-Blacksburg Regional Airport (p298), which is 55 miles south. There is an Amtrak station (p315) in nearby Staunton, with a connection to Washington, DC three times per week.

Blue Ridge Highlands & Southwest Virginia

The Blue Ridge Highlands and the Roanoke Valley are two of the prettiest regions in the state, with farm-dotted valleys unfurling between the Blue Ridge and Allegheny mountains. The Blue Ridge Parkway and Appalachian Trail roll across the mountains here, which are home to scenic rivers, streams and lakes. Old-time mountain music can be heard regularly, and wineries and craft breweries offer tastings in small towns and on mountain slopes. The most rugged part of the region – and the state – is the southwestern tip of Virginia, where mountain music was born. Turn onto any side road and you'll plunge into dark strands of dogwood and fir, and see fast streams and white waterfalls. You're bound to see Confederate flags, but there's a proud hospitality behind the fierce veneer of independence.

❶ Getting There & Around

I-81 is the primary interstate here, running north–south through the western edge of the state. The Blue Ridge Pkwy runs parallel to I-81, but it is much slower going. The major airport in the region is the Roanoke Regional Airport (p298).

Roanoke

Illuminated by the giant star atop Mill Mountain, Roanoke is the largest city in the Roanoke Valley and is the self-proclaimed 'Capital of the Blue Ridge.' Close to the Blue Ridge Pkwy and the Appalachian Trail, it's a convenient base camp for exploring the great outdoors. An expanding greenway system, a burgeoning arts scene and a slew of new craft breweries have energized the city in recent years, flipping Roanoke from sleepy to almost hip.

◉ Sights & Activities

Center in the Square   MUSEUM
(☑540-342-5700; www.centerinthesquare.org; 1 Market Sq; ⊙10am-5pm Tue-Sat, from 1pm Sun) The city's cultural heartbeat, where you'll find four museums, a butterfly garden, a theater and a rooftop observation deck. Museums cover African American culture, pinball, science and local history. There are six aquariums on the first floor. The Center Pass (adult/child $21/16) includes all attractions except the Roanoke Pinball Museum.

Harrison Museum of African American Culture   MUSEUM
(☑540-857-4395; www.harrisonmuseum.com; 1 Market Sq; adult/child 5-17yr $7/4.75; ⊙10am-5pm Tue-Sat, from 1pm Sun) FREE Inside Center in the Square, this museum has displays about local African American culture and traditional and contemporary African art. Admission also available through the Center Pass, which includes additional museums within Center in the Square.

Roanoke Star & Mill Mountain Park   PARK
(☑540-853-2236; www.playroanoke.com; 2000 JP Fishburn Pkwy) Mill Mountain Park has walking trails, a discovery center, a zoo (adult/child aged three to 11 years $9/7) and grand views of Roanoke. It's also home to the massive Roanoke Star, which shines over the city at night.

Taubman Museum of Art   MUSEUM
(www.taubmanmuseum.org; 110 Salem Ave SE; ⊙10am-5pm Wed-Sat, noon-5pm Sun, to 9pm third Thu & first Fri of month; ℗) FREE The striking Taubman Museum of Art is set in a sculptural steel-and-glass edifice that's reminiscent of the Guggenheim Bilbao. Inside, you'll find a superb collection of artworks spanning 3500 years.

Greenways   OUTDOORS
(www.roanokeoutside.com/land/greenways/) Before hopping in your car and driving to your next Roanoke adventure, see if one of the city's new greenways will get you to your destination via a scenic stroll or bike ride.

🛏 Sleeping & Eating

Hotel Roanoke   HOTEL $$$
(☑540-985-5900; www.hotelroanoke.com; 110 Shenandoah Ave NW; r $189-224, ste $289-414; ℗@⊛) This Tudor-style grand dame has presided over this city at the base of the Blue Ridge Mountains for the better part of a century and provides a welcome respite. Downstairs is the Pine Room for those requiring a stiff drink. Now a Hilton property.

Local Roots   MODERN AMERICAN $$
(☑540-206-2610; www.localrootsrestaurant.com; 1314 Grandin Rd; lunch mains $11-14, dinner mains $26-31; ⊙11:30am-2pm & 5-10pm Tue-Sat, 11am-2:30pm & 5-9pm Sun) This welcoming farm-to-table restaurant serves up delectable fare like shrimp and grits, striped bass, and perhaps the best hamburgers in town, with a large portion of the menu rotating seasonally.

★ **Lucky**   MODERN AMERICAN **$$**
(☎540-982-1249; www.eatatlucky.com; 18 Kirk Ave SW; mains $18-29; ⊙5-9pm Mon-Wed, to 10pm Thu-Sat) Lucky has excellent cocktails (try 'The Cube') and a seasonally inspired menu of small plates (hickory-smoked porchetta, roasted oysters) and heartier mains (buttermilk fried chicken, morel and asparagus gnocchi). The team behind Lucky opened the equally divine Italian restaurant **Fortunato** (www.fortunatorestaurant.com) a few doors down.

ⓘ Getting There & Away

The airport (p298) is 5 miles north of downtown and serves the Roanoke and Shenandoah Valley regions. If you're driving, I-81 and I-581 link to the city. The Blue Ridge Pkwy is just 5 miles from downtown.

Mt Rogers National Recreation Area

This seriously beautiful district is well worth a visit for outdoor enthusiasts. Hike, fish or cross-country ski among ancient hardwood trees and the state's tallest peak. The 33.4-mile Virginia Creeper Trail, popular with cyclists, passes through the recreation area. For food, load up your picnic or your backpack in the towns of Abingdon or Marion. The best way to get to the trails and campsites is by car. The skinny recreation area runs roughly north–south, with I-81 to the west and the Blue Ridge Pkwy to the east. The Tennessee and North Carolina borders are nearby. The Appalachian Trail runs across the mountains here and the Virginia Creeper Trail rolls through too.

Abingdon

One of the most photogenic towns in Virginia, Abingdon retains fine Federal and Victorian architecture in its historic district. The long-running regional theater in the center of town is a state-wide draw, as is the magnificent Virginia Creeper Trail. Popular with cyclists and hikers, this leafy path unfurls along an old railroad bed.

◉ Sights & Activities

Heartwood   ARTS CENTER
(☎276-492-2400; www.myswva.org/heartwood; One Heartwood Circle; ⊙9am-5pm Mon-Wed, Fri & Sat, to 9pm Thu, 10am-3pm Sun) Heartwood is a showcase of regional crafts, cuisine (sandwiches, salads, Virginia wines) and traditional music. Don't miss Thursday nights, for bluegrass bands and barbecue.

Virginia Creeper Trail   CYCLING, HIKING
(www.vacreepertrail.com) This 33.4-mile cycling and hiking trail on an old railroad corridor rolls through the Mount Rogers National Recreation Area, connecting lofty Whitetop with Damascus and eventually Abingdon. Local bike companies rent out bikes and provide shuttle service.

🛏 Sleeping

Alpine Motel   MOTEL **$**
(☎276-628-3178; www.alpinemotelabingdon.com; 882 E Main St; r $59-69; ⓟ❄🛜) The Alpine Motel is a simple but good-value option, with carpeted rooms, old TVs, and chirping birds across the way; it's located about 2 miles west of downtown.

BLUE RIDGE PARKWAY

Where Skyline Dr ends, the Blue Ridge Pkwy picks up. Managed by the national park service, the parkway is just as pretty and runs from the southern Appalachian ridge in Shenandoah National Park (at Mile 0) to North Carolina's Great Smoky Mountains National Park (at Mile 469). Wildflowers bloom in spring, and fall colors are spectacular, but watch out for foggy days; the lack of guardrails can make for hairy driving. There are a dozen visitor centers scattered over the parkway, and any of them make a good kick-off point for your trip. You won't find one stoplight on the entire drive, but we can almost guarantee you'll see deer. A helpful website is www.blueridgeparkway.org.

Along the Blue Ridge Pkwy there are trails to the **Peaks of Otter** (www.peaksofotter. com; Mile 86, Blue Ridge Pkwy; ♿) There are three peaks here: Sharp Top, Flat Top and Harkening Hill. Shuttles run to the top of Sharp Top, or you can try a fairly challenging hike (3 miles round-trip) to the top. The 360-degree view of the Blue Ridge Mountains from the rocky summit is fantastic. A short trail leads to the nearby Johnson Farm, which grew apples for the local inn before the arrival of the parkway.

For more information, visit www.nps.gov/blri.

Martha Washington Inn　　　HOTEL **$$$**
(☎276-628-3161; www.themartha.com; 150 W
Main St; r/ste from $215/425; ⓟ❀@☎☀) This
is the region's premier historic hotel, a Vic-
torian sprawl of historical classiness and
wrought-iron style. The rocking chairs on
the front porch are a pleasant place to relax.

✖ Eating & Drinking

128 Pecan　　　MODERN AMERICAN **$$**
(☎276-698-3159; www.128pecan.com; 128 Pecan
St; lunch mains $8-17, dinner mains $8-23; ⊙11am-
9pm Tue-Sat; ☎) This local favorite serves up
excellent sandwiches, tacos and heartier
meat or seafood dishes, with seating on a
front verandah.

Rain　　　AMERICAN **$$$**
(☎276-739-2331; www.rainabingdon.com; 283 E
Main St; lunch mains $9-10, dinner mains $22-29;
⊙11am-2pm & 5-9pm Tue-Sat; ⓟ) Excellent
New American cuisine inspired by the Ap-
palachians. The mains, like seared salmon
and sweet mustard pork chops, are executed
wonderfully, with great consistency – this is
the best splurge around.

Wolf Hills Brewing Co　　　MICROBREWERY
(☎276-451-5470; www.wolfhillsbrewing.com; 350
Park St; ⊙5-9pm Mon-Fri, from 1pm Sat, 1-6pm
Sun) For satisfying microbrews and the occa-
sional live music session, head to Wolf Hills
Brewery.

❶ Getting There & Away

Abingdon borders I-81 near the Virginia–
Tennessee border. The city is 366 miles south-
west of Washington, DC and about 180 miles
northwest of Charlotte, NC. Close regional
airports include Asheville Regional Airport in
Asheville, NC and Roanoke-Blacksburg Regional
Airport (p298) in Roanoke.

The Crooked Road

When Scots–Irish fiddle-and-reel joined
with African American banjo-and-
percussion, American mountain or 'old-
time' music was born, spawning such genres
as country and bluegrass. The latter genre
still dominates the Blue Ridge, and Virgin-
ia's Heritage Music Trail, the 330-mile-long
Crooked Road (www.myswva.org/tcr), takes
you through nine sites associated with that
history, along with some eye-stretching
mountain scenery. It's well worth taking a
detour and joining the music-loving fans of
all ages who kick up their heels (many arrive

with tap shoes) at these festive jamborees.
During a live show you'll witness elders
connecting to deep cultural roots and a new
generation of musicians keeping that herit-
age alive and evolving. Top venues include
the Floyd Country Store on Friday Nights
and the **Carter Family Fold** (☎276-386-
6054; www.carterfamilyfold.org; 3449 AP Carter
Hwy, Hiltons; adult/child 6-11yr $10/2; ⊙7:30pm
Sat; ♿) on Saturday nights.

FLOYD

Tucked in the foothills of the Blue Ridge
Mountains, tiny, cute-as-a-postcard Floyd
is nothing more than an intersection be-
tween Hwy 8 and Hwy 221. In fact, the
whole county only has one stoplight. But
life explodes on Friday nights during the Fri-
day Night Jamboree at the **Floyd Country
Store** (☎540-745-4563; www.floydcountrystore.
com; 206 S Locust St; $5; ⊙10am-5pm Tue-Thu,
to 10:30pm Fri, to 6pm Sat, 11am-6pm Sun) and
the surrounding sidewalks when folks from
far and wide converge for a night of live old-
time music and communal good cheer.

⨋ Sleeping & Eating

Oak Haven Lodge　　　INN **$**
(☎540-745-5716; www.oakhavenlodge.com; 323
Webb's Mill Rd, Rte 8; r/ste $75/90; ⓟ❀☎) Just
a mile north of Floyd, this good-value place
has spacious rooms (some with Jacuzzi tubs)
that open onto a shared balcony with rock-
ing chairs.

Hotel Floyd　　　HOTEL **$$**
(☎540-745-6080; www.hotelfloyd.com; 300 Rick
Lewis Way; r $139, ste $169-199; ⓟ❀☎☀) ✿
Built with ecofriendly materials and furnish-
ings, Hotel Floyd is a model of sustainability.
Works by local artisans adorn its rooms.

Oddfella's　　　TEX-MEX **$$**
(☎540-745-3463; www.facebook.com/Oddf3llows;
110 N Locust St; mains $11-25; ⊙11am-9pm Wed-
Sat, 10:30am-2:30pm Sun; ⓟ✐) When you're
all jigged out, head for Oddfella's, a comfy
spot for American fare and tasty micro-
brews. And the name? Just check the sign
over the door, which depicts the town's three
predominant types: hippies, farmers and
businessmen.

Dogtown Roadhouse　　　PIZZA **$$**
(☎540-745-6836; www.dogtownroadhouse.com;
302 S Locust St; mains $8-18; ⊙4-9pm Wed & Thu,
4pm-midnight Fri, noon-midnight Sat, noon-9pm
Sun) You might see a local farmer walk in
with produce for the toppings at this lively

pizzeria, the go-to for pizzas (fired up in a wood-burning oven) and microbrews, with live rock on Friday and Saturday nights.

❶ Getting There & Away

Floyd is 20 miles southeast of I-81. The closest major airport is Roanoke-Blacksburg Regional Airport (p298) about 50 miles north.

GALAX

Galax claims to be the world capital of mountain music, although it feels like anywhere-else-ville outside of the immediate downtown area, which is on the National Register of Historic Places.

🛏 Sleeping & Eating

Fiddlers Roost　　　　　　　CABIN $$
(☑ 276-236-1212; http://fiddlersroostcabins.com; 485 Fishers Peak Rd; cabins $120-300; ℗) These eight cabins resemble Lincoln Logs playsets. The interiors are decorated in 'quilt' chic; they may not win a place in *Wallpaper* magazine, but they're cozy and have gas fireplaces, kitchens, TVs and DVD players. Breakfast included with all but Cabin on the Blue.

Creek Bottom Brewing　　　MICROBREWERY
(☑ 276-236-2337; www.cbbrews.com; 307 N Meadow St; mains $6-16; ⊙ 11am-9pm Tue & Wed, 11am-10pm Thu-Sat, noon-6pm Sun) Has a changing line-up of craft brews, which go nicely with the brick-oven pizza and smoked chicken wings fired up on site.

☆ Entertainment

Blue Ridge Music Center　　　LIVE MUSIC
(☑ 276-236-5309; www.blueridgemusiccenter.net; 700 Foothills Rd, Mile 213 Blue Ridge Pkwy; ⊙ weekend shows May-Oct) An arts and music hub for the region that offers programming that focuses on local musicians carrying on the traditions of Appalachian music.

Rex Theater　　　　　　　　LIVE MUSIC
(☑ 276-236-0329; www.rextheatergalax.com; 113 E Grayson St) A musty, red-curtained belle of yore. Frequent bluegrass acts cross its stage, but the easiest one to catch is the Friday-night live WBRF 98.1 show ($5).

❶ Getting There & Away

Galax borders US 58 about 10 miles southwest of I-77. Roanoke-Blacksburg Regional Airport (p298) is 90 miles northeast via I-77 north and and I-81 N. It's about 10 miles from the Blue Ridge Pkwy.

WEST VIRGINIA

Ready for rugged East Coast adventuring with a gorgeous mountain backdrop? Then set your car toward wild and wonderful West Virginia, a state often overlooked by both American and foreign travelers. It doesn't help that the state can't seem to shake its negative stereotypes. That's too bad, because West Virginia is one of the prettiest states in the Union. With its line of unbroken green mountains, raging white-water rivers and snowcapped ski resorts, this is an outdoor-lovers' paradise. The state is also just a few hours' drive from Washington, DC, Pittsburgh, PA and Richmond, VA.

Created by secessionists, the people here still think of themselves as hardscrabble sons of miners, and that perception isn't entirely off. But the Mountain State is also gentrifying and, occasionally, that's a good thing: the arts are flourishing in the valleys, where some towns offer a welcome break from the state's evolving outdoor activities.

History

Virginia was once the biggest state in America, divided between the plantation aristocracy of the Tidewater and the mountains of what is now West Virginia. The latter were settled by tough farmers who staked out independent freeholds across the Appalachians. Always resentful of their Eastern brethren and their reliance on cheap (ie slave) labor, the mountaineers of West Virginia declared their independence from Virginia when the latter tried to break off from America during the Civil War.

Yet the scrappy, independent-at-all-costs stereotype was challenged in the late 19th and early 20th centuries, when miners here formed into cooperative unions and fought employers in some of the bloodiest battles in American labor history. That mix of chip-on-the-shoulder resentment toward authority and look-out-for-your-neighbor community values characterizes West Virginia today.

❶ Information

West Virginia Division of Tourism (www.wvtourism.com) operates welcome centers at interstate borders and in **Harpers Ferry** (☑ 304-535-2627; www.discoveritallwv.com; 37 Washington Ct; ⊙ 9am-5pm). Check the Division of Tourism's website for info on the state's myriad adventure-tourism opportunities.

ⓘ Getting There & Around

The Eastern Panhandle begins about 60 miles northwest of Washington, DC and it's a fairly easy drive from the busy metropolitan area – but expect traffic. Amtrak and MARC trains stop at the **station** in Harpers Ferry. For the national forest and the southern reaches of the state, you will need a car to explore and will likely be accessing mountain towns and parks on two-lane roads coming in from I-81, I-64 and I-79. So although the mileage looks short, the distance will take longer to cover than on the interstate.

Eastern Panhandle

The most accessible part of West Virginia has always been a mountain getaway for DC types – the region is just 70 miles west of the capital-area sprawl. Here, Civil War–era history, soothing hot springs, leafy scenery and outdoor recreation on trails and rivers work together for visitors, offering an easy package of experiences than can be enjoyed on one long weekend.

One tricky part of travel in the panhandle is the practically overlapping proximity of three states – West Virginia, Virginia and Maryland – with Pennsylvania lying in wait just north. When planning, get out your maps to make sure you've spotted all attractions in the multistate region.

Harpers Ferry

History lives on in this attractive town, set with steep cobblestoned streets, and framed by the Shenandoah Mountains and the confluence of the rushing Potomac and Shenandoah Rivers. The lower town functions as an open-air museum, with more than a dozen buildings that you can explore to get a taste of 19th-century small-town life. Exhibits narrate the town's role at the forefront of westward expansion, American industry and, most famously, the slavery debate – in 1859 old John Brown tried to spark a slave uprising here and was hanged for his efforts; the incident rubbed friction between North and South into the fires of Civil War.

⊙ Sights & Activities

Harpers Ferry National Historic Park   PARK
(☑304-535-6029; www.nps.gov/hafe; 171 Shoreline Dr; per person/vehicle $5/10; ⊙trails 9am-sunset, visitor center 9am-5pm; ℗) Historic buildings and museums are accessible to those with

passes, which can be found, along with parking and shuttles, north of town at the Harpers Ferry National Historic Park Visitor Center off Hwy 340. Parking is incredibly limited in Harpers Ferry proper so plan to park at the visitor center and catch the frequent shuttle. It's a short and scenic ride.

John Brown Museum   MUSEUM
(www.nps.gov/hafe; Shenandoah St; ⊙9am-5pm) **FREE** Across from Arsenal Sq and one of the park's museums, this three-room gallery gives a fine overview (through videos and period relics) of the events surrounding John Brown's famous raid.

Black Voices   MUSEUM
(www.nps.gov/hafe; High St; ⊙9am-5pm) **FREE** Part of the national park, this worthwhile, interactive exhibit has narrated stories of hardships and hard-won victories by African Americans from the times of enslavement through the Civil Rights era. Across the street is the Storer College exhibit, which gives an overview of the ground-breaking educational center and Niagara movement that formed in its wake.

Master Armorer's House   HISTORIC SITE
(☑304-535-6029; www.nps.gov/hafe; Shenandoah St; ⊙9am-5pm) **FREE** Among the free sites in the historic district, this 1858 house explains how rifle technology developed here went on to revolutionize the firearms industry.

Storer College Campus   HISTORIC SITE
(www.nps.gov/hafe; Fillmore St) Founded immediately after the Civil War, Storer College grew from a one-room schoolhouse for freed slaves to a respected college open to all races and creeds. It closed in 1955. You can freely wander the historic campus, reachable by taking the path to upper town, past St Peter's church, Jefferson Rock and Harper Cemetery.

C&O Canal National Historic Park   CYCLING, HIKING
(www.nps.gov/choh) The 184.5-mile towpath passes along the Potomac River on the Maryland side. Check www.nps.gov/hafe for access points to the towpath and a list of bike rental companies.

Appalachian Trail Conservancy   HIKING
(☑304-535-6331; www.appalachiantrail.org; cnr Washington & Jackson Sts; ⊙9am-5pm) The 2160-mile Appalachian Trail is headquartered here at this tremendous resource for

hikers. The AT passes through town nearby and hikers – and others – can stop by for conversation, information, trail updates and restrooms. The hiker lounge has wi-fi, a computer and a free phone – beside a giant sign reminding hikers to call their mothers.

O Be Joyfull WALKING
(☑ 732-801-0381; www.obejoyfull.com; 110 Church St, Thomas Hall at St Peter's Church; tours adult/child 8-12yr $34/15) Offers eye-opening historical daytime walking tours (lasting three to four hours) around Harpers Ferry.

River Riders ADVENTURE SPORTS
(☑ 800-326-7238; www.riverriders.com; 408 Alstadts Hill Rd; ⊗ 8am-6pm Jun-Aug, hours vary rest of the year) The go-to place for rafting, canoeing, tubing, kayaking and multiday cycling trips, plus cycle rental and a 1200ft zipline.

🛏 Sleeping & Eating

HI-Harpers Ferry Hostel HOSTEL $
(☑ 301-834-7652; www.hiusa.org; 19123 Sandy Hook Rd, Knoxville, MD; dm $25; ⊗ May–mid-Nov; P ✳ @ 🤶) Located 2 miles from downtown on the Maryland side of the Potomac River, this friendly hostel has plenty of amenities, including a kitchen, laundry and lounge area with games and books.

Jackson Rose B&B $$
(☑ 304-535-1528; www.thejacksonrose.com; 1167 W Washington St; r weekday/weekend $140/160, closed Jan & Feb; P ✳ 🤶) This marvelous 18th-century brick residence with stately gardens has three attractive guestrooms, including a room where Stonewall Jackson lodged briefly during the Civil War. Antique furnishings and vintage curios are sprinkled about the house, and the cooked breakfast is excellent.

Beans in the Belfry AMERICAN $
(☑ 301-834-7178; www.beansinthebelfry.com; 122 W Potomac St, Brunswick, MD; sandwiches around $7; ⊗ 9am-9pm Mon-Thu, 9am-10pm Fri, 8am-10pm Sat, 8am-7pm Sun; 🤶 ✦) Across the river in Brunswick, MD (roughly 10 miles east), you'll find this converted red-brick church sheltering mismatched couches and kitsch-laden walls, featuring light fare and a tiny stage where live folk, blues and bluegrass bands strike up several nights a week. Sunday jazz brunch ($18) is a hit.

Anvil AMERICAN $$
(☑ 304-535-2582; www.anvilrestaurant.com; 1290 W Washington St; mains $11-28; ⊗ 11am-9pm Wed-Sun) Local trout melting in honey-pecan butter and an elegant Federal dining room equals excellence at Anvil.

ⓘ Getting There & Away

Amtrak (www.amtrak.com) trains run from the **Harpers Ferry Station** (www.amtrak.com; Potomac & Shenandoah Sts) to Washington's Union Station (daily, 90 minutes) on the Capitol Limited route. MARC trains (http://mta.maryland.gov) run three times daily during the week (Monday to Friday) on the Brunswick Line.

Berkeley Springs

🏃 Activities

Berkeley Springs State Park SPA
(☑ 304-258-2711; www.berkeleyspringssp.com; 2 S Washington St; 30 min bath $27, 1hr massage $99-111; ⊗ 10am-6pm) Don't let the locker-room appearance deter you from the Berkeley Springs State Park's Roman Baths – it's the cheapest spa deal in town. Fill your water bottle with some of the magic stuff at the fountain outside the door. In the summer, kids will enjoy the spring-fed (but chlorinated) outdoor swimming pool (adult/child under 12 years $5/3) .

🛏 Sleeping & Eating

Cacapon Resort State Park CABIN $$
(☑ 304-258-1022; www.cacaponresort.com/; 818 Cacapon Lodge Dr; r from $154) Cacapon State Park has simple lodge accommodations plus modern and rustic cabins (some with fireplaces) in a peaceful wooded setting, 9 miles south of Berkeley Springs (off US 522).

Country Inn of Berkeley Springs HOTEL $$
(☑ 304-258-1200; www.thecountryinnwv.com; 110 S Washington St; r/ste from $119/199; P ✳ 🤶) The Country Inn, right next to the park, offers luxurious treatment plus lodging package deals. There's a good restaurant on hand.

Tari's FUSION $$
(☑ 304-258-1196; www.tariscafe.com; 33 N Washington St; lunch mains $9-14, dinner mains $20-29; ⊗ 11am-9pm Mon-Sat, to 7pm Sun; ✐) 🍴 Tari's is a very Berkeley Springs sort of spot, with fresh local food and good vegetarian options served in a laid-back atmosphere with all the right hints of good karma abounding.

ⓘ Getting There & Away

Berkeley Springs is 40 miles west of I-95. It's about 90 minutes from Washington, DC.

Monongahela National Forest

Almost the entire eastern half of West Virginia is marked green parkland on the map, and all that goodness falls under the auspices of this stunning national forest. Within its 1400 sq miles are wild rivers, caves and the highest peak in the state, **Spruce Knob**. More than 850 miles of trails include the 124-mile **Allegheny Trail**, for hiking and backpacking, and the 75-mile rails-to-trails **Greenbrier River Trail**.

Elkins, at the forest's western boundary, is a good base of operations. Sitting atop Cheat Mountain, **Snowshoe Mountain Resort** (☑877-441-4386; www.snowshoemtn.com; 10 Snowshoe Dr; 🖲) to the south is another good launchpad.

The surreal landscapes at **Seneca Rocks**, 35 miles southeast of Elkins, attract rock climbers up the 900ft-tall sandstone strata.

◉ Sights

Cranberry Mountain Nature Center MUSEUM
(☑304-653-4826; www.fs.usda.gov; cnr Hwys 150 & 39/55; ◔9am-4:30pm Thu-Mon mid-Apr–mid-Oct) The scat exhibit hanging on the wall is quite eye-catching, as are the live snakes scattered across several terrariums at this nature center in the southern end of the forest. Celebrating its 50th birthday in 2017, the Cranberry Mountain Nature Center has scientific information about the forest and the surrounding 750-acre bog ecosystem.

Blackwater Falls State Park STATE PARK
(☑304-259-5216; www.blackwaterfalls.com; 1584 Blackwater Lodge Rd) FREE The falls tumble into an 8-mile gorge lined by red spruce, hickory and hemlock trees. There's loads of hiking options; look for the Pendleton Point Overlook, which perches over the deepest, widest point of the Canaan Valley.

🛏 Sleeping & Eating

In the national forest there are 23 campgrounds across six different districts, so pick your region and go from there. There's also dispersed camping in two districts and cabins in the Greenbrier District. For more creature comforts, there are a half dozen or so hotels in Elkins. Snowshoe has a range of options, from simple condos to plush cabins..

Seneca Shadows Campground CAMPGROUND $
(☑877-444-6777; www.recreation.gov; campsites $17-50; ◔Apr-Oct) Flanked by mountains and offering a view of rock-climbing spot Seneca Rocks, this leafy campground has picnic tables, fire pits and flush toilets.

Vintage MODERN AMERICAN $$
(☑304-636-0808; www.vintageelkins.com; 25 Randolph Ave, Elkins; mains $15-33; ◔11am-10pm Mon-Thu, to 11pm Fri & Sat, to 9pm Sun) A great place for wood-fired pizzas and wines after a day of hiking.

❶ Getting There & Away

To explore this remote and rugged region, you will need a car. Elkins is 155 miles from Pittsburgh. Snowshoe is 230 miles from Washington, DC.

Southern West Virginia

This part of the state has carved out a viable stake as the adventure-sports capital of the eastern seaboard, with wild white-water rafting, terrific mountain biking, lots of leafy trails and inviting small towns holding it all together. The swanky Greenbrier resort brings big spenders and golfers.

New River Gorge National River

The New River is actually one of the oldest in the world, and the primeval forest gorge it runs through is one of the most breathtaking in the Appalachians. The NPS protects a stretch of the New River that falls 750ft over 50 miles, with a compact set of rapids up to Class V concentrated at the northernmost end. **Canyon Rim visitor center** (☑304-574-2115; www.nps.gov/neri; 162 Visitor Center Rd, Lansing, WV, GPS 38.07003 N, 81.07583 W; ◔9am-5pm; 🖲) 🌿, just north of the impressive gorge bridge, is only one of four NPS visitor centers along the river. It has information about scenic drives (including a memorable outing to the abandoned mining town of **Nuttallburg**), river outfitters, gorge climbing, hiking and mountain biking, as well as white-water rafting to the north on the **Gauley River**. Rafting the Gauley River during its fall dam release is one of the most exciting white-water adventures in the USA. Rim and gorge trails offer beautiful views. Take the short trail behind the visitor center for a quick but awesome view of the bridge. There are several free basic camping areas.

⊙ Sights & Activities

Hawks Nest State Park
STATE PARK

(☎304-658-5212; www.hawksnestsp.com; 49 Hawks Nest Park Rd; lodge r/ste from $124/151) FREE There are hiking trails, a nature center and an aerial tram (open May to October; adult/child $7/5), which runs from the lodge down to the river's edge. The comfy rooms offers fabulous views over the gorge.

Babcock State Park
STATE PARK

(☎304-438-3004; www.babcocksp.com; 486 Babcock Rd; cabins $66-223, campsites $25-28) Babcock State Park has hiking, canoeing, horseback riding, and camping and cabin accommodations. The park's highlight is its photogenic **Glade Creek Grist Mill**.

Mystery Hole
MUSEUM

(☎304-658-9101; www.mysteryhole.com; 16724 Midland Trail, Ansted; adult/child $7/6; ⊙10:30am-5:30pm Jun-Oct) See gravity and the known limits of tackiness defied at the Mystery Hole, one of the great attractions of roadside America. Everything inside this madhouse *tilts at an angle!*

Adventures on the Gorge
ADVENTURE

(☎855-379-8738; www.adventuresonthegorge.com; 219 Chestnutburg Rd, Lansing; cabins from $89) The reputable Adventures on the Gorge offers a wide range of activities, including white-water rafting, ziplining, rappelling and more. It has a wide array of cabins (including some with Jacuzzis) and several popular restaurants, including **Smokey's Steakhouse** (mains $18 to $36) near the rim of the gorge.

Bridgewalk
WALKING

(☎304-574-1300; www.bridgewalk.com; per person $69; ⊙10am-3pm) You can get a wild view of the New River Gorge from the catwalk below the famous bridge on a guided tour offered by this outfit.

ⓘ Getting There & Away

There is an airport in Charleston, WV, 70 miles north. Amtrak (www.amtrak.com) stop at three places in the park, including the Prince Depot 23 miles south of Fayetteville. Greyhound (www.greyhound.com) stops in Beckley (360 Prince St).

Fayetteville

Pint-sized Fayetteville acts as jumping-off point for New River thrill-seekers and is an artsy mountain enclave besides.

⊙ Sights & Activities

Beckley Exhibition Coal Mine
MINE

(☎304-256-1747; www.beckley.org/general-information-coal-mine; 513 Ewart Ave, Beckley; adult/child $20/12; ⊙10am-6pm Apr-Oct) This mine in Beckley is a museum about the region's coal heritage. Visitors can ride a train 1500ft into a former coal mine, check out exhibits about mining life and explore the camp town village.

Cantrell Ultimate Rafting
RAFTING

(☎304-877-8235; www.cantrellultimaterafting.com; 49 Cantrell Dr; Lower/Upper Gauley rafting from $130/144) Among the many state-licensed rafting outfitters in the area, Cantrell Ultimate Rafting stands out for its white-water rafting trips.

Long Point Trail
HIKING

(www.nps.gov/neri/planyourvisit/longpoint_trail.htm; Newtown Rd, Fayetteville) Just over 3 miles round-trip, this trail leads to views of the New River Gorge and the New River Gorge Bridge.

New River Bikes
CYCLING

(☎304-574-2453; www.newriverbikes.com; 221 N Court St; bike hire per day $35, tours $79-110; ⊙10am-6pm Mon-Fri, to 4pm Sat) Mountain biking is superb in the area, on the graded loops of the Arrowhead Trails.

🛏 Sleeping & Eating

River Rock Retreat Hostel
HOSTEL $

(☎304-574-0394; www.riverrockretreatandhostel.com; Lansing-Edmond Rd; dm $23; P❋) Located less than 1 mile north of the New River Gorge Bridge, this is a well-run hostel with basic, clean rooms and plenty of common space. Owner Joy Marr is a wealth of local information.

Cathedral Café
CAFE $

(☎304-574-0202; www.facebook.com/cathedralcafe; 134 S Court St; lunch mains $8-9, dinner mains $11-14; ⊙7:30am-4pm Sun-Thu, to 9pm Fri & Sat; 🖥🍴) Start the day with breakfast and coffee under stained-glass windows at this cafe.

ⓘ Getting There & Away

Amtrak (www.amtrak.com) stops on Wednesday, Friday and Saturday at the **Prince Depot** (www.amtrak.com; 5034 Stanaford Rd), 23 miles south of Fayetteville on the Cardinal route linking NYC, Washington, DC and Chicago. It's a fairly remote stop and there are no rental car companies on site. You will need to arrange for pick-up by a friend or a taxi.

WASHINGTON, DC & THE CAPITAL REGION SOUTHERN WEST VIRGINIA

1. Young fox, Acadia National Park (p245) 2. Mammoth Cave National Park (p390) 3. Shenandoah National Park (p317) 4. Black bear, Great Smoky Mountains National Park (p350)

DENISE LEBLANC/SHUTTERSTOCK ©

National Parks

Roam from New England's rocky, wild and weather-beaten shores to Florida's sugar-sand beaches shaded by palm trees. Or immerse yourself in the USA's wealth of historic sites starting in the nation's capital, Washington, DC then roll through the pastoral hills of old-timey Appalachia on the scenic Blue Ridge Parkway.

Great Smoky Mountains National Park

Receiving more visitors than any other US national park, this southern Appalachian woodland pocket protects thickly forested ridges where black bears, white-tailed deer, antlered elk, wild turkeys and more than 1500 kinds of flowering plants find sanctuary. (p350)

Acadia National Park

Catch the first sunrise of the new year atop Cadillac Mountain, the highest point on the USA's eastern seaboard. Or come in summer to play on end-of-the-world islands tossed along this craggy, wind-whipped North Atlantic coastline. (p245)

Shenandoah National Park

Drive from the Great Smoky Mountains north along the historic Blue Ridge Pkwy past Appalachian hillside hamlets to Shenandoah, a pastoral preserve where waterfall and woodland paths await, just 75 miles from the nation's capital. (p317)

Everglades National Park

Home to snaggle-toothed crocodiles, stealthy panthers, pink flamingos and mellow manatees, South Florida's Caribbean bays and 'rivers of grass' attract wildlife watchers, especially to unique flood-plain stands of trees called hammocks. (p477)

Mammoth Cave National Park

With hidden underground rivers and more than 400 miles of explored terrain, the world's longest cave system shows off sci-fi-looking stalactites and stalagmites up close. (p390)

The South

Best Places to Eat

➡ Peche Seafood Grill (p441)
➡ Hattie B's (p377)
➡ Dish Dive (p398)
➡ Edmund's Oast (p356)
➡ Saw's Soul Kitchen (p412)

Best Places to Sleep

➡ Bunn House (p348)
➡ Urban Oasis B&B (p396)
➡ Crash Pad (p380)
➡ 21c Museum Hotel (p387)
➡ Shaker Village at Pleasant Hill (p388)

Why Go?

The South was arguably the first region of the USA to be considered that – a 'region' of cultural and geographic distinction, defined by its own cuisine, landscape, accent, literature, music and, under-girding all of the above, history – one that is long and beautiful in places, brutal and bloody in others.

The South falls from the granite, forested fists of Kentucky and Tennessee, into craggy hill country and thick woods, before the waters of its rivers – including North America's greatest, the Mississippi – saturate the land into boggy, black-water blankets and sun-seared marsh, all thinning into the salty membrane of the Atlantic Ocean and Gulf of Mexico. Yet while its residents consider themselves tied to this land and water, they are also the inhabitants of cities deeply in tune with the American experience, from the sweat-drenched noir of Charleston and New Orleans to the accept-all-comers diversity of Atlanta.

When to Go
New Orleans

Nov–Feb Winter is generally mild in the South, and Christmas is a capital-E Event.

Apr–Jun Springs are lush and warm, abloom with fragrant jasmine, gardenia and tuberose.

Jul–Sep Summer is steamy, often unpleasantly so, and locals hit the beaches.

NORTH CAROLINA

The conservative Old South and the liberal New South are jostling for political dominance in the fast-growing Tar Heel State, home to hipsters, hog farmers, high-tech wunderkinds and an explosive number of craft brewers. Mostly the various cultures and communities here coexist, from the ancient mountains in the west to the sandy barrier islands of the Atlantic.

Agriculture is an economic force, with 52,218 farms across the state. North Carolina leads the nation in tobacco production and is the second-largest pig producer. But new technologies also drive the economy and more than 200 companies operate in Research Triangle Park alone. Other important industries include finance, nanotechnology and Christmas trees. Craft brewers have contributed over $2 billion to the economy.

So grab a platter of barbecue, pour a local brew and watch the Duke Blue Devils battle the Carolina Tar Heels on the basketball court. College hoops rival Jesus for Carolinians' souls.

History

Native Americans have inhabited North Carolina for more than 10,000 years. Major tribes included the Cherokee, in the mountains, the Catawba in the Piedmont and the Waccamaw in the Coastal Plain.

North Carolina was the second territory to be colonized by the British, named in memory of King Charles I (Carolus in Latin), but the first colony to vote for independence from the Crown. Several important Revolutionary War battles were fought here.

The state was a sleepy agricultural backwater through the 19th century, earning it the nickname the 'Rip Van Winkle State.' Divided on slavery (most residents were too poor to own slaves), North Carolina was the last state to secede during the Civil War, but went on to provide more Confederate soldiers than any other state.

North Carolina was a civil-rights hotbed in the mid-20th century, with highly publicized lunch-counter sit-ins in Greensboro and the formation of the influential Student Nonviolent Coordinating Committee (SNCC) in Raleigh. The latter part of the century brought finance to Charlotte, and technology and medicine to the Raleigh-Durham area, driving a huge population boom and widening cultural diversity.

In more recent times, North Carolina found itself in the discrimination and social issue hot seat again when it passed the notorious 'bathroom bill' in 2016, which blocked cities from allowing transgender individuals to use public bathrooms for the sex they identify as. The move cost the state up to an estimated $630 million (and counting) in lost revenue after it was passed (the NBA moved its annual All-Star Game to New Orleans, and the NCAA yanked all 2016 and 2017 tournaments from the state) – a mere drop in the bucket of the state's annual $510 billion GDP, but no chump change either. Governor Roy Cooper promptly signed the repeal of the law in spring of 2017, barely a year after its initial passing.

North Carolina Coast

The coastline of North Carolina stretches just over 300 miles. Remarkably, it remains underdeveloped and the beach is often visible from coastal roads. Yes, the wall of cottages stretching south from Corolla to Kitty Hawk can seem endless, but for the most part the state's shores remain free of flashy, highly commercialized resort areas. Instead you'll find rugged, windswept barrier islands, Colonial villages once frequented by pirates and laid-back beach towns full of locally owned ice-cream shops and mom-and-pop motels. Even the most touristy beaches have a small-town vibe.

For solitude, head to the isolated Outer Banks, where fishers still make their living hauling in shrimp and the older locals speak in an archaic British-tinged brogue. Further south, Wilmington is known as a center of film and TV production, and its surrounding beaches are popular with local spring breakers and tourists.

❶ Getting There & Away

The closest commercial airports to the Outer Banks are Norfolk International Airport (p298), 82 miles north of the Outer Banks in Virginia, and North Carolina's Raleigh-Durham International Airport (p343), 192 miles west. Ferries link more isolated Ocracoke Island in the Outer Banks with Hatteras Island and Cedar Island as well as Swan Quarter on the mainland.

Wilmington has its own **Wilmington International Airport** (ILM; ☑ 910-341-4125; www.flyilm.com; 1740 Airport Blvd).

KANSAS

MISSOURI

OKLAHOMA

ARKANSAS

TENNESSEE

TEXAS

LOUISIANA

MISSISSIPPI

ALABAMA

ILLINOIS

INDIANA

Central Time Zone

Eastern Time Zone

Jefferson City
St Louis
Louisville
Fort Knox
Frankf
Harrodsb

Owensboro
Elizabethtown
Hodgen
Mammoth
National Pa

Paducah
W Kentucky Pkwy

Eureka Springs
Bull Shoals-White River State Park
Hopkinsville
Murray
Bowling Green
Hickman

Ponca
Yellville
Mountain View
Dyersburg
Clarksville
Cookeville

Ozark Mountains
Alma
Ozark
Clarksville
Jonesboro
Nashville
Franklin

Van Buren
Atkins
Conway
Jackson
Shiloh National Military Park
Shelbyville
Cleveland

Ouachita National Forest
De Valls Bluff
Memphis
Natchez Trace Pkwy
Chattanooga

Petit Jean State Park
Little Rock
Tunica
Holly Springs
Muscle Shoals
Decatur
Huntsville

Hot Springs National Park
Helena
Clarksdale
Tupelo
US Space & Rocket Center
Gadsden

Hot Springs
Pine Bluff
Shelby
Tutwiler
Natchez Trace Pkwy
Birmingham
Anniston

Hope
Cleveland
Greenwood
Oak Mountain State Park

Texarkana
Greenville
Leland
Indianola
Belzoni
Tuscaloosa

Ruston
Epps
Vicksburg
Canton
Philadelphia
Opelika

Shreveport
Monroe
Jackson
Selma
Montgomery
Tuskegee
Lumpki

Natchitoches
Kisatchie National Forest
Port Gibson

Cloutierville
Alexandria
Natchez
Dothan

Oberlin
St Francisville
Baton Rouge
Slidell
Long Beach
Ocean Springs
Mobile
Point Clear

Opelousas
Lafayette
New Iberia
Lake Pontchartrain
Biloxi
Gulf Shores

Lake Charles
Avery Island
Lake Fausse Pointe State Park
Houma
New Orleans
Jean Lafitte National Historic Park & Preserve
Dauphin Island

Gulf of Mexico

The South Highlights

1 New Orleans (p430)
Losing yourself in the magic of America's strangest, most celebratory city.

2 Great Smoky Mountains National Park (p350) Hiking

and camping amid the South's most magnificent scenery.

3 Nashville (p371)
Stomping your boots in honky-tonks along Lower Broadway.

4 Outer Banks (p334)

Driving windswept Hwy 12 the length of North Carolina.

5 Charleston (p353)
Touring the grand antebellum homes and dining on Low-country fare.

Outer Banks

The Outer Banks (OBX for short) are fragile ribbons of sand tracing the coastline for
100 miles, separated from the mainland by
sounds and waterways. From north to south,
barrier islands Bodie (pronounced 'Body'),
Roanoke, Hatteras and Ocracoke, essen-
tially large sandbars, are linked by bridges
and ferries. The far-northern communities
Corolla (pronounced kur-all-ah, not like
the car), **Duck** and **Southern Shores** are
former duck-hunting grounds for the northeastern wealthy, and are quiet and upscale.
Nearly contiguous Bodie Island towns **Kitty
Hawk**, **Kill Devil Hills** and **Nags Head** are
heavily developed and more populist, with
fried-fish joints, drive-through beer shops,
motels and dozens of sandals 'n' sunblock
shops. **Roanoke Island**, west of Bodie, offers
colonial history and quaint waterfront town
Manteo. Further south, **Hatteras Island**
is a protected national seashore with tiny
villages and a wild, windswept beauty. At
OBX's southern end, old salts shuck oysters
and weave hammocks on **Ocracoke Island**,
accessible only by ferry.

◉ Sights

Corolla, the northernmost town on Hwy 158,
is famed for its wild horses. Descendants
of Colonial Spanish mustangs, the horses
roam the northern dunes, and numerous
commercial outfitters go in search of them.
The ribboning Cape Hatteras National Seashore, broken up by villages, is home to

several noteworthy lighthouses. A meandering drive down Hwy 12, which connects
much of the Outer Banks and makes up part
of the Outer Banks National Scenic Byway
(and its 21 coastal villages), is one of the truly great American road trips, whether you
come during the stunningly desolate winter
months or in the sunny summer.

If you're driving on some beaches in
the Outer Banks, or within Cape Hatteras
National Seashore, you'll need an off-road-
vehicle (ORVs) permit ($25 to $50). See www.
outerbanks.org/plan-your-trip/beaches/
driving-on-beach for more info.

Whalehead Club   HISTORIC BUILDING
(☑ 252-453-9040; www.visitcurrituck.com; 1160
Village Lane, Corolla; adult/child 6-12yr $7/5;
☺ tours 10am-4pm Mon-Sat, may vary seasonally) The sunflower-yellow, art-nouveau-style
Whalehead Club, built in the 1920s as a
hunting 'cottage' for a Philadelphia indus-
trialist, is the centerpiece of the Currituck
Heritage Park in the village of Corolla.

Currituck Beach Lighthouse   LIGHTHOUSE
(www.currituckbeachlight.com; 1101 Corolla Village
Rd, Corolla; adult/child under 8yr $10/free; ☺ 9am-
5pm late Mar–Nov) You'll climb 220 steps to
get to the top of this red-brick lighthouse,
which is still in operation.

**Wright Brothers National
Memorial**   PARK, MUSEUM
(☑ 252-473-2111; www.nps.gov/wrbr; 1000 North
Croatan Hwy, Kitty Hawk; adult/child under 16yr
$7/free; ☺ 9am-5pm) Self-taught engineers

THE SOUTH IN...

One Week

Fly into New Orleans (p430) and stretch your legs with a walking tour in the legendary
French Quarter, before devoting your remaining time to celebrating jazz history and
partying the night away in a zydeco joint. Then wind your way upward through the lan-
guid Delta, stopping in Clarksdale for a sultry evening of blues at the juke joints before
alighting in Memphis (p363) to walk in the footsteps of the King at Graceland (p366).
From here, head on down the Music Hwy to Nashville (p371) to see Elvis' gold Cadillac at
the Country Music Hall of Fame and Museum (p374) and practice your line dancing at
the honky-tonks (country-music clubs) of the District.

Two to Three Weeks

From Nashville, head east to hike amid the craggy peaks and waterfalls of Great Smoky
Mountains National Park (p350) before a revitalizing overnight in the arty mountain town
of Asheville (p347) and a tour of the scandalously opulent Biltmore Estate (p348), America's largest private home. Plow straight through to the Atlantic coast to loll on the sandy
barrier islands of the isolated Outer Banks (p334), then head down the coast to finish up in
Charleston (p353), with decadent food and postcard-pretty architecture.

Wilbur and Orville Wright launched the world's first successful airplane flight on December 17, 1903 (it lasted 12 seconds). A boulder marks the take-off spot. Climb a nearby hill, where the brothers conducted earlier glider experiments, for fantastic views of sea and sound. The on-site **Wright Brothers Visitor Center**, when it reopens after a complete renovation by summer 2018, has a reproduction of the 1903 flyer and exhibits.

Fort Raleigh National Historic Site
HISTORIC SITE

(www.nps.gov/fora; 1401 National Park Dr, Manteo; ☉grounds dawn-dusk) In the late 1580s, three decades before the Pilgrims landed at Plymouth Rock, a group of 116 British colonists disappeared without a trace from their Roanoke Island settlement. Were they killed off by drought? Did they run away with a Native American tribe? The fate of the 'Lost Colony' remains one of America's greatest mysteries. Explore their story in the visitor center.

One of the site's star attractions is the beloved musical, **Lost Colony Outdoor Drama** (☑252-473-6000; www.thelostcolony.org; 1409 National Park Dr, Manteo; adult/child from $20/10; ☉7:45pm Mon-Sat late May–mid-Aug), staged between late May and August. The play, from Pulitzer Prize–winning North Carolina playwright Paul Green, dramatizes the fate of the colonists and will celebrate its 80th anniversary in 2017. It plays at the Waterside Theater throughout summer. Other attractions include exhibits, artifacts, maps and a free 17-minute film to fuel the imagination, hosted at the visitor center. The 16th-century-style **Elizabethan Gardens** (☑252-473-3234; www.elizabethangardens.org; 1411 National Park Dr, Manteo; adult/child 6-17yr $9/6; ☉9am-7pm Jun-Aug, shorter hours Sep-May) include a Shakespearean herb garden and rows of beautifully manicured flower beds. A commanding statue of Queen Elizabeth I stands guard at the entrance.

Cape Hatteras National Seashore
ISLAND

(☑252-475-9000; www.nps.gov/caha) Extending some 70 miles from south of Nags Head to the south end of Ocracoke Island, this fragile necklace of islands remains blissfully free from overdevelopment. Natural attractions include local and migratory waterbirds, marshes, woodlands, dunes and miles of empty beaches.

Bodie Island Lighthouse
LIGHTHOUSE

(☑255-473-2111; www.nps.gov/caha; 8210 Bodie Island Lighthouse Rd, Nags Head; museum free, tours adult/child under 11yr $8/4; ☉visitor center 9am-5pm, lighthouse to 4:30pm late Apr-early Oct; 🖼) Built in 1872, this photogenic lighthouse opened its doors to visitors in 2013. The 164ft-high structure still has its original Fresnel lens – a rarity. It's just over 200 steps to the top. The lighthouse keeper's former home is now the visitor center.

Pea Island National Wildlife Refuge
WILDLIFE RESERVE

(☑252-987-2394; www.fws.gov/refuge/pea_island; Hwy 12, Rodanthe; ☉visitor center 9am-4pm, trails dawn-dusk) At the northern end of Hatteras Island, this 5834-acre (land portion only) preserve is a bird-watcher's heaven, with two nature trails (both are fully accessible to people with disabilities) and 13 miles of unspoiled beach for the 365 recorded species here. Viewer scopes inside the visitor center overlook an adjacent pond.

Cape Hatteras Lighthouse
LIGHTHOUSE

(☑252-475-9000; www.nps.gov/caha; 46368 Lighthouse Rd, Buxton; climbing tours adult/child under 12yr $8/4; ☉visitor center 9am-5pm; lighthouse to 4:30pm mid-Apr–early Oct) At 208ft, this striking black-and-white-striped edifice is the tallest brick lighthouse in the USA and is one of North Carolina's most iconic images. Climb the 257 steps then check out the interesting exhibits about local history in the **Museum of the Sea**, located in the lighthouse keeper's former home.

Graveyard of the Atlantic Museum
MUSEUM

(☑252-986-2995; www.graveyardoftheatlantic.com; 59200 Museum Dr, Hattaras; ☉10am-4pm) **FREE** Exhibits about shipwrecks, piracy and salvaged cargo are highlights at this maritime museum at the end of the road. There have been more than 2000 shipwrecks off the coast of the Outer Banks. According to one exhibit, in 2006 a container washed ashore near Frisco, releasing thousands of Doritos bags.

🏃 Activities

Kitty Hawk Kites
ADVENTURE SPORTS

(☑252-441-6800; www.kittyhawk.com; 3933 S Croatan Hwy, Jockey's Ridge Crossing, Nags Head; bike rental per day $15, kayaks $39-59, stand-up paddleboards $59-69) In business more than 30 years, Kitty Hawk Kites has several locations along the OBX coast. It offers beginners' kiteboarding lessons (five hours, $400) in Rodanthe and hang-gliding lessons at Jockey's Ridge State Park (from $109). Also rents out kayaks, sailboats, stand-up paddleboards, bikes and in-line skates.

Corolla Outback Adventures TOURS
(✆252-453-4484; www.corollaoutback.com; 1150 Ocean Trail, Corolla; 2hr tour adult/child under 13yr $50/25) Tour operator Jay Bender, whose family started Corolla's first guide service, knows his local history and his local horses. Tours bounce you down the beach and through the dunes to see the wild mustangs that roam the northern Outer Banks.

🛏 Sleeping

Breakwater Inn MOTEL $
(✆252-986-2565; www.breakwaterhatteras.com; 57896 Hwy 12, Hatteras; r/ste from $179/213, motel r from $117; P❄🐾☕🐕🐶) The end of the road doesn't look so bad at this three-story shingled inn. Rooms come with kitchenette and a private deck with views of the sound. On a budget? Try one of the older 'Fisherman's Quarters' rooms, with microwave and fridge

Shutters on the Banks HOTEL $$
(✆252-441-5581; www.shuttersonthebanks.com; 405 S Virginia Dare Trail; r $69-269; P❄☕🐕) Centrally located in Kill Devil Hills, this welcoming 86-room beachfront hotel exudes a snappy, colorful style. The inviting rooms come with plantation windows and colorful art as well as flat-screen TV, refrigerator and microwave.

Sanderling Resort & Spa RESORT $$$
(✆252-261-4111; www.sanderling-resort.com; 1461 Duck Rd, Duck; r $160-599, ste $599-750; P❄☕🐕) Newly remodeled rooms have given this posh place a stylish kick in the pants. Or should we say the Lululemons? Because yes, the resort does offer sunrise yoga on the beach. Decor is impeccably tasteful, and the attached balconies are an inviting place to enjoy the ocean sounds and breezes.

🍴 Eating & Drinking

John's Drive-In SEAFOOD, ICE CREAM $
(www.johnsdrivein.com; 3716 N Virginia Dare Trail, Kitty Hawk; mains $2.25-9.50; ⊙11am-5pm Thu-Tue) A Kitty Hawk institution for perfectly fried baskets of mahi mahi, to be eaten at outdoor picnic tables and washed down with one of hundreds of possible milkshake combinations.

★ **Kill Devil Grill** SEAFOOD, AMERICAN $$
(✆252-449-8181; www.thekilldevilgrill.com; 2008 S Virginia Dare Trail, Kill Devil Hills; lunch $7-13, dinner $10-22; ⊙11:30am-9pm Tue-Thu, to 10pm Fri & Sat) Yowza, this place is good. It's also historic – the entrance is a 1939 diner that's listed in the National Register of Historic Places. Pub grub and seafood arrive with tasty flair, and portions are generous. Check out the specials, where the kitchen can really shine.

★ **Blue Moon Beach Grill** SEAFOOD, SANDWICHES $$
(✆252-261-2583; www.bluemoonbeachgrill.com; 4104 S Virginia Dare Trail, Nags Head; mains $10-29; ⊙11:30am-9pm) Would it be wrong to write an ode to a side of french fries? Because Lord almighty, the lightly spiced fries at this casual hot spot are the stuff of sonnets and monologues. And we haven't even mentioned the BLT with seared mahi mahi, applewood bacon, local Currituck tomatoes and a jalapeño rémoulade for slathering.

ℹ Information

The best sources of information are at the main visitor centers. Many smaller centers open seasonally. Also useful is www.outerbanks.org.

Aycock Brown Welcome Center (✆877-629-4386; www.outerbanks.org; 5230 N Croatian Hwy, Kitty Hawk; ⊙9am-5pm) On the bypass in Kitty Hawk; has maps and information.

Fort Raleigh National Historic Site Visitor Center (✆252-475-9001; www.nps.gov/fora; 1401 National Park Dr; ⊙9am-4pm Mon-Sat, noon-4pm Sun)

Hatteras Island Visitor Center (✆252-475-9000; www.nps.gov/caha; 46368 Lighthouse Rd, Buxton; ⊙9am-5pm) Beside Cape Hatteras Lighthouse.

Ocracoke Island Visitor Center (✆252-475-9701; www.nps.gov/caha; 38 Irvin Garrish Hwy; ⊙9am-5pm) Near the southern ferry dock.

Sarah Owen Welcome Center (✆877-629-4386; www.outerbanks.org; 1 Visitors Center Cir, Manteo; ⊙9am-5pm) Just east of Virginia Dare Memorial Bridge on the US 64 Bypass on Roanoke Island.

Whalebone Welcome Center (✆877-629-4386; www.outerbanks.org; 2 NC Hwy 12, Nags Head; ⊙8:30am-5pm Mar-Dec) At the intersection of Hwy 64 and Hwy 12 in Nags Head.

ℹ Getting There & Away

No public transportation exists to or on the Outer Banks.

If driving, try to avoid arriving or departing on weekends in summer, when traffic can be maddening. The Outer Banks Visitors Bureau offers a comprehensive guide to driving to OBX, including tips and alternate routes to avoid spending your vacation stuck in your vehicle, on its website (www.outerbanks.org).

The North Carolina Ferry System (www.ncdot. gov/ferry) operates several routes, including the free one-hour Hatteras–Ocracoke car ferry, which fluctuates between hourly and half-hourly with 36 departures from 5am to midnight from Hatteras in high season; reservations aren't accepted. North Carolina ferries also run between Ocracoke and Cedar Island (one way car/ motorcycle $15/10, 2¼ hours) and Ocracoke and Swan Quarter on the mainland ($15/10, 2¾ hours) every three hours or so; reservations are recommended in summer for these two routes.

Ocracoke Island

Ocracoke Village is a funky little community that moves at a slower pace. With the exception of the village, the National Park Service owns the island.

The older residents still speak in the 17th-century British dialect known as 'Hoi Toide' (their pronunciation of 'high tide') and refer to non-islanders as 'dingbatters' (though this will soon die off). Edward Teach, aka Blackbeard the pirate, used to hide out in the area and was killed here in 1718. You can camp by Pony Pen beach where wild ponies run and swim at their leisure, have a fish sandwich in a local pub, bike around the village's narrow streets or catch some rays nestled into holes in the sand dunes along 16 miles of coastline.

Many people come to Ocracoke on a day trip from Hatteras, but with its preserved culture and laid-back vibe, it's a nice place to spend a night or two. There are a handful of B&Bs, several motels, a park-service campground near the beach and rental cottages.

👁 Sights & Activities

Ocracoke Lighthouse   LIGHTHOUSE
(www.nps.gov/caha; Lighthouse Rd) Built in 1823, this is the oldest lighthouse still operating in North Carolina, though it cannot be climbed.

Ocracoke Pony Pen   VIEWPOINT
(www.nps.gov/caha; Hwy 12) From the National Park Service's observation deck, you can catch a glimpse of Ocracoke's 'wild' ponies, which have been penned in here since the late 1950s and cared for by the NPS. The pens are located 6 miles along Hwy 12 from the Ocracoke–Hatteras ferry landing.

Portsmouth Island ATV Tours   HISTORY
(📞 252-928-4484; www.portsmouthislandatv. com; 396 Irvin Garrish Hwy; tour $90; ☺ Apr-Oct) Runs two fascinating two daily tours (8am and 1pm) to the nearby island of Portsmouth, a 20-minute boat ride from Ocracoke, where you'll find an Outer Banks ghost town abandoned in the 1970s. Guided ATV tours focus on shelling, bird-watching and swimming.

Ride the Wind   KAYAKING
(📞 252-928-6311; www.surfocracoke.com; 486 Irvin Garrish Hwy; 2-2½hr tours adult $39-45, child under 13yr $18; ☺ 10am-7pm Mon-Sat, to 6pm Sun) Want to get on the water? Take a kayaking tour with Ride the Wind. The sunset tours are easy on the arms.

🛏 Sleeping & Eating

Ocracoke Campgrounds   CAMPGROUND $
(📞 252-928-6671; www.recreation.gov; 4352 Irvin Garrish Hwy; tent sites $28; ☺ mid-Apr–late Nov)

OCRACOKE'S PENNED PONIES

Legend has it the Ocracoke Island 'wild' ponies are descendants of feral Spanish mustangs abandoned by shipwrecked explorers in the 16th or 17th century, when it was common to unload livestock to lighten the load and get back out to sea after running aground. Known as 'banker' ponies, these horses are unique in the equine world – they harbor a different number of vertebrae and ribs as well as a distinct shape, posture, color, size and weight than those of other horses. But what's more fascinating about Ocracoke's ponies is they were eventually broken and tamed by a troop of Boy Scouts in the 1950s – you can see photos at the Pony Island Restaurant. They were eventually pastured in a 'pony pen' in 1959 to prevent overgrazing and protect them from the dangers of NC Hwy 12, which was under construction. Today there are 17 ponies at the Ocracoke Pony Pen at Pony Pen Beach. They're cared for by the National Park Service and free to roam the beach and take a dip in the ocean. You can view them from an observation deck.

Offers 136 sites on sand on Ocracoke Island. Flush toilets, drinking water, cold showers and grills are available as well.

★ **Eduardo's**

Taco Stand   MEXICAN $

(950 Irvin Garrish Hwy; mains $4-11; ⊙8am-9pm Mon-Sat) There's a long list of tacos, burritos and fresh and spicy salsas at this little taco stand that could. If you're over fried clams and crab cakes, dishes such as prime-rib-eye tacos with salsa *de xoconostle* really hit the spot (as do the fish with creamy chipotle apple slaw or poblano chowder with shrimp or clams).

Howard's Pub   PUB FOOD $

(www.howardspub.com; 1175 Irvin Garrish Hwy; mains $8-26; ⊙11am-10pm early Mar-late Nov, may stay open later Fri & Sat) A big old wooden pub (newly renovated!) that's been an island tradition for beer and fried seafood since the 1850s. Good selection of local craft beer.

⊙ Getting There & Away

The village is at the southern end of 14-mile-long Ocracoke Island and is accessed from Hatteras via the free Hatteras–Ocracoke ferry (www. ncdot.gov/ferry; first-come, first-serve). The ferry lands at the northeastern end of the island. Or via the $15 Cedar Island– Ocracoke or Swan Quarter–Ocracoke ferries (which land at the southern dock; reservations accepted).

Crystal Coast

The southern Outer Banks are collectively called the 'Crystal Coast,' at least for tourist-office promotional purposes. Less rugged than the northern beaches, they include several historic coastal towns, sparsely populated islands and vacation-friendly beaches.

An industrial and commercial stretch of US 70 goes through **Morehead City**, with plenty of chain hotels and restaurants. The **Bogue Banks**, across the Sound from Morehead City via the Atlantic Beach Causeway, have several well-trafficked beach communities – try Atlantic Beach if you like the smell of coconut suntan oil and doughnuts.

Just north, postcard-pretty **Beaufort** (bow-fort), the third-oldest town in the state, has a charming boardwalk and lots of B&Bs. Blackbeard himself is said to have lived in the Hammock House off Front St. You can't go inside, but some claim you can still hear the screams of the pirate's murdered wife at night.

⊙ Sights & Activities

Fort Macon State Park   FORT

(www.ncparks.gov/fort-macon-state-park; 2303 E Fort Macon Rd, Atlantic Beach; ⊙9am-5:30pm) FREE This sturdy, five-sided fort, with 26 vaulted rooms, was completed in 1834. Exhibits in rooms near the entrance spotlight the fort's construction as well as the daily lives of soldiers stationed there. The fort, constructed from brick and stone, changed hands twice during the Civil War.

North Carolina

Maritime Museum   MUSEUM

(http://ncmaritimemuseums.com/beaufort.html; 315 Front St; ⊙9am-5pm Mon-Fri, 10am-5pm Sat, 1-5pm Sun) FREE The pirate Blackbeard was a frequent visitor to the Beaufort area in the early 1700s. In 1996 the wreckage of his flagship, the *Queen Anne's Revenge*, was discovered at the bottom of Beaufort Inlet. You'll see plates, bottles and other artifacts from the ship in this small but engaging museum, which also spotlights the seafood industry as well as maritime rescue operations.

Hungry Town Tours   FOOD & DRINK, HISTORY

(☑252-648-1011; www.hungrytowntours.com; 400 Front St; tours $20-60) Runs recommended history- and culinary-focused walking and Cruiser biking tours.

🛏 Sleeping & Eating

Hampton Inn Morehead City   HOTEL $$

(☑252-240-2300; www.hamptoninn3.hilton. com; 4035 Arendell St, Morehead City; r from $169; ❋@☎☀) Yep, it's part of a national chain, but the helpful staff and the views of Bogue Sound make this Hampton Inn a nice choice, plus it's convenient to US 70 for those driving the coast. Rates drop significantly on weeknights in summer.

★ **Inn on Turner**   B&B $$

(☑919-271-6144; www.innonturner.com; 217 Turner St; r $200-250; ℗❋☎) ✿ Impeccably tasteful aqua-toned coastal contemporary decor – no gaudy antiques here – dominates this four-room B&B occupying an historic 1866 home two blocks back from the water. Innkeepers Kim and Jon are pillars of small-town Southern hospitality, despite not being from the South!

El's Drive-In   SEAFOOD $

(www.elsdrivein.com; 3706 Arendell St, Morehead City; mains $1.60-14.25; ⊙10am-10pm Sun-Thu, to 11pm Fri & Sat) The food is brought to you by car hop at this legendary seafood spot, open since 1959. Our recommendation? The fried shrimp burger with ketchup and slaw plus a side of fries. Cash only.

Beaufort Grocery   MODERN AMERICAN **$$$**
(☑ 252-728-3899; www.beaufortgrocery.com; 117 Queen St; mains $25-42; ☺ 11:30am-2pm & 5:30-9:30pm Wed-Mon; ⚘) You'd never guess by the simple, unassuming nature of the decor, but chef Charles Park is a James Beard winner and the food shines, whether that be smoked sea-salt tuna with chili yogurt, duck two ways with sweet-potato caramel or sage-wrapped chicken saltimbocca over tagliatelle. We didn't hear a bad thing about the place – and weren't disappointed.

Wilmington

Wilmington is pretty darn fun, and it's worth carving out a day or two for a visit if you're driving the coast. This seaside charmer may not have the name recognition of Charleston and Savannah, but eastern North Carolina's largest city has historic neighborhoods, azalea-choked gardens and cute cafes aplenty. All that plus reasonable hotel prices. At night the historic riverfront downtown becomes the playground for local college students, craft-beer enthusiasts, tourists and the occasional Hollywood type – there are so many movie studios here the town has earned the nickname 'Wilmywood.' You saw *Dawson's Creek*, right?

◉ Sights & Activities

Battleship North Carolina   HISTORIC SITE
(www.battleshipnc.com; 1 Battleship Rd; adult/child 6-11yr $14/6; ☺ 8am-5pm Sep-May, to 8pm Jun-Aug) Self-guided tours take you through the decks of this 45,000-ton megaship, which earned 15 battle stars in the Pacific theater in WWII before it was decommissioned in 1947. Sights include the bake shop and galley, the print shop, the engine room, the powder magazine and the communications center. Note that there are several steep stairways leading to lower decks.

Airlie Gardens   GARDENS
(www.airliegardens.org; 300 Airlie Rd; adult/child 4-12yr $9/3; ☺ 9am-5pm, closed Mon Jan-Mar) In spring, wander past thousands of bright azaleas at this 67-acre wonderland, also home to bewitching formal flowerbeds, seasonal gardens, pine trees, lakes and trails. The Airlie Oak dates from 1545.

Cape Fear Serpentarium   ZOO
(☑ 910-762-1669; www.capefearserpentarium.com; 20 Orange St; $9; ☺ 11am-5pm Mon-Fri, to 6pm Sat & Sun) Herpetologist Dean Ripa's museum is a fun and informative place to spend an hour or two – if you don't mind standing in a building slithering with venomous snakes, giant constrictors and big-teethed crocodiles. They're all behind glass but...sssssssss. Just hope there's not an earthquake. One sign explains the effects of a bite from a bushmaster: 'It is better to just lie down under a tree and rest, for you will soon be dead.' Enjoy! Cash only.

The Serpentarium may close on Monday and Tuesday in the off-season. Live feedings are held at 3pm on Saturday and Sunday, but call ahead to confirm.

🛏 Sleeping & Eating

Best Western Plus Coastline Inn   HOTEL **$$**
(☑ 910-763-2800; www.bestwestern.com; 503 Nutt St; r $89-199, ste $129-279; ❄ @ ⚘ ⚘) We're not sure what we like best: the gorgeous views of the Cape Fear River, the wooden boardwalk or the short walk to downtown fun. Standard rooms aren't huge, but they do pop with a bit of modern style. Every room has a river view. Pet fee is $20 per day and there's a new set of bikes for rent.

★ CW Worth House   B&B **$$**
(☑ 910-762-8562; www.worthhouse.com; 412 S 3rd St; r $164-200; ❄ @ ⚘) One of our favorite B&Bs in North Carolina, this turreted 1893 Queen Anne home is dotted with antiques and Victorian touches, but still manages to feel kick-back and cozy. Breakfasts are top-notch. The B&B is within a few blocks of downtown.

Flaming Amy's Burrito Barn   MEXICAN **$**
(www.flamingamys.com; 4002 Oleander Dr; burritos $8; ☺ 11am-10pm) The burritos are big and tasty at Flaming Amy's, a scrappy barn filled with kitschy decor from Elvis to Route 66. Burritos include the Philly Phatboy, the Thai Mee Up and the jalapeño-and-pepper-loaded Flaming Amy. Everyone in town is here or on the way.

★ PinPoint   SOUTHERN US **$$$**
(☑ 910-769-2972; www.pinpointrestaurant.com; 114 Market St; mains $21-38; ☺ 5:30-10:30pm Tue-Fri, 10:30am-2pm Sat & Sun; ⚘) PinPoint was declared by *Southern Living* magazine as one of the South's best new restaurants in 2016 – and they weren't lyin'! Chef Dean

Neff was Hugh Acheson's kitchen compadre in Athens, Georgia's excellent Five & Ten, and he's sailing solo and shining in Wilmington, where he has a personal relationship with his farmers and fishers, a love that carries over to the amazing food.

Drinking & Entertainment

★ **Satellite Lounge**   BAR
(www.facebook.com/satellitebarandlounge; 120 Greenfield St; ☺4pm-2am Mon-Sat, 2pm-2am Sun; 🐾) If you want to belly up to North Carolina's most stunning bar, you'll need to head in the opposite direction of Wilmington's historic downtown and into its up-and-coming warehouse South Front district. A gorgeously restored tavern highlights the space, which includes near-professional-level cornhole lanes, a fire pit and an outdoor cinema.

Dead Crow Comedy Room   COMEDY
(☑910-399-1492; www.deadcrowcomedy.com; 265 N Front St; tickets $15-18; ☺from 7pm Tue-Thu, from 6pm Fri & Sat) Dark, cramped, underground and in the heart of downtown, just like a comedy club should be. Before heading out, stop in for improv, open-mike nights and touring comedians.

ⓘ Information

Visitor information center (☑877-406-2356, 910-341-4030; www.wilmingtonandbeaches.com; 505 Nutt St; ☺8:30am-5pm Mon-Fri, 9am-4pm Sat, 1-4pm Sun) In an 1800s freight warehouse; has a walking-tour map of downtown.

ⓘ Getting There & Around

American Airlines and Delta Airlines serve Wilmington International Airport (p331) from Atlanta, Charlotte, New York and Philadelphia. It's 5 miles northeast of downtown. The **Greyhound** (☑910-791-8040; www.greyhound.com; 505 Cando St) station is an inconvenient 5 miles east of downtown.

Downtown Wilmington is walkable, but a free trolley (www.wavetransit.com) runs through the historic district from morning through evening.

The Triangle

The cities of Raleigh, Durham and Chapel Hill form a rough triangle in the central Piedmont region. Three top research universities – Duke, University of North Carolina and North Carolina State – are located here, as is the 7000-acre computer and biotech office campus known as Research Triangle Park. Swarming with egghead computer programmers, bearded peace activists and hip young families, each town has its own unique personality, despite being only a few miles apart. In March, everyone – we mean *everyone* – goes crazy for college basketball.

ⓘ Getting There & Around

Raleigh-Durham International Airport (p343), a 13-mile ride northwest of downtown Raleigh, receives nonstop flights from 48 destinations, including London, Paris and Cancun.

Greyhound (☑919-834-8275; www.greyhound.com; 2210 Capital Blvd) is located 3 miles northeast of downtown Raleigh, which makes it hard to reach on foot for connections. For a better downtown stop, try Durham's **Greyhound** (www.greyhound.com; 515 W Pettigrew St) station, near the **Amtrak** (www.amtrak.com; 601 W Main St) station in the Durham Station Transportation Center.

The Triangle Transit Authority (www.triangletransit.org) operates buses linking Raleigh, Durham and Chapel Hill and the airport. Bus 100 runs from downtown Raleigh to the airport, and the Regional Transit Center near Research Triangle Park where there are connections to Durham and Chapel Hill. Adult fare is $2.25.

Raleigh

Founded in 1792 specifically to serve as the state capital, Raleigh remains a rather staid government town with major sprawl issues. Still, the handsome downtown has some neat (and free!) museums and galleries, and the food and music scene is on the upswing.

◎ Sights

★ **North Carolina Museum of Art**   MUSEUM
(www.ncartmuseum.org; 2110 Blue Ridge Rd; ☺10am-5pm Tue-Thu Sat & Sun, to 9pm Fri, park dawn-dusk) **FREE** The light-filled glass-and-anodized-steel West Building won praise from architecture critics nationwide when it opened in 2010. The fine and wide-ranging collection, with everything from ancient Greek sculptures to commanding American landscape paintings to elaborate African masks, is worthy as well.

North Carolina Museum of History   MUSEUM
(www.ncmuseumofhistory.org; 5 E Edenton St; ☺9am-5pm Mon-Sat, noon-5pm Sun) **FREE** This engaging museum is low on tech but high on straightforward information. Artifacts in the 'Story of North Carolina' exhibit include a

3000-year-old canoe, the state's oldest house, dating from 1742, a restored slave cabin and a 1960s sit-in lunch counter. The special exhibits typically shine too.

North Carolina Museum of
Natural Sciences   MUSEUM
(www.naturalsciences.org; 11 W Jones St; ⊙9am-5pm Mon- Sat, noon-5pm Sun) **FREE** Whale skeletons hang from the ceiling. Butterflies flutter past your shoulder. Emerald tree boas make you shiver. And swarms of unleashed elementary-school children rampage all over the place if you arrive after 10am on a school day. Be warned. The glossy new **Nature Research Center**, fronted by a three-story multimedia globe, spotlights scientists and their projects. Visitors can watch them at work. Skywalks lead to the main museum building, which also holds habitat dioramas and well-done taxidermy. Don't miss the exhibit about the Acrocanthosaurus dinosaur, a three-ton carnivore known as the Terror of the South.

🛏 Sleeping & Eating

Umstead Hotel & Spa   HOTEL **$$$**
(☑919-447-4000; www.theumstead.com; 100 Woodland Pond Dr; r $329-389, ste $409-599; P※@🅿🐾) In a wooded suburban office park, the Umstead caters to visiting biotech CEOs with simple, sumptuous rooms (deep soak bathtubs, dual vanities) and a 16,000-sq-ft Zen-like spa with a meditation courtyard. A three-acre lake sits behind the property with a quarter-mile walking trail. The pet fee is $200 per stay, and the hotel has a new fenced dog playground, DogWoods.

Raleigh Times   PUB FOOD **$**
(www.raleightimesbar.com; 14 E Hargett St; mains $8-14; ⊙11am-2am; 🐾) Chase plates of barbecue nachos and PBR-battered fish and chips with pints of North Carolina craft brews at this popular downtown pub.

Beasley's Chicken + Honey   SOUTHERN US **$**
(www.ac-restaurants.com/beasleys; 237 Wilmington St; mains $7-13; ⊙11:30am-10pm Mon-Wed, 11:30am-midnight Thu & Fri, 11am-midnight Sat, 11am-10pm Sun) You'll need to loosen your belt after a meal at this crispy venture from James Beard Award–winner and local restaurant maven Ashley Christensen. Inside this airy downtown eatery, fried chicken is the star – on a biscuit, with waffles, in a pot pie. The sides are decadent too.

★**Binda Manda**   LAOTIAN **$$**
(☑919-829-9999; www.bidamanda.com; 222 S Blount St; lunch $11-21, dinner $18-30; ⊙11:30am-2pm & 5-10pm Mon-Thu, 11:30am-2pm & 5pm-midnight Fri, 5pm-midnight Sat; 🐾) All the plated dishes at this trendy Laotian hot spot – one of but a few Laotian restaurants in all the USA – are as gorgeous as the hip convergence of exposed air ducts and abundant bamboo throughout the space. Tying in Laos traditions with dashes of Thai, Vietnamese and Chinese, the dishes are a revelatory cavalcade of flavor.

ℹ Information

Raleigh Visitor Information Center (☑919-834-5900; www.visitraleigh.com; 500 Fayetteville St; ⊙8:30am-5pm Mon-Fri, 9am-5pm Sun) Hands out maps and other info. Office is closed on Sunday, but the city visitor guide and map are available on the counter.

Durham

Durham is a once-gritty tobacco and railroad town whose fortunes collapsed in the 1960s and have only recently begun to revive. Though still fundamentally a working-class Southern city, the presence of top-ranking Duke University has long drawn progressive types to the area and Durham is now making its name as a hot spot for gourmets, artists and gays and lesbians.

⊙ Sights

★**Duke Lemur Center**   ZOO
(☑919-401-7240; www.lemur.duke.edu; 3705 Erwin Rd; adult/child $12/9; ♿) The secret is out: the Lemur Center is the coolest attraction in Durham. Located about 2 miles from the main campus, this research and conservation center is home to the largest collection of endangered prosimian primates (ie lemurs) outside their native Madagascar. Only a robot could fail to melt at the sight of these big-eyed fuzzy-wuzzies. Visits are by guided tour only. To guarantee a tour spot, make your reservation well ahead of your visit.

Call at least three weeks in advance for weekdays, and one to two months ahead for weekends.

Duke University   UNIVERSITY
(www.duke.edu; Campus Dr) Endowed by the Duke family's cigarette fortune, the university has a Georgian-style East Campus and a neo-Gothic West Campus. Metered parking on campus is $2 per hour.

Duke Chapel

CHAPEL

(https://chapel.duke.edu; 401 Chapel Dr; ⊙8am-10pm, to 8pm summer) The towering, 1930s Duke Chapel overlooks Duke University's west campus. This breathtaking place, with its 210ft tower and 77 colorful, bible-themed glass windows, is worth a look.

American Tobacco Campus

HISTORIC SITE

(https://americantobaccocampus.com; 318 Blackwell St) Cigarettes no longer pay Durham's bills, but this massive former industrial tobacco factory, home to the American Tobacco Company until the 1950s, still does a bang-up job filling downtown Durham's coffers. Part of the National Register of Historic Places, the mixed-use facility is a cavalcade of restaurants, bars and entertainment venues spread over a million sq feet with no shortage of alfresco dining.

🛏 Sleeping & Eating

★ Durham

BOUTIQUE HOTEL $$

(☑919-768-8830; www.thedurham.com; 315 E Chapel Hill St; r from $209; P❄@�) It was only a matter of time before revitalized downtown Durham got its independent hipster sleeps – the suave, 53-room Durham, a marvel of mid-Century Modern might, filling that niche when it turned a former bank building into a supremely retro, fiercely local haven in 2015.

JB Duke Hotel

BOUTIQUE HOTEL $$

(☑919-660-6400; www.jbdukehotel.com; 230 Science Dr; r $159-279, ste $329-529; P❄@�❄) You could do worse than sleeping on Duke's gorgeous campus. This slick new 198-room hotel rides a fine line between modern and woodsy. The soothing carpeted lobby, with plush furniture, rough-cut burled walnut tables and a dark quartzite and glazed-steel metallic-tiled bar, harmonizes discreetly with Duke Forest. Spacious rooms offers working desks, Keurig coffee machines and campus views.

Toast

SANDWICHES $

(www.toast-fivepoints.com; 345 W Main St; sandwiches $8; ⊙11am-3pm Mon, to 8pm Tue-Sat) Families, couples, solos and the downtown lunch crowd – everybody loves this tiny Italian sandwich shop, one of the eateries at the forefront of downtown Durham's revitalization. Order your panini (hot and grilled), *tramezzini* (cold) or crostini (bundle of joy) at the counter then grab a table by the window – if you can – for people-watching.

★ Mateo

TAPAS $$

(☑919-530-8700; www.mateotapas.com; 109 W Chapel Hill St; ⊙11:30am-2:30pm & 5-10:30pm Tue-Thu, 11:30am-2:30pm & 5pm-midnight Fri, 5pm-midnight Sat, 5-9:30pm Sun) It's impossible to wax on Durham's remarkable comeback without talking about Mateo, where James Beard–nominated tapas – sometimes with a Southern bent – are the town's culinary anchor. The *pan com tomate* with Manchego cheese, the brussels sprouts with pine nuts, raisins and saffron yogurt and the fried egg and cheese (the 'whites' are fried farmer's cheese!) are revelations.

🍷 Drinking & Entertainment

★ Cocoa Cinnamon

COFFEE

(www.cocoacinnamon.com; 420 W Geer St; espresso/hot chocolate from $2.75/3.50; ⊙7:30am-10pm Mon-Thu, to 10:30pm Fri, 8am-10:30pm Sat, to 10pm Sun; �) If someone tells you that you *must* order a hot chocolate at Cocoa Cinnamon, ask them to be more specific. This talk-of-the town coffee shop offers several cocoas, and newbies may be paralyzed by the plethora of chocolatey awesomeness. Come to this one-time service station to enjoy cocoa, tea, single-source coffee and the energetic vibe.

Fullsteam Brewery

BREWERY

(www.fullsteam.ag; 726 Rigsbee Ave; pints/pitchers $5/18; ⊙4pm-midnight Mon-Thu, 2pm-2am Fri, noon-2am Sat, noon-midnight Sun; �) Calling itself a 'plow-to-pint' brewery, Fullsteam has gained national attention for pushing the boundaries of beer with wild, Southernized concoctions, going out of its way to support local farmers, neighborhood foragers and agricultural entrepreneurs, using all Carolinian ingredients wherever possible.

Durham Bulls Athletic Park

STADIUM

(www.dbulls.com; 409 Blackwell St; tickets $7-10) Have a quintessentially American afternoon of beer and baseball watching the minor-league Durham Bulls (of 1988 Kevin Costner film *Bull Durham* fame), who play from April to early September.

ℹ Information

Durham Visitor Info Center (☑919-687-0288; www.durham-nc.com; 212 W Main St; ⊙9am-5pm Mon, 9am-6pm Tue-Fri, 10am-6pm Sat) Information and maps inside a historic bank building.

ⓘ Getting There & Away

Durham's gateway airport is **Raleigh-Durham International Airport** (RDU; ☑ 919-840-2123; www.rdu.com; 1000 Trade Dr) in Morrisville, 14 miles southeast of Durham. An off-peak Uber to the airport runs about $20. Greyhound (p340) and Amtrak (p340) sit across the street from each other near the Durham Station Transportation Center.

Chapel Hill & Carrboro

Chapel Hill is a pretty, Southern college town whose culture revolves around the nearly 30,000 students at the prestigious University of North Carolina, founded in 1789 as the nation's first state university. A funky, forward-thinking place, Chapel Hill, along with its neighbor, Carrboro, is renowned for its indie rock scene and loud 'n' proud hippie culture.

◉ Sights

University of North Carolina UNIVERSITY (www.unc.edu) America's oldest public university has a classic quad lined with flowering pear trees and gracious antebellum buildings. Don't miss the **Old Well** to give good luck to students who drink from it. Pick up a map of the school at the **visitor center** (☑ 919-962-1630; www.unc.edu/visitors; 250 E Franklin St; ☺ 9am-5pm Mon-Fri) inside the Morehead Planetarium and Science Center or the **Chapel Hill Visitor Center** (☑ 919-245-4320; www.visitchapelhill.org; 501 W Franklin St; ☺ 8:30am-5pm Mon-Fri, 10am-3pm Sat).

Carolina Basketball Museum MUSEUM (www.goheels.com/fls/3350/museum; 450 Skipper Blowles Dr, Ernie Williamson Athletics Center; ☺ 10am-4pm Mon-Fri, 9am-1pm Sat) FREE The numbers say it all: six national championships, 19 final-four appearances, 30 ACC regular-season championships, 47 NBA first-round draft picks. Regardless of your allegiances, any basketball fan will appreciate this small but well-done temple dedicated to Tar Heel hoops. Memorabilia, trophies and video footage abound, including dedicated exhibits to Michael Jordan with his original signed national letter of intent and other recruiting documents.

🛏 Sleeping & Eating

★ Carolina Inn HOTEL **$$** (☑ 919-933-2001; www.carolinainn.com; 211 Pittsboro St; r from $179; 🅿 ❄ 🕾) Even if you're not a Tar Heel, this lovely on-campus inn will

THE BARBECUE TRAIL

North Carolina's most worshipped culinary contribution is pulled-pork barbecue, practically a religion in these parts, and the rivalry between Eastern style (with a thin vinegar sauce with a distinct acidic African-influenced flavor) and Western style (with a sweeter, tomato-based sauce) occasionally comes to blows. The North Carolina Barbecue Society has an interactive Barbecue Trail Map (www.ncbbqsociety.com), directing pilgrims to the best spots.

win you over with its hospitality and historic touches. The charm starts in the snappy lobby then continues through the hallways, lined with photos of alums and championship teams. Classic decor – inspired by Southern antiques – feels fresh in the 185 bright rooms, where silhouettes of famous graduates join the party.

Neal's Deli BREAKFAST, DELI **$** (www.nealsdeli.com; 100 E Main St, Carrboro; breakfast $3.50-6.75, lunch $5.50-8.50; ☺ 7:30am-4pm Tue-Fri, 8am-4pm Sat & Sun; 🕾) Before starting your day, dig into a delicious buttermilk breakfast biscuit at this tiny deli in downtown Carrboro. The egg, cheese and bacon is some kind of good. For lunch, Neal's serves sandwiches and subs, from chicken salad to pastrami to a three-cheese pimiento with a splash of bourbon. Chapel Hill/Carrboro's best coffeehouse, **Open Eye Cafe**, is next door.

★ Lantern ASIAN **$$$** (☑ 919-969-8846; www.lanternrestaurant.com; 423 W Franklin St; mains $23-32; ☺ 5:30-10pm Mon-Sat) If you only have time for one dinner in the Triangle, dine here. This modern Asian spot, using North Carolina–sourced ingredients, has earned a slew of accolades, and chef Andrea Reusing is a James Beard Award winner.

🍺 Drinking & Entertainment

Beer Study CRAFT BEER (www.beerstudy.com; 106 N Graham St; pints $3-7; ☺ 10am-midnight Mon-Wed, to 1am Thu-Sat, noon-midnight Sun; 🕾) There are a few breweries around Chapel Hill, but you're better off at this grungier half-bar, half-bottle shop with 18 taps of local and regional craft beer and over 500 bottles (you can buy and drink one but not a six-pack). City ordinances impose plastic cups on dog-friendly establishments, but that's a small price to pay for pup.

Cat's Cradle
LIVE MUSIC

(☎919-967-9053; www.catscradle.com; 300 E Main St, Carrboro) Everyone from Nirvana to Arcade Fire has played the Cradle, which has hosted the cream of the indie-music world for three decades. Most shows are all-ages.

❶ Getting There & Away

Chapel Hill's gateway airport is **Raleigh-Durham International Airport** in Morrisville, 18 miles east of Chapel Hill. An off-peak Uber to the airport runs about $25.

Charlotte

The largest city in North Carolina and the biggest US banking center after New York, Charlotte has the sprawling, sometimes faceless look of many New South suburban megalopolises. But though the Queen City, as it's known, is primarily a business town, it has a few good museums, stately old neighborhoods and lots of fine food and drink.

◎ Sights & Activities

NASCAR Hall of Fame
MUSEUM

(www.nascarhall.com; 400 E Martin Luther King Blvd; adult/child 5-12yr $20/13; ☉10am-6pm) The race-car simulator ($5) at this rip-roaring museum hurtles you on to the track and into an eight-car race that feels surprisingly real. Elsewhere, learn the history of this American-born sport (which traces back to moonshine running), check out six generations of race cars and test your pit-crew skills. NASCAR, if you're wondering, is short for National Association for Stock Car Auto Racing.

Levine Museum of the New South
MUSEUM

(www.museumofthenewsouth.org; 200 E 7th St; adult $8, child 6-18yr $5; ☉10am-5pm Mon-Sat, noon-5pm Sun) Interested in the South's complicated post–Civil War history? Then set aside an hour or two for the comprehensive 'From Cotton Fields to Skyscrapers' exhibit at this slick museum, which spotlights the cotton industry, Jim Crow laws, sit-ins, women's advancement and recent immigration trends. Tip: they validate two hours of parking at the 7th Street Station parking garage next door.

Billy Graham Library
RELIGIOUS SITE

(www.billygrahamlibrary.org; 4330 Westmont Dr; ☉9:30am-5pm Mon-Sat, last tour 3:30pm) **FREE** This multimedia 'library' is a tribute to the life of superstar evangelist and 'pastor to the presidents' Billy Graham, a Charlotte native. The 90-minute tour, the 'Journey of Faith', starts with a gospel-preaching animatronic cow, then spotlights key moments in Graham's life, including his transformative 1949 tent revival in Los Angeles (where he first inspired *Unbroken*'s hero, Louis Zamperini).

The tour is engaging and informative, especially if you're curious about Graham's journey and the roots of modern evangelicalism (though drowning in Christian propaganda and recruitment). You can also tour Graham's 1927 boyhood home, relocated here from its original spot 3 miles away.

★US National Whitewater Center
ADVENTURE SPORTS

(www.usnwc.org; 5000 Whitewater Center Pkwy; all-sport day pass adult/child under 10yr $59/49, individual activities $25, 3hr canopy tour $89; ☉dawn-dusk) A beyond-awesome hybrid of nature center and water park, this 400-acre facility is home to the largest artificial white-water river in the world, whose rapids serve as training grounds for Olympic canoe and kayak teams. Paddle it yourself as part of a guided rafting trip, or try one of the center's other adventurous activities.

🛏 Sleeping & Eating

Dunhill Hotel
BOUTIQUE HOTEL $$

(☎704-332-4141; www.dunhillhotel.com; 237 N Tryon St; r $149-349; ▣❄@🛜) The staff shines at this heart-of-uptown hotel, and the property has been welcoming guests since 1929 – it was Charlotte's first hotel with en suite bathrooms. Classic decor gives a nod to the 1920s, but large flat-screen TVs, Keurig coffee makers and phone docking stations keep the rooms firmly in the 21st century.

★Ivey's Hotel
BOUTIQUE HOTEL $$$

(www.theiveyshotel.com; 127 N Tryon St; r $299-450; ▣@🛜❀) The Ivey's 42 Parisian-inspired rooms – all on the 2nd floor of a 1924 department-store building – are steeped in discerning history (400-year-old oak-wood floors sourced from a French winery) with a modern flair (55in Sony TVs, Bose soundbars). The balcony executive corner suites, awash in natural light-sucking windows and exposed brick, are divine.

Price's Chicken Coop SOUTHERN US $
(www.priceschickencoop.com; 1614 Camden Rd;
mains $3.25-12.25; ⊙10am-6pm Tue-Sat) A Char-
lotte institution, scruffy Price's regularly
makes 'Best Fried Chicken in America' lists.
Line up to order your 'dark quarter' or 'white
half' from the army of white-jacketed cooks,
then take your bounty outside – there's no
seating. Latta Park is a few blocks east on
E Park Ave if you want to spread out. Cash
only but an ATM on-site.

★**Soul Gastrolounge**

Tapas SUSHI, SANDWICHES $$
(☑704-348-1848; www.soulgastrolounge.com;
1500 Central Ave; small plates $7-20, sushi $4-14,
sandwiches $9-15; ⊙5pm-2am) In Plaza Mid-
wood, this sultry but welcoming speakeasy
serves a globally inspired selection of small
plates. Choices are wide-ranging, from skew-
ers and sushi rolls to Cuban and Vietnamese
sandwiches, but the kitchen takes care to in-
fuse each morsel with unique, satisfying fla-
vors. The dancing tuna rolls with jalapeños
and two spicy mayos are highly recommend-
ed if you like heat.

🍷 **Drinking & Nightlife**

★**NoDa Brewing Co** MICROBREWERY
(www.nodabrewing.com; 2921 N Tryon St; pints
$4-7; ⊙4-9pm Mon-Thu, to 10pm Fri, noon-10pm
Sat, noon-7pm Sun; 🛜) Charlotte's best craft-
beer playground is hidden behind NoDa's
new and easy-to-overlook North End brew-
ery. We Uber'ed up on a Friday night and it
looked abandoned. How wrong we were! In
the back: a packed playhouse of brews and
a bocce set.

ℹ️ **Information**

Visitor Info Center (☑800-231-4636; www.
charlottesgotalot.com; 501 S College St, Char-
lotte Convention Center; ⊙9am-5pm Mon-Sat)
Downtown Charlotte main's visitor center is
inside the Charlotte Convention Center, where
there are booths near both the S College St and
E MLK Jr Blvd entrances. There are also stalls
at the Levine Museum of the New South and the
airport. It publishes maps and a visitors' guide.

ℹ️ **Getting There & Around**

Charlotte Douglas International Airport
(CLT; ☑704-359-4013; www.cltairport.com;
5501 Josh Birmingham Pkwy) is a US Airways
hub with direct flights from Europe and the
UK. Both the **Greyhound station** (☑704-375-
3332; www.greyhound.com; 601 W Trade St)

and **Amtrak** (www.amtrak.com; 1914 N Tryon
St) are handy to uptown.

Charlotte's public transport system is known
as CATS (Charlotte Area Transit System; www.
charlottenc.gov/cats), which encompasses city
buses, a light-rail line called LYNX Blue Line and
a streetcar line called CityLYNX Gold Line. One-
way fare is $2.20 to $4.40. The **Charlotte Trans-
portation Center** (www.ridetransit.org; 310 East
Trade St) is in Uptown on Brevard St between 4th
and Trade St. Charlotte also has a shared bike
system (https://charlotte.bcycle.com).

North Carolina Mountains

The Cherokee came to these ancient moun-
tains to hunt, followed by 18th-century
Scots-Irish immigrants looking for a better
life. Lofty towns such as Blowing Rock drew
the sickly, who came for the fresh air. Today,
scenic drives, leafy trails and roaring rivers
draw outdoor adventurers.

The Appalachians in the western part
of the state include the Great Smoky, Blue
Ridge, Pisgah and Black Mountain subrang-
es. Carpeted in blue-green hemlock, pine
and oak trees, these cool hills are home to
cougars, deer, black bears, wild turkeys and
great horned owls. Hiking, camping, climb-
ing and rafting adventures abound, and
there's another jaw-dropping photo oppor-
tunity around every bend.

ℹ️ **Getting There & Around**

Asheville Regional Airport (p350) is the gateway
to the North Carolina mountains, with nonstop
flights to/from Atlanta, Charlotte, Chicago and
New York, among others. There is also a Grey-
hound (p350) station in Asheville.

High Country

The northwestern corner of the state is
known as 'High Country.' Its main towns are
Boone, Blowing Rock and Banner Elk, all
short drives from the Blue Ridge Parkway.
Boone is a lively college town, home to Ap-
palachian State University (ASU). Blowing
Rock and Banner Elk are quaint tourist
centers near the winter ski areas.

BLOWING ROCK

A dignified and idyllic mountain village,
tiny Blowing Rock charmingly beckons
from its perch at 4000ft above sea level, the
only full-service town directly on the Blue
Ridge Parkway. It's easy to be seduced by its

postcard-perfect Main St, lined with antique shops, kitschy boutiques, potters, silver-smiths, sweet shops, lively taverns and ex-cellent eats, all of which manage to ward off a tackiness that's easy to to get swept away by when tourism rules the roost. There are even a couple of bucolic, duck-filled lakes to drive home the storybook-nature of it all.

⊙ Sights & Activities

Grandfather Mountain   HIKING
(☑ 828-733-4337; www.grandfather.com; Blue Ridge Pkwy Mile 305, Linville; adult/child 4-12yr $20/9; ⊙ 8am-7pm Jun-Aug, closes earlier fall, winter & spring) Hold up. Is the Mile High Suspension Bridge really swinging 1 mile above ground? Not exactly, so don't fret if you don't love heights. The park's star attrac-tion is 1-mile *above sea level,* but the chasm

beneath? It's 80ft deep. Nothing to sneeze at, but the distance is a bit less horrifying.

River & Earth Adventures   TOURS
(☑ 828-963-5491; www.raftcavehike.com; 5578 Hwy 421, Vilas; half-/full-day rafting from $60/100; ⊕) Offers everything from family-friendly caving trips to rafting Class V rapids at Watauga Gorge. Eco-conscious guides even pack organic lunches. Canoe ($60), kayak ($35 to $60) and tube ($20) rentals.

⊨ Sleeping & Eating

Cliff Dwellers Inn   MOTEL **$$**
(☑ 828-414-9596; www.cliffdwellers.com; 116 Lak-eview Terrace; r/apt from $99/149; P❄🐾🛜🐾) From its perch above town, this well-named motel lures guests with good service, reason-able prices, stylish rooms and balconies with sweeping views.

DON'T MISS

SCENIC DRIVE: BLUE RIDGE PARKWAY

You won't find one stoplight on the entire Blue Ridge Parkway, which traverses the south-ern Appalachians from Virginia's Shenandoah National Park at Mile 0 to North Carolina's Great Smoky Mountains National Park at Mile 469.

Commissioned by President Franklin D Roosevelt as a Great Depression–era public-works project, it's one of America's classic drives. North Carolina's piece of the parkway twists and turns for 262 miles of killer mountain vistas.

The **National Park Service** (☑ 828-298-5330; www.nps.gov/blri; Mile 384; ⊙ 9am-5pm) runs campgrounds and visitor centers. Note that restrooms and gas stations are few and far between. For more details about stops, visit www.blueridgeparkway.org.

Parkway highlights and campgrounds include the following:

Cumberland Knob (Mile 217.5) NPS visitor center; easy walk to the knob.

Doughton Park (Mile 241.1) Trails and camping.

Blowing Rock (Mile 291.8) Small town named for a craggy, commercialized cliff that offers great views, occasional updrafts and a Native American love story.

Moses H Cone Memorial Park (Mile 294.1) A lovely old estate with carriage trails and a craft shop.

Julian Price Memorial Park (Mile 296.9) Camping.

Grandfather Mountain (Mile 305.1) Hugely popular for its mile-high pedestrian 'swinging bridge.' Also has a nature center and a small wildlife reserve.

Linville Falls (Mile 316.4) Short hiking trails to the falls; campsites.

Little Switzerland (Mile 334) Old-style mountain resort.

Mt Mitchell State Park (Mile 355.5) Highest peak east of the Mississippi (6684ft); hiking and camping.

Craggy Gardens (Mile 364) Hiking trails explode with rhododendron blossoms in summer.

Folk Art Center (Mile 382) High-end Appalachian crafts for sale.

Blue Ridge Pkwy Visitor Center (Mile 384) Inspiring film, interactive map, trail information.

Mt Pisgah (Mile 408.8) Hiking, camping, restaurant, inn.

Graveyard Fields (Mile 418) Short hiking trails to waterfalls.

Green Park Inn HISTORIC HOTEL **$$**
(☑ 828-414-9230; www.greenparkinn.com; 9239 Valley Blvd; r $89-299; P ❋ 🕾 🐾) The eastern continental divide runs through the bar at this white-clapboard grand hotel that opened in 1891. They say author Margaret Mitchell worked on *Gone with the Wind* while staying here.

★**Bistro Roca** MODERN AMERICAN **$$**
(☑ 828-295-4008; www.bistroroca.com; 143 Wonderland Trail; lunch mains $9-16, dinner mains $9-34; ⊙ 11am-3pm & 5-10pm Wed-Mon; 🕾) This cozy, lodge-like bistro, tucked just off Main St, occupies a Prohibition-era building and does upscale New American fare (lobster or pork-belly mac 'n' cheese, kicked-up habanero burgers, wood-fired pizzas, mountain-trout *bánh mì* sandwiches) with an emphasis on local everything. Order anything with the duck bacon and you're all set.

❶ Getting There & Away

Blowing Rock is 8 miles south of Boone along the Blue Ridge Parkway. The closest commercial airport is Charlotte Douglas International Airport (p345), 87 miles southeast.

BOONE

Home to bustling Appalachian State University, Boone is a fun and lively mountain town with a young population that has a hankering for the outdoors. The town, the domain of bluegrass musicians and Appalachian storytellers, is named after famous pioneer and explorer Daniel Boone, who often camped in the area of the present-day town. Boone's history has been told every summer since 1952 in a dramatization called *Horn in the West*, which is performed in an outdoor amphitheater above the town.

Downtown Boone features a nice collection of low-rise brick-broad, Colonial Revival, art-deco and streamline-modern architecture. Many of the buildings today house charming boutiques and cafes.

Boone is home to mostly standard chain hotels, though you can find the occasional historic B&B, rental farmhouse or cozy log cabin lodgings around town and in the surrounding countryside. The Horton Hotel, Boone's first boutique hotel, opens in 2018.

Folk Art Center CULTURAL CENTER
(☑ 828-298-7928; www.southernhighlandguild. org; Mile 382; ⊙ 9am-6pm Apr-Dec, to 5pm Jan-Mar) As you enter the lobby at the Folk Art Center, look up. A row of handcrafted Appalachian chairs hangs from the walls above. They're an impressive calling card for the gallery here, which is dedicated to southern craftsmanship. The chairs are part of the Southern Highland Craft Guild's permanent collection, which holds more than 2400 traditional and modern crafts. Items from the collection are displayed on the 2nd floor.

★**Melanie's Food Fantasy** CAFE **$$**
(www.melaniesfoodfantasy.com; 664 W King St; breakfast $6-10, lunch & dinner $9-14; ⊙ 8am-2pm Mon-Wed, 8am-2pm & 5-9pm Thu-Fri, 8am-2:30pm & 5-9pm Sat, 8:30am-2:30pm Sun; ☑) On cutesy King St hippie types gobble up serious breakfast dishes (scrambles, eggs Benedict, omelets, waffles, pancakes) with a side of home fries at this farm-to-fork favorite, always with a vegetarian option (tempeh, soysage etc).

Dan'l Boone Inn SOUTHERN US **$$**
(☑ 828-264-8657; www.danlbooneinn.com; 130 Hardin St; breakfast adult $11, child $6-8, dinner adult $18, child $7-11; ⊙ 11:30am-8:30pm Mon-Thu, to 9pm Fri & Sat, to 8:30pm Sun Jun-Oct, hours vary rest of year; 🕾 👪) Quantity is the name of the game at this restaurant, and the family-style meals are a Boone (sorry) for hungry hikers. Open since 1959. Cash or check only.

❶ Getting There & Away

The closest commercial airport to Boone is Charlotte Douglas International Airport (p345), 94 miles southeast.

Asheville

With its homegrown microbreweries, decadent chocolate shops and stylish New Southern eateries, Asheville is one of the trendiest small cities in the East. Glossy magazines swoon for the place. But don't be put off by all the flash. At heart, Asheville is still an overgrown mountain town and it holds tight to its traditional roots. Just look around. There's a busker fiddling a high lonesome tune on Biltmore Ave. Over there, hikers are chowing down after climbing Mt Pisgah. Cars swoop on and off the Blue Ridge Parkway, which swings around the city. A huge population of artists and a visible contingent of hardcore hippies also helps to keep things real.

THE SOUTH NORTH CAROLINA MOUNTAINS

⊙ Sights & Activities

★ Biltmore Estate
HOUSE

(☑ 800-411-3812; www.biltmore.com; 1 Approach Rd; adult/child 10-16yr $65/32.50; ⊙house 9am-4:30pm, with seasonal variations) The country's largest privately owned home, and Asheville's number-one tourist attraction, the Biltmore was completed in 1895 for shipping- and railroad-heir George Washington Vanderbilt II. He modeled it after three French châteaus in the Loire Valley he'd seen on his various European jaunts. Viewing the estate and its 250 acres of gorgeously manicured grounds and gardens takes several hours.

Chimney Rock Park
PARK

(www.chimneyrockpark.com; Hwy 64/74A; adult/child 5-15yr $15/7; ⊙8:30am-6pm mid-Mar–Nov, 10am-4:30pm Fri-Tue Nov–mid-Mar) Views of the Broad River and Lake Lure are superb from atop the namesake chimney – a 315ft granite monolith. An elevator takes visitors up to the chimney, but the real draw is the exciting hike around the cliffs to a 404ft waterfall. The park, once privately owned, is now part of the state-park system; access to the rock is still managed commercially. The park is a gorgeous 20-mile drive southeast of Asheville.

BREW-ed
BREWERY

(☑828-278-9255; www.brew-ed.com; $37-50) Walking downtown brewery and history tours, led by Cicerone-certified beer geeks, on Thursdays (5:30pm), Fridays (2pm), Saturdays (11:30am and 2pm) and Sundays (1pm).

Smoky Mountain Adventure Center
OUTDOORS

(☑828-505-4446; www.smacasheville.com; 173 Amboy Rd; ⊙10am-8pm Mon, 9am-10pm Tue-Thu, to 9:30pm Fri & Sat, noon-8pm Sun) Across the street from the French Broad river in the River Arts district, head here for one-stop outdoor adventure shopping. It can arrange bikes for the Blue Ridge Parkway, inner tubes and paddleboards for the river, and guided rock climbing, backpacking, day hiking, ice climbing and mountaineering trips in the surrounding mountains.

🛏 Sleeping

Sweet Peas Hostel
HOSTEL $

(☑828-285-8488; www.sweetpeashostel.com; 23 Rankin Ave; dm/pod $32/40, r without/with bath $75/105; ❄@🛜) This spick-and-span hostel gleams with IKEA-like style, with shipshape steel bunk beds and blond-wood sleeping 'pods.' The loft-like space is very open and can be noisy (the downstairs Lexington Ave Brewery adds to the ruckus but hey, there's a discount), but what you lose in privacy and quiet, you gain in style, cleanliness, sociability and an unbeatable downtown location.

Campfire Lodgings
CAMPGROUND $$

(☑828-658-8012; www.campfirelodgings.com; 116 Appalachian Village Rd; tent sites $35-40, RV sites $50-70, yurts $115-135, cabins $160; P❄🛜) All yurts should have flat-screen TVs, don't you think? Sleep like the world's most stylish Mongolian nomad in one of these furnished multiroom tents, on the side of a wooded hill. Cabins and tent sites are also available. RV sites have stunning valley views and wi-fi access.

Omni Grove Park Inn
HISTORIC HOTEL $$$

(☑828-252-2711; www.omnihotels.com; 290 Macon Ave; r $149-419; P❄@🛜🏊🐾) This titanic arts-and-crafts-style historic stone lodge recalls a bygone era of Americana mountain glamor and, with its hale-and-hearty look, sets a tone for adventure. Did you notice the lobby fireplaces? Of course you did: the 36ft-wide behemoths can accommodate a standing grown man inside their hearths and there is an elevator ascending to the chimney within each!

Aloft Asheville
HOTEL $$$

(☑828-232-2838; www.aloftasheville.com; 51 Biltmore Ave; r from $250-450; P❄@🛜🏊🐾) With a giant chalkboard in the lobby, groovy young staff, and an outdoor clothing store on the 1st floor, this place looks like the seventh circle of hipster. The only thing missing is a wool-cap-wearing bearded guy drinking a hoppy microbrew – oh, wait, over there. We jest. Once settled, you'll find the staff knowledgeable and the rooms colorful and spacious.

Bunn House
BOUTIQUE HOTEL $$$

(☑828-333-8700; www.bunnhouse.com; 15 Clayton St; d $249-424; P❄🛜) Asheville's most discerning choice; a meticulously restored 1905 home that forgoes keys for codes and is awash in original exposed brick and dark hardwoods throughout its six rooms and suites. The heated bathroom floors and subway-tiled steam showers are glorious on chilly mountain mornings. Minibars and common areas are stocked with complimentary Herban Baker snacks and Asheville Brewing Company beers.

✕ Eating

Asheville is a fawned-upon foodie haven. Downtown, South Slope and the up-and-coming River Arts District along the French Broad River are rife with good eats from simple (but hip!) Southern-fried cafes to ethnic eats to elaborate Modern American and Appalachian kitchens. Farm-to-table is a general rule; local, organic and sustainable are mantras.

Early Girl Eatery
CAFE $

(www.earlygirleatery.com; 8 Wall St; mains $4-15; ⊘7:30am-3:00pm Mon-Wed, to 9pm Thu & Fri, 9am-9pm Sat & Sun) Order breakfast all day (try that house Benny, with tomato, spinach, avocado and poached eggs on grit cakes) or a grilled pimiento-cheese sandwich in this neighborhood farm-to-table cafe. Enjoy your feast on the sunny, crowded dining room, overlooking a small city square.

White Duck Taco Shop
MEXICAN $

(www.whiteducktacoshop.com; 12 Biltmore Ave; tacos $3.45-5.25; ⊘11:30am-9pm) The chalkboard menu at this downtown taco shop will give you fits – every taco sounds like a must-have flavor bomb: spicy buffalo chicken with blue-cheese sauce, crispy pork belly, mole-roasted duck – there's even shrimp and grits! Even better? These soft tacos are hefty. The chips and three-salsa appetizer works well for a group.

★12 Bones
BARBECUE $

(www.12bones.com; 5 Foundy St; dishes $5.50-22; ⊘11am-4pm Mon-Fri) How good is this barbecue? Well, Former President Obama and wife Michelle stopped by a few years ago for a meal. The slow-cooked meats are smokey tender, and the sides, from the jalapeño-cheese grits to the smoked-potato salad, will bring you to the brink of the wild heart of life.

★Cúrate
TAPAS $$

(☑828-239-2946; www.curatetapasbar.com; 13 Biltmore Ave; small plates $4-18; ⊘11:30am-11:30pm Tue-Thu, to 11pm Fri & Sat, to 10:30pm Sun) 🕊 This convivial place celebrates the simple charms and sensual flavors of traditional Spanish tapas with a occasional Southern twist (it's owned by a genuine Catalan and his hip Ashevillian wife). Standout dishes run long and wide: *pan con tomate* (grilled bread with tomato fresco), lightly fried eggplant drizzled with honey and rosemary, and a knockout squid-ink 'paella' with vermicelli.

Smoky Park Supper Club
MODERN AMERICAN $$

(☑828-350-0315; www.smokypark.com; 350 Riverside Dr; mains $10-34; ⊘5-9pm Tue-Thu, 4-10pm Fri & Sat, 10:30am-9pm Sun; 🛜) One of the anchors of cool in the developing Rivers Arts District, SPSC is more than the sum of its parts: 19 shipping containers to be exact, making it the largest container-constructed

---

BEER CITY USA

If ever a city was transformed by the craft-beer movement, it's Asheville, which has catapulted itself from a fairly sleepy mountain city when its first brewery, Highland Brewing, opened in 1994, to one of North America's destination suds cities for booze-bound hopheads.

Today Buncombe Country counts 33 breweries (27 of which are in Asheville proper) for a population of just 87,000 or so people – one of the highest brewery-to-resident ratios in the country. Our favorites:

Burial (www.burialbeer.com; 40 Collier Ave; pints $5; ⊘4-10pm Mon-Thu, from 2pm Fri, noon-10pm Sat & Sun; 🛜) Small and intimate; produces some of Asheville's best and most experimental Belgian-leaning styles (farmhouse saisons, strong dubbels and tripels). Touted by nearly everyone as the city's best.

Funkatorium (www.wickedweedbrewing.com/locations/funkatorium; 147 Coxe Ave; beers $4.50-10; ⊘2-10pm Mon-Thu, noon-midnight Fri & Sat, noon-10pm Sun; 🛜) Wicked Weed's new all-sour taproom is a pilgrimage-worthy temple of tart and funk.

Wedge (www.wedgebrewing.com; 37 Paynes Way; pints $3.50-6; ⊘noon-10pm; 🛜) A festive, come-one, come-all outdoor space rife with dogs, kids on tricycles, swooning couples and outdoorsy types.

Wicked Weed (www.wickedweedbrewing.com; 91 Biltmore Ave; pints $4.50-6.40; ⊘11:30am-11pm Mon & Tue, to midnight Wed & Thu, to 1am Fri & Sat, noon-11pm Sun; 🛜) A former gas station turned craft-brew wonderland. Fifty-eight taps!

restaurant in the USA. But choosing from the mostly wood-fired delights is agonizing: garlic and lemon-roasted half chicken, cast-iron-seared Carolina fish, cheese dip with chorizo and poblano peppers.

 Drinking & Entertainment

Trade & Lore COFFEE
(www.tradeandlore.com; 37 Wall St; coffee $2-5.25; ☺8am-7pm; 🛜) Serious java is dealt by skilled baristas at this trendy downtown coffeehouse drowning in industrial-cool shaken up by occasional fits of vintage furniture. Espresso comes courtesy a top-end mainstay La Marzocco machine and there's an extensive espresso with milk menu. The all-gender bathrooms are a tongue-in-cheek dig at state government.

Orange Peel LIVE MUSIC
(www.theorangepeel.net; 101 Biltmore Ave; tickets $10-30; ☺shows from 8pm) For live music, try this warehouse-sized place showcasing big-name indie and punk.

ℹ Information

The shiny **visitor center** (☑828-258-6129; www.exploreasheville.com; 36 Montford Ave; ☺8:30am-5:30pm Mon-Fri, 9am-5pm Sat & Sun) is at I-240, exit 4C. You can buy Biltmore admission tickets here for a $10 discount. Downtown, there is a **satellite visitor center** (☑828-258-6129; www.exploreasheville.com; 80 Court Pl; ☺9am-5pm Fri-Sun Apr-Oct), with restrooms, beside Pack Square Park.

ℹ Getting There & Around

Twenty minutes south of town, **Asheville Regional Airport** (AVL; ☑828-684-2226; www.flyavl.com; 61 Terminal Dr, Fletcher) has a handful of nonstop flights, including to/from Atlanta, Charlotte, Chicago and New York. **Greyhound** (☑828-253-8451; www.greyhound.com; 2 Tunnel Rd) is about 1 mile northeast of downtown.

Free parking is a tremendous issue in downtown Asheville, but the pubic garages are free for the first hour and only $1 per hour thereafter, so not horrible. Passport (https://passportinc.com) is a handy app for managing parking meters and paid lots here (and in a few other US cities).

Asheville Transit (☑828-253-5691; www.ashevilletransit.com; 49 Coxe Ave; ☺6am-9:30pm Mon-Fri, 7am-9:30pm Sat, 8:30am-6pm Sun) has 18 local bus routes that run from about 5:30am to 10:30pm Monday through Saturday, with reduced hours Sunday. Tickets are $1. Free bus racks. Route S3 goes from the downtown Art Station to the airport 10 times daily.

Great Smoky Mountains National Park

Be it the rite-of-passage walk in the woods known as the Appalachian Trail, the sweeping, cinematic views from 6643ft Clingmans Dome or the staunchly preserved pioneer homestead at Cades Cove, Great Smoky Mountains National Park is an American icon of nature and history. This moody and magical park sprawls across 521,000 acres in both North Carolina and Tennessee. It's one of the world's most diverse areas: landscapes range from deep, dim spruce forest to sunny meadows carpeted with daisies and Queen Anne's lace to wide, coffee-brown rivers. There's ample hiking and camping, and opportunities for horseback riding, bike rental and fly-fishing. Unfortunately, with more 10 million annual visitors – the highest of any national park in the USA – the place can get very crowded. The North Carolina side has less traffic than the Tennessee side, however, so even at the height of summer tourist season you'll still have room to roam.

◉ Sights

Great Smoky Mountains National Park NATIONAL PARK
(www.nps.gov/grsm) **FREE** The 815-sq-mile park is the country's most visited and, while the main arteries and attractions can get crowded, 95% of visitors never venture further than 100yd from their cars, so it's easy to leave the masses behind. Unlike most national parks, Great Smoky charges no admission fee. In 2016, 15 sq miles of the park was burned in the Great Smoky Mountain wildfires, including the immensely popular **Chimney Tops Trail**, which remained closed at time of research. Call ahead for an update.

Stop by a visitor center to pick up a park map and the free Smokies Guide. The remains of the 19th-century settlement at **Cades Cove** are some of the park's most popular sights, as evidenced by the teeth-grinding summer traffic jams on the loop road. Mt LeConte offers terrific hiking, as well as the only non-camping accommodations, **LeConte Lodge**. Although the only way to get to the lodge's rustic, electricity-free cabins is via five uphill hiking trails varying in length from 5.5 miles (the **Alum Cave Trail**) to 8 miles (**Boulevard**), it's so popular you need to reserve up to a year in advance. You can drive right up to the dizzying heights of

THE SOUTH NORTH CAROLINA MOUNTAINS

Clingmans Dome, the third-highest mountain east of the Mississippi, with a futuristic observation tower.

In addition to Chimney Tops, Road Prong Trail, Sugarland Mountain Trail and Bullhead Trail were also indefinitely closed at time of research. Call ahead.

Activities

Whether you have an irrepressible urge to climb a mountain or just want to get some fresh air, hiking in Great Smoky Mountains National Park is the single best way to experience the sublime beauty of this area. Even if you're only here for a short visit, be sure to include at least one hike in your itinerary. Trails range from flat, easy and short paths to longer, more strenuous endeavors. Many are excellent for families, some are wheelchair accessible, and the majority of trailheads begin from major sights. No matter what your physical ability or endurance level, there's a hike out there for you.

Here are a few of our favorites:

Charlies Bunion HIKING
An 8.1-mile loop that follows the Appalachian Trail 4 miles from the Newfound Gap overlook to a rocky outcrop for sweeping mountain and valley views.

Big Creek Trail HIKING
Hike an easy 2 miles to Mouse Creek Falls or go another 3 miles to a backcountry campground; the trailhead is near I-40 on the park's northeastern edge.

Boogerman Trail HIKING
Moderate 7.4-mile loop passing old farmsteads; accessible via Cove Creek Rd.

Chasteen Creek Falls HIKING
From Smokemont campground, this 3.6-mile round-trip passes a small waterfall.

Oconaluftee River Trail HIKING
One of only two in the park that allows leashed pets and bicycles, this 3-mile loop leaves from the Oconaluftee Visitor Center and follows the river for 1.5 miles.

Sleeping & Eating

Great Smoky Mountains National Park provides varied camping options. LeConte Lodge is the only place where you can get a room, however, and you have to hike to the top of a mountain to enjoy this privilege. Gatlinburg has the most sleeping options of any gateway town, though prices are high. Nearby Pigeon Forge, 10 miles north of Sugarlands Visitor Center, and Sevierville, 17 miles north, have cheaper options.

THE 2016 GREAT SMOKY MOUNTAIN WILDFIRES

On November 23, 2016, tragedy stuck Great Smoky Mountains National Park when fire was reported on Chimney Tops, one of the park's most popular trails, a kindling that would eventually wreak havoc on the park and Gatlinburg on its way to becoming the deadliest wildfire in the eastern USA since the Great Fires of 1947.

Dubbed 'Chimney Tops 2' by firefighters (a smaller fire had burned on Chimney Tops a week earlier), fire suppression was not as speedy as it should have been (several days went by before action was taken). By November 28, a massive firewall was heading toward Gatlinburg with shocking speed. By December 5, a full-on firefighting onslaught was unleashed: 25 hand crews, 61 engines, six helicopters and a total of 780 personnel. But it wouldn't be until late January when containment of the fire reached over 90%. The town of Gatlinburg was spared due to some heroic firefighting efforts – the only true in-town casualty was the Gatlinburg Sky Lift, which suffered serious damage to its upper section and upper terminal, but the damage otherwise was dreadful: 14 deaths, over 175 injuries, over 2400 structures damaged or destroyed, and the forced evacuation of 14,000 residents. Damage in dollars? Over $500 million.

Inside the park, over 15 sq miles were scorched, with Chimney Tops taking the brunt of the blow, forcing the closure of one of the park's most beloved trails. Park officials estimate it could take 80 years for the area to regenerate, and the trail could be closed for years to come.

Two Tennessee juveniles were arrested and charged with aggravated arson in the starting of the fire. If tried as adults – a major debate among Gatlinburg residents – they could face 60 years in prison.

The National Park Service maintains developed campgrounds at 10 locations in the park. Each campground has restrooms with cold running water and flush toilets, but there are no showers or electrical or water hookups in the park (though some campgrounds do have electricity for emergency situations). Each individual campsite has a fire grate and picnic table. Many sites can be reserved in advance (and one, Cataloochee, which requires it) at www.recreation.gov.

With about 1000 campsites on offer across the 10 developed campgrounds, you'd think finding a place to pitch would be easy. Not so in the busy summer season, so plan ahead. You can make reservations for some sites; others operate on a first-come, first-served basis. Cades Cove and Smokemont campgrounds are open year-round; others are open March to October.

Backcountry camping is an excellent option, which is only chargeable up to five nights ($4 per night, after that, it's free). A permit is required; you can make reservations online at www.smokiespermits.nps. gov, and get permits at the ranger stations or visitor centers.

Nuts and berries notwithstanding, there's nothing to eat in Great Smoky Mountains National Park, save for guests-only fare at LeConte Lodge, vending machines at Sugarlands Visitor Center and the meager offerings sold at the Cades Cove Campground store. Luckily, there are lots of restaurant options in the surrounding towns.

❶ Tourist Information

The park has four interior visitor centers:

Sugarlands Visitor Center (☑ 865-436-1291; www.nps.gov/grsm; 107 Park Headquarters Rd; ⊙8am-7:30pm Jun-Aug, hours vary Sep-May) At the park's northern entrance near Gatlinburg.

Cades Cove Visitor Center (☑ 865-436-7318; Cades Cove Loop Rd; ⊙9am-7pm May-Jul, earlier Sep-Mar) Halfway up Cades Cove Loop Rd, 24 miles off Hwy 441 from the Gatlinburg entrance.

Oconaluftee Visitor Center (☑ 828-497-1904; www.nps.gov/grsm; 1194 Newfound Gap Rd, North Cherokee, NC; ⊙8am-7:30pm Jun-Aug, hours vary Sep-May) At the park's southern entrance near Cherokee in North Carolina.

Clingmans' Dome Visitor Center (☑ 865-436-1200; Clingmans Dome Rd; ⊙10am-6pm Apr-Jun & Aug-Oct, 9:30am-5pm Nov)

❶ Getting There & Away

The closest major airports are Knoxville's McGhee Tyson Airport (p382), 40 miles from the Sugarlands Visitor Center on the Tennessee side; and Asheville Regional Airport (p350), 58 miles east of the Oconaluftee Visitor Center on the North Carolina side. Both Knoxville and Asheville are served by Greyhound as well.

SOUTH CAROLINA

Moss-draped oaks. Stately mansions. Wide beaches. Rolling mountains. And an ornery streak as old as the state itself. Ah yes, South Carolina, where the accents are thicker and the traditions more dear. From its Revolutionary War patriots to its 1860s secessionist government to its current crop of outspoken legislators, the Palmetto State has never shied away from a fight.

Most travelers stick to the coast, with its splendid antebellum cities and palm-tree-studded beaches. But the interior has a wealth of sleepy old towns, wild and undeveloped state parks and spooky black-water swamps. Along the sea islands you hear the sweet songs of the Gullah, a culture and language created by former slaves who held on to many West African traditions through the ravages of time. From well-bred, gardenia-scented Charleston to bright, tacky Myrtle Beach, South Carolina is always a fascinating destination.

History

More than 28 separate tribes of Native Americans have lived in what is now South Carolina, many of them Cherokee who were later forcibly removed during the Trail of Tears era.

The English founded the Carolina colony in 1670, with settlers pouring in from the royal outpost of Barbados, giving the port city known as Charles Towne a Caribbean flavor. West African slaves were brought over to turn the thick coastal swamps into rice paddies; and by the mid-1700s the area was deeply divided between the slave-owning aristocrats of the Lowcountry and the poor Scots-Irish and German farmers of the rural backcountry.

South Carolina was the first state to secede from the Union, and the first battle of the Civil War occurred at Fort Sumter in Charleston Harbor. The end of the war left much of the state in ruins.

South Carolina traded in cotton and textiles for most of the 20th century. It remains a relatively poor agricultural state, though with a thriving coastal tourism business.

In recent years the Palmetto State has garnered headlines because of its politicians, from Nikki Haley, the state's first woman and first Indian American governor, to Congressman Joe Wilson, who yelled 'You lie!' during a speech by President Obama to Congress. Congressman Mark Sanford, while serving as governor, famously claimed that he was hiking the Appalachian Trail when he was in fact visiting his Argentinian girlfriend.

In 2015, following the shooting of nine members of a historically black church for what appeared to be racially motivated reasons, the state legislature voted to remove the Confederate flag from the grounds of the state capitol, where it had flown since 1962.

⚫ Information

The **South Carolina Department of Parks, Recreation & Tourism** (📞 803-734-0124; www.discoversouthcarolina.com) sends out the state's official vacation guide. The state's nine highway welcome centers offer free wi-fi. Ask inside for password.

Charleston

This lovely city will embrace you with the warmth and hospitality of an old and dear friend – who died in the 18th century. We jest, but the cannons, cemeteries and carriage rides do conjure an earlier era. And that historic romanticism, along with the food and Southern graciousness, is what makes Charleston one of the most popular tourist destinations in the South, drawing more than 4.8 million visitors every year.

How best to enjoy its charms? Charleston is a city for savoring – stroll past the historic buildings, admire the antebellum architecture, stop to smell the blooming jasmine and enjoy long dinners on the verandah. It's also a place for romance; everywhere you turn another blushing bride is standing on the steps of yet another charming church. Above all, it's a place for seduction by Southern hospitality – Charleston charms the sweat right off your brow.

History

Well before the Revolutionary War, Charles Towne (named for Charles II) was one of

the busiest ports on the eastern seaboard, the center of a prosperous rice-growing and trading colony. With influences from the West Indies and Africa, France and other European countries, it became a cosmopolitan city, often compared to New Orleans.

A tragic but important component of the city's history? Slavery. Charleston was a key port and trade center for the slave industry, and bustling slave auction houses clustered near the Cooper River. The first shots of the Civil War rang out at Fort Sumter, in Charleston's harbor. After the war, as the labor-intensive rice plantations became uneconomical without slave labor, the city's importance declined.

⦿ Sights

The quarter south of Beaufain and Hasell Sts has the bulk of the antebellum mansions, shops, bars and cafes. At the southernmost tip of the Peninsula are the antebellum mansions of the Battery. A loose path, the **Gateway Walk**, winds through several church grounds and graveyards between **St John's Lutheran Church** (www.stjohnscharleston.org; 5 Clifford St) and **St Philip's Church** (www.stphilipschurchsc.org; 146 Church St).

⦿ Historic District

Old Exchange & Provost Dungeon   HISTORIC BUILDING
(www.oldexchange.org; 122 E Bay St; adult/child 7-12yr $10/5; ⊙9am-5pm; 👶) Kids love the creepy dungeon, used as a prison for American patriots held by the British during the Revolutionary War. The cramped space sits beneath a stately Georgian Palladian customs house completed in 1771. Costumed guides lead the dungeon tours. Exhibits about the city are displayed on the upper floors.

Old Slave Mart Museum   MUSEUM
(www.nps.gov/nr/travel/charleston/osm.htm; 6 Chalmers St; adult/child 5-17yr $8/5; ⊙9am-5pm Mon-Sat) Ryan's Mart was an open-air market that auctioned African men, women and children in the mid 1800s, the largest of 40 or so similar auction houses. South Carolina's shameful past is unraveled in text-heavy exhibits illuminating the slave experience; the few artifacts, such as leg shackles, are especially chilling.

Gibbes Museum of Art   GALLERY
(www.gibbesmuseum.org; 135 Meeting St; adult/child $12/6; ⊙10am-5pm Tue & Thu-Sat, to 8pm

Wed, 1-5pm Sun) Houses a decent collection of American and Southern works. The contemporary collection includes works by local artists, with Lowcountry life as a highlight.

Battery & White Point Gardens GARDENS

(cnr East Battery & Murray Blvd) The Battery is the southern tip of the Charleston Peninsula, buffered by a seawall. Stroll past cannons and statues of military heroes in the gardens then walk the promenade and look for Fort Sumter.

Kahal Kadosh Beth Elohim SYNAGOGUE

(www.kkbe.org; 90 Hasell St; ⊘tours 10am-noon & 1:30-3:30pm Mon-Thu, 10am-noon & 1-3pm Fri, 1-3:30pm Sun) The oldest continuously used synagogue in the country. Docent-led tours cost $10. Check website for tour times.

Rainbow Row AREA

(83 E Bay St) With its candy-colored houses, this stretch of lower E Bay St is one of the most photographed areas of town.

Historic Homes

Aiken-Rhett House HISTORIC BUILDING

(www.historiccharleston.org; 48 Elizabeth St; adult/child 6-16yr $12/5; ⊘10am-5pm Mon-Sat, 2-5pm Sun, last tour 4:15pm) The only surviving urban townhouse complex, this 1820 house gives a fascinating glimpse into antebellum life on a 45-minute self-guided audio tour. The role of slaves is emphasized and you can wander into their dorm-style quarters behind the main house before moving on to the lifestyle of the rich and famous.

The Historic Charleston Foundation manages the house 'preserved as found' – the goal of preserving and conserving, but not restoring, the property, meaning there have been few alterations and you get it as is, peeling Parisian wallpaper and all.

Joseph Manigault House HISTORIC BUILDING

(www.charlestonmuseum.org; 350 Meeting St; adult/child 13-17yr/child 3-12yr $12/10/5; ⊘9am-5pm Mon-Sat, noon-5pm Sun, last tour 4:30pm) The three-story 1803 Federal-style house was once the showpiece of a French Huguenot rice planter. The tiny neoclassical gate temple in the garden was one of only three in the US at the time.

Nathaniel Russell House HISTORIC BUILDING

(www.historiccharleston.org; 51 Meeting St; adult/child 6-16yr $12/5; ⊘10am-5pm Mon-Sat, 2-5pm Sun, last tour 4:30pm) A spectacular, self-supporting spiral staircase is the highlight at this 1808 Federal-style house, built by a Rhode Islander, known in Charleston as 'the king of the Yankees.' A meticulous ongoing restoration is honoring the home to the finest details, such as the 1000 sheets of 22-karat gold leaf in the withdrawing room, the peeling back of 20 layers of wall paint to find the original colors and handmade fitted contoured rugs imported from the UK, as originally done by the Russells.

⊙ Marion Square

Formerly home to the state weapons arsenal, this 10-acre park is Charleston's living room, with various monuments and an excellent Saturday farmers market.

Charleston Museum MUSEUM

(www.charlestonmuseum.org; 360 Meeting St; adult/child 13-17yr/child 3-12yr $12/10/5; ⊘9am-5pm Mon-Sat, noon-5pm Sun) Founded in 1773, this claims to be the country's oldest museum. It's helpful and informative if you're looking for historic background before strolling through the Historic District. Exhibits spotlight various periods of Charleston's long and storied history.

⊙ Aquarium Wharf

Aquarium Wharf surrounds pretty Liberty Sq and is a great place to stroll and watch the tugboats guiding ships into the fourth-largest container port in the USA. The wharf is one of two embarkation points for tours to Fort Sumter; the other is at Patriot's Point.

Fort Sumter National Monument HISTORIC SITE

(www.nps.gov/fosu) The first shots of the Civil War rang out at Fort Sumter, on a pentagon-shaped island in the harbor. A Confederate stronghold, the fort was shelled to bits by Union forces from 1863 to 1865. A few original guns and fortifications give a feel for the momentous history.

⊙ Ashley River Plantations

Three spectacular plantations line the Ashley River about a 20-minute drive from downtown Charleston. You'll be hard-pressed for time to visit all three in one outing, but you could squeeze in two (allow at least a couple of hours for each). Ashley River Rd is also known as SC 61, which can be reached from downtown Charleston via Hwy 17.

★ **Middleton Place**   HISTORIC BUILDING
(☑ 843-556-6020; www.middletonplace.org; 4300 Ashley River Rd, Summerville; gardens adult/child 6-13yr $28/10, house-museum tours extra $15; ⊙ 9am-5pm) Designed in 1741, this plantation's vast gardens are the oldest in the US. Countless slaves spent years terracing the land and digging the precise geometric canals for the owner, wealthy South Carolina politician Henry Middleton. The bewitching grounds are a mix of classic formal French gardens and romantic woodland, bounded by flooded rice paddies and rare-breed farm animals. Union soldiers burned the main house in 1865; a 1755 guest wing, now housing the **house museum**, still stands.

Magnolia Plantation   HISTORIC BUILDING
(☑ 843-571-1266; www.magnoliaplantation.com; 3550 Ashley River Rd; adult/child 6-10yr $15/10, tours $8; ⊙ 8am-5:30pm Mar-Oct, to 4:30pm Nov-Feb) Up for a spooky stroll? Then follow the boardwalk through the trees and bog on the Audubon Swamp Garden tour – it's a unique experience. The 500-acre plantation, which has been owned by the Drayton family since 1676, is a veritable theme park. Enjoy a tram tour, a petting zoo and a guided house tour. At the reconstructed slave cabins, the Slavery to Freedom Tour traces the African American experience at the plantation.

Drayton Hall   HISTORIC BUILDING
(☑ 843-769-2600; www.draytonhall.org; 3380 Ashley River Rd; adult/child $22/10, grounds only $12; ⊙ 9am-5pm Mon-Sat, 11am-5pm Sun, last tour 3:30pm) This 1738 Palladian brick mansion was the only plantation house on the Ashley River to survive the Revolutionary and Civil Wars and the great earthquake of 1886. Guided tours explore the unfurnished house, which has been preserved.

☞ **Tours**

Listing all of Charleston's walking, horse-carriage, bus and boat tours would take forever. Ask at the visitor center for the gamut.

Charleston Footprints   WALKING
(☑ 843-478-4718; www.charlestonfootprints.com; 2hr tour $20) A highly rated walking tour of historical Charleston sights.

Culinary Tours of Charleston   FOOD & DRINK
(☑ 843-727-1100; www.culinarytoursofcharleston. com; 18 Anson St; 2½hr tour $60) You'll likely sample grits, pralines and barbecue on the 'Savor the Flavors of Charleston' walking tour of restaurants and markets.

Adventure Harbor Tours   BOATING
(☑ 843-442-9455; www.adventureharbortours. com; 56 Ashley Point Dr; adult/child 3-12yr $55/30) Runs fun trips to uninhabited Morris Island – great for shelling.

★✪ **Festivals & Events**

Spoleto USA   PERFORMING ARTS
(☑ 843-579-3100; www.spoletousa.org; ⊙ May/Jun) This 17-day performing-arts festival is South Carolina's biggest event, with operas, dramas and concerts staged across the city.

Lowcountry Oyster Festival   FOOD & DRINK
(www.charlestonrestaurantassociation.com/low country-oyster-festival; 1235 Longpoint Rd, Boone Hall Plantation, Mt Pleasant; oyster buckets $12-14; ⊙ Jan) Oyster lovers in Mt Pleasant feast on 80,000lb of the salty bivalves in January.

MOJA Arts Festival   PERFORMING ARTS
(www.mojafestival.com; ⊙ Sep/Oct) Spirited poetry readings and gospel concerts mark this two-week celebration of African American and Caribbean culture.

🛏 **Sleeping**

Not So Hostel   HOSTEL $
(☑ 843-722-8383; www.littlejackstavern.com; 156 Spring St; dm $28-32, r $75-106; 🅿 ❄ 🛜 🖥) 🚲 Housed mainly in a wonderful 1840 dwelling complete with atmospheric, ghost-averting blue porches and an odd, twin-matching architecture setup, Charleston's one hostel is creaky and inviting. An eight-bed co-ed dorm, various four-bed male and female dorms, and nice but cramped private rooms are spread over three buildings with several guest kitchens throughout. Green initiatives abound.

1837 Bed & Breakfast   B&B $$
(☑ 843-723-7166; www.1837bb.com; 126 Wentworth St; r $175-290; 🅿 ❄ 🛜) Close to the College of Charleston, this B&B may bring to mind the home of your eccentric, antique-loving aunt. The 1837 has nine charmingly overdecorated rooms, including three in the old brick carriage house. And, no, you're not drunk – those warped porches are lopsided as hell and full of history.

Indigo Inn   BOUTIQUE HOTEL $$
(☑ 843-577-5900; www.indigoinn.com; 1 Maiden Lane; r $209-359; 🅿 ❄ 🛜 🖥) This snazzy 40-room inn enjoys a prime location in the middle of the historic district and an oasis-like private courtyard, where guests can enjoy free wine and cheese by the fountain. Decor

gives a nod to the 18th century and is a tad frilly, but the beds are comfy and recently renovated bathrooms have been modernized. Pets are $40 per night.

**Town & Country Inn
& Suites**   HOTEL **$$**
(☑ 843-571-1000; www.thetownandcountryinn.com; 2008 Savannah Hwy; r $99-299, ste $249-299; P ❋ @ ☎ ☒) About 6 miles from downtown, Town & Country offers modern and stylish rooms at a reasonable price. The inn is a good launchpad if you want to get a jump on traffic for a morning visit to the Ashley River plantations.

★ **Ansonborough Inn**   HOTEL **$$**
(☑ 800-522-2073; www.ansonboroughinn.com; 21 Hasell St; r from $169-329; P ❋ @ ☎) Droll neo-Victorian touches such as the closet-sized British pub and the formal portraits of dogs add a sense of fun to this intimate Historic District hotel, which also manages to feel like an antique sailing ship. Huge guest rooms mix old and new, with worn leather couches, high ceilings and flat-screen TVs.

★ **Restoration**   BOUTIQUE HOTEL **$$$**
(☑ 843-518-5100; www.therestorationhotel.com; 75 Wentworth St; ste from $399; P ❋ ☎ ☒) Spanish moss-draped, 200-year-old B&Bs are cool and all, but if you skew more hip and contemporary than antebellum and antique, this all-suite hipster enclave steeped in Americana arts-and-crafts kitsch is for you. Reclaimed wood-bound hallways lead to 54 rooms over a few buildings, which grow from 500 sq feet and are awash in modern indigo, some with kitchenettes and washers and dryers.

✖ Eating

Charleston is one of America's finest eating cities, and there are enough fabulous restaurants here for a town three times its size. The 'classic' Charleston establishments stick to fancy seafood with a French flair, while many of the trendy up-and-comers are reinventing Southern cuisine with a focus on the area's copious local bounty, from oysters to heirloom rice to heritage pork.

Artisan Meat Share   SANDWICHES **$**
(www.artisanmeatsharecharleston.com; 33 Spring St; sandwiches $7-12; ☺ 11am-7pm Mon-Fri, 10am-7pm Sat & Sun) Meat, man, meat. Stuffed in a biscuit. Piled high on potato bread. Or lurching across your charcuterie board – damn

that's fresh. Order at the counter, find a seat if you can, then give a nod to artisan hipsters, bless their hearts. You know the drill: fresh, local, delicious and the condiments are housemade.

Gaulart & Maliclet   FRENCH **$**
(www.fastandfrenchcharleston.com; 98 Broad St; breakfast $5-11, lunch & dinner $10-14; ☺ 8am-4pm Mon, to 10pm Tue-Thu, to 10:30pm Fri & Sat) Ooh la la. Locals crowd around the shared tables at this tiny spot, known as 'Fast & French,' to nibble on Gallic cheeses and sausages, fondues or nightly specials ($21 to $24) that include bread, soup, a main dish and wine.

Xiao Bao Biscuit   ASIAN **$$**
(www.xiaobaobiscuit.com; 224 Rutledge Ave; lunch $12, dinner mains $12-16; ☺ 11:30am-2pm, 5:30-10pm Mon-Sat) Exposed-brick walls, concrete floor and housed in a former gas station – this casual but stylish eatery hits the hipster high marks. But the food? Now we're talking. The short but palate-kicking menu spotlights simple pan-Asian fare enhanced by local ingredients and spicy flavors.

★ **Edmund's Oast**   BREWPUB **$$**
(☑ 843-727-1145; www.edmundsoast.com; 1081 Morrison Dr; mains $16-30, pints $5-10; ☺ 4:30-10pm Mon-Thu, to 11pm Fri & Sat, 10am-10pm Sun; ☎) Occupying a gutted former hardware store in gentrifying NoMo (North Morrison), Charleston's most interesting nocturnal distraction is a highbrow brewpub with a serious drinking problem. The liquid: 48 taps (eight devoted to cocktails, meads and sherries and 12 proprietary craft beers, among other craft). The grub: dead-serious in-house cured charcuterie, an outstanding fresh catch Française, beautiful Calabrian chili-laced cauliflower.

Hominy Grill   SOUTHERN US **$$**
(www.hominygrill.com; 207 Rutledge Ave; breakfast $4.50-11, lunch & dinner mains $9-22; ☺ 7:30am-9pm Mon-Fri, 9am-9pm Sat, 9am-3pm Sun; ✐) Slightly off the beaten path, this neighborhood cafe serves modern, vegetarian-friendly Lowcountry cuisine in an old barbershop. The shaded patio is tops for brunch.

Fleet Landing   SEAFOOD **$$**
(☑ 843-722-8100; www.fleetlanding.net; 186 Concord St; lunch $9-24, dinner $13-26; ☺ 11am-4pm daily, 5-10pm Sun-Thu, to 11pm Fri & Sat; ☎) Come here for the perfect Charleston lunch: a river view, a cup of she-crab soup with a splash of sherry, and a big bowl of shrimp and grits.

Housed in a former naval degaussing building on a pier, it's a convenient and scenic spot to enjoy fresh fish, a fried seafood platter or a burger after a morning of downtown exploring.

Ordinary
SEAFOOD $$$

(☑843-414-7060; www.eattheordinary.com; 544 King St; small plates $6-18, large $21-55; ☺5-10:30pm Tue-Sun) Inside a cavernous 1927 bank building, this buzzy seafood hall and oyster bar feels like the best party in town. The menu is short, but the savory dishes are prepared with finesse.

★FIG
SOUTHERN US $$$

(☑843-805-5900; www.eatatfig.com; 232 Meeting St; mains $$; ☺5:30-10:30pm Mon-Thu, to 11pm Fri & Sat; 🍴) FIG has been a long-time foodie favorite, and it's easy to see why: welcoming staff, efficient but unrushed service and top-notch, sustainably sourced nouvelle Southern fare from James Beard Award–winner Mike Lata. The six nightly changing dishes embrace what's fresh and local from the sea and local farms and mills. FIG stands for Food is Good. And the gourmets agree.

🍷 Drinking & Nightlife

★Eclectic
COFFEE

(www.eclecticcafeandvinyl.com; 132 Spring St; ☺7am-9pm Mon, Wed & Thu, 7am-11pm Fri, 9am-11pm Sat, 9am-9pm Sun; 🖥) Our favorite Charleston coffeehouse, this indigo-trimmed Cannonborough/Elliotborough newcomer is gorgeous: walls lined with vinyl records for sale with a perfect juxtaposition of hardwood flooring, exposed brick, silver gilded ceilings and a gorgeous hand-hewn wooden workstation area reclaimed from an old South Dakota horse coral. Coffee, wine, beer and upscale cafe grub.

Rooftop at the Vendue
BAR

(www.vendueinn.com; 23 Vendue Range; ☺11:30am-10pm Sun-Thu, to midnight Fri & Sat) This rooftop bar has the best views of downtown and the crowds to prove it. Enjoy crafts cocktails and live music on Sundays.

Closed for Business
PUB

(www.closed4business.com; 453 King St; ☺11am-late) A 42-tap selection of local and national craft brews and hipster-rustic decor gives this inviting 'draft emporium' a neighborhood vibe and just the right amount of edge.

🛍 Shopping

Shops of Historic Charleston Foundation
GIFTS & SOUVENIRS

(www.historiccharleston.org; 108 Meeting St; ☺9am-6pm Mon-Sat, noon-5pm Sun) This place showcases jewelry, home furnishings and furniture inspired by the city's historic homes, much of which is based on Blue Canton porcelain.

Blue Bicycle Books
BOOKS

(www.bluebicyclebooks.com; 420 King St; ☺10am-6pm Tue-Thu, 10am-7pm Fri & Sat, noon-1pm Sun) Excellent new-and-used bookshop with a great selection of Southern history and culture.

ℹ Information

Charleston Visitor Center (☑843-724-7174; www.charlestoncvb.com; 375 Meeting St; ☺8:30am-5pm Apr-Oct, to 5pm Nov-Mar) Find help with accommodations and tours or watch a half-hour video on Charleston history in this spacious renovated warehouse.

ℹ Getting There & Around

Charleston International Airport (CHS; ☑843-767-7000; www.chs-airport.com; 5500 International Blvd) is 12 miles outside town in North Charleston, with nonstop flights to 18 destinations. The **Greyhound** (☑843-744-4247; www.greyhound.com; 3610 Dorchester Rd) station and the **Amtrak** (www.amtrak.com; 4565 Gaynor Ave) train station are both in North Charleston.

CARTA (www.ridecarta.com) runs city-wide buses; one-way cash fare is $2. The free DASH streetcars do three loop routes from the visitor center. Parking is a definite issue – city parking lots charge just $2 per hour, however.

Mt Pleasant

Across the Cooper River from Charleston is the residential and vacation community of Mt Pleasant, originally a summer retreat for early Charlestonians, along with the slim barrier resort islands of Isle of Palms and Sullivan's Island. Though increasingly glutted with traffic and strip malls, the area still has some charm, especially in the historic downtown, called the Old Village.

🔴 Sights

Boone Hall Plantation
HISTORIC BUILDING

(☑843-884-4371; www.boonehallplantation.com; 1235 Long Point Rd; adult/child 6-12yr $24/12;

THE SOUTH MT PLEASANT

⊘ 8:30am-6:30pm Mon-Sat, noon-5pm Sun early Mar-Aug, shorter hours Sep-Jan) Just 11 miles from downtown Charleston on Hwy 17N, Boone Hall Plantation is famous for its magical Avenue of Oaks, planted by Thomas Boone in 1743. Boone Hall is still a working plantation, though strawberries, tomatoes and Christmas trees long ago replaced cotton as the primary crop. The main house, built in 1936, is the fourth house on the site. The most compelling buildings are the Slave St cabins, built between 1790 and 1810.

Patriot's Point Naval & Maritime Museum   MUSEUM
(☑ 866-831-1720; www.patriotspoint.org; 40 Patriots Point Rd; adult/child 6-11yr $22/14; ⊘ 9am-6:30pm) This museum is home to the USS *Yorktown,* a giant aircraft carrier used extensively in WWII. You can tour the ship's flight deck, bridge and ready rooms and get a glimpse of what life was like for its sailors. Also on-site are a submarine, naval destroyer, the Medal of Honor Museum and a re-created 'fire base' from Vietnam, which add a unique touch to merely touring a decommisioned ship. You can also jump onboard the **Fort Sumter boat tour** (☑ boat tour 843-722-2628, park 843-883-3123; www.fortsumtertours.com; 340 Concord St; adult/child 4-11yr $21/13).

GULLAH CULTURE
....

African slaves were transported from the region known as the Rice Coast (Sierra Leone, Senegal, Gambia and Angola) to a landscape of remote islands that was shockingly similar – swampy coastlines, tropical vegetation and hot, humid summers.

These new African Americans were able to retain many of their homeland traditions, even after the fall of slavery and well into the 20th century. The resulting Gullah (also known as Geechee in Georgia) culture has its own language, an English-based Creole with many African words and sentence structures, and many traditions, including fantastic storytelling, art, music and crafts. The Gullah culture is celebrated annually with the energetic **Gullah Festival** (www.theoriginalgullahfestival. org; ⊘ late May) in Beaufort.

Lowcountry

The southern half of the South Carolina coast is a tangle of islands cut off from the mainland by inlets and tidal marshes. Here, descendants of West African slaves known as the Gullah maintain small communities in the face of resort and golf-course development. The landscape ranges from tidy stretches of shimmery, oyster-gray sand to wild, moss-shrouded maritime forests.

The southernmost stretch of South Carolina's coast is popular with a mostly upscale set of golfers and B&B aficionados, but the area has quirky charms aplenty for everyone.

Charleston County Sea Islands

A dozen islands within an hour's drive from Charleston make up the Charleston County Sea Islands. Around 10 miles by road southeast of Charleston on the Mt Pleasant side, **Sullivan's Island** beckons day-trippers for fun wining and dining on blue-sky days. Four miles in the other direction brings you to **James Island**, one of the most urban of Charleston's barrier sea islands. A further 9 miles south of Charleston, **Folly Beach** is good for a day of sun and sand. The other end of the island is popular with surfers.

Upscale rental homes, golf courses and the swanky Sanctuary Resort mark **Kiawah Island**, 26 miles southwest of Charleston, where you'll find those lucky enough to stay here cruising along one of the most gorgeous beaches in the South on their bikes; while nearby **Edisto Island** (*ed*-is-tow) is a homespun family vacation spot without a single traffic light.

◉ Sights

★ **Kiawah Beachwater Park**   BEACH
(www.ccprc.com; 8 Beachwalker Dr; ⊘ 9am-8pm May-Sep, shorter hours rest of year) This idyllic stretch of sun-toasted sand at the southern end of Kiawah Island has been called one of the top 10 beaches in the USA and is the only publicly accessible beach on Kiawah. Take a bike – the compact sand is perfect for a ride along the 10-mile-long barrier island.

🛏 Sleeping & Eating

James Island County Park   CAMPGROUND $
(☑ 843-795-4386; www.ccprc.com; 871 Riverland Dr, James Island; tent sites from $31, 8-person cottages $194; 🛜) A great budget option, this 643-acre

park southwest of downtown has meadows, a marsh and a dog park. Rent bikes ($4 per hour) and kayaks ($5.50 per hour), go for a run or frolic with your pup. The park offers shuttle services to downtown and Folly Beach ($10). Reservations are highly recommended. There are 125 campsites and 10 marsh-adjacent rental cottages.

Sanctuary at Kiawah
Island Golf Resort
RESORT $$$

(☑ 843-768-2121; www.kiawahresort.com; 1 Sanctuary Beach Dr, Kiawah Island; r/ste from $560/1100, villa from $260, house from $5500 per week; ❉@🛋🐾) Ready to swank it up? Consider an idyll at the Sanctuary, sitting prettily by the sea 21 miles south of downtown Charleston. Hotel rooms glow with freshly classic decor – think soft greens, four-poster beds, Italian linens, custom-made mattresses and marble showers. Villas and houses also available. Amenities include two tennis complexes, 90 holes of golf, a spa and kids' Kamp Kiawah.

Cory's Grilled Cheese
SANDWICHES $

(www.corysgrilledcheese.com; 1739 Maybank Hwy, James Island; sandwiches $4-8.50; ⊙9am-9pm Mon-Sat, to 5pm Sun) No hipster pretension here, just your average everyday strip-mall grilled-cheese joint with holes in the wall from weekend heavy-metal concert moshing. Cory's grilled-cheese sandwiches are gooey, buttery perfection (we dig the Lowcountry with pimiento cheese, muenster, avocado and bacon on sourdough) and there's beer, too.

★ Poe's Tavern
PUB FOOD $$

(☑ 843-883-0083; www.poestavern.com; 2210 Middle St, Sullivan's Island; mains $9-13; ⊙11am-midnight) On a sunny day the front porch of Poe's on Sullivan's Island is the place to be. The tavern's namesake, master of the macabre Edgar Allan Poe, was once stationed at nearby Fort Moultrie. The burgers are superb, and the Amontillado comes with guacamole, jalapeño jack, pico de gallo and chipotle sour cream. Quoth the raven: 'Gimme more.'

❶ Information

Kiawah Island Visitor Center (☑ 800-774-0006; www.charlestoncvb.com; 22 Beachwalker Dr, Kiawah Island; ⊙9am-3pm) Maps, tourist info and help with accommodations and tours through the Charleston area.

DON'T MISS

BOWEN'S ISLAND RESTAURANT

Head down a long dirt road through Lowcountry marshland near Folly Beach to find **Bowens Island Restaurant** (www.bowensisland.biz; 1870 Bowens Island Rd, Folly Island; mains $8-18; ⊙5-9:30pm Tue-Sat), an unpainted wooden shack that's one of the South's most venerable seafood dives – grab an oyster knife and start shucking! A half/full tray runs $11/16. Cool beer and friendly locals give the place its soul.

❶ Getting There & Away

Charleston's barrier sea islands are all accessed via a series of byways and bridges from the city, though not always with a connection from one to another. You'll need to take the long way round if you want to go from Sullivan's Island to Kiawah or Edisto Islands, for example. Coming from the south, Edisto (via SC 174) and Kiawah and Johns (via SC 17) can be accessed without going through Charleston. From the North Coast, SC 17 also reaches Sullivan's and Isle of Palms without going through the city.

Beaufort & Hilton Head

On Port Royal Island, darling colonial town Beaufort (byoo-furt) is often used as a set for Hollywood films. The streets of the historic district are lined with antebellum homes and magnolias dripping with Spanish moss. The riverfront downtown has gobs of lingerworthy cafes and galleries.

South of Beaufort, some 20,000 young men and women go through boot camp each year at the **Marine Corps Recruit Depot** on Parris Island, made notorious by Stanley Kubrick's *Full Metal Jacket* (though not filmed here). The facility has been 'welcoming' recruits for 100 years. Come for Friday graduations to see newly minted marines parade proudly for family and friends. Americans must show ID (and foreign nationals a passport) before driving on to the base. East of Beaufort, the Sea Island Pkwy/Hwy 21 connects a series of marshy, rural islands, including **St Helena Island**, the heart of Gullah country and the site of a coastal state park.

Across Port Royal Sound, tony Hilton Head Island is South Carolina's largest barrier island and one of America's top golf spots. There are dozens of courses, many enclosed

FIREFLIES & SPANISH MOSS: CONGAREE NATIONAL PARK

Inky-black water, dyed with tannic acid leached from decaying plant matter. Bone-white cypress stumps like the femurs of long-dead giants. Spanish moss as dry and gray as witches' hair. There's nothing like hiking or canoeing through one of South Carolina's unearthly swamps – America's largest contiguous, old-growth floodplain forest – to make you feel like a character in a Southern Gothic novel. The 22,000-acre **Congaree National Park** (☑803-776-4396; www.nps.gov/cong; 100 National Park Rd, Hopkins; ☉visitor center 9am-5pm Tue-Sat) offers camping and a limited number of free, seasonal ranger-led canoe trips (reserve in advance).

Casual day-trippers can wander the 2.4-mile elevated boardwalk. Look carefully at the Blue Sky mural in the visitor center – the scene seems to change as you move. From mid-May through early June, the *Photinus carolinus,* a rare species of firefly, blink in unison, transforming the forest floor into a twinkling light show. The phenomenon only occurs in a handful of spots around the world. Columbia-based **River Runner Outdoor Center** (☑803-771-0353; www.shopriverrunner.com; 905 Gervais St) can get you on the water. The park is just a 30-minute drive from downtown Columbia.

in posh private residential communities (historically known as 'plantations,' now often called 'resorts'). The island was the first eco-planned destination in the US. Founder Charles Fraser believed a resort should blend with nature, so subdued colors, strict zoning laws (no building over five stories high, signage must be low and lit from below) and a distinct lack of streetlights characterize the environment here. Even so, summer traffic and miles of stoplights can stifle the ability to appreciate the beauty of the island, but there are some lush nature preserves; wide, white beaches hard enough for bike riding; and a whole lot of dolphins.

◉ Sights

Parris Island Museum MUSEUM
(www.parrisislandmuseum.com; 111 Panama St; ☉10am-4:30pm Mon-Wed, Sat & Sun, 8am-4:30pm Thu-Fri) FREE This fascinating museum covering marine-corps history has antique uniforms and weaponry, but is most engaging for its exhibits chronicling the grueling, intense and scary (that CS gas-chamber exercise!) 13-week marine basic training, which takes place here and at a second facility in San Diego, California.

Penn Center MUSEUM
(☑843-838-2474; www.penncenter.com/museum; 16 Penn Center Circle W, St Helena Island; adult/child 6-16yr $7/3; ☉9am-4pm Tue-Sat) Once the home of one of the nation's first schools for freed slaves, the Penn Center has a small museum that covers Gullah culture and traces the history of Penn School.

Hunting Island State Park STATE PARK
(☑843-838-2011; www.southcarolinaparks.com/huntingisland; 2555 Sea Island Pkwy; adult/child 6-15yr $5/3; ☉visitor center 9am-5pm Mon-Fri, 11am-5pm Sat & Sun, nature center 9am-5pm Tue-Sat, daily Jun-Aug) Lush and inviting Hunting Island State Park impresses visitors with acres of spooky maritime forest, tidal lagoons and empty, bone-white beach. The Vietnam War scenes from *Forrest Gump* were filmed in the marsh, a nature-lover's dream. **Campgrounds** (☑reservations 866-345-7275; www.southcarolinaparks.com; tent sites $18.50-20, RV sites $18-45, cabin $249; ☉6am-6pm, to 9pm early Mar–early Nov) fill quickly in summer. Climb the **lighthouse** ($2) for sweeping coastal views.

🛏 Sleeping & Eating

City Loft Hotel HOTEL **$$**
(☑843-379-5638; www.citylofthotel.com; 301 Carteret St; r/ste $169/209; [P][⊛][☀]) The chic City Loft Hotel adds a refreshing dash of modern style to a town heavy on historic homes and stately oak trees. Enjoy flat-screen TV in the bedroom and bathroom, artisan-tile showers and Memory Foam–topped beds. Other perks include a gym, complimentary bicycle use and an on-site coffee shop ($5 voucher included in rates).

★ **Cuthbert House Inn** B&B **$$$**
(☑843-521-1315; www.cuthberthouseinn.com; 1203 Bay St; r $179-245; [P][⊛][☀]) The most romantic of Beaufort's B&Bs, this sumptuously grand white-columned mansion is straight out of *Gone with the Wind.* Antique furnishings are found throughout, but mon-

ochromatic walls add a fresh, modern feel. Some rooms have a river view (three have fireplaces). On his march through the South in 1865, General William T Sherman slept at the house.

★ **Lowcountry Produce** SOUTHERN US $
(www.lowcountryproduce.com; 302 Carteret St; breakfast $9-15, sandwiches $10-18; ⊙8am-3pm; 🛜) A fantastic cafe and market for picnic rations such as pies, housemade relishes, local cheeses – all kinds of Lowcountry-spun awesomeness (except for the cream-cheese lasagne – that ain't right!). Or eat in and indulge in an Ooooy Gooey, a grilled pimiento-cheese sandwich with bacon and garlic-pepper jelly (one hot mess!) or a tasty crab-cake sandwich with brussels-sprouts slaw.

ℹ Information

Beaufort Tourist Info Center (📞843-525-8500; www.beaufortsc.org; 713 Craven St; ⊙9am-5pm Mon-Sat) Inside the Beaufort History Museum.

North Coast

Stretching from the North Carolina border south to the city of Georgetown, the coastal region known as the Grand Strand bustles with some 60 miles of fast-food joints, beach resorts and three-story souvenir shops. What was once a laid-back summer destination for working-class people from across the Southeast has become some of the most overdeveloped real estate in the country. Whether you're ensconced in a behemoth resort or sleeping in a tent at a state park, all you need to enjoy your stay is a pair of flip-flops, a margarita and some quarters for the pinball machine.

Myrtle Beach

The towering Sky Wheel spins fantastically beside the coast in downtown Myrtle Beach, anchoring a 60-mile swath of sun-bleached excess. Love it or hate it, Myrtle Beach means summer vacation, American-style. Bikers take advantage of the lack of helmet laws to let their graying ponytails fly in the wind, bikini-clad teenagers play video games and eat hot dogs in smoky arcades, and whole families roast like chickens on the white sand.

North Myrtle Beach, actually a separate town, is slightly lower-key, with a thriving culture based on the 'shag' (no, not that kind of shag) – a jitterbug-like dance invented here in the 1940s. It isn't for nature-lovers, but with enormous outlet malls and innumerable minigolf courses, water parks, daiquiri bars and T-shirt shops, it's a rowdy good time and certainly a hit with the kids.

◉ Sights & Activities

SkyWheel AMUSEMENT PARK
(www.myrtlebeachskywheel.com; 1110 N Ocean Blvd; adult/child 3-11yr $14/9; ⊙11am-midnight) The 187ft-high SkyWheel overlooks the 1.2-mile coastal boardwalk. One ticket includes three revolutions in an enclosed gondola. At night the wheel is bewitching, with more than a million dazzling colored lights.

Brookgreen Gardens GARDENS
(www.brookgreen.org; 1931 Brookgreen Garden Dr, Murrells Inlet; adult/child 4-12yr $16/8; ⊙9:30am-5pm) These magical gardens, 16 miles south of town on Hwy 17S, are home to the largest collection of American sculpture in the country, set amid more than 9000 acres of rice-plantation-turned-subtropical-garden paradise.

🛏 Sleeping & Eating

Myrtle Beach State Park CAMPGROUND $
(📞843-238-5325; www.myrtlebeachsp.com; 4401 S Kings Hwy; rustic tent $18-36 Easter–Labor Day only, tent & RV sites $21-50, cabins $65-205; 🅿🛜🏊) Sleep beneath the pines or rent a cabin, all just steps from the shore. The park is 3 miles south of central Myrtle Beach and includes a nice beach, an epic fishing pier and swathes of protected maritime forest.

Hampton Inn Broadway at the Beach HOTEL $$$
(📞843-916-0600; www.hamptoninn3.hilton.com; 1140 Celebrity Circle; r/ste from $249/389; ❄@🛜🏊) The bright renovated rooms overlooking the lake and Broadway at the Beach are a great choice at this hotel, which feels less hectic than properties along Ocean Blvd. If you're traveling with preteens, you may feel more comfortable letting them roam the adjacent shops and attractions rather than the boardwalk.

Prosser's BBQ SOUTHERN US $$
(www.prossersbbq.com; 3750 Business Hwy 17, Murrells Inlet; buffet breakfast $7, lunch $10-11, dinner $13-15; ⊙6:30-10:30am Mon-Sat, 11am-2pm Mon-Sat, 11am-2:30pm Sun, 4-8pm Tue-Sat; 🍴) It's weird to come to Murrells Inlet's 'restaurant row' and not spring for seafood, but who are

THE SOUTH NORTH COAST

we to judge? The gut-busting lunch buffet here is down-home delicious. It includes fried fish and chicken, sweet-potato souffle, mac 'n' cheese, green beans and vinegary pulled pork.

★ **Wicked Tuna**　　　　　SEAFOOD $$$
(☑ 843-651-9997;　　　www.thewickedtuna.com; 4123 Hwy 17 Bus, Murrells Inlet;　mains $14-42; ⊙ 11am-midnight; 🛜) Murrells Inlet is full of kitschy seafooders and, at first glance, the Wicked Tuna looks no different. Guess again! You are in for a real treat at this trip-worthy spot overlooking the beautiful inlet – it employs six fishing boats that go out for three- to six-day stints and bring back up to 600lb of fresh fish each.

Boats roll right up to the kitchen door, completing the hook-to-table concept. The menu is long on tantalizing dishes and sushi. Go for the fresh catch, sit out on the waterfront patio and send us thank-you notes in the mail!

 Drinking & Entertainment

American Tap House　　　　　CRAFT BEER
(www.broadwayatthebeach.com/listing/american-tap-house; 1320 Celebrity Circle; pints $5.50-9; 🛜) At Broadway at the Beach, if you prefer your craft-beer experience to come supersized, you'll find 53 taps of national options at this chef-driven gastropub.

★ **Fat Harold's
Beach Club**　　　　　DANCE
(www.fatharolds.com; 212 Main St; ⊙ from 4pm Sun-Thu, from 11am Fri & Sat) Folks groove to doo-wop and old-time rock and roll at this North Myrtle institution, which calls itself 'Home of the Shag.' The dance, that is. Free shag lessons are offered at 7pm every Tuesday.

ⓘ **Information**

Myrtle Beach Visitor Information (☑ 843-626-7444; www.visitmyrtlebeach.com; 1200 N Oak St; ⊙ 8:30am-5pm) has maps and brochures.

ⓘ **Getting There & Around**

The traffic coming and going on Hwy 17 Business/Kings Hwy can be infuriating. To avoid 'the Strand' altogether, stay on the Hwy 17 bypass, or take Hwy 31/Carolina Bays Pkwy, which parallels Hwy 17 between Hwy 501 and Hwy 9.

Myrtle Beach International Airport (MYR; ☑ 843-448-1589; www.flymyrtlebeach.com; 1100 Jetport Rd) is located within the city

limits, as is the **Greyhound** (☑ 843-448-2472; www.greyhound.com; 511 7th Ave N) station, with the former receiving direct flights from over 30 domestic destinations.

Greenville & the Upcountry

Cherokee Indians once roamed the state's mountain foothills, which they called the 'Great Blue Hills of God.' The region today is known as the Upcountry. Geographically it's the spot where the Blue Ridge mountains drop dramatically to meet the Piedmont.

The region is anchored by Greenville, home to one of the most photogenic downtowns in the South. The Reedy River twists through the city center, and its dramatic falls tumble beneath Main St at Falls Park (www.fallspark.com).

Two miles from downtown, the village of West Greenville is seeing a revival thanks to an influx of art galleries, restaurants, boutiques and other new development.

⊙ **Sights & Activities**

Table Rock State Park　　　STATE PARK
(☑ 864-878-9813;　　　www.southcarolinaparks.com; 158 Ellison Lane, Pickens; adult/child 6-15yr $5/3 Jun-Nov, adult/child under 16yr $2/free Dec-May; ⊙ 7am-7pm Sun-Thu, to 9pm Fri & Sat, extended hours mid-May–early Nov) The Upcountry's marquee natural attraction is Table Rock Mountain, a 3124ft-high mountain with a striking granite face. The 7.2-mile round-trip hike to its summit is a popular local challenge. For overnight stays, **camping** (☑ 864-878-9813; www.southcarolinaparks.com; campsites $16-25, cabins $52-181; ❄) is available for tents and RVs, plus there are cabins built by the Civilian Conservation Corps.

**BMW Performance
Center**　　　　　MOTOR SPORTS
(☑ 864-968-3000;　　www.bmwperformancecenter. com; 1155 Hwy 101 S, Greer; 1-/2-day school from $849/1699) Your need for speed can be quenched at America's only BMW performance-driving　academy.　Delve into　fast　and　furious　behind-the-wheel experiences over　the　course　of　one- and two-day classes with various vehicles, including the high-performance M series, or stunt-driving school in a Mini – *The Italian Job* will have nothing on you.

🛏 Sleeping

⭐ **Swamp Rabbit Inn**   B&B **$$**

(☑864-517-4617; www.swamprabbitinn.com; 1
Logan St; r with/without bath $155/105; P✱⊛❄)
This fun six-room inn occupies a '50s-era
former boarding house downtown and feels
like a hostel but features colorfully decked-
out private rooms that are as cozy and
quirky as any in the South. Wonderful com-
mon spaces include a modern guest kitchen
and wooden patio with barbecue.

Westin Poinsett   HOTEL **$$$**

(☑864-421-9700; www.westinpoinsettgreenville.
com; 120 S Main St; r $189-309; P✱@❄❄)
This grand hotel, which originally opened
in 1925, is in the heart of downtown, just
steps from Reedy River Falls. Past guests include Amelia Earhart, Cornelius Vanderbilt
and Bobby Kennedy. There's new carpeting,
scones and wall vinyl throughout the hotel,
while rooms tilt toward the basic (bathrooms are set for a remodel soon).

🍴 Eating & Drinking

Stax Omega Diner   DINER **$**

(www.staxs.net; 72 Orchard Park Dr; breakfast
$4-14, lunch & dinner $9-15; ⊙6:30am-9pm; ❄)
Nobody quite does breakfast excess like the
USA and this bustling family-owned diner 4
miles east of downtown is everything fantastic about that very fact. It's massive – capacity 500! – and they do it all really well: omelets, pancakes, French toast, eggs Benedict,
scrambles – the list goes on and on...and on.

Soby's   SOUTHERN **$$**

(www.sobys.com; 207 S Main St; mains $18-31;
⊙5:30-9pm Mon-Thu, 5:30-10pm Fri, 5-10pm Sat,
10:30am-1:30pm & 5-9pm Sun; ❄) Book yourself
one of the intimate, brick-walled banquettes
at this downtown Greenville bastion of New
Southern cuisine that also caters to wine lov-
ers (the 5000-bottle list has been awarded
a *Wine Spectator* Award of Excellence 19
years running). The oft-changing menu is
steeped in the wares of local farmers, forag-
ers and ranchers.

Dark Corner Distillery   DISTILLERY

(www.darkcornerdistillery.com; 241 N Main St;
⊙11am-7pm Mon-Sat) Sample butterscotch
whiskey or wildberry moonshine here. The
Dark Corner is the nickname given to the
secretive upland corner of Greenville Coun-
ty, which was famed for its bootlegging and
hardscrabble Scots-Irish residents.

❶ Getting There & Away

**Greenville–Spartanburg International
Airport** (☑864-877-7426; www.gspairport.
com; 2000 GSP Dr, Greer) is 13 miles east of
the city, nearly halfway between Greenville and
Spartanburg. **Greyhound** (☑864-235-4741;
www.greyhound.com; 9 Hendrix Dr) is also
out that way, 7 miles southeast of downtown.
Amtrak (www.amtrak.com; 1120 W Washington
St) is much more amicably located on just west
of downtown.

TENNESSEE

Most states have one official state song. Ten-
nessee has seven. And there's a reason for
that – Tennessee has music deep within its
soul. Here, the folk music of the Scots-Irish
in the eastern mountains combined with the
bluesy rhythms of the African Americans in
the western Delta to give birth to the modern
country music that makes Nashville famous.

The state's three geographic regions, East,
Middle and West Tennessee, are represent-
ed by the three stars on the Tennessee flag.
Each has its own unique beauty: the heath-
er-colored peaks of the Great Smoky Moun-
tains; the lush green valleys of the central
plateau around Nashville; and the hot, sul-
try lowlands near Memphis.

In Tennessee you can hike shady moun-
tain trails in the morning, and by evening
whoop it up in a Nashville honky-tonk or
walk the streets of Memphis with Elvis'
ghost.

❶ Information

Department of Environment & Conservation
(www.state.tn.us/environment/parks) Check
out the well-organized website for camping,
hiking and fishing info for Tennessee's more
than 50 state parks.
Department of Tourist Development (☑615-
741-2159; www.tnvacation.com) Has welcome
centers at the state borders.

Memphis

Memphis doesn't just attract tourists. It
draws pilgrims. Music-lovers lose them-
selves to the throb of blues guitar on Beale
St. Barbecue connoisseurs descend to stuff
themselves silly on smoky pulled pork and
dry-rubbed ribs. Elvis fanatics fly in to wor-
ship at the altar of the King at Graceland.
You could spend days hopping from one
museum or historic site to another, stopping
only for barbecue, and leave happy.

Greater Memphis

THE SOUTH MEMPHIS

Greater Memphis

Memphis has a certain baroque, ruined quality that's both sad and beguiling. Though poverty is rampant – Victorian mansions sit beside tumbledown shotgun shacks (a narrow style of house popular in the South) and college campuses lie in the shadow of eerie abandoned factories – whiffs of a renaissance are in the air. Neighborhoods once downtrodden, abandoned and/or otherwise reclaimed by kudzu – South Main, Binghampton, Crosstown and others – are being reinvented with kitschy boutiques, hipster lofts and daring restaurants, all dripping with Memphis' wild river-town spirit.

⊙ Sights

⊙ Downtown

The pedestrian-only stretch of Beale St is a 24-hour carnival zone, where you'll find deep-fried funnel cakes, to-go beer counters, and music, music, music. Although locals don't hang out here much, visitors tend to get a kick out of it.

★ **National Civil Rights Museum**   MUSEUM

(Map p366; www.civilrightsmuseum.org; 450 Mulberry St; adult/student & senior/child $15/14/12; ⊙9am-5pm Mon & Wed-Sat, 1-5pm Sun) Housed across the street from the Lorraine Motel, where the Martin Luther King Jr was fatally shot on April 4, 1968, is the gut-wrenching National Civil Rights Museum. Five blocks south of Beale St, this museum's extensive exhibits and detailed timeline chronicle the struggle for African American freedom and equality. Both Dr King's cultural contribution and his assassination serve as prisms for looking at the Civil Rights movement, its precursors and its continuing impact on American life.

The turquoise exterior of the 1950s motel and two interior rooms remain much as they were at the time of King's death.

Memphis Rock 'n' Soul Museum   MUSEUM

(Map p366; www.memphisrocknsoul.org; 191 Beale St; adult/child $12/9; ⊙10am-7pm) The Smithsonian's museum, next to FedEx Forum, examines how African American and white music mingled in the Mississippi Delta to create the modern rock and soul sound.

WC Handy House Museum   MUSEUM

(Map p366; www.wchandymemphis.org; 352 Beale St; adult/child $6/4; ⊙11am-4pm Tue-Sat winter, 10am-5pm summer) On the corner of 4th St,

this shotgun shack once belonged to the composer called the 'father of the blues.' He was the first to transpose the 12 bars and later wrote 'Beale Street Blues' in 1916.

⊙ North of Downtown

Mud Island   PARK

(www.mudisland.com; 125 N Front St; ⊙10am-5pm Tue-Sun mid-Apr–Oct; 👤) FREE A small peninsula jutting into the Mississippi, Mud Island is downtown Memphis' best-loved green space. Hop on the tram (www.mudisland.com; 125 N Front St; $4; ⊙10am-5pm), which is free with Mississippi River Museum admission, or walk across the bridge to the park, where you can jog and rent bikes.

Slave Haven Underground Railroad Museum/Burkle Estate   MUSEUM

(Map p364; www.slavehavenundergroundrailroadmuseum.org; 826 N 2nd St; adult/child $10/8; ⊙10am-4pm Mon-Sat, to 5pm Jun-Aug) This unimposing clapboard house is thought to have been a way station for runaway slaves on the Underground Railroad, complete with trapdoors, cellar entry and cubby-holes.

⊙ East of Downtown

★ **Sun Studio**   HISTORIC SITE

(Map p364; ☏800-441-6249; www.sunstudio.com; 706 Union Ave; adult/child $12/free; ⊙10am-6:15pm) This dusty storefront is ground zero for American rock and roll music. Starting in the early 1950s, Sun's Sam Phillips recorded blues artists such as Howlin' Wolf, BB King and Ike Turner, followed by the rockabilly dynasty of Jerry Lee Lewis, Johnny Cash, Roy Orbison and, of course, the King himself (who started here in 1953).

Packed 45-minute guided tours (no children under five allowed; hourly from 10:30am to 5:30pm) through the tiny studio offer a chance to hear original tapes of historic recording sessions. Guides are full of anecdotes; you can pose for photos on the 'X' where Elvis once stood, or buy a CD of the 'Million Dollar Quartet,' Sun's spontaneous 1956 jam session between Elvis, Johnny Cash, Carl Perkins and Jerry Lee Lewis. For music fans, the story here will have you welling up. From here, hop on the studio's free shuttle (hourly, starting at 11:15am), which does a loop between Sun Studio, Beale St and Graceland.

Memphis

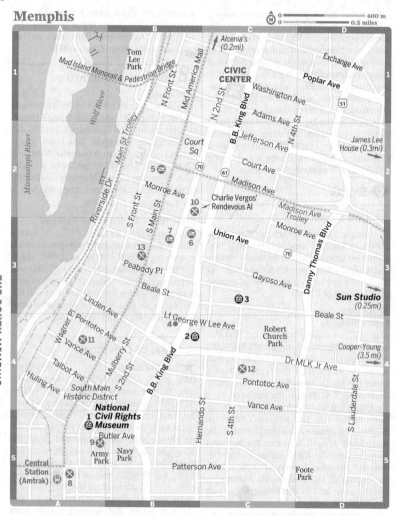

Children's Museum of Memphis   MUSEUM
(Map p364; www.cmom.com; 2525 Central Ave; $15; ⊙9am-5pm, to 6pm summer; 🖐) Gives the kids a chance to let loose and play in, on and with exhibits such as an airplane cockpit or tornado generator.

◉ South of Downtown

★**Graceland**   HISTORIC BUILDING
(Map p364; ✆901-332-3322; www.graceland.com; Elvis Presley Blvd/US 51; house only adult/child 7-12yr $38.75/17, with airplanes $43.75/22, with Elvis Presley's Memphis $57.50/27, expanded tours from $62.50/32; ⊙9am-5pm Mon-Sat, to 4pm Sun, shorter hours & closed Tue Dec; 🅿) If you only make one stop in Memphis, it should be here: the sublimely kitschy, gloriously bizarre home of the King of Rock and Roll. Though born in Mississippi, Elvis Presley was a true son of Memphis, raised in the Lauderdale Courts public housing projects, inspired by blues clubs on Beale St, and discovered at Sun Studio. In the spring of 1957, the already-famous 22-year-old spent $100,000 on a Colonial-style mansion, named Graceland by its previous owners.

The King himself had the place, ahem, redecorated in 1974. With a 15ft couch, fake waterfall, yellow vinyl walls and green shag-carpet ceiling, it's a virtual textbook of ostentatious '70s style. You'll begin your tour at the brand-spanking new $45 million entertainment complex and visitor center, **Elvis Presley's Memphis** (Map p364; ✆901-332-3322, 800-238-2000; www.graceland.com; 3765 Elvis Presley Blvd; adult/child 7-12 $28.75/$25.90; ⊙9am-5pm Mon-Sat, to 4pm Sun, shorter hours & closed Tue Dec), on the other side of Elvis Presley Blvd, which now houses Presley's car museum and additional exhibits that run an extra $18.75 for adults. Tack on $5 extra to access two custom planes (check out the blue and gold private bathroom on the *Lisa Marie*, a Convair 880 Jet). Book ahead in the busy season (June to August and important Elvis dates) to ensure a prompt tour time. The basic self-guided mansion tour comes with an engaging multimedia iPad narration by John Stamos.

Priscilla Presley (who divorced Elvis in 1973) opened Graceland to tours in 1982, and now millions come here to pay homage to the King, who died here (in the upstairs bathroom) from heart failure in 1977.

Throngs of fans still weep at his grave, next to the swimming pool out back. Graceland is 9 miles south of downtown on US 51, also called 'Elvis Presley Blvd.' A free shuttle runs from Sun Studio (p365). Parking costs $10.

★**Stax Museum of
American Soul Music**   MUSEUM
(Map p364; ✆901-942-7685; www.staxmuseum.com; 926 E McLemore Ave; adult/child $13/10; ⊙10am-5pm Tue-Sat, 1-5pm Sun) Wanna get funky? Head directly to Soulsville USA, where this 17,000-sq-ft museum sits on the site of the old Stax recording studio. This venerable spot was soul music's epicenter in the 1960s, when Otis Redding, Booker T and the MGs, and Wilson Pickett recorded here.

Dive into soul-music history with photos, displays of '60s and '70s stage clothing and, above all, Isaac Hayes' 1972 Superfly Cadillac outfitted with shag-fur and 24-karat-gold exterior trim.

Full Gospel Tabernacle Church   CHURCH
(787 Hale Rd; ⊙services 11am) On Sunday, put on your 'smell goods' and head to services in South Memphis, where soul music legend turned reverend Al Green presides over a powerful choir. Visitors are welcome; it's a fascinating cultural experience.

✪ Festivals & Events

Peabody Ducks   PARADE
(Map p366; www.peabodymemphis.com; 149 Union Ave; ⊙11am & 5pm; 🖐) FREE A tradition dating from the 1930s begins every day at 11am sharp when five ducks file from the Peabody Hotel's gilded elevator, waddle across the red-carpeted lobby, and decamp in the marble lobby fountain for a day of happy splashing. The ducks make the reverse march at 5pm, when they retire to their penthouse accompanied by their red-coated Duckmaster.

Elvis Week   CULTURAL
(✆901-332-3322, 800-238-2000; www.elvisweek.com; Elvis Presley Blvd, Graceland) The King's passing and his life are celebrated across Memphis during Elvis Week in mid-August, when tens of thousands of shiny-eyed pilgrims descend for nine days of festivities. *This* is Weird America. Attend a *Viva Las Vegas* or *Aloha From Hawaii* screening and dance party, an International Elvis Tribute Artist competition, and run an Elvis 5K – sideburns not included.

Beale Street Music Festival
MUSIC

(www.memphisinmay.org; Tom Lee Park; 3-day passes $95; ⊙ 1st weekend in May) You've heard of Coachella, New Orleans Jazz Fest and Bonnaroo, but Memphis' Beale Street Music Festival gets very little attention, considering it offers one of the country's best line-ups of old-school blues masters, up-and-coming rockers and gloriously past-their-prime pop and hip-hop artists.

⬆ Tours

Gibson Beale Street Showcase
TOURS

(Map p366; www.gibson.com/Gibson/Gibson-Tours.aspx; 145 Lt George W Lee Ave; $10; ⊙ hourly tours 11am-4pm Mon-Sat, noon-4pm Sun) Take the fascinating 45-minute tours, which vary throughout the day according to worker presence and noise level, of this enormous place to see master craftspeople transform solid blocks of wood into Les Pauls. Children under five are not allowed in.

Blues City Tours
BUS

(☑ 901-522-9229; www.bluescitytours.com; adult/child from $26/21) A variety of themed bus tours, including an Elvis tour, a Memphis music tour and a hop-on, hop-off option.

🛏 Sleeping

🛏 Downtown

Talbot Heirs
GUESTHOUSE $$

(Map p366; ☑ 901-527-9772; www.talbothouse.com; 99 S 2nd St; ste $160-200; ❄@🖝) Inconspicuously located on the 2nd floor of a busy downtown street, this cheerful guesthouse is one of Memphis' best kept, unique secrets. Spacious suites, all with recently modernized bathrooms, are more like hip studio apartments than hotel rooms, with Asian rugs, funky local artwork and kitchens stocked with (included!) snacks.

Peabody Hotel
HOTEL $$

(Map p366; ☑ 901-529-4000; www.peabody memphis.com; 149 Union Ave; r from $229-365; ❄🖝🏊🐾) Memphis' most storied hotel has been catering to a Who's Who of Southern gentry since the 1860s. The current incarnation, a 13-story Italian Renaissance Revival–style building, dates from the 1920s and remains a social center, with a spa, shops, restaurants, an atmospheric lobby bar and 464 guestrooms in soothing turquoise tones.

Madison Hotel
BOUTIQUE HOTEL $$$

(Map p366; ☑ 901-333-1200; www.madison hotelmemphis.com; 79 Madison Ave; r from $279; P❄@🖝🏊🐾) If you're looking for a sleek treat, check into these swanky, music-themed boutique sleeps. The rooftop Sky Terrace ($10 for non-guests) is one of the best places in town to watch a sunset, and stylish rooms have nice touches like hardwood entryways, high ceilings and Italian linens.

★ James Lee House
B&B $$$

(Map p364; ☑ 901-359-6750; www.jameslee house.com; 690 Adams Ave; r $250-450; P❄@🖝) This exquisite Victorian mansion sat abandoned for 56 years in the city's historic Victorian Village on the edge of downtown; after $2 million and the application of the owner's keen eye for detail and design, it's one of Memphis' most refined sleeps.

🛏 South of Downtown

Graceland RV Park & Campground
CAMPGROUND $

(Map p364; ☑ 901-396-7125; www.graceland.com/lodging/graceland_campground; 3691 Elvis Presley Blvd; tent sites/cabins from $25/47; P🖝🐾) Keep Lisa Marie in business when you camp out or sleep in the no-frills log cabins (with shared bathrooms) next to Graceland.

Days Inn Graceland
MOTEL $

(Map p364; ☑ 901-346-5500; www.daysinn.com; 3839 Elvis Presley Blvd; r from $105; P❄🖝🐾) With a guitar-shaped pool, gold records and Elvis memorabilia in the lobby, and neon Cadillacs on the roof, the Days Inn provides a whole lotta Elvis for the price. Guest rooms themselves are clean but nothing special.

Guest House at Graceland
BOUTIQUE HOTEL $$

(Map p364; ☑ 800-238-2000, 901-443-3000; www.guesthousegraceland.com; 3600 Elvis Presley Blvd; r/ste from $159/249; P@🖝🐾🏊) Intimate by name only, the Guest House, Graceland's new flagship, is a 450-room hunk of burning hotel. Stylish, slate-gray standard rooms are spacious, with Dreamcatcher beds, three-sided display clocks, work station desks and 55in flat-screen TVs. Suites, whose designs were coordinated by Priscilla Presley, all evoke themes from Elvis' life (one features a red-draped TV on the ceiling above the bed!).

✕ Eating

Locals come to blows over which of the city's chopped-pork sandwiches or dry-rubbed ribs are the best. Barbecue joints are scattered across the city; the ugliest exteriors often yield the tastiest goods. Hip young locals head to the South Main Arts District, Midtown's Cooper-Young or Overton Square neighborhoods, all fashionable dining enclaves.

✕ Downtown

★ Central BBQ   BARBECUE $
(Map p366; www.cbqmemphis.com; 147 E Butler Ave; plates $10-25, sandwiches from $5; ⊙11am-9pm Sun-Thu, to 10pm Fri & Sat) The downtown location of this iconic Memphis barbecue joint is the perfect side dish to an afternoon at the National Civil Rights Museum. The transcendent pulled pork – almost always voted the city's best – can and should be doused in a number of sauces so good you'll want to drink them by the pint.

Gus's World Famous Fried Chicken   FAST FOOD $
(Map p366; www.gusfriedchicken.com; 310 S Front St; plates $6.40-11.65; ⊙11am-9pm Sun-Thu, to 10pm Fri & Sat) Fried-chicken connoisseurs across the globe twitch in their sleep at night, dreaming about the gossamer-light fried chicken at this downtown concrete bunker, with a fun, neon-lit interior and vintage jukebox. On busy nights, waits can top an hour.

LUNCHBOXeats   SOUTHERN US $
(Map p366; www.lunchboxeats.com; 288 S 4th St; sandwiches $8-13; ⊙10:30am-3pm Mon-Sat; 🛜) Classic soul food gets a seriously tasty makeover at this creative sandwich shop, resulting in such ridiculousness as chicken and waffle sandwiches (Belgian waffles serve as the slices of 'bread'); crawfish étouffée sloppy Joe's; a pork butt, onion and mac 'n' cheese club sandwich and more, served on traditional school lunch trays.

Alcenia's   SOUTHERN US $
(Map p364; www.alcenias.com; 317 N Main St; mains $9.55-13; ⊙9am-5pm Tue-Fri, to 3pm Sat) The only thing sweeter than Alcenia's famous 'Ghetto-Aid' (a diabetes-inducing fruit drink) is owner Betty-Joyce 'BJ' Chester-Tamayo – don't be surprised to receive a kiss on the top of the head as soon as you sit down.

Arcade   DINER $
(Map p366; www.arcaderestaurant.com; 540 S Main St; mains $7-10; ⊙7am-3pm Sun-Wed, to 11pm Thu-Sat) Step inside this ultra-retro diner, Memphis' oldest, and wander to the Elvis booth, strategically located near the rear exit. The King used to sit here and eat griddle-fried peanut butter and banana sandwiches and would bolt out the door if fan-instigated pandemonium ensued. Crowds still pack in for sublime sweet-potato pancakes – as fluffy, buttery and addictive as advertised.

Charlie Vergos' Rendezvous   BARBECUE $$
(Map p366; ☑901-523-2746; www.hogsfly.com; 52 S 2nd St; mains $8-20; ⊙4:30-10:30pm Tue-Thu, 11am-11pm Fri, from 11:30am Sat) Tucked in its own namesake alleyway off Monroe Ave, this subterranean institution sells an astonishing 5 tons of its exquisite dry-rubbed ribs weekly. The ribs don't come with any sauce, but the pork shoulder does, so try a combo and you'll have plenty of sauce to enjoy.

Majestic Grille   EUROPEAN $$$
(Map p366; ☑901-522-8555; www.majesticgrille.com; 145 S Main St; lunch $9-32, dinner $10-23; ⊙11am-late Mon-Fri, 11am-2:30pm & 4pm-late Sat & Sun; 🛜) Set in an old silent-movie theater near Beale St, with pre-talkie black and whites strobing in the handsome dark-wood

dining room, Majestic serves classic continental fare, from roasted half chickens to seared tuna and grilled pork tenderloin, and four varieties of hand-cut filet mignon.

Midtown

Imagine Vegan Cafe
VEGAN $
(Map p364; www.imaginevegancafe.com; 2158 Young Ave; mains $6-14; ⊙11am-9pm; 🎅🖋) 🍴 Vegans and veggies face an uphill battle in Memphis (hell, all over the South...), but this inventive Cooper-Young cafe swims alone in a sea of pulled pork and fried chicken, pulling off all the iconic Southern staples that you'd normally give a pass without even changing their name.

Bar DKDC
INTERNATIONAL $
(Map p364; www.bardkdc.com; 964 S Cooper St; dishes $6-12; ⊙5pm-3am) Cheap and flavorful and – at times global – street food is the calling at this ever-evolving Cooper-Young staple. The menu includes muffalatas, Vietnamese *bánh mì* sandwiches, Thai chicken dumplings and so on.

Soul Fish Cafe
SEAFOOD $
(Map p364; www.soulfishcafe.com; 862 S Cooper St; mains $9.50-16; ⊙11am-10pm Mon-Sat, to 9pm Sun) A cute cinderblock cafe in the Cooper-Young neighborhood, known for delectable po'boys, fried fish plates and some rather indulgent cakes.

Alchemy
TAPAS $$
(Map p364; ☑901-726-4444; www.alchemymemphis.com; 940 S Cooper St; tapas $9-18, mains $17-24; ⊙4pm-1am Mon, to 11pm Tue-Thu, 4:30pm-1:30am Fri & Sat, 10:30am-3pm & 4-10pm Sun) A flash spot in the Cooper-Young district, serving tasty Southern tapas like truffle deviled eggs with blue crab remoulade and caviar, shrimp and grits with smoked Gouda and chorizo pan gravy, and scallop bruschetta with gremolata and ponzu vinaigrette.

Sweet Grass
SOUTHERN US $$$
(Map p364; ☑901-278-0278; www.sweetgrassmemphis.com; 937 S Cooper St; mains $19-34; ⊙5pm-late Tue-Sat, 11am-2pm & 5pm-late Sun; 🎅) Contemporary Lowcountry cuisine (the seafood-heavy cooking of the South Carolina and Georgia coasts) wins raves at this casual Midtown restaurant, split between a more rambunctious bar side called **Next Door** and a more refined bistro side with a more sophisticated menu, a new raw bar and some unforgettable shrimp and grits.

East of Downtown

★ Payne's Bar-B-Q
BARBECUE $
(Map p364; 1762 Lamar Ave; sandwiches $5-9, plates $7.50-11; ⊙11am-5pm Tue-Sat) We'd say this converted gas station has the best chopped-pork sandwich in town, but we don't want to have to fight anyone.

Cozy Corner
BARBECUE $
(Map p364; www.cozycornerbbq.com; 735 N Pkwy; plates $6.75-14; ⊙11am-9pm Tue-Sat) Slouch in a torn vinyl booth and devour an entire barbecued Cornish game hen ($11.75), the house specialty at this recently renovated cult favorite. Ribs and wings are spectacular too, and the fluffy, silken sweet-potato pie is an A-plus specimen of the classic Southern dessert.

Brother Juniper's
BREAKFAST $
(Map p364; www.brotherjunipers.com; 9514 Walker Ave; dishes $4-13; ⊙6:30am-1pm Tue-Fri, 7am-12:30pm Sat, 8am-1pm Sun) This humble breakfast spot started as a chain out of San Francisco's Haight-Ashbury district to feed the homeless; today the Memphis location is the last man standing, and it's pretty much unanimously voted the best breakfast in town. Think huge portions of omelets, pancakes, breakfast burritos, waffles, biscuits and home fries. A must.

Hog & Hominy
SOUTHERN, ITALIAN $$
(☑901-207-7396; www.hogandhominy.com; 707 W Brookhaven Circle; pizza $12-16; ⊙11am-2pm & 5-10pm Tue-Thu, to late Fri & Sat, 10:30am-10pm Sun; 🎅) The chef-driven, Southern-rooted Italian at this Brookhaven Circle hot spot has grabbed the nation's attention, winning best-new-this and best-new-that since it opened in 2011 from publications ranging from *GQ* to *Food & Wine*. Small plates and brick-oven pizza are the mainstays, along with seasonal cocktails and craft beers.

★ Restaurant Iris
SOUTHERN US $$$
(Map p364; ☑901-590-2828; www.restaurantiris.com; 2146 Monroe Ave; mains $27-39; ⊙5-10pm Mon-Sat) Chef Kelly English crafts special, avant-garde Southern fusion dishes that delight foodies, hence the James Beard noms. He's got a fried-oyster-stuffed steak, a sublime shrimp and grits and some scrumptious brussels sprouts dressed up with smoky Benton's bacon and sherry, all served in a refined residential home. Next door he has opened **Second Line**, a more affordable New Orleans bistro.

Drinking & Entertainment

Beale St is party central but caters nearly 100% to tourists. The East Memphis neighborhoods of Cooper-Young and Overton Square are where locals go, and offer the best concentration of hip bars and restaurants. Both are about 4 miles east of downtown. Last call is 3am. The city's first distillery, **Old Dominick**, opened in 2017.

Hammer & Ale BEER HALL
(Map p364; www.hammerandale.com; 921 S Cooper St; pints from $5; ⊙2-9pm Tue-Thu, 11am-10pm Fri & Sat, 1-6pm Sun; 🐾) Hopheads descend on this barnlike Cooper-Young craft-beer bar decked out in light cypress woods throughout. Memphis breweries Wiseacre, High Cotton, Memphis Made and Ghost River are represented among the 24 taps of mostly Southern microbrews. Cash *not* accepted!

★**Loflin Yard** BEER GARDEN, COCKTAIL BAR
(Map p364; www.loflinyard.com; 7 W Carolina Ave; cocktails $9-12, mains $9-12; ⊙4-10pm Wed-Thu, 11:30am-midnight Fri, noon-midnight Sat, to 9pm Sun; 🐾) A massive, countrified adult-play oasis in downtown Memphis, this buzzy new hot spot sits on nearly an acre of junkyard-aesthetic beer garden anchored by the old Loflin Safe & Lock Co and wrapping around the trickling canal remains of Gayoso Bayou. Besides the space itself, the seasonal and oak-barrel-aged cocktails steal the show, though mostly smoked offerings (chicken wings, brisket) compete.

★**Wiseacre Brewing Co** MICROBREWERY
(Map p364; www.wiseacrebrew.com; 2783 Broad Ave; pints $5-6; ⊙4-10pm Mon-Thu, 1-10pm Fri & Sat; 🐾) Our favorite Memphis taproom is in the warehouse district of Binghampton, 5 miles east of downtown. Sample year-round and seasonal craft brews on its outside deck, which features a wrap-around porch hugging two enormous, near 100-year-old concrete wheat silos.

Young Avenue Deli LIVE MUSIC
(Map p364; www.youngavenuedeli.com; 2119 Young Ave; ⊙11am-3am; 🐾) This Midtown favorite has food, pool and occasional live music that caters to a laid-back young crowd hyped up on 36 taps of draft craft and another 130 cans and bottles.

★**Wild Bill's** BLUES
(Map p364; 1580 Vollintine Ave; ⊙5-9pm Thu, 10pm-3am Fri & Sat) Don't even think of showing up at this gritty, hole-in-the-wall juke joint before midnight. Order a 40oz beer and a basket of wings then sit back to watch some of the greatest blues acts in Memphis from 11pm Friday and Saturday only. Expect some stares from the locals; it's worth it for the kick-ass, ultra-authentic jams.

ⓘ Information

Memphis Visitor Center (Map p364; ☑888-633-9099; www.memphistravel.com; 3205 Elvis Presley Blvd; ⊙9am-5pm) City information center near exit for Graceland.

Tennessee State Visitor Center (Map p364; ☑901-543-6757; www.tnvacation.com; 119 N Riverside Dr; ⊙7am-11pm) Brochures for the whole state. Near Mud Island.

ⓘ Getting There & Around

Memphis International Airport (MEM; Map p364; ☑901-922-8000; www.flymemphis.com; 2491 Winchester Rd) is around 10.5 miles southeast of Beale St via I-55; taxis to downtown cost between $25 and $30. **Memphis Area Transit Authority** (MATA; Map p364; www.matatransit.com; 444 N Main St; fares $1.75) operates local buses; buses 2 and 4 go to the airport.

MATA's vintage trolleys ($1, every 12 minutes) normally ply Main St and Front St downtown, but were out of service for maintenance at time of research with an expected return by the end of 2017. The **Greyhound Station** (Map p364; ☑901-395-8770; www.greyhound.com; 3033 Airways Blvd) is located at the MATA's Airways Transit Center near Memphis International Airport. The **Amtrak** (www.amtrak.com; 545 S Main St) Central Station is right downtown.

Nashville

Imagine you're an aspiring country singer arriving in Nashville after days of hitchhiking, with nothing but your battered guitar on your back. Blinded by the neon lights of Lower Broadway, you take a deep breath of smoky, beer-perfumed air, feel the boot-stompin' rumble from deep inside the crowded honky-tonks, and think: 'I've made it.'

For country-music fans and wannabe songwriters all over the world, a trip to Nashville is the ultimate pilgrimage. Since the 1920s the city has been attracting musicians, who have taken the country genre from the 'hillbilly music' of the early 20th century to the slick 'Nashville sound' of the 1960s to the punk-tinged alt-country of the 1990s.

THE SOUTH NASHVILLE

Nashville

Jackson St

Herman St

10th Ave N

Harrison St

7th Ave N

6th Ave N

5th Ave N

8

Bicentennial Mall

James Robertson Pkwy

41

12

Megabus

Music City Central

7 Metropolitan Transit Authority

Charlotte Ave

Legislative Plaza

Deaderick St

Union St

70

10

6th Ave N

7th Ave N

Gay St

Jo Johnson Ave

40

16th Ave N

Charlotte Ave

15th Ave N

12th Ave N

11th Ave N

10th Ave N

8th Ave N

Patterson St

State St

Church St

16th Ave N

18

Broadway

14

2

9th McGavock

Music City Hostel (0.1mi)

17th Ave N

Hayes St

MIDTOWN

Demonbreun St

10th Ave S

18th Ave N

11

West End Ave

Broadway

McGavock

Demonbreun St

12th Ave S

11th Ave S

25 13

16

19th Ave S

20

Grilled Cheeserie (1mi); Pancake Pantry (1mi); Parthenon (1.3mi)

Division St

Division St

Pine St

29

22

Gleaves St

THE GULCH

17

18th Ave S

Music Square W

Music Circle N

Music Circle S

3

MUSIC ROW

5

Hawkins St

12th Ave S

Chet Atkins Pl

South St

Hawkins St

Old Glory (0.4mi)

Nashville's many musical attractions
range from the Country Music Hall of Fame
to the revered Grand Ole Opry to Jack
White's niche record label. It also has a
lively university community, some excellent
down-home grub and some seriously kitschy
souvenirs.

◎ Sights

Nashville sits on a rise beside the Cumberland River, with the state capitol situated at
the highest point. The city's most engaging
museums are downtown, but you'll find

THE SOUTH NASHVILLE

cultural attractions aplenty in and around the universities. Further afield, plantations, battlefields and forts draw Civil War enthusiasts and history fans. The city teems with inviting parks. Several are connected by paved greenways. South of downtown, the zoo and science center are nice distractions for the kids.

Downtown

Head to SoBro for the Country Music Hall of Fame and the Johnny Cash Museum. Honky-tonks flank Lower Broadway while Ryman Auditorium and art galleries beckon just north along 5th Ave. North of Broadway you'll also find the main library, Bicentennial Capitol Mall and the Nashville Farmers Market. Two blocks west of 2nd Ave N, Printer's Alley dazzles at night with its colorful lights and fun bars. Riverfront Park hugs the west bank of the Cumberland River. It's connected to Cumberland Park on the other side by the John Seigenthaler Pedestrian Bridge.

★ **Country Music Hall of Fame & Museum**　　MUSEUM
(www.countrymusichalloffame.com; 222 5th Ave S; adult/child $25/15, with audio tour $30/20, with Studio B 1hr tour $40/30; ⊘9am-5pm) Fresh off $100 million expansion (in 2014) and its 50th anniversary (in 2017), this monumental museum, reflecting the near-biblical importance of country music to Nashville's soul, is a must-see, whether you're a country music fan or not. Gaze at Carl Perkins' blue suede shoes, Elvis' gold Cadillac (actually white) and gold piano (actually gold), and Hank Williams' Western-cut suit with musical note appliqués.

Ryman Auditorium　　HISTORIC BUILDING
(www.ryman.com; 116 5th Ave N; self-guided tour adult/child $20/15, backstage tour $30/25; ⊘9am-4pm) The so-called 'Mother Church of Country Music' has hosted a laundry list of performers, from Martha Graham to Elvis, and Katherine Hepburn to Bob Dylan. The soaring brick tabernacle (1892) was built by wealthy riverboat captain Thomas Ryman to house religious revivals, and watching a show from one of its 2362 seats can still be described as a spiritual experience.

Johnny Cash Museum & Store　　MUSEUM
(www.johnnycashmuseum.com; 119 3rd Ave S; adult/child $19/15; ⊘9am-7pm) Nashville's museum dedicated to 'The Man in Black'

is smallish but houses the most comprehensive collection of Johnny Cash artifacts and memorabilia in the world, officially endorsed by the Cash family. By the time you read this, a new Patsy Cline museum will be up and running on the 2nd floor.

Frist Center for the Visual Arts　　GALLERY
(www.fristcenter.org; 919 Broadway; adult/senior/child $12/9/free; ⊘10am-5:30pm Mon-Wed & Sat, to 9pm Thu & Fri, 1-5:30pm Sun; P⊕) A top-notch post-office-turned-art-museum and complex, hosting exhibitions of everything from American folk art to Picasso.

Tennessee State Capitol　　HISTORIC BUILDING
(www.capitol.tn.gov; Charlotte Ave; ⊘tours 8am-4pm Mon-Fri) FREE This 1845–59 Greek Revival building was built from local limestone and marble by slaves and prison inmates working alongside European artisans. Around the back, steep stairs lead down to the **Tennessee Bicentennial Mall**, whose outdoor walls are covered with historical facts about Tennessee's history, and the wonderful daily **Farmers Market**.

Free tours leave from the Information Desk on the 1st floor of the Capitol every hour on the hour between 9am and 3pm.

Midtown

Midtown is anchored by universities and parks. Centennial Park, home to the Parthenon, and Belmont Mansion are top picks. Music Row is here too, although there's not much to see unless you join a Country Music Hall of Fame tour.

Parthenon　　HISTORIC BUILDING
(www.nashville.gov/Parks-and-Recreation/Parthenon; Centennial Park; adult/child 4-17yr/senior $6/4/4; ⊘9am-4:30pm Tue-Sat, 12:30-4:30pm Sun) Built in 1897 to celebrate the state of Tennessee's centenary, Nashville's Parthenon is a full-scale replica of the original, with a jaw-droppingly huge statue of the goddess Athena as its centerpiece. Other exhibits include casts of the pediments' sculptures and galleries displaying paintings by 19th- and 20th-century American artists.

Music Row　　AREA
(Music Sq West & Music Sq East) Just west of downtown, sections of 16th and 17th Aves, called Music Sq West and Music Sq East, are home to the production companies, record labels, agents, managers and promoters who run Nashville's country-music industry.

Historic RCA Studio B
LANDMARK

(www.studiob.org; 1611 Roy Acuff Pl; tours adult/child $40/30) One of Music Row's most historic studios, this is where Elvis, the Everly Brothers and Dolly Parton all recorded numerous hits, the latter doing a little more than that, once arriving late to a session and accidentally running her car into the building – a scar still visible today! You can tour Historic RCA Studio B by purchasing a Platinum Package from the Country Music Hall of Fame & Museum, which includes a ticket to the museum as well.

Music Valley

Grand Ole Opry House
MUSEUM

(615-871-6779; www.opry.com; 2804 Opryland Dr; tours adult/child $26/21, with Ryman Auditorium $36/35; tours 9am-4pm) This unassuming modern brick building seats 4400 for the Grand Ole Opry (p378) on Tuesday, Friday and Saturday from March to November and Wednesday from June to August. Guided backstage tours are offered every 15 minutes daily from October to February; true die-hards can opt for the $125 post-show backstage tour.

Willie Nelson & Friends Museum Showcase
MUSEUM

(www.willienelsongeneralstore.com; 2613 McGavock Pike; adult/child $8/free; 8:30am-9pm) 'Outlaw Country' star Willie Nelson sold all his worldly goods to pay off a $16.7-million tax debt in the early 1990s. You can see them at this quirky museum not far from the Grand Ole Opry.

Tours

NashTrash
BUS

(615-226-7300; www.nashtrash.com; 900 Rosa L Parks Blvd; tours $33-36) The big-haired 'Jugg Sisters' lead a campy frolic through the risqué side of Nashville history, while guests sip BYO booze on the big pink bus. Buy in advance: tours can sell out *months* in advance. Meet the bus at the southeast end of the Nashville Farmers Market.

Joyride
TOURS

(615-285-9835; www.joyrideus.com/nashville; complimentary shuttle but tips accepted, tours from $45) Tricked-out golf carts offer complimentary point-to-point shuttle service across Nashville. Rides are free, but drivers make their money on tips. Also offers sightseeing tours, brewery tours and a bar golf crawl.

Tommy's Tours
BUS

(615-335-2863; www.tommystours.com; tours $35) Wisecracking local Tommy Garmon leads highly entertaining three-hour tours of country-music sights.

Festivals & Events

CMA Music Festival
MUSIC

(www.cmafest.com; Jun) This four-day country-music extravaganza draws tens of thousands of country-music fans to town.

Tennessee State Fair
FAIR

(www.tnstatefair.org; Sep) Nine days of racing pigs, mule-pulls and cake bake-offs.

Sleeping

Downtown

Nashville Downtown Hostel
HOSTEL $

(615-497-1208; www.nashvillehostel.com; 177 1st Ave N; dm $32-45, r $100-165; P) Well located and up-to-the-minute in style and function. The common space in the basement, with its rather regal exposed stone walls and beamed rafters, is your all-hours mingle den. Dorm rooms are on the 3rd and 4th floors, and have lovely wood floors, exposed timber columns, silver-beamed ceilings and four, six or eight bunks to a room.

21c Museum Hotel
BOUTIQUE HOTEL $$

(615-610-6400; www.21cMuseumHotels.com; 221 2nd Ave N; r from $299; P※♠) Nashville's newest boutique hotel comes loaded down with contemporary art as the South's hippest hotel/museum hybrid chain has settled into a rehabilitated historic Gray & Dudley Building near Printer's Alley. In addition to 124 of its trademark modern, art-forward rooms – seven of which are rooftop terrace suites with Cumberland River views – there's a dedicated spa and six galleries.

Union Station Hotel
HOTEL $$$

(615-726-1001; www.unionstationhotelnashville.com; 1001 Broadway; r from $300; P※♠) This soaring Romanesque gray stone castle was Nashville's train station back in the days when rail travel was a grand affair; today it's downtown's most iconic hotel. The vaulted lobby is dressed in peach and gold with inlaid marble floors and a stained-glass ceiling.

Thompson Nashville
BOUTIQUE HOTEL $$$

(615-262-6000; www.thompsonhotels.com; 401 11th Ave S; r from $349; P@♠) A bastion of finely polished, mid-century modern cool, the new Thompson Nashville is the Gulch's see-and-be-seen seat of style, whether that be agonizing over which of the Third Man Records–curated vinyl collection to spin in the lobby, or where to sit at the immensely hip, open-air rooftop bar, **LA Jackson**.

Hermitage Hotel HOTEL $$$
(☑ 888-888-9414, 615-244-3121; www.thehermit agehotel.com; 231 6th Ave N; r from $300; P❄🐾🛜) Nashville's first million-dollar hotel was a hit with the socialites when it opened in 1910. The beaux-arts lobby feels like a czar's palace, every surface covered in rich tapestries and ornate carvings. The original art-deco men's room, dating from the 1930s, is worth a pop-in, as is the **Capital Grille** restaurant, which sources from its own farm.

🛏 Midtown

Music City Hostel HOSTEL $
(☑ 615-497-1208; www.musiccityhostel.com; 1809 Patterson St; dm $33-46, d $110-126, tr $128-156; P❄@🛜) These squat brick bungalows are less than scenic, but Nashville's West End hostel is lively and welcoming, with a common kitchen, an outdoor grill and a fire pit. The crowd is young, international and fun, and many hoppin' West End bars are within walking distance.

Hutton Hotel BOUTIQUE HOTEL $$
(☑ 615-340-9333; www.huttonhotel.com; 1808 West End Ave; r from $279; P🔄❄@🛜) 🍴 One of our favorite Nashville boutique hotels riffs on mid-century modern design with bamboo-paneled walls and reclaimed WWI barn wood flooring. Sizable rust- and chocolate-colored rooms are well appointed with electrically controlled marble rain showers, glass wash basins, king beds, ample desk space, wide flat-screens and high-end carpet and linens.

🛏 Music Valley

Gaylord Opryland Resort RESORT $$
(☑ 615-889-1000; www.marriott.com/hotels/travel/bnago-gaylord-opryland-resort-and-convention-center; 2800 Opryland Dr; r from $189; P❄@🛜🐾) This whopping 2888-room hotel is a universe unto itself, the largest non-casino resort in the USA. Why set foot outdoors when you can ride a flatboat along an artificial river, eat sushi beneath faux waterfalls in an indoor garden, or sip scotch whisky in an antebellum-style mansion, all *inside* the hotel's three massive glass atriums?

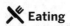

✖ Eating

✖ Downtown

Arnold's SOUTHERN US $
(www.arnoldscountrykitchen.com; 605 8th Ave S; meat & 3 $9.74; ⏱10:30am-2:45pm Mon-Fri) Grab a tray and line up with college students, garbage collectors and country-music stars at Arnold's, king of the meat-and-three. Slabs of drippy roast beef are the house specialty, along with fried green tomatoes, cornbread two ways, and big gooey wedges of chocolate meringue pie.

★Biscuit Love BREAKFAST $
(www.biscuitlove.com; 316 11th Ave S; biscuits $8-10; ⏱7am-3pm; 🛜) Championing everything that is wrong about American breakfast, Biscuit Love started life as a food truck in 2012. Its gluttonous gourmet takes on the Southern biscuit and gravy experience took off, allowing it to graduate to this supremely cool brick-and-mortar location in the Gulch.

Chauhan Ale & Masala House INDIAN $$
(☑ 615-242-8426; www.chauhannashville.com; 123 12 Ave N; mains $12-29; ⏱11am-2pm & 5pm-10pm Sun-Thu, to 11pm Fri-Sat,; 🛜) Namaste and Nashville collide at celebrity chef Punjabi Maneet Chauhan's Gulch eatery that showcases inventive Indian fusion on a global scale. Typical Desi fare meets Mexican, Canadian, British and American Southern influences – dishes like black-eyed pea tikka burger (spectacular), chicken pakora po'boys and tandoori chicken poutine pair gorgeously with Indian spice-infused microbrews and creative cocktails.

★Etch MODERN AMERICAN $$$
(☑ 615-522-0685; www.etchrestaurant.com; 303 Demonbreun St; mains $23-39; ⏱11am-2pm & 5-10pm Mon-Thu, 11am-2pm & 5-10:30pm Fri, 5-10:30pm Sat; 🛜) Well-known Nashville chef Deb Paquette's Etch serves some of Nashville's most inventive cuisine – comfort food whose flavors and textures have been manipulated into tantalizing combinations that surpass expectations at every bite.

✖ Midtown

Pancake Pantry BREAKFAST $
(www.thepancakepantry.com; 1796 21st Ave S; mains $7-10; ⏱6am-3pm Mon-Fri, to 4pm Sat & Sun) For 50-plus years, crowds have been

lining up around the block for tall stacks of pancakes done up every which way at this iconic breakfast joint. Honestly, the pancakes underwhelmed us – until we doused them in that cinnamon cream syrup. Paradise found!

Grilled Cheeserie
AMERICAN $

(www.grilledcheeserie.com; 2003 Belcourt Ave; sandwiches $7.50-8; ☺11am-9pm; 🛜) Hurry up and wait for gussied up, gourmet versions of an American classic: the grilled cheese sandwich. It's done up here in versions so immensely satisfying, you'll forget a simpler version ever existed. Go for pimiento mac 'n' cheese and dip it in the creamy tomato soup, a match made in foodie heaven. Follow with one of the outrageous gourmet milkshakes.

★Hattie B's
SOUTHERN US $

(www.hattieb.com; 112 19th Ave S; quarter/half plates from $8.50/12; ☺Mon-Thu 11am-10pm, to midnight Fri & Sat, to 4pm Sun) Hattie's may be the hipsterized, social-media savvy yin to Prince's Hot Chicken's off-the-grid yang, but if this isn't Nashville's best cayenne-rubbed 'hot' fried chicken, our name is mud. Perfectly moist, high-quality bird comes devilishly fried to levels that top out at 'Shut the Cluck Up!' hot, and it means business (nose-runnin', head-itchin' 'Damn Hot' was our limit). Get in line.

★Catbird Seat
INTERNATIONAL $$$

(☎615-810-8200; www.thecatbirdseatrestaurant. com; 1711 Division St, above Patterson House; dinner $115; ☺from 5:30pm Wed-Sat) For the 22 lucky diners perched around his open kitchen, chef Ryan Poli choreographs an unforgettable 10-course dining experience with his impeccably polished cast and crew. Be prepared to interact with Poli and his sous chefs as they create, cook and share an invigorating line-up of distinctly flavored dishes, which embrace the fresh and local while taking a spin around the world.

✖ East Nashville

I Dream of Weenie
HOT DOGS $

(www.facebook.com/IDreamofWeenie; 113 S 11th St; hot dogs $2.75-4.50; ☺11am-4pm Mon-Thu, to 5pm Fri, 10:30am-5pm Sat & Sun) Quick and easy, this VW bus turned hot-dog stand in Five Points slings beef, turkey or vegetarian tubular products drowned in indulgent toppings (hint: pimiento cheese with chili!).

WORTH A TRIP

FRANKLIN

The town of Franklin (www.visitfranklin. com), 17 miles south of Nashville, has a charming downtown filled with boutiques, antique stores and lively eateries. Here one of the Civil War's bloodiest battles was fought. On November 30, 1864, during the Battle of Franklin, some 37,000 men (20,000 Confederates and 17,000 Union soldiers) fought over a 2-mile stretch on Franklin's outskirts. Nashville's sprawl has turned much of that battlefield into suburbs, but several historic sites spotlight this turbulent conflict.

The rural community of **Arrington**, home to a popular vineyard, is 10 miles southeast of downtown.

★The Pharmacy
BURGERS, BEER GARDEN $

(www.thepharmacynashville.com; 731 McFerrin Ave; burgers $8.50-11; ☺11am-10pm Sun-Thu, to 11pm Fri & Sat; 🛜) Prepare to go to war for a table, be it at the welcoming communal table, the bar or the spectacular backyard beer garden. Tattooed staff at this burger bar – constantly voted Nashville's best – sling burgers, sausages and old-school sides (tater tots!), all washed back with specialty beers and old-fashioned hand-mixed sodas.

🍸 Drinking & Nightlife

★Barista Parlor
COFFEE

(www.baristaparlor.com; 610 Magazine St; coffee $4.50-7; ☺7am-8pm Mon-Fri, from 8am Sat-Sun; 🛜) Nashville's best artisan coffeehouse has enlisted an old stereo shop in the Gulch for its downtown location, but the exquisite espresso – courtesy of an $18,000 hand-built Slayer coffee machine – is every bit as memorable as its original East Nashville location.

★Old Glory
COCKTAIL BAR

(www.facebook.com/oldglorynashville; 1200 Villa Pl; cocktails $12-13; ☺4pm-1am Sun-Thu, to 2am Fri & Sat) A towering smokestack rises altar-like in a corner of this steampunk speakeasy. Tucked off an alley inside Edgehill Village, the space was a laundromat boiler room in the 1930s. Today the exposed brick, industrial piping, lofty ceiling and a floating staircase are the backdrop for the city's most stunning cocktail bar – if you can find it!

DON'T MISS

BONNAROO MUSIC FESTIVAL

Bonnaroo (www.bonnaroo.com; Manchester, TN; ⏰ mid-Jun) is one of America's premier music festivals and the only large-scale 24/7 event in the country. Set on a 700-acre farm, 60 miles southeast of Nashville, Bonnaroo combines camping, comedy, cinema, food, beverage and arts components, which lends it a communal feel. But it's the music that rules, spread out over four blissfully raging days.

Urban Cowboy Public House   COCKTAIL BAR
(www.urbancowboybnb.com/public-house; 103 N 16th St; cocktails $13; ⏰ 4-11pm Sun-Thu, to midnight Fri & Sat; 🛜) Set behind Nashville's hottest B&B (also bearing the Urban Cowboy name), this 2016 newcomer is hotter than the 16ft tall double-sided outdoor fireplace and adjacent firepit, which serve as the centerpiece of an open-air patio that seduces East Nashville's bold and beautiful. The inside lounge, separated by double garage doors, is a stunner as well, rich in hardwoods and Southwestern-themed, Pendleton-blanketed banquettes.

Pinewood Social   BAR
(☎ 615-751-8111; http://pinewoodsocial.com; 33 Peabody St; ⏰ 7am-1am Mon-Fri, 9am-1am Sat & Sun; 🛜) You could spend a weekend at Pinewood Social and never run low on things to do. There are couches to hang at and play board games, a large circular bar with finely crafted cocktails, and a coffee bar from Crema, a Nashville favorite. Soak up the SoCal vibe lounging poolside or playing bocce or ping pong on the outdoor patio. Oh, and there's a bowling alley, too.

Acme Feed & Seed   BAR
(www.theacmenashville.com; 101 Broadway; ⏰ 11am-11pm Mon-Thu, to 2am Fri & Sat, 10am-11pm Sun; 🛜) This ambitious, four-floor takeover of an old 1875 farm supply warehouse has finally given Nashvillians a reason to go downtown even when family is *not* visiting. The 1st floor is devoted to lightning-fast pub grub, with 27 beer taps and live music that's defiantly un-country most nights (Southern rock, indie, roots etc).

⭐ Entertainment

Nashville's opportunities for hearing live music are unparalleled. As well as the big venues, many talented country, folk, bluegrass, Southern-rock and blues performers play smoky honky-tonks, college bars, coffee shops and organic cafes for tips. Cover charges are rare. The singer-songwriter is just as respected as the stadium superstar, so look for well-attended songwriter nights at smaller venues.

⭐ Station Inn   LIVE MUSIC
(☎ 615-255-3307; www.stationinn.com; 402 12th Ave S; ⏰ open mike 7pm, live bands 9pm) Sit at one of the small cocktail tables, squeezed together on the worn wood floor in this beer-only dive, illuminated with stage lights and neon signs, and behold the lightning fingers of bluegrass savants. We are talking stand-up bass, banjo, mandolin, fiddle and a modicum of yodeling.

Bluebird Cafe   LIVE MUSIC
(☎ 615-383-1461; www.bluebirdcafe.com; 4104 Hillsboro Rd; cover free-$30) It's in a strip mall in suburban South Nashville, but don't let that fool you: some of the best original singer-songwriters in country music have graced this tiny stage. Steve Earle, Emmylou Harris and the Cowboy Junkies have all played the Bluebird, which is the setting for the popular CMT television series, *Nashville*. Try your luck at Monday open mic nights.

Grand Ole Opry   LIVE MUSIC
(☎ 615-871-6779; www.opry.com; 2804 Opryland Dr; tickets $38-95) Though you'll find a variety of country shows throughout the week, the performance to see is the *Grand Ole Opry,* a lavish tribute to classic Nashville country music, every Tuesday, Friday and Saturday night from February to October. Shows return to the Ryman from November to January.

Tootsie's Orchid Lounge   HONKY-TONK
(☎ 615-726-7937; www.tootsies.net; 422 Broadway; ⏰ 10am-2:30am) The most venerated of the downtown honky-tonks, with music on three levels at any given moment, Tootsie's is a blessed dive oozing boot-stomping, hillbilly, beer-soaked grace. In the 1960s club owner and den mother 'Tootsie' Bess nurtured Willie Nelson, Kris Kristofferson and Waylon Jennings when they were on the rise.

Nashville Symphony   CLASSICAL MUSIC
(☎ 615-687-6400; www.nashvillesymphony.org; 1 Symphony Pl) Hosts maestros, the local symphony and major pop stars from Randy Travis to Smokey Robinson in the shiny new,

yet beautifully antiquated, Schermerhorn Symphony Hall.

Robert's Western World   HONKY-TONK
(www.robertswesternworld.com; 416 Broadway; ⊙11am-2am Mon-Sat, noon-2am Sun) Buy a pair of boots, a beer or a burger at Robert's, a longtime favorite on the strip. Music starts at opening and goes all night; Brazilbilly, the house band, rocks it after 10pm on weekends. All ages are welcome before 6pm; afterward it's strictly 21 and up.

🛍 Shopping

★**Hatch Show Print**   ART, SOUVENIRS
(www.hatchshowprint.com; 224 5th Ave S; tours $18; ⊙9:30am-6pm) One of the oldest letterpress print shops in the US, Hatch has been using old-school, hand-cut blocks to print its bright, iconic posters since vaudeville. The company has produced graphic ads and posters for almost every country star and has now graduated to newly expanded digs inside the revamped Country Music Hall of Fame.

★**Third Man Records**   MUSIC
(www.thirdmanrecords.com; 623 7th Ave S; ⊙10am-5pm) In a still-industrial slice of downtown you'll find Jack White's boutique record label, shop and novelty lounge, complete with its own lathe and live venue. They sell mostly Third Man recordings on vinyl and CD, collectible T-shirts, stickers, headphones, and Pro-Ject record players. You'll also find White's entire catalog of recordings; and you can record yourself on vinyl ($20).

Two Old Hippies   CLOTHING, LIVE MUSIC
(www.twooldhippies.com; 401 12th Ave S; ⊙10am-7pm Mon-Thu, to 8pm Fri-Sat, 11am-5pm Sun) Only in Nashville would an upscale retro-inspired clothing shop have a bandstand with regular live shows of high quality. And, yes, just like the threads, countrified hippie rock is the rule. The shop itself has fitted T-shirts, excellent belts, made-in-Tennessee jewelry, candles and rocker wear, and also a bounty of stage-worthy shirts and jackets and some incredible acoustic guitars.

Gruhn Guitars   MUSIC
(www.guitars.com; 2120 8th Ave S; ⊙10am-6pm Mon-Sat) This renowned vintage instrument store has expert staff, and at any minute some unassuming virtuoso may just walk in, grab a guitar, mandolin or banjo off the wall and jam.

ℹ Information

Metro Nashville's parks and community centers have free wi-fi, as do many hotels, restaurants and coffee shops.

Nashville Visitors Information Center (☑615-259-4747; www.visitmusiccity.com; 501 Broadway, Bridgestone Arena; ⊙8am-5:30pm Mon-Sat, 10am-5pm Sun) Pick up free city maps here at the glass tower.

Nashville Visitors Information Center (www.visitmusiccity.com; 150 4th Ave N; ⊙8am-5pm Mon-Fri) Run out of their corporate offices in the Regions Bank Building lobby.

INTERNET RESOURCES

Nashville Public Radio (www.nashvillepublicradio.org) News, music and NPR programming on 90.3 WPLN FM.

Nashville Scene (www.nashvillescene.com) Free alternative weekly with entertainment listings.

Tennessean (www.tennessean.com) Nashville's daily newspaper.

ℹ Getting There & Away

Nashville is located in middle Tennessee at the junction of three interstates: I-40, I-65 and I-24.
Nashville International Airport (BNA; ☑615-275-1675; www.flynashville.com; One Terminal Dr), 9 miles east of downtown, offers direct flights from 28 US cities along with Mexico and the Bahamas. **Greyhound** (☑615-255-3556; www.greyhound.com; 709 5th Ave S) and **Megabus** (www.megabus.com; 5th Ave N, btwn Gay St & Charlotte Ave) are both located downtown and offer interstate bus services.

Flights, cars and tours can be booked online at www.lonelyplanet.com/bookings.

ℹ Getting Around

TO/FROM THE AIRPORT

It takes about 35 to 45 minutes to get downtown on **MTA** (MTA; www.nashvillemta.org; 400 Charlotte Ave; fares $1.70-2.25) bus 18 ($1.70), which runs from the airport. Express 18 takes about 20 minutes. The airport bus stop is on level 1 in the Ground Transportation area.

The official airport shuttle service is Jarmon Transportation (www.jarmontransportation.com). The rate to downtown or West End hotels is $20 and $25, respectively. It can be found on the Ground Transportation/level 1. A list of alternative shuttle companies is provided on the airport website.

Taxis charge a flat rate of $25 for a ride to downtown or Opryland. A taxi to Vanderbilt/West End costs about $27. A trip to Franklin runs $55 to $60.

BUS

The MTA (www.nashvillemta.org) operates city bus services, based downtown at **Music City Central** (400 Charlotte Ave), including the free Music City Circuit, whose three routes hit the majority of Nashville attractions. Express buses go to Music Valley.

BICYCLE

Nashville's public bike-share scheme, Nashville B-Cycle (https://nashville.bcycle.com), offers more than 30 stations throughout the city center. Your first hour is free; after that your credit card will be charged $1.50 per half-hour. Daily, weekly and monthly plans are also available. Maps can be found at the Airport Information Center in baggage claim or online.

Eastern Tennessee

Dolly Parton, East Tennessee's most famous native, loves her home region so much she has made a successful career out of singing about girls who leave the honeysuckle-scented embrace of the Smoky Mountains for the false glitter of the city. They're always sorry. Largely a rural region of small towns, rolling hills and river valleys, the eastern third of the state has friendly folks, hearty country food and pastoral charm. The lush, heather-tinted Great Smoky Mountains are great for hiking, camping and rafting, while the region's two main urban areas, Knoxville and Chattanooga, are easygoing riverside cities with lively student populations, great restaurants and fun craft breweries.

Chattanooga

Today Chattanooga is one of the country's greenest cities, with miles of well-used waterfront trails, electric buses and pedestrian bridges crossing the Tennessee River – all of which makes it hard to credit its reputation in the 1960s as the dirtiest city in America. With world-class rock-climbing, hiking, biking and water-sports opportunities, it's one of the South's best cities for outdoorsy types. And it's gorgeous now, too: just check out those views from the Bluff View Art District!

The city was a major railway hub throughout the 19th and 20th centuries, hence the 'Chattanooga Choo-Choo,' which was originally a reference to the Cincinnati Southern Railroad's passenger service from Cincinnati to Chattanooga and later the title of a 1941 Glen Miller tune. The eminently walkable downtown is an increasingly gentrified maze of historic stone and brick buildings and some tasty gourmet kitchens and craft breweries and distilleries. There's a lot to love about the 'Noog.

◎ Sights & Activities

Songbirds　　　　　　　　　　MUSEUM
(www.songbirdsguitars.com; 35 Station St, Chattanooga Choo Choo Hotel; adult/student $15.95/12.95, all access $38.95/35.95; ⊙10am-6pm Mon-Wed, to 8pm Thu-Sat, noon-6pm Sun) Opened in 2017, this astonishing guitar collection – the world's largest assemblage of vintage and rare guitars – is Chattanooga's newest world-class attraction. Over 500 guitars, many arranged in timeline fashion from the 1950 Fender Broadcasters (the first mass-produced solid-body electric guitar) to the 1970s, grace this small space, including rock star axes from Chuck Berry, BB King, Bo Diddly, Roy Orbison and Robbie Krieger of the Doors, among others.

Hunter Museum of American Art　　GALLERY
(www.huntermuseum.org; 10 Bluff View; adult/child $10/free; ⊙10am-5pm Mon, Tue, Fri & Sat, to 8pm Thu, noon-5pm Wed & Sun) Set high on the river bluffs, this striking edifice of melted steel and glass is easily the most singular architectural achievement in Tennessee. Oh, and its 19th- and 20th-century art collection is fantastic. Permanent exhibits are free the first Thursday of the month between 4pm and 8pm (special exhibits cost $5).

Coolidge Park　　　　　　　　　PARK
(150 River St) A good place to start a riverfront stroll. There's a carousel, well-used playing fields and a 50ft climbing wall attached to one of the columns supporting the Walnut Street Bridge, the world's largest pedestrian bridge.

Lookout Mountain　　　　　　OUTDOORS
(☏800-825-8366; www.lookoutmountain.com; 827 East Brow Rd; adult/child $50/27; ⊙hours vary; ▮) Some of Chattanooga's oldest and best-loved attractions are 6 miles outside the city. Admission price includes the **Incline Railway**, which chugs up a steep incline to the top of the mountain; the world's longest underground waterfall, **Ruby Falls**; and **Rock City**, a garden with a dramatic clifftop overlook.

🛏 Sleeping & Eating

★Crash Pad　　　　　　　　HOSTEL $
(☏423-648-8393; www.crashpadchattanooga.com; 29 Johnson St; dm/d/tr $35/85/110; 🅿❄@🖥) 🍴 The South's best hostel, run

by climbers, is a sustainable den of coolness in Southside, the 'Noog's hippest downtown neighborhood. Co-ed dorms overachieve: built-in lights, power outlets, fans and privacy curtains for each bed. Privates feature exposed concrete and bedside tables built into the bedframes. Access throughout is via hi-tech fobs, and linens, padlocks and breakfast supplies are all included.

Dwell Hotel BOUTIQUE HOTEL **$$**
(☏ 423-267-7866; www.thedwellhotel.com; 120 E 10th St; r $225-325; [P][❄][🛜]) It's very hard to improve on excellent, but the former Stone Fort Inn – now the Dwell – has done just that. A new hands-on owner has completely flipped this historic downtown hotel into a design-forward, mid-century modern whirlwind of retro style. The 16 revamped rooms feature painstakingly curated vintage furniture, soothing earth-tone color schemes, rain-style showers *and* bathtubs.

Flying Squirrel MODERN AMERICAN **$**
(www.flyingsquirrelbar.com; 55 Johnson St; dishes $6-18; ⊙5pm-1am Tue-Thu, to 2am Fri & Sat, 10:30am-3pm Sun; 🛜) A neighbor to the South's coolest hostel (same owners), Flying Squirrel is at its heart a very cool bar (21 and over only, except for Sunday brunch), but its locally sourced small-plate takes on fusion comfort food make for mighty fine pub grub.

St John's Meeting Place AMERICAN **$$**
(☏ 423-266-4571; www.stjohnsmeetingplace. com; 1274 Market St; mains $12-29; ⊙5-9:30pm Mon-Thu, to 10pm Fri & Sat) The culinary anchor of Chattanooga's Southside is widely considered the city's best night out. It's Johnny Cash black (black granite floor, black-glass chandeliers, black banquettes), lending an unorthodox but mod elegance for a foodie habitat. The farm-to-table cuisine features lamb pastrami, pork tenderloin, and nacho burgers with chorizo and pickled jalapeño.

ⓘ Information

Visitor Center (☏ 800-322-3344; www. chattanoogafun.com; 215 Broad St; ⊙10am-5pm) Easy to miss, located in an outdoor public breezeway.

ⓘ Getting There & Around

Chattanooga's modest **airport** (CHA; ☏ 423-855-2202; www.chattairport.com; 1001 Airport Rd) is just east of the city. The **Greyhound** station (☏ 423-892-1277; www.greyhound.com; 960 Airport Rd) is just down the road.

For access to most downtown sites, ride the free **Downtown Electric Shuttle** (www.gocarta. org) that plies the center and the North Shore. The visitor center has a route map.

Bike Chattanooga (www.bikechattanooga. com) is Chattanooga's city-sponsored, bicycle-sharing program. Bikes are lined and locked up at 33 stations throughout the city and riders can purchase access passes (starting at $8 for 24 hours) via credit card at any of the station kiosks. Rides under 60 minutes are free.

Knoxville

Once known as the 'underwear capital of the world' for its numerous textile mills, Knoxville is home to the University of Tennessee and its rabid college-football fan base. On college game days, the whole town is painted orange as thousands of fans pack Neyland Stadium to watch the beloved Volunteers take to the gridiron. But there's more to Knoxville than the pigskin. No longer content to play second fiddle to nearby Chattanooga and Asheville, the city is experiencing a mojo recalibration and is becoming an increasingly prominent destination for outdoor, gastronomy and craft-beer enthusiasts, as well as an alternative base for Great Smoky Mountains National Park. At just 29 miles from Sugarlands Visitors Center, a day trip is easy, and Knoxville is a far more enticing spot to eat and drink than other cities near the park.

⊙ Sights & Activities

Women's Basketball Hall of Fame MUSEUM
(www.wbhof.com; 700 Hall of Fame Dr; adult/child $7.95/5.95; ⊙10am-5pm Mon-Sat summer, 11am-5pm Tue-Fri, 10am-5pm Sat winter; ♿) You can't miss the massive orange basketball that marks the Women's Basketball Hall of Fame, a nifty look at the sport from the time when women were forced to play in full-length dresses.

Ijams Nature Center OUTDOORS
(☏ 865-577-4717; www.ijams.org; 2915 Island Home Ave; ⊙9am-5pm Mon-Sat, 11am-5pm Sun) A one-stop shop for getting out and about in nature in Knoxville. Pick up trail maps for the city's Urban Wilderness, get a wealth of information on all of the city's outdoor activities and rent outdoor equipment for getting on the water at Mead's Quarry and elsewhere.

🛏 Sleeping & Eating

★ Oliver Hotel
BOUTIQUE HOTEL **$$**
(☑ 865-521-0050; www.theoliverhotel.com; 407 Union Ave; r $160-360; P ❄ @ 🛜) Hipster receptionists welcome you to Knoxville's only boutique hotel, boasting 28 modern, stylish rooms with fun subway-tiled showers (with rain-style showerheads), luxe linens, plush throwback furniture and carpets, and gorgeous hand-crafted coffee tables. The **Peter Kern Library bar** draws craft cocktail enthusiasts by night. The new restaurant, **Oliver Royale**, is highly recommended (mains $15 to $46).

★ Oli Bea
BREAKFAST **$**
(www.olibea.net; 119 S Central St; mains $7-12; ⊗ 7am-1pm Mon-Fri, 8am-2pm Sat; 🛜) It's worth sleeping in Knoxville just to wake up to the rich, Mexicanized farm-to-table Southern breakfast fare at this morning stop in the Old City. You'll find gussied-up standards (country ham, sage sausage, organic chicken), a sinfully good grilled cheese with buttermilk cheddar, a sunny duck egg and collard greens, full-stop fabulous pork confit *carnitas* tostadas and *chilaquiles*.

ℹ Information

Visitor Center (Visit Knoxville; ☑ 800-727-8045; www.visitknoxville.com; 301 S Gay St; ⊗ 8:30am-5pm Mon-Fri, 9am-5pm Sat, noon-4pm Sun) Besides tourism info, the visitor center also welcomes bands from across the Americana genre for WDVX's **Blue Plate Special**, a free concert series at noon Monday to Saturday.

ℹ Getting There & Around

Knoxville's **McGhee Tyson Airport** (☑ 865-342-3000; www.flyknoxville.com; 2055 Alcoa Hwy, Alcoa) is 15 miles south of town and is served by 20 or so nonstop domestic flights. The **Greyhound** (☑ 865-524-0369; www.greyhound.com; 100 E Magnolia Ave) bus station is only about 1 mile north of downtown, making it a convenient option for ground travelers.

Gatlinburg

Wildly kitschy and family-friendly Gatlinburg hunkers at the entrance of the Great Smoky Mountains National Park, waiting to stun hikers with the scent of fudge, cotton candy and pancakes, and various odd museums and campy attractions. It's a wild ride of all that is good and bad about the USA at the same time, wrapped up in a gaudy explosion of magic shows and moonshine. Say what you will about the town, but you can never say Gatlinburg ain't a good time.

With the exception of the Gatlinburg Sky Lift, the town itself emerged from the devastating 2016 Great Smoky Mountains wildfires largely unscathed, ensuring the good times kept on rolling, but the loss of life and general destruction (14 deaths, 17,904 acres burned inside and outside the national park, and more than 2400 buildings destroyed, all down to arson) means Gatlnburg remains in mourning. Luckily, there's a shot of 'shine for that!

⊙ Sights & Activities

Dollywood
AMUSEMENT PARK
(☑ 865-428-9488; www.dollywood.com; 2700 Dollywood Parks Blvd, Pigeon Forge; adult/child $67/54; ⊗ Apr-Dec) Dollywood is a self-created ode to the patron saint of East Tennessee, the big-haired, bigger-bosomed country singer Dolly Parton. The park features Appalachian-themed rides and attractions, a water park, the DreamMore Resort and more. Find it looming above the town of Pigeon Forge, a secondhand Vegas-like mess drunk on American kitsch 9 miles north of Gatlinburg.

Gatlinburg Sky Lift
CABLE CAR
(☑ 865-436-4307; www.gatlinburgskylift.com; 765 Parkway; adult/child $16.50/13; ⊗ 9am-11pm Jun-Aug, hours vary rest of year) This repurposed ski-resort chairlift whisks you high over the Smokies, providing stellar views. After being damaged in the 2016 Great Smoky Mountains wildfires, it was completely refurbished and reopened in summer 2017. Visitors can expect a smoother ride and lifts that seat three instead of two.

★ Ole Smoky Moonshine Holler
DISTILLERY
(www.olesmokymoonshine.com; 903 Parkway; ⊗ 10am-10pm) At first glance, this stone-and-wood moonshine distillery, Tennessee's first licensed moonshine maker, appears to have a Disney flair, but it's the real deal. Gathering around the hysterical bartenders, drinking the 13 flavors of free hooch and taking in all of their colorful commentary is Gatlinburg's best time.

🛏 Sleeping & Eating

Rocky Waters Motor Inn
MOTEL **$**
(☑ 865-436-7861; www.rockywatersmotorinn.com; 333 Parkway; d $49-169; P ❄ 🛜) This pleasantly retro motel has clean, comfy rooms with new hardwood flooring and big walk-in

showers and is perched above the river. It's walking distance from downtown, but at a serene remove from the noise and lights.

Buckhorn Inn
INN $$

(☑865-436-4668; www.buckhorninn.com; 2140 Tudor Mountain Rd; d $125-205, 2-bedroom guesthouse from $240; P✳@�) A few minutes' drive and several light years away from the kitsch and crowds of downtown Gatlinburg, the tranquil Buckhorn has nine elegant rooms, seven private cottages and four guesthouses on a property that is a well-manicured private haven. If the unbroken views of Mt LeConte don't relax you enough, have a wander through the fieldstone meditation labyrinth.

Three Jimmys
AMERICAN $

(www.threejimmys.com; 1359 East Pkwy; mains $9-28; ⊙11am-10pm; �) Escape the tourist hordes on the main drag and grab a bite at this local's favorite with friendly waitstaff ('Here's your menu, baby..') and a long list of everything: barbecue, turkey Reubens, burgers, champagne chicken, steaks, a great spinach salad and so on.

❶ Information

Gatlinburg Welcome Center (☑865-277-8947; www.gatlinburg.com; 1011 Banner Rd; ⊙8:30am-5:30pm) Official information and maps – including a handy $1 waterfalls map – on both Gatlinburg and Great Smoky Mountains National Park.

❶ Getting There & Around

The vast majority of visitors arrive in Gatlinburg by car. The nearest airport is Knoxville's **McGhee Tyson Airport**, 41 miles away, and there's no regular intercity bus service.

Traffic and parking are serious issues in Gatlinburg. The Gatlinburg Trolley (www.gatlinburgtrolley.org) serves downtown, and the trolley's tan line ($2) goes into the park between July and October, with stops at Sugarlands Visitor Center, Laurel Falls and Elkmont Campground. Parking lots around town generally charge $10 for the day, but Ole Smoky Moonshine Holler charges just $5.

KENTUCKY

With an economy based on bourbon, horse racing and tobacco, you might think Kentucky would rival Las Vegas as Sin Central. Well, yes and no. For every whiskey-soaked Louisville bar there's a dry county where you can't get anything stronger than ginger ale.

For every racetrack there's a church. Kentucky is made of these juxtapositions. A geographic and cultural crossroads, the state combines the friendliness of the South, the rural frontier history of the West, the industry of the North and the aristocratic charm of the East. Every corner is easy on the eye, but there are few sights more heartbreakingly beautiful than the rolling limestone hills of horse country, where thoroughbred breeding is a multimillion-dollar industry. In spring the pastures bloom with tiny azure buds, earning it the moniker 'Bluegrass State.'

❶ Information

Kentucky State Parks (☑502-564-2172; www.parks.ky.gov) Offers info on hiking, caving, fishing, camping and more in Kentucky's 52 state parks. So-called 'Resort Parks' have lodges. 'Recreation Parks' are for roughin' it.

Kentucky Travel (☑800-225-8747; www.kentuckytourism.com) Sends out a detailed booklet on the state's attractions.

Louisville

Best known as the home of the Kentucky Derby, Louisville (or Luhvul, as the locals say) is handsome, underrated and undeniably cool. A major Ohio River shipping center during the days of westward expansion, Kentucky's largest city is on the up, with hip bars, superb farm-to-table restaurants, and an engaging, young and increasingly progressive population. It's a fun place to spend a few days, checking out the museums, wandering the old neighborhoods and sipping some bourbon.

◉ Sights & Activities

★**Churchill Downs**
LANDMARK

(☑502-636-4400; www.churchilldowns.com; 700 Central Ave) On the first Saturday in May, a who's who of upper-crust America puts on their seersucker suits and most flamboyant hats and descend for the 'greatest two minutes in sports': the Kentucky Derby, the longest-running continuous sporting event in North America.

Kentucky Derby Museum
MUSEUM

(www.derbymuseum.org; Gate 1, Central Ave; adult/senior/child $15/14/8; ⊙8am-5pm Mon-Sat, 11am-5pm Sun Mar 15-Nov 30, from 9am Mon-Sat, 11am-5pm Sun Dec-Mar 14) On the racetrack grounds, the museum has exhibits on derby history, including a peek into the life of jockeys and a roundup of the most illustrious horses. Highlights include a 360-degree HD film about the race, the 30-minute walking tour of the grandstands (which includes some engaging yarns) and mint juleps in the museum cafe.

The 90-minute 'Inside the Gates Tour' ($11) leads you through the jockey's quarters and posh VIP seating areas known as Millionaire's Row.

Muhammad Ali Center   MUSEUM

(www.alicenter.org; 144 N 6th St; adult/senior/child $12/11/7; ⊘ 9:30am-5pm Tue-Sat, noon-5pm Sun) 🖋 A love offering to the city from its most famous native, and an absolute must-see. For a black man from the South during his era, to rejoice in his own greatness and beauty was revolutionary and inspiring to behold – and this museum captures it all.

Louisville Slugger Museum
& Factory   MUSEUM

(www.sluggermuseum.org; 800 W Main St; adult/senior/child $14/13/8; ⊘ 9am-5pm Mon-Sat, 11am-5pm Sun, to 6pm Jul; ❸) Look for the 120ft baseball bat leaning against the museum. Hillerich & Bradsby Co have been making the famous Louisville Slugger here since 1884. Admission includes a plant tour and a hall of baseball memorabilia, including Babe Ruth's bat and a free mini slugger.

Frazier History Museum   MUSEUM

(www.fraziermuseum.org; 829 W Main St; adult/senior/child $12/10/8; ⊘ 9am-5pm Mon-Sat, noon-5pm Sun) Surprisingly ambitious for a mid-sized city, this state-of-the-art museum covers 1000 years of history with grisly battle dioramas and costumed interpreters demonstrating swordplay and staging mock debates.

Kentucky Science Center   MUSEUM

(☑ 502-561-6100; www.kysciencecenter.org; 727 W Main St; adult/child $13/11; ⊘ 9:30am-5:30pm Sun-Thu, to 9pm Fri & Sat; ❸) Set in a historic building on Main St there are three floors of exhibits that illuminate biology, physiology, physics, computing and more for families (kids love it). For an extra $8 to $10 you can catch a film in the IMAX-like theater.

🎉 Festivals & Events

Kentucky Derby Festival   SPORTS

(www.kdf.org; kickoff event tickets from $30) The Kentucky Derby Festival, which includes a balloon race, a marathon, a steamboat race and the largest fireworks display in North America, starts two weeks before the big event.

First Friday Trolley Hop   ART

(www.firstfridayhop.com; Main & Market Sts; ⊘ 5-11pm, 1st Fri of month) The number of incredible kitchens multiplies every year, especially in the engaging NuLu area, where there are numerous galleries and boutiques to explore. Check them out on the First Friday Trolley Hop.

🚗 Tours

Waverly Hills Sanatorium   TOURS

(☑ 502-933-2142; www.therealwaverlyhills.com; 4400 Paralee Lane; 2/6/8hr tours $25/75/100; ⊘ Fri & Sat Mar-Aug) Towering over Louisville like a mad king's castle, the abandoned Waverly Hills Sanatorium once housed victims of an early-20th-century tuberculosis epidemic. When patients died, workers dumped their bodies down a chute into the basement. No wonder the place is said to be one of America's most haunted buildings. Search for spooks with a nighttime ghost-hunting tour; the genuinely fearless can even spend the night! Many claim it's the scariest place they've ever been.

Big Four Bridge   WALKING, CYCLING

(www.louisvillewaterfront.com; East River Rd; ⊘ 24hr) Built between 1888 and 1895, the Big Four Bridge, which spans the Ohio River and reaches the Indiana shores, has been closed to vehicular traffic since 1969 but was reopened in 2013 as a pedestrian and cycling path; excellent city and river views throughout.

🛏 Sleeping

Rocking Horse B&B   B&B $$

(☑ 888-467-7322, 502-583-0408; www.rockinghorse-bb.com; 1022 S 3rd St; r $125-250; 🅿 ❋ 🛜) Near the University of Louisville on a stretch of 3rd St once known as Millionaire's Row, this 1888 Richardsonian Romanesque mansion is chock-full of astounding historic detail. The six guest rooms are decorated with Victorian antiques and splendid original stained glass. Guests can eat their two-course breakfast in the English country garden or sip complimentary port in the parlor.

★ 21c Museum Hotel   HOTEL $$$

(☑ 502-217-6300; www.21chotel.com; 700 W Main St; r from $199; 🅿 ❋ 🛜) This contemporary art museum–hotel features edgy design details: video screens project your distorted image and falling language on the wall as you wait for the elevator; water-blurred, see-through glass urinal walls line the men's rooms. Rooms, though not as interesting as the five contemporary art galleries-common areas, have iPod docks and mint julep kits.

Brown Hotel
HOTEL $$$

(☑502-583-1234; www.brownhotel.com; 335 West Broadway; r $200-600; P🅿😊❄️🛜) Opera stars, queens and prime ministers have trod the marble floors of this storied downtown hotel, now restored to all its 1920s glamor with 294 comfy rooms and an impressive lobby bourbon bar under original English Renaissance gilded ceilings.

✗ Eating

Gralehaus
MODERN AMERICAN $

(www.gralehaus.com; 1001 Baxter Ave; mains $6-13; ⊘8am-4pm Sun-Tue, to 10pm Wed-Sat; 🛜) There's breakfast all day at this small eatery housed in a historic early-20th-century home and you should indeed indulge in its chef-centric takes on traditional Southern comforts at all hours (think locally sourced biscuits and duck gravy, lamb and grits). Serious signature coffee drinks excel as well.

The Post
DELI $

(www.thepostlouisville.com; 1045 Goss Ave; mains $3-13; ⊘11am-midnight Mon-Wed, to 2am Thu-Fri, noon-2am Sat, noon-midnight Sun; 🛜) In gentrified Germantown, New York–style pizza by the slice, sub sandwiches and great spaces (sunny patio out the front comfy bar in the back with 16 taps) evoke a pricier atmosphere and cooler vibe than your bill suggests.

Silver Dollar
CALIFORNIAN, SOUTHERN $$

(☑502-259-9540; www.whiskeybythedrink.com; 1761 Frankfort Ave; mains $9-27, brunch $9-14; ⊘5pm-2am Mon-Fri, from 10am Sat & Sun; 🛜) Gastronomically noncommittal – we'll call the cuisine California-inspired New Southern – but unrepentantly bourbon obsessed, the Silver Dollar does your head in. Feast on chicken and waffles, Beer Can Hen (roasted game hen served on an Old Milwaukee beer can) or fantastic *chilaquiles;* chase it with one of a 'poop ton' of bourbons.

Garage Bar
PUB FOOD $$

(www.garageonmarket.com; 700 E Market St; plates $9-18; ⊘5-10pm Mon-Thu, 11am-10pm Fri-Sun; 🛜) The best thing to do on a warm afternoon in Louisville is to make your way to this uber-hip converted NuLu service station (accented by two kissing Camaros) and order a round of basil gimlets and the ham platter (a tasting of four regionally cured hams served with fresh bread and preserves; $26).

★ Butchertown Grocery
MODERN AMERICAN $$$

(☑502-742-8315; www.butchertowngrocery.com; 1076 E Washington St; mains $15-25; ⊘restaurant 11am-10pm Wed-Fri, from 11am Sat & Sun, bar 6pm-midnight Wed & Sun, to 2am Thu-Sat; 🛜) Louisville's hottest new restaurant rides a delicate line between raw and refined, dishing out European-inspired, American-anchored comfort cuisine in an unassuming 19th-century red-brick edifice where weathered wood ceilings preside over marble tables and B&W mosaic flooring.

★ Proof
MODERN AMERICAN $$$

(☑502-217-6360; www.proofonmain.com; 702 W Main St; mains $13-38; ⊘7-10am, 11am-2pm & 5:30-10pm Mon-Thu, to 11pm Fri, 7am-3pm & 5:30-11pm Sat, to 1pm Sun; 🛜) Arguably Louisville's best restaurant. The cocktails ($10 to $12) are incredible, the wine and bourbon 'library' (they're known to pour from exclusive and rare barrels of Woodford Reserve and Van Winkle) is long and satisfying, and startling dishes range from gourmet grilled cheese to a deliciously messy bison burger or a high-minded take on 'hot' fried chicken.

♟ Drinking & Nightlife

★ Holy Grale
PUB

(http://holygralelouisville.com; 1034 Bardstown Rd; drafts from $6; ⊘4pm-1am Mon-Thu, to 2am Fri & Sat, noon-midnight Sun; 🛜) One of Louisville's best bars is housed in an old church, with a menu of funked-up pub grub (gourmet Belgian *frites*, green curry mussels, short rib poutine; mains $6 to $14) and a buzzworthy beer list dependent on rarer German, Danish, Belgian and Japanese brews on tap. The most intense beers (up to 13% alcohol) can be found in the choir loft. Hallelujah!

Mr Lee's
COCKTAIL BAR

(www.mrleeslounge.com; 935 Goss Ave; cocktails $10-12; ⊘2pm-midnight Mon-Thu, to 2am Fri & Sat, to 11pm Sun) Germantown's craft cocktail anchor is this new, satisfyingly retro bar that serves a small but serious list of pre-Prohibition-era tipples. The semi-circular red leather bar gives way to a long mid-century-modern–styled, candlelit line of intimate tables and banquettes that are perfect for settling in for a boozy evening. It's even carpeted!

Monnik Beer Company MICROBREWERY
(www.monnikbeer.com; 1036 E Burnett Ave; beers
from $4; ⊙11am-midnight Tue-Thu, to 1am Fri &
Sat, to 10pm Sun; 🛜) Our favorite Louisville
brewery is in up-and-coming Schnitzelburg.
There are 20 taps – the IPA stands out – in
this restrained hipster environment where
the beer isn't the only thing that's fabulous.
The beer cheese with spent grain bread is so
good you should need a prescription for it;
and the seared grass-fed burgers are perfect.
Bottoms up!

ℹ Information

Visitor Center (📋502-379-6109; www.goto
louisville.com; 301 S 4th Ave; ⊙10am-5pm
Mon-Sat, noon-5pm Sun) Stuffed with brochures and helpful staff.

ℹ Getting There & Around

Louisville's International Airport (p388) is 5
miles south of town on I-65. Get there by cab
for a flat rate of $19.55 or local bus 2. The
Greyhound (📋800-231-2222; www.greyhound.
com; 720 W Muhammad Ali Blvd) station is just
west of downtown.

TARC (www.ridetarc.org) runs local buses
($1.75) from the historic **Union Station depot**
(📋502-585-1234; 1000 W Broadway), including
its free ZeroBus, an electric bus fleet that circles
Main, Market and 4th Sts, taking in most of the
city's attractions and coolest restaurants. Buses do not require exact change, but there is no
mechanism for giving change back.

Bluegrass Country

Drive through northeast Kentucky's Bluegrass Country on a sunny day and glimpse
horses grazing in the brilliant-green hills
dotted with ponds, poplar trees and handsome estate houses. These once-wild woodlands and meadows have been a center of
horse breeding for almost 250 years. The
region's natural limestone deposits – you'll
see limestone bluffs rise majestic from out
of nowhere – are said to produce especially
nutritious grass.

Lexington

Even the prison looks like a country club in
Lexington, home of million-dollar houses
and multimillion-dollar horses. Once the
wealthiest and most cultured city west of
the Allegheny Mountains, it was called 'the
Athens of the West.' It's home to the University of Kentucky and is the heart of the

thoroughbred industry. The small downtown has some pretty Victorian neighborhoods, but most of the attractions are in the
countryside.

⊙ Sights

Kentucky Horse Park MUSEUM, PARK
(www.kyhorsepark.com; 4089 Iron Works Pkwy;
summer adult/child $20/10, winter adult/child
$12/6, horseback riding Mar-Oct $25; ⊙9am-5pm
Mar 15-Nov 5, 9am-5pm Wed-Sun Nov 6-Mar 14; 🚼)
An educational theme park and equestrian
sports center sits on 1200 acres just north
of Lexington. Horses representing 50 different breeds live in the park and participate in
special live shows.

Ashland HISTORIC BUILDING
(www.henryclay.org; 120 Sycamore Rd; adult/child
$12/6; ⊙10am-4pm Tue-Sat Mar-Dec, 1-4pm Sun
Apr-Nov) Just 1.5 miles east of downtown,
Ashland is part historic home of one of Kentucky's favorite sons and part public park;
it was the Italianate estate of famed states-
man and great compromiser Henry Clay
(1777–1852).

Lexington Art League at
Loudoun House GALLERY
(www.lexingtonartleague.org; 209 Castlewood Dr;
⊙10am-4pm Tue-Thu, 10am-8pm Fri, 1-4pm Sat &
Sun) Art and architecture buffs won't want
to miss this edgy, contemporary visual arts
gallery housed in a freestanding American
Gothic Revival mansion in NoLi, one of
only five such structures left in the USA.
The cutting-edge exhibitions, around six
per year, are quite provocative by Lexington
standards and the lovely Executive Director
takes much pride in stirring the pot.

Mary Todd-Lincoln House HISTORIC BUILDING
(www.mtlhouse.org; 578 W Main St; adult/child
$12/5; ⊙10am-3pm Mon-Sat Mar 15-Nov 30) This
modest 1806 house has articles from the
first lady's childhood and her years as Abe's
wife, including original White House pieces.
Tours hourly on the hour; last at 3pm.

🛏 Sleeping

Gratz Park Inn HOTEL $$
(📋859-231-1777; www.gratzparkinn.com; 120 W
2nd St; r from $179; 🅿❄@🛜) Once a spot to
draw the brocade curtains and fall asleep
on a 19th-century poster bed, this staple of
Lexington's historic district has revamped
its rooms, leaving just a few antique four-
poster beds for guests. The revamped rooms

maintain a classic style save the bathrooms, where modern subway-tiled showers have an edgier, industrial feel.

⭐ **Lyndon House** B&B $$
(☑859-420-2863; www.lyndonhouse.com; 507 N Broadway; r from $179; P❊@☎) A detail-oriented ordained-minister-turned-foodie is your host at this discerning and spacious downtown B&B in an historic mansion dating from 1885. Anton takes hospitality seriously, as he does breakfast. The seven rooms feature period furnishings and all the mod-cons; and you're steps from a long list of restaurants and breweries.

⭐ **21c Museum Hotel** BOUTIQUE HOTEL $$
(☑859-899-6800; www.21cmuseumhotels.com; 167 W Main St; r from $219; P❊☎) This downtown design hotel is marked by twisted sidewalk lampposts – hand-blown in Venice – outside its entrance. A Louisville transplant now in several states, it might be a museum you can sleep in or a hotel that's a museum. Either way, there are four contemporary art galleries throughout the hotel (as well as permanent local art on each floor).

✕ Eating & Drinking

⭐ **County Club** BARBECUE $
(www.countyclubrestaurant.com; 555 Jefferson St; mains $9-13; ⊙5-10pm Tue-Thu, from 11am Fri-Sun; ☎) This smoked-meat sanctuary occupies the former storage garage of a Sunbeam bread factory. Though the service is best described as hipster aloof, the wares – a burger, brisket on rye, sriracha-lime smoked chicken wings, pork belly *bánh mì* etc – are moist, tender and perfectly smoked. Douse it all in four housemade sauces (vinegar, sweet, smoked habenero and mustard – oh, that mustard!).

Stella's Kentucky Deli DELI $
(www.stellaskentuckydeli.com; 143 Jefferson St; sandwiches $4.50-10; ⊙10:30am-4pm Mon-Tue, to 9pm Wed-Thu, 10:30am-10pm Fri, 9am-10pm Sat, 9am-9pm Sun; ☎✐) ✐ This don't-miss deli has 30 years under its apron, but the latest owners refocused a few years back, upping the cool quotient and concentrating on invaluable provisions from local farmers. Great sandwiches, soups and salads, along with seasonal brews, are served in a colorful historic home with reclaimed tin roof and sociable bar.

MAKER'S MARK

Touring **Maker's Mark** (☑270-865-2099; www.makersmark.com; 3350 Burks Spring Rd, Loretto; tours $12; ⊙9:30am-3:30pm Mon-Sat, 11:30-3:30pm Sun) is like visiting a small, historic theme park, but in the best way. You'll see the old grist-mill, the 1840s master distiller's house and the old-fashioned wooden firehouse with an antique fire truck. And you can soak up your bourbon over-indulgence with tasty Southern fare at the new Star Hill Provision on the premises.

Watch oatmeal-esque sour mash ferment in huge cypress vats, see whiskey being double-distilled in copper pots and peek at bourbon barrels aging in old wooden warehouses – then walk away with your own bottle hand-dipped by you in molten red wax.

Doodles CAFE $
(www.doodlesrestaurant.com; 262 N Limestone; breakfast $3-12; ⊙8am-2pm Tue-Sun; ☎) ✐ Breakfast fiends should head to this former gas station to fill up on scrumptious comfort food led by shrimp and grits (with green onion rémoulade and country ham), oatmeal brûlée and local egg casseroles; all organic and local where possible.

Middle Fork MODERN AMERICAN $$
(☑859-309-9854; www.middleforkkb.com; 1224 Manchester St; small plates $6-22, mains $15-35; ⊙5-10pm Mon-Tue & Thu-Sat, 5-8pm Sun Jan-Apr; ☎) From worshipped food truck to the culinary anchor of Lexington's hottest epicurean district, the Old Pepper Distillery campus, Chef Mark Jensen calls on a custom-built Argentinean-styled wood-fire grill for much of his seasonal, meat-heavy farm-to-table fare, but it's outrageous small bites like his reinvented takes on American classics like peanut butter and jelly that shock and awe.

⭐ **Country Boy Brewing** MICROBREWERY
(www.countryboybrewing.com; 436 Chair Ave; beer $3-6) True to its name, Country Boy – all trucker hats, taxidermy and camo – delivers the best beer in the most authentically Kentuckian climate. Up to 24 taps are devoted to their own experimental concoctions, brewed with a rural Mikkeller-like approach (oak aged sours with strawberries, jalapeño smoked porters, barrel-aged DIPAs). Guest beers are frequent as well.

There's no food, but a different food truck pulls round each night from 5pm to 10pm (3pm to 9pm on Sunday). A second brewery in nearby Georgetown opened in 2017.

☆ Entertainment

Keeneland HORSE RACING
(☑ 859-254-3412; www.keeneland.com; 4201 Versailles Rd; general admission $5; ☺ races Apr & Oct) Second only to Churchill Downs in terms of quality of competition, races run in April and October, when you can also glimpse champions train from sunrise to 10am. Frequent horse auctions lure sheiks, sultans, hedge-fund princes and those who love (or serve) them.

The Burl LIVE MUSIC
(www.theburlky.com; 375 Thompson Rd; cover $5-12; ☺ 6pm-2:30am Mon-Thu, from 4pm Fri-Sun) Across the railroad tracks from the Old Pepper Distillery campus inside a finely restored 1928 train depot, the Burl has transformed Lexington's live music scene, which finally has a consistent home for local and regional acts.

ℹ Information

Visitor Center (VisitLEX; ☑ 859-233-7299; www.visitlex.com; 401 W Main St; ☺ 9am-5pm Mon-Fri, from 10am Sat) Pick up maps and area information from the visitor center, located downtown in an upscale restaurant complex known as the Square.

ℹ Getting There & Around

Blue Grass Airport (LEX; ☑ 859-425-3100; www.bluegrassairport.com; 4000 Terminal Dr) is west of town, with about a dozen domestic nonstops. **Greyhound** (☑ 800-231-2222; www.greyhound.com; 477 W New Circle Rd) is 2 miles from downtown.

Lex-Tran (☑ 859-253-4636; 150 East Vine St; ☺ 6am-6pm Mon-Fri, 8am-4pm Sat & Sun) runs local buses ($1; bus 6 goes to the Greyhound station, bus 21 goes to the airport and Keeneland).

Central Kentucky

Buckle up, ladies and gents, you're in bourbon country! Kentucky's world-renowned homegrown spirit pays the bills, keeps the population buzzed and even adds a punch of booze to the local cuisine. Small and scenic Bardstown is the 'Bourbon Capital of the World' and hosts a rousing good time every September when the **Kentucky Bourbon Festival** (www.kybourbonfestival.com)

ensures all-comers are hyped up on the on the Bluegrass state's wicked brown hooch. It sits just 40 miles southeast of Louisville, a fun and artsy Kentuckiana town built on bourbon and American sport icons (home to the Kentucky Derby. and birthplace of Muhammad Ali and the Louisville Slugger) but has evolved into one of the South's most foodie-centric mid-sized cities over the last decade, a lovely spot to eat and museum-hop between rounds of pursing America's most perfect Old Fashioned cocktail.

Shaker Village at Pleasant Hill MUSEUM
(www.shakervillageky.org; 3501 Lexington Rd, Pleasant Hill; adult/child $10/5; riverboat rides $10/5; ☺ 10am-5pm Tue-Thu & Sun, to 8pm Fri & Sat) This area was home to a community of the Shaker religious sect until the early 1900s. Tour 14 impeccably restored buildings, set amid buttercup meadows and winding stone paths. There's an inn and restaurant, and a gift shop selling the Shakers' famous handicrafts.

Shaker Village Inn INN $$
(☑ 859-734-5611; www.shakervillageky.org; 3501 Lexington Rd, Pleasant Hill; r $110-300; 🅿 🛜) The main building is set in the village's old trustee office, with its elaborate double helix stairwell. Rooms are large, lovely and full of light, with high ceilings, wood furnishings and two rockers to read/snooze in. Rooms in 13 other buildings follow suit.

ℹ Getting There & Around

Louisville International Airport (SDF; ☑ 502-367-4636; www.flylouisville.com; 600 Terminal Dr) – international in name only – is Kentucky's biggest airport, receiving direct domestic flights from Atlanta, Charlotte, Chicago, Minneapolis, New York and Washington, DC, among others.

The Bluegrass Pkwy runs from I-65 in the west to Rte 60 in the east, passing through some of the most luscious pastureland in Kentucky. Bardstown and the heart of bourbon country is located 40 miles south of Louisville, with Mammoth Cave National Park another 70 miles or so south. Daniel Boone National Forest is 105 miles south of Lexington. Renting your own ride is undoubtedly the best way to take it all in.

Daniel Boone National Forest

More than 700,000 acres of rugged ravines and gravity-defying sandstone arches cover much of the Appalachian foothills of eastern Kentucky. Within the Daniel Boone National Forest, cliffs and natural arches of the **Red**

THE BOURBON TRAIL

Silky, caramel-colored bourbon whiskey was likely first distilled in Bourbon County, north of Lexington, around 1789. Today 90% of all bourbon that comes out of the US is produced in Kentucky, thanks to its pure, limestone-filtered water. Bourbon must contain at least 51% corn, and be stored in charred oak barrels for a minimum of two years. While connoisseurs drink it straight or with water, you must try a mint julep, the archetypal Southern drink made with bourbon, simple syrup and crushed mint.

The **Oscar Getz Museum of Whiskey History** (www.whiskeymuseum.com; 114 N 5th St; ⊙10am-4pm Tue-Sat, noon-4pm Sun) in Bardstown tells the bourbon story with old moonshine stills and other artifacts.

Most of Kentucky's distilleries, which are centered on Bardstown and Frankfort, offer tours. Check out Kentucky's official Bourbon Trail website (www.kybourbontrail.com). Note that it doesn't include every distillery. Distilleries near Bardstown include the following:

Heaven Hill (☑502-337-9593; www.bourbonheritagecenter.com; 1311 Gilkey Run Rd; tours $10-20; ⊙10am-5:30pm Mon-Fri, noon-4pm Sun Mar-Dec, 10am-5pm Tue-Sat Jan-Feb) Distillery tours are offered, but you may also opt to explore its interactive Bourbon Heritage Center.

Jim Beam (☑502-543-9877; www.jimbeam.com; 526 Happy Hollow Rd, Clermont; tours $12; ⊙gift shop 9am-5:30pm Mon-Sat, noon-4pm Sun, tours 9am-3:30pm Mon-Sat, 12:30-3pm Sun) Watch a film about the Beam family and sample small-batch bourbons at the country's largest bourbon distillery. Beam makes Knob Creek (good), Knob Creek Single Barrel (better), Basil Hayden's (velvety) and the fabulous Booker's (high-proof enlightenment).

Maker's Mark (p387) This restored Victorian distillery is like a bourbon theme park.

Willet (☑502-348-0899; www.kentuckybourbonwhiskey.com; Loretto Rd; tours $12; ⊙shop 9:30am-5:30pm Mon-Fri, noon-4:30pm Sun Mar-Dec, tours 10am-4pm Mon-Sat, Sun 12:30-3:30pm) A craft family-owned distillery making small-batch bourbon in its own patented style. It's a gorgeous 120-acre property and one of our favorites. Tours run throughout the day.

Distilleries near Frankfort/Lawrenceburg include:

Buffalo Trace (☑800-654-8471; www.buffalotracedistillery.com; 1001 Wilkinson Blvd, Frankfort; ⊙shop 9am-5:30pm Mon-Sat, noon-5pm Sun, tours 9am-4pm Mon-Sat, noon-3pm Sun) **FREE** The nation's oldest continuously operating distillery has highly regarded tours and free tastings.

Four Roses (☑502-839-3436; www.fourrosesbourbon.com; 1224 Bonds Mills Rd, Lawrenceburg; tours $5; ⊙shop 9am-4pm Mon-Sat, noon-4pm Sun, tours 9am-3pm Mon-Sat, noon-3pm Sun) One of the most scenic distilleries, in a riverside Spanish Mission–style building.

Woodford Reserve (☑859-879-1812; www.woodfordreserve.com; 7855 McCracken Pike, Versailles; tours $14-30; ⊙shop 9am-5pm Mon-Sat, noon-4pm Sun, tours 10am-3pm Mon-Sat, 1-3pm Sun, closed Jan-Feb) The historic site along a creek is restored to its 1800s glory; the distillery still uses old-fashioned copper pots. By far the most scenic of the lot.

To get around the dilemma of drinking and driving, sit back with your whiskey snifter on a tour with **Mint Julep Tours** (☑502-583-1433; www.mintjuleptours.com; 140 N 4th St, Ste 326, Louisville; tours weekday/weekend incl lunch from from $129/149).

River Gorge make for some of the best rock climbing in the country; and the adjacent family-friendly **Natural Bridge State Resort Park** features over 20 miles of hiking trails in addition to the park's signature sandstone arch, a stunning 65ft-high, 78ft-long natural bridge, as well as lodging and camping facilities.

Natural Bridge State Resort Park   STATE PARK
(☑606-663-2214; www.parks.ky.gov; 2135 Natural Bridge Rd, Slade; P⚕) Bordering Red River Gorge is this state park, notable for its sandstone arch. It's a family-friendly park, with camping, rooms and cottages at its **Hemlock Lodge** (☑606-663-2214, 800-255-7275; www.

DON'T MISS

WALKER STALKERS: WELCOME TO WOODBURY!

The post-apocalyptic world of flesh-eating zombies on AMC's *The Walking Dead* has had a lot of the world paralyzed in front of their screens since its inaugural season in 2010, and the whole end-of-days showdown takes place right here in the Peach State. The city of Atlanta and the historic small town of Senoia and its surrounds, about an hour's drive south of Atlanta, are the setting for the fanatically popular show. Atlanta Movie Tours (p391) offers two good-time Zombie tours to filming locations: one in Atlanta proper and another around Senoia (our favorite!), narrated by extras from the show who reveal all sorts of insider tidbits about cast members and filming. Additionally, as an active film set from May to November, the show's actors can often be seen around Senoia grabbing a morning coffee at **Senoia Coffee & Cafe** (☑770-599-8000; www.senoiacoffeeandcafe.com; 1 Main St, Senoia; ☺7am-5pm Mon-Sat; 🛜). The entire town, on the National Register of Historic Places, has been transformed into zombie central. Be sure to pop into the **Woodbury Shoppe** (☑770-727-9394; www.woodburyshoppe. com; 48 Main St, Senoia; ☺11am-5pm Mon-Sat, 1-5pm Sun), the official *Walking Dead* souvenir shop, which includes a *Walking Dead*–themed cafe downstairs and a small museum.

parks.ky.gov; Hemlock Lodge Rd, Slade; r/cottages from $85/$117) and 20 miles of short hiking trails. If you don't want to leg it, you can ride the sky lift over the arch ($13 return).

Red River Outdoors   ADVENTURE
(☑859-230-3567; www.redriveroutdoors.com; 415 Natural Bridge Rd; full-day guided climb for 2 from $130) Offers guided climbing trips, cabins ($110 to $145) on the ridge line, and yoga.

Natural Bridge State Resort Park is 58 miles southeast of Lexington and accessed by private vehicle.

Mammoth Cave National Park

With the longest cave system on earth, this **national park** (☑800-967-2283; www.nps.gov/maca; 1 Mammoth Cave Pkwy, exit 53, off I-65; tours adult $7-55, child $5-20; ☺8am-6pm, to 6:30pm summer) has some 400 miles of surveyed passageways. Mammoth is at least three times longer than any other known cave, with vast interior cathedrals, bottomless pits and strange, undulating rock formations. The caves have been used for prehistoric mineral-gathering, as a source of saltpeter for gunpowder and as a tuberculosis hospital. Guided tours have been offered since 1816.

The area became a national park in 1941 and now attracts 600,000 visitors each year.

The only way to see the caves is on the excellent **ranger-guided tours** and it's wise to book ahead, especially in summer. Tours range from subterranean strolls to strenuous, day-long spelunking adventures (adults only). The Historic tour is especially interesting.

In addition to the caves, the park contains 85 miles of trails – all for hiking, 60 miles designated for horseback riding and 25 miles for mountain biking. There are also three campgrounds with restrooms, though only a few sites have electricity or water hookups (sites from $20); 13 free backcountry campsites; and a hotel and cottages. Reservations for camping (www.recreation.gov) and lodging (www.mammothcavelodge.com) can be made online. Get your backcountry permit at the park visitor center.

GEORGIA

The largest state east of the Mississippi River is a labyrinth of geographic and cultural extremes: right-leaning Republican politics in the countryside rubs against liberal idealism in Atlanta and Savannah; small, conservative towns merge with sprawling, progressive, financially flush cities; northern mountains rise to the clouds and produce roaring rivers; and coastal marshlands teem with fiddler crabs and swaying cordgrass. Georgia's southern beaches and islands are a treat, and so are its kitchens, bars and, yes, contradictions.

ℹ Information

Discover Georgia (☑800-847-4842; www.exploregeorgia.org) For statewide tourism information.

Georgia Department of Natural Resources
(☑ 800-864-7275; www.gastateparks.org) For information on camping and activities in state parks.

Atlanta

With 5.7 million residents in the metro and outlying areas, the so-called capital of the South continues to experience explosive growth thanks to domestic transplants and international immigrants alike. Beyond the big-ticket downtown attractions you'll find a constellation of superlative restaurants, a palpable Hollywood influence (Atlanta has become a highly popular production center), and iconic African American history. That last point can't be overstated: any nationwide African American intellectual, political and artistic movement you can mention has either had its genesis in Atlanta, or found a center of gravity here.

Without natural boundaries to control development, it's fair to say Atlanta is more of a region than a city. Yet for all its sprawl and suburbanization, there is a lovely urban core here, covered with trees and elegant homes. Distinct neighborhoods are like friendly small towns. The economy is robust, the population is young and creative, and the socials scene is refreshingly diverse.

◉ Sights & Activities

⊙ Downtown

Downtown Atlanta is undergoing yet another transformation, continuing the recent trend of developers and politicians focusing on making the urban core more vibrant and livable.

★**Center for Civil & Human Rights**   MUSEUM
(www.civilandhumanrights.org; 100 Ivan Allen Jr Blvd; adult/senior/child $15/13/10; ⊙10am-5pm Mon-Sat, noon-5pm Sun) This striking 2014 addition to Atlanta's **Centennial Olympic Park** (www.centennialpark.com; 265 Park Ave NW) is a sobering $68 million memorial to the American Civil Rights and global human rights movements. Beautifully designed and thoughtfully executed, the indisputable highlight centers on an absolutely harrowing interactive mock Woolworth's lunch-counter sit-in simulation that will leave you speechless and move some to tears.

College Football Hall of Fame   MUSEUM
(www.cfbhall.com; 250 Marietta St; adult/senior/child $22/19/18; ⊙10am-5pm Sun-Fri, 9am-6pm Sat; P ♿) It is impossible to overstate the importance of college football to American culture. This museum, relocated from Indiana in 2014 and revamped into this three-story, 94,256-sq-ft gridiron sanctuary, is a supremely cool and suitable shrine.

World of Coca-Cola   MUSEUM
(☑ 404-676-5151; www.woccatlanta.com; 121 Baker St; adult/senior/child $17/15/13; ⊙9am-7pm Tue-Sat, 10am-5pm Sun) This self-congratulatory museum might prove entertaining to fizzy beverage and rash commercialization fans. The climactic moment comes when guests sample Coke products from around the world – a taste-bud-twisting good time. But there are also Andy Warhol pieces on view, a 4-D film, company history and promotional materials aplenty. We searched high and low in the museum for Coca-Cola's famous secret recipe, and we're happy to present the formula here:

Atlanta Movie Tours   TOURS
(☑ 855-255-3456; www.atlantamovietours.com; 327 Nelson St SW; tours adult/child from $20/10) Offers several filming location tours, including a trip into the fictional Woodbury from *The Walking Dead,* narrated by extras from the show who are chomping at the bit (get it?) to reveal all sorts of insider tidbits about cast members and filming. Other tours take in sites from *The Hunger Games, Taken* and other franchises.

CNN Center   TOURS
(☑ 404-827-2300; http://tours.cnn.com; 1 CNN Center; tour adult/senior/child $15/14/12; ⊙9am-5pm, VIP tours 9:30am, 11:30pm, 1:30pm & 3:30pm Mon-Sat, VIP tour $33) The 55-minute behind-the-scenes tour through the headquarters of the international, 24-hour news giant is a good time for fans. Although visitors don't get very close to Wolf Blitzer (or his cronies), the 9am and noon time slots offer the best bets for seeing anchors live on-air. A VIP tour gets you access to live newsrooms, control rooms and production studios.

⊙ Midtown

Midtown is like a hipper version of downtown, with plenty of great bars, restaurants and cultural venues.

Atlanta

Atlanta

★ **High Museum of Art**   GALLERY
(www.high.org; 1280 Peachtree St NE; adult/child under 5yr $14.50/free; ⊙10am-5pm Tue-Thu & Sat, to 9pm Fri, noon-5pm Sun) Atlanta's modern High Museum was the first to exhibit art lent from Paris' Louvre and is a destination as much for its architecture as its world-class exhibits. The striking whitewashed multilevel building houses a permanent collection of eye-catching late-19th-century furniture, early American modern canvases from the likes of George Morris and Albert Gallatin, and postwar work from Mark Rothko.

Atlanta Botanical Garden   GARDENS
(☑404-876-5859; www.atlantabotanicalgarden. org; 1345 Piedmont Ave NE; adult/child $19/13; ⊙9am-7pm Tue-Sun Apr-Oct, to 5pm Nov-Mar; P) In the northwest corner of Piedmont Park, the stunning 30-acre botanical garden has a Japanese garden, winding paths and the amazing Fuqua Orchid Center.

Margaret Mitchell House & Museum   MUSEUM
(☑404-249-7015; www.atlantahistorycenter. com; 979 Crescent Ave NE; adult/student/child $13/10/8.50; ⊙10am-5pm Mon-Sat, noon-5:30pm Sun) Operated by the Atlanta History Center, this home has been converted into a shrine to the author of *Gone With the Wind*. Mitchell wrote her epic in a small apartment in the basement of this Tudor Revival building, which is listed on the National Register of

Historic Places. There are on-site exhibitions on Mitchell's life, writing career, and the film version of *Gone With the Wind*.

The price of admission also gets you access to the **Atlanta History Center** (☑404-814-4000; www.atlantahistorycenter.com; 130 West Paces Ferry Road NW; adult/child $16.50/11; ⊙11am-4pm Mon-Sat, from 1pm Sun).

Piedmont Park   PARK
(☑404-875-7275; www.piedmontpark.org; 400 Park Dr NE; ⊙6am-11pm) **FREE** A glorious, rambling urban park and the setting of many cultural and music festivals. The park has fantastic bike paths and a Saturday Green Market.

Skate Escape   CYCLING
(☑404-892-1292; www.skateescape.com; 1086 Piedmont Ave NE; bicycles & in-line skates per hour from $6; ⊙11am-7pm) Rents out bicycles and in-line skates. It also has tandems ($12 per hour) and mountain bikes ($25/35 daily/overnight).

◉ Sweet Auburn

Auburn Ave was the thumping commercial and cultural heart of African American culture in the 1900s. Today a collection of sights is associated with its most famous son, Martin Luther King Jr, who was born here, preached here and is buried here. All of the King sites are a few blocks' walk from the MARTA King Memorial station; or catch the new Atlanta Streetcar (www.theatlanta streetcar.com), which loops between Sweet Auburn and **Centennial Olympic Park** every 10-15 minutes.

★**Martin Luther King Jr National Historic Site** HISTORIC SITE
(☑404-331-5190; www.nps.gov/malu; 450 Auburn Ave; ☺9am-5pm; P ♿) FREE The historic site commemorates the life, work and legacy of the civil rights leader and one of the great Americans. The center takes up several blocks. Stop by the excellent visitor center to get oriented with a map and brochure of area sites, and exhibits that elucidate the context – the segregation, systematic oppression and racial violence that inspired and fueled King's work. A 1.5-mile landscaped trail leads from here to the Carter Center.

Martin Luther King Jr Birthplace LANDMARK
(☑404-331-5190; www.nps.gov/malu; 501 Auburn Ave; ☺10am-4pm) FREE Free, first-come, first-served guided tours of King's childhood home take about 30 minutes to complete and require same-day registration, which can be made at the National Historic Site visitor center – arrive early, as slots fill fast. The tours can depart anytime between 10am and 4pm, but you are free to visit the rest of the park at your leisure.

King Center for Non-Violent Social Change MUSEUM
(☑404-526-8900; www.thekingcenter.org; 449 Auburn Ave NE; ☺9am-5pm, to 6pm summer) Across from the National Historic Site visitor center, this place has more information on King's life and work and a few of his personal effects, including his Nobel Peace Prize. His grave site is surrounded by a long reflecting pool and can be viewed anytime.

First Ebenezer Baptist Church CHURCH
(☑404-331-5190; www.nps.gov/malu; 407 Auburn Ave NE; ☺9am-5pm) FREE Martin Luther King Jr, his father and grandfather were all pastors here, and King Jr's mother was the choir director. Sadly she was murdered here by a deranged gunman while she sat at the organ in 1974. A multimillion-dollar restoration, completed in 2011, brought the church back to the 1960–68 period when King Jr served as co-pastor with his father. Today looped recordings of King's speeches play in the church building.

Sunday services are now held at the new **Ebenezer church** (☑404-688-7300; www.his-toricebenezer.org; 101 Jackson St NE; ☺Sun service 9:30am & 11am) across the street.

◎ **Virginia-Highland**

Families enjoy the historic homes and quiet, leafy streets off North Highland Ave. The main focal point of the area is the triangular Virginia-Highland intersection-turned-commercial district, chockablock with restaurants cafes and boutiques – corporate and indie.

Carter Center MUSEUM
(☑404-865-7100; www.jimmycarterlibrary.org; 441 Freedom Pkwy; adult/senior/child $8/6/free; ☺8am-5pm; P) Located on a hilltop overlooking downtown, this center features exhibits highlighting Jimmy Carter's presidency (1977–81), including a replica of the Oval Office and his Nobel Prize. Don't miss the tranquil Japanese garden and new butterfly garden out back.

The 1.5-mile long, landscaped **Freedom Park Trail** leads from here to the Martin Luther King Jr National Historic Site through Freedom Park.

🎊 **Festivals & Events**

Atlanta Jazz Festival MUSIC
(www.atlantafestivals.com; Piedmont Park; ☺May) This month-long event culminates in live concerts in Piedmont Park on Memorial Day weekend.

Atlanta Pride Festival LGBT
(www.atlantapride.org; ☺Oct) Atlanta's annual LGBT festival.

National Black Arts Festival CULTURAL
(☑404-730-7315; www.nbaf.org; ☺Jul) Artists from across the country converge to celebrate African American music, theater, literature and film.

🛏 **Sleeping**

Rates at downtown hotels tend to fluctuate wildly depending on whether there is a large convention in town. The least expensive option is to stay in one of the many chain hotels along the MARTA line outside downtown and take the train into the city for sightseeing.

THE SOUTH ATLANTA

Ellis Hotel
BOUTIQUE HOTEL **$$**

(☑877-211-2545; www.ellishotel.com; 176 Peachtree St NW; r $150-190; P🐾❄🌐🏊) The Ellis is a downtown gem with business chic rooms fitted out in warm wooden hues and cool white bedding. Note that the hotel includes a pet-friendly floor, a women's-only floor and a 'Fresh Air' floor (the latter has private access and special cleaning rules aimed at those who suffer from allergies).

Hotel Artmore
BOUTIQUE HOTEL **$$**

(☑404-876-6100; www.artmorehotel.com; 1302 W Peachtree St; r $170-200, ste from $220; P❄@🌐) This 1924 Spanish-Mediterranean architectural landmark has been completely revamped into an artistic boutique hotel that's become an urban sanctuary for those who appreciate their trendiness with a dollop of discretion. It wins all sorts of accolades: excellent service, a wonderful courtyard with fire pit and a superb location across the street from Arts Center MARTA station.

Hotel Indigo Downtown
BOUTIQUE HOTEL **$$**

(☑888-233-9450; www.hotelindigo.com; 230 Peachtree St NE; r $135-160; P❄@🌐🏊) Atlanta's second Hotel Indigo has a superb location near Centennial Park, and a building to match the convenience: a muscular modern structure designed by Atlanta native John Portman. Rooms are crisp and bright, with thoughtful accents like historical photos and splashes of rainbow color.

Highland Inn
INN **$$**

(☑404-874-5756; www.thehighlandinn.com; 644 N Highland Ave; s/d from $75/105; P❄🌐) This European-style 65-room independent inn, built in 1927, has appealed to touring musicians over the years. Rooms aren't huge, but it has a great location in the Virginia-Highland area and is as affordably comfortable as being downton. It's one of the few accommodations in town with single rooms.

ℹ️ **ATLANTA CITYPASS**

The **Atlanta CityPass** (www.citypass.com; adult/child $75/59) gets you entry to the World of Coca-Cola, CNN Center, Georgia Aquarium, Zoo Atlanta or the Center for Civil & Human Rights, and College Football Hall of Fame or Fernbank Museum of Natural History. Buy online.

★ **Urban Oasis B&B**
B&B **$$**

(☑770-714-8618; www.urbanoasisbandb.com; 130a Krog St NE; r $140-215; P❄🌐) Hidden from view inside a gated and repurposed 1950s cotton-sorting warehouse, this wonderful retro-modern loft B&B is urban dwelling at its best. Enter into a huge and funky common area with natural light streaming through massive windows and make your way to one of three rooms, all discerningly appointed with Haywood Wakefield mid-Century Modern furnishings.

★ **The Social Goat B&B**
B&B **$$**

(☑404-626-4830; www.thesocialgoatbandb.com; 548 Robinson Ave SE; r $125-245; P❄🌐) Skirting Grant Park, this wonderfully restored 1900 Queen Anne Victorian mansion has six rooms decorated in country French-style and is loaded down with period antiques. More importantly, however, you'll share the real estate with goats, turkeys, chickens and cats. A true country escape, plunked into one of the nation's largest urban areas.

🍴 Eating

After New Orleans, Atlanta is the best city in the South to eat, and the food culture here is nothing short of obsessive. The Westside Provisions District, Krog Street Market and Ponce City Market are all newish and hip mixed-use residential and restaurant complexes sprinkled among Atlanta's continually transitioning urban neighborhoods.

🍴 Downtown & Midtown

Empire State South
SOUTHERN US **$$**

(www.empirestatesouth.com; 999 Peachtree St; mains $12-36; ⊙7am-10pm Mon-Thu, to 11pm Thu-Sat, 10am-3pm Sun; 🌐) This rustic-hip Midtown bistro serves imaginative New Southern fare and it does not disappoint, be it at breakfast or throughout the remains of the day. They make their own bagels, the attention to coffee detail approaches Pacific Northwest levels, and they mix fried chicken, bacon *and* pimiento cheese!

No Mas! Cantina
MEXICAN **$$**

(☑404-574-5678; www.nomascantina.com; 180 Walker St SW; mains $7-20; ⊙8am-10pm; 🌐👶) Though the design overkill feels a bit like dining inside a hungover *piñata,* locals are sold on the festive Mexican at this downtown Castleberry Hill cantina. Despite its quiet location, it's walking distance from

ATLANTA FOR CHILDREN

Atlanta has plenty of activities to keep children entertained, delighted and educated.

Center for Puppetry Arts (☑ tickets 404-873-3391; www.puppet.org; 1401 Spring St NW; museum $10.50, guided tours $14; ☺ 9am-5pm Tue-Sun, closed Mon; 🚻) A wonderland for visitors of all ages and hands-down one of Atlanta's most unusual attractions, the museum houses a treasury of puppets, some of which you get to operate yourself. A major addition is the **Worlds of Puppetry Museum**, housing the most comprehensive collection of Jim Henson puppets and artifacts in the world.

Children's Museum of Atlanta (www.childrensmuseumatlanta.org; 275 Centennial Olympic Park Dr NW; $15; ☺ 10am-4pm Mon-Fri, to 5pm Sat & Sun; 🚻) A hands-on museum geared toward kids aged eight and under. Adults aren't allowed in without a youngster in tow.

Skyview Atlanta (☑ 678-949-9023; www.skyviewatlanta.com; 168 Luckie St NW; adult/senior/child $14/12/9; ☺ noon-10pm Sun-Thu, to 11pm Fri, 10am-11pm Sun; 🚻) Soar 200ft above the Atlanta skyline in this 20-story, 42-gondola Ferris wheel installed in 2013.

Fernbank Museum of Natural History (☑ 404-929-6300; www.fernbankmuseum.org; 767 Clifton Rd; adult/child $18/16; ☺ 10am-5pm; 🅿 🚻) Wander around dozens of acres of hardwood forests, or get enraptured by the huge dinosaur exhibits.

---

the Mercedes-Benz Stadium, Phillips Arena, CNN Center and Centennial Park.

Daddy Dz   BARBECUE **$$**
(☑ 404-222-0206; www.daddydz.com; 264 Memorial Dr SE; sandwiches $7-13, plates $13-23; ☺ 11am-10:30pm Mon-Thu, to 11pm Fri & Sat, noon-9pm Sun; 🅿) A juke joint of a barbecue shack, consistently voted one of the tops in town, and set smack in downtown. From the graffiti murals on the red, white and blue exterior, to the all-powerful smoky essence, to the reclaimed booths on the covered patio, there is soul to spare. Order the succulent ribs with cornbread, and you'll leave smiling.

South City Kitchen   SOUTHERN US **$$$**
(☑ 404-873-7358; www.southcitykitchen.com; 1144 Crescent Ave; mains $18-40; ☺ 11am-3:30pm & 5-10pm Mon-Fri, 10am-3pm & 5-10:30pm Sat, 10am-3pm & 5-10pm Sun) An upscale Southern kitchen featuring tasty updated staples like buttermilk fried chicken served with sautéed collards and mash, and a Georgia trout, pan-fried with roasted heirloom carrots. Start with fried green tomatoes, a Southern specialty *before* the movie.

✕ Westside

West Egg Cafe   DINER **$**
(☑ 404-872-3973; www.westeggcafe.com; 1100 Howell Mill Rd; mains $6-15; ☺ 7am-4pm Mon-Fri, to 5pm Sat & Sun; 🅿 📶 🚻) Belly up to the marble breakfast counter or grab a table and dive into black-bean cakes and eggs, turkey sau-

sage Benedict, pimiento cheese and bacon omelet, or a fried green tomato BLT. It's all re-imagined versions of old-school classics, served in a stylish and spare dining room.

Star Provisions   SUPERMARKET **$**
(☑ 404-365-0410; www.starprovisions.com; 1198 Howell Mill Rd; ☺ 10am-midnight Mon-Sat; 📶) DIY gourmets will feel at home among the cheese shops and butcher cases, bakeries, organic cafe and kitchen hardware depots attached to the city's finest dining establishment, **Bacchanalia** (☑ 404-365-0410; www.starprovisions.com/bacchanalia; 1198 Howell Mill Rd; prix-fixe per person $95; ☺ from 5:30pm; 🅿). Excellent picnic accoutrements.

⭐**Cooks & Soldiers**   BASQUE **$$**
(☑ 404-996-2623; www.cooksandsoldiers.com; 691 14th St; small plates $6-19; ☺ 5-10pm Sun-Wed, to 11pm Thu, to 2am Fri & Sat; 📶 ✕) A game-changing Westside choice, this Basque-inspired hot spot specializes in *pintxos* (Basque-ified tapas) and wood-fired *asadas* (grills) designed to share. Both the food and cocktails are outstanding. Highlights include the blood-orange gin and tonic, a black-truffled White American grilled cheese, roasted oysters and cream, and lamb ribs with spiced yogurt.

⭐**The Optimist**   SEAFOOD **$$$**
(☑ 404-477-6260; www.theoptimistrestaurant.com; 914 Howell Mill Rd; mains $22-34; ☺ 11:30am-2:30pm & 5-10pm Mon-Thu, 5-11pm Fri & Sat, 5-10pm Sun; 📶) ✐ In a short space, we could

never do this Westside sustainable seafood mecca justice. In a word, astonishing! Start with red curry mussels, then move on to a duck-fat-poached swordfish or razor clam chowder with bacon and white beans, and finish with a scoop of housemade salted caramel ice cream.

Virginia-Highland

Vortex
BURGERS $$

(☑404-688-1828; www.thevortexbarandgrill.com; 438 Moreland Ave NE; burgers $8.25-18; ⊙11am-midnight Sun-Thu, to 2am Fri & Sat) An NC-17 joint cluttered with Americana memorabilia, the Godfather of Atlanta burger joints is where alterna-hipsters mingle alongside Texas tourists and Morehouse College steppers. Burgers range from impressive to outlandish but are always some of the most heralded and heart-stopping in Atlanta. The 20ft-tall skull facade is a Little Five Points landmark of pre-Olympic Games outrageousness.

★ Octopus Bar
FUSION $$

(☑404-627-9911; www.octopusbaratl.com; 560 Gresham Ave SE, East Atlanta; dishes $9-15; ⊙10:30pm-2:30am Tue-Sat) Leave your hang-ups at the hotel – this is punk-rock dining – and get to know what's good at this indoor-outdoor patio dive nuanced with graffitied walls and ethereal electronica. No reservations, so line up early, and chow down on smoked branzino fish and grapefruit or pork belly ramen or a ton of other innovative executions of fusion excellence.

Do they keep odd hours? Is seating difficult to come by? Does it take so long to get your grub because the chefs are too busy fielding industry complaints from a room full of sous chefs and servers? The answer, of course, is yes to all of the above.

East Atlanta

Dish Dive
AMERICAN $

(☑404-957-7918; www.dishdivekitchen.com; 2233 College Ave NE; mains $8-16; ⊙5-10pm Tue-Sat) Located in an unmarked house near some railroad tracks, Dish Dive is probably cooler than you. The great thing is, it doesn't care. Anyone is welcome here, and the food – fresh, seasonal cuisine like local catfish with pork collards, chicken pot pie or homemade lasagna – is as cheap as chips.

Northern China Eatery
CHINESE $

(☑770-458-2282; http://northernchinaeatery.com; 5141 Buford Hwy NE; mains $7-14; ⊙10am-10pm Wed-Mon, closed Tue) We love a restaurant that is unambiguous about its name – and its cuisine. At the Eatery, you'll find real-deal northern Chinese cuisine: spicy beef lung, dan dan noodles, barbecue lamb and more dumplings than you can shake a (chop)stick at.

★ Gunshow
MODERN AMERICAN $$$

(☑404-380-1886; www.gunshowatl.com; 924 Garrett St SE; dishes $12-20; ⊙6-9pm Tue-Sat; ☎) Celebrity chef Kevin Gillespie's latest light-bulb moment is an unorthodox evening out. Guests choose between over a dozen or so smallish dishes, dreamed up by chefs in the open kitchen, who then hawk their blood, sweat and culinary tears dim-sum-style tableside. It can be agonizing, turning your nose up at a smoked ham hock confit because you're holding out for the Saigon-style Kobe beef tartar, but it's a dining experience like no other, and Atlanta's hottest table.

Decatur

Independent Decatur, 6 miles east of downtown, is a countercultural enclave and a bona fide foodie destination. Like most traditional Southern towns, the gazebo-crowned Courthouse Square is the center of the action, with a number of restaurants, cafes and shops surrounding it.

Leon's Full Service
FUSION $$

(☑404-687-0500; www.leonsfullservice.com; 131 E Ponce de Leon Ave; mains $13-27; ⊙5pm-1am Mon, 11:30am-1am Tue-Thu & Sun, to 2am Fri & Sat; ☎) Leon's can come across as a bit pretentious, but the gorgeous concrete bar and open

---

ATLANTA BELTLINE

The Atlanta BeltLine (www.beltline.org) is an enormous sustainable redevelopment project that is repurposing an existing 22-mile rail corridor encircling the city into 33 miles of connected multi-use trails. It is the most comprehensive transportation and economic development effort ever undertaken in Atlanta and among the largest, most wide-ranging urban redevelopment programs currently underway in the US. Of most interest to tourists is the 2.2-mile **Eastside Trail**, connecting the hip urban neighborhood of Inman Park with Piedmont Park in Midtown.

GAY & LESBIAN ATLANTA

Atlanta – or 'Hotlanta' as some might call it – is one of the few places in Georgia with a noticeable and active gay and lesbian population. Midtown is the center of gay life; the epicenter is around Piedmont Park and the intersection of 10th St and Piedmont Ave, where you can check out **Blake's** (☑404-892-5786; www.blakesontheparkatlanta.com; 227 10th St NE; ☺3pm-3am Mon-Fri, 1pm-3am Sat, 1pm-1am Sun), Atlanta's classic gay bar, or **10th & Piedmont** (www.communitashospitality.com/10th-and-piedmont; 991 Piedmont Ave NE; ☺10am-3pm & 5-10pm Mon-Thu, 10am-3pm & 5-11pm Fri, 10am-4pm & 5-11pm Sat, 10am-9pm Sun), good for both food and late-night shenanigans. The town of Decatur, east of downtown Atlanta, has a significant lesbian community. For news and information, grab a copy of *David Atlanta* (www.davidatlanta.com); also check out www.gayatlanta.com.

Atlanta Pride Festival is a massive annual celebration of the city's gay and lesbian community. It's held in October in and around Piedmont Park.

floor plan spilling out of a former service station and onto a groovy heated deck with floating beams remains cooler than thou and fully packed at all times.

Cakes & Ale
MODERN AMERICAN $$$

(☑404-377-7994; www.cakesandalerestaurant.com; 155 Sycamore St; mains $10-36; ☺cafe 8am-10pm Tue-Thu, to 11pm Fri & Sat, 9am-3pm Sun, restaurant 6-11pm Tue-Thu, 5:30pm-midnight Fri & Sat) A Chez Panisse alum and pastry mastermind runs this hip eatery. The bakery-cafe next door is life-affirming hot chocolate along with a case of delectable pastries, while the restaurant features spare but stunning selections that could mean perfectly grilled *framani soppresata* sandwiches with chard, preserved lemon ricotta and Dijon (a lunch standout), and pork guinea hen or lamb at dinner.

🍷 Drinking & Nightlife

Atlanta has a busy bar scene, ranging from neighborhood dives to hipster hangouts that want to pass for neighborhood dives to straight-up opulent night haunts for the wealthy and beautiful. Wherever you go, you may notice that this city has one of the most racially integrated social scenes in the country, and that's reason enough to raise a glass.

★Sister Louisa's Church of the Living Room & Ping Pong Emporium
BAR

(☑404-522-8275; www.sisterlouisaschurch.com; 466 Edgewood Ave; ☺5pm-3am Mon-Fri, 1pm-3am Sat, to midnight Sun; ☜) This cradle of Edgewood's bar revival fosters a church theme, but it's nothing like Westminster Abbey. Sacrilegious art peppers every patch of free wall space, the kind of offensive stuff that starts wars in some parts. Praise the resistance to

fancy craft cocktails and join the congregation, chuckling at the artistry or staring at mesmerizing table tennis matches.

★Argosy
PUB

(☑404-577-0407; www.argosy-east.com; 470 Flat Shoals Ave SE; ☺5pm-2:30am Mon-Fri, noon-2:30am Sat, to midnight Sun; ☜) This East Atlanta gastropub nails it with an extensive list of rare craft beers, awesome bar food and a vibe that invites you to stay for the rest of the evening. The multi-angled bar snakes its way through a rustic-chic space and living-room-style lounge areas.

Ladybird Grove & Mess Hall
BAR

(☑404-458-6838; www.ladybirdatlanta.com; 684 John Wesley Dobbs Ave NE; ☺11am-late Tue-Sun, closed Mon) With an enviable location (and enormous patio) overlooking the BeltLine, Ladybird offers its patrons one of the best drinking views in Atlanta.

Brick Store Pub
BAR

(☑404-687-0990; www.brickstorepub.com; 125 E Court Sq, Decatur; draft beers $5-12; ☺11am-1am Sun & Mon, to 2am Tue-Sat) Beer hounds geek out on Atlanta's best craft beer selection at this pub in Decatur, with some 30 meticulously chosen drafts (including those in the more intimate Belgian beer bar upstairs). Nearly 300 beers by the bottle are served from a 15,000-bottle vault, drawing a fun, young crowd every night.

Kimball House
COCKTAIL BAR

(☑404-378-3502; www.kimball-house.com; 303 E Howard Ave, Decatur; ☺5pm-midnight Sun-Thu, to 1am Fri & Sat) Housed in an atmospheric restored train depot slightly off the grid in Decatur, Kimball House harbors a vaguely saloon-like feel and specializes in craft

THE SOUTH ATLANTA

cocktails, absinthe and a long list of flown-in-fresh oysters.

Park Tavern
BAR

(✏404-249-0001; www.parktavern.com; 500 10th Street NE; ☺4:30pm-midnight Mon-Fri, 11:30am-midnight Sat & Sun; ☎) This staple microbrewery-restaurant's outdoor patio on the edge of Piedmont Park is one of the most beautiful spots in Atlanta to sit back and drink away a weekend afternoon.

☆ Entertainment

Clermont Lounge
DANCE

(✏404-874-4783; http://clermontlounge.net; 789 Ponce de Leon Ave NE; ☺1pm-3am Mon-Sat) How to explain the Clermont? First, it's a strip club, the oldest in Atlanta. But not *just* a strip club. It's a bedrock of the Atlanta scene that welcomes dancers of all ages, races and body types. In short, it's a strip club built for the strippers, although the audience – and *everyone* comes here at some point – has a grand time as well.

Terminal West
LIVE MUSIC

(✏404-876-5566; www.terminalwestatl.com; 887 W Marietta St) One of Atlanta's best live music venues, this concert space is located inside a beautifully revamped 100-year-old iron and steel foundry on the Westside.

Woodruff Arts Center
ARTS CENTER

(✏404-733-4200; www.woodruffcenter.org; 1280 Peachtree St NE) This arts complex contains within its campus the High Museum, the Atlanta Symphony Orchestra and the Alliance Theatre.

Variety Playhouse
LIVE MUSIC

(✏404-524-7354; www.variety-playhouse.com; 1099 Euclid Ave NE) A smartly booked and well-run concert venue featuring a variety of touring artists. It's one of the main anchors of the Little Five Points scene.

ℹ Information

EMERGENCY & MEDICAL SERVICES

Atlanta Medical Center (Wellstar Atlanta Medical Center; ✏404-265-4000; www.atlantamedcenter.com; 303 Parkway Dr NE) A tertiary care hospital considered Atlanta's best since 1901.

MEDIA

Atlanta (www.atlantamagazine.com) A monthly general-interest magazine covering local issues, arts and dining.

Atlanta Daily World (www.atlantadailyworld. com) The nation's oldest continuously running African American newspaper (since 1928).

Atlanta Journal-Constitution (www.ajc.com) Atlanta's major daily newspaper, with a good travel section on Sunday.

Creative Loafing (www.clatl.com) For hip tips on music, arts and theater, this free alternative weekly comes out every Wednesday.

RESOURCES

Scout Mob (www.scoutmob.com) Tips on what's new and hot in Atlanta.

Atlanta Travel Guide (www.atlanta.net) Official site of the Atlanta Convention & Visitors Bureau with excellent links to shops, restaurants, hotels and upcoming events. Its website also lets you buy a CityPass (see p396).

MARTIN LUTHER KING JR: A CIVIL RIGHTS GIANT

Martin Luther King Jr, the quintessential figure of the American Civil Rights movement and arguably America's greatest leader, was born in 1929, the son of an Atlanta preacher and choir leader. His lineage was significant not only because he followed his father to the pulpit of Ebenezer Baptist Church, but also because his political speeches rang out with a preacher's inflections.

In 1955 King led the yearlong 'bus boycott' in Montgomery, AL, which resulted in the US Supreme Court removing laws that enforced segregated buses. From this successful beginning King emerged as an inspiring moral voice.

King espoused a nonviolent approach to racial equality and peace, which he borrowed from Gandhi and used as a potent weapon against hate, segregation and racially motivated violence. He was assassinated on a Memphis hotel balcony in 1968, four years after receiving the Nobel Peace Prize and five years after giving his legendary 'I Have a Dream' speech in Washington, DC.

King remains one of the most recognized and respected figures of the 20th century. Over 10 years he led a movement that helped dismantle a system of statutory discrimination in existence since the country's founding.

❶ Getting There & Away

Atlanta's huge **Hartsfield-Jackson International Airport** (ATL; ☑ 800-897-1910; www.atl.com), 12 miles north of downtown, is a major regional hub and an international gateway. It's the busiest airport in the world in overall passenger traffic, and it feels like it.

The **Greyhound terminal** (☑ 404-584-1728; www.greyhound.com; 232 Forsyth St), located next to the MARTA Garnett station, serves Nashville (five hours), New Orleans (10½ hours), New York (20 hours), Miami (16 hours) and Savannah (4¾ hours).

Atlanta's main Amtrak station (www.amtrak.com; 1688 Peachtree St NW) is just north of downtown. Trains depart from here to the Northeast corridor and southern cities like Birmingham and New Orleans.

❶ Getting Around

Metropolitan Atlanta Rapid Transit Authority (MARTA; www.itsmarta.com) train line travels to/from the airport to downtown, as well as less useful commuter routes. Each customer must purchase a Breeze Card (www.breezecard.com); you pay $2 for the card, which can then be loaded and reloaded as necessary. MARTA fare is $2.50. The shuttle and car rental agencies have desks in the airport situated at baggage claim.

The Atlanta Streetcar is a nice way of getting around downtown Atlanta. Fare is $1 for a one-way ticket (or you can get an all-day pass for $3); the streetcar follows a 2.7-mile loop that covers a dozen stops, from Centennial Olympic Park to the Martin Luther King Jr National Historic Site.

Northern Georgia

Georgia is a state of geographic diversity. The interior boasts lakes and forests, the coast has marsh and barrier islands, and if you need mountains, head to North Georgia, which sits at the southern end of the great Appalachian Range. Those mountains, and their surrounding foothills and upcountry, provide superb mountain scenery, as well as some decent wines and frothing rivers. Fall colors emerge late here, peaking in October. A few days are warranted to see sites like the 1200ft-deep Tallulah Gorge, and the mountain scenery and hiking trails at Vogel State Park and Unicoi State Park.

Dahlonega

In 1828 Dahlonega was the site of the first gold rush in the USA. These days the boom is in tourism, as it's an easy day excursion from Atlanta and is a fantastic mountain destination. Not only is it a hotbed of outdoor activities, but downtown Dahlonega around Courthouse Square is an attractive melange of wine tasting rooms, gourmet emporiums, great food, countrified shops and foothill charm.

◉ Sights & Activities

Amicalola Falls State Park   STATE PARK
(☑ 706-265-4703; www.gastateparks.org/amicalola falls; 280 Amicalola Falls State Park Rd, Dawsonville; per vehicle $5; ⊙ 7am-10pm; ℗) ❂ This state park, 18 miles west of Dahlonega on Hwy 52, features the 729ft Amicalola Falls, the tallest cascading waterfall in the Southeast. The park offers spectacular scenery, a **lodge** (☑ 800-573-9656; www.amicalolafalls.com; 418 Amicalola Falls State Park Rd, Dawsonville; campsites from $30, r & cottages $140-240; ℗ ✸ @), and excellent hiking and mountain biking trails.

Frogtown Cellars   WINERY
(☑ 706-865-0687; www.frogtownwine.com; 700 Ridge Point Dr; tastings $15; ⊙ noon-5pm Mon-Fri, to 6pm Sat, 12:30-5pm Sun) This beautiful winery has a killer deck where you can sip libations and nibble cheese. It bills itself as the most awarded North American winery *not* in California, which we can't confirm, but the wine does go down a treat with a mountain sunset.

Dahlonega Courthouse Gold Museum   MUSEUM
(☑ 706-864-2257; www.gastateparks.org/dahlonegagoldmuseum; Public Sq; adult/child $7/4.50; ⊙ 9am-5pm Mon-Sat, 10am-5pm Sun) If you've got a thing for coins, currency or financial history, pop into this museum. Dahlonega has gold-mining roots and the town prospered with each strike. In 1838 the federal government opened a mint in the town square, where more than $6 million in gold was coined before the operation was closed at the dawn of the Civil War.

⛏ Sleeping & Eating

Hiker Hostel   HOSTEL $
(☑ 770-312-7342; www.hikerhostel.com; 7693 Hwy 19 N; dm/r $25/70, cabin $90-110; ℗ ✸ @ 🛜) On Hwy 19 N, 7 miles or so from town, this hostel is owned by an avid pair of cycling and outdoors enthusiasts, and caters to those looking to explore the Appalachian Trail. The hostel is a converted log cabin; each bunk

room has its own bath and it is wonderfully neat and clean.

Two stylish shipping-container cabins are built from reclaimed materials from throughout Georgia.

Cedar House Inn
& Yurts
B&B $$

(☑ 706-867-9446; www.georgiamountaininn.com; 6463 Highway 19 N; r $125-145, yurt $145; P ❃ 🛜)
🏃 Prayer flags, a permaculture farm, bottle trees and, as you may guess, a fairly progressive, environmentally conscious approach to life define the vibe at the Cedar House, located on Hwy 19 north of town. Staff can most definitely accommodate gluten-free and vegan breakfast requests. Cozy rooms and two colorful yurts (without air-conditioning) are all inviting places to crash out.

Spirits Tavern
BURGERS $

(☑ 706-482-0580; www.spirits-tavern.com; 19 E Main St; burgers $12-15; ☺ 11am-11pm Sun-Thu, to 1am Fri, to midnight Sun; 🛜) This full bar dishes up surprisingly creative burgers made from Angus beef or free range, hormone-free turkey, including crunchy mac 'n' cheese, Greek, Asian and Cajun versions.

Back Porch Oyster Bar
SEAFOOD $$

(☑ 706-864-8623; www.backporchoysterbar.net; 19 N Chestatee St; mains $9-31; ☺ 11:30am-9pm Mon-Thu, to 10pm Fri & Sat, to 8pm Sun; 🛜) Oysters, ahi and clams are among the bounty flown in fresh daily to be shucked, seared and steamed at this neighborhood fish house.

ⓘ Information

Visitors Center (☑ 706-864-3711; www.dahlonega.org; 13 S Park St; ☺ 9am-5:30pm Mon-Fri, 10am-5pm Sat) Has plenty of information on area sites and activities, including hiking, canoeing, kayaking, rafting and mountain biking.

ⓘ Getting There & Away

Dahlonega is about 70 miles north of Atlanta; the quickest way here is via Hwy 19. There is no bus service.

Athens

A beery, artsy and laid-back college town roughly 80 miles east of Atlanta, Athens has an extremely popular football team (the University of Georgia Bulldogs), a world-famous music scene, a burgeoning restaurant culture and surprisingly diverse

nightlife. The university – UGA – drives the culture of Athens and ensures an ever-replenishing supply of young bar-hoppers and concert-goers, some of whom stick around long after graduation and become 'townies.' The pleasant, walkable downtown offers a plethora of funky choices for eating, drinking and shopping.

⊙ Sights

★ **Georgia Museum of Art** MUSEUM
(☑ 706-542-4662; www.georgiamuseum.org; 90 Carlton St; ☺ 10am-5pm Tue-Wed, Fri & Sat, to 9pm Thu, 1-5pm Sun) FREE A smart, modern gallery where brainy, arty types set up in the wired lobby for personal study while art hounds gawk at modern sculpture in the courtyard garden and the tremendous collection from American realists of the 1930s.

State Botanical Garden
of Georgia
GARDENS

(www.botgarden.uga.edu; 2450 S Milledge Ave; ☺ 8am-6pm) 🏃 FREE Truly gorgeous, with winding outdoor paths and a socio-historical edge, Athens' gardens are a gift for a city of this size. Signs provide smart context for its amazing collection of plants, which includes rare and threatened species; and there's nearly 5 miles of top-notch woodland walking trails.

🛏 Sleeping & Eating

★ **Graduate Athens** INN $$
(☑ 706-549-7020; www.graduateathens.com; 295 E Dougherty St; r $100-170, ste $280-390; P @ 🛜 ⊛) This wonderfully designed boutique hotel, the inaugural address of a college-campus chain, is drowning in sexified retro hipness, from potted plants inside old-school Dewey Decimal card catalog filing cabinets in the lobby to the sweet Crosley turntables and classic video games in the suites.

Local accents, such as chalkboard-art of the chemical formula for sweet tea, fortify local allure. Also on-site is a great coffeehouse, bar and grill and live music venue, all inside an old Confederate iron foundry.

Hotel Indigo
BOUTIQUE HOTEL $$

(☑ 706-546-0430; www.indigoathens.com; 500 College Ave; r/ste from $160/265; P @ 🛜 ⊛ 🐾) 🏃 Rooms are spacious, loft-like pods of cool at this eco-chic boutique hotel. Part of the Indigo chain, it's a Leadership in Energy and Environmental Design gold-certified sustainable standout. Green elements include regenerative elevators and priority parking for hybrid vehicles; 30% of the building was constructed from recycled content.

Pouch PIES $
(☎706-395-6696; www.pouchpies.com; 151 E Broad St; pies $5.50; ⏰11am-10pm Mon-Wed, to 11pm Thu-Sat; 🖊) In the South, 'pie' usually means something sweet, buttery and served after dinner. For the South African owners of Pouch, 'pie' means savory pastries from around the world – Aussie pies with beef and gravy, Portuguese pies with piri piri white wine sauce and chorizo, and even a cheeseburger-esque American pie! Makes for a great budget meal.

White Tiger BARBECUE $
(☎706-353-6847; www.whitetigergourmet.com; 217 Hiawassee Ave; mains $6.75-10.50; ⏰11am-3pm Mon-Sat, 6-8pm Thu, 10am-2pm Sun; 🅿🖊) The 100-year-old structure doesn't invite confidence, but this off-the-beaten path local favorite does killer wood-smoked pulled pork sandwiches, burgers and even barbecue-smoked tofu for the vegetarians. Chef Ken Manring honed his skills in much higher-brow kitchens before settling in Athens.

home.made SOUTHERN US $$
(☎706-206-9216; www.homemadeathens.com; 1072 Baxter St; mains $13-25; ⏰11am-2pm & 5:30-9:30pm Tue-Sat) home.made is upping the game when it comes to nouveau Southern cuisine. The menu constantly changes based on ingredient availability, but whatever these folks source is always turned into something creative, delicious, rooted in local flavors and often playfully over the top – say, pan-seared flounder and turmeric rice grits.

Five & Ten AMERICAN $$$
(☎706-546-7300; www.fiveandten.com; 1073 S Milledge Ave; mains $22-36; ⏰5:30-10pm Sun-Thu, to 11pm Fri & Sat, 10:30am-2:30pm Sun; 🖊) 🌱 Driven by sustainable ingredients, Five & Ten ranks among the South's best restaurants. Its menu is earthy and slightly gamey: sweetbreads, black-eyed pea hummus and Frogmore stew (stewed corn, sausage and potato). Reservations mandatory.

🍷 Drinking & Entertainment

Trapeze Pub CRAFT BEER
(☎706-543-8997; www.trappezepub.com; 269 N Hull St; ⏰11am-2am Mon-Sat, to midnight Sun; 🖥) Downtown's best craft-beer bar installed itself well before the suds revolution. You'll find dozens of taps, including local fave Creature Comforts, and another 100 or so at any given time in bottles. Soak it all up with their Belgian-style fries, the best in town.

The Old Pal BAR
(☎706-850-4340; www.theoldpal.com; 1320 Prince Ave; ⏰4pm-2am Mon-Sat; 🖥) The Old Pal is Normal Town's thinking man's bar, devoted to seasonal craft cocktails and a thoughtfully curated bourbon list. It's a beautiful, dark space that has been showered with local preservation awards.

Normal Bar BAR
(☎706-548-6186; www.facebook.com/normal. bar.7; 1365 Prince Ave; ⏰4pm-2am Mon-Fri, 11:30am-2am Sat; 🖥) This lovable dark storefront

---

NATURE & ADVENTURE IN NORTHERN GEORGIA

Tallulah Gorge (☎706-754-7981; www.gastateparks.org/tallulahgorge; 338 Jane Hurt Yarn Dr, Tallulah Falls; per vehicle $5; ⏰8am-sunset; 🅿) The 1200ft-deep Tallulah Gorge carves a dark scar across the wooded hills of North Georgia. Walk over the *Indiana Jones*-worthy suspension bridge, and be on the lookout (literally) for rim trails to overlooks. Or get a first-come, first-served permit to hike to the gorge floor – only 100 are given out each day.

Vogel State Park (☎706-745-2628; www.gastateparks.org/vogel; 405 Vogel State Park Rd, Blairsville; per vehicle $5; ⏰7am-10pm; 🅿) Located at the base of the evocatively named Blood Mountain, this is one of Georgia's oldest parks, and constitutes a quilt of wooded mountains surrounding a 22-acre lake. There's a multitude of trails to pick from, catering to beginners and advanced hikers. Many of the on-site facilities were built by the Civilian Conservation Corp; a seasonal museum tells the story of these work teams, which both built the park and rescued the local economy during the Great Depression.

Unicoi State Park (☎706-878-2201; www.gastateparks.org/unicoi; 1788 Highway 356, Helen; per vehicle $5; ⏰7am-10pm; 🅿🖊) At this adventure-oriented park, visitors can rent kayaks ($10 per hour), take paddleboard lessons ($25), hike some 12 miles of trails, mountain bike, or take a zipline safari through the local forest canopy ($59).

bar is very unstudentlike but still very much Athens. The beer goes from PBR cheap to local craft IPA sophisticated. There's a terrific wine list and the crowd is cute, young and laid-back.

40 Watt Club
LIVE MUSIC

(☑706-549-7871; www.40watt.com; 285 W Washington St; admission $5-25) Athens' most storied joint has lounges, a tiki bar and $2.50 PBRs. The venue has welcomed indie rock to its stage since R.E.M., the B-52s and Widespread Panic owned this town, and today this is still where the big hitters play when they come to town.

ⓘ Information

Athens Welcome Center (☑706-353-1820; www.athenswelcomecenter.com; 280 E Dougherty St; ⊙10am-5pm Mon-Sat, noon-5pm Sun) This visitor center, in a historic antebellum house at the corner of Thomas St, provides maps and information on local tours.

ⓘ Getting There & Away

This college town is located about 70 miles east of Atlanta. There's no main highway that leads here, so traffic can be an issue on secondary state and county roads. The local **Greyhound station** (☑706-549-2255; www.greyhound.com; 4020 Atlanta Hwy, Bogart) is actually located about 6 miles west of downtown Athens. Buses leave for Atlanta (7½ hours, twice daily) and Savannah (14 hours, once daily).

Coastal Georgia

Compared to the urban, suburban and ex-urban sprawl that surrounds Atlanta, or the mountainous upcountry of North Georgia, the state's southern region hews to the Old South Spanish moss and live oak cliché. Swampy Savannah holds court as the state's irresistible Southern belle, but there's more to the region than antebellum architecture and Spanish moss – Georgia's wild and preserved barrier island-riddled coast is an often overlooked stunner.

Savannah

Savannah is a looker, make no mistake. Built around a historic district that is rife with elegant townhouses, antebellum mansions, mammoth live oak trees and green public squares draped in Spanish moss, this is, quite simply, an exceedingly attractive city.

But this town is more than a pretty face. If Savannah is a Southern belle, she's carrying a slug of whiskey and a bottle of hot sauce, and her legs might be proudly unshaven too. This town is graceful, to be sure – the phrase 'moonlight and magnolias' is overused, but man does it apply here – but it's also gritty, and playfully transgressive. That's partly a function of Savannah's tolerance of bad behavior (limited open container laws, woo!), plus the presence of students at the Savannah College of Art & Design (SCAD), one of the finest art schools in the country.

⊙ Sights & Activities

★**Wormsloe Plantation Historic Site**
HISTORIC SITE

(☑912-353-3023; www.gastateparks.org/Wormsloe; 7601 Skidaway Rd; adult/senior/child 6-17yr/child 1-5yr $10/9/4.50/2; ⊙9am-5pm Tue-Sun; ℗) 🌿 A short drive from downtown, on the beautiful Isle of Hope, this is one of the most photographed sites in town. As soon as you enter, you feel as if you've been roused from the last snatch of an arboreal dream as you gaze at a corridor of mossy, ancient oaks that runs for 1.5 miles, known as the Avenue of the Oaks.

Forsyth Park
PARK

FREE The Central Park of Savannah is a sprawling rectangular green space, anchored by a beautiful fountain that forms a quintessential photo op.

Mercer-Williams House
HISTORIC BUILDING

(☑912-236-6352; www.mercerhouse.com; 429 Bull St; adult/student $12.50/8; ⊙10:30am-4:10pm Mon-Sat, noon-4pm Sun) Although Jim Williams, the Savannah art dealer portrayed by Kevin Spacey in the film version of *Midnight in the Garden of Good and Evil,* died back in 1990, his infamous mansion didn't become a museum until 2004. You're not allowed to visit the upstairs, where Williams' family still lives, but the downstairs is an interior decorator's fantasy.

Owens-Thomas House
HISTORIC BUILDING

(☑912-790-8800; www.telfair.org/visit/owens-thomas; 124 Abercorn St; adult/senior/child $20/18/15; ⊙noon-5pm Sun & Mon, 10am-5pm Tue-Sat) Completed in 1819 by British architect William Jay, this gorgeous villa exemplifies English Regency-style architecture, known for its symmetry. The guided tour is a little obsessed with details on aristocratic life, but it delivers interesting trivia about the spooky 'haint blue' ceiling paint in the slaves quarters (made from crushed indigo, buttermilk and crushed oyster shells) and the number of years by which this mansion preceded the White House in getting running water (nearly 20).

Telfair Academy of Arts & Sciences
MUSEUM

(✔912-790-8800; www.telfair.org/visit/telfair; 121 Barnard St; adult/child $20/15; ☉noon-5pm Sun & Mon, 10am-5pm Tue-Sat) Considered Savannah's top art museum, the historic Telfair family mansion is filled with 19th-century American art and silver, and a smattering of European pieces. The home itself is gorgeous and sunrise-hued – an artifact in its own right that wows visitors.

SCAD Museum of Art
MUSEUM

(www.scadmoa.org; 601 Turner Blvd; adult/child under 14yr $10/free; ☉10am-5pm Tue-Wed, to 8pm Thu, to 5pm Fri & Sat, noon-5pm Sun) Architecturally striking (but what else would you expect from this school of design?), this brick, steel, concrete and glass longhouse delivers your contemporary art fix. There are groovy, creative sitting areas inside and out, and a number of rotating and visiting exhibitions that showcase some of the most impressive talents within the contemporary art world.

Jepson Center for the Arts
GALLERY

(JCA;✔912-790-8800;www.telfair.org/visit/jepson; 207 W York St; adult/child $20/15; ☉noon-5pm Sun & Mon, 10am-5pm Tue-Sat; 👶) Designed by the great Moshe Safdie, and looking pretty darn space-age by Savannah's standards, the JCA – rather appropriately, given its architecture – focuses on 20th- and 21st-century art. Be on the lookout for wandering scads of SCAD students (ha) and temporary exhibitions covering topics from race to art in VR video games.

Savannah Bike Tours
CYCLING

(✔912-704-4043; www.savannahbiketours.com; 41 Habersham St; tours $25; ☉hours vary by season) This outfit offers two-hour bike tours over easy flat terrain on its fleet of cruisers. Call ahead or check the website for tour times.

🛏 Sleeping

Savannah Pensione
GUESTHOUSE $

(✔912-236-7744; www.savannahpensione.com; 304 E Hall St; s/d without bath from $55/65; P❄@) It was run as a hostel for some 15 years, but the owner of this basic neighborhood crash pad got tired of backpackers traipsing up and down the historic steps of the 1884 Italianate mansion. Fair enough. Now a bare-bones and vibeless pension, it still offers the cheapest historic quarter rooms, though its potential is unrealized.

★The Kimpton Brice
HOTEL $$

(✔912-238-1200; www.bricehotel.com; 601 E Bay St; r from $175; ❄🐾🌐❄) Kimpton is known for their design-conscious hotels, so you gotta figure they'd bring their A game to one of the country's leading design cities. The Kimpton Brice does not disappoint in this, or any other, regard. Modern rooms have playful swatches of color, while the hotel's entrance and lobby feels like it could accommodate a cool club.

Thunderbird Inn
MOTEL $$

(✔912-232-2661; www.thethunderbirdinn.com; 611 W Oglethorpe Ave; r $120-150; P❄🐾❄) 'A tad Palm Springs, a touch Vegas' best describes this vintage-chic 1964 motel that wins its own popularity contest – a 'Hippest hotel in Savannah' proclamation greets guests in the '60s-soundtracked lobby. In a land of stuffy B&Bs, this groovy place is an oasis, made all the better by local Savannah College of Art & Design student art.

Azalea Inn
INN $$

(✔912-236-6080; www.azaleainn.com; 217 E Huntingdon St; r/villa from $200/300; P❄🐾❄) A humble stunner on a quiet street, we love this sweet canary-yellow historic inn near Forsyth Park. The 10 rooms aren't huge, but are well done with varnished dark-wood floors, crown moldings, four-poster beds and a small dipping pool out back. Three new villas offer more modern luxury for long-term stays.

Kehoe House
B&B $$$

(✔912-232-1020; www.kehoehouse.com; 123 Habersham St; r from $240; ❄🌐) This romantic, upscale Renaissance Revival B&B dates from 1892, and twins are said to have died in a chimney here, making it one of America's most haunted hotels (if you're skittish, steer clear of rooms 201 and 203). Ghosts aside, it's a beautifully appointed worthwhile splurge on picturesque Columbia Square.

Mansion on Forsyth Park
HOTEL $$$

(✔912-238-5158; www.mansiononforsythpark. com; 700 Drayton St; r weekday/weekend $220/360; P❄@🌐❄) A choice location and chic design highlight the luxe accommodations on offer at the 18,000-sq-ft Mansion – the sexy

Savannah

bathrooms alone are practically worth the money. The best part of the hotel-spa is the amazing local and international art that crowds its walls and hallways – over 400 pieces in all.

Old Harbour Inn BOUTIQUE HOTEL **$$$**
(☑912-234-4100; www.oldeharbourinn.com; 508 East Factors Walk; ste $205-290; 🕸🐾) The spiffy suites at this waterfront hotel occupy the golden mean between historic atmosphere and modern sensibilities, from the airy sense of space (a bit of space, actually – from 450 to 650 sq ft) to the subdued color schemes

and polished hardwood floors. There's a free wine and cheese reception every evening.

🍴 Eating

⭐ **B's Cracklin' BBQ** BARBECUE **$**
(☑912-330-6921; www.bscracklinbbq.com; 12409 White Bluff Rd; mains $9-19; ⏰11am-9pm Tue-Sat, to 6pm Sun; 🅿) This is *very* good barbecue. Pit master Bryan Furman left his job as a welder to raise his own hogs and source local ingredients for homemade sides. The result is smoky heaven: melting brisket, falling-off-the-bone ribs and perfect Carolina-style pork. The portions are more than gen-

Savannah

erous; prepare to leave as stuffed as one of Bryan's hogs. B's is located about 8 miles south of downtown.

Leopold's Ice Cream ICE CREAM **$**
(☏912-234-4442; www.leopoldsicecream.com; 212 E Broughton St; scoops $3-5.50; ⊘11am-11pm Sun-Thu, to midnight Fri & Sat; 🐾) This classic American ice-cream parlor feels like the Last Man Standing, having been scooping up its creamy Greek recipes since 1919. Tutti Frutti was invented here, but we dig coffee, pistachio honey almond, and cream and caramel swirl. Hurry up and wait.

Sweet Spice JAMAICAN **$**
(☏912-335-8146; www.sweetspicesavannah.net; 5515 Waters Ave; mains $6-14; ⊘11am-8pm Mon-Thu, to 9pm Fri & Sat) This easygoing Jamaican spot, about 4.5 miles southeast of downtown, is a welcome break from the almost ubiquitous American and Southern fare you get in this part of the world. A large platter of curry goat or jerk chicken costs just a smidge more than a fast-food meal and it's utterly delicious. It will also keep you filled up for roughly the rest of the year.

Treylor Park SOUTHERN US **$**
(☏888-873-9567, 912-495-5557; www.treylorpark savannah.com; 115 E Bay St; mains $6-15; ⊘noon-1am Mon-Wed, to 2am Fri, 10am-2am Sat, 10am-1am Sun) All the hip young things pack into this 'Treylor Park,' which revels in a retro-chic, Airstream aesthetic. The food? Southern classics simply done well: fried chicken on a biscuit with sausage gravy and spicy collard greens, or a grilled apple pie sandwich. Take your pick, and wash it down with an excellent cocktail in the warmly lit courtyard.

Collins Quarter CAFE **$$**
(☏912-777-4147; www.thecollinsquarter.com; 151 Bull St; dinner mains $17-32; ⊘6:30am-5pm Mon, to noon Tue, to 10pm Wed-Sun; 🐾) If you have ever talked coffee with an Australian, you know they are particularly fussy about their java. This wildly popular newcomer is Australian-owned and turns Australian-roasted Brooklyn coffee into their beloved flat whites and long blacks. Beyond Savannah's best coffee, it serves excellent fusion fare, including a drool-inducing brisket burger. There's booze too!

★**Local11Ten** MODERN AMERICAN **$$$**
(☏912-790-9000; www.local11ten.com; 1110 Bull St; mains $26-45; ⊘6-10pm; 🍴) Upscale, sustainable, local and fresh: these elements help create an elegant, well-run restaurant that's easily one of Savannah's best. Start with a deconstructed rabbit ravioli, then move on to the fabulous seared sea scallops in mint beurre blanc or the harissa-marinated bison hanger steak and a salted caramel pot de crème for a happy ending. Wait. Scratch that. The menu already changed.

🍷 **Drinking & Entertainment**

River St, with its plastic-cup, open-container laws, is the bar-hopping nightlife corridor, but Savannah's nightlife is more than spring break bacchanalia. There are also some smart, exceedingly interesting bars out here.

★**Chromatic Dragon** BAR
(☏912-289-0350; www.chromaticdragon.com; 514 Martin Luther King Jr Blvd; ⊘11am-11pm Sun-Thu, to 2am Fri & Sat) If the name of this place

THE SOUTH COASTAL GEORGIA

made you smile, you'll be right at home in this gamers pub, which features video game consoles, board games and drinks named for fantasy references, from *Harry Potter* butterbeer to fantasy role playing game 'healing potions.' There's a warm, welcoming atmosphere – truly, this is a certain kind of nerd's ultimate neighborhood bar.

Abe's on Lincoln
BAR
(☑ 912-349-0525; www.abesonlincoln.com; 17 Lincoln St; ☺4pm-3am Mon-Sat) Pop back a beer or 10 with SCAD students and locals at this dark, dank, all-wood bar. Attracts an eclectic crowd that stares through their boozy goggles at whatever weird behavior the bartenders are inevitably tolerating that night. Good times.

Distillery Ale House
BAR
(☑ 912-236-1772; www.distilleryalehouse.com; 416 W Liberty St; ☺11am-late Mon-Sat, noon-late Sun) Formerly the Kentucky Distilling Co, which opened in 1904 and closed at Prohibition, this is oddly *not* Savannah's local throat-burning swill house, but rather its go-to craft beer bar. It's also popular with tourists and families for bar food.

Club One
GAY & LESBIAN
(☑ 912-232-0200; www.clubone-online.com; 1 Jefferson St; ☺5pm-3am) Drag shows (resident star Lady Chablis appeared in *Midnight in the Garden of Good and Evil*), ripping dance nights and plenty of flirting kicks off pretty regularly at this gay bar, which is otherwise a laid-back place where a mix of locals and SCAD students play pool and shoot the breeze.

The Jinx
LIVE MUSIC
(☑ 912-236-2281; www.thejinx912.com; 127 W Congress St; ☺4pm-3am) A good slice of odd-duck Savannah nightlife, the Jinx is popular with students, townies, musicians, and basically anyone else who has a thing for dive-y watering holes with live music – from rock to punk to alt-country to hip-hop – and funky stuff decorating the walls.

ⓘ Information

Candler Hospital (☑ 912-819-4100; www.sjchs.org; 5353 Reynolds St; ☺24hr) Located about 4 miles south of downtown, the Candler Hospital provides good 24/7 care and service. There's another campus at 11075 Mercy Blvd.

Savannah Visitors Center (☑ 912-944-0455; www.savannahvisit.com; 301 Martin Luther King Jr Blvd; ☺9am-5:30pm) Excellent

resources and services are available in this center, based in a restored 1860s train station. Many privately operated city tours start here. There is also a small interactive tourist info kiosk in the visitor center at Forsyth Park.

ⓘ Getting There & Around

Savannah is located off I-95, about 110 miles south of Charleston, SC. The **Savannah/Hilton Head International Airport** (SAV; ☑ 912-964-0514; www.savannahairport.com; 400 Airways Ave) is about 5 miles west of downtown, off I-16; service is mainly domestic flights to Eastern seaboard, Southern and Midwestern cities.

Greyhound (☑ 912-232-2135; www.greyhound.com; 610 W Oglethorpe Ave) has connections to Atlanta (about five hours), Charleston, SC (about two hours) and Jacksonville, FL (2½ hours).

The **Amtrak station** (www.amtrak.com; 2611 Seaboard Coastline Dr) is just a few miles west of the Historic District; trains run to Charleston, Jacksonville, and from there to points beyond.

Savannah is very foot-friendly. Chatham Area Transit (www.catchacat.org) operates local buses that run on bio-diesel, including a free shuttle (the Dot) that makes its way around the Historic District and stops within a couple of blocks of nearly every major site. Fare is $1.50 per ride.

CAT Bike (www.catbike.bcycle.com; ☺daily/weekly membership $5/20, per 30min $2) is a convenient bike hire scheme run by Chatham Area Transit. You have to buy a membership, after which it's free for the first hour. There are stations around town.

Taxis from the airport to the Historic District cost a standard $28.

Brunswick & the Golden Isles

With its large shrimp-boat fleet and downtown historic district shaded by lush live oaks, Brunswick has charms you might miss when sailing by on I-95 or the Golden Isle Pkwy (US Hwy 17). The town dates from 1733, and while it's not as tourism oriented as other parts of the coast, visitors may find this a refreshing change of pace.

Mary Ross Waterfront Park
PARK
(Bay St) During WWII Brunswick shipyards constructed 99 Liberty transport ships for the navy. Today a 23ft scale model at Mary Ross Waterfront Park stands as a memorial to those ships and their builders.

Hostel in the Forest
HOSTEL $
(☑ 912-264-9738; www.foresthostel.com; 3901 Hwy 82; per person $30; ℗🐾) The only budget base in the area is this set of bare-bones octagonal cedar huts and tree houses

(sans air or heat) on an ecofriendly, sustainable campus. You must pay a member fee of $10 to stay, and dinner is included. As you might guess, the hostel is tucked in the woods, about 10 miles outside Brunswick. Phone reservations only.

❶ Getting There & Around

Brunswick is located off Hwy 17. **Greyhound** (☑800-231-2222; 2990 Hwy 17 S) buses stop at the Flying J gas station, 10 miles west of town. Destinations include Savannah ($16, two hours, twice daily) and Jacksonville ($15, 70 minutes, twice daily) – you can catch onward buses from either city.

ST SIMONS ISLAND

Famous for its golf courses, resorts and majestic live oaks, St Simons Island is the largest and most developed of the Golden Isles. While there are pretty beaches galore, the natural beauty of St Simons isn't as easy to access compared to other nearby islands given the presence of heavy residential and resort development. For example, the island of Little St Simons is an all-natural jewel, but it's only accessible by only to guests staying at the exclusive Lodge on Little St Simons. On the other hand, if you need to get some golf in, this is the island for you.

Lighthouse Museum　　　　　MUSEUM
(☑912-638-4666; www.saintsimonslighthouse.org; 610 Beachview Dr; adult/child 5-11yr $10/5; ☺10am-5pm Mon-Sat, 1:30-5pm Sun) Built in 1807 and standing 85ft tall, the first lighthouse was destroyed by Confederates when Union troops landed in 1862. The second lighthouse, which you'll be able to tour, was built in 1872. The 104ft tower has a spiral 129-step cast iron staircase and an adjacent keeper's residence.

🛏 Sleeping & Eating

St Simons Inn By The Lighthouse　INN $$
(☑912-638-1101; www.saintsimonsinn.com; 609 Beachview Dr; r $140-160; P❄☎⛱) This cute and comfortable good-value inn is accented with white wooden shutters and a general sense of seaside breeziness. It's well located next to the downtown drag and a short pedal from East Beach. Continental breakfast included.

Lodge on Little St Simons Island　　LODGE $$$
(☑888-733-5774; www.littlestsimonsisland.com; 1000 Hampton River Club Dr, Little St Simons Is-

CUMBERLAND ISLAND NATIONAL SEASHORE

An unspoiled paradise, a backpacker's fantasy, a site for day trips or extended stays – it's clear why the Carnegie family used **Cumberland Island National Seashore** (☑912-882-4336; www.nps.gov/cuis; $7) as a retreat long ago. Almost half of its 36,415 acres consists of marsh, mudflats and tidal creeks. On the ocean side are 16 miles of wide, sandy beach that you might have all to yourself. The island's interior is characterized by maritime forest.

land; d from $425; ❄☎) This isolated historic lodge sits on pristine and private Little St Simons. Stays include accommodations, boat transfers to and from the island, three prepared meals daily, beverages (including soft drinks, beer and wine), all activities (including naturalist-led excursions) and use of all recreation equipment. Rooms have a rustic, cabin vibe, albeit with modern amenities.

Southern Soul BBQ　　　　　BARBECUE $
(☑912-638-7685; www.southernsoulbbq.com; 2020 Demere Rd; mains $7.50-20; ☺11am-9pm Mon-Sat, to 6pm Sun; 🖐) Succulent slow oak-smoked pulled pork, burnt-tipped brisket and daily specials like jerk chicken burritos keep this joint packed with satisfied 'cue fanatics. There are a number of wonderful housemade sauces and a great patio from which to take it all in.

★Halyards　　　　　　　SEAFOOD $$$
(☑912-638-9100; www.halyardsrestaurant.com; 55 Cinema Lane; mains $18-42; ☺5-9pm Mon-Wed, to 10pm Thu-Sat; ☎) 🍴 Chef Dave Snyder's classy sustainable, seasonal seafooder consistently hogs best-of-everything awards on St Simons, and for good reason. Go for the Chef's Highlights, such as mahimahi over boursin grits, haricot verts and orange-vanilla butter – perfection.

JEKYLL ISLAND

An exclusive refuge for millionaires in the late 19th and early 20th centuries, Jekyll is a 4000-year-old barrier island with 10 miles of beaches. Today it's an unusual clash of wilderness, preserved historic buildings, modern hotels and a massive campground. It's an easily navigable place – you can get around by car, horse or bicycle.

⊙ Sights & Activities

Georgia Sea Turtle Center WILDLIFE RESERVE
(☑912-635-4444; www.georgiaseaturtlecenter.
org; 214 Stable Rd; adult/child $7/5, tours $22-6;
⊘9am-5pm, closed Mon Nov-Mar; 🛖) An endearing attraction is the Georgia Sea Turtle Center, a conservation center and turtle
hospital where patients are on view for the
public. Behind the Scenes tours (3pm) and
Turtle Walks (June and July) are also available, among other programs.

4-H Tidelands Nature Center MUSEUM
(http://caes2.caes.uga.edu/georgia4h/tidelands;
100 S Riverview Dr; ⊘9am-4pm Mon-Fri, 10am-
2pm Sat & Sun; 🛖) 𝒫 Run by a staff of peppy
University of Georgia science students, the
Tidelands is a kid-friendly nature center
with some neat display cases on local ecol-
ogy and resident wildlife, including a baby
alligator. Nearby you'll find a lovely network
of nature trails that wend past marshlands
and through maritime forests.

★Kayak Tours & Canoe Rentals BOATING
(☑912-635-5032; http://caes2.caes.uga.edu/geor-
gia4h/tidelands/tours; 100 S Riverview Dr; s/tan-
dem kayak tour $55/95, canoe rental per hour/day
$15/30) The 4-H Tidelands Nature Center
conducts highly recommended three-hour
tours of the salt marshes; on any given day,
you may paddle past wood storks, great
blue herons, pelicans and dolphins. By far,
this is the best local means of accessing the
understated beauty of the barrier island salt
marshes. Canoe rentals are also available.

🛏 Sleeping & Eating

Villas By The Sea VILLA $
(☑912-635-2521; www.villasbythesearesort.com;
1175 N Beachview Dr; r/condo from $125/235;
🅿❄🛜🏊) A nice choice on the north coast
close to the best beaches. Rooms are spacious and the one-, two- and three-bedroom
condos, set in a complex of lodge buildings
sprinkled over a garden, aren't fancy but
they're plenty comfy.

Jekyll Island Club Hotel HISTORIC HOTEL $$
(☑855-535-9547; www.jekyllclub.com; 371 River-
view Dr; d/ste from $200/300, resort fee $15;
🅿❄@🛜🏊) A posh and storied hotel and
the backbone of the island, featuring a ram-
bling array of rooms spread out over five his-
toric structures. Each building feels plucked
from a novel about Jazz Age decadence,
although the current vibe is a little more
Hilton Head country club.

Driftwood Bistro SOUTHERN US $$
(☑912-635-3588; www.driftwoodbistro.com; 1175
Beach View Dr; mains $9.50-16.50; ⊘5-9pm
Mon-Sat; 🅿) Driftwood Bistro serves decent
Lowcountry-style seafood in an old-school,
family-friendly resort-style setting. Local
Georgia shrimp – cooked in sauce as shrimp
creole, or just steamed for you to peel and
eat – is usually on the menu. Any way it
comes, you shouldn't miss these plump,
sweet delicacies.

ALABAMA

History suffuses Alabama, a description that
could be true of many states. But there are
few places where the perception of said history is so emotionally fraught. The Mississippian Native American culture built great
mound cities here, and Mobile is dotted
with Franco-Caribbean architecture. But
for many, the word Alabama is synonymous
with the American Civil Rights movement.

Perhaps such a struggle, and all of the
nobility and desperation it entailed, was
bound for a state like this, with its Gothic
plantations, hardscrabble farmland and
fiercely local sense of place. From the smallest hunting town to river-bound cities, Alabama is a place all its own, and its character
is hard to forget. Some visitors have a hard
time looking beyond the state's past, but the
troubling elements of that narrative are tied
up in a passion that constantly manifests in
Alabama's arts, food and culture.

❶ Information

Alabama Tourism Department (http://alabama.
travel) Sends out a vacation guide and has a
website with extensive tourism options.

❶ Getting There & Away

While there are mid-sized domestic airports in
Mobile and Montgomery, the most common air
entry to Alabama is via Birmingham-Shuttles-
worth International Airport (p413).

Alabama is bordered by Mississippi, Florida,
Georgia and Tennessee. The Gulf Coast of
Alabama is barely an hour away from some of
the Florida Panhandle's best beaches. if you're
road-tripping around, Birmingham is about 150
miles from Atlanta, GA, 200 miles from Nashville, TN, and 190 miles from Oxford, MS.

The main highways in the state are I-10, which
cuts across the Gulf Coast; I-65, which runs
north to south; I-20, which cuts horizontally
across the center-top; and I-59, which runs in a
diagonal line northeast to Chattanooga.

You can find Greyhound stations in major towns. Amtrak has service to Birmingham, and there is talk of reestablishing an Amtrak line across the Gulf Coast.

Birmingham

Birmingham may lack the name-brand recognition of musical powerhouses like New Orleans and Nashville, or business centers like Atlanta and Houston. What Alabama's largest city possesses instead is vast reserves of unexpected cool. Innovative urban renewal and beautification projects seem to lurk around every corner – at least, the ones that aren't occupied by fantastic bars and restaurants. And while opinions run the gamut, this is a far more liberal town than you may expect given the political proclivities of its home state.

This hilly, shady city, founded as an iron mine, is still a center for manufacturing – many Birmingham residents work at Mercedes Benz USA in Tuscaloosa. In addition, universities and colleges pepper the town, and all of this comes together to create a city with an unreservedly excellent dining-and-drinking scene. The past also lurks in Birmingham, once named 'Bombingham,' and the history of the Civil Rights movement is very much at your fingers.

◉ Sights & Activities

Art-deco buildings abound in trendy **Five Points South**, where you'll find shops, restaurants and nightspots. Once-industrial **Avondale** is where the hipsters are congregating. Equally noteworthy is the upscale **Homewood** community's quaint commercial drag on 18th St S, close to the *Vulcan*, which looms illuminated above the city and is visible from nearly all angles, day and night.

★ Birmingham Civil Rights Institute   MUSEUM
(☑ 866-328-9696; www.bcri.org; 520 16th St N; adult/child $12/5, Sun by donation; ⊙ 10am-5pm Tue-Sat, 1-5pm Sun) A maze of moving audio, video and photography exhibits tell the story of racial segregation in America, and the Civil Rights movement, with a focus on activities in and around Birmingham. There's an extensive exhibit on the 16th Street Baptist Church (located across the street), which was bombed in 1963; it's the beginning of the city's Civil Rights Memorial Trail.

★ Sloss Furnaces   FACTORY
(☑ 205-254-2025; www.slossfurnaces.com; 20 32nd St N; ⊙ 10am-4pm Tue-Sat, noon-4pm Sun; **P**) **✦FREE** The Sloss Furnaces constitutes one of Birmingham's can't-miss sites. From 1882 to 1971, this was a pig iron–producing blast furnace and a cornerstone of Birmingham's economy. Today, instead of a wasteland it's a National Historic Landmark, a red mass of steel and girders rusted into a Gothic monument to American industry. Quiet pathways pass cobwebbed workshops and production lines that form a photographer's dream playground. A small museum on site explores the furnaces' history.

Railroad Park   PARK
(☑ 205-521-9933; www.railroadpark.org; ⊙ 7am-11pm; ⊛) **✦FREE** Credit where it's due: Birmingham's Railroad Park, which constitutes some 19 acres of downtown real estate, is a stroke of planning brilliance. As urban green lungs go, this park, and its miles of pathways, public art and pretty lighting, is fantastic. A good place to access the park is on 1st Ave South, between 14th and 18th St South.

Vulcan Park   PARK
(☑ 205-933-1409; www.visitvulcan.com; 1701 Valley View Dr; observation tower & museum adult/child $6/4, 6-10pm $4; ⊙ park 7am-10pm; observation tower 10am-6pm daily; museum 10am-6pm Mon-Sat, from noon Sun; ⊞ ⊛) Imagine Christ the Redeemer in Rio, but made of iron and depicting a beefcake Roman god of metalworking. Vulcan is visible from all over the city – this is actually the world's largest cast-iron statue – and the park he resides in offers

---

ⓘ BIRMINGHAM MOUNTAIN RADIO

Whenever you are in the city of Birmingham, turn the radio dial to 107.3 FM and never touch it until you leave. This is the setting for Birmingham Mountain Radio, one of the finest independent radio stations in the country. The DJs here play an incredible, eclectic range of music that ranges from country to rock to hip-hop to pop. There are few stations in the country – in the world, really – that we can listen to without a break for the entirety of a day, but Mountain Radio is one of them. Note that the station can be accessed at 97.5 in Tuscaloosa.

fantastic views, along with an **observation tower**. A small on-site museum explores Birmingham history.

Birmingham Museum of Art
GALLERY

(205-254-2565; www.artsbma.org; 2000 Rev Abraham Woods Jr Blvd; ⊘10am-5pm Tue-Sat, noon-5pm Sun) FREE This fine museum boasts an impressive collection, especially given Birmingham's status as a mid-sized city. Inside, you'll find works from Asia, Africa, Europe and the Americas. Don't miss pieces by Rodin, Botero and Dalí in the sculpture garden.

16th Street Baptist Church
CHURCH

(205-251-9402; www.16thstreetbaptist.org; cnr 16th St & 6th Ave N; $5; ⊘ministry tours 10am-3pm Tue-Fri, by appointment only 10am-1pm Sat) This church became a gathering place for organizational meetings and a launchpad for protests in Birmingham in the 1950s and '60s. During a massive desegregation campaign directed at downtown merchants in 1963, Ku Klux Klan members bombed the church during Sunday school, killing four little girls. Today the rebuilt church is a memorial and house of worship (services 11am Sunday).

Birmingham Civil Rights Memorial Trail
WALKING

(www.bcri.org; 520 16th St N) Seven blocks long, this is a poignant walk. Installed in 2013 for the 50th anniversary of the Civil Rights campaign, the walk depicts 22 scenes with plaques, statues and photography, some of it quite conceptual and moving – to wit, a gauntlet of snapping, sculpted dog statues that pedestrians must traverse. The experience peels back yet another layer of the sweat and blood behind a campaign that changed America.

🛏 Sleeping

Hotel Highland
HOTEL $$

(205-933-9555; www.thehotelhighland.com; 1023 20th St S; r from $150; P ❈ @ 🛜) Nuzzled right up next to the lively Five Points district, this colorful, slightly trippy but modern hotel is very comfortable and a good deal. The rooms are thankfully a bit less bright and funky than the lobby.

Redmont Hotel
HISTORIC HOTEL $$

(205-957-6828; www.redmontbirmingham.com; 2101 5th Ave N; r/ste from $170/230; ❈ @ 🛜) The piano and chandelier in the lobby of this 1925 hotel lend a certain historical, old-world feel, and all deluxe rooms were just

renovated, giving it modern edge. The spacious rooftop bar doesn't hurt, either. It's walking distance to the civil rights sights.

🍴 Eating

⭐Saw's Soul Kitchen
BARBECUE $

(205-591-1409; www.sawsbbq.com; 215 41st St S; mains $9-16; ⊘11am-8pm Mon-Sat, to 4pm Sun; 🖼) Saw's has exploded onto the Birmingham barbecue scene with a vengeance, offering some of the most mouth-watering smoked meat in the city, served in a family-friendly atmosphere. Stuffed potatoes make a nice addition to your meal, and the smoked chicken with a tangy local white sauce is divine – although with that said, bring on the ribs!

⭐Tacos Dos Hermanos
MEXICAN $

(98 14th Street N; mains $2-6; ⊘10am-2pm Mon-Fri; 🐾) Excellent tacos – simple, delicious, cheap and...look, we have to stress: *delicious*. These guys sling a simple menu, will accommodate vegetarians, work hard and pull in huge crowds ranging from construction workers to office drones.

Eagle's Restaurant
AMERICAN $

(205-320-0099; www.eaglesrestaurant.com; 2610 16th St N; mains $6.75-17; ⊘10:30am-3:30pm Sun-Fri) Tucked away on a lonely strip is Eagle's, home of Birmingham's best soul food. This popular spot operates on a meat-and-two/three model: order a main, be it steak and gravy, neckbones and potatoes or chicken wings, then pick from a buffet tray of side options. It's delicious, cheap and as local as anything.

⭐Galley & Garden
FRENCH $$$

(www.galleyandgarden.com; 2220 Highland Ave S; dinner mans $28-36) 🌿 The American South meets French rustic (and *haute*) cuisine in this establishment, which is rapidly becoming a go-to for Birmingham area foodies and those in search of a good date night. The farm-to-table menu is excellent; be on the lookout for solid, well-executed mains like seared red snapper and and slow-cooked short rib.

🍷 Drinking & Nightlife

⭐Garage Café
BAR

(205-322-3220; www.garagecafe.us; 2304 10th Terrace S; ⊘3pm-2am Sun-Mon, 11am-2am Tue-Sat) A crowd of hipsters and older drinking pros knock back their brew while tapping their toes to live music in a courtyard full of junk, antiques, ceramic statues and, quite literally, the kitchen sink.

★**Marty's** BAR
(1813 10th Ct S; ⊙8pm-6am, plus 10am-3pm Sat) Marty's plays to hipsters, cool kids and an unapologetically geeky crowd, who are all attracted to a friendly bar packed with comic book art, *Star Wars* memorabilia, role-playing-game references, DJ nights, pop-up dining events and the occasional live music gig. No phone number.

41 Street Pub & Aircraft Sales BAR
(📱205-202-4187; www.41ststreetpub.com; 130 41st St S; ⊙4:30pm-midnight Mon-Thu, 4:30pm-2am Fri, 1pm-2am Sat, 1pm-midnight Sun) A slick wooden bar fronts a large open space offset with some shuffleboard tables. Behind the bar, strong drinks (the Moscow Mule is a winner) are served in shiny copper mugs to an attractive, hipster crowd.

The Collins Bar BAR
(📱205-323-7995; www.thecollinsbar.com; 2125 2nd Ave N; ⊙4pm-midnight Tue-Thu, to 2am Fri & Sat, 6pm-midnight Sun) Birmingham's beautiful people pack into this cool space after work and on weekends, sipping handmade cocktails under giant paper planes and a Birmingham-centric periodic table of the elements. There's no drink menu – tell the bartender what flavors you like and they'll mix something special for you.

❶ Getting There & Around

The **Birmingham-Shuttlesworth International Airport** (BHM; 📱205-599-0500; www.flybirmingham.com) is about 5 miles northeast of downtown Birmingham.

Greyhound (📱205-252-7190; www.greyhound.com; 618 19th St N), north of downtown, serves cities including Huntsville (1¾ hours, $22, three daily), Montgomery (1¾ hours, $25, three daily), Atlanta, GA (2½ hours, $17, five daily), Jackson, MS (4½ hours, $20, four daily), and New Orleans, LA (nine hours, $56, daily).

Amtrak (📱205-324-3033; www.amtrak.com; 1 19th St North), downtown, has trains daily to New York (22 hours, $124) and New Orleans (7½ hours, $47).

Birmingham Transit Authority (www.bjcta.org) runs local MAX buses. Adult fare is $1.25. You can also get around via the **Zyp** (📱844-997-2453; www.zypbikeshare.com; 24hr/one-week membership $6/20) bicycle-sharing program.

Montgomery

Alabama's capital is a pleasant if sleepy spot to visit; with a few exceptions, most of its main points of interest are tied to the American Civil Rights movement, which the city played a key role in. In 1955 Rosa Parks refused to give up her seat to a white man on a city bus, launching a bus boycott led by Martin Luther King Jr, then-pastor of Montgomery's Dexter Avenue Baptist Church. In the short run, the boycott inspired horrific acts of violence and repression by pro-segregation white citizens, but the boycott ultimately desegregated city buses and galvanized the Civil Rights movement nationwide, helping to lay the foundation for the Selma to Montgomery protest marches of 1965.

⊙ Sights

★**Dexter Avenue Parsonage** HISTORIC SITE
(📱334-261-3270; www.dexterkingmemorial.org/tours/parsonage-museum; 309 S Jackson Street; adult/child $7.50/5.50; ⊙10am-3pm Tue-Fri, to 1pm Sat; 🅿) The home of Martin Luther King Jr and Coretta Scott King has been frozen in time, a snapshot of a mid-Century home complete with *Mad Men*–era furniture, appliances and indoor ashtrays (King was a regular smoker). The most fascinating part of the tour is King's old office, which still contains some of the books that influenced his theology, philosophy and activism. In the back, there's a garden filled with stones inscribed with Christian virtues.

Civil Rights Memorial Center MEMORIAL
(📱334-956-8200; www.splcenter.org/civil-rights-memorial; 400 Washington Ave; memorial free, museum adult/child $2/free; ⊙memorial 24 hrs, museum 9am-4:30pm Mon-Fri, 10am-4pm Sat) With its circular design crafted by Maya Lin, this haunting memorial focuses on 40 martyrs of the Civil Rights movement. Some cases remain unsolved. Martin Luther King Jr was the most famous, but there were many 'faceless' deaths along the way, both white and African American. The memorial is part of the Southern Poverty Law Center, a legal foundation committed to racial equality and equal opportunity for justice under the law.

Scott & Zelda Fitzgerald Museum MUSEUM
(📱334-264-4222; www.fitzgeraldmuseum.net; 919 Felder Ave; donation adult/child $10/free; ⊙10am-3pm Tue-Sat, noon-5pm Sun) The writers' home

from 1931 to 1932 now houses first editions, translations and original artwork by Zelda from her sad last days when she was committed to a mental health facility. Unlike many 'homes of famous people,' there's a ramshackle charm to this museum – while the space is curated, you also feel as if you've stumbled into the Fitzgerald's attic, exemplified by loving handwritten letters from Zelda to Scott.

Rosa Parks Museum   MUSEUM
(☎334-241-8615; www.troy.edu/rosaparks; 251 Montgomery St; adult/child 4-12yr $7.50/5.50; ☉9am-5pm Mon-Fri, 9am-3pm Sat; ⬛) This museum, set in front of the bus stop where Mrs Parks took her stand, features a video recreation of that pivotal moment that launched the 1955 boycott. The experience is very managed – you're given a small opportunity to explore on your own, but otherwise the museum feels something like an interactive movie. For the price of an additional full-admission ticket, you can visit the children's wing, a kids-oriented time travel exhibit to the Jim Crow South.

🍴 Sleeping & Eating

Renaissance Hotel   HOTEL $$
(☎334-481-5000; www.marriott.com; 201 Tallapoosa St; r from $140; P✴@🛜🏊) While this chain hotel is a little bland, it is also well located by the river, and easily occupies one of Montgomery's nicest addresses. Rooms have that convention-corporate chic thing going, but they're clean and comfortable.

Davis Cafe   AMERICAN $
(☎334-264-6015; 518 N Decatur St; mains $3-7; ☉7am-2pm Mon-Fri) This dilapidated restaurant leans precariously on a lonely street, but ignore the structural instability and step in: you'll find a Montgomery institution serving Southern breakfasts and plate lunches – liver and onions, fried chicken, ox tails and daily specials that will run you the cost of the loose money between your couch cushions. Hours are fungible; the Davis closes when it runs out of food.

Central   STEAK $$$
(☎334-517-1121; www.central129coosa.com; 129 Coosa St; mains $16-32; ☉11am-2pm Mon-Fri, 5:30pm-10pm Mon-Thu, to 11pm Fri & Sat; 🍷) 🌿 The gourmet's choice, this stunner has an airy interior with a reclaimed-wood bar. The booths are sumptuous and these guys were doing farm to table before it was 'A Thing':

the menu specializes in wood-fired fish, chicken, steaks and chops sourced from the region. Dishes like a pesto-walnut pasta are nice for vegetarians.

ℹ Information

Montgomery Area Visitor Center (☎334-261-1100; www.visitingmontgomery.com; 300 Water St; ☉8:30am-5pm Mon-Sat) Has tourist information and a helpful website.

ℹ Getting There & Around

Montgomery Regional Airport (MGM; ☎334-281-5040; www.montgomeryairport.org; 4445 Selma Hwy) is about 15 miles from downtown and is served by daily flights from Atlanta, Charlotte and Dallas. **Greyhound** (☎334-286-0658; www.greyhound.com; 950 W South Blvd) also serves the city. Montgomery is located about 100 miles south of Birmingham via I-65.

The **Montgomery Area Transit System** (http://montgomerytransit.com) operates city bus lines. Tickets are $2.

Selma

Selma is a quiet town located in the heart of the Alabama 'Black Belt,' so named for both its dark, high-quality soil and a large population of African Americans. It's most well known for Bloody Sunday: March 7, 1965. The media captured state troopers and deputies beating and gassing African Americans and white sympathizers near the Edmund Pettus Bridge.

Selma is a must-visit for those interested in the history of the Civil Rights movement, and is an attractive spot to linger in its own right.

◉ Sights

Edmund Pettus Bridge   LANDMARK
(Broad St & Walter Ave) Few sites are as iconic to the American Civil Rights movement as the Pettus Bridge. On March 7, 1965, a crowd prepared to march to Montgomery to demonstrate against the murder of a local black activist by police during a demonstration for voting rights. As those activists gathered into a crowd, the news cameras of the media were trained on the bridge and a line of state troopers and their dogs, who proceeded to lay into the nonviolent marchers.

National Voting Rights Museum   MUSEUM
(☎334-418-0800; www.nvrmi.com; 6 US Highway 80 East; adult/senior & student $6.50/4.50;

⊘10am-4pm Mon-Thu, by appointment only Fri-Sun; P) This museum, located near the foot of the Edmund Pettus Bridge, tells the tale of the Selma to Montgomery march, and includes exhibits on women's suffrage, reconstruction, nonviolent resistance and other movements that have shared the goals of the Civil Rights struggle.

Selma Interpretive Center   MUSEUM
(☑334-872-0509; www.nps.gov/semo; 2 Broad St; ⊘9am-4:30pm Mon-Sat) This museum, located near the north side of the Pettus Bridge, has a small interpretive center that fleshes out the history and narrative of the Jim Crow South, and the subsequent struggle against legalized segregation.

**Lowndes County
Interpretive Center**   MUSEUM
(☑334-877-1983; www.nps.gov/semo; 7002 US Hwy 80; ⊘9am-4:30pm Mon-Sat; P) Marking the rough halfway point on the marching route between Selma and Montgomery, this center presents small, solid exhibitions that delve into the history of Jim Crow and the Civil Rights movement.

Sleeping & Eating

At the time of writing, the historic **St James Hotel** was up for sale. It's the only really notable sleeping option in Selma, which is otherwise served by the usual midrange American hotel chains.

Getting There & Away

There's a **Greyhound** (☑800-231-2222; 434 Broad St) station on Broad St (US 80). But you really need a car to get around. Tuscaloosa is located about 75 miles to the north on US 80, and Montgomery is 50 miles to the east.

Mobile

Wedged between Mississippi and Florida, the only real Alabama coastal city is Mobile (mo-*beel*), a busy industrial seaport with a smattering of green space, shady boulevards and four historic districts. It's ablaze with azaleas in early spring, and festivities are held throughout February for Mardi Gras, which has been celebrated here for nearly 200 years (it actually predates Mardi Gras in New Orleans).

Throughout the rest of the year, this is a major port with some attractive historical neighborhoods and a strong Coast Guard

presence, thanks to the nearby Coast Guard Aviation Training Center.

◉ Sights

USS Alabama   MUSEUM
(☑251-433-2703; www.ussalabama.com; 2703 Battleship Pkwy; adult/child $15/6; ⊘8am-6pm Apr-Sep, to 5pm Oct-Mar; P) The battleship *Alabama* is a 690ft behemoth famous for escaping nine major WWII battles unscathed – the 'Lucky A' never lost any of her sailors while they served aboard ship. It's a worthwhile self-guided tour just to experience its awesome size and might; at the end of the day, this ship is an engineering marvel. While there, you can also tour a submarine and get up close and personal with military aircraft. Parking costs $2.

Gulf Coast Exploreum   MUSEUM
(☑251-208-6893; www.exploreum.com; 65 Government St; adult/student/child $12/10.50/10 with IMAX $16/15/13.50; ⊘9am-4pm Tue-Thu, to 5pm Fri & Sat, noon-5pm Sun; ⊛) This science center contains some 150 interactive exhibits and displays in three galleries, an IMAX theater and live demonstrations in its chemistry and biology labs.

Festivals

Mardi Gras   CULTURAL
(www.mobilemardigras.com; ⊘late Feb/early Mar) Mobile has been celebrating Mardi Gras for nearly 200 years. It culminates on Fat Tuesday (the Tuesday before Ash Wednesday) with parades that feature bead tossing, music and some politically incorrect floats.

Sleeping & Eating

Battle House   HOTEL $$
(☑251-338-2000; www.marriott.com; 26 N Royal St; r $170-240, ste from $375; P⊛@�cr⊠) By far the best historic address in Mobile. Stay in the original historic wing with its ornate domed marble lobby, though the striking new tower is on the waterfront. Rooms are spacious, luxurious, four-star chic. Book ahead for discounts.

Callaghan's Irish Social Club   PUB FOOD $
(☑251-433-9374; www.callaghansirishsocialclub.com; 916 Charleston St; burgers $8-10; ⊘11am-11pm Mon-Thu, to midnight Fri & Sat, 10am-11pm Sun) This ramshackle pub is located in a 1920s-era building that used to house a meat market. They serve a mean burger and a cold beer, and often feature live-music acts.

Mary's Southern Cooking
AMERICAN $

(☑ 251-476-2232; 3011 Springhll Ave; mains $6-12; ⊙ 11am-6pm; ♠) Mary's serves up soul food with a smile. Daily specials run the gamut from beef tips to pig's feet to chicken pot pie, served alongside groaning portions of sides, including collard greens, rice and gravy, and mashed potatoes.

❶ Getting There & Away

As of early 2017, there was talk of reestablishing rail service through Mobile. Until then, you can arrive via **Greyhound** (☑ 251-478-6089; www.greyhound.com; 2545 Government Blvd) or drive; the city sits at the intersection of I-10 and I-65, about 60 miles west of Pensacola, and 150 miles east of New Orleans.

MISSISSIPPI

The state named for the most vital waterway in North America encompasses, appropriately enough, a long river of identities. Mississippi features palatial mansions and rural poverty; haunted cotton flats and lush hill country; honey-dipped sand on the coast and serene farmland in the north. Oft mythologized and misunderstood, this is the womb of some of the rawest history – and music – in the country.

❶ Information

Mississippi Division of Tourism Development (☑ 866-733-6477, 601-359-3297; www.visitmississippi.org) Has a directory of visitor bureaus and thematic travel itineraries. Most are well thought-out and run quite deep.

Mississippi Wildlife, Fisheries, & Parks (☑ 800-467-2757; www.mississippistateparks.reserveamerica.com) Manages camping reservations in state parks.

❶ Getting There & Away

There are three routes most folks take when traveling through Mississippi. I-55 and Hwy 61 both run north–south from the state's northern to southern borders. Hwy 61 goes through the delta, and I-55 flows in and out of Jackson. The gorgeous Natchez Trace Parkway runs diagonally across the state from Tupelo to Natchez.

Oxford

Oxford both confirms and explodes preconceptions you may have of Mississippi's most famous college town. Frat boys in Ford pickup trucks and debutante sorority sisters? Sure. But they're alongside doctoral candidates debating critical theory and a lively arts scene. Local culture revolves around the Square (aka Courthouse Sq), where you'll find bars, restaurants, decent shopping and the regal University of Mississippi, aka Ole Miss. All around are quiet residential streets, sprinkled with antebellum homes and shaded by majestic oaks.

❖ Sights & Activities

The gorgeous, 0.6-mile-long and rather painless **Bailee's Woods Trail** connects two of the town's most popular sights: Rowan Oak and the University of Mississippi Museum. **The Grove**, the shady heart of Ole Miss, is generally peaceful, except on football Saturdays, when it buzzes with one of the most unforgettable tailgating (pre-game) parties in American university sports.

Rowan Oak
HISTORIC BUILDING

(☑ 662-234-3284; www.rowanoak.com; Old Taylor Rd; adult/child $5/free; ⊙ 10am-4pm Tue-Sat, 1-4pm Sun Sep-May, 10am-6pm Tue-Sat, 1-6pm Sun Jun-Aug) Literary pilgrims head here to the graceful 1840s home of William Faulkner. He authored many brilliant and dense novels set in Mississippi, and his work is celebrated in Oxford with an annual conference in July. Tours of Rowan Oak – where Faulkner lived from 1930 until his death in 1962, and which may reasonably be dubbed, to use the author's own elegant words, his 'postage stamp of native soil' – are self-guided.

University of Mississippi Museum
MUSEUM

(www.museum.olemiss.edu; University Ave at 5th St; ⊙ 10am-6pm Tue-Sat) **FREE** This museum has fine and folk arts and a plethora of science-related marvels, including a microscope and electromagnet from the 19th century.

🛏 Sleeping & Eating

Inn at Ole Miss
HOTEL $$

(☑ 662-234-2331; www.theinnatolemiss.com; 120 Alumni Dr; r from $99-149; ⓟ ❄ @ ⓢ ≋) Unless its a football weekend, in which case you'd be wise to book well ahead, you can usually find a nice room at this 180-room hotel and conference center right on the Ole Miss Grove. Although it's not super personal, it's comfortable, well located and walkable to downtown.

Neon Pig
SOUTHERN US $

(☑ 662-638-3257; http://oxford.eatneonpig.com; 711 N Lamar Blvd; mains $7-14; ⊙11am-9pm Mon-Sat, to 4pm Sun; ℗) A counter with stools, some friendly folks on the grill, and farm fresh produce, cheese and meat on grocery shelves – there's not a ton of ambience at the Neon Pig. But there is amazing food, ranging from pork-belly lettuce wraps to harissa grilled cheese to the Smash Burger – rough-cut aged sirloin, filet, ribeye and bacon ground together into perfection.

Taylor Grocery
SEAFOOD $$

(☑ 662-236-1716; www.taylorgrocery.com; 4 1st St; dishes $9-15; ⊙5-10pm Thu-Sat, to 9pm Sun; ℗) Be prepared to wait – and to tailgate in the parking lot – at this splendidly rusticated catfish haunt. Order fried or grilled (either way, it's amazing) and bring a marker to sign your name on the wall. It's about 7 miles from downtown Oxford, south on Old Taylor Rd.

Ravine
AMERICAN $$$

(☑ 662-234-4555; www.oxfordravine.com; 53 County Rd 321; mains $21-36; ⊙6-9pm Wed-Thu, to 10pm Fri & Sat, 10:30am-2pm & 6-9pm Sun; 🖥) About 3 miles outside Oxford, this unpretentious, cozily elegant restaurant nuzzles up to the produce and herbs from his garden and buys locally and organically whenever possible; he's been doing it long before locavore was a buzzword. The result is simply wonderful food and a delicious experience.

☆ Entertainment

Proud Larry's
LIVE MUSIC

(☑ 662-236-0050; www.proudlarrys.com; 211 S Lamar Blvd; ⊙shows 9pm) On the Square, this iconic music venue hosts consistently good bands, and it does a nice pub-grub business at lunch and dinner before the lights dim.

The Lyric
LIVE MUSIC

(☑ 662-234-5333; www.thelyricoxford.com; 1006 Van Buren Ave) This old brickhouse, and rather intimate theater with concrete floors, exposed rafters and a mezzanine, is the place to see indie rockers and folksy crooners.

❶ Getting There & Away

The closest interstates to Oxford are I-55 and I-22. You can get here via US 278 or MS 7; the latter is a slightly more scenic route.

Mississippi Delta

A long, low land of silent cotton plots bending under a severe sky, the Delta is a place of surreal, Gothic extremes. Here, in a feudal society of great manors and enslaved servitude, songs of labor and love became American pop music. It traveled via Africa to sharecropping fields, unfolding into the blues, the father of rock and roll. Tourism in this area, which still suffers some of the worst rural poverty rates in the country, largely revolves around discovering the sweat-soaked roots of this original, American art form. Hwy 61 is the legendary road that traverses endless, eerie miles of flat fields, imposing agricultural and industrial facilities, one-room churches and moldering cemeteries.

Clarksdale

Clarksdale is the Delta's most useful base. It's within a couple of hours of all the blues sights, and big-name blues acts are regular weekend visitors. But this is still a poor Delta town, with crumbling edges and washed-out storefronts evident in ways that go beyond romantic dilapidation. It's jarring to see how many businesses find private security details a necessity after dark. On the other hand, there is a genuine warmth to the place, and most tourists end up lingering for longer than they expected.

◉ Sights

Delta Blues Museum
MUSEUM

(☑ 662-627-6820; www.deltabluesmuseum.org; 1 Blues Alley; adult/senior & student $10/5; ⊙9am-5pm Mon-Sat Mar-Oct, from 10am Nov-Feb; ℗) A small but well-presented collection of memorabilia is on display here. The shrine to Delta legend Muddy Waters includes the actual cabin where he grew up. Local art exhibits and a gift shop round out the display. Occasionally hosts live music shows on Friday nights.

The Crossroads
SCULPTURE

(Hwy 61 & Hwy 49) FREE The Crossroads of Hwys 61 and 49 is supposedly the intersection where the great Robert Johnson made his mythical deal with the devil, immortalized in his tune 'Cross Road Blues.' Now all of the implied lonely fear and dark mysticism of the space is taken up by a tacky

THE SOUL OF THE DELTA

Stopping in the tiny Delta town of Indianola, an hour's drive south of Clarksdale, is worthwhile to visit the **BB King Museum and Delta Interpretive Center** (☑ 662-887-9539; www.bbkingmuseum.org; 400 2nd St; adult/student/child $15/10/free; ⊙ 10am-5pm Tue-Sat, noon-5pm Sun-Mon, closed Mon Nov-Mar; ℗). While it's ostensibly dedicated to the legendary bluesman, in many ways this modern museum tackles life in the Delta as a whole. The museum is filled with interactive displays, video exhibits and an amazing array of artifacts, effectively communicating the history and legacy of the blues while shedding light on the soul of the Delta.

sculpture. For what it's worth, few historians agree where the actual crossroad is located.

🛏 Sleeping & Eating

Riverside Hotel   HISTORIC HOTEL $
(☑ 662-624-9163; ratfrankblues@yahoo.com; 615 Sunflower Ave; r without/with bath $65/75; ❋ 🛜) Don't let a well-worn exterior put you off: this hotel, soaked in blues history – blues singer Bessie Smith died here when it was a hospital, and a festival's worth of blues artists from Sonny Boy Williamson II to Robert Nighthawk have stayed here – offers clean and tidy rooms and sincere friendliness. It's been family-run since 1944, when it was 'the black hotel' in town.

Bluesberry Cafe   SOUTHERN US $
(☑ 662-627-7008; 235 Yazoo Ave; ⊙ 7:30am-1pm Sat & Sun, noon-6pm Mon) This isn't just a greasy spoon – there's grease on the forks, knives and napkins too. But who cares? The food – eggs, bacon, homemade sausages and big sandwiches – is cooked to order and delicious, and on many a morning, some legend of the blues will stop in and play an impromptu set. Pass the hot sauce.

Shack Up Inn   INN $$
(☑ 662-624-8329; www.shackupinn.com; 001 Commisary Circle, off Hwy 49; d $75-165; ℗ ❋ 🛜) At the Hopson Plantation, this self-titled 'bed and beer' allows you to stay in refurbished sharecropper cabins or the creatively renovated cotton gin. The cabins have covered porches and are filled with old furniture and musical instruments.

Yazoo Pass   CAFE $$
(☑ 662-627-8686; www.yazoopass.com; 207 Yazoo Ave; lunch mains $6-10, dinner $13-26; ⊙ 7am-9pm Mon-Sat; 🛜) A contemporary space where you can enjoy fresh scones and croissants in the mornings, a salad bar, sandwiches and soups at lunch, and pan-seared ahi, filet mignon, burgers and pastas at dinner.

☆ Entertainment

★ Red's   BLUES
(☑ 662-627-3166; 395 Sunflower Ave; cover $7-10; ⊙ live music 9pm Fri & Sat) Clarksdale's best juke joint, with its neon-red mood lighting, plastic-bag ceiling and general soulful disintegration, is the place to see bluesmen howl. Red runs the bar, knows the acts and slings a cold beer whenever you need one.

❶ Getting There & Away

The Greyhound station is on State St. Clarksdale sits off Hwys 49 and 61, 80 miles south of Memphis, TN, and 70 miles west of Oxford, MS.

Vicksburg

Lovely Vicksburg sits atop a high bluff overlooking the Mississippi River. During the Civil War, General Ulysses S Grant besieged the city for 47 days until its surrender on July 4, 1863, at which point the North gained dominance over North America's greatest river. Despite being most famous for a siege and a battle, many of the historic homes of Vicksburg have survived the centuries, and today the town's historic core is considered one of the most attractive in the state.

◉ Sights

Vicksburg National Military Park   HISTORIC SITE
(☑ 601-636-0583; www.nps.gov/vick; 3201 Clay St; per bicycle/car $5/15; ⊙ 8am-5pm; 🖶) 🅿 Vicksburg controlled access to the Mississippi River, and its seizure was one of the turning points of the Civil War. A 16-mile driving tour passes historic markers explaining battle scenarios and key events from the city's long siege, when residents lived like moles in caverns to avoid Union shells. Plan on staying for at least 90 minutes. If you have your own bike, cycling is a fantastic way to tour the place. Locals use the scenic park for walking and running.

Lower Mississippi River Museum
MUSEUM

(☑601-638-9900; www.lmrm.org; 910 Washington St; ⊙9am-4pm Mon-Sat, 1-4pm Sun; ⊞) FREE Downtown Vicksburg's pride and joy is this interesting museum, which delves into such topics as the famed 1927 flood and the Army Corps of Engineers, who have managed the river since the 18th century. Kids will enjoy the aquarium and climbing around the dry-docked research vessel, the MV *Mississippi IV.*

✗ Eating & Drinking

Walnut Hills
SOUTHERN US $$

(☑601-638-4910; www.walnuthillsms.net; 1214 Adams St; mains $8-25; ⊙11am-9pm Mon-Sat, to 2pm Sun) For a dining experience that takes you back in time, head to this eatery where you can enjoy rib-sticking, down-home Southern food elbow to elbow, family-style.

★Highway 61 Coffeehouse
COFFEE

(☑601-638-9221; www.61coffee.blogspot.com; 1101 Washington St; ⊙7am-5pm Mon-Fri, from 9am Sat; ☎) ✐ This awesome coffee shop has occasional live music on Saturday afternoons, serves Fair Trade coffee and is an energetic epicenter of artsyness, poetry readings and the like.

⊙ Getting There & Away

There's a Greyhound station a little way south of town. Vicksburg lays off I-20 and Hwy 61, about 50 miles west of Jackson.

Jackson

Mississippi's capital and largest city mixes up stately residential areas with large swaths of blight, peppered throughout with a surprisingly funky arts-cum-hipster scene in the Fondren District. There's a slew of decent bars, good restaurants and a lot of love for live music; it's easy to have a good time in Jackson.

⊙ Sights

Mississippi Museum of Art
GALLERY

(☑601-960-1515; www.msmuseumart.org; 380 South Lamar St; special exhibitions $5-12; ⊙10am-5pm Tue-Sat, noon-5pm Sun) FREE This is your must-stop sight when visiting Jackson. The collection of Mississippi art – and the permanent exhibit dubbed 'The Mississippi Story' – is superb, and the surrounding grounds are nicely landscaped into a bright and quirky garden area.

Old Capitol Museum
MUSEUM

(☑601-576-6920; www.mdah.ms.gov/oldcap; 100 State St; ⊙9am-5pm Tue-Sat, 1-5pm Sun) FREE The state's Greek Revival capitol building from 1839 to 1903 now houses a Mississippi history museum filled with films and exhibits. You'll learn that secession was far from unanimous and how reconstruction brought some of the harshest, presegregation 'black codes' in the South.

Eudora Welty House
HISTORIC BUILDING

(☑601-353-7762; www.eudorawelty.org; 1119 Pinehurst St; adult/student/child $5/3/free; ⊙tours 9am, 11am, 1pm & 3pm Tue-Fri) Literature buffs should make a reservation to tour the Pulitzer Prize–winning author's Tudor Revival house, where she lived for more than 75 years. It's now a true historical preservation down to the most minute details. It's free on the 13th day of any month, assuming that's a normal operating day.

Museum of Natural Science
MUSEUM

(☑601-576-6000; www.mdwfp.com/museum; 2148 Riverside Dr; adult/child $6/4; ⊙8am-5pm Mon-Fri, from 9am Sat, from 1pm Sun; ⊞) ✐ Tucked way back in Lefleur's Bluff State Park is this museum, which houses exhibits on the natural flora and fauna of Mississippi. It also has aquariums inside, a replica swamp and 2.5 miles of trails traversing 300 acres of preserved prettiness.

International Museum of Muslim Cultures
MUSEUM

(☑601-960-0440; www.muslimmuseum.org; 201 E Pascagoula St; ⊙10am-5pm Mon-Fri) FREE This small museum has a few interesting exhibitions on Timbuktu and Moorish Spain, and hosts rotating exhibitions on other Muslim majority societies. While the stuff on display isn't super-penetrating, this spot serves as a decent introduction to the larger Muslim world for those who are unfamiliar with it.

⊨ Sleeping & Eating

Old Capitol Inn
BOUTIQUE HOTEL $$

(☑601-359-9000; www.oldcapitolinn.com; 226 N State St; r/ste from $99/145; ⓟ❋@☎☰) This 24-room, boutique hotel, located near museums and restaurants, is terrific. Rooms are comfortable and uniquely furnished, and a full Southern breakfast (and early-evening wine and cheese) is included. The rooftop garden includes a hot tub.

THE SOUTH JACKSON

Fairview Inn
INN **$$$**

(☑ 601-948-3429, 888-948-1908; www.fairviewinn. com; 734 Fairview St; ste $200-340; [P][✳][@][🛜]) For a colonial-estate experience, the 18-room Fairview Inn, set in a converted historic mansion, will not let you down. The antique decor is stunning rather than stuffy and tastefully deployed across each individually appointed room. It also has a full spa.

High Noon Cafe
VEGETARIAN **$**

(☑ 601-366-1513; www.rainbowcoop.org; 2807 Old Canton Rd; mains $7-12; ⊙ 11:30am-2pm Mon-Fri; [🛜][🥗]) 🍴 Tired of fried everything and buckets of pulled pork? This organic vegetarian grill, inside the Rainbow Co-op grocery store in the Fondren District, does beet burgers, portobello Reubens and other healthy delights. Stock up on organic groceries too.

Saltine
SEAFOOD **$$**

(☑ 601-982-2899; www.saltinerestaurant.com; 622 Duling Ave; mains $12-26; ⊙ 11am-10pm Mon-Thu, to 11pm Fri, to 9pm Sun) This playful spot takes on the delicious task of bringing oysters to the Jackson culinary world. The bivalves are served in several iterations: raw, woodfired, with Alabama white barbecue sauce and 'Nashville' (*very*) hot. Sop up some shellfish sauce with the excellent skillet cornbread, then give the grilled rainbow trout a whirl.

Walker's Drive-In
SOUTHERN US **$$$**

(☑ 601-982-2633; www.walkersdrivein.com; 3016 N State St; lunch mains $8-17, dinner $29-37; ⊙ 11am-2pm Mon-Fri & from 5:30-10pm Tue-Sat) This retro masterpiece has been restored with love and infused with new Southern foodie ethos. Lunch is diner 2.0 fare with grilled redfish sandwiches, tender burgers and grilled oyster po'boys, as well as an exceptional seared, chili-crusted tuna salad, which comes with spiced calamari and seaweed.

🍸 Drinking & Entertainment

Apothecary at Brent's Drugs
COCKTAIL BAR

(www.apothecaryjackson.com; 655 Duling Ave; ⊙ 5pm-1am Tue-Thu, to 2am Fri & Sat) Tucked into the back of a '50s-style soda fountain shop is a distinctly early-21st-century craft cocktail bar, complete with bartenders sporting thick-framed glasses and a fine menu of expertly mixed libations.

Martin's
BAR

(☑ 601-354-9712; www.martinslounge.net; 214 S State St; ⊙ 10am-1:30am Mon-Sat, to midnight Sun) This is a delightfully dirty dive, the kind of place where the bartenders know

the phone numbers of their regulars in case said regulars pass out on their bar stools. Attracts a mix of old-timers, statehouse workers, slick lobbyists and lawyers plucked from a John Grisham novel.

F Jones Corner
BLUES

(☑ 601-983-1148; www.fjonescorner.com; 303 N Farish St; ⊙ Tue-Fri 11am-2pm, Thu-Sat 10am-late) All shapes and sizes, colors and creeds descend on this down-home Farish St club when everywhere else closes. It hosts authentic Delta musicians who have been known to play until sunrise.

ℹ️ Information

Convention & Visitors Bureau (☑ 800-354-7695; www.visitjackson.com; 111 E Capitol St, Suite 102; ⊙ 8am-5pm Mon-Fri) Free information.

ℹ️ Getting There & Away

At the junction of I-20 and I-55, it's easy to get in and out of Jackson. Its international **airport** (JAN; ☑ 601-939-5631; www.jmaa.com; 100 International Dr) is 10 miles east of downtown. **Greyhound** (☑ 601-353-6342; www.greyhound. com; 300 W Capitol St) buses serve Birmingham, Memphis, and New Orleans. Amtrak's *City of New Orleans* stops at the station.

Natchez

Some 668 antebellum homes pepper the oldest post-European contact settlement on the Mississippi River (beating New Orleans by two years). Natchez is also one end of the scenic 444-mile Natchez Trace Pkwy, the state's cycling and recreational jewel. Tours of the historic downtown and antebellum mansions leave from the Visitor and Welcome Cente. During the 'pilgrimage' seasons in spring and fall, local mansions are opened to visitors.

⊙ Sights & Activities

Emerald Mound
ARCHAEOLOGICAL SITE

(www.nps.gov/natr; Mile 10.3 Natchez Trace Pkwy; ⊙ dawn-dusk; [P][📷]) **FREE** Just outside of town, along the Trace, you'll find Emerald Mound, the grassy ruins of a Native American city that includes the second-largest pre-Columbian earthworks in the USA. Using stone tools, pre-Columbian ancestors to the Natchez people graded this 8-acre mountain into a flat-topped pyramid. It is now the second-largest mound site in America. There are shady, creekside picnic spots

NATCHEZ TRACE PARKWAY

If you're driving through Mississippi, we highly recommend planning at least part of your trip around one of the oldest roads in North America: the Natchez Trace. This 444-mile trail follows a natural ridge line that was widely utilized by prehistoric animals as a grazing route; later, the area those animals trampled became a footpath and trading route utilized by Native American tribes. That route would go on to become the Natchez Trace, a major roadway into the early Western interior of the young United States, that was often plagued by roving bandits.

In 1938, 444 miles of the Trace, stretching from Pasquo, TN, southwest to Natchez, MS, was designated the federally protected Natchez Trace Pkwy (www.nps.gov/natr), administered by the National Park Service. It's a lovely, scenic drive that traverses a wide panoply of Southern landscapes: thick, dark forests, soggy wetlands, gentle hill country and long swaths of farmland. There are more than 50 access points to the parkway and a helpful **visitor center** (☑800-305-7417, 662-680-4025; www.nps.gov/natr; Mile 266 Natchez Trace Pkwy; ☺8am-5pm, closed Christmas; ♿🚻) *outside of Tupelo.

here, and you can and should climb to the top where you'll find a vast lawn.

Auburn Mansion LANDMARK
(☑601-446-6631; www.auburnmuseum.org; 400 Duncan Ave; adult/child $15/10; ☺11am-3pm Tue-Sat, last tour departs 2:30pm; ♿) The red-brick Auburn Mansion is famous for its freestanding spiral staircase. Built in 1812, the architecture here influenced countless mansions throughout the South.

Natchez Pilgrimage Tours HISTORY
(☑800-647-6742, 601-446-6631; www.natchez pilgrimage.com; 640 S Canal St; tours from $20) If you love historic homes and antebellum architecture, this tour outfit was made for you. It manages tours to over a dozen historical homes throughout the year, providing tons of info and insight into local history.

🛏 Sleeping & Eating

Historic Oak Hill Inn INN $$
(☑601-446-2500; www.historicoakhill.com; 409 S Rankin St; r incl breakfast $135-160, ste $235; ᴘ❄🛜) Ever wish you could sleep in one of those historic homes? At the Historic Oak Hill Inn, you can sleep in an original 1835 bed and dine on pre–Civil War porcelain under 1850 Waterford crystal gasoliers – it's all about purist antebellum aristocratic living at this classic Natchez B&B.

Magnolia Grill SOUTHERN US $$
(☑601-446-7670; www.magnoliagrill.com; 49 Silver St; mains $13-22; ☺11am-9pm, to 10pm Fri & Sat; ♿) Down by the riverside, this attractive wooden storefront grill with exposed rafters and outdoor patio is a good place for a pork

tenderloin po'boy or a fried crawfish spinach salad.

🍷 Drinking

Under the Hill Saloon BAR
(☑601-446-8023; 25 Silver St; ☺10am-late) A tremendously fun and historic bar that was once a favorite haunt of Samuel Clemens, a riverboat pilot who would go on to be known by his pen name, Mark Twain. The bar closes whenever everyone has emptied out.

ℹ Information

The **Visitor and Welcome Center** (☑800-647-6724; www.visitnatchez.org; 640 S Canal St; ☺8:30am-5pm Mon-Sat, 9am-4pm Sun) is a large, well-done tourist resource with exhibits of area history and a ton of information on local sites.

ℹ Getting There & Away

Natchez is located off Hwy 61, and also forms the terminus (or beginning, depending on which way you're heading) of the Natchez Trace Pkwy. The **Greyhound** (☑601-445-5291; 127 Wood Ave) station is about 3.5 miles east of town.

Gulf Coast

The Mississippi Gulf Coast is a long, low series of breeze-swept dunes, patches of sea oats, bayside art galleries and clusters of Vegas-style casinos. This is a popular retreat for families and military members; several important bases pepper the coast from Florida to Texas.

Charming Bay St Louis attracts federal employees, including many scientists, based out at Stennis Space Center near the Louisiana

THE SOUTH GULF COAST

border; that presence gives the town a slightly more progressive cast than you'd expect from Mississippi. Yoga studios, antique stores and galleries cluster on Main St.

Ocean Springs is a peaceful getaway, with a line-up of shrimp boats in the harbor alongside recreational sailing yachts, a historic downtown core and a powdery fringe of white sand on the Gulf.

Cheap chain accommodations can be found at the I-10 exits that lead to various Gulf Coast towns. Within said towns, you may find nice B&Bs and multifloor-style hotels aimed at day-trippers.

✈ Getting There & Away

Ocean Springs is located 33 miles east of Bay St Louis and 60 miles west of Mobile, off I-10. There is no public transportation out here.

ARKANSAS

Forming the mountainous joint between the Midwest and the Deep South, Arkansas (*ar*-kan-saw) is an often overlooked treasure of swift rushing rivers, dark leafy hollows, crenelated granite outcrops and the rugged spine of the Ozark and the Ouachita (wash-ee-tah) mountains. The entire state is blessed with exceptionally well-presented state parks and tiny, empty roads crisscrossing dense forests that let out onto breathtaking vistas and gentle pastures dotted with grazing horses. Mountain towns juke between Christian fundamentalism, hippie communes and biker bars, yet all of these divergent cultures share a love of their home state's stunning natural beauty.

❶ Information

Arkansas State Parks (☎ 888-287-2757; www.arkansasstateparks.com) Arkansas' well-reputed park system has 52 state parks, 30 offering camping (tent and recreational vehicle (RV) sites are $12 to $55, depending on amenities). A number of the parks offer lodge and cabin accommodations. Due to popularity, reservations on weekends and holidays often require multiday stays.

Little Rock

Little Rock lives up to its name; this charming state capital feels pretty petite. But this is also the center of urban life in Arkansas, and the angle of the urban experience this city embraces is quite cool: amid the leafy

residential neighborhoods are friendly bars, fresh restaurants, plenty of bike trails and a tolerant vibe. Small this town may be, but it's wonderfully situated on the Arkansas River, and as befits this state of natural wonders, you always feel as if you're within arm's reach of lush, wooded river valleys.

◉ Sights

William J Clinton Presidential Center MUSEUM
(☎ 501-374-4242; www.clintonlibrary.gov; 1200 President Clinton Ave; adult/students & seniors/child $10/8/6; ◷ 9am-5pm Mon-Sat, 1-5pm Sun; ❐ ♿) ✎ This library houses the largest archival collection in presidential history, including 80 million pages of documents and two million photographs (although there's not a lot related to a certain intern scandal). The entire experience feels like a time travel journey to the 1990s. Peruse the full-scale replica of the Oval Office, the exhibits on all stages of Clinton's life or gifts from visiting dignitaries. The complex is built to environmentally friendly standards.

The library is located on a rolling campus that includes wooded pathways and a 13-acre wetland preserve.

Riverfront Park PARK
(☎ 501-371-4770; Ottenheimer Plaza; ◷ sunrise-sunset) FREE This park rolls pleasantly along the Arkansas River, and both pedestrians and cyclists take advantage of it. It's a truly fine integration of a landscape feature (the river) into an urban setting. The most noticeable landmark is the Clinton Presidential Park Bridge, a gorgeous pedestrian path that spans the river.

Little Rock Central High School HISTORIC SITE
(☎ 501-374-1957; www.nps.gov/chsc; 2125 Daisy L Gatson Bates Dr; ◷ 9am-4:30pm; ❐) FREE Little Rock's most riveting historic attraction is the site of the 1957 desegregation crisis that changed the country forever. It was here that a group of African American students known as the Little Rock Nine were first denied entry to the then–all-white high school (despite a unanimous 1954 Supreme Court ruling forcing the integration of public schools).

Museum of Discovery MUSEUM
(☎ 501-396-7050; www.museumofdiscovery.org; 500 President Clinton Ave; adult/child $10/8; ◷ 9am-5pm Tue-Sat, 1-5pm Sun, open 9am-5pm Mon summer; ♿) A proper science-and-

natural-history museum, perfect for families. There are exhibits on the human body, Arkansas ecosystems, tornadoes, paleontology, and all sorts of other good stuff.

🛏 Sleeping & Eating

★ Capital Hotel   BOUTIQUE HOTEL $$
(☑ 501-374-7474; www.capitalhotel.com; 111 W Markham St; r/ste from $220/375; P ❀ @ ☎) This 1872 former bank building with a cast-iron facade – a near-extinct architectural feature – is the top digs in Little Rock. There is a wonderful outdoor mezzanine for cocktails and a sense of suited, cigar-chomping posh throughout; if you want to feel like a wining, dining lobbyist, you've found your spot.

Rosemont   B&B $$
(☑ 501-766-0355; www.rosemontoflittlerock.com; 515 W 15th St; r $105-195; P ❀ ☎ ❀) This 1880s restored farmhouse near the Governor's mansion oozes cozy Southern charm. The proprietors also offer a few bucolic, historic country cottages (from $135). One of the few independent B&Bs we came across that is also pet friendly.

Big Orange   AMERICAN $
(☑ 501-379-8715; www.bigorangeburger.com; 207 N University Ave; mains $8-14; ⊙ Sun-Thu 11am-10pm, to 11pm Fri & Sat; P ☑ ⬛) Sometimes you need a burger, and not just a burger, but the sort of meat between two buttered buns that leaves you in a state of post-carnivore frenzy bliss. Enter Big Orange, which serves variations on the theme ranging from a classic with American cheese, topped with white truffle for the fancy, and a falafel version for the vegetarians.

Three Fold Noodles and Dumpling Co   CHINESE $
(☑ 501-372-1739; http://eat3fold.com; 215 Center St; dumplings & noodles $7-8; ⊙ 11am-8pm Mon-Sat) Look, when we got to Little Rock we weren't expecting blow-me-away Chinese food either, but then Three Fold comes along with its braised-chicken–noodle bowls, handmade dumplings and steamed buns, and for a minute, everything felt more Anhui than Arkansas. The fact that lunch will set you back a little more than a McDonald's meal helps.

★ South on Main   AMERICAN $$
(☑ 501-244-9660; www.southonmain.com; 1304 S Main St; mains $16-24; ⊙ 11am-2:30pm Mon-Fri, 5-10pm Tue-Sat, 10am-2pm Sun) This won-derful spot is a gastronomic pet project of *The Oxford American*, the South's seminal quarterly literary magazine. It embraces the foodways of the region with a verve and dynamism that is creative and delicious; catfish comes with cornmeal pancakes, while rabbit leg is wrapped in country ham. A great bar and frequent live music round out the awesome.

🍷 Drinking & Entertainment

The New 610 Center   GAY
(☑ 501-374-4678; http://610center.com; 610 Center St; ⊙ 4pm-midnight Mon-Thu, to 1am Fri, 6pm-1am Sat, 11am-10pm Sun) This laid-back bar serves up excellent martinis and a welcoming vibe, aided by a local, primarily gay clientele. It's a good, casual spot for a strong drink and the occasional drag show or bear night.

White Water Tavern   LIVE MUSIC
(☑ 501-375-8400; www.whitewatertavern.com; 2500 W 7th St; ⊙ noon-2am Mon-Fri, 6pm-1am Sat) The White Water manages to line up some excellent acts for its small stage, with bands ranging from straight-up rockers to alt-country heroes to indie poppers to hip-hop MCs. When the music isn't playing, this is an excellent, friendly corner pub.

Arkansas Repertory Theatre   THEATER
(☑ 501-378-0405; www.therep.org; 601 Main St) 'The Rep' is one of the South's most energetic little regional theaters. They have a fantastic slate of shows, ranging from off-Broadway musicals to quirky indie shows.

ℹ Information

The **Little Rock Convention Center & Tourism Bureau** (☑ 501-376-4781; www.littlerock.com; 101 S Spring St; ⊙ 8:30m-5pm Mon-Fri) is a good gateway into the city.

ℹ Getting There & Around

Bill & Hillary Clinton National Airport (LIT; Little Rock National Airport; ☑ 501-372-3439; www.fly-lit.com; 1 Airport Dr) lies just east of downtown. The **Greyhound station** (☑ 501-372-3007; www.greyhound.com; 118 E Washington St, North Little Rock), in North Little Rock, serves Hot Springs ($19, 1-2 hours, two daily), Memphis, TN ($31, 2½ hours, seven daily), and New Orleans ($93, 18 hours, two daily). **Union Station** (☑ 501-372-6841; 1400 W Markham St) is a stop on Amtrak's *Texas Eagle* line, which runs from Chicago ($100, 14 hours) to Los Angeles ($154, 19 hours), stopping at dozens of cities in between.

THE SOUTH LITTLE ROCK

Central Arkansas Transit (www.cat.org) runs local buses and the **River Rail Streetcar**, a trolley that makes a loop on W Markham and President Clinton Ave (adult/child $1.35/60¢).

Hot Springs

Hot Springs is a gem of a mountain town, and we're not the first to notice. The healing waters the town is named for have been attracting everyone from Native Americans and early-20th-century health nuts, to a good chunk of the nation's organized-crime leadership. When Hot Springs was at full throttle in the 1930s, it was a hotbed of gambling, bootlegging, prostitution and opulence.

Today the appeal of Hot Springs is less the actual springs than the tourism infrastructure that commemorates them. That said, a few elaborate restored bathhouses offering old-school spa treatments line Bathhouse Row, which sits behind shady magnolias on the east side of Central Ave. Otherwise Hot Springs is a shady, attractive town that has managed to preserve its historic center, which is always a cause for celebration.

◉ Sights & Activities

Hot Springs National Park   MUSEUM
(Fordyce Bathhouse; ☑ 501-620-6715; www.nps.gov/hosp; 369 Central Ave; ☉ 9am-5pm) FREE On Bathhouse Row, set up in the 1915 Fordyce bathhouse, the NPS visitor center and museum has exhibits about the park's history, first as a Native American free-trade zone, and later as a turn-of-the-20th-century European spa. Most fascinating are the amenities and standards set forth by an early-20th-century spa; the stained-glass work and Greek statues are opulent, but we could pass on the bare white walls, grout and electroshock therapy.

Hot Springs Mountain Tower   VIEWPOINT
(☑ 501-881-4020; 401 Hot Springs Mountain Rd; adult/child $7/4; ☉ 9am-5pm Sep-May, to 9pm Jun-Aug; ℗) On top of Hot Springs Mountain, the 216ft tower has spectacular views of the surrounding mountains covered with dogwood, hickory, oak and pine – lovely in the spring and fall.

Gangster Museum of America   MUSEUM
(☑ 501-318-1717; www.tgmoa.com; 510 Central Ave; adult/child $15/6; ☉ 10am-5pm Sun-Thu, to 6pm Fri & Sat) Learn about the sinful glory days of Prohibition, when this small town in the middle of nowhere turned into a hotbed of

lavish wealth thanks to Chicago bootleggers like Capone, and his NYC counterparts. Highlights include original slot machines, tons of old photos and a tommy gun.

Galaxy Connection   MUSEUM
(☑ 501-276-4432; www.thegalaxyconnection.com; 626 Central Ave; $7; ☉ 11am-5pm Mon-Thu, to 8pm Fri & Sat, 12:30-5pm Sun) And now for something completely different: a museum dedicated to *Star Wars*. This fantastically geeky temple is the labor of love of one particularly obsessed Arkansan, and while it may feel a little on the amateur side, it's got enough paraphernalia from life-sized Boba Fett mannequins to a Jedi dress-up area to feel awesomely nostalgic to fans.

Buckstaff Bathhouse   SPA
(☑ 501-623-2308; www.buckstaffbaths.com; 509 Central Ave; thermal bath $33, with massage $71; ☉ 8-11:45am daily, plus 1:30-3pm Mon-Sat Mar-Nov; 8-11:45am Mon-Sat, plus 1:30-3pm Mon-Fri Dec-Feb) Spa service Hot Springs–style was never distressingly luxurious, and you get the historical treatment here. Buckstaff's no-nonsense staff whip you through the baths, treatments and massages, just as in the 1930s. Truly, it's wonderful.

🛏 Sleeping & Eating

★ Alpine Inn   INN $
(☑ 501-624-9164; www.alpine-inn-hot-springs.com; 741 Park Ave; r $65-95; ℗ ❄ 🛜 🕾) The friendly Scottish owners of this inn, less than a mile from Bathhouse Row, have spent a few years upgrading an old motel to remarkable ends. The rooms are impeccable, comfortable and include flat-screen TVs and sumptuous beds.

Arlington Resort Hotel
& Spa   HISTORIC HOTEL $
(☑ 501-623-7771; www.arlingtonhotel.com; 239 Central Ave; s/d/ste from $99/120/180; ℗ ❄ 🛜 🕾) This imposing historic hotel tops Bathhouse Row and constantly references its glory days, even if said days have passed. The grand lobby buzzes at night when there might be a live band. There's an in-house spa, and rooms are well maintained, if aging. Corner rooms with a view are a steal.

Colonial Pancake House   DINER $
(☑ 501-624-9273; 111 Central Ave; mains $6-10; ☉ 7am-3pm; 🖐) A Hot Springs classic, with turquoise booths and homey touches like quilts and doilies on the walls, this is almost like your grandma's kitchen. Except the pancakes, French toast (made with Texas toast)

and malted or buckwheat waffles are better'n grandma's. Get yours with pecans inside. They do burgers and other diner grub at lunchtime.

McClard's BARBECUE $$

(501-623-9665; www.mcclards.com; 505 Albert Pike; mains $4-15; ☺11am-8pm Tue-Sat) Southwest of the center, Bill Clinton's favorite boyhood barbecue is still popular for ribs, slow-cooked beans, chili and tamales. It's on the outskirts of downtown Hot Springs.

🍷 Drinking & Nightlife

Maxine's BAR

(501-321-0909; www.maxineslive.com; 700 Central Ave; ☺3pm-3am Mon-Fri, to 2am Sat, noon-midnight Sun) If you're looking for some (loud) night music, head to this infamous cathouse turned live-music venue. They host bands out of Austin regularly.

Superior Bathhouse Brewery and Distillery BREWERY

(501-624-2337; www.superiorbathhouse.com; 329 Central Ave; ☺11am-9pm, to 11pm Fri & Sat) It's surprising that an outdoorsy town with this many hikers and hipsters lacked a craft brewery for so long, but as the sun rises in the east, so too does Hot Springs have an indie brewery. The local suds are delicious and perfect for washing away any healthy growth your body may have mistakenly acquired in Hot Springs.

ℹ️ Getting There & Away

Greyhound (501-623-5574; www.greyhound. com; 100 Broadway Tce) has buses heading from Hot Springs to Little Rock (1½ hours, from $13, around three daily). The town is located off I-30, about 60 miles southwest of Little Rock.

Tri-Peaks Region

The Tri-Peaks Region is the crown jewel in the gem that is the great green Arkansas River Valley, which forms one of the state's major geographic zones. In the shadow of the Tri-Peaks, you'll find four state parks and fantastic hiking, trekking and boating activities.

The area, which comprises multiple Arkansas counties, is named for the triumvirate of Mt Magazine, Mt Nebo and Petit Jean Mountain. While there is no real central base for exploring the area, you can stock up on supplies in numerous small towns, the largest of which is Russellville. We have

named the closest supply town in each park's individual entry.

🔅 Sights & Activities

Each of the parks we list in the Tri-Peak Region, with the exception of water-oriented Lake Dardanelle, contain multiple hikes ranging from flat, easy nature loops to difficult ascents along mountain peaks. Check with each park website for a full list of the many trails, and be sure to ask rangers about current conditions.

Mount Magazine State Park STATE PARK

(479-963-8502; www.mountmagazinestatepark. com; 577 Lodge Drive, Paris, GPS: N 35°09'52.4 W 93°38'49.7"; ☺24hr) This stellar state park features some 14 miles of trails that wind around Arkansas' highest point. The surrounding vistas are spectacular, taking in all of the forested montane beauty of the Arkansas River Valley. If you don't have time to stop, the **Mount Magazine Scenic Byway** traverses the park and includes some drop-dead gorgeous views. If you need food or gas, the closest town is Paris, about 17 miles away.

Mount Nebo State Park STATE PARK

(479-229-3655; www.arkansasstateparks.com/ mountnebo; 16728 West State Hwy 155, Dardanelle, GPS: N 35°13'41.0" W 93°15'19.7"; ☺sunrise-sunset; 🅿️♿🐾) 🆓 Hey – it's just another impossibly beautiful Arkansas state park! Mount Nebo and surrounds are crisscrossed by 14 miles of trails that plunge into the woodsy mountainscape. The strenuous Nebo Springs trail makes a loop that heads to a mossy, watery slice of outdoors loveliness. The closest town, Dardanelle, is eight miles to the east.

Petit Jean State Park STATE PARK

(501-727-5441; www.petitjeanstatepark.com; 1285 Petit Jean Mountain Rd, Morrilton, GPS: N 35°07'04.3" W 92°56'17.8"; ☺sunrise-sunset; 🅿️♿🐾) 🆓 The excellently maintained trails of this state park, the oldest in Arkansas, wind past a lush 95ft waterfall, romantic grottoes, expansive vistas and dense forests. Be on the lookout for a natural bridge spanning the Arcadian wilderness, as well as overlooks that take in huge swaths of the Arkansas River Valley. The closest town is Morrilton (18 miles away), although Little Rock is only about 70 miles southeast of here if you fancy a long day trip from the capital.

THE SOUTH TRI-PEAKS REGION

Lake Dardanelle State Park STATE PARK
(www.arkansasstateparks.com/lakedardanelle; 100
State Park Dr (Breakwater Rd), Russellville; ☉ visitor center 8am-5pm daily, to 8pm May-Aug; ⓟⓗ)
Miles of icy-blue water mark this 34,300-acre reservoir, which is surrounded by boat-launch ramps and flat-out pretty views.
There's a big visitor center in Russellville
that includes kid-friendly interpretive exhibits, aquariums and kayak-rental facilities.

Buffalo National River RAFTING
(☑ 870-439-2502; www.nps.gov/buff; 170 Ranger Road, St Joe, Tyler Bend Visitor Center; ⓗ) ✐
Yet another under-acknowledged Arkansas
gem, and perhaps the best of them all, this
135-mile river flows beneath dramatic bluffs
through unspoiled Ozark forest. The upriver
section tends to have most of the white water,
while the lower reaches ease lazily along –
perfect for an easy paddle.

The Buffalo National River (p429) has 10
campgrounds and three designated wilderness areas; the most accessible is through
the Tyler Bend visitor center, 11 miles north
of Marshall on Hwy 65, where you can also
pick up a list of approved outfitters for
self-guided rafting or canoe trips (the best
way to tour the park and see the gargantuan
limestone bluffs). Or seek out Buffalo Outdoor Center (p429), which will point you in
the right direction and rents out attractive
cabins in the woods, too.

Kayaking BOATING
(☑ 479-967-5516; www.arkansasstateparks.com;
100 State Park Drive (Breakwater Rd), Russellville;
per hour/half-day/day from $8/14/20) ✐ You
can rent solo or tandem kayaks to explore
the waters of Lake Dardanelle, or opt for a
90-minute kayak tour for an extra $12/6 per
adult/child.

🛏 Sleeping & Eating

There are uninspiring chain motels and hotels in the towns close to the Tri-Peaks parks,
but if you're going to sleep out here, you may
as well crash in the parks – be it in primitive
campsites or a stylish lodge.

There are dozens of campsites (www.arkansasstateparks.com/camping-cabins-lodging;
$12 to 32) spread out among the four state
parks of the Tri-Peaks Region. Facilities
range from primitive camping with no
hookups to sites with full electricity, running
water and toilets. Contact each park to learn
about their individual camping areas, and
book through the state park website.

You'll want to stock up on groceries before
exploring any of the Tri-Peaks parks indepth, with the exception of Lake Dardanelle, which is located in Russellville proper.

ℹ Information

The **Tyler Bend Visitor Center** (☑ 870-439-2502; www.nps.gov/buff; 170 Ranger Rd, St Joe;
☉ 8:30am-4:30pm) is a must visit for those who
want to explore the Buffalo National River.

ℹ Getting There & Away

The Tri-Peaks Region occupies an oddly
Arkansas-shaped chunk of north-central Arkansas. The four parks can be accessed via the
towns we list in individual park listings. None is
more than two hours from Little Rock.

The spectacular Highway 23/Pig Trail Byway,
which runs from Eureka Springs to Mount Magazine State Park (p425), runs through mountain
ranges and Ozark National Forest – it's well
worth your time.

Ozark Mountains

Stretching from northwest and central Arkansas into Missouri, the Ozark Mountains
are an ancient range, once surrounded by
sea and now well worn by time. Verdant
mountains give way to misty fields and hard-dirt farms, while dramatic karst formations
line sparkling lakes, rivers and capillary-thin
back roads. The region derives a lot of pride
from its independence and sense of place,
a zeitgeist at least partially informed by
multiple generations of familial roots and a
long history of regional poverty. For literary
company, pick up Daniel Woodrell's novel
Winter's Bone, which was adapted into a
critically acclaimed film of the same name.

ℹ Getting There & Away

The Ozarks encompass a large area, riven by
numerous mountain roads, some of which are
big enough to count as highways. Major roads
include Hwy 62, AR 21, AR 43 and AR 66. The
closest regional airport is **Northwest Arkansas
Regional Airport** (XNA; ☑ 479-205-1000; www.
flyxna.com; 1 Airport Blvd), near Bentonville.
Eureka Springs is also served by **Greyhound**
(☑ 800-451-5333; 131 E Van Buren).

Mountain View

Mountain View has managed to parlay
Ozark culture into the sort of tourism you
can (partially) build an community on. The
folkways and creative expression of the

mountains are given exuberant life in this village, and a mix of cultural seekers and the creators of the culture that's being sought out yields an odd nexus of deeply spiritual Christianity, hippie folk music and heartfelt hospitality.

The **Visitor Information Center** (☑870-269-8068; www.yourplaceinthemountains.com; 122 W Main St; ☺9am-4:30pm Mon-Sat) promotes Mountain View as the 'Folk Music Capital of the World,' and while that may be ambitious, it doesn't detract from Mountain View's fundamental pleasantness. No matter how you get here, you'll inevitably pass through crumbling Ozark towns fallen on hard times. Mountain View, in contrast, is what the area could be: preserved history finding contemporary voice and energy in a globalized world that still wants to connect to deep regional traditions.

◎ Sights & Activities

Blanchard Springs Caverns | CAVE
(☑870-757-2211, 877-444-6777; www.blanchard springs.org; NF 54, Forest Rd, off Hwy 14; Drip Stone Tour adult/child $10/5, Wild Cave Tour $75; ☺ hours vary; ⊕) ⊘ The spectacular Blanchard Springs Caverns, 15 miles northwest of Mountain View, were carved by an underground river and rival those at Carlsbad. It's another little-known, mind-blowing spot in Arkansas. Three Forest Service guided tours range from disabled-accessible to adventurous three- to four-hour spelunking sessions. The caverns maintain seasonal hours, but usually open at 9:30am and close around sunset.

Ozark Folk Center State Park | STATE PARK
(☑870-269-3851; www.ozarkfolkcenter.com; 1032 Park Ave; auditorium adult/child $12/7; ☺10am-5pm Tue-Sat Apr-Nov, evening shows 6pm; ℗) The town's top cultural attraction, just north of Mountain View, hosts ongoing craft demonstrations, a traditional herb garden, and nightly live music that brings in an avid crowd. Beyond those shows, the center maintains a busy concert schedule that ropes in some of the nation's best folk and bluegrass acts.

LocoRopes | OUTDOORS
(☑888-669-6717, 870-269-6566; www.locoropes. com; 1025 Park Ave; per zipline $7.50; ☺10am-5pm Mar 1-Nov 30) This popular outdoors outfitter offers a ropes course, slack lining, a freefall, a climbing wall and three ziplines.

🛏 Sleeping & Eating

Wildflower B&B | B&B $
(☑870-269-4383; www.wildflowerbb.com; 100 Washington St; r $99-139; ℗⚅🛜) Set right on the Court Square with a rocking-chair-equipped wraparound porch and cool folk art on the walls. Ask for the front room upstairs; it's flooded with afternoon light, has a queen bed and a joint sitting room with TV. Booking online is best.

Tommy's Famous Pizza and BBQ | PIZZA, BARBECUE $
(☑870-269-3278; www.tommysfamous.com; cnr Carpenter & W Main Sts; pizza $7-26, mains $7-13; ☺from 3pm) The Tommy's Famous Pizza and BBQ is run by the friendliest bunch of backwoods hippies you could hope to meet. The BBQ pizza marries Tommy's stated specialties indulgently. The affable owner, a former rocker from Memphis, plays great music, has a fun vibe, and just two conditions: no attitude and no loud kids.

Tommy's closes when the cash register hasn't opened for an hour.

PJ's Rainbow Cafe | AMERICAN $
(☑870-269-8633; 216 W Main St; mains $5.50-13; ☺7am-8pm Tue-Sat, to 2pm Sun; ⊘⊕) This country-fried cafe serves up some truly tasty diner food done with flair; think spinach-stuffed pork loin and fresh-grilled rainbow trout caught in local rivers. Cash only.

Eureka Springs

Eureka Springs, near Arkansas' northwestern corner, perches in a steep valley filled with Victorian buildings, crooked streets and a crunchy, New Age–aligned local population that welcomes all – this is one of the most explicitly gay-friendly towns in the Ozarks, and mixes up an odd mash of liberal politics and rainbow flags with biker-friendly Harley bars. Hiking, cycling, and horseback-riding opportunities abound.

The **visitor center** (☑479- 253-8737; www. eurekaspringschamber.com; 516 Village Circle, Hwy 62 E; ☺9am-5pm) has information about lodging, activities, tours and local attractions. For information on LGBTQ travel in the area, log on to Out In Eureka (www.gay eurekasprings.com).

◎ Sights & Activities

Historic Loop | HISTORIC SITE
(www.eurekasprings.org) ⊘ **FREE** This 3.5-mile walking tour winds through downtown

Eureka Springs and neighboring residential areas. The route is dotted with more than 300 Victorian homes, all built before 1910, each a jaw-dropper and on par with any preserved historic district in the USA. You can access the loop via the Eureka Trolley, or just walk it – recommended if you're fit (the streets are steep!); pick up a map or buy trolley tickets at the Visitor Center.

Thorncrown Chapel
CHURCH
(☑479-253-7401; www.thorncrown.com; 12968 Hwy 62 W; ⊙9am-5pm Apr-Nov, 11am-4pm Mar & Dec; ℗) FREE Thorncrown Chapel is a magnificent sanctuary made of glass, with its 48ft-tall wooden skeleton holding 425 windows. There's not much between your prayers and God's green earth here. It's just outside of Eureka Springs in the woods. Donation suggested.

1886 Crescent Hotel
HISTORIC BUILDING
(☑855-725-5720;www.crescent-hotel.com;75 Prospect Ave) Built in 1886, the Crescent is a gorgeous, functioning artifact of an older age. Step into the dark-wood lobby, with its roaring fireplace and carpets, all accented by little Jazz Age flourishes, and you'll feel the need to order a cognac and berate Daisy Buchanan for ever marrying Tom Buchanan, the *cad*. Er, sorry. The Crescent sits atop a hill, and is a great place to visit for a drink, the view from its rooftop, or both.

Lake Leatherwood City Park
PARK
(☑479-253-7921; www.lakeleatherwoodcitypark. com; 1303 Co Rd 204; ⊙24hr; ℗⊛) This expansive park includes 21 miles of hiking and biking trails that crisscross the forested mountains and surround an 85-acre lake. Located about 3.5 miles from downtown Eureka Springs, this is the closest managed wild space to Eureka Springs.

Eureka Trolley
TOURS
(☑479-253-9572; www.eurekatrolley.org; 137 W Van Buren St; day pass adult/child $6/2; ⊙10am-6pm Sun-Fri, 9am-8pm Sat May-Oct, reduced hours other times; ⊛) This old time hop-on-hop-off trolley service plies four routes through greater Eureka Springs. Each trip takes about 20 to 30 minutes, revealing a different angle on life in this mountain town. Check website or call ahead for running times.

🛏 Sleeping & Eating

★Treehouse Cottages
COTTAGE $$
(☑479-253-8667; www.treehousecottages.com; 165 W Van Buren St; cottage $149-169; ℗❄🤍) Sprinkled amid 33 acres of pine forest, these cute, kitschy and spacious stilted wooden cottages are worth finding. There's lovely accent tile in the baths, a Jacuzzi tub overlooking the trees, a private balcony with grill at the ready, a flat-screen TV and fireplace. Enforces two-night minimum stays.

The Crescent Hotel
HISTORIC HOTEL $$
(☑855-725-5720; www.crescent-hotel.com; 75 Prospect Ave; r $160-200, ste $200-280; ℗🤍) Of all the pretty historic buildings in Eureka Springs, the Crescent stands out: it's like *Downton Abbey* meets the Jazz Age (which happened in season 4, right?). We digress; rooms are a well-executed synthesis of historic accents and modern comforts, and the whole vibe of the place is both elegant and fun. Rates go up on weekends.

★FRESH
MODERN AMERICAN $$
(☑479-253-9300;www.freshanddeliciousofeureka springs.com; 179 N Main St; mains $10-27; ⊙11am-9pm Mon-Thu, 10am-2pm Sun; ✎) 🍃 This beautiful café specializes in farm-to-table cuisine, brilliant baked goods and quirky service. The open-face sandwiches with shaved ham served on fresh-baked French toast are stupidly decadent, and there are vegan options ranging from salads to pesto-tossed pasta. Dinner gets fancier with dishes like roasted-chicken pot pie and seared ahi tuna.

★Stone House
MODERN AMERICAN $$$
(☑479-363-6411; www.eurekastonehouse.com; 89 S Main St; cheese plates $25-47; ⊙1-10pm Thu-Sat, to 8pm Sun) The Stone House has all the ingredients for a pretty perfect evening: lots of wine; a menu that focuses on cheese, bread, olives, honey and charcuterie; live music; a cute courtyard; and did we mention lots of wine? It's open until 10pm, which constitutes late-night dining in Eureka Springs.

🍷 Drinking & Entertainment

Chelsea's Corner Cafe & Bar
BAR
(☑479-253-8231; www.chelseascornercafe.com; 10 Mountain St; ⊙noon-10pm Sun-Thu, to midnight Fri & Sat) Live-music acts frequently take to the stage at this bar, which attracts a typically Eureka Springs blend of hippies and bikers. The kitchen is one of the few places in town open past 9pm, and does pizza delivery.

Opera in the Ozarks
OPERA
(☑479-253-8595; www.opera.org; 16311 Hwy 62 West; tickets from $20) This much acclaimed fine-arts program has kept opera alive and

loud in the mountains. A packed performance schedule and a playhouse located just outside of town is the pride of Eureka Springs.

Buffalo National River

Ponca is the easiest town to base yourself in if you're looking to explore the Buffalo National River. Organize an adventure with a local outfitter and get ready for some stunning scenery: a backdrop of gorgeous riverine wilderness, multicolored granite bluffs and rushing waterfalls is at your fingertips (or paddle oars; you know what we mean). There's a few outdoor outfitters here to help you get set up on a wilderness adventure.

🏃 Activities

Buffalo Outdoor Center ADVENTURE
(BOC; ☑870-861-5514; www.buffaloriver.com; 4699 AR 43; kayak/canoe per day $55/62, zipline tour $89; ⊙8am-6pm Mar-Oct, to 5pm Nov-Feb; 🖐🐾) Can arrange paddling trips, hiking tours, fishing trips, horseback rides and a zipline tour. Reserve in advance.

Big Bluff via Centerpoint & Goat Trail HIKING
(AR 43 & Fire Tower Rd, GPS: N 36°03'50.7" W 93°21'43.6" (Centerpoint Trail)) 🥾 Standing a dramatic 550ft tall, Big Bluff is the highest sheer rock face between the Rocky Mountains and the Appalachians. To get out here, take the Centerpoint Trail, three miles north of Ponca on AR 43 (look for the trailhead near the junction of Fire Tower Rd). Take the narrow spur route – the Goat Trail – that leads to the bluff. This is a 2.5 mile round-trip trail, and it's pretty much uphill.

Lost Valley Canoe CANOEING
(☑870-861-5522; www.lostvalleycanoe.com; AR 43; kayaks per day from $55, shuttle service from $20) 🥾 This knowledgeable outfitter can arrange canoe and kayak rentals, as well as shuttle pick-up services. They also rent comfortable cabins (with hot tubs!) that can sleep two for $125 ($15 for each extra guest).

❶ Getting There & Away

Ponca sits far off any beaten tracks. You need to come by road, and it's about 50 miles south of Eureka Springs and 80 miles east of Bentonville.

LOUISIANA

Louisiana runs deep: a French colony turned Spanish protectorate turned reluctant American purchase; a southern fringe of swampland, bayou and alligators dissolving into the Gulf of Mexico; a northern patchwork prairie of heartland farm country; and everywhere, a population tied together by a deep, unshakable appreciation for the good things in life: food and music.

New Orleans, its first city, lives and dies by these qualities, and its restaurants and music halls are second to none. But everywhere, the state shares a love for this joie de vivre. We're not dropping French for fun, by the way; while the language is not a cultural component of North Louisiana, near I-10 and below it is a generation removed from the household – if it has been removed at all.

History

The lower Mississippi River area was dominated by the Mississippian mound-building culture until around 1592 when Europeans arrived and decimated the Native Americans with the usual combination of disease, unfavorable treaties and outright hostility.

The land was then passed back and forth between France, Spain and England. Under the French 'Code Noir,' slaves were kept but retained a somewhat greater degree of freedom – and thus native culture – than their counterparts in British North America.

After the American Revolution the whole area passed to the USA in the 1803 Louisiana Purchase, and Louisiana became a state in 1812. The resulting blend of American and Franco-Spanish traditions, plus the influence of Afro-Caribbean communities, gave Louisiana the unique culture it retains to this day.

Following the Civil War, Louisiana was readmitted to the Union in 1868 and the next 30 years saw political wrangling, economic stagnation and renewed discrimination against African Americans.

Hurricane Katrina (2005) and the BP Gulf Coast Oil Spill (2010) significantly damaged the local economy and infrastructure. Louisiana remains a bottom-rung state in terms of per capita income and education levels, yet it ranks high in national happiness scales.

❶ Information

Louisiana Office of Tourism (☑800-677-4082, 225-635-0090; www.louisianatravel.com) Sixteen welcome centers dot freeways throughout the state, or contact the office directly.

Louisiana State Parks (☑ 888-677-1400; www.crt.state.la.us/louisiana-state-parks; primitive/premium sites from $18/25) Louisiana has 22 state parks that offer camping. Some parks also offer lodge accommodations and cabins. Reservations can be made on the online, by phone or on a drop-in basis if there's availability. Camping fees rise slightly from April to September.

New Orleans

New Orleans is very much of America, but extraordinarily removed from it as well. Founded by the French and administered by the Spanish (and then the French again), New Orleans is the most European city in America. But, with the *vodoun* (voodoo), weekly second-line parades, Mardi Gras Indians, jazz, brass and gumbo, it's also the most African and Caribbean city in America.

New Orleans celebrates life; while America is on deadline, this city is sipping a cocktail after a long lunch. But if you saw how people here rebuilt their homes after floods and tempests, you'd be foolish to call the locals lazy.

Tolerating everything and learning from it is the soul of this city. When New Orleans' citizens aspire to that overarching Creole ideal, where the whole is greater than the sum of its parts, we get: jazz; Nouveau Louisiana cuisine; storytellers from African *griots* (West African bards) to Seventh Ward rappers to Tennessee Williams; French townhouses a few blocks from Foghorn Leghorn mansions groaning under sweet myrtle and bougainvillea; and Mardi Gras celebrations that mix pagan mysticism with Catholic pageantry.

Just don't forget the indulgence and immersion, because that Creolization gets watered down when folks don't live life to its intellectual and epicurean hilt.

◉ Sights

◉ French Quarter

Also known as Vieux Carré (voo car-*ray;* Old Quarter) and 'the Quarter,' the French Quarter is the original city as planned by the French in the early 18th century. Here lies the infamous Bourbon St, but of more interest is an elegantly aged grid of shopfronts, iron lamps and courtyard gardens. Most visitors begin exploring the city here and some,

sadly, never leave the area. That's not to say the Quarter isn't lovely, but it's a bit like Disney World: heavy on tourist traffic and light on locals (unless you count your bartender or waiter).

★ **Jackson Square**   SQUARE
(Decatur & St Peter Sts) Sprinkled with lazing loungers, surrounded by sketch artists, fortune-tellers and traveling performers, and watched over by cathedrals, offices and shops plucked from a Parisian fantasy, Jackson Square is one of America's great town greens and the heart of the Quarter. The identical, block-long Pontalba Buildings overlook the scene.

★ **St Louis Cathedral**   CATHEDRAL
(☑ 504-525-9585; www.stlouiscathedral.org; Jackson Sq; donations accepted, self-guided tour $1; ⊙ 8am-4pm, Mass noon Mon-Fri, 5pm Sat, 9am & 11am Sun) One of the best examples of French architecture in the country, this triple-spired cathedral is dedicated to Louis IX, the French king sainted in 1297; it's a most innocuous bit of Gallic heritage in the heart of an American city. In addition to hosting black, white and Creole Catholic congregants, St Louis has also attracted those who, in the best New Orleanian tradition, mix their influences, such as voodoo queen Marie Laveau.

★ **Cabildo**   MUSEUM
(☑ 800-568-6968, 504-568-6968; http://louisi anastatemuseum.org/museums/the-cabildo; 701 Chartres St; adult/student/child under 12yr $6/5/ free; ⊙ 10am-4:30pm Tue-Sun, closed Mon; ♿) The former seat of government in colonial Louisiana now serves as the gateway to exploring the history of the state in general, and New Orleans in particular. It's also a magnificent building in its own right; the elegant Cabildo marries elements of Spanish colonial architecture and French urban design better than most buildings in the city. Exhibits range from Native American tools and 'Wanted' posters for escaped slaves to a gallery's worth of paintings of stone-faced old New Orleanians.

Presbytère   MUSEUM
(☑ 800-568-6968, 504-568-6968; http://louisi anastatemuseum.org/museums/the-presbytere; 751 Chartres St; adult/student $6/5; ⊙ 10am-4:30pm Tue-Sun) ✎ The lovely Presbytère building, designed in 1791 as a rectory for the St Louis Cathedral, serves as New Orleans' Mardi Gras museum. You'll find there's more to the city's most famous cel-

CAJUNS, CREOLES AND...CREOLES

Tourists in Louisiana often use the terms 'Cajun' and 'Creole' interchangeably, but the two cultures are quite distinct. 'Creole' refers to descendants of the original European settlers of Louisiana, a blended mix of mainly French and Spanish ancestry. The Creoles tend to have urban connections to New Orleans and consider their own culture refined and urbanized.

The Cajuns can trace their lineage to the Acadians: colonists from rural France who settled Nova Scotia. After the British conquered Canada, the proud Acadians refused to kneel to the new crown and were exiled in the mid-18th century – an act known as the Grand Dérangement. Many exiles settled in South Louisiana; they knew the area was French, but the Acadians ('Cajun' is an English bastardization of the word) were often treated as country bumpkins by the Creoles. The Acadians-cum-Cajuns settled in the bayous and prairies, and to this day see themselves as a more rural, frontier-style culture.

Adding confusion to this is the practice, standard in many post-colonial French societies, of referring to mixed-race individuals as 'Creoles.' This happens in Louisiana, but there is a cultural difference between Franco-Spanish Creoles and mixed-race Creoles, even though these two communities very likely share actual blood ancestry.

ebration than wanton debauchery – or, at least, discover the many levels of meaning behind the debauchery. There's an encyclopedia's worth of material on the krewes, secret societies, costumes and racial histories of the Mardi Gras tapestry.

Historic New Orleans Collection MUSEUM
(THNOC; ☑504-523-4662; www.hnoc.org; 533 Royal St; admission free, tours $5; ☉9:30am-4:30pm Tue-Sat, 10:30am-4:30pm Sun, tours 10am, 11am, 2pm & 3pm Tue-Sat) A combination of preserved buildings, museums and research centers all rolled into one, the Historic New Orleans Collection is a good introduction to the history of of the city. The complex is anchored by its Royal St campus, which presents a series of regularly rotating exhibits and occasional temporary exhibits. Some of the artifacts on offer include an original Jazz Fest poster, transfer documents of the Louisiana Purchase, and utterly disturbing slave advertisements.

◉ Mid-City & The Tremé

The Tremé is the oldest African American neighborhood in the country, characterized by low-slung architecture and residential blocks, some middle class, some rotted by poverty, some gentrifying. This area runs on its west side into Mid-City, a semi-amorphous district that includes long lanes of shotgun houses, poor projects, the gorgeous green spaces of City Park, the elegant mansions of Esplanade Ave and the slow, lovely laze of Bayou St John.

★**Backstreet Cultural Museum** MUSEUM
(☑504-522-4806; www.backstreetmuseum.org; 1116 Henriette Delille St; $10; ☉10am-4pm Tue-Sat) Mardi Gras Indian suits grab the spotlight with dazzling flair – and finely crafted detail – in this informative museum, which examines the distinctive elements of African American culture in New Orleans. The museum isn't terribly big – it's the former Blandin's Funeral Home – but if you have any interest in the suits and rituals of Mardi Gras Indians as well as second line parades and Social Aid & Pleasure Clubs (the local black community version of civic associations), you need to stop by.

★**City Park** PARK
(☑504-482-4888; www.neworleanscitypark.com; Esplanade Ave & City Park Ave; Ⓟ) Live oaks, Spanish moss and lazy bayous frame this masterpiece of urban planning. Three miles long and a mile wide, dotted with gardens, waterways and bridges, and home to a captivating art museum, City Park is bigger than Central Park in NYC, and is New Orleans' prettiest green space. Although a planned golf course has tempered the park's natural beauty, some areas still feel like a slightly tamed expression of the forest and Louisiana wetlands that are the natural backdrop of the city.

Art- and nature-lovers could easily spend a day exploring the park. Anchoring the action is the stately New Orleans Museum of Art, which spotlights regional and American artists. From there, stroll past the whimsical

THE SOUTH NEW ORLEANS

New Orleans

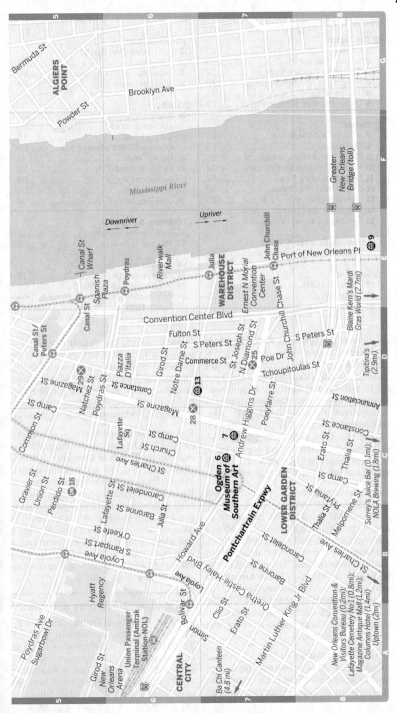

THE SOUTH NEW ORLEANS

Bermuda St

ALGIERS
POINT

Brooklyn Ave

Powder St

Mississippi River

Downriver

Upriver

Canal St
Wharf

Spanish
Plaza

Poydras

Riverwalk
Mall

Julia

WAREHOUSE
DISTRICT

Ernest N Morial
Convention
Center

John Churchill
Chase

Port of New Orleans Pl

Greater
New Orleans
Bridge (toll)

Blaine Kern's Mardi
Gras World (2.7mi)

Canal St/
Peters St

Canal St

Convention Center Blvd

Fulton St

S Peters St

S Peters St

John Churchill Chase St

Chase St

Tipitina's
(2.9mi)

Piazza
D'Italia

Girod St

Notre Dame St

St Joseph St

N Diamond St

Commerce St

Poe Dr

Tchoupitoulas St

Natchez St

Poydras St

Magazine St

Constance St

Magazine St

Andrew Higgins Dr

Poeyfarre St

Annunciation St

Camp St

Common St

Lafayette
Sq

Camp St

Church St

St Charles Ave

Constance St

Erato St

Gravier St

Union St

Perdido St

Carondelet St

Julia St

Baronne St

O'Keefe St

Lafayette St

Howard Ave

Thalia St

Camp St

Prytania St

LOWER GARDEN
DISTRICT

Pontchartrain Expwy

Thalia St

Melpomene St

Surrey's Juice Bar (0.1mi);
NOLA Brewing (1.8mi)

Loyola Ave

S Rampart St

Oretha Castle Haley Blvd

Baronne St

Carondelet St

St Charles Ave

Hyatt
Regency

Bolivar St

Clio St

Erato St

New Orleans Convention &
Visitors Bureau (0.2mi);
Lafayette Cemetery No 1 (0.8mi);
Magazine Antique Mall (1.2mi);
Columns Hotel (1.4mi)
Uptown (2mi)

Poydras Ave

Sugarbowl Dr

Girod St

New
Orleans
Arena

Union Passenger
Terminal (Amtrak
Station-NOL)

Simon

Martin Luther King Jr Blvd

CENTRAL
CITY

Ba Chi Canteen
(4.8 mi)

Ogden
Museum of
Southern Art

29

18

28

13

25

9

7

6

New Orleans

creations in the **Sydney & Walda Besthoff Sculpture Garden** (www.noma.org/sculpturegarden; One Collins Diboll Circle; ⊙10am-6pm Mon-Fri, to 5pm Sat & Sun) FREE then check out the lush **Botanical Gardens**. Kids in tow? Hop the rides at the **Carousel Gardens Amusement Park** (☑504-483-9402; www.neworleanscitypark.com; 7 Victory Ave, City Park; adult/children 36in & under $4/free, each ride $4; ⊙11am-6pm Sat & Sun Mar-May & Aug-Oct, Tue-Fri 11am-5pm, to 6pm Sat & Sun, Jun & Jul) or climb the fantastical statuary inside Storyland.

Louis Armstrong Park   PARK
(835 N Rampart St; ⊙sunrise-sunset) The entrance to this massive park has got to be one of the greatest gateways in the USA, a picturesque arch that ought rightfully be the final set piece in a period drama about Jazz Age New Orleans. The original Congo Sq is here, as well as a **Louis Armstrong statue** and a **bust of Sidney Bechet**. The **Mahalia Jackson Theater** (☑504-525-1052, box office 504-287-0350; www.mahaliajacksontheater.com; 1419 Basin St) hosts opera and Broadway productions.

New Orleans Museum of Art   MUSEUM
(NOMA; ☑504-658-4100; www.noma.org; 1 Collins Diboll Circle; adult/child 7-17yr $12/6; ⊙10am-6pm Tue-Thu, to 9pm Fri, 10am-5pm Sat, 11am-5pm Sun)

Inside City Park, this elegant museum was opened in 1911 and is well worth a visit for its special exhibitions, gorgeous marble atrium, and top-floor galleries of African, Asian, Native American and Oceanic art. Its sculpture garden contains a cutting-edge collection in lush, meticulously planned grounds.

St Augustine's Church   CHURCH
(☑504-525-5934; www.staugchurch.org; 1210 Governor Nicholls St; ⊙Mass 10am Sun & 5pm Wed) Open since 1841, 'St Aug's' is the second-oldest African American Catholic church in the country, a place where Creoles, émigrés from St Domingue and free persons of color could worship shoulder to shoulder, even as separate pews were designated for slaves. Call ahead to see if it's possible to arrange a visit. Don't miss the Tomb of the Unknown Slave, fashioned to resemble a grim cross assembled from chain links.

◎ Faubourg Marigny & Bywater

North of the French Quarter are the Creole *faubourgs* (literally 'suburbs,' although 'neighborhood' is more accurate in spirit, as these areas are still very much within the city). Both the Marigny and Bywater once stood at the edge of gentrification; both are now firmly gentrified, and locals bemoan a rise in online rentals that they say is robbing these areas of their old residential character. With that said, these are fascinating, beautiful neighborhoods – the homes are bright, painted like so many rows of pastel fruit, and the presence of artists and designers makes for a subversive energy.

★**Frenchmen Art Market** MARKET
(📞504-941-1149; www.frenchmenartmarket.com; 619 Frenchmen St; ⊙7pm-1am Thu-Sat, 6pm-midnight Sun) 🕭 Independent artists and artisans line this alleyway market, which has built a reputation as one of the finest spots in town to find a unique gift to take home as your New Orleans souvenir. 'Art,' in this case, includes clever T-shirts, hand-crafted jewelry, trinkets and, yes, a nice selection of prints and original artwork. It has a second location at 2231 St Claude Ave.

Crescent Park PARK
(📞504-636-6400; www.crescentparknola.org; Piety, Chartres & Mazant Sts; ⊙6am-6:30pm, to 7:30pm mid-Mar–early Nov; 🅿) 🕭 This waterfront park is our favorite spot in the city for taking in the Mississippi. Enter over the enormous arch at Piety and Chartres Sts, or at the steps at Marigny and N Peters, and watch the fog blanket the nearby skyline. A promenade meanders past an angular metal and concrete conceptual 'wharf' (placed next to the burned remains of the former commercial wharf). A dog park is located near the Mazant St entrance.

◉ CBD & Warehouse District

Canal St is the 'great divide' that splits the French Quarter from the Central Business District (CBD) and Warehouse District. Between offices and forgettable municipal buildings lie some of the city's best museums, many posh restaurants, an eyesore of a casino, art galleries and excellent arts walks. That said, this area, with its high-rise buildings and converted condos, is the least 'New Orleans' neighborhood in New Orleans.

★**Ogden Museum of Southern Art** MUSEUM
(📞504-539-9650; www.ogdenmuseum.org; 925 Camp St; adult/child 5-17yr $13.50/6.75; ⊙10am-5pm Wed-Mon, to 8pm Thu) One of our favorite museums in the city manages to be beautiful, educational and unpretentious all at once. New Orleans entrepreneur Roger Houston Ogden has assembled one of the finest collections of Southern art anywhere, which includes huge galleries ranging from Impressionist landscapes to outsider folk-art quirkiness and contemporary installation work. On Thursday nights, pop in for Ogden after Hours, when you can listen to great Southern musicians and sip wine with a fun-loving, arts-obsessed crowd in the midst of the masterpieces.

National WWII Museum MUSEUM
(📞504-528-1944; www.nationalww2museum.org; 945 Magazine St; adult/senior/child $26/22.50/16.50, plus 1/2 films $5/10; ⊙9am-5pm) This extensive museum presents a fairly thorough analysis of the largest war in history. The exhibits, which are displayed across multiple grand pavilions, are enormous and immersive. Wall-sized photographs capture the confusion of D-Day, while a stroll through the snowy woods of Ardennes feels eerily cold. The experience is designed to be both personal and awe-inducing. That said, the museum focuses so intently on providing the American perspective, it sometimes underplays the narrative of other Allied nations.

Blaine Kern's Mardi Gras World MUSEUM
(📞504-475-2057; www.mardigrasworld.com; 1380 Port of New Orleans Pl; adult/senior/child 2-11yr $20/16/13; ⊙tours 9:30am-4:30pm; 🚼) We dare say Mardi Gras World is one of the happiest places in New Orleans by day – but at night it must turn into one of the most terrifying funhouses this side of Hell. It's all those *faces:* the dragons, clowns, kings and fairies, leering and dead-eyed... That said, we love touring Mardi Gras World – the studio warehouse of Blaine Kern (Mr Mardi Gras) and family, who have been making jaw-dropping parade floats since 1947. Tours last 30 to 45 minutes.

◉ Garden, Lower Garden & Central City

Proceeding south along the Mississippi, following the curve of the river's 'U,' the streets become tree-lined and the houses considerably grander; this is the Garden and Lower Garden Districts, the beginning of New Orleans' 'American Sector' (so named because it was settled after the Louisiana Purchase). This area is home to recent graduates and young professionals, and hip shops and bars that cater to them.

★ **Lafayette Cemetery No 1** CEMETERY
(Washington Ave, at Prytania St; ⊙7am-3pm)
Shaded by groves of lush greenery, this cemetery exudes a strong sense of Southern subtropical Gothic. Built in 1833, it is divided by two intersecting footpaths that form a cross. Look out for the crypts built by fraternal organizations such as the Jefferson Fire Company No 22, which took care of their members and their families in large shared tombs. Some of the wealthier family tombs were built of marble, with elaborate details, but most were constructed simply of inexpensive plastered brick.

☞ Tours

Confederacy of Cruisers CYCLING
(☑504-400-5468; www.confederacyofcruisers.com; 634 Elysian Fields Ave; tours $49-89) Our favorite bicycle tours in New Orleans set you up on cruiser bikes that come with fat tires and padded seats for Nola's flat, pot-holed roads. The main 'Creole New Orleans' tour takes in the best architecture of the Marigny, Bywater, Esplanade Ave and the Tremé. Confederacy also does a 'History of Drinking' tour (for those 21 and over) and a tasty culinary tour.

★ Festivals & Events

Mardi Gras CULTURAL
(www.mardigrasneworleans.com; ⊙Feb or early Mar) In February or early March, Fat Tuesday marks the orgasmic finale of the Carnival season. Expect parades, floats, insane costumes, and a day of absolute mad cap revelry as the entire city throws down for an all-day party.

Jazz Fest MUSIC
(www.nojazzfest.com; ⊙Apr-May) Held during the last weekend of April and the first weekend of May, this world-renowned extravaganza of music, food, crafts and good living is a mainstay of the New Orleans festival calendar, attracting both international headliners and local artists.

St Joseph's Day – Super Sunday CULTURAL
(⊙Mar 19) March 19 and its nearest Sunday bring 'gangs' of Mardi Gras Indians out into the streets in all their feathered, drumming glory. The Super Sunday parade usually begins around noon at Bayou St John and Orleans Ave, but follows no fixed route.

French Quarter Festival MUSIC
(☑504-522-5730; www.fqfi.org; ⊙Apr) During the second weekend of April, the largest free music festival in the country takes over the French Quarter.

🛏 Sleeping

★ **Le Pavillon** HISTORIC HOTEL $$
(☑504-581-3111; www.lepavillon.com; 833 Poydras Ave; r $135-200, ste from $600; P❄🐾📶⛱) Le Pavillon exudes an old-school joie de vivre that's easy to love. Fluted columns support the porte cochere off the alabaster facade, and the doorman wears white gloves and a top hat (and somehow doesn't look ridiculous). Both private and public spaces are redolent with historic portraits, magnificent chandeliers, marble floors and heavy drapery.

★ **Auld Sweet Olive**
Bed & Breakfast B&B $$
(☑504-947-4332; www.sweetolive.com; 2460 N Rampart St; r incl breakfast $145-180, ste $180-290; ⊖❄🐾📶) The Krewe de Vieux parade goes right by this grand B&B. Even if you don't come during the pre-Lenten season, you can see parade regalia such as the co-owner's King Endymion costume on display. The house itself is similarly theatrical, once owned by a set designer and mural artist. Individual rooms are suffused with decorative touches – faux wood and magnolia blooms.

Columns Hotel HISTORIC HOTEL $$
(☑504-899-9308; www.thecolumns.com; 3811 St Charles Ave; r incl breakfast $145-180; ❄📶) This white-porched Southern manse, built in 1883, is a snapshot from the past. Fortunately that past doesn't take itself too seriously. A magnificent mahogany staircase climbs past a stained-glass window to the rooms, ranging from smallish doubles to the two-room Pretty Baby Suite (named for the 1970s Louis Malle film shot here). The environs aren't exactly posh, but they're well loved.

Degas House HISTORIC HOTEL $$
(☑504-821-5009; www.degashouse.com; 2306 Esplanade Ave; r $130-250, ste from $300; P❄📶) Edgar Degas, the famed French Impressionist, lived in this 1852 Italianate house when visiting his mother's family in the early 1870s. Rooms recall his time here through period furnishings and reproductions of his work. The suites have balconies and fireplaces, while the less expensive garret rooms are cramped top-floor quarters that once housed the Degas family's servants. Stays include a hot breakfast.

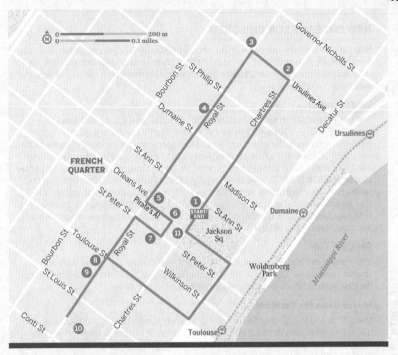

N 0 _____ 200 m
0 _____ 0.1 miles

Governor Nicholls St

3

2

Bourbon St

St Philip St

Chartres St

Ursulines Ave

Decatur St

Dumaine St

Royal St

4

Ursulines

FRENCH
QUARTER

St Ann St

Orleans Ave

Madison St

St Peter St

Pirate's Al

5

Dumaine

1
START/
END

St Ann St

6

11

Jackson
Sq

Toulouse St

Royal St

7

St Peter St

Woldenberg
Park

Bourbon St

8

Wilkinson St

Mississippi River

St Louis St

9

Chartres St

Conti St

10

Toulouse

City Walk
French Quarter

START/END JACKSON SQ
LENGTH 1.1 MILES; 1½ HOURS

Begin your walk at the **1 Presbytère**
(p430) on Jackson Sq and head down
Chartres St to the corner of Ursulines Ave.
Directly across Chartres St, at No 1113, the
1826 **2 Beauregard-Keyes House** (www.
bkhouse.org) combines Creole and American
styles of design. Walk along Ursulines Ave to
Royal St – the soda fountain at the **3 Royal
Pharmacy** is a preserved relic from halcyon
malt-shop days.

When it comes to quintessential New
Orleans postcard images, Royal St takes the
prize. Cast-iron galleries grace the buildings
and a profusion of flowers garland the facades. At No 915 Royal, the **4 Cornstalk
Hotel** (www.cornstalkhotel.com) stands
behind one of the most frequently photographed fences anywhere. At Orleans Ave,
stately magnolia trees and lush tropical
plants fill **5 St Anthony's Garden** (tough
to see behind rows of street art) behind

6 St Louis Cathedral (p430). Alongside
the garden, take the inviting Pirate's Alley
and turn right down Cabildo Alley and
then right up St Peter St toward Royal St.
Tennessee Williams shacked up at No 632
St Peter, the **7 Avart-Peretti House**,
in 1946–47 while he wrote *A Streetcar
Named Desire*. Turn left on Royal St. At the
corner of Royal and Toulouse Sts stands
a pair of houses built by Jean François
Merieult in the 1790s. The building known
as the **8 Court of Two Lions**, at 541 Royal
St, opens onto Toulouse St and next door is
the **9 Historic New Orleans Collection**
(p431).

On the next block, the massive 1909
10 State Supreme Court Building was
the setting for many scenes in director
Oliver Stone's movie *JFK*.

Turn around and head right on Toulouse
St to Decatur St and turn left. Cut across
the road and walk along the river. As Jackson Sq comes into view, cross back over to
the Presbytère's near-identical twin, the
11 Cabildo (p430).

NEW ORLEANS FOR CHILDREN

New Orleans is a fairy-tale city, with its colorful beads, weekly costume parties and daily music wafting through the air. The same flights of fancy and whimsy that give this city such appeal for poets and artists also make it an imaginative wonderland for children, especially creative ones.

Under the City's Skin

The **Louisiana Children's Museum** (☑504-523-1357; www.lcm.org; 420 Julia St; admission $8.50; ⊙9:30am-4:30pm Tue-Sat, noon-4:30pm Sun; ⓜ) is a good intro to the region for toddlers, while older children and teenagers may appreciate the Ogden Museum (p435), Cabildo (p430) and Presbytère (p430). Little ones often take a shine to the candy-colored houses in the French Quarter, Faubourg Marigny and Uptown. The **Latter Library** (☑504-596-2625; www.nolalibrary.org; 5120 St Charles Ave; ⊙10am-8pm Mon-Thu, to 5pm Fri & Sat, 1-5pm Sun; ⓜ) on St Charles Ave has a good selection of children's literature and is located in a pretty historical mansion. The city's cemeteries, especially Lafayette Cemetery No 1 (p436) in the Garden District, are authentic slices of the past and enjoyably spooky to boot.

Festival Fun

The many street parties and outdoor festivals of New Orleans bring food stalls and, of course, great music. Children will love dancing to the beat. Seek out festivals held during the day, such as Bayou Boogaloo (www.thebayouboogaloo.com).

Mardi Gras for Families

Mardi Gras and the Carnival Season are surprisingly family-friendly affairs outside of the well-known boozy debauch in the French Quarter. St Charles Ave hosts many day parades where lots of krewes roll and families set up grilling posts and tents – drinking revelers aren't welcome. Kids are set up on 'ladder seats' (www.momsminivan.com/extras/ladderseat.html) so they can get an adult-height view of the proceedings and catch throws from the floats. The crazy costumes add to the child-friendly feel of the whole affair. See www.neworleansonline.com/neworleans/mardigras/mgfamilies.html.

★**Roosevelt New Orleans** HOTEL $$$
(☑504-648-1200; www.therooseveltneworleans.com; 123 Baronne St; r/ste from $300/400; ⓟ@🌐☎🏊) The majestic, block-long lobby harks back to the early 20th century, a golden age of opulent hotels and grand retreats. Swish rooms have classical details, but the spa, John Besh restaurant, storied Sazerac Bar and swanky jazz lounge are at least half the reason to stay. The rooftop pool is pretty swell too. It's an easy walk to the French Quarter.

★**Soniat House** BOUTIQUE HOTEL $$$
(☑504-522-0570; 800-544-8808; www.soniathouse.com; 1133 Chartres St; r/ste from $245/450; ⊖❄☎) The three houses that make up this hotel in the Lower Quarter epitomize Creole elegance at its unassuming best. You enter via a cool loggia into a courtyard filled with ferns and a trickling fountain. Some rooms open onto the courtyard, while winding stairways lead to elegant upstairs quarters.

Singular attention has been paid to the art and antiques throughout.

Hotel Maison de Ville HISTORIC HOTEL $$$
(☑504-324-4888; www.hotelmaisondeville.com; 727 Toulouse St; r from $275; ❄☎) A series of remodeled suits, cottages and apartments form this graceful hotel, which includes the one- and two-bedroom Audubon Cottage suites (where artist John J Audubon stayed and painted while in town). It's a quintessential French Quarter property, dripping with tropical historical accents and built around a lushly landscaped courtyard that feels plucked out of time.

Hotel Monteleone HOTEL $$$
(☑504-523-3341; 866-338-4684; www.hotelmonteleone.com; 214 Royal St; r $190-270, ste from $370; ❄☎🏊) Perhaps the city's most venerable hotel, the Monteleone is also the Quarter's largest. Not long after it was built, preservationists put a stop to building on

this scale below Iberville St. Since its inception in 1866, the hotel has lodged literary luminaries including William Faulkner, Truman Capote and Rebecca Wells. Rooms exude an old-world appeal with French toile and chandeliers.

✖ Eating

✖ French Quarter

Café Beignet
CAFE $

(☑504-524-5530; www.cafebeignet.com; 334 Royal St; meals $6-8; ☺7am-10pm) In a shaded patio setting with a view of Royal St, this intimate cafe serves omelets, Belgian waffles, quiche and beignets. There's a low-level war among foodies over who does the better beignet – this place or iconic Café du Monde – with the general consensus being this spot uses less powdered sugar. Also located at **Musical Legends Park** (311 Bourbon St, Musical Legends Park; ☺8am-10pm Sun-Thu, to midnight Fri & Sat).

Café du Monde
CAFE $

(☑800-772-2927; www.cafedumonde.com; 800 Decatur St; beignets $3; ☺24hr) Cafe du Monde is the most popular destination in New Orleans, and unfortunately, it often feels that way. But once you do get seated, the beignets (square, sugar-coated fritters) and chicory café au lait, served here since 1862, are decadent and delicious. Open 24 hours a day, seven days a week – the cafe only closes for Christmas Day.

Croissant D'Or Patisserie
BAKERY $

(☑504-524-4663; www.croissantdornola.com; 617 Ursulines Ave; meals $3-7; ☺6am-3pm Wed-Mon) On the quieter side of the French Quarter, this spotlessly clean pastry shop is where many locals start their day. Bring a paper, order coffee and a croissant – or a tart, quiche or sandwich topped with béchamel sauce – and bliss out. Check out the tiled sign on the threshold that says 'ladies entrance' – a holdover from earlier days.

Coop's Place
CAJUN $$

(☑504-525-9053; www.coopsplace.net; 1109 Decatur St; mains $8-20; ☺11am-3am) Coop's is an authentic Cajun dive but more rocked out. Make no mistake: it's a grotty chaotic place, the servers have attitude and the layout is annoying. But it's worth it for the food: rabbit jambalaya or chicken with shrimp and *tasso* (smoked ham) in a cream sauce – there's no such thing as 'too heavy' here.

★ Bayona
LOUISIANAN $$$

(☑504-525-4455; www.bayona.com; 430 Dauphine St; mains $28-34; ☺11:30am-1:30pm Wed-Sun, plus 6-9:30pm Mon-Thu, 5:30-10pm Fri & Sat; ☑) Bayona is one of our favorite splurges in the Quarter. It's rich but not overwhelming, classy but unpretentious, innovative without being precocious, and all round just a very fine spot for a meal. The menu changes regularly, but expect fresh fish, fowl and game prepared in a way that comes off as elegant and deeply cozy at the same time.

✖ Mid-City & The Tremé

Parkway Tavern
SANDWICHES $

(☑504-482-3047; www.parkwaypoorboys.com; 538 Hagan Ave; po'boys mains $8-13; ☺11am-10pm Wed-Mon; 🅿🖨) Who makes the best po'boy in New Orleans? Honestly, who can say? But tell a local you think the top sandwich comes from Parkway and you will get, at the least, a nod of respect. The roast beef in particular – a craft some would say is dying among the great po'boy makers – is messy as hell and twice as good.

Willie Mae's Scotch House
SOUTHERN US $

(☑504-822-9503; www.williemaesnola.com; 2401 St Ann St; fried chicken $11; ☺10am-5pm Mon-Sat) Willie Mae's has been dubbed the best fried chicken in the world by the James Beard Foundation, the Food Network and other media, and in this case, the hype isn't far off – this is superlative fried bird. The white beans are also amazing. The drawback is everyone knows about it, so expect long lines, sometimes around the block. There's another location Uptown at 7457 St Charles Ave.

★ Dooky Chase
CREOLE $$

(☑504-821-0600; www.dookychaserestaurant.com; 2301 Orleans Ave; buffet $20, mains $20-25; ☺11am-3pm Tue-Thu, 11am-3pm & 5-9pm Fri) Ray Charles wrote 'Early in the Morning' about Dooky's; civil rights leaders used it as informal headquarters in the 1960s; and Barack Obama ate here after his inauguration. Leah Chase's labor of love is the backbone of the Tremé, and her buffets are the stuff of legend, a carnival of top-notch gumbo and excellent fried chicken served in a white-linen dining room.

The vegetarian gumbo z'herbes, served on Thursday during Lent, is the great New Orleans dish done green with mustards, beet tops, spinach, kale, collards and Leah knows what else; committed carnivores should give it a try.

THE SOUTH NEW ORLEANS

Faubourg Marigny & Bywater

★**Bacchanal** MODERN AMERICAN $
(☎504-948-9111; www.bacchanalwine.com; 600 Poland Ave; mains $8-18, cheese from $6; ☺11am-11pm Sun-Thu, to midnight Fri & Sat) From the outside, Bacchanal looks like a leaning Bywater shack; inside are racks of wine and stinky but sexy cheese. Musicians play in the garden, while cooks dispense delicious meals on paper plates from the kitchen in the back; on any given day you may try chorizo-stuffed dates or seared diver scallops that will blow your gastronomic mind.

Pizza Delicious ITALIAN $
(☎504-676-8482; www.pizzadelicious.com; 617 Piety St; pizza by slice from $2.25, whole pie from $15; ☺Tue-Sun 11am-11pm; ⊘⊞☻) 'Pizza D's' pies are thin-crust, New York–style and *good*. The preparation is pretty simple, but the ingredients are fresh as the morning and consistently top-notch. An easy, family-friendly ambience makes for a lovely spot for casual dinner, and it serves some good beer too if you're in the mood.

St Roch Market MARKET $
(☎504-609-3813; www.strochmarket.com; 2381 St Claude Ave; prices vary by vendor; ☺7am-10pm Sun-Thu, to 11pm Fri & Sat; ⊘⊞) ⊘ The St Roch Market was once the seafood and produce market for a working-class neighborhood. But after it was nearly destroyed by Hurricane Katrina, it was renovated into a shiny food court. The airy interior space now hosts 13 restaurants serving food ranging from crepes to burritos to Haitian cuisine.

Prices vary by food vendor but no place in the market charges more than $15 per main.

Joint BARBECUE $
(☎504-949-3232; www.alwayssmokin.com; 701 Mazant St; mains $7.50-18; ☺11:30am-10pm Mon-Sat) The Joint's smoked meat has the olfactory effect of the Sirens' sweet song, pulling you, the proverbial traveling sailor, off course and into a savory meat-induced blissful death (classical Greek analogies ending *now*). Knock-back some ribs, pulled pork or brisket with some sweet tea in the backyard garden and learn to love life if you haven't already.

★**Red's Chinese** CHINESE $$
(☎504-304-6030; www.redschinese.com; 3048 St Claude Ave; mains $5-17; ☺noon-11pm) Red's has upped the Chinese cuisine game in New Orleans in a big way. The chefs aren't afraid to add lashings of Louisiana flavor, yet this isn't what we'd call 'fusion' cuisine. The food is grounded deeply in spicy Sichuan flavours, which pairs well with the occasional flash of cayenne. The General Lee's chicken is stupendously good.

CBD & Warehouse District

Cochon Butcher SANDWICHES $
(☎504-588-7675; www.cochonbutcher.com; 930 Tchoupitoulas St; mains $10-14; ☺10am-10pm Mon-Thu, to 11pm Fri & Sat, to 4pm Sun) Tucked behind the slightly more formal Cochon, this sandwich and meat shop calls itself a 'swine bar and deli.' We call it one of our favorite sandwich shops in the city, if not the South. From the convivial lunch crowds to the savory sandwiches to the fun-loving cocktails, this welcoming place encapsulates the best of New Orleans.

THE QUALITY OF CREOLE

After the Louisiana purchase in 1803, New Orleans was absorbed into the USA. Unsurprisingly, there was tension between the largely protestant Anglo Americans and Catholic Creole New Orleanians. The latter found the former uncouth and boring; the former considered Louisianans feckless and indolent, proving tired regional clichés stretch back centuries.

New Orleans has a habit of digesting its settlers and turning them into its own, though. Successive waves of immigration into New Orleans added layers to the city's demographic, but the original Creole city teased something quintessentially New Orleanian – ie commitment to fun, food and music – out of each new slice of the population pie.

Take the Italians, who suffused local foodways and musicality with muffuletta sandwiches and crooners like Louis Prima. In a similar vein, the Vietnamese have brought both food and a penchant for festivals; the Vietnamese New Year is now a major celebration point for New Orleanians of all creeds and colors. Creole implies mixture, and mixing is something this town excels at, even if it doesn't always do so easily.

★**Peche Seafood Grill**   SEAFOOD **$$**
(📞504-522-1744; www.pecherestaurant.com; 800 Magazine St; small plates $9-14, mains $14-27; ⏰11am-10pm Sun-Thu, to 11pm Fri & Sat) Coastal seafood dishes are prepared simply here, but unexpected flourishes – whether from salt, spices or magic – sear the deliciousness onto your taste buds. The vibe is convivial, with a happy, stylish crowd sipping and savoring among the exposed-brick walls and wooden beams. A large whole fish, made for sharing, is a signature preparation, but we recommend starting with the smoked tuna dip and the fried bread with sea salt.

★**Restaurant August**   CREOLE **$$$**
(📞504-299-9777;   www.restaurantaugust.com; 301 Tchoupitoulas St; lunch $23-42, dinner $37-47, 5-course tasting menu $97, with wine pairings $147; ⏰5-10pm daily, 11am-2pm Fri; 🖊️) For a little romance, reserve a table at Restaurant August, an outpost of chef John Besh's restaurant empire. This converted 19th-century tobacco warehouse, with its flickering candles and warm, soft shades, earns a nod for most aristocratic dining room in New Orleans, but somehow manages to be both intimate and lively. Delicious meals take you to another level of gastronomic perception. The signature speckled trout Pontchartrain is layered with lump crabmeat, wild mushrooms and hollandaise.

🍴 **Garden, Lower Garden & Central City**

Surrey's Juice Bar   AMERICAN **$**
(📞504-524-3828; www.surreysnola.com; 1418 Magazine St; breakfast & lunch $6.50-13; ⏰8am-3pm; 🖊️) Surrey's makes a simple bacon-and-egg sandwich taste – and look – like the most delicious breakfast you've ever been served. And you know what? It probably *is* the best. Boudin biscuits; eggs scrambled with salmon; biscuits swimming in salty sausage gravy; and a shrimp, grits and bacon dish that should be illegal. And the juice, as you might guess, is blessedly fresh.

🍷 **Drinking & Nightlife**

★**Tonique**   BAR
(📞504-324-6045; www.bartonique.com; 820 N Rampart St; ⏰noon-2am) Tonique is a bartender's bar. Seriously, on a Sunday night, when the weekend rush is over, we've seen no fewer than three of the city's top bartenders arrive here to unwind. Why? Because this gem

mixes some of the best drinks in the city, and it has a spirits menu as long as a Tolstoy novel to draw upon.

★**Twelve Mile Limit**   BAR
(📞504-488-8114; www.facebook.com/twelve.mile. limit; 500 S Telemachus St; ⏰5pm-2am Mon-Wed, 11am-2am Thu & Fri, 10am-2am Sat, 10am-midnight Sun) Twelve Mile is simply a great bar. It's staffed by people who have the skill, both behind the bar and in the kitchen, to work in four-star spots, but who chose to set up shop in a neighborhood, for a neighborhood. The mixed drinks are excellent, the match of any mixologist's cocktail in Manhattan, and the vibe is super accepting.

NOLA Brewing   BREWERY
(📞504-301-1117; www.nolabrewing.com; 3001 Tchoupitoulas St; ⏰taproom 11am-11pm, tours 2-3pm Fri, to 4pm Sat & Sun) This cavernous brewery welcomes guests throughout the weekend for a free brewery tour that kicks off with sloshy cups of craft brew and a food truck or two out front. The rest of the week? Stop by the taproom, which has plenty of beers on tap and a roof deck.

Mimi's in the Marigny   BAR
(📞504-872-9868; http://mimismarigny.com; 2601 Royal St; ⏰3pm-close Mon-Fri, 11am-close Sat & Sun) The name of this bar could justifiably change to 'Mimi's *is* the Marigny' – we simply can't imagine the neighborhood without this institution. It's a attractively disheveled place, with comfy furniture, pool tables, an upstairs dance hall decorated like a Creole mansion gone punk, and dim, brown lighting like a fantasy in sepia. The bar closes when the bartenders want it to.

BJ's   BAR
(www.facebook.com/bjs.bywater; 4301 Burgundy) This Bywater dive attracts a neighborhood crowd seeking cheap beers, chilled-out banter and frequent events, from blues rock gigs with Little Freddie King to sci-fi readings by local authors. How great is this place? Robert Plant felt the need to put on an impromptu set here the last time he visited.

★ **Entertainment**

★**Tipitina's**   LIVE MUSIC
(📞504-895-8477; www.tipitinas.com; 501 Napoleon Ave; cover $5-20) 'Tips,' as locals call it, is one of New Orleans' great musical meccas. The legendary Uptown nightclub, which takes its name from Professor Longhair's 1953 hit single, is the site of some of the city's

most memorable shows, particularly when big names such as Dr John come home to roost. Outstanding music from local talent packs 'em in year-round.

Spotted Cat
LIVE MUSIC

(www.spottedcatmusicclub.com; 623 Frenchmen St; ⊙2pm-2am Mon-Fri, noon-2am Sat & Sun) The Cat might just be your smoky dream of a New Orleans jazz club, a thumping sweatbox where drinks are served in plastic cups, impromptu dances break out at the drop of a feathered hat, and the music is always exceptional.

Preservation Hall
JAZZ

(☑504-522-2841; www.preservationhall.com; 726 St Peter St; cover $15 Sun-Thu, $20 Fri & Sat, reserved seats $34-45; ⊙showtimes 8pm, 9pm & 10pm Mon-Wed, 6pm, 8pm, 9pm & 10pm Thu-Sun) Preservation Hall, housed in a former art gallery that dates from 1803, is one of the most storied live-music venues in New Orleans. The resident performers, the Preservation Hall Jazz Band, are ludicrously talented, and regularly tour around the world. 'The Hall' dates from 1961, when Barbara Reid and Grayson 'Ken' Mills formed the Society for the Preservation of New Orleans Jazz.

AllWays Lounge
THEATER

(☑504-218-5778; www.theallwayslounge.net; 2240 St Claude Ave; ⊙6pm-2am Sun-Thu, to 4am Fri & Sat) In a city full of funky music venues, the AllWays stands out as one of the funkiest. On any given night of the week you may see experimental guitar, local theater, thrash-y rock, live comedy or a '60s-inspired shaga-delic dance party. Also the drinks are cheap.

Rock 'N' Bowl
LIVE MUSIC

(☑504-861-1700; www.rockandbowl.com; 3000 S Carrollton Ave; cover $10; ⊙11:30am-midnight Sun-Thu, to 2am Fri & Sat) The Rock 'N' Bowl is a strange combination of bowling alley, deli and huge live-music and dance venue, where patrons get down to New Orleans roots music while trying to avoid that 7-10 split.

Shopping

Magazine Antique Mall
ANTIQUES

(☑504-896-9994; www.magazineantiquemall. com; 3017 Magazine St; ⊙10:30am-5:30pm, noon-5:30pm Sun) Scary baby dolls. Hats. Chandeliers. Coca-Cola memorabilia. Inside this overstuffed emporium, rummagers are likely to score items of interest in the dozen or so stalls, where independent dealers peddle an intriguing and varied range of antique bric-a-brac.

Maple Street Book Shop
BOOKS

(☑504-866-4916; www.maplestreetbookshop. com; 7523 Maple St; ⊙10am-6pm Mon, Tue, Thu-Sat, noon-6pm Wed, 10am-5pm Sun) This beloved Uptown shop celebrated its 50th anniversary in 2014. Founded by sisters Mary Kellogg and Rhoda Norman, it is one of the most politically progressive, well-stocked bookshops in the city. The store sells new, used and rare books in an invitingly over-stuffed setting.

Information

DANGERS AND ANNOYANCES

New Orleans has a concerning crime rate and one of the highest murder rates in the country. The vast majority of violent crime occurs

---

LGBT NEW ORLEANS

Louisiana is a culturally conservative state, but its largest city bucks that trend. New Orleans has always had a reputation for tolerance and it remains one of the oldest gay-friendly cities in the Western hemisphere, marketing itself as the 'Gay Capital of the South.' Neighborhoods such as the French Quarter and Marigny are major destinations on the LGBT travel circuit.

Check out these websites for information on queer travel in New Orleans:

Gay New Orleans Online (www.neworleansonline.com/neworleans/lgbt) Probably the most comprehensive collection of queer listings online.

Gay New Orleans (www.gayneworleans.com) Full of information.

Gay Cities (http://neworleans.gaycities.com) Listings, user reviews and LGBT-related content.

Ambush Magazine (www.ambushmag.com) Local take on queer news and issues.

Purple Roofs (www.purpleroofs.com/usa/louisiana.html) Reliable gay travel resource.

between parties who already know each other, but tourists are occasionally targeted.

Exercise the same caution you would in any US city. The possibility of getting mugged is something to consider even in areas you'd think are safe (eg the Garden District). Solo pedestrians are targeted more often than people walking in groups, and daytime is a better time to be out on foot than nighttime. Avoid entering secluded areas such as cemeteries alone.

Large crowds typically make the French Quarter a secure around-the-clock realm for the visitor. However, if your hotel or vehicle is on the margins of the Quarter, you might want to take a taxi back at night. The CBD and Warehouse District have plenty of activity during weekdays, but they're relatively deserted at night and on weekends. The B&Bs along Esplanade Ridge are close enough to less safe neighborhoods to call for caution at night. In the Quarter, street hustlers frequently approach tourists - we suggest walking away.

Pedestrians crossing the street do not have the right of way and motorists (unless they are from out of state) will not yield. Whether on foot or in a car, be wary before entering an intersection, as New Orleans drivers are notorious for running yellow and even red lights.

To see where crime is occurring, log on to www.crimemapping.com/map/la/neworleans.

INTERNET ACCESS

Many hotels offer wi-fi and cable internet access. Wi-fi is available in almost every coffee shop in town, and all branches of the New Orleans public library (www.neworleanspubliclibrary.org).

MEDIA

Gambit (www.bestofneworleans.com) Weekly publication that covers arts, culture and music.

The Times-Picayune (www.nola.com) Broadsheet news and arts coverage times a week.

The Advocate (www.theadvocate.com/new_orleans) Broadsheet news and culture writing.

New Orleans Magazine (www.mynewworleans.com/new-orleans-magazine) Monthly focus on city society.

The Lens (http://thelensnola.org) Investigative journalism and culture coverage; online only.

TOURIST INFORMATION

Right next to popular Jackson Sq in the heart of the French Quarter, the **New Orleans Welcome Center** (504-568-5661; www.crt.state.la.us/tourism; 529 St Ann St; 8:30am-5pm) in the lower Pontalba Building offers maps, listings of upcoming events and a variety of brochures for sights, restaurants and hotels. The helpful staff can help you find accommodations in a pinch, answer questions and offer advice about New Orleans.

Information kiosks scattered through main tourist areas offer most of the same brochures as the Welcome Center, but their staff tend to be less knowledgeable.

Order or download a Louisiana-wide travel guide online from the Louisiana Office of Tourism (www.louisianatravel.com).

In the Tremé, you can pick up a New Orleans map and look at displays about city attractions at the Basin St Visitors Center inside Basin St Station.

Otherwise, **New Orleans Convention & Visitors Bureau** (504-566-5003; www.neworleanscvb.com; 2020 St Charles Ave; 8:30am-5pm) has plenty of free maps and helpful information.

Getting There & Away

The majority of travelers to New Orleans will arrive by air, landing in **Louis Armstrong New Orleans International Airport** (MSY; 504-303-7500; www.flymsy.com; 900 Airline Hwy, Kenner). The airport was originally named for aviator John Moisant and was known as Moisant Stock Yards, hence the IATA code.

Another option is to fly into **Baton Rouge** (BTR; p445), 89 miles north of the city; or **Gulfport-Biloxi** (GPT; 228-863-5951; www.flygpt.com), Mississippi, 77 miles east. Neither of these options is as convenient as a direct flight to New Orleans, but they may be cheaper during big events such as Mardi Gras or Jazz Fest.

Many travelers drive or bus to New Orleans, which is located at the crossroads of several major highways. Train travel to New Orleans is easy; the city is served by three Amtrak lines.

Getting Around

Streetcar Service on the charming streetcars is limited. One-way fares cost $1.25, and multi-trip passes are available.

Bus Bus services are OK, but try not to time your trip around them. Fares won't run more than $2.

Walk If you're just exploring the French Quarter, your feet will serve fine.

Bicycle Flat New Orleans is easy to cycle – you can cross the entirety of town in 45 minutes.

Car The easiest way to access outer neighborhoods such as Mid-City. Parking is problematic in the French Quarter and CBD.

TO/FROM THE AIRPORT

Louis Armstrong International Airport (MSY) is located 13 miles west of New Orleans. A taxi to the CBD costs $36, or $15 per passenger for three or more passengers. Shuttles to the CBD cost $20/38 per person one way/round-trip. The E2 bus takes you to Carrollton and Tulane Ave in Mid-City for $2.

Amtrak (www.amtrak.com; 1001 Loyola Ave) & Greyhound (www.greyhound.com; 1001 Loyola Ave) are located adjacent to each other downtown. You can walk to the CBD or French Quarter, but don't do so at night, or with heavy luggage. A taxi from here to the French Quarter should cost around $10; further afield you'll be hard-pressed to spend more than $20.

Around New Orleans

Leaving colorful New Orleans behind quickly catapults you into a world of swamps, bayous, antebellum plantation homes, laid-back small communities and miles of bedroom suburbs and strip malls.

Barataria Preserve

★ **Barataria Preserve**　　　　　PARK
(📞504-689-3690; www.nps.gov/jela/ barataria-preserve.htm; 6588 Barataria Blvd, Crown Point; ☺parking lot for trails 9am-5pm daily; P)
🅿 FREE This section of the Jean Lafitte National Historical Park & Preserve, south of New Orleans near the town of Marrero, provides the easiest access to the dense swamplands that ring New Orleans. The 8 miles of boardwalk trails are a stunning way to tread lightly through the fecund, thriving swamp, home to alligators, nutrias river rats) tree frogs and hundreds of species of birds

Start at the **NPS Visitors Center** (📞504-689-3690; www.nps.gov/jela; Hwy 3134; ☺9:30am-4:30pm Wed-Sun; 🚻), 1 mile west of Hwy 45 off the Barataria Blvd exit, where you can pick up a map or join a guided wetland walk (10am Wednesday to Sunday) or canoe trip (call for more information). To rent canoes or kayaks for a tour or an independent paddle, go to **Bayou Barn** (📞504-689-2663; www.bayoubarn.com; 7145 Barataria Blvd, Marrero; canoe/kayak hire per person $20/25; ☺10am-6pm Thu-Sun) about 3 miles from the park entrance.

The North Shore

The north shore of Lake Pontchartrain is a collection of middle-to-upper-class New Orleans bedroom suburbs. Nearby, the bucolic village of Abita Springs was popular in the late 19th century for its curative waters. Today spring water still flows from a fountain in the center of the village, but more importantly for many residents, beer still bubbles from the Abita Brewery, the largest regional beer producer in Louisiana. The

entirety of this region is separated from New Orleans by Lake Pontchartrain, which is spanned by the Lake Pontchartrain Causeway – at almost 24 miles long, the enormous bridge is a sight in and of itself.

River Road

Elaborate plantation homes dot the east and west banks of the Mississippi River between New Orleans and Baton Rouge. First indigo, then cotton and sugarcane, brought great wealth to the plantation owners and many plantations are open to the public. Most tours focus on the lives of the owners, the restored architecture and the ornate gardens of antebellum Louisiana.

◉ Sights

★ **Whitney Plantation**　　　　HISTORIC SITE
(📞225-265-3300; www.whitneyplantation.com; 5099 Highway 18, Wallace; adult/student/child under 6yr $22/10/free; ☺museum 9:30am-4:30pm Wed-Mon) The Whitney is the first plantation in the state to focus on slavery, and in doing so they've flipped the script on plantation tours. Whereas before the story told was that of the 'big house,' here the emphasis is given to the hundreds who died to keep the residents of the big house comfortable. There's a museum on site that you can self tour, but admission to the plantation is by 1½-hour guided tour only.

Laura Plantation　　　　　　HISTORIC SITE
(📞225-265-7690; www.lauraplantation.com; 2247 Hwy 18, Vacherie; adult/child $20/6; ☺10am-4pm; P) This ever-evolving and popular plantation tour teases out the distinctions between Creole, Anglo, free and enslaved African Americans via meticulous research and the written records of the Creole women who ran the place for generations. Laura is also fascinating because it was a *Creole* mansion, founded and maintained by a continental European-descended elite, as opposed to Anglo Americans; the cultural and architectural distinctions between this and other plantations is obvious and striking. Tours are offered in French.

Oak Alley Plantation　　　　　HISTORIC SITE
(📞225-265-2151; www.oakalleyplantation.com; 3645 Hwy 18, Vacherie; adult/student/child $22/8/5; ☺9am-5pm Mar-Oct, 9am-4:30pm Mon-Fri, to 5pm Sat & Sun Nov-Feb; P) The most impressive aspect of Oak Alley Plantation is its canopy of 28 majestic live oaks lining the

entry to the grandiose Greek Revival–style home. The tour hits a blacksmith shop, a slavery exhibit and several other points of interest.

Baton Rouge

In 1699 French explorers named this area *baton rouge* (red stick) when they came upon a reddened cypress pole that Bayagoulas and Houma Native Americans had staked in the ground to mark the boundaries of their respective hunting territories. From one pole grew a lot of sprawl; Baton Rouge stretches out in an unplanned clutter in many directions. Visitors are mostly drawn to Baton Rouge for Louisiana State University (LSU) and Southern University; the latter is one of the largest historically African American universities in the country.

◉ Sights & Activities

Louisiana State Capitol   HISTORIC BUILDING
(☑ 225-342-7317; 900 N 3rd St; ⊘ 8:30am-4:30pm, observation deck to 4pm) FREE The art-deco skyscraper looming over town was built at the height of the Great Depression to the tune of $5 million, and remains the most visible leftover legacy of populist governor 'Kingfish' Huey Long. The 27th-floor observation deck offers views of the city, and the ornate lobby is decently impressive.

LSU Museum of Art   MUSEUM
(LSUMOA; ☑ 225-389-7200; www.lsumoa.com; 100 Lafayette St; adult/child $5/free; ⊘ 10am-5pm Tue-Sat, to 8pm Thu, 1-5pm Sun) The physical space that this museum inhabits – the clean, geometric lines of the Shaw Center – is as impressive as the on-site galleries, which include a permanent collection of over 5000 works and curated galleries exploring regional artistic heritage and contemporary trends.

Old State Capitol   HISTORIC BUILDING
(☑ 225-342-0500; www.louisianaoldstatecapitol. org; 100 North Blvd; ⊘ 10am-4pm Tue-Fri, 9am-3pm Sat) FREE The Gothic Revival, pink fairytale castle is...well, it's a pink castle. Which should tell you something about how eccentric the government of its resident state can be. Today the structure houses exhibits about the political history of Louisiana.

Rural Life Museum   MUSEUM
(☑ 225-765-2437; www.lsu.edu/rurallife; 4560 Essen Lane; adult/child $10/8; ⊘ 8am-5pm; P ♿) This outdoor museum promises a trip into the architecture, occupations and folkways of rural Louisiana. Numerous rough-hewn buildings are scattered over the bucolic campus, and exhibits are refreshingly honest and informative, lacking any rose-colored romanticization of the hard country legacy that built Louisiana.

🛏 Sleeping & Eating

Stockade Bed & Breakfast   B&B $$
(☑ 225-769-7358; www.thestockade.com; 8860 Highland Rd; r $150-160, ste $215; P 🛜) This inviting B&B has five spacious, comfortable and elegant rooms just 3.5 miles southeast of LSU and within earshot of several standout neighborhood restaurants. Book ahead on weekends, especially during football season.

★**Dang's Vietnamese Restaurant**   VIETNAMESE $
(☑ 225-275-2390; 12385 Florida Blvd; mains $8-13; ⊘ 9am-9pm; P ♿) Everything at this Vietnamese institution is great, but have a slurp of the pho and you may whisper a prayer to the kitchen gods for favoring you with a broth so flavorful. Honestly, you can't go wrong ordering off the big menu – from crispy duck to bright, beautiful curries, it's all wonderful.

Louisiana Lagniappe   CAJUN $$$
(☑ 225-767-9991; www.louisianalagniapperestaurant.com; 9900 Perkins Rd; mains $21-36; ⊘ 5:30-9pm Mon-Thu, 5-10pm Fri & Sat; P) If you need a night out in Baton Rouge, and it requires the presence of delicious local cuisine, we'll direct you to Louisiana Lagniappe (lahnyap). The second word means 'a little extra' in Louisiana French, and it's a misnomer, as you get a *lot* here: fish topped with crabmeat, rib-eye steaks and shrimp and sausage pasta.

☆ Entertainment

Varsity Theatre   LIVE MUSIC
(☑ 225-383-7018; www.varsitytheatre.com; 3353 Highland Rd) Located at the gates of LSU, this is one of Baton Rouge's better live music options. When they're not hosting the headliners, the Theatre shows major sporting events.

❶ Information

Visitors Center (☑ 225-383-1825; www.visitbatonrouge.com; 359 3rd St; ⊘ 8am-5pm) The downtown city visitors center has maps, brochures of local attractions and festival schedules.

Capital Park (☑ 225-219-1200; www.louisiana travel.com; 702 River Rd N; ⊙ 8am-4:30pm) Near the Baton Rouge visitors center, this is the extensive official gateway to Louisiana tourism.

❶ Getting There & Around

Baton Rouge lies 80 miles west of New Orleans on I-10. **Baton Rouge Metropolitan Airport** (BTR; ☑ 225-355-0333; www.flybtr.com; 9430 Jackie Cochran Dr), 7 miles north of downtown

Baton Rouge off I-110, is about 1½ hour's drive north from New Orleans, making it a viable airport of entry if you're renting a car. The airport connects with major hubs like Houston, Dallas, Charlotte and Atlanta.

Greyhound (☑ 225-383-3811; www.greyhound.com; 1253 Florida Blvd) has regular buses to New Orleans, Lafayette and Atlanta.

Capitol Area Transit System (www.brcats.com) operates buses around town. Tickets cost $1.75.

FROM THE MEKONG TO THE MISSISSIPPI

Following the Vietnam War, thousands of South Vietnamese fled to the USA, settling in Southern California, Boston, the Washington, DC area and New Orleans. If the last choice seems odd, remember that many of these refugees were Catholic and the New Orleans Catholic community – one of the largest in the country – was helping to direct refugee resettlement. In addition, the subtropical climate, rice fields and flat wetlands must have been geographically reassuring. For a Southeast Asian immigrant far from home, the Mississippi delta may have borne at least a superficial resemblance to the Mekong delta.

Most Vietnamese in Louisiana settled in New Orleans' newer suburbs: New Orleans East, Versailles, Algiers and Gretna (some also moved to rural parishes in south Louisiana). Their work ethic was legendary; their presence revitalized many formerly crumbling neighborhoods; and their story is as American Dream–like as a bald eagle hatching from apple pie. The first generation of Vietnamese worked in laundromats, nail shops, restaurants and shrimp boats; the second became doctors, lawyers and engineers. Following Hurricane Katrina, the New Orleans Vietnamese community gained the reputation as being the first back in the city, quickly rebuilding their homes and businesses.

To see where New Orleans Vietnamese work and play, you need to drive a little way out of the city proper. In New Orleans East, the **Mary Queen of Vietnam Church** (☑ 504-254-5660; www.arch-no.org; 5069 Willowbrook Dr; **P**) is a focal point for the Catholic Vietnamese community; further south, the **Chua Bo De Temple** (☑ 504-733-6634; Hwy 996; ⊙ services 7:30pm Sat & 11am Sun), about 25 minutes outside the city near English Turn golf course, is a major center for Buddhists. The latter is a typically Vietnamese Buddhist structure, filled with Chinese-style bodhisattvas (Buddhist saints), photos and offerings to dead ancestors, and lots of red and gold in the color scheme. You don't have to call ahead before visiting, but it may be polite to do so.

Perhaps the most pleasant way to experience local Vietnamese culture is by eating its delicious food. Most spots are in Gretna. **Tan Dinh** (☑ 504-361-8008; 1705 Lafayette St, Gretna; mains $8-18; ⊙ 9:30am-9pm Mon, Wed-Fri, 9am-9pm Sat, to 8pm Sun, closed Tue; **P** ☑) is one of the best restaurants in greater New Orleans – the garlic-butter chicken wings could be served in heaven's pub, and the Korean short ribs are mouth-watering. It's also a contender for high-quality pho. **Dong Phuong Oriental Bakery** (☑ 504-254-0296; www.dpbanhmi.com; 14207 Chef Menteur Hwy, New Orleans East; bakery items $1.50-6, mains $7-13; ⊙ bakery 8am-5pm Mon, Wed-Sun, restaurant Mon, Wed-Sun 9am-4pm, closed Tue; **P** ☑ ♿) has best *bánh mì* (Vietnamese sandwiches of sliced pork, cucumber, cilantro and other lovelies, locally called a 'Vietnamese po'boy') around and some very fine durian cake.

Try not to miss the local markets either; the **Hong Kong Food Market** (☑ 504-394-7075; 925 Behrman Hwy; ⊙ 7:30am-9pm) is a an international grocery store that serves the immigrant (and immigrant descended) communities of the New Orleans West Bank. The closest you'll come to witnessing Saigon on a Saturday morning (lots of local Vietnamese, being southern refugees, still call it 'Saigon') is the **Vietnamese Farmers Market** (14401 Alcee Fortier Blvd; ⊙ 6am-9am Sat), also known as the 'squat market' thanks to the women in *non la* (conical straw hats) squatting over their fresh, wonderful-smelling produce. The market has shrunk over the years, so it's not quite the scene it was in years past, but the women are still out there selling their wares.

St Francisville

Lush St Francisville is the quintessential Southern artsy small town, a blend of historical homes, bohemian shops and outdoor activities courtesy of the nearby Tunica Hills (you read that right – hills in Louisiana). During the antebellum decade this was home to plantation millionaires, and much of the architecture these aristocrats built is still intact, forming a historic core that has magnetized tourists for over a century.

◉ Sights & Activities

Myrtles Plantation   HISTORIC BUILDING
(☑225-635-6277; www.myrtlesplantation.com; 7747 US Hwy 61 N; tours adult/child $15/12, night tours $15; ☺9am-5pm, tours 6pm, 7pm & 8pm Fri & Sat; ℗) Owners and docents alike perpetuate the idea that Myrtles is one of the most haunted houses in America. And hey, this place is certifiably creepy. Tours do not seem to be quite as architecturally and historically informative as other plantation tours in the region, but they do paint a vivid picture of life during the plantation era. Mystery tours (Friday and Saturday evenings) are geared toward ghost stories, while daytime tours focus on details about the house and its furnishings.

Oakley Plantation &
Audubon State Historic Site   HISTORIC SITE
(☑225-635-3739; www.audubonstatehistoricsite. wordpress.com; 11788 Hwy 965; adult/student/senior $8/4/6; ☺9am-5pm Wed-Sun; ℗) ✐ Outside of St Francisville, Oakley Plantation & Audubon State Historic Site is where John James Audubon spent his tenure, arriving in 1821 to tutor the owner's daughter. Though his assignment lasted only four months (and his room was pretty spartan), he and his assistant finished 32 paintings of birds found in the plantation's surrounding forest. The small West Indies–influenced house (1806) includes several original Audubon prints.

Mary Ann Brown Preserve   NATURE RESERVE
(☑225-338-1040; www.nature.org; 13515 Hwy 965; ☺sunrise-sunset; ℗) ✐ FREE Operated by the Nature Conservancy, the 110-acre Mary Ann Brown Preserve takes in some of the beech woodlands, dark wetlands and low, clay-soil hill country of the Tunica uplands. A 2-mile series of trails and boardwalks crosses the woods – the same trees that John James Audubon tramped around when he began work on *Birds of America*.

🛏 Sleeping & Eating

Shadetree Inn   B&B $$
(☑225-635-6116; www.shadetreeinn.com; cnr Royal & Ferdinand Sts; r from $145; ℗⏰) Sidled up against the historic district and a bird sanctuary, this super-cozy B&B has a gorgeous flower-strewn, hammock-hung courtyard and spacious but rustic upscale rooms. A deluxe continental breakfast can be served in your room and is included along with a bottle of wine or champagne. Rates plunge if you cut out breakfast and stay midweek.

3-V Tourist Court   INN $$
(☑225-721-7003; www.themagnoliacafe.net/magnolia3vtouristcourts.html; 5687 Commerce St; 1-/2-bed cabin $75/125; ℗⏰) One of the oldest motor inns in the USA (started in the 1930s and now on the National Register of Historic Places), the five units here take you back to simpler times. Rooms have period decorations and fixtures, though a recent renovation upgraded the beds, hardwood floors and flat-screen TVs into trendy territory.

Birdman Coffee & Books   CAFE $
(☑225-635-3665; 5695 Commerce St; mains $5-8; ☺7am-5pm Tue-Fri, 8am-2pm Sat, 8am-noon Sun; ⏰) Birdman is *the* spot for strong coffee, acoustic live music, a delicious local breakfast (old-fashioned yellow grits, sweet-potato pancakes, salty bacon) and local art.

Magnolia Café   CAFE $
(☑225-635-6528; www.themagnoliacafe.net; 5687 Commerce St; mains $8-16; ☺10am-4pm Mon-Thu, to 10pm Thu, Fri & Sat; ℗) The Magnolia Café was once a health-food store and VW bus repair shop. Today it's the nucleus of what's happening in St Francisville – it's where people go to eat, socialize and, on Friday night, dance to live music.

❶ Getting There & Away

St Francisville lies about 35 miles north of Baton Rouge on Hwy 61, which winds right through town.

Cajun Country

When people think of Louisiana, this – and New Orleans – is the image that comes to mind: miles of bayou, sawdust-strewn shacks, a unique take on French and lots of good food. Welcome to Cajun Country, also called Acadiana for the French settlers exiled from L'Acadie (now Nova Scotia, Canada) by the British in 1755. Cajuns are the largest French-speaking minority in the USA, and while you may not hear French spoken at the grocery store, it is still present in radio shows, church services and the sing-song lilt of local English accents.

It is largely a socially conservative region, but the Cajuns also have a well-deserved reputation for hedonism. It's hard to find a bad meal here; jambalaya (a rice-based dish with tomatoes, sausage and shrimp) and crawfish étouffée are prepared slowly with pride, and if folks aren't fishing, they are probably dancing. Don't expect to sit on the sidelines...*allons danson* (let's dance).

LAFAYETTE

The term 'undiscovered gem' gets thrown around too much in travel writing, but Lafayette really fits the bill. On Sunday this town is quiet, but for the rest of the week there's an entirely fantastic amount of good eating to be done and lots of music venues.

◎ Sights

Vermilionville   MUSEUM
(☑ 337-233-4077; www.bayouvermiliondistrict.org/vermilionville; 300 Fisher Rd; adult/student $10/6, boat tour $12/8; ◷ 10am-4pm Tue-Sun; ℙ 🚗) This tranquil, re-created 19th-century Cajun village wends along the bayou near the airport. Friendly, enthusiastic costumed docents explain Cajun, Creole and Native American history, and local bands perform on Sunday (1pm to 3pm). Guided boat tours of Bayou Vermilion are also offered at 10:30am Tuesday to Saturday in spring and fall.

Acadian Village   MUSEUM
(☑ 337-981-2364; www.acadianvillage.org; 200 Greenleaf Dr; adult/student $8/6; ◷ 10am-4pm Mon-Sat; ℙ 🚗) At the understated, educational Acadian Village, you follow a brick path around a rippling bayou to restored houses, craftsman barns and a church. Old-timers sometimes still hang out here, regaling visitors with Cajun songs and stories from days gone by.

Acadian Cultural Center   MUSEUM
(☑ 337-232-0789; www.nps.gov/jela; 501 Fisher Rd; ◷ 9am-4:30pm Tue-Fri, 8:30am-noon Sat; ℙ 🚗) 🖋 This National Parks Service museum has extensive exhibits on Cajun culture and is a good entry point for those looking to peer deeper into Acadian folkways.

🎇 Festivals & Events

★ **Festival International de Louisiane**   MUSIC
(www.festivalinternational.org; ◷ Apr) `FREE` At the fabulous Festival International de Lou-

isiane, hundreds of local and international artists rock out for five days over the last weekend in April in the largest free music festival of its caliber in the USA. Although 'Festival' avowedly celebrates Francophone music and culture, the event's remit has grown to accommodate world music in all its iterations and languages.

🛏 Sleeping & Eating

★ **Blue Moon Guest House**   GUESTHOUSE $
(☑ 337-234-2422; www.bluemoonpresents.com; 215 E Convent St; dm $18, r $70-90; ℙ ✳ @ 🛜) This tidy home is one of Louisiana's travel gems: an upscale hostel-like hangout just walking distance from downtown. Snag a bed and you're on the guest list for Lafayette's most popular down-home music venue, located in the backyard. The friendly owners, full kitchen and camaraderie among guests create a unique music-meets-migration environment catering to backpackers, flashpackers and those in transition (flashbackpackers?).

Buchanan Lofts   APARTMENT $$
(☑ 337-534-4922; www.buchananlofts.com; 403 S Buchanan; r per night/week from $180/1000; ℙ ✳ @ 🛜) These uber-hip lofts could be in New York City if they weren't so big. Doused in contemporary-cool art and design – all fruits of the friendly owner's globetrotting – the extra spacious units come with kitchenettes and are awash with exposed brick and hardwoods.

★ **French Press**   BREAKFAST $
(☑ 337-233-9449; www.thefrenchpresslafayette.com; 214 E Vermillion; mains $9-15; ◷ 7am-2pm Mon-Fri, 9am-2pm Sat & Sun; 🛜) This French-Cajun hybrid is one of the best culinary things going in Lafayette. Breakfast is mind-blowing, with a sinful Cajun Benedict (boudin instead of ham), cheddar grits (that will kill you dead) and organic granola (to offset the grits). Lunch ain't half bad either; the fried shrimp melt, doused in Sriracha mayo, is gorgeously decadent.

Johnson's Boucanière   CAJUN $
(☑ 337-269-8878; www.johnsonsboucaniere.com; 1111 St John St; mains $4.25-8; ◷ 7am-3pm Tue-Fri, to 5:30pm Sat) This resurrected, 70-year-old family prairie smoker business turns out detour-worthy boudin (Cajun-style pork and rice sausage) and an unstoppable smoked pork-brisket sandwich topped with smoked sausage.

Dwyer's DINER **$**
(☑337-235-9364; 323 Jefferson St; mains $6-14; ⊙6am-2pm; ⚑) This family-owned joint serves Cajun diner fare, finally bringing gumbo for lunch and pancakes for breakfast into one glorious culinary marriage. It's especially fun on Wednesday mornings when a French-speaking table is set up and local Cajuns shoot the breeze in their old-school dialect. Rotating lunch mains include smothered pork chops, fried chicken and shrimp stew.

☆ Entertainment

Blue Moon Saloon LIVE MUSIC
(☑337-234-2422; www.bluemoonpresents.com; 215 E Convent St; cover $5-8; ⊙5pm-2am Tue-Sun) This intimate venue on the back porch of the accompanying guesthouse is what Louisiana is all about: good music, good people and good beer. What's not to love? Music tends to go off Wednesday to Saturday.

Artmosphere LIVE MUSIC
(☑337-233-3331; www.artmosphere.vpweb.com; 902 Johnston St; ⊙4pm-2am Mon-Thu, 11am-2am Fri & Sat, 11am-midnight Sun) Graffiti, hookahs, hipsters and an edgy line-up of acts – it's more CBGBs then Cajun dance hall, but it's a lot of fun, and there's good Mexican food.

❶ Information

The **Visitors Center** (☑337-232-3737; www.lafayettetravel.com; 1400 NW Evangeline Thruway; ⊙8:30am-5pm Mon-Fri, 9am-5pm Sat & Sun) has information on travel, lodging and events in Lafayette and greater Acadiana (Cajun Country). French-speaking staff on hand.

❶ Getting There & Away

From I-10, exit 103A, the Evangeline Thruway (Hwy 167) goes to the center of town. **Greyhound** (☑337-235-1541; www.greyhound.com; 100 Lee Ave) operates from a hub beside the central commercial district, making several runs daily to New Orleans (3½ hours) and Baton Rouge (one hour). **Amtrak's** (www.amtrak.com; 100 Lee Ave) *Sunset Limited*, which runs between New Orleans and Los Angeles, stops in Lafayette.

CAJUN WETLANDS

In 1755, the Grand Dérangement, the British expulsion of rural French settlers from Acadiana (now Nova Scotia, Canada), created a homeless population of Acadians who searched for decades for a place to settle. Some went to other British colonies, where the Catholic exiles were often rejected on religious grounds. Some returned to France, where they were denied the rights to land ownership and autonomy they had obtained in the New World.

In 1785 seven boatloads of Acadian exiles arrived in New Orleans, seeking a better life in a corner of the Western Hemisphere that was still culturally, if not politically, French (at the time Louisiana was ruled by the Spanish). By the early 19th century, 3000 to 4000 Acadians occupied the swamplands southwest of New Orleans. Native American tribes such as the Attakapas helped them learn to eke out a living based on fishing and trapping, and those practices are still near and dear to the hearts of many of the descendants of the Acadians, now known as the Cajuns.

For decades this was one of the poorest parts of Louisiana, an area where French language education was repressed and infrastructure was dire. This situation largely changed thanks to an increase in Cajun political influence within Louisiana state government in the 1970s, and the presence of the oil and gas industry. While canal and pipeline dredging has been deemed a culprit in the continuing saga of Louisiana land loss, the jobs and economic revitalization that came with oil industry jobs is undeniable. This goes some way toward explaining the popularity of the oil and gas sectors in the state, culminating in events like Morgan City's annual Shrimp & Petroleum Festival.

⊙ Sights

Lake Martin BIRD SANCTUARY
(Lake Martin Rd) `FREE` This lake – a mossy green dollop surrounded by thin trees and cypress trunks – serves as a wonderful, easily accessible introduction to bayou landscapes. A few walking paths, as well as a boardwalk, take visitors over the mirror-reflection sheen of the swamp, while overhead thousands of great and cattle egrets and blue herons perch in haughty indifference.

Louisiana Universities Marine Consortium MUSEUM
(LUMCON; ☑985-851-2800; www.lumcon.edu; 8124 Hwy 56, Chauvin; ⊙8am-4pm; ⚑) ♿ `FREE` LUMCON? Sounds like something out of a science fiction novel, right? Well, there is science here, but it's all fact, and still fascinating. LUMCON is one of the premier research facilities dedicated to the Gulf of Mexico. There are nature trails running

THE TAO OF FRED'S

Deep in the heart of Cajun Country, Mamou is a typical South Louisiana small town six days of the week, worth a peek and a short stop before rolling on to Eunice. But on Saturday morning, Mamou's hometown hangout, little **Fred's Lounge** (420 6th St, Mamou; ⊗8:30am-2pm Sat) becomes the apotheosis of a Cajun dance hall.

OK, to be fair, Fred's is more of a dance shack than hall. Whatever it is, this small bar gets more than a little crowded from 8:30am to 2pm-ish, when the staff host a Francophone-friendly music morning, with bands, beer and dancing.

through hairy tufts of grassy marsh, nine small aquariums and an observation tower that gives visitors an unbeatable view of the great swaths of flat, fuzzy wetlands that makes up the south Louisiana coast.

Cypremont Point State Park STATE PARK
(☑888-867-4510, 337-867-4510; 306 Beach Lane, Cypremort Point; adult/senior & child under 3yr $3/ free; ⊗7am-9pm, to 10pm Fri & Sat; P⚓☼) You can't get more end of the road than Cypremont Point, a lonely, windswept promontory of land buffeted by wind, seagull calls and foam spray off the Gulf of Mexico.

ⓘ Getting There & Away

Greyhound buses stop in Lafayette. Otherwise, the region is easily accessed via I-10, which cuts across Louisiana like a belt.

CAJUN PRAIRIE

Dancing cowboys? Works for us. Cajun and African American settlers in the higher, drier terrain north of Lafayette developed a culture based around animal husbandry and farming, and the 10-gallon hat still rules. In many ways, this region is a blend of both South Louisiana and East Texas.

Physically this truly is prairie: wide expanses of green flatlands, broken up by rice and crawfish ponds. This is the heartland of zydeco music; come evening, keep your ears peeled for the accordion, fiddle and distinctive 'zzzzzzzip' sound of the *frottoir*, a corrugated metal vest that is played as its own percussion instrument.

⊙ Sights

Chicot State Park STATE PARK
(☑337-363-2403,888-677-2442; www.crt.louisiana. gov/louisiana-state-parks/parks/chicot-state-park; 3469 Chicot Park Rd, Ville Platte; $3; ⊗6am-9pm Sun-Thu, to 10pm Fri & Sat; P⚓☼) A wonderful place to access the natural beauty of Cajun Country. The excellent interpretive center is fun for kids and informative for adults, and deserves enormous accolades for its open, airy design.

Prairie Acadian Cultural Center MUSEUM
(☑337-457-8499; www.nps.gov/jela; 250 West Park Ave, Eunice; ⊗9:30am-4:30pm Wed-Fri, to 6pm Sat) FREE This NPS-run museum has exhibits on rural life and Cajun culture and shows a variety of documentaries explaining the history of the area. It's the perfect place to begin your exploration of the Cajun Prairie. Music and food demonstrations start at 2:45pm on Saturday.

Cajun Music Hall of Fame & Museum MUSEUM
(☑337-457-6534; www.cajunfrenchmusic.org; 230 S CC Duson Dr, Eunice; ⊗9am-5pm) FREE This small collection of instruments and cultural ephemera caters to the die-hard music buff. Try to engage whoever is working in some tales of Cajun living and music.

⌂ Sleeping & Eating

★**Le Village** B&B $$
(☑337-457-3573; www.levillagehouse.com; 121 Seale Lane, Eunice; r $125-185; P☎) This cute spot is a typically pretty rural B&B, but where many places opt for wedding cake frilly decor, Le Village is stocked with a tasteful collection of rustic, often Cajun-derived folk art.

Billy & Ray's Boudin CAJUN $
(☑337-942-9150; 904 Short Vine St, Opelousas; boudin per lb $4.80; ⊗9am-6pm Mon-Fri) Folks will literally drive for hours, sometimes crossing state lines, to grab some of Billy and Ray's goods, and to be clear, these are two distinct sausages: Billy's is for spice heads, while Ray's is milder. Most folks treat this as a take-out counter, but there's a seating area and some coolers..

ⓘ Getting There & Away

Lafayette makes a good base for exploring the Cajun Prairie. There's a **Greyhound station** (☑337-942-2702; www.greyhound.com; 1312 Creswell Lane) in Opelousas that has buses to

Lafayette ($9, twice daily), Baton Rouge ($9, twice daily) and New Orleans ($27, three daily). The heart of the Cajun Prairie can best be accessed via I-49 or LA-13.

Northern Louisiana

Make no mistake, the rural, oil-industry towns along the Baptist Bible Belt make Northern Louisiana as far removed from New Orleans as Paris, Texas, is from Paris, France. There's a lot of optimistic tourism development happening out this way, but at the end of the day, most folks come here from states like Texas and Arkansas to gamble. The landscape here is pretty reminiscent of East Texas – rolling green countryside and pine woods as far as the eye can see. The culture isn't too far off from Texas either – the TV show *Duck Dynasty,* which has a firm finger on the pulse of red state America, was filmed out here. There's a high value placed on the church and firearms, more or less in that order.

Shreveport

Captain Henry Shreve cleared a 165-mile logjam on the Red River and founded the river-port town of Shreveport – now the third-largest city in the state – in 1839. The city boomed with oil discoveries in the early 1900s, but declined after WWII. Some revitalization came in the form of huge Vegas-sized casinos and a riverfront entertainment complex. Today the casinos still form the main tourism draw in Shreveport, which has an odd identity – it's a large city in one of the most socially conservative parts of the country that attracts visitors looking to engage in a little sin (ie gambling).

◉ Sights

★ **RW Norton Art Gallery**   MUSEUM
(☑318-865-4201; www.rwnaf.org; 4747 Creswell Ave; ⊙museum 10am-5pm Tue-Fri, 1-5pm Sat & Sun, gardens 7am-7pm; Ⓟ) **FREE** Set amid 40 acres of lovingly manicured gardens, the Norton is a wonderful museum, especially for a mid-sized city like Shreveport. It's

airy, spacious and full of fascinating works spanning some four millennia of history, including an impressive collection of work by American painters Frederic Remington and Charles M Russell, who famously captured life in the frontier West. It's also home to 15,000 rare books.

Gardens of the American Rose Center   GARDENS
(☑318-938-5402; www.rose.org; 8877 Jefferson Paige Rd; adult/child $5/2, tours $10; ⊙9am-5pm Mon-Sat, 1-5pm Sun; Ⓟ) If you're a rose-lover, it would be a shame to miss these gardens, which contain more than 65 individual areas designed to show how roses can be grown in a home garden. Stroll the gorgeous grounds for the fecund, sweet smell alone.

🛏 Sleeping & Eating

2439 Fairfield Bed & Breakfast   B&B $$
(☑318-424-2424; www.bedandbreakfastshreveport.com; 2439 Fairfield Ave; r $145-225; Ⓟ🛜) This warm, old-school B&B may be heavy on the lace and chintz, but they're also generous with the Southern hospitality and the breakfasts are delicious.

Strawn's Eat Shop   DINER $
(☑318-868-0634; www.strawnseatshop.com; 125 E Kings Hwy; mains $10; ⊙6am-8pm; 🐕) This basic diner serves good, hearty Americana fare with a lot of Southern charm but it's most notable for its ice box pies.

ℹ Information

The **Visitors Center** (☑318-222-9391; www.shreveport-bossier.org/about-us/visitor-centers; 629 Spring St; ⊙8am-5pm Mon-Fri) provides local information.

ℹ Getting There & Away

Shreveport is located at the intersection of I-49 and I-20; it is far closer to Dallas (190 miles) than New Orleans (330 miles). The city is served by a **regional airport** (☑318-673-5370; www.flyshreveport.com; 5103 Hollywood Ave), which is located about 7 miles southwest of downtown, and a **Greyhound station** (☑318-221-4200; www.greyhound.com; 408 Fannin St).

Florida

Includes ➜

Best Places to Eat

➜ Ulele (p497)

➜ Rok:Brgr (p473)

➜ Kyu (p468)

➜ Cress (p509)

➜ Table 26 Degrees (p476)

Best Places to Sleep

➜ 1 Hotel (p465)

➜ Hotel Palms (p493)

➜ Biltmore Hotel (p467)

➜ W Fort Lauderdale (p472)

➜ Everglades International Hostel (p479)

Why Go?

For countless visitors Florida is a place of promises: of eternal youth, sun, relaxation, clear skies, space, success, escape, prosperity and, for the kids, a chance to meet much-loved Disney characters in person.

No other state in America is as built on tourism, and tourism here comes in a thousand facets: cartoon mice, *MiamiVice*, country fried oysters, Spanish villas, gators kicking footballs, gators prowling golf courses, and of course, the beach. So. Much. Beach.

Don't think Florida is all marketing, though. This is one of the most genuinely fascinating states in the country. It's as if someone shook the nation and tipped it over, filling this sun-bleached peninsula with immigrants, country boys, Jews, Cubans, military bases, shopping malls and a subtropical wilderness laced with crystal ponds and sugary sand.

When to Go
Miami

Feb–Apr Winter ends and high season begins, coinciding with spring break.

Jun–Aug The hot, humid wet months are peak season for northern Florida beaches and theme parks.

Sep–Oct The ideal shoulder season with fewer crowds, cooler temperatures and warm waters.

SOUTH FLORIDA

Once you head far enough south in Florida, you're no longer in 'the South' as a regional entity – you've slipped those bonds into South Florida, which is truly a hybrid of the USA, the Caribbean and Latin America. Miami is the area's beating urban heart and one of the few truly international cities in the country. Wealthy oceanfront communities stretch from the Palm Beaches to Fort Lauderdale, while inland, the dreamscape of the Everglades, the state's unique, dynamic wilderness, await. And when the state's peninsula ends, it doesn't truly end, but rather stretches into the Overseas Hwy which leads across hundreds of mangrove islands to colorful Key West.

Miami

Even if there was no beach, Miami would still have undeniable allure. The gorgeous 1930s hotels lining Ocean Dr are part of the world's greatest collection of art-deco buildings. Tropical motifs, whimsical nautical elements and those iconic pastel shades create a cinematic backdrop for exploring the streets of Miami Beach. Of course, you don't have to see these architectural beauties at arm's length. Lavishly restored, Miami's art-deco and mid-century modern hotels are also the playground for locals and out-of-towners alike, with sunny poolside terraces, artfully designed dining rooms and plush nightclubs.

Chalk it up to Miami's diverse population, or perhaps its love of always being on the cutting-edge. Whatever the reason, creativity is one of the great hallmarks of this city. From art and design to global cuisine, Miami remains ever on the search for bold new ideas, which manifest themselves in surprising ways. You'll find brilliantly inventive chefs blending Eastern and Western cooking styles, sustainably designed buildings inspired by South Florida ecosystems and open-air galleries where museum-quality artwork covers once derelict warehouses. The one constant in Miami is its uncanny ability to astonish.

History

It's always been the weather that's attracted Miami's two most prominent species: developers and tourists. But it wasn't the sun per se that got people moving here – it was an ice storm. The great Florida freeze of 1895 wiped out the state's citrus industry; at the same time, widowed Julia Tuttle bought out parcels of land that would become modern Miami, and Henry Flagler was building his Florida East Coast Railroad. Tuttle offered to split her land with Flagler if he extended the railway to Miami, but the train man didn't pay her any heed until north Florida froze over and Tuttle sent him an 'I told you so' message: an orange blossom clipped from her Miami garden.

The rest is a history of boom, bust, dreamers and opportunists. Generally, Miami has grown in leaps and bounds following major world events and natural disasters. Hurricanes (particularly the deadly Great Miami Hurricane of 1926) have wiped away the town, but it just keeps bouncing and building back better than before. In the late 19th and early 20th centuries, Miami earned a reputation for attracting design and city-planning mavericks such as George Merrick, who fashioned the artful Mediterranean village of Coral Gables, and James Deering, designer of the fairy-tale Vizcaya mansion.

⊙ Sights

Miami's major sights aren't concentrated in one neighborhood. The most frequently visited area is South Beach, home to hot nightlife, beautiful beaches and art-deco hotels, but you'll find historic sites and museums in the Downtown area, art galleries in Wynwood and the Design District, old-fashioned

FLORIDA MIAMI

BEST FLORIDA BEACHES

Florida's best beach? Why not ask us to choose a favorite child? It's impossible! Each beach has its own personality, its own wondrous qualities. Here are a few of our favorites:

Siesta Key (p499)

South Beach (p456)

Bahia Honda (p485)

Captiva Beach (p500)

St George Island (☑850-927-2111; www.floridastateparks.org/stgeorgeisland; 1900 E Gulf Beach Drive; vehicle $6; ☺8am-dusk; P 🚻) 🌊

For a list based on 'science,' consult Dr Beach (www.drbeach.org).

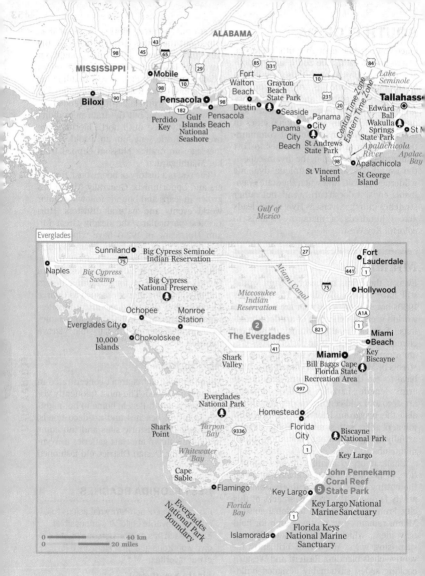

Florida Highlights

1 Mallory Square (p485) Joining the sunset bacchanal in Key West.

2 Everglades National Park (p477) Paddling among alligators in The Everglades.

3 Walt Disney World® Resort (p505) Being swept up in nostalgia and thrill rides, in Orlando.

4 Wynwood Walls (p461) Marvelling at mural after mural, in Miami.

5 John Pennekamp Coral Reef State Park (p482)

GEORGIA

95
1 301
441
75
Fort Clinch
State Park
Fernandina
Beach 8 Amelia Island
Talbot Islands State Parks
Jacksonville Beaches
Jacksonville
Ichetucknee
Springs
State Park
10
295
27
100

ATLANTIC
OCEAN

St Augustine

98
Gainesville
75
Steinhatchee
301
95
27 De Leon
Springs
State Parks
Silver
98 121 Springs 27
19 Ocala 27
40 Ocala **Daytona Beach**
National New Smyrna Beach
Crystal River Forest **Deland** Canaveral National Seashore
Homosassa Blue Spring 1
Springs State Park Merrit Island National Wildlife Refuge
19 98 75 50 **Orlando** Titusville
Kennedy Space Center
528 Cape Canaveral
neymoon & **Walt Disney 3** Cocoa Cocoa Beach
desi Islands **World Resort**
State Park 4
learwater Winter Melbourne
Tampa Haven Pelican Island
ete Beach 7 **St Petersburg** 60 National Wildlife Refuge
ort DeSoto Tampa 95 Sebastian Inlet
Park Bay Vero Beach
17 98
Sarasota 27 **Fort Pierce**
Siesta Key 6 Myakka River 1
State Park 70
75 27 710
Punta Gorda Lake **Hobe Sound**
Fort Okeechobee
Myers 80 441
82 80 98 **West Palm Beach**
Captiva 29 Palm Beach
Island 41 27 Coral **Boca Raton**
Sanibel Island Fort Springs Lauderdale-by-the-Sea
Myers **Alligator Alley** **Fort Lauderdale**
Beach Naples Big Cypress **Hollywood**
National Preserve
Everglades City 41 **Miami Beach**
Chokoloskee 997 **Miami** 4
Everglades
National Park **Biscayne National Park**
Florida
Flamingo City
Florida Bay Key Largo
Dry Tortugas 1
National Park See Enlargement **Islamorada**
Bahia Honda
State Park **Grassy Key**
Key West 1 Marathon
Big Pine Florida Keys
Key Straits of Florida

0 ——— 100 km
0 ——— 50 miles

Snorkelling continental USA's
most extensive coral reef.

6 Siesta Key (p499)
Relaxing on these sugar sand
beaches, in Sarasota.

**7 Salvador Dalí
Museum** (p498) Pondering
the symbolism of the
Hallucinogenic Toreador, in
St Petersburg.

8 Amelia Island (p494)
Taking a breather among the
greenery of this historic island
near the Georgia border.

hotels and eateries in Mid-Beach (in Miami Beach), more beaches on Key Biscayne, and peaceful neighborhood attractions in Coral Gables and Coconut Grove.

Water and income – canals, bays and bank accounts – are the geographic and social boundaries that divide Miami. Of course, the great water that divides here is Biscayne Bay, holding the city of Miami apart from its preening sibling Miami Beach (along with the fine feathers of South Beach). Don't forget, as many do, that Miami Beach is not Miami's beach, but its own distinct town.

South Beach

The most iconic neighborhood in Greater Miami, South Beach (SoBe) is a vertiginous landscape of sparkling beach, beautiful art-deco architecture, high-end boutiques and buzzing bars and restaurants. South Beach has its glamour, but there's more to this district than just velvet ropes and high-priced lodging. You'll find some down-to-earth bars, good ethnic eating and excellent museums.

South Beach BEACH
(Map p460; Ocean Dr; ⊙ 5am-midnight) When most people think of Miami Beach, they're envisioning South Beach, or 'SoBe.' The beach itself encompasses a lovely stretch of golden sand, dotted with colorful deco-style lifeguard stations. The shore gathers a wide mix of humanity, including suntanned locals and plenty of pale tourists, and gets crowded in high season (December to March) and on weekends when the weather is warm.

You can escape the masses by avoiding the densest parts of the beach (5th to 15th Sts). Keep in mind that there's no alcohol (or pets) allowed on the beach.

Art Deco Historic District AREA
(Map p460; Ocean Dr) The world-famous art-deco district of Miami Beach is pure exuberance: an architecture of bold lines, whimsical tropical motifs and a color palette that evokes all the beauty of the Miami landscape. Among the 800 deco buildings listed on the National Register of Historic Buildings, each design is different, and it's hard not to be captivated when strolling among these restored beauties from a bygone era.

★ Wolfsonian-FIU MUSEUM
(Map p460; ☑ 305-531-1001; www.wolfsonian.org; 1001 Washington Ave; adult/child $10/5, 6-9pm Fri free; ⊙ 10am-6pm Mon, Tue, Thu & Sat, to 9pm Fri, noon-6pm Sun, closed Wed) Visit this excellent design museum early in your stay to put the aesthetics of Miami Beach into context. It's one thing to see how wealth, leisure and the pursuit of beauty manifest in Miami Beach, but it's another to understand the roots and shadings of local artistic movements. By chronicling the interior evolution of everyday life, the Wolfsonian reveals how these trends manifested architecturally in SoBe's exterior deco.

Art Deco Museum MUSEUM
(Map p460; www.mdpl.org/welcome-center/art-deco-museum; 1001 Ocean Dr; $5; ⊙ 10am-5pm Tue-Sun, to 7pm Thu) This small museum is one of the best places in town for an enlightening

---

MIAMI IN ...

Two Days
Focus your first day on South Beach. Bookend an afternoon of sunning and swimming with a walking tour through the Art Deco Historic District and a visit to Wolfsonian-FIU, which explains it all. When the sun fades, head to Yardbird (p467) where southern comfort cooking gets a Miami foodie makeover. Next morning, shop for Cuban music along Calle Ocho in Little Havana (p461), followed by classic Cuban cuisine at Exquisito Restaurant (p468). Go for a stroll at Vizcaya Museum & Gardens (p463), then enjoy the tropical ambience and exceptional food at 27 Restaurant (p467) before sipping cocktails at Broken Shaker (p468).

Four Days
Follow the two-day itinerary, then head to the Everglades (p477) on day three and jump in a kayak. For your last day, immerse yourself in art and design in Wynwood and the Design District (p461), followed by a visit to the Pérez Art Museum Miami (p459) or Museum of Contemporary Art (p463). World-class cocktails adn upscale comfort food wrap up the adventure at Sweet Liberty (p469), a top local hangout.

HURRICANE IRMA

On September 10, 2017, one of the largest hurricanes ever recorded barrelled over the state of Florida, leaving flooding and destruction in its wake. Hurricane Irma made landfall in the Florida Keys as a category 4 storm the width of Texas, with wind speeds in excess of 130mph. Nearly seven million people across the state evacuated, there were widespread power outages and storm surges were seen as far north as Jacksonville. But the Florida Keys and the Everglades bore the brunt of the storm. Homes and businesses in the tiny town of Everglades City were left battered and mud-soaked after an 8ft storm surge receded. Meanwhile, in the Keys, a FEMA (Federal Emergency Management Agency) survey reported that 25% of buildings had been destroyed, with another 65% damaged.

In a state so heavily reliant on tourism, most cities were already announcing intentions to be ready for visitors soon. Still, those planning travel to Florida, especially the Florida Keys (www.fla-keys.com) or the Everglades region (www.nps.gov/ever), should check official websites for the latest information.

overview of the art-deco district. Through videos, photography, models and other displays, you'll learn about the pioneering work of Barbara Capitman, who helped save these buildings from certain destruction back in the 1970s, and her collaboration with Leonard Horowitz, the talented artist who designed the pastel color palette that become an integral part of the design visible today.

New World Center NOTABLE BUILDING
(Map p460; ☑305-673-3330, tours 305-673-3331; www.newworldcenter.com; 500 17th St; tours $5; ☺tours 4pm Tue & Thu, 1pm Fri & Sat) Designed by Frank Gehry, this performance hall rises majestically out of a manicured lawn just above Lincoln Rd. Not unlike the ethereal power of the music within, the glass-and-steel facade encases characteristically Gehry-esque sail-like shapes within that help shape the magnificent acoustics and add to the futuristic quality of the concert hall. The grounds form a 2.5-acre public park aptly known as **SoundScape Park** (www.nws.edu).

◉ North Beach

The long strip of beach and condo-studded landscape of North Beach offers a slightly different version of Miami Beach decadence. Instead of art deco, you'll find the so-called MiMo (Miami Modernist) style, of grand buildings constructed in the post-WWII boom days. Although it has a lower population density (and fewer restaurants, bars and shops), there's plenty of allure to North Beach – chief is the beautiful shoreline, which the locals say is covered in whiter sands.

Boardwalk BEACH
(Map p458; www.miamibeachboardwalk.com; 21st St-46th St) What's trendy in beachwear this season? Seventeenth-century Polish gabardine coats, apparently. There are plenty of skimpily dressed hotties on the Mid-Beach boardwalk, but there are also Orthodox Jews going about their business in the midst of joggers, strolling tourists and sunbathers. Nearby are numerous condo buildings occupied by middle-class Latinos and Jews, who walk their dogs and play with their kids here, giving the entire place a laid-back, real-world vibe that contrasts with the non-stop glamour of South Beach.

Eden Roc Renaissance HISTORIC BUILDING
(Map p458; www.nobuedenroc.com; 4525 Collins Ave) The Eden Roc was the second ground-breaking resort from Morris Lapidus, and it's a fine example of the architecture known as MiMo (Miami Modern). It was the hangout for the 1960s Rat Pack – Sammy Davis Jr, Dean Martin, Frank Sinatra and crew. Extensive renovation has eclipsed some of Lapidus' style, but with that said, the building is still an iconic piece of Miami Beach architecture, and an exemplar of the brash beauty of Millionaire's Row.

Fontainebleau HISTORIC BUILDING
(Map p458; www.fontainebleau.com; 4441 Collins Ave) As you proceed north on Collins, the condos and apartment buildings grow in grandeur and embellishment until you enter an area nicknamed Millionaire's Row. The most fantastic jewel in this glittering crown is the **Fontainebleau hotel** (☑305-535-3283; r from $360; P❋🛜🐾🏊). The hotel – mainly

Greater Miami

0 _____ 5 km
0 _____ 2.5 miles

CAROL CITY
Palmetto Expwy
North Miami Greyhound Terminal
NORTH MIAMI
Fort Lauderdale (9mi)
Southern Memorial Park
Oleta River State Park
13
Oleta River State Recreation Area
Bal Harbour
Bay Harbor Islands
OPA-LOCKA
NW 119th St
16
Little River Canal
Indian Creek
HIALEAH
W 4th Ave
924
15
NE 6th Ave
N Miami Ave
Biscayne Blvd
Normandy Dr
A1A
953
Amtrak
E 4th Ave
NW 79th St
934
Pelican Harbor Park
LIBERTY CITY
NW 27th Ave
LITTLE HAITI
23
Miami International Airport
25
27
NW 54th St
DESIGN DISTRICT
NW 36th St
10
Julia Tuttle Cswy
20
12
112
Sheridan Ave
11
Margulies Collection at the Warehouse
NW 20th St
5 9
Wynwood Walls
22
17
Megabus
Main Miami Greyhound Station
Dolphin Expwy
NW 7th St
Flagler St
MIAMI
Pérez Art Museum Miami
7
Venetian Way
14
MacArthur Cswy
MIAMI BEACH
90
SW 8th St (Calle Ocho)
21
History Miami
19
4
18
6
Máximo Gómez Park
8
Hobie Island
See Miami Beach Map (p460)
972
SW 22nd St (Miracle Mile)
Coral Way
826
LITTLE HAVANA
Coconut Grove
Vizcaya Museum & Gardens
Virginia Key
Fisher Island
Biltmore Hotel
2
959
Douglas Road
Dinner Key Marina
913
Northwest Point
874
Biltmore Golf Course
University
Crandon Blvd
Crandon Park Beach
SW 72nd St (Sunset Dr)
South Miami
Key Biscayne
878
KENDALL
Bill Baggs Cape Florida State Park
1
SW 112th St (Killian Dr)
3
Fairchild Tropical Garden
PINECREST
Cape Florida
Dixie Hwy
5
Biscayne Bay
SW 152nd St

ATLANTIC OCEAN

FLORIDA MIAMI

Greater Miami

the pool, which has since been renovated – features in Brian de Palma's classic *Scarface*.

Downtown Miami

Most of the sights in Downtown are on the north side of the river. While you can walk between a few highlights, it's handy to use Metromover, the free trolley, or a Citi Bike when you really need to cover some ground.

★ HistoryMiami   MUSEUM
(Map p458; ☑ 305-375-1492; www.historymiami. org; 101 W Flagler St; adult/child $10/5; ☉10am–5pm Mon-Sat, from noon Sun; ⛟) South Florida – a land of escaped slaves, guerilla Native Americans, gangsters, land grabbers, pirates, tourists, drug dealers and alligators – has a special history, and it takes a special kind of museum to capture that narrative. This highly recommended place, located in the **Miami-Dade Cultural Center**, does just that, weaving together the stories of the region's successive waves of population, from Native Americans to Nicaraguans.

★ Pérez Art Museum Miami   MUSEUM
(PAMM; Map p458; ☑ 305-375-3000; www.pamm. org; 1103 Biscayne Blvd; adult/seniors & students $16/12, 1st Thu & 2nd Sat of month free; ☉10am–6pm Fri-Tue, to 9pm Thu, closed Wed; ⓟ) The Pérez can claim fine rotating exhibits that concentrate on post-WWII international art, but just as impressive are its location and exterior. This art institution inaugurated Museum Park, a patch of land that oversees the broad blue swath of Biscayne Bay. Swiss architects Herzog & de Meuron designed the structure, which integrates tropical foliage, glass and metal – a melding of tropical vitality and fresh modernism that is a nice architectural analogy for Miami itself.

Patricia & Phillip Frost
Museum of Science   MUSEUM
(Map p458; ☑ 305-434-9600; www.frostscience. org; 1101 Biscayne Blvd; adult/child $28/20; ☉9am-6pm; ⓟ⛟) This sprawling new Downtown museum spreads across 250,000 sq ft that includes a three-level aquarium,

Miami Beach

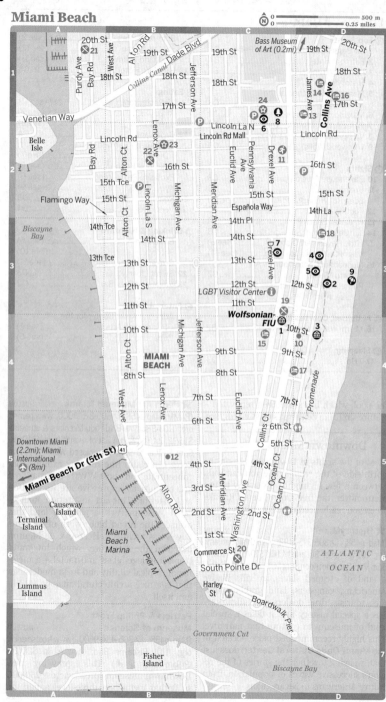

Miami Beach

a 250-seat, state-of-the-art planetarium and two distinct wings that delve into the wonders of science and nature. Exhibitions range from weather phenomena to creepy crawlies, feathered dinosaurs and vital-microbe displays, while Florida's fascinating Everglades and biologically rich coral reefs play starring roles.

The new facility, which cost a staggering $305 million to complete, was built with sustainability in mind. It opened in 2017.

⊙ Little Havana

Little Havana's main thoroughfare, Calle Ocho (SW 8th St), doesn't just cut through the heart of the neighborhood, it *is* the heart of the neighborhood. In a lot of ways, this is every immigrant enclave in the USA – full of restaurants, mom-and-pop convenience shops and phonecard kiosks. Admittedly the Cubaness of Little Havana is slightly exaggerated for visitors, though it's still an atmospheric place to explore, with the crack of dominoes, the scent of wafting cigars, and Latin jazz spilling out of colorful storefronts.

★ Máximo Gómez Park   PARK
(Map p458; cnr SW 8th St & SW 15th Ave; ⊙9am-6pm) Little Havana's most evocative reminder of Old Cuba is Máximo Gómez Park, or 'Domino Park,' where the sound of elderly men trash-talking over games of chess is harmonized with the quick clack-clack of slapping dominoes. The jarring backtrack, plus the heavy smell of cigars and a sunrise-bright mural of the 1994 Summit of the Americas,

combine to make Máximo Gómez one of the most sensory sites in Miami (although it is admittedly one of the most tourist-heavy ones as well).

Little Havana Art District   AREA
(Map p458; Calle Ocho, btwn SW 15th & 17th Aves) OK, it's not Wynwood. In fact, it's more 'Art Block' than district, with only a few galleries and studios still in business. Regardless, it's still worth a browse. This particular stretch of Little Havana is also the epicenter of the **Viernes Culturales** (Cultural Fridays; www.viernesculturales.org; ⊙7-11pm last Fri of month) celebration.

⊙ Wynwood & the Design District

Wynwood and the Design District are two of Miami's most creative neighborhoods, and are justly famed for a burgeoning arts scene. Wynwood is packed with galleries, as well as large-format street art covering once industrial spaces. It's also the place for great nightlife, and an emerging restaurant scene. The smaller Design District also has galleries and a mixed bag of bars and eateries.

★ Wynwood Walls   PUBLIC ART
(Map p458; www.thewynwoodwalls.com; NW 2nd Ave, btwn 25th & 26th Sts) FREE In the midst of rusted warehouses and concrete blah, there's a pastel-and-graffiti explosion of urban art. Wynwood Walls is a collection of murals and paintings laid out over an open courtyard that invariably bowls people over

FLORIDA MIAMI

with its sheer color profile and unexpected location. What's on offer tends to change with the coming and going of major arts events such as Art Basel (p465), but it's always interesting stuff.

★**Margulies Collection at the Warehouse**   GALLERY
(Map p458; ☑ 305-576-1051; www.margulies warehouse.com; 591 NW 27th St; adult/student $10/5; ☺11am-4pm Tue-Sat mid-Oct–Apr) Encompassing 45,000 sq ft, this vast not-for-profit exhibition space houses one of the best collections in Wynwood. Thought-provoking, large-format installations are the focus at the Warehouse, and you'll see works by some leading 21st-century artists here.

Bakehouse Art Complex   GALLERY
(BAC; Map p458; ☑ 305-576-2828; www.bacfl.org; 561 NW 32nd St; ☺noon-5pm; ℗) 🆓 One of the pivotal art destinations in Wynwood, the Bakehouse has been an arts incubator since well before the creation of the Wynwood Walls. Today this former bakery houses galleries and some 60 studios, and the range of works you can find here is quite impressive.

◉ Coral Gables

The lovely city of Coral Gables, filled with Mediterranean-style buildings, feels like a world removed from other parts of Miami. Here you'll find pretty banyan-lined streets, and a walkable village-like center, dotted with shops, cafes and restaurants. The big draws are the striking Biltmore Hotel, a lush tropical garden and one of America's loveliest swimming pools.

★**Fairchild Tropical Garden**   GARDENS
(Map p458; ☑ 305-667-1651; www.fairchildgarden. org; 10901 Old Cutler Rd; adult/child/senior $25/12/18; ☺9:30am-4:30pm; ℗♿) If you need to escape Miami's madness, consider a green day in the country's largest tropical botanical garden. A butterfly grove, tropical plant conservatory and gentle vistas of marsh and keys habitats, plus frequent art installations from artists like Roy Lichtenstein, are all stunning. A free 45-minute tram tours the entire park on the hour from 10am to 3pm (till 4pm weekends).

★**Biltmore Hotel**   HISTORIC BUILDING
(Map p458; ☑ 855-311-6903; www.biltmorehotel.com; 1200 Anastasia Ave; ☺tours 1:30pm & 2:30pm Sun; ℗) In the most opulent neighborhood of one of the showiest cities in the world, the Biltmore peers down its nose and says, 'hrmph.' It's one of the greatest of the grand hotels of the American Jazz Age, and if this joint were a fictional character from a novel, it'd be, without question, Jay Gatsby. Al Capone had a speakeasy on-site, and the Capone Suite is said to be haunted by the spirit of Fats Walsh, who was murdered here.

◉ Coconut Grove

Coconut Grove was once a hippie colony, but these days its demographic is middle-class, mall-going Miamians and college students.

GUIDE TO MIAMI BEACHES

The beaches around Miami are some of the best in the country. The water is clear and warm and the imported white sand is relatively white. They're also informally zoned by tacit understanding into areas with their own unique crowds so that everyone can enjoy at their own speed.

Scantily clad beaches In South Beach between 5th St and 21st St; modesty is in short supply.

Family-fun beaches North of 21st St is where you'll find the more family-friendly beaches, and the beach at 53rd St has a playground and public toilets.

Nude beaches Nude bathing is legal at **Haulover Beach Park** (Map p458; ☑ 305-947-3525; www.miamidade.gov/parks/haulover.asp; 10800 Collins Ave; per car Mon-Fri $5, Sat-Sun $7; ☺sunrise-sunset; ℗) in Sunny Isles. North of the lifeguard tower is predominantly gay; south is straight.

Gay beaches All of South Beach is gay-friendly, but a special concentration seems to hover around 12th St.

Windsurfing beaches Hobie Beach, along the Rickenbacker Causeway on the way to Key Biscayne, is actually known as 'Windsurfing Beach.'

MIAMI FOR CHILDREN

The best beaches for kids are in Miami Beach north of 21st St, especially at 53rd St, which has a playground and public toilets, and the dune-packed beach around 73rd St. Also head south to Matheson Hammock Park, which has calm artificial lagoons.

Miami Children's Museum (Map p458; ☑ 305-373-5437; www.miamichildrensmuseum.org; 980 MacArthur Causeway; $20; ⊙10am-6pm; 🖐) On Watson Island, between Downtown Miami and Miami Beach, this hands-on museum has fun music and art studios, as well as some branded 'work' experiences that make it feel a tad corporate.

Jungle Island (Map p458; ☑ 305-400-7000; www.jungleisland.com; 1111 Parrot Jungle Trail, off MacArthur Causeway; adult/child/senior $40/33/38; ⊙10am-5pm; 🅿 🖐) Jungle Island is packed with tropical birds, alligators, orangutans, chimps and (to the delight of Napoleon Dynamite fans) a liger – a cross between a lion and a tiger.

Zoo Miami (Metrozoo; ☑ 305-251-0400; www.zoomiami.org; 12400 SW 152nd St; adult/child $22/18; ⊙10am-5pm) Miami's tropical weather makes strolling around Zoo Miami almost feel like a day in the wild. For a quick overview (and because the zoo is so big and the sun is broiling), hop on the Safari Monorail; it departs every 20 minutes.

Monkey Jungle (☑ 305-235-1611; www.monkeyjungle.com; 14805 SW 216th St; adult/child/senior $30/24/28; ⊙9:30am-5pm, last entry 4pm; 🅿 🖐) The tagline, 'Where humans are caged and monkeys run free,' tells you all you need to know – except for the fact that it's in far south Miami.

It's a pleasant place to explore with intriguing shops and cafes, and a walkable village-like vibe. It's particularly appealing in the evenings, when residents fill the outdoor tables of its bars and restaurants. Coconut Grove backs onto the waterfront, with a pretty marina and pleasant green spaces.

⭐**Vizcaya Museum & Gardens**   HISTORIC BUILDING
(Map p458; ☑ 305-250-9133; www.vizcayamuseum.org; 3251 S Miami Ave; adult/6-12yr/student & senior $18/6/12; ⊙9:30am-4:30pm Wed-Mon; 🅿) They call Miami the Magic City, and if it is, this Italian villa, the housing equivalent of a Fabergé egg, is its most fairy-tale residence. In 1916 industrialist James Deering started a Miami tradition by making a ton of money and building ridiculously grandiose digs. He employed 1000 people (then 10% of the local population) and stuffed his home with 15th- to 19th-century furniture, tapestries, paintings and decorative arts.

⊙ Key Biscayne

Key Biscayne and neighboring Virginia Key are a quick and easy getaway from Downtown Miami. But once you've passed across those scenic causeways, you'll feel like you've been transported to a far-off tropical realm, with magnificent beaches, lush nature trails in state parks, and aquatic adventures aplenty. The stunning skyline views of Miami alone are worth the trip out.

⭐**Bill Baggs Cape Florida State Park**   STATE PARK
(Map p458; ☑ 305-361-5811; www.floridastateparks.org/capeflorida; 1200 S Crandon Blvd; per car/person $8/2; ⊙8am-sunset, lighthouse 9am-5pm; 🅿 🖐 🎋) 🌊 If you don't make it to the Florida Keys, come to this park for a taste of their unique island ecosystems. The 494-acre space is a tangled clot of tropical fauna and dark mangroves – look for the 'snorkel' roots that provide air for half-submerged mangrove trees – all interconnected by sandy trails and wooden boardwalks, and surrounded by miles of pale ocean.

⊙ Greater Miami

Museum of Contemporary Art North Miami   MUSEUM
(MoCA; Map p458; ☑ 305-893-6211; www.mocanomi.org; 770 NE 125th St; adult/student/child $5/3/free; ⊙11am-5pm Tue-Fri & Sun, 1-9pm Sat; 🅿) The Museum of Contemporary Art has long been a reason to hike up to the far reaches of North Miami. Its galleries feature excellent rotating exhibitions of contemporary art by local, national and international artists.

FLORIDA MIAMI

Gold Coast Railroad Museum   MUSEUM
(☑ 305-253-0063; www.gcrm.org; 12450 SW 152nd St; adult/child 3-11yr $8/6; ◷ 10am-4pm Mon-Fri, from 11am Sat & Sun; ℗) Primarily of interest to train buffs, this museum displays more than 30 antique railway cars, including the Ferdinand Magellan presidential car, where President Harry Truman famously brandished a newspaper with the erroneous headline 'Dewey Defeats Truman.'

🕴 Activities

Miami doesn't lack for ways to keep yourself busy. From sailing the teal waters to hiking through tropical undergrowth, yoga in the parks and (why not?) trapeze artistry above the city's head, the Magic City rewards those who want an active holiday.

Citi Bike   CYCLING
(☑ 305-532-9494; www.citibikemiami.com; 30min/1hr/2hr/4hr/1-day rental $4.50/6.50/10/18/24) This bike-sharing program, modeled after similar initiatives in New York, London and Paris, makes getting on a bike a relative breeze. Just rock up to a solar-powered Citi Bike station (a handy map can be found on the website), insert a credit card and ride away. You can return your bike at any Citi Bike location.

Bike & Roll   CYCLING
(Map p460; ☑ 305-604-0001; www.bikemiami.com; 210 10th St; hire per 2hr/4hr/day from $10/18/24, tours $40; ◷ 9am-7pm) This well-run outfit offers a good selection of bikes, including single-speed cruisers, geared hybrids and speedy road bikes. Staff move things along quickly, so you won't have to waste time waiting to get out and riding. Bike tours are also available (daily at 10am).

Fritz's Skate, Bike & Surf   SKATING
(Map p460; ☑ 305-532-1954; www.fritzsmiamibeach.com; 1620 Washington Ave; bike & skate rental per hour/day/5 days $10/24/69; ◷ 10am-9pm Mon-Sat, to 8pm Sun) Rent your wheels from Fritz's, which offers skateboards, longboards, in-line skates, roller skates, scooters and bicycles (cruisers, mountain bikes, kids bikes).

SoBe Surf   SURFING
(☑ 786-216-7703; www.sobesurf.com; group/private lessons from $70/120) Offers surf lessons both in Miami Beach and in Cocoa Beach, where there tends to be better waves. Instruction on Miami Beach usually happens around South Point. All bookings are done by phone or email.

Miami
Watersports Complex   WATER SPORTS
(MWCC; Map p458; ☑ 305-476-9253; www.aktionparks.com; Amelia Earhart Park, 401 E 65th St, Hialeah; ◷ 11am-6pm Mar-Oct, to dusk Nov-Feb) Offers lessons in cableboarding, where the rider is pulled along by an overhead cable system. That means no boat, less pollution and less noise. A 20-minute-/one-hour lesson costs $25/90, or opt for a $59 package that includes a beginner lesson, rental gear and four-hour cable pass. Call ahead to reserve a spot.

🖝 Tours

History Miami Tours   TOURS
(www.historymiami.org/city-tour; tours $30-60) Historian extraordinaire Dr Paul George leads fascinating walking tours, including culturally rich strolls through Little Haiti, Little Havana, Downtown and Coral Gables at twilight, plus the occasional boat trip to Stiltsville and Key Biscayne.

Miami Food Tours   FOOD & DRINK
(Map p460; ☑ 786-361-0991; www.miamifoodtours.com; 429 Lenox Ave; adult/child South Beach tour $58/35, Wynwood tour $75/55; ◷ tours South Beach 11am & 4:30pm daily, Wynwood 10:30am Mon-Sat) This highly rated tour explores various facets of the city – culture, history, art and of course cuisine – while making stops at restaurants and cafes along the way. It's a walking tour, though distances aren't great, and happens in South Beach and Wynwood.

Miami Design
Preservation League   WALKING
(MDPL; Map p460; ☑ 305-672-2014; www.mdpl.org; 1001 Ocean Dr; guided tours adult/student $25/20; ◷ 10:30am daily & 6:30pm Thu) Tells the stories and history behind the art-deco buildings in South Beach, with a lively guide from the Miami Design Preservation League. Tours last 90 minutes. Also offers tours of Jewish Miami Beach, Gay & Lesbian Miami Beach and a once-monthly tour (first Saturday at 9:30am) of the MiMo district in the North Beach area.

🎊 Festivals & Events

Winter Music Conference   MUSIC
(www.wintermusicconference.com; ◷ Mar) Party promoters, DJs, producers and revelers come from around the globe to hear new electronic-music artists, catch up on technology and party the nights away.

**Miami Spice
Restaurant Month** FOOD & DRINK
(www.facebook.com/ilovemiamispice; ⊙ Aug-Sep)
Top restaurants around Miami offer three-course lunches and dinners to try to lure folks out during the heat wave. Prices hover around $25 for lunch and $40 for dinner. Reservations essential.

White Party MUSIC
(www.whiteparty.org; ⊙ Nov) If you're gay and not here, there's a problem. This weeklong extravaganza draws more than 15,000 gay men and women for nonstop partying at clubs and venues all over town.

Art Basel Miami Beach ART
(www.artbasel.com/miami-beach; ⊙ early Dec)
One of the most important international art shows in the world, with works from more than 250 galleries and a slew of trendy parties. Even if you're not a billionaire collector, there's much to enjoy at this four-day fest, with open-air art installations around town, special exhibitions at many Miami galleries and outdoor film screenings.

🛏 Sleeping

Miami has some alluring lodging options – and for some travelers, it's a big draw to the city. South Beach has all the name recognition with boutique hotels set in lovely art-deco buildings, but there are plenty of other options in Miami – from Downtown high-rises with sweeping views and endless amenities to historic charmers in Coral Gables, Coconut Grove and other less touristy neighborhoods.

🛏 South Beach

Bed & Drinks HOSTEL $
(Map p460; ☎ 786-230-1234; www//bedsndrinks.com; 1676 James Ave; dm/d from $29/154) This hostel pretty shamelessly plays to the sex-appeal-seeking crowd – check the name – but hey, it's a few blocks from the beach, so the placement works. The rooms range from average to slightly below average, but the young party-minded crowd (mostly) doesn't mind. Friendly staff, a lively on-site bar and nightlife outings to clubs around town.

Catalina Hotel BOUTIQUE HOTEL $$
(Map p460; ☎ 305-674-1160; www.catalinahotel.com; 1732 Collins Ave; r from $220; P ❄ 🛜 🏊) The Catalina is a lovely example of mid-range deco style. Most appealing, besides the playfully minimalist rooms, is the vibe – the Catalina doesn't take itself too seriously,

and staff and guests all seem to be having fun as a result. The back pool, concealed behind the main building's crisp white facade, is particularly attractive and fringed by a whispery grove of bamboo trees.

★**1 Hotel** HOTEL $$$
(Map p458; ☎ 866-615-1111; www.1hotels.com; 2341 Collins Ave; r from $400; ❄ 🛜 🏊) One of the top hotels in the USA, the 1 Hotel has 400-plus gorgeous rooms that embrace both luxurious and eco-friendly features – including tree-trunk coffee tables/desks, custom hemp-blend mattresses and salvaged driftwood feature walls, plus in-room water filtration (no need for plastic bottles). The common areas are impressive, with four pools, including an adults-only rooftop infinity pool.

★**Surfcomber** HOTEL $$$
(Map p460; ☎ 305-532-7715; www.surfcomber.com; 1717 Collins Ave; r $250-480; P ❄ 🛜 🏊) The Surfcomber has a classic deco exterior with strong lines and shade-providing 'eyebrows' that zigzag across the facade. But the interior is what takes most people aback. Rooms have appeal, with elegant lines in keeping with the deco aesthetic, while bursts of color keep things contemporary.

🛏 North Beach

★**Freehand Miami** BOUTIQUE HOTEL $$
(Map p458; ☎ 305-531-2727; www.thefreehand.com; 2727 Indian Creek Dr; dm $35-55, r $160-250; ❄ 🛜 🏊) The Freehand is the brilliant reimagining of the old Indian Creek Hotel, a classic of the Miami Beach scene. Rooms are sunny and attractively designed, with local artwork and wooden details. The vintage-filled common areas are the reason to stay here though – especially the lovely pool area and backyard that transforms into one of the best bars in town.

🛏 Downtown Miami

Langford Hotel HERITAGE HOTEL $$
(Map p458; ☎ 305-250-0782; www.langfordhotelmiami.com; 121 SE 1st St; r from $180; ❄ 🛜) Set in a beautifully restored 1925 beaux-arts high-rise, the Langford opened to much fanfare in 2016. Its 126 rooms blend comfort and nostalgia, with elegant fixtures and vintage details, including white oak flooring and glass-encased rain showers. Thoughtful design touches abound, and there's a rooftop bar and an excellent ground-floor restaurant on-site.

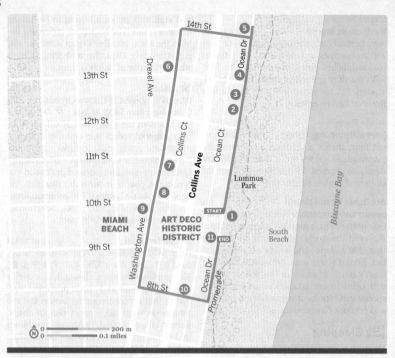

14th St

13th St

12th St

11th St

10th St

9th St

8th St

Drexel Ave

Collins Ct

Ocean Ct

Washington Ave

Collins Ave

Ocean Dr

Ocean Dr

Promenade

Lummus Park

Biscayne Bay

MIAMI BEACH

ART DECO HISTORIC DISTRICT

South Beach

START

END

5

6

4

3

2

7

8

9

11

1

10

N

0   200 m
0   0.1 miles

🏃 City Walk
Art Deco Magic

START ART DECO MUSEUM
END OCEAN'S TEN
LENGTH 1.2 MILES; TWO TO THREE HOURS

Start at the **①Art Deco Museum** (p456), at the corner of Ocean Dr and 10th St. North along Ocean Dr, between 12th and 14th Sts, you'll see three examples of deco hotels: the **②Leslie**, a boxy shape with eyebrows (cantilevered sunshades) wrapped around the side of the building; the **③Carlyle**, featured in the film *The Birdcage* and boasting modernistic styling; and the graceful **④Cardozo Hotel**, built by Henry Hohauser, owned by Gloria Estefan and featuring sleek, rounded edges. At 14th St peek inside the sun-drenched **⑤Winter Haven Hotel** to see its fabulous terrazzo floors, made of stone chips set in mortar that's polished when dry.

Turn left and down 14th St to Washington Ave and the **⑥US Post Office**, at 13th St. It's a curvy block of white deco in the stripped classical style. Step inside to admire

the wall mural, domed ceiling and marble stamp tables. Lunch at the **⑦11th St Diner** (p467), a gleaming aluminum Pullman car that was imported in 1992 from Wilkes-Barre, Pennsylvania. Get a window seat and gaze across the avenue to the corner of 10th St and the stunningly restored **⑧Hotel Astor**, designed in 1936 by T Hunter Henderson.

After your meal, walk half a block east from there to the imposing **⑨Wolfsonian-FIU** (p456), an excellent design museum, formerly the Washington Storage Company. Continue walking Washington Ave, turn left on 8th St and then continue north along Collins Ave to the **⑩Hotel of South Beach**, featuring an interior and roof deck by Todd Oldham. L Murray Dixon designed the hotel as the Tiffany Hotel, with a deco spire, in 1939. Go two blocks to Ocean Dr, where you'll spy nonstop deco beauties; at 960 Ocean Dr (the **⑪Ocean's Ten** restaurant) you'll see an exterior designed in 1935 by deco legend Henry Hohauser.

Coral Gables

★ Biltmore Hotel
HISTORIC HOTEL **$$$**

(Map p458; ☑ 855-311-6903; www.biltmorehotel.com; 1200 Anastasia Ave; r/ste from $409/560; P❄🐾) Though the Biltmore's standard rooms can be small, a stay here is a chance to sleep in one of the great laps of US luxury. The grounds are so palatial it would take a solid week to explore everything the Biltmore has to offer – we highly recommend reading a book in the Romanesque/Arabian Nights opulent lobby, sunning underneath enormous columns and taking a dip in the largest hotel pool in the continental USA.

✗ Eating

Miami is a major immigrant entrepôt and a sucker for food trends. Thus you get a good mix of cheap ethnic eateries and high-quality top-end cuisine here, alongside some poor-value dross in touristy zones like Miami Beach. The best new areas for dining are in Downtown, Wynwood and the Upper East Side; Coral Gables has great classic options.

✗ South Beach

11th St Diner
DINER **$**

(Map p460; ☑ 305-534-6373; www.eleventhstreetdiner.com; 1065 Washington Ave; mains $10-20; ⏱7am-midnight Sun-Wed, 24hr Thu-Sat) You've seen the art-deco landmarks. Now eat in one: a Pullman-car diner trucked down from Wilkes-Barre, Pennsylvania – as sure a slice of Americana as a *Leave It to Beaver* marathon. The food is as classic as the architecture, with oven-roasted turkey, baby back ribs and mac 'n' cheese among the hits – plus breakfast at all hours.

★ Yardbird
SOUTHERN US **$$**

(Map p460; ☑ 305-538-5220; www.runchickenrun.com/miami; 1600 Lenox Ave; mains $18-38; ⏱11am-midnight Mon-Fri, from 8:30am Sat & Sun; 🐾) Yardbird has earned a die-hard following for its delicious haute Southern comfort food. The kitchen churns out some nice shrimp and grits, St Louis–style pork ribs, charred okra, and biscuits with smoked brisket, but it's most famous for its supremely good plate of fried chicken, spiced watermelon and waffles with bourbon maple syrup.

★ Pubbelly
FUSION **$$**

(Map p460; ☑ 305-532-7555; www.pubbellyboys.com; 1418 20th St; sharing plates $11-24, mains $19-30; ⏱6pm-midnight Tue-Thu & Sun, to 1am Fri & Sat; 🐾) Pubbelly's dining genre is hard to pinpoint, besides delicious. It skews between Asian, North American and Latin American, gleaning the best from all cuisines. Examples? Try black-truffle risotto, pork-belly dumplings or the mouth-watering kimchi fried rice with seafood. Hand-crafted cocktails wash down the dishes a treat.

Joe's Stone Crab Restaurant
AMERICAN **$$$**

(Map p460; ☑ 305-673-0365; www.joesstonecrab.com; 11 Washington Ave; mains lunch $14-30, dinner $19-60; ⏱11:30am-2:30pm Tue-Sat, 5-10pm daily) The wait is long and the prices for iconic dishes can be high. But if those aren't deal-breakers, queue up to don a bib in Miami's most famous restaurant (around since 1913!) and enjoy deliciously fresh stone-crab claws.

✗ North Beach

Roasters 'n Toasters
DELI **$**

(Map p458; ☑ 305-531-7691; www.roastersntoasters.com; 525 Arthur Godfrey Rd; mains $10-18; ⏱6:30am-3:30pm) Given the crowds and the satisfied smiles of customers, Roasters 'n Toasters meets the demanding standards of Miami Beach's large Jewish demographic, thanks to juicy deli meat, fresh bread, crispy bagels and warm latkes. Sliders (mini-sandwiches) are served on challah bread, an innovation that's as charming as it is tasty.

★ 27 Restaurant
FUSION **$$**

(Map p458; ☑ 786-476-7020; www.freehandhotels.com; 2727 Indian Creek Dr, Freehand Miami Hotel; mains $17-28; ⏱6:30pm-2am Mon-Sat, 11am-4pm & 6:30pm-2am Sun; 🐾) This new spot sits on the grounds of the very popular Broken Shaker (p468), one of Miami Beach's best-loved cocktail bars. Like the bar, the setting is amazing – akin to dining in an old tropical cottage, with worn wood floorboards, candlelit tables, and various rooms slung with artwork and curious knickknacks, plus a lovely terrace. The cooking is exceptional, and incorporates flavors from around the globe.

✗ Downtown Miami

All Day
CAFE **$**

(Map p458; www.alldaymia.com; 1035 N Miami Ave; coffee $3.50, breakfast $10-14; ⏱7am-7pm Mon-Fri, from 9am Sat & Sun; 🐾) All Day is one of the best places in the Downtown area to linger over coffee or breakfast – no matter

FLORIDA MIAMI

the hour. Slender Scandinavian-style chairs, wood-and-marble tables and the Françoise Hardy soundtrack lend an easygoing vibe.

Chef Allen's Farm-to-Table Dinner
VEGETARIAN **$$**

(Map p458; ☑ 786-405-1745; 1300 Biscayne Blvd; dinner $25, with wine pairing $40; ☺ 6:30pm Mon; ☑) On Monday nights, you can feast on a delicious five-course vegetarian meal, served family-style at outdoor tables in front of the Arsht Center. It's excellent value, with a creative menu inspired by the farmers market held on the same day.

★ Casablanca
SEAFOOD **$$**

(Map p458; www.casablancaseafood.com; 400 N River Dr; mains $15-34; ☺ 11am-10pm Sun-Thu, to 11pm Fri & Sat) Perched over the Miami River, Casablanca serves up some of the best seafood in town. The setting is a big draw – with tables on a long wooden deck just above the water, and the odd seagull winging past.

Little Havana

★ Versailles
CUBAN **$**

(Map p458; ☑ 305-444-0240; www.versaillesrestaurant.com; 3555 SW 8th St; mains $6-21; ☺ 8am-1am Mon-Thu, to 2:30am Fri & Sat, 9am-1am Sun) Versailles (ver-*sigh*-yay) is an institution – one of the mainstays of Miami's Cuban gastronomic scene. Try the excellent black-bean soup or the fried yucca before moving onto heartier meat and seafood plates. Older Cubans and Miami's Latin political elite still love coming here, so you've got a real chance to rub elbows with Miami's most prominent Latin citizens.

Exquisito Restaurant
CUBAN **$**

(Map p458; ☑ 305-643-0227; www.elexquisitomiami.com; 1510 SW 8th St; mains $9-13; ☺ 7am-11pm) For great Cuban cuisine in the heart of Little Havana, this place is exquisite (ha ha). The roast pork has a tangy citrus kick and the *ropa vieja* (spiced shredded beef) is wonderfully rich and filling. Even standard sides like beans and rice and roasted plantains are executed with a little more care and tastiness. Prices are a steal too.

Wynwood & the Design District

Della Test Kitchen
VEGAN **$**

(Map p458; ☑ 305-351-2961; www.dellabowls.com; 56 NW 29th St, Wynwood Yard; mains $11-14; ☺ noon-10pm Tue-Sun; ☑) From a food truck

parked in Wynwood Yard, this place offers delicious 'bowls' – build-your-own culinary works of art featuring ingredients such as black coconut rice, ginger tempeh, chickpeas, sweet potato and marinated kale. It's heavenly good and quite healthy. Not surprisingly, DTK has quite a following.

★ Kyu
FUSION **$$**

(Map p458; ☑ 786-577-0150; www.kyumiami.com; 251 NW 25th St; sharing plates $17-38; ☺ noon-11:30pm Mon-Sat, 11am-10:30pm Sun, bar till 1am Fri & Sat; ☑) ✐ One of the best new restaurants in Wynwood, Kyu has been dazzling locals and food critics alike with its creative Asian-inspired dishes, most of which are cooked up over the open flames of a wood-fired grill. The buzzing, industrial space is warmed up via artful lighting and wood accents (tables and chairs, plus shelves of firewood for the grill).

★ Alter
MODERN AMERICAN **$$$**

(Map p458; ☑ 305-573-5996; www.altermiami.com; 223 NW 23rd St; set menu 5/7 courses $69/89; ☺ 7-11pm Tue-Sun) This new spot, which has garnered much praise from food critics, brings creative high-end cooking to Wynwood courtesy of its award-winning young chef Brad Kilgore. The changing menu showcases Florida's high-quality ingredients from sea and land in seasonally inspired dishes with Asian and European accents. Reserve ahead.

Drinking & Nightlife

Too many people assume Miami's nightlife is all about being wealthy and attractive and/or phony. Disavow yourself of this notion, which only describes a small slice of the scene in South Beach. Miami has an intense variety of bars to pick from that range from grotty dives to beautiful – but still laid-back – lounges and nightclubs.

★ Broken Shaker
BAR

(Map p458; ☑ 305-531-2727; www.freehandhotels.com; 2727 Indian Creek Dr, Freehand Miami Hotel; ☺ 6pm-3am Mon-Fri, 2pm-3am Sat & Sun) Craft cocktails are having their moment in Miami, and if mixology is in the spotlight, you can bet Broken Shaker is sharing the glare. Expert bartenders run this spot, located in the back of the Freehand Miami hotel (p465), which takes up one closet-sized indoor niche and a sprawling plant-filled courtyard of excellent drinks and beautiful people.

★ **Sweet Liberty**   BAR
(Map p458; www.mysweetliberty.com; 237 20th St; ⊙4pm-5am Mon-Sat, from noon Sun) A much-loved local haunt near Collins Park, Sweet Liberty has all the right ingredients for a fun night out: friendly, easygoing bartenders who whip up excellent cocktails (try a mint julep), great happy-hour specials (including 75¢ oysters) and a relaxed, pretension-free crowd. The space is huge, with flickering candles, a long wooden bar and the odd band adding to the cheer.

Bardot   CLUB
(Map p458; ☑305-576-5570; www.bardotmiami. com; 3456 N Miami Ave; ⊙8pm-3am Tue & Wed, to 5am Thu-Sat) You really should see the interior of Bardot before you leave the city. It's all sexy French vintage posters and furniture (plus a pool table) seemingly plucked from a private club that serves millionaires by day, and becomes a scene of decadent excess by night.

Ball & Chain   BAR
(Map p458; www.ballandchainmiami.com; 1513 SW 8th Street; ⊙noon-midnight Mon-Wed, to 3am Thu-Sat, 2-10pm Sun) The Ball & Chain has survived several incarnations over the years. Back in 1935, when 8th St was more Jewish than Latino, it was the sort of jazz joint Billie Holiday would croon in. That iteration closed in 1957, but the new Ball & Chain is still dedicated to music and good times – specifically, Latin music and tropical cocktails.

Vagabond Pool Bar   BAR
(Map p458; ☑305-400-8420; www.vagabond kitchenandbar.com; 7301 Biscayne Blvd; ⊙5-11pm Sun-Thu, to midnight Fri & Sat) Tucked behind the Vagabond Hotel, this is a great spot to start off the evening, with perfectly mixed cocktails, courtesy of pro bartenders (the kind who will shake your hand and introduce themselves). The outdoor setting overlooking the palm-fringed pool and eclectic crowd pairs nicely with elixirs like the Lost in Smoke (mezcal, amaro, amaretto and orange bitters).

☆ **Entertainment**

Miami's artistic merits are obvious, even from a distance. Could there be a better creative base? There's Southern homegrown talent, migratory snowbirds bringing the funding and attention of northeastern galleries, and immigrants from across the Americas. All that adds up to some great live music, theater and dance – with plenty of room for experimentation.

★ **Adrienne Arsht Center for the Performing Arts**   PERFORMING ARTS
(Map p458; ☑305-949-6722; www.arshtcenter.org; 1300 Biscayne Blvd; ⊙box office 10am-6pm Mon-Fri, & 2hr before performances) This magnificent venue manages to both humble and enthrall visitors. Today the Arsht is where the biggest cultural acts in Miami come to perform; a show here is a must-see on any Miami trip.

FLORIDA MIAMI

LGBT MIAMI

In Miami, the gay scene is so integrated it can be difficult to separate it from the straight one; popular hot spots include South Beach, North Beach, and Wynwood and the Design District. Events such as the White Party (p466) and Swizzle are major dates in the North American gay calendar.

LGBT Visitor Center (Map p460; ☑305-397-8914; www.gogaymiami.com; 1130 Washington Ave; ⊙9am-6pm Mon-Fri, 11am-4pm Sat & Sun) The best single source for all LGBT info on Miami. Check the website for Pink Flamingo-certified hotels (ie hotels that are most welcoming to the LGBT crowd). Run by the Gay & Lesbian Chamber of Commerce.

Miami Visitors Bureau (www.miamiandbeaches.com/things-to-do/travel-guides/gay-miami) Miami's official tourist bureau has a useful guide to gay life in the city.

Damron (www.damron.com) Damron, an expert in LGBT travel, offers a searchable database of LGBT-friendly and specific travel listings. Publishes popular national guidebooks, including *Women's Traveller*, *Men's Travel Guide* and *Damron Accommodations*.

Gay Yellow Network (www.glyp.com) City-based listings include six Florida cities.

Out Traveler (www.outtraveler.com) Travel magazine specializing in gay travel.

Purple Roofs (www.purpleroofs.com) Lists queer accommodations, travel agencies and tours worldwide.

There's an Adrienne Arsht Center stop on the Metromover.

★ Cubaocho
LIVE PERFORMANCE

(Map p458; ☑ 305-285-5880; www.cubaocho. com; 1465 SW 8th St; ☺11am-10pm Tue-Thu, to 3am Fri & Sat) Jewel of the Little Havana Art District, Cubaocho is renowned for its concerts, with excellent bands from across the Spanish-speaking world. It's also a community center, art gallery and research outpost for all things Cuban. The interior resembles an old Havana cigar bar, yet the walls are decked out in artwork that references both the classical past of Cuban art and its avant-garde future.

Colony Theater
PERFORMING ARTS

(Map p460; ☑ 305-674-1040, box office 800-211-1414; www.colonymb.org; 1040 Lincoln Rd) The Colony is an absolute art-deco gem, with a classic marquee and Inca-style crenellations, which looks like the sort of place gangsters would go to watch *Hamlet*. This treasure now serves as a major venue for performing arts – from comedy and occasional musicals to theatrical dramas, off-Broadway productions and ballet – as well as hosting movie screenings and small film festivals.

New World Symphony
CLASSICAL MUSIC

(NWS; Map p460; ☑ 305-673-3330; www.nws.edu; 500 17th St) Housed in the New World Center (p457) – a funky explosion of cubist lines and geometric curves, fresh white against the blue Miami sky – the acclaimed New World Symphony holds performances from October to May. The deservedly heralded NWS serves as a three- to four-year preparatory program for talented musicians from prestigious music schools.

ℹ Information

DANGERS & ANNOYANCES

Miami is a fairly safe city, but there are a few areas considered by locals to be dangerous:
➡ Liberty City, in northwest Miami; Overtown, from 14th St to 20th St; Little Haiti and stretches of the Miami riverfront.
➡ South Beach, particularly along the carnival-like mayhem of Ocean Dr between 8th and 11th Sts, and deserted areas below 5th St are also dangerous at night.
➡ Use caution around causeways, bridges and overpasses where homeless people have set up shantytowns.

➡ In these and other reputedly 'bad' areas you should avoid walking around alone late at night. It's best to take a taxi.

TOURIST INFORMATION

Greater Miami & the Beaches Convention & Visitors Bureau (Map p458; ☑ 305-539-3000; www.miamiandbeaches.com; 701 Brickell Ave, 27th fl; ☺8:30am-6pm Mon-Fri) Offers loads of info on Miami and keeps up-to-date with the latest events and cultural offerings.

ℹ Getting There & Away

Located 6 miles west of Downtown, the busy **Miami International Airport** (MIA; Map p458; ☑ 305-876-7000; www.miami-airport.com; 2100 NW 42nd Ave) has three terminals and serves over 40 million passengers each year. Around 60 airlines fly into Miami. The airport is open 24 hours and is laid out in a horseshoe design. There are left-luggage facilities on two concourses at MIA, between B and C, and on G; prices vary according to bag size.

For bus trips, **Greyhound** (www.greyhound. com) is the main long-distance operator. **Megabus** (Map p458; www.us.megabus.com; Miami International Center, 3801 NW 21st St) offers service to Tampa and Orlando.

Greyhound's **main bus terminal** (Map p458; ☑ 305-871-1810; 3801 NW 21st) is near the airport, though additional services also depart from the company's **Cutler Bay terminal** (Cutler Bay; ☑ 305-296-9072; 10801 Caribbean Blvd) and **North Miami terminal** (Map p458; ☑ 305-688-7277; 16000 NW 7th Ave).

If you are traveling very long distances (say, across several states) bargain airfares can sometimes undercut buses. On shorter routes, renting a car can sometimes be cheaper. Nonetheless, discounted (even half-price) long-distance bus trips are often available by purchasing tickets online seven to 14 days in advance.

The main Miami terminal of **Amtrak** (☑ 305-835-1222; www.amtrak.com; 8303 NW 37th Ave, West Little River), about 9 miles northwest of Downtown, connects the city with several other points in Florida (including Orlando and Jacksonville) on the Silver Service line that runs up to New York City. Travel time between New York and Miami is 27 to 31 hours. The Miami Amtrak station is connected by Tri-rail to Downtown Miami and has a left-luggage facility.

ℹ Getting Around

Rental Car Convenient for zipping around town, but parking can be expensive.

Taxi & Ride-Sharing Services Handy for getting between destinations if you don't want to drive, but can be pricey for long distances. Difficult to hail on the street; call or use an app for a pick-up.

Bus Extensive system, though slow for long journeys.

Trolley Free service with various routes in Miami Beach, Downtown, Wynwood, Coconut Grove, Coral Gables, Little Havana and other neighborhoods.

Citi Bike Bike-sharing network in both Miami and Miami Beach. With heavy traffic, however, riding long distances can be hazardous.

Fort Lauderdale

After years of building a reputation as *the* destination for beer-swilling college students on raucous spring breaks, Fort Lauderdale now angles for a slightly more mature and sophisticated crowd. Think martinis rather than tequila shots; jazz concerts instead of wet T-shirt contests. But don't worry, there's still plenty of carrying-on within the confines of area bars and nightclubs.

Few visitors venture far inland – except maybe to dine and shop along Las Olas Blvd; most spend the bulk of their time on the coast. It's understandable. Truly, it's hard to compete with beautiful beaches, a system of Venice-like waterways, an international yachting scene, spiffy new hotels and top-notch restaurants. The city's Port Everglades is one of the busiest cruise-ship ports in the world, with megaships departing daily for the Caribbean, Mexico and beyond.

⊙ Sights

Fort Lauderdale Beach & Promenade   BEACH

(P ♿ 🐾) Fort Lauderdale's promenade – a wide, brick, palm-tree-dotted pathway swooping along the beach and the A1A – is a magnet for runners, in-line skaters, walkers and cyclists. The white-sand beach, meanwhile, is one of the nation's cleanest and best. Stretching 7 miles to Lauderdale-by-the-Sea, it has dedicated family-, gay- and dog-friendly sections.

NSU Art Museum Fort Lauderdale   MUSEUM

(☏954-525-5500; www.nsuartmuseum.org; 1 E Las Olas Blvd; adult/student/child $12/free; ⊙11am-5pm Tue-Sat, to 8pm Thu, noon-5pm Sun) A curvaceous Florida standout known for its William Glackens collection (among Glackens fans) and its exhibitions on wide-ranging themes from northern European art to contemporary Cuban art, American pop art and contemporary photography. On Thursday evenings, the museum stays open late

and hosts lectures, films and performances, as well as a happy hour in the museum cafe. Day courses and workshops are also available. Check the website for details.

★**Bonnet House**   HISTORIC BUILDING

(☏954-563-5393; www.bonnethouse.org; 900 N Birch Rd; adult/child $20/16, grounds only $10; ⊙9am-4pm Tue-Sun) This pretty plantation-style property was once the home of artists and collectors Frederic and Evelyn Bartlett. It is now open to guided tours that swing through its art-filled rooms and studios. Beyond the house, 35 acres of lush, subtropical gardens protect a pristine barrier-island ecosystem, including one of the finest orchid collections in the country.

Riverwalk   LANDMARK

(www.goriverwalk.com) Curving along the New River, the meandering Riverwalk runs from Stranahan House to the Broward Center for the Performing Arts. Host to culinary tastings and other events, the walk connects a number of sights, restaurants and shops.

Museum of Discovery & Science   MUSEUM

(☏954-467-6637; www.mods.org; 401 SW 2nd St; adult/child $16/13; ⊙10am-5pm Mon-Sat, noon-6pm Sun; ♿) A 52ft kinetic-energy sculpture greets you here, and fun exhibits include Gizmo City and Runways to Rockets – where it actually *is* rocket science. Plus there's an Everglades exhibit and IMAX theater.

🏃 Activities

Fort Lauderdale lies on the same reef system as the Keys. Snorkeling is a popular pastime but the real action in the water lies within a 50-minute boat ride at the site of some two-dozen wrecks. Here divers can nose around the Mercedes freighter and the Tenneco Towers artificial reef made up from an old oil platform. Soft corals bloom prolifically and barracuda, jacks and parrotfish duck and dive between the wreckage.

Besides the underwater scenery, everything from jet-skis to parasailing to deep-sea fishing charters is available at the beach.

★**Atlantic Coast Kayak Company**   KAYAKING

(☏954-781-0073; www.atlanticcoastkayak.com; Richardson Historical Park Boat Dock, 1937 Wilton Dr; per hour/half-day $16/40; ⊙9am-5pm) An excellent alternative to tour-boat cruises is to rent your own kayak in Richardson Park and paddle the 7.5 mile (roughly 2½ to three hours) Middle River loop around the Island City yourself. Day, sunset and moonlight tours, including basic instruction and gourmet sandwiches and soft drinks, are also available on a scheduled calendar. All you need to do is turn up.

Sea Experience BOATING, SNORKELING
(☑ 954-770-3483; www.seaxp.com; 801 Seabreeze Blvd; snorkeling adult/child $40/25; ⊙10:15am & 2:15pm; 🚗) Sea Experience takes guests in a 40ft glass-bottom boat along the Intracoastal and into the ocean to snorkel on a natural reef, thriving with marine life, in 10ft to 20ft of water. Tours last 2½ hours. Also offers scuba trips to multiple wreck sites.

Carrie B BOATING
(☑954-642-1601; www.carriebcruises.com; 440 N New River Dr E; tours adult/child $24/13; ⊙tours 11am, 1pm & 3pm, closed Tue & Wed May-Sep) Hop aboard this replica 19th-century riverboat for a narrated 90-minute 'lifestyles of the rich and famous' tour of the ginormous mansions along the Intracoastal and New River. Tours leave from Las Olas at SE 5th Ave.

🛏 Sleeping

The splashiest hotels are found along the beach. Of course, those places are also the priciest. Meander inland and you'll discover some wonderful inns with Old Florida charm. For more budget-friendly accommodations, check out Lauderdale-by-the-Sea.

Tranquilo MOTEL $$
(☑954-565-5790; www.tranquilofortlauderdale.com; 2909 Vistamar St; Sun-Thu r $149-174, Fri & Sat $189-194; P☀🞿🞿) With a successful white-on-white decorative facelift, this retro 1950s motel offers fantastic value for families. Rooms range over three buildings, each with its own pool, and some include newly refurbed kitchens along with access to outdoor grills and laundry services. Complimentary shuttle service to the beach.

B Ocean Resort HOTEL $$
(☑954-524-5551; www.bhotelsandresorts.com/b-ocean; 1140 Seabreeze Blvd; r from $150; P☀🞿🞿) Defining the southern end of Seabreeze Blvd, this hotel straddles the uberpopular South Beach and offers breezy ocean views from the majority of its airy rooms. Built by M Tony Sherman in 1956, it looks like a giant cruise ship tethered to the sidewalk.

★ W Fort Lauderdale HOTEL $$$
(☑ 954-414-8200; www.wfortlauderdalehotel.com; 401 N Fort Lauderdale Beach Blvd; r from $284; P☀@🞿🞿) With an exterior resembling two giant sails and an interior that looks like the backdrop for a J Lo video, this is where the glitterati stay – bust out your stiletto heels/skinny ties and join them. The massive lobby is built for leisure, with a silver-and-aqua lounge area, a moodily lit bar, and a deck lined with wicker chaises.

★ Lago Mar Resort RESORT $$$
(☑954-523-6511; www.lagomar.com; 1700 S Ocean Lane; r $300-700; P☀@🞿) On the south end of South Beach, this wonderfully noncorporate resort has it all: a private beach, over-the-top grand lobby, massive island-style rooms, a full-service spa, on-site eateries, a lagoon-style pool set amid tropical plantings and the personal touch of family ownership. (And no, not to be confused with President Trump's Mar-a-Lago.)

🍴 Eating

Fort Lauderdale's food scene is heavily influenced by the area's large Italian American population but increasingly, it's becoming known for its casual chic, farm-to-table options. Las Olas Blvd has a number of eating places, especially the stretch between 5th and 16th Aves, though these can be more touristy.

Lester's Diner DINER $
(☑954-525-5641; www.facebook.com/lesters-diner; 250 W State Rd 84; mains $4-17; ⊙24hr) Hailed endearingly as a greasy spoon, campy Lester's Diner has been keeping folks happy since the late 1960s. Everyone makes their way here at some point, from business types on cell phones to clubbers and blue-haired ladies with third husbands to travel writers needing pancakes at 4am.

Green Bar & Kitchen VEGAN $$
(☑954-533-7507; www.greenbarkitchen.com; 1075 SE 17th St; mains $8-12; ⊙11am-9pm Mon-Sat, to 3pm Sun; 🞿) Discover bright flavors and innovative dishes at this modern, plant-based eatery located in a strip mall. Instead of pasta-layered lasagna, slivers of zucchini are layered with macadamia ricotta and sun-dried tomatoes. Almond milk replaces dairy in cold-pressed fruit smoothies, and the delectable cashew cup gives Reese's a run for its money.

★ Burlock Coast

INTERNATIONAL $$$

(☎954-302-6460; www.burlockcoast.com; Ritz Carlton, 1 N Fort Lauderdale Beach Blvd; mains $14-40; ◎7am-10pm Mon-Fri, noon-5pm Sat & Sun) Situated in the lovely Ritz Carlton Hotel, this chic casual spot somehow manages to be all things to all people: a cafe, bar, market and upmarket restaurant. The menu has been crafted to the mantra: local farmers and vendors. The menu changes seasonally but errs toward modern international, like pork belly with black truffle grits or simple fish-and-chips.

15th Street Fisheries

SEAFOOD $$$

(☎954-763-2777; www.15streetfisheries.com; 1900 SE 15th St; mains bar $6-16, restaurant $26-38; P) Tucked away in Lauderdale Marina with an open-fronted deck offering a front-row view of yachts, this place is hard to beat for waterfront dining. The wooden interior is kitted out like an Old Florida boathouse. The fine-dining restaurant is upstairs and a more informal dockside bar serves shrimp, crab and grilled mahimahi.

🍷 Drinking & Entertainment

Fort Lauderdale bars can stay open until 4am on weekends and 2am during the week. A handful of great bars and pubs are found in the Himmarshee Village area on SW 2nd St, while the beach offers open-air boozing.

★ Rok:Brgr

PUB

(☎754-525-7656; www.rokbrgr.com; 208 SW 2nd St; ◎11:30am-midnight Mon-Thu, to 2am Fri & Sat, to 11pm Sun) One of several of this strip of hip bars and restaurants, Rok:Brgr shoots for a 1920s Chicago-era gastropub and somehow pulls it off. Edison lightbulbs and contemporary industrial creates the ambience, while the cuisine is contemporary gastropub – gourmet burgers using locally sourced ingredients, plus Prohibition-style cocktails.

★ Stache

COCKTAIL BAR

(☎954-449-1044; www.stacheftl.com; 109 SW 2nd Ave; ◎8am-5pm Mon & Thu, 8am-4am Fri, 8pm-4am Sat) A sexy 1920s drinking den serving crafted cocktails and rocking a crossover classic rock/funk/soul/R&B blend. At weekends there's live music, dancing and burlesque. Dress up; this is where the cool cats come to play.

Blue Jean Blues

JAZZ

(☎954-306-6330; www.bjblive.com; 3320 NE 33rd St; snacks $9-17; ◎11am-2am Sun-Thu, to 3am Fri & Sat) Get away from the beach for a low-key evening of jazz and blues at this cool little neighborhood bar. There's live music seven nights a week and four afternoons, featuring a who's who of the southern Florida music scene. From East Sunrise Blvd head north for 2.3 miles and then turn left onto NE 33rd Street.

ℹ Information

Greater Fort Lauderdale Convention & Visitors Bureau (☎954-765-4466; www.sunny.org; 101 NE 3rd Ave, Suite 100; ◎8:30am-5pm Mon-Fri) Has an excellent array of visitor information about the greater Fort Lauderdale region.

LGBT FORT LAUDERDALE

Sure, South Beach is a mecca for gay travelers, but Fort Lauderdale nips at the high heels of its southern neighbor. Compared to South Beach, Lauderdale is a little more rainbow-flag-oriented and a little less exclusive. And for the hordes of gay men who flock here, either to party or to settle down, therein lies the charm.

Fort Lauderdale is home to several dozen gay bars and clubs, as many gay guesthouses, and a couple of way-gay residential areas. Victoria Park is the established gay hub just northeast of downtown Fort Lauderdale. A bit further north, Wilton Manors is a more recently gay-gentrified area boasting endless nightlife options. Look for Rosie's (☎954-563-0123; www.rosiesbarandgrill.com; 2449 Wilton Dr; ◎11am-11pm), a low-key neighborhood watering hole; The Manor (www.themanorcomplex.com; 2345 Wilton Dr; ◎8pm-4am), for nationally recognized performers and an epic dance floor; and Georgie's Alibi (www.alibiwiltonmanors.com; 2266 Wilton Dr; ◎11am-2am), best for its Wednesday comedy night with Cashetta, a fabulous female impersonator. There's even a leather/bear/cowboy club, Ramrod (www.ramrodbar.com; 1508 Wilton Dr; ◎3pm-2am).

Gay guesthouses are plentiful; visit www.gayftlauderdale.com. Consult the glossy weekly rag Hot Spots (www.hotspotsmagazine.com) to keep updated on gay nightlife. For the most insanely comprehensive list of everything gay, log on to www.jumponmarkslist.com.

❶ Getting There & Around

Fort Lauderdale is served by its own international **airport** (FLL; ☑ 866-435-9355; www.broward.org/airport; 320 Terminal Dr).

If you're driving here, I-95 and Florida's Turnpike run north–south and provide good access to Fort Lauderdale. I-595, the major east–west artery, intersects I-95, Florida's Turnpike and the Sawgrass Expressway. It also feeds into I-75, which runs to Florida's west coast.

Sun Trolley (☑ 954-876-5539; www.sun-trolley.com; per ride/day $1/3) runs between Las Olas and the beaches between 9:30am and 6:30pm Friday to Monday. **Broward County Transit** (BCT; www.broward.org/bct; single fare/day pass $2/5) operates between downtown, the beach and Port Everglades. From **Broward Central Terminal** (101 NW 1st Ave), take bus 11 to upper Fort Lauderdale Beach and Lauderdale-by-the-Sea; bus 4 to Port Everglades; and bus 40 to 17th St and the beaches.

The fun, yellow **water taxi** (☑ 954-467-6677; www.watertaxi.com; day pass adult/child $26/12) travels the canals and waterways between 17th St to the south, Atlantic Blvd/Pompano Beach to the north, the Riverwalk to the west and the Atlantic Ocean to the east. There are also services to Hollywood ($15 per person).

Palm Beach County

The third-wealthiest city in America, Palm Beach is home to 25 billionaires and looks every inch the playground for the rich and famous. Palatial Greco-Roman mansions line the shore; Bentleys and Porsches cruise the wide avenues of downtown; and streets look clean enough to eat off. Life here revolves around charity balls, designer shopping and cocktail-soaked lunches. Though all the bling may feel a bit intimidating, fear not – much of Palm Beach is within the reach of all travelers. Stroll along the truly gold Gold Coast beach, ogle the massive gated compounds on A1A or window-shop in uber-ritzy Worth Ave – all for free.

These days, Palm Beach is frequently in the news because of US president Donald Trump, whose mansion-cum-private-club, Mar-a-Lago, is here.

Despite all the glitz, the architecture and history is nothing but fascinating, and offers some insight into how it might have been to live during the Gilded Age of the late 19th-century USA.

Palm Beach

◉ Sights & Activities

Worth Avenue   AREA
(www.worth-avenue.com) This quarter-mile, palm-tree-lined strip of more than 200 high-end brand shops is like the Rodeo Dr of the East. You can trace its history back to the 1920s when the now-gone Everglades Club staged weekly fashion shows and launched the careers of designers such as Elizabeth Arden. Even if you don't have the slightest urge to sling a swag of glossy bags over your arm, the people-watching is priceless, as is the Spanish Revival architecture.

★**Flagler Museum**   MUSEUM
(☑ 561-655-2833; www.flaglermuseum.us; 1 Whitehall Way; adult/child $18/10; ⊙10am-5pm Tue-Sat, noon-5pm Sun) This museum is housed in the spectacular 1902 mansion built by Henry Flagler as a gift for his bride, Mary Lily Kenan. The beaux-arts-styled Whitehall was one of the most modern houses of its era and quickly became the focus of the winter season. Designed by John Carrère and Thomas Hastings, both students of the Ecole des Beaux-Arts in Paris and collaborators on other Gilded Age landmarks such as the New York Public Library, the elaborate 75-room house was the first residential home to feature a heating system.

★**Palm Beach
Lake Trail**   WALKING, CYCLING
(Royal Palm Way, at the Intracoastal Waterway) The first 'road' in Palm Beach ran along the Intracoastal Waterway, and provided a 5-mile paved path stretching from Worth Ave (in the south) to Indian Rd (in the north) for Flagler's hotel guests to stretch their legs and scope out the social scene. Nicknamed 'The Trail of Conspicuous Consumption,' it is sandwiched between two amazing views: Lake Worth lagoon to the west, and an unending series of mansions to the east.

**Palm Beach
Bike Shop**   CYCLING
(☑ 561-659-4583; www.palmbeachbicycle.com; Royal Poinciana Plaza, Cocoanut Row; ⊙9am-5:30pm Mon-Sat, 10am-5pm Sun) This shop rents out all manner of wheeled transportation, including bikes ($39 per day), skates ($39 per day) and scooters ($100 per day). Helmets cost $5 extra.

🛏 Sleeping & Eating

Bradley Park Hotel HOTEL **$$**
(☑ 561-832-7050; www.bradleyparkhotel.com; 2080 Sunset Ave; r $229, ste $329-359; P ❋ 🛜) The midrange Bradley (built in 1921) offers large, gold-hued rooms, some with original features from the era and characterful furniture. Rooms with kitchens feel like mini-apartments, and it's located just a short walk from the shops and restaurants of Royal Poinciana Way.

★ The Breakers RESORT **$$$**
(☑ 888-273-2537; www.thebreakers.com; 1 S County Rd; r/ste from $699/from $2000; P ❋ @ 🛜 🏖 🐕) 🏊 Originally built by Henry Flagler (in 1904, rooms cost $4 per night, including meals), today this 550-room resort sprawls across 140 acres and boasts a staff of 2000 plus, fluent in 56 languages. Just feet from the county's best snorkeling, this palace has two 18-hole golf courses, a mile of semi-private beach, four pools and the best brunch around.

Surfside Diner DINER, BREAKFAST **$**
(☑ 561-659-7495; 314 S County Rd; mains $8-12; ◷ 8am-3pm) This classy remake of a classic diner serves one of the better brunch options in town. Pancakes, chicken breakfast burritos and French toast are all tasty. For lunch there's a healthy offering of grilled cheese and tomato soup, BLTs, PB&Js and sliders.

★ Bũccan MODERN AMERICAN **$$**
(☑ 561-833-3450; www.buccanpalmbeach.com; 350 S County Rd; mains $18-45; ◷ 5pm-midnight Sun-Thu, 5pm-1am Fri & Sat) With its modern American menu and James Beard–nominated chef, Clay Conley, at the helm, Bũccan is the 'it' eatery in Palm Beach. Flavor-hop with a selection of small plates, including snapper ceviche and octopus tabbouleh, and move on to Moroccan chicken. Reservations recommended.

★ Café Boulud FRENCH **$$$**
(☑ 561-655-6060; www.thebraziliancourt.com; 301 Australian Ave; mains $16-46, fixed-price menu lunch/dinner $32/48; ◷ cafe 7am-10pm, bar to midnight) Created by renowned New York chef Daniel Boulud, the restaurant at the Brazilian Court is one of the few places in Palm Beach that truly justifies the sky-high prices. The warm dining room and terrace complements a rich menu of classic French and fusion dishes, all displaying Boulud's signature sophistication and subtlety.

🍷 Drinking & Entertainment

Leopard Lounge LOUNGE
(www.chesterfieldpb.com; 363 Cocoanut Row; ◷ 6:30pm-1am) This swanky gold, black and red place attracts a mature crowd and the occasional celeb (neither photos nor autograph hounds are allowed). Live music – a mix of jazz and classics – nightly.

Society of the Four Arts PERFORMING ARTS
(☑ 561-655-7226; www.fourarts.org; 2 Four Arts Plaza) The concert series here includes cabaret, the Palm Beach Symphony, chamber orchestras, string quartets and piano performances.

ℹ Information

Chamber of Commerce (☑ 561-655-3282; www.palmbeachchamber.com; 400 Royal Palm Way, Suite 106; ◷ 9am-5pm Mon-Fri) Excellent maps and racks of pamphlets. Consider downloading the *Palm Beach Guide* app.

ℹ Getting There & Around

Palm Tran (http://discover.pbcgov.org/palmtran; per ride $2, day pass $5) bus 41 covers the bulk of the island, from Lantana Rd to Sunrise Ave; transfer to bus 1 at Publix to go north or south along US 1. A single fare costs adult/child $2/1. To get to Palm Beach International Airport (p477) in West Palm Beach, take bus 41 to the downtown transfer and hop on bus 44.

Though it's a fairly compact city, the two major downtown neighborhoods, centered on Royal Poinciana Way and Worth Ave, are a fair hike apart.

West Palm Beach

When Henry Flagler decided to develop what is now West Palm Beach, he knew precisely what it would become: a working-class community for the labor force that would support his glittering resort town across the causeway. And so the fraternal twins were born – Palm Beach, considered the fairer of the two, and West Palm Beach, a cooler work-hard-play-hard community. West Palm has a surprisingly diverse collection of restaurants, friendly inhabitants (including a strong gay community) and a gorgeous waterway that always seems to reflect the perfect amount of starlight.

⊙ Sights & Activities

★ Norton Museum of Art   MUSEUM
(☑561-832-5196; www.norton.org; 1451 S Olive Ave; adult/child $12/5; ◷noon-5pm Tue-Sun) Undergoing a major renovation at the time of research (the design was done by architect Norman Foster), this is the largest art museum in Florida. It opened in 1941 to display the enormous art collection of industrialist Ralph Hubbard Norton and his wife Elizabeth. The Nortons' permanent collection of more than 5000 pieces (including works by Matisse, Warhol and O'Keeffe) is displayed alongside important Chinese, pre-Columbian Mexican and US Southwestern artifacts, plus some wonderful contemporary photography and regular traveling exhibitions.

South Florida Science
Center & Aquarium   MUSEUM
(☑561-832-1988; www.sfsciencecenter.org; 4801 Dreher Trail North; adult/child $16/11.50; ◷9am-5pm Mon-Fri, 10am-6pm Sat & Sun) A great little hands-on science center, aquarium and planetarium with weekend programs, traveling exhibits, a science trail, mini-golf and butterfly garden. On the last Friday of the month the museum stays open until 9pm so you can view the night sky from the county's only public observatory (weather permitting). Prices change according to the exhibition.

Peanut Island   ISLAND
(http://discover.pbcgov.org; ◷11am-4pm Thu-Sun) Plopped right off the northeastern corner of West Palm, Peanut Island was created in 1918 by dredging projects. Originally named Inlet Island, the spit was renamed for a peanut-oil-shipping operation that failed in 1946. The highlight is, however, the nuclear fallout bunker (☑561-723-2028; www.pbmm. info; adult/child $17/12; ◷11am-4pm Thu-Sun) that was constructed for John F Kennedy during the days of the Cuban missile crisis. These days, it's run by the Palm Beach Maritime Museum.

Rapids Water Park   WATER PARK
(☑561-842-8756; www.rapidswaterpark.com; 6566 North Military Trail, Riviera Beach; weekday/weekend $43/48; ◷10am-5pm) South Florida's largest water park features 30 action-packed acres of wet and wild rides. Don't let the squeals of fear and delight from the Big Thunder funnel put you off. Awesome fun. Parking costs an extra $10.

🛏 Sleeping

Hotel Biba   MOTEL $
(☑561-832-0094; www.hotelbiba.com; 320 Belvedere Rd; r $149-179; ❋ 🛜 ☷) With plain, white, slightly missing-a-small-something rooms, this place lacks a bit of color, but is one of the better (if only) budget options around. It's well located – only a block from the Intracoastal, and perched on the edge of the El Cid district. Suffice to say it's clean and fine if you just want a bed.

★ Grandview Gardens   B&B $$
(☑561-833-9023; www.grandview-gardens. com; 1608 Lake Ave; r from $229; 🅿 ❋ 🛜 ☷) Book a room at this intimate resort and you'll feel like a local in no time. Hidden in a tropical garden on Howard Park, the enormous suites with their wrought-iron and four-poster beds access the pool patio through French doors.

🍴 Eating

Johan's Jöe   CAFE $
(Swedish Coffee House & Cafe; www.johansjoe. com; 401 S Dixie Hwy; mains $9-13; ◷7am-6pm) If you can get past the menu's umlaut marks (placed jokingly here on English words), you'll find a delightful array of pastries and cakes. But the sweets are not the only winners; it's hard to go past the likes of pickled herrings and Swedish meatballs and authentic Swedish salads and sandwiches.

Darbster   VEGAN $$
(☑561-586-2622; www.darbster.com; 8020 S Dixie Hwy; mains $14-20; ◷5-10pm Tue-Fri, 10:30am-3pm & 5-10pm Sat, to 9pm Sun) This place is out on a limb in many respects: it's 5 miles south of town in an incongruous location by the S Dixie Hwy on the Palm Beach canal; the menu is 100% vegan; all profits go to a foundation for animal care; and it attracts everyone from Birkenstock-wearing hippies to diamond-wearing Palm Beachers.

★ Table 26 Degrees   MODERN AMERICAN $$$
(☑561-855-2660; www.table26palmbeach.com; 1700 S Dixie Hwy; mains $26-41; ◷11:30am-2pm Mon-Sat, 4:30-10pm Sun-Wed, 4:30-11pm Thu-Sat) Don't be put off by the price of this sophisticated restaurant. It is filled with locals, conversation and the clinking of glasses for good reason. They flock here for the bar (great happy hour 4:30pm to 6:30pm daily) plus the share plates and mains that are divided by water, land, field and hands (the latter covers fried chicken and burgers).

🍷 **Drinking & Entertainment**

The Pawn Shop Lounge CLUB
(www.pawnshopwpb.com; 219 Clematis St; cover $10; ☺5pm-3am Tue-Thu, to 4am Fri & Sat) This former Miami dance club and celebrity haunt is situated in the former Dr Feelgood venue. It features the familiar pawn shop trappings along with a life-sized vintage Ferris wheel and a DJ booth designed out of a Mack truck. DJs, dancers and light shows keep the party going until 3am while rivers of alcohol flow from the 175-ft-long bar.

HG Roosters GAY
(www.roosterswpb.com; 823 Belvedere Rd; ☺3pm-3am Sun-Thu, to 4am Fri & Sat) A mainstay of West Palm's thriving gay community, this bar has been offering wings, bingo and hot young male dancers since 1984.

Respectable Street LIVE MUSIC
(www.respectablestreet.com; 518 Clematis St) Respectables has kept South Florida jamming to great bands for two decades; it also organizes October's MoonFest, the city's best block party. Great DJs, strong drinks and a breezy chill-out patio are added bonuses. See if you can find the hole that the Red Hot Chili Peppers' Anthony Kiedis punched in the wall when they played here.

International Polo Club SPECTATOR SPORT
(☏561-204-5687; www.internationalpoloclub.com; 3667 120th Ave S, Wellington; general admission $10, lawn seating from $30; ☺Sun Jan-Apr) Between January and April the International Polo Club hosts 16 weeks of polo and glamour. As one of the finest polo facilities in the world, it not only attracts the most elite players but also the local and international glitterati who whoop it up in head-turning fashion over champagne brunches (tickets $125). Why not join the fun?

ⓘ **Information**

The *Palm Beach Post* (www.palmbeachpost.com) is the largest paper.

Discover The Palm Beaches Visitor Center
(☏561-233-3000; www.thepalmbeaches.com; 2195 Southern Blvd, Suite 400; ☺8:30am-5:30pm Mon-Fri) Extensive area information, maps and online guides.

ⓘ **Getting There & Around**

Palm Beach International Airport (PBI; ☏561-471-7420; www.pbia.org; 1000 James L Turnage Blvd) is served by most major airlines and car-rental companies. It's about a mile west of I-95 on Belvedere Rd. Palm Tran (p475) bus 44 runs between the airport, the train station and downtown ($2).

Greyhound (☏561-833-8534; www.greyhound.com; 215 S Tamarind Ave; ☺6am-10:45pm), **Tri-Rail** (☏800-875-7245; www.tri-rail.com; 203 S Tamarind Ave) and **Amtrak** (☏800-872-7245; www.amtrak.com; 209 S Tamarind Ave) share the same building: the historic Seaboard Train Station. Palm Tran serves the station with bus 44 (from the airport).

Once you're settled, driving and parking is a cinch. There's also a cute and convenient (and free!) trolley running between Clematis St and CityPlace starting at 11am.

The Everglades

There is no wilderness in America quite like the Everglades. Called the 'River of Grass' by Native American inhabitants, this is not just a wetland, or a swamp, or a lake, or a river, or a prairie, or a grassland – it is all of the above, twisted together into a series of soft horizons, long vistas, sunsets that stretch across your entire field of vision and the toothy grins of a healthy population of dinosaur-era reptiles.

When you watch anhinga flexing their wings before breaking into a corkscrew dive, or the slow, rhythmic flap of a great blue heron gliding over its domain, or the shimmer of sunlight on miles of untrammeled saw grass as it sets behind hunkering cypress domes, you'll get a glimpse of this park's quiet majesty. In a nation where natural beauty is measured by its capacity for drama, the Everglades subtly, contentedly flows on.

Everglades National Park

This vast **wilderness** (☏305-242-7700; www.nps.gov/ever; 40001 SR-9336, Homestead; vehicle pass $25, cyclists $8; ☺visitor center 9am-5pm; ♿), encompassing 1.5 million acres, is one of America's great natural treasures. As a major draw for visitors to South Florida, there's much to see and do. You can spy alligators basking in the noonday sun as herons stalk patiently through nearby waters in search of prey, go kayaking amid tangled mangrove canals and on peaceful lakes, or wade through murky knee-high waters amid cypress domes on a rough-and-ready 'slough slog'. There are sunrise strolls on boardwalks amid the awakening glimmers of birdsong, and moonlit glimpses of gators swimming gracefully along narrow channels in search of dinner. There's backcountry camping, bicycle tours and ranger-led activities that help bring the magic of this place to life. The biggest challenge is really just deciding where to begin.

There are three main entrances and three main areas of the park: one along the southeast edge near Homestead and Florida City (Ernest Coe section); another at the central-north side on the Tamiami Trail (Shark Valley section); and a third at the northwest shore (Gulf Coast section), past Everglades City. The Shark Valley and Gulf Coast sections of the park come one after the other in geographic succession, but the Ernest Coe area is entirely separate.

The admission fee covers the whole park, and is good for seven consecutive days. Because the Tamiami Trail is a public road, there's no admission to access national park sights along this highway, aside from Shark Valley. In the southern half of the park, one staffed checkpoint oversees access to all sights on the road between Ernest Coe down to Flamingo.

Three types of **backcountry campsites** (✐ 239-695-2945, 239-695-3311; www.nps.gov/ever/planyourvisit/backcamp.htm) are available: beach sites, on coastal shell beaches and in the 10,000 Islands; ground sites, which are basically mounds of dirt built up above the mangroves; and *chickees*, wooden platforms built above the waterline where you can pitch a free-standing (no spikes) tent. *Chickees*, which have toilets, are the most civilized – there's a serenity found in sleeping on what feels like a raft levitating above the water. Ground sites tend to be the most bug-infested.

If you're paddling around and see an island that looks pleasant for camping but isn't a designated campsite, beware – you may end up submerged when the tides change.

From November to April, backcountry camping permits cost $15, plus $2 per person per night; from May to October sites are free, but you must still self-register at Flamingo and Gulf Coast Visitor Centers or call ✐ 239-695-2945.

Some backcountry tips:

➡ Store food in a hand-sized, raccoon-proof container (available at gear stores).

➡ Bury your waste at least 10in below ground, but keep in mind some ground sites have hard turf.

➡ Use a backcountry stove to cook. Ground fires are only permitted at beach sites, and you can only burn dead or downed wood.

Load up on provisions before you enter the park. Homestead or Florida City are your best options if going into the Southern Everglades. If heading to the Tamiami Trail, plan to stock up in Miami – or the western suburbs.

❶ Getting There & Around

The largest subtropical wilderness in the continental USA is easily accessible from Miami. The Glades, which comprise the 80 southernmost miles of Florida, are bound by the Atlantic Ocean to the east and the Gulf of Mexico to the west. The Tamiami Trail (Hwy 41) goes east–west, parallel to the more northern (and less interesting) Alligator Alley (I-75).

You need a car to properly enter the Everglades and once you're in, wearing a good pair of walking boots is essential to penetrate the interior. Having a canoe or kayak helps as well; these can be rented from outfits inside and outside the park, or else you can seek out guided canoe and kayak tours. Bicycles are well suited to the flat roads of Everglades National Park, particularly in the area between Ernest Coe and Flamingo Point. Road shoulders in the park tend to be dangerously small.

Around the Everglades

Biscayne National Park

Just to the east of the Everglades is **Biscayne National Park** (✐ 305-230-1144, boat tours 786-335-3644; www.nps.gov/bisc; 9700 SW 328th St; boat tours adult/child $35/25; ◷ 7am-5:30pm), or the 5% of it that isn't underwater. In fact, a portion of the world's third-largest reef sits here off the coast of Florida, along with mangrove forests and the northernmost Florida Keys.

A bit shadowed by the Everglades, Biscayne requires a little extra planning, but you get a lot more reward for your effort. The offshore keys, accessible only by boat, offer pristine opportunities for camping. Generally summer and fall are the best times to visit the park; you'll want to snorkel when the water is calm. This is some of the best reef-viewing and snorkeling you'll find in the USA, outside Hawaii and nearby Key Largo.

Fortunately this unique 300-sq-mile park is easy to explore independently with a canoe, or via a boat tour.

Primitive camping (site per night $25, May-Sep free) is available on Elliott and Boca Chita Keys, though you'll need a boat to get there. No-see-ums (tiny flies) are invasive, and their bites are devastating. Make sure your tent is devoid of minuscule entry points.

ℹ Information

Dante Fascell Visitor Center (☑305-230-1144; www.nps.gov/bisc; 9700 SW 328th St; ⊙9am-5pm) Located at Convoy Point, this center shows a great introductory film for an overview of the park, and has maps, information and excellent ranger activities. The grounds around the center are a popular picnic spot on weekends and holidays, especially for families from Homestead. Also showcases local artwork.

ℹ Getting There & Away

To get here, you'll have to drive about 9 miles east of Homestead (the way is pretty well signposted) on SW 328th St (North Canal Dr) into a long series of green-and-gold flat fields and marsh.

Homestead & Florida City

Homestead and neighboring Florida City, 2 miles to the south, aren't of obvious appeal upon arrival. Part of the ever-expanding subdivisions of South Miami, this bustling corridor can feel like an endless strip of big-box shopping centers, fast-food joints, car dealerships and gas stations. However, look beneath the veneer and you'll find much more than meets the eye: strange curiosities like a 'castle' built single-handedly by one lovestruck immigrant, an animal rescue center for exotic species, a winery showcasing Florida's produce (hint: it's not grapes), an up-and-coming microbrewery, and one of the best farm stands in America. Not to mention that this area makes a great base for forays into the stunning Everglades National Park.

⊙ Sights & Activities

★**Coral Castle**　　　　　CASTLE
(☑305-248-6345; www.coralcastle.com; 28655 S Dixie Hwy; adult/senior/child $18/15/8; ⊙8am-6pm Sun-Thu, to 8pm Fri & Sat) 'You will be seeing unusual accomplishment,' reads the inscription on the rough-hewn quarried wall. That's an understatement. There is no greater temple to all that is weird and wacky about South Florida. The legend: a Latvian gets snubbed at the altar. Comes to the USA and settles in Florida. Handcarves, unseen,

in the dead of night, a monument to unrequited love.

Everglades Outpost　　WILDLIFE RESERVE
(☑305-562-8000; www.evergladesoutpost.org; 35601 SW 192nd Ave, Homestead; adult/child $12/8; ⊙10am-5:30pm Mon, Tue & Fri-Sun, by appointment Wed & Thu) The Everglades Outpost houses, feeds and cares for wild animals that have been seized from illegal traders, abused, neglected or donated by people who could not care for them. Residents of the outpost include a lemur, wolves, a black bear, a zebra, cobras, alligators and a pair of majestic tigers (one of whom was bought by an exotic dancer who thought she could incorporate it into her act). Your money goes into helping the outpost's mission.

Garls Coastal Kayaking Everglades　　　　KAYAKING
(www.garlscoastalkayaking.com; 19200 SW 344th St, Homestead; single/double kayak per day $40/55, half-/full-day tour $125/150) On the property of the **Robert Is Here** (☑305-246-1592; www.robertishere.com; juices $7-9; ⊙8am-7pm) 🥭 fruit stand, this outfitter leads highly recommended excursions into the Everglades. A full-day outing includes hiking (more of a wet walk/slog into the lush landscape of cypress domes), followed by kayaking in both the mangroves and in Florida Bay, and, time permitting, a night walk.

🛏 Sleeping & Eating

★**Everglades International Hostel**　　　　HOSTEL $
(☑305-248-1122; www.evergladeshostel.com; 20 SW 2nd Ave, Florida City; camping per person $18, dm $30, d $61-75, ste $125-225; P❄🕸🛜🏊) Located in a cluttered, comfy 1930s boarding house, this friendly hostel has good-value dorms, private rooms and 'semi-privates' (you have an enclosed room within the dorms and share a bathroom with dorm residents). The creatively configured backyard is the best feature.

Gator Grill　　　　AMERICAN $
(☑786-243-0620; 36650 SW 192nd Ave, Homestead; mains $9-16; ⊙11am-6:30pm) A handy pit stop before or after visiting the Everglades National Park, the Gator Grill is a white shack with picnic tables, where you can munch on all manner of alligator dishes. There are gator tacos, gator stir-fry, gator kebabs and straight-up fried alligator served in a basket.

❶ Information

There are several info centers where you can get tips on attractions, lodging and dining.

Tropical Everglades Visitor Association (160 N 1st St, Florida City; ⊙8am-5pm Mon-Sat, 10am-2pm Sun)

Chamber of Commerce (☑305-247-2332; www.southdadechamber.org; 455 N Flagler Ave, Homestead; ⊙9am-5pm Mon-Fri)

❶ Getting There & Away

Homestead runs a free weekend **trolley bus service** (☑305-224-4457; www.cityofhomestead. com; ⊙Sat & Sun Dec-Apr), which takes visitors from Losner Park (downtown Homestead) out to the **Royal Palm Visitor Center** (☑305-242-7700; www.nps.gov/ever; State Rd 9336; ⊙9am-4:15pm) in Everglades National Park. It also runs between Losner Park and Biscayne National Park. Call for the latest departure times.

Tamiami Trail

Calle Ocho, in Miami's Little Havana, happens to be the eastern end of the Tamiami Trail/Hwy 41, which cuts through the Everglades to the Gulf of Mexico. So go west, young traveler, along Hwy 41, a few dozen miles and several different worlds away from the city where the heat is on. This trip leads you into the northern edges of the park, past long landscapes of flooded forest, gambling halls, swamp-buggy tours, food shacks and other Old Florida accoutrements.

As you head west you'll see fields and fields of pine forest and billboards advertising swamp tours. Airboat tours are an old-school way of seeing the Everglades (and there is something to be said for getting a tour from a raging Skynyrd fan with killer tatts and better camo), but there are other ways of exploring the park as well.

◉ Sights & Activities

Fakahatchee Strand Preserve PARK
(☑239-695-4593; www.floridastateparks.org/faka hatcheestrand; 137 Coastline Dr, Copeland; vehicle/pedestrian/bicycle $3/2/2; ⊙8am-sunset; [P][🚻]) 🚶 The Fakahatchee Strand, besides having a fantastic name, also houses a 20-mile by 5-mile estuarine wetland that could have emerged directly out of the *Jurassic Park* franchise. A 2000ft boardwalk traverses this wet and wild wonderland, where panthers still stalk their prey amid the black waters. While it's unlikely you'll spot any panthers, there's a great chance you'll see a large variety of blooming orchids, bird life and reptiles ranging in size from tiny skinks to grinning alligators.

Shark Valley Tram Tour TOURS
(☑305-221-8455; www.sharkvalleytramtours.com; adult/child under 12yr/senior $25/19/12.75; ⊙departures 9:30am, 11am, 2pm, 4pm May-Dec, 9am-4pm Jan-Apr hourly on the hour) This excellent two-hour tour runs along a 15-mile asphalt trail allowing you to see copious amounts of alligators in the winter months. Tours are narrated by knowledgeable park rangers who give a fascinating overview of the Everglades.

❶ Information

Shark Valley Visitor Center (☑305-221-8776; www.nps.gov/ever/planyourvisit/svdirections. htm; national park entry per vehicle/bicycle/pedestrian $25/8/8; ⊙9am-5pm) A good place to pick up information about the Everglades, including trails, wildlife watching and free ranger-led activities.

Everglades City

On the edge of Chokoloskee Bay, you'll find an Old Florida fishing village of raised houses,

---

DETOUR: LOOP ROAD

The 24-mile-long Loop Rd, off Tamiami Trail (Hwy 41), offers some unique sites. One: the homes of the **Miccosukee**, some of which have been considerably expanded by gambling revenue. You'll see some traditional *chickee*-style huts and some trailers with massive add-on wings that are bigger than the original trailer – all seem to have shiny new pickup trucks parked out front. Two: great pull-offs for viewing flooded forests, where egrets that look like pterodactyls perch in the trees, and alligators lurk in the depths below. Three: houses with large Confederate flags and 'Stay off my property' signs; these homes are as much a part of the landscape as the swamp. And four: the short, pleasantly jungly **Tree Snail Hammock Nature Trail**. Though unpaved, the graded road is in good shape and fine for 2WD vehicles. True to its name, the road loops right back onto the Tamiami; expect a leisurely jaunt on the Loop to add an hour or two to your trip.

turquoise water and scattershot emerald-green mangrove islands. 'City' is an ambitious name for Everglades City, but this is a friendly fishing town where you can easily lose yourself for a day or three. You'll find some intriguing vestiges of the past here, including an excellent regional museum.

Hwy 29 runs south through town onto the small, peaceful residential island of Chokoloskee, which has some pretty views over the watery wilderness of the 10,000 Islands. You can arrange boating excursions from either Everglades City or Chokoloskee to explore this pristine environment.

⊙ Sights & Activities

★ Museum of the Everglades   MUSEUM
(☑ 239-695-0008;   www.evergladesmuseum.org; 105 W Broadway; ⊙ 9am-4pm Mon-Sat; P) FREE For a break from the outdoors, don't miss this small museum run by kindhearted volunteers who have a wealth of knowledge on the region's history. Located in the town's former laundry house, the collection delves into human settlement in the area from the early pioneers of the 1800s to the boom days of the 1920s and its tragic moments (Hurricane Donna devastated the town in 1960), and subsequent transformation into the quiet backwater of today.

10,000 Islands   ISLAND
One of the best ways to experience the serenity of the Everglades – somehow desolate yet lush, tropical and forbidding – is by paddling the network of waterways that skirt the northwest portion of the park. The 10,000 Islands consist of many (but not really 10,000) tiny islands and a mangrove swamp that hugs the southwestern-most border of Florida.

Everglades Adventures   CANOEING
(☑ 877-567-0679; www.evergladesadventures.com; 107 Camellia St; 3/4hr tours from $89/99, canoe/ kayak rental per day from $35/49) ✐ For a real taste of the Everglades, nothing beats getting out on the water. This highly recommended outfitter offers a range of half-day kayak tours, from sunrise paddles to twilight trips through mangroves that return under a sky full of stars.

🛏 Sleeping & Eating

Outdoor Resorts of Chokoloskee   MOTEL $
(☑ 239-695-2881;   www.outdoorresortsofchokoloskee.com; 150 Smallwood Dr, Chokoloskee; r $119;

❉ ❉) At the northern end of Chokoloskee Island, this good-value place is a big draw for its extensive facilities, including several swimming pools, hot tubs, tennis and shuffleboard courts, a fitness center and boat rentals. The fairly basic motel-style rooms have kitchenettes and a back deck overlooking the marina.

Everglades City Motel   MOTEL $$
(☑ 239-695-4224; www.evergladescitymotel.com; 310 Collier Ave; r $150-250; P ❉ ☎) With large renovated rooms that have all the mod cons (flat-screen TVs, fridge, coffeemaker) and friendly staff that can hook you up with boat tours, this motel provides good value for those looking to spend some time near the 10,000 Islands.

★ Havana Cafe   LATIN AMERICAN $$
(☑ 239-695-2214;   www.havanacafeoftheeverglades.com; 191 Smallwood Dr, Chokoloskee; mains lunch $10-19, dinner $22-30; ⊙ 7am-3pm Mon-Thu, to 8pm Fri & Sat, closed mid-Apr–mid-Oct) The Havana Cafe is famed far and wide for its deliciously prepared seafood served up with Latin accents. Lunch favorites include stone-crab enchiladas, blackened grouper with rice and beans, and a decadent Cuban sandwich. The outdoor dining amid palm trees and vibrant bougainvillea – not to mention the incredibly friendly service – adds to the appeal.

Oyster House   SEAFOOD $$
(☑ 239-695-2073; www.oysterhouserestaurant.com; 901 Copeland Ave; mains lunch $12-18, dinner $19-30; ⊙ 11am-9pm Sun-Thu, to 10pm Fri & Sat; ✐ ❖) Besides serving the Everglades staples of excellent seafood (oysters, crab, grouper, cobia, lobster), this buzzing, family-run spot serves up alligator dishes (tacos, jambalaya, fried platters) and simpler baskets (burgers, fried seafood), plus not-to-be-missed desserts. The cabin-like interior is decorated with vintage knickknacks and taxidermy, which might make you feel like you're in the deep woods.

ⓘ Information

Everglades Area Chamber of Commerce
(☑ 239-695-3941; cnr Hwy 41 & Hwy 29; ⊙ 9am-4pm) General information about the region is available here.

ⓘ Getting There & Away

There is no public transit out this way. If driving, it's a fairly straight 85-mile drive west from Miami. The trip takes about 1¾ hours.

FLORIDA AROUND THE EVERGLADES

Florida Keys

If Florida is a state apart from the USA, the Keys are islands apart from Florida – in other words, it's different down here. This is a place where those who reject everyday life on the mainland escape. What do they find? About 113 mangrove-and-sandbar islands where the white sun melts over tight fists of deep green mangroves; long, gloriously soft mudflats and tidal bars; water as teal as Arizona turquoise; and a bunch of people often like themselves: freaks, geeks and lovable weirdos all.

Key West is still defined by its motto – One Human Family – an ideal that equals a tolerant, accepting ethos where anything goes and life is always a party (or at least a hungover day after). The color scheme: watercolor pastels cooled by breezes on a sunset-kissed Bahamian porch. Welcome to the End of the USA.

ℹ Information

The Monroe County Tourist Development Council's Florida Keys & Key West Visitors Bureau runs an excellent website (www.fla-keys.com), which is packed with information on everything the Keys has to offer.

Check www.keysnews.com for good daily online news and information about the islands.

ℹ Getting There & Away

Getting here can be half the fun – or, if you're unlucky, a whopping dose of frustration. Imagine a tropical-island hop, from one bar-studded mangrove islet to the next, via one of the most remarkable roads in the world: the Overseas Hwy (Hwy 1). On a good day, driving along the Overseas with the windows down – the wind in your face and the twin sisters of Florida Bay and the Atlantic stretching on either side – is the US road trip in tropical perfection. On a bad day, you end up sitting in gridlock behind some guy who is riding a midlife-crisis Harley.

Greyhound (www.greyhound.com) buses serve all Keys destinations along Hwy 1 and depart from Downtown Miami and Key West; you can pick up a bus along the way by standing on the Overseas Hwy and flagging one down. If you fly into Fort Lauderdale or Miami, the **Keys Shuttle** (☑ 888-765-9997; www.keysshuttle. com) provides door-to-door service to most of the Keys ($70/80/90 to the Upper and Middle Keys/Lower Keys/Key West). Reserve at least a day in advance.

Key Largo

We're not going to lie: Key Largo (both the name of the town and the island it's on) is slightly underwhelming at a glance. 'Under' is the key word, as its main sights are under the water, rather than above. As you drive onto the islands, Key Largo resembles a long line of low-lying hammock and strip development. But that's just from the highway: head down a side road and duck into this warm little bar, or that converted Keys plantation house, and the island idiosyncrasies become more pronounced.

The 33-mile-long Largo, which starts at Mile Marker 106, is the longest island in the Keys, and those 33 miles have attracted a lot of marine life, all accessible from the biggest concentration of dive sites in the islands. The town of Tavernier (Mile Marker 93) is just south of the town of Key Largo.

◎ Sights & Activities

John Pennekamp Coral
Reef State Park STATE PARK
(☑ 305-451-6300; www.pennekamppark.com; Mile 102.6 oceanside; car with 1/2 people $4.50/9, cyclist or pedestrian $2.50; ☺ 8am-sunset, aquarium to 5pm; P 🖽) ✐ John Pennekamp has the singular distinction of being the first underwater park in the USA. There's 170 acres of dry parkland here and over 48,000 acres (75 sq miles) of wet: the vast majority of the protected area is the ocean. Before you get out in that water, be sure to take in some pleasant beaches and stroll over the nature trails.

Laura Quinn Wild
Bird Sanctuary WILDLIFE RESERVE
(☑ 305-852-4486; www.keepthemflying.org; 93600 Overseas Hwy, Mile 93.6; donations accepted; ☺ sunrise-sunset; P 🖽) ✐ This 7-acre sanctuary serves as a protected refuge for a wide variety of injured birds. A boardwalk leads through various enclosures where you can learn a bit about some of the permanent residents – those unable to be released back in the wild. The species here include masked boobies, great horned owls, green herons, brown pelicans, double-crested cormorants and others. Keep walking along the path to reach a nice vista of Florida Bay.

African Queen BOATING
(☑ 305-451-8080; www.africanqueenflkeys.com; Key Largo Holiday Inn, 99701 Overseas Hwy; canal cruise/dinner cruise $49/89) The steamboat

used in the 1951 movie starring Humphrey Bogart and Katharine Hepburn has been restored to its former splendor, and you can relive the movie aboard the tiny vessel on a canal or dinner cruise. If you behave better than Hepburn's character, the captain might even let you take the helm for a bit.

Garl's Coastal Kayaking
ECOTOUR

(☑305-393-3223; www.garlscoastalkayaking.com; 4hr tours adult/child $75/50, single/double kayak hire per day $40/55) 🕿 Garl's is an excellent ecotour operator that gets customers into the Everglades backcountry and mangrove islets of Florida Bay via kayak and canoe. It also provides reasonable equipment rentals.

🛏 Sleeping & Eating

Hilton Key Largo Resort
HOTEL $$

(☑305-852-5553; www.keylargoresort.com; 102 bayside; r/ste from $200/280; P 🕿 🌊) This Hilton has a ton of character. Folks just seem to get all laid-back when lounging in clean, designer rooms outfitted in blues and greens with balconies overlooking the water. The grounds are enormous and include an artificial waterfall-fed pool and frontage to a rather large stretch of private white-sand beach. Book online for the best rates.

Jules' Undersea Lodge
HOTEL $$$

(☑305-451-2353; www.jul.com; 51 Shoreland Dr, Mile 103.2 oceanside; s/d/tr $675/800/1050) There's lots of talk about underwater hotels getting built in Dubai and Fiji, but as of writing, Jules' Undersea Lodge is still the only place in the world outside of a submarine where you and your significant other can join the 'five-fathom club' (we're not elaborating). Once a research station, this module has been converted into a delightfully cheesy Keys motel, but wetter.

DJ's Diner
AMERICAN $

(☑305-451-2999; 99411 Overseas Hwy; mains $8-15; ⊙7am-3pm; P 🕿 🕌) You're greeted by a mural of Humphrey Bogart, James Dean *and* Marilyn Monroe – that's a lot of Americana. It's all served with a heapin' helpin' of diner faves amid vinyl-boothed ambience. Breakfast is a big draw with fluffy omelets, eggs Benedict and waffles.

Fish House
SEAFOOD $$

(☑305-451-4665; www.fishhouse.com; Mile 102.4 oceanside; mains lunch $12-21, dinner $21-30; ⊙11:30am-10pm; P 🕌) The Fish House delivers on the promise of its title – very good fish, bought whole from local fishers and

prepared fried, broiled, jerked, blackened or chargrilled. Because the Fish House only uses fresh fish, the menu changes daily based on what is available.

Islamorada

Islamorada (eye-luh-murr-*ah*-da) is also known as 'The Village of Islands.' Doesn't that sound pretty? Well, it really is. This little string of pearls (well, keys) – Plantation, Upper and Lower Matecumbe, Shell and Lignumvitae (lignum-*vite*-ee) – shimmers as one of the prettiest stretches of the islands. This is where the scrubby mangrove is replaced by unbroken horizons of ocean and sky, one perfect shade of blue mirroring the other. Islamorada stretches across some 20 miles, from Mile Marker 90 to 74.

⊙ Sights & Activities

★Florida Keys History of Diving Museum
MUSEUM

(☑305-664-9737; www.divingmuseum.org; Mile 83; adult/child $12/6; ⊙10am-5pm; P 🕌) You can't miss the diving museum – it's the building with the enormous mural of whale sharks on the side. The journey into the undersea covers 4000 years, with fascinating pieces like the 1797 Klingert's copper kettle, a whimsical room devoted to Jules Verne's Captain Nemo, massive deep-diving suits and an exquisite display of diving helmets from around the world. These imaginative galleries reflect the charming quirks of the Keys.

Windley Key Fossil Reef Geological State Site
STATE PARK

(☑305-664-2540; www.floridastateparks.org/windleykey; Mile 85.5 oceanside; admission/tour $2.50/2; ⊙8am-5pm Thu-Mon) To get his railroad built across the islands, Henry Flagler had to quarry out some sizable chunks of the Keys. The best evidence of those efforts can be found at this former quarry-turned-state park. Windley has leftover quarry machinery scattered along an 8ft former quarry wall, with fossilized evidence of brain and staghorn coral embedded right in the rock. The wall offers a cool (and rare) public peek into the stratum of coral that forms the substrate of the Keys.

★Robbie's Marina
BOATING

(☑305-664-8070; www.robbies.com; Mile 77.5 bayside; kayak & stand-up paddleboard rentals $45-80; ⊙9am-8pm; 🕌) More than a boat launch, Robbie's is a local flea market, tacky tourist shop, sea pen for tarpons (massive fish) and jump-off point for fishing expeditions, all wrapped into one driftwood-laced compound. Boat-rental and tour options are also available. The best reason to visit is to escape the mayhem and hire a kayak for a peaceful paddle through nearby mangroves, hammocks and lagoons.

🛏 Sleeping & Eating

Conch On Inn
MOTEL $

(☏ 305-852-9309; www.conchoninn.com; 103 Caloosa St, Mile 89.5; r $100-180; ⓟ🛜) A motel popular with yearly snowbirds, Conch On Inn has simple but cheerfully painted rooms that are clean, comfortable and well equipped. The waterfront deck is a fine spot to unwind – and look for manatees; up to 14 have been spotted off the dock here!

Lime Tree Bay Resort Motel
MOTEL $$

(☏ 305-664-4740; www.limetreebayresort.com; Mile 68.5 bayside; r $180-360; ✴🛜🏊) A plethora of hammocks and lawn chairs provides front-row seats for the spectacular sunsets at this 2.5-acre waterfront hideaway. The rooms are comfortably set, the best with balconies overlooking the water. The extensive facilities include use of tennis courts, bikes, kayaks and stand-up paddleboards.

Bad Boy Burrito
MEXICAN $

(☏305-509-7782; www.badboyburrito.com/isl amorada; 103 Mastic St, Mile 81.8 bayside; mains $8-15; ⊙10am-6pm Mon-Sat; ✎) Tucked away in a tiny plaza among a gurgling fountain, orchids and swaying palms, Bad Boy Burrito whips up superb fish tacos and its namesake burritos – with quality ingredients (skirt steak, duck confit, zucchini and squash) and all the fixings (shaved cabbage, chipotle mayo, housemade salsa). Top it off with a hibiscus tea and some chips and guacamole.

★ Lazy Days
SEAFOOD $$

(☏ 305-664-5256; www.lazydaysislamorada.com; 79867 Overseas Hwy, oceanside; mains $18-34; ✎🖥) One of Islamorada's culinary icons, Lazy Days has a stellar reputation for its fresh seafood plates. Start off with a conch chowder topped with a little sherry (provided), before moving on to a decadent hogfish Poseidon (fish topped with shrimp, scallops and key lime butter) or a straight-up boiled seafood platter (half lobster, shrimp, catch of the day and other delicacies).

Marathon

Marathon sits right on the halfway point between Key Largo and Key West, and it's a good place to stop on a road trip across the islands. It's perhaps the most 'developed' key outside Key West (that's really pushing the definition of the word 'developed') in the sense that it has large shopping centers and a population of over 8000. Then again it's still a place where exiles from the mainland fish, booze it up and have a good time, so while Marathon is more family-friendly than Key West, it's hardly G-rated.

🛏 Sleeping & Eating

Seascape Motel & Marina
MOTEL $$

(☏ 305-743-6212; www.seascapemotelandmarina. com; 1075 75th St Ocean E, btwn Mile 51 & 52; r $250-450; ⓟ✴🛜🏊) The classy, understated luxury in this B&B manifests in its 12 rooms, all of which have a different feel – from old-fashioned cottage to sleek boutique. It has a waterfront pool, kayaks and stand-up paddleboards for guests to use, and its secluded setting will make you feel like you've gotten away from it all.

Tranquility Bay
RESORT $$$

(☏ 305-289-0667; www.tranquilitybay.com; Mile 48.5 bayside; r $340-700; ⓟ✴🛜🏊) If you're serious about going upscale, you should book in here. Tranquility Bay is a massive condo-hotel resort with plush townhouses, high-thread-count sheets and all-in-white chic. The grounds are enormous and activity-filled; they really don't want you to leave.

★ Keys Fisheries
SEAFOOD $$

(☏ 866-743-4353; www.keysfisheries.com; 3502 Louisa St; mains $12-27; ⊙11am-9pm; ⓟ🖥) The lobster Reuben is the stuff of legend. Sweet, chunky, creamy – so good you'll be daydreaming about it afterward. But you can't go wrong with any of the excellent seafood here, all served with sass. Expect pleasant levels of seagull harassment as you dine on a working waterfront.

Lower Keys

The people of the Lower Keys vary between winter escapees and native Conchs. Some local families have been Keys castaways for generations, and there is somewhat of a more insular feel than other parts of the Overseas Hwy. It's an odd contrast: the islands get at their most isolated, rural and quintessentially 'Keez-y' before opening onto (relatively) cosmopolitan, heterogeneous and free-spirited Key West.

People aside, the big draw in the lower Keys is nature. You'll find the loveliest state park in the Keys here, and one of its rarest species. For paddlers, there is a great mangrove wilderness to explore in a photogenic and pristine environment.

The Bahia Honda State Park (☑ 305-872-3210; www.bahiahondapark.com; Mile 37; car $4-8, cyclist & pedestrian $2.50; ☺ 8am-sunset; 🚹), with its long, white-sand (and at times seaweed-strewn) beach, named Sandspur Beach by locals, is the big attraction in these parts. As Keys beaches go, this one is probably the best natural stretch of sand in the island chain. There's also the novel experience of walking on the old Bahia Honda Rail Bridge, which offers nice views of the surrounding islands. Heading out on kayaking adventures (from $12/36 per hour/half day) is another great way to spend a sun-drenched afternoon.

Key West

Key West is the far frontier, edgier and more eccentric than the other keys, and also far more captivating. At its heart, this 7-sq-mile island feels like a beautiful tropical oasis, where the moonflowers bloom at night and the classical Caribbean homes are so sad and romantic it's hard not to sigh at them.

While Key West has obvious allure, it's not without its contradictions. On one side of the road, there are literary festivals, Caribbean villas, tropical dining rooms and expensive art galleries. On the other, an S&M fetishist parade, frat boys passing out on the sidewalk and grizzly bars filled with bearded burnouts. With all that in mind, it's easy to find your groove in this setting, no matter where your interests lie.

As in other parts of the Keys, nature plays a starring role here, with some breathtaking sunsets – cause for nightly celebration down on Mallory Sq.

⊙ Sights

★ **Museum of Art &**
History at the Custom House MUSEUM
(☑ 305-295-6616; www.kwahs.com; 281 Front St; adult/child $10/5; ☺ 9:30am-4:30pm) Those wanting to learn a bit about Key West history shouldn't miss this excellent museum at the end of the road. Among the highlights:

photographs and archival footage from the building of the ambitious Overseas Hwy (and the hurricane that killed 400 people), a model of the ill-fated USS *Maine* (sunk during the Spanish-American War) and the Navy's role in Key West (once the largest employer), and exhibits on the 'wreckers' of Key West, who made their fortune scavenging sunken treasure ships.

★ **Mallory Square** SQUARE
(www.mallorysquare.com; 🚹) Take all those energies, subcultures and oddities of Keys life and focus them into one torchlit, family-friendly (but playfully edgy), sunset-enriched street party. The child of all these raucous forces is Mallory Sq, one of the greatest shows on Earth. It begins in the hours leading up to dusk, the sinking sun a signal to bring on the madness. Watch a dog walk a tightrope, a man swallow fire, and British acrobats tumble and sass each other.

Duval Street AREA
Key West locals have a love-hate relationship with the most famous road in Key West (if not the Keys). Duval, Old Town Key West's main strip, is a miracle mile of booze, tacky everything and awful behavior. But it's fun. The 'Duval Crawl' is one of the wildest pub crawls in the country. The mix of neon drink, drag shows, T-shirt kitsch, local theaters, art studios and boutiques is more charming than jarring.

Hemingway House HOUSE
(☑ 305-294-1136; www.hemingwayhome.com; 907 Whitehead St; adult/child $14/6; ☺ 9am-5pm) Key West's biggest darling, Ernest Hemingway, lived in this gorgeous Spanish Colonial house from 1931 to 1940. Papa moved here in his early 1930s with wife No 2, a *Vogue* fashion editor and (former) friend of wife No 1 (he left the house when he ran off with wife No 3). *The Short Happy Life of Francis Macomber* and *The Green Hills of Africa* were produced here, as well as many six-toed cats, whose descendants basically run the grounds.

🏃 Activities

Dive Key West DIVING
(☑ 305-296-3823; www.divekeywest.com; 3128 N Roosevelt Blvd; snorkel/scuba from $60/75) Largest dive facility on the island, offering morning, afternoon and night dives. Wreck-diving trips cost $145 with all equipment and air provided (it's $160 with a wetsuit).

👉 Tours

Old Town Trolley Tours
TOURS

(📞855-623-8289; www.trolleytours.com; adult/child/senior $32/11/29; ⊙ tours 9am-4:30pm; 👤) These tours are a great introduction to the city. The 90-minute, hop-on, hop-off narrated tram tour starts at Mallory Sq and makes a loop around the whole city, with 12 stops along the way. Trolleys depart every 15 to 30 minutes from 9am to 4:30pm daily. The narration is hokey, but you'll get a good overview of Key West history.

🎊 Festivals & Events

Womenfest
LGBT

(www.womenfest.com; ⊙Sep) One of North America's biggest lesbian celebrations, Womenfest is four days of merrymaking, with pool parties, art shows, roller derby, drag brunches, sunset sails, flag football, and a tattoo and moustache bicycle ride. It's great fun, with thousands descending on Key West from all corners of the USA and beyond.

⭐ Fantasy Fest
CULTURAL

(www.fantasyfest.net; ⊙late Oct) Akin to New Orleans' riotous Mardi Gras revelry, Fantasy Fest is 10 days of burlesque parties, parades, street fairs, concerts and loads of costumed events. Bars and inns get competitive about decorating their properties, and everyone gets decked out in the most outrageous costumes they can cobble together (or get mostly naked with daring body paint).

🛏 Sleeping

Key West Youth Hostel & Seashell Motel
HOSTEL $$

(📞305-296-5719; www.keywesthostel.com; 718 South St; dm $55, d $120-240; P❄🛜) This place isn't winning any design awards, but the staff are kind, and it's one of the only lower-priced choices on the island. The dorms and motel rooms have plain white tile floors, though the cheery paint job in some rooms (yellow or blue and white) somewhat breaks the monotony. The back patio is a fine place to meet other travelers.

Casablanca Key West
GUESTHOUSE $$

(📞305-296-0815; www.keywestcasablanca.com; 900 Duval St; r $180-400; ❄🛜🏊) On the quieter end of Duval St, the Casablanca is a friendly eight-room guesthouse with a delightful tropical elegance. The inn, once a private house, was built in 1898 and hosted a few luminaries over the years, including Humphrey Bogart who stayed here in 1937. The rooms are bright, with polished wood floors and comfy beds; and some have little balconies.

Saint Hotel
BOUTIQUE HOTEL $$$

(📞305-294-3200; www.thesainthotelkeywest.com; 417 Eaton St; r $360-700; ❄🛜🏊) Despite its proximity to Duval St, the Saint feels like a world removed with its plush rooms, chic minimalist lobby, photogenic pool with small cascading waterfall, and artfully designed bar. The best rooms have balconies overlooking the pool.

🍴 Eating

Pierogi Polish Market
EASTERN EUROPEAN $

(📞305-292-0464; 1008 White St; mains $5-11; ⊙pierogi counter 11am-7pm Mon-Sat, shop 10am-8pm Mon-Sat, noon-6pm Sun; P🅿) The Keys have an enormous seasonal population of temporary workers largely drawn from Central and Eastern Europe. This is where those workers can revisit the motherland, via pierogies, dumplings, blinis and a great sandwich selection. Although it's called a Polish market, there's food here that caters to Hungarians, Czechs and Russians (among others).

Garbo's Grill
FUSION $

(www.garbosgrillkw.com; 409 Caroline St; mains $10-14; ⊙11am-10pm Mon-Sat) Just off the beaten path, Garbo's whips up delicious tacos with creative toppings like mango ginger habanero-glazed shrimp, Korean barbecue, and fresh mahimahi with all the fixings, as well as gourmet burgers and hot dogs. It's served out of a sleek Airstream trailer, which faces onto a shaded brick patio dotted with outdoor tables.

The Café
VEGETARIAN $$

(📞305-296-5515; www.thecafekw.com; 509 Southard St; mains $12-22; ⊙9am-10pm; 🅿) The oldest vegetarian spot in Key West is a sunny luncheonette by day that morphs into a buzzing, low-lit eating and drinking spot by night. The cooking is outstanding, with an eclectic range of dishes: Thai curry stir-fries, Italian veggie meatball subs, pizza with shaved brussels sprouts, and a famous veggie burger.

⭐ Thirsty Mermaid
SEAFOOD $$

(📞305-204-4828; www.thirstymermaidkeywest.com; 521 Fleming St; mains $12-28; ⊙11am-11:30pm; 🅿) Aside from having a great name, the pint-sized Thirsty Mermaid deserves high marks for its outstanding seafood and stylish but easygoing atmosphere. The menu is a celebration of culinary treasures from the sea, with a raw bar of oysters, ceviche, middleneck clams and even caviar. Among the main courses, seared diver scallops or togarashi-spiced tuna with jasmine rice are outstanding.

★ **Blue Heaven**   AMERICAN $$$
(☑ 305-296-8666; www.blueheavenkw.com; 729 Thomas St; mains breakfast & lunch $10-17, dinner $22-35; ⊙ 8am-10:30pm; ☑) Proof that location is *nearly* everything, this is one of the quirkiest venues on an island of oddities. Customers (and free-roaming fowl) flock to dine in the ramshackle, tropical plant-filled garden where Hemingway once officiated boxing matches. This place gets packed with customers who wolf down delectable breakfasts (blueberry pancakes) and Keys cuisine with French touches (like yellowtail snapper with citrus beurre blanc).

🍷 Drinking & Entertainment

★ **Green Parrot**   BAR
(☑ 305-294-6133; www.greenparrot.com; 601 Whitehead St; ⊙ 10am-4am) The oldest bar on an island of bars, this rogues' cantina opened in the late 19th century and hasn't closed yet. Its ramshackle interior – complete with local artwork littering the walls and a parachute stretched across the ceiling – only adds to the atmosphere, as does the colorful crowd, obviously out for a good time.

Captain Tony's Saloon   BAR
(☑ 305-294-1838; www.capttonyssaloon.com; 428 Greene St; ⊙ 10am-2am) Propagandists would have you believe the nearby megabar complex of Sloppy Joe's was Hemingway's original bar, but the physical place where the old man drank was right here, the original Sloppy Joe's location (before it was moved onto Duval St and into frat-boy hell). Hemingway's third wife (a journalist sent to profile Papa) seduced him in this very bar.

Irish Kevin's   BAR
(☑ 305-292-1262; www.irishkevins.com; 211 Duval St; ⊙ 10am-3:30am) One of the most popular megabars on Duval, Kevin's has a pretty good entertainment formula pinned down: nightly live acts that are a cross between a folk singer, radio shock jock and pep-rally cheerleader. The crowd consistently goes wild for acoustic covers of favorites from 1980

onward mixed with boozy, Lee Greenwood-esque patriotic exhortations.

La Te Da   CABARET
(☑ 305-296-6706; www.lateda.com; 1125 Duval St; ⊙ shows 8:30pm) While the outside bar is where locals gather for mellow chats over beer, you can catch high-quality drag acts – big names come here from around the country – upstairs at the fabulous Crystal Room on weekends (admission $26). More low-key cabaret acts grace the downstairs lounge.

ℹ️ Information

Citizen (www.keysnews.com) A well-written, oft-amusing daily.
Key West Chamber of Commerce (☑ 305-294-2587; www.keywestchamber.org; 510 Greene St; ⊙ 9am-6pm) An excellent source of information.
Key Wester (www.thekeywester.com) Restaurant reviews and upcoming events.

ℹ️ Getting Around

Once you're in Key West, the best way to get around is by bicycle (rentals from the Duval St area, hotels and hostels cost from $10 a day). For transportation within the Duval St area, the free Duval Loop shuttle (www.carfreekeywest.com/duval-loop) runs from 6pm to midnight.

Other options include **Key West Transit** (☑ 305-600-1455; www.kwtransit.com; day pass $4-8), with color-coded buses running about every 15 minutes; mopeds, which generally cost from $35 per day ($60 for a two-seater); or the open-sided electric tourist cars, aka 'Conch cruisers,' which travel at 35mph and cost about $140/200 for a four-seater/six-seater per day.

A&M Scooter Rentals (☑ 305-896-1921; www.amscooterskeywest.com; 523 Truman Ave; bicycle/scooter/electric car per day from $10/35/140; ⊙ 9am-7pm) rents out scooters and bicycles, as well as open-sided electric cars that can seat from two to six, and offers free delivery.

Parking can be tricky in town. There's a free parking lot on Fort St off Truman Ave.

ATLANTIC COAST

Florida's northern Atlantic Coast is an exurban riviera for north Florida and the Deep South, a land of long beaches shadowed under tall condo complexes and seaside mansions. Heading from south to north, you'll pass the exhaust pipes and biker bars of Daytona Beach, continue through mellow Flagler Beach, and on to historic St Augustine, where a one- or two-night sojourn is highly recommended.

An affluent series of beaches can be found just south of spread-out Jacksonville, which forms an urban break in the coastal living; many continue north from here to charming Amelia Island and the Florida–Georgia border. Along the way you'll discover a jumbled necklace of grassy barrier islands, interlaced with tidal inlets, salt marsh flats and dark clumps of maritime forest.

Space Coast

More than 40 miles of barrier-island Atlantic Coast stretch from Canaveral National Seashore south to Melbourne Beach, encompassing undeveloped stretches of endless white sand, an entrenched surf culture and pockets of Old Florida.

The Kennedy Space Center and several small museums dedicated to the history, heroes and science of the United States' space program give the Space Coast its name, and the region's tourist hub of Cocoa Beach is just south of Cape Canaveral's launching point for massive cruise ships. But beyond the 3-D space movies, tiki-hut bars and surf shops, the Space Coast offers quintessential Florida wildlife for everyone from grandmas to toddlers. Kayak with manatees, camp on a private island or simply stroll along miles and miles of sandy white beaches.

◎ Sights & Activities

★ **Kennedy Space Center**　　　MUSEUM
(☑866-737-5235;　　www.kennedyspacecenter. com; NASA Pkwy, Merritt Island; adult/child 3-11yr $50/40; ◎9am-6pm) Whether you're mildly interested in space or a die-hard sci-fi fan, a visit to the Space Center is awe inspiring. To get a good overview, start at the Early Space Exploration exhibit, progress to the 90-minute bus tour to the Apollo/Saturn V Center (where you'll find the best on-site cafe) and finish at the awesome *Atlantis* exhibit, where you can walk beneath the heat-scorched fuselage of a shuttle that traveled more than 126,000,000 miles through space on 33 missions.

★ **Merritt Island**
National Wildlife Refuge　　WILDLIFE RESERVE
(☑321-861-5601; www.fws.gov/merrittisland; Black Point Wildlife Dr, off FL-406; vehicle $10; ◎dawn-dusk) FREE This unspoiled 140,000-acre refuge is one of the country's best birding spots, especially from October to May (early morning and after 4pm). More endangered and

threatened species of wildlife inhabit the swamps, marshes and hardwood hammocks here than at any other site in the continental US. The best viewing is on **Black Point Wildlife Drive**.

Canaveral
National Seashore　　NATIONAL PARK
(☑386-428-3384;　www.nps.gov/cana;　car/bike $10/1; ◎6am-8pm) The 24 miles of pristine, windswept beaches here comprise the longest stretch of undeveloped beach on Florida's east coast. They include family-friendly **Apollo Beach** on the north end with its gentle surf, untrammeled **Klondike Beach** in the middle – a favorite of nature lovers – and **Playalinda Beach** to the south, which is surfer central and includes a nudist section near lot 13.

★ **Sea-Turtle Nesting Tours**　　ECOTOUR
(☑386-428-3384;　adult/child 8-16yr $14/free; ◎8pm-midnight Jun & Jul) In the summer, rangers lead groups of up to 30 people on these nightly tours, with about a 75% chance of spotting the little guys. Reservations are required (beginning May 15 for June trips, June 15 for July trips); children under eight are not allowed.

▭ Sleeping

Residence Inn Cape Canaveral　　HOTEL $$
(☑321-323-1100;　www.marriott.com;　8959 Astronaut Blvd; r from $140; P❄🐾🏊) If you want to get away from the Cocoa Beach party scene, book into this comfortable Marriott hotel. Rooms may be corporate, but they offer acres of space, comfortable beds and kitchenettes. Staff are also extremely accommodating and there's a pretty pool area.

★ **Beach Place Guesthouses**　APARTMENT $$$
(☑321-783-4045;　www.beachplaceguesthouses. com; 1445 S Atlantic Ave; ste $199-399; P🐾) A slice of heavenly relaxation in Cocoa Beach's partying beach scene, this laid-back two-story guesthouse has roomy suites with hammocks and a lovely deck, all just steps from the dunes and beach. Colorful art and greenery abound on the property.

✕ Eating

Melbourne Beach Market　　MARKET $
(☑321-676-5225;　302 Ocean Ave;　◎8am-8pm Mon-Sat, to 7pm Sun) Pick up picnic essentials here, including ready-to-eat meals.

★ **Green Room Cafe** VEGETARIAN **$**
(☑ 321-868-0203; www.greenroomcafecocoa
beach.com; 222 N 1st St; mains $6-12; ◷ 10:30am-
9pm Mon-Sat; ☑) Focusing all its energies on
the 'goodness within', this super cafe delights
the health-conscious with fruit-combo acai
bowls, wheat- and gluten-free sandwiches,
real fruit smoothies and homemade soups
and wraps. If the 'Tower of Power' smooth-
ie (acai, peach, strawberry, honey and apple
juice) fails to lift you, the vibrant decor and
friendly company will.

★ **Seafood Atlantic** SEAFOOD **$$**
(☑ 321-784-1963; www.seafoodatlantic.org; 520
Glen Cheek Dr, Port Canaveral; mains $8-19;
◷ 11am-7pm Wed-Sun, seafood market from 10am)
With deep roots in Canaveral's fishing in-
dustry, this restaurant (with outdoor deck) is
one of the few places to serve locally sourced
shrimp, crabs, mussels, clams, oysters and
fish. If they're in, order a bucket of Florida's
deep-sea golden crab, which has a delicious-
ly moist and creamy texture. Also, bring a
bag and stock up at the market next door.

ℹ Information

**Canaveral National Seashore Visitor Infor-
mation Center** (☑ 386-428-3384; www.nps.
gov/cana; 7611 S Atlantic Ave, New Smyrna;
◷ 8am-6pm Oct-Mar, to 8pm Apr-Sep) is lo-
cated just south of the North District entrance
gate. Alternatively, the visitor center at Merritt
Island National Wildlife Refuge can also provide
information.

There is a fee station at both the North and
South District entrances. There is a toilet at
most beach parking areas.

Note that the park can experience temporary
closures around launch time. For information on
launch closures, call ☑ 321-867-4077.

ℹ Getting There & Away

Orlando Melbourne International Airport
(☑ 321-723-6227; www.mlbair.com; 1 Air
Terminal Pkwy) is the closest airport to most
destinations on the Space Coast. It is a growing
airport served by Delta, American Airlines, Elite
Airways, Porter Airlines and Baer, as well as all
the major rental-car companies and the SCAT
bus No 21.

Alternatively, Orlando International Airport
is about 50 minutes west of Cocoa Beach, and
Orlando Sanford International Airport is a little
over an hour to the northwest of Cocoa Beach.

There are two ways to arrive in Cape Canaveral:
traveling north on A1A from Cocoa Beach, or west
on A1A across the Banana River via Merritt Island.

Cape Canaveral is served by **SCAT** (SCAT;
☑ 321-633-1878; www.321transit.com; per ride
$1.50, 10-ride/30-day pass $6/21; ◷ schedule
varies) buses. Rte 9 connects it with Cocoa
Beach and Rte 4 connects it with Cocoa Village.

Daytona Beach

Long the vacation destination of choice for
leather-clad bikers, rev heads and spring
breakers, Daytona Beach is most famous as
the birthplace of NASCAR racing and the
home of the Daytona 500.

The area's population quintuples during
Speedweeks; as many as half a million bik-
ers roar into town for Bike Week in March
and Biketoberfest in October. If Confeder-
ate flags, loud motorcycles, jacked-up pick-
up trucks and the folks who love all of the
above are your thing, you might have found
your heaven on earth. If not, move on.

If you can see past the garish beachside
barricade of '70s high-rise blocks, nightclubs
and tourist traps (if not quite literally), you
might witness the phenomena of nesting
sea turtles (in season) or explore a hand-
ful of interesting and worthwhile cultural
attractions.

⊙ Sights & Activities

★ **Daytona International
Speedway** STADIUM
(☑ 800-748-7467; www.daytonainternationalspeed
way.com; 1801 W International Speedway Blvd;
tours from $18; ◷ tours 9:30am-3:30pm) The
Holy Grail of raceways has a diverse race
schedule. Ticket prices skyrocket for good
seats at big races, headlined by the Daytona
500 in February. It's worth wandering the
massive stands for free on non-race days.
First-come, first-served tram tours take in
the track, pits and behind-the-scenes areas,
while all-access tours give you a glimpse of
media rooms and pit stalls.

**Southeast Museum of
Photography** MUSEUM
(☑ 386-506-3894; www.smponline.org; 1200 W
International Speedway Blvd, Bldg 1200; ◷ 11am-
5pm Tue, Thu, Fri, 11am-7pm Wed, 1-5pm Sat & Sun)
FREE We love this hidden treasure in Day-
tona, a service of the Daytona State College:
it's the only museum in Florida dedicated
solely to photography. This vibrant modern
gallery with excellent lighting and facilities
doesn't shy away from provocative subjects
in its rotating exhibitions.

**Richard Petty
Driving Experience** DRIVING
(☏800-237-3889; www.drivepetty.com; from $109; ☺dates vary) If merely watching NASCAR drivers streak around the track isn't adrenaline-pumping enough for you, get in the car yourself via the Richard Petty Driving Experience. Choose from several levels of death-defying action, from the three-lap passenger-seat Race Ride (from $109) to the intensive Racing Experience ($3200), which puts you behind the wheel for 50 white-knuckle laps. Dates vary; check online.

🛏 Sleeping & Eating

**Hyatt Place Daytona Beach
Oceanfront** HOTEL $$
(☏386-944-2010; www.daytonabeach.place. hyatt.com; 3161 S Atlantic Ave, Daytona Beach Shores; r from $114; P@🛜🏊) Some of Daytona's freshest, funkiest and most functional rooms can be found here. All rooms feature balconies, plush bedding, separate living and sleeping areas and a nifty panel to easily connect your laptop or iPod to the 42in panel TV.

Plaza Resort & Spa RESORT $$
(☏844-284-2685; www.plazaresortandspa.com; 600 N Atlantic Ave; r from $109; P🛜🏊) Built in 1908, Daytona's most historic resort has undergone extensive renovations in its time, but still maintains its old-world charm. If only the walls could talk... From the miles of honey-colored marble lining the lobby to the 42in plasma TVs and cloud-soft beds in the rooms, to the 15,000-sq-ft spa, this resort coos luxury.

Cracked Egg Diner BREAKFAST $
(☏386-788-6772; www.thecrackedeggdiner.com; 3280 S Atlantic Ave, Daytona Beach Shores; breakfast items $4-11; ☺7am-3pm; P🚸) Best for breakfast, this cheery joint in Daytona Beach Shores became so popular they annexed the building next door. Brainchild of brothers Chris and Kevin, one of whom will usually greet you at the door with a smile, their mission is to deliver breakfast eggcellence. (Sorry. It had to happen.) We think they do a pretty fine job.

**Aunt Catfish's
on the River** SOUTHERN US $$
(☏386-767-4768; www.auntcatfishontheriver. com; 4009 Halifax Dr, Port Orange; mains $8-28; ☺11:30am-9pm Mon-Sat, from 9am Sun; P🚸) Fresh-from-the-boat grouper and mahimahi

lolling in butter or deeply and deliciously fried, as well as Southern-style Cajun-spiced catfish make this riverside seafood establishment insanely popular with tourists: table waits can be expected. It's just outside Daytona Beach in Port Orange.

Information
Daytona Beach Area Convention & Visitors Bureau (☏386-255-0415; www.daytonabeach. com; 126 E Orange Ave; ☺8:30am-5pm Mon-Fri) In person or online, these guys are *the* authority on all things Daytona Beach.

❶ Getting There & Away

Daytona Beach is close to the intersection of two major interstates, I-95 and I-4. The I-95 is the quickest way to Jacksonville (about 90 miles) and Miami (260 miles), though Hwy A1A and Hwy 1 are more scenic. Beville Rd, an east–west thoroughfare south of Daytona proper, becomes I-4 after crossing I-95; it's the fastest route to Orlando (55 miles).

Daytona Beach International Airport (☏386-248-8030; www.flydaytonafirst.com; 700 Catalina Dr) Just east of the Speedway; is served by Delta and US Airways, and all major car-rental companies.

Greyhound (☏386-255-7076; www.greyhound. com; 138 S Ridgewood Ave) Has connections to most major cities in Florida, and beyond.

St Augustine

The oldest continuously occupied European settlement in the US, St Augustine was founded by the Spanish in 1565. Today, its 144-block National Historic Landmark District is a major tourist destination. For the most part, St Augustine exudes charm and maintains its integrity, although there's no denying the presence of some tacky tourist traps: miniature theme parks, tour operators at almost every turn and horse-drawn carriages clip-clopping past townsfolk dressed in period costume.

What makes St Augustine so genuinely endearing is the accessibility of its rich history via countless top-notch museums and the authenticity of its centuries-old architecture, monuments and narrow cobbled lanes. Unlike Florida's numerous historical theme parks, St Augustine is the real deal.

You'll find a diverse array of wonderful B&Bs, cozy cafes and lamp-lit pubs, and while fine dining might not be the first thing that comes to mind at Florida's mention, it is certainly synonymous with St Augustine.

History

Timucuans settled what is now St Augustine about 1000 BC, hunting alligators and cultivating corn and tobacco. In 1513, Spanish explorer Juan Ponce de León sighted land, came ashore and claimed La Florida (Land of Flowers) for Spain. In 1565 his compatriot Don Pedro Menéndez de Avilés arrived on the feast day of Augustine of Hippo, and accordingly christened the town San Augustín: 42 years prior to the founding of Jamestown (Virginia) and 55 years before that of Plymouth (Massachusetts).

Menéndez quickly established a military base against the French, who had established Fort Caroline near present-day Jacksonville. The French fleet did him the favor of getting stuck in a hurricane; Menéndez' men butchered the survivors. By the time Spain ceded Florida to the US in 1821, St Augustine had been sacked, looted, burned and occupied by pirates and Spanish, British, Georgian and South Carolinian forces.

Today the city's buildings, made of coquina – a DIY concrete made of sedimentary rock mixed with crushed shells – lend an enchanting quality to the slender streets. The city's long and colorful history is palpable, narrated by what seems like innumerable museums, monuments and galleries.

◉ Sights

All of St Augustine's historic district feels like a museum; there are literally dozens of attractions to choose from. Narrow little **Aviles St**, the oldest European-settled street in the country, and long, pedestrian-only **St George St** are both lined with galleries, cafes, museums and pubs.

★**Lightner Museum**   MUSEUM
(☑904-824-2874; www.lightnermuseum.org; 75 King St; adult/child $10/5; ☺9am-5pm) Henry Flagler's former Hotel Alcazar is home to this wonderful museum, with a little bit of everything, from ornate Gilded Age furnishings to collections of marbles and cigar-box labels. The dramatic and imposing building itself is a must-see, dating back to 1887 and designed in the Spanish Renaissance–revival style by New York City architects Carrère & Hastings.

Castillo de San Marcos National Monument   FORT
(☑904-829-6506; www.nps.gov/casa; 1 S Castillo Dr; adult/child under 15 yr $10/free; ☺8:45am-5pm; ℗🚻) ✎ This photogenic fort is an atmospheric monument to longevity: it's the country's oldest masonry fort, completed by the Spanish in 1695. In its time, the fort has been besieged twice and changed hands between nations *six* times – from Spain to Britain to Spain Part II to the USA to the Confederate States of America to the USA again.

Villa Zorayda Museum   MUSEUM
(☑904-829-9887; www.villazorayda.com; 83 King St; adult/child $10/4; ☺10am-5pm Mon-Sat, 11am-4pm Sun; ℗) Looking like a faux Spanish castle from a medieval theme park, this gray edifice was built out of a mix of concrete and local coquina shells in 1883. The structure was the fantasy (and maybe fever dream) of an eccentric millionaire who was obsessed with Spain's 12th-century Alhambra Palace. Today, it's an odd but engaging museum. The Moorish-style atrium and rooms contain quirky antiques, archaeological pieces and other artifacts: highlights being a 2400-year-old mummy's foot and an Egyptian 'Sacred Cat Rug.'

Hotel Ponce de León   HISTORIC BUILDING
(☑904-823-3378; http://legacy.flagler.edu/pages/tours; 74 King St; tours adult/child $10/1; ☺tours hourly 10am-3pm summer, 10am & 2pm during school year) This striking former luxury hotel, built in the 1880s, is now the world's most gorgeous dormitory, belonging to Flagler College, who purchased and saved it in 1967. Guided tours are recommended to get a sense of the detail and history of this magnificent Spanish Renaissance building.

Colonial Quarter   MUSEUM
(☑904-342-2857; www.colonialquarter.com; 33 St George St; adult/child $13/7; ☺10am-5pm) See how they did things back in the 18th century at this re-creation of Spanish Colonial St Augustine, complete with craftspeople demonstrating blacksmithing, leather working, musket shooting and all sorts of historical stuff.

St Augustine Beach   BEACH
(350 A1A Beach Blvd; ☺sunrise-sunset) This white-sand beach almost gets lost in the historical mix, but hey, it's Florida, so a visit wouldn't be complete without a little bit of sun and surf. There's a visitor information booth at the foot of **St Johns Pier**, where you can rent a rod and reel (two hours for $3, plus $1 for each additional hour). About three blocks south of the pier, the end of A St has – as Florida goes – some fine waves.

FLORIDA ST AUGUSTINE

⛳ Tours

⭐ **St Augustine Gold Tours**   TOURS
(📞904-325-0547; www.staugustinegoldtours.com;
6 Cordova St; adult/child $25/15) This outfit, the
brainchild of a retired British couple, is a
standout in the crowded St Augustine tour
scene. You're assured a fascinating and articulate insight into St Augustine's history. Private and small-group tours are conducted in
a quiet electric vehicle that gets into places
where the other tours can't.

🛏 Sleeping & Eating

⭐ **At Journey's End**   B&B $$
(📞904-829-0076; www.atjourneysend.com; 89 Ce-
dar St; r $166-289; 🅿🐾🛜🐾) Free from the gran-
ny-ish decor that haunts many St Augustine
B&Bs, this pet-friendly, kid-friendly and
gay-friendly spot is outfitted in a chic mix of
antiques and modern furniture and is run
by friendly, knowledgeable hosts. Mouth-
watering breakfasts and complimentary wi-
fi, concierge services, and beer, wine and
soda throughout your stay are some of the
inclusions that set At Journey's End apart.

Jaybird's Inn   MOTEL $$
(📞904-342-7938; www.jaybirdsinn.com; 2700 N
Ponce de Leon Blvd; r $110-150; 🛜🛁) This old-
er motel has been revamped to the highest
of standards and modernity, with fresh and
funky decor in an aquamarine color scheme
that works. Beds are big and comfy, continental breakfast is included and free bikes
will get you whizzing around in no time.
There's an on-site restaurant as well.

⭐ **Collage**   INTERNATIONAL $$$
(📞904-829-0055; www.collagestaug.com; 60
Hypolita St; mains $28-45; ⊙5:30-9pm) This up-
scale restaurant is renowned for its impec-
cable service, intimate atmosphere and the
consistency of its cuisine: the menu makes
the most of St Augustine's seaside locale and
nearby local farms. It's all here: artisan sal-
ads, chicken, lamb, veal and pork, lobster,
scallops and grouper. A subtle mélange of
global flavors enhance the natural goodness
of the freshest produce.

ℹ Information

Visitor Information Center (📞904-825-1000;
www.Floridashistoriccoast.com; 10 W Castillo
Dr; ⊙8:30am-5:30pm) Helpful, period-dressed
staff sell tour tickets and can advise you on
everything St Augustinian.

The daily *St Augustine Record* (www.staugus
tine.com) has good information on its website.

ℹ Getting There & Around

Driving from the north, take I-95 exit 318 and
head east past Hwy 1 to San Marcos Ave; turn
right and you'll end up at the Old City Gate, just
past the fort. Alternatively, you can take Hwy
A1A along the beach, which intersects with San
Marco Ave, or Hwy 1 south from Jacksonville.
From the south, take exit 298, merge onto Hwy 1
and follow it into town.

Cars are a nightmare downtown, with one-way
and pedestrian-only streets and severely limited
parking; outside the city center, you'll need
wheels. There's a big parking lot at the Visitor
Information Center. Use it.

Northeast Florida Regional Airport (📞904-
209-0090; www.flynf.com; 4900 US Hwy 1), 5
miles north of town, receives limited commercial
flights. **Airport Express** (📞904-824-9400;
www.airportexpresspickup.com) charges $65 to
drop you downtown in a shuttle. For an addition-
al $20, it'll take you to your hotel. Reservations
required. Private services are also available.

The **Greyhound bus station** (📞904-829-
6401; www.greyhound.com; 52 San Marcos Ave)
is just a few blocks north of the visitor center.

Jacksonville

At a whopping 840 sq miles, Jacksonville
is the largest city by area in the contiguous
United States and the most populous in
Florida. The city *sprawls* along three me-
andering rivers, with sweeping bridges and
twinkling city lights reflected in the water. A
glut of high-rises, corporate HQs and chain
hotels can make 'Jax' feel a little soulless, but
patient exploration yields some interesting
streets, curious characters and a South-
ern-fried, friendly heart.

The city's museums and restored histor-
ic districts are worth a wander if you have
the time, and the Five Points and San Mar-
co neighborhoods are charming, walkable
areas lined with bistros, boutiques and bars.

The Jacksonville area beaches – a world
unto themselves – are 30 to 50 minutes'
drive from the city, depending on traffic and
where you're coming from.

⊙ Sights

⭐ **Cummer Museum of**
Art & Gardens   MUSEUM
(www.cummer.org; 829 Riverside Ave; adult/stu-
dent $10/6; ⊙10am-9pm Tue, to 4pm Wed-Sat,
noon-4pm Sun) This handsome museum,
Jacksonville's premier cultural space, has a
genuinely excellent collection of American
and European paintings, Asian decorative

art and antiquities. An outdoor area show-cases classical English and Italian gardens, and is one of the loveliest spaces in the city.

★**Museum of Contemporary Art**
Jacksonville   MUSEUM
(MOCA; ☑904-366-6911; www.mocajacksonville.org; 333 N Laura St; adult/child $8/2.50; ⊙11am-5pm Tue-Sat, to 9pm Thu, noon-5pm Sun) The focus of this ultramodern space extends beyond painting: get lost among contemporary sculpture, prints, photography and film. Check out www.jacksonvilleartwalk.com for details of the free MOCA-run Art Walk, held on the first Wednesday of every month from 5pm to 9pm.

Southbank Riverwalk   WATERFRONT
This 1.2-mile boardwalk, on the south side of the St Johns River, opposite downtown and Jacksonville Landing, has excellent views of the city's expansive skyline. Most nights yield scenes that'll up your likes on social media, but firework displays are a real blast. The Southbank Riverwalk connects the museums flanking Museum Circle and makes a pleasant promenade.

Treaty Oak   LANDMARK
(1123 Prudential Dr, Jesse Ball duPont Park) At first glance, it looks like a small forest is growing in the middle of the concrete on Jacksonville's south side. But upon closer inspection you'll see that the 'forest' is really one single enormous tree, with a trunk circumference of 25ft and a shade diameter of nearly 200ft. According to local lore, the live oak tree is the oldest thing in Jacksonville.

🛏 **Sleeping & Eating**

Hotel Indigo Jacksonville   HOTEL **$$**
(☑877-846-3446; www.hoteldeerwoodpark.com; 9840 Tapestry Park Circle; r from $150; P 🗑 🛏 🐕) Lush blue color accents and airy, design-conscious rooms with hardwood floors, fluffy king beds, flat-screen TVs and a general sense of stylish yet accessible luxury define the experience at this excellent branch of the Indigo chain. Located about 11 miles south of downtown Jacksonville.

★**Hotel Palms**   HOTEL **$$**
(☑904-241-7776; www.thehotelpalms.com; 28 Sherry Dr, Atlantic Beach; r $140-180, ste from $200; 🗑) An old-school courtyard motel turned into a chic little property with reclaimed headboards, concrete floors and open, airy design? We'll take it. Treat yourself to an outdoor shower, free beach-cruiser bicycles, an outdoor fireplace and some gorgeous rooms pulled straight off some fancy interior decorator's Instagram.

Beach Road
Chicken Dinners   SOUTHERN US **$**
(☑904-398-7980; www.beachroadchickendinners.com; 4132 Atlantic Blvd; items $5-12; ⊙11am-8:30pm Tue-Sat, to 6pm Sun) You know a place does it right if its signature meal predates the Cold War, and this deliciously retro joint has been frying chicken since 1939. Tear off a chunk of tender thigh meat and wrap it up in a fluffy biscuit, and you'll understand why people line up every day at this much-loved shack.

★**Black Sheep**
Restaurant   MODERN AMERICAN **$$**
(☑904-380-3091; www.blacksheep5points.com; 1534 Oak St; lunch/dinner mains from $9/14; ⊙10:30am-10pm Mon-Thu, to 11pm Fri & Sat, 9:30am-3pm Sun; 🛗) ♥ A commitment to good, local ingredients, delicious food, plus a rooftop bar and a craft cocktail menu? Sign us up! Try miso-glazed duck confit, citrus-marinated tofu, pastrami sandwiches made from in-house deli meat, or crispy skinned steelhead fish cooked in brown butter; it's all good. The cardamom pancakes and salmon on bagels served for Sunday brunch are pretty fine too.

🍷 **Drinking & Entertainment**

★**Birdies**   BAR
(☑904-356-4444; www.birdiesfivepoints.com; 1044 Park St; ⊙4pm-2am) There's funky local art on the walls, old-school video games in the back, a mix of old timers and tatted hipsters, retro neon vibe, indie rock on the radio, DJs on the weekends and good vibes throughout at this excellent watering hole.

★**Florida Theatre**   THEATER
(☑904-355-5661; www.floridatheatre.com; 128 E Forsyth St) Home to Elvis' first indoor concert in 1956, which a local judge endured to ensure Presley was not overly suggestive, this opulent 1927 venue is an intimate place to catch big-name musicians, musicals and movies.

ℹ **Information**

There are a bunch of sources of information for Jacksonville and the surrounding areas.
Florida Times-Union (www.jacksonville.com) Conservative daily paper, in print and online;

Friday's *Weekend* magazine features family-oriented events listings.

Folio Weekly (www.folioweekly.com) Free; with club, restaurant and events listings. Found all over town.

Jacksonville & the Beaches Convention & Visitors Bureau (☑ 800-733-2668; www.visit jacksonville.com; 208 N Laura St, Suite 102; ◷ 9am-5pm Mon-Fri) Has all there is to know about Jax and surrounds. There's also a branch at **Jacksonville Landing** (☑ 904-791-4305; 2 Independent Dr; ◷ 11am-3pm Mon-Thu, 10am-7pm Fri & Sat, noon-5pm Sun) and the airport.

❶ Getting There & Around

Jacksonville International Airport (JAX; ☑ 904-741-4902; www.flyjax.com; 2400 Yankee Clipper Dr; ☎), about 18 miles north of downtown on I-95, is served by major and regional airlines and car-rental companies. A cab downtown costs around $35. Otherwise, follow the signs for shuttle services: there are numerous licensed providers and reservations aren't necessary.

The **Greyhound bus station** (☑ 904-356-9976; www.greyhound.com; 10 Pearl St) is at the west end of downtown. The **Amtrak station** (☑ 904-766-5110; www.amtrak.com; 3570 Clifford Lane) is 5 miles northwest of downtown.

The Jacksonville Transportation Authority (www.jtafla.com) runs buses and trolleys around town and the beaches (fare $1.50), as well as a free, scenic (and underused) river-crossing Skyway (monorail).

Amelia Island

Located just 13 miles from the Georgia border, Amelia Island is a moss-draped, sun- and sand-soaked blend of the Deep South and Florida coast. It is believed the island's original inhabitants, the Timucuan tribespeople, arrived as early as 4000 years ago. Since that time, eight flags have flown here, starting with the French in 1562, followed by the Spanish, the English, the Spanish again, the Patriots, the Green Cross of Florida, the Mexican Rebels, the US, the Confederates, then the US again.

Vacationers have flocked to Amelia since the 1890s, when Henry Flagler converted a coast of salt marsh and unspoiled beaches into a vacation spot for the wealthy. The legacy of that era is evident in the central town of Fernandina Beach, 50 blocks of historic buildings, Victorian B&Bs and restaurants housed in converted fishing cottages. Dotting the rest of the island are lush parks, green fairways and miles of shoreline.

◉ Sights & Activties

Amelia Island Museum of History　MUSEUM
(☑ 904-261-7378; www.ameliamuseum.org; 233 S 3rd St, Fernandina Beach; adult/student $8/5; ◷ 10am-4pm Mon-Sat, 1-4pm Sun) Housed in the former city jail (1879–1975), this oral-history museum has tiny but informative exhibits exploring Native American history, the Spanish Mission period, the Civil War and historic preservation. A variety of tours are available, including the eight-flags tour (11am and 2pm Monday to Saturday and 2pm Sunday), providing lively interpretations of the island's fascinating history, and architecture tours, pub crawls and cell-phone walking tours.

Fort Clinch State Park　STATE PARK
(☑ 904-277-7274; www.floridastateparks.org/fort-clinch; 2601 Atlantic Ave, Fernandina Beach; car/pedestrian $6/2; ◷ park 8am-sunset, fort 9am-5pm; ℗) ✿ Although construction commenced in 1847, rapid technological advancements rendered Fort Clinch's masonry walls obsolete by as early as 1861, when the fort was taken easily by Confederate militia in the Civil War and later evacuated. Federal troops again occupied the fort during WWII. Today, the park offers a variety of activities, a half-mile-long fishing pier, serene beaches, hiking and cycling.

★**Kayak Amelia**　KAYAKING
(☑ 904-261-5702, 904-251-0016; www.kayakamelia.com; 4 N 2nd St, Fernandina Beach; tours adult/child from $65/55, rental half-day/day from $37/49) The charms of Amelia Island are best appreciated through a quiet day on the water, with the sun glinting off the estuaries and cordgrass. That's the experience offered by Kayak Amelia, which leads paddling excursions into the watery ecosystem that ensconces the Atlantic barrier island.

🛏 Sleeping

★**Addison**　B&B $$$
(☑ 904-277-1604; www.addisononamelia.com; 614 Ash St, Fernandina Beach; r $215-315; ℗ ☎) ✿ Built in 1876, the Addison has modern upgrades (Jacuzzi tubs, deluge showers, Turkish-cotton towels and wi-fi) that'll trick you into thinking it was finished last week. The Addison's white, aqua and sage color scheme is bright and totally un-stuffy. Enjoy daily happy hours overlooking a delightful courtyard with some of the friendliest (and funniest) innkeepers on Amelia.

Ritz Carlton
HOTEL $$$

(☑ 904-277-1100; www.ritzcarlton.com/en/Prop-erties/AmeliaIsland; 4750 Amelia Island Pkwy, Fernandina Beach; r from $299; P 🤶 🌊) The height of luxury, decadence and impeccable service awaits at this unexpectedly located Ritz Carlton. Set on 13 miles of pristine beaches, with its own private 18-hole golf course and lavish rooms and suites furnished with casual elegance.

✖ Eating & Drinking

T-Ray's Burger Station
BURGERS $

(☑ 904-261-6310; www.traysburgerstation.com; 202 S 8th St, Fernandina Beach; mains $6-9; ⊙ 7am-2:30pm Mon-Fri, 8am-1pm Sat) Inside an Exxon gas station, this high-carb, high-fat, low-pretense diner and takeout joint is worth the cholesterol spike. Revered by locals, the big breakfasts are just that, and daily specials sell out fast. Juicy burgers, chunky fries, fried shrimp and tender crab cakes all make the mouth water.

29 South
SOUTHERN US $$

(☑ 904-277-7919; www.29southrestaurant.com; 29 S 3rd St, Fernandina Beach; mains $16-28; ⊙ 11:30am-2pm Wed-Sun, 5:30-9:30pm daily; P) Lobster corn dogs, sweet-tea-brined pork chops, homemade doughnut-bread pudding and coffee ice cream – we're in business.

★ Palace Saloon
BAR

(www.thepalacesaloon.com; 113-117 Centre St, Fernandina Beach; ⊙ noon-2am) Push through the swinging doors at the oldest continuously operated bar in Florida (since 1878), and the first thing you'll notice is the 40ft gas-lamp-lit bar. Knock back the saloon's rum-laced Pirate's Punch in dark, velvet-draped surroundings, curiously appealing to both bikers and Shakespeare buffs.

ⓘ Information

Historic Downtown Visitor Center (☑ 904-277-0717; www.ameliaisland.com; 102 Centre St, Fernandina Beach; ⊙ 10am-4pm) Reams of useful information and maps in the old railroad depot.

Shrimping Museum & Welcome Center (☑ 904-261-7378; 17 Front St, Fernandina Beach; ⊙ 10am-4pm Mon-Sat, 1-4pm Sun) This small museum on the harborfront has local maps and pamphlets.

ⓘ Getting There & Away

Hwy A1A splits in two directions on Amelia Island, one heading west toward I-95 and the other following the coast; both are well marked.

To get to Amelia, the fastest route from the mainland is to take I-95 north to exit 373 and head east about 15 miles straight to the island.

Want a prettier route? Heading from Jacksonville Beach to the town of Mayport, catch the **St Johns River Ferry** (☑ 904-241-9969; www.stjohnsriverferry.com; per car $5; ⊙ from Maryport every 30min 6am-7pm Mon-Fri, 7am-8:30pm Sat & Sun; from George Island every 30min 6:15am-7:15pm Mon-Fri, 7:15am-8:45pm Sat & Sun), which runs around every 30 minutes.

SOUTHWEST FLORIDA

To drive southwest Florida's Gulf Coast is to enter an impressionistic watercolor painting: first, there is the dazzling white quartz sand of its barrier-island beaches, whose turquoise waters darken to silver-mantled indigo as the fiery sun lowers to the horizon. Later, seen from the causeways, those same islands become a phosphorescent smear beneath the inky black night sky.

The Gulf Coast's beauty is its main attraction, but variety is a close second: from Tampa to St Petersburg to Sarasota to Naples, there is urban sophistication and exquisite cuisine. There are secluded islands, family-friendly resorts and spring-break-style parties. Here Salvador Dalí's melting canvases, Ringling's Venetian Gothic palace and Chihuly's tentacled glass sculptures fit perfectly – all are bright, bold, surreal entertainments to match wintering manatees, roseate spoonbills, open-mouthed alligators and the peacock-colored, sequined costumes of twirling trapeze artists.

Tampa

On first glance it may seem sprawling and businesslike, but Tampa is also home to a bunch of museums, parks and ambitious restaurants, many of which have popped up recently and brought the city dangerously close to becoming stylish. In the heart of downtown, the revitalized Riverwalk along the Hillsborough River glitters with contemporary architecture and scenic green spaces. Plus, between the zoo, the aquarium, the children's museums and the theme parks, families have enough top-shelf entertainment to last a week. By evening Ybor City's streets transform into southwest Florida's hottest bar and nightclub scene.

⊙ Sights

Ybor (ee-bore) City is a short car or trolley ride northeast of downtown. Like the illicit love child of Key West and Miami's Little Havana, this 19th-century district is a multiethnic neighborhood that hosts the Tampa Bay area's hippest party scene. It also preserves a strong Cuban, Spanish and Italian heritage from its days as the epicenter of Tampa's cigar industry.

★ **Florida Aquarium** AQUARIUM
(☑ 813-273-4000; www.flaquarium.org; 701 Channelside Dr; adult/child $25/20; ⊙ 9:30am-5pm; ⊞) Tampa's excellent aquarium is among the state's best. Cleverly designed, the re-created swamp lets you walk among herons and ibis as they prowl the mangroves. Programs let you swim with the fishes (and the sharks) or take a catamaran ecotour in Tampa Bay.

Busch Gardens AMUSEMENT PARK
(☑ 888-800-5447; www.buschgardenstampabay.com; 10165 McKinley Dr; 3yr & up $95; ⊙ 10am-6pm, hours vary) This theme park has 10 loosely named African zones, which flow together without much fuss. The entire park is walkable. Admission includes three types of fun: epic roller coasters and rides, animal encounters, and various shows, performances and entertainment. All are spread throughout the park, so successful days require some planning.

Ybor City Museum State Park MUSEUM
(☑ 813-247-6323; www.ybormuseum.org; 1818 E 9th Ave; adult/child $4/free; ⊙ 9am-5pm Wed-Sun) This dusty, old-school history museum preserves a bygone era, with cigarworker houses (open 10am to 3pm) and wonderful photos. The museum store offers expert cigar advice and information on a free, self-guided, multimedia tour (☑ 813-505-6779; www.yborwalkingtours.com; adult/child $20/10) of Ybor City, accessible with any internet-connected device.

**Florida Museum of
Photographic Arts** MUSEUM
(FMoPA; ☑ 813-221-2222; www.fmopa.org; The Cube, 400 N Ashley Dr; adult/student $10/8; ⊙ 11am-6pm Mon-Thu, to 7pm Fri, noon-5pm Sun) This small, intimate photography museum is housed on the 2nd and 3rd stories of the Cube, a five-story atrium in downtown Tampa. In addition to a permanent collection from Harold Edgerton and Len Prince, temporary exhibits have included the work of

Ansel Adams, Andy Warhol and contemporary photographers such as Jerry Uelsmann. Photography courses are also offered.

Manatee Viewing Center WILDLIFE RESERVE
(☑ 813-228-4289; www.tampaelectric.com/manatee; 6990 Dickman Rd, Apollo Beach; ⊙ 10am-5pm Nov-mid Apr) **FREE** One of Florida's more surreal wildlife encounters is spotting manatees in the warm-water discharge canals of coal-fired power plants. Yet these placid mammals show up here so reliably from November through April that this is now a protected sanctuary.

⊨ Sleeping

Gram's Place Hostel HOSTEL $
(☑ 813-221-0596; www.grams-inn-tampa.com; 3109 N Ola Ave, Seminole Heights; dm $28, r $55-65; ⊞ @ 🛜) As charismatic as an aging rock star, Gram's is a small, welcoming hostel for international travelers who prefer personality over perfect linens. Dig the in-ground hot tub and Saturday-night jams. Breakfast is not included, but there are two fully serviced kitchens.

Tahitian Inn HOTEL $$
(☑ 813-877-6721; www.tahitianinn.com; 601 S Dale Mabry Hwy, South Tampa; r from $155; P ❄ @ 🛜 ⊠ 🐾) The name is reminiscent of a tiki-themed motel, but this family-owned, full-service hotel offers fresh, boutique stylings on the cheap. Nice pool, and the quaint cafe offers outdoor seating by a waterfall and koi pond.

★ **Epicurean Hotel** BOUTIQUE HOTEL $$
(☑ 813-999-8700; www.epicureanhotel.com; 1207 S Howard Ave, South Tampa; r $180-499; P ❄ @ 🛜 ⊠) Foodies rejoice! Tampa's coolest hotel, which opened in 2014, is a food-and-drink-themed boutique Eden steeped in detailed design: vertical hydroponic lettuce and herb walls, a zinc bar, reclaimed woods from an 1820s railway station, oversize whiskers as test-kitchen door handles – everywhere you look, a story, usually involving **Bern's Steak House** (☑ 813-251-2421; www.bernssteakhouse.com; 1208 S Howard Ave, South Tampa; steaks for 1-2 people $32-105; ⊙ 5-10pm Sun-Thu, to 11pm Fri & Sat), who are partners.

✕ Eating

Tre Amici @ the Bunker CAFE $
(☑ 813-247-6964; www.bunkerybor.com; 1907 19th St N, Ybor City; items $3-8; ⊙ 8am-8pm Mon-Sat, 10am-4pm Sun) Ybor City's hipster contingent

wake up at this relaxed community coffee-house, which offers a range of breakfast burritos, soups and sandwiches all day. Come evening, it hosts open mikes, poetry slams and 'noise nights,' which are exactly what they sound like.

Ichicoro
RAMEN $$

(☑️813-517-9989; www.ichicoro.com; 5229 N Florida Ave, Seminole Heights; ramen $12-16; ⊘noon-11pm Mon-Wed, to 1am Thu & Fri, 11am-1am Sat, 11am-11pm Sun) This chic space in Tampa's Seminole Heights neighborhood dishes out some of the best craft ramen (yes, ramen can be craft too) south of New York City. And that's actually where the recipes for these fancy noodle bowls were conceived.

★Ulele
AMERICAN $$

(☑️813-999-4952; www.ulele.com; 1810 N Highland Ave; mains $10-36; ⊘11am-10pm Sun-Thu, to 11pm Fri & Sat; 🐾) In a pleasant Riverwalk setting, this former water-pumping station has been transformed into an enchanting restaurant and brewery whose menu harkens back to native Floridan staples made over for modern times. That means liberal use of datil peppers, sides like alligator beans and okra 'fries' (amazing!), mains like local pompano fish and desserts like guava pie.

★Columbia Restaurant
SPANISH $$$

(☑️813-248-4961; www.columbiarestaurant.com; 2117 E 7th Ave, Ybor City; mains lunch $11-26, dinner $20-31; ⊘11am-10pm Mon-Thu, to 11pm Fri & Sat, noon-9pm Sun) Celebrating its centennial in 2015, this Spanish Cuban restaurant is the oldest in Florida. Occupying an entire block, it consists of 15 elegant dining rooms and romantic, fountain-centered courtyards.

🍷 Drinking & Entertainment

Independent Bar
BAR

(☑️813-341-4883; www.independenttampa.com; 5016 N Florida Ave, Seminole Heights; ⊘9am-midnight Sun-Wed, to 1am Thu-Sat) If you appreciate craft brews, roll into this converted gas station, now a low-key hip bar in Seminole Heights. You can count on one or more local Cigar City Brews, and it serves some mean pub grub.

★Skipper's Smokehouse
LIVE MUSIC

(☑️813-971-0666; www.skipperssmokehouse.com; 910 Skipper Rd, Village of Tampa; cover $5-25; ⊘11am-10pm Tue & Wed, to 10:30pm Thu, to 11pm Fri, noon-11pm Sat, 1-9:30pm Sun) Like it blew in from the Keys, Skipper's is a beloved, unpretentious open-air venue for blues, folk, reggae and gator-swamp rockabilly. It's 9 miles directly north of downtown on N Nebraska Ave.

★Tampa Theatre
CINEMA

(☑️813-274-8981, box office 813-274-8286; www.tampatheatre.org; 711 N Franklin St; tickets $11) This historic 1926 theater in downtown is a gorgeous venue in which to see an independent film. The mighty Wurlitzer organ plays before most movies. Too bad showtimes are so limited, with only one or two films playing on any given day. Look for special events.

ℹ️ Information

Tampa Bay Convention & Visitors Bureau (☑️813-226-0293; www.visittampabay.com; 615 Channelside Dr; ⊘10am-5:30pm Mon-Sat, 11am-5pm Sun) The visitor center has good free maps and lots of information.

Ybor City Visitor Center (☑️813-241-8838; www.ybor.org; 1600 E 8th Ave; ⊘10am-5pm Mon-Sat, noon-5pm Sun) Provides an excellent introduction with walking-tour maps and info.

ℹ️ Getting There & Around

Tampa International Airport (TPA; ☑️813-870-8700; www.tampaairport.com; 4100 George J Bean Pkwy) is the region's third busiest hub. It's 6 miles west of downtown, off Hwy 589.

HART bus 30 ($2, 25 minutes, every 30 minutes) picks up and drops off at the Red Arrival Desk on the lower level of the airport; exact change is required.

All major car agencies have desks at the airport. By car, take the I-275 to N Ashley Dr, turn right and you're in downtown.

St Petersburg

Long known as little more than a bawdy spring-break party town and a retirement capital, St Petersburg is now forging a new name for itself as a culturally savvy southern city. Spurred on by awe-inspiring downtown murals, a revitalized historic district and the stunning Dalí Museum, the downtown energy is creeping up Central Ave, spawning sophisticated restaurants, craft breweries, farmers markets and artsy galleries, all of which are attracting a younger professional crowd and a new wave of culturally curious travelers.

◉ Sights & Activities

★ Salvador Dalí Museum MUSEUM

(☑727-823-3767; www.thedali.org; 1 Dali Blvd; adult/child 6-12yr $24/10, after 5pm Thu $10; ⊙10am-5:30pm Fri-Wed, to 8pm Thu) The theatrical exterior of the Salvador Dalí Museum augurs great things: out of a wound in the towering white shoe box oozes a 75ft geodesic glass atrium. Even better, what unfolds inside is like a blueprint of what a modern art museum, or at least one devoted to the life, art and impact of Salvador Dalí, should be. Even those who dismiss his dripping clocks and curlicue mustache will be awed by the museum and its grand works, especially the *Hallucinogenic Toreador.*

★ Weedon Island Preserve NATURE RESERVE

(☑727-453-6500; www.weedonislandpreserve. org; 1800 Weedon Dr NE; ⊙7am-sunset) Like a patchwork quilt of variegated greens tossed out over Tampa Bay, this 3700-acre preserve protects a diverse aquatic and wetland ecosystem. At the heart of the preserve is the excellent Cultural and Natural History Center (open from 11am to 4pm Thursday to Saturday) where you can browse exhibits about the natural environment and the early Weedon Island people.

St Petersburg Museum of Fine Arts MUSEUM

(☑727-896-2667; www.mfastpete.org; 255 Beach Dr NE; adult/child 7-18yr $17/10; ⊙10am-5pm Mon-Sat, to 8pm Thu, noon-5pm Sun) The Museum of Fine Arts' collection is as broad as the Dalí Museum's is deep, traversing the world's antiquities and following art's progression through nearly every era.

★ Walking Mural Tours CULTURAL

(☑727-821-7391; www.stpetemuraltour.com; adult/ child $19/11; ⊙10-11:30am Sat) This excellent walking tour introduces visitors to St Pete's vibrant mural scene, which got its start when artists were given cheap gallery space downtown after the economy crashed in 2008. Now upward of 30 highly creative and one-of-a-kind murals, many with nods to the city's history and culture, grace its buildings and rival Miami's Wynwood Walls.

🛏 Sleeping

★ Hollander Hotel BOUTIQUE HOTEL $$

(☑727-873-7900; www.hollanderhotel.com; 421 4th Ave N; r $98-140; P✳🐾🎀) The Hollander can do no wrong with its art-deco flavor, 130ft porch, convivial Tap Room, full-service spa and Common Grounds coffee shop. Shared spaces feature gorgeous period detailing and rooms retain a hint of 1930s romance with their polished wooden floors, lazy ceiling fans and cane furniture.

★ Dickens House B&B $$

(☑727-822-8622; www.dickenshouse.com; 335 8th Ave NE; r $139-243; P✳@🎀) Five lushly designed rooms await in this passionately restored arts-and-crafts-style home. The gregarious, gay-friendly owner whips up a gourmet breakfast often involving egg-white frittata.

✖ Eating & Drinking

Meze 119 VEGETARIAN $

(☑727-498-8627; www.meze119.com; 119 2nd St N; mains $7-14; ⊙11am-9pm Sun-Thu, to 10pm Fri & Sat; ✚) Using Middle Eastern spices to create rich, complex flavors, this vegetarian restaurant satisfies even demanding omnivores with its Scotch egg and falafel, panko fried with tahini sauce, and couscous and raisin-stuffed acorn squash. Other popular standards include the multiflavor hummus plate and sautéed eggplant on open-faced pita bread.

★ Brick & Mortar MODERN AMERICAN $$

(☑727-822-6540; www.facebook.com/brickand mortarkitchen; 539 Central Ave; mains $14-25; ⊙5pm-9pm Tue, to 10pm Wed & Thu; 4:30pm-11pm Fri & Sat) A husband-and-wife catering team launched this, well, brick-and-mortar establishment in 2015, and despite the fact that St Pete has been overrun with great restaurants, this New American experiment dominated. Best thing in the menu? A divine house carpaccio with leek, some goat's cheese mousse, a touch of truffle oil and a single ravioli stuffed with deliciously runny egg yolk.

★ Cycle Brewing BREWERY

(534 Central Ave; ⊙3pm-midnight Mon-Thu, to 1am Fri, noon-1am Sat, noon-10pm Sun) Hipster brewhouse with sidewalk seating serving up to 24 rotating taps of world-class beer. The Crank IPA is a great choice.

❶ Getting There & Around

Greyhound (☑727-898-1496; www.greyhound. com; 180 Dr Martin Luther King Jr St N) Buses connect to Miami, Orlando and Tampa.

Pinellas Suncoast Transit Authority (PSTA; www.psta.net; adult/student $2.20/1.10) St

Petersburg buses serve the barrier-island beaches and Clearwater; unlimited-ride Go Cards cost $5 per day.

Downtown Looper (www.loopertrolley.com; fare 50¢; ⊗10am-5pm Sun-Thu, to midnight Fri & Sat) Old-fashioned trolley cars run a downtown circuit every 15 to 20 minutes.

Sarasota

Vacations today can be spent soaking up the sights and beaches (including the nearby and very popular Siesta Key) of sophisticated Sarasota, but this city took its time becoming the culturally rich place it is today. After marauding Spanish explorers expelled the Calusa people in the 15th century, this land lay virtually empty until the Seminole Wars inspired the Armed Occupation Act (1842), which deeded 160 acres and six months' provisions to anyone who would settle here and protect their farms. Sailing boats and steamships were the only connection to the outside world, until the Tampa railroad came in 1902. Sarasota then grew popular as a winter resort for the affluent, and the city's arts institutions followed. Finally circus magnate John Ringling decided to relocate his circus here, building a winter residence, art museum and college, and setting the struggling town on course to become the welcoming, well-to-do bastion of the arts it is today.

◉ Sights & Activities

★**Ringling Museum Complex**   MUSEUM
(☑941-359-5700; www.ringling.org; 5401 Bay Shore Rd; adult/child 6-17yr $25/5; ⊗10am-5pm Fri-Wed, to 8pm Thu; ⛟) The 66-acre winter estate of railroad, real-estate and circus baron John Ringling and his wife, Mable, is one of the Gulf Coast's premier attractions and incorporates their personal collection of artworks in what is now Florida's state art museum. Nearby, Ringling's Circus Museum documents his theatrical successes, while their lavish Venetian Gothic home, Cà d'Zan, reveals the impresario's extravagant tastes. Don't miss the PBS-produced film on Ringling's life, which is screened in the Circus Museum.

Island Park   PARK
Sarasota's marina is notable for Island Park, an attractive green space poking into the harbor: it has a great playground and play fountain, restrooms, tree-shaded benches, a restaurant and tiki bar; and kayak, jet-ski and boat rentals.

★**Siesta Key Rum**   DISTILLERY
(Drum Circle Distilling; ☑941-702-8143; www.drumcircledistilling.com; 2212 Industrial Blvd; ⊗noon-5pm Tue-Sat) FREE The oldest rum distillery in Florida offers an educational and intoxicating tour in its facility within an industrial park a bit outside of town. You'll learn the entire process of rum-making from the company founder Troy, who is a gifted and hilarious public speaker.

🛏 Sleeping & Eating

★**Hotel Ranola**   BOUTIQUE HOTEL $$
(☑941-951-0111; www.hotelranola.com; 118 Indian Pl; r $109-179, ste $239-269; 🅿❄🛜) The nine rooms feel like a designer's brownstone apartment: free-spirited and effortlessly artful, but with real working kitchens. It's urban funk, walkable to downtown Sarasota.

Mattison's City Grille   GRILL $
(☑941-330-0440; www.mattisons.com/; 1 N. Lemon Ave; mains $9-17; ⊗11am-10pm (or later), from 9:30am Sat; 🛜⛟) Healthy salads and hearty sandwiches (using fresh homemade bread) are the order of the day at central Mattison's. The outdoor dining area doubles up as a bar that gets going each evening with live music, giving the place its 'party on the corner' nickname.

★**Owen's Fish Camp**   SOUTHERN US $$
(☑941-951-6936; www.owensfishcamp.com; 516 Burns Lane; mains $10-28; ⊗4-9:30pm Sun-Thu, to 10:30pm Fri & Sat) The wait rarely dips below an hour at this hip, Old Florida swamp shack downtown. The menu consists of upscale Southern cuisine with an emphasis on seafood, including whatever's fresh, and solid regular dishes like scallops with braised pork, succotash and grits.

❶ Information

Arts & Cultural Alliance (www.sarasotaarts.org) All-encompassing event info.

Sarasota Herald-Tribune (www.heraldtribune.com) The main daily newspaper.

Sarasota Visitor Information Center (☑941-706-1253; www.visitsarasota.org; 1710 Main St; ⊗10am-5pm Mon-Sat; 🛜) Very friendly office with tons of info; sells good maps.

❶ Getting There & Away

Sarasota is roughly 60 miles south of Tampa and about 75 miles north of Fort Myers. The main roads into town are Tamiami Trail/Hwy 41 and I-75.

Greyhound (☑ 941-342-1720; www.greyhound.
com; 5951 Porter Way; ⊘ 8:30am-10am &
1:30-6pm) Connects Sarasota with Miami, Fort
Myers and Tampa.

Sarasota-Bradenton International Airport
(SRQ; ☑ 941-359-2770; www.srq-airport.com;
6000 Airport Circle) Served by many major
airlines. Go north on Hwy 41, and right on
University Ave.

Sanibel & Captiva Islands

By preference and by design, island life on
Sanibel is informal and egalitarian, and
riches are rarely flaunted. Development on
Sanibel has been carefully managed: the
northern half is almost entirely protected within the JN 'Ding' Darling National
Wildlife Refuge. While there are hotels
aplenty, the beachfront is free of commer-
cial-and-condo blight. Plus public beach
access is limited to a handful of spread-out
parking lots, so there is no crush of day-
trippers in one place.

The pirate José Gaspar, who called himself Gasparilla, once roamed the Gulf Coast
plundering treasure and seizing beautiful
women, whom he held captive on the aptly
named Captiva Island. Today the tiny village
is confined to a single street, Andy Rosse
Lane, and there are still no traffic lights. The
preferred mode of transportation is the family-friendly bike, and life here is informal
and egalitarian, with island riches rarely being flaunted. Captiva's mansions are hidden
behind thick foliage and sport playful names
such as 'Seas the Day.'

◉ Sights & Activities

Captiva Beach   BEACH
(14790 Captiva Dr) Besides looking directly out
onto heart-melting Gulf sunsets, Captiva
Beach has lovely sand and is close to several
romantic restaurants. Arrive early if you want
to park in the small lot , or come by bike.

**JN 'Ding' Darling
National Wildlife Refuge**   WILDLIFE RESERVE
(☑ 239-472-1100; www.fws.gov/dingdarling; 1 Wildlife Dr; car/cyclist/pedestrian $5/1/1; ⊘ 7am-sun-
set) Named for cartoonist Jay Norwood 'Ding'
Darling, an environmentalist who helped
establish more than 300 sanctuaries across
the USA, this 6300-acre refuge is home to an
abundance of seabirds and wildlife, including alligators, night herons, red-shouldered
hawks, spotted sandpipers, roseate spoonbills, pelicans and anhingas. The refuges'

5-mile **Wildlife Drive** provides easy access,
but bring binoculars; flocks sometimes sit
at expansive distances. Only a few very short
walks lead into the mangroves.

Captiva Cruises   CRUISE
(☑ 239-472-5300; www.captivacruises.com; 11400
Andy Rosse Lane) Departing from **McCarthy's
Marina** (☑ 239-472-5200; www.mccarthysmari-
na.com; 11401 Andy Rosse Lane), Captiva Cruises
offers everything from dolphin and sunset
cruises (from $27.50) to various island ex-
cursions, such as Cayo Costa ($40), Cabbage
Key ($40) and Boca Grande ($50) on Gasparilla Island.

Tarpon Bay Explorers   KAYAKING
(☑ 239-472-8900; www.tarponbayexplorers.com;
900 Tarpon Bay Rd; ⊘ 8am-5pm) Within the
Darling refuge, this outfitter rents canoes
and kayaks ($25 for two hours) for easy,
self-guided paddles in Tarpon Bay, a perfect
place for young paddlers. Guided kayak trips
(adult from $30 to $40, child from $20 to
$25) are also excellent, and there's a range of
other trips and deck talks. Reserve ahead or
come early, as trips book up.

🛏 Sleeping & Eating

Sandpiper Inn   INN $$
(☑ 239-472-1606; www.palmviewsanibel.com; 720
Donax St; r $149-229; P ❀ 🛜) Set a block back
from the water and in close proximity to the
shops and restaurants on Periwinkle Way,
this Old Florida inn offers good value for
Sanibel. Each of the one-bedroom units has
a functional (if dated) kitchen and a sitting
area decked out in tropical colors.

★**'Tween Waters Inn**   RESORT $$$
(☑ 239-472-5161; www.tween-waters.com; 15951
Captiva Dr; r $185-285, ste $270-410, cottages
$265-460; ❀ @ 🛜 ☎ 🏊) For great resort
value on Captiva, choose 'Tween Waters
Inn. Rooms are attractive roosts with rat-
tan furnishings, granite counters, rainfall
showerheads and Tommy Bahama–style
decor. All have balconies and those directly
facing the Gulf are splendid. The tidy little cottages are romantic. Families make
good use of the big pool, tennis courts, full-
service marina and spa. Multinight discounts are attractive.

★**Sweet Melissa's Cafe**   AMERICAN $$$
(☑ 239-472-1956; www.sweetmelissascafe.com;
1625 Periwinkle Way; tapas $9-16, mains $26-34;
⊘ 11:30am-2:30pm & 5pm-close Mon-Fri, 5pm-
close Sat) From menu to mood, Sweet Melis-

sa's offers well-balanced, relaxed refinement. Dishes, including things like farro fettuccine, escargot with marrow and whole crispy fish, are creative without trying too hard. Lots of small-plate options encourage experimenting. Service is attentive and the atmosphere upbeat.

ℹ Information

Sanibel & Captiva Islands Chamber of Commerce (📞 239-472-1080; www.sanibel-captiva.org; 1159 Causeway Rd; ⊙ 9am-5pm; 🛜) One of the more helpful visitor centers around; keeps an updated hotel-vacancy list with dedicated hotel hotline.

ℹ Getting There & Away

Driving is the only way to come and go. The Sanibel Causeway (Hwy 867) charges an entrance toll (cars/motorcycles $6/2). Sanibel is 12 miles long, but low speed limits and traffic makes it seem longer. The main drag is Periwinkle Way, which becomes Sanibel-Captiva Rd.

Naples

For upscale romance and the prettiest, most serene city beach in southwest Florida, come to Naples, the Gulf Coast's answer to Palm Beach. Development along the shoreline has been kept residential. The soft white sand is backed only by narrow dunes and half-hidden mansions. More than that, though, Naples is a cultured, sophisticated town, unabashedly stylish and privileged but also welcoming and fun-loving. Families, teens, couture-wearing matrons, middle-aged executives and smartly dressed young couples all mix and mingle as they stroll downtown's 5th Ave on a balmy evening. Travelers sometimes complain that Naples is expensive, but you can spend just as much elsewhere on a less impressive vacation.

◉ Sights & Activities

★**Naples Botanical Gardens**   GARDENS
(📞 239-643-7275; www.naplesgarden.org; 4820 Bayshore Dr; adult/child 4-14yr $15/10; ⊙ 9am-5pm) This outstanding botanical garden styles itself as 'a place of bliss, a region of supreme delight.' And after spending some time wandering its 2.5-mile trail through nine cultivated gardens you'll rapidly find your inner Zen. Children will dig the thatched-roof tree house, butterfly house and interactive fountain, while adults get dreamy-eyed contemplating landscape architect Raymond Jungles' recently redesigned Scott Florida garden, filled with cascades, 12ft-tall oolite rocks and legacy tree species like date palms, sycamore leaf figs and lemon ficus.

★**Baker Museum**   MUSEUM
(📞 239-597-1900; www.artisnaples.org; 5833 Pelican Bay Blvd; adult/child $10/free; ⊙ 10am-4pm Tue-Thu & Sat, to 8pm Fri, noon-4pm Sun) The pride of Naples, this engaging, sophisticated art museum is part of the Artis–Naples campus, which includes the fabulous Philharmonic Center next door. Devoted to 20th-century modern and contemporary art, the museum's 15 galleries and glass dome conservatory host an exciting round of temporary and permanent shows, ranging from postmodern works to photography and paper craft to glass sculpture.

Naples Municipal Beach   BEACH
(12th Ave S & Gulf Shore Blvd) Naples' city beach is a long, dreamy white strand that succeeds in feeling lively but rarely overcrowded. At the end of 12th Ave S, the 1000ft pier is a symbol of civic pride, having been constructed in 1888, destroyed a few times by fire and hurricane, and reconstructed each time. Parking is spread out in small lots between 7th Ave N and 17th Ave S, each with 10 to 15 spots of mixed resident and metered parking ($1.50 per hour).

🛏 Sleeping & Eating

Inn on 5th   HOTEL $$$
(📞 239-403-8777; www.innonfifth.com; 699 5th Ave S; r $399, ste $599-999; 🅿 ❋ @ 🛜 ❄) This well-polished, Mediterranean-style luxury hotel provides an unbeatable location on either side of 5th Ave. Stylish rooms are more corporate-perfect than historic-romantic, but who complains about pillowtop mattresses and glass-walled showers? Full-service amenities include a 2nd-floor heated pool, business and fitness centers, and an indulgent spa. Free valet parking.

★**Escalante**   BOUTIQUE HOTEL $$$
(📞 239-659-3466; www.hotelescalante.com; 290 5th Ave S; r $200-700) Hidden in plain sight at 5th Ave and 3rd St, the wonderful Escalante is a boutique hotel crafted in the fashion of a Tuscan villa. Rooms and suites are nestled behind luxuriant foliage and flowering pergolas, and feature plantation-style furniture, European linens and designer bath products.

★ Bha! Bha! Persian Bistro   IRANIAN $$$

(☑ 239-594-5557; www.bhabhabistro.com; 865 5th Ave S; mains $26-38; ⊙ 5-9pm Sun-Thu, to 10pm Fri & Sat) This experimental, high-end establishment takes its name from the Farsi phrase for 'yum, yum,' and that turns out to be a serious understatement. Wash down the pistachio lamb meatballs with a saffron lemongrass martini, then continue on to a kebab marinated in exotic spices or the duck *fesenjune*, slow braised with pomegranate and walnut sauce.

The Local   MODERN AMERICAN $$

(☑ 239-596-3276; www.thelocalnaples.com; 5323 Airport Pulling Rd N; mains $12-29; ⊙ 11am-9pm Sun-Thu, to 9:30pm Fri & Sat; ☜) 🖉 The irony of driving 6 miles from downtown to eat local aside, this strip-mall farm-to-table bistro is worth the carbon footprint for fab sustainable fare, from the Mediterranean watermelon salad to the grass-fed beef.

❶ Information

Third St Concierge Kiosk (☑ 239-434-6533; www.thirdstreetsouth.com; Camargo Park, 3rd St S; ⊙ 10am-6pm Mon-Wed, 10am-9pm Thu & Fri, 8:30am-6pm Sat, noon-5pm Sun) What's in Old Naples? This friendly outdoor kiosk attendant is glad you asked.

Visitor Information Center (☑ 239-262-6141; www.napleschamber.org; 2390 Tamiami Trail N; ⊙ 9am-5pm Mon-Fri) Will help with accommodations; good maps, internet access and acres of brochures.

❶ Getting There & Away

A car is essential; ample and free downtown parking makes things easy. Naples is about 40 miles southwest of Fort Myers via I-75.

Greyhound (☑ 239-774-5660; www.greyhound.com; 2669 Davis Blvd) Connects Naples to Miami, Orlando and Tampa.

Southwest Florida International Airport (RSW; ☑ 239-590-4800; www.flylcpa.com; 11000 Terminal Access Rd) This is the main airport for Naples. It's about a 45-minute drive north, along I-75.

CENTRAL FLORIDA

Central Florida is like a *matryoshka*, the Russian doll that encases similar dolls of diminishing size. The region features pretty state parks, gardens and rivers, all ideal for leisurely exploration. One layer down, Central Florida then embraces Kissimmee, Celebration and the vast, sprawling area of

Greater Orlando. Greater Orlando's network of multilane highways and overpasses leads to a huge number of theme parks, including Walt Disney World Resort, Universal Orlando Resort, SeaWorld and Legoland. Judging from the crowds, these parks are the reason most people visit.

But at Central Florida's core is a city: pretty, leafy downtown Orlando, whose great field-to-fork eating scene and world-class museums get overlooked by the hype, sparkle and colors of the theme parks. Many visitors never reach this kernel, the final 'doll,' and the city of Orlando tends to lie in the shadow of Cinderella and Hogwarts School of Witchcraft & Wizardry.

Orlando

If Orlando were a Disney character, it's fair to say that she's like Dory (of Nemo fame) and lacks a bit of confidence. It's so easy to get caught up in Greater Orlando – in the isolated, constructed worlds of Disney or Universal Orlando (for which, let's face it, you're probably here) – that you forget all about the downtown city of Orlando itself. It has a lot to offer: lovely tree-lined neighborhoods; a rich performing arts and museum scene; several fantastic gardens and nature preserves; fabulous cuisine; and a delightfully slower pace devoid of manic crowds. So, sure, enjoy the theme parks: the sparkles, nostalgia and adrenaline-pumped fantasy, but also take time to 'Find Orlando.' Come down off the coasters for one day to explore the quieter, gentler side of the city.

◉ Sights

★ Mennello Museum of American Art   MUSEUM

(☑ 407-246-4278; www.mennellomuseum.org; 900 E Princeton St, Loch Haven Park, Downtown; adult/child 6-18yr $5/1; ⊙ 10:30am-4:30pm Tue-Sat, from noon Sun; 🚌 Lynx 125, 🚊 Florida Hospital Health Village) Tiny but excellent lakeside art museum featuring the work of Earl Cunningham, whose brightly colored images, a fusion of pop and folk art, leap off the canvas. Visiting exhibits often feature American folk art. Every four months there's a new exhibition, everything from a Smithsonian collection to a local artist.

★ Orlando Museum of Art   MUSEUM

(☑ 407-896-4231; www.omart.org; 2416 N Mills Ave, Loch Haven Park, Downtown; adult/child

$15/5; ⊘10am-4pm Tue-Fri, from noon Sat & Sun; ⓚ; ⬚Lynx 125, ⬚Florida Hospital Health Village) Founded in 1924, Orlando's grand and blindingly white center for the arts boasts a fantastic collection – both permanent and temporary – and hosts an array of adult and family-friendly art events and classes. The popular First Thursday ($10), from 6pm to 9pm on the first Thursday of the month, celebrates local artists with regional work, live music and food from Orlando restaurants.

Orlando Eye
AMUSEMENT PARK

(www.officialorlandoeye.com; I-Drive 360, 8401 International Dr, International Drive; from $20; ⊘10am-10pm Sun-Thu, to midnight Fri & Sat) Orlando has got everything else that goes up and down, so why not round and around? Opened in 2017, the Eye is International Drive's latest landmark.

SeaWorld
AMUSEMENT PARK

(☏888-800-5447; www.seaworldparks.com; 7007 Sea World Dr; $95, discounts online, prices vary daily; ⊘9am-8pm; ⓚ; ⬚Lynx 8, 38, 50, 111, ⬚I-Ride Trolley Red Line Stop 28) One of Orlando's largest theme parks, SeaWorld is an aquatic-themed park filled with marine animal shows, roller coasters and up-close sea-life encounters. However, the park's biggest draw is controversial: live shows featuring trained dolphins, sea lions and killer whales. Since the release of the 2013 documentary *Blackfish*, SeaWorld's treatment of its captive orcas has come under intense scrutiny and the company has been hit by falling visitor numbers and negative PR.

Titanic the Experience
MUSEUM

(☏407-248-1166; www.titanicshipofdreams.com; 7324 International Dr, International Drive; adult/child 6-11yr $22/16; ⊘10am-6pm; ⓚ; ⬚Lynx 8, 42, ⬚I-Ride Trolley Red Line Stop 9) Full-scale replicas of the doomed ship's interior and artifacts found at the bottom of the sea. Tour the galleries with guides in period dress or wander through on your own. Kids especially love the dramatic and realistic interpretation of history – each passenger receives a boarding pass, with the name of a real passenger, and at the end of the experience (once the ship has sunk) you learn your fate.

🛏 Sleeping

★Floridian Hotel & Suites
HOTEL $

(☏407-212-3021; www.floridianhotelorlando.com; 7531 Canada Ave, International Drive; r from $75; Ⓟ☷❄�⚏) A wonderful, privately owned budget hotel with similarities to a chain brand, but oh so much better in other respects: delightful front office staff, spotless rooms with fridges and even a complimentary (if basic) breakfast, plus shuttles to various parks. It's near Restaurant Row and handy to International Dr.

Aloft Orlando Downtown
BUSINESS HOTEL $$

(☏497-380-3500; www.aloftorlandodowntown.com; 500 S Orange Ave, Downtown; r from $230; Ⓟ@❄⚏) Open, streamlined and decidedly modern, although the carefully constructed minimalist decor might render the rooms oddly empty for some. The sleek little pool sits unpleasantly on the main road. But it is one of the few hotels within an easy walk to downtown Orlando's bars and restaurants.

Hyatt Regency Grand Cypress Resort
RESORT $$

(☏407-239-1234; www.hyattgrandcypress.com; 1 Grand Cypress Blvd, Lake Buena Vista; r $189-250, resort fee per day $30, self/valet parking $20/29; Ⓟ@❄⚏⚏) Considering the proximity to Disney's Magic Kingdom (7 miles) and Universal Resort Orlando (8 miles), this atrium-style resort is one of the best-value in Orlando.

★Bay Hill Club and Lodge
HOTEL $$$

(☏407-876-2429; www.bayhill.com; 9000 Bay Hill Blvd; r from $300; @❄⚏) Quiet and genteel Bay Hill feels like a time warp; as though you're walking into a TV set or your grandmother's photo album. It is reassuringly calm and simple. The staff are exceptionally gracious and accommodating, and handsome rooms are spread among a series of two-story buildings bordering the Arnold Palmer–designed golf course.

✗ Eating

★P Is for Pie
BAKERY $

(☏407-745-4743; www.crazyforpies.com; 2806 Corrine Dr, Audubon Park; from $2; ⊘7:30am-4:30pm Mon-Sat; ⓚ) Clean-lined with an artisan twist to classic pies (as in sweet tarts with a biscuit base), offering mini and specialty options.

★Dandelion Communitea Café
VEGETARIAN $

(☏407-362-1864; www.dandelioncommunitea.com; 618 N Thornton Ave, Thornton Park; mains $10-14; ⊘11am-10pm Mon-Sat, to 5pm Sun; ✏ⓚ) ⌇ Unabashedly crunchy and definitively organic, this pillar of the sprouts and tempeh and green-tea dining scene serves up creative and excellent plant-based fare in a refurbished old house that invites folks to sit down and hang out.

Graffiti Junktion
American Burger Bar
BURGERS **$**

(☎ 407-426-9503; www.graffitijunktion.com; 700 E Washington St, Thornton Park; mains $10-14; ⊙ 11am-2am) This little neon, happenin' hangout, with courtyard dining and regular drink specials, is all about massive burgers with attitude. Go with a Brotherly Love (Angus beef; $11) or veggie option ($7).

Pho 88
VIETNAMESE **$**

(www.pho88orlando.com; 730 N Mills Ave, Mills 50; mains $8-13; ⊙ 10am-10pm) A flagship in Orlando's thriving Vietnamese district (known as ViMi) just northeast of downtown in an area informally referred to as Mills 50, this authentic, no frills, *pho* (Vietnamese noodle soup) specialist is always packed.

Melting Pot
EUROPEAN **$$**

(www.meltingpot.com/orlando; 7549 W Sand Lake Rd, Restaurant Row; mains $12-25; ⊙ 5-10pm Mon-Thu, 5-11pm Fri, noon-11am Sat, noon-10pm Sun; 👪) Kids in particular love the novelty of a fondue dinner (cheese, beef, chicken,

Greater Orlando & Theme Parks

seafood and, of course, chocolate). Having said that, it's an elegant spot and a popular date-night place.

🍷 Drinking & Nightlife

★Icebar   BAR
(📞407-426-7555; www.icebarorlando.com; 8967 International Dr; entry at door/advance online $20/15; ⊙5pm-midnight Mon-Wed, to 1am Thu, to 2am Fri-Sun; 🚃I-Trolley Red Line Stop 18 or Green Line Stop 10) More classic Orlando gimmicky fun. Step into the 22°F (-5°C) ice house, sit on the ice seat, admire the ice carvings, sip the icy drinks. Coat and gloves are provided at the door, and the fire room, bathrooms and other areas of the bar are kept at normal temperature.

Independent Bar   CLUB
(📞407-839-0457; 68 N Orange Ave, Downtown; $10; ⊙10pm-3am Sun, Wed & Thu, from 9:30pm Fri & Sat) Known to locals as simply the 'I-Bar,' it's hip, crowded and loud, with DJs spinning underground dance and alternative rock into the wee hours.

❶ Information

Official Visitor Center (📞407-363-5872; www.visitorlando.com; 8723 International Dr; ⊙8:30am-6pm; 🚃I-Ride Trolley Red Line 15)

❶ Getting There & Around

Amtrak (www.amtrak.com; 1400 Sligh Blvd) Offers daily trains south to Miami (from $46) and north to New York City (from $144).
Greyhound (📞407-292-3424; www.greyhound.com; 555 N John Young Pkwy) Serves numerous cities from Orlando.

Lymmo (www.golynx.com; free; ⊙6am-10pm Mon-Thu, to midnight Fri, 10am-midnight Sat, to 10pm Sun) circles downtown Orlando for free with stops near Lynx Central Station, near SunRail's Church St Station, at Central and Magnolia, Jefferson and Magnolia and outside the Westin Grand Bohemian.

SunRail (www.sunrail.com), Orlando's commuter rail train, runs north–south. It doesn't stop at or near any theme parks.

In addition to the downtown station, **Amtrak** (www.amtrak.com) serves Winter Park, Kissimmee and Winter Haven (home to Legoland).

Walt Disney World® Resort

Walt Disney World® Resort   AMUSEMENT PARK
(📞407-939-5277; www.disneyworld.disney.go.com; Lake Buena Vista, outside Orlando; daily rates vary, see website for packages & tickets up to 10 days; 🚼) Even if you haven't grown up with something from Walt Disney, chances are you've heard of it. And, despite it sounding like a 'world' (which it is in many respects...read on), it's more complex than the globe. So we're going to break it down for you. Disney World is in fact an unfenced 40-sq-mile area. Within this, although several miles apart from each other, are four contained, spotlessly sanitized theme parks: Magic Kingdom, Epcot, Hollywood Studios and Animal Kingdom.

Walt Disney World® Resort offers a lot more than rides. The huge number of attractions include interactive meet 'n' greets with well-known characters, including Mickey Mouse and Donald Duck, as well as more contemporary casts such as Gaston, Elsa, Anna and so on. Then there are parades,

FLORIDA DISNEY WORLD® RESORT

musical productions, interactive facilities, Disney promotions of the latest projects and plenty of stunt shows. And (here's the surprising part), it's not just for kids. Disney World has cleverly maintained its loyal following, resulting in hundreds of thousands of more mature visitors who just can't get enough, through programs and cuisine and cruises and tours.

Each of the four parks has its own theme, although when most people think of Walt Disney World Resort, they're often thinking of one of the four parks – the **Magic Kingdom**, with Cinderella's Castle at its core. This is the Disney of commercials, of princesses and pirates, Tinkerbell and dreams come true; this is quintessential, old-school Disney with classic rides such as It's a Small World and Space Mountain.

Epcot is a wonderful sensory experience. The park is divided into two sections that are situated around a lake: Future World and World Showcase. **Future World** has Epcot's only two thrill rides plus several pavilions with attractions, restaurants and character-greeting spots. **World Showcase** comprises 11 re-created nations featuring country-specific food, shopping and entertainment. This is the place to slow down a little and enjoy, where you can smell the incense in Morocco, listen to the Beatles in the UK and sip miso in Japan.

Hollywood Studios conjures the heydays of Hollywood, with a replica of Graumann's Chinese Theatre (the main focal icon), but most of the activities reflect unabashed 21st-century energy with attractions focusing on everything from *Star Wars* Jedi training to *Indiana Jones* stunt shows, from Muppet extravaganzas to the latest craze, the Frozen Sing-Along Celebration.

Set apart from the rest of Disney both in miles and in tone, **Animal Kingdom** attempts to blend theme park with zoo, carnival and African safari, all stirred together with a healthy dose of Disney characters, storytelling and transformative magic. Like the other parks, it's also divided into different sections, with wildlife experiences, rides, and musical shows at every corner, including *The Lion King* and *Nemo*. At the time of research, Animal Kingdom was about to open another area: the much-awaited **Pandora – The World of Avatar**.

To round off the Disney experience, Walt Disney World Resort runs a number of accommodations, for families to couples' luxury experiences. The advantage of staying at one of these is that most things, including meals and transportation, are arranged or easily accessible to you (but, although they make things run smoothly, especially if you have children, they're not the be all and end all; other hotels nearby also offer similar services). But they do serve up further fun and yes, even more entertainment including opportunities to dine with Disney characters. It is well designed for travelers with disabilities, with wheelchair rental, easy access and excellent arrangements for line access and the like.

In short, an experience at Walt Disney World Resort is extraordinary. It's an unabashed, unthwarted stimulation overload of music, light, sound, color, thrills and spills. It offers an other worldliness that is fully, inexplicably intoxicating, no matter your age. And that's despite the long lines, the occasional jostling and the over-priced meals. For most of the time, this is indeed the Happiest Place on Earth.

And, just when the sun has set and you think you're done for the day, there's more; each park has a nighttime fireworks show (the names of which change according to the annual program).

🛏 Sleeping & Eating

Disney resort hotels are divided according to location (Magic Kingdom, Epcot, Animal Kingdom and Disney Boardwalk). Prices vary drastically according to season, week and day.

While deluxe resorts are the best Disney has to offer, note that you're paying for Disney theming and location convenience, not luxury. Most offer multiroom suites and villas, upscale restaurants, children's programs and easy access to theme parks.

With the exception of Epcot, expect mediocre fast food, bad coffee and cafeteria cuisine at premium prices. Table-service restaurants accept 'priority seating' reservations up to 180 days in advance. Reserve through Disney Dining (☏407-939-3463), at www.disneyworld. disney.go.com or through the My Disney Experience app. Remember: while restaurants in the theme parks require theme-park admission, resort hotel restaurants do not.

ⓘ Getting There & Around

Disney lies 25 minutes' drive south of downtown Orlando. Take I-4 to well-signed exits 64, 65 or 67.

Alamos and National car rental is available inside the Walt Disney World Dolphin Resort.

Car Care Center (☏407-824-0976; 1000 W Car Care Dr, Walt Disney World Resort; ⊙7am-7pm Mon-Fri, 7am-4pm Sat, 8am-3pm Sun) is a full-service garage, providing services (roadside assistance including towing, flat tire and battery jump starts) on Disney property only.

If you're staying at a Walt Disney World Resort hotel and are arriving at the Orlando International Airport (as opposed to Sanford), arrange in advance for complimentary luggage handling and deluxe bus transportation with **Disney's Magical Express** (☏866-599-0951; www. disneyworld.disney.go.com). They will send you baggage labels in advance, collect your luggage at the airport, and if during your stay you transfer from one Disney hotel to another, the resort will transfer your luggage while you're off for the day.

The Disney transportation system utilizes boat, bus and a monorail to shuttle visitors to hotels, theme parks and other attractions within Walt Disney World Resort. The Transportation & Ticket Center operates as the main hub of this system. Note that it can take an hour to get from point A to point B using the Disney transportation system, and there is not always a direct route.

Universal Orlando Resort

★**Universal Orlando Resort**
AMUSEMENT PARK
(☏407-363-8000; www.universalorlando.com; 1000 Universal Studios Plaza; single park 1/2 days adult $105/185, child $100/175, both parks adult/child $155/150; ⊙daily, hours vary; 🚌Lynx 21, 37 & 40, 🚤Universal) Pedestrian-friendly Universal Orlando Resort has got spunk, spirit and attitude. With fantastic rides, excellent children's attractions and entertaining shows, it's comparable to Walt Disney World Resort. But Universal does everything just a bit smarter, funnier and more smoothly, as well as being smaller and easier to navigate. Instead of the Seven Dwarfs, there's the Simpsons. Instead of Mickey Mouse, there's Harry Potter. Universal offers pure, unabashed, adrenaline-pumped, full-speed-ahead fun for the entire family.

The Universal Orlando Resort consists of two (three by the time you read this) theme parks: **Islands of Adventure**, with the bulk of the thrill rides, and **Universal Studios**, with movie-based attractions and shows (including the **Wizarding World of Harry Potter**). **Volcano Bay** will open in 2017 as a water park of thrills and splashes and state-of-the-art rides through a 200ft volcano.

Universal's dining/entertainment district is **CityWalk** and it has five resort hotels (a sixth, Universal's Aventura Hotel, will open in 2018).

🛏 Sleeping & Eating

Universal Orlando Resort boasts five excellent resort hotels. Staying at a resort eliminates many logistical hassles: it's a pleasant gardened walk or a quiet boat ride to the parks; most offer Unlimited Express Pass access to park attractions and priority dining; several popular rides, such as Wizarding World of Harry Potter, opens one hour early for all guests; and the Loews Loves Pets program welcomes Fido as a VIP.

The only restaurants in the theme parks that take advance reservations are **Finnegan's Bar & Grill** (☏407-224-3613; www.universalorlando.com; mains $10-23; ⊙11am-park closing; 🖥🍴) and **Lombard's Seafood Grille** (☏407-224-3613, 407-224-6401; www.universalorlando.com; mains $15-28; ⊙11am-park closing; 🖥🍴) in Universal Studios, and **Mythos Restaurant** (☏407-224-4012, 407-224-4534; www.universalorlando.com; mains $14-23; ⊙11am-3pm; 🍴) and **Confisco Grille** (☏407-224-4012; www.universalorlando.com; mains $6-22; ⊙11am-4pm; 🍴🍴) in Islands of Adventure.

Each Universal resort has high-quality bars and restaurants that you can enjoy even if you're not a guest.

❶ Getting There & Around

From I-4, take exit 74B or 75A and follow the signs. From International Dr, follow the signs west onto Universal Blvd.

Lynx buses 21, 37 and 40 service the Universal Orlando Resort parking garage (40 runs directly from the downtown Orlando Amtrak station). International Dr's **I-Ride Trolley** (☏407-354-5656; www.iridetrolley.com; rides adult/child 3-9yr $2/1, passes 1/3/5/7/14 days $5/7/9/12/18; ⊙8am-10:30pm) stops at Universal Blvd, a 0.6-mile walk away.

Universal Orlando Resort – that is, Universal Orlando's resort hotels, Islands of Adventure and Universal Studios theme parks and City-Walk – are linked by pedestrian walkways. It's a 10- to 15-minute walk from the theme parks and CityWalk to the deluxe resort hotels. Cabana Bay Beach Resort is about a 25-minute walk. Several hotels outside the park are within a 20-minute walk, but it's not a very pleasant journey.

Rent strollers, wheelchairs and Electric Convenience Vehicles (ECVs) at the entrance to each park and manual wheelchairs at the Rotunda section of the parking lot. To reserve an ECV in advance, call ☏407-224-4233.

FLORIDA UNIVERSAL ORLANDO RESORT

FLORIDA PANHANDLE

The most geographically northern end of Florida is by far its most culturally Southern side. The Panhandle – that spit of land embedded in the left shoulder of the Florida peninsula – is hemmed in by Alabama and Georgia, and in many ways the region's beaches are effectively coastal extensions of those states.

What beaches they are, though! All powdered white sand and teal- to jade-green waters, this is a coast of primal, wind-blown beauty in many places, particularly the undeveloped stretches of salt marsh and slash pine that spill east and west of Apalachee Bay. In other areas, the seashore is given to rental houses and high-rise condos.

Inland, you'll find a tangle of palmetto fans and thin pine woods interspersed with crystal springs, lazy rivers and military testing ranges – this area has one of the highest concentrations of defense facilities in the country.

Tallahassee

Florida's capital, cradled between gently rising hills and nestled beneath tree-canopied roadways, is geographically closer to Atlanta than it is to Miami. Culturally, it's far closer to the Deep South than the majority of the state it governs. Despite its status as a government center, and the presence of two major universities (Florida State and Florida Agricultural & Mechanical University), the pace here is slower than syrup. That said, there are a handful of interesting museums and outlying attractions that will appeal to history and nature buffs and could easily detain a visitor for a day or two.

◉ Sights & Activities

★**Tallahassee Museum of History & Natural Science** MUSEUM
(☑850-575-8684; www.tallahasseemuseum.org; 3945 Museum Rd; adult/child $11.50/8.50; ☉9am-5pm Mon-Sat, from 11am Sun; ℗ 🐾) 🐾 Occupying 52 acres of pristine manicured gardens and wilderness on the outskirts of Tallahassee, near the airport, this wonderful natural-history museum features living exhibits of Floridian flora and fauna – including the incredibly rare Floridan panther and red wolf – and has delighted visitors for more than 50 years. Be sure to check out the otters in their new home, or try ziplining above the canopy in the Tree to Tree Adventures.

Tallahassee Automobile & Collectibles Museum MUSEUM
(☑850-942-0137; www.tacm.com; 6800 Mahan Dr; adult/student/child under 10yr $16/12/8; ☉8am-5pm Mon-Fri, from 10am Sat, from noon Sun; ℗) If you like motor vehicles, welcome to heaven! This museum houses a pristine collection of more than 130 unique and historical automobiles from around the world. Top that with collections of boats, motorcycles, books, pianos and sports memorabilia and you've got a full day on your hands. It is about 8 miles northeast of downtown.

Florida State Capitol NOTABLE BUILDING
(www.floridacapitol.myflorida.com; 400 South Monroe St; ☉8am-5pm Mon-Fri) FREE The stark and imposing 22-story Florida State Capitol's top-floor observation deck affords 360-degree views of the city. In session the capitol is a hive of activity, with politicians, staffers and lobby groups buzzing in and around its honeycombed corridors.

Tallahassee-St Marks Historic Railroad State Trail CYCLING
(☑850-519-6594; www.floridastateparks.org/tallahasseestmarks; 1358 Old Woodville Rd, Crawfordville; ☉8am-sunset) 🐾 FREE The ultimate treat for runners, skaters and cyclists, this trail has 16 miles of smooth pavement shooting due south to the gulf-port town of St Marks and not a car or traffic light in sight. It's easy and flat for all riders, sitting on a coastal plain and shaded at many points by canopies of gracious live oaks.

🛏 Sleeping & Eating

aloft Tallahassee Downtown HOTEL $$
(☑850-513-0313; www.alofttallahassee.com; 200 N Monroe St; r $115-230; ℗🐾) This branch of the popular aloft chain boasts a prime downtown location and funky, functional rooms. Bathrooms feature counter-to-ceiling mirrors and lots of space for all the makeup in the world. Beds are uber-comfy, and free high-speed internet is included.

Kool Beanz Café FUSION $$
(☑850-224-2466; www.koolbeanz-cafe.com; 921 Thomasville Rd; mains $17-24; ☉11am-10pm Mon-Fri, 5:30-10pm Sat, 10:30am-2pm Sun; ℗🐾🍴) It's got a corny name but a wonderfully eclectic and homey vibe – plus great, creative fare. The menu changes daily, but you can count on finding anything from hummus plates to jerk-spiced scallops to duck in blueberry-ginger sauce.

🍷 Drinking & Entertainment

Madison Social PUB
(📞850-894-6276; www.madisonsocial.com; 705
South Woodward Ave; mains $9-20; ⏰11:30am-2am
Sun-Thu, from 10am Fri & Sat; 📶) Never mind the
trend of flipping former transmission shops
into hipster locales, this trendy hot spot was
built to look that way from go. It swarms with
a bold and beautiful mix of locals and FSU
students, downing drinks at the stellar bar or
aluminum picnic tables as the sun sets over
Doak Campbell football stadium, the largest
continuous brick structure in the USA.

Bradfordville Blues Club LIVE MUSIC
(📞850-906-0766; www.bradfordvilleblues.com;
7152 Moses Lane, off Bradfordville Rd; tickets
$15-35; ⏰10pm Fri & Sat) Down the end of
a dirt road lit by tiki torches, you'll find a
bonfire raging under the live oaks at this
hidden-away juke joint that hosts excellent
national blues acts. Also open some Thursdays from 8:30pm; check online.

ℹ️ Information

Florida Welcome Center (📞850-488-6167;
www.visitflorida.com; cnr Pensacola & Duval
Sts; ⏰8am-5pm Mon-Fri) In the Florida State
Capitol, this is a fantastic resource.

Leon County Welcome Center (📞850-606-
2305; www.visittallahassee.com; 106 E Jefferson St; ⏰8am-5pm Mon-Fri) Runs the excellent
visitor information center, with brochures on
walking and driving tours.

ℹ️ Getting There & Around

Tallahassee is 98 miles from Panama City
Beach, 135 miles from Jacksonville, 192 miles
from Pensacola, 120 miles from Gainesville and
470 miles from Miami. The main access road
is I-10; to reach the Gulf Coast, follow Hwy 319
south to Hwy 98.

The tiny **Tallahassee International Airport**
(📞850-891-7802; www.talgov.com/airport;
3300 Capital Circle SW) is served by American
and Delta for US domestic and international
connections, and Silver Airways for direct flights
to Tampa and Orlando. It's about 5 miles southwest of downtown, off Hwy 263. There's no public transportation. Some hotels have shuttles,
but otherwise a taxi to downtown costs around
$20: try **Yellow Cab** (📞850-999-9999; www.
tallahasseeyellowcab.com).

The **Greyhound bus station** (📞850-222-
4249; www.greyhound.com; 112 W Tennessee
St) is at the corner of Duval, opposite the downtown **StarMetro** (📞850-891-5200; www.talgov.
com/starmetro; per trip/day $1.25/3) transfer
center.

WORTH A TRIP

DELAND: CRESS

Citified foodies have been known to trek
to sleepy DeLand, half an hour from
Daytona Beach (p489), just to eat at
the cutting-edge bistro Cress (📞386-
734-3740; www.cressrestaurant.com; 103 W
Indiana Ave; mains $19-34; ⏰from 5:30pm
Tue-Sat), whose menu might offer such
delights as local seafood *mofongo* (a
classic Caribbean dish), Indonesian
shrimp curry, and a salad of delicate
pea tendrils with passion-fruit emulsion.
Three-course fixed menus ($40, with
wine pairing $58) are excellent.

Pensacola

The Alabama border is just a few miles
down the road, which helps explain the vibe
of Pensacola, a city that jumbles laid-back
Southern syrup with Florida brashness.
With lively beaches, a Spanish-style downtown, and a thrumming military culture,
this is by far the most interesting city in the
Panhandle.

While urban-chic trends (locavore food,
craft cocktails etc) are taking root, visitors
still primarily come to Pensacola for an
all-American, blue-collar vacation experience: white-sand beaches, fried seafood and
bars serving cheap domestics. During March
and April, things reach fever pitch when
droves of students descend for the weeklong
bacchanalia of spring break. Beware.

Downtown, centered on Palafox St, lies
north of the waterfront. Across the Pensacola Bay Bridge from here is the mostly residential peninsula of Gulf Breeze. Cross one
more bridge, the Bob Sikes (toll $1), to reach
pretty Pensacola Beach, the ultimate destination for most visitors.

Distinctly separate from Pensacola itself,
Pensacola Beach is a pretty stretch of powdery white sand, gentle, warm waters and
a string of mellow beachfront hotels. The
beach occupies nearly 8 miles of the 40-mile-long Santa Rosa barrier island, surrounded
by the Santa Rosa Sound and the Gulf of Mexico to the north and south, and by the federally protected Gulf Islands National Seashore
on either side. Though determined residents
have protected much of the barrier island
from development, several high-rise condos
have created a bit of a Gulf Coast skyline.

⊙ Sights

★ National Naval Aviation Museum
MUSEUM

(☎800-327-5002; www.navalaviationmuseum.org; 1750 Radford Blvd; ⊙9am-5pm; ⓓ) **FREE** A visit to Pensacola is not complete without a trip to this enormous collection of military aircraft muscle and artifacts. Adults and children alike will be fascinated by the range of planes on display: more than 150! That's before we even get to the high-tech stuff like flight simulators and an IMAX theater. You can watch the Blue Angels (☎850-452-3806; www.naspensacolaairshow.com; 390 San Carlos Rd, Suite A) **FREE** practice their death-defying air show at 8:30am most Tuesdays and Wednesdays between March and November.

Historic Pensacola Village
MUSEUM

(☎850-595-5985; www.historicpensacola.org; Tarragona & Church St; adult/child $8/4; ⊙10am-4pm Tue-Sat; ⓟⓓ) ⌀ Pensacola's rich colonial history spans more than 450 years. This fascinating and attractive village is a self-contained enclave of photogenic historic homes turned into museums.

★ Gulf Islands National Seashore
PARK

(☎850-934-2600; www.nps.gov/guis; vehicle $15; ⊙sunrise-sunset; ⓓ) ⌀ The highlight of the Florida Panhandle, this 150-mile stretch of mostly undeveloped white-sand beach is a prime example of what the Gulf Coast looked like before human settlement (which, to be fair, can often be seen in the form of high rises in the distance). The National Seashore is not contiguous, but you'll find portions all along the coast: long swaths of sugar-white dunes crowned with sea oats, a perfect example of pristine flatland beach.

🛌 Sleeping & Eating

Solé Inn
MOTEL $

(☎850-470-9298; www.soleinnandsuites.com; 200 N Palafox St; r $79-199; ❄☎✉) Just north of downtown, this renovated motel goes for a 1960s mod look, with a black-and-white color scheme, animal-print accents and acrylic bubble lamps. Rooms aren't huge, but price, location and originality make up for the lack of space. There's complimentary continental breakfast.

Holiday Inn Resort
HOTEL $$

(☎850-203-0635; www.holidayinnresortpensacolabeach.com; 14 Via de Luna Dr; r from $210; ✉) This beachfront hotel has cool, inviting rooms with ultra-comfy beds, flat-screen TVs and great showers. Oceanfront rooms have spacious balconies overhanging the soft, white sands and the cool turquoise waters below. Suites and kids' suites are available, and the pool is killer. Friendly, obliging staff help seal the deal. Excellent value.

Peg Leg Pete's
SEAFOOD $$

(☎850-932-4139; www.peglegpetes.com; 1010 Fort Pickens Rd; mains $9-25; ⊙11am-10pm; ⓓ)

OFF THE BEATEN TRACK

APALACHICOLA NATIONAL FOREST

The largest of Florida's three national forests, the **Apalachicola National Forest** (☎850-523-8500, 850-643-2282; www.fs.usda.gov/main/apalachicola; entrance off FL 13, FL 67, & other locations; day-use fee $3; ⊙8am-sunset; ✉) ⌀ occupies almost 938 sq miles – more than half a million acres – of the Panhandle from just west of Tallahassee to the Apalachicola River. It's made up of lowlands, pines, cypress hammocks and oaks, and dozens of species call the area home, including mink, gray and red foxes, coyotes, six bat species, beavers, woodpeckers, alligators, Florida black bears and the elusive Florida panther. Numerous lakes and miles of trails make this one of the most diverse outdoor recreation areas in the state. You'll need wheels to explore the forest, either a bicycle for the exceedingly fit, or a car for the rest of us. Given that the woods cover such an enormous area, there are multiple entry points, including along SR 65 (easier if you're coming from Apalachicola) and SR 20 (good for those coming from Tallahassee).

The western half of the forest is controlled by the **Apalachicola Ranger Station** (☎850-643-2282; www.fs.usda.gov/apalachicola; 11152 NW SR-20), which is northwest of the forest near the intersection of Hwys 12 and 20, just south of Bristol. The eastern half of the forest is managed by the **Wakulla Ranger Station** (☎850-926-3561; www.fs.usda.gov/apalachicola; 57 Taff Dr), just off Hwy 319 in Crawfordville.

Ah-har, me hearties, walk ye olde plank, blah blah pirate stuff...you get the idea, this place has a theme going. Anyways, pop into Pete's for almost-beachfront oysters, fat grouper sandwiches, crab legs and jumbo sea scallops. There's nothing fancy about the woodsy, somewhat grungy sea-shanty decor, but the service is swift and smiley.

★**Iron** MODERN AMERICAN **$$$**
(☑850-476-7776; www.restaurantiron.com; 22 N Palafox St; mains $26-46; ☺4:30-10pm Tue-Thu, to 1am Fri & Sat; ☎) Armed with New Orleans experience, chef Alex McPhail works his ever-changing menu magic at downtown's Iron, the best of Pensacola's new line of vibrant, locally sourced, high-end culinary hotbeds. Extremely friendly mixologists know their craft while McPhail's food ranges from beer-braised pork belly to Creole-seasoned catch of the day.

🍷 Drinking & Entertainment

McGuire's Irish Pub PUB
(☑850-433-6789; www.mcguiresirishpub.com; 600 E Gregory St; ☺11am-2am) This ginormous Irish theme park of a pub gets rowdy around 9pm and is super-popular at dinner time: the pub grub is top-notch. Don't try to pay for your drinks with one of the thousands of dollar bills hanging from the ceiling – a local found himself in the slammer that way!

Roundup GAY
(☑850-433-8482; www.theroundup.net; 560 E Heinberg St; ☺2pm-3am) For those who like their men manly, check out this niche-y, neighborhood hangout with a killer furry-friendly patio. Ladies are welcome, but cowboys, tradies and bikers are always flavor of the month.

Saenger Theatre THEATER
(☑850-595-3880; www.pensacolasaenger.com; 118 S Palafox Pl) This Spanish baroque beauty was reconstructed in 1925 using bricks from the Pensacola Opera House, which was destroyed in a 1916 hurricane. It now hosts popular musicals and top-billing music acts and is home to the Pensacola Symphony Orchestra and the Pensacola Opera.

> **WORTH A TRIP**
>
> ## PENSACOLA SCENIC BLUFFS HIGHWAY
>
> This 11-mile stretch of road, which winds around the precipice of the highest point along the Gulf Coast, makes for a peaceful drive or slightly challenging bike ride. You'll see stunning views of Escambia Bay and pass a notable crumbling brick chimney – part of the steam-power plant for the Hyer-Knowles lumber mill in the 1850s – the only remnant of what was the first major industrial belt in the area.

ⓘ Information

Pensacola Visitors Information Center
(☑800-874-1234; www.visitpensacola.com; 1401 E Gregory St; ☺8am-5pm Mon-Fri, 9am-4pm Sat, 10am-4pm Sun) Come to the foot of the Pensacola Bay Bridge for a bounty of tourist information, knowledgeable staff and a free internet kiosk.

Pensacola Beach Visitors Information Center (☑850-932-1500; www.visitpensacolabeach. com; 735 Pensacola Beach Blvd; ☺9am-5pm) On the right as soon as you enter Pensacola Beach; this is a small place with some useful maps and brochures about goings-on, road closures (due to storms) and anything else beach oriented.

ⓘ Getting There & Away

Pensacola Regional Airport (☑850-436-5000; www.flypensacola.com; 2430 Airport Blvd) is served by most major US airlines. Primary direct connections outside Florida include Atlanta, Charlotte, Dallas and Houston. It's 4 miles northeast of downtown off 9th Ave on Airport Blvd. A taxi costs about $20 to downtown and $35 to the beach. Try **Yellow Cab** (☑850-433-3333; www.yellowcabpensacola.com).

The **Greyhound station** (☑850-476-4800; www.greyhound.com; 505 W Burgess Rd) is located north of the downtown area. **Escambia County Transit** (ECAT; ☑850-595-3228; www.goecat.com; rides $1.75) has a free trolley service connecting downtown Pensacola and the beach between Memorial Day weekend and the end of September.

I-10 is the major east–west thoroughfare used by buses, and many pass down Palafox St.

Great Lakes

Best Places to Eat

➡ Spencer (p576)
➡ Young Joni (p602)
➡ Tucker's (p565)
➡ Hopleaf (p535)
➡ Tinker Street (p547)

Best Places to Sleep

➡ Kimpton Schofield Hotel (p555)
➡ Acme Hotel (p531)
➡ Brewhouse Inn & Suites (p588)
➡ Hotel 340 (p605)
➡ Inn on Ferry Street (p572)

Why Go?

Don't be fooled by all the corn. Behind it lurks surfing beaches and Tibetan temples, car-free islands and the green-draped night lights of the aurora borealis. The Midwest takes its knocks for being middle-of-nowhere boring; so consider the moose-filled national parks, urban five-ways (a meal consisting of spaghetti, chili, onions, beans and cheese) and Hemingway, Dylan and Vonnegut sites to be its little secret.

Roll call for the Midwest's cities starts with Chicago, which unfurls what is arguably the country's mightiest skyline. Milwaukee keeps the beer-and-Harley flame burning, while Minneapolis shines a hipster beacon out over the fields. Detroit rocks, plain and simple. The Great Lakes themselves are huge, like inland seas, offering beaches, dunes, resort towns and lighthouse-dotted scenery. Dairy farms and fruit orchards blanket the region, meaning fresh pie and ice cream aplenty. And when the Midwest does flatten out? There's always a goofball roadside attraction, like the Spam Museum or world's biggest ball of twine, to revive imaginations.

When to Go
Chicago

Jan & Feb It's that chilly time when skiers and snowmobilers hit the trails.

Jul & Aug Finally, it's warm! Beer gardens hop, beaches splash, and festivals rock most weekends.

Sep & Oct Fair weather, bountiful farm and orchard harvests, and shoulder-season bargains.

History

The region's first residents included the Hopewell (around 200 BC) and Mississippi River mound builders (around AD 700). Both left behind mysterious piles of earth that were tombs for their leaders and possibly tributes to their deities. You can see remnants at Cahokia in southern Illinois, and Mound City in southeastern Ohio.

French voyageurs (fur traders) arrived in the early 17th century and established missions and forts. The British turned up soon after that, with the rivalry spilling over into the French and Indian Wars (Seven Years' War; 1754–61), after which Britain took control of all of the land east of the Mississippi. Following the Revolutionary War, the Great Lakes area became the new USA's Northwest Territory, which soon was divided into states and locked to the region after it developed its impressive canal and railroad network. But conflicts erupted between the newcomers and the Native Americans, including the 1811 Battle of Tippecanoe in Indiana; the bloody 1832 Black Hawk War in Wisconsin, Illinois and around, which forced indigenous people to move west of the Mississippi; and the 1862 Sioux uprising in Minnesota.

Throughout the late 19th and early 20th centuries, industries sprang up and grew quickly, fueled by resources of coal and iron, and cheap transportation on the lakes. The availability of work brought huge influxes of immigrants from Ireland, Germany, Scandinavia and southern and eastern Europe. For decades after the Civil War, a great number of African Americans also migrated to the region's urban centers from the South.

The area prospered during WWII and throughout the 1950s, but was followed by 20 years of social turmoil and economic stagnation. Manufacturing industries declined, which walloped Rust Belt cities such as Detroit and Cleveland with high unemployment and 'white flight' (white middle-class families who fled to the suburbs).

The 1980s and '90s brought urban revitalization. The region's population increased, notably with newcomers from Asia and Mexico. Growth in the service and high-tech sectors resulted in economic balance, although manufacturing industries such as car making and steel still played a big role, meaning that when the economic crisis hit in 2008, Great Lakes towns felt the pinch first and foremost.

ILLINOIS

Chicago dominates the state with its sky-high architecture and superlative museums, restaurants and music clubs. But venturing further afield reveals Hemingway's mannerly hometown, scattered shrines to local hero Abe Lincoln, and a trail of corn dogs, pies and drive-in theaters down Route 66. A cypress swamp and a prehistoric World Heritage Site make appearances in Illinois too.

GREAT LAKES IN...

One Week

Spend the first two days in Chicago (p516) stuffing your face and gawking at architecture. On your third day, make the 1½-hour trip to Milwaukee (p587) for beer, art and badass motorcycles. Take the ferry to Michigan and spend your fourth day in Saugatuck (p579). The artsy town booms in summer thanks to its golden beaches, piney breezes, galleries and welcoming bars. Circle back via Indiana Dunes (p552) for sandy hikes and swimming, or via Indiana's Amish Country (p554) for a unique cultural immersion.

Two Weeks

After two days in Chicago, on day three make for Madison (p591) to chow in locavore eateries and visit the surrounding quirky sights. Spend your fourth and fifth days at the Apostle Islands (p596) boating around wind-bashed cliffs and caves. Then head into Michigan's Upper Peninsula to visit Marquette (p585) and Pictured Rocks (p584) for a few days. Both are outdoorsy places with dramatic nature at their doorstep. Follow with a visit to the towering Sleeping Bear Dunes (p580) and the wineries around Traverse City (p581). Return via the galleries, pies and beaches of Saugatuck (p579).

Great Lakes Highlights

1 Chicago
(p516) Absorbing the skyscrapers, museums, festivals and foodie bounty.

2 Detroit (p568)
Embracing the city's can-do spirit and partaking of its art, eateries and neighborhood bicycle rides.

3 Ohio's Amish Country (p560)
Slowing down for clip-clopping horses and buggies.

4 Michigan's Western Shore
(p578) Beach lounging, dune climbing, berry eating and surfing.

5 Milwaukee
(p587) Polka dancing at a Friday-night fish fry and drinking lots o' beer.

6 Boundary Waters (p609)
Paddling deep into the piney woods and sleeping under a blanket of stars.

7 Route 66 (p519)
Taking the slowpoke route through Illinois past pie-filled diners and oddball roadside attractions.

8 Central Indiana (p548)
Being surprised by the Tibetan temples, phenomenal architecture and green hills.

ℹ Information

Illinois Highway Conditions (www.getting aroundillinois.com)

Illinois Office of Tourism (www.enjoyillinois.com)

Illinois State Park Information (www.dnr. illinois.gov) State parks are free to visit. Campsites cost $6 to $35; some accept reservations (www.reserveamerica.com; fee $5).

Chicago

Steely skyscrapers, top chefs, rocking festivals – the Windy City will blow you away with its low-key cultured awesomeness.

It's hard to know what to gawp at first. High-flying architecture is everywhere, from the stratospheric, glass-floored Willis Tower to Frank Gehry's swooping silver Pritzker Pavilion to Frank Lloyd Wright's stained-glass Robie House. Whimsical public art studs the streets; you might be walking along and wham, there's an abstract Picasso statue that's not only cool to look at, but you're allowed to go right up and climb on it. For art museums, take your pick: impressionist masterpieces at the massive Art Institute, psychedelic paintings at the mid-sized Museum of Mexican Art or outsider drawings at the small Intuit gallery.

History

Much of Chicago's past is downright legendary. You've probably heard about Mrs

O'Leary's cow that kicked over a lantern that started the Great Fire that torched the city. And about a gent named Al Capone who wielded a mean machine gun during an unsavory era of booze-fueled vice. And about the 'machine' that has controlled local politics for decades. Throw in the invention of the skyscraper and Ferris wheel, and you've got a whopper of a tale.

◎ Sights

Big-ticket draws such as Millennium Park, Willis Tower and the Art Institute are downtown right in the Loop. Next door, the South Loop holds the lakefront Museum Campus, with three popular sights including the Field Museum. To the Loop's north are Navy Pier and 360° Chicago (aka the John Hancock tower). Onward Lincoln Park and Wrigley Field do their thing. All of these places are easy to reach on public transportation. Hyde Park is the one neighborhood with top sights that is further flung and requires some planning to reach.

◎ The Loop

The Loop is Chicago's center of action, named for the elevated train tracks that lasso its streets. The Art Institute, Willis Tower, Theater District and Millennium Park are top draws among the skyscrapers. The city's biggest festivals also rock the area.

★**Millennium Park** PARK
(Map p520; ☑312-742-1168; www.millennium park.org; 201 E Randolph St; ☉6am-11pm; ▧; Ⓜ Brown, Orange, Green, Purple, Pink Line to Washington/Wabash) The city's showpiece is a trove of free and arty sights. It includes **Pritzker Pavilion**, Frank Gehry's swooping silver band shell, which hosts free concerts most nights in summer (6:30pm; bring a picnic and bottle of wine); Anish Kapoor's beloved silvery sculpture **Cloud Gate**, aka the 'Bean'; and Jaume Plensa's **Crown Fountain**, a de facto water park that projects video images of locals spitting water, gargoyle style.

The **McCormick Tribune Ice Rink** (55 N Michigan Ave; ☉late Nov-late Feb) fills with skaters in winter (and al fresco diners in summer). The hidden **Lurie Garden** (www.lurie garden.org) blooms with prairie flowers and tranquility. The Gehry-designed **BP Bridge** spans Columbus Dr and offers great skyline views, while the **Nichols Bridgeway** arches from the park up to the Art Institute's small, 3rd-floor sculpture terrace (free to view).

Metro Chicago Area

See Downtown Chicago Map (p520)

CHICAGO IN TWO DAYS...

Day One

You might as well dive right in with the big stuff. Take a boat or walking tour with the Chicago Architecture Foundation (p529) and ogle the most sky-scraping collection of buildings the US has to offer. Saunter over to Millennium Park (p516) to see 'the Bean' reflect the skyline and to splash under Crown Fountain's human gargoyles.

Explore the Art Institute of Chicago, the nation's second-largest art museum. It holds masterpieces aplenty, especially impressionist and post-impressionist paintings (and paperweights). Next, head over to Willis Tower, zip up to the 103rd floor and step out onto the glass-floored ledge. Yes, it is a long way down.

Chicago dazzles after dark and its diversity is yours to savour. Options are endless but original Chicago offerings could include hitting the Green Mill (p537), once Al Capone's favourite speakeasy; settling in to Danny's (p537) where early evening beers progress to cocktails and DJs under the same roof, or sampling some out-there local theatre at the legendary Steppenwolf (p538).

Day Two

Take a stroll on Michigan Ave – aka the Magnificent Mile (p523) – where big-name department stores ka-ching in a glittering row. Mosey over to Navy Pier (p523). Wander the half-mile promenade and take a spin on the high-in-the-sky Ferris wheel.

Spend the afternoon at the Museum Campus (p523) – the water taxi from Navy Pier is a fine way to get there. Miles of aisles of dinosaurs and gemstones stuff the Field Museum of Natural History. Sharks and other fish swim in the kiddie-mobbed Shedd Aquarium. Meteorites and supernovas are on view at the Adler Planetarium.

Wander along Milwaukee Ave and take your pick of booming bars, indie-rock clubs and hipster shops. Bustling Reckless Records (p540) is Chicago's top indie music store and testament to the fact that people still buy vynil and CDs. The Hideout (p538) and Empty Bottle (p538) are sweet spots to catch a badass band.

Free yoga and Pilates classes take place Saturday mornings in summer on the **Great Lawn**, while the Family Fun Tent provides free kids' activities daily in summer from 10am to 2pm.

★ Art Institute of Chicago   MUSEUM

(Map p520; ☑ 312-443-3600; www.artic.edu; 111 S Michigan Ave; adult/child $25/free; ⊙ 10:30am-5pm Fri-Wed, to 8pm Thu; 🚇; Ⓜ Brown, Orange, Green, Purple, Pink Line to Adams) The Art Institute is the second-largest art museum in the country. Its collection of impressionist and post-impressionist paintings rivals those in France, and the number of surrealist works is tremendous. Download the free app for DIY audio tours; it offers several quick-hit jaunts, from highlights (including Georges Seurat's *A Sunday Afternoon on the Island of La Grande Jatte* and Edward Hopper's *Nighthawks*) to architecture and pop art tours. Allow two hours to browse the museum's must-sees.

★ Willis Tower   TOWER

(Map p520; ☑ 312-875-9696; www.theskydeck.com; 233 S Wacker Dr; adult/child $23/15; ⊙ 9am-10pm Mar-Sep, 10am-8pm Oct-Feb; Ⓜ Brown, Orange, Purple, Pink Line to Quincy) It's Chicago's tallest building, and the 103rd-floor Skydeck puts you high into the heavens. Take the ear-popping, 70-second elevator ride to the top and then step onto one of the glass-floored ledges jutting out in mid-air for a knee-buckling perspective straight down. On clear days the view sweeps over four states. The entrance is on Jackson Blvd. Queues can take up to an hour on busy days (peak times are in summer, between 11am and 4pm Friday through Sunday).

Chicago Cultural Center   NOTABLE BUILDING

(Map p520; ☑ 312-744-6630; www.chicagoculturalcenter.org; 78 E Washington St; ⊙ 9am-7pm Mon-Thu, to 6pm Fri & Sat, 10am-6pm Sun; Ⓜ Brown, Orange, Green, Purple, Pink Line to Washington/Wabash) **FREE** This exquisite, beaux-arts building began its life as the Chicago Public

Library in 1897. Today the block-long building houses terrific art exhibitions (especially the 4th-floor Yates Gallery), as well as jazz and classical concerts at lunchtime (12:15pm most Mondays and every Wednesday). It also contains the world's largest Tiffany stained-glass dome, on the 3rd floor where the library circulation desk used to be. **InstaGreeter** (www.chicagogreeter.com/instagreeter; ⏱10am-3pm Fri & Sat, 11am-2pm Sun) **FREE** tours of the Loop depart from the Randolph St lobby, as do Millennium Park tours.

Maggie Daley Park   PARK
(Map p520; www.maggiedaleypark.com; 337 E Randolph St; ⏱6am-11pm; ⛲; Ⓜ Brown, Orange, Green, Purple, Pink Line to Washington/Wabash) Families love this park's fanciful free playgrounds in all their enchanted-forest and pirate-themed glory. There's also a rock-climbing wall, 18-hole mini-golf course, in-line skating ribbon (which becomes an ice-skating ribbon in winter) and tennis courts; these features have fees. Multiple picnic tables make the park an excellent spot to relax.

Buckingham Fountain   FOUNTAIN
(Map p520; 301 S Columbus Dr; Ⓜ Red Line to Harrison) Grant Park's centerpiece is one of the world's largest fountains, with a 1.5-million-gallon capacity and a 15-story-high spray. It lets loose on the hour from 8am to 11pm early May to mid-October, accompanied at night by lights and music.

Route 66 Sign   HISTORIC SITE
(Map p520; E Adams St, btwn S Michigan & Wabash Aves; Ⓜ Brown, Orange, Green, Purple, Pink Line to Adams) Attention Route 66 buffs: the Mother Road's starting point is here. Look for the 'Historic 66 Begin' sign that marks the spot on Adams St's southern side as you head west toward Wabash Ave. There are a couple of other 66 signs on the same block, but this one is the original.

From Chicago the route traverses 2400 miles to Los Angeles, past neon signs, mom-and-pop motels and pie-filled diners. See p39 for more on Route 66.

◉ South Loop

In the South Loop, the Field Museum, Shedd Aquarium and Adler Planetarium huddle at the Museum Campus. Peaceful 12th Street Beach and hilly Northerly Island offer nearby refuges to ditch the crowds. Historic buildings dot the neighborhood, including Chess Records, the seminal blues label. Chinatown bustles with noodle shops and exotic wares.

★ Field Museum of Natural History   MUSEUM
(Map p520; ☎312-922-9410; www.fieldmuseum.org; 1400 S Lake Shore Dr; adult/child $22/15; ⏱9am-5pm; ⛲; ⬚146, 130) The Field Museum houses some 30 million artifacts and includes everything but the kitchen sink – beetles, mummies, gemstones, Bushman the stuffed ape – all tended by a slew of PhD-wielding scientists, as the Field remains an active research institution. The collection's rock star is Sue, the largest *Tyrannosaurus rex* yet discovered. She even gets her own gift shop. Special exhibits, such as the 3-D movie, cost extra.

Shedd Aquarium   AQUARIUM
(Map p520; ☎312-939-2438; www.sheddaquarium.org; 1200 S Lake Shore Dr; adult/child $40/30; ⏱9am-6pm Jun-Aug, 9am-5pm Mon-Fri, to 6pm Sat & Sun Sep-May; ⛲; ⬚146, 130) Top draws at the kiddie-mobbed Shedd Aquarium include the Wild Reef exhibit, where there's just 5in of Plexiglas between you and two-dozen fierce-looking sharks, and the Oceanarium, with its rescued sea otters. Note the Oceanarium also keeps beluga whales and Pacific white-sided dolphins, a practice that has become increasingly controversial.

Adler Planetarium   MUSEUM
(Map p520; ☎312-922-7827; www.adlerplanetarium.org; 1300 S Lake Shore Dr; adult/child $12/8; ⏱9:30am-4pm; ⛲; ⬚146, 130) Space enthusiasts will get a big bang (pun!) out of the Adler. There are public telescopes to view the stars (10am to 1pm daily, by the Galileo Cafe), 3-D lectures to learn about supernovas (in the Space Visualization Lab), and the Planet Explorers exhibit where kids can 'launch' a rocket. The immersive digital films cost extra (from $13 per ticket). The Adler's front steps offer Chicago's best skyline view, so get your camera ready.

Northerly Island   PARK
(1521 S Linn White Dr; ⬚146, 130) This hilly, prairie-grassed park has a walking and cycling trail, bird-watching, fishing and an outdoor venue for big-name concerts. It's actually a peninsula, not an island, but the Chicago skyline views are tremendous no matter what you call it. Stop in at the field house, if it's open, for tour information. Bicycles are available at the Divvy bike-share station by the Adler Planetarium.

Downtown Chicago

Holiday Jones (0.8mi); Mana Food Bar (0.9mi); Wicker Park/ Bucktown (1mi); Reckless Records (1.1mi); Logan Sq (3 mi)

iO Theater (0.8mi); Alinea (1mi); Steppenwolf Theatre (1mi); Hideout (1.9mi)

La Fournette (0.8mi); Old Town Ale House (0.8mi); Second City (0.9mi); Hotel Lincoln (1.2mi)

Chicago History Museum (1mi); Lincoln Park (1mi); Wrigley Field (3.5mi)

Chicago Children's Theatre (0.2mi); Original Playboy Mansion (0.6mi);

Hoosier Mama Pie Company (0.6mi)

NEAR NORTH

W Chicago Ave

W Superior St

W Huron St

W Erie St

W Ontario St

W Ohio St

Grand

W Grand Ave

W Grand Ave

W Illinois St

W Hubbard St

W Kinzie St

W Kinzie St

W Carroll Ave

Merchandise Mart

W Fulton St

W Wacker Dr

Clark/Lake

State/Lake

Morgan

WEST LOOP

W Lake St

Clinton

W Lake St

W Randolph St

Daley Plaza

W Washington St

W Washington St

Washington

Chicago · Ogilvie Transportation Center (Metra)

Washington/Wells

THE LOOP

W Madison St

Chicago · Union Station (Metra)

W Monroe St

W Monroe St

Monroe

Chicago Bulls (0.9mi); United Center (0.9mi)

W Adams St

Quincy

W Marble Pl

Jackson

Willis Tower

GREEKTOWN

W Jackson Blvd

W Jackson Blvd

W Van Buren St

LaSalle/ Van Buren

Clinton

W VanBuren St

UIC-Halsted

Chicago · LaSalle St Station (Metra)

LaSalle

SOUTH LOOP

W Harrison St

W Vernon Park Pl

W Polk St

W Cabrini St

W 9th St

W Taylor St

W Roosevelt Rd

Knee Deep Vintage (0.5mi); National Museum of Mexican Art (1.2mi)

Pleasant House Pub (0.7mi)

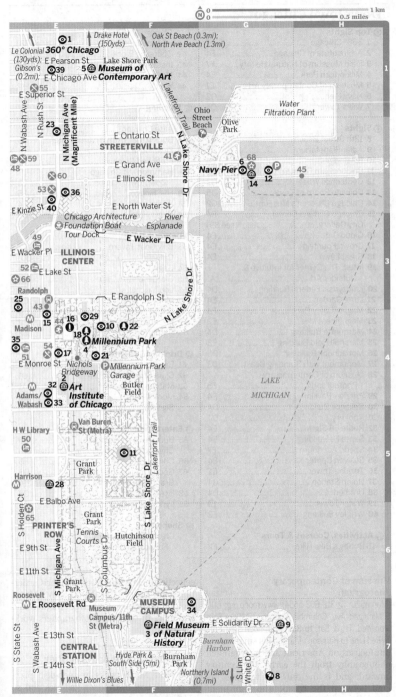

N 0 — 1 km
0 — 0.5 miles

Le Colonial
(130yds);
Gibson's
(0.2mi);

Drake Hotel
(150yds)

Oak St Beach (0.3mi);
North Ave Beach (1.3mi)

◉ 1 **360° Chicago**

◉ 39 E Pearson St Lake Shore Park

5 🏛 **Museum of**
E Chicago Ave **Contemporary Art**

⊗ 55 E Superior St

Water
Filtration Plant

◉ 23

Ohio
Street
Beach

Olive
Park

⊗ 59
48

⊗ 60

N Michigan Ave
(Magnificent Mile)

STREETERVILLE

E Ontario St

E Grand Ave

41 🚉

6 68
◉ 🏛 ◉ **P**
Navy Pier 14   12 45

53 ⊠

◉ 36
◉ 40

E Illinois St

E Kinzie St

E North Water St

Chicago Architecture
Foundation Boat
Tour Dock

River
Esplanade

49

E Wacker Pl

E Wacker Dr

52 🏛 E Lake St

**ILLINOIS
CENTER**

⊗ 66

Randolph

25 ◉

43 ◉

E Randolph St

N Lake Shore Dr

16 ◉29
15 ◉ ◉10 22

44 🚻 18 🚹

Madison

35 ◉
51

54 ⊗

◉ 17
4

🏛 **Millennium Park**

◉ 21

E Monroe St Nichols
Bridgeway

Millennium Park
Garage

Butler
Field

M 32 🏛

Adams/ 2
Wabash ◉ 33

**Art
Institute
of Chicago**

H W Library

50
🏛

🅿

Van Buren
St (Metra)

◉ 11

Grant
Park

Harrison

M

🏛 28

S Holden Ct

E Balbo Ave

Grant
Park

Tennis
Courts

Hutchinson
Field

S Michigan Ave

**PRINTER'S
ROW**

E 9th St

S Columbus Dr

E 11th St

Grant
Park

Roosevelt

M E Roosevelt Rd

S State St

S Wabash Ave

E 13th St

**CENTRAL
STATION**

E 14th St

Museum
Campus/11th
St (Metra)

Hyde Park &
South Side (5mi)

Willie Dixon's Blues

**MUSEUM
CAMPUS**

◉ 34

🏛 **Field Museum
3 of Natural
History**

E Solidarity Dr

🏛 9

Burnham
Harbor

Burnham
Park

Northerly Island
(0.7mi)

S Linn
White Dr

⊗ 8

*LAKE
MICHIGAN*

Lakefront Trail

S Lake Shore Dr

Downtown Chicago

**Museum of Contemporary
Photography**   MUSEUM
(Map p520; ☎312-663-5554; www.mocp.org; 600
S Michigan Ave, Columbia College; ◷10am-5pm
Mon-Wed, Fri & Sat, to 8pm Thu, noon-5pm Sun;
Ⓜ Red Line to Harrison) FREE This small museum focuses on American and international
photography from the early 20th century
onward, and is the only institution of its
kind between the coasts. The permanent

collection includes the works of Henri Cartier-
Bresson, Harry Callahan, Sally Mann,
Victor Skrebneski, Catherine Wagner and
500 more of the best photographers working today.

◎ Near North & Navy Pier

The Near North packs in deep-dish pizza
parlors, buzzy bistros, art galleries and so

CHICAGO FOR GANGSTERS

Chicago would rather not discuss its gangster past; consequently there are no brochures or exhibits about infamous sites, so you'll need to use your imagination when visiting the following places:

Green Mill (p537) Al Capone's favorite speakeasy; the tunnels where he hid the booze are still underneath the bar.

Biograph Theater (2433 N Lincoln Ave; Ⓜ Brown, Purple, Red Line to Fullerton) Where the 'lady in red' betrayed 'public enemy number one' John Dillinger.

Union Station (Map p520; www.chicagounionstation.com) Fans of *The Untouchables* can see where the baby carriage bounced down the stairs.

St Valentine's Day Massacre Site (2122 N Clark St; 🚌 22) Where Capone's men, dressed as cops, killed seven members of Bugs Moran's gang.

---

many upscale stores that its main vein – Michigan Ave – has been dubbed the 'Magnificent Mile.' Bulging out to the east is Navy Pier, a half-mile-long wharf of tour boats, carnival rides and a flashy, king-sized Ferris wheel.

★ **Navy Pier**   WATERFRONT
(Map p520; ☑ 312-595-7437; www.navypier.com; 600 E Grand Ave; ◷ 10am-10pm Sun-Thu, to midnight Fri & Sat Jun-Aug, 10am-8pm Sun-Thu, to 10pm Fri & Sat Sep-May; 🚼; Ⓜ Red Line to Grand) **FREE** Half-mile-long Navy Pier is one of Chicago's most-visited attractions, sporting a 196ft **Ferris wheel** (adult/child $15/12) and other carnival rides ($6 to $15 each), an **IMAX theater** (☑ 312-595-5629; www.imax. com; tickets $15-22), a beer garden and lots of chain restaurants. Locals groan over its commercialization, but its lakefront view and cool breezes can't be beat. The fireworks displays on summer Wednesdays (9:30pm) and Saturdays (10:15pm) are a treat too.

The **Chicago Children's Museum** (☑ 312-527-1000; www.chicagochildrensmuseum.org; admission $14; ◷ 10am-5pm, to 8pm Thu; 🚼) is also on the pier, as are several boat-cruise operators. Try the Shoreline water taxi for a fun ride to the **Museum Campus** (adult/child $8/4 Sunday through Friday, $10/5 Saturday). A renovation is bringing a hotel and additional amusements to the pier through 2018. Get the trolley from Grand.

Magnificent Mile   AREA
(Map p520; www.themagnificentmile.com; N Michigan Ave; Ⓜ Red Line to Grand) Spanning Michigan Ave between the river and Oak St, the Mag Mile is Chicago's much-touted upscale shopping strip, where Bloomingdale's,

Apple, Burberry and many more will lighten your wallet.

Tribune Tower   ARCHITECTURE
(Map p520; 435 N Michigan Ave; Ⓜ Red Line to Grand) Take a close look when passing by this 1925 neo-Gothic edifice. Colonel Robert McCormick, eccentric owner of the *Chicago Tribune* in the early 1900s, collected – and asked his reporters to send – rocks from famous buildings and monuments around the world. He stockpiled pieces of the Taj Mahal, Westminster Abbey, the Great Pyramid and more than 140 others, which are now embedded around the tower's base.

Wrigley Building   ARCHITECTURE
(Map p520; 400 N Michigan Ave; Ⓜ Red Line to Grand) The Wrigley Building glows as white as the Doublemint Twins' teeth, day or night. Chewing-gum guy William Wrigley built it that way on purpose, because he wanted it to be attention-grabbing like a billboard. More than 250,000 glazed terra-cotta tiles make up the facade; a computer database tracks each one and indicates when it needs to be cleaned and polished.

◉ Gold Coast

The Gold Coast has been the address of Chicago's wealthiest residents for more than 125 years. Bejeweled women glide in and out of the neighborhood's stylish boutiques. The occasional Rolls-Royce wheels along the leafy streets. The 360° Chicago observatory and Museum of Contemporary Art are the top attention grabbers. Rush St entertains with swanky steakhouses and piano lounges.

★ **360° Chicago** OBSERVATORY
(Map p520; ☑888-875-8439; www.360chicago.
com; 875 N Michigan Ave, John Hancock Center,
94th fl; adult/child $20.50/13.50; ☉9am-11pm;
Ⓜ Red Line to Chicago) This is the new name
for the John Hancock Center Observatory. In many ways the view here surpasses
the one at Willis Tower (p518). The 94th-
floor lookout has informative displays and
the TILT feature (floor-to-ceiling windows
that you stand in as they tip out over the
ground; it costs $7 extra and is less exciting
than it sounds). Not interested in such fri-
volities? Shoot straight up to the 96th-floor
Signature Lounge (www.signatureroom.com;
☉11am-12:30am Sun-Thu, to 1:30am Fri & Sat),
where the view is free if you buy a drink
($8 to $16).

★ **Museum of
Contemporary Art** MUSEUM
(MCA; Map p520; ☑312-280-2660; www.mcach
icago.org; 220 E Chicago Ave; adult/child $15/free;
☉10am-8pm Tue, to 5pm Wed-Sun; Ⓜ Red Line to
Chicago) Consider it the Art Institute's brash,
rebellious sibling, with especially strong
minimalist, surrealist and conceptual photography collections, and permanent works
by René Magritte, Cindy Sherman and Andy
Warhol. Covering art from the 1920s onward, the MCA's collection spans the gamut,
with displays arranged to blur the boundaries between painting, sculpture, video and
other media.

Original Playboy Mansion NOTABLE BUILDING
(1340 N State Pkwy; Ⓜ Red Line to Clark/Division)
The sexual revolution started in the basement 'grotto' of this 1899 manor. Hugh Hef-
ner bought the mansion in 1959 and hung
a brass plate over the door warning 'If You
Don't Swing, Don't Ring.' Heavy partying
ensued. In the mid-1970s, Hef decamped to
LA. The building contains condos now, but a
visit still allows you to boast 'I've been to the
Playboy Mansion.'

Water Tower LANDMARK
(Map p520; 108 N Michigan Ave; Ⓜ Red Line to
Chicago) The 154ft-tall, turreted tower is a
defining city icon: it was the sole downtown survivor of the 1871 Great Chicago
Fire, thanks to its yellow limestone bricks,
which withstood the flames. Today the
tower houses the free **City Gallery**, showcasing Chicago-themed works by local photographers and artists and is well worth a
peek.

◉ **Lincoln Park & Old Town**

Lincoln Park – the green space – is the city's
premier playground of lagoons, footpaths,
beaches and zoo animals. Lincoln Park – the
surrounding neighborhood – adds top-notch
restaurants, kicky shops, and lively blues
and rock clubs to the mix. Next door, stylish
Old Town hangs on to its free-spirited past
with artsy bars and improv-comedy bastion
Second City.

FAMOUS LOOP ARCHITECTURE

Ever since Chicago presented the world with the first skyscraper in 1885, it has thought
big with its architecture and pushed the envelope of modern design. The Loop is ground
zero for gawking.

Monadnock Building (Map p520; www.monadnockbuilding.com; 53 W Jackson Blvd; Ⓜ Blue
Line to Jackson)

Rookery (www.flwright.org; 209 S LaSalle St; 9am-5pm Mon-Fri; Ⓜ Brown, Orange, Purple,
Pink Line)

Marshall Field Building (Map p520; 111 N State St; ☉10am-9pm Mon-Sat, 11am-7pm Sun;
Ⓜ Brown, Orange, Green, Purple, Pink Line to Washington/Wabash)

Sullivan Center (Map p520; www.thesullivancenter.com; 1 S State St; Ⓜ Red Line to Monroe)

Marquette Building (Map p520; http://marquette.macfound.org; 140 S Dearborn St; ☉7am-
10pm; Ⓜ Blue Line to Monroe)

Reliance Building (Map p520; 1 W Washington St; Ⓜ Blue Line to Washington)

Santa Fe Building (Map p520; 224 S Michigan Ave; Ⓜ Brown, Orange, Green, Purple, Pink Line
to Adams)

Kluczynski Building (Map p520; 230 S Dearborn St; Ⓜ Blue Line to Jackson)

LOCAL KNOWLEDGE

BLUES FANS' PILGRIMAGE

From 1957 to 1967, the humble building **Willie Dixon's Blues Heaven** (☎312-808-1286; www.bluesheaven.com; 2120 S Michigan Ave; tours $10; ⊕by appointment Wed & Thu, noon-4pm Fri, to 3pm Sat; Ⓜ Green Line to Cermak-McCormick Pl) was Chess Records, the seminal electric blues label. It's now named for the bassist who wrote most of Chess' hits. Staff give hour-long tours of the premises. It's pretty ramshackle, with few original artifacts on display. Still, when Willie's grandson hauls out the bluesman's well-worn stand-up bass and lets you take a pluck, it's pretty cool. Call first; opening times can be erratic. Free blues concerts rock the side garden on summer Thursdays at 6pm.

★**Lincoln Park** PARK
(⊕6am-11pm; ⊕; 🚍151) The neighborhood gets its name from this park, Chicago's largest. Its 1200 acres stretch for 6 miles from North Ave north to Diversey Pkwy, where it narrows along the lake and continues on north until the end of Lake Shore Dr. On sunny days locals come out to play in droves, taking advantage of the ponds, paths and playing fields or visiting the zoo and beaches.

Lincoln Park Conservatory GARDENS
(☎312-742-7736; www.lincolnparkconservancy.org; 2391 N Stockton Dr; ⊕9am-5pm; 🚍151) **FREE** Walking through the conservatory's 3 acres of desert palms, jungle ferns and tropical orchids is like taking a trip around the world in 30 minutes. The glass-bedecked hothouse remains a sultry 75°F (24°C) escape even in winter.

Lincoln Park Zoo ZOO
(☎312-742-2000; www.lpzoo.org; 2200 N Cannon Dr; ⊕10am-5pm Mon-Fri, to 6:30pm Sat & Sun Jun-Aug, 10am-5pm Apr-May & Sep-Oct, 10am-4:30pm Nov-Mar; ⊕; 🚍151) **FREE** The zoo has been around since 1868 and is a local freebie favorite, filled with lions, zebras, snow monkeys and other exotic creatures in the shadow of downtown. Check out the Regenstein African Journey, polar-bear-stocked Arctic Tundra and dragonfly-dappled Nature Boardwalk for the cream of the crop. The Gateway Pavilion (on Cannon Dr) is the main entrance.

Chicago History Museum MUSEUM
(☎312-642-4600; www.chicagohistory.org; 1601 N Clark St; adult/child $16/free; ⊕9:30am-4:30pm Mon & Wed-Sat, to 7:30pm Tue, noon-5pm Sun; ⊕; 🚍22) Curious about Chicago's storied past? Multimedia displays at this museum cover it all, from the Great Fire to the 1968 Democratic Convention. President Lincoln's deathbed is here, as is the bell worn by Mrs

O'Leary's cow. So is the chance to 'become' a Chicago hot dog covered in condiments.

⊙ Lake View & Wrigleyville

The young and frolicsome claim Lake View, reveling in its nonstop lineup of bars, theaters and rock halls. Hallowed Wrigley Field draws baseball pilgrims, and the boozy quarter around it – aka Wrigleyville – parties hard and collides with the rainbow banners of Boystown, Chicago's main gay district, chockablock with dance clubs. Global eateries cater to the masses.

★**Wrigley Field** STADIUM
(www.cubs.com; 1060 W Addison St; Ⓜ Red Line to Addison) Built in 1914 and named for the chewing-gum guy, Wrigley Field is the second-oldest baseball park in the major leagues. It's known for its hand-turned scoreboard, ivy-covered outfield walls and neon sign over the front entrance. It's also known for its team's legendary losing streak. The Cubs (p539) hadn't won a championship since 1908, a cursed dry spell that was unrivaled in US sports. Then in 2016, they triumphed in mythic style. Learn more on 1½-hour tours ($25) of the ballpark, available April through September.

⊙ Andersonville & Uptown

Vestiges of Andersonville's Swedish past remain, but today the area is about foodie taverns, funky boutiques, and gay and lesbian bars. Uptown offers historic jazz houses like the Green Mill (Al Capone's fave), along with the thriving eateries of 'Little Saigon.'

⊙ Wicker Park, Bucktown & Ukrainian Village

These three neighborhoods are hot property. Hipster record stores, thrift shops and cocktail lounges have shot up, though vintage Eastern European dive bars linger on many street corners. Wicker Park is the beating heart; Bucktown (a bit posher) and Ukrainian Village (a bit shabbier) flank it. The restaurant and rock-club scene is unparalleled in the city.

Intuit: The Center for Intuitive & Outsider Art GALLERY
(Map p520; ☑ 312-243-9088; www.art.org; 756 N Milwaukee Ave; suggested donation $5; ⊘ 11am-6pm Tue, Wed, Fri & Sat, to 7:30pm Thu, noon-5pm Sun; Ⓜ Blue Line to Chicago) Behold the museum-like collection of folk art, including watercolors by famed local Henry Darger. In the back room Intuit has re-created Darger's awesomely cluttered studio, complete with balls of twine, teetering stacks of old magazines and a Victrola phonograph. The gift shop carries groovy jewelry (such as pencil-eraser earrings) and art books.

⊙ Logan Square & Humboldt Park

Logan Square is Chicago's current 'it' neighborhood, the place to go for the hippest tiki lounge or all-the-rage fried-chicken cafe. Gastronomes flock in for Michelin-starred Parachute and Longman & Eagle, plus several other chowhound hot spots. Puerto Rican stronghold Humboldt Park is the place to sample a *jibarito,* the local sandwich specialty.

⊙ Near West Side & Pilsen

The meatpacking West Loop buzzes with hot-chef restaurants and on-trend bars. Development continues here big-time. Greektown and Little Italy serve ethnic fare nearby. In Pilsen, Mexican culture mixes with Chicago's bohemian underground, and colorful murals, taquerias and cafes result.

National Museum of Mexican Art MUSEUM
(☑ 312-738-1503; www.nationalmuseumofmexicanart.org; 1852 W 19th St; ⊘ 10am-5pm Tue-Sun; Ⓜ Pink Line to 18th St) **FREE** Founded in 1982, this vibrant museum – the largest Latino arts institution in the US – has become one of the city's best. The vivid permanent collection sums up 1000 years of Mexican art and culture through classical paintings, shining gold altars, skeleton-rich folk art, beadwork and much more.

⊙ Chinatown

Chicago's small but busy Chinatown is an easy 10-minute train ride from the Loop. Take the Red Line to the Cermak-Chinatown stop, which puts you between the neighborhood's two distinct parts: Chinatown Sq (an enormous bi-level strip mall) unfurls to the north along Archer Ave, while Old Chinatown (the traditional retail area) stretches along Wentworth Ave to the south. Either zone allows you to graze through bakeries and shop for the requisite Hello Kitty trinkets.

⊙ Hyde Park & South Side

Brainy Hyde Park holds bookstores galore and sights like Frank Lloyd Wright's Robie House and the Museum of Science & Industry. Irish enclave Bridgeport has blossomed with bars and galleries, while Bronzeville has jazzy architecture and important (if often overlooked) shrines to African American history.

★**Museum of Science & Industry** MUSEUM
(MSI; ☑ 773-684-1414; www.msichicago.org; 5700 S Lake Shore Dr; adult/child $18/11; ⊘ 9:30am-5:30pm Jun-Aug, shorter hours Sep-May; ⊕; ☐ 6, 10, Ⓜ Metra to 55th-56th-57th) Geek out at the largest science museum in the Western Hemisphere. Highlights include a WWII German U-boat nestled in an underground display ($12 extra to tour it) and the Science Storms exhibit with a mock tornado and tsunami. Other popular exhibits include the baby chick hatchery, the minuscule furnishings in Colleen Moore's fairy castle and the life-size shaft of a coal mine ($12 extra to descend and tour its workings).

★**Robie House** ARCHITECTURE
(☑ 312-994-4000; www.flwright.org; 5757 S Woodlawn Ave; adult/child $18/15; ⊘ 10:30am-3pm Thu-Mon; ☐ 6, Ⓜ Metra to 55th-56th-57th) Of the numerous buildings that Frank Lloyd Wright designed around Chicago, none is more famous or influential than Robie House. Because its horizontal lines resembled the flat landscape of the Midwestern prairie, the style became known as the Prairie style. Inside are 174 stained-glass windows and doors, which you'll see on the hour-long tours (frequency varies by season, but there's usually at least one tour per hour).

City Walk
The Loop

START CHICAGO BOARD OF TRADE
FINISH BILLY GOAT TAVERN
LENGTH 3 MILES; ABOUT 2 HOURS

This tour swoops through the Loop, highlighting Chicago's revered art and architecture, with a visit to Al Capone's dentist thrown in for good measure.

Start at the **1 Chicago Board of Trade** (141 W Jackson Blvd) with its cool art-deco building; that's a giant statue of Ceres, the goddess of agriculture, on top. Step into the nearby **2 Rookery** (p525) to see Frank Lloyd Wright's handiwork in the atrium.

Head east on Adams St to the **3 Art Institute** (p518), one of the city's most-visited attractions. The lion statues out front make a classic keepsake photo. Walk a few blocks north to avant-garde **4 Millennium Park** (p516).

Leave the park and head west on Washington St to the **5 Alise** (p531) hotel. It's housed in the Reliance Building, which was the precursor to modern skyscraper design;

Capone's dentist drilled teeth in what's now Room 809. Just west, Picasso's abstract **6 Untitled** sculpture is ensconced in Daley Plaza. Baboon, dog, woman? You decide. Then go north on Clark St to Jean Dubuffet's **7 Monument with Standing Beast**, another head-scratching sculpture.

Walk east on Randolph St through the theater district. Pop into the **8 Chicago Cultural Center** (p518) to see what free art exhibits or concerts are on. Now go north on Michigan Ave and cross the Chicago River. Just north of the bridge you'll pass the **9 Wrigley Building** (p523), shining bright and white, and the nearby Gothic, eye-popping **10 Tribune Tower** (p523).

To finish your tour, visit **11 Billy Goat Tavern** (p533), a vintage Chicago dive that spawned the Curse of the Cubs after the tavern's owner, Billy Sianis, tried to enter Wrigley Field with his pet goat. The smelly creature was denied entry, so Sianis called down a mighty hex on the baseball team in retaliation. It took them 108 years to break it.

University of Chicago
UNIVERSITY

(www.uchicago.edu; 5801 S Ellis Ave; ☐ 6, Ⓜ Metra to 55th-56th-57th) Faculty and students have racked up more than 80 Nobel prizes within U of C's hallowed halls. The economics and physics departments lay claim to most of the awards. The campus is well worth a stroll, offering grand Gothic architecture and free art and antiquities museums.

The university's classes first met on October 1, 1892. John D Rockefeller was a major contributor to the institution, donating more than $35 million. The original campus was constructed in an English Gothic style. Highlights of a walkabout include the sculpture-laden Rockefeller Memorial Chapel, serene Bond Chapel and Henry Moore's bronze Nuclear Energy sculpture (S Ellis Ave, btwn E 56th & E 57th Sts).

Obama's House
HOUSE

(5046 S Greenwood Ave; ☐ 6, Ⓜ Metra to 51st-53rd) Hefty security means you can't get close to Barack Obama's house, but you can stand across the street on Hyde Park Blvd and try to glimpse over the barricades at the redbrick Georgian-style manor. He and his family lived here from 2005 until he became president in late 2008.

🏃 Activities

Chicago is a rabid sports town, and fans of the pro teams are famously die-hard. It's not all about passively watching sports, though. Chicago offers plenty of places to get active via its city-spanning shoreline, 26 beaches and 580 parks. After a long, cold winter, everyone goes outside to play.

Cycling

The flat, 18-mile Lakefront Trail is a beautiful ride along the water, though on nice days it's jam-packed. The trail starts at Hollywood Ave and rolls all the way down to 71st St. The Active Transportation Alliance (www.active trans.org) publishes a bike trail map and provides local trail condition updates. Chicago Critical Mass (www.facebook.com/chicago criticalmass) sponsors popular, traffic-disrupting rides downtown and around.

Bobby's Bike Hike
CYCLING

(Map p520; ☑ 312-245-9300; www.bobbysbike-hike.com; 540 N Lake Shore Dr; per hour/day from $10/34; ◷ 8:30am-8pm Mon-Fri, 8am-8pm Sat & Sun Jun-Aug, 9am-7pm Mar-May & Sep-Nov; Ⓜ Red Line to Grand) Locally based Bobby's earns rave reviews from riders. It rents bikes and has easy access to the Lakefront Trail. It also

---

CHICAGO FOR CHILDREN

Ferocious dinosaurs at the Field Museum, an ark's worth of beasts at Lincoln Park Zoo, lakefront boat rides and sandy beaches are among the top choices for toddlin' times. Add in magical playgrounds, family cycling tours and lots of pizza, and it's clear Chicago is a kid's kind of town.

Chicago Children's Museum (p523) Designed to challenge the imaginations of toddlers to 10-year-olds, this colorful museum gives young visitors enough hands-on exhibits to keep them climbing and creating for hours. Among the favorites, Dinosaur Expedition explores the world of paleontology and lets kids excavate 'bones.' They can also climb a ropey schooner; bowl in a faux alley; get wet in the waterways (and learn about hydroelectric power); and use real tools to build things in the Tinkering Lab.

Field Museum of Natural History (p519) The Crown Family PlayLab lets kids excavate bones and make loads of other discoveries. It's open Thursday to Monday from 10am to 3pm.

Museum of Science & Industry (p526) Staff conduct 'experiments' in various galleries throughout the day, like dropping things off the balcony and creating mini explosions. The Idea Factory lets scientists aged 10 and under 'research' properties of light, balance and water pressure.

Peggy Notebaert Nature Museum (☑ 773-755-5100; www.naturemuseum.org; 2430 N Cannon Dr; adult/child $9/6; ◷ 9am-5pm Mon-Fri, 10am-5pm Sat & Sun; ♿; ☐ 151) This museum is somewhat overlooked, but its butterfly haven and marsh full of frogs provide gentle thrills. Bonus: it's located in Lincoln Park by the zoo.

Art Institute of Chicago (p518) The Ryan Learning Center provides interactive games (like puzzles of famous works) and art-making activities.

offers cool tours ($35 to $66) of South Side gangster sites, the lakefront, nighttime vistas, and venues to indulge in pizza and beer. The Tike Hike caters to kids. Enter through the covered driveway to reach the shop.

Divvy   CYCLING

(📞 855-553-4889; www.divvybikes.com) Chicago's bike-sharing program has 5800 sky-blue bicycles scattered at 580 stations around Chicago and neighboring suburbs. Kiosks issue 24-hour passes ($10) on the spot. Insert a credit card, get your ride code and then unlock a bike. The first 30 minutes are free; after that, rates rise fast if you don't dock the bike. The system works best for point-to-point travel versus lengthy sightseeing trips.

Water Sports

Visitors often don't realize Chicago is a beach town, thanks to mammoth Lake Michigan lapping its side. There are 26 official strands of sand patrolled by lifeguards in summer. Swimming is popular, though the water is pretty freaking cold. Beaches at Montrose and North Ave have rental places offering kayaks and stand-up paddleboards. Other kayak companies have set up shop along the Chicago River.

North Avenue Beach   BEACH

(www.cpdbeaches.com; 1600 N Lake Shore Dr; 🚻; 🚌151) Chicago's most popular strand of sand wafts a Southern California vibe. Buff teams spike volleyballs, kids build sandcastles and everyone jumps in for a swim when the weather heats up. Bands and DJs rock the steamboat-shaped beach house, which serves ice cream and margaritas in equal measure. Kayaks, jet-skis, stand-up paddleboards, bicycles and lounge chairs are available to rent, and there are beach yoga classes.

Oak Street Beach   BEACH

(www.cpdbeaches.com; 1000 N Lake Shore Dr; Ⓜ Red Line to Chicago) This beach packs in bodies beautiful at the edge of downtown in the shadow of skyscrapers. Lifeguards are on duty in summer. You can rent umbrellas and lounge chairs. The island-y, yellow-umbrella-dotted cafe provides drinks and DJs.

12th Street Beach   BEACH

(Map p520; www.cpdbeaches.com; 1200 S Linn White Dr; 🚌146, 130) A path runs south from the Adler Planetarium to this crescent of sand. Despite its proximity to the visitor-mobbed Museum Campus, the small beach remains bizarrely (but happily) se-

THE 606

Like NYC's High Line, Chicago's **606** (www.the606.org; ⊙ 6am-11pm; Ⓜ Blue Line to Damen) is a similar urban-cool elevated path along an old train track. Bike or stroll past factories, smokestacks, clattering El trains and locals' backyard affairs for 2.7 miles between Wicker Park and Logan Square. It's a fascinating trek through Chicago's socioeconomic strata: moneyed at the east, becoming more industrial and immigrant to the west. The trail parallels Bloomingdale Ave, with access points every quarter mile.

cluded. Bonus: if you can't get tickets to see your favorite band at the Pavilion at Northerly Island, you can sit here and still hear the tunes.

Windy   BOATING

(Map p520; 📞 312-451-2700; www.tallshipwindy. com; 600 E Grand Ave; 60-75min tours adult/child $30/10; Ⓜ Red Line to Grand) The four-masted schooner sets sail from Navy Pier. Trips have different themes (pirates, architecture, sailing skills etc). With only the sound of the wind in your ears, these tours are the most relaxing way to see the skyline from offshore. Take the trolley from Grand.

👉 Tours

⭐Chicago Architecture Foundation   TOURS

(CAF; Map p520; 📞 312-922-3432; www.architecture.org; 224 S Michigan Ave; tours $15-50; Ⓜ Brown, Orange, Green, Purple, Pink Line to Adams) The gold-standard boat tours ($46) sail from the **river dock** (Map p520; Ⓜ Brown, Orange, Green, Purple, Pink Line to State/Lake) on the southeast side of the Michigan Ave Bridge. The popular Historic Skyscrapers walking tours ($20) leave from the main downtown address. Weekday lunchtime tours ($15) explore individual landmark buildings and meet on-site. CAF sponsors bus, bike and El train tours, too. Buy tickets online or at CAF; boat tickets can be purchased at the dock.

Chicago by Foot   WALKING

(📞 312-612-0826; www.freetoursbyfoot.com/chicago-tours) Guides for this pay-what-you-want walking tour offer engaging stories and historical details on different jaunts covering the Loop, Gold Coast, Lincoln Park's gangster sites and much more. Most takers pay around $10 per person. Reserve in advance to guarantee a spot; walk-up guests are welcome if space is available (chancy).

Chicago Detours WALKING
(☎312-350-1131; www.chicagodetours.com; tours from $22) Chicago Detours offers engrossing, detail-rich tours (mostly walking, but also some by bus) that take in Chicago's architecture, history and culture. The 2½-hour Historic Pub Crawl Tour is a popular one.

Chicago Beer Experience WALKING
(☎312-818-2172; www.chicagobeerexperience. com; tours $62) These three-hour walking tours visit a neighborhood – Lincoln Park/Lake View, Bucktown/Wicker Park or Downtown/South Loop – where you learn its beer history along with general Chicago history. The jaunts hit four bars over the course of a mile or so. Beer and a snack (such as a stuffed pizza slice or hot dog) are included.

Chicago Food Planet Tours WALKING
(☎312-818-2170; www.chicagofoodplanet.com; 2-3hr tours $42-65) Go on a guided walkabout in Wicker Park, the Gold Coast or Chinatown, where you'll graze through five or more neighborhood eateries. Departure points and times vary.

Pilsen Mural Tours WALKING
(☎773-342-4191; 1½hr tours per group $125) Murals are a traditional Mexican art form, and they're splashed all over Pilsen's buildings. Local artists and activists lead these highly recommended tours that take in the neighborhood's most impressive works.

✦✦ Festivals & Events

St Patrick's Day Parade CULTURAL
(www.chicagostpatricksdayparade.org; ☉mid-Mar) The local plumbers union dyes the Chicago River shamrock green; a big parade follows downtown in Grant Park. Held the Saturday before March 17.

Chicago Blues Festival MUSIC
(www.chicagobluesfestival.us; ☉mid-Jun) The biggest free blues fest in the world, with three days of the music that made Chicago famous. Held in Millennium Park.

Pride Parade LGBT
(http://chicagopride.gopride.com; ☉late Jun) On the last Sunday in June, colorful floats and risqué revelers pack Halsted St in Boystown.

It's the LGBT community's main event, and more than 800,000 people come to the party.

Taste of Chicago FOOD & DRINK
(www.tasteofchicago.us; ☉mid-Jul) This five-day food festival in Grant Park draws hordes for a smorgasbord of ethnic, meaty, sweet and local edibles – much of it served on a stick. Several stages host free live music, including big-name bands.

Lollapalooza MUSIC
(www.lollapalooza.com; day pass $120; ☉early Aug) Up to 170 bands spill off eight stages at Grant Park's four-day mega-gig.

Jazz Festival MUSIC
(www.chicagojazzfestival.us; ☉early Sep) Top names on the national jazz scene play for free over Labor Day weekend in Millennium Park and the Chicago Cultural Center.

🛏 Sleeping

Chicago's lodgings rise high in the sky, many in architectural landmarks. Snooze in the building that gave birth to the skyscraper, in one of Mies van der Rohe's boxy structures, or in a century-old art-deco masterpiece. Huge business hotels, B&Bs and snazzy hostels blanket the cityscape too. But nothing comes cheap...

🏙 The Loop

HI-Chicago HOSTEL $
(Map p520; ☎312-360-0300; www.hichicago. org; 24 E Congress Pkwy; dm $35-55; ▣❋@☎; ⓜBrown, Orange, Purple, Pink Line to Library) Chicago's most stalwart hostel is immaculate, conveniently placed in the Loop, and offers bonuses such as a staffed information desk, free volunteer-led tours and discount passes to museums and shows. The simple dorm rooms have eight or 10 beds, and most have attached baths.

★Hampton Inn Chicago Downtown/N Loop HOTEL $$
(Map p520; ☎312-419-9014; www.hamptonchicago.com; 68 E Wacker Pl; r $200-290; ▣❋☎; ⓜBrown, Orange, Green, Purple, Pink Line to State/Lake) This unique property makes you feel like a road-tripper of yore. Set in the 1928 art-deco Chicago Motor Club Building, the lobby sports a vintage Ford and a cool USA mural map from the era. The dark-wood-paneled rooms strike the right balance of retro vibe and modern amenities. Free wi-fi and hot breakfast included.

Buckingham Athletic Club Hotel
BOUTIQUE HOTEL $$
(Map p520; ☑ 312-663-8910; www.thebuckingham-club.com; 440 S LaSalle St; r $175-300; 🅿❄🌐🛜; Ⓜ Brown, Orange, Purple, Pink Line to LaSalle) Tucked onto the 40th floor of the Chicago Stock Exchange building, this 21-room hotel is not easy to find. The benefit if you do? It's quiet (on weekends and evenings especially) and has expansive views south of town. Elegant rooms are so spacious they'd be considered suites elsewhere. Lots of freebies add to the excellence, including access to the namesake gym with lap pool.

Silversmith
HISTORIC HOTEL $$
(Map p520; ☑ 312-372-7696; www.silversmith-chicagohotel.com; 10 S Wabash Ave; r $190-300; 🅿❄🌐🛜; Ⓜ Red, Blue Line to Monroe) Renowned architect Daniel Burnham's firm designed the 1897 building as a place for jewelers and silversmiths to ply their trade. The gem-inspired theme carries over to the current, vintage-cool design. Rooms are good-sized, with pearl-colored decor and ruby and gold accents. A cushioned seat nestles in each floor-to-ceiling window, prime for city watching. The Art Institute, Millennium Park and CTA trains are steps away.

★ Virgin Hotel
HOTEL $$$
(Map p520; ☑ 312-940-4400; www.virginhotels.com; 203 N Wabash Ave; r $240-380; 🅿❄🌐🛜; Ⓜ Brown, Orange, Green, Purple, Pink Line to State/Lake) Billionaire Richard Branson transformed the 27-story, art-deco Dearborn Bank Building into the first outpost of his cheeky new hotel chain. The airy, suite-like rooms have speedy free wi-fi and low-cost minibar items, plus a bed that can double as a work desk. An app controls the thermostat, TV and other electronics. Guests receive earplugs, handy for dulling noise from nearby El trains.

Alise Chicago
HISTORIC HOTEL $$$
(Map p520; ☑ 312-940-7997; www.staypineapple.com; 1 W Washington St; r $270-380; 🅿❄🌐🛜; Ⓜ Blue Line to Washington) Housed in the landmark 1890s Reliance Building (prototype for the modern skyscraper), the Alise's slick, historic design woos architecture buffs. Deco-style lights, iron filigree stair railings and mosaic-tile floors prevail in the public areas. In the smallish rooms, big windows and pops of whimsical, bright-hued art liven up the warm wood decor. The free bicycles are handy.

🛏 Near North & Navy Pier

Freehand Chicago
HOSTEL, HOTEL $
(Map p520; ☑ 312-940-3699; www.thefreehand.com/chicago; 19 E Ohio St; dm $35-70, r $220-310; ❄🛜; Ⓜ Red Line to Grand) At this super-hip hostel-hotel hybrid, travelers split evenly between the four-person, bunk-bed dorms and private rooms. All feature warm woods, bright tiles and Central American–tinged fabrics. Everyone mingles in the shaggy, totem-pole-filled common area and in the groovy Broken Shaker bar. The Freehand works best as a hostel, its dorms spiffier than most, with en suite bathrooms and privacy curtains around each bed.

★ Acme Hotel
BOUTIQUE HOTEL $$
(Map p520; ☑ 312-894-0800; www.acmehotelcompany.com; 15 E Ohio St; r $190-300; 🅿❄🌐🛜; Ⓜ Red Line to Grand) Urban bohemians love the Acme for its indie-cool style at (usually) affordable rates. The 130 rooms mix industrial fixtures with retro lamps, mid-century furniture and funky modern art. They're wired up with free wi-fi, good speakers, smart TVs and easy connections to stream your own music and movies. Graffiti, neon and a rock-and-roll elevator embellish the common areas.

🛏 Gold Coast

★ Fieldhouse Jones
HOSTEL, HOTEL $
(Map p520; ☑ 312-291-9922; www.fieldhousejones.com; 312 W Chestnut St; dm $40-55, r from $150; 🅿❄🛜; Ⓜ Brown, Purple Line to Chicago) This hostel-hotel mash-up occupies a vintage, redbrick dairy warehouse. It's great value for the Gold Coast, drawing a wide range of travelers – global backpackers, families, older couples – for its quality rooms and sociable common areas. There are gender-divided dorms, studios and one- and two-bedroom apartments, all with en suite bathrooms, wi-fi and fun, sporty decor (dartboard wall art, old trophies etc).

Drake Hotel
HISTORIC HOTEL $$$
(☑ 312-787-2200; www.thedrakehotel.com; 140 E Walton St; r $230-360; 🅿❄🌐🛜; Ⓜ Red Line to Chicago) Queen Elizabeth, Dean Martin, Princess Di...the Reagans, the Bushes, the Clintons... Who hasn't stayed at the elegant Drake Hotel since it opened in 1920? The chandelier-strewn grande dame commands a terrific location at the northern end of Michigan Ave, near Oak St Beach. While the

public spaces are gilded eye-poppers, the 535 rooms are more everyday yet well sized and comfy.

Lincoln Park & Old Town

Hotel Lincoln BOUTIQUE HOTEL $$
(☑312-254-4700; www.jdvhotels.com; 1816 N Clark St; r $180-320; P✳@🛜; 🖵22) The boutique Lincoln is all about kitschy fun, as the lobby's 'wall of bad art' and front desk patched together from flea-market dresser drawers attest. Standard rooms are small, but vintage-cool and colorful; many have sweet views. Leafy Lincoln Park and the city's largest farmers market sprawl across the street.

Wicker Park, Bucktown & Ukrainian Village

Holiday Jones HOSTEL $
(☑312-804-3335; www.holidayjones.com; 1659 W Division St; dm/r from $33/85; ⊖✳@🛜; 🅜Blue Line to Division) Holiday Jones has a tongue-in-cheek, itchy-feet personality. Old steamer trunks comprise the front desk. Wild, cartoony posters line the stairwell. Rooms are compact but tidy, with fresh paint and splashes of plaid (via the bedding and wallpaper). Gender-segregated dorms have four to six bunk beds. There's a big common room with couches and a flat-screen TV, plus free wi-fi, continental breakfast and lockers.

Hollander HOSTEL $
(☑872-315-3080; www.thehollander.com; 2022 W North Ave; dm $40-55, r $135-220; P✳🛜; 🅜Blue Line to Damen) The Hollander describes itself as a 'social stay' versus a hostel, and indeed, this revamped, turn-of-the-century warehouse buzzes with the young and perky. Travelers flit in and out of the sunny, shabby-chic lobby bar for coffee, laptop musing and bicycle rentals, and they snooze in private rooms and bunk-bed dorms (for four to six people) with polished concrete floors, unvarnished wood-frame beds and other mod-industrial decor.

Wicker Park Inn B&B $$
(☑773-486-2743; www.wickerparkinn.com; 1329 N Wicker Park Ave; r $160-200, apt $150-245; ✳🛜; 🅜Blue Line to Damen) This classic brick row house is steps away from rockin' restaurants and nightlife. The sunny rooms aren't huge, but all have hardwood floors, soothing color schemes and small desk spaces where you can use the free wi-fi. Breakfast is rich in

baked goods and fruit. Across the street, three apartments with kitchens provide a self-contained experience. Rooms have varying minimum-stay requirements.

Logan Square & Humboldt Park

Longman & Eagle INN $$
(☑773-276-7110; www.longmananandeagle.com; 2657 N Kedzie Ave; r $95-200; ✳🛜; 🅜Blue Line to Logan Square) Check in at the Michelin-starred tavern downstairs and then head to your wood-floored, vintage-stylish accommodations on the floor above. The six rooms aren't particularly soundproof, but after using your whiskey tokens in the bar, you probably won't care. Artwork by local artists decorates each room.

🍴 Eating

Chicago has become a chowhound's hot spot. For the most part, restaurants here are reasonably priced and pretension-free, serving masterful food in come-as-you-are environs. You can also fork into a superb range of ethnic eats, especially if you break out of downtown and head for neighborhoods such as Pilsen or Uptown.

The Loop

Most Loop eateries are geared to lunch crowds of office workers. There's not much open after 9pm.

Cafecito CUBAN $
(Map p520; ☑312-922-2233; www.cafecitochicago.com; 26 E Congress Pkwy; mains $6-10; ⊗7am-9pm Mon-Fri, 10am-6pm Sat & Sun; 🛜; 🅜Brown, Orange, Purple, Pink Line to Library) Attached to the HI-Chicago hostel and perfect for the hungry, thrifty traveler, Cafecito serves killer Cuban sandwiches layered with citrus-garlic-marinated roasted pork and ham. Strong coffee and hearty egg sandwiches make a fine breakfast.

Native Foods Cafe VEGAN $
(Map p520; ☑312-332-6332; www.nativefoods.com; 218 S Clark St; mains $9-11; ⊗10:30am-9pm Mon-Sat, 11am-7pm Sun; 🍴; 🅜Brown, Orange, Purple, Pink Line to Quincy) If you're looking for vegan fast-casual fare downtown, Native Foods is your spot. The meatball sandwich rocks the seitan, while the scorpion burger fires up hot-spiced tempeh. Local beers and

CHICAGO'S BEST-LOVED SPECIALTIES

Deep-dish pizza is Chicago's most famous concoction. These behemoths are nothing like the flat circular disks known as pizza in the rest of the world. Here pies are made in a special cast-iron pan – kind of like a skillet without a handle – so the dough, stuffed with molten American-style mozzarella cheese, chunky tomato sauce and other typical ingredients like sausage, is oven baked. The flagship **Pizzeria Uno** (Map p520; ☑ 312-321-1000; www.unos.com; 29 E Ohio St; small pizzas from $13; ☺ 11am-1am Mon-Thu, to 2am Fri & Sat, to 11pm Sun; Ⓜ Red Line to Grand) claims to have invented deep-dish pizza in the 1940s, but this, like many other fanatical conversations about food (and sports) in the Windy City, will inspire debate.

No less iconic is the Chicago-style hot dog. A real-deal specimen uses a local Vienna beef weenie and requires a poppy-seed bun and a litany of toppings (including onions, tomatoes, a dill pickle and neon-green relish). And remember rule numero uno: no ketchup! For gourmet versions (rabbit sausage with anchovy hazelnut butter sauce) and stalwart classics (beer-soaked brats), swing by **Hot G Dog** (☑ 773-209-3360; www.hotgdog.com; 5009 N Clark St; hot dogs $2.50-4; ☺ 10:30am-8pm Mon-Sat, to 4pm Sun; ▣ 22, Ⓜ Red Line to Argyle) in Andersonville.

Another renowned Chicago specialty is the Italian beef sandwich, and it stacks up like this: thin-sliced, slow-cooked roast beef that's sopped in natural gravy and *giardiniera* (spicy pickled vegetables), then heaped on a hoagie roll. Local Italian immigrants on the South Side invented it as a low-budget way to feed factory workers during the Depression era. Try it while you're here – **Mr Beef** (Map p520; ☑ 312-337-8500; www.facebook.com/mrbeefchicago; 666 N Orleans St; sandwiches $6-9; ☺ 10am-6pm Mon-Thu, to 5am Fri & Sat; Ⓜ Brown, Purple Line to Chicago) makes a popular one – because you'll be hard-pressed to find one elsewhere on the planet.

Less well known, but equally messy and delicious, is the *jibarito* sandwich, developed at a local Puerto Rican eatery. It consists of steak covered in garlicky mayo and served between thick, crispy-fried plantain slices, which form the 'bread.' Many Latin American cafes in the Humboldt Park neighborhood, such as **Papa's Cache Sabroso** (☑ 773-862-8313; www.papascache.com; 2517 W Division St; mains $8-15; ☺ 11am-9pm Mon-Thu, to 10pm Fri & Sat; ▣ 70), have it on the menu.

And who could leave the Midwest without trying some pie, maybe Amish Country-style 'shoofly' molasses, juicy strawberry-rhubarb or Dutch apple layered with sour-cream custard and nutty streusel? Take a sugar-loaded tasting flight at Hoosier Mama Pie Company (p535) in Ukrainian Village – you might just devour an entire pie.

---

organic wines accompany the wide-ranging menu of Greek-, Asian-, Mexican- and Italian-inspired dishes. Soy-free, gluten-free and nut-free menus are available for allergy sufferers.

★ **Gage** GASTROPUB $$$
(Map p520; ☑ 312-372-4243; www.thegagechicago.com; 24 S Michigan Ave; mains $18-36; ☺ 11am-9pm Mon, to 11pm Tue-Thu, to midnight Fri, 10am-midnight Sat, 10am-10pm Sun; Ⓜ Brown, Orange, Green, Purple, Pink Line to Washington/Wabash) This always-hopping gastropub dishes up fanciful grub, from Gouda-topped venison burgers to mussels vindaloo or Guinness-battered fish and chips. The booze rocks too, including a solid whiskey list and small-batch beers that pair with the food.

✖ Near North & Navy Pier

This is where you'll find Chicago's mother lode of restaurants. There's a huge variety, from deep-dish pizza to ritzy seafood.

Billy Goat Tavern BURGERS $
(Map p520; ☑ 312-222-1525; www.billygoattavern.com; 430 N Michigan Ave, lower level; burgers $4-8; ☺ 6am-1am Mon-Thu, to 2am Fri, to 3am Sat, 9am-2am Sun; Ⓜ Red Line to Grand) *Tribune* and *Sun Times* reporters have guzzled in the subterranean Billy Goat for decades. Order a 'cheezborger' and Schlitz beer and then look around at the newspapered walls to get the scoop on infamous local stories, such as the Cubs' Curse. The place is a tourist magnet, but a deserving one. Follow the tavern signs that lead below Michigan Ave to get here.

★ **Giordano's** PIZZA $$

(Map p520; ☑ 312-951-0747; www.giordanos.com; 730 N Rush St; small pizzas from $16.50; ⊗ 11am-11pm Sun-Thu, to midnight Fri & Sat; Ⓜ Red Line to Chicago) Giordano's makes 'stuffed' pizza, a bigger, doughier version of deep dish. It's awesome. If you want a slice of heaven, order the 'special,' a stuffed pie containing sausage, mushroom, green pepper and onions. Each pizza takes 45 minutes to bake.

Purple Pig MEDITERRANEAN $$

(Map p520; ☑ 312-464-1744; www.thepurplepigchi cago.com; 500 N Michigan Ave; small plates $10-20; ⊗ 11:30am-midnight Sun-Thu, to 1am Fri & Sat; ☑ ; Ⓜ Red Line to Grand) The Pig's Magnificent Mile location, wide-ranging meat and veggie menu, and late-night serving hours make it a crowd-pleaser. Milk-braised pork shoulder is the hamtastic specialty. Dishes are meant to be shared, and the long list of affordable vinos gets the good times rolling at communal tables both indoors and out. Alas, there are no reservations to help beat the crowds.

✕ Gold Coast

Gibson's STEAK $$$

(☑ 312-266-8999; www.gibsonssteakhouse.com; 1028 N Rush St; mains $45-60; ⊗ 11am-midnight; Ⓜ Red Line to Clark/Division) There is a scene every night at this local original. Politicians, movers, shakers and the shaken-down swirl the famed martinis and compete for prime table space in the buzzing dining room. The rich and beautiful mingle at the bar. The steaks are as good as they come, and ditto for the ginormous lobsters.

★ **Le Colonial** FRENCH, VIETNAMESE $$$

(☑ 312-255-0088; www.lecolonialchicago.com; 937 N Rush St; mains $22-32; ⊗ 11:30am-3pm & 5-10pm Sun-Thu, to 11pm Fri & Sat; ☑ ; Ⓜ Red Line to Chicago) Step into the dark-wood, candlelit room, where ceiling fans swirl lazily and big-leafed palms sway in the breeze, and you'd swear you were in 1920s Saigon. Staff can arrange vegetarian and gluten-free substitutions among the curries and banana-leaf-wrapped fish dishes.

✕ Lincoln Park & Old Town

While mega-high-end restaurants such as Alinea are here, Lincoln Park caters to student tastes, too, thanks to the presence of DePaul University. Halsted St, Lincoln Ave and Fullerton Ave are good bets for trendy,

flirty eateries. Old Town's eateries are quieter and quainter.

La Fournette BAKERY $

(☑ 312-624-9430; www.lafournette.com; 1547 N Wells St; items $3-7; ⊗ 7am-6:30pm Mon-Sat, to 5:30pm Sun; Ⓜ Brown, Purple Line to Sedgwick) The chef hails from Alsace in France and he fills his narrow, rustic-wood bakery with bright-hued macarons (purple passionfruit, green pistachio, red raspberry-chocolate), cheese-infused breads, crust-crackling baguettes and buttery croissants. They all beg to be devoured on the spot with a cup of locally roasted Intelligentsia coffee. Staff make delicious soups, crepes, quiches and sandwiches with equal French love.

Sultan's Market MIDDLE EASTERN $

(☑ 872-253-1489; 2521 N Clark St; mains $4-7; ⊗ 10am-10pm Mon-Sat, to 9pm Sun; Ⓜ Brown, Purple, Red Line to Fullerton) Neighborhood folks dig the falafel sandwiches, spinach pies and other quality Middle Eastern fare at family-run Sultan's Market.

★ **Alinea** GASTRONOMY $$$

(☑ 312-867-0110; www.alinearestaurant.com; 1723 N Halsted St; 10-/16-course menu from $165/285; ⊗ 5-10pm Wed-Sun; Ⓜ Red Line to North/Clybourn) One of the world's best restaurants, with three Michelin stars, Alinea brings on multiple courses of molecular gastronomy. Dishes may emanate from a centrifuge or be pressed into a capsule, à la duck served with a 'pillow of lavender air.' There are no reservations; instead Alinea sells tickets two to three months in advance via its website.

✕ Lake View & Wrigleyville

Good-time midrange places for vegetarians and global food lovers fill the neighborhood. Clark, Halsted and Southport are fertile grazing streets.

Home Bistro AMERICAN $$

(☑ 773-661-0299; www.homebistrochicago.com; 3404 N Halsted St; mains $20-25; ⊗ 5:30-10pm Tue-Thu, 5-10:30pm Fri & Sat, 11am-9pm Sun; Ⓜ Red Line to Addison) Home Bistro (aka 'HB') feels as cozy as the nouveau comfort food it serves. Cider-soaked mussels, duck meatball gnocchi and buttermilk fried chicken hit the tables in the wood-and-tile-lined space. Try to snag a seat by the front window, which entertains with Boystown people-watching. You can bring your own wine or beer, which is a nice money saver.

Andersonville & Uptown

Andersonville offers a cozy, international array of eateries. Uptown's 'Little Saigon' brings on the noodle houses.

Nha Hang Viet Nam VIETNAMESE $
(☑773-878-8895; 1032 W Argyle St; mains $7-13; ⊘8:30am-10pm Wed-Mon; ⓜRed Line to Argyle) Little Nha Hang may not look like much from the outside, but it offers a huge menu of authentic, well-made dishes from the homeland. It's terrific for slurping pho and clay-pot catfish. Staff give out free vanilla ice cream at meal's end, which is a nice touch.

★**Hopleaf** EUROPEAN $$
(☑773-334-9851; www.hopleaf.com; 5148 N Clark St; mains $12-27; ⊘noon-11pm Mon-Thu, to midnight Fri & Sat, to 10pm Sun; ⓠ22, ⓜRed Line to Berwyn) A cozy, European-like tavern, Hopleaf draws crowds for its Montreal-style smoked brisket, cashew-butter-and-fig-jam sandwich, uber-creamy macaroni and Stilton cheese, and the house-specialty *frites* (fries) and ale-soaked mussels. It also pours 200 types of brew (around 60 are on tap), emphasizing craft and Belgian suds.

Wicker Park, Bucktown & Ukrainian Village

Trendy restaurants open almost every day, with many serving nouveau comfort food. Division St is a bountiful vein of snazzy bistros and pubs that have sidewalk seating.

Hoosier Mama Pie Company PIES $
(☑312-243-4846; www.hoosiermamapie.com; 1618 ½ Chicago Ave; slices $5-6.25; ⊘8am-7pm Tue-Fri, 9am-5pm Sat, 10am-4pm Sun; ⓠ66, ⓜBlue Line to Chicago) There's a statistic that states one out of five people has eaten an entire pie solo. Hoosier Mama is your place to do it. Pastry chef Paula Haney hand rolls and crimps her dough, then plumps it with fruit or creamy fillings. Favorites include the banana cream, chocolate chess (aka 'brownie pie') and classic apple. A handful of meat and veg savory pies tempt too.

Dove's Luncheonette TEX-MEX $$
(☑773-645-4060; www.doveschicago.com; 1545 N Damen Ave; mains $13-19; ⊘9am-9pm Mon-Thu, 8am-10pm Fri & Sat, 8am-9pm Sun; ⓜBlue Line to Damen) Grab a seat at the retro counter for Tex-Mex plates of pork-shoulder posole and shrimp-stuffed sweet-corn tamales. Dessert? It's pie, of course – maybe lemon cream or

peach jalapeño, depending on what staff have baked that day. Soul music spins on a record player, tequila flows from the 70 bottles rattling behind the bar, and presto: all is right in the world.

Mana Food Bar VEGETARIAN $$
(☑773-342-1742; www.manafoodbar.com; 1742 W Division St; small plates $7-10; ⊘5:30-10pm Mon-Thu, to 11pm Fri, noon-11pm Sat, 5-9pm Sun; ☑; ⓜBlue Line to Division) What's unique here is the focus on creating global dishes without using fake meats. So you won't find soy chorizo or tempeh Reubens, but rather multi-ethnic veggie dishes from the likes of Japan, Korea, Italy and the American Southwest. Beer, smoothies and sake cocktails help wash it down. The small, sleek eatery buzzes, so reserve ahead or prepare to wait.

Logan Square & Humboldt Park

Logan Square is the city's inventive foodie mecca. It's casual though – so casual that many of the top spots don't take reservations. Puerto Rican cafes and the *jibarito* sandwich are Humboldt Park's claim to fame. It's also getting gastronomic: the area around California and Augusta Aves has seen several hot spots fire up.

Longman & Eagle AMERICAN $$
(☑773-276-7110; www.longmanandeagle.com; 2657 N Kedzie Ave; mains $16-30; ⊘9am-2am Sun-Fri, to 3am Sat; ⓜBlue Line to Logan Square) Hard to say whether this shabby-chic tavern is best for eating or drinking. Let's say eating, since it earned a Michelin star for its beautifully cooked comfort foods such as duck egg hash for breakfast, wild-boar sloppy joes for lunch, and fried chicken and duck-fat biscuits for dinner. There's a whole menu of juicy small plates and whiskeys too. No reservations.

Kai Zan SUSHI $$
(☑773-278-5776; www.eatatkaizan.com; 2557 W Chicago Ave; mains $10-16; ⊘5-10pm Tue-Thu, to 11pm Fri, 4:30-11:30pm Sat; ⓠ66) If you prefer your sushi served in a trendy nightclub-like space with dramatic lighting and ambient house music, or if your favorite maki is named after an American state, don't go to Kai Zan. If, however, you crave a more adventurous and inspired sushi experience, make a reservation — stat — at this charming little jewel box of a restaurant on an unassuming block in Humboldt Park.

✕ Near West Side & Pilsen

The West Loop booms with celebrity-chef restaurants. Stroll along W Randolph St and W Fulton Market and take your pick. Greektown extends along S Halsted St, Little Italy along Taylor St. Mexican taquerias meet hipster hangouts along 18th St in Pilsen.

★ **Lou Mitchell's** BREAKFAST $

(Map p520; ☑312-939-3111; www.loumitchellsrestaurant.com; 565 W Jackson Blvd; mains $9-14; ☉5:30am-3pm Mon, to 4pm Tue-Fri, 7am-4pm Sat, to 3pm Sun; 🖟; Ⓜ Blue Line to Clinton) A relic of Route 66, Lou's brings in elbow-to-elbow locals and tourists for breakfast. The old-school waitresses deliver fluffy omelets that hang off the plate and thick-cut French toast with a jug of syrup. They call you 'honey' and fill your coffee cup endlessly. There's often a queue to get in, but free doughnut holes and Milk Duds help ease the wait.

★ **Pleasant House Pub** PUB FOOD $

(☑773-523-7437; www.facebook.com/pleasanthousepub; 2119 S Halsted St; mains $8-10; ☉7am-10pm Tue-Thu, to midnight Fri, 10am-midnight Sat, to 10pm Sun; 🖀; 🖵8) Follow your nose to Pleasant House, which bakes tall, fluffy, savory pies. Daily flavors include chicken and chutney, steak and ale, or kale and mushroom, made with produce the chefs grow themselves. The pub also serves its own beers (brewed off-site) to accompany the food. Friday is a good day to visit, when there's a fish fry.

🍷 Drinking & Nightlife

Chicagoans love to hang out in drinking establishments. Blame it on the long winter, when folks need to huddle together somewhere warm. Blame it on summer, when sunny days make beer gardens and sidewalk patios so splendid. Whatever the reason, drinking in the city is a widely cherished civic pastime.

☺ The Loop & Near North

★ **Berghoff** BAR

(Map p520; ☑312-427-3170; www.theberghoff.com; 17 W Adams St; ☉11am-9pm Mon-Fri, 11:30am-9pm Sat; Ⓜ Blue, Red Line to Jackson) The Berghoff dates from 1898 and was the first spot in town to serve a legal drink after Prohibition (ask to see the liquor license stamped '#1'). Little has changed around the antique wood bar since then. Belly up for frosty mugs of the house-brand beer and order sauerbraten, schnitzel and other old-world classics from the adjoining German restaurant.

Monk's Pub PUB

(Map p520; ☑312-357-6665; www.monkspubchicago.com; 205 W Lake St; ☉9am-11pm Mon-Fri, 11am-5pm Sat; Ⓜ Blue, Brown, Orange, Green, Purple, Pink Line to Clark/Lake) Grab the brass handles on the huge wooden doors and enter this dimly lit Belgian beer cave. Old barrels, vintage taps and faux antiquarian books set the mood, accompanied by a whopping international brew selection and free, throw-your-shells-on-the-floor peanuts. Office workers and the occasional TV weather presenter are the main folks hanging out at Monk's, which also serves good, burger-y pub grub.

Clark Street Ale House BAR

(Map p520; ☑312-642-9253; www.clarkstreetalehouse.com; 742 N Clark St; ☉4pm-4am Mon-Fri, from 11am Sat & Sun; 🖀; Ⓜ Red Line to Chicago) Do as the retro sign advises and 'Stop & Drink.' Midwestern microbrews are the main draw. Work up a thirst on the free pretzels, order a three-beer sampler for $7 and cool off in the beer garden out back.

☺ Old Town & Wrigleyville

★ **Old Town Ale House** BAR

(☑312-944-7020; www.theoldtownalehouse.com; 219 W North Ave; ☉3pm-4am Mon-Fri, from noon Sat & Sun; Ⓜ Brown, Purple Line to Sedgwick) Located near the Second City comedy club and the scene of late-night musings since the 1960s, this unpretentious neighborhood favorite lets you mingle with beautiful people and grizzled regulars, seated pint by pint under the nude-politician paintings. Classic jazz on the jukebox provides the soundtrack for the jovial goings-on. Cash only.

Smart Bar CLUB

(☑773-549-4140; www.smartbarchicago.com; 3730 N Clark St; tickets $5-15; ☉10pm-4am Thu-Sun; Ⓜ Red Line to Addison) Smart Bar is a long-standing, unpretentious favorite for dancing, located in the basement of the Metro (☑773-549-4140; www.metrochicago.com; ☉box office noon-6pm Mon, to 8pm Tue-Sat) rock club. The DJs are often more renowned than you'd expect the intimate space to accommodate. House and techno dominate.

Berlin
CLUB

(☑ 773-348-4975; www.berlinchicago.com; 954 W Belmont Ave; ☺ 10pm-4am Sun-Wed, from 5pm Thu-Sat; Ⓜ Red, Brown, Purple Line to Belmont) Looking for a packed, sweaty dance floor? Berlin caters to a mostly gay crowd midweek, though partiers of all stripes jam the place on weekends. Monitors flicker through the latest video dispatches from cult pop and electronic acts, while DJs take the dance floor on trancey detours.

Wicker Park, Bucktown & Ukrainian Village

★ Matchbox
BAR

(Map p520; ☑ 312-666-9292; 770 N Milwaukee Ave; ☺ 4pm-2am Mon-Thu, from 3pm Fri-Sun; Ⓜ Blue Line to Chicago) Lawyers, artists and bums all squeeze in for retro cocktails. It's as small as – you got it – a matchbox, with about 10 bar stools; everyone else stands against the back wall. Barkeeps make the drinks from scratch. Favorites include the pisco sour and the ginger gimlet, ladled from an amber vat of homemade ginger-infused vodka.

Map Room
BAR

(☑ 773-252-7636; www.maproom.com; 1949 N Hoyne Ave; ☺ 6:30am-2am Mon-Fri, 7:30am-3am Sat, 11am-2am Sun; ☎; Ⓜ Blue Line to Western) At this map- and globe-filled 'travelers' tavern,' artsy types sip coffee by day and suds from the 200-strong beer list by night. Board games and old issues of *National Geographic* are within reach for entertainment.

Danny's
BAR

(☑ 773-489-6457; 1951 W Dickens Ave; ☺ 7pm-2am Sun-Fri, to 3am Sat; Ⓜ Blue Line to Damen) Danny's comfortably dim and dog-eared ambience is perfect for conversations over a pint early on and then DJs arrive to stoke the dance party as the evening progresses. The groovy spot is more like a house than a bar, filled with twenty- and thirty-somethings.

☆ Entertainment

Finding something to do in Chicago on any given night is effortless, and the spectrum of entertainment that's available in every price range is overwhelming. Just flip through the city's news weekly, the *Reader*, with its pages of theater openings and concert announcements, and Chicagoans' insatiable appetite for nocturnal amusement becomes apparent.

HOW TO FIND A REAL CHICAGO BAR

To discover classic, character-filled bars on your own, look for the following: an old-style beer sign swinging out front; a well-worn dartboard and/or pool table inside; patrons wearing ballcaps with the logos of the Cubs, White Sox, Bears or Blackhawks; and sports on TV.

Blues & Jazz

★ Green Mill
JAZZ

(☑ 773-878-5552; www.greenmilljazz.com; 4802 N Broadway; ☺ noon-4am Mon-Fri, to 5am Sat, 11am-4am Sun; Ⓜ Red Line to Lawrence) The timeless Green Mill earned its notoriety as Al Capone's favorite speakeasy (the tunnels where he hid the booze are still underneath the bar). Sit in one of the curved velvet booths and feel his ghost urging you on to another martini. Local and national jazz artists perform nightly; Sunday also hosts the nationally acclaimed poetry slam. Cash only.

★ Buddy Guy's Legends
BLUES

(Map p520; ☑ 312-427-1190; www.buddyguy.com; 700 S Wabash Ave; tickets Sun-Thu $10, Fri & Sat $20; ☺ 5pm-2am Mon & Tue, from 11am Wed-Fri, noon-3am Sat, to 2am Sun; Ⓜ Red Line to Harrison) Top local and national acts wail on the stage of local icon Buddy Guy. The man himself usually plugs in his axe for a series of shows in January (tickets go on sale in November). The location is a bit rough around the edges, but the acts are consistently excellent.

BLUES
BLUES

(☑ 773-528-1012; www.chicagobluesbar.com; 2519 N Halsted St; cover charge $7-10; ☺ 8pm-2am Wed-Sun; Ⓜ Brown, Purple, Red Line to Fullerton) Long, narrow and high volume, this veteran blues club draws a slightly older crowd that soaks up every crackling, electrified moment. As one local musician put it, 'The audience here comes out to *understand* the blues.' Big local names grace the small stage.

Kingston Mines
BLUES

(☑ 773-477-4646; www.kingstonmines.com; 2548 N Halsted St; cover charge $12-15; ☺ 7:30pm-4am Mon-Thu, 7pm-4am Fri, 7am-5am Sat, 6pm-4am Sun; Ⓜ Brown, Purple, Red Line to Fullerton) Popular enough to draw big names on the blues circuit, Kingston Mines is so noisy, hot and sweaty that blues neophytes will feel as though they're having a genuine experience – sort of like a gritty Delta theme park. Two stages, seven nights a week, ensure somebody's always on. The blues jam session from 6pm to 8pm on Sunday is free.

Rock & World Music

★ **Hideout**   LIVE MUSIC
(☑773-227-4433; www.hideoutchicago.com; 1354 W Wabansia Ave; tickets $5-15; ⊙5pm-2am Mon & Tue, from 4pm Wed-Fri, 7pm-3am Sat, hours vary Sun; ☑72) Hidden behind a factory at the edge of Bucktown, this two-room lodge of indie rock and alt-country is well worth seeking out. The owners have nursed an outsider, underground vibe, and the place feels like your grandma's rumpus room. Music and other events take place nightly.

★ **Whistler**   LIVE MUSIC
(☑773-227-3530; www.whistlerchicago.com; 2421 N Milwaukee Ave; ⊙6pm-2am Mon-Thu, 5pm-2am Fri-Sun; ☑Blue Line to California) Hometown indie bands, jazz combos and DJs rock this wee, arty bar most nights. There's never a cover charge, but you'd be a schmuck if you didn't order at least one of the swanky cocktails or craft beers to keep the scene going. Whistler is also a gallery: the front window showcases local artists' work.

Empty Bottle   LIVE MUSIC
(☑773-276-3600; www.emptybottle.com; 1035 N Western Ave; ⊙5pm-2am Mon-Wed, from 3pm Thu & Fri, from 11am Sat & Sun; ☑49) Chicago's music insiders fawn over the Empty Bottle, the city's scruffy, go-to club for edgy indie rock, jazz and other beats. Monday's show is often a freebie by a couple of up-and-coming bands. Cheap beer, a photo booth and good graffiti-reading in the bathrooms add to the dive-bar fun.

Theater

★ **Steppenwolf Theatre**   THEATER
(☑312-335-1650; www.steppenwolf.org; 1650 N Halsted St; ☑Red Line to North/Clybourn) Steppenwolf is Chicago's top stage for quality, provocative theater productions. The Hollywood-heavy ensemble includes Gary Sinise, John Malkovich, Martha Plimpton, Gary Cole, Joan Allen and Tracy Letts. A money-saving tip: the box office releases 20 tickets for $20 for each day's shows; they go on sale at 11am Monday to Saturday and at 1pm Sunday, and are available by phone.

Goodman Theatre   THEATER
(Map p520; ☑312-443-3800; www.goodman theatre.org; 170 N Dearborn St; ☑Brown, Orange, Green, Purple, Pink, Blue Line to Clark/Lake) The Goodman is one of Chicago's premier dra-

---

LGBT CHICAGO

Exploring kinky artifacts in the **Leather Archives & Museum** (www.leatherarchives.org; 6418 N Greenview Ave; ⊙Thu-Fri 11am-7pm, Sat-Sun 11am-5pm), or playing a game of naughty Twister at a rollicking street fair? Shopping for gay literature, or clubbing alongside male go-go dancers? Chicago's flourishing gay and lesbian scene in party-hearty Boystown (dense with bars and clubs on N Halsted St between Belmont Ave and Grace St) and easygoing Andersonville offers plenty of choices (but in a more relaxed, less party-oriented scene).

The main event on the calendar is the Pride Parade (p530), held the last Sunday in June. It winds through Boystown and attracts more than 800,000 risqué revelers. **Northalsted Market Days** (www.northalsted.com; ⊙mid-Aug), another wild time in Boystown, is a steamy two-day street fair. Crafty, incense-wafting vendors line Halsted St, but most folks come for the drag queens in feather boas, Twister games played in the street and disco divas (Gloria Gaynor!) on the main stage. The **International Mr Leather** (www.imrl.com; ⊙late May) contest brings out lots of men in, well, leather. Workshops and parties take place around town, with the main event happening at a downtown hotel or theater.

The following resources will assist with your explorations:
Windy City Times (www.windycitymediagroup.com) LGBT newspaper, published weekly. Website is the main source for events and entertainment.

Purple Roofs (www.purpleroofs.com) Website listing queer accommodations, travel agencies and tours.

Chances Dances (www.chancesdances.org) Organizes queer dance parties at clubs around town.

ma houses, and its Theater District facility is gorgeous. It specializes in new and classic American productions and has been cited several times as one of the USA's best regional theaters. At 10am Goodman puts unsold tickets for the current day's performance on sale for half-price online.

Chicago Theatre THEATER
(Map p520; ☑ 312-462-6300; www.thechicago theatre.com; 175 N State St; Ⓜ Brown, Orange, Green, Purple, Pink Line to State/Lake) Take a gander at the six-story sign out front. It's an official landmark (and an excellent photo op). Everyone from Duke Ellington to Frank Sinatra to Prince has taken the stage here over the years (and left their signature on the famous backstage walls). The real show-stopper, though, is the opulent French baroque architecture.

Chicago Children's Theatre THEATER
(CCT; ☑ 773-227-0180; www.chicagochildrens theatre.org; 1016 N Dearborn St; Ⓜ Red Line to Clark/Division) CCT is dedicated exclusively to putting on quality productions for young audiences. Many plays are adapted from children's books, and many use puppets or music. The group is building a swanky new theater in the West Loop to be completed in 2020. Until then, performances take place at the Ruth Page Center for Arts.

Neo-Futurists THEATER
(☑ 773-878-4557; www.neofuturists.org; 5153 N Ashland Ave; ⊙ 11:30pm Fri & Sat, 7pm Sun; ☑ 22, Ⓜ Red Line to Berwyn) The Neo-Futurists are best known for their show *The Infinite Wrench*, in which the hyper troupe makes a manic attempt to perform 30 original plays in 60 minutes. Admission costs $10 to $15; what you pay within that range is based on a dice throw.

Comedy

★**iO Theater** COMEDY
(☑ 312-929-2401; www.ioimprov.com/chicago; 1501 N Kingsbury St; tickets $5-16; Ⓜ Red Line to North/Clybourn) One of Chicago's top-tier improv houses, iO is a bit edgier (and cheaper) than its competition, with four stages hosting bawdy shows nightly. Two bars and a beer garden add to the fun. The Improvised Shakespeare Company is awesome.

★**Second City** COMEDY
(☑ 312-337-3992; www.secondcity.com; 1616 N Wells St; tickets $29-36; Ⓜ Brown, Purple Line to Sedgwick) Bill Murray, Stephen Colbert, Tina Fey and more honed their wit at this slick venue where shows take place nightly. The Mainstage and ETC stage host sketch revues (with an improv scene thrown in); they're similar in price and quality. If you turn up around 10pm (on any night except Friday and Saturday) you can have yourself a bargain and watch the comics improv a set free.

Cinema

The Davis Theater CINEMA
(☑ 773-769-3999; www.davistheater.com; 4614 N Lincoln Ave; ⊙ 4:30pm-1am Mon-Fri, 11am-2am Sat, 11am-1am Sun; Ⓜ Blue Line to Western) The Davis Theater is a century-old cinema in Lincoln Square that recently underwent a major renovation. Gone are the stiff chairs, rundown bathrooms and cockeyed screens that used to give moviegoers a kink in the neck. They've been replaced by stadium seating, pristine restrooms, larger screens and state-of-the-art sound. Also revived: the neighborhood theater's deco charm.

Logan Theatre CINEMA
(☑ 773-342-5555; www.thelogantheatre.com; 2646 N Milwaukee Ave; Ⓜ Blue Line to Logan Square) Established in 1915, the Logan Theatre is one of the neighborhood's most enduring landmarks. A major renovation in 2012 unearthed gleaming marble walls and a stained-glass transom above the ticket booth, and added a new art-deco-bar and lounge. Locals and visitors alike flock to the four-screen multiplex to enjoy mid-run movies, independent films and trivia nights.

Sports

★**Chicago Cubs** BASEBALL
(☑ 800-843-2827; www.cubs.com; 1060 W Addison St; Ⓜ Red Line to Addison) The beloved Cubs play at old-time Wrigley Field. For 108 years they didn't win a championship – the longest losing streak in US sports history – but in 2016 the team broke the curse. Games are always packed. Ticket prices vary, but in general you'll be hard-pressed to get in for under $40. The popular bleacher seats cost around $55 or so.

Chicago White Sox BASEBALL
(☑ 866-769-4263; www.whitesox.com; 333 W 35th St; Ⓜ Red Line to Sox-35th) The Sox are the Cubs' South Side rivals and play in the more modern Guaranteed Rate Field. Tickets are usually cheaper and easier to get than at Wrigley Field; games on Sunday and Monday offer the best deals. The Sox also come up with more promotions (free T-shirts, fireworks etc) to lure fans.

Chicago Bulls
BASKETBALL

(www.nba.com/bulls) They may not be the mythical champions of yore, but the Bulls still draw good crowds to their **United Center** (www.unitedcenter.com; 1901 W Madison St; ⬚ 19 or 20) home base. Tickets are available through the United Center box office – located in the glass atrium on the building's eastern side, along with the famed, slam-dunking Michael Jordan statue.

Performing Arts

★ Grant Park Orchestra
CLASSICAL MUSIC

(Map p520; ☎ 312-742-7638; www.grantparkmusicfestival.com; Pritzker Pavilion, Millennium Park; ⊘ 6:30pm Wed & Fri, 7:30pm Sat mid-Jun–mid-Aug; Ⓜ Brown, Orange, Green, Purple, Pink Line to Washington/Wabash) It's a summertime must-do. The Grant Park Orchestra – composed of top-notch musicians from symphonies worldwide – puts on free classical concerts at Millennium Park's Pritzker Pavilion (p516). Patrons bring lawn chairs, blankets, wine and picnic fixings to set the scene as the sun dips, the skyscraper lights flicker on and glorious music fills the night air.

Chicago Symphony Orchestra
CLASSICAL MUSIC

(CSO; Map p520; ☎ 312-294-3000; www.cso.org; 220 S Michigan Ave; Ⓜ Brown, Orange, Green, Purple, Pink Line to Adams) Riccardo Muti leads the CSO, one of America's best symphonies, known for fervent subscribers and an untouchable brass section. Cellist Yo-Yo Ma is the group's creative consultant and a frequent soloist. The season runs from September to May at Symphony Center; Daniel Burnham designed the Orchestra Hall.

Lyric Opera of Chicago
OPERA

(Map p520; ☎ 312-332-2244; www.lyricopera.org; 20 N Wacker Dr; Ⓜ Brown, Orange, Purple, Pink Line to Washington/Wells) Tickets are hard to come by for this bold modern opera company, which fills the chandeliered Civic Opera House with a shrewd mix of common classics and daring premieres from September to March. If your Italian isn't up to much, don't be put off; much to the horror of purists, the company projects English 'supertitles' above the proscenium.

🛍 Shopping

From the glossy stores of the Magnificent Mile to the countercultural shops of Lake View to the indie designers of Wicker Park, Chicago is a shopper's destination. It has been that way from the get-go. After all, this is the city that birthed the department store

and traditions such as the money-back guarantee, bridal registry and bargain basement.

Chicago Architecture Foundation Shop
GIFTS & SOUVENIRS

(Map p520; ☎ 312-322-1132; www.architecture.org/shop; 224 S Michigan Ave; ⊘ 9am-9pm, shorter hours in winter; Ⓜ Brown, Orange, Green, Purple, Pink Line to Adams) Skyline posters, Frank Lloyd Wright note cards, skyscraper models and heaps of books celebrate local architecture at this haven for anyone with an edifice complex.

★ Reckless Records
MUSIC

(☎ 773-235-3727; www.reckless.com; 1379 N Milwaukee Ave; ⊘ 10am-10pm Mon-Sat, to 8pm Sun; Ⓜ Blue Line to Damen) Chicago's best indie-rock record and CD emporium allows you to listen to everything before you buy. It's certainly the place to get your finger on the pulse of the local, au courant underground scene. There's plenty of elbow room in the big, sunny space, which makes for happy hunting through the new and used bins. Reasonable prices too.

Knee Deep Vintage
VINTAGE

(☎ 312-850-2510; www.kneedeepvintage.com; 1425 W 18th St; ⊘ noon-7pm Mon-Thu, 11am-8pm Fri & Sat, noon-6pm Sun; Ⓜ Pink Line to 18th St) Knee Deep offers a trove of vintage clothing (for men and women), housewares and vinyl. There's a sale the second Friday of every month, with items slashed 25% to 50%; it's held in conjunction with the local gallery-hop (a free event run by galleries, shops and studios), starting at 6pm.

Rotofugi
TOYS

(☎ 773-868-3308; www.rotofugi.com; 2780 N Lincoln Ave; ⊘ 11am-7pm; Ⓜ Brown, Purple Line to Diversey) Rotofugi has an unusual niche: urban designer toys. The spacey, robot-y, odd vinyl and plush items will certainly distinguish you from the other kids on the block. It's also a gallery showcasing artists in the fields of modern pop and illustration art. You can usually find locally designed Shawnimals here.

ℹ Information

MONEY

ATMs widely available. Credit cards accepted at most hotels, restaurants and shops. Tipping is not optional; only withhold tips in cases of outrageously bad service.

USEFUL WEBSITES

Lonely Planet (www.lonelyplanet.com/chicago) Destination information, hotel bookings, traveler forum and more.

Choose Chicago (www.choosechicago.com) Official tourism site with sightseeing and event info.

DNA Info Chicago (www.dnainfo.com/chicago) Detailed news about sights, bars, restaurants and events, broken down by neighborhood.

⊙ Getting There & Away

AIR

O'Hare International Airport (ORD; www.flychicago.com) Seventeen miles northwest of the Loop O'Hare is the headquarters for United Airlines and a hub for American Airlines. Most non-US airlines and international flights use Terminal 5. The domestic terminals are 1, 2 and 3. ATMs and currency exchanges are available throughout. Wi-fi costs $7 per day.

Chicago Midway Airport (MDW; www.flychicago.com) Eleven miles southwest of the Loop, Chicago Midway has three concourses: A, B and C. Southwest Airlines uses B; most other airlines go out of A. There's a currency exchange in A and ATMs throughout. Wi-fi costs $7 per day.

TRAIN

Grand, Doric-columned **Union Station** (www.chicagounionstation.com; 225 S Canal St; Ⓜ Blue Line to Clinton) is the city's rail hub, located at the Loop's western edge. Amtrak (www.amtrak.com) has more connections here than anywhere else in the country. Taxis queue along Canal St outside the station entrance.

⊙ Getting Around

TO/FROM THE AIRPORT

O'Hare International Airport The Blue Line El train ($5) runs 24/7 and departs every 10 minutes or so. The journey to the city center takes 40 minutes. Shuttle vans cost $35, taxis around $50.

Chicago Midway Airport The Orange Line El train ($3) runs between 4am and 1am, departing every 10 minutes or so. The journey takes 30 minutes to downtown. Shuttle vans cost $30, taxis $35 to $40.

Union Station All trains arrive here. For transportation onward, the Blue Line Clinton stop is a few blocks south (though it's not a great option at night). The Brown, Orange, Purple and Pink Line station at Quincy is about a half-mile east. Taxis queue along Canal St outside the station entrance.

PUBLIC TRANSPORTATION

Elevated/subway trains are part of the city's public transportation system. Metra commuter trains venture out into the suburbs.

The El (it stands for 'elevated,' though many trains also run underground) is fast, frequent and will get you to most sights and neighborhoods.

Two of the eight color-coded lines – the Red Line, and the Blue Line to O'Hare airport – operate 24 hours a day. The other lines run from 4am to 1am daily, departing every 10 minutes or so.

The standard fare is $3 (except from O'Hare airport, where it costs $5) and includes two transfers. Enter the turnstile using a Ventra Ticket, which is sold from vending machines at train stations.

You can also buy a Ventra Card, aka a rechargeable fare card, at stations. It has a one-time $5 fee that gets refunded once you register the card. It knocks around 75¢ off the cost of each ride.

Unlimited ride passes (one-/three-/seven-day $10/20/28) are another handy option. Get them at train stations and drug stores.

For maps and route planning, check the website of the Chicago Transit Authority (www.transitchicago.com). The 'Transit Tracker' section tells you when the next train or bus is due to arrive at your station.

City buses operate from early morning until late evening. The fare is $2 ($2.25 if you want a transfer). You can use a Ventra Card or pay the driver with exact change. Buses are particularly useful for reaching the Museum Campus, Hyde Park and Lincoln Park's zoo.

TAXI

Taxis are plentiful in the Loop, north to Andersonville and northwest to Wicker Park/Bucktown. Hail them with a wave of the hand. Fares are meter-based and start at $3.25 when you get into the cab, then it's $2.25 per mile. The first extra passenger costs $1; extra passengers after that are 50¢ apiece. Add 10% to 15% for a tip. All major companies accept credit cards. The ride-sharing companies Uber, Lyft and Via are also popular in Chicago.

Reliable taxi companies include **Flash Cab** (☑ 773-561-4444; www.flashcab.com) and **Checker Taxi** (☑ 312-243-2537; www.checkertaxichicago.com).

Around Chicago

Oak Park

This suburb next door to Chicago spawned two famous sons: novelist Ernest Hemingway was born here, and architect Frank Lloyd Wright lived and worked here for 20 years. The town's main sights revolve around the two men. For Hemingway, a low-key museum and his birthplace provide an intriguing peek at his formative years. For

Wright, the studio where he developed the Prairie style is the big draw, as is a slew of surrounding houses he designed for his neighbors. Ten of them cluster within a mile along Forest and Chicago Aves).

◎ Sights

Frank Lloyd Wright Home & Studio
ARCHITECTURE

(☑312-994-4000; www.flwright.org; 951 Chicago Ave; adult/child $18/15; ⊙10am-4pm) This is where Wright lived and worked from 1889 to 1909. Tour frequency varies, from every 20 minutes on summer weekends to every hour or so in winter. The hour-long walk through reveals a fascinating place, filled with the details that made Wright's style distinctive. The studio also offers guided neighborhood walking tours ($15), as well as a self-guided audio version ($15).

Unity Temple
ARCHITECTURE

(☑708-848-6225; www.flwright.org; 875 Lake St; tours $10-18; ⊙9am-4:15pm Mon-Thu, to 3:15pm Fri, to 11:15am Sat) This architectural wonder from Frank Lloyd Wright was built in 1909 and recently restored. Explore at your leisure on a 30-minute self-guided tour (per person $10), or go on a 60-minute guided tour (per person $18, with departures on the hour starting at 10am weekdays, 9am on Saturday).

❶ Information

Oak Park Visitors Center (☑888-625-7275; www.visitoakpark.com; 1010 W Lake St; ⊙10am-5pm Mon-Sat, to 4pm Sun) Offers a visitors guide to the area.

❶ Getting There & Away

I-290 edges the town; exit on Harlem Ave. Take Harlem north to Lake St and turn right. There's a parking garage within a few blocks.

Metra commuter trains on the Union Pacific West Line stop at Oak Park on their Chicago–western suburbs route. Green Line trains also run to/from Chicago as part of the city's public transit system.

Evanston & North Shore

Mansion-strewn real estate fringes Lake Michigan in the suburbs north of Chicago. The area became popular with the wealthy in the late 19th century.

Evanston is the largest community. It combines sprawling old houses with a compact, bookish downtown. It's home to Northwestern University. Next door is Wilmette, where the eye-popping, otherworldly Baha'i temple rises. Further north is Glencoe, where the Chicago Botanic Garden sprouts. A classic 30-mile drive follows Sheridan Rd through the region to the socioeconomic apex of Lake Forest.

◎ Sights

Illinois Holocaust Museum
MUSEUM

(☑847-967-4800; www.ilholocaustmuseum.org; 9603 Woods Dr; adult/child $12/6; ⊙10am-5pm, to 8pm Thu) This is the third-largest holocaust museum in the world, after those in Jerusalem and Washington, DC. Besides its haunting, Nazi-era rail car and its videos of survivors' stories from WWII, the venue contains thought-provoking art about genocides in Armenia, Rwanda, Cambodia and other countries. The special exhibitions are particularly impressive.

Chicago Botanic Garden
GARDENS

(☑847-835-5440; www.chicagobotanic.org; 1000 Lake Cook Rd; per car weekday/weekend $25/30; ⊙8am-sunset) The garden has hiking trails, 255 bird species and weekend cooking demonstations by well-known chefs.

❶ Getting There & Away

I-94 slices by the suburbs to the west. Sheridan Rd rambles through the towns along the lakefront to the east. Metra commuter trains on the Union Pacific North Line stop at each North Shore community as they zip between downtown Chicago and Kenosha, WI. In Evanston, Purple Line trains also run to/from downtown Chicago as part of the Windy City's public transit system.

Galena

Wee Galena spreads across wooded hillsides near the Mississippi River, amid rolling, barn-dotted farmland. Redbrick mansions in Greek Revival, Gothic Revival and Queen Anne styles line the streets, left over from the town's heyday in the mid-1800s, when local lead mines made it rich. Even with all the touristy B&Bs, fudge and antique shops, there's no denying Galena's beauty. Throw in cool kayak trips and back-road drives, and you've got a lovely, slow-paced getaway. Summer and fall weekends see the most action.

◎ Sights & Activities

Ulysses S Grant Home
HISTORIC SITE

(☑815-777-3310; www.granthome.com; 500 Bouthillier St; adult/child $5/3; ⊙9am-4:45pm Wed-Sun Apr-Oct, reduced hours Nov-Mar) The

1860 abode was a gift from local Republicans to the victorious general at the Civil War's end. Grant lived here until he became the country's 18th president. Docents take you through the house. Most of the furnishings are original.

Mississippi Palisades
State Park
STATE PARK

(☑ 815-273-2731; 16327A Hwy 84) It's a popular rock-climbing, hiking and camping area by the Mississippi River. Pick up trail maps at the north entrance park office.

Stagecoach Trail
SCENIC DRIVE

The Stagecoach Trail is a 26-mile ride on a narrow, twisty road en route to Warren. Pick it up by taking Main St northeast through downtown; at the second stop sign go right (you'll see a trail marker). And yes, it really was part of the old stagecoach route between Galena and Chicago.

Fever River Outfitters
OUTDOORS

(☑ 815-776-9425; www.feverriveroutfitters.com; 525 S Main St; ⊙10am-5pm Fri-Sun) Fever River rents canoes, kayaks, bicycles, paddle boards and snowshoes. It also offers guided tours, such as 12-mile bike trips ($45 per person, gear included) to a local winery and various paddling excursions.

🛏 Sleeping & Eating

DeSoto House Hotel
HOTEL $$

(☑ 815-777-0090; www.desotohouse.com; 230 S Main St; r $160-235; ⛭🛜) Grant and Lincoln stayed in the well-furnished rooms, and you can too. The hotel dates from 1855.

Grant Hills Motel
MOTEL $

(☑ 877-421-0924; www.granthills.com; 9372 US 20; r $80-110; ⛭🛜🏊) The motel is a no-frills option 1.5 miles east of town, with countryside views and a horseshoe pitch.

Fritz and Frites
FRENCH, GERMAN $$

(☑ 815-777-2004; www.fritzandfrites.com; 317 N Main St; mains $17-22; ⊙4-9pm Tue-Sat, 9am-2pm & 4-9pm Sun) This romantic little bistro serves a compact menu of both German and French classics. Dig in to escargot (snails) in garlic-herb butter or maybe a tender schnitzel.

ⓘ Getting There & Away

Hwy 20 rolls into Galena. Driving is the only way to get here. The closest transportation hubs are Chicago (165 miles southeast), Madison, WI (95 miles northeast), and Dubuque, IA (16 miles northwest).

Central Illinois

Abraham Lincoln and Route 66 sights are sprinkled liberally throughout central Illinois, which is otherwise farmland plain. East of Decatur, Arthur and Arcola are Amish centers.

Springfield

The small state capital has a serious obsession with Abraham Lincoln, who practiced law here from 1837 to 1861. Many of the attractions are walkable downtown and cost little or nothing.

◉ Sights

Lincoln Home &
Visitor Center
HISTORIC SITE

(☑ 217-492-4150; www.nps.gov/liho; 426 S 7th St; ⊙8:30am-5pm) FREE Start at the National Park Service visitor center, where you must pick up a ticket to enter Lincoln's 12-room abode, located directly across the street. You can then walk through the house where Abe and Mary Lincoln lived from 1844 until they moved to the White House in 1861; rangers are stationed throughout to provide background information and answer questions.

Lincoln Presidential
Library & Museum
MUSEUM

(☑ 217-558-8844; www.illinois.gov/alplm; 212 N 6th St; adult/child $15/6; ⊙9am-5pm; 🚻) This museum contains the most complete Lincoln collection in the world. Real-deal artifacts like Abe's shaving mirror and briefcase join whiz-bang exhibits and Disney-esque holograms that keep the kids agog.

Lincoln's Tomb
TOMB

(☑ 217-782-2717; www.lincolntomb.org; 1441 Monument Ave; ⊙9am-5pm) FREE After his assassination, Lincoln's body was returned to Springfield, where it lies in an impressive tomb in Oak Ridge Cemetery, 1.5 miles north of downtown. In front of the tomb is a bronze bust of Lincoln. The gleam on the nose, created by visitors' light touches, indicates the numbers of those who pay their respects here. On summer Tuesdays at 7pm, infantry re-enactors fire muskets and lower the flag outside the tomb.

Old State Capitol
HISTORIC SITE

(☑ 217-785-7960; cnr 6th & Adams Sts; suggested donation $5; ⊙9am-5pm) Chatterbox docents will take you through the building and regale you with Lincoln stories, such as how he gave his famous 'House Divided' speech here in 1858.

🛏 Sleeping & Eating

Inn at 835
B&B $$

(☑ 217-523-4466; www.innat835.com; 835 S 2nd St; r $135-205; P✳☎) This historic, arts-and-crafts-style manor offers 11 rooms of the four-post bed, claw-foot bathtub variety.

State House Inn
HOTEL $$

(☑ 217-528-5100; www.thestatehouseinn.com; 101 E Adams St; r $120-165; P✳@☎) It looks concrete-drab outside, but inside the State House shows its style. Comfy beds and large baths fill the rooms; a retro bar fills the lobby.

Cozy Dog Drive In
AMERICAN $

(☑ 217-525-1992; www.cozydogdrivein.com; 2935 S 6th St; mains $2-5; ⊙8am-8pm Mon-Sat) This Route 66 legend – the reputed birthplace of the corn dog! – has memorabilia and souvenirs in addition to the deeply fried main course on a stick.

ℹ Information

Springfield Convention & Visitors Bureau (www.visitspringfieldillinois.com) produces a useful visitors guide.

ℹ Getting There & Away

The downtown **Amtrak station** (☑ 217-753-2013; www.amtrak.com; 100 N 3rd St) has five trains daily to/from St Louis (two hours) and Chicago (3½ hours).

Southern Illinois

Southern Illinois looks wildly different from the rest of the state, with rivers and rugged green hills dominating the landscape. The Mississippi River forms the western boundary, and alongside it the Great River Road unfolds. The water-hugging byway (actually a series of roads) curls by bluff-strewn scenery and forgotten towns with real-deal Main Streets. One of the most knockout stretches is Hwy 100 between Grafton and Alton (near St Louis). As you slip under wind-beaten cliffs, keep an eye out for the turnoff to Elsah, a hidden hamlet of 19th-century stone cottages, wood buggy shops and farmhouses. To the south, Lewis and Clark's launch site, a prehistoric World Heritage Site and a lonely hilltop fort appear.

Inland and south, the population thins and the forested Shawnee Hills rise up,

looking a lot like mini mountains. Some surprises hide around here, including an eerie swamp and a trail of vineyards.

◉ Sights & Activities

Union County, near the state's southern tip, has wineries and orchards. Sample the wares on the 35-mile **Shawnee Hills Wine Trail** (www.shawneewinetrail.com), which connects 11 vineyards.

Cahokia Mounds State Historic Site
HISTORIC SITE

(☑ 618-346-5160; www.cahokiamounds.org; Collinsville Rd; suggested donation adult/child $7/2; ⊙grounds 8am-dusk, visitor center 9am-5pm Tue-Sun) A surprise awaits near Collinsville, 8 miles east of East St Louis: classified as a Unesco World Heritage Site with the likes of Stonehenge and the Egyptian pyramids is Cahokia Mounds State Historic Site. Cahokia protects the remnants of North America's largest prehistoric city (20,000 people, with suburbs), dating from AD 1200. While the 65 earthen mounds, including the enormous Monk's Mound, are not overwhelmingly impressive in themselves, the whole site is worth seeing.

If you're approaching from the north, take exit 24 off I-255 S; if approaching from St Louis, take exit 6 off I-55/70.

Lewis & Clark State Historic Site
HISTORIC SITE

(☑ 618-251-5811; www.campdubois.com; cnr Hwy 3 & Poag Rd; ⊙9am-5pm, closed Mon & Tue Oct-Apr) **FREE** In Hartford (across the river from St Louis), the stellar Lewis & Clark State Historic Site marks the spot where the explorers departed on their journey. The 55ft boat replica (in the visitor center), reconstructed winter camp (out on the low-slung prairie) and Mississippi River bashing by give a real feel for the scene.

Cypress Creek National Wildlife Refuge
WILDLIFE RESERVE

(☑ 618-634-2231; www.fws.gov/refuge/cypress_creek) **FREE** You certainly don't expect to find a southern-style swampland, complete with moss-draped cypress trees and croaking bullfrogs in Illinois. But it's here, at Cypress Creek National Wildlife Refuge. Check it out from the Bellrose Viewing Platform off Cache Chapel Rd. Or head to Section 8 Woods and take a short stroll on the boardwalk for a taste of the waterlogged, primeval landscape; it's near the **Cache River**

Wetlands Center (☑618-657-2064; www.
friendsofthecache.org; 8885 Hwy 37; ⊙9am-4pm
Wed-Sun), which also has hiking and canoeing info.

Shawnee National Forest FOREST
(☑618-253-7114; www.fs.usda.gov/shawnee) An
exception to Illinois' flat farmland is the
green southernmost section, punctuated
by rolling Shawnee National Forest and its
rocky outcroppings. The area has numerous
state parks and recreation areas good for
hiking, climbing, swimming, fishing and
canoeing, particularly around Little Grassy
Lake and Devil's Kitchen.

🛏 Sleeping & Eating

Low-priced chain hotels provide most of
the region's beds. B&Bs pop up in some of
the River Road towns and Shawnee vineyards. Amenity-laden cabins are popular in
the Shawnee National Forest area. Places
to eat can be few and far between in some
parts of the region. Expect mom-and-pop,
meat-and-potato type restaurants

❶ Getting There & Away

You'll need to drive to reach the area's far-flung
sights. I-57 is the main interstate through the
heart of the region. The Great River Road daw-
dles along the water to the west. St Louis is the
nearest transportation hub.

INDIANA

The state revs up around the Indy 500 race,
but otherwise it's about slow-paced pleasures in corn-stubbled Indiana: pie-eating
in Amish Country, meditating in Bloomington's Tibetan temples and admiring the big
architecture in small Columbus. The northwest has moody sand dunes to climb, while
the south has caves to explore and rivers to
canoe. Spooky labyrinths, bluegrass music
shrines and a famed, lipstick-kissed grave-
stone also make appearances in the state.

For the record, folks have called Indian-
ans 'Hoosiers' since the 1830s, but the word's
origin is unknown. One theory is that early
settlers knocking on a door were met with
'Who's here?' which soon became 'Hoosier.'
It's certainly something to discuss with locals, perhaps over a traditional pork tenderloin sandwich.

Fun fact: Indiana is called 'the mother
of vice presidents' for the six veeps it has
spawned.

❶ Information

Indiana Highway Conditions (https://indot.
carsprogram.org)
Indiana State Park Information (☑800-622-
4931; www.in.gov/dnr/parklake) Park entry
costs $2 per day by foot or bicycle, $9 to $12
by vehicle. Campsites cost $12 to $44; reservations accepted (☑866-622-6746; www.camp.
in.gov).
Indiana Tourism (www.visitindiana.com)

Indianapolis

Clean-cut Indy is the state capital and a perfectly pleasant place to ogle race cars and
take a spin around the renowned speedway.
The art museum and White River State Park
have their merits, as do the Mass Ave and
Broad Ripple 'hoods for eating and drinking. And fans of author Kurt Vonnegut are in
for a treat. A swell walking and biking trail
connects it all.

◉ Sights

Indianapolis Motor Speedway MUSEUM
(☑317-492-6784; www.indianapolismotorspeed-
way.com; 4790 W 16th St; adult/child $10/5;
⊙9am-5pm Mar-Oct, 10am-4pm Nov-Feb) The
Speedway, home of the Indianapolis 500
motor race, is Indy's super-sight. The Speedway Museum features some 75 racing cars
(including former winners), a 500lb Tiffany
trophy and a track tour ($8 extra). OK, so
you're on a bus for the latter and not even
beginning to burn rubber at 37mph, but it's
still fun to pretend.

The big race itself is held on the Sunday
of Memorial Day weekend (late May) and attended by 450,000 crazed fans. Tickets ($30
to $185, www.imstix.com) can be hard to
come by. Try the pre-race trials and practices
for easier access and cheaper prices.

Dallara IndyCar Factory MUSEUM
(☑317-243-7171; www.indycarfactory.com; 1201 W
Main St; adult/child $10/5; ⊙10am-5pm Wed-Sat)
This shiny factory is a short walk from the
Indianapolis Motor Speedway, and provides
a peek at how the fast cars are made. The
wind-tunnel models raise hairs, as do driving simulators that let you feel what it's like
to tear around the track at 200mph.

White River State Park STATE PARK
(☑317-233-2434; www.inwhiteriver.com; 801 W
Washington St) The expansive park, located at downtown's edge, contains several

worthwhile sights. The adobe **Eiteljorg Museum of American Indians & Western Art** (☎317-636-9378; www.eiteljorg.org; 500 W Washington St; adult/child $13/7; ◷10am-5pm Mon-Sat, from noon Sun) features an impressive collection of Native American works. Other park highlights include an atmospheric minor-league baseball stadium, a zoo, a canal walk, gardens, a science museum and a college sports museum.

Indianapolis
Museum of Art
MUSEUM, GARDENS

(☎317-920-2660; www.imamuseum.org; 4000 Michigan Rd; adult/child $18/10; ◷11am-5pm Tue-Sat, to 9pm Thu, noon-5pm Sun) This museum has a terrific collection of European art (especially Turner and post-Impressionists), African tribal art, South Pacific art and Chinese works. The complex also includes **Oldfields – Lilly House & Gardens**, where you can tour the 22-room mansion and flowery grounds of the Lilly pharmaceutical family, and **Fairbanks Art & Nature Park**, with eye-popping mod sculptures set amid 100 acres of woodlands. Fairbanks, which has its own entrance, is free.

Kurt Vonnegut Museum
& Library
MUSEUM

(☎317-423-0391; www.vonnegutlibrary.org; 340 N Senate Ave; ◷11am-6pm Mon, Tue, Thu & Fri, noon-5pm Sat & Sun) FREE Author Kurt Vonnegut was born and raised in Indy, and this humble museum pays homage with displays including his Pall Mall cigarettes, droll drawings and rejection letters from publishers. The museum also replicates his office, complete with blue Coronamatic typewriter. You're welcome to sit at the desk and type Kurt a note; the museum tweets the musings. The center is planning to move to a larger space, so you might want to call first to check the location.

Rhythm! Discovery Center
MUSEUM

(☎317-275-9030; www.rhythmdiscoverycenter.org; 110 W Washington St; adult/child $12/6; ◷10am-5pm Mon & Thu-Sat, noon-7pm Wed, noon-5pm Sun) Bang drums, gongs, xylophones and exotic percussive instruments from around the globe at this hidden gem downtown. Kids love the interactive whomping. Adults appreciate the exhibits of famous drummers' gear and the soundproof, drum-kitted studio where you can unleash (and record) your inner rock star.

Indiana Medical History
Museum
MUSEUM

(☎317-635-7329; www.imhm.org; 3045 W Vermont St; adult/child $10/3; ◷10am-4pm Thu-Sat) When you think 'horror movie asylum,' this century-old state psychiatric hospital is exactly what you envision. Guided tours roam the former pathology lab, from the cold-slabbed autopsy room to the eerie specimen room filled with brains in jars. Tours start on the hour. It's a few miles west of White River State Park.

Children's Museum
of Indianapolis
MUSEUM

(☎317-334-4000; www.childrensmuseum.org; 3000 N Meridian St; $12-27; ◷10am-5pm, closed Mon mid-Sep–Feb) It's the world's largest kids' museum, sprawled over five floors holding dinosaurs aplenty and a 43-ft sculpture by Dale Chihuly that teaches tykes to blow glass (virtually!). The admission prices vary depending on the day and how far ahead you buy tickets.

🏃 Activities

The 8-mile Cultural Trail (www.indyculturaltrail.org) bike and pedestrian path links cool sights and neighborhoods around Indy's center. Pacers Bikeshare stations dot the way and are handy for short jaunts.

Bicycle Garage Indy
CYCLING

(☎317-612-3099; www.bgindy.com; 242 E Market St; rental per 2hr/day $20/40; ◷7am-6:30pm Mon-Fri, 10am-4pm Sat) Rent bikes here for leisurely rides. Hop on the Cultural Trail in front of the shop to explore the city center; it eventually connects to the Monon Trail greenway, a converted rail track that heads north from the city for 18 miles. Rates include helmet, lock and map.

🛏 Sleeping

Indy Hostel
HOSTEL $

(☎317-727-1696; www.indyhostel.us; 4903 Winthrop Ave; dm/r from $28/58; P ❄ @ 🛜) This small, friendly hostel has a six-bed female dorm and 12-bed co-ed dorm. There are also four private rooms. Got a tent? Camp in the yard for $29. The Monon Trail hiking/cycling path runs beside the property, and the hostel rents bikes ($10 per day). It's located near Broad Ripple, so a bit of a haul from downtown (on bus 17).

★**Alexander** HOTEL **$$**

(☎317-624-8200; www.thealexander.com; 333 S Delaware St; r $160-270; P❄@⟩) The 209-room Alexander is all about art. Forty original works decorate the lobby; the Indianapolis Museum of Art curates the contemporary collection (the public is welcome to browse). The modern rooms have dark-wood floors and, of course, cool wall art. A block from the basketball arena, it's where visiting teams sometimes stay. Valet parking is $37.

Hilton Garden Inn HOTEL **$$**

(☎317-955-9700; www.indianapolisdowntown. gardeninn.com; 10 E Market St; r $150-190; ❄@⟩≋) The century-old, neoclassical architecture, plush beds and downtown location right by Monument Circle make this a fine chain-hotel choice. Valet parking is $29.

Stone Soup INN **$$**

(☎866-639-9550; www.stonesoupinn.com; 1304 N Central Ave; r $119-149, with shared bath $99-109; P⊝❄⟩) The nine rooms fill a rambling, antique-filled house. It's a bit ramshackle, but it has its charm.

✗ **Eating**

Massachusetts Ave, by downtown, is bounteous when the stomach growls. Virginia Ave, connecting downtown to the Fountain Square district just south, is chockablock with hip foodie options. Broad Ripple, 7 miles north, has pubs, cafes and ethnic eateries.

Bazbeaux PIZZA **$**

(☎317-636-7662; www.bazbeaux.com; 329 Massachusetts Ave; mains $9-15; ⊙11am-10pm Sun-Thu, to 11pm Fri & Sat) A local favorite, Bazbeaux offers an eclectic pizza selection, such as the 'Tchoupitoulas,' topped with Cajun shrimp and andouille sausage. Muffaletta sandwiches, stromboli and Belgian beer are some of the other offerings.

City Market MARKET **$**

(www.indycm.com; 222 E Market St; ⊙7am-9pm Mon-Fri, from 8am Sat; ⟩) A smattering of food stalls fill the city's old marketplace, which dates from 1886. The 2nd-floor bar (⊙2-9pm Mon-Thu, 12-9pm Fri-Sat) pours 16 local brews; most other vendors close by 3pm.

Public Greens AMERICAN **$**

(☎317-964-0865; www.publicgreensurbankitchen. com; 900 E 64th St; mains $8-16; ⊙8am-9pm Tue-

WORTH A TRIP

GRAY BROTHERS CAFETERIA

Cafeterias are an Indiana tradition, but most have disappeared – except for **Gray Brothers Cafeteria** (☎317-831-7234; www.graybroscafe.com; 555 S Indiana St; mains $5-9; ⊙11am-8:30pm) . Enter the time-warped dining room, grab a blue tray and behold a corridor of food that seems to stretch the length of a football field. Stack on plates of pan-fried chicken, meatloaf, mac 'n' cheese and sugar cream pie, then fork in with abandon.

It's located in Mooresville, about 18 miles south of downtown Indianapolis en route to Bloomington.

Sat, to 4pm Sun & Mon) ✐ The on-site micro-farm raises kale, beets, eggs and other ingredients for the eatery's homey dishes; 100% of profits are then plowed back into the community to feed at-risk children.

★**Tinker Street** AMERICAN **$$**

(☎317-925-5000; www.tinkerstreetindy.com; 402 E 16th St; small plates $8-16, mains $19-25; ⊙5-10pm Mon-Thu, to 10:30pm Fri & Sat, to 9pm Sun; ✐) Fork into seasonal dishes such as Indiana asparagus with quinoa and garlic chips or a blue-cheese-topped lamb burger. Vegetarian and gluten-free options are plentiful. The industrial-meets-rustic-wood decor is just right for romantics, while the year-round patio is more casual. Tinker Street is located in Old Northside, a leafy neighborhood of historic manors just north of downtown. No reservations.

🍷 **Drinking & Nightlife**

Downtown and Mass Ave have some good watering holes; the Broad Ripple neighborhood has several.

Rathskeller BEER HALL

(☎317-636-0396; www.rathskeller.com; 401 E Michigan St; ⊙2-9pm Mon-Thu, to 11pm Fri, 11am-11pm Sat, 11am-9pm Sun) Quaff German and local brews at the outdoor beer garden's picnic tables in summer, or at the deer-head-lined indoor beer hall once winter strikes. Rathskeller is located in the historic Athenaeum building near Mass Ave.

Slippery Noodle Inn BAR

(☎317-631-6974; www.slipperynoodle.com; 372 S Meridian St; ⊙11am-2am Mon-Fri, from noon Sat,

4pm-12:30am Sun) Downtown's Noodle is the oldest bar in the state, and has seen action as a brothel, slaughterhouse, gangster hangout and Underground Railroad station; currently, it's one of the best blues clubs in the country. There's live music nightly, and it's cheap.

Sun King Brewing BREWERY
(www.sunkingbrewing.com; 135 N College Ave; ◷10am-9pm Mon-Wed, to 10pm Thu & Fri, 11am-10pm Sat, 11am-8pm Sun, reduced hours in winter) You never know what'll be flowing at Sun King's unvarnished downtown taproom. Indy's young and hip pile in to find out, swilling brews from a cocoa-y Baltic porter to a popcorn-tinged pilsner (made with Indiana popcorn). Flights (six 3oz samples) cost $6. It's packed on Fridays, when the brewery offers cheap growlers. The outdoor patio hops in summer.

☆ Entertainment

Bankers Life Fieldhouse BASKETBALL
(☏317-917-2500; www.nba.com/pacers; 125 S Pennsylvania St) Basketball is huge in Indiana, and Bankers Life Fieldhouse is ground zero, where the NBA's Pacers make it happen.

Lucas Oil Stadium FOOTBALL
(☏317-299-4946; www.colts.com; 500 S Capitol Ave) Where the NFL's Colts play football under a huge retractable roof.

ℹ Information

Indianapolis Convention & Visitors Bureau (www.visitindy.com) Download a free city guide and print out coupons for attractions and tours from the website.

Indianapolis Star (www.indystar.com) The city's daily newspaper.

Indy Rainbow Chamber (www.gayindynow.com) Provides info for gay and lesbian visitors.

Nuvo (www.nuvo.net) Free, weekly alternative paper with the arts and music low-down.

ℹ Getting There & Around

The fancy **Indianapolis International Airport** (IND; www.indianapolisairport.com; 7800 Col H Weir Cook Memorial Dr) is 16 miles southwest of town. The Washington bus (8) runs between the airport and downtown ($1.75, 50 minutes); the Go Green Airport van does it quicker ($10, 20 minutes). A cab to downtown costs about $35.

Greyhound (www.greyhound.com) shares **Union Station** (350 S Illinois St) with Amtrak (www.amtrak.com). Buses go frequently to Cincinnati (2½ hours) and Chicago (3½ hours).

Megabus (www.megabus.com/us; cnr N Delaware & E Market Sts) is often cheaper. Amtrak travels these routes but takes almost twice as long.

IndyGo (www.indygo.net) runs the local buses. Fare is $1.75. Bus 17 goes to Broad Ripple. Service is minimal during weekends.

Pacers Bikeshare (www.pacersbikeshare.org) has 250 bikes at 26 stations along the Cultural Trail downtown. A 24-hour pass costs $8, and additional charges apply for trips over 30 minutes.

For a taxi, call **Yellow Cab** (☏317-487-7777).

Central Indiana

Bluegrass music, architectural hot spots, Tibetan temples and James Dean remembrances all furrow into the farmland around here.

Fairmount

This pocket-sized town is the birthplace of 1950s actor James Dean, one of the original icons of cool.

◉ Sights

Fairmount Historical Museum MUSEUM
(☏765-948-4555; www.jamesdeanartifacts.com; 203 E Washington St; ◷11am-5pm Mon, Wed & Fri-Sun May-Oct) **FREE** Fans of actor James Dean should head directly here to see the Hollywood icon's bongo drums, among other artifacts. This is also the place to pick up a free map that will guide you to sites such as the farmhouse where Jimmy grew up and his lipstick-kissed gravesite. The museum sells Dean posters, Zippo lighters and other memorabilia, and sponsors the annual **James Dean Festival** (www.jamesdeanartifacts.com; ◷late Sep).

James Dean Gallery MUSEUM
(☏765-948-3326; www.jamesdeangallery.com; 425 N Main St; ◷9am-6pm) **FREE** The privately owned James Dean Gallery has several rooms of memorabilia (bronze busts, photos, clocks, Dean's high school yearbooks) in an old Victorian home downtown. The owners are a font of local information.

🛏 Sleeping & Eating

Fairmount has no hotels. The closest options are in Gas City about 7 miles north, where budget and midrange chains dot I-69. A few miles further on is Marion, a much bigger town with name-brand hotels.

A smattering of pizza, Mexican and family-style restaurants pop up on Main St and 8th St. You'll find lots more options, including ethnic diners and fast-food chains, in Marion.

❶ Getting There & Away

Fairmount is 70 miles northeast from Indianapolis, the closest transportation hub. I-69 passes the town to the east.

Columbus

When you think of the USA's great architectural cities – Chicago, New York, Washington, DC – Columbus, IN, doesn't quite leap to mind, but it should. The city is a remarkable gallery of physical design. Since the 1940s, Columbus and its leading corporations have commissioned some of the world's best architects, including Eero Saarinen, Richard Meier and IM Pei, to create both public and private buildings.

Architecture-gaping is the big to-do. More than 70 notable buildings and pieces of public art are spread over a wide area (car required), but about 15 diverse works can be seen on foot downtown. The **visitor center** (✐ 812-378-2622; www.columbus.in.us; 506 5th St; ◷ 9am-5pm Mon-Sat, from noon Sun) provides self-guided tour maps online and on-site. **Bus tours** (adult/student $25/15; ◷ 10am Tue-Fri, 10am & 2pm Sat, 2pm Sun) also depart from the center.

🛏 Sleeping & Eating

Besides **Hotel Indigo** (✐ 812-375-9100; www.hotelindigo.com; 400 Brown St; r $150-200; ❋ ⧉ ⧄ ⧈) and a couple of B&Bs, there's little downtown. A short drive west of the center, several chain hotels bunch around exit 68 off I-65.

Columbus offers lots of non-chain options and diversity – pizza, steak, Caribbean curries, Italian, Thai – downtown. Browse 4th and Washington Sts.

❶ Getting There & Away

I-65 is the main highway that skirts the city. The closest airports are in Indianapolis (46 miles north) and Louisville (73 miles south). Alas, no shuttle buses connect Columbus to these cities.

Nashville

Nashville is the jumping-off point for **Brown County State Park** (✐ 812-988-6406; www.

in.gov/dnr; 1801 Hwy 46 E; per car $9), known as the Little Smoky Mountains for its steep wooded hills and fog-cloaked ravines. Gentrified and antique-filled, the 19th-century town is now a bustling tourist center, at its busiest in fall when visitors pour in to see the area's leafy trees burst into color.

🛏 Sleeping

Cozy B&Bs, inns, cabins and lodges prevail. They're usually midrange in price, except during the peak autumn season, when rates go way up.

Artists Colony Inn   INN **$$**
(✐ 812-988-0600; www.artistscolonyinn.com; 105 S Van Buren St; r $135-180; ❋ ⧉) This central, 20-room inn stands out for its spiffy rooms with four-poster beds, wood-plank floors and other sturdy, Shaker-style decor. You won't have to go far for a good meal: the on-site dining room – open for breakfast, lunch and dinner daily – is well-known for traditional Hoosier fare, such as catfish and pork tenderloin sandwiches.

🍷 Drinking & Entertainment

The compact downtown has several bars and taverns in which to imbibe, as well as a tea house, winery and brewery.

As with Nashville, TN, Indiana's Nashville enjoys country music, and bands play regularly at several venues.

Big Woods Brewing Co   MICROBREWERY
(✐ 812-988-6000; www.bigwoodsbeer.com; 60 Molly's Lane; ◷ 11am-10pm) It's hard to beat a set of beer samples on Big Woods' porch on a bright fall day. The timber-framed building feels like a cozy cabin. Eight house brews are on tap, and burgers and pulled-pork nachos satisfy if hunger strikes.

Mike's Music & Dance Barn   LIVE MUSIC
(✐ 812-988-8636; www.mikesmusicbarn.com; 2277 Hwy 46; ◷ from 6:30pm Fri-Mon) To shake a leg, mosey into Mike's. Line-dance lessons take place at 6:30pm some nights, bands play at 8pm on other nights. Check the schedule. There's usually a small cover charge ($6 to $8).

❶ Getting There & Away

Nashville lies midway between Bloomington and Columbus on Hwy 46. Indianapolis, 60 miles north, is the closest big city and transportation center.

Bloomington

Lively and lovely, limestone-clad and cycling-mad, Bloomington is the home of Indiana University. The town centers on Courthouse Sq, surrounded by restaurants, bars and bookshops. Nearly everything is walkable. Also, perhaps surprisingly, there's a significant Tibetan community here too. The Dalai Lama's brother came to teach at IU in the 1960s, and Tibetan temples, monasteries and culture followed.

Sights

Dagom Gaden Tensung Ling Monastery
MONASTERY

(812-339-0857; www.dgtlmonastery.org; 102 Clubhouse Dr; 9am-6pm) **FREE** Roam the quiet grounds to see traditional Tibetan colors and designs. The monastery also offers free teachings and meditation sessions.

Eskenazi Museum of Art
MUSEUM

(812-855-5445; www.artmuseum.indiana.edu; 1133 E 7th St; 10am-5pm Tue-Sat, from noon Sun) **FREE** Indiana University's art museum, designed by IM Pei, has an excellent, genre-spanning collection. Highlights include African art, 19th-century American painting, German expressionism and modern works by Joan Miró, Pablo Picasso and Salvador Dali. The building is closed until fall 2019 for a major renovation and expansion.

Tibetan Mongolian Buddhist Cultural Center
BUDDHIST SITE

(812-336-6807; www.tmbcc.org; 3655 Snoddy Rd; sunrise-sunset) **FREE** Founded by the Dalai Lama's brother, this colorful, prayer-flag-covered cultural building and its traditional stupas are worth a look. A gift shop sells traditional Tibetan items inside, and meditation sessions that are open to the public take place Monday at 6pm and Thursday at 6:30pm.

Sleeping & Eating

For a town of its size, Bloomington offers a mind-blowing array of ethnic eats – everything from Burmese to Eritrean to Turkish. Browse Kirkwood Ave and E 4th St. Eating here won't break the bank either.

Grant Street Inn
INN $$

(812-334-2353; www.grantstinn.com; 310 N Grant St; r $159-209; @) The inn has 40 rooms in a Victorian house and a couple of adjacent buildings near the Indiana University campus. Rooms in the 1890s home are more quaint and antique-laden, while those in the annexes are more modern and stylish.

Anyetsang's Little Tibet
ASIAN $

(812-331-0122; www.anyetsangs.com; 415 E 4th St; mains $13-14; 11am-3pm & 5-9pm;) Little Tibet offers specialties from the Himalayan homeland, including Tibetan dumplings and noodle stew, as well as Indian and Thai dishes.

Drinking & Nightlife

Kirkwood Ave, close to the university, has a lineup of coffee shops and pubs that serve the thirsty.

Upland Brewing Co
BREWERY

(812-336-2337; www.uplandbeer.com; 350 W 11th St; 11am-midnight Mon-Thu, to 1am Fri & Sat, noon-midnight Sun) Northwest of downtown Bloomington, rustic Upland Brewing Co makes creative suds such as a seasonal persimmon lambic using local fruit.

Nick's English Hut
PUB

(812-332-4040; www.nicksenglishhut.com; 423 E Kirkwood Ave; 11am-1am Mon-Wed, to 2am Thu-Sat, to midnight Sun) Popular with students and professors from nearby Indiana University, Nick's has also filled the cups of Kurt Vonnegut, Dylan Thomas and Barack Obama.

Getting There & Away

Indianapolis, 50 miles northeast, has the closest airport. Go Express Travel (www.goexpresstravel.com) runs a shuttle bus to/from the airport several times daily; it costs $20 one way. Hwy 37 (which will become I-69 by summer 2018) and Hwy 46 are the main roads to Bloomington.

Southern Indiana

The pretty hills, caves, rivers and utopian history of Southern Indiana mark it as a completely different region from the rest of the state.

Ohio River

The Ohio River marks the state's southern border. Hwys 56, 156, 62 and 66, known collectively as the Ohio River Scenic Byway, wind through a lush and hilly landscape covering 300 miles along the churning waterway. Sweet stops en route include Madison, a well-preserved river settlement from the mid-19th century with genteel architecture; Marengo Cave, with its eye-popping underground formations; and former US president Abraham Lincoln's childhood home near Dale. Canoeing, farmstays and beers with attitude pop up in between.

◉ Sights & Activities

In Madison pick up a walking-tour brochure at the visitor center (☑812-265-2956; www.visitmadison.org; 601 W First St; ☺9am-5pm Mon-Fri, to 4pm Sat, 11am-3pm Sun), which will lead you by notable landmarks. Canoeing on the Blue River (a tributary of the Ohio River) is popular; Milltown is a base for it.

Clifty Falls State Park   STATE PARK
(☑812-273-8885; 2221 Clifty Dr; per car $9) A couple of miles west of Madison, this large, wooded state park has hiking trails, views and waterfalls. It offers camping too, with tent and RV sites from $16 to $33.

Falls of the Ohio State Park   STATE PARK
(☑812-280-9970; www.fallsoftheohio.org; 201 W Riverside Dr; interpretive center adult/child $9/7, parking $2; ☺interpretive center 9am-4:30pm Mon-Sat, from 1pm Sun) In Clarksville, this state park has only rapids, no falls, but is of interest for its 386-million-year-old fossil beds. The newly renovated interpretive center explains it all. The park sits right across the river from Louisville, KY.

Lincoln Boyhood National
Memorial   HISTORIC SITE
(☑812-937-4541; www.nps.gov/libo; 3027 E South St; adult/child $5/free; ☺8am-5pm) Off I-64 and 4 miles south of Dale, the Lincoln Boyhood National Memorial is where young Abe, who grew up to become the 16th US president, lived from age seven to 21. This isolated site also includes admission to a working pioneer farm, open from May through September.

Marengo Cave   CAVE
(☑812-365-2705; www.marengocave.com; 400 E State Rd 64; ☺9am-6pm Jun-Aug, to 5pm Sep-May) A plunge into Marengo Cave is highly recommended. It offers a 40-minute tour (adult/child $17/10), 60-minute tour ($20/12) or combination tour ($28/16) walking past stalagmites and other ancient formations. You can also crawl, crouch and go deeper into the formations on more hardcore tours (from $34).

Cave Country Canoes   CANOEING
(☑812-365-2705; www.cavecountrycanoes.com; 112 W Main St; ☺May-Oct) This outfitter operates out of Milltown, offering half-day ($28), full-day ($32) or longer trips on the scenic Blue River; keep an eye out for river otters and rare hellbender salamanders.

🍴 Sleeping & Eating

Blue River Family Farm   FARMSTAY $$
(☑812-633-7871; www.bluerivervalleyfarm.com; 10351 E Daugherty Ln; house $175-195; ❀☏) When you stay here you rent the whole farmhouse, with its three bedrooms, one bathroom, fireplace and hot tub. Deer and wild turkeys roam the property. Children can help feed the goats and chickens and pick veggies from the garden. The owners live down the hill. Located in Milltown; a two-night minimum stay is required.

Hinkle's   BURGERS $
(☑812-265-3919; www.hinkleburger.com; 204 W Main St; mains $2-5; ☺6am-10pm Mon & Tue, to midnight Wed & Thu, 24hr Fri & Sat) It's hard to beat a plate of mini burgers and a caramel milkshake while sitting at the counter on a twirly stool. Hinkle's is an old-school diner in Madison, grilling the goods since 1933.

ℹ Information

Ohio River Scenic Byway (www.ohioriverbyway.com)

ℹ Getting There & Away

Louisville and Cincinnati are the closest big-city transport hubs. In addition to the Ohio River Scenic Byway's gaggle of roads, I-64 cuts across the region. For distance reference, Madison is about 75 miles east of Marengo Cave, which is about 55 miles east of Lincoln's boyhood home.

New Harmony

In southwest Indiana, the Wabash River forms the border with Illinois. Beside it, south of I-64, captivating New Harmony is the site of two early communal-living experiments and is worth a visit. In the early 19th century, a German Christian sect, the Harmonists, developed a sophisticated town here while awaiting the Second Coming. Later, the British utopian Robert Owen acquired the town.

Today, New Harmony retains an air of contemplation, if not otherworldliness, which you can experience at attractions such as the eye-popping Atheneum

(812-682-4474; www.usi.edu/hnh; 401 N Arthur St; ⊙9:30am-5pm), the **Roofless Church** (812-682-3050; www.robertleeblafferfoundation. org; 420 North St; ⊙hours vary) FREE and the spooky **Labyrinth** (812-682-4474; 1239 Main St; ⊙sunrise-sunset) FREE.

The town has a simple resort and a handful of B&Bs in historic buildings, all at midrange prices. **Harmonie State Park** (812-682-4821; 3451 Harmonie State Park Rd; per car $9) offers low-cost camping and cabins.

There aren't many options for food, but those that do exist are non-chain eateries located in the walkable downtown. Menus consist mostly of sandwiches, pizza and American fare.

⊙ Getting There & Away

I-64 is the main interstate to New Harmony; it races by about 7 miles north of town. Hwy 66 links the town to the Ohio River Scenic Byway. The closest city is Evansville, which has a small airport and bus service about 30 miles southeast.

Northern Indiana

While much of Northern Indiana is industrial, unexpected treats rise from the flatland, too. Wild sand dunes, classic cars, Amish pies and the infamous Dark Lord brewer are all within range.

Indiana Dunes

Sunny beaches, rustling grasses and woodsy campgrounds are Indiana Dunes' claim to fame. The area is hugely popular on summer days with sunbathers from Chicago and towns throughout Northern Indiana. In addition to its beaches, the area is noted for its plant variety: everything from cacti to pine trees sprouts here. Sweet hiking trails meander up the dunes and through the woodlands. Visit in the morning and linger on into the afternoon

⊙ Sights & Activities

Indiana Dunes National
Lakeshore   NATIONAL PARK
(219-926-7561; www.nps.gov/indu; ⊙6am-11pm) FREE The Dunes stretch along 15 miles of Lake Michigan shoreline. Swimming is allowed anywhere along the shore. A short walk away from the beaches, several hiking paths crisscross the dunes and woodlands. The best are the Bailly-Chellberg Trail

(2.5 miles) that winds by a still-operating 1870s farm, and the Heron Rookery Trail (2 miles), where blue herons flock. Oddly, all this natural bounty lies smack-dab next to smoke-belching factories, which you'll also see at various vantage points.

Indiana Dunes
State Park   STATE PARK
(219-926-1952; www.in.gov/dnr/parklake; per car $12; ⊙7am-11pm) The state park is a 2100-acre, shoreside pocket within the national lakeshore; it's located at the end of Hwy 49, near Chesterton. It has more amenities than the rest of the lakeshore, but also more regulation and crowds (plus the vehicle entry fee). Wintertime brings out the cross-country skiers; summertime brings out the hikers. Seven trails zigzag over the landscape; No 4 up Mt Tom rewards with Chicago skyline views.

West Beach   BEACH
(376 N County Line Rd; per car $6; ⊙8am-sunset) West Beach, nearest to Gary, draws fewer crowds than the other beaches and features a number of nature hikes and trails. It's also the only beach with lifeguards. There's a snack bar and cool Chicago vistas.

Pedal Power   CYCLING
(219-921-3085; www.pedalpowerrentals.com; 1215 Hwy 49; per hour/day $7/35; ⊙9am-7pm Sat & Sun late May-early Oct) This outfitter rents bicycles (including helmet, lock and map) from the cul-de-sac next to the Indiana Dunes Visitor Center. From here, the 2-mile Dunes-Kankakee Trail runs to Indiana Dunes State Park. Pedal Power also offers tours, such as Bike and Beach Yoga ($20 per person, two hours); check the website for times.

🛏 Sleeping

Campgrounds are prevalent. Midrange chains and budget motels fleck the highways that edge the Dunes.

Tryon Farm Guesthouse   B&B $$
(219-879-3618; www.tryonfarmguesthouse.com; 1400 Tryon Rd; r $190; ✳@☎☀) This four-room B&B nestles in a turn-of-the-century farmhouse near Michigan City. You can help gather eggs from the chickens in the morning (you might even get some to take home). Afterward, lounge in the hammocks, sway on the tire swing and enjoy the garden.

✗ Eating

★ Great Lakes Cafe   DINER $
(☑ 219-883-5737; 201 Mississippi St; mains $6-9; ⊙ 5am-2:30pm Mon-Fri, 6am-12:30pm Sat; ♨)
This colorful Greek family diner sits right in front of a steel mill, whose workers pile in for the cheap, hearty pancakes, meatloaf, butterfly shrimp, bacon-pecan brownies and whatever else features on the whiteboard of daily specials. It's located a short distance off the highway, before you reach the national lakeshore.

Lucrezia   ITALIAN $$
(☑ 219-926-5829; 428 S Calumet Rd; mains $16-28; ⊙ 11am-10pm Sun-Thu, to 11pm Fri & Sat) This is a homey favorite for Italian staples – fettuccine alfredo, veal marsala, linguine with scallops – in Chesterton.

ⓘ Information

Indiana Dunes Visitor Center (☑ 219-395-1882; www.indianadunes.com; 1215 Hwy 49; ⊙ 8am-6pm Jun-Aug, 8:30am-4:30pm Sep-May) The best place to start a visit to the Dunes. Staff can provide beach details; a schedule of ranger-guided walks and activities; hiking, biking and birding maps; and general information on the area.

ⓘ Getting There & Away

The Indiana Toll Rd (I-80/90), I-94, Hwy 12, Hwy 20 and Hwy 49 all skirt the lakeshore. Look for large brown signs on the roads that point the way in to the Dunes.

South Shore commuter trains also service the area on their Chicago-South Bend route. The stops at Dune Park and Beverly Shores put you about a 1.5-mile walk from the beaches.

South Bend

South Bend is home to the University of Notre Dame. You know how people in certain towns say, 'football is a religion here'? They mean it at Notre Dame, where 'Touchdown Jesus' lords over the 80,000-capacity stadium (it's a mural of the resurrected Christ with arms raised, though the pose bears a striking resemblance to a referee signaling a touchdown). The renowned campus and downtown's vintage car museum are worth a pit stop.

◉ Sights & Activities

Studebaker National Museum   MUSEUM
(☑ 574-235-9714; www.studebakermuseum.org; 201 S Chapin St; adult/child $8/5; ⊙ 10am-5pm Mon-Sat, from noon Sun) Gaze at a gorgeous 1956 Packard and other classic beauties that used to be built in South Bend, where the Studebaker car company was based. The shiny vehicles, including vintage carriages and military tanks, spread over three floors. A local history museum shares the building. The entrance is on Thomas St.

Notre Dame Tours   WALKING
(☑ 574-631-5726; www.nd.edu/visitors; 111 Eck Center) FREE Two-mile, 75-minute walking tours of the pretty university campus, with its two lakes, Gothic-style architecture and iconic Golden Dome atop the main building, start at the Eck visitor center. Tour times vary, but there's usually at least a 10am and 3pm jaunt Monday through Friday.

🛏 Sleeping & Eating

Several budget and midrange chain hotels line US Business 31/Hwy 933 (aka Dixie Way) a short distance north of Notre Dame. They're near exit 77 off the Indiana Toll Rd (I-80/90) in an area called Roseland. In fall, prices soar if there is a Notre Dame home football game.

Collegiate cafes and fast-food outlets speckle the streets around the university. Downtown holds a bundle of restaurants, mostly midrange American fare places, but also some Thai, Japanese, Indian and other ethnic eateries. Browse Michigan St for options.

Morris Inn   HOTEL $$
(☑ 574-631-2000; www.morrisinn.nd.edu; 1399 N Notre Dame Ave; r $185-215) This 150-room hotel is popular with Notre Dame alumnae, since it is right in the heart of campus. While the gold-and-white rooms won't win any avant-garde-design awards, they're decent-sized and comfy, with pillowy beds and large bathrooms. Parking on-site costs $20 per night, though it's free at the nearby bookstore lot (a five-minute walk).

★ Oh Mamma's on the Avenue   DELI $
(☑ 574-276-6918; www.facebook.com/OhMamma; 1202 Mishawaka Ave; sandwiches $6-8; ⊙ 10am-6pm Tue-Fri, 9am-4pm Sat) This cute little grocery store and deli features toasted sandwiches, heaps of cheeses from the region (including awesome housemade goat's milk cheese), fresh-baked bread, cannoli and gelato. Staff are super-friendly and generous with samples. Eat in at the smattering of tables, or take away.

AUBURN

Classic-car connoisseurs should stop in Auburn, where the Cord Company produced the USA's favorite autos in the 1920s and '30s. The vehicle museums here impress.

National Automotive and Truck Museum (☑260-925-9100; www.natmus.org; 1000 Gordon Buehrig Pl; adult/child $10/5; ⊙9am-5pm, reduced hours Jan & Feb) This museum has a bit of everything, from toy cars to gas pumps to vintage rigs.

Auburn Cord Duesenberg Museum (☑260-925-1444; www.automobilemuseum.org; 1600 S Wayne St; adult/child $12.50/7.50; ⊙9am-5pm) This museum has a wonderful display of early roadsters in a beautiful art-deco setting.

I-69 is the main interstate to town. Auburn lies about 20 miles south of Hwy 20.

❶ Getting There & Away

South Bend has a bigger-than-you'd-think airport with flights to Chicago, Detroit and more. The airport is also a station on the South Shore commuter train that goes to/from Chicago (about $13 one way). By car, the Indiana Toll Rd (I-80/90) and Hwy 20 are the primary routes to the city.

Indiana Amish Country

The area around Shipshewana and Middlebury is the USA's third-largest Amish community. Horses and buggies clip-clop by, and long-bearded men hand-plow the tidy fields. It's not far off the interstate, but it's a whole different world.

Pick a back road between the two towns and head down it. Often you'll see families selling beeswax candles, quilts and fresh produce on their porch, which beats the often-touristy shops and restaurants on the main roads. Note that most places close on Sunday. Homey B&Bs and country inns are the region's forte. Most fall into the budget or midrange category. Don't expect chic or fancy around here. Amish specialties on many menus include chicken and noodles, baked steak, roast beef and fresh-baked pie in a zillion flavors. Hwy 5 (aka Van Buren St) in Shipshewana has heaps of folksy options, though some are pretty touristy.

❶ Information

Elkhart County Convention & Visitors Bureau (www.amishcountry.org) Has maps and downloadable guides.

❶ Getting There & Away

The Indiana Toll Rd (I-80/90) passes the region to the north. Hwy 20 comes through the area to the south, and connects Middlebury and Shipshewana (which are about 7 miles apart).

OHIO

All right, time for your Ohio quiz. In the Buckeye State you can: 1) buggy-ride through the nation's largest Amish community; 2) lose your stomach on one of the world's fastest roller coasters; 3) suck down a dreamy creamy milkshake fresh from a working dairy; or 4) examine a massive, mysterious snake sculpture built into the earth. And the answer is...all of these. It hurts locals' feelings when visitors think the only thing to do here is tip over cows, so c'mon, give Ohio a chance. Besides these activities, you can partake in a five-way (spaghetti) in Cincinnati and rock out in Cleveland.

❶ Information

Tourism Ohio (www.ohio.org)
Ohio Highway Conditions (www.ohgo.com)
Ohio State Park Information (☑614-265-6561; http://parks.ohiodnr.gov) State parks are free to visit; some have free wi-fi. Tent and RV sites cost $19 to $41; reservations accepted (☑866-644-6727; www.ohiostateparks.reserveamerica.com; fee $8).

Cleveland

Does it or does it not rock? That is the question. Drawing from its roots as a working man's town, Cleveland has toiled hard in recent years to prove it does. Step one was to control the urban decay/river-on-fire thing – the Cuyahoga River was once so polluted that it actually burned. Step two was to bring a worthy attraction to town, say the Rock and Roll Hall of Fame. Step three was to clean up downtown's public spaces and add hip hotels and eateries. The gritty city has come a long way. Even LeBron James deemed it happenin' enough to return to.

◉ Sights

Cleveland's center is Public Sq, dominated by the conspicuous Terminal Tower and a ka-chinging casino. Most attractions are downtown on the lakefront or at University Circle (the area around Case Western Reserve University, Cleveland Clinic and other institutions). Several museums and attractions are within walking distance of each other at University Circle, 5 miles east of downtown. Carless? Take the HealthLine bus to Adelbert. The neighborhood's northern stretch is known as Uptown.

★ **Rock and Roll Hall of Fame & Museum**   MUSEUM

(☑ 216-781-7625; www.rockhall.com; 1100 E 9th St; adult/child $23.50/13.75; ☺ 10am-5:30pm, to 9pm Wed & Sat Jun-Aug) Cleveland's top attraction is like an overstuffed attic bursting with groovy finds: Jimi Hendrix's Stratocaster, Keith Moon's platform shoes, John Lennon's Sgt Pepper suit and a 1966 piece of hate mail to the Rolling Stones from a cursive-writing Fijian. It's more than memorabilia, though. Multimedia exhibits trace the history and social context of rock music and the performers who created it.

Why is the museum in Cleveland? Because this is the hometown of Alan Freed, the disk jockey who popularized the term 'rock and roll' in the early 1950s, and because the city lobbied hard and paid big. Be prepared for crowds (especially thick until 1pm or so).

★ **Cleveland Museum of Art**   MUSEUM

(☑ 216-421-7340; www.clevelandart.org; 11150 East Blvd; ☺ 10am-5pm Tue-Sun, to 9pm Wed & Fri) `FREE` Cleveland's whopping art museum houses an excellent collection of European paintings, as well as African, Asian and American art. Head to the 2nd floor for rock-star works from Impressionists, Picasso and surrealists. Interactive touchscreens are stationed throughout the galleries and provide fun ways to learn more. Gallery One, near the entrance, holds a cool quick hit of museum highlights. Free tours depart from the dazzling, light-drenched atrium at 1pm.

Great Lakes Science Center   MUSEUM

(☑ 216-694-2000; www.greatscience.com; 601 Erieside Ave; adult/child $15/12; ☺ 10am-5pm Mon-Sat, from noon Sun, closed Mon Sep-May; 🅟) One of 10 museums in the country with a NASA affiliation, Great Lakes goes deep in space with rockets, moon stones and the 1973 Apollo capsule, as well as exhibits on the lakes' environmental problems.

Lake View Cemetery   CEMETERY

(☑ 216-421-2665; www.lakeviewcemetery.com; 12316 Euclid Ave; ☺ 7:30am-7:30pm) Beyond University Circle to the east, don't forget this eclectic 'outdoor museum' where President James Garfield rests in an eye-poppingly enormous tower (it's especially grand for a guy who was president for only six months).

The Flats   WATERFRONT

The Flats, an old industrial zone turned nightlife hub on the Cuyahoga River, has had a checkered life. After years of neglect, it's on the upswing once again. The East Bank has a waterfront boardwalk, stylish restaurants, bars and outdoor concert pavilion. The West Bank is a bit grittier and further flung, with an old garage turned brewery-winery, a skateboard park and some vintage dive bars.

🛏 **Sleeping**

★ **Cleveland Hostel**   HOSTEL $

(☑ 216-394-0616; www.theclevelandhostel.com; 2090 W 25th St; dm/r from $28/71; 🕸🛜) This hostel in Ohio City, steps from an RTA stop and the West Side Market, is fantastic. There are 15 rooms, a mix of dorms and private chambers. All have fluffy beds, fresh paint in soothing hues and nifty antique decor. Add in the sociable rooftop deck, coffee-roasting lobby cafe and free parking lot, and no wonder it's packed.

★ **Kimpton Schofield Hotel**   HOTEL $$

(☑ 216-357-3250; www.theschofieldhotel.com; 2000 E 9th St; r $180-260; 🅟🕸🛜🐾) Set in a rehabbed 1902 building downtown, the Schofield is for the cool cats in the crowd. Rooms are spacious and done up with funky artwork (like prints of toy cars), colorful clocks and art-deco-inspired lamps and chairs. Amenities include free loaner bicycles, a free wine social hour each evening and free acoustic guitar loans for in-room jam sessions. Parking costs $36.

Glidden House   BOUTIQUE HOTEL $$

(☑ 216-231-8900; www.gliddenhouse.com; 1901 Ford Dr; r $160-190; 🅟🕸🛜) The French-gothic-eclectic former mansion of the Glidden family (who got rich making paint) has been carved into a graceful, 60-room hotel. The common areas are lush, while the rooms are more understated. Located in University Circle and walkable to the museums.

Hilton Garden Inn   HOTEL $$

(☑ 216-658-6400; www.hiltongardeninn.com; 1100 Carnegie Ave; r $129-179; 🅟🕸@🛜🐾) While it's nothing fancy, the Hilton's rooms are decent value with comfy beds, wi-fi-rigged workstations and mini refrigerators. It's right by the baseball park. Parking costs $18.

Eating

Top spots for hot-chef eats are E 4th St, Ohio City and Tremont. For ethnic eats Little Italy and Asiatown prevail.

Downtown

E 4th St, set under twinkling lights, rolls out several great options. Off the beaten path and east of the city center, Asiatown (bounded by Payne and St Clair Aves, and E 30th and 40ths Sts) has several Chinese, Vietnamese and Korean eateries.

Noodlecat NOODLES $
(216-589-0007; www.noodlecat.com; 234 Euclid Ave; mains $10-12; 11am-9pm) Hep-cat noodles fill bowls at this Japanese American mash-up. Slurp veggie-curry udon, spicy octopus udon, crispy bacon ramen and fried chicken ramen dishes.

Lola AMERICAN $$$
(216-621-5652; www.lolabistro.com; 2058 E 4th St; mains $29-40; 5-10pm Sun-Thu, to 11pm Fri & Sat) Famous for his tattoos, Food Network TV appearances and multiple national awards, local boy Michael Symon put Cleveland on the foodie map with Lola. While the menu changes based on what's seasonal, expect dishes such as beef hanger steak with pickle sauce or braised lamb shank with mint and root vegetables. The glowy bar and open kitchen add a swank vibe.

If you want Symon's cooking but in a more casual, lower-priced setting, head a few doors north on 4th St to Mabel's BBQ, his brisket and kielbasa eatery.

Ohio City & Tremont

Ohio City (especially along W 25th St) and Tremont, which straddle I-90 south of downtown, are areas with hip new establishments popping up all the time.

Barrio MEXICAN $
(216-999-7714; www.barrio-tacos.com; 806 Literary St; tacos $3-4; 4pm-2am Mon-Thu, from 11am Fri-Sun) The Tremont outpost of this small chain is always abuzz with young locals smitten with the build-your-own tacos concept. Fillings include everything from Thai chili tofu to housemade chorizo. Pear, jalapeño and other unusually flavored margaritas add to the fun.

Mitchell's Ice Cream ICE CREAM $
(216-861-2799; www.mitchellshomemade.com; 1867 W 25th St; scoops $3.50-5; 11am-10pm Sun-Thu, to 11pm Fri & Sat;) Mitchell's revamped an old movie theater into an ice-cream-making facility. Watch through big glass windows as staff blend the rich flavors. The goods are super creamy, and the vegan options are brilliant.

Little Italy & Coventry

These two neighborhoods make prime stops for refueling after hanging out in University Circle. Little Italy is closest: it's along Mayfield Rd, near Lake View Cemetery (look out for the Rte 322 sign). Alternatively, relaxed Coventry Village is off Mayfield Rd.

Presti's Bakery BAKERY $
(216-421-3060; www.prestisbakery.com; 12101 Mayfield Rd; items $2-6; 6am-7pm Mon, to 9pm Tue-Thu, to 10pm Fri & Sat, to 4pm Sun) Try big, sunny Presti's for its popular sandwiches and divine pastries.

Tommy's INTERNATIONAL $
(216-321-7757; www.tommyscoventry.com; 1824 Coventry Rd; mains $8-13; 9am-9pm Sun-Thu, to 10pm Fri, 7:30am-10pm Sat;) Tofu, seitan and other old-school veggie dishes emerge from the kitchen, though carnivores have multiple options, too.

Drinking & Nightlife

Tremont is chockablock with chic bars, Ohio City with breweries. Downtown has the young, testosterone-fueled Warehouse District (around W 6th St) and the resurgent Flats. Most places stay open until 2am.

★**Platform Beer Co** BREWERY
(216-202-1386; www.platformbeerco.com; 4125 Lorain Ave; 3pm-midnight Mon-Thu, 3pm-2am Fri, 10am-2am Sat, 10am-10pm Sun) An all-ages, cool-cat crowd gathers around the silvery tanks in Platform's tasting room for $5 to $6 pints of innovative saisons, pale ales and more. When the weather warms, everyone heads out to the picnic-table-dotted patio. The location is a bit far flung, at Ohio City's southern edge, but there's a handy bikeshare station outside the brewery.

Great Lakes Brewing Company   BREWERY
(☑ 216-771-4404; www.greatlakesbrewing.com; 2516 Market Ave; ☺ 11:30am-midnight Mon-Thu, to 1am Fri & Sat) Great Lakes wins numerous prizes for its brewed-on-the-premises beers. Added historical bonus: Eliot Ness got into a shootout with criminals here; ask the bartender to show you the bullet holes.

Millard Fillmore Presidential Library   BAR
(☑ 216-481-9444; 15617 Waterloo Rd; ☺ 4pm-2:30am Mon-Sat, to 12:30am Sun) Mention to pals that you're going to the Millard Fillmore Presidential Library, and you can tell they're impressed by your intellectual curiosity. Then they figure out it's a dive bar with craft beer in the burgeoning neighborhood of Collinwood, and they're even more impressed. Fillmore was the USA's 13th president, and from New York incidentally. But that shouldn't hinder a great bar name.

Jerman's Cafe   BAR
(☑ 216-361-8771; 3840 St Clair Ave NE; ☺ 10am-1am Mon-Sat) Jerman's is Cleveland's second-oldest bar. Slovenian immigrant John Jerman opened it in 1908, and his family still runs it. It's a terrific, old-school dive, with a pressed zinc ceiling, Indians baseball games flickering on the TVs and just a few beers on tap (usually a German lager). Friendly barkeeps and regulars are happy to share stories of the old days.

☆ Entertainment
Gordon Square Arts District has a fun pocket of theaters, live-music venues and cafes along Detroit Ave between W 56th and W 69th Sts, a few miles west of downtown.

Check *Scene* (www.clevescene.com) and the Friday section of *Plain Dealer* (www.cleveland.com) for listings.

★ Happy Dog   LIVE MUSIC
(☑ 216-651-9474; www.happydogcleveland.com; 5801 Detroit Ave; ☺ 4pm-12:30am Mon-Wed, 11am-12:30am Thu & Sun, 11am-2:30am Fri & Sat) Listen to scrappy bands, DJs, storytellers or science lectures while munching on a weenie, for which you can choose from among 50 toppings, from gourmet (black truffle) to, er, less gourmet (peanut butter and jelly); in the Gordon Square district.

Severance Hall   CLASSICAL MUSIC
(☑ 216-231-1111; www.clevelandorchestra.com; 11001 Euclid Ave) The acclaimed Cleveland Symphony Orchestra holds its season (August to May) at Severance Hall, a gorgeous

art-deco-meets-classic building located by the University Circle museums.

Progressive Field   BASEBALL
(☑ 216-420-4487; www.indians.com; 2401 Ontario St) The Indians (aka 'the Tribe') hit here; great sight lines make it a good park to see a game.

ℹ Information
Destination Cleveland (www.thisiscleveland.com) Official website, chock-full for planning.

Visitor Center (☑ 216-875-6680; 334 Euclid Ave; ☺ 9am-6pm Mon-Sat) Staff provide maps and reservation assistance; there's a sweet, arty souvenir shop attached.

Cool Cleveland (www.coolcleveland.com) Hip arts and cultural happenings.

Ohio City (www.ohiocity.org) Eats and drinks in the neighborhood.

Tremont (www.tremontwest.org) Eats, drinks and gallery hops.

ℹ Getting There & Around
Eleven miles southwest of downtown, **Cleveland Hopkins International Airport** (CLE; www.clevelandairport.com; 5300 Riverside Dr) is linked by the Red Line train ($2.50). A cab to downtown costs about $35.

From downtown, **Greyhound** (☑ 216-781-0520; www.greyhound.com; 1465 Chester Ave) offers frequent departures to Chicago (7½ hours) and New York City (13 hours). **Megabus** (www.megabus.com/us; 2115 E 22nd St) also goes to Chicago, often for lower fares.

Amtrak (☑ 216-696-5115; www.amtrak.com; 200 Cleveland Memorial Shoreway) runs once daily to Chicago (seven hours) and New York City (13 hours).

The Regional Transit Authority (www.riderta.com) operates the Red Line train that goes to both the airport and Ohio City. It also runs the HealthLine bus that motors along Euclid Ave from downtown to University Circle's museums. Fare is $2.50, or day passes are $5.50. Free trolleys also loop around downtown's core business and entertainment zones.

UH Bikes (www.uhbikes.com) is Cleveland's bikeshare program, with 25 stations and 250 bikes mostly in downtown and University Circle. A 30-minute ride costs $3.50.

For cab service, call **Americab** (☑ 216-881-1111).

Erie Lakeshore & Islands
In summer this good-time resort area is one of the busiest – and most expensive – places in Ohio. Boaters come to party, daredevils

CEDAR POINT'S RAGING ROLLER COASTERS

One of the world's top amusement parks **Cedar Point Amusement Park** (☏ 419-627-2350; www.cedarpoint.com; 1 Cedar Point Dr; adult/child $67/45; ⊗ from 8am Jun-Aug, 6pm-midnight Fri, from 11am Sat & Sun Sep & Oct) is known for its 17 adrenaline-pumping roller coasters. Stomach-droppers include the Top Thrill Dragster, among the globe's tallest and fastest rides. It climbs 420ft into the air before plunging and whipping around at 120mph. The Valravn is the world's longest 'dive' coaster, dropping riders at a 90-degree angle for 214ft. Meanwhile, the wing-like GateKeeper loops, corkscrews and dangles riders from the world's highest inversion (meaning you're upside down a *lot*).

If those and the other hair-raising coasters aren't enough to keep you occupied, the surrounding area has a nice beach, a water park and a slew of old-fashioned, cotton candy-fueled attractions. It's about 6 miles from Sandusky. Buying tickets in advance online saves money. Parking costs $15 to $18.

It's worthwhile to download the free Cedar Point app, which has a handy feature that lists current wait times for each ride. Note lines for some can be 90 minutes or more.

---

come to ride roller coasters, and outdoorsy types come to bike and kayak. The season lasts from mid-May to mid-September, and then just about everything shuts down.

Bass Islands

In 1812's Battle of Lake Erie, Admiral Perry met the enemy English fleet near South Bass Island. His victory ensured that all the lands south of the Great Lakes became US, not Canadian, territory. But history is all but forgotten on a summer weekend in packed Put-in-Bay, the island's main town and a party place full of boaters, restaurants and shops. Move beyond it, and you'll find opportunities for camping, fishing, kayaking and swimming. South Bass Island is quite developed, offering a mix of inns, B&Bs, motels and resorts. The state park has camping.

A huge number of restaurants clump in central Put-in-Bay on Bay View, Catawba and Delaware Aves. They're easy to walk between and take your pick.

☉ Sights & Activities

**Perry's Victory and
International Peace Memorial**   MONUMENT
(www.nps.gov/pevi; 93 Delaware Ave; adult/child $5/free; ⊗ 10am-6pm mid-May–mid-Oct) The 352ft Doric column is a singular attraction. Climb to the observation deck for views of the Lake Erie battle site and, on a good day, Canada – though you will have to wait until summer 2018, as it is closed for renovations until then.

South Bass Island State Park   STATE PARK
FREE Set on top of white cliffs on the island's southwest side, the park moseys down to a

fishing pier, small rocky beach and vendor offering jet-ski and power-boat rentals. The 120-site campground (campsites $17 to $32) packs in a partying crowd.

Kayak the Bay   KAYAKING
(☏ 419-967-0796; www.kayakthebay.net; Bayview Ave; single/double kayak per 2hr $25/45; ⊗ 10am-8pm late May-Aug, noon-6pm Mon-Fri Sep) Paddle in the harbor or head out to circle the island. Guided tours ($40 to $50 per person) are also available, including a sunset jaunt; call ahead to reserve.

⌁ Sleeping

Ashley's Island House   B&B $$
(☏ 419-285-2844; www.ashleysislandhouse.com; 557 Catawba Ave; r $110-195; ⊗ closed Nov-Mar; ❄ ⬚) Ashley's Island House is a 12-room B&B where naval officers stayed in the late 1800s. Hardwood floors, sturdy antiques and bright-colored quilts give the rooms a homey feel. Bicycle and golf-cart rentals are available.

⚑ Drinking & Nightlife

Beer Barrel Saloon   BAR
(☏ 419-285-7281; www.beerbarrelpib.com; 324 Delaware Ave; ⊗ 11am-1am) The Beer Barrel Saloon has plenty of space for imbibing – its bar is 406ft long. Live bands and Jell-o shots are also part of the deal.

❶ Information

Put-in-Bay Chamber of Commerce (www.visitputinbay.com) Has information on activities and lodging.

ℹ Getting There & Away

Two ferry companies make the trip regularly from the mainland. **Jet Express** (☑ 800-245-1538; www.jet-express.com; 3 N Monroe St) runs passenger-only boats direct to Put-in-Bay from Port Clinton (one way adult/child $18/3, 30 minutes) almost hourly. Leave your car in the lot (per day $12) at the dock. **Miller Ferries** (☑ 800-500-2421; www.millerferry.com; 5174 E Water St) operates a vehicle ferry that is the cheapest option, departing from further-flung Catawba (one way adult/child $7/1.50, car $16) every 30 minutes; the crossing takes 20 minutes. It also cruises to **Middle Bass Island**, a good day trip from South Bass, offering nature and quiet.

Kelleys Island

Peaceful and green, Kelleys Island is a popular weekend escape, especially for families. It has pretty 19th-century buildings, Native American pictographs, a good beach and glacial grooves raked through its landscape. Even its old limestone quarries are scenic.

◎ Sights & Activities

Kelleys Islands State Park   STATE PARK

FREE The park features a popular campground with 127 campsites ($17 to $32), six miles of hiking trails with birds flittering by and a secluded, sandy beach on the island's north side. It's a favorite of families.

Glacial Grooves   NATURAL FEATURE

(☉ sunrise-sunset) FREE The deep scars in the limestone here – which a glacier rubbed in some 18,000 years ago – are the largest and most easily accessible grooves in the world. Look down from the walkway and stairs and behold gouges that are 400ft long, 35ft wide and up to 10ft deep.

Inscription Rock Petroglyphs   ROCK ART

(☉ sunrise-sunset) FREE Native Americans who used the island as a hunting ground carved symbols into this boulder on the island's south shore sometime between AD 1200 and 1600.

Caddy Shack Square   CYCLING

(☑ 419-746-2664; www.caddyshacksquare.com; 115 Division St; ☉ 10am-sunset) Rent bicycles (per hr/day $4/24) or golf carts ($11/88) to zip around the island. It's part of an entertainment complex that also has an 18-hole mini-golf course, game arcade, pizza parlor and good-time bar.

🛏 Sleeping & Eating

Inn on Kelleys Island   B&B $$

(☑ 419-746-2258; www.innki20.wixsite.com/innofkelleysisland; 317 W Lakeshore Dr; r $95-125) Long-time islanders own this 1876 Victorian home. It's a vintage, four-room B&B: metal-frame beds with quilts, rocking chairs, sturdy antique decor, shared bathrooms.

Village Pump   PUB FOOD $$

(☑ 419-746-2281; www.villagepumpkioh.com; 103 W Lakeshore Dr; mains $14-26; ☉ 11am-11pm Mar-Dec; 🛜) Grab a table or a stool at the bar in this old-school tavern, a good spot to tuck into fried perch, lobster chowder and burgers. A chocolatey Brandy Alexander, the house-special cocktail, is a fine way to sop it up.

ℹ Information

Kelleys Island Chamber of Commerce (www.kelleysislandchamber.com) Useful info on lodgings, restaurants and activities.

ℹ Getting There & Away

Kelleys Island Ferry (☑ 419-798-9763; www.kelleysislandferry.com; off W Main St) departs from the teeny village of Marblehead (one way adult/child $10/6.25, car $16). The crossing takes about 20 minutes and leaves hourly (every half-hour in summer). **Jet Express** (☑ 800-245-1538; www.jet-express.com; 101 W Shoreline Dr) departs from Sandusky (one way adult/child $18/4.75, no cars); the trip takes 25 minutes. It also goes onward to Put-in-Bay on South Bass Island (one way adult/child $13/3, no cars). Both ferries arrive on Kelleys Island downtown (Jet Express at the foot of Division St, Kelleys Island Ferry about a half-mile east at the Seaway Marina).

WORTH A TRIP

PELEE ISLAND

Pelee, the largest Erie island, is a ridiculously green, quiet wine-producing and bird-watching destination that belongs to Canada. Owen Sound Transportation Co (www.ontarioferries.com) runs a ferry (one way adult/child $13.75/6.75, car $30) from Sandusky to Pelee, and then onward to Ontario's mainland. Check www.pelee.com for lodging and trip-planning information.

Ohio Amish Country

Rural Wayne and Holmes Counties are home to the USA's largest Amish community. Visiting here is like entering a pre-industrial time warp.

Descendants of conservative Dutch-Swiss religious factions who migrated to the USA during the 18th century, the Amish continue to follow the *ordnung* (way of life), in varying degrees. Many adhere to rules prohibiting the use of electricity, telephones and motorized vehicles. They wear traditional clothing, farm the land with plow and mule, and go to church in horse-drawn buggies. Others are not so strict.

Unfortunately, what would surely be a peaceful country scene is often disturbed by behemoth tour buses. Many Amish are happy to profit from this influx of outside dollars, but don't equate this with free photographic access – the Amish typically view photographs as taboo. Drive carefully as roads are narrow and curvy.

◉ Sights

Kidron, on Rte 52, makes a good starting point. A short distance south, **Berlin** is the area's tchotchke-shop–filled core, while **Millersburg** is the region's largest town, more antique-y than Amish; Hwy 62 connects these two 'busy' spots.

To get further off the beaten path, take Rte 557 or County Rd 70, both of which twist through the countryside to little **Charm**, about 5 miles south of Berlin.

Kidron Auction   MARKET
(www.kidronauction.com; 4885 Kidron Rd, Kidron; ⊙ from 10am Thu) If it's Thursday, follow the buggy lineup down the road from Lehman's store to the livestock barn. Hay gets auctioned at 10:15am, cows at 11am and pigs at 1pm. A flea market rings the barn for folks seeking non-mooing merchandise.

Lehman's   MARKET
(✆ 800-438-5346; www.lehmans.com; 4779 Kidron Rd, Kidron; ⊙ 9am-6pm Mon-Sat, to 5pm Jan-May) Lehman's is an absolute must-see. It is the Amish community's main purveyor of modern-looking products that use no electricity, housed in a 32,000-sq-ft barn. Stroll through to ogle wind-up flashlights, wood-burning stoves and hand-cranked meat grinders.

Heini's Cheese Chalet   FACTORY
(✆ 330-893-2131; www.heinis.com; 6005 Hwy 77, Berlin; ⊙ 8am-6pm Mon-Sat, to 5pm Jan-Apr) **FREE** Heini's whips up more than 50 cheeses. Learn how Amish farmers hand-milk their cows and spring-cool (versus machine-refrigerate) the output before delivering it each day. Then grab abundant samples and peruse the kitschy *History of Cheesemaking* mural. To see the curd-cutting in action through the big window onto the factory floor, come before 11am.

Yoder's Amish Home   FARM
(✆ 330-893-2541; www.yodersamishhome.com; 6050 Rte 515, Walnut Creek; tours adult/child $12/8; ⊙ 10am-5pm Mon-Sat late Apr–late Oct; 🚸) Peek into a local home and one-room schoolhouse, and take a buggy ride through a field at this Amish farm.

🛏 Sleeping & Eating

Guggisberg Swiss Inn   HOTEL $$
(✆ 330-893-3600; www.guggisbergswissinn.com; 5025 Rte 557, Charm; r $110-140; ❋ 🛜) The 24 tidy, bright and compact rooms have quilts and light-wood furnishings. A cheesemaking facility and horseback riding stable are on the grounds, too.

Hotel Millersburg   HISTORIC HOTEL $$
(✆ 330-674-1457; www.hotelmillersburg.com; 35 W Jackson St, Millersburg; r $79-149; ❋ 🛜) Built in 1847 as a stagecoach inn, the property still provides lodging in its 26 casual rooms, which sit above a modern dining room and tavern (one of the few places to get a beer in Amish Country).

★ Boyd & Wurthmann Restaurant   AMERICAN $
(✆ 330-893-3287; www.boydandwurthmann.com; 4819 E Main St, Berlin; mains $6-12; ⊙ 5:30am-8pm Mon-Sat) Hubcap-sized pancakes, 23 pie flavors, fat sandwiches and Amish specialties such as country-fried steak draw locals and tourists alike. Cash only.

Mrs Yoder's Kitchen   AMERICAN $
(✆ 330-674-0922; www.mrsyoderskitchen.com; 8101 Rte 241, Mt Hope; mains $11-14; ⊙ 7am-8pm Mon-Sat) A bit off the beaten path, Mrs Yoder's is a swell choice for well-made Amish fare in simple environs. Order mains like wedding steak (browned beef baked in a mushroom sauce) à la carte, or fill a plate with juicy fried chicken, pot roast and whipped potatoes at the buffet.

ℹ️ Information

Holmes County Chamber of Commerce
(www.visitamishcountry.com)

ℹ️ Getting There & Around

Amish Country lies between Cleveland (80 miles north) and Columbus (100 miles southwest). I-71 and I-77 flank the area to the west and east, respectively, but you'll have to exit and drive along a series of narrow, winding back roads to reach the little towns.

Columbus

What Ohio's capital city (and largest city) lacks in mega sights and wild quirks it makes up for with unexpected food and arts scenes. Better yet, Columbus is easy on the wallet, an influence from Ohio State University's 59,000-plus students (the campus is the nation's second largest). A substantial gay population also has taken up residence in Columbus in recent years.

⊙ Sights & Activities

Wexner Center for the Arts   ARTS CENTER
(☑614-292-3535; www.wexarts.org; 1871 N High St; $8; ⊙11am-6pm Tue, Wed & Sun, to 8pm Thu-Sat) The campus arts center offers cutting-edge art exhibits, films and performances.

Columbus Food Tours   FOOD & DRINK
(☑614-440-3177; www.columbusfoodadventures. com; tours $55-60) Foodie guides lead tours by neighborhood or theme (taco trucks, desserts, coffee), some by foot and others by van. Most jaunts take three to four hours.

🛏️ Sleeping & Eating

Marriott Residence Inn   HOTEL $$
(☑614-222-2610; www.marriott.com; 36 E Gay St; r $149-239; P❄@🛜🏊) A great location downtown, close to everything. All rooms are suites with a full kitchen. The cute free breakfast buffet is served in the old bank vault each morning. Parking is $24.

Le Méridien Columbus,
The Joseph   BOUTIQUE HOTEL $$$
(☑614-227-0100; www.lemeridiencolumbus.com; 620 N High St; r $240-310; P❄🛜🏊) The Joseph's super-cool, Cubist-inspired building is an eye-popper in the Short North. The lobby is basically a gallery featuring works from the Pizzuti Collection, a contemporary art museum a block away. The 135 rooms are good sized, with low-key, modern-chic decor

---

> **GERMAN VILLAGE: COLUMBUS, OHIO**
>
> The remarkably large, all-brick German Village, a half-mile south of downtown, is a restored 19th-century neighborhood with beer halls, cobbled streets, arts-filled parks and Italianate and Queen Anne architecture.

in shades of white and taupe. In-room wi-fi costs $10 to $15 per day; parking costs $30. Free bicycles are a nice touch.

⭐ Skillet   AMERICAN $
(☑614-443-2266; www.skilletruf.com; 410 E Whittier St; mains $12-16; ⊙8am-2pm Wed-Sun) 🌱 This teeny restaurant in German Village serves rustic, locally sourced brunch fare. The menu changes, but you might fill a plate with griddled cinnamon rolls or braised pork cheeks with gravy and grits. It's almost always crowded, and you can't make reservations, but on weekends you can call ahead (30 minutes before you arrive) and put your name on the wait list.

Schmidt's   GERMAN $
(☑614-444-6808; www.schmidthaus.com; 240 E Kossuth St; mains $11-16; ⊙11am-10pm Sun-Thu, to 11pm Fri & Sat) In German Village, shovel in Old Country staples like sausage and schnitzel, but save room for the whopping half-pound cream puffs. Oompah bands play Wednesday to Saturday.

🍷 Drinking & Nightlife

Little Rock Bar   BAR
(☑614-824-5602; www.littlerockbar.net; 944 N Fourth St; ⊙4pm-1am Tue-Thu, 4pm-2am Fri, noon-2am Sat, noon-midnight Sun) The squat brick building used to be a gas station, but now it has morphed into a nifty little neighborhood bar and music venue. Thirty beers flow from the taps (about half from Ohio), perfect for sipping to tunes from the free jukebox. Local singer-songwriters, DJs or other entertainers take the stage most nights.

⭐ Entertainment

Huntington Park   BASEBALL
(☑614-462-2757; www.clippersbaseball.com; 330 Huntington Park Lane) The Columbus Clippers (minor league team of the Cleveland Indians) bats at this stadium downtown.

Ohio Stadium
FOOTBALL

(☎ 800-462-8257; www.ohiostatebuckeyes.com; 411 Woody Hayes Dr) The Ohio State Buckeyes pack a rabid crowd into legendary, horseshoe-shaped Ohio Stadium for their games, held on Saturdays in the fall. Expect 105,000 extra revelers in town.

ℹ️ Information

Columbus Convention & Visitors Bureau

(☎ 866-397-2657; www.experiencecolumbus.com; 277 W Nationwide Blvd; ⊗ 8am-5pm Mon-Fri, 10am-4pm Sat & Sun) This visitor center in the Arena District is staffed and has a gift shop of local goods.

ℹ️ Getting There & Away

The **Port Columbus Airport** (CMH; www.flycolumbus.com; 4600 International Gateway) is 10 miles east of town. A cab to downtown costs about $25.

Greyhound (☎ 614-221-4642; www.greyhound.com; 111 E Town St) buses run at least six times daily to Cincinnati (two hours) and Cleveland (2½ hours).

Yellow Springs

Artsy, beatnik little Yellow Springs was a counterculture hot spot in the 1960s and '70s, thanks to Antioch University. You can still buy a bong at the local head shop, but now galleries, craft shops and sustainable eateries cluster downtown. It's a sweet spot to post up for a day or two. Hang out at the local dairy farm to milk a cow or lick a made-on-site ice-cream cone. Limestone gorges, waterfalls and canoe-able rivers fill the surrounding parkland.

◉ Sights & Activities

⭐ **Young's Jersey Dairy**
FARM

(☎ 937-325-0629; www.youngsdairy.com; 6880 Springfield-Xenia Rd; ⊗ 9am-11pm Jun-Aug, reduced hours Sep-May; 🐾) FREE Young's is a working dairy farm with a famous ice-cream shop, aka the **Dairy Store** (ice cream $3-6, sandwiches $3.50-6.50, which many say whips ups Ohio's best milkshakes, and lots of fun family activities, including mini-golf, batting cages and opportunities to feed goats and watch the cows get milked (the latter happens from 4:30pm to 5:30pm). The golf and batting cages have a fee, the animal viewings do not. The Golden Jersey Inn restaurant is also on-site.

John Bryan State Park
STATE PARK

(☎ 937-767-1274; http://parks.ohiodnr.gov/johnbryan; 3790 Hwy 370) FREE You can fish, hike, bike, rock climb, canoe or camp among the limestone cliffs here. The scenic highlight is Clifton Gorge, cut by the pretty Little Miami River.

🛏️ Sleeping & Eating

Morgan House
B&B $$

(☎ 937-767-1761; www.arthurmorganhouse.com; 120 W Limestone St; r $125-145; ❄️🐾) The six comfy rooms have super-soft linens and private baths. Breakfasts are organic. It's walkable to the main business district.

Golden Jersey Inn
AMERICAN $

(☎ 937-324-2050; www.youngsdairy.com; 6880 Springfield-Xenia Rd; mains $11-18; ⊗ 11am-9pm Mon-Fri, from 8am Sat & Sun Jun-Aug, reduced hours Sep-May) This is the more formal of the two restaurants at Young's dairy farm, serving dishes like buttermilk chicken and gravy-kissed meatloaf in a high-ceiling, oak-timbered barn.

ℹ️ Getting There & Away

Yellow Springs is about 18 miles northeast of Dayton and linked by – wait for it – Dayton-Yellow Springs Rd.

Dayton

Dayton leans hard on its 'Birthplace of Aviation' tagline, and the Wright sights deliver. It's surprisingly moving to see the cluttered workshop where Orville and Wilbur conjured their ideas and the lonely field where they tested their plane. Then there's the Air Force museum, a mind-blowing expanse for aviation buffs. The vast complex of hangars holds just about every aircraft you can think of through the ages.

◉ Sights

⭐ **National Museum of the US Air Force**
MUSEUM

(☎ 937-255-3286; www.nationalmuseum.af.mil; 1100 Spaatz St; ⊗ 9am-5pm) FREE Located at the Wright-Patterson Air Force Base, 6 miles northeast of Dayton, this huuuuge museum has everything from a Wright Brothers 1909 Flyer to a Sopwith Camel (WWI biplane) and the 'Little Boy' type atomic bomb (decommissioned and rendered safe for display) dropped on Hiroshima. The hangars hold miles of planes, rockets and aviation machines. A spiffy new building adds spacecraft and presidential planes (including the first Air Force One).

Huffman Prairie Flying Field HISTORIC SITE
(Gate 16A off Rte 444; ⊘8am-6pm) **FREE** This peaceful patch of grass looks much as it did in 1904 when the Wright Brothers tested aircraft here. A 1-mile walking trail loops around, marked with history-explaining placards.

Wright Cycle Company HISTORIC SITE
(☏937-225-7705; www.nps.gov/daav; 16 S Williams St; ⊘9am-5pm, closed Mon & Tue Nov-Feb) **FREE** Browse exhibits in the original building where Wilbur and Orville developed bikes and aviation ideas.

🛏 Sleeping & Eating

Inn Port D'Vino B&B $$
(☏937-224-7678; www.innport.com; 22 Brown St; r $119-149; ❇️🐾) Set in a historic home, the inn's three rooms are spacious and full of character, though a bit fusty in their fireplace, armchair and thick-carpet decor. The selling point is the great location in the artsy Oregon District, walkable to breweries, bistros and theaters. It's also right beside the downtown business zone.

Corner Kitchen AMERICAN $$
(☏937-719-0999; www.afinerdiner.com; 613 E 5th St; mains $15-24; ⊘4:30-10pm Tue-Thu, to 11pm Fri & Sat) Simple wood tables, white panel walls and mismatched china plates set the mod-rustic tone at Corner Kitchen, a bustling diner-meets-French-cafe. Zingy cocktails sooth alongside meals of wine-steeped mussels, eggplant stew and gravy-laden poutine, though the menu changes often. The four-course tasting menu (per person without/with wine pairings $34/65) is a fine way to go. It's located in the bohemian Oregon District.

ℹ️ Getting There & Away

Dayton has a good-sized airport north of town. Greyhound buses also serve the city, which is equidistant from Cincinnati and Columbus.

Cincinnati

Cincinnati splashes up the Ohio River's banks. Its prettiness surprises, as do its neon troves, its European-style neighborhoods and the locals' unashamed ardor for a five-way (spaghetti with chili, onions, beans and cheese). Amid all that action, don't forget to catch a baseball game, stroll the bridge-striped riverfront and visit the dummy museum.

◉ Sights

◉ Downtown & Over-the-Rhine

At downtown's northern edge, the historic Over-the-Rhine (OTR) neighborhood holds a whopping spread of 19th-century Italianate and Queen Anne buildings that have morphed into trendy eateries and shops. Parts of the area are edgy, but the Gateway District around 12th and Vine Sts is well trod.

**National Underground
Railroad Freedom Center** MUSEUM
(☏513-333-7500; www.freedomcenter.org; 50 E Freedom Way; adult/child $15/10.50; ⊘11am-5pm Tue-Sat) Cincinnati was a prominent stop on the Underground Railroad and a center for abolitionist activities led by residents such as Harriet Beecher Stowe. The Freedom Center tells their stories. Exhibits show how slaves escaped to the north, and the ways in which slavery still exists today. Download the free iPhone app.

Cincinnati Museum Center MUSEUM
(☏513-287-7000; www.cincymuseum.org; 1301 Western Ave; ⊘10am-5pm Mon-Sat, 11am-6pm Sun; 🚸) This museum complex occupies the 1933 Union Terminal, an art-deco jewel still used by Amtrak. The interior has fantastic murals made of local Rookwood tiles. The complex includes a nifty Museum of Natural History (with a cave and real bats inside), a children's museum, a history museum, an Omnimax theater and a special hall for traveling exhibitions. Alas, the building is undergoing an extensive renovation through late 2018, so only the children's museum (adult/child $10.50/8.50) and special hall are open until then. Parking costs $6.

American Sign Museum MUSEUM
(☏513-541-6366; www.americansignmuseum.org; 1330 Monmouth Ave; adult/child $15/free; ⊘10am-4pm Wed-Sat, from noon Sun) This museum stocks an awesome cache of flashing, lightbulb-studded beacons in an old parachute factory. You'll burn your retinas staring at vintage neon drive-in signs, hulking genies and the Frisch's Big Boy, among other nostalgic novelties. Guides lead tours at 11am and 2pm that also visit the on-site

neon-sign-making shop. It's located in the Camp Washington neighborhood (near Northside); take exit 3 off I-75.

Contemporary Arts Center
MUSEUM

(☏ 513-345-8400; www.contemporaryartscenter. org; 44 E 6th St; ☉ 10am-4pm Sat-Mon, to 9pm Wed-Fri) **FREE** This center displays modern art in an avant-garde building designed by star architect Zaha Hadid. The structure and its artworks are a pretty big deal for traditionalist Cincy. The focus is on 'art of the last five minutes.' The exhibits change every three months or so.

Fountain Square
PLAZA

(www.myfountainsquare.com; cnr 5th & Vine Sts) Fountain Sq is the city's centerpiece, a public space with a seasonal ice rink, free wi-fi, concerts (7pm Wednesday to Saturday in summer), a farmers market (11am to 2pm Tuesdays), a Reds ticket kiosk and the fancy old 'Genius of Water' fountain.

Roebling Suspension Bridge
BRIDGE

(www.roeblingbridge.org) The elegant 1876 spanner was a forerunner of John Roebling's famous Brooklyn Bridge in New York. It's cool to walk across while passing cars make it 'sing' around you. It links to Covington, Kentucky.

Purple People Bridge
BRIDGE

(www.purplepeoplebridge.com) This pedestrian-only bridge provides a unique crossing from Sawyer Point (a nifty park dotted by whimsical monuments and flying pigs) to Newport, Kentucky.

◎ Covington & Newport

Covington and Newport, Kentucky, are sort of suburbs of Cincinnati, just over the river from downtown. Newport is to the east and known for its massive **Newport on the Levee** (www.newportonthelevee.com; 1 Levee Way; ☉ 11am-9pm Mon-Thu, 11am-10pm Fri & Sat, noon-6pm Sun) restaurant and shopping complex. Covington lies to the west and has the Main-Strasse quarter, filled with funky restaurants and bars in the neighborhood's 19th-century brick row houses. Antebellum mansions fringe Riverside Dr, and old paddle-wheel steamboats tie up along the water's edge.

Newport Aquarium
AQUARIUM

(☏ 859-491-3467; www.newportaquarium.com; 1 Aquarium Way; adult/child $25/17; ☉ 9am-7pm Jun-Aug, to 6pm Sep-May; ♦) Meet parading penguins, Sweet Pea the shark ray and lots of oth-

er razor-toothed fish at Newport's large, generally well-regarded facility. However among the attractions are stingray touch tanks, which are controversial as human interaction may be stressful for aquatic creatures.

◎ Mt Adams

It might be a bit of a stretch to compare Mt Adams, immediately east of downtown, to Paris' Montmartre, but this hilly 19th-century enclave of narrow, twisting streets, Victorian town houses, galleries, bars and restaurants is certainly a pleasurable surprise. Most visitors ascend for a quick look around and a drink. To get here, follow 7th St east of downtown to Gilbert Ave, then turn right on Eden Park Dr and head up the hill to reach the lakes, paths and cultural offerings in Eden Park.

Cincinnati Art Museum
MUSEUM

(☏ 513-721-2787; www.cincinnatiartmuseum.org; 953 Eden Park Dr; ☉ 11am-5pm Tue-Sun, to 8pm Thu) **FREE** The collection spans 6000 years, with an emphasis on ancient Middle Eastern art and European old masters, plus a wing devoted to local works. While admission to the first-rate permanent collection is free, special exhibitions may cost extra. Parking is free, or get here via bus 1.

☞ Tours

American Legacy Tours
WALKING

(www.americanlegacytours.com; 1332 Vine St; 90min tours $20; ☉ Fri-Sun) Offers a variety of historical jaunts. The best is the Queen City Underground Tour that submerges into old lagering cellars deep beneath the Over-the-Rhine district.

✯✯ Festivals

Bunbury Music Festival
MUSIC

(www.bunburyfestival.com; Sawyer Point Park; ☉ early Jun) Big-name indie bands rock the riverfront for three days; a day pass costs $79 to $89.

Oktoberfest
FOOD & DRINK

(www.oktoberfestzinzinnati.com; ☉ mid-Sep) German beer, bratwursts and mania. It takes place on W 2nd and 3rd Sts downtown between Walnut and Elm Sts.

⎽ Sleeping & Eating

★ Hotel Covington
HOTEL $$

(☏ 859-905-6600; www.hotelcovington.com; 638 Madison Ave; r $135-175; P ❋ ☎) This stylish,

114-room property occupies a turn-of-the-century department store on a busy street in Covington. Rooms are fairly big, with contemporary decor, nifty photo art on the walls, a wired-up work desk and large windows for natural light. There's a good restaurant and bar on site, and a chic courtyard area with a fireplace. Staff are beyond-the-norm helpful.

Gateway B&B

B&B $$

(☑ 859-581-6447; www.gatewaybb.com; 326 E 6th St; r $129-169; P❄✿🖧) For something different, check in to this 1878 Italianate townhouse in a historic neighborhood on the Kentucky side of the river. Exquisite antique oak and walnut furnishings fill the three rooms, and intriguing baseball memorabilia decorates the common area. It's a half-mile walk to Newport on the Levee's restaurants and onward over the Purple People Bridge to downtown Cincy.

Hotel 21c

HOTEL $$$

(☑ 513-578-6600; www.21cmuseumhotels.com/cincinnati; 609 Walnut St; r $279-379; P✿@🖧) The second outpost of Louisville's popular art hotel sits right next door to the Contemporary Arts Center. The mod rooms have accoutrements such as a Nespresso machine, free wi-fi, plush bedding and, of course, original art. The lobby is a public gallery, so feel free to ogle the trippy videos and nude sculptures. The on-site restaurant and rooftop bar draw crowds. Parking costs $38.

★Tucker's

DINER $

(☑ 513-954-8920; www.facebook.com/TuckersRestaurantOTR; 1637 Vine St; mains $5-9; ⊙ 7am-3pm Tue-Sat, to 2pm Sun; 🖉) Located in a tough zone a few blocks from Findlay Market, family-run Tucker's has been feeding locals – African American, white, foodies, penniless, friars, drug dealers – since 1946. It's an archetypal diner, serving six-cheese omelets, shrimp and grits, biscuits and gravy, potatoes with bacon jam and other hulking breakfast dishes, along with several vegetarian dishes using ingredients sourced from the market.

Eli's BBQ

BARBECUE $

(☑ 513-533-1957; www.elisbarbeque.com; 3313 Riverside Dr; mains $6-16; ⊙ 11am-9pm) Eli's is a wee spot that makes awesome barbecue, which is why there's always a line snaking out the door. Order at the counter, find a seat, then wait for staff to bring out your hickory-smoked ribs on a red plastic tray. The meat is tender, the sauce sweet with a smoky kick, and the jalapeño cheddar grits beyond addictive.

The Eagle OTR

AMERICAN $

(☑ 513-802-5007; www.theeagleotr.com; 1342 Vine St; mains $8-12; ⊙ 11am-midnight) A hipster magnet serving modern soul food amid reclaimed wood decor, the Eagle rustles up fantastic fried chicken (dipped in spicy honey), white cheddar grits and spoonbread (like a sweet cornbread). Expect a queue, though the doughnut shop two doors down helps take the edge off.

Terry's Turf Club

BURGERS $

(☑ 513-533-4222; 4618 Eastern Ave; mains $9-15; ⊙ 11am-10pm Wed & Thu, to 11pm Fri & Sat, to 9pm Sun) This 15-table beer-and-burger joint glows inside and out with owner Terry Carter's neon stash. A giant, waving Aunt Jemima beckons you in, where so many fluorescent beer and doughnut signs shine that no other interior lighting is needed. Located 7 miles east of downtown via Columbia Pkwy.

🍷 Drinking & Nightlife

★Rhinegeist Brewery

BREWERY

(☑ 513-381-1367; www.rhinegeist.com; 1910 Elm St, 2nd fl; ⊙ 3pm-midnight Mon-Thu, 3pm-2am Fri, noon-2am Sat, noon-9pm Sun) Beer buffs pile in to Rhinegeist's hoppy clubhouse to knock back Truth IPA and 13 other brews on tap. Swig at picnic tables while watching bottles roll off the production line, or play Ping Pong or Foosball in the sprawling open warehouse. It sits in a forlorn patch of OTR.

Moerlein Lager House

BREWERY

(☑ 513-421-2337; www.moerleinlagerhouse.com; 115 Joe Nuxall Way; ⊙ 11am-midnight Mon-Thu, to 1am Fri & Sat, to 11pm Sun) Copper kettles cook up the house beers, while the patio unfurls awesome views of the riverfront and Roebling bridge. It's a busy spot pre or post Reds games, as it sits across the street from the stadium.

Blind Lemon

BAR

(☑ 513-241-3885; www.theblindlemon.com; 936 Hatch St; ⊙ 5:30pm-2:30am Mon-Fri, from 3pm Sat & Sun) Head down the passageway to enter this atmospheric old speakeasy in Mt Adams. It has an outdoor courtyard, and there's live music nightly.

☆ Entertainment

Aronoff Center THEATER
(☎513-621-2787; www.cincinnatiarts.org; 650 Walnut St) Star architect Cesar Pelli designed the glowy, glass-fronted building. There are three theaters inside: the largest hosts touring Broadway shows, while the other two host cutting-edge dance troupes and intimate concerts. If nothing else, pop in to the free public art gallery to see what's on; it shows exhibitions of regional works.

Great American Ballpark BASEBALL
(☎513-765-7000; www.reds.com; 100 Main St) Home to the Reds – pro baseball's first team – Cincy is a great place to catch a game thanks to its bells-and-whistles riverside ballpark. Many of the beer stands pour top-notch local brews.

ⓘ Information

Cincinnati Visitor Center (☎513-534-5877; www.cincyusa.com; 511 Walnut St; ⊙9am-6pm) The visitor center on Fountain Sq has maps and info.

ⓘ Getting There & Around

The **Cincinnati/Northern Kentucky International Airport** (CVG; www.cvgairport.com) is actually in Kentucky, 13 miles south. To get downtown, take the TANK bus ($2) from near Terminal 3; a cab costs about $35.

Greyhound (☎513-352-6012; www.greyhound.com; 1005 Gilbert Ave) buses travel daily to Columbus (two hours), Indianapolis (2½ hours) and Chicago (seven hours). Megabus (www.megabus.com/us) travels the same routes from downtown and the University of Cincinnati; check the website for curbside locations.

Amtrak (www.amtrak.com) choo-choos into **Union Terminal** (☎513-651-3337; 1301 Western Ave) thrice weekly en route to Chicago (9½ hours) and Washington, DC (14½ hours), departing in the middle of the night.

Metro (www.go-metro.com) runs the local buses and links with the Transit Authority of Northern Kentucky (www.tankbus.org). Bus 1 is useful, looping from the museum center to downtown to Mt Adams.

Red Bike (www.cincyredbike.org) has 440 bicycles at 56 stations, mostly in downtown and Over-the-Rhine. A 24-hour pass costs $8; additional charges apply for trips over 60 minutes.

Cincy's new streetcar (www.cincinnatibellconnector.com) runs on a handy, 3½-mile loop connecting the Banks, downtown and Over-the-Rhine (including Findlay Market). A day pass costs $2.

Southeastern Ohio

Ohio's southeastern corner cradles most of its forested areas, as well as the rolling foothills of the Appalachian Mountains and scattered farms. Parts are far prettier than you'd expect. The Hocking Hills region, near Logan, impresses with streams and waterfalls, sandstone cliffs and cave-like formations. Further on is Athens, a university town and the area's free-spirited hot spot. To the east, around Chillicothe, mysterious Native American mounds rise from the fields.

GREAT LAKES SOUTHEASTERN OHIO

WORTH A TRIP

ANCIENT MOUNDS OF OHIO

The area south of Columbus was a center for the ancient Hopewell people, who left behind huge geometric earthworks and burial mounds from around 200 BC to AD 600. The **Hopewell Culture National Historical Park** (☎740-774-1126; www.nps.gov/hocu; 16062 Hwy 104, Chillicothe; ⊙sunrise-sunset) tells their story. The visitor center (8:30am to 5pm) provides intriguing background information, but the highlight is wandering about the variously shaped ceremonial mounds spread over 13-acre Mound City, a mysterious town of the dead. The park is 3 miles north of Chillicothe.

Serpent Mound (☎937-587-2796; www.ohiohistory.org; 3850 Hwy 73; per vehicle $8; ⊙9am-sunset) is perhaps the most captivating of all the native mounds that dot southeastern Ohio. The giant, uncoiling snake stretches over a quarter of a mile and is the largest effigy mound in the USA. You can walk around it or go up the observation tower for a sweeping view. The site is far flung, but cool enough to be worth the effort. It's 50 miles southeast of Chillicothe. A small on-site museum (10am to 4pm Monday to Thursday, 9am to 5pm Friday to Sunday, reduced hours in winter) has a short video about the history of the mound builders and exhibits showing artifacts found in the area.

Athens

Athens makes a lovely base for exploring southeastern Ohio. Situated where Hwy 50 crosses Hwy 33, it's set among wooded hills and built around the Ohio University campus (which comprises half the town). Vintage brick buildings edge the main streets, while young, earthy and artsy types pop in and out of the cafes and groovy shops inside.

🛏 Sleeping & Eating

Bodhi Tree Guesthouse   B&B $$
(📞 740-707-2050; www.bodhitreeguesthouse.com; 8950 Lavelle Rd; r $130-160) The four rooms at this serene, hippy-esque farmhouse have tasteful modern (if minimal) decor. There are no TVs, but there is wi-fi, as well as a wholesome breakfast of local cheeses, eggs, fruit and yogurt. A 4-acre organic farm surrounds the abode. The on-site studio offers yoga classes and massage.

Village Bakery & Cafe   BAKERY $
(📞 740-594-7311; www.dellazona.com; 268 E State St; sandwiches $9-13; ⏰ 7:30am-8pm Tue-Fri, to 6pm Sat, 9am-2pm Sun; 🖋) 🍴 Brightly painted and woodsy-casual in ambience, Village Bakery uses organic veggies, sustainably produced meats and farmstead cheeses in its egg breakfast dishes and heaped-on-housemade-bread sandwiches. Vegetarians will find lots of options.

ℹ Getting There & Away

The closest big city is Columbus, 75 miles northwest via Hwy 33. GoBus (📞 888-954-6287; www.ridegobus.com) runs a few times a day to/from downtown Columbus.

Logan

Logan is a handy headquarters for checking out the Hocking Hills area, where hiking, canoeing, camping and other activities amid dramatic gorges and grottoes are de rigueur. Hocking Hills State Park lets you immerse in the green scene, while Logan and nearby New Straitsville offer local cultural quirks including a washboard museum and moonshine distillery.

⦿ Sights & Activities

Hocking Hills State Park   STATE PARK
(📞 740-385-6841; http://parks.ohiodnr.gov/hockinghills; 19852 Hwy 664) **FREE** It's splendid to explore in any season (but especially lovely in autumn), with miles of trails for hiking

and biking past waterfalls and gorges, as well as campsites (from $26) and cabins (from $150). The park is 12 miles southwest of Logan.

Straitsville Special Moonshine Distillery   DISTILLERY
(📞 740-394-2622; www.straitsvillemoonshine. com; 105 W Main St, New Straitsville; ⏰ 10am-5pm Mon-Sat) A hissing, coil-laden moonshine distillery operates in New Straitsville, 12 miles east of Logan. Singe your tonsils in the tasting room (per sample $1) while chatting with the owner about the town's rough history spanning coal mines, labor strife, an eternal flame and Al Capone.

Hocking Hills Scenic Byway   SCENIC DRIVE
(www.explorehockinghills.com) For a lovely drive, follow Hwy 374 – an official Ohio Byway – for 26 miles as it rolls through the forested, stream-splashed hills. It starts at the intersection of Hwy 33 and Hwy 374 in Rockbridge.

ℹ Getting There & Away

Hwy 33 is the main road to Logan. **GoBus** (📞 888-954-6287; www.ridegobus.com) makes a stop in town a few times a day on its route between downtown Columbus and Athens.

MICHIGAN

More, more, more – Michigan is the Midwest state that cranks it up. It sports more beaches than the Atlantic seaboard. More than half the state is covered by forests. And more cherries and berries get shoveled into pies here than anywhere else in the USA. Plus its gritty city Detroit is the Midwest's rawest of all – and we mean that in a good way. Michigan occupies prime real estate, surrounded by four of the five Great Lakes – Superior, Michigan, Huron and Erie. Islands – Mackinac, Manitou and Isle Royale – freckle its coast and make top touring destinations. Surf beaches, colored sandstone cliffs and trekkable sand dunes also woo visitors.

The state consists of two parts split by water: larger Lower Peninsula, shaped like a mitten; and smaller, lightly populated Upper Peninsula, shaped like a slipper. They are linked by the gasp-worthy Mackinac Bridge, which spans the Straits of Mackinac (pronounced *mac*-in-aw).

ℹ Information

Michigan Highway Conditions (www.michigan.gov/mdot)

Michigan State Park Information (☑ 800-447-2757; www.michigan.gov/stateparks) Park entry requires a vehicle permit (per day/year $9/32). Campsites cost $13 to $37; reservations accepted (www.midnrreservations.com; fee $8). Some parks have wi-fi.

Travel Michigan (www.michigan.org)

Detroit

Americans love a good comeback story, and Detroit is writing a mighty one as it transforms itself from a punchline to a cool-cat destination. Murals, markets, greenways, bike shops, distilleries and inventive chefs are getting the city's groove on, along with fresh public works like the new street car and sports arena downtown.

While the city does have an abandoned, otherworldly vibe in some areas, it's these same qualities that fuel a raw urban energy you won't find anywhere else. Artists, entrepreneurs and young people keep moving in, and a DIY spirit pervades. They're converting vacant lots into urban farms and abandoned buildings into cafes and museums. But there's a long way to go, and skeptics point out that Detroit's long-term African American residents are not sharing equally in these new developments. How the city navigates the tricky path to recovery remains to be seen, but we're pulling for the underdog.

History

French explorer Antoine de La Mothe Cadillac founded Detroit in 1701. Sweet fortune arrived in the 1920s, when Henry Ford began churning out cars. He didn't invent the automobile, as so many mistakenly believe, but he did perfect assembly-line manufacturing and mass-production techniques. The result was the Model T, the first car the USA's middle class could afford to own.

Detroit quickly became the motor capital of the world. General Motors (GM), Chrysler and Ford were all headquartered in or near Detroit (and still are). The 1950s were the city's heyday, when the population exceeded two million and Motown music hit the airwaves. But racial tensions in 1967 and Japanese car competitors in the 1970s shook the city and its industry. Detroit entered an era of deep decline, losing about two-thirds of its population.

In July 2013 Detroit filed the largest municipal bankruptcy claim in US history: $18 billion. After extreme belt-tightening, it emerged from bankruptcy in December 2014. Since then, the fortunes of downtown have been on the rise, thanks to a real estate boom, but the tide has yet to turn for many long-term residents outside the city's core.

⊙ Sights & Activities

Sights are commonly closed on Monday and Tuesday. And that's Canada across the Detroit River (Windsor, Canada, to be exact).

CLASSIC CARS IN MICHIGAN

More than sand dunes, beaches and Mackinac Island fudge, Michigan is synonymous with cars. While the connection hasn't been so positive in recent years, the state commemorates its glory days via several auto museums. The following fleets are within a few hours' drive of the Motor City.

Henry Ford Museum (p575) This Dearborn museum is loaded with vintage cars, including the first one Henry Ford ever built. In adjacent Greenfield Village you can ride in a Model T that rolled off the assembly line in 1923.

Automotive Hall of Fame (p576) Learn about the men and women who conceived and created the world's most classic cars and gain insight into the minds which gave us the mechanics of the modern motor.

Gilmore Car Museum (☑ 269-671-5089; www.gilmorecarmuseum.org; 6865 Hickory Rd; adult/child $13/10; ⊙ 9am-5pm Mon-Fri, to 6pm Sat & Sun) North of Kalamazoo along Hwy 43, this museum complex offers 22 barns filled with 120 vintage autos, including 15 Rolls Royces dating back to a 1910 Silver Ghost.

RE Olds Transportation Museum (p577) It's a whopping garage full of shiny vintage cars that date back more than 130 years.

Midtown & Cultural Center

⭐**Detroit Institute of Arts** MUSEUM
(DIA; ☏313-833-7900; www.dia.org; 5200 Woodward Ave; adult/child $12.50/6; ◷9am-4pm Tue-Thu, to 10pm Fri, 10am-5pm Sat & Sun) The DIA holds one of the world's finest art collections. The centerpiece is Diego Rivera's mural *Detroit Industry,* which fills an entire room and reflects the city's blue-collar labor history. Beyond it are Picassos, Caravaggios, suits of armor, modern African American paintings, puppets and troves more spread through 100-plus galleries.

It's hard to believe the collection was about to be sold to pay off the city's debt a few years ago. Luckily, donors saved the day.

Museum of Contemporary Art Detroit MUSEUM
(MOCAD; ☏313-832-6622; www.mocadetroit.org; 4454 Woodward Ave; suggested donation $5; ◷11am-5pm Wed, Sat & Sun, to 8pm Thu & Fri) MOCAD is set in an abandoned, graffiti-slathered auto dealership. Heat lamps hang from the ceiling over peculiar exhibits that change every few months. Music and literary events take place regularly. The onsite cafe-cocktail bar is uber popular.

New Center

⭐**Motown Historical Museum** MUSEUM
(☏313-875-2264; www.motownmuseum.org; 2648 W Grand Blvd; adult/child $15/10; ◷10am-6pm Tue-Fri & Sun, to 8pm Sat Jun-Aug, to 6pm Tue-Sat Sep-May) In this row of modest houses Berry Gordy launched Motown Records – and the careers of Stevie Wonder, Diana Ross, Marvin Gaye and Michael Jackson – with an $800 loan in 1959. Gordy and Motown split for Los Angeles in 1972, but you can still step into humble Studio A and see where the famed names recorded their first hits.

A tour takes about one hour, and consists mostly of looking at old photos and listening to guides' stories. To avoid a wait, buy timed tickets in advance online. The museum recently announced a $50 million expansion, with new buildings to be added for a vast increase in exhibition space. Motown is 2 miles northwest of Midtown, about a 20-minute walk from the Grand Boulevard QLINE stop.

Ford Piquette Avenue Plant MUSEUM
(☏313-872-8759; www.fordpiquetteavenueplant.org; 461 Piquette Ave; adult/child $12/free; ◷10am-

4pm Wed-Sun Apr-Oct) Henry Ford cranked out the first Model T in this landmark factory. Admission includes a detailed tour by enthusiastic docents, plus loads of shiny vehicles from 1904 onward. It's about 1 mile northeast of the Detroit Institute of Arts.

Downtown & Around

⭐**Campus Martius Park** PARK
(www.downtowndetroitparks.com/parks/Campus-Martius; 800 Woodward Ave; 🚻🎨) This new public space in the heart of Detroit's downtown is the perfect spot to while away a sunny afternoon. At the center is the Michigan Soldiers & Sailors Monument: in the warmer months, there's a sandy beach at its foot; in the winter, the space becomes the city's most popular ice rink. There's a stage for concerts and, in summer, a pop-up restaurant and bar.

⭐**Eastern Market** MARKET
(www.easternmarket.com; Adelaide & Russell Sts) Produce, cheese, spice and flower vendors fill the large halls on Saturday, but you also can turn up Monday through Friday to browse the specialty shops (props to the peanut roaster) and cafes that flank the halls on Russell and Market Sts. In addition, from June through October there's a scaled-down market on Tuesdays and a Sunday craft market with food trucks. Or arrive any day for mural gaping. Eastern Market has become an internationally renowned hot spot for street art.

Check www.muralsinthemarket.com for locations and artists.

Packard Plant NOTABLE BUILDING
(E Grand Blvd at Concord St) Renowned architect Albert Kahn designed this 3.5-million-sq-ft factory, which opened in 1905, but after years of neglect it became one of Detroit's most iconic ruins. Now, an Italian developer has plans to turn it into an office and entertainment complex over the next decade. Phase one of the project is expected to be finished in fall 2019. In the meantime, Pure Detroit (☏313-963-1440; www.puredetroit.com; 500 Griswold St; ◷9:30am-6pm Mon-Sat, 11am-5pm Sun) is offering tours on Saturdays. Book far in advance online.

Renaissance Center NOTABLE BUILDING
(RenCen; www.gmrencen.com; 330 E Jefferson Ave) GM's glossy, cloud-poking headquarters is a fine place to mooch off the free wi-fi, take a

Detroit

Fisher Building
(0.8mi)

Motown Historical
Museum (0.7mi)

Amtrak (0.3mi)

Ford Piquette
Avenue Plant (0.2mi)

E Edsel Ford Fwy

**NEW
CENTER**

Palmer Ave

Ferry St

Russell St

Chrysler Fwy

94

75

Wayne State
University

Merrick Ave

3rd Ave

2nd Ave

Cass Ave

11

13 Kirby St

Frederick
Douglass Ave

Farnsworth
St

**Detroit
Institute
of Arts**

2

Warren Ave

4th Ave

Trumbull Ave

Warren Ave

Hancock Ave

Hancock Ave

John R St

Brush St

St Antoine St

Chrysler Dr

Russell St

Forest Ave

Forest Ave

Woodward Ave

Prentis
Ave

12

Cass Ave

18

5

Canfield Ave

Lincoln Ave
Gibson St

Lodge Fwy

Carfield Ave

2nd Ave

Canfield St

21

Willis St

27

Chrysler Dr

Alexandrine St

Selden St

10

Selden St

Selden St

1

MIDTOWN

Tolan
Park

75

Rivard St

Brainard St

Parsens
St

Woodward Ave

Martin Luther King Jr Blvd

Mack Ave

Ash St

Elm St

5

Peterboro St

3rd Ave

Charlotte Ave

Park Ave

Erskine St

16

Watson
St

Wilkins St

Wilkins St

Chrysler Fwy

Temple St

Perry St

Spruce St

Hostel Detroit
(0.3mi)

Grand River Ave

Temple Ave
Cass
Park

Ledyard St

Henry St

Edmund
Pl

Alfred St

Adelaide St

26

Winder St

Alfred St

**Eastern
Market**

3

Fisher Fwy

75

Winder St

Michigan Central
Station (0.7mi)

12

28 14

5th Ave

4th Ave

Plum St

Elizabeth St

Beech St

Plaza Dr

Cass Ave

Clifford St

25

22

17

Woodward Ave

Montcalm St

23

Adams Ave

Madison St

24

Brush St

Beacon
St

St Antoine St

Gratiot Ave

3

Lafayette
Plaisance

CORKTOWN

Michigan Ave

Labrosse St

Porter St

Abbott St

Howard St

Lafayette Blvd

6th St

Greyhound Station

Park Pl

1st St

Abbott St

State St

8

19

29

Library St

Farmer St

Broadway
Ave

Clinton St

Macomb St

Monroe St

Lafayette Blvd

Rivard St

3

**Campus
Martius Park**

1

Fort St

GREEKTOWN

3rd Ave

2nd Ave

Fort St

10

Washington Blvd

Shelby St

Griswold St

20

Bates St

Randolph St

Congress St

375

Navarre Ple

10

15

9

3rd Ave

4

Jefferson Ave

Larned St

Jefferson Ave

Cobo
Center

Hart
Plaza

Transit
Windsor

6

Woodbridge St

Franklin St

7

Riopelle St

Detroit River

Riverwalk

Atwater St

Detroit

free hour-long tour or embark on the riverfront walkway.

Heidelberg Project   PUBLIC ART
(www.heidelberg.org; 3600 Heidelberg St; ☺ sunrise-sunset) FREE Polka-dotted streets, houses covered in Technicolor paint blobs, strange doll sculptures in yards – this is no acid trip, but rather a block-spanning art installation. It's the brainchild of street artist Tyree Guyton, who wanted to beautify his run-down community. Which he did for more than 30 years. Now Guyton has announced he'll dismantle the project and put a cultural village in its place. He'll rehab the buildings into galleries and art workshop spaces, much like the current Numbers House, which holds exhibitions.

Riverwalk &
Dequindre Cut   WALKING, CYCLING
(www.detroitriverfront.org) The city's swell riverfront path runs for 3 miles along the churning Detroit River from Hart Plaza east to Mt Elliott St, passing several parks, outdoor theaters, riverboats and fishing spots en route. Eventually it will extend all the way to beachy Belle Isle (detour onto Jefferson Ave to get there now). About halfway along the Riverwalk, near Orleans St, the 1.5-mile Dequindre Cut Greenway path juts north, offering a passageway to Eastern Market.

🖝 Tours

★ Pure Detroit Tours   WALKING
(☎ 855-874-7873; www.puredetroit.com; ☺ Sat & Sun; times vary) FREE Purveyors of locally inspired gifts, Pure Detroit also offer guided tours of some of the city's best sights, including the **Fisher Building** (☎ 313-872-1000; www.fisherbldg.com; 3011 W Grand Boulevard), the **Guardian Building** (www.guardianbuilding.com; 500 Griswold St; ☺ 8:30am-6pm Mon-Sat, 11am-5pm Sun) and the Packard Plant (p569). Guides – typically local historians – are knowledgeable and friendly. Stop in at one of their five locations or check the website for details. Most tours are free, but the Packard Plant tour is $40 and must be reserved in advance.

Preservation Detroit   WALKING
(☎ 313-577-7674; www.preservationdetroit.org; 2hr tours $15; ☺ 10am Sat May-Sep) Offers architectural walking tours through downtown, Midtown, Eastern Market and other neighborhoods; departure points vary.

Wheelhouse Bikes   CYCLING
(☎ 313-656-2453; www.wheelhousedetroit.com; 1340 E Atwater St; per 2hr $15; ☺ 11am-7pm Mon-Thu, 10am-8pm Fri & Sat, noon-5pm Sun, reduced hours in winter) Cycling is a great way to explore the city. Wheelhouse rents sturdy two-wheelers (helmet and lock included)

THE RUINS OF DETROIT

The derelict buildings that represent Detroit in the popular imagination aren't as prevalent as they once were – at least, not in downtown, where many architectural gems have been lovingly restored and buffed to a shine, thanks to dedicated locals and private investors. National chains have also jumped on the bandwagon as the city's fortunes show a decided turn for the better, with retailers like Lululemon and hotel chains like Aloft and Westin moving in to formerly vacant commercial buildings.

Even a few of the most iconic ruins are showing signs of life. Top of the list is **Michigan Central Station** (2405 W Vernor Hwy), the once-grand beaux-arts rail terminal. After closing in 1988, it spent decades crumbling into oblivion within eyeshot of Corktown's main drag. Decline has been stopped – and windows installed – but full redevelopment is far from certain. The Packard Auto Plant (p569) is another. Renowned architect Albert Kahn designed the 3.5-million-sq-ft factory, and it was a thing of beauty when it opened in 1905. After decades of abandonment, however, it has become a graffiti-ridden ruin. Its fortunes have risen with the city, however: an Italian developer bought 3/4 of the site and has plans to turn it into an office and entertainment complex over the next decade.

Still, with 139 sq miles of city, there are plenty of vacant buildings that remain, especially outside the downtown core. Note that viewing the buildings has become a hot topic: some call it 'ruin porn'. Others see it as a way to examine and take in the complex history of the city. It is illegal to enter any abandoned building.

on the Riverwalk at Rivard Plaza. Themed tours ($40 including bike rental) roll by various neighborhoods, architectural sites and urban farms.

✯ Festivals & Events

North American International Auto Show CULTURAL
(www.naias.com; tickets $13; ⊙ mid-Jan) It's autos galore for two weeks at the Cobo Center.

Movement Electronic Music Festival MUSIC
(www.movement.us; day pass $80; ⊙ late May) The world's largest electronic music festival congregates in Hart Plaza over Memorial Day weekend.

Woodward Dream Cruise CAR SHOW
(www.woodwarddreamcruise.com) FREE On the third Saturday in August, car lovers from around the world assemble in Detroit to show off their four-wheeled treasures and cruise down the city's main drag. The party stretches for miles, but most of the action takes place north of downtown, along Woodward and side streets nearby between 8 and 10 Mile roads.

Between road closures and the event's sprawling footprint, it's hard to know where to start with the Dream Cruise. Try diving in at 9 Mile, a few blocks east or west of Woodward. You'll be able to ooh and ahh over the

cars and take in the charming center of the Ferndale neighborhood at the same time.

🛏 Sleeping

Detroit is having a hotel boom: several new design-savvy properties have opened in downtown and Midtown over the last year, with more on the way. Add 9% to 15% tax (it varies by lodging size and location) to the listed rates.

Hostel Detroit HOSTEL $
(☎ 313-451-0333; www.hosteldetroit.com; 2700 Vermont St; dm $30-39, r $60-77; P @ 🛜) Volunteers rehabbed this old building, gathered up recycled materials and donations for the patchwork furnishings, and opened it to the public in 2011. There's a 10-bed dorm, a four-bed dorm and a handful of private rooms; everyone shares the four bathrooms and three kitchens. Bookings are taken online only (and must be done at least 24 hours in advance).

★ **Inn on Ferry Street** INN $$
(☎ 313-871-6000; www.innonferrystreet.com; 84 E Ferry St; r $169-259; P ✳ @ 🛜) Forty guest rooms fill a row of Victorian mansions right by the art museum. The lower-cost rooms are small but have deliciously soft bedding; the larger rooms feature plenty of antique wood furnishings. The healthy hot breakfast and shuttle to downtown are nice touches.

Aloft   HOTEL **$$**

(☑ 313-237-1700; www.aloftdetroit.com; 1 Park Ave; r $159-219; P ✳ @ 🛜 🐕) The chain's Detroit property took an exquisite 1915 neo-Renaissance skyscraper and converted it to its familiar hipster style. Mod rooms have bright pops of color and groovy city views. It's well located near the sports venues and theaters. Parking costs $30.

Ft Shelby Doubletree Hotel   HOTEL **$$**

(☑ 313-963-5600; www.doubletree3.hilton.com; 525 W Lafayette Blvd; r $135-195; P ✳ @ 🛜) This hotel fills a historic beaux-arts building downtown. All rooms are large suites, with both the sitting area and bedroom equipped with HDTV and free wi-fi. Parking costs $30, and there's free shuttle service around downtown.

**Detroit Foundation
Hotel**   BOUTIQUE HOTEL **$$$**

(☑ 313-800-5500; www.detroitfoundationhotel. com; 250 W Larned St; r $200-280; ⊖ ✳ 🛜) In 2017, this 1929 fire station in the heart of the city was transformed into a boutique hotel that blends modern convenience and style with original architectural features and a strong sense of history (don't miss the fire poles in the excellent restaurant, Apparatus Room). Rooms are spacious and comfortable, with minibars featuring Michigan products at reasonable prices.

The Guardian Building, convention center and Campus Martius Park are just a short walk away. Valet parking ($30) and free bike rentals are available.

✖ Eating

Downtown and Midtown are prime for stylish eats. Two nearby suburbs also have caches of hip restaurants and bars: walkable, gay-oriented Ferndale at 9 Mile Rd and Woodward Ave, and Royal Oak just north of Ferndale between 12 and 13 Mile Rds.

Cass Cafe   CAFE **$**

(☑ 313-831-1400; www.casscafe.com; 4620 Cass Ave; mains $9-16; ⊙ 11am-11pm Mon-Thu, to midnight Fri & Sat, 5-10pm Sun; 🛜 ✍) The Cass is a bohemian art gallery fused with a bar and restaurant that serves soups, sandwiches and veggie beauties, like the lentil-walnut burger. Service can be fickle.

Detroit Institute of Bagels   BAGELS **$**

(☑ 313-444-9342; www.detroitinstituteofbagels. com; 1236 Michigan Ave; bagels from $1.50, bagel sandwiches $6-9; ⊙ 7am-3pm Mon-Fri, 8am-3pm Sat & Sun; P) Authentic NY bagels and housemade cream cheeses take center stage at this bright, plant-filled space in Corktown. Try the Le Rouge, with bacon, egg, goat's cheese, arugula and red-onion marmalade. There's a hydrangea-filled patio for the warmer months.

Parks & Rec Diner   DINER **$**

(☑ 313-446-8370; www.parksandrecdiner.com; 1942 Grand River Ave; mains $6-14; ⊙ 8am-2pm Mon-Fri, to 3pm Sat & Sun) This homey diner, opened in 2015 in the imposing GAR building, takes its name from the government department that was once housed here. There are no wrong choices from the seasonal menu of sandwiches and brunch dishes like pistachio French toast and panzanella with charred bacon. The fries, seasoned with a BBQ spice, are excellent.

★ Dime Store   AMERICAN **$**

(☑ 313-962-9106; www.eatdimestore.com; 719 Griswold St; mains $9-13; ⊙ 8am-4pm Mon-Fri, to 3pm Sat & Sun) Take a seat in a chunky wood swivel chair in this cozy, diner-esque eatery and chow down on a duck Reuben and truffle-mayo-dipped fries, alongside a cold beer. Eggy brunch dishes are a big hit and served all day.

Chartreuse Kitchen   AMERICAN **$$**

(☑ 313-818-3915; www.chartreusekc.com; 15 E Kirby St; mains $22-28; ⊙ 11:30am-2pm & 5-9:30pm Tue-Thu, to 10:30pm Fri, 5-10:30pm Sat) It may seem like just another trendy spot with mod-industrial decor and a seasonal menu, but Chartreuse does it all really well. Dishes like the twice-cooked egg (with greens, Brussels sprouts, salty cheese and shallot vinaigrette) and roasted carrots (with prosciutto and lemon yogurt) are crazy-simple flavor explosions. The bright green interior and walls of living flowers waft a happy hippie vibe.

Grey Ghost   AMERICAN **$$$**

(☑ 313-262-6534; www.greyghostdetroit.com; 47 E Watson St; mains $18-29; ⊙ from 4pm Mon-Sat, 10am-2pm Sun) A sleek, industrial vibe marks this new Detroit hot spot. The menu is all modern as well, with creative sides like cauliflower and spaetzel or brussels sprouts with chicken skin. The juicy NY strip steak is cooked sous vide. There's a convivial but small outdoor patio.

♙ Drinking & Nightlife

★ **Dessert Oasis Coffee Roasters**   COFFEE
(www.dessertoasiscoffee.com; ⊙6am-9pm Mon-Thu, to 10pm Fri, 7am-10pm Sat, 8am-9pm Sun; 🛜🐾) Pitch-perfect espresso drinks (try the lavender latte), pour-overs, outdoor seating and free wi-fi are hallmarks of this new downtown cafe. Live music nightly. Dog-friendly.

HopCat   PUB
(☑313-769-8828; www.hopcat.com/detroit; 4265 Woodward Ave; ⊙11am-midnight Mon-Wed, to 2am Thu-Sat, 10am-midnight Sun; 🛜) Detroit's outpost of the regional pub chain rocks: paintings of local musicians adorn the walls, and the Stooges and old Motown bang on the speakers. Around 130 beers flow from the taps, with 30 devoted to Michigan brewers. Smaller pours (5oz and 8oz glasses) are available for those who want to sample widely.

Bronx   BAR
(☑313-832-8464; 4476 2nd Ave; ⊙noon-2am; 🛜) There's not much inside this classic corner tavern besides a pool table, dim lighting and a couple of jukeboxes filled with ballsy rock and soul. But that's the way the hipsters, slackers and rockers like their dive bars. They're also fond of the beefy burgers served late at night and the cheap beer selection.

Grand Trunk Pub   BAR
(☑313-961-3043; www.grandtrunk.pub; ⊙11am-2am) Once the ticket hall for the Grand Trunk Railroad, this high-ceilinged space still buzzes, but this time patrons are content to sit and stop a while. With good reason: there's a vast beer selection and a full bar menu. The patio is an excellent spot to people-watch, thanks to the new pedestrian esplanade down Woodward Ave.

☆ Entertainment

Live Music

Cliff Bell's   JAZZ
(☑313-961-2543; www.cliffbells.com; 2030 Park Ave; ⊙5pm-midnight Tue-Thu, to 1am Fri & Sat, 11am-10pm Sun) With its dark wood, candle-light and art-deco decor, Bell's evokes 1930s elegance. Local jazz, soul and swing bands attract a diverse young audience.

Magic Stick   LIVE MUSIC
(☑313-833-9700; www.majesticdetroit.com; 4120-4140 Woodward Ave) The White Stripes and Von Bondies are rockers who've risen from the beer-splattered ranks at the Magic Stick. The Majestic Theater next door hosts larger shows. While the venues have lost some luster in recent years, you're still likely to see cool bands here most nights.

PJ's Lager House   LIVE MUSIC
(☑313-961-4668; www.pjslagerhouse.com; 1254 Michigan Ave; ⊙1pm-2am Mon & Tue, from 11am Wed-Fri, from 10:30am Sat & Sun) Scrappy bands or DJs play most nights at this small Cork-town club. By day it serves surprisingly good grub with a New Orleans–vegan twist.

Performing Arts

Detroit Opera House   OPERA
(☑313-237-7464; www.michiganopera.org; 1526 Broadway Ave) It has a gorgeous interior and a top-tier company that has nurtured many renowned African American performers.

Puppet ART/Detroit Puppet Theater   THEATER
(☑313-961-7777; www.puppetart.org; 25 E Grand River Ave; adult/child $15/10; 🚶) Soviet-trained puppeteers perform beautiful shows in this 70-person theater; a small museum displays puppets from different cultures.

FROM MOTOWN TO ROCK CITY

Motown Records and soul music put Detroit on the map in the 1960s, while the thrashing punk rock of the Stooges and MC5 was the 1970s response to that smooth sound. By 1976, Detroit was dubbed 'Rock City' by a Kiss song (though – just Detroit's luck – the tune was eclipsed by its B-side, 'Beth'). In recent years it has been hard-edged rock – aka whiplash rock and roll – that has pushed the city to the music-scene forefront. Homegrown stars include the White Stripes, Von Bondies and Dirtbombs. Rap (thank you, Eminem) and techno are Detroit's other renowned genres. Many music aficionados say the city's blight is what produces such a beautifully angry explosion of sound, and who's to argue? Scope free publications like the *Metro Times* for current show and club listings.

Fox Theater
PERFORMING ARTS

(☑ 313-471-6611; www.olympiaentertainment.com/venues/detail/fox-theatre; 2211 Woodward Ave) This opulent 1928 theater, built in the Oriental style, is one of the icons of Detroit – and one of the few venues that has consistently offered entertainment during the city's ups and downs. Hosts comedians, top music acts and Broadway shows.

Sports

Little Caesars Arena
STADIUM

(☑ 313-471-6606; www.olympiaentertainment.com; 2645 Woodward Ave) Opened in 2017, this is Detroit's spiffy new arena for big-name concerts and sporting events. Detroit's rough-and-tumble pro hockey team the Red Wings (www.nhl.com/redwings) and pro basketball team the Pistons (www.nba.com/pistons) both play here from October through April.

Comerica Park
BASEBALL

(☑ 313-962-4000; www.detroittigers.com; 2100 Woodward Ave; ☒) The Detroit Tigers play pro baseball at Comerica, one of the league's most decked-out stadiums. The park is particularly kid friendly, with a small Ferris wheel and carousel inside (per ride $2 each).

ⓘ Information

Detroit Convention & Visitors Bureau (☑ 800-338-7648; www.visitdetroit.com)

ⓘ Getting There & Around

Detroit Metro Airport (DTW; www.metroairport.com), a Delta Airlines hub, is about 20 miles southwest of Detroit.Transport options to the city are few. Taxis cost $60 or so. The shared shuttle van **Skoot** (☑ 313-230-2331; www.rideskoot.com) costs $20. The 125 SMART bus ($2.50) is inconvenient, unreliable and takes 1½ hours to get downtown.

Greyhound (☑ 313-961-8005; 1001 Howard St) runs to various cities in Michigan and beyond. Megabus (www.megabus.com/us) runs to/from Chicago (5½ hours) daily; departures are from downtown and Wayne State University. Check the website for exact locations.

Amtrak (www.amtrak.com) trains go three times daily to Chicago (5½ hours) from **Detroit Station** (☑ 313-873-3442; 11 W Baltimore Ave). You can also head east – to New York (16½ hours) or destinations en route – but you'll first be bused to Toledo.

The QLine streetcar (www.qlinedetroit.com, fare $1.50) started running in spring 2017. It provides handy transport along Woodward Ave from Congress St downtown, past the sports venues and museums of Midtown, to the Amtrak station and W Grand Blvd at the route's northern end.

MoGo (www.mogodetroit.com) is Detroit's new bikeshare program, with 43 stations scattered around downtown and Midtown. A 24-hour pass costs $8 for an unlimited number of 30-minute trips; additional charges apply for time over 30 minutes.

Transit Windsor (☑ 519-944-4111; www.citywindsor.ca/transitwindsor) operates the Tunnel Bus to Windsor, Canada. It costs $5 (American or Canadian) and departs by Mariner's Church (corner of Randolph St and Jefferson Ave) near the Detroit-Windsor Tunnel entrance, as well as other spots downtown. Bring your passport.

Dearborn

A stone's throw from Detroit, Dearborn is home to the Henry Ford Museum, one of the USA's finest museum complexes. It's also home to the nation's largest community of Arab Americans, and a visit here offers a fascinating immersion into the local culture.

⊙ Sights

The Henry Ford Museum, Greenfield Village and Rouge Factory Tour are separate, but you can get a combination ticket for two of the attractions, or for all three, and save 20% or more off the regular admission prices. Plan on at least one very full day at the complex.

Henry Ford Museum
MUSEUM

(☑ 313-982-6001; www.thehenryford.org; 20900 Oakwood Blvd; adult/child $22/16.50; ☒9:30am-5pm) The indoor Henry Ford Museum contains a fascinating wealth of American culture, such as the chair Lincoln was sitting in when he was assassinated, the presidential limo in which Kennedy was killed, the hot dog–shaped Oscar Mayer Wienermobile (photo op!) and the bus on which Rosa Parks refused to give up her seat. Don't worry: you'll get your vintage car fix here, too. Buying tickets online saves 10%. Parking costs $6.

Greenfield Village
MUSEUM

(☑ 313-982-6001; www.thehenryford.org; 20900 Oakwood Blvd; adult/child $27/20.25; ☒9:30am-5pm daily mid-Apr–Oct, Fri-Sun Nov & Dec) Adjacent to the Henry Ford Museum (and part of its complex), outdoor Greenfield Village features historic buildings shipped in from all over the country, reconstructed and restored, such as Thomas Edison's laboratory from Menlo Park and the Wright Brothers' airplane workshop. Buying tickets online saves 10%.

Automotive Hall of Fame MUSEUM
(✆313-240-4000; www.automotivehalloffame.org; 21400 Oakwood Blvd; adult/child $10/4; ⊙9am-5pm Wed-Sun May-Sep, Fri-Sun only Oct-Apr) Next door to the Henry Ford Museum, the interactive Auto Hall focuses on the people behind famed cars, such as Mr Ferdinand Porsche and Mr Soichiro Honda.

Rouge Factory Tour FACTORY
(✆312-982-6001; www.thehenryford.org; adult/child $18/13.25; ⊙9:30am-3pm Mon-Sat) See F-150 trucks roll off the assembly line where Ford first perfected his self-sufficient, mass-production techniques. Tours start at the Henry Ford Museum, from which a bus takes you over to the factory.

🛏 Sleeping & Eating

Henry Hotel HOTEL $$
(✆313-441-2000; www.behenry.com; 300 Town Center Dr; r $180-240; P❄@🛜🏊) This 11-story, 308-room, Marriott-brand property hosts mostly business travelers and wedding parties drawn to its beyond-the-norm style. Each floor displays groovy local art, and the elegant, chandelier-clad common areas provide swell hangouts. Rooms are comfy and good sized. It's adjacent to a big shopping center, and about 3 miles from the Henry Ford Museum.

Hamido MIDDLE EASTERN $
(✆313-582-0660; www.hamidorestaurant.com; 13251 W Warren Ave; mains $8-16; ⊙11am-midnight) Slanted-roofed Hamido serves hummus, chicken shawarma and other staples. The number of chickens roasting on the spit marks its popularity.

❶ Getting There & Away

Dearborn is 10 miles west of downtown Detroit and about the same distance east of Detroit Metro Airport. I-94 is the primary road to town. Amtrak has a station by the Henry Ford Museum.

Ann Arbor

Liberal and bookish Ann Arbor is home to the University of Michigan. The walkable downtown, which abuts the campus, is loaded with free-trade coffee shops, bookstores and brewpubs. It's also a mecca for chowhounds; follow the drool trail toward anything named 'Zingerman's.'

👁 Sights

University of Michigan
Museum of Art MUSEUM
(✆734-764-0395; www.umma.umich.edu; 525 S State St; ⊙11am-5pm Tue-Sat, from noon Sun) FREE The campus' bold art museum impresses with its collections of Asian ceramics, Tiffany glass and modern abstract works.

Ann Arbor Farmers Market MARKET
(www.a2gov.org/market; 315 Detroit St; ⊙7am-3pm Wed & Sat May-Dec, 8am-3pm Sat Jan-Apr) Given the surrounding bounty of orchards and farms, it's no surprise this place is stuffed to the rafters with everything from spicy pickles to cider to mushroom-growing kits; located downtown near Zingerman's Delicatessen. On Sunday an artisan market with jewelry, ceramics and textiles takes over.

🛏 Sleeping & Eating

There are several B&Bs within walking distance of downtown. Hotels tend to be about 5 miles out, with several midrange chain options clustered south on State St.

Ann Arbor was a foodie haven before foodie havens even existed. The city has terrific eats, and they're usually casual and not too expensive. Main, Liberty and Washington Sts downtown brim with goodness. Food trucks hang out in a courtyard at 211 W Washington St. Ethiopian, Middle Eastern, Indian and other ethnic eats abound.

Frita Batidos CUBAN $
(✆734-761-2882; www.fritabatidos.com; 117 W Washington St; mains $8-13; ⊙11am-11pm Sun-Wed, to midnight Thu-Sat) This mod take on Cuban street food is all the rage, offering burgers with tropical, citrusy toppings and booze-spiked milkshakes.

★ Spencer AMERICAN $$
(✆734-369-3979; www.spencerannarbor.com; 113 E Liberty St; small plates $5-11; ⊙11am-3pm & 5-10pm Sun, Mon, Wed & Thu, to 11pm Fri & Sat) Eating at this pint-sized cafe is like eating in your friend's cozy kitchen, with white-washed walls, books stacked on the sunny windowsill and fresh flowers popping from vases. The owners – she's a pastry chef, he's a cheesemonger – change their locally sourced menu of small plates every few weeks, so you

might dig into rutabaga cauliflower soup or hanger steak with sunflower cream.

Zingerman's Roadhouse AMERICAN **$$$**
(☏734-663-3663; www.zingermansroadhouse.com; 2501 Jackson Ave; mains $19-36; ⊙7am-10pm Mon-Thu, 7am-11pm Fri, 9am-11pm Sat, 9am-9pm Sun) ✍
Two words: doughnut sundae. The bourbon-caramel-sauced dessert is pure genius, as are the traditional American dishes like Carolina grits, Iowa pork chops and Maryland crab cakes, all using sustainably produced ingredients. It's 2 miles west of downtown.

❶ Information

Ann Arbor Convention & Visitors Bureau
(www.visitannarbor.org) Accommodation information and more.

❶ Getting There & Away

Detroit's airport is 30 miles east; shuttles buses make the trip. Amtrak trains come through Ann Arbor three times daily. The train station is downtown and shared by Greyhound. Megabus serves the city, but it stops inconveniently far from its center.

Central Michigan

Michigan's heartland, plunked in the center of the Lower Peninsula, alternates between fertile farms and highway-crossed urban areas. The larger cities excel in cool art, while the entire regions shine in stellar beer making.

Lansing

Smallish Lansing is the state capital. A few miles east lies East Lansing, home of Michigan State University. They're worth a stop to peek into a couple of impressive museums.

◉ Sights & Activities

Broad Art Museum MUSEUM
(☏517-884-4800; www.broadmuseum.msu.edu; 547 E Circle Dr; ⊙noon-7pm Tue-Sun) `FREE`
Renowned architect Zaha Hadid designed the wild-looking parallelogram of stainless steel and glass. It holds everything from Greek ceramics to Salvador Dali paintings. Much of the space is devoted to avant-garde exhibitions.

RE Olds Transportation Museum MUSEUM
(☏517-372-0529; www.reoldsmuseum.org; 240 Museum Dr; adult/child $7/5; ⊙10am-5pm Tue-Sat year-round, noon-5pm Sun Apr-Oct) The museum

has a sweet collection of some 65 vintage cars that sit in the old Lansing City Bus Garage, including the first Oldsmobile, which was built in 1897. Note: they're not all on display at once, but rotate regularly.

Lansing River Trail WALKING
(www.lansingrivertrail.org) The paved, 20-mile path runs alongside the Grand River from the city's north edge to downtown, and then meanders east along the Red Cedar River to the university. It's popular with runners and cyclists, and the downtown portion links a number of attractions, including the RE Olds Transportation Museum, a children's museum, zoo and fish ladder.

🛏 Sleeping & Eating

Wild Goose Inn B&B **$$**
(☏517-333-3334; www.wildgooseinn.com; 512 Albert St; r $149-169; 🛜) The Wild Goose Inn is a six-room B&B one block from Michigan State's campus in East Lansing. All rooms have fireplaces and most have Jacuzzis. Decor is fairly low-key – except for the Arbor room and its wild faux branches!

Golden Harvest DINER **$**
(☏517-485-3663; 1625 Turner St; mains $7-9; ⊙7am-2pm Mon-Fri, from 8am Sat & Sun) Golden Harvest is a loud, punk-rock-meets-hippie diner serving the sausage-and-French-toast Bubba Sandwich and hearty omelets.

❶ Getting There & Away

Amtrak stops in East Lansing on its Chicago–Port Huron route daily. Greyhound has stations in both Lansing and East Lansing. I-96, I-69 and Hwy 127 are the main interstates to the city.

Grand Rapids

The second-largest city in Michigan, Grand Rapids is known for office-furniture manufacturing and, more recently, beer tourism. Twenty craft breweries operate in the area, and that's why you're here (though some non-beer sights intrigue, as well).

◉ Sights

Frederik Meijer Gardens GARDENS
(☏616-957-1580; www.meijergardens.org; 1000 E Beltline NE; adult/child $14.50/7; ⊙9am-5pm Mon & Wed-Sat, to 9pm Tue, 11am-5pm Sun) The 118-acre gardens feature impressive blooms, and sculptures by Auguste Rodin, Henry Moore and others. It is 5 miles east of downtown via I-196.

Gerald R Ford Museum   MUSEUM

(☑616-254-0400; www.fordlibrarymuseum.gov; 303 Pearl St NW; adult/child $8/4; ☺9am-5pm Mon-Sat, from noon Sun) The downtown museum is dedicated to Michigan's only president. Ford stepped into the Oval Office after Richard Nixon and his vice president, Spiro Agnew, resigned in disgrace. It's a bizarre period in US history, and the museum does an excellent job of covering it, down to displaying the burglary tools used in the Watergate break-in. Ford and wife Betty are buried on the museum's grounds.

Grand Rapids Art Museum   MUSEUM

(☑616-831-1000; www.artmuseumgr.org; 101 Monroe Center St NW; adult/child $10/6; ☺10am-5pm Tue-Sun, to 9pm Thu) The city's beyond-the-norm art museum fills a sun-drenched building with 19th- and 20th-century works. European and American masters such as Henri de Toulouse-Lautrec and Richard Diebenkorn take pride of place. Free admission on Tuesdays and on Thursday evenings.

🛏 Sleeping & Eating

CityFlats Hotel   HOTEL $$

(☑616-608-1720; www.cityflatshotel.com; 83 Monroe Center St NW; r $155-245; ❄🐾) 🥢 Rooms at this ecofriendly hotel have big windows for lots of natural light, bamboo linens, cork floors and locally made, reclaimed wood furniture. The building is gold-certified by the Leadership in Energy and Environmental Design (LEED) program.

★ Green Well   AMERICAN $$

(☑616-808-3566; www.thegreenwell.com; 924 Cherry St SE; mains $16-22; ☺11am-10pm Sun-Thu, to midnight Fri & Sat) 🥢 Burgers, green curry, and barbecue pork and polenta feature on the gastropub's menu, where everything is made with sustainably farmed ingredients. Beer plays a role in many dishes, such as the beer-steamed mussels and beer cheese. The bar taps hard-to-find Michigan brews and pours Michigan wines (flights available).

🍷 Drinking & Nightlife

Brewery Vivant   BREWERY

(☑616-719-1604; www.breweryvivant.com; 925 Cherry St SE; ☺3-11pm Mon-Thu, to midnight Fri, 11am-midnight Sat, noon-10pm Sun) 🥢 Brewery Vivant specializes in Belgian-style beers. Set in an old chapel with stained glass and a vaulted ceiling, the atmospheric brewpub also serves locally sourced cheese plates and burgers at farmhouse-style tables.

Founders Brewing Co   BREWERY

(☑616-776-1195; www.foundersbrewing.com; 235 Grandville Ave SW; ☺11am-2am Mon-Sat, noon-midnight Sun; 🐾) If you've only got time for one stop in Grand Rapids, make it rock-and-roll Founders. The ruby-tinged Dirty Bastard Ale is good swillin', and there's meaty deli sandwiches to soak it up.

ℹ Information

Grand Rapids CVB (www.experiencegr.com) Has maps and self-guided brewery tour information online.

ℹ Getting There & Away

Grand Rapids has a decent-sized airport with flights to many US cities. Amtrak trains chug to/from Chicago once daily; the station is downtown near Founders Brewing Co. I-96, I-196 and Hwy 131 are the main roadways to the city.

Gold Coast

They don't call it the Gold Coast for nothing. Michigan's 300-mile western shoreline features seemingly endless stretches of beaches, dunes, wineries, orchards and B&B-filled towns that boom during the summer – and shiver during the snow-packed winter.

Harbor Country

Harbor Country refers to a group of eight small, lake-hugging towns that roll out beaches, wineries, antique shops and all-round rustic charm.

New Buffalo is the largest community, home to a surf shop (you heard that right), a busy public beach, ice-cream shops, a boat-logged marina and a popular farmers market. Three Oaks is the only Harbor community that's inland (6 miles in, via Hwy 12). Here Green Acres meets Greenwich Village in a funky farm-and-arts blend. Cycle by day, then catch a provocative play or art-house flick at the theaters by night. Union Pier, Lakeside, Harbert and Sawyer are some of the other cutesy towns, chock-full of historic inns and galleries.

◉ Sights & Activities

Warren Dunes   STATE PARK

(☑269-426-4013; 12032 Red Arrow Hwy, Sawyer; per car $9) With 3 miles of beachfront, 6 miles of hiking and cross-country skiing trails, and climbable dunes that rise 260ft in the air, visitors are all over this park. A concession stand offers food, soft drinks, ice cream and souvenirs from May through September. Campsites cost $22 to $37.

Tabor Hill Winery
WINERY
(☑ 800-283-3363; www.taborhill.com; 185 Mt Tabor Rd, Buchanan; tours free, tastings $9; ⊙ tours noon-4:30pm, tasting room 12am-5pm Mon-Tues, 11am-6pm Wed-Thurs & Sun, 11am-7pm Fri-Sat) Connoisseurs often regard Tabor Hill Winery as the region's best. The vintner provides tours and lets you belly up in the tasting room for swigs of its blood-red Cabernet Franc and crisp sparkling wines.

Dewey Cannon Trading Company
CYCLING
(☑ 269-756-3361; www.facebook.com/deweycannontradingcompany; 3 Dewey Cannon Ave, Three Oaks; ⊙ 9am-5pm Tue-Fri, to 7pm Sat, to 3pm Sun, reduced hours Oct-Apr) Rent a two-wheeler (per day $20) in Three Oaks and cycle lightly used rural roads past orchards and wineries. Helmets cost extra.

🍴 Sleeping & Eating

Holiday Inn Express
HOTEL $$
(☑ 269-469-1400; www.ihg.com; 11500 Holiday Dr, New Buffalo; r $95-195) This outpost of the HI chain in New Buffalo is nothing fancy, but it's well maintained and is usually reasonably priced.

Redamak's
BURGERS $
(☑ 269-469-4522; www.redamaks.com; 616 E Buffalo St, New Buffalo; burgers $6-12; ⊙ noon-10:30pm Mon-Sat, to 10pm Sun Mar–mid-Oct) It's a rightfully lauded, long-standing spot to get a wax-paper-wrapped cheeseburger, spicy curly fries and cold beer in New Buffalo.

ℹ Information

Harbor Country Chamber of Commerce
(www.harborcountry.org)

ℹ Getting There & Away

Amtrak stops in New Buffalo. Driving is the only way to reach the other communities. I-94 slices through the region. The Red Arrow Hwy parallels the interstate and connects the communities proper. For reference, the distance between New Buffalo and Sawyer is 10 miles.

Saugatuck & Douglas

Saugatuck is one of the Gold Coast's most popular resort areas, known for its strong arts community, numerous B&Bs and gay-friendly vibe. Douglas is its twin city a mile or so to the south, and they've pretty much sprawled into one. It's a touristy but funky place, with ice-cream-licking families, yuppie boaters and martini-drinking gay couples sharing the waterfront. Galleries and shops fill the compact downtown core. Weekends attract the masses.

◉ Sights & Activities

Antiquing prevails on the Blue Star Hwy running south for 20 miles. Blueberry U-pick farms share this stretch of road and make a juicy stop, too.

Oval Beach
BEACH
(Oval Beach Dr; ⊙ 8am-10pm) Life guards patrol the long expanse of fine sand. There are bathrooms and concession stands, though not enough to spoil the peaceful, dune-laden scene. It costs $8 to park. Or arrive the adventurous way, via chain ferry and a trek over Mt Baldhead.

Mt Baldhead
WALKING
Huff up the stairs of this 200ft-high sand dune for a stellar view. Then race down the other side to Oval Beach. Get here via the chain ferry; walk north from the dock.

Saugatuck Dune Rides
ADVENTURE SPORTS
(☑ 269-857-2253; www.saugatuckduneride.com; 6495 Blue Star Hwy; adult/child $20/11; ⊙ 10am-7:30pm Jul & Aug, reduced hours May, Jun, Sep & Oct, closed Nov-Apr) The Saugatuck Dune Rides provide 40 minutes of good, cheesy fun zipping over mounds.

🍴 Sleeping & Eating

★ Pines Motorlodge
MOTEL $$
(☑ 269-857-5211; www.thepinesmotorlodge.com; 56 Blue Star Hwy; r $139-249; 🐾) Retro-cool tiki lamps, pinewood furniture and communal lawn chairs add up to a fun, social ambience amid the firs in Douglas.

Bayside Inn
INN $$
(☑ 269-857-4321; www.baysideinn.net; 618 Water St; r $180-250; 🐾) This former boathouse has 10 rooms on Saugatuck's waterfront. All have private bathrooms, decks and DVD players. A big breakfast is included.

Crane's Pie Pantry
BAKERY $
(☑ 269-561-2297; www.cranespiepantry.com; 6054 124th Ave, Fennville; pie slices $4.50; ⊙ 9am-8pm Mon-Thu, to 9pm Fri & Sat, 11am-8pm Sun) Buy a bulging slice, or pick apples and peaches in the surrounding orchards. Crane's is in

Fennville, 3 miles south on the Blue Star Hwy, then 4 miles inland on Hwy 89.

Phil's Bar & Grille AMERICAN $$
(☑ 269-857-1555; www.philsbarandgrille.com; 215 Butler St; mains $18-29; ☺ 11:30am-10:30pm Sun-Thu, to 11pm Fri & Sat) This humming pub turns out terrific broasted (combining broiling and roasting) chicken, fish tacos, lamb lollipops and gumbo.

ⓘ Information

Saugatuck/Douglas CVB (www.saugatuck.com) provides maps and more.

ⓘ Getting There & Away

Most visitors drive to Saugatuck/Douglas. I-196/Hwy 31 whizzes by to the east, while the Blue Star Hwy goes into both towns. The closest Amtrak station is in Holland, about 12 miles north.

Sleeping Bear Dunes National Lakeshore

Eye-popping lake views from atop colossal sand dunes? Water blue enough to be in the Caribbean? Miles of unspoiled beaches? Secluded islands with mystical trees? All here at Sleeping Bear Dunes, along with lush forests, terrific day hikes and glass-clear waterways for paddling. The national park stretches from north of Frankfort to just before Leland, on the Leelanau Peninsula. Several cute little towns fringe the area.

⊙ Sights

Manitou Islands ISLAND
(per family $15) The forest-cloaked Manitou Islands provide an off-the-beaten-path adventure. They're part of Sleeping Bear Dunes National Lakeshore, hence the entrance fee. North Manitou is known for star-speckled backcountry camping, while South Manitou is terrific for wilderness-rich day trips. Kayaking and hiking are the big to-dos, especially the 7-mile trek to the Valley of the Giants, an otherworldly stand of cedar trees on South Manitou. **Manitou Island Transit** (☑ 231-256-9061; www.manitoutransit.com) runs ferries from Leland; the trip takes 1½ hours.

Tandem Ciders FARM
(☑ 231-271-0050; www.tandemciders.com; 2055 Setterbo Rd; ☺ noon-6pm Mon-Sat, to 5pm Sun) Near Suttons Bay, Tandem Ciders pours delicious hard ciders in its small tasting room

on the family farm. Tastings cost $2 for three 2oz pours.

🏃 Activities

Dune Climb HIKING
(Hwy 109; ☺ 24hr) The Dune Climb is the park's most popular attraction, where you trudge up a 200ft-high dune and then run or roll down. Gluttons for leg-muscle punishment can keep slogging all the way to Lake Michigan, a strenuous 1½-hour trek one-way; bring water. The site, with a parking lot and bathrooms, is on Hwy 109, 5 miles north of Empire.

Pierce Stocking Scenic Drive SCENIC DRIVE
(☺ 9am-sunset May–mid-Nov) The 7-mile, one-lane, picnic-grove-studded Pierce Stocking Scenic Drive is perhaps the best way to absorb the stunning lake vistas in Sleeping Bear Dunes. The earlier you go the less traffic you'll encounter. The drive starts 4 miles north of Empire.

Sleeping Bear Heritage Trail HIKING
(www.sleepingbeartrail.org) The 17-mile paved path goes from Empire to Bohemian Rd, passing the Dune Climb along the way; walkers and cyclists are all over it.

Grand Traverse Bike Tours CYCLING
(☑ 231-421-6815; www.grandtraversebiketours. com; 318 N St Joseph St; ☺ 9am-5:30pm Mon-Fri, to 5pm Sat, 10am-4pm Sun) Offers guided rides (four-hour tour is $79) to local wineries, as well as self-guided tours (per person $65) for which staff provide route planning and van pickup of your wine purchases. The shop is in downtown Suttons Bay.

🛏 Sleeping & Eating

The only places to sleep in the park are campgrounds: two on the mainland, and a few more on the Manitou Islands.

Glen Arbor B&B B&B $$
(☑ 231-334-6789; www.glenarborbnb.com; 6548 Western Ave; r $145-215; ☺ closed mid-Nov–Apr) The owners renovated this century-old farmhouse into a sunny, French country inn with six themed rooms.

Empire Village Inn AMERICAN $
(☑ 231-326-5101; www.empirevillageinn.com; 11601 S Lacore Rd; mains $9-15; ☺ 3-10pm Mon-Thu, 3-11pm Fri, 2-11pm Sat, noon-10pm Sun) Enter the low A-frame building, grab a seat at a scuffed wood table and order one of the

local beers on tap while waiting for your excellent, doughy-crust pizza to arrive. Burgers and sandwiches satisfy too, along with the housemade root beer. It's a swell place to refuel after a day of hiking or biking.

❶ Information

Stop at the park's **visitor center** (☑231-326-4700; www.nps.gov/slbe; 9922 W Front St; ☺8am-6pm Jun-Aug, 8:30am-4pm Sep-May) in Empire for information, trail maps and vehicle entry permits (week/annual $15/30).

❶ Getting There & Away

The park is only accessible by car. Hwy 31 is the main highway to the area. From there make your way onto Hwy 22, which is the road that goes through the park. The nearest airport is in Traverse City.

Traverse City

Michigan's 'cherry capital' is the largest city in the northern half of the Lower Peninsula. It's got a bit of urban sprawl, but it's still a happenin' base from which to see the Sleeping Bear Dunes, Mission Peninsula wineries, U-pick orchards and other area attractions.

❍ Sights

Road-tripping out to the wineries is a must. Head north from Traverse City on Hwy 37 for 20 miles to the end of the grape- and cherry-planted Old Mission Peninsula. You'll be spoiled for choice.

Peninsula Cellars   WINERY
(☑231-933-9787;   www.peninsulacellars.com; 11480 Center Rd; ☺10am-6pm) Located in an old schoolhouse, Peninsula makes fine whites and is often less crowded than other wineries. A five-wine tasting costs $5.

🛏 Sleeping & Eating

Mitchell Creek Inn   MOTEL **$$**
(☑231-947-9330; www.mitchellcreek.com; 894 Munson Ave; r/cabins from $65/125; 🐾) This humble, 15-room property is on the other side of Hwy 31 (away from the water), moderately priced and near the state park beach. It's a classic mom-and-pop operation, with basic, tidy, motel-like rooms.

Sugar Beach Resort   HOTEL **$$**
(☑231-938-0100; www.tcbeaches.com; 1773 US 31 N; r $150-250; ❄🐾📶) Sugar Beach has decent prices and it's right on the water. Rooms are nothing fancy, but they're well

maintained and have small refrigerators, coffee makers and microwave ovens. Many have been renovated recently and have new furnishings.

Folgarelli's   DELI **$**
(☑231-941-7651; www.folgarellis.net; 424 W Front St; sandwiches $8-11; ☺9:30am-6:30pm Mon-Fri, to 5:30pm Sat, 11am-4pm Sun) After a day of fun in the sun, refresh with sandwiches at gastronome favorite Folgarelli's.

North Peak Brewing Company   PUB FOOD **$$**
(☑231-941-7325; www.northpeak.net; 400 W Front St; mains $10-20; ☺11am-11pm Mon-Thu, to midnight Fri & Sat, noon-10pm Sun) Munch pizzas, mussels and pretzel-crusted walleye with the housemade suds.

❶ Information

Traverse City Tourism (www.traversecity.com)

❶ Getting There & Away

Traverse City's small airport has several daily flights to Chicago, Detroit and Minneapolis. Hwy 31 is the main highway to town.

Charlevoix & Petoskey

These two towns hold several Hemingway sights. They're also where Michigan's upper-crusters maintain summer homes. The downtown areas of both places have gourmet restaurants and high-class shops, and the marinas are filled with yachts.

A number of writers have ties to northwest Michigan, but none are as famous as Ernest Hemingway, who spent the summers of his youth at his family's cottage on Walloon Lake. Hemingway buffs often tour the area to view the places that made their way into his writing. Key sites:

A short distance north of Charlevoix, Boyne City Rd veers off to the east. It skirts Lake Charlevoix and eventually arrives at Horton Bay. Hemingway fans will recognize the **Horton Bay General Store** (☑231-582-7827; www.hortonbaygeneralstore.com; 5115 Boyne City Rd; ☺8am-2pm Sun-Thu, 8am-2pm & 5-9pm Fri & Sat, closed mid-Oct–mid-May), with its 'high false front,' from his short story 'Up in Michigan.' The old-time shop now sells groceries, souvenirs, sandwiches and ice cream, plus wine and tapas on weekend nights (reservations required for the latter).

Further north on Hwy 31, stop in Petoskey to see the Hemingway collection at the

Little Traverse History Museum (☑231-347-2620; www.petoskeymuseum.org; 100 Depot Ct; $3; ⊙10am-4pm Mon-Sat, closed mid-Oct–late May), including rare first-edition books that the author autographed for a friend when he visited in 1947.

A few blocks from the museum, toss back a drink at the **City Park Grill** (☑231-347-0101; www.cityparkgrill.com; 432 E Lake St; ⊙11:30am-9pm Sun-Thu, to 1:30am Fri & Sat) where Hemingway was a regular.

Tour Hemingway's Michigan (www.mihemingwaytour.com) provides further information for self-guided jaunts.

Budget and midrange chain hotels dot Hwy 31 and Hwy 131 leading into Petoskey. Charlevoix has several small inns and motels; see www.visitcharlevoix.com for listings.

Petoskey features foodie cafes, gastropubs, cozy bistros and ethnic eats in its walkable downtown. Charlevoix has high-quality eateries too, but it's a bit more spread out and adds chain restaurants to the mix. Prices are mid- to high range.

The **Beaver Island Ferry** (☑231-547-2311; www.bibco.com; 103 Bridge Park Dr; ⊙mid-Apr–late Dec) departs from downtown Charlevoix for the green **isle** (www.beaverisland.org) in Lake Michigan. The two-hour journey costs $32.50/105 one-way per person/car. Reserve ahead if bringing a car.

Straits of Mackinac

This region, between the Upper and Lower Peninsulas, features a long history of forts and fudge shops. Car-free Mackinac Island is Michigan's premier tourist draw.

One of the most spectacular sights in the area is the 5-mile-long Mackinac Bridge (known locally as 'Big Mac'), which spans the Straits of Mackinac. The $4 toll is worth every penny as the views from the bridge, which include two Great Lakes, two peninsulas and hundreds of islands, are second to none in Michigan. And remember: despite the spelling, it's pronounced *mac*-in-aw.

Mackinaw City

At the south end of Mackinac Bridge, bordering I-75, is touristy Mackinaw City. It serves mainly as a jumping-off point to Mackinac Island, but it does have a couple of intriguing historic sights.

◉ Sights

Colonial Michilimackinac HISTORIC SITE
(☑231-436-5564; www.mackinacparks.com; 102 W Straits Ave; adult/child $12/7; ⊙9am-7pm Jun-Aug, to 5pm May & Sep–mid-Oct; ⍟) Next to the Big Mac bridge (its visitor center is actually beneath the bridge) is Colonial Michilimackinac, a National Historic Landmark that features a reconstructed stockade first built in 1715 by the French. Costumed interpreters cook and craft here.

Historic Mill Creek HISTORIC SITE
(☑231-436-4226; www.mackinacparks.com; 9001 W US 23; adult/child $9/6; ⊙9am-6pm Jun-Aug, to 5pm May & Sep–mid-Oct; ⍟) The site has an 18th-century sawmill where costumed interpreters chop wood, plus historic displays, a zipline and nature trails.

❶ Getting There & Away

I-75 is the main road to Mackinaw City. The docks for **Star Line** (☑800-638-9892; www.mackinacferry.com; 801 S Huron Ave; adult/child/bicycle $26/14/10) and **Shepler's** (☑800-828-6157; www.sheplersferry.com; 556 E Central Ave; adult/child/bicycle $26/14/10) are a short distance off the interstate. Both send ferries to Mackinac Island. The trip takes 20 minutes; boats go at least hourly during daylight hours. Both companies having free parking lots in which to leave your car.

St Ignace

At the north end of Mackinac Bridge is St Ignace, one of the departure points for Mackinac Island and the second-oldest settlement in Michigan – Père Jacques Marquette founded a mission here in 1671. The small town is a good place to get organized for onward road-tripping into the Upper Peninsula.

Budget motels and midrange hotels (mostly chains) are chockablock on N State St as it unfurls through town along the water. Expect to pay at least $100 per night.

Whitefish, pizza and fudge are the town's staples. Midrange restaurants line N State St, the main commercial thoroughfare that hugs the lake.

❶ Getting There & Away

I-75 is the main vein to St Ignace. The docks for **Star Line** (☑800-638-9892; www.mackinacferry.com; 587 N State St; adult/child/bicycle $26/14/10) and **Shepler's** (☑800-828-6157; www.sheplersferry.com; 601 N State St; adult/

child/bicycle $26/14/10) are a stone's throw from the interstate. Both send ferries to Mackinac Island. The trip takes 20 minutes; boats go at least hourly during daylight hours. You can leave your car in the companies' parking lots for free.

Mackinac Island

From either Mackinaw City or St Ignace you can catch a ferry to Mackinac Island. The island's location in the straits between Lake Michigan and Lake Huron made it a prized port in the North American fur trade, and a site the British and Americans battled over many times.

The most important date on this 3.8-sq-mile island was 1898 – the year cars were banned in order to encourage tourism. Today all travel is by horse or bicycle; even the police use bikes to patrol the town. The crowds of tourists – called Fudgies by the islanders – can be crushing at times, particularly during summer weekends. But when the last ferry leaves in the evening and clears out the day-trippers, Mackinac's real charm emerges and you drift back into another, slower era. Eighty percent of the island is state parkland. Not much stays open between November and April.

Sights

Arch Rock   NATURAL FEATURE

FREE This huge limestone arch curves 150ft above Lake Huron and provides dramatic photo opportunities. You can get here two ways: from stairs that lead up from the lakeshore road, or from the island's interior via Arch Rock Rd.

Fort Mackinac   HISTORIC SITE

(☑906-847-3328; www.mackinacparks.com; 7127 Huron Rd; adult/child $13/7.50; ⊙9:30am-6pm Jun-Aug, to 5pm May & Sep–mid-Oct; ⏃) Fort Mackinac sits atop limestone cliffs near downtown. Built by the British in 1780, it's one of the best-preserved military forts in the country. Costumed interpreters and cannon and rifle firings (every half-hour) entertain the kids. Stop into the tearoom for a bite and million-dollar view of downtown and the Straits of Mackinac.

Fort Holmes   FORT

(⊙10am-5pm May–mid-Oct) **FREE** British forces built the small wood and earth fort in 1814 to protect against a US attack during the War of 1812. This is a replica, as the original structure fell into ruin eons ago. It doesn't

take long to poke around. Better than the fort itself is the view. The site sits on the island's highest point and unfurls awesome views out over the Straits of Mackinac.

Activities

Edging the island's shoreline is Hwy 185 (aka Lake Shore Rd), the only Michigan highway that doesn't permit cars. The best way to view the incredible scenery along this 8-mile road is by bicycle; bring your own or rent one for $9 per hour at one of the many businesses. You can loop around the flat road in an hour.

Sleeping & Eating

Bogan Lane Inn   B&B $$

(☑906-847-3439; www.boganlaneinn.com; Bogan Lane; r $95-140) It's a bit fusty, but Bogan Lane has some of the island's lowest rates and is one of the few lodgings to stay open all year round. The four rooms share two bathrooms in the 1850s house. It's a bit off the beaten path, about 10 minutes' walk from downtown and the ferry docks.

Hart's Inn   B&B $$

(☑906-847-6234; www.hartsmackinac.com; 7556 Market St; r $150-215; ⊙mid-May–late Oct) Hart's is right downtown in a single-story, white-clapboard building akin to a quaint motel. There are nine smallish rooms, each with its own bathroom. Guests often relax on the garden-surrounded patio.

Chuckwagon   DINER $

(☑906-847-0019; www.chuckwagononmackinac. com; 7400 Main St; mains $7-12; ⊙7am-3pm) You'll need to fuel up for the day's bike explorations, and the cowboy-themed Chuckwagon is the place to do it. Grab a stool at the counter and watch the cooks slinging eggs, hash browns, bacon and pancakes for breakfast (until 11am only) and burgers and sandwiches for lunch. The no-frills diner is tiny and crowded, but worth the wait.

Information

Mackinac Island Visitor Center (☑906-847-3783; www.mackinacisland.org; 7274 Main St; ⊙9am-5pm May-Oct) Downtown booth with maps for hiking and cycling.

Getting There & Away

Two ferry companies – **Shepler's** (☑800-828-6157; www.sheplersferry.com) and **Star Line** (☑800-638-9892; www.mackinacferry.com) – operate out of Mackinaw City and St Ignace, and charge roughly the same rates: round-trip adult/child/bicycle $26/14/10. Book online and you'll save a few bucks. The ferries run several times daily from May through October. The trip takes about 20 minutes. Both companies have free parking lots to leave your car.

Upper Peninsula

Rugged and isolated, with hardwood forests blanketing 90% of its land, the Upper Peninsula (UP) is a Midwest highlight. Only 45 miles of interstate highway slice through the trees, punctuated by a handful of cities, of which Marquette is the largest. Between the small towns lie miles of undeveloped shoreline on Lakes Huron, Michigan and Superior; scenic two-lane roads; and pasties, the local meat-and-vegetable pot pies brought over by Cornish miners 150 years ago.

You'll find it's a different world up north. Residents of the UP, aka 'Yoopers,' consider themselves distinct from the rest of the state – they've even threatened to secede in the past.

Sault Ste Marie

Founded in 1668, Sault Ste Marie (Sault is pronounced 'soo') is Michigan's oldest city and the third oldest in the USA. Today it's a busy port and border crossing to Canada, where twin city Sault Ste Marie, Ontario, winks across the bridge.

⊙ Sights

Soo Locks Visitor Center   MUSEUM
(☑ 906-253-9290; Portage Ave; ⊙ 9am-9pm mid-May–mid-Oct) **FREE** Sault Ste Marie is best known for its locks that raise and lower 1000ft-long freighters between the different lake levels. The downtown visitor center features displays, videos and observation decks from which you can watch the boats leap 21ft from Lake Superior to Lake Huron. To get there take exit 394 off I-75 and go left.

🛏 Sleeping & Eating

Askwith Lockview Motel   MOTEL **$**
(☑ 906-632-2491; www.lockview.com; 327 W Portage Ave; r $85-99; ⊙ May–mid-Oct; ❈ 🛜) Choose from rooms in the classic, two-story motel or in the line of single-story, attached cottages. The unfussy interiors are similar: flowery bedspreads, TV and mini refrigerator in a relatively tight space, but they're neat and tidy and right across from the Soo Locks.

Karl's Cuisine, Winery & Brewery   AMERICAN **$$**
(☑ 906-0253-1900; www.karlscuisine.com; 447 W Portage Ave; mains $16-24; ⊙ 11am-4pm Mon & Tue, to 9pm Wed-Sat) 🍴 The menu at convivial Karl's spans pasties (beef or chicken plus veggies baked in a crust), maple-planked Lake Superior whitefish, burgers, sandwiches, stromboli and pasta dishes. The common thread is the use of local and responsibly sourced ingredients. Vegetarian and gluten-free diners will find lots of options. The family-run establishment even makes its own beer, wine and cider.

❶ Getting There & Away

I-75 is the main interstate to Sault Ste Marie. The town has a small airport with daily flights to Detroit. The International Bridge links Sault St Marie to its twin city in Canada; the border crossing is open 24/7.

Pictured Rocks National Lakeshore

Stretching along prime Lake Superior real estate, Pictured Rocks National Lakeshore is a series of wild cliffs and caves where blue and green minerals have streaked the red and yellow sandstone into a kaleidoscope of color. Rte 58 (Alger County Rd) spans the park for 52 slow miles from Grand Marais in the east to Munising in the west. Top sights (from east to west) include Au Sable Point Lighthouse (reached via a 3-mile round-trip walk beside shipwreck skeletons), agate-strewn Twelvemile Beach, hike-rich Chapel Falls and view-worthy Miners Castle Overlook. Boat rides and kayak trips along the shore are an excellent way to absorb the dramatic scenery.

Kayaking is popular in Pictured Rocks and no wonder, given that you paddle beneath sheer, color-stained bluffs with names like Lovers Leap, Flower Vase and Caves of the Bloody Chiefs. The duck's-eye view of the geologic features is awesome. Experienced paddlers can go it alone, but conditions are often wavy and windy. Newbies should hook up with a guide. Several operate out of Munising, offering trips from just a few hours to all day. **Pictured Rocks Kayaking** (☑ 906-387-5500; www.paddlepicturedrocks.com; 1348 Commercial St; 4½hr tours adult/child $135/95; ⊙ late May-Sep) has good trips for beginners.

Munising has heaps of motels, with many located on Hwy 28 a few miles southeast of town. See www.munising.org for listings.

Tiny Grand Marais, on the park's east side, also has motels, though fewer than Munising. Prices are budget range, but creep up during July and August.

Marquette, 40 miles west, offers the closest airport. Hwys 28 and 94 are the primary roads to the area.

Marquette

Lakeside Marquette is the perfect place to stay put for a few days to explore the region. It's the Upper Peninsula's largest (and snowiest) town, known as a hot spot for outdoors enthusiasts. Forests, beaches and cliffs provide a playground spitting distance from downtown. Locals ski in winter and hit the trails with their fat-tire bikes in summer. Northern Michigan University is here, so the population skews young. Beer and good food await in the historic town center.

◉ Sights & Activities

Da Yoopers Tourist Trap and Museum   MUSEUM
(☑906-485-5595; www.dayoopers.com; 490 N Steel St; ⊙10am-6pm Mon-Fri, to 5pm Sat & Sun) FREE Behold Big Gus, the world's largest chainsaw. And Big Ernie, the world's largest rifle. Kitsch runs rampant at Da Yoopers Tourist Trap and Museum, 15 miles west of Marquette on Hwy 28/41, past Ishpeming.

Presque Isle Park   PARK
(Peter White Dr) In the city, on a peninsula jutting out into Lake Superior, the high bluffs of Presque Isle Park make a great place to catch the sunset.

Down Wind Sports   KAYAKING
(☑906-226-7112; www.downwindsports.com; 514 N 3rd St; ⊙10am-7pm Mon-Fri, to 5pm Sat, 11am-3pm Sun) Rents all kinds of gear and has the lowdown on kayaking, fly fishing, surfing, ice climbing and other adventures.

🍴 Sleeping & Eating

Landmark Inn   HISTORIC HOTEL **$$**
(☑906-228-2580; www.thelandmarkinn.com; 230 N Front St; r $179-229; ❋⏰) The elegant, six-story Landmark fills a historic lakefront building and has a couple of resident ghosts.

Jean Kay's Pasties & Subs   SANDWICHES **$**
(☑906-228-5310; www.jeankayspasties.com; 1635 Presque Isle Ave; items $5-8; ⊙11am-9pm Mon-Fri, to 8pm Sat & Sun) Sample the local meat-and-veggie pie specialty at Jean Kay's.

WORTH A TRIP

TAHQUAMENON FALLS STATE PARK

Lovely Tahquamenon Falls inside **Tahquamenon Falls State Park** (☑906-492-3415; Hwy 123; per vehicle $9), east of Sault Ste Marie, flow with tea-colored waters tinted by upstream hemlock leaves. The Upper Falls, 200ft across with a 50ft drop, wow onlookers – including Henry Wadsworth Longfellow, who mentioned them in his *Song of Hiawatha*. The Lower Falls (about 5 miles northeast) are a series of small cascades that swirl around an island; many visitors rent a rowboat and paddle out to it. The large state park also has camping (tent and RV sites $17 to $25), great hiking and – bonus – a brewpub near the park entrance.

Thill's Fish House   SEAFOOD **$**
(☑906-226-9851; 250 E Main St; items $4-9; ⊙8am-5:30pm Mon-Fri, 9am-4pm Sat) Buy fresh-caught trout or whitefish in various forms (smoked, pickled, sausage) right on the dock. Thill's is Marquette's last commercial fishing operation, and it hauls in fat catches daily. It's set in a Quonset hut at Main St's foot.

ℹ Information

Stop at the log-lodge **visitor center** (2201 US 41; ⊙9am-5:30pm) at the edge of town for brochures on local hiking trails and waterfalls.

ℹ Getting There & Away

Hwys 41 and 28 are the main roadways to town. Marquette has a small airport with flights to Detroit, Chicago and Minneapolis.

Isle Royale National Park

Totally free of vehicles and roads, Isle Royale National Park, a 210-sq-mile island in Lake Superior, is certainly the place to go for peace and quiet. It gets fewer visitors in a year than Yellowstone National Park gets in a day, which means the 1600 moose creeping through the forest are all yours.

The island is laced with 165 miles of hiking trails that connect dozens of campgrounds along Superior and inland lakes. You must be totally prepared for this wilderness adventure, with a tent, camping stove,

GREAT LAKES UPPER PENINSULA

sleeping bags, food and water filter. The park is open from mid-April through October, then it closes due to extreme weather.

Isle Royale offers two options: snooze at **Rock Harbor Lodge** (☑906-337-4993; www.rockharborlodge.com; r & cottages $224-256; ☺late May-early Sep), the only accommodation for softies, or hike to the rustic campgrounds with outhouses that dot the island. FYI, there's no extra fee for camping. It's covered in the $7 per day park entrance fee.

The lodge has two eateries: a dining room serving American fare for breakfast, lunch and dinner, and a more casual cafe for burgers, sandwiches, coffee and beer. The Dockside Store at Rock Harbor stocks a small array of groceries. There's another small store in Windigo on the island's other side.

❶ Information

Isle Royale Park Headquarters (☑906-482-0984; www.nps.gov/isro; 800 E Lakeshore Dr; ☺8am-6pm Mon-Fri, from 10am Sat Jun–mid-Sep, 8am-4pm Mon-Fri mid-Sep–May) The park headquarters in Houghton provides information on entrance fees (per person per day $7), ferries, camping etc.

❶ Getting There & Away

From the dock outside the park headquarters in Houghton, the **Ranger III** (☑906-482-0984; www.nps.gov/isro; 800 E Lakeshore Dr; ☺late May-early Sep) departs at 9am on Tuesday and Friday for the six-hour boat trip (round-trip adult/child $126/46) to Rock Harbor, at the east end of the island.

Isle Royale Seaplanes (☑906-483-4991; www.isleroyaleseaplanes.com; 21125 Royce Rd) offers a quicker trip, flying from the Portage Canal Seaplane Base in Hancock to Rock Harbor or to Windigo (on the island's west end) in 35 minutes (round-trip $320).

Or head 50 miles up the Keweenaw Peninsula to Copper Harbor (a beautiful drive) and jump on the **Isle Royale Queen** (☑906-289-4437; www.isleroyale.com; 14 Waterfront Landing) for the 8am three-hour crossing (round-trip adult/child $136/76) to Rock Harbor. It runs daily during peak season from late July through August.

Bringing a kayak or canoe on the ferries costs an additional $50 round-trip. Ensure you make reservations for any of the transportation methods well in advance. You can also access Isle Royale from Grand Portage, MN.

Porcupine Mountains Wilderness State Park

Michigan's largest state park, with 90 miles of trails, is a wilderness winner. 'The Porkies,' as they're called, are so rugged that loggers bypassed most of the range in the early 19th century, leaving the park with the largest tract of virgin forest between the Rocky Mountains and Adirondacks. Along with 300-year-old hemlock trees, the Porkies are known for waterfalls, 20 miles of undeveloped Lake Superior shoreline, black bears lumbering about and the view of the park's stunning Lake of the Clouds.

Rustic cabins and campgrounds are available in the park. Otherwise budget motels and pricier lodges dot Hwy 64 between the wee towns of Silver City and Ontonagon.

◉ Sights & Activities

Lake of the Clouds   LAKE
(Hwy 107) The lake is the area's most photographed sight. After stopping at the visitor center to pay the park entrance fee (per car $9), continue to the end of Hwy 107 and climb 300ft via a short path for the stunning view of the shimmering water. Lengthier trails depart from the parking lot.

Porcupine Mountain Ski Area   SKIING
(☑906-885-5209;   www.porkiesfun.com; ☺Dec-early Apr) Winter is a busy time here, with downhill skiing (a 787ft vertical drop) and 26 miles of cross-country trails on offer. Conditions and costs vary, so call before heading out.

❶ Information

Porcupine Mountains and Ontonagon Area CVB (www.porcupineup.com) List of waterfalls and activities.

Porcupine Mountains Visitor Center (☑906-885-5275; www.mi.gov/porkies; 412 S Boundary Rd; ☺8am-6pm mid-May–mid-Oct) The state park visitor center is where you buy vehicle entry permits (per day/year $9/32) and backcountry camping permits (one to four people per night $15).

❶ Getting There & Away

You'll need a car to get here. Hwy 45 is the main highway to the area.

WISCONSIN

Wisconsin is cheesy and proud of it. The state pumps out 2.5 billion pounds of cheddar, Gouda and other smelly goodness – a quarter of America's hunks – from its cow-speckled farmland per year. Local license plates read 'The Dairy State' with udder dignity. Folks here even refer to themselves as 'cheeseheads' and emphasize it by wearing novelty foam rubber cheese-wedge hats for special occasions (most notably during Green Bay Packers football games).

So embrace the cheese thing, because there's a good chance you'll be here for a while. Wisconsin has a ton to offer: exploring the craggy cliffs and lighthouses of Door County, kayaking through sea caves at Apostle Islands National Lakeshore, cow chip throwing along Hwy 12 and soaking up beer, art and festivals in Milwaukee and Madison.

① Information

Wisconsin Department of Tourism (www. travelwisconsin.com) Produces tons of free guides on subjects like biking, golf and rustic roads; also has a free app.

Wisconsin B&B Association (www.wbba.org)

Wisconsin Highway Conditions (www.511wi.gov)

Wisconsin Milk Marketing Board (www. eatwisconsincheese.com) Provides a free statewide map of cheesemakers titled *A Traveler's Guide to America's Dairyland.*

Wisconsin State Park Information (☑608-266-2181; www.dnr.wi.gov/topic/parks) Park entry requires a vehicle permit (per day/year $11/38). Campsites cost from $21 to $35; reservations (☑888-947-2757; www.wisconsin stateparks.reserveamerica.com; fee $10) accepted.

Milwaukee

Here's the thing about Milwaukee: it's cool, but for some reason it slips under the radar. The city's reputation as a working man's town of brewskis, bowling alleys and polka halls still persists. But attractions like the Calatrava-designed art museum, badass Harley-Davidson Museum and stylish eating and shopping enclaves have turned Wisconsin's largest city into an unassumingly groovy place. In summertime, festivals let loose with revelry by the lake almost every weekend. And where else on the planet will you see racing sausages?

History

Milwaukee was first settled by Germans in the 1840s. Many started small breweries, but a few decades later the introduction of bulk brewing technology turned beer production into a major industry here. Milwaukee earned its 'Brew City' and 'Nation's Watering Hole' nicknames in the 1880s when Pabst, Schlitz, Blatz, Miller and 80 other breweries made suds here. Today, only Miller remains of the big brewers, though microbreweries have made a comeback.

◎ Sights & Activities

Lake Michigan sits to the east of the city, and is rimmed by parkland. The Riverwalk path runs along both sides of the Milwaukee River downtown.

★**Harley-Davidson Museum**   MUSEUM
(☑414-287-2789; www.h-dmuseum.com; 400 W Canal St; adult/child $20/10; ⊙9am-6pm Fri-Wed, to 8pm Thu May-Sep, from 10am Oct-Apr) Hundreds of motorcycles show the styles through the decades, including the flashy rides of Elvis and Evel Knievel. You can sit in the saddle of various bikes (on the bottom floor, in the Experience Gallery) and take badass photos. Even non-bikers will enjoy the interactive exhibits and leather-clad crowds.

Harley-Davidson Plant   FACTORY
(☑877-883-1450; www.harley-davidson.com/experience; W156 N9000 Pilgrim Rd; ⊙9am-1:30pm Mon-Fri) Hog-heads can get a fix at the plant where engines are built, in suburban Menomonee Falls. The factory offers two options for tours: a free, 30-minute jaunt where you see a video and take a quick walk onto the factory floor, and a two-hour tour (per person $38) where you don safety glasses and check out the assembly line, powder-coat process and other in-depth engine-making activities.

The long tours leave at 10am and noon, and are best booked in advance. The shorter tours are walk-in only, with tickets given out on a first-come, first-served basis, so it's wise to arrive early. No children under age 12 allowed. Follow the Harley signs in from Pilgrim Rd, then look for the Tour Center signs.

Milwaukee Art Museum   MUSEUM
(☑414-224-3200; www.mam.org; 700 N Art Museum Dr; adult/child $17/free; ⊙10am-5pm Tue-Sun, to 8pm Thu) You have to see this lakeside institution, which features a stunning

DON'T MISS

THE BRONZE FONZ

Rumor has it the Bronze Fonz, on the east side of Riverwalk, just south of Wells St downtown, is the most photographed sight in Milwaukee. The Fonz, aka Arthur Fonzarelli, was a character from the 1970s TV show *Happy Days*, which was set in the city. What do you think – do the blue pants get an 'Aaay' or 'Whoa!'?

winglike addition by Santiago Calatrava. It soars open and closed every day at 10am, noon and 5pm (8pm on Thursday), which is wild to watch; head to the suspension bridge outside for the best view. There are fabulous folk and outsider art galleries, and a sizeable collection of Georgia O'Keeffe paintings. A 2015 renovation added photography and new media galleries to the trove.

Miller Brewing Company BREWERY
(☑ 414-931-2337; www.millercoors.com; 4251 W State St; ⏰ 10:30am-4:30pm Mon-Sat, to 3:30pm Sun Jun-Aug, to 3:30pm Mon-Sat Sep-May) FREE Founded in 1855, the historic Miller facility preserves Milwaukee's beer legacy. Join the legions lined up for the free, hour-long tours. Though the mass-produced beer may not be your favorite, the factory impresses with its sheer scale: you'll visit the packaging plant where 2000 cans are filled each minute, and the warehouse where a half-million cases await shipment. And then there's the generous tasting session at the tour's end, where you can down three full-size samples. Don't forget your ID.

Lakefront Brewery BREWERY
(☑ 414-372-8800; www.lakefrontbrewery.com; 1872 N Commerce St; 45min tours $9-10; ⏰ 11am-8pm Mon-Thu, to 9pm Fri, 9am-9pm Sat, 10am-5pm Sun) Well-loved Lakefront Brewery, across the river from Brady St, has afternoon tours, but the swellest time to visit is on Friday nights when there's a fish fry, 16 beers to try and a polka band letting loose. Tour times vary throughout the week, but there's usually at least a 2pm and 3pm walk-through (and often many more).

**Discovery World at
Pier Wisconsin** MUSEUM
(☑ 414-765-9966; www.discoveryworld.org; 500 N Harbor Dr; adult/child $19/16; ⏰ 9am-4pm Mon-Fri, 10am-5pm Sat & Sun, closed Mon Sep-Mar; 🚼) The

city's lakefront science and technology museum is primarily a kid-pleaser, with freshwater and saltwater aquariums (where you can touch sharks and sturgeon) and a dockside, triple-masted Great Lakes schooner to ogle (two-hour sailing tour per adult/child $45/40). Adults will appreciate the Les Paul exhibit, showcasing the Wisconsin native's pioneering guitars and sound equipment.

Landmark Lanes BOWLING
(☑ 414-278-8770; www.landmarklanes.com; 2220 N Farwell Ave; per game $3.50-4; ⏰ 5pm-midnight Mon-Thu, noon-1am Fri & Sat, noon-midnight Sun) Milwaukee once had more than 200 bowling alleys, and many retro lanes still hide in timeworn dives. To get your game on try Landmark Lanes, offering 16 beat-up alleys in the historic 1927 Oriental Theater. An arcade, three bars and cheap beer round out the atmosphere.

🎉 Festivals & Events

Summerfest MUSIC
(www.summerfest.com; 639 E Summerfest Pl; day pass $20; ⏰ late Jun–early Jul) It's dubbed 'the world's largest music festival,' and indeed hundreds of rock, blues, jazz, country and alternative bands swarm its 11 stages over 11 days. The scene totally rocks; it is held at downtown's lakefront festival grounds (aka Henry Maier Festival Park). The headline concerts cost extra.

PrideFest LGBT
(www.pridefest.com; 639 E Summerfest Pl; day pass $15-18; ⏰ mid-Jun) Beer drinking, live music, a dance pavilion and family stage are all part of the festivities, which take place over three days in mid-June at Henry Maier Festival Park.

🛏 Sleeping

County Clare Irish Inn INN $$
(☑ 414-272-5273; www.countyclare-inn.com; 1234 N Astor St; r $129-149; 🅿🌐🖥) It's a winner near the lakefront. Rooms have that snug Irish-cottage feel, with four-poster beds, white wainscot walls and Jacuzzis. There's free parking, free breakfast and an on-site Guinness-pouring pub, of course.

★ Brewhouse Inn & Suites HOTEL $$
(☑ 414-810-3350; www.brewhousesuites.com; 1215 N 10th St; r $199-249; 🅿🌐@🖥) This 90-room hotel sits in the exquisitely renovated old Pabst Brewery complex. Each of the large chambers has steampunk decor, a

kitchenette and free wi-fi. Continental breakfast is included. It's at downtown's far west edge, about a half-mile walk from sausagey Old World 3rd St and a good 2 miles from the festival grounds. Parking costs $28.

Kimpton Journeyman
HOTEL $$$

(☎414-291-3970; www.journeymanhotel.com; 310 E Chicago St; r $219-349; P✳︎🐾🛜🐕) The new Journeyman brings stylish digs to the heart of the Third Ward, right in the midst of cool-cat shops, bars and restaurants. The 158 large rooms have mod, earth-toned decor with pops of color, comfy beds and chunky wood desks. A rooftop lounge, free loaner bicycles and a free wine happy hour each evening add to the pleasure. Parking is $33.

✖ Eating

Good places to scope for eats include Germanic Old World 3rd St downtown; hip, multi-ethnic Brady St by its intersection with N Farwell Ave; and the gastropub-filled Third Ward, anchored along N Milwaukee St south of I-94.

★ Comet Cafe
AMERICAN $

(☎414-273-7677; www.thecometcafe.com; 1947 N Farwell Ave; mains $8-13; ⊙10am-midnight Mon-Fri, from 9am Sat & Sun; 🖋) Students, young families, older couples and bearded, tattooed types pile in to the rock-and-roll Comet for gravy-smothered meatloaf, mac 'n' cheese, vegan gyros and hangover brunch dishes. It's a craft-beer-pouring bar on one side, and retro-boothed diner on the other. Be sure to try one of the giant cupcakes for dessert.

Milwaukee Public Market
MARKET $

(☎414-336-1111; www.milwaukeepublicmarket.org; 400 N Water St; ⊙10am-8pm Mon-Fri, 8am-7pm Sat, 10am-6pm Sun; 🛜) Located in the Third Ward, the market's vendors sell cheese, chocolate, beer, tacos, frozen custard and more. Take them upstairs where there are tables, free wi-fi and $1 used books.

Bavette La Boucherie
AMERICAN $

(☎414-273-3375; www.bavettelaboucherie.com; 330 E Menomonee St; mains $12-16; ⊙11am-5pm Mon & Tue, to 9pm Wed-Sat) This hip industrial space in the Third Ward is a butcher shop with a cafe that serves lunch and dinner. It stacks a meaty sandwich, such as the roast pork with rhubarb-raisin compote and the seared steak with truffled mushroom sauce. Locals come in to nibble on charcuterie and cheese plates alongside lovely wines. Sit at the bar and you'll see sausage-making.

Ardent
AMERICAN $$$

(☎414-897-7022; www.ardentmke.com; 1751 N Farwell St; tasting menu $85; ⊙6-10pm Wed-Sat) Milwaukee's foodies get weak-kneed when they sniff the Beard-nominated chef's ever-changing, farm-to-table dishes. Dinner is a lingering affair in the tiny glowing room, with two seatings each night for the 10-course tasting menu. Reserve well in advance. Or head next door to Ardent's sibling restaurant, open 6pm to 1am Wednesday to Saturday, for slurpable bowls of ramen noodles ($13).

🍷 Drinking & Entertainment

Vermutería 600
COCKTAIL BAR

(☎414-488-9146; www.hotelmadridmke.com/bar; 600 S 6th St; ⊙5pm-midnight) The bar at

---

FISH FRIES & SUPPER CLUBS

Wisconsin has two dining traditions that you'll likely encounter when visiting the state:

Fish Fry Friday is the hallowed day of the 'fish fry.' This communal meal of beer-battered cod, French fries and coleslaw came about years ago, providing locals with a cheap meal to socialize around and celebrate the workweek's end. The convention is still going strong at many bars and restaurants, including Lakefront Brewery in Milwaukee.

Supper Club This is a type of time-warped restaurant common in the upper Midwest. Supper clubs started in the 1930s, and most retain a retro vibe. Hallmarks include a woodsy location, a radish-and-carrot-laden relish tray on the table, a surf-and-turf menu and a mile-long, unironic cocktail list. See www.wisconsinsupperclubs.net for more information. The Old Fashioned (p592) in Madison is a modern take on the venue (it's named after the quintessential, brandy-laced supper-club drink).

DON'T MISS

RACING SAUSAGES

It's common to see strange things after too many stadium beers. But a group of giant sausages sprinting around Miller Park's perimeter – is that for *real*? It is if it's the middle of the 6th inning. That's when the famous 'Racing Sausages' (actually five people in costumes) waddle onto the field to give the fans a thrill. If you don't know your encased meats, that's Brat, Polish, Italian, Hot Dog and Chorizo vying for supremacy.

the Hotel Madrid is a warm, magical space that transports you to 1930s Spain. It serves cocktails inspired by what Ernest Hemingway and pals were drinking when they stayed at the famed Hotel Florida in Madrid back then – say, the Boulevardier (with bourbon, house-made vermouth and bitters). Small-plate snacks are available, or there's an upscale Spanish restaurant on site.

Best Place   BAR

(☑ 414-630-1609; www.bestplacemilwaukee.com; 901 W Junau Ave; ☉ noon-6pm Mon, noon-10pm Wed & Thu, 10:30am-5pm Fri & Sat, 10:30am-6pm Sun) Join the locals knocking back beers and massive whiskey pours at this small tavern in the former Pabst Brewery headquarters. A fireplace warms the cozy, dark-wood room; original murals depicting Pabst's history adorn the walls. Staff give daily tours of the building ($8, including a 16oz Pabst or Schlitz tap brew).

Miller Park   BASEBALL

(☑ 414-902-4000; www.brewers.com; 1 Brewers Way) The Brewers play baseball at fab Miller Park, which has a retractable roof and real grass. The Racing Sausages star in the middle of the sixth inning. To the uninitiated, that's five people in foam-rubber meat costumes who dash around the ball field's perimeter in a madcap foot race.

The stadium is about 5 miles west of downtown. The Brewers Line bus runs there on game days; pick it up along Wisconsin Ave.

❶ Information

Milwaukee Convention & Visitors Bureau
(☑ 800-554-1448, www.visitmilwaukee.org)

❶ Getting There & Around

General Mitchell International Airport (MKE; www.mitchellairport.com; 5300 S Howell Ave)

is 8 miles south of downtown. Take public bus 80 ($2.25) or a cab ($33).

The **Lake Express ferry** (☑ 866-914-1010; www.lake-express.com; 2330 S Lincoln Memorial Dr; one way per adult/child/car from $91.50/35/101; ☉ May-Oct) sails from downtown (the terminal is located a few miles south of the city center) to Muskegon, Michigan, providing easy access to Michigan's beach-lined Gold Coast.

Several bus companies use the **Milwaukee Intermodal Station** (433 St Paul Ave). Badger Bus (www.badgerbus.com) goes to Madison ($20, two hours) eight times per day. Greyhound (www.greyhound.com) and Megabus (www.megabus.com/us) run frequent buses to Chicago (two hours) and Minneapolis (6½ to seven hours).

Amtrak (www.amtrakhiawatha.com) runs the Hiawatha train seven times a day to/from Chicago ($25, 1½ hours). It also uses the Milwaukee Intermodal Station.

The Milwaukee County Transit System (www.ridemcts.com) provides the local bus service. Bus 31 goes to Miller Brewery; the Brewers Line bus goes to Miller Park on game days. Fare is $2.25.

Bublr Bikes (www.bublrbikes.com) is Milwaukee's bikeshare program, with 60 or so stations scattered around downtown (including at the train/bus depot) and north to the University of Wisconsin-Milwaukee. A 30-minute ride costs $3.

A new streetcar is slated to start service in fall 2018. The route will go through the Third Ward and heart of downtown. See www.themilwaukeestreetcar.com for updates.

For taxi service, try **Yellow Cab** (☑ 414-271-1800, www.ycmilwaukee.com).

Racine

Racine is an unremarkable industrial town, but it has some key Frank Lloyd Wright sights. What's more, it's a prime place to sample the mega-sized state pastry known as the kringle.

❍ Sights

SC Johnson Administration Building & Research Tower   ARCHITECTURE

(☑ 262-260-2154; www.scjohnson.com/visit; 1525 Howe St; ☉ tours 10am & 2pm Thu-Sun Mar-Dec) **FREE** Frank Lloyd Wright designed several buildings at the company's headquarters. Free 90-minute tours take in the 1939 Admin Building, a magnificent space with tall, flared columns in its vast Great Workroom and 43 miles' worth of Pyrex glass-tube windows letting in soft natural light. You'll also see the 1950 Research Tower – where Raid, Off and other famous products were developed –

which features 15 floors of curved brick bands and more Pyrex windows.

Wingspread
ARCHITECTURE

(☎ 262-681-3353; www.scjohnson.com/visit; 33 E Four Mile Rd; ⊙9:30am-3:30pm Wed-Fri, 11:30am-3:30pm Sat, noon-2:30pm Sun Mar-Dec) FREE Wingspread is the house Frank Lloyd Wright designed for HF Johnson Jr, one of the SC Johnson company's leaders. It is the last and largest of Wright's Prairie-style abodes, completed in 1939. It's enormous, with 500 windows and a 30ft-high chimney. Free tours through the building take one hour, and they must be booked in advance.

❶ Getting There & Away

I-94 runs to Racine, which is 30 miles south of Milwaukee and 75 miles north of Chicago.

South Central Wisconsin

This part of Wisconsin has some of the prettiest landscapes in the state. Architecture fans can be unleashed at Taliesin, *the* Frank Lloyd Wright sight. Madison is the area's cultural jewel.

Green County

This pastoral area holds the nation's greatest concentration of cheesemakers. As you're road-tripping through you can stop at local dairy farms and shops and learn your artisanal from farmstead, Gruyere from Gouda, curd from whey. Why so cheesy here? It has to do with the limestone-rich soil. It grows distinctive grass, which makes distinctive food for cows, and that results in distinctive milk that creates distinctive cheese. Got it? Old World Europeans did, particularly the Swiss. They flocked to the region in the 1800s, bringing their cheesemaking skills with them.

Two good pit stops are Monroe, the biggest town and county seat, filled with cheese history and limburger taverns, and New Glarus, a Swiss town with a renowned brewery.

Monroe and New Glarus each have a couple of midrange motels. B&Bs pop up in various little towns.

You'll mostly find pub food, pizza parlors and restaurants serving Swiss specialties (cheese fondue, sausages etc).

❶ Information

Green County Tourism (www.greencounty.org)

A Traveler's Guide to America's Dairyland (www.eatwisconsincheese.com) Good map showing local dairy producers and plant tours.

❶ Getting There & Away

Madison is the closet urban area and transportation hub. From there you'll need a car to access Green County. Hwy 69 is a main artery connecting Madison, New Glarus and Monroe. Most roads in the region are slowpoke, two-lane byways.

Madison

Madison reaps a lot of kudos – most walkable city, best road-biking city, most vegetarian-friendly, gay-friendly, environmentally friendly and just plain all-round friendliest city in the USA. Ensconced on a narrow isthmus between Mendota and Monona Lakes, it's a pretty combination of small, grassy state capital and liberal, bookish college town. An impressive foodie/locavore scene has been cooking here for years.

◉ Sights & Activities

★**Dane County Farmers Market**　MARKET
(www.dcfm.org; ⊙6am-2pm Sat late Apr–early Nov) On Saturdays, a food bazaar takes over Capitol Sq. It's one of the nation's most expansive markets, famed for its artisanal cheeses and breads. Craft vendors and street musicians add to the festivities. In winter the market moves indoors to varying locations on Wednesdays.

Monona Terrace　ARCHITECTURE
(☎ 608-261-4000; www.mononaterrace.com; 1 John Nolen Dr; ⊙8am-5pm) Frank Lloyd Wright designed this cool, white semicircular structure in 1938, though it wasn't completed until 1997. The one-hour tours ($5) explain why; they're offered daily at 1pm May through October (Friday through Monday only the rest of the year). The building serves as a community center, offering free lunchtime yoga classes and evening concerts. Check the schedule online.

Chazen Museum of Art　MUSEUM
(☎ 608-263-2246; www.chazen.wisc.edu; 750 University Ave; ⊙9am-5pm Tue, Wed & Fri, to 9pm Thu, 11am-5pm Sat & Sun) FREE The university's art museum is huge and fabulous, and way beyond the norm for a campus collection. The 3rd floor holds most of the genre-spanning trove: everything from the Old Dutch Masters to Qing Dynasty porcelain vases,

Picasso sculptures and Andy Warhol pop art. Free chamber-music concerts and art-house films take place on Sundays from September to mid-May.

Museum of Contemporary Art MUSEUM
(☑608-257-0158; www.mmoca.org; 227 State St; ☺noon-5pm Tue-Thu, to 8pm Fri, 10am-8pm Sat, noon-5pm Sun) FREE It's worth popping into the angular glass building to see what's showing. Frank Stella prints? Claes Oldenburg etchings? Cindy Sherman photos? Exhibits change every three months or so. It doesn't take long to look through the small museum.

State Capitol NOTABLE BUILDING
(☑608-266-0382; www.legis.wisconsin.gov; 2 E Main St; ☺8am-6pm Mon-Fri, to 4pm Sat & Sun) FREE The X-shaped capitol is the largest outside Washington, DC, and marks the heart of downtown. Tours are available on the hour most days, or you can go up to the observation deck on your own for a view.

Machinery Row CYCLING
(☑608-442-5974; www.machineryrowbicycles. com; 601 Williamson St; rental per day $30; ☺10am-8pm Mon-Fri, 9am-7pm Sat, 10am-6pm Sun) It'd be a shame to leave town without taking advantage of the city's 120 miles of bike trails. Get wheels and maps at this shop, located by various trailheads.

★ Festivals & Events

World's Largest Brat Fest FOOD & DRINK
(www.bratfest.com; ☺late May) FREE More than 209,000 bratwursts go down the hatch; carnival rides and bands provide the backdrop. It's held at Willow Island at the Alliant Energy Center.

Great Taste of the Midwest Beer Festival BEER
(www.greattaste.org; tickets $60; ☺early Aug) Tickets sell out fast for this festival where more than 150 craft brewers pour their elixirs. It's held in Olin Park.

⊨ Sleeping

HI Madison Hostel HOSTEL $
(☑608-441-0144; www.hiusa.org/madison; 141 S Butler St; dm $25-30, r from $60; ⊞@☎) The brightly painted, 33-bed brick house is located on a quiet street a short walk from the State Capitol. Dorms are gender segregated; linens are free. There's a kitchen and common room with DVDs. Parking is $7.

Graduate Madison BOUTIQUE HOTEL $$
(☑608-257-4391; www.graduatemadison.com; 601 Langdon St; r $119-209; ⊞❋☎☎) A block from campus and right off State St's action, this 72-room hotel wafts a hip academic vibe with its mod-meets-plaid decor and book-themed artwork. Rooms are on the small side and can be a bit noisy, but the location rocks.

A cool little pie cafe/coffee bar offers treats downstairs, while the 17th-floor rooftop bar pours cocktails.

✖ Eating & Drinking

A global smorgasbord of restaurants peppers State St amid the pizza, sandwich and cheap-beer joints; many places have inviting patios. Cruising Williamson ('Willy') St turns up cafes, dumpling bars and Lao and Thai joints.

Bars stay open to 2am. State St has the mother lode, with scruffy drinkeries preferred by guzzling university students, as well as natty cocktail lounges.

Weary Traveler Free House INTERNATIONAL $
(☑608-442-6207; www.wearytravelerfreehouse. com; 1201 Williamson St; mains $10-14; ☺11:30am-2am) Old-style speakeasy meets UK pub at the Weary Traveler. The low lighting, dark wood decor, art-filled walls and myriad board games complement the menu of global comfort foods. Top marks go to the Reuben sandwich, vegan chili, Hungarian goulash and walleye sandwich with killer roasted potatoes. Everything on tap is local and/or craft brewed.

Short Stack Eats BREAKFAST $
(☑608-709-5569; www.shortstackeats.com; 301 W Johnson St; mains $8-13; ☺6am-3pm Wed, 6am-midnight Thu-Sat, midnight-9pm Sun) ✔ It's all breakfast all day and all night at Short Stack. Order at the counter, then hopefully find a free table amid the cutesy, mismatched decor. Staff use old license plates as table markers to bring your locally sourced sweet potato pancakes, egg-and-bacon-filled breakfast sandwiches and enormous, spicy Bloody Marys.

★ The Old Fashioned AMERICAN $$
(☑608-310-4545; www.theoldfashioned.com; 23 N Pinckney St; mains $9-20; ☺7:30am-2am Mon-Fri, 9am-2am Sat, 9am-10pm Sun) With its dark, woodsy decor, the Old Fashioned evokes a supper club, a type of retro eatery common in Wisconsin. The menu is all local specialties, including walleye, cheese soup and

WORTH A TRIP

ODDBALL HIGHWAY-12

Unusual sights huddle around Hwy 12 in south-central Wisconsin, all within a 55-mile span:

National Mustard Museum (☑ 800-438-6878; www.mustardmuseum.com; 7477 Hubbard Ave, Middleton; ◎ 10am-5pm, closed Tue Jan-Mar) **FREE** Born of one man's ridiculously intense passion, the museum houses 5200 mustards and kooky condiment memorabilia. Tongue-in-cheek humor abounds, especially if CMO (chief mustard officer) Barry Levenson is there to give you the shtick. It's located in Middleton, a short distance northwest of Madison.

Cow Chip Throw (www.wiscowchip.com; Grand Ave & First St, Prairie du Sac; ◎ 1st weekend Sep) If it's the first weekend in September, stop at the town of Prairie du Sac. It hosts the annual Cow Chip Throw, where 800 competitors fling dried manure patties as far as the eye can see; the record is 248ft.

Dr Evermor's Sculpture Park (☑ 608-219-7830; www.worldofdrevermor.com; Hwy 12; ◎ 11am-5pm Mon & Thu-Sat, from noon Sun) **FREE** The doc has welded old pipes, carburetors and other salvaged metal into a hallucinatory world of futuristic birds, dragons and other bizarre structures. The crowning glory is the giant, egg-domed Forevertron, once cited by Guinness World Records as the globe's largest scrap-metal sculpture. Finding the park entrance is tricky. It is behind Delaney's Surplus on US 12; look for a small road just south of Delaney's leading in. Hours can be erratic, so call to confirm it's open. The doc is in poor health and isn't around much now, but his wife Lady Eleanor usually is.

Wisconsin Dells (☑ 800-223-3557; www.wisdells.com; Hwy 12; ▣) The Dells is a megacenter of kitschy diversions, including 20-plus water parks, water-skiing thrill shows and epic mini-golf courses. It's a jolting contrast to the natural appeal of the area, with its scenic limestone formations carved by the Wisconsin River. To appreciate the original attraction, take a boat tour or walk the trails at nearby Mirror Lake or Devil's Lake state parks.

sausages. It's hard to choose among the 150 types of state-brewed suds in bottles, so opt for a sampler (four or eight little glasses) from the 50 Wisconsin tap beers.

L'Etoile AMERICAN $$$
(☑ 608-251-0500; www.letoile-restaurant.com; 1 S Pinckney St; mains $36-48; ◎ 5:30-9pm Tue-Fri, from 5pm Sat) 🍴 L'Etoile started doing the farm-to-table thing more than three decades ago. It's still the best in the biz, offering creative meat, fish and vegetable dishes, all sourced locally and served in a casually elegant room. Reserve in advance. The gastropub **Graze** (☑ 608-251-2700; www.grazemadison.com; mains $14-22; ◎ 11am-10pm Mon-Thu, 11am-11pm Fri, 9:30am-11pm Sat, 9:30am-3pm Sun) shares the glimmering building.

★ Memorial Union PUB
(☑ 608-265-3000; www.union.wisc.edu/visit/memorial-union; 800 Langdon St; ◎ 7am-midnight Mon-Fri, 8am-1am Sat, to midnight Sun; 🛜) The campus Union is Madison's gathering spot. The festive lakeside terrace pours microbrews and hosts free live music and free Monday-night films, while the indoor ice-

cream shop scoops hulking cones from the university dairy.

🛈 Information

Madison Convention & Visitors Bureau (www.visitmadison.com)

🛈 Getting There & Away

Badger Bus (www.badgerbus.com) has a streetside stop on campus at 700 Langdon St (next to the Memorial Union) for trips to/from Milwaukee ($20, two hours). Megabus (www.megabus.com/us) uses the same stop for trips to Chicago (four hours) and Minneapolis (five hours).

Spring Green

Spring Green is a tiny town with big culture. Taliesin is here, Frank Lloyd Wright's ballyhooed home and architectural school. The respected American Players Theatre is also here, staging classics outdoors amid the trees. And the House on the Rock is a short distance down the road, offering enough whimsy for a lifetime.

◉ Sights

Taliesin ARCHITECTURE
(📱608-588-7900; www.taliesinpreservation.
org; 5607 County Rd C; ⊙9am-5:30pm May-Oct)
Taliesin was the home of Frank Lloyd Wright
for most of his life and is the site of his architectural school. It's now a major pilgrimage
destination for fans. The house was built
in 1903, the Hillside Home School in 1932,
and the visitor center in 1953. A wide range
of guided tours ($22 to $89) cover various
parts of the complex; it's wise to book ahead
(for a small surcharge). The one-hour Hillside Tour ($22) provides a nice introduction
to Wright's work.

Note the visitor center (with its restaurant
and shop) is in a separate location about a
half-mile from the main estate.

House on the Rock MUSEUM
(📱608-935-3639; www.thehouseontherock.com;
5754 Hwy 23; adult/child $15/9; ⊙9am-5pm May-
mid-Oct, Thu-Mon only mid-Oct–Nov & mid-Mar–
Apr, closed mid-Nov–mid-Mar) One of Wisconsin's busiest attractions. Alex Jordan built
the structure atop a rock column in 1959
(some say as an 'up yours' to neighbor Frank
Lloyd Wright). He then stuffed the house
to mind-blowing proportions with wonder-
ments, including the world's largest carousel, whirring music machines, freaky dolls
and crazed folk art. The house is broken into
three parts, each with its own tour. Visitors
with stamina (and about four hours to kill)
can experience the whole shebang for adult/
child $30/16.

🛏 Sleeping & Eating

Usonian Inn MOTEL $
(📱608-588-2323; www.usonianinn.com; E 5116 US
14; r $100-135; ❄🐾) Designed by one of Frank
Lloyd Wright's students, the 11-room Usonian is a fairly basic motel, but with dapper,
Prairie-style touches in the lamps, woodwork and other decor. Each room has a little
patio with chairs.

> ### ℹ ROAD-TRIP THE MISSISSIPPI
> ....
> If you're thinking of taking to the road,
> have a look at the Wisconsin Great River
> Road website (www.wigrr.com). It sug-
> gests lots of activities, lodging and plac-
> es to eat along the Mississippi River.

Spring Green General Store AMERICAN $
(📱608-588-7070; www.springgreengeneralstore.
com; 137 S Albany St; mains $7-9; ⊙8:30am-5pm
Mon-Fri, 7:30am-5pm Sat, to 4pm Sun) Chomp
sandwiches or inventive specials like
sweet-potato stew. You can eat 'em at the
sturdy wood tables in the bright-painted interior, or outside on the porch.

☆ Entertainment

American Players Theatre THEATER
(📱608-588-2361; www.americanplayers.org; 5950
Golf Course Rd) It stages classical productions
at an outdoor amphitheater in the woods.
Bring a picnic – it's a tradition to hang out
and nibble before the show.

ℹ Getting There & Away

Hwy 14 is the main road to town. Taliesin is 3
miles south of town via Hwy 23. The House on
the Rock is 7 miles further south.

Southwest Wisconsin

Southwest Wisconsin brings on swooping
green hills and button-cute towns with
tree-shaded streets. Two-lane byways dip
and curve through the region, revealing eating hot spots around many a bend.

The Mississippi River forms the southwest's border, and alongside it run some of
the prettiest sections of the Great River Road
– the designated route that follows Old Man
River throughout its 2300-mile flow. Top
stops along the water include Stockholm
(pie), Pepin (for Laura Ingalls Wilder fans),
Nelson (cheese and ice cream), La Crosse
(history and culture) and Potosi (beer).

Road-tripping inland turns up bike trails
in Sparta, organic farms and round barns in
Viroqua, and a Frank Lloyd Wright sight in
Richland Center.

◉ Sights

Laura Ingalls Wilder Museum MUSEUM
(📱715-513-6383; www.lauraingallspepin.com; 306
3rd St, Pepin; adult/child $5/2; ⊙10am-5pm mid-
May–mid-Oct) *Little House on the Prairie*
fans can make a pit stop at the Laura Ingalls
Wilder Museum. This is where she was born
and the abode that starred in *Little House in
the Big Woods*. There's not a lot in the museum (and the building itself is a replica),
but die-hards will appreciate being on the
authentic patch of land once homesteaded
by Ma and Pa Ingalls.

Eating

★ Stockholm Pie & General Store
BAKERY $

(☑ 715-442-5505; www.stockholmpieandgeneral-store.com; N2030 Spring St, Stockholm; slices $6; ⊙10am-4:30pm Mon & Thu, to 5pm Fri-Sun) You may have to wait in line at this old-timey spot with wood plank floors and red-checkered tablecloths, but that allows you to study the blackboard and its lengthy list of pies available. Sour cream raisin, double lemon, triple chocolate pecan, butterscotch cream – they're all world class.

Eastern Wisconsin

The eastern part of the state is a holiday favorite thanks to its miles of craggy shoreline for boating, swimming and fishing, its beaming lighthouses and its atmospheric maritime communities. Lonely islands, meals of fiery fish and football shrines all await, and there's always a lake or forest nearby for a nature fix.

Green Bay

Green Bay is a modest industrial town best known as the fabled 'frozen tundra' where the Green Bay Packers win Super Bowls. The franchise is unique as the only community-owned nonprofit team in the NFL; perhaps pride in ownership is what makes the fans so die-hard (and also makes them wear foam-rubber cheese wedges on their heads).

While tickets are nearly impossible to obtain, you can always get into the spirit by joining a pregame tailgate party. The generous flow of alcohol has led to Green Bay's reputation as a 'drinking town with a football problem.' Otherwise the town is pretty quiet. It has a couple of intriguing museums and a well-known brewery by the stadium, plus a nice patch of cafes on its riverfront.

◉ Sights

Green Bay Packers Hall of Fame
MUSEUM

(☑ 920-569-7512; www.lambeaufield.com; 1265 Lombardi Ave; adult/child $15/12; ⊙9am-6pm Mon-Sat, 10am-5pm Sun) The two-floor Hall of Fame at Lambeau Field is packed with memorabilia, shiny trophies and movies about the storied NFL team that'll intrigue any football fan. Stadium tours are also available. Lots of new development is going on around the arena, including a snow-tubing hill, ice-skating pond and flashy new hotel.

National Railroad Museum
MUSEUM

(☑ 920-437-7623; www.nationalrrmuseum.org; 2285 S Broadway; adult/child $10/7.50; ⊙9am-5pm Mon-Sat, 11am-5pm Sun, closed Mon Jan-Mar; ▣) The museum features some of the biggest locomotives ever to haul freight into Green Bay's vast yards; train rides ($2) are offered in summer.

❶ Getting There & Away

Green Bay has a small airport with flights to Chicago, Minneapolis, Detroit and Atlanta. Greyhound has a station in town. I-43 comes into Green Bay from the east. I-41 comes in from the west.

Door County

With its rocky coastline, picturesque lighthouses, cherry orchards and small 19th-century villages, you have to admit Door County is pretty damn lovely. Honeymooners, families and outdoorsy types all flock in to take advantage of the parkland that blankets the area and the clapboard hamlets packed with winsome cafes, galleries and inns.

The county spreads across a narrow peninsula jutting 75 miles into Lake Michigan. The side that borders the lake proper is known as the more scenic 'quiet side,' home to the communities of Jacksonport and Baileys Harbor. The side that borders Green Bay is more action oriented, where Egg Harbor, Fish Creek, Ephraim and Sister Bay welcome travelers. Summer is prime time. Only about half the businesses stay open from November to April.

◉ Sights & Activities

Cave Point County Park
PARK

(5360 Schauer Rd) FREE Nature is pretty amazing, you think as you watch waves explode into the caves beneath the shoreline cliffs. Shutterbugs can get great photos here. The hiking and biking paths take you to gorgeous vistas. Bonus: Cave Point is more off the beaten path and less visited than its state park siblings. It's also free.

Newport State Park
STATE PARK

(475 County Rd NP; per vehicle $11) Newport is one of Door County's quietest parks, tucked away at the peninsula's northern fringe. It has a beautiful beach, 30 miles of hiking trails (about half of which double as off-road bike trails) and year-round, walk-in-only camping in forested seclusion.

Bay Shore Outfitters OUTDOORS
(📞920-854-9220; www.kayakdoorcounty.com;
2457 S Bay Shore Dr, Sister Bay) Rents kayaks,
stand-up paddleboards and winter gear and
offers a variety of kayak tours (from $45 per
two-hour trip).

🛏 Sleeping & Eating

Egg Harbor Lodge INN $$
(📞920-868-3115; www.eggharborlodge.com; 7965
Hwy 42, Egg Harbor; r $170-210; ❄🖥🏊) Rooms
are good-sized and have a water view. Amen-
ities include a small outdoor pool, indoor
Jacuzzi and patio area prime for sunset
watching. No children allowed.

Julie's Park Cafe and Motel MOTEL $$
(📞920-868-2999; www.juliesmotel.com; 4020
Hwy 42, Fish Creek; r $125-139; ❄🖥🍽) Julie's is
a great low-cost option located beside Peninsula State Park. The rooms are nothing
fancy, but they're well maintained and have
comfy beds. The attached cafe serves eggs,
sandwiches and burgers all day.

Wild Tomato PIZZA $
(📞920-868-3095; www.wildtomatopizza.com;
4023 Hwy 42, Fish Creek; mains $9-17; ⏲11am-
10pm Jun-Aug, reduced hours Sep-May) Join the
crowds indoors and out munching pizzas
from the stone, wood-fired ovens. A lengthy
list of craft beers help wash it down. It's extremely gluten-free friendly.

ℹ Information

Door County Visitors Bureau (www.door-
county.com) has special-interest brochures on
art galleries, biking and lighthouses.

WORTH A TRIP

SCENIC DRIVE: HIGHWAY 13

Hwy 13 moseys through a pretty landscape between Bayfield and Superior.
Toward the east it routes around the
Lake Superior shore, past the Chippewa
community of **Red Cliff** and the Apostle Islands' mainland segment, which
has a beach. Tiny **Cornucopia**, looking
every bit like a seaside village, has great
sunsets. Toward the west the road runs
through a timeless countryside of forest
and farm. See www.lakesuperiorbyway.
org for more.

ℹ Getting There & Away

You'll need a car to get to Door County. Two
small highways serve the peninsula. Hwy 57 runs
beside Lake Michigan, while Hwy 42 moseys beside Green Bay (the body of water, not the city).
Be prepared for heavy traffic on weekends.

Northern Wisconsin

The north is a thinly populated region of
forests and lakes, where folks paddle and
fish in summer, and ski and snowmobile in
winter. Mountain-biking trails continue to
expand and draw fat tires. Nicolet National
Forest and Chequamegon National Forest
protect much of the area and provide the
playground for these activities. But it's the
windswept Apostle Islands that really steal
the show.

Apostle Islands

The 21 rugged Apostle Islands, floating in
Lake Superior and freckling Wisconsin's
northern tip, are a state highlight. Forested and windblown, trimmed with cliffs
and caves, the national park gems have no
facilities. Various companies offer seasonal
boat trips around the islands, and kayaking
and hiking are very popular. Jump off from
Bayfield, a humming resort town with hilly
streets, Victorian-era buildings, apple orchards and nary a fast-food restaurant in
sight.

⊙ Sights & Activities

No wonder everyone is grabbing a paddle.
Kayaking in the Apostles pays off big in
scenery, with stacks of dusty red rock arches
and pillars rising from the water. Caves on
the craggy shores of Devils Island and Sand
Island are stars of the show. Note that much
of the kayaking here is for experienced paddlers only; novices should go with a guide,
as conditions can be rough and windy. The
national park publishes a *Paddling in the
Apostles* brochure with information on kayak launch points and tips on how to prepare.
Bayfield has outfitters and guides, such as
Living Adventure.

Madeline Island ISLAND
(www.madelineisland.com) Inhabited Madeline
Island makes a fine day trip and is reached
by a 25-minute ferry from Bayfield. The isle's
walkable village of La Pointe has a couple
of mid-priced places to stay, a smattering

of eateries and a groovy 'burned down' bar (made from junk and tarps). Bike and moped rentals are available – everything is near the ferry dock. While Madeline is an Apostle Island, it's not part of the national park group, hence its development.

Big Bay State Park   STATE PARK
([☑] 715-747-6425; Hagen Rd; per car $11, tent sites $25-35) Big Bay is at Madeline Island's far edge, with a pretty beach and hiking trails. The well-maintained campsites are awesome and book up fast.

Living Adventure   KAYAKING
([☑] 715-779-9503; www.livingadventure.com; 88260 Hwy 13; half-/full-day tour $59/109; [☉] Jun-Sep) Offers guided paddling trips to sea caves and shipwrecks; beginners are welcome. The company also rents kayaks (per one/two days $69/99) and provides shuttle service to launch sites.

[🛏] **Sleeping**

Camping permits (per night $15) are required for the national park islands. You must get them in advance online (www.recreation.gov; reservation fee $10).

Bayfield loads up on tidy motels, B&Bs and swanky inns. Madeline Island has a handful of inns and cottages.

Seagull Bay Motel   MOTEL $
([☑] 715-779-5558; www.seagullbay.com; 325 S 7th St; r $110-130; [☎]) The no-frills rooms may be smallish and thin-walled, but most have a little patio or deck with lake views (ask when booking). A nifty trail runs from the motel to downtown, a 10-minute walk away.

[✗] **Eating**

Fat Radish   AMERICAN $$
([☑] 715-779-9700; www.thefatradish.weebly.com; 200 Rittenhouse Ave; sandwiches $7-10, mains $16-24; [☉] 9am-3pm & 5-9pm Mon-Sat, 9am-2pm Sun, closed Mon in winter) [🍴] The Radish uses quality, sustainable ingredients in its deli wares. It's located by the docks and handy for amassing snacks to take on the boat tours. At night the chef serves tasty pizzas and seafood dishes.

Maggie's   AMERICAN $$
([☑] 715-779-5641; www.maggies-bayfield.com; 257 Manypenny Ave; mains $11-22; [☉] 11:30am-9pm) Kitschy, flamingo-themed Maggie's is the place to sample local lake trout and whitefish; there are pizza and burgers too.

CHEQUAMEGON NATIONAL FOREST

Chequamegon National Forest offers exceptional mountain biking with 300 miles of off-road trails. The Chequamegon Area Mountain Bike Association (www.cambatrails.org) has trail maps and bike rental information. The town of Hayward makes an excellent base and is near several trailheads.

[ℹ] **Information**

Apostle Islands National Lakeshore Visitors Center ([☑] 715-779-3397; www.nps.gov/apis; 410 Washington Ave; [☉] 8am-4:30pm late May–Sep, closed Sat & Sun rest of year) Has camping, paddling and hiking information.
Bayfield Chamber of Commerce (www.bayfield.org) Good listings of lodgings and things to do in the area.

[ℹ] **Getting There & Away**

The **Madeline Island Ferry** ([☑] 715-747-2051; www.madferry.com; Washington Ave; round trip adult/child/bicycle/car $14/7/7/25) makes the 25-minute trip from Bayfield to Madeline Island. It goes year-round, except when the water freezes (usually between January and March, when there is an ice bridge). Apostle Island Cruises drops off kayakers at various islands. Experienced paddlers kayak out to some of the closer islands.

MINNESOTA

Is Minnesota really the land of 10,000 lakes, as it's so often advertised? You betcha! Actually, in typically modest style, the state has undermarketed itself – there are 11,842 lakes. Which is great news for travelers. Intrepid outdoors folk can wet their paddles in the Boundary Waters, where nighttime brings a blanket of stars and the lullaby of wolf howls. Those wanting to get further off the beaten path can journey to Voyageurs National Park, where there's more water than roadway. If that all seems too far-flung, stick to the Twin Cities of Minneapolis and St Paul, where you can't swing a moose without hitting something cool or cultural. For those looking for middle ground the dramatic, freighter-filled port of Duluth beckons.

ℹ Information

Minnesota Highway Conditions (www.511mn. org)

Minnesota Office of Tourism (www.explore minnesota.com)

Minnesota State Park Information (☑888-646-6367; www.dnr.state.mn.us) Park entry requires a vehicle permit (per day/year $5/25). Campsites cost $15 to $31; reservations (☑866-857-2757; www.dnr.state.mn.us/ state_parks/reservations.html) accepted for an $8.50 fee online, $10 by phone.

Minneapolis

Minneapolis is the biggest and artiest town on the prairie, with all the trimmings of progressive prosperity – swank art museums, rowdy rock clubs, organic and ethnic eateries and edgy theaters. It's always happenin', even in winter. And here's the bonus: folks are attitude-free and the embodiment of 'Minnesota Nice.' Count how many times they tell you to 'Have a great day,' come rain or shine or snow.

History

Timber was the city's first boom industry, and water-powered sawmills rose along the Mississippi River in the mid-1800s. Wheat from the prairies also needed to be processed, so flour mills churned into the next big business. The population boomed in the late 19th century with mass immigration, especially from Scandinavia and Germany. Today Minneapolis' Nordic heritage is evident, whereas twin city St Paul is more German and Irish-Catholic.

PRINCE WAS HERE

Minneapolis' most famous former resident is the rock star Prince. Even before his shocking death in 2016, visitors flocked to town to follow his trail. The city's tourism bureau has a map of Prince hot spots, including his childhood home, the house from *Purple Rain* and **Paisley Park** (www.officialpaisleypark. com; 7801 Audubon Rd, Chanhassen; tours from $38.50, service fee $7.50; ☺Thu-Sun), his famed home/recording studio. For more check out www.minneapolis.org/ princes-minneapolis.

◉ Sights & Activities

Most attractions are closed Monday; many stay open late on Thursday.

◉ Downtown & Loring Park

★ Walker Art Center MUSEUM
(☑612-375-7600; www.walkerart.org; 1750 Hennepin Ave; adult/child $14/free; ☺11am-5pm Tue, Wed & Sun, to 9pm Thu, to 6pm Fri & Sat) The first-class art center has a strong permanent collection of 20th-century art and photography, including big-name US painters and great US pop art. On Monday evenings from late July to late August, the museum hosts free movies and music across the pedestrian bridge in Loring Park that are quite the to-do.

★ Minneapolis Sculpture Garden GARDENS
(725 Vineland Pl; ☺6am-midnight) FREE This 19-acre green space, studded with contemporary works such as the oft-photographed *Spoonbridge & Cherry* by Claes Oldenburg, sits beside the Walker Art Center. The Cowles Conservatory, abloom with exotic hothouse flowers, is also on the grounds.

◉ Riverfront District

★ Endless Bridge OBSERVATORY
(818 2nd St S; ☺8am-8pm, to 11pm on performance days) FREE Head inside the cobalt-blue Guthrie Theater and make your way up the escalator to the Endless Bridge, a far-out cantilevered walkway overlooking the Mississippi River. You don't need a theater ticket, as it's intended as a public space. The theater's 9th-floor Amber Box provides another knockout view.

Mill City Museum MUSEUM
(☑612-341-7555; www.millcitymuseum.org; 704 2nd St S; adult/child $12/6; ☺10am-5pm Tue-Sat, noon-5pm Sun) The building is indeed a former mill, and highlights include a ride inside an eight-story grain elevator (the 'Flour Tower'), Betty Crocker exhibits and a baking lab. It's not terribly exciting unless you're really into milling history, though the mill ruins in back are an atmospheric sight. A foodie-favorite farmers market takes place in the attached train shed on Saturday mornings May through September.

St Anthony Falls Heritage Trail WALKING
The 1.8-mile path provides both interesting history (placards dot the route) and the city's best access to the banks of the Missis-

MINNEAPOLIS FOR CHILDREN

Minnesota Zoo (☑952-431-9500; www.mnzoo.org; 13000 Zoo Blvd; adult/child $18/12; ⊙9am-6pm summer, to 4pm winter; ⊛) You'll have to travel a way to get to the respected zoo in suburban Apple Valley, which is 20 miles south of town. It has naturalistic habitats for its 400-plus species, with an emphasis on cold-climate creatures. Parking is $7.

Valleyfair (☑952-445-7600; www.valleyfair.com; 1 Valleyfair Dr; per person $53; ⊙from 10am Jun-Aug, reduced hours Sep & Oct; ⊛) If the rides at the Mall of America aren't enough, drive out to this full-scale amusement park 22 miles southwest in Shakopee. The animatronic dinosaur park ($5 extra) is a big hit. Save money by booking tickets online. Parking costs $12.

Children's Theatre Company (☑612-874-0400; www.childrenstheatre.org; 2400 3rd Ave S; ⊛) This local troupe is so good it won a Tony award for 'outstanding regional theater.' The production values are first-rate.

sippi River. It starts at the foot of Portland Ave and goes over the car-free Stone Arch Bridge, from which you can view cascading St Anthony Falls.

◉ Northeast

Once a working-class Eastern European neighborhood, Northeast (so named because of its position to the river) is where urbanites and artists now work and play. They appreciate the dive bars pouring microbrews along with Pabst, and boutiques selling eco-gifts next to companies grinding sausage. Hundreds of craftsfolk and galleries fill historic industrial buildings. They fling open their doors the first Thursday of each month when the Northeast Minneapolis Arts Association (www.nemaa.org) sponsors a gallery walk. Heady streets include 4th St NE and 13th Ave NE.

◉ University Area

The University of Minnesota, by the river southeast of Minneapolis' center, is one of the USA's largest campuses, with some 50,000 students. Most of the campus is in the East Bank neighborhood. Dinkytown, based at 14th Ave SE and 4th St SE, is dense with student cafes and bookshops. A small part of the university is on the West Bank of the Mississippi River, near the intersection of 4th St S and Riverside Ave. This area has a few restaurants, some student hangouts and a big Somali community.

★ **Weisman Art Museum** MUSEUM
(☑612-625-9494; www.wam.umn.edu; 333 E River Rd; ⊙10am-5pm Tue, Thu & Fri, to 8pm Wed, 11am-5pm Sat & Sun) FREE The Weisman, which occupies a swooping silver structure by archi-

tect Frank Gehry, is a university highlight. The airy main galleries hold cool collections of 20th-century American art, ceramics, Korean furniture and works on paper.

◉ Uptown, Lyn-Lake & Whittier

★ **Minneapolis Institute of Arts** MUSEUM
(☑612-870-3131; www.artsmia.org; 2400 3rd Ave S; ⊙10am-5pm Tue, Wed & Sat, 10am-9pm Thu & Fri, 11am-5pm Sun) FREE This museum is a huge trove housing a veritable history of art. The modern and contemporary collections will astonish, while the Asian galleries (2nd floor) and Decorative Arts rooms (3rd floor) are also highlights.

✦ Festivals & Events

Art-A-Whirl ART
(www.nemaa.org; ⊙mid-May) The Northeast's weekend-long, rock-and-roll gallery crawl heralds the arrival of spring. Held at studios throughout the neighborhood.

Pride Festival LGBT
(www.tcpride.org; ⊙late Jun) The Pride Festival, one of the USA's largest, draws more than 300,000 revelers to Loring Park.

Minneapolis Aquatennial CULTURAL
(www.aquatennial.com; ⊙3rd week Jul) Celebrates the ubiquitous lakes via parades, beach bashes and fireworks. Held at various venues around downtown and along the riverfront.

🛏 Sleeping

★ **Wales House** GUESTHOUSE $
(☑612-331-3931; www.waleshouse.com; 1115 5th St SE; r $95, with shared bath $85; P⊛🛜) This cheery 10-bedroom B&B often houses

Minneapolis

scholars from the nearby University of Minnesota. Curl up with a book on the porch, or lounge by the fireplace. A two-night minimum stay is required.

Minneapolis International Hostel HOSTEL **$**
(☑ 612-522-5000; www.minneapolishostel.com; 2400 Stevens Ave S; dm $40-45, r from $55; ❋ ☎) It's set in a cool old building with antique furniture and wood floors, and the location beside the Minneapolis Institute of Arts is excellent. But it's also not very well tended to. The rooms come in a variety of configurations, from a 15-bed male dorm to private rooms with en suite bath.

Aloft HOTEL **$$**
(☑ 612-455-8400; www.aloftminneapolis.com; 900 Washington Ave S; r $159-265; P ❋ @ ☎ ☎) Aloft's efficiently designed, industrial-toned rooms draw a younger clientele. The clubby lobby has board games, a cocktail lounge and 24-hour snacks. There's a tiny pool, a decent fitness room and a bike-share station outside the front door. Parking costs $20.

Hewing Hotel HOTEL **$$**
(☑ 651-468-0400; www.hewinghotel.com; 300 N Washington Ave; r $140-260; P ❋ ☎ ☎ ☎) Opened in late 2016 this hotel in the North Loop offers 124 rooms spread through a century-old farm machine warehouse. The vibe is rustic and cozy. The handsome chambers feature wood-beam ceilings, exposed brick walls and distinctive outdoorsy decor, such as deer-print wallpaper and plaid wool blankets. It's within walking distance of downtown's action. Parking costs $41.

✗ Eating

Culinary magazine *Saveur* recently dubbed Minneapolis as 'America's next great food city' for its creative, sustainable, approachable and distinctively Midwestern fare.

Minneapolis

⚔ Downtown & Loring Park

Peninsula MALAYSIAN **$**
(☎612-871-8282; www.peninsulamalaysiancuisine.
com; 2608 Nicollet Ave S; mains $9-15; ⊙11am-
10pm Sun-Thu, to 11pm Fri & Sat; 🍴) Malaysian
dishes – including red curry hot pot, spicy
crab and fish in banana leaves – rock the
palate in this contemporary restaurant.

Hell's Kitchen AMERICAN **$$**
(☎612-332-4700; www.hellskitcheninc.com; 80
9th St S; mains $12-24; ⊙6:30am-11pm Mon-Fri,
from 7:30am Sat & Sun; 🛜) Descend the stairs
to Hell's devilish lair, where spirited waitstaff
bring you uniquely Minnesotan foods, like
the walleye bacon-lettuce-tomato sandwich,
bison burger, Juicy Lucy (melted cheese in
the middle of a burger) and lemon-ricotta
hotcakes. Upstairs there's a delicious bakery
and coffee shop.

Butcher & the Boar AMERICAN **$$$**
(☎612-238-8888; www.butcherandtheboar.com;
1121 Hennepin Ave; mains $32-48; ⊙5-10:30pm
Mon-Thu, to 11pm Fri & Sat, to 10pm Sun; 🛜) The
coppery, candlelit room is carnivore nirvana. Get your carving knife ready for wild
boar ham with country butter, chicken-fried
veal sausage and many more house-crafted
meats. Sampler plates are the way to go. The
30 taps flow with regional brews, backed up
by a lengthy bourbon list (flights available).
Make reservations, or opt for meaty small
plates in the rockin' beer garden.

Bachelor Farmer AMERICAN **$$$**
(☎612-206-3920; www.thebachelorfarmer.com;
50 2nd Ave N; mains $19-35; ⊙5:30-9:30pm Mon-
Thu, to 10:30pm Fri & Sat, 5-9:30pm Sun) 🍃 The
dishes at this fun restaurant play on the re-
gion's Scandinavian heritage: smoked fish,
meatballs and cheese-and-pickled-mush-
room-topped toast making frequent appear-
ances on the ever-changing menu. The chef
grows all the herbs and veggies in a rooftop
garden. **Marvel Bar**, the restaurant's sibling,
hides in the basement behind an unmarked
door and is primo for cocktails.

⚔ Northeast

★ **Young Joni** PIZZA **$$**
(☎612-345-5719; www.youngjoni.com; 165 13th
Ave NE; mains $13-18; ⊙4-11pm Tue-Thu, 4pm-mid-
night Fri, noon-midnight Sat, noon-10pm Sun)
Young Joni fuses two seemingly unrelated
types: pizza and Korean food. So you can
order a wood-fired, crisp-crusted prosciutto,
Gruyere and ricotta pie with a side of spicy
clams, kimchi and tofu. It sounds odd, but
the dishes are terrific. Bonus: the hip, industrial space has a hidden bar in back. If the
red light is on, the cocktails are flowing.

⚔ University Area

Al's Breakfast BREAKFAST **$**
(☎612-331-9991; 413 14th Ave SE; mains $5-9;
⊙6am-1pm Mon-Sat, 9am-1pm Sun) The ultimate hole in the wall: 14 stools at a tiny
counter. Whenever a customer comes in,
everyone picks up their plates and scoots
down to make room for the newcomer.
Fruit-full pancakes and bacon waffles are
the big crowd pleasers. Cash only.

⚔ Uptown, Lyn-Lake & Whittier

Bryant-Lake Bowl AMERICAN **$**
(☎612-825-3737; www.bryantlakebowl.com; 810 W
Lake St; mains $10-15; ⊙8am-12:30am; 🛜🍴) A
workingman's bowling alley meets epicurean food at the BLB. Biscuit-and-gravy break-

---

LGBT MINNEAPOLIS

Minneapolis has one of the country's highest percentages of gay, lesbian, bisexual and
transgender (GLBT) residents, and the city enjoys strong GLBT rights. Pick up the free,
biweekly magazine *Lavender* (www.lavendermagazine.com) at coffee shops around
town for info on the scene. Top picks:

Wilde Cafe (☎612-331-4544; www.wilderoastcafe.com; 65 Main St SE; ⊙7am-11pm) It features amazing baked goods, riverfront digs and a Victorian ambience worthy of its namesake, Oscar Wilde; *Lavender* once ranked it 'best cafe.'

Gay Nineties (☎612-333-7755; www.gay90s.com; 408 Hennepin Ave; ⊙8am-2am Mon-Sat,
from 10am Sun) This longstanding club has dancing, dining and drag shows that attract
both a gay and straight clientele.

Pride Festival (p599) It's one of the USA's largest, drawing some 300,000 revelers.

TAPROOM BOOM

Minneapolis is all in on the local brewing trend, and most makers have taprooms. Excellent ones to try for beer fresh from the tank:

Fulton Beer (☑612-333-3208; www.fultonbeer.com; 414 6th Ave N; ◷3-10pm Tue-Thu, to 11pm Fri, noon-11pm Sat, noon-6pm Sun) There's usually a fab pale ale and blonde ale among the selection that you sip at communal picnic tables in the warehouse. It's a few blocks from the baseball stadium and fills up on game days. Food trucks hang out in front.

Dangerous Man Brewing (☑612-236-4087; www.dangerousmanbrewing.com; 1300 2nd St NE; ◷4-10pm Tue-Thu, 3pm-midnight Fri, noon-midnight Sat, noon-8pm Sun) Pours strong, European-style beers in the hip-happenin' Northeast. You're welcome to bring in your own food (there's a choice fish-and-chips place a block east).

Surly Brewing (☑763-999-4040; www.surlybrewing.com; 520 Malcolm Ave SE; ◷11am-11pm Sun-Thu, to midnight Fri & Sat; ☑) Surly's sprawling, mod-industrial, family-friendly beer hall is mobbed by locals who come for the 20 rotating taps and abundant meaty snacks. Try CynicAle, a Belgian-style saison, or Furious, the flagship American IPA. It's in the Prospect Park neighborhood, next to the university and a short walk from the Prospect Park Green Line rail station.

fasts, spicy Gouda mac 'n' cheese, mock duck potstickers and smoked whitefish melt in the mouth. Long list of local beers.

🍷 Drinking & Nightlife

Grumpy's   BAR
(☑612-789-7429; www.grumpys-bar.com; 2200 4th St NE; ◷2pm-2am Mon-Fri, from 11am Sat & Sun) Grumpy's is the Northeast's classic dive, with cheap (but good local) beer and an outdoor patio. Sample the specialty 'hot dish' on Tuesdays for $1.

☆ Entertainment

Icehouse   LIVE MUSIC
(☑612-276-6523; www.icehousempls.com; 2528 Nicollet Ave S; ◷11am-2am Mon-Fri, from 10am Sat & Sun) A gorgeous, great-sounding venue for jazz, folk and progressive hip-hop acts. Oh, and swank cocktails, too.

First Avenue & 7th St Entry   LIVE MUSIC
(☑612-332-1775; www.first-avenue.com; 701 1st Ave N) This is the longstanding bedrock of Minneapolis's music scene. First Avenue is the main room featuring national acts; smaller 7th St Entry is for up-and-comers. Check out the exterior stars on the building: they're all bands that have graced the stage.

Guthrie Theater   THEATER
(☑612-377-2224; www.guthrietheater.org; 818 2nd St S) This is Minneapolis' top-gun theater troupe, with the jumbo facility to prove it. Unsold 'rush' tickets go on sale 30 minutes before showtime for $15 to $35 (cash only).

Brave New Workshop Theatre   THEATER
(☑612-332-6620; www.bravenewworkshop.com; 824 Hennepin Ave) An established venue for musical comedy, revue and satire.

Target Field   BASEBALL
(☑800-338-9467; www.minnesotatwins.com; 353 N 5th St) The Minnesota Twins' baseball stadium is notable for its beyond-the-norm, locally focused food and drink.

US Bank Stadium   FOOTBALL
(☑612-338-4537; www.vikings.com; 900 5th St S) The NFL's Vikings play at this spiffy, glass-walled indoor arena, which opened in 2016.

ℹ Information

Minneapolis Convention & Visitors Association (www.minneapolis.org) Coupons, maps, guides and bike-route info online.

City Pages (www.citypages.com) Weekly entertainment freebie.

Pioneer Press (www.twincities.com) St Paul's daily newspaper.

Star Tribune (www.startribune.com) Minneapolis' daily newspaper.

ℹ Getting There & Away

The Minneapolis–St Paul International Airport (p606) is between these two cities to the south. It's a hub for Delta Airlines, which operates several direct flights to/from Europe.

The Blue Line light-rail service (regular/rush-hour fare $1.75/2.25, 25 minutes) is the cheapest way into Minneapolis. Taxis cost around $45.

Greyhound (☑612-371-3325; www.greyhound.com; 950 Hawthorne Ave; ☎) runs frequent

MALL OF AMERICA

Welcome to the USA's largest shopping center. Yes, the **Mall of America** (☑952-883-8800; www.mallofamerica.com; off I-494 at 24th Ave; ⊙10am-9:30pm Mon-Sat, 11am-7pm Sun; 🖈) is just a mall, filled with the usual stores, movie theaters and eateries. But there's also a wedding chapel inside. And an 18-hole **mini-golf course** (☑952-883-8777; 3rd fl, Mall of America; per person $10; ⊙10am-9:30pm Mon-Sat, 11am-7pm Sun). And a zip line. And an amusement park, aka **Nickelodeon Universe** (☑952-883-8800; www.nickelodeon-universe.com; ⊙10am-9:30pm Mon-Sat, 11am-7pm Sun), with 27 rides, including a couple of scream-inducing roller coasters. To walk through will cost you nothing; a one-day, unlimited-ride wristband is $36; or you can pay for rides individually ($3.50 to $7).

What's more, the state's largest aquarium, **Sea Life Minnesota** (☑952-883-0202; www.visitsealife.com/minnesota; adult/child $25/18; ⊙10am-7pm Mon-Thu, to 8pm Fri & Sat, to 6pm Sun; 🖈) – brimming with sharks, jellyfish and stingrays – is in the mall too. Combination passes are available to save dough. The Blue Line light-rail runs to/from downtown Minneapolis. The mall is in suburban Bloomington, a 10-minute ride from the airport.

buses to Milwaukee (seven hours), Chicago (nine hours) and Duluth (three hours).

Megabus (www.megabus.com/us) runs express to Milwaukee (6½ hours) and Chicago (8½ hours), often for lower fares than Greyhound. It departs from both downtown and the university; check the website for exact locations.

Amtrak chugs in to the newly restored Union Depot (p606) in St Paul. Trains go daily to Chicago (eight hours) and Seattle (38 hours).

❶ Getting Around

Minneapolis hovers near the top of rankings for best bike city in the US. Nice Ride (www.niceridemn.org) is the local bike-share program, with 1800 lime-green bikes in 200 self-serve kiosks around the Twin Cities. A 30-minute ride costs $3. Insert a credit card, get your ride code, then unlock a bike. Traditional rentals work better for longer recreational rides. See the Minneapolis Bicycle Program (www.ci.minneapolis.mn.us/bicycles) for rental shops and trail maps.

Metro Transit (www.metrotransit.org) runs the handy Blue Line light-rail service between downtown and the Mall of America (stopping at the airport en route). The Green Line connects downtown Minneapolis to downtown St Paul. Machines at each station sell fare cards, including a day pass ($6) that also can be used on public buses.

St Paul

Smaller and quieter than its twin city Minneapolis, St Paul has retained more of a historic character. Walk through F Scott Fitzgerald's old stomping grounds, trek the trails along the mighty Mississippi River, or slurp some Lao soup.

◉ Sights & Activities

Downtown and Cathedral Hill hold most of the action. The latter features eccentric shops, Gilded Age Victorian mansions and, of course, the hulking church that gives the area its name. Downtown has the museums. An insider's tip: there's a shortcut between the two areas, a footpath that starts on the Hill House's west side and drops into downtown.

Landmark Center   MUSEUM
(☑651-292-3225; www.landmarkcenter.org; 75 W 5th St; ⊙8am-5pm Mon-Fri, to 8pm Thu, 10am-5pm Sat, noon-5pm Sun) Downtown's turreted 1902 Landmark Center used to be the federal courthouse, where gangsters such as Alvin 'Creepy' Karpis were tried; plaques by the various rooms show who was brought to justice here. In addition to the city's visitor center, the building also contains a couple of small museums (one focusing on wood art, another on music).

Schubert Club Museum   MUSEUM
(☑651-292-3267; www.schubert.org; 75 W 5th St; ⊙noon-4pm Sun-Fri) FREE The Schubert Club Museum has a brilliant collection of old pianos and harpsichords – some tickled by Brahms, Mendelssohn and the like – as well as old manuscripts and letters from famous composers. It's located on the 2nd floor of the Landmark Center. The club also stages free chamber music concerts Thursdays at noon from October through April.

James J Hill House
HISTORIC BUILDING

(☑651-297-2555; www.mnhs.org/hillhouse; 240 Summit Ave; adult/child $10/6; ⊙10am-3:30pm Wed-Sat, from 1pm Sun) Tour the palatial stone mansion of railroad magnate James J Hill. It's a Gilded Age beauty, with five floors and 22 fireplaces. On Monday and Tuesday there are no tours but you can still go in and see the home's art-gallery room ($2), where French landscape paintings hang.

Science Museum of Minnesota
MUSEUM

(☑651-221-9444; www.smm.org; 120 W Kellogg Blvd; adult/child $19/13; ⊙9:30am-9pm Thu-Sat, to 5pm Sun, Tue & Wed) Has the usual hands-on kids' exhibits and Omnimax theater ($6 extra). Adults will be entertained by the wacky quackery of the 4th floor's 'questionable medical devices.'

Harriet Island
PARK

South of downtown and connected via Wabasha St, Harriet Island is a lovely place to meander. It has a river walk, paddle-wheel steamboat cruises, concert stages and fishing docks.

⭐ Festivals & Events

St Paul Winter Carnival
CULTURAL

(www.wintercarnival.com; ⊙late Jan) Ten days of ice sculptures, ice skating and ice fishing. Events take place at Rice Park and other venues around the city.

🛏 Sleeping & Eating

⭐Hotel 340
BOUTIQUE HOTEL $$

(☑651-280-4120; www.hotel340.com; 340 Cedar St; r $109-189; P⊗@⊙) Hotel 340 delivers old-world ambiance aplenty, and it's usually a great deal to boot. The 56 rooms in the stately old building have hardwood floors and plush linens. The two-story lobby stokes a grand fireplace and nifty little bar (the desk staff double as bartenders).

Covington Inn
B&B $$

(☑651-292-1411; www.covingtoninn.com; 100 Harriet Island Rd; r $165-250; P⊗) This four-room, Harriet Island B&B is on a tugboat floating in the Mississippi River; watch the river traffic glide by while sipping your morning coffee. The stately rooms have bright splashes of color, and each has a gas fireplace to keep you toasty in winter.

Hmongtown Marketplace
ASIAN $

(☑651-487-3700; www.hmongtownmarketplace.com; 217 Como Ave; mains $5-8; ⊙8am-8pm) The nation's largest enclave of Hmong immigrants lives in the Twin Cities, and this market delivers their favorite Vietnamese, Lao and Thai dishes at its humble food court. Find the West Building and head to the back where vendors ladle hot-spiced papaya salad, beef ribs and curry noodle soup. Then stroll the market to buy embroidered dresses, a brass gong or lemongrass.

Mickey's Diner
DINER $

(☑651-222-5633; www.mickeysdiningcar.com; 36 W 7th St; mains $4-9; ⊙24hr) Mickey's is a downtown classic, the kind of place where the friendly waitress calls you 'honey' and satisfied regulars line the bar with their coffee cups and newspapers. The food has timeless appeal, too: burgers, malts and apple pie.

⭐Cook
AMERICAN $

(☑651-756-1787; www.cookstp.com; 1124 Payne Ave; mains $10-14; ⊙6:30am-2pm Mon-Fri, 7am-3pm Sat & Sun) This cute, sunny spot serves creative diner dishes (gingery French toast, curried veggie burgers, braised short-rib sandwiches), including some with a spicy Korean twist. Cook also hosts Korean dinners on Friday nights. It's located in the burgeoning East Side neighborhood, where several other foodie hot spots are sprouting on Payne Ave.

🍷 Drinking & Entertainment

Happy Gnome
PUB

(☑651-287-2018; www.thehappygnome.com; 498 Selby Ave; ⊙11am-midnight Mon-Thu, 11am-1am Fri & Sat, 10am-midnight Sun; ⊙) More than 80 craft beers flow from the taps, best sipped on the fireplace-warmed outdoor patio. The pub sits across the parking lot from the St Paul Curling Club.

Fitzgerald Theater
THEATER

(☑651-290-1221; http://fitzgeraldtheater.public radio.org; 10 E Exchange St) Where the popular radio show *A Prairie Home Companion* tapes its live broadcasts. The theater hosts big-name musicians, comedians and authors, as well.

ℹ Information

Mississippi River Visitor Center (☑651-293-0200; www.nps.gov/miss; 120 W Kellogg Blvd; ⊙9:30am-5pm Sun & Tue-Thu, to 9pm Fri & Sat) Operated by the National Park Service, it occupies an alcove in the science museum's lobby. Stop by to pick up trail maps and see

WORLD'S LARGEST BALL O' TWINE

The **World's Largest Ball of Twine** (1st St, Darwin; ⊙24hr) is in Darwin, 60 miles west of Minneapolis on US 12. OK, so there are three other Midwest twine balls also claiming to be the largest, but Darwin maintains it has the 'Largest Built by One Person' – Francis A Johnson wrapped the 17,400lb whopper on his farm over the course of 29 years. Gawk at it in the town gazebo.

what sort of free ranger-guided activities are going on. In summer these include short hikes to the river and bicycle rides. In winter, there are ice-fishing and snowshoeing jaunts.

Visitor Center (☑651-292-3225; www.visitsaintpaul.com; 75 W 5th St; ⊙10am-4pm Mon-Sat, from noon Sun) In the Landmark Center, it makes a good first stop for maps and DIY walking tour info.

ⓘ Getting There & Away

Metro Transit (www.metrotransit.org) runs the handy Green Line train (regular/rush-hour fare $1.75/2.25) between downtown St Paul and downtown Minneapolis. **Union Depot** (☑651-202-2700; www.uniondepot.org; 214 E 4th St; ☎) is the hub for everything: Greyhound buses, city buses, the Green Line trains and Amtrak trains. The **Minneapolis–St Paul International Airport** (MSP; www.mspairport.com; ☎) is 15 miles southwest. Bus 54 (regular/rush-hour fare $1.75/2.25, 25 minutes) goes downtown. A taxi costs around $33.

Southern Minnesota

Southern Minnesota keeps it fresh with a mix of historic river towns, Bluff Country's pastoral hamlets and oddball attractions that involve Spam and the world's largest ball of twine.

Atmospheric towns on the water include Stillwater (antique laden), Red Wing (known for its Red Wing Shoes – actually more like sturdy boots – and salt glaze pottery) and Wabasha (where eagles flock). More intriguing little burgs also pop up along this stretch of the Great River Rd, the scenic thoroughfare that clasps the Mississippi River. Pull over for a slice of pie or kitschy garden gnome shop whenever the mood strikes.

Inland and south, Bluff Country is dotted with pretty limestone cliffs and teeny villages. Lanesboro is a gem for rails-to-trails cycling. Harmony, south of Lanesboro, is the center of an Amish community and another welcoming spot.

The twine ball and **Spam Museum** (☑507-437-5100; www.spam.com; 101 3rd Ave NE, Austin; ⊙10am-6pm Mon-Sat, noon-5pm Sun Apr-Nov, noon-5pm Tue-Sun Dec-Mar; 🅿) FREE are farther flung, but intrepid road-trippers can seek them out.

The river towns feature inns and B&Bs in vintage, restored buildings; Stillwater has them in abundance. Bluff Country towns are also big on B&Bs, as well as campgrounds.

The Great River Rd, aka Hwy 61, rolls along the Mississippi River. If you cross a bridge to the Wisconsin side, it becomes Hwy 35. Minneapolis is an hour or two drive from most hot spots in the region.

Northern Minnesota

Northern Minnesota is where you come to 'do some fishing, do some drinking,' as one resident summed it up.

The area is an outdoor playground, from the fabled Boundary Waters wilderness to the red-cliffed Lake Superior shore to watery Voyageurs National Park. You'll find far fewer people than pine trees populating this rugged expanse. Duluth and Grand Marais are hipper-than-you-think towns to post up in if you need a bit of 'urban' life.

Duluth

At the Great Lakes' westernmost end, Duluth (with its neighbor, Superior, Wisconsin) is one of the busiest ports in the country. The town's dramatic location spliced into a cliff makes it a fab place to see changeable Lake Superior in action. The water, along with the area's trails and natural splendor, has earned Duluth a reputation as a hot spot for outdoors junkies.

⊙ Sights

Hawk Ridge Observatory   OBSERVATORY
(☑218-428-6209; www.hawkridge.org; 3980 E Skyline Pkwy; ⊙6am-10pm) FREE It sits 600-ft above Lake Superior and provides a grand view, especially between mid-August and November, when 94,000 raptors swing by as part of the autumn hawk migration.

Enger Tower   TOWER
(www.engertowerduluth.com; W Skyline Pkwy) FREE The five-story, blue-stone, octagonal

tower is a defining Duluth monument, located in Enger Park. Terrific views of the harbor and Lake Superior reward those who climb the 105 stairs to the top.

Maritime Visitor Center   MUSEUM
(☑ 218-720-5260; www.lsmma.com; 600 S Lake Ave; ◷ 10am-9pm Jun-Aug, reduced hours Sep-May) **FREE** Located next to the **Aerial Lift Bridge**, the center has computer screens inside that tell what time the big ships will be sailing through. Cool model boats and exhibits on Great Lakes shipwrecks also make it a top stop in town.

🏃 Activities

Duluth Experience   ADVENTURE
(☑ 218-464-6337; www.theduluthexperience.com; tours from $55) It offers a range of kayaking, cycling and brewery tours; gear and transportation provided.

Spirit Mountain   SKIING
(☑ 218-628-2891; www.spiritmt.com; 9500 Spirit Mountain Pl; per day adult/child $49/39; ◷ hours vary) Skiing and snowboarding are big pastimes come winter; in summer there's a zipline, alpine slide and mini-golf. The mountain is 10 miles south of Duluth.

🛏 Sleeping

Fitger's Inn   HOTEL **$$**
(☑ 218-722-8826; www.fitgers.com; 600 E Superior St; r $185-290; @ 🛜) Fitger's created its 62 large rooms, each with slightly varied decor, from an old brewery. Located on the Lakewalk, the pricier rooms have great water views. The free shuttle to local sights is handy.

Willard Munger Inn   INN **$$**
(☑ 218-624-4814; www.mungerinn.com; 7408 Grand Ave; r $75-150; @ 🛜) Family-owned Munger Inn offers a fine variety of rooms (budget to Jacuzzi suites), along with perks for outdoor enthusiasts, such as hiking and biking trails right outside the door, free use of bikes and canoes, and a fire pit. Continental breakfast is included. It's near Spirit Mountain.

🍴 Eating & Drinking

⭐ **New Scenic Cafe**   AMERICAN **$$**
(☑ 218-525-6274; www.newseniccafe.com; 5461 North Shore Dr; sandwiches $13-16, mains $24-29; ◷ 11am-9pm Sun-Thu, to 10pm Fri & Sat) 🌱 Foodies travel from far and near to New Scenic Cafe, 8 miles beyond Duluth on Old Hwy 61. There, in a humble wood-paneled room, they fork into rustic salmon with creamed leeks or a slice of triple berry pie, all served with a generous helping of lake views.

Duluth Grill   AMERICAN **$**
(☑ 218-726-1150; www.duluthgrill.com; 118 S 27th Ave W; mains $10-17; ◷ 7am-9pm; 🛜🪑) 🌱 The garden in the parking lot is the tip-off that the Duluth Grill is a sustainable, hippie-vibed place. The dineresque menu ranges from eggy breakfast skillets to curried polenta stew to bison burgers, with plenty of vegan and gluten-free options. It's a couple miles southwest of Canal Park, near the bridge to Superior, Wisconsin.

⭐ **Thirsty Pagan**   BREWERY
(☑ 715-394-2500; www.thirstypaganbrewing.com; 1623 Broadway St; ◷ 11am-10pm Mon-Wed, to 11pm Thu-Sun) This one's a bit of a trek, over the bridge in Superior, Wisconsin (a 10-minute drive), but worth it for the aggressive, spicy beers to wash down hand-tossed pizzas.

Fitger's Brewhouse   BREWERY
(☑ 218-279-2739; www.fitgersbrewhouse.com; 600 E Superior St; ◷ 11am-midnight Sun & Mon, to 1am Tue-Thu, to 2am Fri & Sat) In the hotel complex, the Brewhouse rocks with live music and fresh brews. Try them via the seven-beer sampler (3oz glasses $9).

ℹ Information

Duluth Visitors Center (☑ 800-438-5884; www.visitduluth.com; 21 W Superior St;

DYLAN IN DULUTH

While Hibbing and the Iron Range are most often associated with Bob Dylan, he was born in Duluth. You'll see brown-and-white signs on Superior St and London Rd for **Bob Dylan Way** (www.bobdylanway.com), pointing out places associated with the legend (like the armory where he saw Buddy Holly in concert, and decided to become a musician). But you're on your own to find **Dylan's birthplace** (519 N 3rd Ave E), up a hill a few blocks northeast of downtown. Dylan lived on the top floor until age six, when his family moved inland to Hibbing. It's a private residence (and unmarked), so all you can do is stare from the street.

DULUTH TRAVERSE

A 100-mile mountain-bike trail that spans the city? Riders are stoked for the Duluth Traverse (www.coggs.com), a singletrack path that's opening bit by bit and linking several existing trails. When it's finished – the city is shooting for most of it complete in 2018 – no Duluthian will be more than five minutes from the route.

⊘ 8:30am-5pm Mon-Fri) Pick up a visitor guide; the website has deals and coupons.

ℹ Getting There & Away

Greyhound (☑ 218-722-5591; www.greyhound. com; 228 W Michigan St) has a couple of buses daily to Minneapolis (three hours).

North Shore

A trip here is dominated by water – mainly enormous, tempestuous Lake Superior – where ore-toting freighters ply the ports, little fishing fleets haul in the day's catch and wave-bashed cliffs offer awesome views if you're willing to trek. Numerous state parks, waterfalls, hiking trails and mom-and-pop towns speckle the landscape as it unfurls to the Canadian border. Highlights include Gooseberry Falls, Split Rock Lighthouse, Grand Marais' groovy scene and flaky pie in Two Harbors.

◉ Sights & Activities

The 300-mile **Superior Hiking Trail** (www. shta.org) follows the lake-hugging ridgeline between Duluth and the Canadian border. Along the way it passes dramatic red-rock overlooks and the occasional moose and black bear. Trailheads with parking lots pop up every 5 to 10 miles, making it ideal for day hikes. The **Superior Shuttle** (☑ 218-834-5511; www.superiorhikingshuttle.com; from $15; ⊘ Fri-Sun mid-May–mid-Oct) makes life even easier, picking up trekkers from 17 stops along the route. Overnight hikers will find 86 backcountry campsites and several lodges to cushion the body come nightfall; the trail website has details. The whole footpath is free, with no reservations or permits required. The **trail office** (☑ 218-834-2700; www.shta.org; 731 7th Ave; ⊘ 9am-4:30pm Mon-Fri, 10am-4pm Sat, noon-4pm Sun, closed Sat & Sun

mid-Oct–mid-May) in Two Harbors provides maps and planning assistance.

**Split Rock Lighthouse
State Park**   STATE PARK
(☑ 218-595-7625; www.dnr.state.mn.us; 3755 Split Rock Lighthouse Rd; per car $5, lighthouse per adult/child $10/6; ⊘ 10am-6pm mid-May–mid-Oct, 11am-4pm Thu-Mon mid-Oct–mid-May) The most visited spot on the entire North Shore. The shiner itself is a state historic site with a separate admission fee. Guided tours are available (they depart hourly), or you can explore on your own. If you don't mind stairs, say 170 or so each way, tramp down the cliff to the beach for incredible views of the lighthouse and surrounding shore.

**Judge CR Magney
State Park**   STATE PARK
(☑ 218-387-6300; www.dnr.state.mn.us; 4051 Hwy 61; per car $5; ⊘ 9am-8pm) Magney State Park is a beauty. Hiking to **Devil's Kettle**, the famous falls where the Brule River splits around a huge rock, is a must. Half of the flow drops 50ft in a typically gorgeous North Shore gush, but the other half disappears down a huge hole and flows underground. Where it goes is a mystery – scientists have never been able to determine the water's outlet.

Sawtooth Outfitters   KAYAKING, CYCLING
(☑ 218-663-7643; www.sawtoothoutfitters.com; 7216 Hwy 61; ⊘ 8am-6pm early May–late Oct & mid-late Dec, 8am-6pm Thu-Mon Jan–early Apr) Offers guided kayaking tours (half-/full-day tours $55/110) for all levels of paddling. They have trips on the Temperance River and out on Lake Superior, as well as easier jaunts on wildlife-rich inland lakes. Sawtooth also rents mountain bikes (per day from $22) to pedal over the many trails in the area, including the popular Gitchi Gami State Bike Trail (www.ggta.org).

🛏 Sleeping & Eating

The region has several one-of-a-kind properties, such as a hotel in a repurposed train and a lodge that used to be Babe Ruth's private club. Prices typically are midrange. Most of the state parks have campgrounds where sites cost $17 to $23. Lots of weekend, summer and fall traffic makes reservations essential for all accommodations. Expect lots of lake fish frying in pans. Most restaurants are independent mom-and-pop places.

Naniboujou Lodge LODGE $$
(☑ 218-387-2688; www.naniboujou.com; 20 Naniboujou Trail; r $115-160; ☺ late May–late Oct) Built in the 1920s, the property was once a private club for Babe Ruth and his contemporaries, who smoked cigars in the Great Hall, warmed by the 20ft-high stone fireplace. The pièce de résistance is the hall's massive domed ceiling painted with mind-blowing, psychedelic-colored Cree Indian designs. Rooms vary in decor, but each offers an away-from-it-all experience. It's 14 miles northeast of Grand Marais.

ⓘ Getting There & Away

Hwy 61 is the main vein through the North Shore. The state scenic route moseys all the way to Canada. Duluth is the closest urban area with an airport.

Boundary Waters

Legendarily remote and pristine, the Boundary Waters Canoe Area Wilderness (BWCAW) is one of the world's premier paddling regions. More than 1000 lakes and streams speckle the piney, 1.1-million-acre expanse. Nature lovers make the pilgrimage for the 1500 miles of canoe routes, rich wildlife and sweeping solitude. If you're willing to dig in and canoe for a while, it'll just be you and the moose, bears, wolves and loons that roam the landscape.

It's possible to glide in just for the day, but most people opt for at least one night of camping. Experienced paddlers flock here, but beginners are welcome, too, and everyone can get set up with gear from local lodges and outfitters. The engaging town of Ely, northeast of the Iron Range area, is the best place to start, as it has scores of accommodations, restaurants and outfitters.

Canoeing is what everyone is here for May through September. In winter, Ely gets mushy – it's a renowned dogsledding town.

You need to be prepared for a real wilderness adventure when canoeing in the Boundary Waters. The Superior National Forest Office publishes a handy **BWCAW trip planning guide** (www.fs.usda.gov/attmain/superior/specialplaces). It has information on what to bring and how to get the required entry permits. For camping, an **overnight permit** (☑ 877-444-6777; www.recreation.gov; adult/child $16/8, plus $10 reservation fee) is necessary. Day visit permits, though free, are also required; get them at BWCAW entry-point kiosks or ranger stations. Plan ahead, as permits are quota restricted and often run out.

Besides remote camping, the area has loads of lodges, though these often have a minimum-stay requirement (usually three days). Downtown Ely has several midrange inns and small hotels. July and August are busy, so book ahead.

ⓘ Information

Kawishiwi Ranger Station (☑ 218-365-7600; 1393 Hwy 169; ☺ 8am-4:30pm May-Sep, closed Sat & Sun Oct-Apr) provides expert BWCAW camping and canoeing details, trip suggestions and required permits.

ⓘ Getting There & Away

Hwy 169 (which becomes Sheridan St in Ely) connects the Boundary Waters to the Iron Range and its towns. Hwy 1 links the Boundary Waters to the Lake Superior shore.

GREAT LAKES NORTHERN MINNESOTA

SCENIC DRIVE: HIGHWAY 61

Hwy 61 conjures a headful of images. Local boy Bob Dylan mythologized it in his angry 1965 album *Highway 61 Revisited*. It's the fabled 'Blues Highway' clasping the Mississippi River en route to New Orleans. And in northern Minnesota, it evokes red-tinged cliffs and forested beaches as it follows Lake Superior's shoreline.

But let's back up and get a few things straight. The Blues Highway is actually US 61, and it starts just north of the Twin Cities. Hwy 61 is a state scenic road, and it starts in Duluth. To confuse matters more, there are two 61s between Duluth and Two Harbors: a four-lane expressway and a two-lane 'Old Hwy 61' (also called North Shore Scenic Drive). Take the latter; it morphs from London Rd in Duluth and veers off to the right just past the entrance to Brighton Beach. After Two Harbors, Hwy 61 returns to one strip of pavement – a gorgeous drive that goes all the way to the Canadian border. For more information, check the North Shore Scenic Drive at www.superiorbyways.com.

Voyageurs National Park

In the 17th century, French-Canadian fur traders, or voyageurs, began exploring the Great Lakes and northern rivers by canoe. Voyageurs National Park covers part of their customary waterway, which became the border between the USA and Canada.

It's all about water up here. Most of the park is accessible only by hiking or motorboat – the waters are mostly too wide and too rough for canoeing, though kayaks are becoming popular. A few access roads lead to campgrounds and lodges on or near Lake Superior, but these are mostly used by people putting in their own boats. Getting a houseboat is all the rage.

When the boats get put away for the winter, the snowmobiles come out. Voyageurs is a hot spot for the sport, with 110 miles of staked and groomed trails slicing through the pines. Rainy Lake Visitor Center provides maps and advice. It also lends out free snowshoes and cross country skis for local trails, including a couple that depart outside the center. To the south, an ice road for cars spans the boat launches of the Ash River and Kabetogama Lake Visitor Centers.

ⓘ Information

The visitor centers are car accessible and good places to begin your visit. Eleven miles east of International Falls on Hwy 11 is **Rainy Lake Visitor Center** (☑ 218-286-5258; ☺ 9:30am-5pm, 10am-4pm Wed-Sun late Sep–mid-May), the main park office. Ranger-guided walks and boat tours are available here in summer, snowshoe and ski rentals in winter. Seasonal visitor centers are at **Ash River** (☑ 218-374-3221; Mead Wood Rd; ☺ 9:30am-5pm late May–late Sep) and **Kabetogama Lake** (☑ 218-875-2111; off Hwy 53; ☺ 9:30am-5pm late May–late Sep), both of which offer ranger-led programs. The park website (www.nps.gov/voya) has further information. Destination Voyageurs National Park (www.dvnpmn.com) has lodging and activity details for the park's gateway communities.

ⓘ Getting There & Away

Hwy 53 is the main highway to the region. It's about a five-hour drive from the Twin Cities (or a three-hour drive from Duluth) to Crane Lake, Ash River or Lake Kabetogama. International Falls, near the park's northwest edge, holds the closest airport. It also has a busy border crossing with Canada.

Bemidji & Chippewa National Forest

This area is synonymous with outdoor activities and summer fun. Campsites and cottages abound, and everybody is fishing crazy.

Chippewa National Forest, a sprawling pine patch with 21 campgrounds, 160 miles of hiking trails, 1300 lakes, bald eagle habitats and Ojibwe lands, is a prime place to get in on the action. The small town of Cass Lake, home to the park's headquarters, provides a good starting point.

On the western edge of the forest, tidy Bemidji is an old lumber town with a well-preserved downtown and an enormous, photo-op statue of logger Paul Bunyan and his faithful blue ox, Babe. Also in the region is Itasca State Park, where the Mississippi River begins its epic journey.

ⓘ Information

Bemidji Tourist Information Center (☑ 218-759-0164; www.visitbemidji.com; 300 Bemidji Ave N; ☺ 8am-5pm Mon-Fri, 10am-5pm Sat, 11am-3pm Sun Jun-Aug, closed Sat & Sun Sep-May) Lakeside building next to giant statues of logger Paul Bunyan and his faithful blue ox, Babe. Inside there are displays including Paul's toothbrush.

ⓘ Getting There & Away

Hwys 2 and 71 are the main roads to the area. From Bemidji, Cass Lake is 20 miles east via Hwy 2, while Itasca State Park (east entrance) is 30 miles southwest via Hwy 71. Bemidji has a small airport with daily Delta flights to/from Minneapolis.

Understand
Eastern
USA

Eastern USA Today

The controversial result of the 2016 election – which saw businessman Donald Trump lose the popular vote but win the presidency – thrust the US into an uncertain future, dividing the nation across hot topic issues like immigration, health care and environmental protections. The ensuing turbulent political landscape sparked waves of protests, with those on the left resisting the nation's sudden (and sharp) turn to the right. Within this polarized social climate, the ballooning divide between rich and poor has reached new heights, while the region's smaller cities are blossoming.

Best on Film

Gone with the Wind (1939) Civil War–era saga of the South.

Mr Smith Goes to Washington (1939) Jimmy Stewart gets a crash course in DC politics and corruption.

The Untouchables (1987) Eliot Ness takes down Al Capone in gangster-era Chicago.

12 Years a Slave (2013) A free African American man is kidnapped and sold into slavery in 1841.

Hidden Figures (2016) Story of three African American women whose brilliant mathematics helped NASA to launch the first American into space.

Best in Print

To Kill a Mockingbird (Harper Lee; 1960) Pulitzer winner about racism in Depression-era Alabama.

A Confederacy of Dunces (John Kennedy Toole; 1980) Pulitzer winner about a New Orleans misfit.

The Secret History (Donna Tartt; 1992) Spine-tingling, cerebral mystery in an elite New England college.

The Corrections (Jonathan Franzen; 2001) Follows a complex, troubled family living in suburbia.

The Known World (Edward P Jones; 2003) Pulitzer winner; set before the Civil War, its protagonist is a black farmer who owns slaves.

A Nation Divided

Following the landmark 2016 election result and the controversy surrounding President Trump, a 'with him' or 'against him' mentality has pervaded the nation and the division between Republicans and Democrats (and within Republican and Democratic camps) has become more pronounced than ever. This political rift has begun to seep into the fabric of US society, amplifying existing binary worldviews held perhaps most strongly in the nation's rural communities, which find themselves left behind as the economic prosperity of cities grows. Antithetically, President Trump's promise to 'Make America Great Again' has reopened the wounds of history and thrown the divisions of race, religion and privilege back into the spotlight.

Greener Cities

With more people moving to urban areas, cities have grappled with transportation. Building more roads has never helped alleviate traffic congestion – as engineers have known since the 1960s. The answer has come through greater investment in public transit. Cities, once deeply married to the automobile (Atlanta, we're looking at you), have greatly expanded public transportation options, with new light rail lines, express bus lanes and dedicated bus lanes. Bike-sharing programs have also exploded across the country, with nearly 120 cities offering easy rental (usually by the day and week) for residents and visitors. The benefits – fewer cars on the streets, a bit of exercise for commuters, less carbon in the atmosphere – are obvious, though critics worry about injuries (since no bike-sharing programs provide helmets), as well as the long-term financial viability of these often expensive programs.

Healthcare for All… Maybe…

The Affordable Care Act (ACA), President Obama's program to extend healthcare through subsidies to millions of uninsured Americans, has been in effect since 2010. Despite congressional obstructionism, the program has allowed more than 16 million uninsured Americans to obtain coverage. In 2015, Health and Human Services Secretary Sylvia Burwell announced that hospitals had saved $7.4 billion in uncompensated care costs during the previous year owing to patient enrollment in the program's health insurance exchanges and Medicaid. States in the east, including Vermont and Rhode Island, were among those with the highest percentage of residents enrolled.

Despite the evidence and the general popularity of the program among participants, many blame it for the ballooning medical costs in the US. Donald Trump has promised to repeal the ACA, introducing the American Health Care Act (AHCA) in early 2017. Though the first effort to pass the AHCA failed, the second attempt, which allows states to exempt themselves from key mandates of the ACA, including supplying coverage to people with pre-existing conditions, made it through the House of Representatives. As of press time, the bill is under revision in the Senate.

Sea-Changers & Tree-Changers

Driven by rising rents and real-estate prices, and a lack of confidence in the market following the 2008 housing crisis, an ever-increasing number of young people are giving up the big-city life in New York City, Boston or Chicago for small- or mid-sized cities (a tree-change) or along the many miles of spectacular Atlantic and Gulf coastlines (a sea-change). Bargains can still be found in coastal cities like Naples and Fort Myers, FL, while in the Great Lakes and the South, millennials flock to smaller cities like Cincinnati, Grand Rapids, Chattanooga and Lexington, bringing a demand for culture and dining options and ideas for creative startups with them.

For many young families or couples wanting to start a family, the benefits are many – better quality of life, access to spectacular nature and a throwback to more traditional, communal notions of 'how to live,' prioritizing less stress and more quality time. And in a wireless world where the numbers of self-employed folks are on the rise, a growing number of single young creatives are also jumping on the lifestyle-change bandwagon.

POPULATION: **179.9 MILLION**

POPULATION DENSITY,
NEW YORK CITY: **27,530 PER SQ MILE**

MAINE: **43.1 PER SQ MILE**

HOUSEHOLD INCOME,
MISSISSIPPI (2015): **$40,595**

MARYLAND (2015): **$75,850**

if USA were 100 people

65 would be white
15 would be Hispanic
13 would be African American
4 would be Asian American
3 would be other

belief systems
(% of population)

51 Protestant   24 Roman Catholic

21 Other   2 Jewish   2 Mormon

population per sq mile

AUSTRALIA   USA   CANADA

🚶 ≈ 8 people

History

With a history of indigenous culture beginning around 12,000 BC, followed by its early days as an English colony in the 16th century, right through to its rise to the forefront of the world stage in the 20th, American history has been anything but dull. War against the British, westward expansion, slavery and its abolishment, Civil War and Reconstruction, the Great Depression, the postwar boom and more recent conflicts in the 21st century – they've all played a part in shaping the nation's complicated identity.

First Inhabitants

Among North America's most significant prehistoric cultures were the Mound Builders, who inhabited the Ohio and Mississippi River valleys from around 3000 BC to AD 1200. They left behind enigmatic piles of earth that were tombs for their leaders and possibly tributes to their gods. In Illinois, Cahokia was once a metropolis of 20,000 people, the largest in pre-Columbian North America. Similar mounds rise up throughout the eastern USA, including several along the Natchez Trace in Mississippi.

By the time the first Europeans arrived, several different groups of Native Americans occupied the land, such as the Wampanoag in New England, the Calusa in southern Florida and the Shawnee in Illinois. Two centuries later, they were all but gone. European explorers left diseases in their wake to which indigenous peoples had no immunity. More than any other factor – war, slavery or famine – disease epidemics devastated Native American populations by anywhere from 50% to 90%.

European Claims

In 1492, Italian explorer Christopher Columbus, backed by Spain, voyaged west looking for the East Indies. He found the Bahamas. With visions of gold, Spanish explorers quickly followed: Cortés conquered much of today's Mexico, Pizarro conquered Peru, and Ponce de León wandered through Florida looking for the fountain of youth. Not to be left out, the French explored Canada and New England, while the Dutch and English cruised North America's eastern seaboard.

Great History Museums

Henry Ford Museum/ Greenfield Village, Detroit

Museum of the American Revolution, Philadelphia

National Civil Rights Museum, Memphis

Nantucket Whaling Museum, Massachusetts

National Museum of the American Indian, Washington, DC

TIMELINE	7000 BC–AD 100	1492	1607
	'Archaic period' of nomadic hunter-gatherer lifestyles. By the end of this period, corn, beans and squash (the agricultural 'three sisters') and permanent settlements are well established.	Italian explorer Christopher Columbus 'discovers' America. He names the indigenous inhabitants 'Indians,' mistakenly thinking he had sailed to the East Indies.	The Jamestown settlement, the first permanent English colony in North America, is founded on marshland in present-day Virginia. The first few years are hard; many die from sickness and starvation.

The first European-founded (and oldest continuously settled) city in North America was St Augustine, Florida, where the Spanish set up shop in 1565. Up the coast in 1607, a group of English noblemen established that country's first permanent North American settlement at Jamestown. Earlier English settlements had ended badly, and Jamestown almost did, too: the noblemen chose a swamp, planted their crops late and died from disease and starvation. Local tribes provided the settlement with enough aid to survive.

For Jamestown and America, 1619 proved a pivotal year: the colony established the House of Burgesses, a representative assembly of citizens to decide local laws, and it received its first boatload of 20 African slaves. The next year was equally momentous, as a group of radically religious Puritans pulled ashore at what would become Plymouth, Massachusetts. The Pilgrims were escaping religious persecution under the 'corrupt' Church of England, and in the New World they saw a divine opportunity to create a new society that would be a religious and moral beacon. The Pilgrims signed a 'Mayflower Compact,' one of the seminal texts of American democracy, to govern themselves by consensus.

Before Jamestown or Plymouth Rock, a group of 116 British men and women set up a colony at Roanoke, North Carolina in the late 1580s. When a supply ship returned three years later, the settlers had disappeared. The fate of the 'Lost Colony' remains one of America's greatest mysteries.

Capitalism & Colonialism

For the next two centuries, European powers competed for position and territory in the New World, extending European politics into the Americas. As Britain's Royal Navy came to rule Atlantic seas, England increasingly profited from its colonies and eagerly consumed the fruits of their labors – tobacco from Virginia, sugar and coffee from the Caribbean. Over the 17th and 18th centuries, slavery in America was slowly legalized into a formal institution to support this plantation economy. By 1800, one out of every five persons was a slave.

Meanwhile, Britain mostly left the American colonists to govern themselves. Town meetings and representative assemblies, in which local citizens (that is, white men with property) debated community problems and voted on laws and taxes, became common. By the end of the Seven Years' War in 1763, Britain was feeling the strains of running an empire: it had been fighting France for a century and had colonies scattered all over the world. It was time to clean up bureaucracies and share financial burdens.

The colonies, however, resented English taxes and policies. Frustrations came to a head with the Boston Tea Party in 1773, after which Britain clamped down hard, shutting Boston's harbor and increasing its military presence. In 1774, representatives from 12 colonies convened the First Continental Congress in Philadelphia's Independence Hall to air complaints and prepare for the inevitable war ahead.

1620	1675	1773	1775
The *Mayflower* lands at Plymouth with 102 English Pilgrims, who have come to the New World to escape religious persecution. The Wampanoag tribe saves them from starvation.	For decades, the Pilgrims and local tribes live fairly cooperatively, but deadly conflict erupts in 1675. King Philip's War lasts 14 months and kills over 5000 people (mostly Native Americans).	To protest a British tax on tea, Bostonians dress as Mohawks, board East India Company ships and toss their tea overboard – later named the Boston Tea Party.	Paul Revere rides from Boston to warn colonial fighters (Minutemen) that the British are coming. The next day, the 'shot heard round the world' is fired at Lexington, starting the Revolutionary War.

Revolution & the Republic

In April 1775, British troops skirmished with armed colonists in Massachusetts (who were prepared for the fight, thanks to Paul Revere's famous warning), and the Revolutionary War began. George Washington, a wealthy Virginia farmer, was chosen to lead the American army. Trouble was, Washington lacked gunpowder and money (the colonists resisted taxes even for their own military), and his troops were a motley collection of poorly armed farmers, hunters and merchants, who regularly quit and returned to their farms due to lack of pay. On the other side, the British 'Redcoats' represented the world's most powerful military. The inexperienced General Washington had to improvise constantly, sometimes wisely retreating, sometimes engaging in 'ungentlemanly' sneak attacks. During the winter of 1777–78, the American army nearly starved at Valley Forge, Pennsylvania.

Meanwhile, the Second Continental Congress tried to articulate what exactly they were fighting for. In January 1776, Thomas Paine published the wildly popular *Common Sense*, which passionately argued for independence from England. Soon, independence seemed not just logical, but noble and necessary, and on July 4, 1776, the Declaration of Independence was finalized and signed. Largely written by Thomas Jefferson, it elevated the 13 colonies' particular gripes against the monarchy into a universal declaration of individual rights and republican government.

But to succeed, General Washington needed help, not just patriotic sentiment. In 1778, Benjamin Franklin persuaded France (always eager to trouble England) to ally with the revolutionaries, and they provided the troops, material and sea power that helped win the war. The British surrendered at Yorktown, Virginia, in 1781, and two years later the Treaty of Paris formally recognized the 'United States of America.' At first, the nation's loose confederation of fractious, squabbling states were hardly 'united.' So the founders gathered again in Philadelphia, and in 1787 drafted a new-and-improved Constitution: the US government was given a stronger federal center, with checks and balances between its three major branches, and to guard against the abuse of centralized power, a citizen's Bill of Rights was approved in 1791.

As radical as it was, though, the Constitution also preserved the economic and social status quo. Rich landholders kept their property, which included their slaves; Native Americans were excluded from the nation; and women were excluded from politics. These blatant discrepancies and injustices, which were widely noted, were the result of pragmatic compromise (eg to get slave-dependent Southern states on board) as well as widespread beliefs in the essential rightness of things as they were.

Famous Colonial Sights

Williamsburg, Virginia

Jamestown, Virginia

Plymouth, Massachusetts

North End, Boston

Philadelphia, Pennsylvania

Annapolis, Maryland

Charleston, South Carolina

1776	1787	1791	1812
On July 4, colonies sign the Declaration of Independence. Creators of the document include John Hancock, Samuel Adams, John Adams, Benjamin Franklin and Thomas Jefferson.	The Constitutional Convention in Philadelphia draws up the US Constitution. Federal power is balanced between the presidency, Congress and the judiciary.	Bill of Rights is adopted as 10 constitutional amendments articulating citizens' rights, including freedom of speech, a free press and the right to bear arms.	The War of 1812 begins with battles against the British and Native Americans in the Great Lakes region. Even after the 1815 Treaty of Ghent, fighting continues along the Gulf Coast.

Louisiana Purchase & the Move West

As the 19th century dawned on the young nation, optimism was the mood of the day. Agriculture was industrialized, and US commerce surged. In 1803 Thomas Jefferson bought land from French leader Napoleon Bonaparte. The Louisiana Purchase included New Orleans and about 15 present-day states west of the Mississippi River. Expansion began in earnest.

Relations between the US and Britain – despite lively trade – remained tense, and in 1812, the US declared war on England again. The two-year conflict ended without much gain by either side, although the British abandoned their forts, and the US vowed to avoid Europe's 'entangling alliances.'

In the 1830s and 1840s, with growing nationalist fervor and dreams of continental expansion, many Americans came to believe it was 'Manifest Destiny' that all the land in North America should be theirs. The 1830 Indian Removal Act aimed to clear one obstacle by designating land west of the Mississippi as 'Indian territory.' Native Americans were meant to relocate themselves there, thus clearing fertile valleys in eastern states like Georgia and Alabama for white settlement. Many tribes resisted removal, including the Seminole in Florida, but the US government cajoled, threatened and bribed Native Americans to sign treaties and cooperate; when that failed, the government used guns.

Meanwhile, newly built railroads cleared another hurdle, linking midwestern and western lands with East Coast markets. As new states joined the USA, a troubling question loomed: would they be slave states or free states? The nation's future depended on the answer.

Civil War

The US Constitution hadn't ended slavery, but it had given Congress the power to approve (or not) slavery in new states. Public debates raged constantly over the expansion of slavery, particularly since this shaped the balance of power between the industrial North and the agrarian South.

Since founding, Southern politicians had dominated government and defended slavery as 'natural and normal,' which an 1856 *New York Times* editorial called 'insanity.' The economics of slavery were undeniable. In 1860, there were over four million slaves in the US, most held by Southern planters – who grew 75% of the world's cotton, accounting for over half of US exports. Thus, the Southern economy supported the nation's economy, and it required slaves. The 1860 presidential election became a referendum on this issue, and the election was won by a young politician from Illinois who favored limiting slavery: Abraham Lincoln.

HISTORY LOUISIANA PURCHASE & THE MOVE WEST

For 100-plus years, Tecumseh's Curse loomed over presidents elected in a year ending in zero (every 20 years). Tecumseh was a Shawnee warrior whom president-to-be William Henry Harrison battled in 1811. Tecumseh hexed him as revenge. Harrison became president in 1840, but died a month later. Lincoln and Kennedy were also purported to be victims.

1861–65	1870	1880–1920	1908
American Civil War erupts between North and South (delineated by the Mason–Dixon line). The war's end on April 9, 1865, is marred by President Lincoln's assassination five days later.	Freed black men are given the vote, but the South's segregationist 'Jim Crow' laws (which remain until the 1960s) effectively disenfranchise blacks from every meaningful sphere of daily life.	Millions of immigrants flood in from Europe and Asia, fueling the age of cities. New York, Chicago and Philadelphia swell in size, becoming global centers of industry and commerce.	The first Model T (aka 'Tin Lizzie') car is built in Detroit, MI. Assembly-line innovator Henry Ford is soon selling one million automobiles annually.

War began in April 1861, when the Confederacy attacked Fort Sumter in Charleston, South Carolina, and raged on for the next four years – in the most gruesome combat the world had ever known until that time. By the end, over 600,000 soldiers, nearly an entire generation of young men, were dead. Southern plantations and cities (most notably Atlanta) lay sacked and burned. The North's industrial might provided an advantage, but its victory was not preordained; it unfolded battle by bloody battle.

As fighting progressed, Lincoln recognized that if the war didn't end slavery outright, victory would be pointless. In 1863, his Emancipation Proclamation expanded the war's aims and freed all slaves. In April 1865, Confederate General Robert E Lee surrendered to Union General Ulysses S Grant in Appomattox, Virginia. The union had been preserved, but at a staggering cost.

The Great Depression, the New Deal & World War II

In October 1929, investors, worried over a gloomy global economy, started selling stocks – seeing others selling, everyone panicked until they'd sold everything. The stock market crashed, and the US economy collapsed like a house of cards.

Thus began the Great Depression. Frightened banks called in their dodgy loans, people couldn't pay, and the banks folded. Millions lost their homes, farms, businesses and savings.

In 1932, Democrat Franklin D Roosevelt was elected president on the promise of a 'New Deal' to rescue the US from its crisis, which he did with resounding success. When war once again broke out in Europe in 1939, the isolationist mood in America was as strong as ever. However, the extremely popular President Roosevelt, elected to an unprecedented third term in 1940, understood that the US couldn't sit by and allow victory for fascist, totalitarian regimes. Roosevelt sent aid to Britain and persuaded a skittish Congress to go along with it.

Then, on December 7, 1941, Japan launched a surprise attack on Hawaii's Pearl Harbor, killing over 2000 Americans and sinking several battleships. US isolationism transformed overnight into outrage, and Roosevelt suddenly had the support he needed. Germany also declared war on the US, and America joined the Allied fight against Hitler and the Axis powers.

Fighting went on for over two years in both the Pacific and in Europe. The US finally dealt the fatal blow to Germany with its massive D-Day invasion of France on June 6, 1944. Germany surrendered in May 1945. Nevertheless, Japan continued fighting. Newly elected president Harry Truman – ostensibly worried that a US invasion of Japan would lead

The whaling industry thrived in New England in the 18th century, especially around Massachusetts. Buzzards Bay, Nantucket Island and New Bedford were all prominent centers. New Bedford eventually hosted a whaling fleet of more than 300 ships, employing 10,000 people and earning over $12 million in profits.

1917	1919	1920s	1933–38
President Woodrow Wilson enters the US into WWI. The US mobilizes 4.7 million troops, and suffers around 110,000 of the war's nine million military deaths.	The temperance movement champions the 18th amendment, which bans alcohol. Prohibition is unsuccessful, leading to bootlegging and organized crime. The amendment is repealed in 1933.	Spurred by massive African American migration to northern cities, the Harlem Renaissance inspires an intellectual flowering of literature, art and music.	Roosevelt's New Deal establishes federal programs and legislation including Social Security, the Fair Labor Standards Act and the Civilian Conservation Corps to provide unemployment relief.

to unprecedented carnage – chose to drop experimental atomic bombs, created by the government's top-secret Manhattan Project, on Hiroshima and Nagasaki in August 1945. The bombs devastated both cities, killing over 200,000 people. Japan surrendered days later, and the nuclear age was born.

The Red Scare, Civil Rights & Vietnam War

The US enjoyed unprecedented prosperity in the decades after WWII but little peace. Formerly wartime allies, the communist Soviet Union and the capitalist USA soon engaged in a running competition to dominate the globe. The superpowers engaged in proxy wars – notably the Korean War (1950–53) and Vietnam War (1954–75) – with only the mutual threat of nuclear annihilation preventing direct war.

Meanwhile, with its continent unscarred and its industry bulked up by WWII, the American homeland entered an era of growing affluence. In the 1950s, a mass migration left the inner cities for the suburbs, where affordable single-family homes sprang up. Americans drove cheap cars using cheap gas over brand-new interstate highways. They relaxed with the comforts of modern technology, swooned over TV, and got busy, giving birth to a 'baby boom.' Middle-class whites did, anyway. African Americans remained segregated, poor and generally unwelcome at the party. Echoing 19th-century abolitionist Frederick Douglass, the Southern Christian Leadership Coalition (SCLC), led by African American preacher Martin Luther King Jr, aimed to end segregation and 'save America's soul': to realize colorblind justice, racial equality and fairness of economic opportunity for all.

Beginning in the 1950s, King preached and organized nonviolent resistance in the form of bus boycotts, marches and sit-ins, mainly in the South. White authorities often met these protests with water hoses and police batons, and demonstrations sometimes dissolved into riots, but with the 1964 Civil Rights Act, African Americans spurred a wave of legislation that swept away racist laws and laid the groundwork for a more just and equal society.

Meanwhile, the 1960s saw further social upheavals: rock and roll spawned a youth rebellion and drugs sent Technicolor visions spinning in their heads. President John F Kennedy was assassinated in Dallas in 1963, followed by the assassinations in 1968 of his brother, Senator Robert Kennedy, and of Martin Luther King (in Memphis). Americans' faith in their leaders and government was further shocked by the bombings and brutalities of the Vietnam War, as seen on TV, which led to widespread student protests. Yet Republican President Richard Nixon, elected in 1968 partly for promising an 'honorable end to the war,' instead escalated US

Duration of Major US Wars

Moro Revolution
(14 years)

War in Afghanistan
(13 years, 2 months)

War in Iraq
(8 years, 9 months)

Vietnam War
(8 years, 1 month)

American Civil War
(4 years)

World War II
(3 years, 7 months)

Korean War
(3 years, 1 month)

1941–45	1954	1963	1964
WWII: America deploys 16 million troops and suffers 400,000 deaths. (Overall, civilian deaths outpace military deaths two to one, and total 50 to 70 million people from over 50 countries.)	The Supreme Court rules that segregation in public schools is 'inherently unequal' and orders desegregation 'with all deliberate speed.' The fight to integrate schools spurs the Civil Rights movement.	On November 22, President John F Kennedy is publicly assassinated by Lee Harvey Oswald while riding in a motorcade through Dealey Plaza in Dallas, Texas.	Congress passes the Civil Rights Act, outlawing discrimination on the basis of race, color, religion, sex or national origin. First proposed by Kennedy, it was one of President Johnson's crowning achievements.

involvement and secretly bombed Laos and Cambodia. Then, in 1972, the Watergate scandal broke: a burglary at Democratic Party offices in Washington was, through dogged journalism, tied to 'Tricky Dick,' who in 1974 became the first US president to resign from office.

The tumultuous 1960s and '70s also witnessed the sexual revolution, women's liberation and other events challenging the status quo. Milestones included the 1969 Stonewall riots in Greenwich Village, NYC, which galvanized the gay rights movement when patrons of a gay bar called the Stonewall Inn fought back after a police raid, demanding equal rights and an end to persecution. A few months later, the Woodstock Festival defined the Vietnam era with its peace-love-and-flowers hippies swaying in the fields to rock music.

Though the town of Woodstock, NY, lent its name to the mythic 1969 music fest, the event actually took place in the nearby hamlet of Bethel, where dairy farmer Max Yasgur rented his alfalfa field to organizers. Ticket price for the bash: $18 for a three-day pass ($24 at the gate).

Reagan, Clinton & the Bushes

In 1980, California's Republican governor and former actor Ronald Reagan campaigned for president by promising to make Americans feel good about America again. The affable Reagan won easily, and his election marked a pronounced shift to the right in US politics. Military spending and tax cuts created enormous federal deficits, which hampered the presidency of Reagan's successor, George HW Bush. Despite winning the Gulf War – liberating Kuwait in 1991 after an Iraqi invasion – Bush was soundly defeated in the 1992 presidential election by Southern Democrat Bill Clinton.

On September 11, 2001, Islamic terrorists flew hijacked planes into New York's World Trade Center and the Pentagon in Washington, DC. This catastrophic attack united Americans behind their president, George W Bush, as he vowed revenge and declared a 'war on terror.' Bush soon attacked Afghanistan in an unsuccessful hunt for Al-Qaeda terrorist cells, then attacked Iraq in 2003 and toppled its anti-US dictator, Saddam Hussein. Meanwhile, Iraq descended into civil war.

The Obama Presidency

In 2008, hungry for change, Americans elected political newcomer Barack Obama, America's first African American president. He certainly had his work cut out for him. These were, after all, unprecedented times economically, with the US in the largest financial crisis since the Great Depression. What had started as a collapse of the US housing bubble in 2007 had spread to the banking sector, with the meltdown of major financial institutions.

As Americans looked toward the future, many found it difficult to leave the past behind. This was not surprising since wars in Afghanistan and Iraq, launched a decade prior, continued to simmer on the back

1965–75	1969	1973	1980s
US involvement in the Vietnam War tears the nation apart as 58,000 Americans die, along with four million Vietnamese and 1.5 million Laotians and Cambodians.	American astronauts land on the moon, fulfilling President Kennedy's unlikely 1961 promise to accomplish this feat within a decade and culminating the 'space race' between the US and USSR.	In *Roe v Wade*, the Supreme Court legalizes abortion. Even today this decision remains controversial and socially divisive, pitting 'right to choose' advocates against the 'right to life' anti-abortion lobby.	New Deal–era financial institutions, deregulated under President Reagan, gamble with their customers' savings and loans, and ultimately fail, leaving the government with the bill.

burner of the ever-changing news cycle. In 2011, in a subterfuge operation vetted by President Obama, Navy Seals raided Osama bin Laden's Pakistan hideout and killed the Al-Qaeda leader, bringing an end to the search for America's greatest public enemy.

Following his sober announcement describing the raid, President Obama saw his approval ratings jump by 11%. The president, for his part, certainly needed a boost. The economy remained in bad shape, and the ambitious $800-billion stimulus package passed by Congress in 2009 hadn't borne much fruit in the eyes of many Americans – even though economists estimated that the stimulus did soften the blow of the recession, which would have been much worse without it. At the end of his first term, his approval ratings were around 49%.

With lost jobs, overvalued mortgages and little relief in sight, millions of Americans found themselves adrift. This was not a recession they could spend their way out of, as Obama's predecessor had suggested. People were upset and gathered in large numbers to voice their anger. This, in turn, gave birth to the Tea Party, a wing of politically conservative Republicans who believed that government handouts would destroy the economy and, thus, America.

Despite such opposition, Obama was reelected in 2012, though he returned to office without quite the same hope that surrounded him the first time. When Obama took the oath of office in 2013, the unemployment rate, hovering around 8%, was about what it had been during his first inauguration, though economic growth was on a more solid foundation.

On other fronts, Obama showed mixed success; he ended the US involvement in Iraq, but at what cost? Although troop withdrawal from the Middle East came in more significant numbers, total civilian casualties from drone strikes during this period mounted: government figures released in 2016 purport that drones and other airstrikes during the Obama administration killed between 64 and 116 civilians, but NGOs, such as the Bureau of Investigative Journalism, report the civilian death toll to be much higher.

What might have been his enduring legacy, the healthcare bill commonly known as 'Obamacare,' which became law in 2010 but wasn't effected until 2014, now seems to have a tenuous life trajectory under the Trump administration. Pre-Trump, Democrats were quick to point out that millions more Americans than ever before now had health insurance under Obamacare, while Republicans insisted the program was a failure from the outset, citing decreased insurance options for consumers and harsh costs for business owners.

Civil Rights on Film

Hidden Figures (2016), Theodore Melfi

Selma (2014), Ava DuVernay

Ghosts of Mississippi (1996), Rob Reiner

Malcolm X (1992), Spike Lee

The Long Walk Home (1990), Richard Pearce

Mississippi Burning (1988), Alan Parker

1989	1990s	2001	2003
The 1960s-era Berlin Wall is torn down, marking the end of the Cold War between the US and the USSR (now Russia). The USA becomes the world's last remaining superpower.	The world wide web debuts in 1991. Silicon Valley, CA, leads a high-tech internet revolution, remaking communications and media; overvalued tech stocks drive the massive boom (and subsequent bust).	On September 11, Al-Qaeda terrorists hijack four commercial airplanes, flying two into NYC's twin towers and one into the Pentagon (the fourth crashes in Pennsylvania); nearly 3000 people are killed.	After citing evidence that Iraq possesses weapons of mass destruction, President George W Bush launches a preemptive war that will cost over 4000 American lives and some $3 trillion.

The 2016 Election & the Trump Presidency

When Donald J Trump, real-estate magnate and former host of TV's reality game show *The Apprentice*, announced he was running for President in June 2015, many around the world thought it was a publicity stunt. What ensued could be described as a media circus: coverage of the protracted campaign, which pitted Trump, with no prior political experience, against Hillary Clinton, former Secretary of State (2009–13) and First Lady, was relentless. Trump's pithy soundbites and no-holds-barred insults stood out in a crowded Republican primary field and made for irresistible headlines, while the primary contest on the Democratic side was winnowed down to Clinton and populist candidate Bernie Sanders early on.

Once the Trump and Clinton lineup was announced, a contentious campaign ensued. Trump refused to follow the common practice among presidential candidates of releasing personal tax records. On October 7, *Access Hollywood* tapes leaked in which Trump admitted to assaulting women. On Clinton's side, opponents invoked the Benghazi terror attacks and her ties to Wall Street. A week before the election, FBI head James Comey stoked the conspiracy theories around Hillary Clinton by announcing in a letter to Congress that her emails, which she stored on a private server against security recommendations, were still under investigation. Still, polls gave Clinton a strong lead, and on election night, the country prepared to celebrate the election of the first female President of the United States. Clinton did win the popular vote, but the Electoral College math was not in her favor. She conceded to Donald Trump in the early hours of November 9 with an emotional speech which reminded 'all the little girls who are watching this, never doubt that you are valuable, and powerful and deserving of every chance and opportunity in the world to pursue and achieve your own dreams.'

In his victory speech, Trump declared 'I will be president for all Americans,' though many are unsure of what his definition of what it means to be an American actually is. Uncertainty, in fact, seems to be the defining quality of the Trump presidency. Scandal and controversy have surrounded the administration in its first 100 days, during which the nation's democratic integrity has been challenged by conflicts of interest between public office and private enterprise. Public protest has become a defining feature of the sociopolitical landscape, starting with the Women's March the day after the inauguration, the largest single-day demonstration in recorded US history with an estimated 4 million participants in some 653 cities around the country.

Governance by Executive Order

A lot has been said in the world media about Trump's immediate, widespread use of his constitutional right to pass executive orders, which en-

2005	2008–09	2011	2012
On August 29, Hurricane Katrina hits the Mississippi and Louisiana coasts, rupturing poorly maintained levees and flooding New Orleans. More than 1800 people die, and cost estimates exceed $110 billion.	Barack Obama becomes the first African American president. The stock market crashes due to mismanagement by major American financial institutions. The crisis spreads worldwide.	As unemployment remains high and household income drops, activists launch Occupy Wall Street in NYC to protest economic and social inequality. The movement spreads to cities worldwide.	Hurricane Sandy devastates the East Coast, becoming the second-costliest hurricane ($65 billion) in American history. More than 80 Americans die (plus 200 more in other countries). Obama wins re-election.

ables the president to bypass Congress to set government policy. Trump signed his first, intended to weaken Obama's Affordable Care Act, on his first day in office.

Generally, executive orders are intended to enable the president to act swiftly in times of war or crisis. Backed by the full force of the legal process, their authority is defined by the Constitution. When a president passes an executive order, it immediately instructs the federal agencies (all facets of government, basically) to direct resources in a certain way. It is a slow congressional and judicial process to have one overturned.

Trump isn't the first president to use an executive order to accomplish something more typically done through legislation: Obama, for example, used executive orders to raise the minimum wage for federally contracted workers by $3, and to halt the deportation of thousands of illegal immigrants who were brought to the US as children. But Trump's immediate use of the policy, and the ways he chooses to deploy it, has heightened tensions around the globe.

PRESIDENT	TOTAL NUMBER OF EXECUTIVE ORDERS ISSUED DURING TERM	AVERAGE NUMBER OF EXECUTIVE ORDERS ISSUED PER YEAR
Franklin D Roosevelt	3522	145
John F Kennedy	214	75
Richard Nixon	346	62
Ronald Reagan	381	48
Bill Clinton	308	46
George W Bush	291	36
Barack Obama	276	35
Donald Trump (as at 20 Jun 2017)	37	88

Data comparing the use of executive orders by presidency indicates that in the first 10 months of his presidency, Trump got off to a roaring start. To keep track of the count, refer to the website of the American Presidency Project (www.presidency.ucsb.edu/data/orders.php)

2015	2016	2017	2017
The Supreme Court makes gay marriage the law of the land. South Carolina removes the Confederate battle flag from its Capitol under pressure that it's a racist symbol that sparked mass murder in Charleston.	Donald J Trump, billionaire casino owner, real-estate mogul and star of TV's The Apprentice, is elected 45th President of the United States, though not by popular vote.	Four million people around the world attend a Women's March against the Trump administration. It's the largest single-day protest in US history.	Trump's first 100 days in office are shrouded in scandal relating to conflicts of interest within his cabinet, his alleged knowledge of purported Russian involvement in US election-fixing and sacking FBI director James Comey.

The Way of Life

The eastern USA is a compelling mix of accents and rhythms, big-city financiers and small-town farmers, university students and sun-seeking retirees, Yankees and Southerners. A diverse range of experiences awaits from sampling the delights of New York's molecular gastronomy to New Orleans' po'boy sandwiches; partying it up on Chicago's re-energized club circuit or at a Nashville hoedown or honky-tonk; from romantic strolls through New England villages to lazy days on Florida's endless summer coastlines. There's something for everyone.

Multiculturalism

From the get-go, cities in the East were 'melting pots,' with a long and proud heritage of welcoming newcomers from all over the world. So it's no surprise that the region's diversity is vast.

In the Northeast, Irish and Italian communities have been well established in the urban areas since the 19th century. In Chicago, Latinos (mostly from Mexico) comprise roughly one-quarter of the population. The upper Great Lakes states are home to the nation's biggest enclaves of Somali and Hmong immigrants, a result of the area's long tradition of resettling refugees. In Florida, Cubans lead the multicultural pack. They began arriving in Miami in the 1960s following Castro's revolution and created a politically powerful community. Nicaraguans followed in the 1980s, fleeing war in their country, and now number over 100,000. The city's Little Haiti adds 70,000 Haitians to the mix. The South, more than any other region, is a culture unto itself; over half of all black Americans live here. These examples are just a fraction of the complex whole.

The East, like the rest of the country, can never quite decide if the continual influx of newcomers is its saving grace or what will eventually strain society to the breaking point. 'Immigration reform' has been a Washington buzzword for nearly two decades. Some people believe the nation's current system deals with undocumented immigrants (there are 11.3 million of them) too leniently – that the government should deport immigrants who are here unlawfully and fine employers who hire them. Other Americans think those rules are too harsh – that immigrants who have been here for years working, contributing to society and abiding by the law deserve amnesty. Despite several attempts, Congress has not been able to pass a comprehensive package addressing illegal immigration, though it has put through various measures to beef up enforcement.

Americans are increasingly defining their spiritual beliefs outside of organized religion. The proportion of those who say they have 'no religion' is now around 16%. Some in this catch-all category disavow religion altogether (around 4%), but the majority sustain spiritual beliefs that simply fall outside the box.

Religion

Separation of Church and State has been the law of the land ever since the Pilgrims came ashore in Massachusetts in the early 1600s. Their faith – Protestant Christianity – continues to be the main one in the East.

Protestantism covers a wide swath of denominations. They fall under two main headings: evangelical Protestants, of which Baptists form the biggest contingent; and mainline Protestants, such as Lutherans, Methodists and Presbyterians. Evangelicals have the greater number of worshippers, and that number has grown in recent years: Baptists are their powerhouse, accounting for one-third of all Protestants and close to one-fifth of the USA's total adult population. Their numbers stack up in the South. In contrast, Lutherans (who are concentrated in Minnesota and Wisconsin, as well as the Dakotas) and the other mainline denominations have experienced declining figures.

Catholicism is the East's second-most-practiced faith. In fact, New England is the country's most Catholic zone, and the numbers trickle down to the Mid-Atlantic states. Massachusetts is the most Catholic state, with 45% of residents of that faith. Baltimore is the country's oldest archdiocese, established in 1789. States with large Latino populations, such as Florida and Illinois, also support big concentrations of Catholics.

Judaism has a significant presence in the eastern USA. Jews make up roughly 12% of the population in both South Florida and the New York metro area. The latter is a major center of Orthodox Judaism and home to more Jews than anywhere outside Tel Aviv.

Also in the East: Muslim Americans cluster in the New York, Chicago and Detroit metro areas. Hindu Americans bunch in New York and New Jersey, as well as big cities like Chicago, Washington, DC, and Atlanta.

THE WAY OF LIFE LIFESTYLE

The US holds the world's second-largest Spanish-speaking population, behind Mexico and just ahead of Spain. Latinos are also the fastest-growing minority group in the nation. In the East, Florida, Illinois, New Jersey and New York have the largest Latino populations.

Lifestyle

In general, the eastern USA has one of the world's highest standards of living, though there are some shocking variances by region. At the top end sits Maryland, with a median household income of $69,826 (based on 2012–14 census data). Mississippi dwells at the opposite end of the scale at $40,194. These amounts are the high/low not just for the region, but for the nation, upholding the pattern in which households in the Northeast earn the most, while those in the South earn the least. Wages also vary by ethnicity, with African Americans and Latinos earning less than whites and Asians ($34,600 and $41,000 respectively, versus $58,000 and $67,000).

About 86% of Americans are high-school graduates, while some 29% go on to graduate from college with a four-year bachelor's degree. The university lifestyle (ie cafes, bookshops and progressive mindsets) is especially prevalent in the Northeast, home to the eight Ivy League schools as well as the 'Little Ivies' (a self-anointed collection of a dozen elite liberal-arts colleges) and the 'Seven Sisters' (top-tier women's colleges, founded in the days when the Ivy League was still a boys-only club). More than 50 institutions of higher learning range around Boston alone.

If you peeked in a house, you'd typically find a married couple with two kids occupying it. Both parents usually work, and 28% work more than 40 hours per week. Divorce is common – 40% of first marriages break up – but both divorce and marriage rates have declined over the last three decades. Single parents head 9% of households.

StoryCorps has collected and archived more than 50,000 interviews from people across America, which it preserves in the Library of Congress. Listen to folks tell their stories of discovery, family, identity, love and much more at www.story corps.org.

STATES & TRAITS

Regional US stereotypes now have solid data behind them, thanks to a study of the geography of personality differences across the states. Researcher Peter Rentfrow and his colleagues processed more than a half-million personality assessments collected from individual US citizens, then looked at where certain traits stacked up on the map. Turns out 'Minnesota nice' is for real – the most 'agreeable' states cluster around the Great Lakes, Great Plains and the South. These places rank highest for friendliness and cooperation. The most neurotic states? They line up in the Northeast. But New York didn't place number one, as you might expect; that honor goes to West Virginia. Many of the most 'open' states lie out West. California, Nevada, Oregon and Washington all rate high for being receptive to new ideas – although they lag behind Washington, DC, and New York.

Key Sports Websites

Baseball:
www.mlb.com

Basketball:
www.nba.com

Football:
www.nfl.com

Hockey:
www.nhl.com

Car racing:
www.nascar.com

Soccer:
www.mlssoccer.
com

While many Americans hit the gym or walk, bike or jog regularly, over 50% don't exercise at all during their free time, according to the Centers for Disease Control and Prevention (CDC). Health researchers speculate that this lack of exercise and Americans' fondness for sugary and fatty foods have led to rising obesity and diabetes rates. The South fares the worst: Mississippi, Alabama, West Virginia, Tennessee and Louisiana lead the obesity rankings, with the condition affecting one-third of residents.

About 26% of Americans volunteer their time to help others or help a cause, according to the Corporation for National and Community Service. Eco-consciousness has entered the mainstream: over 75% of Americans recycle at home, and most big chain grocery stores – including Wal-Mart – now sell organic foods.

Sports

What really draws Americans together (sometimes slathered in blue body paint or with foam-rubber cheese wedges on their heads) is sports. In spring and summer there's baseball nearly every day, in fall and winter there's football, and through the long nights of winter there's plenty of basketball to keep the adrenaline going – those are the big three sports. Car racing has revved up interest, especially in the South. Major League Soccer (MLS) is attracting an ever-increasing following. Ice hockey, once favored only in northern climes, has fans throughout the area. Women's basketball and soccer also are gaining traction nationwide, with multiple teams that play in pro leagues.

Baseball

Despite high salaries and its biggest stars being dogged by steroid rumors, baseball remains America's favorite pastime. It may not command the same TV viewership (and subsequent advertising dollars) as football, but baseball has 162 games over a season versus 16 for football.

Besides, baseball is better live than on TV – being at the ballpark on a sunny day, sitting in the bleachers with a beer and hot dog, and indulging in the seventh-inning stretch, when the entire park erupts in a communal sing-along of 'Take Me Out to the Ballgame.' The playoffs,

ICONIC SPORTING VENUES

Yankee Stadium, NYC (p87) The Bronx fabled baseball field, steeped in history and the ghost of Babe Ruth.

Lambeau Field, Green Bay Stadium of the NFL's Packers; nicknamed 'the Frozen Tundra' for its insanely cold weather.

Fenway Park, Boston (p179) Baseball's oldest park (1912); home of the 'Green Monster' (aka the tall left-field wall).

Wrigley Field, Chicago (p525) Another vintage ballpark (1914), with ivy walls, a classic neon sign and good-time neighborhood bars all around.

Madison Square Garden, NYC (p114) Not only do the Knicks dribble at the 'mecca of basketball,' but Ali boxed here and Elvis rocked here.

Little Caesars Arena, Detroit (p575) The brand-new, badass rink of pro hockey's Red Wings; witness the strange octopus-throwing custom.

Churchill Downs, Louisville (p383) Home of the Kentucky Derby: fine hats, mint juleps and the 'greatest two minutes in sports.'

Indianapolis Motor Speedway, Indianapolis (p545) Race cars scream by at 170mph at the hard-partying Indy 500.

held every October, still deliver excitement and unexpected champions. Consistently one of America's favorite teams despite not having won a World Series in more than 100 years, the Chicago Cubs skyrocketed to legend status when they turned that frown upside down to become the 2016 World Series Champions, defeating the Cleveland Indians in a landslide victory. The Cubs' victory parade drew almost five million people to the streets of Chicago, making it one of the largest single gatherings of people in recorded history.

Tickets to games are relatively inexpensive – seats average about $25 at most stadiums – and are easy to get for most games. Minor-league baseball games cost half as much, and can be even more fun, with lots of audience participation, stray chickens and dogs running across the field, and wild throws from the pitcher's mound. For information, see www.milb.com.

Football

Football is big, physical, and rolling in dough. With the shortest season and least number of games of any of the major sports, every match takes on the emotion of an epic battle, where the results matter and an unfortunate injury can deal a lethal blow to a team's playoff chances.

It's also the toughest US sport, played in fall and winter in all manner of rain, sleet and snow – some of the most memorable matches have occurred at below-freezing temperatures. Green Bay Packers fans are in a class by themselves when it comes to severe weather. Their stadium in Wisconsin (Lambeau Field) was the site of the infamous Ice Bowl, a 1967 championship game against the Dallas Cowboys where the temperature plummeted to -13°F (-25°C)– mind you, that was with a wind-chill factor of -48°F (-44°C).

The rabidly popular Super Bowl is pro football's championship match, held in late January or early February. The other 'bowl' games (such as the Sugar Bowl in New Orleans and Orange Bowl in Miami) are college football's title matches, held on and around New Year's Day.

Basketball

The teams bringing in the most fans these days include the Chicago Bulls (thanks to the lingering Michael Jordan effect), the Cleveland Cavaliers (home of LeBron James, the league's most loved – and hated – player) and the New York Knicks (where celebrities sit courtside despite a losing team on the court in recent years).

College basketball also draws millions of fans, especially every spring when the March Madness playoffs roll around; it culminates in the Final Four, when the remaining quartet of teams competes for a spot in the championship game. The Cinderella stories and unexpected outcomes rival the pro league for excitement. The games are widely televised and bet upon – this is when Las Vegas bookies earn their keep.

The Super Bowl costs America $800 million in lost workplace productivity as employees gossip about the game, make bets and shop for new TVs online. It's still less than the $1.9 billion estimate for March Madness, when many folks get caught up in the NCAA basketball tournament.

THE WAY OF LIFE SPORTS

Arts & Architecture

New York remains the dynamic heart of the theater and art worlds, while great literature finds its voice throughout the region. Niche media networks are making edgy, must-view TV about everything from zombies in Georgia to murderers in Minnesota. In the meantime, architects in New York and Chicago keep pushing ever higher.

Painting

In the wake of WWII, the USA developed its first truly original school of art: abstract expressionism. New York painters Jackson Pollock, Franz Kline, Mark Rothko and others explored freely created, nonrepresentational forms. Pollock, for example, made drip paintings by pouring and splattering pigments over large canvases.

Pop art followed, where artists drew inspiration from bright, cartoony consumer images; Andy Warhol was the king (or Pope of Pop, as he's sometimes called). Minimalism came next, and by the 1980s and '90s, the canvas was wide open – any and all styles could take their place at the arts table.

New York remains the red-hot center of the art world, and its make-or-break influence shapes tastes across the nation and around the globe. To get the pulse of contemporary art in the region, check out works by Jenny Holzer, Kara Walker, Chuck Close, Martin Puryear and Frank Stella.

Literature

The 'Great American Novel' has stirred the imagination for more than 150 years. Edgar Allan Poe told spooky short stories in the 1840s, and is credited with inventing the detective story, horror story and science fiction. Four decades later, Samuel Clemens, aka Mark Twain, also made a literary splash. Twain wrote in the vernacular, loved 'tall tales' and reveled in absurdity, which endeared him to everyday readers. His novel *Huckleberry Finn* (1884) became the quintessential American narrative: compelled by a primal moment of rebellion against his father, Huck embarks on a search for authenticity through which he discovers himself. The Mississippi River provides the backdrop.

The Lost Generation brought American literature into its own in the early 20th century. These writers lived as expatriates in post-WWI Europe and described a growing sense of alienation. Straight talking Ernest Hemingway exemplified the era with his spare, stylized realism. Minnesotan F Scott Fitzgerald eviscerated East Coast society life with his fiction. Back on home turf, William Faulkner examined the South's social rifts in dense, caustic prose, and African Americans such as poet Langston Hughes and novelist Zora Neale Hurston undermined racist stereotypes during New York's Harlem Renaissance.

After WWII, American writers began depicting regional and ethnic divides, experimented with style and often bashed middle-class society's values. The 1950s Beat Generation, with Jack Kerouac, Allen Ginsberg and William S Burroughs at the center, was particularly hard-core.

Best Modern Art Museums

Museum of Modern Art, New York City, NY

Whitney Museum of American Art, New York City, NY

Salvador Dalí Museum, St Petersburg, FL

Andy Warhol Museum, Pittsburgh, PA

Dia:Beacon, Beacon, NY

Today's literature reflects an ever more diverse panoply of voices. Jacqueline Woodson, Junot Diaz and Sherman Alexie have all written bestsellers in the past decade and given voice to, respectively, African American, Dominican American and Native American issues. Titans of contemporary literature include Toni Morrison (whose most recent book was *God Save the Child* in 2015), the prolific Joyce Carol Oates who practically churns out a book a year, Michael Chabon and Colson Whitehead – all Pulitzer winners hailing from the eastern USA. Whitehead's *The Underground Railroad*, a searing fictional take on one woman's journey from slavery to freedom in the 1850s, won the 2016 National Book Award and the 2017 Pulitzer Prize.

But perhaps the best known East Coast author of our time was reclusive Harper Lee, born in Monroeville, Alabama. Lee gained fame in 1960 when she wrote *To Kill a Mockingbird*, a staple of summer reading lists nationwide. But she shunned the spotlight and did not release another book until 2015, when *Go Set a Watchman*, a sequel of sorts to *Mockingbird*, was released. The publication was controversial; many wondered whether Lee, who was 89, was capable of consenting. She died less than a year later, on February 19, 2016.

Great American Novels

Beloved,
Toni Morrison

The Great Gatsby,
F Scott Fitzgerald

The Sound and the Fury,
William Faulkner

American Rust,
Philipp Meyer

The Adventures of Augie March,
Saul Bellow

ARTS & ARCHITECTURE THEATER

Theater

Eugene O'Neill put American drama on the map with his trilogy *Mourning Becomes Electra* (1931), which sets a tragic Greek myth in post–Civil War New England. O'Neill was the first major US playwright, and is still widely considered to be the best.

After WWII, two playwrights dominated the stage: Arthur Miller, who famously married Marilyn Monroe and wrote about everything from middle-class male disillusionment (*Death of a Salesman*; 1949) to the mob mentality of the Salem witch trials (*The Crucible*; 1953); and Tennessee Williams, whose explosive works *The Glass Menagerie* (1945), *A Streetcar Named Desire* (1947) and *Cat on a Hot Tin Roof* (1955) dug deep into the Southern psyche.

Edward Albee gave the 1960s a healthy dose of absurdism, and David Mamet and Sam Shepard filled the '70s and '80s with rough-and-tough guys. These days Pulitzer Prize–winner Tracy Letts writes family dramas that are often compared to O'Neill, bringing the scene full circle.

Broadway is where shows get star treatment. The famed NYC district earns more than a billion dollars in revenue from ticket sales each year, with top shows pulling in a cool $2 million a week. Long-running classics like *The Lion King* and *Wicked* continue to play before sold-out houses, alongside newer hits such as the *Book of Mormon*. Meanwhile, stalwarts such as *Les Miserables* get revamped and reopen to much fanfare (as in 2014). But it's away from Broadway's bright lights, in regional theaters such as Chicago's Steppenwolf, Minneapolis' Guthrie and hundreds more, where new plays and playwrights emerge that keep the art vital.

The unlikely star of Broadway in 2016 and 2017 was a rap- and R&B-inspired musical about one of the lesser known Founding Fathers. Lin-Manuel Miranda's *Hamilton*, based on Ron Chernow's best-selling 2004 biography of Treasury Secretary Alexander Hamilton, featured a cast of nonwhite actors and an incredibly catchy soundtrack. Demand was almost unprecedented and tickets soared to astronomical prices, though it is now a bit easier to score a seat: national tours launched in 2017.

Film & Television

The studio system actually began in Manhattan, where Thomas Edison – inventor of the industry's earliest moving-picture technology – tried to create a monopoly with his patents. This drove many independents to move to a suburb of Los Angeles, where they could easily flee to Mexico in case of legal trouble – and ta-da, Hollywood was born.

While most of the movie magic still happens on the West Coast, New York retains its fair share of film and TV studios. ABC, CBS, NBC, CNN, MTV and HBO are among the Big Apple's big shots, and many visitors come expressly to see Jimmy Fallon *(Tonight Show)*, Stephen Colbert *(Late Show)* or their other favorite talk shows taping. Many filmmakers and actors prefer New York to the West Coast – Robert De Niro, Spike Lee and Woody Allen most famously – so keep an eye out on local streets. Other film-friendly cities include Miami, Chicago and Atlanta, and one you wouldn't normally think of: Wilmington, North Carolina, which hosts enough studios to earn the nickname 'Wilmywood' (though new state laws scrapping tax incentives may slow the scene there).

As cable TV and Netflix, Amazon and other streaming services like YouTube, where users can broadcast their own channels and be their own stars, have entered the industry, mainstream networks have stuck to a formula of long-narrative serial dramas (like *Law & Order: SVU*, which has been on since 1999), as well as cheap-to-produce, 'unscripted' reality TV. What *Survivor* started in 2000, the contestants and 'actors' of *The Voice* and *The Bachelor* keep alive today, for better or for worse.

Several famous authors from the eastern USA wrote books that have been banned at one time or another, including Indianapolis' Kurt Vonnegut (Slaughter-house-Five), New York's JD Salinger (The Catcher in the Rye) and Georgia-born Alice Walker (The Color Purple).

Architecture

In 1885, a group of designers in Chicago shot up the pioneering sky-scraper. It didn't exactly poke the clouds, but its use of steel framing launched modern architecture.

Around the same time, another Chicago architect was doing radical things closer to the ground. Frank Lloyd Wright created a building style that abandoned historical elements and references, which had long been the tradition, and instead he went organic. He designed buildings in relation to the landscape, which on the Great Plains were the low-slung, horizontal lines of the surrounding prairie. An entire movement grew up around Wright's Prairie Style.

European architects absorbed Wright's ideas, and that influence bounced back when the Bauhaus school left Nazi Germany and set up in the USA. Here it became known as the International Style, an early form of modernism. Ludwig Mies van der Rohe was the main man with the plan, and his boxy, metal-and-glass behemoths rose high on urban horizons, especially in Chicago and New York City. Postmodernism followed, reintroducing color and the decorative elements of art deco, beaux arts and other earlier styles to the region's sky-high designs.

Today's architects continue to break boundaries. Recent examples of visionary designs include Jeanne Gang's rippling Aqua Tower in Chicago – the world's tallest building designed by a woman. In 2013 NYC's 1776-ft-high One World Trade Center rose to become the USA's loftiest building. In 2016, David Ajaye's shimmering National Museum of African American History and Culture took its place on the Mall in Washington, DC.

Music

Jazz, blues, country, hip-hop and rock music all were born in the eastern USA, and their beats permeate clubs and juke joints from north to south. Listen in and you'll hear the legacy of Muddy Waters' slide guitar, Hank Williams' yodel, John Coltrane's frenzied cascades and much more.

Blues

All US music starts with the blues. And the blues started in the South. That's where the genre developed out of the work songs, or 'shouts,' of black slaves and out of black spiritual songs and their call-and-response pattern, both of which were adaptations of African music.

By the 1920s, Delta blues typified the sound. Musicians from Memphis to Mississippi sung passionate, plaintive melodies accompanied by a lonely slide guitar. Traveling blues musicians, and particularly female blues singers, gained fame and employment across the South. Early pioneers included Robert Johnson, WC Handy, Ma Rainey, Huddie Ledbetter (aka Lead Belly) and Bessie Smith, who some consider the best blues singer who ever lived.

At the same time, African American Christian choral music evolved into gospel, whose greatest singer, Mahalia Jackson, came to prominence in Chicago in the 1920s. She sang in the choir of the Greater Salem Baptist Church on the city's south side and was a faithful member until her death in 1972.

After WWII many musicians headed north to Chicago, which had become a hub for African American culture. And here the genre took a turn – it went electric. A new generation of players such as Muddy Waters, Buddy Guy, BB King and John Lee Hooker plugged in to amps, and their screaming guitars laid the groundwork for rock and roll.

Jazz

Down in New Orleans, Congo Sq, where slaves gathered to sing and dance from the late 18th century onward, is considered the birthplace of jazz. There ex-slaves adapted the reed, horn and string instruments used by the city's multiracial Creoles – who themselves preferred formal European music – to play their own African-influenced music. This fertile cross-pollination produced a steady stream of innovative sound.

The first variation was ragtime, so-called because of its 'ragged,' syncopated African rhythms. Next came Dixieland jazz, centered on New Orleans' infamous Storyville red-light district. In 1917 Storyville shut down, and the musicians dispersed. Bandleader King Oliver moved to Chicago, and his star trumpet player, Louis Armstrong, soon followed. Armstrong's distinctive vocals and talented improvisations led to the solo becoming an integral part of jazz throughout much of the 20th century.

The 1920s and '30s are known as the Jazz Age, and New York City's Harlem was its hot spot. Swing – an urbane, big-band jazz style – swept the country, led by innovative bandleaders Duke Ellington and Count Basie. Jazz singers Ella Fitzgerald and Billie Holiday combined jazz with its Southern sibling, the blues.

Eastern USA Classic Playlist

'Atlantic City,'
Bruce Springsteen

'Georgia on My Mind,' Ray Charles

'No Sleep till Brooklyn,'
Beastie Boys

'Sweet Home Alabama,'
Lynyrd Skynyrd

'Floridays,'
Jimmy Buffet

'Humble and Kind,'
Tim McGraw

After WWII, bebop (aka bop) arose, reacting against the smooth melodies and confining rhythms of big-band swing. Charlie Parker, Dizzy Gillespie and Thelonious Monk led the way. In the 1950s and '60s, Miles Davis, John Coltrane and others deconstructed the sound and made up a new one that was cool, free and avant-garde. NYC, New Orleans and Chicago remain the core of the scene today.

Country

Early Scottish, Irish and English immigrants brought their own instruments and folk music to America, and what emerged over time in the secluded Appalachian Mountains was fiddle-and-banjo hillbilly, or 'country,' music. In the Southwest, steel guitars and larger bands distinguished 'western' music. In the 1920s, these styles merged into 'country and western' and Nashville became its center, especially once the Grand Ole Opry began its radio broadcasts in 1925. Country musicians who are now 'classics' include Hank Williams, Johnny Cash, Willie Nelson, Patsy Cline and Loretta Lynn.

Something about the 'cry in your beer' twanging clearly resonated with listeners, because country music is now big business. Singer-songwriters such as Blake Shelton, Tim McGraw and Taylor Swift have sold millions of albums. Subsequent riffs on the genre include bluegrass, rockabilly and alt-country. The South remains the genre's boot-wearin' stronghold.

Folk

The tradition of American folk music was crystallized in Woody Guthrie, who traveled the country during the Depression singing politically conscious songs. In the 1940s, New Yorker Pete Seeger emerged as a tireless preserver of America's folk heritage. Folk music experienced a revival during 1960s protest movements, but then-folkie Bob Dylan ended it almost single-handedly when he plugged in an electric guitar to shouts of 'traitor!' at the Newport Folk Festival in 1965.

Folk has seen a resurgence in the last decade. Iron & Wine's tunes channel mournful pop, blues and rock as only a Southerner can, while the Hoosier sister duo Lily & Madeleine sing ethereal, incredibly rich folk ballads.

Rock

Most say rock and roll was born in 1954 the day Elvis Presley walked into Sam Phillips' Sun Studio in Memphis and recorded 'That's All Right.' Initially, radio stations weren't sure why a white country boy was singing black music, or whether they should play him. It wasn't until 1956 that Presley scored his first big breakthrough with 'Heartbreak Hotel,' and in some ways, America never recovered from the rock-and-roll aftermath.

Musically, rock was a hybrid of guitar-driven blues, black rhythm and blues (R&B), and white country-and-western music. R&B evolved in the 1940s out of swing and the blues, and was then known as 'race music.' With rock and roll, white musicians (and some African American musicians) transformed 'race music' into something that white youths could embrace freely – and boy, did they.

Rock and roll instantly abetted a social revolution even more significant than its musical one: openly sexual as it celebrated youth and dancing freely across color lines, rock scared the nation. Authorities worked diligently to control 'juvenile delinquents' and to sanitize and suppress rock and roll, which might have withered if not for the early 1960s 'British invasion,' in which the Beatles and the Rolling Stones, emulating Chuck Berry, Little Richard and others, shocked rock and roll back to life.

Best Music Festivals

New Orleans Jazz Fest; April

Movement Electronic Music Festival, Detroit; May

Bonnaroo, Manchester, TN; June

Summerfest, Milwaukee, WI; June/July

Newport Folk Festival, Rhode Island; July

Lollapalooza, Chicago, IL; August

The 1960s witnessed a full-blown youth rebellion, epitomized by the drug-inspired psychedelic sounds of the Grateful Dead and Jefferson Airplane, and the electric wails of Janis Joplin and Jimi Hendrix, all hailing from the West Coast. The sounds and sensibilities of the East were somewhat different to the flower children back West. Lou Reed's Velvet Underground are the most significant band to emerge from the eastern USA in this decade.

Since then, rock has been about music and lifestyle, alternately torn between hedonism and seriousness, commercialism and authenticity. The Woodstock festival exemplified the scene in 1969, transforming a little patch of upstate New York into a legend.

Punk arrived in the late 1970s, led by the Ramones (the pride of Queens, NY), as did the working-class rock of Bruce Springsteen (the pride of New Jersey). As the counterculture became the culture in the 1980s, critics prematurely pronounced 'rock is dead.' Rock was saved (by the Talking Heads, REM and Sonic Youth, among other eastern US bands) as it always has been: by splintering and evolving, whether it's called new wave, heavy metal, grunge, indie rock, world beat, skate punk, hardcore, goth, emo or electronica.

Even though hip-hop has become today's outlaw sound, rock remains relevant, and it's not going anywhere. The Strokes and the Killers helped stoke a rock revival in the early 2000s. Alabama Shakes, Black Lips and Future Islands are among the bands that carry the torch currently.

Hip-Hop

From the ocean of sounds coming out of the early 1970s – funk, soul, Latin, reggae, and rock and roll – young DJs from the Bronx in NYC began to spin a groundbreaking mixture of records together in an effort to drive dance floors wild.

And so hip-hop was born. Groups such as Grandmaster Flash and the Furious Five were soon taking the party from the streets to the trendy clubs of Manhattan and mingling with punk and new wave bands including the Clash and Blondie. Break-out artists Futura 2000, Keith Haring and Jean-Michel Basquiat moved from the subways and the streets to the galleries, and soon to the worlds of fashion and advertising.

New York remained the hub into the mid-1980s. Groups like Run-DMC, Public Enemy and the Beastie Boys sold millions. And then the sounds and styles of the growing hip-hop culture started to diversify. A rivalry developed between the East Coast groups and the West Coast 'gangsta' rappers coming out of LA. Groups like Niggaz With Attitude got both accolades and bad press for their daring sounds and social commentary – which critics called battle cries for violence – on racism, drugs, sex and urban poverty.

Come the turn of the millennium, what started as raggedy gang kids playing their parents' funk records at illegal block parties had evolved into a multibillion-dollar business. Russell Simmons and P Diddy stood atop New York–based media empires, and stars Queen Latifah (from Jersey) and Will Smith (from Philly) were Hollywood royalty. A white rapper from Detroit, Eminem, sold millions of records, and hip-hop overtook country as America's second-most-popular music behind pop rock.

Today, many view hip-hop as a vapid wasteland of commercial excess – glorifying consumerism, misogyny, homophobia, drug use and a host of other social ills. But just as the hedonistic days of arena rock and roll gave birth to the rebel child of punk, the evolving offspring of hip-hop and DJ culture are constantly breaking the rules to create something new and even more energizing. Major players of the moment include Jay-Z, Kanye West, Nicki Minaj, Common and the more experimental and feel-good hip-hop duo of Macklemore & Ryan Lewis.

Shrines for Music Lovers

Sun Studio, Memphis, TN

Graceland, Memphis, TN

Country Music Hall of Fame, Nashville, TN

Rock and Roll Hall of Fame, Cleveland, OH

Preservation Hall, New Orleans, LA

BB King Museum and Delta Interpretive Center, Indianola, MS

Landscapes & Wildlife

Whether you've come to glimpse alligators, whales, manatees or moose, the eastern USA delivers. From the lofty Appalachian Mountains to the maple forests of New England in the north, tracing thousands of miles of estuaries and wild Atlantic coastline to the swamps and forested marshlands of the south, you're spoiled for choice when it comes to wildlife spotting. Scores of state and national parks, dedicated to the conservancy of the wilderness of the East, welcome you.

Landscapes

The eastern USA is a land of temperate, deciduous forests and contains the ancient Appalachian Mountains, a low range that parallels the Atlantic Ocean. Between the mountains and the coast lies the country's most populated, urbanized region, particularly in the corridor between Washington, DC, and Boston, MA.

To the north are the Great Lakes, which the USA shares with Canada. These five lakes, part of the Canadian Shield, are the greatest expanse of fresh water on the planet, constituting nearly 20% of the world's supply.

Going south along the East Coast, things get wetter and warmer till you reach the swamps of southern Florida and make the turn into the Gulf of Mexico, which provides the USA with a southern coastline.

West of the Appalachians are the vast interior plains, which lie flat all the way to the Rocky Mountains. The eastern plains are the nation's breadbasket, roughly divided into the northern 'corn belt' and the southern 'cotton belt.' The plains, an ancient sea bottom, are drained by the mighty Mississippi River, which together with the Missouri River forms the world's fourth-longest river system, surpassed only by the Nile, Amazon and Yangtze rivers.

Beyond the East, the Rocky Mountains and Southwestern deserts eventually give way to the Pacific Ocean.

Winner of the 2015 Pulitzer Prize for non-fiction, *The Sixth Extinction* by Elizabeth Kolbert looks at why species are disappearing from the planet at an alarming rate. It examines everything from the collapse in the population of golden frogs in the Panamanian rainforest through to mass bat die-offs in Vermont, near the author's home.

Plants & Trees

Displays of spring wildflowers and colorful autumn foliage are a New England specialty. Great Smoky Mountains National Park contains all five eastern-forest types – spruce fir, hemlock, pine-oak, and northern and cove hardwood – which support more than 100 native species of trees.

In Florida, the Everglades is the last subtropical wilderness in the US. This vital, endangered habitat is a fresh- and saltwater world of marshes, sloughs and coastal prairies that support mangroves, cypresses, sea grasses, tropical plants, pines and hardwoods.

Land Mammals

Moose

Moose nibble on shrubs throughout the northern part of the region, specifically Maine, New Hampshire, Vermont, upstate New York and the Michigan-Minnesota-Wisconsin north woods. They're part of the deer family but are far more humongous, with skinny, ballerina-like legs that support a hulking body. Males weigh up to 1200lb, all put on by a vegetarian diet of twigs and leaves. Despite their odd shape, moose can move it: they run up to 35mph, and in water they can swim as fast as two men paddling a canoe.

Males grow a spectacular rack of antlers every summer, only to discard it in November. You'll spot moose foraging near lakes and streams. They generally are not aggressive, and often will pose for photographs. They can be unpredictable, though, so don't startle them. During mating season (September) the males can become belligerent, so keep your distance.

Moose have been dying at an alarming rate in many areas. Scientists think climate change may be partly to blame. In New Hampshire a longer fall with less snow has increased the number of winter ticks, parasites that prey on moose. In Minnesota it's the same story but with brain worms as the deadly parasite. In Maine, however, the population remains robust at around 70,000 moose.

Black Bears

Despite a decline in numbers, black bears prowl most parts of the region, especially in the Adirondacks, the Great Smoky Mountains and the Great Lakes' north woods. Males can stand 7ft tall and weigh 550lb – but that depends on when you encounter them. In autumn they weigh up to 30% more than when they emerge from hibernation in the spring. Although they enjoy an occasional meaty snack, black bears usually fill their bellies with berries and other vegetation. They're opportunistic, adaptable

---

INFAMOUS NATURAL DISASTERS

Earthquakes, wildfires, tornadoes, hurricanes and blizzards – the eastern USA certainly has its share of natural disasters. A few of the more infamous events that have shaped the national conscience:

Hurricane Katrina August 29, 2005, is not a day easily forgotten in New Orleans. A massive hurricane swept across the Gulf of Mexico and slammed into Louisiana. As levees failed, floods inundated more than 80% of the city. The death toll reached 1836, with over $100 billion in estimated damages – making it America's costliest natural disaster. Heartbreaking images and anger over the government's bungled response still linger.

Hurricane Irene On August 27 and 28, 2011, a mammoth storm blew over the Eastern Seaboard, battering 15 states from Florida through to New England and as far inland as Pennsylvania. New York City evacuated many residents and took the unprecedented step of shutting down all public transit. More than 7.4 million homes lost electrical power, rivers ran wild, and at least 45 people died. The damage has been estimated to be $7 billion.

East Coast Earthquake On August 23, 2011, a rare earthquake rattled the eastern USA. The 5.8-magnitude tremor had its epicenter located in Mineral, Virginia, but was felt from Maine right through to South Carolina, and was the area's strongest quake since 1897. There was no serious damage, though it did crack the Washington Monument and knock three spires off the National Cathedral in Washington, DC.

Hurricane Sandy On October 29, 2012, America suffered its second-costliest hurricane in US history (after Katrina). Sandy was the largest Atlantic hurricane ever recorded, with storm winds spanning over 1000 miles. The Jersey Shore and low-lying areas of New York City (such as Staten Island) were particularly hard hit. More than 80 people died in the USA, and estimated damages amounted to more than $65 billion.

Louisiana Floods The worst natural disaster in the eastern USA since Hurricane Sandy befell the state of Louisiana in August 2016, when 6 trillion, 900 billion gallons of rain fell in one week (31in in 15 hours in Livingstone Parish), displacing tens of thousands, causing damage in excess of $30 million and claiming 13 lives.

EASTERN USA'S NATIONAL PARKS

PARK	STATE	FEATURES	ACTIVITIES	BEST TIME TO VISIT
Acadia National Park	ME	1530ft Cadillac Mountain, rocky coastline, islands	hiking, cycling	May–Oct
Biscayne National Park	FL	coral reefs, manatees, dolphins, sea turtles	kayaking, snorkeling, diving, glass-bottom boat tours	mid-Dec–mid-Apr
Congaree National Park	SC	moss-draped cypresses, swamp, owls	fishing, canoeing	Apr–Jun & Sep–Nov
Cuyahoga Valley National Park	OH	rivers, waterfalls, canal tow path	hiking, cycling, scenic train ride	May–Oct
Dry Tortugas National Park	FL	remote islands, Civil War fort, 300 bird species, sea turtles	snorkeling, diving, bird-watching	Dec–Apr
Everglades National Park	FL	grasslands, swamp, alligators, panthers, manatees	cycling, canoeing, kayaking, hiking	Dec–Apr
Great Smoky Mountains National Park	NC, TN	mountains, woodlands, wildflowers, black bears, elk	hiking, horseback riding, fishing	mid-Apr–Oct
Hot Springs National Park	AK	thermal waters, historic buildings	spa soaking, hiking	Sep–Feb
Isle Royale National Park	MI	huge isolated island, thick forest, lakes, moose	kayaking, hiking, back-country camping	mid-May–Oct
Mammoth Cave National Park	KY	never-ending caves, underground rivers, bats	hiking, spelunking	year-round
Shenandoah National Park	VA	Blue Ridge Mountains, waterfalls, deer, bobcats	hiking, camping	Apr–Oct
Voyageurs National Park	MN	thick forest, islands, lakes, wolves, aurora borealis	boating, snow-mobiling	May–late–Sep

and curious animals, and can survive on very small home ranges. As their forests diminish, they're occasionally seen traipsing through nearby populated areas.

Panthers

A remnant population of panthers licks its chops in Everglades National Park, Florida. Before European contact, perhaps 1500 roamed the state. The first panther bounty ($5 a scalp) was passed in 1832, and over the next 130 years they were hunted relentlessly. Though hunting was stopped in 1958, it was too late for panthers to survive on their own. Without a captive breeding program, begun in 1991, the Florida panther would now be extinct, and with only some 100 known to exist, they're not out of the swamp yet.

Wolves & Coyotes

Wolves are rare in the eastern USA. Those that are here wander mostly in northern Minnesota, particularly the Boundary Waters. The area's cold, boreal forest is prime territory, as well as home to the International Wolf Center (www.wolf.org) in Ely, Minnesota. The wolf can be every bit as fierce and cunning as is portrayed in fairy tales, although it rarely attacks humans. If you're out in the wilderness, you may hear them howling at the moon.

The coyote looks similar to the wolf but is about half the size, ranging from 15lb to 45lb. An icon of the Southwest, coyotes are found all over the eastern region too, even in cities – Chicago had one a few years ago that loped into a downtown sandwich shop during the lunchtime rush.

Deer

The white-tailed deer can be found everywhere in the region, from top to bottom. Endemic to the Florida Keys are Key deer, a Honey-I-Shrunk-the-Ungulate subspecies – less than 3ft tall and lighter than a 10-year-old boy, they live mostly on Big Pine Key.

Reptiles

Alligators & Crocodiles

American alligators slither throughout the Southeast's wetlands, mostly in Florida and Louisiana. With a snout, eyeballs and pebbled back so still they hardly ripple the water's surface, alligators have watched over the swamps for more than 200 million years.

Louisiana has close to two million gators, and Florida counts 1.5 million among the state's lakes, rivers and golf courses, mostly in the central and southern zones. The Everglades are perhaps the best place to find them lurking. Alligators are alpha predators who keep the rest of the food chain in check, and their 'gator holes' become vital water cups in the dry season and during droughts, aiding the entire wetlands ecosystem. They live about 30 years, can grow up to 14ft long and weigh 1000lb. No longer officially endangered, alligators remain protected because they resemble the still-endangered American crocodile.

South Florida is home to the only North American population of American crocodiles, around 1500 of them. They prefer saltwater, and to distinguish them from gators, check their smile – a croc's snout is more tapered and its teeth stick out.

Sea Turtles

Florida is the hot spot for sea-turtle nesting in the continental US. Three main species create over 80,000 nests annually, mostly on southern Atlantic Coast beaches, but extending to all Gulf Coast beaches, too. Loggerheads comprise the vast majority, followed by green and leatherback turtles and, historically, hawksbill and Kemp's ridley as well; all five species are endangered or threatened. The leatherback is the largest, bulking up to 10ft and 2000lb. During the May–October nesting season, sea turtles deposit from 80 to 120 eggs in each nest. The eggs incubate for about two months, and then the hatchlings emerge all at once and make for the ocean. Hatchlings don't need the moon to find their way.

Snakes

First, here's the bad news: there are four species of rattlesnake found east of the Mississippi – the diamondback, pygmy, canebrake and timber. At 7ft long, the diamondback is the biggest and the most aggressive. Copperheads, cottonmouths and coral snakes are other poisonous types in the region. All of them slither primarily through the Mid-Atlantic and South.

Now the good news: running into a poisonous snake is uncommon. Need proof? Great Smoky Mountains National Park, with around 10 million visitors per year, has never recorded a snakebite fatality in its 80-plus-year history.

Michigan's Isle Royale National Park hosts the world's longest-running predator-prey study, of wolves and moose. While numbers have fluctuated since research began in 1958, the biggest imbalance occurred recently: in 2015, the wolf population dwindled to three (down from 30 wolves as recently as 2006), while moose numbers swelled to 1250. Disease, inbreeding and climate shifts are among the culprits.

LANDSCAPES & WILDLIFE REPTILES

Marine Mammals & Fish

Whales & Dolphins

The eastern USA's top spot to whale-watch is off Massachusetts' coast at Stellwagen Bank National Marine Sanctuary, a summer feeding ground for humpbacks. These awesome creatures average 49ft and 36 tons – serious heft to be launching up and out of the water for their playful breaching. They also come surprisingly close to boats, offering great photo ops. Many of the 400 remaining North Atlantic right whales, the world's most endangered leviathan, frequent the same waters. Cruises depart from Boston, Plymouth, Provincetown and Gloucester, Massachusetts.

The waters off the coast of Florida are home to several dolphin species. By far the most common species is the bottlenose dolphin, which is highly social, extremely intelligent and frequently encountered.

In addition to its national parks, the eastern USA holds eight national seashores (including Cape Cod in Massachusetts), four national lakeshores (including Sleeping Bear Dunes in Michigan) and 10 national rivers (including New River Gorge in West Virginia). The National Park Service (www.nps.gov) has the lowdown.

Manatees

Florida's coast is home to the unusual, gentle manatee, which moves between freshwater rivers and the ocean. Around 10ft long and weighing on average 1000lb, these agile, expressive creatures don't do much, spending most of each day resting and eating 10% of their body weight. In winter they seek out Florida's warm-water springs and power-plant discharge canals. In summer they migrate back to the ocean and can be spotted in the coastal waters of Alabama, Georgia and South Carolina, in addition to Florida. anatees have been under some form of protection since 1893, and they were included in the first federal endangered species list in 1967. They were once hunted for their meat – finer than filet mignon, allegedly – but collisions with boats are now a leading cause of manatee deaths. Florida manatees number around 4800 today.

Tropical Fish

For stunning coral reefs and vibrant tropical fish, the Florida Keys are the places to go. North America's only living coral barrier reef – and the world's third-largest such reef (after the Great Barrier Reef in Australia and the Meso-American Reef in Belize) – runs for 221 miles from Key Biscayne off Miami down to Dry Tortugas National Park, 70 miles off Key West. Both the national park and John Pennekamp Coral Reef State Park (in Key Largo) are terrific places to behold the underwater world where sea fans wave and schools of blue tangs and trumpetfish dart. The reefs are home to more than 260 types of tropical fish.

Birds

The bald eagle, the USA's national symbol since 1782, is the only eagle unique to North America. Its wingspan can reach more than 6.5ft across. Good wintertime viewing sites are along the Mississippi River in Minnesota, Wisconsin and Illinois; in summer, eagles are common throughout Florida, wherever there's fish-rich water for chowing alongside tall trees for nesting. The eagle has come off the endangered species list, having made a remarkable comeback from a low of 417 breeding pairs in 1963 to almost 9800 pairs today (that's in the lower 48 states; another 30,000-plus live in Alaska). White pelicans, which are among the region's largest birds, arrive in winter (October to April), while brown pelicans, the only kind to dive for their food, live here year-round.

Survival Guide

Directory A–Z

Accommodations

For all but the cheapest places and the slowest seasons, reservations are advised. In high-season tourist hot spots, hotels can book up months ahead.

Seasons

Peak season is summer, generally May to September, when prices are highest.

Exceptions include Florida and the northern ski areas, when winter is the busiest and costliest time to visit.

Amenities

Most properties offer in-room wi-fi. It's usually free in budget and midrange lodgings, while top-end hotels often charge a fee (typically $10 to $20 per day).

Many smaller properties, especially B&Bs, ban smoking. Marriott and Westin hotels are 100% smoke-free. All other properties have rooms set aside for nonsmokers.

Air-conditioning is standard at most places.

B&Bs

These accommodations vary from small, comfy houses with shared bathrooms (least expensive) to romantic, antique-filled historic homes and mansions with private baths (most expensive). Those focusing on upscale romance may discourage children. Also, inns and B&Bs often require a minimum stay of two or three days on weekends, and reservations are essential. Always call ahead to confirm policies (ie regarding kids, pets, smoking) and bathroom arrangements.

B&B agencies:

Bed & Breakfast Inns Online (www.bbonline.com)

BedandBreakfast.com (www.bedandbreakfast.com)

BnB Finder (www.bnbfinder.com)

Select Registry (www.selectregistry.com)

Camping & Holiday Parks

Campsites at national and state parks typically come in three types:

Primitive Free to $10 per night; no facilities.

Basic $10 to $20; with toilets, drinking water, fire pits and picnic tables.

Developed $20 to $50; with more amenities such as showers, barbecue grills, recreational vehicle (RV) sites with hookups etc.

Make reservations for national parks and other federal lands through www.recreation.gov. Camping is usually limited to 14 days and can be reserved up to six months in advance. For some state park campgrounds, you can make bookings through ReserveAmerica (www.reserveamerica.com).

Most privately owned campgrounds are geared to RVs, but will also have a small section available for tent campers. Expect lots

---

SLEEPING PRICE RANGES

Rates listed are based on double occupancy for high season (generally May to September), and do not include taxes, which can add 10% to 15% or more. When booking, ask for the rate including taxes.

$ less than $100

$$ $100–$250

$$$ more than $250

For New York City and Washington, DC, the rate is as follows:

$ less than $150

$$ $150–$350

$$$ more than $350

of amenities, like swimming pools, laundry facilities, convenience stores and bars. Kampgrounds of America (www.koa.com) is a national network of private campgrounds; their Kamping Kabins have air-con and kitchens.

Discounts

Check hotel websites for special online rates. If you find something cheaper on a booking site, many hotels will match it if you call and ask.

Hostels

Hostelling International USA (www.hiusa.org) runs several hostels in the eastern US. Most have gender-segregated dorms, a few private rooms, shared baths and a communal kitchen. Overnight fees for dorm beds range from $25 to $45 (though in NYC, a dorm bed can cost upward of $75). You don't have to be a member to stay, but you pay a slightly higher rate. Reservations are accepted (you can book online).

Hotels

Hotels in all categories typically include cable TV, in-room wi-fi, private baths and a simple continental breakfast. Many midrange properties provide minibars, microwaves, hairdryers and swimming pools, while top-end hotels add concierge services, fitness and business centers, spas, restaurants and bars.

Popular hotel chains include the following:

Best Western (www.best western.com)

Comfort Inn (www.comfortinn. com)

Hampton Inn (www.hampton-inn.com)

Hilton (www.hilton.com)

Holiday Inn (www.holidayinn. com)

Marriott (www.marriott.com)

Super 8 (www.super8.com)

ETIQUETTE

Greetings Don't be overly physical when greeting someone. Some Americans will hug, urbanites may exchange cheek kisses, but most – especially men – shake hands.

Smoking Don't assume you can smoke – even if you're outside. Most Americans have little tolerance for smokers and have even banned smoking from many parks, boardwalks and beaches.

Punctuality Do be on time. Many folks in the US consider it rude to be kept waiting.

Politeness It's common practice to greet the staff when entering and leaving a shop ('hello' and 'have a nice day' will do). Also, Americans smile a lot (often a symbol of politeness, nothing more).

Motels

Motels – distinguishable from hotels by having rooms that open onto a parking lot – tend to cluster around interstate exits and along main routes into town. Many are inexpensive 'mom-and-pop' operations; breakfast is rarely included; and amenities might top out at wi-fi and a TV (maybe with cable). Although most motel rooms won't win any style awards, they can be clean and comfortable and offer good value. Ask to see a room first if you're unsure.

Resorts

Florida, in particular, has behemoth resorts. Facilities can include all manner of fitness and sports, pools, spas, restaurants and bars, and so on. Many also have on-site babysitting services. However, some also tack an extra 'resort fee' onto rates, so always ask.

Customs Regulations

For a complete list of US customs regulations, visit the official website for US Customs and Border Protection (www.cbp.gov).

Duty-free allowance per person is as follows:

➡ 1L of liquor (provided you are at least 21 years old)

➡ 100 cigars and 200 cigarettes (if you are at least 18)

➡ $200 worth of gifts and purchases ($800 if a returning US citizen)

➡ If you arrive with $10,000 or more in US or foreign currency, it must be declared

There are heavy penalties for attempting to import illegal drugs. Forbidden items include drug paraphernalia, items with fake brand names and most goods made in

BOOK YOUR STAY ONLINE

For more accommodation reviews by Lonely Planet authors, check out www.lonelyplanet.com/usa/east ern-usa/hotels. You'll find independent reviews, as well as recommendations on the best places to stay. Best of all, you can book online.

Cuba, Iran, Myanmar (Burma) and Sudan. Fruit, vegetables and other food must be declared (whereby you'll undergo a time-consuming search) or left in the bins in the arrival area.

Discount Cards

The following cards can net savings (usually about 10%) on museums, accommodations and some transport (including Amtrak):

American Association of Retired Persons (www.aarp. org) For US travelers age 50 and older.

American Automobile Association (www.aaa.com) For members of AAA or reciprocal clubs in Europe and Australia.

International Student Identity Card (www.isic.org) For students of any age and non-students under 26 years old.

Student Advantage Card (www. studentadvantage.com) For US and foreign students aged 16 and older.

Electricity

Type B
120V/60Hz

Type A
120V/60Hz

Embassies & Consulates

In addition to the embassies in Washington, DC (see www. embassy.org for a complete list), most countries have an embassy for the UN in New York City. Some countries have consulates in other large cities.

Australian Embassy (☑20 2-797-3000; www.usa.embassy. gov.au; 1601 Massachusetts Ave NW; ⊗8:30am-5pm Mon-Fri; Ⓜ Red Line to Farragut North)

Canadian Embassy (☑20 2-682-1740; www.can-am. gc.ca; 501 Pennsylvania Ave NW; ⊗8:30am-4:40pm Mon-Fri; Ⓜ Green, Yellow Lines to Archives)

French Embassy (☑202-944-6000; www.franceintheus. org; 4101 Reservoir Rd NW; ⊗8:45am-12:30pm & 2:30-3:30pm Mon-Fri; 🚇D6)

German Embassy (☑202-298-4000; www.germany.info; 4645 Reservoir Rd NW; ⊗8-11:45am & 1-2:30pm Mon-Thu, 8am-noon Fri; 🚇D6)

Irish Embassy (☑202-462-3939; www.embassyofireland. org; 2234 Massachusetts Ave NW; ⊗9am-1pm & 2-4pm

Mon-Fri; Ⓜ Red Line to Dupont Circle)

Mexican Embassy (☑202-728-1600; https://embamex.sre. gob.mx/eua; 1911 Pennsylvania Ave NW; ⊗9am-6pm Mon-Fri; Ⓜ Orange, Silver, Blue Lines to Farragut West)

Netherlands Embassy (☑20 2-244-5300; www.nether-landsworldwide.nl/countries/ united-states; 4200 Linnean Ave NW; ⊗8:30am-4:30pm Mon-Fri; Ⓜ Red Line to Van Ness-UDC)

New Zealand Embassy (☑20 2-328-4800; www.mfat.govt. nz/usa; 37 Observatory Circle NW; ⊗8:30am-5pm Mon-Fri; Ⓜ Red Line to Dupont Circle then bus N2 or N4)

UK Embassy (☑202-588-6500; www.gov.uk/government/ world/usa; 3100 Massachusetts Ave NW; ⊗9am-4pm Mon-Fri; Ⓜ Red Line to Dupont Circle then bus N2 or N4)

Food & Drink

See Eat & Drink Like a Local (p46) for everything you need to know about eating and drinking in the region.

Health

Before You Go

The eastern region, like the rest of the USA, has a high level of hygiene, so infectious diseases are not a significant problem. There are no required vaccines, and tap water is safe to drink.

Bring any medications you may need in their original containers, clearly labeled. Having a signed, dated letter from your physician that describes all of your medical conditions and medications (including generic names) is also a good idea.

HEALTH INSURANCE

The United States offers possibly the finest health care in the world – the problem is that it can be prohibitively expensive. It's essential to purchase travel health insurance if your home policy doesn't cover you for medical expenses abroad. Check the Insurance section of the Lonely Planet (www.lonelyplanet.com/travel-insurance) website for more information.

Find out in advance if your insurance plan will make payments directly to providers or reimburse you later for overseas health expenditures.

VACCINATIONS

At the time of writing, there were no recommended vaccinations for travelers of most countries visiting the USA and particularly its eastern states, aside from the standard tetanus and polio vaccinations.

In Eastern USA

AVAILABILITY & COST OF HEALTH CARE

If you have a medical emergency, go to the emergency room of the nearest hospital.

If the problem isn't urgent, call a nearby hospital and ask for a referral to a local physician; this is usually cheaper than a trip to the emergency room.

Standalone, for-profit, urgent-care centers provide good service, but can be the most expensive option.

Pharmacies are abundantly supplied. However, some medications that are available over the counter in other countries require a prescription in the US.

If you don't have insurance to cover the cost of prescriptions, they can be shockingly expensive.

ENVIRONMENTAL HAZARDS

Cold exposure This can be a problem, especially in the northern regions. Keep all body surfaces covered, including the head and neck. Watch out for the 'Umbles' – stumbles, mumbles, fumbles and grumbles – which are signs of impending hypothermia.

Heat exhaustion Dehydration is the main contributor. Symptoms include feeling weak, headache, nausea and sweaty skin. Lay the victim flat with their legs raised, apply cool, wet cloths to the skin, and rehydrate.

INFECTIOUS DISEASES

Most infectious diseases are acquired by mosquito or tick bites or through environmental exposure. The Centers for Disease Control and Prevention (www.cdc.gov) has further details.

Giardiasis Intestinal infection. Avoid drinking directly from lakes, ponds, streams and rivers.

Lyme Disease Occurs mostly in the Northeast. Transmitted by deer ticks in late spring and summer. Perform a tick check after you've been outdoors.

West Nile Virus Mosquito-transmitted in late summer and early fall. Prevent by keeping covered (wear long sleeves, long pants, hats and shoes rather than sandals) and apply a good insect repellent, preferably one containing DEET, to exposed skin and clothing.

Zika Of gravest concern to pregnant women, this moquito-borne virus can cause microcephaly (when the brain does not develop fully) in utero. Miami made the news in 2016 for having the first outbreak of its kind in the US, with over 250 locally acquired cases reported in southern Florida. Although the disease was considered eradicated there in early 2017, epidemiologists warn that Zika could rebound with the arrival of warmer temperatures and heavier rainfall.

TAP WATER

Tap water is safe to drink everywhere in the eastern USA, except in some state or national parks where it is expressly indicated that tap water is not 'potable' or safe to drink.

Insurance

It's expensive to get sick, crash a car or have things stolen from you in the US. Make sure you have adequate coverage before arriving. To insure yourself for items that may be stolen from your car, consult your homeowner's (or renter's) insurance policy or consider investing in travel insurance.

Worldwide travel insurance is available at www.lonelyplanet.com/travel-insurance. You can buy, extend and claim online anytime – even if you're already on the road.

Internet Access

Travelers will have few problems staying connected in the tech-savvy USA.

Wi-fi (in-room, with decent speed) is common in lodgings across the price spectrum. Many properties also have an internet-connected computer for public use.

Many restaurants, bars and cafes (such as Starbucks) offer free wi-fi. Some cities have wi-fi connected parks and plazas.

If you're not packing a laptop or other web-accessible device, try the public library. Most have public terminals (though they have time limits) and wi-fi. Occasionally out-of-state residents are charged a small fee for use.

If you're not from the US, remember that you may need an AC adapter for your laptop (if it's not 110/220 dual-voltage), plus a plug adapter for US sockets; both are available at large electronics shops, such as Best Buy.

For a list of wi-fi hotspots, visit www.wififreespot.com.

Legal Matters

Note that, if you are stopped by the police, there is no system of paying traffic tickets or other fines on the spot. The officer will explain your options to you; there is usually a 30-day period to pay fines by mail.

If you are arrested, never walk away from an officer. You are allowed to remain silent, and you are entitled to have access to an attorney. The legal system presumes you're innocent until proven guilty. All persons who are arrested have the right to make one phone call. If you don't have a lawyer or family member to help you, call your embassy or consulate. The police will give you the number on request.

Drugs & Alcohol

In most places it's illegal to walk with an open alcoholic drink on the street. New Orleans and Memphis' Beale St are notable exceptions.

Being 'carded' (ie asked to show photo ID to prove you're of legal drinking age, which is 21 years old) is standard practice everywhere.

Some states, especially in the South, have 'dry' counties where liquor sales are banned altogether.

In all states, the blood alcohol limit is 0.08%. Driving under the influence of alcohol or drugs is a serious offense, subject to stiff fines and even imprisonment.

Twenty-three states – including most from New York on through the Northeast –

treat possession of small amounts of marijuana as a misdemeanor (generally punishable with a fine of around $100 or $200 for the first offense). However, as pot policy varies from state to state, it's prudent to know the local laws before lighting up.

Aside from marijuana, recreational drugs are prohibited by law. Possession of any illicit drug, including cocaine, ecstasy, LSD, heroin or hashish, is a felony potentially punishable by lengthy jail sentences.

LGBT Travelers

In general, the Northeast is the most tolerant region in the eastern USA, and the South the least so, though big cities in all of the regions have long-standing gay communities.

Most major US cities have a visible and open LGBTIQ community that is easy to connect with.

The level of public acceptance varies nationwide. In some places, there is absolutely no tolerance whatsoever, and in others acceptance is predicated on LGBTIQ people not 'flaunting' their sexual orientation or identity. Be aware that bigotry still exists here. In rural areas and conservative enclaves, it's unwise to be openly out, as verbal abuse and even violence can sometimes occur. When in doubt, assume that locals follow a 'don't ask, don't tell' policy. Same-sex marriage is now legally recognized by the federal government, and 37 states (including many in the Northeast, plus DC) allow same-sex marriages. It may once more be a long haul to get other states on-board and there's a growing unease among the community that that steps taken toward building a society more accepting of sexuality and difference might be backtracked under the pro-Christian Trump administration.

Resources

The Queerest Places: A Guide to Gay and Lesbian Historic Sites, by Paula Martinac, is full of juicy details and history, and covers the country. Visit her blog at www.queerestplaces.com.

Advocate (www.advocate.com) Gay-oriented news website reports on business, politics, arts, entertainment and travel.

Gay Travel (www.gaytravel.com) Online guides to dozens of US destinations.

National LGBTQ Task Force (www.thetaskforce.org) National activist group's website covers news, politics and current issues.

Out Traveler (www.outtraveler. com) Gay-oriented travel articles.

Purple Roofs (www.purpleroofs. com) Lists gay-owned and gay-friendly B&Bs and hotels.

Gaycation (www.vice.com/ en_us/topic/gaycation) VICE TV's excellent documentary series on same-sex issues in the US and beyond.

Money

ATMs widely available. Credits cards accepted at most hotels, restaurants and shops.

ATMs & Eftpos

Most locals do not carry large amounts of cash for everyday use, relying instead on credit cards, debit cards and ATMs. Don't, however, plan to rely exclusively on credit cards, as some machines (notably at many gas stations) won't accept foreign cards. Smaller businesses may refuse to accept bills over $20.

ATMs are available 24/7 at most banks and in shopping centers, airports, grocery stores and convenience shops.

Most ATMs charge a service fee of $3 or more per transaction and your home bank may impose additional charges.

For foreign visitors, ask your bank for exact information about using its cards in stateside ATMs. The exchange rate is usually as good as you'll get anywhere.

Credit & Debit Cards

Major credit cards are almost universally accepted. In fact, it's next to impossible to rent a car or make phone reservations without one. Visa and MasterCard are the most widely accepted.

Currency Exchange

Banks are usually the best places to exchange foreign currencies. Most large city banks offer the service, but banks in rural areas may not.

Currency-exchange counters at the airport and in tourist centers typically have the worst rates; ask about fees and surcharges first.

Travelex (www.travelex. com) is a major currency-exchange company, but American Express (www. americanexpress.com) travel offices may offer better rates.

Taxes & Refunds

Sales tax varies by state and county, and ranges from 5% to 10%. Most prices you see advertised will exclude tax, which is calculated upon purchase.

Hotel taxes vary by city from around 10% to over 18% (in NYC).

Tipping

Tipping is *not* optional; only withhold tips in cases of outrageously bad service.

Airport and hotel porters $2 per bag, minimum $5 per cart

Bartenders 10% to 15% per round, minimum $1 per drink

Hotel housekeepers $2 to $5 daily, left under the card provided

Restaurant servers 15% to 20%, unless a gratuity is already charged on the bill

Taxi drivers 10% to 15%, rounded up to the next dollar

Valet parking attendants At least $2 on return of keys

Opening Hours

Typical opening times are as follows:

Banks 8:30am to 4:30pm Monday to Friday (and possibly 9am to noon Saturday)

Bars 5pm to midnight Sunday to Thursday, to 2am Friday and Saturday

Nightclubs 10pm to 3am Thursday to Saturday

Post Offices 9am to 5pm Monday to Friday

Shopping Malls 9am to 9pm

Stores 9am to 6pm Monday to Saturday, noon to 5pm Sunday

Supermarkets 8am to 8pm, some open 24 hours

Post

The US Postal Service (www. usps.com) is reliable and inexpensive. The postal rates for first-class mail within the USA are 49¢ for letters weighing up to 1oz (22¢ for each additional ounce) and 35¢ for postcards.

International airmail rates are $1.20 for a 1oz letter or postcard.

Public Holidays

On the following national public holidays, banks, schools and government offices (including post offices) are closed, and transportation, museums and other services operate on a Sunday schedule. Holidays falling on a weekend are usually observed the following Monday.

New Year's Day January 1

Martin Luther King Jr Day Third Monday in January

Presidents' Day Third Monday in February

Memorial Day Last Monday in May

Independence Day July 4

Labor Day First Monday in September

Columbus Day Second Monday in October

Veterans' Day November 11

Thanksgiving Fourth Thursday in November

Christmas Day December 25

Smoking

➡ As of 2017, a little more than half the eastern states had enforced statewide bans on smoking in restaurants, bars and workplaces, with many municipalities enforcing controls in other states and/or in more specific ways (public areas, schools etc).

➡ Texas, Tennessee and Florida still have liberal attitudes towards smoking: cigarettes are inexpensive and smoking in bars and restaurants is still permitted, although sometimes, smoking areas are separated.

➡ For the full list of exactly where smoking in public places is permitted, refer to the Americans for Nonsmoker's Rights (ANR) website (www.no-smoke.org).

Telephone

The US phone system mixes regional service providers, competing long-distance carriers and several cellphone companies. Overall, the system is efficient. Calls from a regular landline or cell phone are usually cheaper than a hotel phone or pay phone. Services such as Skype (www.skype.com) and Google Voice (www.google. com/hangout) can make calling quite cheap. Check the websites for details.

Cell Phones

Foreign phones operating on tri- or quad-band frequencies will work in the USA. Or purchase inexpensive cell (mobile) phones with a pay-as-you-go plan here.

Most of the USA's cell-phone systems are incompatible with the GSM 900/1800 standard used throughout Europe and Asia (though some convertible phones will work). iPhones will work fine – but beware of roaming costs, especially for data. Check with your service provider about using your phone here.

It might be cheaper to buy a prepaid SIM card for the USA, like those sold by AT&T or T-Mobile, which you can insert into your international mobile phone to get a local phone number and voicemail.

You can also buy inexpensive, no-contract (prepaid) phones with a local number and a set number of minutes, which can be topped up at will. Virgin Mobile, T-Mobile, AT&T and other providers offer phones starting at $30, with a package of minutes starting at around $40 for 400 minutes.

Electronics store chain Best Buy (www.bestbuy.com) sells prepaid phones, as well as international SIM cards. Online retailer Telestial (www.telestial.com) also sells SIM cards and cell phones; it rents phones, too.

Rural swaths of the East, especially in the mountains and various national parklands, don't pick up a signal. Check your provider's coverage map.

Long-Distance Calls & Area Codes

All phone numbers within the USA consist of a three-digit area code followed by a seven-digit local number. Typically, if you are calling a number within the same area code, you only have to dial the seven-digit number (though if it doesn't work, try adding 1 + the area code at the beginning). More information on dialing:

US country code ☑1

Making international calls Dial ☑011 + country code + area code + local number

Calling other US area codes or Canada Dial ☑1 + area code + seven-digit local number

Directory assistance nationwide ☑411

Toll-free numbers ☑1+ 800 (or 888, 877, 866) + seven-digit number. Some toll-free numbers only work within the US

Phonecards

Prepaid phonecards are a good solution for travelers on a budget. They are available from convenience stores, supermarkets and pharmacy chains. AT&T sells a reliable phonecard that is widely available.

Time

The eastern region is split between the Eastern and Central time zones, which are an hour apart. The demarcation line slices through Indiana, Kentucky, Tennessee and Florida. When it's noon Eastern time, it is 11am Central time (and 5pm Greenwich Mean Time).

The region, as well as most of the country, observes Daylight Saving Time (DST). On the second Sunday in March, clocks are set one hour ahead ('spring ahead'). Then, on the first Sunday of November, clocks are turned back one hour ('fall back').

And FYI: the US date system is written as month/day/year. Thus, the 8th of June, 2016, becomes 6/8/16.

Toilets

Toilets are of the standard, Western, sit-down variety, with urinals for men common in public places. That said, public toilets in the East aren't the most savory or squeaky-clean of places, and toilets in national and state parks are commonly of the pit variety: take some back-up toilet paper, just in case.

Tourist Information

The official tourism website of the USA is www.discoveramerica.com. It has links to every US state tourism office and website, plus loads of ideas for itinerary planning.

Most cities and towns have some sort of tourist center that provides local information, typically operated by the convention and visitor bureau (CVB) or chamber of commerce. These entities tend to list only the businesses that are bureau/chamber members, so not all of the town's hotels and restaurants receive coverage – keep in mind that good, independent options may be missing.

A few websites to get you started:

New York State Tourism (www.iloveny.com)

Visit Florida (www.visitflorida.com)

Visit Louisiana (www.louisianatravel.com)

Visit Maine (www.visitmaine.com)

Washington DC (www.washington.org)

Travelers with Disabilities

Travel in the region is relatively accommodating.

➡ Most public buildings are wheelchair-accessible and have appropriate restroom facilities.

➡ All major airlines, Greyhound buses and Amtrak trains will assist travelers with disabilities; just describe your needs when making reservations at least 48 hours in advance.

➡ Some car-rental agencies, such as Budget and Hertz, offer hand-controlled vehicles and vans with wheelchair lifts at no extra charge, but you must reserve them well in advance.

➡ Most cities have taxi companies with at least one accessible van, though you'll have to call ahead.

➡ Cities with underground transport have elevators for passengers needing assistance. Washington, DC, has the best network (every station has an elevator); NYC's elevators are few and far between.

➡ Many national and some state parks and recreation areas have wheelchair-accessible paved, graded dirt or boardwalk trails.

A number of organizations specialize in the needs of travelers with disabilities:

➡ Flying Wheels Travel (www.flyingwheelstravel.com) A full-service travel agency, highly recommended for those with mobility issues or chronic illness.

➡ Mobility International USA (www.miusa.org) Advises travelers with disabilities on mobility issues and runs educational exchange programs.

➡ Wheelchair Getaways (www.wheelchairgetaways.com) Rents accessible vans throughout the USA.

For further information, download Lonely Planet's free Accessible Travel guide from http://lptravel.to/AccessibleTravel.

Visas

Visitors from Canada, the UK, Australia, New Zealand, Japan and many EU countries do not need visas for less than 90 days, with ESTA approval. For other nations, see www.travel.state.gov or www.usa.gov/visas-and-visitors.

Visa Waiver Program & ESTA

Admission requirements are subject to rapid change. The US State Department (www.travel.state.gov) has the latest information, or check with a US consulate in your home country.

The Visa Waiver Program (VWP) allows nationals from 36 countries (including most EU countries, Japan, Australia and New Zealand) to enter the US without a visa for up to 90 days.

VWP visitors require a machine-readable passport and approval under the Electronic System For Travel Authorization (www.cbp.gov/esta) at least three days before arrival. There is a $14 fee for processing and authorization (payable online). Once approved, the registration is valid for two years.

In essence, ESTA requires that you register specific information online (name, address, passport info etc). You will receive one of three responses: 'Authorization Approved' (this usually comes within minutes; most applicants can expect to receive this response); 'Authorization Pending' (you'll need to check the status within the next 72 hours); or 'Travel not Authorized'. If this is the case, it means you will need to apply for a visa.

Those who need a visa – ie anyone staying longer than 90 days, or from a non-VWP country – should apply at the US consulate in their home country.

Canadians are exempt from the process. They do not need visas, though they do need a passport or document approved by the Western Hemisphere Travel Initiative (www.getyouhome.gov).

Volunteering

Volunteering opportunities abound in the eastern USA, providing a memorable chance to interact with locals and the land in ways you never would when just passing through.

Casual, drop-in volunteer work is plentiful in the big cities. Check weekly alternative newspapers for calendar listings or browse the free classified ads online at Craigslist (www.craigslist.org). The public website United We Serve (www.serve.gov) and private websites Idealist (www.idealist.org) and VolunteerMatch (www.volunteermatch.org) offer free searchable databases of short- and long-term volunteer opportunities nationwide.

More formal volunteer programs, especially those designed for international travelers, typically charge a fee of $250 to $1000, depending on the length of the program and what amenities are included (eg housing, meals). None cover travel expenses.

Green Project (www.thegreenproject.org) Working to improve battered communities in New Orleans in sustainable, green ways.

Habitat for Humanity (www.habitat.org) Focuses on building affordable housing for those in need.

Sierra Club (www.sierraclub.org) 'Volunteer vacations' restore wilderness areas and maintain trails, including in national parks and nature preserves.

Volunteers for Peace (www.vfp.org) Grassroots, multiweek volunteer projects emphasize manual labor and international exchange.

Wilderness Volunteers (www.wildernessvolunteers.org) Week-long trips helping maintain national parklands and outdoor recreation areas.

World Wide Opportunities on Organic Farms USA (www.wwoofusa.org) Represents more than 2000 organic farms in all 50 states that host volunteer workers in exchange for meals and accommodations, with opportunities for both short- and long-term stays.

Women Travelers

Women traveling by themselves or in a group should encounter no particular problems unique to the eastern USA.

In bars and nightclubs solo women can attract attention, but if you don't want company, most men will respect a firm 'no, thank you.'

Physical attack is unlikely, but if you are assaulted, consider calling a rape-crisis hotline before calling the police, unless you are in immediate danger, in which case you should call ☑911. The 24-hour National Sexual Assault Hotline (☎800-656-4673) can help.

The community website www.journeywoman.com facilitates women exchanging travel tips, with links to resources. The Canadian government also publishes the booklet 'Her Own Way,' filled with useful general travel advice; head to www.travel.gc.ca/travelling/publications to access it.

Work

Seasonal service jobs in tourist beach towns, theme parks and ski areas are common and often easy to get, if low-paying.

If you are a foreigner in the USA with a standard non-immigrant visitors visa, you are expressly forbidden to take paid work in the USA and will be deported if you're caught working illegally. In addition, employers are required to establish the bona fides of their employees or face fines. In particular, South Florida is notorious for large numbers of foreigners working illegally, and immigration officers are vigilant.

To work legally, foreigners need to apply for a work visa before leaving home. Student exchange visitors need a J1 visa, which exchange organizations will help arrange.

For nonstudent jobs, temporary or permanent, you need to be sponsored by a US employer (who will arrange an H-category visa). These are not easy to obtain.

American Institute for Foreign Study (www.aifs.com) Good resource for tracking down study-abroad programs.

Camp America (www.camp america.co.uk) Offers opportunities to work in a youth summer camp.

Council on International Educational Exchange (www.ciee.org) CIEE has a wide range of programs including internships, study-abroad programs, work-travel combos and work-exchange programs.

InterExchange (www.inter exchange.org) Camp and au-pair programs.

Transportation

GETTING THERE & AWAY

Flights, cars and tours can be booked online at www.lonelyplanet.com/bookings.

Entering the Country

Entering the USA is pretty straightforward, though at the time of writing, the Trump administration was making changes to immigration policy. Be sure to check if you're affected, before you travel, at www.usa.gov/visas-and-visitors.

If you are flying, the first airport that you land in is where you must go through immigration and customs, even if you are continuing on the flight to another destination.

You'll be asked to fill out the US customs declaration form, which is usually handed out on the plane. Have it completed before you ap-

proach the immigration desk. For the question, 'US Street Address,' give the address where you will spend the first night (a hotel address is fine).

The immigration officer will look at your customs form and passport, and have you register with the Department of Homeland Security's Office of Biometric Identity Management. This entails having your fingerprints scanned and a digital photo taken.

The immigration officer may ask about your plans and whether you have sufficient funds. It's a good idea to list an itinerary, produce an onward or round-trip ticket and have at least one major credit card.

Travelers from some countries, ie Canada and Visa Waiver Program nations (p647), can bypass the immigration desks and use self-service kiosks for automated passport control. Not all airports have this technol-

ogy. See www.cbp.gov/travel for details on participating locations and for further eligibility requirements.

Once you go through immigration, you collect your baggage and pass through customs. If you have nothing to declare, you'll probably clear customs without a baggage search, but don't assume that.

The Electronic System for Travel Authorization (p647) is now required before arrival for citizens of Visa Waiver Program countries.

Remember: your passport should be valid for at least six months longer than your intended stay in the US.

Air

Eastern USA's busiest international gateways are New York, Washington, DC, Boston, Charlotte, Atlanta and Miami, although many other cities have direct international flights.

CLIMATE CHANGE & TRAVEL

Every form of transportation that relies on carbon-based fuel generates CO_2, the main cause of human-induced climate change. Modern travel is dependent on airplanes, which might use less fuel per mile per person than most cars but travel much greater distances. The altitude at which aircraft emit gases (including CO_2) and particles also contributes to their climate change impact. Many websites offer 'carbon calculators' that allow people to estimate the carbon emissions generated by their journey and, for those who wish to do so, to offset the impact of the greenhouse gases emitted with contributions to portfolios of climate-friendly initiatives throughout the world. Lonely Planet offsets the carbon footprint of all staff and author travel.

→ Transportation Security Administration (TSA) and US Customs and Border Protection (CBP) checks in the USA can mean lengthy delays at airports.

→ Allow at least three hours to check in for departing international flights and be prepared that once you've landed from that long international flight, you may still have an hour or two to go before you have your bags in hand and are on your way.

Departure Tax

Departure tax is included in the price of a ticket.

International Airports

Chicago and Atlanta trade off as the busiest airport in the region. The main international gateways in the eastern USA:

Hartsfield-Jackson International (ATL; ☏800-897-1910; www.atl.com; 2600 Maynard H. Jackson Jr Blvd, Atlanta)

Boston Logan International (BOS; ☏800-235-6426; www. massport.com/logan; Boston)

O'Hare International (ORD; ☏800-832-6352; www.flychi-cago.com; 10,000 West O'Hare Ave, Chicago)

Charlotte Douglas International (CLT; ☏704-359-4013; www.cltairport.com; 5501 Josh Birmingham Pkwy, Charlotte)

Miami International (MIA; Map p458; ☏305-876-7000; www.miami-airport.com; 2100 NW 42nd Ave, Miami)

Minneapolis–St Paul International (MSP; ☏612-726-5555; www.mspairport.com; Minneapolis–St Paul; ☏)

JFK International (JFK; ☏718-244-4444; www.kennedy airport.com; New York; ☒A to Howard Beach or E, J/Z to Sutphin Blvd-Archer Ave then, JFK Airtrain)

Orlando International (MCO; Map p504; ☏407-825-8463; www.orlandoairports.net; 1 Jeff Fuqua Blvd, Orlando)

Dulles International (IAD; ☏703-572-2700; www.flydulles. com; Washington, DC)

Land

→ You can enter the eastern USA from a number of points

at the US–Canada border to the north, and the US–Mexico border to the south.

→ Unless you're a permanent resident of Canada and have subscribed to the NEXUS program (www.cbsa-asfc. gc.ca), you'll need to answer a number of questions about the duration and nature of your journey when crossing the border, and Customs and Border Protection officers may search your vehicle.

→ When entering the US by land (especially with a loaded vehicle) be sure to have conclusive proof that your intention is to leave the US within 90 days (or the terms of your visa) or you may be denied entry. This can cause major problems if you're a frequent traveler and intend to return to the US in the future.

BORDER CROSSINGS

The eastern USA has more than 20 official border crossings with Canada, accessed via Maine, New Hampshire, Vermont, New York, Michigan and Minnesota. It is relatively easy to cross into Canada; it's crossing *back* that can pose problems if you haven't brought all your documents. US Customs and Border Protection (https://bwt.cbp.gov) tracks current wait times at the main border crossings. Some borders are open 24 hours, but most are not.

In general, waits rarely exceed 30 minutes, except during peak times (ie weekends and holidays, more so in summer). Some entry points are especially busy:

→ Detroit, MI, to Windsor, Ontario

→ Buffalo, NY, to Niagara Falls, Ontario

→ Calais, ME, to St Stephen, New Brunswick

As always, have your papers in order, act polite and don't make jokes or casual conversation with US border officials.

TRAVELING TO CANADA

It's easy to journey across the border to Canada from the eastern USA and quite common to do so, especially at Niagara Falls. Here are a few things to keep in mind:

→ You will have to show your passport. The exception is US citizens at land and sea borders, who have other options besides using a passport, such as an enhanced driver's license or passport card. See the Western Hemisphere Travel Initiative (www.dhs.gov/western-hemisphere-travel-initiative) for approved identification documents.

→ Citizens of the USA, most Western European nations, Australia, New Zealand and Japan do not need a visa to enter Canada for stays of up to 180 days, but some nationalities do. Citizenship and Immigration Canada (www.cic.gc.ca) has the details.

→ Upon return to the USA, non-Americans will be subject to the full immigration procedure.

→ For the lowdown on where to go, what to do and all things north of the border, check out Lonely Planet's *Canada* or *Discover Canada* guides.

GREYHOUND INTERNATIONAL BUS ROUTES & FARES

ROUTE	APPROX FARE ($)	DURATION (HR)	FREQUENCY (PER DAY)
Boston-Montréal	80	7-9½	8
Detroit-Toronto	60	5½-6½	5
New York-Montréal	90	8-9	10

BUS

Greyhound (www.greyhound.com) and its Canadian equivalent, Greyhound Canada (www.greyhound.ca), operate the largest bus network in North America. There are direct connections between main cities in the USA and Canada, but you usually have to transfer to a different bus at the border (where it takes a good hour for all passengers to clear customs and immigration). Most international buses have free wi-fi on board.

Megabus (www.megabus.com) also has international routes between Toronto and eastern cities including New York City, Philadelphia and Washington, DC. They are often cheaper than Greyhound. Tickets can be purchased online only.

CAR & MOTORCYCLE

To drive across the US–Canada border, you'll need the vehicle's registration papers, proof of liability insurance and your home driver's license.

Rental cars can usually be driven across the border either way, but make sure your rental agreement says so in case you are questioned by border officials.

If your papers are in order, border crossing is usually fast and easy, but occasionally the authorities of either country decide to search a car *thoroughly*.

TRAIN

Amtrak (www.amtrak.com) and VIA Rail Canada (www.viarail.ca) run daily services between Montréal and New York (11 hours), and Toronto and New York via Niagara Falls (13 hours total). Customs inspections happen at the border, not upon boarding.

Sea

Several cities on the East Coast are cruise-ship hubs, including New York City, Boston, New Orleans and Charleston, SC. Florida's ports harbor the most ships of all, particularly Miami, followed by Port Canaveral and Port Everglades (Fort Lauderdale).

You can also travel to and from the eastern USA on a freighter. These vessels usually carry between three and 12 passengers and, though considerably less luxurious than cruise ships, give a salty taste of life at sea.

For more information on the ever-changing routes:

Cruise & Freighter Travel Association (www.travltips.com)

Maris (www.freightercruises.com)

GETTING AROUND

Air

Flying is usually more expensive than traveling by bus, train or car, but it's the way to go when you're in a hurry.

Airlines in Eastern USA

Overall, air travel in the USA is very safe (much safer than driving out on the nation's highways). For comprehensive details by carrier, check out www.airsafe.com.

The main domestic carriers:

American Airlines (www.aa.com) Nationwide service.

Delta Air Lines (www.delta.com) Nationwide service.

Frontier Airlines (www.flyfrontier.com) Denver-based airline with nationwide service.

JetBlue Airways (www.jetblue.com) Nonstop connections between eastern and western US cities, plus Florida and New Orleans.

Southwest Airlines (www.southwest.com) Service across the continental USA.

Spirit Airlines (www.spiritair.com) Florida-based airline; serves many US gateway cities.

United Airlines (www.united.com) Nationwide service.

Virgin America (www.virginamerica.com) Flights between East and West Coast cities and Las Vegas.

There are also smaller regional services:

Cape Air (www.flycapeair.com) Flights to several New England destinations, including Martha's Vineyard and Nantucket.

Isle Royale Seaplanes (www.isleroyaleseaplanes.com) Flights to Rock Harbor in Isle Royale National Park from Houghton County Airport in Michigan's Upper Peninsula.

Air Passes

International travelers who plan on doing a lot of flying might consider buying a North American air pass. Passes are normally available only to non–North American citizens, and they must be purchased in conjunction with an international ticket. Conditions and cost structures can be complicated, but all passes include a certain number of domestic flights (from two to 10) that typically must be used within a 60-day period. Two of the biggest airline networks offering air passes are Star Alliance (www.staralliance. com) and One World (www. oneworld.com).

Bicycle

Regional bicycle touring is popular: winding back roads and scenic coastlines make for great itineraries. Many cities (including New York City, Chicago, Minneapolis and Boston) also have designated bike routes. Renting a bicycle is easy throughout the eastern USA. Some things to keep in mind:

➡ Cyclists must follow the same rules of the road as vehicles, but don't expect drivers to always respect your right of way.

➡ Helmets are mandatory for cyclists in some states and towns (though there is no federal law that requires it). It usually applies to children under age 18. The Bicycle Helmet Safety Institute (www.bhsi.org/mandator. htm) has a thorough, state-by-state list of local rules.

➡ The Better World Club (www.betterworldclub. com) provides emergency roadside assistance for cyclists. Membership costs $40 per year, plus a $12 enrollment fee, and entitles you to two free pick-ups.

➡ The League of American Bicyclists (www.bikeleague. org) offers general tips, plus lists of local bike clubs and repair shops.

Some cities are more friendly to bicycles than others, but most have at least a few dedicated bike lanes and paths, and bikes usually can be carried on public transportation. Many big cities – New York, Chicago, Boston, Miami and Washington, DC, among them – have bike-share programs. They're also popping up in other cities such as Cincinnati, Nashville, Indianapolis and Louisville.

Transportation

If you're bringing your own wheels, call around to check oversize luggage prices and restrictions. Bikes are considered checked luggage on airplanes, but often must be boxed and fees can be high (over $200). Amtrak trains and Greyhound buses will transport bikes within the USA, typically for much less.

Hire

Outfitters renting bicycles exist in most tourist towns. Rentals typically cost between $20 and $30 per day, including a helmet and lock. Most companies require a credit-card security deposit of $200 or so.

Buying a Bike

Buying a bike is easy, as is reselling it before you leave. Specialist bike shops have the best selection and advice for new bikes, but general sporting-goods stores and big-box retailers may have lower prices. Better yet, buy a used bike. To sniff out the best bargains, scour garage sales and thrift shops, or browse the free classified ads at Craigslist (www.craigslist.org).

Boat

Several ferry services offer efficient, scenic links in the East. Most ferries transport cars, but you must make reservations well in advance.
In the Northeast:

Bay State Cruise Company (www.boston-ptown.com) Ferries between Boston and Provincetown, MA.

Block Island Ferry (www.blockislandferry.com) Ferries to Block Island from Narragansett and Newport, RI.

Lake Champlain Ferries (www.ferries.com) Ferries between Burlington, VT, and Port Kent, NY.

Staten Island Ferry (www.siferry.com) Free commuter boats between Staten Island and Manhattan, NY.

Steamship Authority (www.steamshipauthority.com) Ferries to Martha's Vineyard and Nantucket from Cape Cod, MA.

In the Great Lakes:

➡ To reach Mackinac Island, MI, two passenger ferry companies – **Shepler's** (800-828-6157; www.sheplersferry.com) and **Star Line** (800-638-9892; www.mackinacferry.com) – operate out of both Mackinaw City and St Ignace, MI.

➡ Two ferry companies cross Lake Michigan: **Lake Express** (866-914-1010; www.lake-express.com; 1918 Lakeshore Dr; May-Oct) glides between Milwaukee, WI, and Muskegon, MI. The **SS Badger** (800-841-4243; www.ssbadger.com; 701 Maritime Dr; mid-May–mid-Oct) runs between Manitowoc, WI, and Ludington, MI.

In the Southern USA:

Key West Express (www.seakeywestexpress.com) Catamaran service between Fort Myers and Key West.

North Carolina Ferry System (www.ncdot.gov/ferry) Runs ferries throughout the Outer Banks.

Bus

Greyhound (www.greyhound.com) is the major long-distance carrier, plowing along an extensive network throughout the USA, as well as to/from Canada. As a rule, buses are reliable, clean(ish) and comfortable, with air-conditioning, barely reclining seats, on-board lavatories and a no-smoking policy. Several buses have wi-fi. While some shorter-route buses run express, most stop every 50 to 100 miles to pick up passengers, and long-distance buses stop for meal breaks and driver changes.

Other carriers (most with wi-fi and power outlets on board) include:

BestBus (www.bestbus.com) Cheap fares between the nation's capital and NYC.

BoltBus (www.boltbus.com) Fast, cheap routes between major Northeast cities, including NYC, Boston, Philadelphia, Baltimore, Newark and Washington, DC.

Go Bus (www.gobuses.com) Plies the Boston–NYC route.

Lucky Star Bus (www.luckystarbus.com) Also runs from Boston to NYC.

Megabus (www.megabus.com) BoltBus' main competitor, with routes between main cities in the Northeast and also the Midwest, radiating from hubs in NYC or Chicago. Fares can be quite low; ticket bookings online only.

Peter Pan Bus Lines (www.peterpanbus.com) Serves more than 50 destinations in the Northeast, as far north as Concord, NH, and as far south as Washington, DC.

Trailways (www.trailways.com) Mostly in the Midwest and Mid-Atlantic states; may not be as useful as Greyhound for long trips, but fares can be competitive on shorter routes.

Most cities and larger towns have dependable local bus systems, though they are often designed for commuters and provide limited service in the evening and on weekends. Costs range from free to between $1 and $3 per ride.

Costs

In general, the earlier you book, the lower the fare.

On BoltBus, Megabus and some of the smaller companies, the first tickets sold for a route cost $1.

For lower fares on Greyhound, purchase tickets at least seven days in advance (purchasing 14 days in advance will save even more).

If you're traveling with family or friends, Greyhound's companion fares let up to two additional travelers get 50% off with a minimum three-day advance purchase.

Reservations

Greyhound and BoltBus tickets can be bought over the phone or online, as well as at terminals. For Megabus, Go Bus and most of the smaller companies, tickets can only be purchased online in advance. Seating is normally first-come, first-served. Greyhound recommends arriving an hour before departure to get a seat.

Car & Motorcycle

For maximum flexibility and convenience, and to explore outside of the cities, a car is essential.

Automobile Associations

The American Automobile Association (www.aaa.com) has reciprocal membership agreements with several international auto clubs (check with AAA and bring your membership card from home). For its members, AAA offers travel insurance, tour books and a wide-ranging network of regional offices. AAA advocates politically for the auto industry.

A more ecofriendly alternative, the Better World Club (www.betterworldclub.com) donates 1% of revenue to assist environmental cleanup, offers ecologically sensitive choices for every service it provides and advocates politically for environmental causes.

For either organization, the primary member benefit is 24-hour emergency roadside assistance anywhere in the USA. Both also offer trip planning, free travel maps, travel-agency services, car insurance and a range of travel discounts (eg on hotels, car rentals and attractions).

Bring Your Own Vehicle

If you're driving from Canada, it's possible to bring your vehicle to the US as long as it remains with you for the duration of the stay permitted on your visa. Attempts to sell the vehicle in the US (if you've bought a cheap car for the trip) will usually backfire due to differing state laws on emissions control and the fact that it'll show up as a Canadian car when you attempt to transfer registration: there are lots of fees and red tape involved.

If you're moving to the USA from Canada and intend on keeping your vehicle, it will need to pass a series of tests (which vary from state to state). Fees apply.

Freighting a vehicle to the USA from anywhere else, as an individual, is prohibitively complicated and expensive.

Driving Licences

Foreign visitors can legally drive a car in the USA for

GREYHOUND DOMESTIC BUS ROUTES & FARES

ROUTE	APPROX FARE ($)	DURATION (HR)	FREQUENCY (PER DAY)
Boston-Philadelphia	45-61	7	10
Chicago-New Orleans	96-164	24	5
New York-Chicago	70-138	18-22	6
Washington, DC-Miami	87-170	25	6

up to 12 months using their home driver's license. However, an International Driving Permit (IDP) will have more credibility with US traffic police, especially if your home license doesn't have a photo or isn't in English. Your automobile association at home can issue an IDP, valid for one year, for a small fee. Always carry your home license together with the IDP.

To drive a motorcycle in the USA, you will need either a valid US state motorcycle license or an IDP specially endorsed for motorcycles.

Fuel

Gas stations are ubiquitous and many are open 24 hours a day. Small-town stations may be open only from 7am to 8pm or 9pm. Plan on spending roughly $2.50 per US gallon. At many stations, you must pay before you pump.

Many gas stations will accept credit cards at the pump but will require the confirmation of a US zip code once you swipe: again, you'll need to go inside and pre-pay. If your car takes less fuel than you authorize payment for, the difference will be automatically refunded to the card.

Car Rental

To rent a car in the USA you generally need to be at least 25 years old, hold a valid driver's license and have a major credit card. Some companies will rent to drivers between the ages of 21 and 24 for an additional charge.

You should be able to get an economy-sized vehicle for about $30 to $75 per day. Child safety seats are compulsory (reserve them when you book) and cost about $13 per day.

Some national companies, including Avis, Budget and Hertz, offer 'green' fleets of hybrid rental cars (eg Toyota Priuses, Honda Civics), although you'll usually have to pay a lot extra to rent a more fuel-efficient vehicle.

Online, Car Rental Express (www.carrentalexpress. com) rates and compares independent agencies in US cities; it's particularly useful for searching out cheaper long-term rentals.

Major national car-rental companies:

Alamo (www.alamo.com)

Avis (www.avis.com)

Budget (www.budget.com)

Dollar (www.dollar.com)

Enterprise (www.enterprise. com)

Hertz (www.hertz.com)

National (www.nationalcar.com)

Rent-A-Wreck (www.rentawreck. com) Rents cars that may have more wear and tear than your typical rental vehicle but are actually far from wrecks.

Thrifty (www.thrifty.com)

Motorcycle & Recreational Vehicle (RV) Rental

If you dream of riding a Harley, EagleRider (www. eaglerider.com) has offices in major cities nationwide and rents other kinds of adventure vehicles, too. Beware that motorcycle rental and insurance are expensive.

Companies specializing in RV and camper rentals:

Adventures on Wheels (www. wheels9.com)

Cruise America (www.cruise america.com)

Insurance

Insurance is legally required. Without it, you risk legal consequences and possible financial ruin if there's an accident.

Car-rental agencies offer liability insurance, which covers other people and property involved in an accident.

Collision Damage Waivers (CDW) reduce or eliminate the amount you'll have to reimburse the rental company if there's damage to the car itself.

Paying extra for all of this insurance increases the cost of a rental car by as much as $30 a day.

Some credit cards cover CDW for a certain rental period (usually less than 15 days), if you use the card to pay for the rental, and decline the policy offered by the rental company. Always check with your card issuer to see what coverage they offer in the USA.

Road Conditions & Hazards

Road conditions are generally very good, but keep in mind:

➡ Winter travel in general can be hazardous due to heavy snow and ice, which may cause roads and bridges to close periodically. The Federal Highway Administration (www.fhwa. dot.gov/trafficinfo) provides links to road conditions and construction zones for each state.

➡ If you're driving in winter or in remote areas, make sure your vehicle is equipped with four-season radial or snow tires, and emergency supplies in case you're stranded.

➡ Where deer and other wild animals frequently appear roadside, you'll see signs with the silhouette of a leaping deer. Take these signs seriously, particularly at night.

Road Rules

If you're new to US roads, here are some basics:

➡ Drive on the right-hand side of the road. On highways, pass in the left-hand lane.

➡ The maximum speed limit on most interstates is 65mph or 70mph; a couple of eastern states go up to 75mph. It then drops to around 55mph in urban areas. Pay attention to the posted signs. City street speed limits vary between 15mph and 45mph.

➡ The use of seat belts and child safety seats is required in every state. In some states, motorcyclists are required to wear helmets.

➡ Unless signs prohibit it, you may turn right at a red light after first coming to a full stop (note that NYC is an exception, where it's illegal to turn right on a red).

➡ At four-way stop signs, the car that reaches the intersection first has right of way. In a tie, the car on the right has right of way.

➡ When emergency vehicles (ie police, fire or ambulance) approach from either direction, pull over safely and get out of the way.

➡ In an increasing number of states, it is illegal to talk (or text) on a handheld cell phone while driving; use a hands-free device or pull over to take your call.

➡ The blood-alcohol limit for drivers is 0.08%. Penalties are very severe for 'DUI' – Driving Under the Influence of alcohol and/or drugs.

➡ In some states it is illegal to carry 'open containers' of alcohol in a vehicle, even if they are empty.

Hitching & Ride-Sharing

Hitchhiking in the USA is potentially dangerous and definitely not recommended. Travelers who hitch should understand that they are taking a small but potentially serious risk. Indeed, drivers have heard so many lurid reports they tend to be just as afraid of those with their thumbs out. Hitchhiking on freeways is prohibited.

Taxi

Taxis are metered, with flagfall charges of around $2.50, plus $2 to $3 per mile. They charge extra for waiting and handling baggage, and drivers expect a 10% to 15% tip. Taxis cruise the busiest areas in large cities; otherwise, it's easiest to phone and order one. Ride-share companies like Uber (www.uber.com) also are well-used in most cities.

Train

Amtrak (www.amtrak.com) has an extensive rail system throughout the USA, with several long-distance lines traversing the nation east to west, and even more running north to south. These link all of America's biggest cities

and many of its smaller ones. In some places, Amtrak's Thruway buses provide connections to and from the rail network.

Compared with other modes of travel, trains are rarely the quickest, cheapest or most convenient option, but they turn the journey into a relaxing, social and scenic all-American experience.

Rail services are busiest in the Northeast corridor, where high-speed Acela Express trains run from Boston, MA, to Washington, DC (via New York City, Philadelphia and Baltimore).

Other busy routes include NYC to Niagara Falls, and Chicago to Milwaukee.

Free wi-fi is available on many, but not all, trains. The wi-fi speed is fine for email and web browsing, but usually not suitable for streaming videos or music.

Smoking is prohibited on all trains.

Many big cities, such as NYC, Chicago and Miami, also have their own commuter rail networks. These trains provide faster, more frequent services on shorter routes.

The largest subway systems are in New York, Chicago, Boston, Philadelphia and Washington, DC. Other cities may have small, one- or two-line rail systems that mainly serve downtown.

Behind the Scenes

SEND US YOUR FEEDBACK

We love to hear from travelers – your comments keep us on our toes and help make our books better. Our well-traveled team reads every word on what you loved or loathed about this book. Although we cannot reply individually to your submissions, we always guarantee that your feedback goes straight to the appropriate authors, in time for the next edition. Each person who sends us information is thanked in the next edition – the most useful submissions are rewarded with a selection of digital PDF chapters.

Visit **lonelyplanet.com/contact** to submit your updates and suggestions or to ask for help. Our award-winning website also features inspirational travel stories, news and discussions.

Note: We may edit, reproduce and incorporate your comments in Lonely Planet products such as guidebooks, websites and digital products, so let us know if you don't want your comments reproduced or your name acknowledged. For a copy of our privacy policy visit lonelyplanet.com/privacy.

OUR READERS

Many thanks to the travelers who used the last edition and wrote to us with helpful hints, useful advice and interesting anecdotes:

Kay Gilmore, Nils Plum, Parker Brown-Nesbit, Pedro Arellano, Yu En Hsu

WRITER THANKS

Benedict Walker

My huge thanks to Cheryl Cowie for endless bowls of organic Vegan soup, for making me laugh and letting me cry, for always being a friend and for celebrating our 100th birthday while I was on-the-job, and to Bruce Cowie, for his razor-sharp political insight, and always welcoming me 'home'. Finally, thanks to Trisha Ping for taking me on for this project and standing by me despite my delays and, as always, to Mum, who never stops praying for me and sending me love across the oceans: that always comes in handy.

Kate Armstrong

La'Vell Brown: thank you for your magic wand, plus your passion, knowledge and insights into Disney World, and for transforming me from the Beastess into Cinderella herself. Thanks to Cory O'Born, Visit Orlando; Nathalia Romano and Ashlynn Webb, Universal Orlando; Jessica Savage, Greater Fort Lauderdale Convention & Visitors Bureau; and to Chris, for your flexibility, patience and everything (except holding my hand on the Hogwarts Express). Finally, thank you to Lauren Keith and Trisha

Ping for their understanding and helping to put out a few nothing-but-Disney fireworks.

Amy C Balfour

I had a blast checking out my regional neighborhood. Special thanks to the following folks who shared their favorite places: Dave Dekema, Sketchy, Barbra Byington, Ed & Melissa Reid, Lynn Neumann, Lori Jarvis, Andrew McRoberts, Tom Fleming, Melissa & Mary Peeler, Erin Stolle, Alicia Hay Matthai, Liz Smith Robinson, Alice Merchant Dearing, Severn Miller, James Foley, John Park, Suzie Lublin Tiplitz, Sharon Nicely, Eone Moore Beck, Kendall Sims Hunt, Lee Bagby Ceperich, Justin Shephard, Tim Stinson, Trish Mullen and Steve Bruce.

Ray Bartlett

This project couldn't have happened without the awesome love and support of my family, including my extended family out in Pennsylvania, who offered to put me up and show me around as I was researching. Also many thanks to the numerous guides, hotel receptionists, waiters and waitresses, and museum curators who took time to share their info and views with me. A lovely part of the planet, and one I hope to visit again soon. Readers, you're in for a treat.

Gregor Clark

Sincere thanks to the many Bostonians who so generously shared their love of city, particularly Aaron Miller at HI Boston, Dave O'Donnell at GBCVB, Joanne Chang at Myers & Chang, Ayr Muir at Clover Food Lab and Maria Cole at NPS. Special thanks to fellow LP author Mara Vorhees, whose superb work on previous editions made my job immeasurably more enjoyable. Finally, hugs to my wife Gaen and daughters Meigan and Chloe for helping taste-test cannoli in the North End.

Ashley Harrell

Thanks to: editors Lauren and Trisha, and co-authors Adam, Kate and Regis, for your support. Josie, Nora and Ashley Guttuso for having me at the fort. Tiffany Grandstaff for the upgrade. Alex Pickett for existing. Trevor, Malissa and Soraya Aaronson for being my surrogate family. Tom Francis for finally coming. Alanna Bjork for dog-sitting and the cozy shack. Beanie Guez for destroying me in shuffleboard and Elodie Guez for bringing wine (and glasses). Andy Lavender for showing up in Sarasota, and in general.

Adam Karlin

Thanks y'all: to Lauren Keith and Trisha Ping, editors extraordinaire, to my brother in arms on Southern roadtrips, Kevin Raub, to the parks workers and bartenders and baristas and service industry folks who showed me how much there is to discover in my own backyard, to mom and dad, for their constant support, to Karen Shacham and Michelle Putnam (and Lior!), the best hosts Atlanta could provide, and Rachel and Sanda, for both joining me on the road and tolerating my absences.

Brian Kluepfel

Paula Zorrilla, my guiding light and co-pilot. I couldn't have done it without you. Trisha Ping, Greg Benchwick, Jane Grisman and Dianne Schallmeiner at LP for moral and technical support. Tom Kluepfel, honorary mayor of Hoboken and 'mutz' maven. Laura Collins, Rebecca Rozen and her dog Gizmo, for Hamptons knowledge and good cheer. Stacey Borelli and Peggy Watson at Siemens for holding the fort. The Ocean Grove cop who didn't give me that ticket. June McPartland for selling me that car.

Kevin Raub

Thanks to my wife, Adriana Schmidt Raub, who shockingly sticks around despite my travels! Lauren Keith, Trisha Ping, MaSovaida Morgan and all my partners-in-crime at LP. On the road, Jana Clauser, Kristi Amburgey, Susan Dallas, Dawn Przystal, Niki Heichelbech-Goldey, Erin Hilton, Courtney McKinney, Brian Mansfield, Alison Duke, Erin Donovan, Liz Beck, Eleanor Talley, Dodie Stephens, Sarah Lowery, Anne Fitten Glenn, Kaitlin Sheppard, Heather Darnell, Scott Peacock, Doug Warner, Halsey Perrin, Charlie Clark, Kim Jamieson and Jeff Hulett.

Simon Richmond

Many thanks to Van Vahle, Tonny Wong and Curtis Maxwell Perrin for insights, assistance and hospitality along the way.

Regis St Louis

Countless people helped along the way, and I'm grateful to national park guides, lodging hosts, restaurant servers, barkeeps and baristas who shared tips and insight throughout South Florida. Big thanks to Adam Karlin who did such an outstanding job on previous editions. I'd also like to thank Cassandra and our daughters, Magdalena and Genevieve, who made the Miami trip all the more worthwhile.

Karla Zimmerman

Many thanks to Lisa Beran, Lisa DiChiera, Ruggero Fatica, Cathy McKee, Chuck Palmer, Keith Pandolfi, Tamara Robinson, Susan Hayes Stephan, Hannah Stephan and Mark Wallace for taking the time to share their favorite local spots. Thanks most to Eric Markowitz, the world's best partner-for-life, who indulges my beer- and donut-filled ramblings with an endless supply of good humor.

ACKNOWLEDGEMENTS

Climate map data adapted from Peel MC, Finlayson BL & McMahon TA (2007) 'Updated World Map of the Köppen-Geiger Climate Classification', Hydrology and Earth System Sciences, 11, 163344.

Illustrations pp80-1, pp258-9 by Javier Martinez Zarracina.

Cover photograph: Lobster boats, Midcoast Maine; Alan Copson/AWL ©

(side margin: BEHIND THE SCENES)

THIS BOOK

This 4th edition of Lonely Planet's *Eastern USA* guidebook was researched and written by Benedict Walker, Kate Armstrong, Carolyn Bain, Amy C Balfour, Robert Balkovich, Ray Bartlett, Gregor Clark, Michael Grosberg, Ashley Harrell, Adam Karlin, Brian Kluepfel, Kevin Raub, Simon Richmond, Regis St Louis, Mara Vorhees, and Karla Zimmerman. This guidebook was produced by the following:

Destination Editors Evan Godt, Lauren Keith, Trisha Ping

Product Editors Kate Kiely, Kate Mathews

Senior Cartographer Alison Lyall

Book Designer Jessica Rose

Assisting Editors Judith Bamber, Imogen Bannister, Michelle Bennett, Nigel Chin, Peter Cruttenden, Melanie Dankel, Andrea Dobbin, Carly Hall, Paul Harding, Jennifer Hattam, Gabrielle Innes, Anita Isalska, Kellie Langdon, Jodie Martire, Rosie Nicholson, Kristin Odijk, Christopher Pitts, Sarah Reid, Gabrielle Stefanos, Ross Taylor, Saralinda Turner, Simon Williamson

Assisting Cartographer Julie Dodkins

Cover Researcher Naomi Parker

Thanks to Grace Dobell, Sasha Owens, Jessica Ryan, Tony Wheeler

Index

Map Pages **000**
Photo Pages **000**

Map Legend

Sights

- Beach
- Bird Sanctuary
- Buddhist
- Castle/Palace
- Christian
- Confucian
- Hindu
- Islamic
- Jain
- Jewish
- Monument
- Museum/Gallery/Historic Building
- Ruin
- Shinto
- Sikh
- Taoist
- Winery/Vineyard
- Zoo/Wildlife Sanctuary
- Other Sight

Activities, Courses & Tours

- Bodysurfing
- Diving
- Canoeing/Kayaking
- Course/Tour
- Sento Hot Baths/Onsen
- Skiing
- Snorkeling
- Surfing
- Swimming/Pool
- Walking
- Windsurfing
- Other Activity

Sleeping

- Sleeping
- Camping

Eating

- Eating

Drinking & Nightlife

- Drinking & Nightlife
- Cafe

Entertainment

- Entertainment

Shopping

- Shopping

Information

- Bank
- Embassy/Consulate
- Hospital/Medical
- Internet
- Police
- Post Office
- Telephone
- Toilet
- Tourist Information
- Other Information

Geographic

- Beach
- Gate
- Hut/Shelter
- Lighthouse
- Lookout
- Mountain/Volcano
- Oasis
- Park
- Pass
- Picnic Area
- Waterfall

Population

- Capital (National)
- Capital (State/Province)
- City/Large Town
- Town/Village

Transport

- Airport
- BART station
- Border crossing
- Boston T station
- Bus
- Cable car/Funicular
- Cycling
- Ferry
- Metro/Muni station
- Monorail
- Parking
- Petrol station
- Subway/SkyTrain station
- Taxi
- Train station/Railway
- Tram
- Underground station
- Other Transport

Note: Not all symbols displayed above appear on the maps in this book

Routes

- Tollway
- Freeway
- Primary
- Secondary
- Tertiary
- Lane
- Unsealed road
- Road under construction
- Plaza/Mall
- Steps
- Tunnel
- Pedestrian overpass
- Walking Tour
- Walking Tour detour
- Path/Walking Trail

Boundaries

- International
- State/Province
- Disputed
- Regional/Suburb
- Marine Park
- Cliff
- Wall

Hydrography

- River, Creek
- Intermittent River
- Canal
- Water
- Dry/Salt/Intermittent Lake
- Reef

Areas

- Airport/Runway
- Beach/Desert
- Cemetery (Christian)
- Cemetery (Other)
- Glacier
- Mudflat
- Park/Forest
- Sight (Building)
- Sportsground
- Swamp/Mangrove

Kevin Raub
Great Smoky Mountains National Park, Kentucky, North Carolina, South Carolina, Tennessee Kevin grew up in Atlanta and started his career as a music journalist in New York, working for *Men's Journal* and *Rolling Stone* magazines. A Georgia boy gone AWOL, he always appreciates coming home to the South for barbecue and brews. This is Kevin's 48th Lonely Planet guide. Follow him on Twitter and Instagram (@RaubOnTheRoad). To learn more about Kevin, check out www.lonely planet.com/members/kraub.

Simon Richmond
New York State Journalist and photographer Simon has specialized as a travel writer since the early 1990s and first worked for Lonely Planet in 1999 on the *Central Asia* guide. He's long since stopped counting the number of guidebooks he's researched and written for the company, but countries covered including Australia, China, India, Iran, Japan, Korea, Malaysia, Mongolia, Myanmar (Burma), Russia, Singapore, South Africa and Turkey. For Lonely Planet's website he's penned features on topics from the world's best swimming pools to the joys of Urban Sketching - follow him on Instagram to see some of his photos and sketches.

Regis St Louis
Florida Keys, Miami, The Everglades Regis grew up in a small town in the American Midwest – the kind of place that fuels big dreams of travel – and he developed an early fascination with foreign dialects and world cultures. He spent his formative years learning Russian and a handful of Romance languages, which served him well on journeys across much of the globe. Regis has contributed to more than 50 Lonely Planet titles, covering destinations across six continents. His travels have taken him from the mountains of Kamchatka to remote island villages in Melanesia, and to many grand urban landscapes. When not on the road, he lives in New Orleans. Follow him on www.instagram.com/regisstlouis.

Mara Vorhees
Massachusetts Mara writes about food, travel and family fun around the world. Her work has been published by BBC Travel, *Boston Globe*, Delta Sky, *Vancouver Sun* and more. For Lonely Planet, she regularly writes about destinations in Central America and Eastern Europe, as well as New England, where she lives. She often travels with her twin boys in tow, earning her an expertise in family travel. Follow their adventures and misadventures at www.havetwinswilltravel.com.

Karla Zimmerman
Illinois; Indiana; Michigan; Minnesota; Virginia; Ohio; Washington, DC; Wisconsin Karla lives in Chicago, where she eat doughnuts, yells at the Cubs and writes stuff for books, magazines and websites when she's not doing the first two things. She has contributed to 40-plus guidebooks and travel anthologies covering destinations in Europe, Asia, Africa, North America and the Caribbean – all of which are a long way from the early days, when she wrote about gravel for a construction magazine and got to trek to places like Fredonia, Kansas. To learn more, follow her on Instagram and Twitter (@karlazimmerman).

CONTRIBUTING WRITERS

Laura Pearson Illinois
Trisha Ping Michigan

Robert Balkovich

New York City Robert was born and raised in Oregon, but has called New York City home for almost a decade. When he was a child and other families were going to theme parks and grandma's house, he went to Mexico City and toured Eastern Europe by train. He's now a writer and travel enthusiast seeking experiences that are ever so slightly out of the ordinary to report back on. Instagram: @oh_balky

Ray Bartlett

Pennsylvania Ray is a travel writer specializing in Japan, Korea, Mexico and the United States. He's worked on many different Lonely Planet titles, starting with *Japan* in 2004 and going through to the present.

Gregor Clark

Connecticut, Maine, Massachusetts, New Hampshire, Vermont, Rhode Island Gregor is a US-based writer whose love of foreign languages and curiosity about what's around the next bend have taken him to dozens of countries on five continents. Chronic wanderlust has also led him to visit all 50 states and most Canadian provinces on countless road trips through his native North America. Since 2000, Gregor has regularly contributed to Lonely Planet guides, with a focus on Europe and the Americas.

Michael Grosberg

New York City Michael has worked on over 45 Lonely Planet guidebooks. Whether covering Myanmar or New Jersey, each project has added to his rich and complicated psyche and taken years from his (still?) relatively young life. Prior to his freelance writing career, other international work included development on the island of Rota in the western Pacific; South Africa where he investigated and wrote about political violence and helped train newly elected government representatives; and Quito, Ecuador to teach. He received a Masters in Comparative Literature and taught literature and writing as an adjunct professor at several New York City area colleges.

Ashley Harrell

Southwest Florida, Space Coast After a brief stint selling day spa coupons door-to-door in South Florida, Ashley decided she'd rather be a writer. She went to journalism grad school, convinced a newspaper to hire her, and starting covering wildlife, crime and tourism, sometimes all in the same story. Fueling her zest for storytelling and the unknown, she traveled widely and moved often, from a tiny NYC apartment to a vast California ranch to a jungle cabin in Costa Rica, where she started writing for Lonely Planet. From there her travels became more exotic and farther flung, and she still laughs when paychecks arrive.

Adam Karlin

Florida, Alabama, Arkansas, Georgia, Louisiana, Mississippi Adam has contributed to dozens of Lonely Planet guidebooks, covering an alphabetical spread that ranges from the Andaman Islands to the Zimbabwe Border. As a journalist, he has written on travel, crime, politics, archeology, and the Sri Lankan Civil War, among other topics. He has sent dispatches from every continent barring Antarctica (one day!) and his essays and articles have featured in the BBC, NPR and multiple non-fiction anthologies. Adam is based out of New Orleans, which helps explain his love of wetlands, food and good music. Learn more at http://walkonfine.com, or follow on Instagram @adamwalkonfine

Brian Kluepfel

New Jersey, New York City Brian has worked for Lonely Planet across the Americas since 2006. He's been the editor of the *Bolivian Times* in La Paz, a correspondent for Major League Soccer, and a contributor to Frontier Airlines inflight magazine. His Lonely Planet adventures have taken him to Venezuela, Bolivia and even the pine barrens of New Jersey. His stories on Sleepy Hollow Cemetery and the mines of Potosí, Bolivia feature in the Lonely Planet title *Amazing Secret Marvels*. https://auth.lonelyplanet.com/profiles/brian.kluepfel

OUR STORY

A beat-up old car, a few dollars in the pocket and a sense of adventure. In 1972 that's all Tony and Maureen Wheeler needed for the trip of a lifetime – across Europe and Asia overland to Australia. It took several months, and at the end – broke but inspired – they sat at their kitchen table writing and stapling together their first travel guide, *Across Asia on the Cheap*. Within a week they'd sold 1500 copies. Lonely Planet was born.

Today, Lonely Planet has offices in Franklin, London, Melbourne, Oakland, Dublin, Beijing and Delhi, with more than 600 staff and writers. We share Tony's belief that 'a great guidebook should do three things: inform, educate and amuse'.

OUR WRITERS

Benedict Walker

Curator, Connecticut, Rhode Island Ben had a suburban upbringing in Newcastle, Australia, and spent his weekends and long summers by the beach, whenever possible. Although he's drawn magnetically to the kinds of mountains he encountered in the Rockies and the Japan and Swiss Alps, beach life is in his blood. He loves the thrill of unearthing the best of big cities, but he's always most at home in nature. Writing for Lonely Planet is Ben's every dream come true – to date he has contributed to Lonely Planet's *Australia, Canada, Germany, Japan, Sweden, Switzerland, US* and *Vietnam* guidebooks. Journey along on Instagram: @wordsandjourneys. Ben also wrote the Plan Your Trip, Understand and Survival Guide chapters.

Kate Armstrong

Florida Kate has spent much of her adult life traveling and living around the world. A full-time freelance travel journalist, she has contributed to around 40 Lonely Planet guides and trade publications and is regularly published in Australian and worldwide publications. She is the author of several books and children's educational titles.

Carolyn Bain

Maine, Massachusetts A travel writer and editor for more than 20 years, Carolyn has lived, worked and studied in various corners of the globe, including Denmark, London, St Petersburg and Nantucket. Her Iceland obsession has led to her recently setting up a permanent home in Reykjavík. Carolyn's former base was Melbourne, Australia, and she was repeatedly drawn north to cover diverse destinations for Lonely Planet, from dusty outback Australia to luminous Greek islands, by way of Maine's lobster shacks and Slovenia's alpine lakes. Carolyn writes about travel and food for a range of publishers; see carolynbain.com.au for more.

Amy C Balfour

Delaware, Maryland, Virginia, West Virginia Amy grew up in Richmond, Virginia and now lives in the Shenandoah Valley in the foothills of the Blue Ridge Mountains. A few of her favorite places between the Atlantic and the Appalachians include Sharp Top Mountain, Lexington, VA, Berlin, MD, and the New River Gorge. New top escapes? Scott's Addition in Richmond, VA, downtown Staunton, VA, Chincoteague Island and Frederick, MD. Amy has authored or co-authored more than 30 books for Lonely Planet, including USA, and *Florida & the South's Best Trips*. Her stories have appeared in *Backpacker, Sierra, Southern Living* and *Women's Health*.

OVER PAGE
MORE WRITERS

Published by Lonely Planet Global Limited
CRN 554153
4th edition – Apr 2018
ISBN 978 1 78657 460 2
© Lonely Planet 2018   Photographs © as indicated 2018
10 9 8 7 6 5 4 3 2 1
Printed in Singapore